# Black Writers

## SECOND EDITION

# Black Writers

## A Selection of Sketches from Contemporary Authors

## SECOND EDITION

*Contains more than four hundred entries on twentieth-century black writers, all updated or originally written for this volume.*

*Sharon Malinowski*

**Editor**

**Gale Research Inc.** • *DETROIT* • *WASHINGTON, D.C.* • *LONDON*

Sh‍ ‍tor

Joanna Brod, Bruce Ching, Elizabeth A. Des Chenes, Kathleen J. Edgar, Marie Ellavich, David M. Galens, Denise E. Kasinec, Mark F. Mikula, Terrie M. Rooney, Pamela L. Shelton, Deborah A. Stanley, Polly A. Vedder, and Thomas Wiloch, *Associate Editors*

Pamela S. Dear, Jeff Hill, Jane K. Kosek, Thomas F. McMahon, Mary L. Onorato, Scot Peacock, Anders Ramsay, Ken Rogers, Geri J. Speace, Aarti D. Stephens, Linda Tidrick, Brandon Trenz, Roger M. Valade III, and Kathleen Wilson, *Assistant Editors*

Todd Ableser, Joseph O. Aimone, Robert Anderson, Diane Andreassi, Alexis Avery, Sara Bader, Jane Ball, David Banush, Billy Bergman, Suzanne Bezuk, Muriel Wright Brailey, Michael Broder, Julie Catalano, Terry Cole, Ken Cuthbertson, Rita B. Dandridge, Leonard Deutsch, Marcie Epstein, Judith Farer, Jim Gerard, Mary Gillis, Margaret Glynn, Valerie Grim, Virginia Guilford, Elizabeth Henry, Janet Hile, Radcliffe Joe, Leota Lawrence, John E. Little, Meg Macdonald, Gordon Mayer, Lynda Morris, Susan Noguera, Pat Onorato, Cindy Pritchard, Megan Ratner, Thomas Riggs, Lillian Roland, Sharon Rose, John A. Shanks, John Simecek, James Stephens, Australia Tarver, Steve Vedder, Wendy Walters, Carol Was, Julie Was, Mel Wathen, Denise Wiloch, Karen Withem, and Jon Woodson, *Sketchwriters*

James G. Lesniak, *Senior Editor*

Victoria B. Cariappa, *Research Manager*
Mary Rose Bonk, *Research Supervisor*

Reginald A. Carlton, Andrew Guy Malonis, and Norma Sawaya, *Editorial Associates*
Laurel Sprague Bowden, Rachel A. Dixon, Eva Marie Felts, Shirley Gates, Doris Lewandowski, Sharon McGilvray, Dana R. Schleiffers, and Amy B. Wieczorek, *Editorial Assistants*

Cynthia Baldwin, *Art Director*

*Cover photos:* Maya Angelou, © Gamma Liaison; Walter Mosley, Terry McMillan, and Derek Walcott, © Jerry Bauer.

♾ ™ This book is printed on acid-free paper that meets the minimum requirements of American National Standard for Information Sciences- Permanence Paper for Printed Library Materials, ANSI Z39.48-1984.
Library of Congress Catalog Card Number 81-640179

ISBN 0-8103-7788-8

Printed in the United States of America.
Published simultaneously in the United Kingdom
by Gale Research International Limited
(An affiliated company of Gale Research Inc.)

I(T)P™

The trademark ITP is used under license.
10 9 8 7 6 5 4 3 2 1

# Contents

v

# Preface

The first and second editions of *Black Writers* cumulatively provide extensive and accurate biographical, bibliographical, and critical information on nearly 700 black authors active during the twentieth century. This second edition does not replace the previous edition but complements it by:

- Providing completely updated information on approximately 150 authors selected from the first edition of *Black Writers,* based upon the need for significant revision (e.g., bibliographical additions, changes in addresses or career, major awards, or personal information such as changes in name, or the addition of a death date). These revised entries have been extensively rewritten, and many include informative new sidelights.

- Presenting nearly 250 new entries, which include selections that have appeared in Gale's acclaimed *Contemporary Authors* series since 1989 and have been completely updated for the publication of *Black Writers,* as well as entries that will appear in future volumes of *Contemporary Authors.*

## Scope

Before preparing the first edition of *Black Writers,* the editors of *Contemporary Authors* conducted a telephone survey of librarians, mailed a print survey to more than four thousand libraries, and met with an advisory board composed of librarians from university, high school, and public libraries throughout the country.

The librarian advisors expressed a need for an information source that specifically covered black writers of the twentieth century, one that would contain the type of in-depth, primary information not found in other works on black writers as well as critical material and sources when available. These librarians also indicated that the inclusion criteria for this volume should be broad, rather than narrow, in terms of the types of writers and the predominant periods of activity featured.

Following their advice, the editors of the first edition not only included entries for contemporary pre-eminent black novelists, poets, short story writers, dramatists, and journalists, but also sketched those individuals active in the earlier portion of the century, particularly writers prominent during the Harlem Renaissance. The editors also included individuals who had written books but were better known for their work in the political or social arena. For the second edition of *Black Writers,* we secured the assistance of an advisory board that reviewed the list of revisions from the first edition and ranked more than 450 additional names of black authors, and made suggestions of other names, from which the nearly 250 new entries were selected.

Because our advisors thought the volume should reflect an international scope, we have included important African and Caribbean black writers of interest to an American audience (and, of course, who have written in English or have had their works translated into English). The first and second editions together provide information on nearly 200 such authors from more than 35 countries.

## Format

Entries in *Black Writers* provide in-depth information that is unavailable in any other single reference source. The format of each entry is designed for ease of use--for students, teachers, scholars, and librarians. Individual paragraphs, labelled with descriptive rubrics, ensure that a reader seeking specific information can quickly focus on the pertinent portion of an entry.

Sketches in *Black Writers* contain the following, biographical and bibliographical information:

- **Entry heading:** the most complete form of author's name, plus any pseudonyms or name variations used for writing.

- **Personal information:** author's date and place of birth, family data, educational background, political and religious affiliations, and hobbies and leisure interests.

- **Addresses:** author's home, office, or agent's addresses as available.

- **Career summary:** name of employer, position, and dates held for each career post; resume or other vocational achievements, military service.

- **Awards and honors:** military and civic citations, major prizes and nominations, fellowships, grants, and honorary degrees.

- **Membership information:** professional, civic, and other association memberships and any official posts held.

- **Writings:** a comprehensive list of titles, publishers, dates of original publication and revised editions, and production information for plays, televised scripts, and screenplays.

- **Adaptations:** a list of films, plays, and other media which have been adapted from the author's work.

- **Work in progress:** current or planned projects, with dates of expected completion and/or publication, and publisher, when known.

- **Sidelights:** a biographical portrait of the author's development, information about the critical reception of the author's work, revealing comments (often by the author) on personal interests, aspirations, motivations, and thoughts on writing.

- **Biographical and critical sources:** a list of books and periodicals in which additional information on an author's life and/or writings appears.

### New Features

This edition of *Black Writers* provides indexing to the entries in both the first and second editions and directs the reader to the most current entry:

- **Cumulative Index:** Lists the names, name variations, and pseudonyms of authors featured in both the first and second editions of *Black Writers*.

- **Nationality Index:** Lists alphabetically the authors featured in both the first and second editions of *Black Writers* according to country of origin and/or country of citizenship.

- **Gender Index:** Lists the authors featured in both the first and second editions of *Black Writers* alphabetically according to gender.

## Acknowledgments

The editor gratefully acknowledges the members of the advisory board for their expertise and collaboration; Roger M. Valade III for his indispensable editorial support; Kenneth R. Shepherd for his technical assistance; Michael LaBlanc, Emily McMurray, Laura Standley Berger, Shelly Andrews, and Nicholas Jakubiak for their desktop publishing assistance; Peter Gareffa, senior editor of biographical directories, and Donna Olendorf and Susan Trosky, editors of *Contemporary Authors* series for their cooperation and assistance, and for that of their staffs.

## Suggestions Are Welcome

The editor hopes that you find *Black Writers* a useful reference tool and welcomes comments and suggestions on any aspects of this work. Please send comments to: The Editor, *Black Writers,* 835 Penobscot Building, Detroit, MI 48226-4094; or call toll-free at 800-347-GALE; or fax to 313-961-6599.

# Advisory Board

**Emily Belcher**
General and Humanitites Reference Librarian
Princeton University Libraries
Princeton, New Jersey

**Doris H. Clack**
Professor of Library and Information Studies
Florida State University, Tallahassee

**Henry Louis Gates, Jr.**
W. E. B. DuBois Professor of the Humanities
Harvard University
Cambridge, Massachusetts

**Will Gibson**
President
American Black Book Writers Association
Marina Del Rey, California

**Alton Hornsby, Jr.**
Fuller E. Callaway Professor of History
Morehouse College
Atlanta, Georgia

# Black Writers

## SECOND EDITION

# **B**lack **W**riters

**ABDUL-JABBAR, Kareem 1947-**

*PERSONAL:* Original name, Ferdinand Lewis Alcindor; name legally changed in 1971; born April 16, 1947, in New York, NY; son of Ferdinand Lewis (a police officer and jazz musician) and Cora Alcindor; married Janice (name changed to Habiba) Brown, 1971 (divorced, 1973); children: Habiba, Sultana, Kareem, Amir. *Education:* University of California, Los Angeles, B.A., 1969. *Avocational interests:* Wind surfing, jazz, yoga. *Religion:* Hanafi Muslim.

*ADDRESSES: Home*—Hawaii. *Office*—c/o Los Angeles Lakers, P.O. Box 10, Inglewood, CA 90306.

*CAREER:* Professional basketball player with Milwaukee Bucks, 1969-75, and Los Angeles Lakers, 1975-89. Actor in motion pictures, including *Airplane, Enter the Dragon, The Fish That Saved Pittsburgh,* and *Fletch;* actor in television productions, including *Mannix* and *Diff'rent Strokes.* President of Cranberry Records.

*AWARDS, HONORS:* Most Valuable Player of Playoffs Award, National Collegiate Athletic Association, 1967, 1968, and 1969; named best collegiate basketball player, 1967 and 1969; National Basketball Association (NBA) Rookie of the Year Award, 1970; selected for inclusion in NBA All Star Game, 1970-87 and 1989; NBA Most Valuable Player Award, 1971, 1972, 1974, 1976, 1977, and 1980; NBA Playoffs Most Valuable Player Award, 1971 and 1985; named to NBA Thirty-Fifth Anniversary All Star Team, 1980; Sportsman of the Year Award, *Sports Illustrated,* and Jackie Robinson Award, both 1985.

*WRITINGS:*

(With Peter Knobler) *Giant Steps: An Autobiography of Kareem Abdul-Jabbar,* Bantam, 1983.
(With Mignon McCarthy) *Kareem,* Random, 1990.

Contributor to periodicals, including *TV Guide.*

*SIDELIGHTS:* Kareem Abdul-Jabbar is the author of two autobiographies, *Giant Steps* and *Kareem.* Both books recount the life of the man whom many rank among basketball's greatest players. *Giant Steps* traces Abdul-Jabbar's earliest exposure to sports, relating his experiences playing high school, college, and professional basketball. *Kareem* is structured primarily in diary form and recounts Abdul-Jabbar's final season in the NBA, along with anecdotes about the people and places that he encountered in his long and successful career.

Abdul-Jabbar was born Ferdinand Lewis ("Lew") Alcindor in New York City in 1947. An unusually tall youth—he was more than six feet tall by his early teens—he readily proved himself an extraordinary athlete. Baseball, ice skating, and swimming were merely a few of the sports in which he excelled. But by the time he reached high school and was nearing a height of seven feet, he clearly exhibited a natural gift for basketball. At Power Memorial Academy he played varsity basketball for four years, and in that time he scored more than two thousand points and led his team to more than ninety victories.

Receiving enormous publicity as a high school player, Alcindor was considered an excellent prospect for the collegiate game, and he was faced with offers from all over the United States. He settled on the University of California at Los Angeles (UCLA), a school whose basketball team, under coach John Wooden, consistently ranked among the nation's best. Joining the varsity squad in his sophomore year, Alcindor quickly gained national attention. His considerable speed and agility—in conjunction with his great height—rendered him a formidable scorer, even when two or three players were guarding him. In his very first game for UCLA he established a new school record by scoring fifty-six points, and in the ensuing years he continued to produce at an unparalleled pace. During his three varsity years UCLA won the national championship three times and lost only two games in total.

In 1969 Alcindor was drafted by the Milwaukee Bucks, a relatively new team that had accomplished little during its term in the National Basketball Association. With Alcindor's talent, though, the team quickly emerged among the league's finest. And though the league was rife with talented centers—including Wilt Chamberlain, Willis Reed, and Nate Thurmond—Alcindor soon surpassed them with his balanced combination of scoring, rebounding, and shot blocking. Alcindor's achievements earned him the NBA's Rookie of the Year Award and served notice throughout the league that the Bucks would be a considerable foe in the coming seasons.

Although Alcindor quickly established himself as the dominant player in the NBA, he was incapable of leading the Bucks to the championship without greater support. To rectify that situation, the team traded for Oscar Robertson, who had long been one of the NBA's greatest shooters and passers. With the combination of Robertson and Alcindor—who had developed a virtually unstoppable hook shot, dubbed the "skyhook," which he could execute with either hand and from a variety of locations on the court—the Bucks turned into the league's best team. They won the 1971 championship and brought Robertson, who had long languished on poor teams, a particularly deserved triumph. And for his own considerable achievements, Alcindor was named Most Valuable Player for both the regular season and the playoffs.

In 1971 Alcindor, who had become a Muslim while at UCLA, changed his name to Kareem Abdul-Jabbar. Many years later, when asked by *Playboy* why he converted to the Muslim faith, Abdul-Jabbar noted that "black people are attracted to Islam in this country because the religion espouses egalitarianism, and the morality is basically the same that you find in Christianity."

In the next few seasons the Bucks continued to fare well in the NBA, but without Robertson, who had retired, Abdul-Jabbar was once again compelled to assume an overwhelming amount of responsibility for the team's success at both offensive and defensive ends of the court. He continued to score at an impressive rate, leading the league by averaging thirty-five points in 1971-72 (a season in which he again was named Most Valuable Player), but the Bucks were unable to make it to the NBA championship. Furthermore, he missed life on the West Coast, and he longed to return to the Los Angeles area. In 1975 the Bucks, complying with Abdul-Jabbar's wishes, traded him to the Los Angeles Lakers.

Throughout the remainder of the 1970s the Lakers ranked among the better teams in the NBA, but with their nearly exclusive reliance on Abdul-Jabbar as their leading scorer and defender they failed to match up against the league's more well-rounded squads. As in Milwaukee, though, Abdul-Jabbar maintained his distinction as the league's most imposing force, and by the end of the decade he had won two more Most Valuable Player awards.

Despite his extraordinary individual success, Abdul-Jabbar longed for another NBA championship. The opportunity presented itself in the 1979-80 season when the Lakers, with impressive rookie Earvin "Magic" Johnson, made it to the finals, where they faced the Philadelphia 76ers. The Lakers triumphed in six games to win the title, and Johnson—who replaced the injured Abdul-Jabbar for the decisive sixth game—was named the playoff's Most Valuable Player. But Abdul-Jabbar's great contributions as scorer, rebounder, and shot blocker were hardly ignored by the league, which accorded him still another Most Valuable Player award.

Throughout the remainder of the 1980s the Lakers maintained their position as the NBA's most consistently winning team. During that decade the team realized the championship on five occasions. Particularly memorable among the Lakers' triumphs are the team's mid-1980s skirmishes against the Boston Celtics, a team that featured Larry Bird. The Lakers emerged as the winners on two of those occasions, including a stirring 1987 series in which—during the decisive contest—Abdul-Jabbar substantially maintained the Lakers' offensive presence before the entire team united in overcoming their foes.

The year 1984 was an especially significant one for Abdul-Jabbar; it was during this time that he became both the league's oldest player and its all-time leading scorer. He would remain the league's oldest player until his retirement after the 1989 championship finals. In that memorable series, the Lakers, playing without two of their injured starters, succumbed quickly to the Detroit Pistons, but the forty-two-year-old Abdul-Jabbar gamely led his team, and in game three he once again proved the dominant player, leading the Lakers in both scoring and rebounding.

Although he retired from professional basketball in 1989, Abdul-Jabbar nonetheless remained an active force in basketball. In 1991 he lead a squad on an exhibition tour of Saudi Arabia. The same year he participated against fellow legend Julius Erving in a one-on-one basketball contest designed to raise funds for AIDS research.

Aside from his basketball endeavors, Abdul-Jabbar has also worked as an actor, appearing as a martial-arts fighter opposite Bruce Lee in the action film *Enter the Dragon* and as a poisoned pilot in the comedy *Airplane!* In addition he has presided over Cranberry Records. A renowned jazz aficionado, Abdul-Jabbar has shown an interest in encouraging new musical talents.

Besides his many accolades for basketball, Abdul-Jabbar has also received praise for his work as a memoirist. *Giant Steps* was described by *Sports Illustrated* writer Bruce Newman as "an intelligent, thoughtful autobiography." In the book Abdul-Jabbar recounts his experiences with racism and candidly discusses drug abuse. In addition he relates his acquaintances with several memorable figures, including UCLA's legendary coach Wooden. Mary Pjerrou Huckaby, writing in the *Los Angeles Times Book Review,* declared that *Giant Steps* is a work "by a great athlete who has some important things to say about himself, his profession and life at large."

Abdul-Jabbar followed *Giant Steps* with *Kareem.* Here he provides his thoughts as he makes one last tour of the league, one in which honors were inevitably bestowed by teammates and opponents alike. In addition, he provides more candid comments and insights on life both inside and outside the game of basketball. *Washington Post* reviewer Jonathan Yardley deemed *Kareem* "the best book 'by' a sports figure in many years," and George Plimpton, writing in the *New York Times Book Review,* ranked Abdul-Jabbar's second memoir among the few "worthy books about basketball." Still another reviewer, Steve Rushin, affirmed in *Sports Illustrated* that in *Kareem* "Abdul-Jabbar is offering that rarity among sports autobiographies—an unvarnished opinion."

Despite enjoying a basketball career of unmatched longevity and substantial individual and team success, Abdul-Jabbar maintains a balanced perspective on his achievements. When asked by a *Playboy* interviewer how he felt about being considered the game's greatest player ever, Abdul-Jabbar responded, "It's very flattering, and it's nice to be considered in that light, but I don't get too excited about it." Elsewhere in the interview, he added: "I've played professional basketball longer than anyone else.... I just hope that in remembering me, people will acknowledge my professionalism and consistency."

*BIOGRAPHICAL/CRITICAL SOURCES:*

*BOOKS*

Abdul-Jabbar, Kareem, and Peter Knobler, *Giant Steps: An Autobiography of Kareem Abdul-Jabbar,* Bantam, 1983.
Abdul-Jabbar, Kareem, and Mignon McCarthy, *Kareem,* Random, 1990.
Doucette, Eddie, *The Milwaukee Bucks and the Remarkable Abdul-Jabbar,* Prentice-Hall, 1974.
Hano, Arnold, *Kareem!: Basketball Great,* Putnam, 1975.
Haskins, James, *From Lew Alcindor to Kareem Abdul-Jabbar,* Lothrop, 1978.
Jackson, H. C., *Jabbar: Giant of the NBA,* Walck, 1972.
Klein, Dave, *Pro Basketball's Big Men,* Random, 1973.
Margolies, Jacob, *Kareem Abdul-Jabbar: Basketball Great,* F. Watts, 1992.
May, Julian, *Kareem Abdul-Jabbar: Cage Superstar,* Crestwood, 1973.
Pepe, Phil, *Stand Tall: The Lew Alcindor Story,* Grosset & Dunlap, 1970.

*PERIODICALS*

*Ebony,* April, 1988.
*Jet,* July 8, 1991, p. 15; August 5, 1991, p. 48.
*Los Angeles Times Book Review,* November 27, 1983, pp. 1, 6.
*Maclean's,* May 22, 1989, p. 51.
*New York Times Book Review,* January 29, 1984, p. 23; March 25, 1990, p. 9.
*Playboy,* June, 1986, pp. 55-68.
*Rolling Stone,* April 10, 1986, p. 17.
*Sporting News,* June 29, 1987, p. 7; February 8, 1988, p. 27; July 3, 1989, p. 40.
*Sports Illustrated,* December 26, 1983, p. 6; February 12, 1990; March 26, 1990, p. 6.
*Time,* February 20, 1989, p. 82.
*Washington Post,* March 28, 1990.

\*   \*   \*

## ACHEBE, (Albert) Chinua(lumogu) 1930-

*PERSONAL:* Born November 16, 1930, in Ogidi, Nigeria; son of Isaiah Okafo (a Christian churchperson) and Janet N. (Iloegbunam) Achebe; married Christie Chinwe Okoli, September 10, 1961; children: Chinelo (daughter), Ikechukwu (son), Chidi (son), Nwando (daughter). *Education:* Attended Government College, Umuahia, 1944-47; attended University College, Ibadan, 1948-53; London University, B.A., 1953; studied broadcasting at the British Broadcasting Corp., London, 1956. *Avocational interests:* Music.

*ADDRESSES: Home*—P.O. Box 53 Nsukka, Anambra State, Nigeria. *Office*—Institute of African Studies, University of Nigeria, Nsukka, Anambra State, Nigeria; and University of Massachusetts, Amherst, MA 01003.

*CAREER:* Writer. Nigerian Broadcasting Corp., Lagos, Nigeria, talks producer, 1954-57, controller of Eastern Region in Enugu, 1958-61, founder and director of Voice of Nigeria, 1961-66; University of Nigeria, Nsukka, senior research fellow, 1967-72, professor of English, 1976-81, professor emeritus, 1985—; Anambra State University of Technology,

Enugu, pro-chancellor and chair of council, 1986—; University of Massachusetts—Amherst, professor, 1987-88. Served on diplomatic missions for Biafra during the Nigerian Civil War, 1967-69. Visiting professor of English at University of Massachusetts—Amherst, 1972-75, and University of Connecticut, 1975-76. Lecturer at University of California, Los Angeles, and at universities in Nigeria and the United States; speaker at events in numerous countries throughout the world. Chair, Citadel Books Ltd., Enugu, Nigeria, 1967; director, Heinemann Educational Books Ltd., Ibadan, Nigeria, 1970—; director, Nwamife Publishers Ltd., Enugu, Nigeria, 1970—. Founder and publisher, *Uwa Ndi Igbo: A Bilingual Journal of Igbo Life and Arts,* 1984—. Governor, Newsconcern International Foundation, 1983. Member, University of Lagos Council, 1966, East Central State Library Board, 1971-72, Anambra State Arts Council, 1977-79, and National Festival Committee, 1983; director, Okike Arts Centre, Nsukka, 1984—. Deputy national president of People's Redemption Party, 1983; president of town union, Ogidi, Nigeria, 1986—.

*MEMBER:* International Social Prospects Academy (Geneva), Writers and Scholars International (London), Writers and Scholars Educational Trust (London), Commonwealth Arts Organization (member of executive committee, 1981—), Association of Nigerian Authors (founder; president, 1981-86), Ghana Association of Writers (fellow), Royal Society of Literature (London), Modern Language Association of America (honorary fellow), American Academy and Institute of Arts and Letters (honorary member).

*AWARDS, HONORS:* Margaret Wrong Memorial Prize, 1959, for *Things Fall Apart;* Rockefeller travel fellowship to East and Central Africa, 1960; Nigerian National Trophy, 1961, for *No Longer at Ease;* UNESCO fellowship for creative artists for travel to United States and Brazil, 1963; Jock Campbell/ *New Statesman* Award, 1965, for *Arrow of God;* D.Litt., Dartmouth College, 1972, University of Southampton, 1975, University of Ife, 1978, University of Nigeria, Nsukka, 1981, University of Kent, 1982, Mount Allison University, 1984, University of Guelph, 1984, and Franklin Pierce College, 1985; Commonwealth Poetry Prize, 1972, for *Beware, Soul-Brother, and Other Poems;* D.Univ., University of Stirling, 1975; Neil Gunn international fellow, Scottish Arts Council, 1975; Lotus Award for Afro-Asian Writers, 1975; LL.D., University of Prince Edward Island, 1976; D.H.L., University of Massachusetts—Amherst, 1977; Nigerian National Merit Award, 1979; named to the Order of the Federal Republic of Nigeria, 1979; Commonwealth Foundation senior visiting practitioner award, 1984; *A Man of the People* was cited in Anthony Burgess's 1984 book *Ninety-nine Novels: The Best in England since 1939;* Booker Prize nomination, 1987, for *Anthills of the Savannah.*

*WRITINGS:*

*Things Fall Apart* (novel), Heinemann, 1958, McDowell Obolensky, 1959, reprinted, Fawcett, 1988.
*No Longer at Ease* (novel), Heinemann, 1960, Obolensky, 1961, second edition, Fawcett, 1988.
*The Sacrificial Egg, and Other Stories,* Etudo (Onitsha, Nigeria), 1962.
*Arrow of God* (novel), Heinemann, 1964, John Day, 1967.
*A Man of the People* (novel), John Day, 1966, published with an introduction by K. W. J. Post, Doubleday, 1967.
*Chike and the River* (juvenile), Cambridge University Press, 1966.
*Beware, Soul-Brother, and Other Poems,* Nwankwo-Ifejika (Enugu, Nigeria), 1971, Doubleday, 1972, revised edition, Heinemann, 1972.
(With John Iroaganachi) *How the Leopard Got His Claws* (juvenile), Nwankwo-Ifejika, 1972, (bound with *Lament of the Deer,* by Christopher Okigbo), Third Press, 1973.
*Girls at War* (short stories), Heinemann, 1973, reprinted, Fawcett, 1988.
*Christmas in Biafra, and Other Poems,* Doubleday, 1973.
*Morning Yet on Creation Day* (essays), Doubleday, 1975.
*The Flute* (juvenile), Fourth Dimension Publishers (Enugu), 1978.
*The Drum* (juvenile), Fourth Dimension Publishers, 1978.
(Editor with Dubem Okafor) *Don't Let Him Die: An Anthology of Memorial Poems for Christopher Okigbo,* Fourth Dimension Publishers, 1978.
(Co-editor) *Aka Weta: An Anthology of Igbo Poetry,* Okike (Nsukka, Nigeria), 1982.
*The Trouble with Nigeria* (essays), Fourth Dimension Publishers, 1983, Heinemann, 1984.
(Editor with C. L. Innes) *African Short Stories,* Heinemann, 1984.
*Anthills of the Savannah* (novel), Anchor Books, 1988.
*Hopes and Impediments* (essays), Heinemann, 1988.

Also author of essay collection *Nigerian Topics,* 1988.

*CONTRIBUTOR*

Ellis Ayitey Komey and Ezekiel Mphahlele, editors, *Modern African Stories,* Faber, 1964.
Neville Denny, compiler, *Pan African Stories,* Nelson, 1966.
Paul Edwards, compiler, *Through African Eyes,* two volumes, Cambridge University Press, 1966.
Mphahlele, editor, *African Writing Today,* Penguin Books (Baltimore), 1967.
Barbara Nolen, editor, *Africa and Its People: Firsthand Accounts from Contemporary Africa,* Dutton, 1967.
Ime Ikiddeh, compiler, *Drum Beats: An Anthology of African Writing,* E. J. Arnold, 1968.

Ulli Beier, editor, *Political Spider: An Anthology of Stories
   from "Black Orpheus,"* Africana Publishing, 1969.
John P. Berry, editor, *Africa Speaks: A Prose Anthology with
   Comprehension and Summary Passages,* Evans, 1970.
Joseph Conrad, *Heart of Darkness,* edited by Robert
   Kimbrough, third edition, Norton, 1987.
Innes, L., and Achebe, Chinua, editors, *The Heinemann Book
   of Contemporary African Short Stories,* Heinemann,
   1992.

*OTHER*

Founding editor, "African Writers Series," Heinemann, 1962-
72; editor, *Okike: A Nigerian Journal of New Writing,* 1971—;
editor, *Nsukkascope,* a campus magazine.

*Things Fall Apart* has been translated into forty-five languages.

*ADAPTATIONS: Things Fall Apart* was adapted for the stage
and produced by Eldred Fiberesima in Lagos, Nigeria; it was
also adapted for radio and produced by the British Broadcasting Corp. in 1983, and for television in English and Igbo and
produced by the Nigerian Television Authority in 1985.

*SIDELIGHTS:* Since the 1950s, Nigeria has witnessed "the
flourishing of a new literature which has drawn sustenance
both from traditional oral literature and from the present and
rapidly changing society," writes Margaret Laurence in her
book *Long Drums and Cannons: Nigerian Dramatists and
Novelists.* Thirty years ago, Chinua Achebe was among the
founders of this new literature and over the years many critics have come to consider him the finest of the Nigerian novelists. His achievement has not been limited to his native country or continent, however. As Laurence maintains in her 1968
study of his novels, "Chinua Achebe's careful and confident
craftsmanship, his firm grasp of his material and his ability to
create memorable and living characters place him among the
best novelists now writing in any country in the English language."

Unlike some African writers struggling for acceptance among
contemporary English-language novelists, Achebe has been
able to avoid imitating the trends in English literature. Rejecting the European notion "that art should be accountable to no
one, and [needs] to justify itself to nobody," as he puts it in
his book of essays, *Morning Yet on Creation Day,* Achebe has
embraced instead the idea at the heart of the African oral tradition: that "art is, and always was, at the service of man. Our
ancestors created their myths and legends and told their stories for a human purpose." For this reason, Achebe believes
that "any good story, any good novel, should have a message,
should have a purpose."

Achebe's feel for the African context has influenced his aesthetic of the novel as well as the technical aspects of his works.
As Bruce King comments in *Introduction to Nigerian Literature:* "Achebe was the first Nigerian writer to successfully
transmute the conventions of the novel, a European art form,
into African literature." In an Achebe novel, King notes, "European character study is subordinated to the portrayal of communal life; European economy of form is replaced by an aesthetic appropriate to the rhythms of traditional tribal life." Kofi
Awoonor writes in *The Breast of the Earth* that, in wrapping
this borrowed literary form in African garb, Achebe "created
a new novel that possesses its own autonomy and transcends
the limits set by both his African and European teachers."

On the level of ideas, Achebe's "prose writing reflects three
essential and related concerns," observes G. D. Killam in his
book *The Novels of Chinua Achebe,* "first, with the legacy of
colonialism at both the individual and societal level; secondly, with the *fact* of English as a language of national and international exchange; thirdly, with the obligations and responsibilities of the writer both to the society in which he lives and
to his art." Over the past century, Africa has been caught in a
war for its identity between the forces of tradition, colonialism, and independence. This war has prevented many nations
from raising themselves above political and social chaos to
achieve true independence. "Most of the problems we see in
our politics derive from the moment when we lost our initiative to other people, to colonizers," Achebe observes in his
book of essays. He goes on to explain: "What I think is the
basic problem of a new African country like Nigeria is really
what you might call a 'crisis in the soul.' We have been subjected—we have subjected ourselves too—to this period during which we have accepted everything alien as good and
practically everything local or native as inferior."

In order to reestablish the virtues of precolonial Nigeria, chronicle the impact of colonialism on native cultures, and expose
present day corruption, Achebe needed to clearly communicate these concerns to his fellow countrymen and to those
outside his country. The best channel for these messages was
writing in English, the language of colonialism. It is the ways
in which Achebe transforms language to achieve his particular ends, however, that many feel distinguishes his writing
from the writing of other English-language novelists. To convey the flavor of traditional Nigeria, Achebe translates Ibo
proverbs into English and weaves them into his stories.
"Among the Ibo the art of conversation is regarded very highly," he writes in his novel *Things Fall Apart,* "and proverbs
are the palm-oil with which words are eaten." "Proverbs are
cherished by Achebe's people as tribal heirlooms, the treasure
boxes of their cultural heritage," explains Adrian A. Roscoe
in his book *Mother Is Gold: A Study of West African Literature.* "Through them traditions are received and handed on;
and when they disappear or fall into disuse ... it is a sign that

a particular tradition, or indeed a whole way of life, is passing away." Achebe's use of proverbs also has an artistic aim, as Bernth Lindfors suggests in *Folklore in Nigerian Literature*. "Achebe's proverbs can serve as keys to an understanding of his novels," comments the critic, "because he uses them not merely to add touches of local color but to sound and reiterate themes, to sharpen characterization, to clarify conflict, and to focus on the values of the society he is portraying."

To engender an appreciation for African culture in those unfamiliar with it, Achebe alters English to reflect native Nigerian languages in use. "Without seriously distorting the nature of the English," observes Eustace Palmer in *The Growth the African Novel*, "Achebe deliberately introduces the rhythms, speech patterns, idioms and other verbal nuances of Ibo.... The effect of this is that while everyone who knows English will be able to understand the work and find few signs of awkwardness, the reader also has a sense, not just of black men using English, but of black Africans speaking and living in a genuinely black African rural situation." In the opinion of *Busara* contributor R. Angogo, this "ability to shape and mould English to suit character and event and yet still give the impression of an African story is one of the greatest of Achebe's achievements." The reason, adds the reviewer, is that "it puts into the reader a kind of emotive effect, an interest, and a thirst which so to say awakens the reader."

Finally, Achebe uses language, which he sees as a writer's best resource, to expose and combat the propaganda generated by African politicians to manipulate their own people. "Language is our tool," he told Anthony Appiah in a *Times Literary Supplement* interview, "and language is the tool of the politicians. We are like two sides in a very hostile game. And I think that the attempt to deceive with words is countered by the efforts of the writer to go behind the words, to show the meaning."

Faced with his people's growing inferiority complex and his leaders' disregard for the truth, the African writer cannot turn his back on his culture, Achebe believes. "A writer has a responsibility to try and stop [these damaging trends] because unless our culture begins to take itself seriously it will never ... get off the ground." He states his mission in his essay "The Novelist As Teacher": "Here then is an adequate revolution for me to espouse—to help my society regain belief in itself and to put away the complexes of the years of denigration and self-abasement. And it is essentially a question of education, in the best sense of that word. Here, I think, my aims and the deepest aspirations of society meet."

Although he has also written poetry, short stories, and essays—both literary and political—Achebe is best known for his novels: *Things Fall Apart, No Longer at Ease, Arrow of God, A Man of the People,* and *Anthills of the Savannah.* Considering Achebe's novels, Anthony Daniels writes in the *Specta-*

*tor,* "In spare prose of great elegance, without any technical distraction, he has been able to illuminate two emotionally irreconcilable facets of modern African life: the humiliations visited on Africans by colonialism, and the utter moral worthlessness of what replaced colonial rule." Set in this historical context, Achebe's novels develop the theme of "tradition verses change," and offer, as Palmer observes, "a powerful presentation of the beauty, strength and validity of traditional life and values and the disruptiveness of change." Even so, the author does not appeal for a return to the ways of the past. Palmer notes that "while deploring the imperialists' brutality and condescension, [Achebe] seems to suggest that change is inevitable and wise men ... reconcile themselves to accommodating change. It is the diehards ... who resist and are destroyed in the process."

Two of Achebe's novels—*Things Fall Apart* and *Arrow of God*—focus on Nigeria's early experience with colonialism, from first contact with the British to widespread British administration. "With remarkable unity of the word with the deed, the character, the time and the place, Chinua Achebe creates in these two novels a coherent picture of coherence being lost, of the tragic consequences of the African-European collision," offers Robert McDowell in a special issue of *Studies in Black Literature* dedicated to Achebe's work. "There is an artistic unity of all things in these books which is rare anywhere in modern English fiction."

*Things Fall Apart,* Achebe's first novel, was published in 1958 in the midst of the Nigerian renaissance. Achebe explained his motivation to begin writing at this time in an interview with Lewis Nkosi published in *African Writers Talking: A Collection of Radio Interviews:* "One of the things that set me thinking [about writing] was Joyce Cary's novel set in Nigeria, *Mr. Johnson,* which was praised so much, and it was clear to me that this was a most superficial picture ... not only of the country, but even of the Nigerian character.... I thought if this was famous, then perhaps someone ought to try and look at this from the inside." Charles R. Larson, in his book *The Emergence of African Fiction,* details the success of Achebe's effort, both in investing his novel of Africa with an African sensibility and in making this view available to African readers. "In 1964,... *Things Fall Apart* became the first novel by an African writer to be included in the required syllabus for African secondary school students throughout the English-speaking portions of the continent." Later in that decade, it "became recognized by African and non-African literary critics as the first 'classic' in English from tropical Africa," adds Larson.

The novel tells the story of an Ibo village of the late 1800s and one of its great men, Okonkwo. Although the son of a ne'er-do-well, Okonkwo has achieved much in his life. He is a champion wrestler, a wealthy farmer, a husband to three wives, a title-holder among his people, and a member of the select *egwugwu* whose members impersonate ancestral spirits at tribal rituals. "The most impressive achievement of *Things Fall Apart* ...," maintains David Carroll in his book *Chinua Achebe,* "is the vivid picture it provides of Ibo society at the end of the nineteenth century." He explains: "Here is a clan in the full vigor of its traditional way of life, unperplexed by the present and without nostalgia for the past. Through its rituals the life of the community and the life of the individual are merged into significance and order."

This order is disrupted, however, with the appearance of the white man in Africa and with the introduction of his religion. "The conflict in the novel, vested in Okonkwo, derives from the series of crushing blows which are levelled at traditional values by an alien and more powerful culture causing, in the end, the traditional society to fall apart," observes Killam. Okonkwo is unable to adapt to the changes that accompany colonialism. In the end, in frustration, he kills an African employed by the British, and then commits suicide, a sin against the tradition to which he had long clung. The novel thus presents "two main, closely intertwined tragedies," writes Arthur Ravenscroft in his study *Chinua Achebe,* "the personal tragedy of Okonkwo ... and the public tragedy of the eclipse of one culture by another."

Although the author emphasizes the message in his novels, he still receives praise for his artistic achievement. As Palmer comments, "Chinua Achebe's *Things Fall Apart* ... demonstrates a mastery of plot and structure, strength of characterization, competence in the manipulation of language and consistency and depth of thematic exploration which is rarely found in a first novel." Achebe also achieves balance in recreating the tragic consequences of the clash of two cultures. Killam notes that "in showing Ibo society before and after the coming of the white man he avoids the temptation to present the past as idealized and the present as ugly and unsatisfactory." And, as Killam concludes, Achebe's "success proceeds from his ability to create a sense of real life and real issues in the book and to see his subject from the point of view which is neither idealistic nor dishonest."

*Arrow of God,* the second of Achebe's novels of colonialism, takes place in the 1920s after the British have established a presence in Nigeria. The "arrow of god" mentioned in the title is Ezeulu, the chief priest of the god Ulu who is the patron deity of an Ibo village. As chief priest, Ezeulu is responsible for initiating the rituals that structure village life, a position vested with a great deal of power. In fact, the central theme of this novel, as Laurence points out, is power: "Ezeulu's testing of his own power and the power of his god, and his effort to maintain his own and his god's authority in the face of village factions and of the [Christian] mission and the British administration." "This, then, is a political novel in which different systems of power are examined and their dependence

upon myth and ritual compared," writes Carroll. "Of necessity it is also a study in the psychology of power."

In Ezeulu, Achebe presents a study of the loss of power. After his village rejects his advice to avoid war with a neighboring village, Ezeulu finds himself at odds with his own people and praised by the British administrators. The British, seeking a candidate to install as village chieftain, make him an offer, which he refuses. Caught in the middle with no allies, Ezeulu slowly loses his grip on reality and slips into senility. "As in Achebe's other novels," observes Gerald Moore in *Seven African Writers,* "it is the strong-willed man of tradition who cannot adapt, and who is crushed by his virtues in the war between the new, more worldly order, and the old, conservative values of an isolated society."

The artistry displayed in *Arrow of God,* Achebe's second portrait of cultures in collision, has drawn a great deal of attention, adding to the esteem in which the writer is held. Charles Miller comments in a *Saturday Review* article that Achebe's "approach to the written word is completely unencumbered with verbiage. He never strives for the exalted phrase, he never once raises his voice; even in the most emotion-charged passages the tone is absolutely unruffled, the control impeccable." Concludes this reviewer, "It is a measure of Achebe's creative gift that he has no need whatever for prose fireworks to light the flame of his intense drama."

Killam recognizes this novel as more than a vehicle for Achebe's commentary on colonialism. He suggests in his study that "Achebe's overall intention is to explore the depths of the human condition and in this other more important sense *Arrow of God* transcends its setting and shows us characters whose values, motivations, actions and qualities are permanent in human kind." Laurence offers this evaluation in her 1968 book: "*Arrow of God,* in which [Achebe] comes into full maturity as a novelist, ... is probably one of the best novels written anywhere in the past decade."

Achebe's three other novels—*No Longer at Ease, A Man of the People,* and *Anthills of the Savannah*—examine Africa in the era of independence. This is an Africa less and less under direct European administration, yet still deeply affected by it, an Africa struggling to regain its footing in order to stand on its own two feet. Standing in the way of realizing its goal of true independence is the corruption pervasive in modern Africa, an obstacle Achebe scrutinizes in each of these novels.

In *No Longer at Ease,* set in Nigeria just prior to independence, Achebe extends his history of the Okonkwo family. Here the central character is Obi Okonkwo, grandson of the tragic hero of *Things Fall Apart.* This Okonkwo has been raised a Christian and educated at the university in England. Like many of his peers, he has left the bush behind for a position as a civil servant in Lagos, Nigeria's largest city. "*No Longer at Ease* deals with the plight of [this] new generation of Nigerians," observes Palmer, "who, having been exposed to education in the western world and therefore largely cut off from their roots in traditional society, discover, on their return, that the demands of tradition are still strong, and are hopelessly caught in the clash between the old and the new."

Many, faced with this internal conflict, succumb to corruption. Obi is no exception. "The novel opens with Obi on trial for accepting bribes when a civil servant," notes Killam, "and the book takes the form of a long flashback." "In a world which is the result of the intermingling of Europe and Africa ... Achebe traces the decline of his hero from brilliant student to civil servant convicted of bribery and corruption," writes Carroll. "It reads like a postscript to the earlier novel [*Things Fall Apart*] because the same forces are at work but in a confused, diluted, and blurred form." In *This Africa: Novels by West Africans in English and French,* Judith Illsley Gleason points out how the imagery of each book depicts the changes in the Okonkwo family and the Nigeria they represent. As she points out, "The career of the grandson Okonkwo ends not with a machet's swing but with a gavel's tap."

Here again in this novel Achebe carefully shapes language, to inform, but also to transport the reader to Africa. "It is through [his characters'] use of language that we are able to enter their world and to share their experiences," writes Shatto Arthur Gakwandi in *The Novel and Contemporary Experience in Africa.* Gakwandi adds: "Through [Achebe's] keen sensitivity to the way people express themselves and his delicate choice of idiom the author illuminates for us the thoughts and attitudes of the whole range of Nigerian social strata." The impact of Achebe's style is such that, as John Coleman observes in the *Spectator,* his "novel moves towards its inevitable catastrophe with classic directness. Nothing is wasted and it is only after the sad, understated close that one realises, once again how much of the Nigerian context has been touched in, from the prejudice and corruption of Lagos to the warm, homiletic simplicities of life."

*A Man of the People* is "the story of the yokel who visits the sinful city and emerges from it scathed but victorious," writes Martin Tucker in *Africa in Modern Literature,* "while the so-called 'sophisticates' and 'sinners' suffer their just desserts." In this novel, Achebe casts his eye on African politics, taking on, as Moore notes, "the corruption of Nigerians in high places in the central government." The author's eyepiece is the book's narrator Odili, a schoolteacher; the object of his scrutiny is Chief the Honorable M. A. Nanga, Member of Parliament, Odili's former teacher and a popular bush politician who has

risen to the post of Minister of Culture in his West African homeland.

At first, Odili is charmed by the politician; but eventually he recognizes the extent of Nanga's abuses and decides to oppose the minister in an election. Odili is beaten, both physically and politically, his appeal to the people heard but ignored. The novel demonstrates, according to Gakwandi, that "the society has been invaded by a wide range of values which have destroyed the traditional balance between the material and the spiritual spheres of life, which has led inevitably to the hypocrisy of double standards." Odili is a victim of these double standards.

Despite his political victory, Nanga, along with the rest of the government, is ousted by a coup. "The novel is a carefully plotted and unified piece of writing," writes Killam. "Achebe achieves balance and proportion in the treatment of his theme of political corruption by evoking both the absurdity of the behavior of the principal characters while at the same time suggesting the serious and destructive consequences of their behavior to the commonwealth." The seriousness of the fictional situation portrayed in *A Man of the People* became real very soon after the novel was first published in 1966 when Nigeria itself was racked by a coup.

Two decades passed between the publications of *A Man of the People* and Achebe's 1988 novel, *Anthills of the Savannah.* During this period, the novelist wrote poetry, short stories, and essays. He also became involved in Nigeria's political struggle, a struggle marked by five coups, a civil war, elections marred by violence, and a number of attempts to return to civilian rule. *Anthills of the Savannah* represents Achebe's return to the novel, and as Nadine Gordimer comments in the *New York Times Book Review,* "it is a work in which 22 years of harsh experience, intellectual growth, self-criticism, deepening understanding and mustered discipline of skill open wide a subject to which Mr. Achebe is now magnificently equal." It also represents a return to the themes informing Achebe's earlier novels of independent Africa. "This is a study of how power corrupts itself and by doing so begins to die," writes *Observer* contributor Ben Okri. "It is also about dissent, and love."

Three former schoolmates have risen to positions of power in an imaginary West African nation, Kangan. Ikem is editor of the state-owned newspaper; Chris is the country's minister of information; Sam is a military man become head of state. Sam's quest to have himself voted president for life sends the lives of these three and the lives of all Kangan citizens into turmoil. "In this new novel ... Chinua Achebe says, with implacable honesty, that Africa itself is to blame," notes Neal Ascherson in the *New York Review of Books,* "and that there is no safety in excuses that place the fault in the colonial past or in the commercial and political manipulations of the First World." Ascherson continues that the novel becomes "a tale about responsibility, and the ways in which men who should know better betray and evade that responsibility."

The turmoil comes to a head in the novel's final pages. All three of the central characters are dead. Ikem, who spoke out against the abuses of the government, is murdered by Sam's secret police. Chris, who flees into the bush to begin a journey of transformation among the people, is shot attempting to stop a rape. Sam is kidnapped and murdered in a coup. "The three murders, senseless as they are, represent the departure of a generation that compromised its own enlightenment for the sake of power," writes Ascherson. And, as Okri observes, "The novel closes with the suggestion that power should reside not within an elite but within the awakened spirit of the people." Here is the hope offered in the novel, hope that is also suggested in its title, as Charles Trueheart relates in the *Washington Post:* "When the brush fires sweep across the savanna, scorching the earth, they leave behind only anthills, and inside the anthills, the surviving memories of the fires and all that came before."

*Anthills of the Savannah* has been well received and has earned for Achebe a nomination for the Booker Prize. In Larson's estimation, printed in the *Tribune Books,* "No other novel in many years has bitten to the core, swallowed and regurgitated contemporary Africa's miseries and expectations as profoundly as 'Anthills of the Savannah'." It has also enhanced Achebe's reputation as an artist; as *New Statesman* contributor Margaret Busby writes, "Reading [this novel] is like watching a master carver skillfully chiselling away from every angle at a solid block of wood: at first there is simply fascination at the sureness with which he works, according to a plan apparent to himself. But the point of all this activity gradually begins to emerge—until at last it is possible to step back and admire the image created."

Despite the fact that Achebe's next book, *Hopes and Impediments,* is a collection of essays and speeches written over a period of twenty-three years, it was perceived in many ways to be a logical extension of the ideas he examined in *Anthills of the Savannah.* In this collection, however, he is not addressing the way in which Africans view themselves but rather the manner in which Africa is viewed by the outside world. The central theme of the essays is the corrosive impact of the racism that pervades the traditional western appraisal of Africa. The collection opens with an examination of Joseph Conrad's 1902 story *Heart of Darkness;* Achebe criticizes Conrad for projecting an image of Africa as "the other world"—meaning non-European and, therefore, uncivilized. Achebe argues that to this day, the Condradian myth persists that Africa is a dark and bestial land. The time has come, Achebe states, to sweep away the old prejudices in favor of new myths and

socially "beneficent fiction" which will enable Africans and non-Africans alike to redefine the way they look at the continent.

Some reviewers are highly critical of Achebe's premise in *Hopes and Impediments.* Craig Raine, writing in the *London Review of Books,* objects to Achebe's efforts to "place art at the service of propaganda and social engineering." Other reviewers, however, are untroubled by this notion and see the collection as highly worthwhile. Observes Adam Lively in the *New Statesman & Society,* "Western writers could learn much from these African visions ... not because they radiate universal truths in a way that Europe has seen itself as doing, but precisely because they are so divergent from, so seemingly irrelevant to, our own head-down anxieties." Says Joe Wood of the *New York Times Book Review,* "Mr Achebe aims to nudge readers to think past their stubborn preconceptions, and he succeeds marvelously."

In his writings—particularly his novels—Achebe has created a significant body of work in which he offers a close and balanced examination of contemporary Africa and the historical forces that have shaped it. "His distinction is to have [looked back] without any trace either of chauvinistic idealism or of neurotic rejection, those twin poles of so much African mythologizing," maintains Moore. "Instead, he has recreated for us a way of life which has almost disappeared, and has done so with understanding, with justice and with realism." And Busby commends the author's achievement in "charting the socio-political development of contemporary Nigeria." However, Achebe's writing reverberates beyond the borders of Nigeria and beyond the arenas of anthropology, sociology, and political science. As literature, it deals with universal qualities. And, as Killam writes in his study: "Achebe's novels offer a vision of life which is essentially tragic, compounded of success and failure, informed by knowledge and understanding, relieved by humour and tempered by sympathy, embued with an awareness of human suffering and the human capacity to endure." Concludes the critic, "Sometimes his characters meet with success, more often with defeat and despair. Through it all the spirit of man and the belief in the possibility of triumph endures."

*BIOGRAPHICAL/CRITICAL SOURCES:*

*BOOKS*

Achebe, Chinua, *A Man of the People,* introduction by K. W. J. Post, Doubleday, 1967.
Achebe, *Hopes and Impediments,* Heinemann, 1988.
Achebe, *Morning Yet on Creation Day,* Doubleday, 1975.
Achebe, *Things Fall Apart,* Fawcett, 1977.
Awoonor, Kofi, *The Breast of the Earth,* Doubleday, 1975.

Baldwin, Claudia, *Nigerian Literature: A Bibliography of Criticism,* G. K. Hall, 1980.

Carroll, David, *Chinua Achebe,* Macmillan, 1990.

*Contemporary Literary Criticism,* Gale, Volume 1, 1973; Volume 3, 1975; Volume 5, 1976; Volume 7, 1977; Volume 11, 1979; Volume 26, 1983; Volume 51, 1988.

Duerden, Dennis and Cosmo Pieterse, editors, *African Writers Talking: A Collection of Radio Interviews,* Africana Publishing, 1972.

Gakwandi, Shatto Arthur, *The Novel and Contemporary Experience in Africa,* Africana Publishing, 1977.

Gikandi, Simon, *Reading Chinua Achebe: Language and Ideology in Fiction,* Heinemann, 1991.

Gleason, Judith Illsley, *This Africa: Novels by West Africans in English and French,* Northwestern University Press, 1965.

Killam, G. D., *The Novels of Chinua Achebe,* Africana Publishing, 1969.

King, Bruce, *Introduction to Nigerian Literature,* Africana Publishing, 1972.

King, Bruce, *The New English Literatures: Cultural Nationalism in a Changing World,* Macmillan, 1980.

Larson, Charles R., *The Emergence of African Fiction,* Indiana University Press, 1972.

Laurence, Margaret, *Long Drums and Cannons: Nigerian Dramatists and Novelists,* Praeger, 1968.

Lindfors, Bernth, *Folklore in Nigerian Literature,* Africana Publishing, 1973.

McEwan, Neil, *Africa and the Novel,* Humanities Press, 1983.

Moore, Gerald, *Seven African Writers,* Oxford University Press, 1962.

Njoku, Benedict Chiaka, *The Four Novels of Chinua Achebe: A Critical Study,* Peter Lang, 1984.

Omotoso, Kole, *Achebe or Soyinka?: A Reinterpretation and a Study in Contrasts,* Hans Zell Publishers, 1992.

Palmer, Eustace, *The Growth of the African Novel,* Heinemann, 1979.

Petersen, K. H., *Chinua Achebe: A Celebration,* Heinemann, Dangeroo Press, 1991.

Ravenscroft, Arthur, *Chinua Achebe,* Longmans, Green, for the British Council, 1969.

Roscoe, Adrian A., *Mother Is Gold: A Study of West African Literature,* Cambridge University Press, 1971.

Tucker, Martin, *Africa in Modern Literature,* Ungar, 1967.

Wren, Robert M., *Achebe's World: The Historical and Cultural Context of the Novels,* Three Continents, 1980.

*PERIODICALS*

*Afro-American and African Journal of Arts and Letters,* winter, 1990.

*America,* June 22-29, 1991.

*Boston Globe,* March 9, 1988.

*Busara,* Volume 7, number 2, 1975.

*Commonweal,* December 1, 1967.

*Commonwealth Essays and Studies,* fall, 1990.

*Economist,* October 24, 1987.

*English Studies in Africa,* September, 1971.

*Listener,* October 15, 1987.

*Lively Arts and Book Review,* April 30, 1961.

*London Review of Books,* August 7, 1986; October 15, 1981; June 22, 1989, p. 16-17.

*Los Angeles Times Book Review,* February 28, 1988.

*Massachusetts Review,* spring, 1987.

*Michigan Quarterly Review,* fall, 1970.

*Modern Fiction Studies,* fall, 1991.

*Nation,* October 11, 1965; April 16, 1988.

*New Africa,* November, 1987.

*New Statesman,* January 4, 1985; September 25, 1987.

*New Statesman and Society,* July 22, 1988, p. 41-42.

*New York Review of Books,* March 3, 1988.

*New York Times,* August 10, 1966; February 16, 1988.

*New York Times Book Review,* December 17, 1967; May 13, 1973; August 11, 1985; February 21, 1988; November 12, 1989, p. 55.

*Observer,* September 20, 1987.

*Parabola,* fall, 1992.

*Saturday Review,* January 6, 1968.

*Spectator,* October 21, 1960; September 26, 1987.

*Studies in Black Literature: Special Issue; Chinua Achebe,* spring, 1971.

*Times Educational Supplement,* January 25, 1985.

*Times Literary Supplement,* February 3, 1966; March 3, 1972; May 4, 1973; February 26, 1982; October 12, 1984; October 9, 1987.

*Tribune Books* (Chicago), February 21, 1988.

*Utne Reader,* March/April, 1990.

*Village Voice,* March 15, 1988.

*Wall Street Journal,* February 23, 1988.

*Washington Post,* February 16, 1988.

*Washington Post Book World,* February 7, 1988.

*World Literature Today,* summer, 1985.

*World Literature Written in English,* November, 1978.

\* \* \*

## AKAR, John J(oseph)   1927-1975

*PERSONAL:* Born May 20, 1927, in Rotifunk, Sierra Leone; died of heart disease, June 23, 1975; son of Joseph Philip and Tikidankay (Mansaray) Akar; married Constance Eleanor Wright, November 24, 1956; children: Jacqueline Jasmin, Pamela Juli, Melissa Dankay, Michelle Mayilla, Cynthia Collette, Emily Yama. *Education:* Attended Otterbein College, 1946-49; University of California at Berkeley, B.A., 1950; attended Lincoln's Inn, London, 1950-53; attended London School of Economics, 1950-52.

*CAREER:* Free-lance broadcaster, 1950-55; affiliated with the Voice of America, 1955-56; Sierra Leone Broadcasting System, director, 1957-67; Sierra Leone Hotels and Tourist Board, secretary, 1960-67; Commonwealth Broadcasting Secretariat, London, England, secretary, 1967-69; Ambassador to the United States from Sierra Leone, 1969-75; High Commissioner to Canada, 1970-75. Danforth visiting lecturer to the United States, 1964-66; member of Sierra Leone Museum Committee; chair of Sierra Leone National Museums, Monuments, and Relics Commission; founder of National Dance Troupe of Sierra Leone. Chiefdom counsellor, Bumpeh Chiefdom, Rotifunk, Sierra Leone; actor on stage and in films.

*MEMBER:* American Federation of Television and Radio Artists, Rotary Club.

*AWARDS, HONORS:* Honorary Trustee, Baker University, Baldwin, KS; Order of the British Empire (OBE); chevalier Cedars of Lebanon, 1959; received Sierra Leone Independence Medal, 1961; Independence Competition prize, Congress for Cultural Freedom, 1961, for *Cry Tamba;* honorary doctorates, Albright College, Reading, PA, and Otterbein College, Westerville, OH; Neuffield Scholar, University of Edinburgh, Scotland.

*WRITINGS:*

*Cry Tamba* (play), West African Review, 1954.

Also author of additional plays, including 1949s *Valley Without Echo,* produced by the British Council in 1954, and *The Second Chance,* 1954. Contributor to periodicals in Jamaica. Also composer of the Sierra Leone national anthem.

*SIDELIGHTS:* John J. Akar was a diplomat, broadcaster, actor, and author of the play *Valley Without Echo,* one of the first African plays to be produced in Europe in 1954. For his second play, *Cry Tamba,* Akar won the Independence Competition prize, awarded by the Congress for Cultural Freedom in 1961. After completing his education at colleges in the United States and England, Akar worked as a broadcaster with the Voice of America and with the Sierra Leone Broadcasting System. In 1969, Akar joined the diplomatic service as ambassador to the United States and High Commissioner to Canada. During his career, he appeared on stage as an actor in London and on Broadway, and was the composer of the music for the Sierra Leone national anthem.

*BIOGRAPHICAL/CRITICAL SOURCES:*

BOOKS

*African Authors: A Companion to Black African Writing, Volume 1: 1300-1973,* Black Orpheus Press, 1973.

PERIODICALS

*West African Review,* July, 1954.

*OBITUARIES:*

PERIODICALS

*New York Times,* July 1, 1975, p. 32.

\* \* \*

## ALBA, Nanina   1915(?)-1968

*PERSONAL:* Name originally Nannie Williemenia Champney; born November 21, 1915 (some sources say 1917), in Montgomery, AL; died of cancer, June 24, 1968; daughter of I. C. Champney (a Presbyterian minister); married Reuben Andres Alba, November 27, 1937; children: Panchita Alba Crawford, Andrea. *Education:* Attended Haines Institute, Augusta, GA; Knoxville College, B.A., 1935; Alabama State College, M.A., 1955; additional graduate study at Indiana University. *Avocational interests:* Piano, civil rights activism.

*CAREER:* Poet and teacher. Teacher of English, French, and music at public schools in Alabama; instructor at Alcorn State College, Alabama State College, and Tuskegee Institute. Cofounder of *Omnibus: A Journal of Creative Writing,* 1957.

*AWARDS, HONORS:* Second place award, Ester R. Beer Memorial Poetry Prize, National Writers' Club.

*WRITINGS:*

*The Parchments: A Book of Verse,* Merchants Press, 1962.
*The Parchments II: A Book of Verse,* illustrated by daughter Panchita Alba Crawford, privately printed, 1967.

Also author of the "Miss Lucy" series of short stories. Contributor to anthologies, including *For Malcolm,* edited by Dudley Randall and Margaret G. Burroughs, Broadside Press, 1969; *Poetry of Black America,* edited by Arnold Adoff, Harper, 1973; and *The Poetry of the Negro 1746-1970.* Contributor of poems and short stories to periodicals, including *Crisis, Phylon,* and *Negro Digest.* Many poems included in *Parchments* were previously published in various newspapers and periodicals.

*SIDELIGHTS:* A poet of versatility, Nanina Alba embraces many themes and utilizes varied forms in her work. Religion and spirituality, modern technology, music, and the despair and beauty of being human and being black in America are all subjects which find a voice in her poetry. "With dexterity she meshes Christian imagery, Greek mythology, black folkways, global and local concerns into a tapestry," maintains Enid Bogle in *Dictionary of Literary Biography* (*DLB*).

The *Parchments* series was so named after Alba heard a sermon by the Reverend William Lloyd Imes comparing the "parchments" of the apostle Paul to his creative work for Christ. Numerous poems in the series pay tribute to her heroes, including musicians, writers, and scientists. One work, "Carver," praises the modesty of botanist George Washington Carver. The role of pain in music making is described in "The Holy Blues," which reverently depicts a man playing harmonica: "And close / his eyes / And slowly pat his feet / And make his sorrows moan / until his worldly blues went holy / circling his head in a halo of relief."

Alba was strongly influenced by American poet and author Langston Hughes, with whom she corresponded. Hughes encouraged her and gave her an autographed copy of his 1955 nonfiction work *The Sweet Flypaper of Life*. She wrote poetic tributes to Hughes and to Countee Cullen, another writer whom she acknowledged had a major influence on her own work. Other poems are odes to Ernest Hemingway and John Donne.

But public figures and the literary world were not the exclusive domain for Alba's creations. Like many poets who are also mothers, Alba found inspiration in her children. "Prayer," written for her daughter Andrea, expresses both gratitude for the gift of her child as well as a plea for divine strength for Andrea. Alba's other daughter, Panchita Alba Crawford, illustrated the second *Parchments* volume. In this work, Alba departs from the more traditional form which characterized her first *Parchments* book to include free verse and haiku. Some poems in the second volume possess a delicate, dreamlike rhythm, while others have a disturbing, stark cadence, as in "Psychosis." Alba also makes adept use of both standard English and folk dialect.

Alba's premier work may be the critically acclaimed poem "Be Daedalus." The poet was inspired by the Greek myth of Daedalus, who escaped the Cretan Labyrinth by creating wings with wax. Daedalus's escape was successful, but his son Icarus flew too close to the sun, melting his wings and causing his death. Alba cautioned the black individual, in his quest for freedom and salvation, to emulate not Icarus, but his father. Alba dedicated her poem to the "struggle that the Negro has always had to make in adjusting to the myriad and complex problems of his living."

Alba created memorable satire in prose form in her "Miss Lucy" series. The narrator of "So Quaint," the first of the se-

ries, is an anonymous black woman who is employed by Miss Lucy, a southern white woman. Although Miss Lucy champions the cause of the Negro in the 1950s setting, she also patronizes her helper as well as other blacks. The hero speaks out against harassment and segregation of Negroes, but she also shows her lack of understanding by remarking to the narrator, "Your people, they are so quaint." Miss Lucy is killed with a gunshot after expressing condemnation of white prejudice.

The Miss Lucy character reappears in two stories that are "prequels"—written after "So Quaint" but with action that precedes the first story. Miss Lucy's relationships with black and white intimates are recounted in "The Satin-Back Crepe Dress" and "A Scary Story." Of Alba's prose style, Bogle writes in *DLB*: "Her astute use of folk expressions and dialect, impeccable attention to detail, significant diversion, and subtle humor elevates the simple plot of each story."

*BIOGRAPHICAL/CRITICAL SOURCES:*

*BOOKS*

Alba, Nanina, *The Parchments: A Book of Verse,* Merchants Press, 1962.

Alba, *The Parchments II: A Book of Verse,* illustrated by daughter Panchita Alba Crawford, privately printed, 1967.

*Dictionary of Literary Biography,* Volume 41: *Afro-American Poets since 1955,* Gale, 1985, pp. 3-8.

Randall, Dudley, and Margaret G. Burroughs, editors, *For Malcolm,* Broadside Press, 1969.

Redmond, Eugene B., *Drumvoices: The Mission of Afro-American Poetry, A Critical History,* Doubleday, 1976, pp. 319, 332-33.

\*    \*    \*

## ALCAYAGA, Lucila Godoy
## See GODOY ALCAYAGA, Lucila

\*    \*    \*

## ALCINDOR, (Ferdinand) Lew(is)
## See ABDUL-JABBAR, Kareem

\*    \*    \*

## ALDRIDGE, Delores P(atricia)

*PERSONAL:* Born in Tampa, FL; daughter of Willie L. and

Mary (Bennett) Aldridge; married Kwame Essuon, June 17, 1972; children: Kwame G. Essuon, Aba D. Essuon. *Education:* Clark College, B.A., 1963; Atlanta University, M.S.W., 1966; University of Ireland, psychology certificate, 1967; Purdue University, Ph.D., 1971.

*ADDRESSES: Office*—Department of Sociology, Emory University, 201 B Candler Library Bldg., Atlanta, GA 30322.

*CAREER:* Tampa Urban League, Tampa, FL, associate director, 1966; Greater Lafayette Community Centers, director of community development, 1969-70, executive director, 1969-71; Shaw University, Raleigh, NC, and Spelman College, Atlanta, GA, adjunct associate professor of sociology, 1971-75; Emory University, Atlanta, GA, founding director of the department of Afro-American and African studies, 1971-90, assistant professor, 1971-75, associate professor, 1975-88, professor of sociology, 1988—, Grace Towns Hamilton Distinguished Professor of Sociology, 1990—. Consultant and panelist for the National Science Foundation, the National Endowment of the Humanities, and the Department of Health, Education, and Welfare, 1971—; consultant for organizations including, Southern Regulatory Council, 1972-78, Southern Association of College and Schools, 1973—, and Center for the Study of Black Family Life, 1975—.

*MEMBER:* National Council for Black Studies (member of board, 1979—; president, 1984-88), Association of Social and Behavioral Scientists (vice president, 1980; president, 1982-83), Clark Atlanta University (member of board of trustees, 1988—).

*AWARDS, HONORS:* Grants and fellowships from National Institute of Mental Health, National Defense Education Act, and National Institute of Education; W. E. B. DuBois Distinguished Scholar Award, Association of Social and Behavioral Scientists, 1986; Distinguished Alumni Award, Purdue University, 1988; Presidential Award, National Council for Black Studies, 1989; Oni Award, International Black Women's Congress, 1990.

*WRITINGS:*

*A Statement on Racial Ethnic,* Presbyterian Church (USA), 1987.
(Editor) *Black Male-Female Relationships: A Resource Book of Selected Materials,* Kendall/Hunt, 1989.
*Focusing: Black Male-Female Relationships,* Third World Press, 1991.

Member of editorial board of *Journal of Afro-American Issues, Journal of Social & Behavioral Sciences, Umoja,* and *Journal of Black Studies.*

## ALEXANDER, Estella Conwill 1949-

*PERSONAL:* Born January 19, 1949, in Louisville, KY; children: Patrice Sales, Dominic. *Education:* University of Louisville, B.A., 1975, M.A., 1976; University of Iowa, Ph.D., 1984.

*ADDRESSES: Office*—Department of English, Hunter College of the City University of New York, 695 Park Ave., New York, NY 10021.

*CAREER:* University of Iowa, Iowa City, instructor and director of black poetry, 1976-79; Grinnell College, Grinnell, IA, assistant professor, 1979-80; professor of English at Kentucky State University and Hunter College of the City University of New York.

*AWARDS, HONORS:* Grants from Kentucky Arts Council and Kentucky Foundation for Women, both 1986.

*WRITINGS:*

*Jiva Telling Rites: An Initiation,* Third World Press, 1989.

\* \* \*

## ALEXANDER, Ric
## See LONG, Richard A(lexander)

\* \* \*

## ALI, Shahrazad 1947-

*PERSONAL:* Born February 5, 1947, in Cincinnati, OH; daughter of Harry and Lucy (Marshall) Levy; married Solomon Ali, August 17, 1965; children: Pamela, Hassan, Fatima. *Education:* Attended Xavier University, 1964-66, and Georgia State University, 1979-80.

*ADDRESSES: Office*—P.O. Box 50377, Atlanta, GA 30302.

*CAREER: Cincinnati Enquirer,* Cincinnati, OH, contributing editor, 1965-67; *Cincinnati Call Newspaper,* Cincinnati, news and feature editor, 1966-67; *Cincinnati Post,* Cincinnati, news and feature editor, 1966-67; *Cincinnati Herald,* Cincinnati, editor, 1966-67; affiliated with *Cincinnati Hi-Lites Magazine,* 1967-75. Staff member at Temple University, Philadelphia, PA, Philadelphia and Clark College, Atlanta, GA, and Philadelphia Community College, Philadelphia. Nutritionist; freelance writer.

*AWARDS, HONORS:* Named one of the top Georgia authors, Atlanta-Fulton Public Library, 1985.

*WRITINGS:*

*How Not to Eat Pork: or Life Without the Pig,* Civilized Publications, 1985.
*The Blackman's Guide to Understanding the Blackwoman,* Civilized Publications, 1990.
*The Blackwoman's Guide to Understanding the Blackman,* Civilized Publications, 1992.

*SIDELIGHTS:* Shahrazad Ali is the author of *The Blackman's Guide to Understanding the Black Woman,* published in 1990. The work focuses on male-female relationships, and, as quoted in *Essence,* Ali asserts she wrote the book to "enlighten the Blackman and create a revolution of positive change in Black relationships." Ali discusses the crisis in modern black American families that is due to many situations and people, but she finds the behavior of black females especially at fault, citing an inferior intellect among black women (when compared to black men), poor personal hygiene, and "keeping a nasty house." According to the author, black women must recognize the authority and control of black men. In the book, Ali advocates a penalty when the female "becomes viciously insulting" to a man—she recommends that the black man "soundly slap her in the mouth" for her offense. Ali's philosophy has proved controversial; many black women have reacted to the book with confusion and anger while some black men have taken the opposite viewpoint and "loved" it. After inviting Ali to discuss *The Blackman's Guide* on a New York City radio program, the host received such a violent reaction from the audience that he feared for Ali's future safety. Iyanla Vanzant in *Essence* declared that Ali's "message is anti-African and anticultural," and calls for healing and unity emphasizing respect for one another, not oppression. Vanzant concluded that African Americans must recognize "both the positive and the negative" within "the culture and tradition of our ancestors," and "gain from the experience of interaction with one another and with our men."

*BIOGRAPHICAL/CRITICAL SOURCES:*

*BOOKS*

Ali, Shahrazad, *The Blackman's Guide to Understanding the Blackwoman,* Civilized Publications, 1990.

*PERIODICALS*

*Essence,* September, 1990, p. 55.

**ALLEN, Sarah A.**
**See HOPKINS, Pauline Elizabeth**

\*　　\*　　\*

**ANDERSON, Henry L(ee Norman) 1934-**

*PERSONAL:* Born May 23, 1934, in Ogeechee, GA; son of Lee and Louise Anderson; married Agnes A. Fox, 1961; children: three. *Education:* Cheyney State College, B.S., 1957; University of California, Los Angeles, Ed.D., 1972; Yale University, M.A.R., 1973. *Politics:* Republican. *Religion:* Episcopalian.

*ADDRESSES: Office*—City University, 3960 Wilshire Blvd., Suite 501, Los Angeles, CA 90010.

*CAREER:* Academic administrator, free-lance writer, lecturer, radio and television host, and licensed marriage, family and child counsellor. Los Angeles County Schools, teacher, 1961-66; Los Angeles Unified Schools District, instructor, administrator, 1967-68; University of California, Los Angeles, Department of Special Education Programs, associate director, 1968-69; Loyola University, Los Angeles, CA, Graduate School of Education, and California State University, Los Angeles, supervisor of student teachers, 1972-73; Windsor University, Los Angeles, CA, vice-president, 1973-75; City University, Los Angeles, CA, chancellor, 1974—. Evaluations & Management International, Inc., director, 1971. Hosts weekly talk radio and wellness television series. Founder and chancellor of the Martin Luther King Memorial Urban Core Multi-Versity. Founder of the Organic Wellness Crusade, Imahe Wellness Village. Consultant and lecturer in wellness and other fields; real estate developer.

*MEMBER:* World Federation, National Association for the Advancement of Colored People (life member), National Speakers' Association, American Natural Hygiene Society (life member), Wilshire Chamber of Commerce, University of California, Los Angeles Alumni Association (life member), Cheyney Alumni Association, Yale Club of Southern California, Million Dollar Club.

*AWARDS, HONORS:* Recipient of Renaissance Award, best talk show, 1991, for wellness television series.

*WRITINGS:*

*You and Race ... A Christian Reflects,* Western, 1960.
*No Use Cryin'* (novel), Western, 1961, International Scope, 1967.
*Helping Hand: Eight-Day Diet Programs for People Who Care about Wellness,* Publius, 1986.

*Ihre gesundheit liegt in ihrer hand,* Waldthausen (West Germany), 1992.

*Organic Wellness Fasting Technique,* BLI Publishers, 1992.

*African: Born in America,* BLI Publishers, 1993.

Also author of *Revolutionary Urban Teaching,* 1973. Contributor of articles to professional journals.

\* \* \*

## ANDERSON, Jervis (B.) 1936-

*PERSONAL:* Born October 1, 1936, in Jamaica, West Indies; son of Peter (a contractor and builder) and Ethlyn (Allen) Anderson; married Eugenia Kemble, September 24, 1969 (divorced, 1979). *Education:* New York University, B.A., 1963, M.A., 1966. *Religion:* Protestant.

*ADDRESSES: Home*—New York, NY. *Office*—New Yorker, 20 West 43rd St., New York, NY 10036. *Agent*—Robert Lescher, Lescher & Lescher Ltd., 67 Irving Place, New York, NY 10003.

*CAREER: Daily Gleaner,* Kingston, Jamaica, West Indies, reporter and copy editor, 1952-56; *Public Opinion,* Kingston, feature writer, 1956-58; John Wiley (publisher), New York City, copy editor, 1966-67; A. Philip Randolph Institute, New York City, research director, 1967-68; *New Yorker,* staff writer, 1968—.

*MEMBER:* PEN, Authors Guild, Society of American Historians.

*AWARDS, HONORS:* Sidney Hillman Foundation Award, 1973, for *A. Philip Randolph: A Biographical Portrait;* Guggenheim Fellowship, 1978-79; National Endowment for the Humanities grant, 1992, to support work on a biography of Bayard Rustin.

*WRITINGS:*

*A. Philip Randolph: A Biographical Portrait,* Harcourt, 1973.
*This Was Harlem: A Cultural Portrait, 1900-50,* Farrar, Straus, 1982.
*Guns in American Life,* Random House, 1984.

Contributor to numerous magazines, including *New Yorker, New Republic, New York Review of Books, Dissent, New York Times Book Review, Commentary, American Scholar,* and *New Leader.*

*WORK IN PROGRESS:* A biography of Bayard Rustin.

*SIDELIGHTS:* Jamaican-born Jervis Anderson, a staff writer for the *New Yorker,* worked as a journalist in Kingston before coming to New York City in 1958 to study literature at New York University. After writing a biography of civil-rights leader A. Philip Randolph and a study of the New York district of Harlem in its heyday, Anderson wrote *Guns in American Life,* a book which, according to Ralph Sipper in the *Los Angeles Times Book Review,* discusses "the history of firearms in America, with its recoiling social effects."

Anderson's *A. Philip Randolph: A Biographical Portrait* examines the life of the black labor leader who founded and led the Brotherhood of Sleeping Car Porters, a union of railroad employees. Anderson charts his subject's career and also remarks on how Randolph conceived the 1963 civil rights March on Washington. Reviewing Anderson's biography for the *New York Times,* A. H. Raskin calls the book "something of a joyous voyage of discovery, a circumstance that adds measurably to its qualities of excitement and illumination for the reader." Critic Nathan Irvin Huggins in the *New York Times Book Review* finds in this portrayal of A. Philip Randolph "a view of personal integrity, character, and dedication that ... seems to have vanished entirely from the American scene."

In *This Was Harlem: A Cultural Portrait, 1900-50,* Anderson portrays the vitality of an older Harlem that, in his words, was "crowded with energy, crowded with talent, crowded with style." This was the era when caucasian groups began patronizing such Harlem nightspots as the Cotton Club. According to Anderson, the blacks who lived there were "blessed or cursed with a wonderful optimism." What Anderson is attempting, avers David Bradley in the *New York Times Book Review,* "is not a history of Harlem, or even a depiction of it, but a re-creation of its spirit." Robert Dawidoff, writing in the *Los Angeles Times Book Review* praises the book as "marvelous reading, typical of the best nonfiction in the *New Yorker,* where it was serialized."

Jervis Anderson has noted that editors often want black writers to write only on black subjects, although the *New Yorker,* in his many years there, never imposed such restrictions. Anderson's third book, *Guns in American Life,* approaches the broad topic of the proliferation of handguns in the United States, exploring the curious love affair of Americans with their weaponry. He writes of the romanticizing of murder by guns in movies and on television: "Unless it was the blowing of a kiss, nothing looked easier on the screen than pulling a trigger that released an invisible and impersonal bullet," Jervis declares in *Guns in American Life.* "No human contact was necessary." Writing in the *New York Times Book Review,* former New York City police commissioner Patrick V. Murphy—who during his first year on the job, attended the burial of eight police officers who had been murdered with illegal handguns—calls Anderson's book "a quick yet penetrating look at the history, social significance and political realities of guns in American society."

*BIOGRAPHICAL/CRITICAL SOURCES:*

*BOOKS*

Anderson, Jervis, *Guns in American Life,* Random House, 1984.
Anderson, *This Was Harlem: A Cultural Portrait, 1900-50,* Farrar, Straus, 1982.

*PERIODICALS*

*Los Angeles Times Book Review,* July 18, 1982, p. 3; January 13, 1985, p. 2.
*New Republic,* February 25, 1985, p. 38.
*New York Review of Books,* October 7, 1982, p. 29.
*New York Times,* May 3, 1973; May 29, 1982; June 10, 1982.
*New York Times Book Review,* May 27, 1973; May 9, 1982, p. 7; February 24, 1985, p. 9.
*Time,* May 10, 1982, p. 117.
*Times Literary Supplement,* December 31, 1982, p. 1441.
*Village Voice Literary Supplement,* December, 1982, p. 11.
*Washington Post,* January 30, 1985.
*Washington Post Book World,* May 16, 1982, p. 3.

\*     \*     \*

**ANDREW, Joseph Maree**
**See OCCOMY, Marita Odette**

\*     \*     \*

**ANDREWS, Raymond   1934-1991**

*PERSONAL:* Born June 6, 1934, in Madison, GA; son of George Cleveland (a sharecropper) and Viola (Perryman) Andrews; married Adelheid Wenger (an airline sales agent), December 28, 1966 (divorced June 2, 1980); died November 26, 1991, in Athens, GA, from a self-inflicted gunshot wound. *Education:* Attended Michigan State University, 1956-57. *Politics:* None. *Religion:* None.

*ADDRESSES: Home*—2013 Morton Rd., Athens, GA 30605. *Agent*—Susan Ann Protter, 110 West 40th St., Suite 1408, New York, NY 10018.

*CAREER:* Writer. Worked variously as sharecropper, 1943-49, hospital orderly, 1949-51, bartender, busboy, dishwash-

er, and stockroom worker, 1951-52, postal mail sorter, 1956, and stockroom clerk, 1957; KLM Royal Dutch Airlines, New York City, airline employee, 1958-66; photograph librarian, 1967-72; Archer Courier, New York City, messenger, telephone operator, night dispatcher, and bookkeeper, 1972-84. *Military service:* U.S. Air Force, 1952-56.

*AWARDS, HONORS:* James Baldwin Prize for Fiction, 1978, for *Appalachee Red.*

*WRITINGS:*

*FICTION*

*Appalachee Red* (novel), illustrations by brother, Benny Andrews, Dial, 1978.
*Rosiebelle Lee Wildcat Tennessee* (novel), illustrations by B. Andrews, Dial, 1979.
*Baby Sweet's* (novel), illustrations by B. Andrews, Dial, 1983.
*Jessie and Jesus* [and] *Cousin Claire* (novellas), illustrations by B. Andrews, Peachtree, 1991.

*MEMOIRS*

*The Last Radio Baby: A Memoir,* Peachtree, 1990.

*OTHER*

(Illustrator) Lily Mathieu LaBraque, *Man from Mono,* LaBraque, 1991.

Contributor to *Sports Illustrated* and *Ataraxia.*

*SIDELIGHTS:* Raymond Andrews once commented: "As children, my brother and I drew, with him continuing on and becoming an artist, while I stopped drawing and became more interested in reading. To me, there was nothing better than a *good* story. But in the farming—sharecropping—community I came from, most people couldn't read. This, along with a poor school system, did not encourage budding authors. Yet in the back of my head a writer was what I wanted to be most of all, and I couldn't help but feel that someday, *somehow,* I would write.

"It wasn't until the day of my thirty-second birthday that I finally got around to doing something about this nagging in the back of my head which down through the years had absolutely refused to shut up. At the time I was working for an airline and was being given what I felt was an uncalled-for hard time over the telephone by a client. I told him to wait and put the call on hold. At precisely 12:36, after eight years, two months, two weeks, and three days, I walked out, never to return. I went home and had my telephone disconnected. The next morning upon rising at my usual early hour, I told myself, 'you *are* going to write.' And I've been at it ever since."

In his writing, Andrews draws upon his personal experience as a youth in a small sharecropping community in the South. He has set each of his novels in the town of Appalachee, the county seat of the fictional Muskhogean county in northern Georgia. The close connection between Andrews's stories and their setting is part of their appeal. "Andrews has a deep and intricate understanding of the small southern town," writes David Guy in the *Washington Post Book World*, "and displays this understanding not only in passages of exposition but also in the hearts of his narratives." The author's choice of a small southern town with its population of blacks and whites living in close proximity also allows him to examine, as Janet Boyarin Blundell notes in *Library Journal*, the "complex interracial relationships" that occur.

Andrews's first novel, *Appalachee Red*, won for its author the first James Baldwin Prize for Fiction. It is the story of a young black woman who, while her husband is in jail, has the child of one of the town's most influential white men. The child, Appalachee Red, is sent north to be raised. Years later he returns to take revenge upon his father and the town. Although *Best Sellers* contributor Russ Williams finds that "the thin line between sociological trauma and stark fiction is not drawn," he does admit, "Raymond Andrews has an especial gift and skill of narrative, one which enables him to compel the reader through even the most unlikely passages." A *Publishers Weekly* reviewer also comments upon the author's ability: "Andrews is an extremely gifted storyteller in the best Southern revivalist tradition." Concludes Blundell, "This is a pungent, witty, and powerful first novel, deserving winner of the first James Baldwin Prize for Fiction."

The title of the author's second novel, *Rosiebelle Lee Wildcat Tennessee*, is also the name of its main character, a part American Indian, part black woman who comes to Appalachee, goes to work for the town's richest man, becomes first the mistress of the man's son, and much later the matriarch to the town's black population. "Andrews has skillfully created a portrait of an aggressive, life-hungry black woman, her four children, and the surrounding community," comments Blundell. Once again, reviewers note the author's capacity to fashion a good tale. A reviewer for the *New Yorker* writes, "Mr. Andrews is well versed in the rights and duties of the traditional storyteller, and he knows just how far to stretch his audience's memory and credulity as he spins and weaves his colorful yarns." And a *Publishers Weekly* contributor adds, "Raymond Andrews is an extraordinary writer—a true and absolutely original American voice."

In *Baby Sweet's* "the characters are larger than life and often seem to represent phenomena as much as they do flesh and

blood human beings," observes David Guy in the *Washington Post Book World*. Baby Sweet's is the name given to the brothel opened by the eccentric son of Appalachee's leading citizen to provide black prostitutes for the white population. Once again, Andrews examines how the intermingling of the races affects the entire community. Reviewers also note the folksy style evident in *Baby Sweet's*. "Andrews' writing stems from a black oral tradition and could effectively be read aloud," notes Guy. In the *New York Times Book Review* Frederick Busch writes that *Baby Sweet's* "is a novel chanted to achieve the feeling of blues ... [and] it is the music of Mr. Andrews's narrative that makes this book a pleasure to read." Finally, Guy commends Andrews "for his raucous and robust humor, his really profound knowledge of the South, his ultimately accepting and benign vision ... and most of all for the entertaining voice that tells the stories."

Andrews returns to his rural Georgia home of the '30s and '40s for *The Last Radio Baby: A Memoir*, which *People Magazine* calls "a cross between *Roots* and *'Prairie Home Companion'*." In this memoir, Andrews remembers the special qualities of the radio—not only did it link rural America to the outside world, it was a cornerstone of family entertainment. He recalls, for example, hiking more than a mile to listen to the first Joe Louis and Billy Conn heavyweight fight at an uncle's house because the batteries in his own radio were dead. Noting that "fantastic" characters fill Andrews' work, a *Washington Post Book World* contributor points to Mrs. Hill, who was born into slavery and when she was in her nineties, ran around with a "set of fast girls in their sixties."

In Andrews' two novellas, *Jessie and Jesus* [and] *Cousin Claire*, he continues his style of telling a story as if his readers were personally nearby. Placing the action in fictional downstate Georgia's Muskhogean County, Andrews paints a pair of portraits that Al Young, in his *Washington Post Book World* review, says "reveals that both of these determined *femmes fatales* are as cunning as they are attractive. The flies in these powerful women's ointment take the form of male treachery and neglect." Both of these woman, rural Jesse and city-bred Claire, are dark-hearted ladies who in their own eccentric ways, Young believes, are "sisters under the skin, determined to keep their ointment flyless."

*BIOGRAPHICAL/CRITICAL SOURCES:*

*PERIODICALS*

*Best Sellers*, February, 1979.
*Chicago Tribune Book World*, February 8, 1981.
*Ebony*, September, 1980.
*Essence*, December, 1980.
*New Yorker*, August 11, 1980.
*New York Times Book Review*, August 17, 1980; July 24, 1983.

*People Magazine,* February 25, 1991.
*Publishers Weekly,* July 24, 1978; May 2, 1980; August 30, 1991.
*Synergos,* spring, 1981.
*Washington Post Book World,* July 31, 1983; February 3, 1991; February 16, 1992.

*OBITUARIES:*

*PERIODICALS*

*Chicago Tribune,* December 12, 1991.

\*   \*   \*

## ANGELOU, Maya  1928-

*PERSONAL:* Name originally Marguerita Johnson; surname is pronounced "*An*-ge-lo"; born April 4, 1928, in St. Louis, MO; daughter of Bailey (a naval dietician) and Vivian (Baxter) Johnson; married Tosh Angelou (divorced); married Paul Du Feu, December, 1973 (divorced); children: Guy. *Education:* Attended public schools in Arkansas and California; studied music privately; studied dance with Martha Graham, Pearl Primus, and Ann Halprin; studied drama with Frank Silvera and Gene Frankel.

*ADDRESSES: Home*—Sonoma, CA. *Office*—c/o Dave La Camera, Lordly and Dame, Inc., 51 Church St., Boston, MA 02116.

*CAREER:* Author, poet, playwright, professional stage and screen producer, director, performer, and singer. Appeared in *Porgy and Bess* on twenty-two-nation tour sponsored by the U.S. Department of State, 1954-55; appeared in Off-Broadway plays *Calypso Heatwave,* 1957, and *The Blacks,* 1960; produced and performed in *Cabaret for Freedom,* with Godfrey Cambridge, Off-Broadway, 1960; University of Ghana, Institute of African Studies, Legon-Accra, Ghana, assistant administrator of School of Music and Drama, 1963-66; appeared in *Mother Courage* at University of Ghana, 1964, and in *Medea* in Hollywood, 1966; made Broadway debut in *Look Away,* 1973; directed film *All Day Long,* 1974; directed her play *And Still I Rise* in California, 1976; appeared in film *Roots,* 1977; directed Errol John's *Moon on a Rainbow Shawl* in London, England, 1988; also appeared on numerous television programs. Television narrator, interviewer, and host for African American specials and theatre series, 1972. Modern Dance instructor at The Rome Opera House and Hambina Theatre, Tel Aviv, c. 1955; lecturer at University of California, Los Angeles, 1966; writer in residence at University of Kansas, 1970; distinguished visiting professor at Wake Forest University, 1974, Wichita State University, 1974, and California State University, Sacramento, 1974; first Reynolds professor of American Studies (lifetime appointment), Wake Forest University, 1981—. Northern coordinator of Martin Luther King, Jr.'s Southern Christian Leadership Conference, 1959-60; appointed member of American Revolution Bicentennial Council by President Gerald R. Ford, 1975-76; member of National Commission on the Observance of International Women's Year.

*MEMBER:* American Federation of Television and Radio Artists, American Film Institute (member of board of trustees, 1975—), Directors Guild, Harlem Writers Guild, Equity, Women's Prison Association (member of advisory board).

*AWARDS, HONORS:* Nominated for National Book Award, 1970, for *I Know Why the Caged Bird Sings;* Yale University fellowship, 1970; Pulitzer Prize nomination, 1972, for *Just Give Me a Cool Drink of Water 'fore I Diiie;* Antoinette Perry ("Tony") Award nomination, League of New York Theatres and Producers, 1973, for performance in *Look Away;* Rockefeller Foundation scholar in Italy, 1975; named Woman of the Year in Communications, 1976; Tony Award nomination for best supporting actress, 1977, for *Roots;* honorary degrees from Smith College, 1975, Mills College, 1975, and Lawrence University, 1976; named one of the Top 100 Most Influential Women by *Ladies' Home Journal,* 1983; Matrix award, 1983; North Carolina Award in Literature, 1987.

*WRITINGS:*

*I Know Why the Caged Bird Sings* (autobiography), Random House, 1970.
*Just Give Me a Cool Drink of Water 'fore I Diiie* (poetry), Random House, 1971.
*Gather Together in My Name* (autobiography), Random House, 1974.
*Oh Pray My Wings Are Gonna Fit Me Well* (poetry), Random House, 1975.
*Singin' and Swingin' and Gettin' Merry Like Christmas* (autobiography), Random House, 1976.
*And Still I Rise* (poetry), Random House, 1978.
*The Heart of a Woman* (autobiography), Random House, 1981.
*Shaker, Why Don't You Sing?* (poetry), Random House, 1983.
*All God's Children Need Traveling Shoes* (autobiography), Random House, 1986.
*Mrs. Flowers: A Moment of Friendship* (fiction), illustrations by Etienne Delessert, Redpath Press, 1986.
*Poems: Maya Angelou,* four volumes, Bantam, 1986.
*Now Sheba Sings the Song,* illustrations by Tom Feelings, Dial Books, 1987.
*Selected from I Know Why the Caged Bird Sings and The Heart of A Woman,* Literacy Volunteers of New York City, 1989.

*I Shall Not Be Moved* (poetry), Random House, 1990.
*On the Pulse of Morning* (inaugural poem), Random House, 1993.

Also author of *All Day Long* (short stories) and (with Abbey Lincoln) *The True Believers* (poetry). Contributor of poetry to film *Poetic Justice,* Columbia, 1993. Contributor and author of foreword, *Double Stitch: Black Women Write about Mothers and Daughters,* edited by Patricia Bell-Scott, Beacon Press, 1991; author of foreword, *Dust Tracks on the Road: An Autobiography,* Zora Neale Hurston, HarperCollins, 1991.

### PLAYS

(With Godfrey Cambridge) *Cabaret for Freedom* (musical revue), first produced in New York at Village Gate Theatre, 1960.
*The Least of These* (two-act drama), first produced in Los Angeles, 1966.
(Adaptor) Sophocles, *Ajax* (two-act drama), first produced in Los Angeles at Mark Taper Forum, 1974.
*And Still I Rise* (one-act musical), first produced in Oakland, CA, at Ensemble Theatre, 1976.

Also author of two-act drama *The Clawing Within,* 1966, and of two-act musical *Adjoa Amissah,* 1967, both as yet unproduced.

### SCREENPLAYS

*Georgia, Georgia,* Independent-Cinerama, 1972.
*All Day Long,* American Film Institute, 1974.

### TELEVISION PLAYS

*Blacks, Blues, Black* (ten one-hour programs), National Educational Television (NET-TV), 1968.
(With Leonora Thuna and Ralph B. Woolsey) *I Know Why the Caged Bird Sings* (based on Angelou's book), Columbia Broadcasting System, Inc. (CBS-TV), 1979.
*Sister, Sister* (drama), National Broadcasting Co. (NBC-TV), 1982.

Also author of *Assignment America* series, 1975, and two Afro-American specials *The Legacy* and *The Inheritors,* 1976.

### RECORDINGS

*Miss Calypso* (songs), Liberty Records, 1957.
*The Poetry of Maya Angelou,* GWP Records, 1969.
*Women in Business,* University of Wisconsin, 1981.

### OTHER

*Conversations with Maya Angelou,* edited by Jeffrey M. Elliot, University Press of Mississippi, 1989.

Composer of songs, including two songs for movie *For Love of Ivy,* and composer of musical scores for both her screenplays. Contributor to Ghanaian Broadcasting Corp., 1963-65. Contributor of articles, short stories, and poems to periodicals, including *Harper's, Cosmopolitan, Ebony, Ghanaian Times, Mademoiselle, Essence, Redbook,* and *Black Scholar.* Associate editor, *Arab Observer* (English-language news weekly in Cairo, Egypt), 1961-62; feature editor, *African Review* (Accra, Ghana), 1964-66.

*SIDELIGHTS:* By the time she was in her early twenties, Maya Angelou had been a Creole cook, a streetcar conductor, a cocktail waitress, a dancer, a madam, and an unwed mother. The following decades saw her emerge as a successful singer, actress, and playwright, an editor for an English-language magazine in Egypt, a lecturer and civil rights activist, and a popular author of four collections of poetry and five autobiographies. Lynn Z. Bloom in *Dictionary of Literary Biography* wrote that Angelou "is forever impelled by the restlessness for change and new realms to conquer that is the essence of the creative artist, and of exemplary American lives, white and black."

Angelou is hailed as one of the great voices of contemporary black literature and as a remarkable Renaissance woman. She began producing books after some notable friends, including author James Baldwin, heard Angelou's stories of her childhood spent shuttling between rural, segregated Stamps, Arkansas, where her devout grandmother ran a general store, and St. Louis, Missouri, where her worldly, glamorous mother lived. *I Know Why the Caged Bird Sings,* a chronicle of her life up to age sixteen (and ending with the birth of her son, Guy) was published in 1970 with great critical and commercial success. Although many of the stories in the book are grim, as in the author's revelation that she was raped at age eight by her mother's boyfriend, the volume also recounts the self-awakening of the young Angelou. "Her genius as a writer is her ability to recapture the texture of the way of life in the texture of its idioms, its idiosyncratic vocabulary and especially in its process of image-making," reports Sidonie Ann Smith in *Southern Humanities Review.* "The imagery holds the reality, giving it immediacy. That [the author] chooses to recreate the past in its own sounds suggests to the reader that she accepts the past and recognizes its beauty and its ugliness, its assets and its liabilities, its strengths and its weaknesses. Here we witness a return to the final acceptance of the past in the return to and full acceptance of its language, the language a symbolic construct of a way of life. Ultimately Maya Angelou's style testifies to her reaffirmation of self-acceptance, [which] she achieves within the pattern of the autobiography."

Her next two volumes of autobiography, *Gather Together in My Name* and *Singin' and Swingin' and Gettin' Merry Like*

*Christmas,* take Angelou from her late adolescence, when she flirted briefly with prostitution and drug addiction, to her early adulthood as she established a reputation as a performer among the avant-garde of the early 1950s. Not as commercially successful as *I Know Why the Caged Bird Sings,* the two books were guardedly praised by some critics. Lynn Sukenick, for example, remarks in *Village Voice* that *Gather Together in My Name* is "sculpted, concise, rich with flavor and surprises, exuding a natural confidence and command." Sukenick adds, however, that one fault lies "in the tone of the book.... [The author's] refusal to let her earlier self get off easy, and the self-mockery which is her means to honesty, finally becomes in itself a glossing over; although her laughter at herself is witty, intelligent, and a good preventative against maudlin confession, ... it eventually becomes a tic and a substitute for a deeper look." Annie Gottlieb has another view of *Gather Together in My Name.* In her *New York Times Book Review* article, Gottlieb states that Angelou "writes like a song, and like the truth. The wisdom, rue and humor of her storytelling are borne on a lilting rhythm completely her own, the product of a born writer's senses nourished on black church singing and preaching, soft mother talk and salty street talk, and on literature."

The year 1981 brought the publication of *The Heart of a Woman,* a book that "covers one of the most exciting periods in recent African and Afro-American history," according to Adam David Miller in *Black Scholar.* Miller refers to the era of civil rights marches, the emergence of Martin Luther King, Jr., and Malcolm X, and the upheaval in Africa following the assassination of the Congolese statesman Patrice Lumumba. The 1960s see Angelou active in civil rights both in America and abroad; at the same time she enters into a romance with African activist Vusumzi Make, which dissolves when he cannot accept her independence or even promise fidelity. In a *Dictionary of Literary Biography* piece on Angelou, Lynn Z. Bloom considers *The Heart of a Woman* the author's best work since *I Know Why the Caged Bird Sings:* "Her enlarged focus and clear vision transcend the particulars and give this book a fascinating universality of perspective and psychological depth that almost matches the quality of [Angelou's first volume].... Its motifs are commitment and betrayal."

*Washington Post Book World* critic David Levering Lewis also sees a universal message in *The Heart of a Woman.* "Angelou has rearranged, edited, and pointed up her coming of age and going abroad in the world with such just-rightness of timing and inner truthfulness that each of her books is a continuing autobiography of Afro-America. Her ability to shatter the opaque prisms of race and class between reader and subject is her special gift," he says. To Bloom, "it is clear from [this series of autobiographies] that Angelou is in the process of becoming a self-created Everywoman. In a literature and a culture where there are many fewer exemplary lives of women than of men, black or white, Angelou's autobiographical self, as it matures through successive volumes, is gradually assuming that exemplary stature."

In her fifth autobiographical work, *All God's Children Need Traveling Shoes,* Angelou describes her four-year stay in Ghana, "just as that African country had won its independence from European colonials," according to Barbara T. Christian in the *Chicago Tribune Book World.* Christian indicates that Angelou's "sojourn in Africa strengthens her bonds to her ancestral home even as she concretely experiences her distinctiveness as an Afro-American."

*All God's Children Need Traveling Shoes* has also received praise from reviewers. Wanda Coleman in the *Los Angeles Times Book Review* calls it "a thoroughly enjoyable segment from the life of a celebrity," while Christian describes it as "a thoughtful yet spirited account of one Afro-American woman's journey into the land of her ancestors." In Coleman's opinion, *All God's Children Need Traveling Shoes* is "an important document drawing more much needed attention to the hidden history of a people both African and American."

"As [Angelou] adds successive volumes to her life story," writes Bloom, "she is performing for contemporary black American women—and men, too—many of the same functions that escaped slave Frederick Douglass performed for his nineteenth-century peers through his autobiographical writings and lectures. Both became articulators of the nature and validity of a collective heritage as they interpret the particulars of a culture for a wide audience of whites as well as blacks.... As people who have lived varied and vigorous lives, they embody the quintessential experiences of their race and culture."

*I Shall Not Be Moved* is Angelou's fifth collection of poetry. The title is drawn from the poem "Our Grandmothers," in which an elderly woman refuses to be moved from her "heartfelt stand," as Jacqueline Gropman writes in the *School Library Journal.* Angelou "is able to command our ear," declares Gloria T. Hull in *Belles Lettres.* "As I listen, what I hear in her open, colloquial poems is racial wit and earthy wisdom, honest black female pain and strength, humor, passion, and rhetorical force." Other themes include "loss of love and youth, human oneness in diversity, the strength of blacks in the face of racism and adversity," notes a reviewer in *Publishers Weekly.* *Library Journal* contributor Lenard D. Moore judges the poems to be "highly controlled and yet powerful," using language that is "precise and filled with imagery." Gropman concludes that the poems in *I Shall Not Be Moved* "possess the drama of the storyteller and the imagery and soul of the poet."

*BIOGRAPHICAL/CRITICAL SOURCES:*

*BOOKS*

Angelou, Maya, *I Know Why the Caged Bird Sings,* Random House, 1970.

Angelou, *Gather Together in My Name,* Random House, 1974.

Angelou, *Singin' and Swingin' and Gettin' Merry Like Christmas,* Random House, 1976.

Angelou, *The Heart of a Woman,* Random House, 1981.

Angelou, *All God's Children Need Traveling Shoes,* Random House, 1986.

*Contemporary Literary Criticism,* Gale, Volume 12, 1980, Volume 35, 1985.

*Dictionary of Literary Biography,* Volume 38: *Afro-American Writers after 1955: Dramatists and Prose Writers,* Gale, 1985.

*PERIODICALS*

*Belles Lettres,* spring, 1991, pp. 2-4.
*Black Scholar,* summer, 1982.
*Black World,* July, 1975.
*Chicago Tribune,* November 1, 1981.
*Chicago Tribune Book World,* March 23, 1986.
*Detroit Free Press,* May 9, 1986.
*Harper's,* November, 1972.
*Harvard Educational Review,* November, 1970.
*Ladies' Home Journal,* May, 1976.
*Library Journal,* June 1, 1990, p. 132.
*Los Angeles Times,* May 29, 1983.
*Los Angeles Times Book Review,* April 13, 1986; August 9, 1987.
*Ms.,* January, 1977.
*New Republic,* July 6, 1974.
*New Statesman,* September, 15, 1989, p. 37.
*Newsweek,* March 2, 1970.
*New York Times,* February 25, 1970.
*New York Times Book Review,* June 16, 1974.
*Observer* (London), April 1, 1984.
*Parnassus: Poetry in Review,* fall-winter, 1979.
*Poetry,* August, 1976.
*Publishers Weekly,* March 23, 1990, p. 69.
*School Library Journal,* September, 1990, p. 268.
*Southern Humanities Review,* fall, 1973.
*Time,* March 31, 1986.
*Times* (London), September 29, 1986.
*Times Literary Supplement,* February 17, 1974; June 14, 1985; January 24, 1986.
*Village Voice,* July 11, 1974, October 28, 1981.
*Washington Post,* October 13, 1981.
*Washington Post Book World,* October 4, 1981; June 26, 1983; May 11, 1986.

## ANOZIE, Sunday O(gbonna) 1942-

*PERSONAL:* Born in 1942 in Owerri, Nigeria. *Education:* University of Nsukka, B.A., 1963; attended Sorbonne, University of Paris.

*ADDRESSES: Agent*—c/o Evans Brothers Ltd., 2A Portman Mansions, Chiltern St., London W1M 1LE, England.

*CAREER: Conch* (magazine), Paris, France, founder and managing editor, beginning 1969; critic and writer. University of Texas, Austin, visiting professor of English.

*AWARDS, HONORS:* Scholarship from United Nations Educational, Scientific, and Cultural Organization (UNESCO).

*WRITINGS:*

*Sociologie du roman africaine,* Aubier-Montaigne, 1970.
*Christopher Okigbo: Creative Rhetoric,* Africana Publishing, 1972.
*Structural Models and African Poetics: Towards a Pragmatic Theory of Literature,* Routledge & Kegan Paul, 1981.
(Editor) *Phenomenology in Modern African Studies,* Conch Magazine, 1982.

Contributor to *Black Literature and Literary Theory,* edited by Henry Louis Gates, Jr., Methuen, 1984. Contributor to journals, including *Presence Africaine.*

\*   \*   \*

## ANSA, Tina McElroy 1949-

*PERSONAL:* Born November, 18, 1949, in Macon, GA; daughter of Walter J. McElroy (in business) and Nellie McElroy (a teacher's assistant; maiden name, Lee); married Jonee Ansa, May 1, 1978. *Education:* Spelman College, B.A., 1971. *Avocational interests:* Gardening, the environment.

*ADDRESSES: Office*—P.O. Box 20602, St. Simons Island, GA 31522.

*CAREER:* Copy editor, editor, feature writer, and news reporter for Atlanta *Constitution* and *Charlotte Observer;* Clark College, Atlanta, GA, instructor on mass media; Spelman College, Brunswick, GA, writing workshop supervisor.

*MEMBER:* Authors Guild.

*AWARDS, HONORS:* Georgia Authors Series Award, for *Baby of the Family;* American Library Association award for best literature for young adults.

*WRITINGS:*

*Not Soon Forgotten: Cotton Planters and Plantations of the Golden Isles of Georgia, 1784-1812,* Coastal Georgia Historical Society, c. 1987.
*Baby of the Family* (novel), Harcourt, 1989.
*Ugly Ways* (novel), Harcourt, 1993.

Contributor to newspapers, including *New York Newsday, Los Angeles Times Book Review,* and the *Florida Times-Union.*

*WORK IN PROGRESS: The Mulberry Tales,* a collection of short stories; a screenplay version of *Baby of the Family;* another novel set in fictional Mulberry, Georgia.

*SIDELIGHTS:* Georgia native Tina McElroy Ansa is author of the novels *Baby of the Family* and *Ugly Ways. Baby of the Family,* set in the 1950s, tells of a black girl coming of age in a small town in Georgia. The girl, Lena McPherson, is born with a caul on her face, which is believed to be a sign that she possesses special wisdom and the ability to see and talk to ghosts. Lena's mother is too modern to accept her daughter's supposed powers, however, and Lena—who does encounter ghosts—grows up confused and sometimes fearful of her gift. By adolescence, she has generated an aversion toward her special ability, feeling a strong desire to be "normal."

*Baby of the Family* is about more than Lena's second sight, however, and as Deb Robertson explained in *Booklist,* the author manages to interject Lena's magic "without distracting from an otherwise affecting and entertaining tale." "Along the way," observed Nina Burleigh in *Tribune Books,* "Lena discovers all the things children learn whether they are supposed to or not: lessons about the fleeting nature of girlhood friendships, the pleasures of sex, a mother's broken heart, the insidiousness of racism and the effects of alcohol." Commenting on the style of the work, *New York Times Book Review* contributor Valerie Sayers found that "the story has a nubby, homespun texture that is unpretentious and engaging" and that "Ms. Ansa's rich descriptive passages are evocative, often poetic, but they are sometimes broken by unnecessary shifts in point of view or by the sudden interruption of exposition in intense emotional scenes." Sayers concluded that the novel "offers dense rich scenes of black Southern life, scenes deeply felt by the characters who act them out. Tina McElroy Ansa tells a good quirky story, and she tells it with humor, grace and great respect for the power of the particular."

In *Ugly Ways,* the three daughters of Mudear Lovejoy prepare for the funeral of their recently deceased mother, reflecting on their upbringing and how it affected their lives. Reacting to her husband's tyranny, Mudear had abandoned all cooking and cleaning activity when her daughters were young, would only leave her house under the cover of darkness, and

spent her time watching television and ordering her children around. Mudear's daughters find that although their mother's behavior may have impaired their ability to love, they have her to thank for their self-reliance and sense of dignity. Describing the work as "jangling, slightly mystical, [and] extremely feminine," *Booklist* contributor Donna Seaman concluded that Ansa "has once again infused African American family life with a curious sense of magic and destiny."

Ansa commented: "I plan to remain in the little fictional middle Georgia town of Mulberry my entire writing career. It is here, in the heart of the South and the heart of Georgia, I explore the African American family and the African American community of this decade and earlier ones. It is an infinitely fascinating and rich subject.

"In my latest novel, *Ugly Ways,* I try to expand the canvas of American literature to include a mother, a black mother, who challenges the 'conventional wisdom,' the accepted line on what 'mother' is and means in African American culture. To record, examine, and push the parameters of our lives is, I believe, the job and duty of literature."

*BIOGRAPHICAL/CRITICAL SOURCES:*

*PERIODICALS*

*Booklist,* November 1, 1989, p. 524; July, 1993.
*Essence,* March, 1990, p. 48.
*Kirkus Reviews,* September 1, 1989, p. 1265.
*New York Times Book Review,* November 26, 1989, p. 6.
*Publishers Weekly,* September 8, 1989, p. 56.
*Tribune Books* (Chicago), December 24, 1989, p. 5.
*Voice Literary Supplement,* May, 1990, pp. 26-29.

\*    \*    \*

## ANTHONY, Michael 1930-

*PERSONAL:* Born February 10, 1930, in Mayaro, Trinidad and Tobago; son of Nathaniel (a drain-digger) and Eva (Jones) Anthony; married Yvette Francesca (a homemaker), February 8, 1958; children: two sons, two daughters. *Education:* Attended Mayaro Roman Catholic School and Junior Technical School, San Fernando, Trinidad. *Politics:* "Uncategorized."

*ADDRESSES: Home*—99 Long Circular Rd., St. James, Port-of-Spain, Trinidad and Tobago.

*CAREER:* Author and lecturer. Held a number of factory jobs after immigrating to England; Reuters news agency, London,

England, sub-editor, 1964-68; lived in Brazil, 1968-70; *Texas Star,* Texaco Trinidad, Pointe-a-Pierre, Trinidad and Tobago, assistant editor, 1970-72; Ministry of Culture, Port-of-Spain, Trinidad and Tobago, researcher, 1972-88; University of Richmond, Richmond, VA, teacher of creative writing, 1992. Broadcast historical radio programs, 1975-89.

*WRITINGS:*

*The Games Were Coming* (novel), Deutsch, 1963, Houghton, 1968, expanded edition with introduction by Kenneth Ramchand, Heinemann and Deutsch, 1977.

*The Year in San Fernando* (novel), Deutsch, 1965, published with introduction by Paul Edwards and Ramchand, Heinemann, 1970.

*Green Days by the River* (novel), Deutsch, 1965, Houghton, 1967.

*Cricket in the Road, and Other Stories,* Heinemann Educational, 1973.

*Sandra Street, and Other Stories,* Heinemann Educational, 1973.

*Glimpses of Trinidad and Tobago, with a Glance at the West Indies,* Columbus (Trinidad), 1974.

*Profile Trinidad: A Historical Survey from the Discovery to 1900,* Macmillan, 1975.

(Editor with Andrew Carr, and contributor) *David Frost Introduces Trinidad and Tobago,* Deutsch, 1975.

*Streets of Conflict* (novel), Deutsch, 1976.

*Folk Tales and Fantasies* (short stories), illustrated by Pat Chu Foon, Columbus, 1977.

*King of the Masquerade,* Thomas Nelson, 1977.

*The Making of Port-of-Spain, 1757-1939,* Key Caribbean, 1978.

*Bright Road to El Dorado* (novel), Nelson Caribbean, 1981.

*All That Glitters* (novel), Deutsch, 1982.

*Port-of-Spain in a World at War, 1939-1945,* Ministry of Sports, Culture, and Youth Affairs (Port-of-Spain), 1984.

*First in Trinidad,* Circle Press, 1985.

*Heroes of the People of Trinidad and Tobago,* Circle Press, 1986.

(Editor) *The History of Aviation in Trinidad and Tobago, 1913-1962,* Paria, 1987.

*A Better and Brighter Day,* Circle Press, 1987.

*Towns and Villages of Trinidad and Tobago,* Circle Press, 1988.

*Parade of the Carnivals of Trinidad, 1839-1989,* Circle Press, 1989.

*The Golden Quest: The Four Voyages of Christopher Columbus,* Macmillan, 1992.

*The Chieftain's Carnival and Other Stories,* Longman, 1993.

Also contributor to periodicals.

*WORK IN PROGRESS:* A historical dictionary of Trinidad and Tobago, for Scarecrow Press.

*SIDELIGHTS:* Michael Anthony writes apparently simple tales of life on the island of Trinidad that convey deep insights into human relationships. Often told from the viewpoint of a child, these tales also give the reader a taste of Caribbean life. *New York Times* contributor Martin Levin claims, "Mr. Anthony has perfect pitch and an artist's eye for the finer shadings of the native scene he knows so intimately." Writing of Anthony's short story collection *Cricket in the Road* in *Books and Bookmen,* James Brockway finds "an evocative power I have rarely come across, a power drawn not merely from observation, but from observing *the things that matter,* and conveying them in exactly the right words and not a word too many." Brockway concludes, "Mr. Anthony reminds us that there are simpler, more essential things in life than getting and spending and he writes about them with a serenity that can only come from strength."

Daryl Cumber Dance comments in *Fifty Caribbean Writers,* "The genius of Anthony ... is that despite the apparent simplicity of his plot, his stories are narrated with such power that not only does the reader never doubt the significance of whatever seemingly trite experience the protagonist is undergoing, but he is also irresistibly caught up in it." Dance also remarks on Anthony's treatment of women in his novels and short stories. "There are several of the strong, enduring mother figures so familiar in West Indian literature...; but there are also some beautiful young Black women, whom Anthony develops with uncharacteristic sensitivity and empathy.... [T]here is no denying that he has created some memorable and unusual portraits of attractive, often passionate, sometimes surprisingly resilient and resourceful Black women." *Dictionary of Literary Biography* contributor Harold Barratt notes, "One of Anthony's most important contributions to the continuing development of West Indian fiction is his emphasis on strong, dour personalities. The abused or abandoned wives and mothers are particularly tenacious, and many of these women are their families' only bulwark against destitution." Anthony remarked to Dance, "The close family relationships [which appear in my works result from] a little bit of nostalgia because my father died when I was very young. I loved him very much and I really missed the fact that he wasn't there, and I thought that our relationship would have been a very meaningful one, and so I believe that I have projected this into my work."

Barratt described *The Games Were Coming,* the author's first published work, as "one of Anthony's most artistically controlled pieces of fiction." The story follows cyclist Leon Seal as he trains for the Southern Games, eschewing the pleasures of the annual carnival and neglecting his girlfriend. "Leon's rigid discipline sometimes turns him into a callous, rather rebarbative young man;" Barratt remarks, "yet there is something admirable about Leon's unswerving commitment to the rigors of his training.... Self-discipline, the novel implies, is essential for the achievement of excellence." In *The Year in San Fernando,* twelve-year-old Francis must work as a servant and companion for a bitter old woman to pay for his schooling. The year spent in the Chandles household proves to be pivotal in Francis' maturation. *Contemporary Novelists* contributor Jeremy Poynting finds *The Year in San Fernando* "much more than a sensitive novel about growing up" and adds, "none of Anthony's other novels quite achieves the same degree of understated but unflawed art."

Barratt notes that in both *The Year in San Fernando* and *Green Days by the River* "Anthony's skill in exploring a youngster's maturation can be seen at its most consummate." Discussing the protagonist of *Green Days by the River* Barratt comments, "Like Francis in *The Year in San Fernando,* Shellie ... is also receptive to the changing rhythms of his world." The story follows Shellie's friendship with Mr. Gidharee, whose generosity towards the boy turns to violent rage when Shellie seduces Rosalie, Mr. Gidharee's daughter. The *New York Times*'s Levin finds that the author "makes his characters appealing without overly romanticizing them, and his ear for dialogue is magnificently accurate."

"In a more intense way than in any earlier novel, Anthony focuses on a child's attempts to discern whether people are being sincere or false" in *All That Glitters,* Poynting notes. The return of young Horace Lumpers's Aunty Roomeen to his village leads to various lessons for Horace, and he finds that "being an adult means wearing different faces," Poynting observes. The boy's discovery of his talent as a writer brings further complications, which his teacher finally resolves with the advice, "'Make it colourful and vivid—and true' which both Horace and Michael Anthony follow," Poynting concludes.

Anthony once said, "I am essentially a novelist and since I hold that the novel tells a story I feel strongly that I should not use the medium to air my philosophies. However, I feel very strongly about the brotherhood of mankind and as a consequence abominate war. One of my main hopes is that human beings will find a way to live together without friction, and my feeling is that the most distressing thing in this world is the inhumanity of man to man on the grounds of race. I feel that if the racial problem is solved man will have found the key to peace on this planet. Although I am not hopeful about any immediate change in the Southern African situation, I think the thousands of people who are trying to solve the problem in the United States must make a great difference to the basic situation there. Yet, though I feel this way, the books I write have nothing (on the surface) to do with race or war."

Anthony also wrote that he is extremely interested in space exploration "as I sometimes find the mystery of the Universe too much to bear. I often wonder if space exploration will one day explode our present theories about God, and about the origin and formation of the matter about us. I do consider man's quest for knowledge vital and, in fact, inevitable." He also commented that he would "like to see this world of rich and poor nations, powerful and weak nations, superseded by a world of one strong nation formed out of all. In other words I am advocating World Government. I sometimes think that I am merely being idealistic, but being an optimist I am not surprised."

*BIOGRAPHICAL/CRITICAL SOURCES:*

*BOOKS*

*Contemporary Authors Autobiography Series,* Volume 18, Gale, 1993.
*Contemporary Novelists,* fifth edition, St. James Press, 1991, pp. 46-48.
*Dictionary of Literary Biography,* Volume 125: *Twentieth-Century Caribbean and Black African Writers,* Gale, 1993.
*Fifty Caribbean Writers,* Greenwood Press, 1986, pp. 19-25.
Ramchand, Kenneth, *The West Indian Novel and Its Background,* Faber, 1970.

*PERIODICALS*

*Books and Bookmen,* February, 1974.
*London Magazine,* April, 1967.
*New York Times Book Review,* August 6, 1967; April 14, 1968.
*Observer,* July 26, 1981.
*Punch,* February 22, 1967.
*Spectator,* February 21, 1976.
*Times Literary Supplement,* March 4, 1965; April 13, 1967.
*World Literature Today,* spring, 1984.
*World Press Review,* January, 1987, p. 62.

\*    \*    \*

## APPIAH, (K.) Anthony 1954-

*PERSONAL:* Born May 8, 1954, in London, England; son of Joseph Emmanuel (a lawyer, diplomat, and politician) and Enid Margaret (an art historian and writer; maiden name, Cripps) Appiah. *Education:* Clare College, Cambridge, B.A., 1975, M.A., 1980, Ph.D., 1982. *Politics:* "Complicated." *Religion:* None. *Avocational interests:* Music, reading.

*ADDRESSES: Office*—Department of African American Studies, Harvard University, 1430 Massachusetts Ave., Cambridge, MA 02138. *Agent*—Carl D. Brandt, Brandt & Brandt, 1501 Broadway, New York, NY 10036.

*CAREER:* University of Ghana, Legon, teaching assistant, 1975-76; Yale University, New Haven, CT, visiting fellow, 1979, assistant professor, became associate professor of philosophy, 1981-86; Cornell University, Ithaca, NY, associate professor, 1986-89, professor of philosophy, 1989; Duke University, Durham, NC, professor of philosophy and literature, 1990-91; Harvard University, Cambridge, MA, professor of African American studies, 1991—. Cambridge University, visiting fellow of Clare College, 1983-84. Social Science Research Council and American Council of Learned Societies, chair of Joint Committee on African Studies, 1991—. Boston Algebra in the Middle Schools, member of community board; Facing History, member of advisory board; consultant to International Labor Organization.

*MEMBER:* Society for African Philosophy in North America (founding member; president, 1991-92), African Literature Association, American Philosophical Association, Aristotelian Society, Modern Language Association of America, English Institute.

*AWARDS, HONORS:* Morse fellow, 1983-84; Woodrow Wilson fellow at Florida A & M University, 1989, and Dillard University, 1991; Andrew W. Mellon fellow, National Humanities Center, 1990-91; honorary degree, Harvard University, 1991.

*WRITINGS:*

*Assertion and Conditionals,* Cambridge University Press, 1985.
*For Truth in Semantics,* Basil Blackwell, 1986.
*Necessary Questions: An Introduction to Philosophy,* Prentice-Hall, 1989.
(Editor and author of introduction) *Early African-American Classics,* Bantam, 1990.
*Avenging Angel* (novel), Constable, 1990, St. Martin's, 1991.
*In My Father's House: Africa in the Philosophy of Culture,* Oxford University Press, 1992.

Contributor to periodicals. Editor, with Henry L. Gates, Jr., of "Amistad Critical Studies in African American Literature" series, 1993. Guest co-editor, *Critical Inquiry,* Volume XVIII, number 4; assistant editor, *Theoria to Theory,* 1974-79; associate editor, *Philosophical Review,* 1987-89; editor, *Transition,* 1991—. Member of editorial board, *Universitas,* 1976, *Perspectives in Auditing and Information Systems,* 1986—, *Diacritics,* 1987—, *Common Knowledge,* 1990—, and *GLQ: A Journal of Lesbian and Gay Studies,* 1992—; member of editorial collective, *Public Culture,* 1989—; member of editorial advisory board, *Callaloo,* 1990—.

*WORK IN PROGRESS: The Oxford Book of African Literature,* for Oxford University Press; *A Dictionary of Global Literacy,* with Henry L. Gates, Jr., Knopf; *Bu Me Be: The Proverbs of the Akan,* with mother Enid Margaret Appiah and others; *Tolerable Falsehoods: Idealization and Human Understanding; Nobody Loves Letitia: A Patrick Scott Mystery;* research on multiculturalism, the significance of race, idealization in the social sciences, and the African novel.

*SIDELIGHTS:* Anthony Appiah commented: "In the preface to *In My Father's House,* I wrote: 'My first memories are of a place called Mbrom, a small neighborhood in Kumasi, capital of Asante, as that kingdom turned from being part of the British Gold Coast colony to being a region of the Republic of Ghana.... We went from time to time to my mother's native country, to England, to stay with my grandmother in the rural West Country ... and the life there ... seems, at least now, to have been mostly not too different.' Later I took degrees in philosophy at Cambridge and came to the United States in the early eighties to teach philosophy and African-American studies.

"All of this is relevant because, though I write—and enjoy writing—about many things, most of my publications have grown out of my philosophical training, my upbringing in Europe and in Africa, my explorations of African-American culture and history, and my love of reading. (Professors of literature these days are supposed to hide their enjoyment of fiction. I'm a philosopher, so I don't have to be coy.)

"My first publications, outside school magazines and newspapers, were poems, published privately in the 1970s by my mother, in a volume of family poetry for my grandmother. I was in my early twenties, and I was thrilled. Then came a long hiatus, in which I published only reviews and set about the life of a graduate student. (It is an axiom of graduate student life that one avoids writing at all costs.) Only with the pressure created by the imminence of my first 'proper' job and the refusal of my graduate adviser to grant me more extensions, did I finally settle down to write a dissertation.

"I've now published my first novel, a mystery set at Cambridge University, titled *Avenging Angel.* Another, set this time on a Scottish island, rather like one I used to visit, is on the way. The mystery is a wonderful genre for an academic dabbler."

\*   \*   \*

## ARCHER, Chalmers, Jr. 1938-

*PERSONAL:* Born April 21, 1938, in Tchula, MS; son of Chalmers and Eva (an educator; maiden name, Ratharford)

Archer. *Education:* Saints Junior College, A.A., 1969; Tuskegee Institute, B.S., 1971, M.Ed., 1972; Auburn University, Ph.D., 1979; University of Alabama, Postdoctoral Certificate in Research and Statistics, 1980; Massachusetts Institute of Technology, Certificate, 1982. *Politics:* Democrat. *Religion:* Baptist. *Avocational interests:* Gardening, exercise, reading.

*ADDRESSES: Home*—4522 Commons Dr., No. 40, Annandale, VA 22003-4959. *Office*—Office of the Director of Financial Aid, Northern Virginia Community College, Alexandria Campus, 3001 North Beauregard St., Alexandria, VA 22311.

*CAREER:* Saints Junior College, Lexington, MS, assistant to the president and registrar, 1968-70; Tuskegee Institute, Tuskegee Institute, AL, career and placement counselor and coordinator of cooperative program, 1972-74, assistant dean for admissions and records, 1974-76, assistant to the vice-president for administration, 1976-79, associate dean for admissions and records and assistant professor of educational administration and counseling, 1979-83; Northern Virginia Community College, coordinator of admissions and records at Annandale Campus, 1983-85, director of financial aid at Alexandria Campus, 1985—. Cambridge University, lecturer, 1988-89. National Consortium for the Recruitment of Black Students from Northern Cities, past chair and member of board of directors; Alabama State Steering Committee for Advanced Placement of High School Students, past chair. *Military service:* U.S. Army, Airborne, General Military Administration, and Special Forces (Green Berets), served for ten years; became captain.

*MEMBER:* National Association of College Deans, Registrars, and Admissions Officers, American Association of Collegiate Registrars and Admissions Officers, American Personnel and Guidance Association, American Association of University Professors, Southeastern Association of Community Colleges, Phi Delta Kappa, Kappa Delta Pi, National Association for the Advancement of Colored People, Kiwanis International (charter member of Macon College chapter), Saints Junior College Alumni Association (vice president).

*AWARDS, HONORS:* H.D.L., Saints Junior College, 1970; Award for Leadership, Phi Delta Kappa, 1981.

*WRITINGS:*

*Growing up Black in Rural Mississippi: Memoirs of a Family, Heritage of a Place,* Walker and Co., 1992.

Author of a weekly newspaper column. Contributing editor, *Jackson Advocate.*

*WORK IN PROGRESS:* Research on "getting an education in rural Mississippi during separate but unequal times."

\*   \*   \*

## ASANTE, Molefi Kete 1942-
### (Arthur L[ee] Smith)

*PERSONAL:* Original name, Arthur Lee Smith, Jr.; name legally changed in 1975; born August 14, 1942, in Valdosta, GA; son of Arthur L. and Lillie (Wilkson) Smith; married second wife, Kariamu Welsh; children: Kasina Eka, Daahoud Ali, Molefi Khumalo. *Education:* Southwestern Christian College, A.A., 1962; Oklahoma Christian College, B.A. (cum laude), 1964; Pepperdine College (now Pepperdine University), M.A., 1965; University of California, Los Angeles, Ph.D., 1968. *Religion:* Ancestralism.

*ADDRESSES: Home*—707 Medary Ave., Philadelphia, PA 19126. *Office*—Department of African American Studies, Gladfelter Hall 025-26, Temple University, Philadelphia, PA 19122.

*CAREER:* California State Polytechnic College (now California State Polytechnic University), Pomona, instructor, 1966-67; San Fernando Valley State College (now California State University, Northridge), instructor, 1967; Purdue University, Lafayette, IN, assistant professor of communication, 1968-69; University of California, Los Angeles, assistant professor, 1969-70, associate professor of speech, 1971-73, director of Center for Afro-American Studies, 1970-73; State University of New York at Buffalo, professor of communication, beginning in 1973, chair of department, 1973-79. Howard University, Washington, DC, visiting professor, 1979-80; Fulbright professor, Zimbabwe Institute of Mass Communication, 1981-82; Temple University, Philadelphia, PA, professor and chair of African American Studies. Indiana State Civil Rights Commission on Higher Education and the Afro-American, chair, 1968-69. Member of selection committee, Martin Luther King and Woodrow Wilson fellowships, 1970-72; member of advisory board, *Black Law Journal,* 1971-73, and *Race Relations Abstract,* 1973-76.

*MEMBER:* International Communication Association, International Association for Symbolic Analysis, International Society for General Semantics, National Association for Dramatic and Speech Art, National Afrocentric Institute, Speech Communication Association (member of legislative assembly, 1971-73), African Studies Association, African Heritage Studies Association, Society for Intercultural Education, Training and Research, Western Speech Association, Central State Speech Association, Southern Speech Association, Institute of Black Peoples, African Continental University, Ouagadougou, Anyabwile Angaza.

*AWARDS, HONORS:* Christian Education Guild Writer's Award, 1965; L.H.D., University of New Haven, 1976; named Outstanding Community Scholar, Jackson State University, 1980; L.H.D., Sojourner-Douglass College, 1989; National Council of Black Studies, outstanding scholar, 1990; Pan-African Society Excellence Award, 1992.

*WRITINGS:*

*African and Afro-American Communication Continuities,* State University of New York at Buffalo Center for International Affairs, 1975.

(With Eileen Newmark) *Intercultural Communication: Theory Into Practice,* Speech Communication Association, 1976.

(With J. Frye) *Contemporary Public Communication,* Harper, 1976.

(Editor with Mary B. Cassata) *The Social Uses of Mass Communication,* Communication Research Center, State University of New York at Buffalo, 1977.

(With Jerry K. Frye) *Contemporary Public Communication: Applications,* Harper, 1977.

(With Cassata) *Mass Communication: Principles and Practices,* Macmillan, 1979.

(With Kariamu Welsh) *A Guide to African and African American Art and Antiquities,* Museum of African and African American Art, 1979.

(Editor with Eileen Newmark and Cecil A. Blake) *Handbook of Intercultural Communication,* Sage Publications, 1979.

*Afrocentricity: The Theory of Social Change,* Amulefi, 1980, third edition, Africa World Press, 1987.

(Editor with Abdulai S. Vandi) *Contemporary Black Thought: Alternative Analyses in Social and Behavioral Science,* Sage Publications, 1980.

*Research in Mass Communication: Guide to Practice,* Zimbabwe Institute of Mass Communication, 1982.

*African Myths: New Frames of Reference,* Zimbabwe Institute of Mass Communications, 1982.

(With others) *Media Training Needs in Zimbabwe,* Mass Media Trust and Friedrich Naumann Foundation, 1982.

(Editor with Kariamu Welsh Asante) *African Culture: The Rhythms of Unity,* Greenwood Press, 1985.

*The Afrocentric Idea,* Temple University Press, 1987.

*Umfundalai: Afrocentric Rite of Passage,* National Afrocentric Institute, 1989.

(Editor with William B. Gudykunst and Eileen Newmark) *Handbook of Intercultural and International Communication,* Sage Publications, 1989.

*Kemet, Afrocentricity, and Knowledge,* Africa World Press, 1990.

(With Mark Mattson) *Historical and Cultural Atlas of African Americans,* Macmillan, 1991.

*The Book of African Names,* Africa World Press, 1991.

(With Dhyana Ziegler) *Thunder and Silence: The Mass Media in Africa,* Africa World Press, 1991.

*Classical Africa,* Peoples Publishing, 1993.

*Malcolm X as Cultural Hero and Other Afrocentric Essays,* Africa World Press, 1993.

*Fury in the Wilderness,* Scribner, 1994.

(Editor with Abu Abarry) *The Sources of the African Tradition,* Temple University Press, 1994.

*UNDER NAME ARTHUR L. SMITH*

*The Break of Dawn* (poetry), Dorrance, 1964.

*Rhetoric of Black Revolution,* Allyn and Bacon, 1969.

(With Andrea Rich) *Rhetoric of Revolution: Samuel Adams, Emma Goldman, Malcolm X,* Moore Publishing, 1970.

*Toward Transracial Communication,* Afro-American Studies Center, University of California, Los Angeles, 1970.

(Editor with Stephen Robb) *The Voice of Black Rhetoric,* Allyn and Bacon, 1971.

(With Anne Allen and Deluvina Hernandez) *How to Talk with People of Other Races, Ethnic Groups, and Cultures,* Transcultural Educational Foundation, 1971.

*Language, Communication and Rhetoric in Black America,* Harper, 1972.

*Transracial Communication,* Prentice-Hall, 1973.

*OTHER*

Also author of *Mfecane* (a novel), 1984. Author of foreword, *The Nubian,* by Duane Smith, Azimuth Press, 1992. Contributor to numerous books and periodicals. Associate editor of *Nigerian Journal of Political Economy, Afrodiaspora, Afrique Histoire, Africa and the World, Urban African Quarterly,* and *Journal of African Civilization.* Member of board of editors, "Black Men in America" reprint series, 1969-70; founding editor, *Journal of Black Studies,* 1969—; editorial associate, *Speech Teacher,* 1970-73; contributing editor, *Encore,* 1970-72; book reviewer, *Journal of Communication,* 1970-72. Reviewer for scholarly books, *UNESCO,* 1985.

*SIDELIGHTS:* Molefi Kete Asante is known for his specialization in intercultural communication, both as an instructor and a writer. A proponent of the Afrocentric philosophy that focuses on the importance of African people as agents of history and culture. "Asante seeks pluralism without hierarchy," explained Alex Boyd and Catherine J. Lenix-Hooker in the *Library Journal.* Asante believes that "Afrocentrism should take its place not above but alongside other cultural and historical perspectives." Many of Asante's books concentrate on communication and Afrocentricity, and provide reference sources on the historical contributions made by people of African descent.

Asante's 1987 title, *The Afrocentric Idea,* is an exploration of the concept that cultural ethics originating in Africa have a direct effect on speech and behavior in black communities in the Western Hemisphere. Aware of the way in which speech has at times been used to perpetuate racial division, "Asante stresses the significance of rhetoric and rhythm in black life," according to Andrew Hacker in the *New York Review of Books.* Asante also emphasizes the prominence in black culture of oral dialogue over the written word. Moreover, the heritage of African Americans is manifest in the achievements of African Americans in music and sports, according to Asante. Some reviewers, such as Hacker, noted that "Asante's attempts to show that their talents derive from African culture are certainly suggestive." But "the problem is that this African emphasis supports a more insidious aspect of white racism," by not emphasizing more intellectual achievements. However, Melvin Dixon in the *New York Times Book Review* added that Asante makes the Afrocentric perspective and ideal crucial not only to an enriched awareness but also to any noteworthy analysis of the lives of blacks. Dixon concluded that "Asante's discussion ends by promoting spiritual balance as the key to an Afrocentric ideal in America. Such balance is crucial to our African-American identity; neither Africa nor Europe *alone* provides sufficient scope for our collective experience."

Asante's *Historical and Cultural Atlas of African Americans,* published in 1991, is a chronological history presenting experiences from African origins to the present day, illustrated with maps by cartographer Mark T. Mattson. In the book, Asante provides several resources for the reader, including charts, lists of important dates to remember, statistical data, highlights of selected events, brief biographies of important people, and a practical atlas format. R. C. Dickey in *Choice* described Asante's *Historical and Cultural Atlas of African Americans* as a "helpful overall view of black American history."

*BIOGRAPHICAL/CRITICAL SOURCES:*

*PERIODICALS*

*Choice,* September, 1991, p. 51.
*Library Journal,* July, 1991, p. 86; November 1, 1992, pp. 46-49.
*New York Review of Books,* March 3, 1988, pp. 36-41.
*New York Times Book Review,* January 7, 1990, p. 35.
*Wilson Library Bulletin,* September, 1991, pp. 123-24.

\*    \*    \*

**ASARE, Bediako**
  **See KONADU, S(amuel) A(sare)**

## ASHE, Arthur (Robert, Jr.)   1943-1993

*PERSONAL:* Born July 10, 1943, in Richmond, VA; died of pneumonia, February 6, 1993, in Richmond, VA; son of Arthur Robert, Sr. (a park superintendent) and Mattie (Cunningham) Ashe; married Jeanne-Marie Moutoussamy (a photographer), February 20, 1977; children: Camera Elizabeth. *Education:* University of California, Los Angeles, B.S., 1966.

*CAREER:* Amateur tennis player, 1958-69; professional tennis player, 1969-80. U.S. Davis Cup Tennis Team, member, beginning 1963. Played in numerous tennis championships, including National Indoor Junior Tennis Championship, 1960 and 1961; U.S. Men's Hard Court Championship, 1963; U.S. intercollegiate championships, 1965; U.S. Men's Clay Court Championship, 1967; U.S. Amateur Title, 1968; U.S. Open Championship, 1968; Australian Open Championship, 1970; and Wimbledon Singles Championship, 1975. President of Players Enterprises, Inc., beginning in 1969; lecturer and writer. American Broadcasting Company (ABC) Sports and Home Box Office (HBO), correspondent; Le Coq Sportif, vice-president; Doral Resort and Country Club, Miami, FL, tennis director. National campaign chair, American Heart Association, 1981-82; member of board of directors, Aetna Life and Casualty; chair of advisory staff, Head Sports. *Military service:* U.S. Army, 1967-69; became first lieutenant.

*AWARDS, HONORS:* Named Player of the Year, Association of Tennis Profiles, 1975; inducted into the International Tennis Hall of Fame, 1985; Sportsman of the Year, *Sports Illustrated,* 1992; honorary doctorates from Princeton University, Dartmouth College, Le Moyne University, Virginia Commonwealth University, Bryant College, and Trinity University.

*WRITINGS:*

(With Clifford G. Gewecke, Jr.) *Advantage Ashe* (autobiography), Coward, 1967.
(With Frank Deford) *Arthur Ashe: Portrait in Motion* (autobiography), Houghton, 1975.
(With Louie Robinson, Jr.) *Getting Started in Tennis,* photographs by wife, Jeanne Moutoussamy, Atheneum, 1977.
*Mastering Your Tennis Strokes,* Macmillan, 1978.
(With Neil Amdur) *Off the Court* (autobiography), New American Library, 1981.
*Arthur Ashe's Tennis Clinic,* Simon & Schuster, 1981.
(With Kip Branch, Ocania Chalk, and Francis Harris) *A Hard Road to Glory: A History of the African-American Athlete,* 3 volumes, Warner, 1988.
(With Arnold Rampersad) *Days of Grace: A Memoir,* Knopf, 1993.

Contributor to newspapers and magazines, including the *New*

*York Times, Tennis Magazine, Washington Post,* and *People.*
Author, with Stan Smith and Vic Braden, of video "Tennis
Our Way," 1986.

*ADAPTATIONS: A Hard Road to Glory* has been adapted for
television.

*SIDELIGHTS:* "It's not merely because he is the only black
male thus far to achieve superstardom in professional tennis
that Arthur Ashe stands out from the crowd," says Jonathan
Yardley in *Sports Illustrated.* "It's also because he is one of
the few genuinely multidimensional individuals ever to
achieve superstardom in any sport." Indeed, Ashe's life and
career provided material enough to fill a number of biographies and autobiographies. After working his way through the
amateur and professional tennis circuits during the 1960s and
1970s, Ashe attained worldwide acclaim in his 1975 Wimbledon singles triumph over Jimmy Connors.

Tennis was Ashe's top priority from an early age. As the son
of a playground superintendent in then-segregated Richmond,
Virginia, Ashe showed promise in tennis by age seven. A few
years later, he studied the game under the tutelage of Robert
Walter Johnson, a black physician who dedicated himself to
developing young black tennis players in an era when the sport
was the bastion of upper-class whites.

In his writings, Ashe often mentioned the admiration he had
for Johnson and discussed the racism black athletes encountered before the days of the civil rights movement. Although
he was a top-ranked teenage player, for example, Ashe was
barred from some tennis clubs when he toured. Later, as a
member of the University of California, Los Angeles tennis
team, Ashe alone was excluded from the team's invitation to
compete at an exclusive country club tournament. But, far
from openly retaliating, Ashe demonstrated a grace under
pressure and a sense of self-control that he attributed to
Johnson's training.

In 1979 Ashe was a member of the Davis Cup team and ranked
as one of America's leading players when, after returning from
a tournament, he began experiencing chest pains that culminated in a heart attack. He underwent quadruple bypass surgery and then endured a slow, but steady, recovery. While high
blood pressure and heart disease run in Ashe's family, the
athlete admitted that he thought himself immune to their effects. "Why should I have worried?" Ashe remarked in an
interview with Judy Kessler and Allan Ripp of *People* magazine. "My blood pressure and cholesterol are low, I don't
smoke or take drugs, and with all the tennis I play, I'm as
physically fit as a 36-year-old man can be. People like me
simply don't get heart attacks." As Ashe later explained to
Richard K. Rein in *People,* "One thing I've learned is that it's
not so much the heart attack that kills most people, though

there are a few who die on the spot. Most people die because
they deny it; they say it's indigestion or heartburn. A heart
attack is not something that goes click, boom. A heart attack
can occur in a few minutes or over a period of days. If we could
just get people not to go through the denial stage, then we
would save even more lives." The incident ended Ashe's professional tennis career, but he remained active in the sport,
serving as captain of the Davis Cup team. Ashe also became
campaign chair of the American Heart Association. "There's
a hell of a lot I can do," he told Kessler and Ripp in *People.* "I
am a determined person. I expect to live a long time."

Ashe discovered writing as therapy after his second coronary
bypass surgery in 1983, when he began *A Hard Road to Glory: A History of the African-American Athlete.* Spanning the
years from 1619 to 1986, the three-volume history focuses on
black athletes and their struggles to overcome prejudice as they
excelled in their sport. Alex Ward in the *New York Times Book
Review* relates that when Ashe began his research, "he was
astounded to discover that there was only a single 'comprehensive' volume on the history of American black athletes....
So for the next five years [Ashe] worked to fill that void."
Athletes featured include Joe Louis, Jack Johnson, Wilma
Rudolph, Kenny Washington, Jackie Robinson, and Willie
Mays. "The project," Ashe told the *Chicago Tribune,* "brought
both sides of me, the bookish and the sports-minded, togeth-
er." *A Hard Road to Glory* met with critical acclaim and earned
Ashe a great number of honorary degrees from colleges and
universities throughout the nation.

It is ironic that the very medical procedure that saved Ashe's
life after his heart attack, a blood transfusion, would also cause
his later demise. Well aware of the social stigma attached to
contracting the Acquired Immune Deficiency Syndrome
(AIDS) virus, Ashe kept his secret until a news reporter confronted him on April 7, 1992, for confirmation. Christopher
Lehman-Haupt reports in the *New York Times* that Ashe argued vehemently for his right to privacy, but when he realized that the newspaper would not honor his request, he called
a press conference to announce that he had contracted AIDS
through a blood transfusion after heart surgery in 1983. Ashe
was concerned about his reputation and wanted the public to
know that he had contacted AIDS not through moral turpi-
tude or irresponsible behavior but through a medical procedure. He explained in his autobiography *Days of Grace: A
Memoir:* "Did I feel a sense of shame, however subdued, about
having AIDS, although I was guilty of nothing in contracting
it? Very little. I could not shake off completely that irrational
sense of guilt ... to recognize that it was based on nothing substantial." Ashe's reflections on his life include self-recrimi-
nations for not having done or said enough on the issues of
race and racism, an examination of his shortcomings, and a
reprimand to basketball superstar Earvin (Magic) Johnson for
neglecting the importance of "religion and morality" in dis-

cussions on the prevention of AIDS. Equally important to Ashe during his last days were the quiet moments when he "centered down," a phrase taken from Howard Thurman, an admired theologian. During these times, Ashe cherished music, memories, contemplation on the Bible, and reading. Usually not prone to emotional exuberance, Ashe broke his usual pattern of restraint in the last chapter of his memoir, an open letter to his daughter, Camera.

Ashe, the first black man to win at Wimbledon and the first to be inducted into the International Tennis Hall of Fame, was a successful writer, lecturer, and a spokesperson for equality. Described as "the very personification of the educated gentleman-athlete" by *Contemporary Black Biography,* he was eulogized by Paul A. Witteman in *Time* as a gentle man, "a paradigm of understated reason and elegance" and "a man of fire and grace."

*BIOGRAPHICAL/CRITICAL SOURCES:*

*BOOKS*

Ashe, Arthur, and Clifford G. Gwecke, Jr., *Advantage Ashe,* Coward, 1967.
Ashe, Arthur, and Frank Deford, *Arthur Ashe: Portrait in Motion,* Houghton, 1975.
Ashe, Arthur, and Arnold Rampersad, *Days of Grace: A Memoir,* Knopf, 1993.
Ashe, Arthur, and Neil Amdur, *Off the Court,* New American Library, 1981.
*Contemporary Black Biography: Profiles from the International Black Community,* volume 1, Gale, 1992.
McPhee, John, *Levels of the Game,* Farrar, Straus, 1969.
Robinson, Louie, Jr., *Arthur Ashe: Tennis Champion,* Doubleday, 1970.

*PERIODICALS*

*Chicago Tribune,* November 28, 1988, p. 3.
*Ebony,* November, 1979.
*Life,* October 15, 1965.
*Newsday,* February 12, 1991.
*Newsweek,* September 7, 1964.
*New Yorker,* June 7, 1969; June 14, 1969; October 13, 1975.
*New York Times,* July, 1985.
*New York Times Book Review,* June 1, 1975; November 22, 1981; December 4, 1988, pp. 11, 46.
*People,* March 12, 1979; March 6, 1989.
*Sports Illustrated,* September 20, 1965; August 29, 1966.
*Time,* August 13, 1965; July 14, 1975.
*Times Literary Supplement,* July 1, 1977.
*Village Voice,* January 6, 1982.
*Wichita Eagle,* February 21, 1990.
*World Tennis,* December, 1980.

*OBITUARIES:*

*PERIODICALS*

*New York Times,* June 10, 1993, p. B2.
*Time,* February 15, 1993, p. 70.

\*   \*   \*

## ATTAWAY, William (Alexander)   1911-1986

*PERSONAL:* Born November 19, 1911, in Greenville, MS; died of heart failure, June 17, 1986, in Los Angeles, CA; son of William S. (a physician) and Florence Parry (a schoolteacher) Attaway; married Frances Settele, December 28, 1962; children: a son and a daughter. *Education:* University of Illinois, B.A., 1936.

*CAREER:* Novelist, playwright, screenwriter, and songwriter. Worked briefly as a seaman, salesman, labor organizer, and actor, touring in *You Can't Take It With You.* Writer and consultant for film industry.

*WRITINGS:*

*Carnival* (play), produced at University of Illinois, Urbana, 1935.
*Let Me Breathe Thunder* (novel), Doubleday, 1939.
*Blood on the Forge* (novel), Doubleday, 1941.
*Hear America Singing,* Lion, 1967.

Contributing editor, *Calypso Song Book,* McGraw-Hill, 1957. Contributor to periodicals, including *Challenge* and *Tiger's Eye.* Arranger of songs for Harry Belafonte. Scriptwriter of *One Hundred Years of Laughter,* American Broadcasting Company (ABC-TV), 1967.

*SIDELIGHTS:* Despite the versatility demonstrated by his career, William Attaway is remembered primarily as a chronicler of the great migration of black Americans from the South to the industrial North during the 1920s and 1930s. This characterization of his writing is based on his second and last novel, *Blood on the Forge,* published in 1941. Attaway's abandonment of this promising genre at age 30 led to a distinguished career as a composer and arranger and a television and film writer.

Attaway moved with his parents from Greenville, Mississippi, to Chicago, Illinois, when he was about 10 years old, and attended public schools in that city. His father and mother, a physician and schoolteacher respectively, wanted him to enter a profession. Instead he decided to become an auto mechanic and attended a vocational high school. But his heart changed when a teacher introduced him to the work of Langston Hughes. Influenced by both the poetry and his sister, Broadway actress Ruth Attaway, the youngster began to write plays and short stories while still in secondary school.

His parents persuaded him to enroll at the University of Illinois in Urbana, but he dropped out after the death of his father and traveled as a hobo for two years. He worked at a series of jobs—seaman, salesman and labor organizer—before returning to the university. There his play *Carnival* was produced in 1935, and he was graduated in 1936. During this time Attaway befriended Richard Wright, whose popular success with *Native Son* would later eclipse that of Attaway's novels.

After receiving his B.A. degree, Attaway moved to New York City where, at 25, he wrote his first novel, *Let Me Breathe Thunder.* He worked at a string of odd jobs while writing, and was touring in George S. Kaufman and Moss Hart's *You Can't Take It With You* when he received word that the novel would be published. Attaway abandoned acting and began his second novel with the help of a grant from the Julius Rosenwald Fund.

*Let Me Breathe Thunder* is the story of two white hoboes, Ed and Step, who take under their wing an innocent Mexican boy who joins the men in their wanderings. Stanley Young in the *New York Times* writes: "All the emotions of the book are direct and primitive, and the bareness of the speech cuts the action to lean and powerful lines." Young compared the story and characters to American novelist John Steinbeck's *Of Mice and Men;* other reviewers compared Attaway's style to that of American author Ernest Hemingway.

The central event of *Let Me Breathe Thunder* is the tragic corruption of the young waif, Hi-Boy, by the two jaded older men. Although the men have a tender love for the boy, the starkness of the world they all inhabit is played out in the relationships among the trio. Step takes Hi-Boy to a prostitute, and during this visit, to prove his courage to the older man, Hi-Boy stabs himself in the hand. The wound ultimately kills him, but not before his moral downfall at a ranch, where he shoots animals and lies to cover up Step's seduction of a young woman. The novel is replete with Biblical metaphor, as in Hi-Boy's hand wound and the setting of apple orchards at the ranch.

Attaway's second novel, like his first, is based on personal experience. *Blood on the Forge* is the story of three black brothers, Big Mat, Chinatown, and Melody Moss, who are sharecroppers in Kentucky until Big Mat badly beats a white overseer for insulting his mother. The three men are forced to accept an offer to travel in a sealed boxcar to a Pennsylvania steel mill, where their attempts to build new lives fail tragi-

cally. Attaway addressed not only obstacles faced by blacks in the South and North, but a tapestry of dilemmas created by the ripening industrial age: Early struggles to organize labor, the uneasy mixture of Irish, Italian and Eastern European immigrants, and the spiritual damage done to men made to work like machines.

The sharply drawn characters of the brothers illustrate three aspects of the human soul, three ways of responding to the uprooting and loss of family which were common in the 1930s. Melody symbolizes the artist, with his love of blues guitar. Chinatown loves pleasure; his greatest pride is his own gold tooth. Big Mat is a man torn from the outset. He is deeply religious, an assiduous student of the Bible who hopes to become a preacher someday. But his wife Hattie's six miscarriages, together with the destruction wreaked by this new, rootless life, gnaw at him.

The noise of the steel mill renders mute the strings of Melody's guitar, and he falls in love with a young Mexican-American prostitute named Anna. But she is drawn instead to Mat, whose strength at a dog fight brawl saved her from harm. Mat, having learned from afar that Hattie lost her seventh baby, gives up on his dream of sending for her to join him, and he moves in with Anna. He begins to erupt in random anger, beating Anna severely, and he is arrested for the attempted murder of a man. Melody badly damages his hand in an accident, and an explosion which kills several other workers blinds Chinatown.

The town is troubled by mounting racial tensions. White union workers are threatening to strike. Steel bosses pit one man against another by preparing to bring in more southern black men, who will work for cheaper wages. In this milieu, the final tragedies of the three brothers unfold.

Attaway's second novel was even more lauded than his first. Wrote critic Milton Rugoff in the *New York Herald Tribune Books:* "[Attaway] writes of the frustration and suffering of his people and does so with crude power and naked intensity." Drake de Kay of the *New York Times Book Review* similarly praised the work of this 29-year-old author: "[*Blood on the Forge*] is a starkly realistic story involving social criticism as searching as any to be found in contemporary literature."

Literary commentators speculate on why Attaway never wrote another novel. Despite the acclaim of reviewers and their anticipation of his next book, *Blood on the Forge* did not sell many copies. In a twist of irony, his success may have been eclipsed by that of his friend Wright. Wright's novel, *Native Son,* published just one year before *Blood on the Forge,* met with both critical and popular success. Some speculate that mainstream America may have been prepared at that time for only one black novelist to burst on the scene.

When *Blood on the Forge* was reprinted in 1969, the country, now widely examining its own relentless racism, was perhaps more prepared to receive it. Cynthia Hamilton wrote in *Black American Literature Forum:* "*Blood on the Forge* is a masterpiece of social analysis." The complexity of Attaway's characters and their story have stood up well to the passage of half a century since its initial publication.

Attaway's two later books were both about music. *Calypso Song Book* was a collection of songs published in 1957, and *Hear America Singing* describes for young readers the history of American popular music. In addition, Attaway composed songs and arranged tunes for his friend, Harry Belafonte.

Attaway took time out from his writing career to march for African American voting rights in Selma, Alabama, in 1965. Among other projects, he subsequently completed *One Hundred Years of Laughter,* a special on the comedy of blacks which aired on ABC-TV in 1967. Attaway was engaged by the producers of *The Man,* the film based on Irving Wallace's novel about a senator who becomes the first black president of the United States. But the script was deemed too rough and Attaway was released from the project, with Rod Serling receiving credit on the final screenplay.

After living for a decade with his family in Barbados, Attaway returned to California where he continued to write scripts for film, radio, and television. He was writing *The Atlanta Child Murders* script when he suffered a heart attack which resulted in his death in Los Angeles, California, on June 17, 1986.

*BIOGRAPHICAL/CRITICAL SOURCES:*

*BOOKS*

*Black Literature Criticism,* Volume 1, Gale, 1992.
*Dictionary of Literary Biography,* Volume 76: *Afro-American Writers, 1940-1955,* Gale, 1988.
Margolies, Edward, *Native Sons: A Critical Study of Twentieth-Century Negro American Authors,* Lippincott, 1968.
Young, James O., *Black Writers of the Thirties,* Louisiana State University Press, 1973.

*PERIODICALS*

*Black American Literature Forum,* spring-summer, 1987, pp. 147-63.
*CLA Journal,* June, 1972, pp. 459-64.
*New York Herald Tribune Books,* August 24, 1941, p. 8.
*New York Times Book Review,* August 24, 1941, pp. 18, 20; June 25, 1939, p. 7.
*Publishers Weekly,* March 30, 1970, p. 66.

*Saturday Review of Literature,* July, 1939, p. 20.
*Studies in Black Literature,* spring, 1973, pp. 1-3.

—*Sketch by Karen Withem*

\*   \*   \*

## AWOLOWO, Obafemi Awo  1909-1987

*PERSONAL:* Born March 6, 1909, in Ikenne, Western Nigeria; died May 10, 1987, in Ikenne; son of David Sopulu (a Yoruba farmer) and Mary (Efunyela) Awolowo; married Hannah Idowu Dideolu, December 26, 1937; children: two sons, three daughters. *Education:* Wesley College, Ibadan, Nigeria, graduate, 1927; University of London, B.Com. (with honors), 1944, LL.B., 1946. *Religion:* Protestant.

*ADDRESSES: Home*—Ikenne-Remo, Ogun State, Nigeria.

*CAREER:* School teacher in Ogbe, Abeokuta, Nigeria, 1928-29; stenographer in Lagos, Nigeria, 1930-32; Wesley College, Ibadan, Nigeria, clerk-stenographer, 1932-34; Nigerian *Daily Times,* reporter, 1934-35; Nigerian Motor Transport Union, assistant secretary, 1936-40, general secretary, 1941-44; *Nigerian Worker,* editor, 1939-44; called to the Bar at Inner Temple, 1947; Supreme Court of Nigeria in Ibadan, solicitor and advocate, 1946-52; Western Region of Nigeria, cabinet minister and leader of government business, 1952-54, premier, 1954-59; leader of the opposition in Federal Parliament, Lagos, Nigeria, 1960-62; elected leader of the Yoruba people, 1966; Government of Nigeria, vice-chairman of the Federal Executive Council and head of the Ministry of Finance, 1967-71; University of Ife, Ile-Ife, Nigeria, chancellor, 1967-75; Ahmadu Bello University, Zaria, Nigeria, chancellor, 1975-78. Member of Nigerian Youth Movement (leading efforts to reform Ibadan Native Authority Council), 1940-43; co-founder, Trades Union Congress of Nigeria, 1943; founder of Egbe Omo Oduduwa (Yoruba cultural movement) in London, England, 1945, general secretary, 1948-51; founder of Action Group of Nigeria (a political party), 1951, and Unity Party of Nigeria (UPN), 1978; UPN presidential candidate, 1979, 1983; senior advocate of Nigeria.

*AWARDS, HONORS:* LL.D., University of Nigeria, 1961, University of Ibadan, 1973, Ahmadu Bello University, 1975, and University of Cape Coast, Ghana, 1976; D.Sc., University of Ife, 1967; D. Litt., University of Lagos, 1970; Grand Commander of the Federal Republic of Nigeria, 1982.

*WRITINGS:*

*Path to Nigerian Freedom,* Faber, 1947.

*Forward to a New Nigeria,* Western Nigeria Information Services, 1957.

*Awo: The Autobiography of Chief Obafemi Awolowo,* Cambridge University Press, 1960.

*Anglo-Nigeria Defence Pact,* Action Group Bureau of Information, 1960.

*Presidential Address Delivered by Chief the Honourable Obafemi Awolowo, Federal President of the Action Group and Leader of the Opposition in the Federal House of Representatives at the Seventh Congress of the Action Group Held at the Abalabi Club, Mushin, on Monday, 19th September, 1960,* African Press, 1960.

*Call to Rededication and Reconstruction* (pamphlet), Union Print, 1961.

*Forward with Democratic Socialism: A Message by Chief Awolowo from Broad Street Prison, Lagos,* Action Group of Nigeria, 1963.

*Thoughts on Nigerian Constitution,* Oxford University Press, 1966.

*An Address Delivered by Chief Obafemi Awolowo on the Occasion of His Installation as the First Chancellor of the University of Ife at Ile-Ife on Monday, 15 May, 1967,* Ibadan University Press, 1967.

*Blueprint for Post-War Reconstruction* (pamphlet), Nigerian Federal Ministry of Information, 1967.

*My Early Life* (autobiography), J. West Publications, 1968.

*The Path to Economic Freedom in Developing Countries,* University of Lagos, 1968.

*The People's Republic,* Oxford University Press, 1968.

*The Strategy and Tactics of the People's Republic of Nigeria,* Macmillan, 1970.

*The Problems of Africa: The Need for Ideological Reappraisal,* Macmillan, 1977.

*Awo on the Nigerian Civil War,* J. West Publications, 1981.

*Path to Nigerian Greatness,* Fourth Dimension Publishers, 1981.

*Voice of Reason,* Fagbamigbe Publishers, 1981.

*Voice of Wisdom,* Fagbamigbe Publishers, 1981.

*Voice of Courage,* Fagbamigbe Publishers, 1981.

*Selected Speeches of Chief Obafemi Awolowo* (includes *Voice of Reason, Voice of Wisdom,* and *Voice of Courage*), Fagbamigbe Publishers, 1981.

*Awo in Urhobo Land,* P.D. Otuedon, 1981.

(With Shehu Usman Aliyu Shagari) *Shagari vs. Awo,* African Press, 1983.

*Adventures in Power,* Macmillan, 1985.

*My March through Prison* (autobiography), Macmillan, 1985.

Also author of *Action Group Fourteen-Point Programme,* 1959, *African Unity,* 1961, *Africa Must be Economically Independent and Self-Reliant,* 1967, *If We Are United, We Shall Succeed Collectively and Separately,* 1968, *Lecture on the Financing of the Nigerian Civil War and Its Implications for the Future Economy of the Nation,* 1970, and *Memorable*

*Quotes from Awo,* edited by Wunmi Adegbonmire, 1978. Contributor to newspapers. Founder, *Nigerian Tribune,* 1949.

*SIDELIGHTS:* Obafemi Awo Awolowo's inherited titles as a descendant of Oduduwo (founder of the Yoruba kingdom) included Ashiwaju of Ijebu-Remo, Losi of Ikenne, Lisa of Ijeun, Apesin of Oshogbo, Odole of Ife, Ajagunla of Ado Ekiti, Odofin of Owo, and Obng Ikpan Isong of Ibibioland. He also had been conferred with Chieftaincy titles in other parts of Nigeria, and was popularly known as Chief Awolowo or simply "Awo". His political activities began while a student in London, England. His party positions, moderate at first, moved steadily toward the left in order to accommodate the members of the party and maintain political unity. He was able to visit India in 1952 and 1953 for political discussions with Nehru (whom Awolowo admired) and other Indian leaders, and to study India's system of symbol voting. Later, as premier of Nigeria's Western Region, Awolowo toured England, the United States, West Germany, Italy, and Japan to promote interest in trade and investment operations in Nigeria.

During a dispute with leaders inside his political party, Awolowo and several others were arrested in 1962; Awolowo himself was detained and tried for treasonable felony and conspiracy, convicted, and sentenced to ten years in prison. He languished there until 1966, when he was pardoned and released, and whereupon he resumed his political career.

Awolowo used his political beliefs and experiences as the subject for his writings, many of which are compilations of his speeches or collections of memoirs. Three works in particular—*Thoughts on Nigerian Constitution, The People's Republic,* and *The Strategy and Tactics of the People's Republic of Nigeria*—are together hailed by scholars as the consummate examination of the challenges facing Nigeria and the responsibilities that that country's government has to its people. A reviewer for the *Times Literary Supplement* describes *The Strategy and Tactics of the People's Republic of Nigeria* as a "kind of ideological blueprint" that, while meticulously detailed, is presented in Awolowo's "flowery, almost biblical style." Though the reviewer admits this combination does not make for easy reading, the book remains "an important—perhaps an essential—key to understanding postwar Nigeria."

*BIOGRAPHICAL/CRITICAL SOURCES:*

*BOOKS*

*Awo: In the Eyes of the People,* Daily Times of Nigeria, 1987.

Awolowo, Obafemi Awo, *Awo: The Chief Autobiography of Chief Obafemi Awolowo,* Cambridge University Press, 1960.

Awolowo, Obafemi Awo, *Awolowo, My Early Life,* J. West Publications, 1968.

Gunther, John, *Inside Africa,* Harper, 1955.

Kaula, Edna Mason, *Leaders of the New Africa,* World Publishing, 1966.

*The New Africans,* Putnam, 1967.

Onibonoje, 'Biodun, compiler and editor, *Awo: The Nigerian Colossus,* A. Onibonoje Agencies, 1987.

Roscoe, Adrian A., editor, *Mother Is Gold: West African Literature,* Cambridge University Press, 1971.

*PERIODICALS*

*Foreign Affairs,* October, 1961, p. 156.

*Guardian,* September 30, 1960, p. 9.

*New Statesman,* October 22, 1960, p. 616.

*Spectator,* October 7, 1960, p. 530.

*Time,* February 16, 1959.

*Times Literary Supplement,* April 10, 1969, p. 379; September 18, 1970, p. 1015.

*U.S. News,* July 4, 1960.

*OBITUARIES:*

*PERIODICALS*

*Chicago Tribune,* May 12, 1987.

*New York Times,* May 11, 1987.

*Times* (London), May 11, 1987.

*Washington Post,* May 11, 1987.

\*   \*   \*

## AWOONOR, Kofi (Nyidevu) 1935-
## (George Awoonor-Williams)

*PERSONAL:* Name originally George Awoonor-Williams; born March 13, 1935, in Wheta, Ghana; son of Atsu E. (a tailor) and Kosiwo (Nyidevu) Awoonor; married; children: three sons, one daughter, including Sika, Dunyo, Kalepe. *Education:* University College of Ghana, B.A., 1960; University College, London, M.A., 1970; State University of New York at Stony Brook, Ph.D., 1972. *Religion:* Ancestralist. *Avocational interests:* Politics, jazz, tennis, herbal medicine (African).

*ADDRESSES: Home and office*—Embassy of Ghana, SQS 111 Bloco B, Apt. 603, Brasilia, Brazil 70466. *Agent*—Harold Ober Associates, Inc., 40 East 49th St., New York, NY 10017.

*CAREER:* University of Ghana, Accra, lecturer and research fellow, 1960-64; Ghana Ministry of Information, Accra, director of films, 1964-67; State University of New York at Stony Brook, assistant professor of English, 1968-75; arrested for suspected subversion, charged with harboring a subversionist, served one year in prison in Ghana, 1975-76; University of Cape Coast, Cape Coast, Ghana, professor of English, beginning 1976; Ghana ambassador to Brazil in Brasilia, with accreditation to Argentina, Uruguay, Venezuela, Surinam, and Guyana, 1983—.

*MEMBER:* African Studies Association of America.

*AWARDS, HONORS:* Longmans fellow at University of London, 1967-68; Fairfield fellow; Gurrey Prize and National Book Council award, both 1979, for poetry.

*WRITINGS:*

(Under name George Awoonor-Williams) *Rediscovery, and Other Poems,* Northwestern University Press, 1964.

(Editor with G. Adali-Mortty) *Messages: Poems from Ghana,* Heinemann, 1970, Humanities, 1971.

*Ancestral Power* [and] *Lament* (plays), Heinemann, 1970.

*This Earth, My Brother: An Allegorical Tale of Africa,* Doubleday, 1971.

*Night of My Blood* (poetry), Doubleday, 1971.

*Ride Me, Memory* (poetry), Greenfield Review Press, 1973.

(Translator) *Guardians of the Sacred Word: Ewe Poetry,* NOK Publishers, 1974.

*The Breast of the Earth: A Survey of the History, Culture, and Literature of Africa South of the Sahara,* Doubleday, 1975.

*The House by the Sea* (poetry), Greenfield Review Press, 1978.

(Translator) *When Sorrow-Song Descends on You* (chapbook), edited by Stanley H. Barkan, Cross-Cultural Communications, 1981.

*Fire in the Valley: Ewe Folktales,* Nok Publishers, 1983.

*The Ghana Revolution: Background Account from a Personal Perspective* (essays), Oasis Publishers, 1984.

*Until the Morning After: Selected Poems, 1963-1985,* Greenfield Review Press, 1987.

*Alien Corn* (novel), Oasis Publishers, 1988.

*Ghana: A Political History from Pre-European to Modern Times,* Sedco Publishing, 1990.

*Comes the Voyager at Last: A Tale of Return to Africa,* Africa World Press, 1992.

Contributor to *Africa Report* and *Books Abroad.* Associate editor of *Transition,* 1967-68, *World View,* and *Okike.*

*WORK IN PROGRESS: Notes from Prison,* a personal account; *The Zambezi Flows Here,* a screenplay.

*SIDELIGHTS:* Noted African poet Kofi Awoonor is also an accomplished novelist, critic, and playwright, as well as Ghana's ambassador to Brazil. Interested in the language of his people, he incorporates the vernacular into much of his poetry. His first book, *Rediscovery,* was "very much an effort to move the oral poetry from which I learnt so much into perhaps a higher literary plane, even if it lost much in the process," explains Awoonor in *Contemporary Authors Autobiography Series* (*CAAS*). Jon M. Warner, writing in the *Library Journal,* notes that "his themes are soul-deep in African identity: his voice is gentle and painfully honest; and he perceives things we perhaps know but have never heard said so concisely."

Awoonor was born in the anteroom of his grandfather's hut in Wheta, Ghana, in 1935. "Childhood, as it must have been for many Africans of my generation and peasant background, was for me a time of general poverty and deprivation, even though it was relieved by the warmth of a doting extended family," writes Awoonor in *CAAS.* Raised with his mother's family, he remembers his maternal grandparents "most lovingly," and his grandmother appears in several pieces of poetry as a focus of childhood memories. As a baby, Awoonor was baptized a Presbyterian due to his father's beliefs, but was raised in traditional African towns with shrines to the thunder gods Yeve and So. He grew up hearing the native stories, war songs, and funeral dirges of his people in their own language, which later influenced his poetry. At the age of nine, Awoonor was sent away to school and boarded with a wealthy family for whom he worked as a domestic servant. The rest of his education followed a similar pattern, always boarding and learning away from home. Eventually, Awoonor's studies took him to England and the United States. "But it is Wheta, my natal village, which remains my spiritual hometown," declares Awoonor in *CAAS.*

In *This Earth, My Brother: An Allegorical Tale of Africa,* Awoonor explores the journey of one man from his native African roots into the contemporary Western world. "It is a journey not only across distances, but also across several hundred years," describes *New York Times Book Review* contributor Jan Carew. From school inspections and the King's Birthday parade to ritual circumcision and home-made gin, Awoonor's protagonist, a lawyer called Amamu, remembers growing up in West Africa. As an adult, Amamu returns to the continent and becomes disillusioned with what he sees around him. "The novel is part visionary, part realistic ... [with] a strongly biographical element," comments a reviewer in *Choice.* The "sketches add up to a mysterious but not wholly opaque portrait of Amamu and an account of his disintegration," judges a critic in the *Times Literary Supplement.* Carew, however, writes: "The author seems intoxicated not only with life but with language. His words assault the senses and the intellect simultaneously. Images leap from the pages ... and yet the book is serious and its message of new and positive forces emerging from the African chaos, unmistakable."

Awoonor takes a closer look at his African heritage in *The Breast of the Earth: A Survey of the History, Culture, and Literature of Africa South of the Sahara.* A collection of essays based on his lectures, *The Breast of the Earth* covers precolonial and colonial history as well as oral tradition and literature, and includes commentary on contemporary African writing. Several critics noted that Awoonor concentrates on literature—"a term which he interprets broadly and constantly relates to other concepts"—using history and culture as "backdrops," as R. Kent Rasmussen notes in the *Library Journal.* As a survey, *The Breast of the Earth* is "necessarily selective and subject to broad generalization," remarks a reviewer in *Choice,* noting that the critical commentary will please readers because of its "perceptive intelligence and wit." Writing in *Publishers Weekly,* Albert H. Johnson judges *The Breast of the Earth* to be "wide-ranging and sensitive," and Rasmussen comments that the book's "significance lies in [Awoonor's] broad, integrative approach."

*Until the Morning After: Selected Poems, 1963-85,* is a collection of Awoonor's poetry from his earliest published work, *Rediscovery,* through *The House by the Sea* and contains nine previously unpublished poems. He also includes a brief autobiographical appendix explaining his relationship with language and writing. *Until the Morning After* traces Awoonor's development as a poet, from his early lyrics about nature and heritage, through his "transitional" period formed by his experiences in a Ghanaian prison, to his more politically oriented, contemporary verse. The title of the volume is based on Awoonor's belief in the basic human need for freedom, and two of his later poems explain that freedom is so important that death will be postponed "until the morning after" it is finally achieved. "The selection is judicious," comments M. Tucker in *Choice,* judging that "this volume is a fine tribute to a significant ... African poet." *World Literature Today* contributor Richard F. Bauerle concludes: "*Until the Morning After* should increase Awoonor's already large audience and further enhance his international stature."

Awoonor once wrote: "The written word came almost as if it had no forebears. So my poetry assays to restate the oral beginnings, to articulate the mysterious relation between the WORD and the magical dimensions of our cognitive world. I work with forces that are beyond me, ancestral and ritualized entities who dictate and determine all my literary endeavors. Simply put, my work takes off from the world of all our aboriginal instincts. It is for this reason that I have translated poetry from my own society, the Ewes, and sat at the feet of ancient poets whose medium is the voice and whose forum is the village square and the market place."

*BIOGRAPHICAL/CRITICAL SOURCES:*

*BOOKS*

Awoonor, Kofi, *Ghana: A Political History from Pre-European to Modern Times,* Sedco Publishing, 1990.

*Contemporary Authors Autobiography Series,* Volume 13, Gale, 1991.

PERIODICALS

*Ariel,* January, 1975.
*Choice,* July, 1971, p. 682; July/August, 1975, p. 690; April, 1988, p. 1253.
*Library Journal,* June 1, 1971, p. 1984; April 15, 1975, p. 763.
*New York Times Book Review,* April 2, 1972, p. 7.
*Publishers Weekly,* February 24, 1975, p. 110.
*Times Literary Supplement,* March 24, 1972, p. 325.
*World Literature Today,* autumn, 1988, p. 715.

\*   \*   \*

## AWOONOR-WILLIAMS, George
### See AWOONOR, Kofi (Nyidevu)

\*   \*   \*

## AYIM, May 1960-
### (May Opitz)

*PERSONAL:* Born May 3, 1960, in Hamburg, Germany; daughter of Emmanuel Nuwokpor Ayim (a medical doctor and university professor) and Ursula Andler (a dancer). *Education:* Received M.A., 1986; speech therapy certification, 1990. *Avocational interests:* Black women in the arts.

*ADDRESSES: Home*—Hohenstaufenstr. 63, 1000 Berlin 30, Germany.

*CAREER:* Free University of Berlin, Berlin, Germany, research assistant, beginning in 1986; free-lance speech therapist, 1990—. Lecturer at the Institute of Educational Sciences of the School for Social Work and Social Pedagogics, the Technological University, and the Free University of Berlin.

*MEMBER:* Association of German Writers, Literatur-Frauen (cofounder, 1989), Initiative of Black Germans (cofounder, 1986).

*WRITINGS:*

(Editor, under name May Opitz, with Katharina Oguntoye and Dagmar Schultz; and contributor) *Farbe Bekennen: Afro-Deutsche Frauen auf den Spuren ihrer Geschichte,* Orlanda, 1986; published as *Showing Our Colors: Afro-German Women Speak Out,* translated by Anne V. Adams, foreword by Audre Lourde, University of Massachusetts Press, 1991.

(Editor and contributor, with others) *Entfernte Verbindungen,* Orlanda, 1992.

Contributor to anthologies, including *Aus Aller Frauen Lander,* edited by Sue O'Sullivan, Orlanda, 1989; *Kreise: Erstes Jahr Deutch im Kontext,* edited by Arendt, Baumann, and Peters, Heinle & Heinle, 1992; and *Daughters of Africa,* edited by Margaret Busby, J. Cape, 1992. Contributor to periodicals, including *Afrekete, The Black Scholar, Isisvivane,* and *Beitrage Zur Feministischen Theorie und Praxis.*

*WORK IN PROGRESS:* A collection of poems, titled *Nachtgesang,* to be published in Berlin, Germany, in 1993.

*SIDELIGHTS:* May Ayim commented: "I am of Ghanian-German descent and was born in Hamburg, Germany. Until 1992, I used the name of my white foster parents in Germany—Opitz. Recently my African father agreed to adopt me and I have started using his surname, Ayim. Since 1984 I have lived in Berlin, working in speech therapy, educational sciences, and as a poet. I am an editor of the book *Showing Our Colors,* which also contains my master's thesis on the history and present situation of blacks in Germany. In 1986 I became one of the founders of the Initiative of Black Germans. In 1989 I was a cofounder of Literatur-Frauen, an association designed to support and promote the written works of women, with particular emphasis on black and immigrant authors.

"After completing my studies in educational sciences, I worked as a research assistant with an interdisciplinary research project at the Free University of Berlin. The title of the project was 'Female Identity in the Process of Change.' In the following years I completed a course of study as a speech therapist and took the state examination in 1990. The subject of my thesis, 'Ethnocentrism and Sexism in Speech Therapy,' became the point of departure for a research project of the psycho-social care system of immigrants and black Germans. I received financial support to continue this research in 1990.

"In 1991 I was actively involved in organizing a conference of Literatur-Frauen members. The event brought together writers from East and West Germany, as well as immigrant writers from more than twenty different countries. The topic of the conference was 'Fatherland—Mothertongue?' Readings, discussions, and workshops focused on how authors of various cultural, social, and political backgrounds have experienced and dealt with the changes in Germany's political climate since the unification of East and West. Other consequences of the unification were also discussed.

"I am currently working as a free-lance speech therapist and as a lecturer. Since 1992 I have also been working on my Ph.D. in education. I have started writing my dissertation on ethnocentrism and racism in the therapeutic field. I have also found time to work as a writer, and, since 1984, a number of my texts and poems have been published in books, journals, and newspapers. I have also given numerous public readings of my work. I am composing my first collection of poems and accompanying texts, which will be published under the title *Nachtgesang.*

"When I am writing, I like to focus, with prose and lyrical verse, on black peoples' lives in the Diaspora. I feel a strong need to express personal experiences in a political and cultural context. At the same time, it is important for me not to limit myself to certain topics. I write about everything!"

# B

## BA, Mariama 1929-1981

*PERSONAL:* Born in 1929 in Dakar, Senegal; died after a long illness in 1981; daughter of a civil servant; married Obeye Diop (a politician), later divorced; children: nine.

*CAREER:* Worked as secretary and primary school teacher; public speaker and writer.

*AWARDS, HONORS:* Noma Award for Publishing in Africa, *African Book Publishing Record,* c. 1980, for *Une si longue lettre.*

*WRITINGS:*

*Une si longue lettre* (novel), Nouvelles Editions Africaines, 1980, translation by Modupe Bode-Thomas published as *So Long a Letter,* Heinemann, 1981.
*Un chant ecarlate* (novel), Nouvelles Editions Africaines, 1981, translation by Dorothy S. Blair published as *Scarlet Song,* Longman, 1986.

Ba's work has been translated into numerous languages.

*SIDELIGHTS:* Lauded as a "writer of rare talent" by *Times Educational Supplement* reviewer Victoria Neumark, Senegalese novelist Mariama Ba published her first book, *Une si longue lettre* (*So Long a Letter*), at the age of fifty-one. Her only other book, *Un chant ecarlate* (*Scarlet Song*), was published after her death. Both books tell the stories of women struggling in an oppressive society, an issue that Ba actively spoke about in her lifetime. She was also concerned with issues such as women's education, polygamy, child custody, and women's legal rights in marriage. Though her literary career was short, it won Ba critical acclaim; she was awarded the first Noma Award for *So Long a Letter.*

*So Long a Letter* is the story of Ramatoulaye, whose husband abandons her after marrying a younger woman. Ramatoulaye's story is revealed as she writes a letter to her friend, Aissatou, while she mourns her husband's death for the lengthy period required by Islamic law. As Ramatoulaye reflects on her life, the reader is introduced to Aissatou, whose husband also married a second time. She, unlike Ramatoulaye, who remained in Senegal, chose to leave her husband, establishing a life and a career independent of him. Ramatoulaye, contemplating the condition of women in her society, is roused to a fury when one of her husband's friends asks her to marry him. Enraged at his assumption that her widowed status makes her vulnerable and an easy addition to his collection of wives, Ramatoulaye responds by saying, "You forget that I have a heart and a head, that I am not just an object that one passes from one hand to the next." And although she chose not to flee her home when her husband left, Ramatoulaye ultimately writes to Aissatou: "I am not against starting my life over again.... It is from offensive, nauseating humus that the green plant springs, and I feel coming up within me, new buds."

Reviewing Ba's books in *Modern Fiction Studies,* Charles Ponnuthurai Sarvan called *So Long a Letter* a feminist novel and noted that one of the issues it touches upon is how women affect each other's lives. "Women play a significant role in breaking up Ramatoulaye's and Aissotou's respective marriages," he wrote. *Black Scholar* contributor Nancy Topping Bazin also discussed this issue, which is resolved, in her opinion, through Ramatoulaye's actions. One of the reasons Ramatoulaye refuses to wed her suitor is that he is already married—she does not want to inflict on his wife the same suffering she had experienced. Bazin suggested that Ramatoulaye's decision illustrates that "this is the kind of female solidarity that can defeat polygamy."

Ramatoulaye transcends the bounds of her society in her own way, according to Sarvan. She admits that her generation may not have achieved all that is needed to ensure fair treatment of women, but that they have made a beginning. When her unmarried daughter becomes pregnant, Ramatoulaye is able to support her through the pain that is inflicted upon her by a traditional society. In Sarvan's opinion, Ramatoulaye has taken "a step in the right direction, and ... her daughters immediately follow and quickly go beyond." Bazin also discussed this progression, citing the story of Daba, one of Ramatoulaye's daughters. Daba is married to a man who values her as someone who shares his life. "Daba is my wife," he says. "She is neither my slave, nor my servant." Ramatoulaye appreciates this feeling and says that Daba and her husband are evolving into her "image of the ideal couple."

*Scarlet Song,* Ba's second novel, is also the story of a woman whose husband marries a second time. Mireille, a French woman, marries Ousmane, her Senegalese classmate. Her father rejects her because she has married a black man. Mireille and Ousmane return to Africa after the marriage, but the relationship soon disintegrates because of cultural differences between the two. Ousmane abandons Mireille and their son for Ouleymatou, a traditional Senegalese woman. Powerless and rejected by both her husband and her family, Mireille goes insane. Realizing that her son will not gain societal acceptance just as she hasn't, Mireille kills him in a fit of anger; later that evening, she attacks and wounds Ousmane. At the end of the book, Mireille is in the custody of the French Embassy.

Sarvan suggested that the tension in *Scarlet Song* "arises from conflicting sympathies for Ousmane as an *African* and Mireille as a *woman* who suffers greatly and undeservedly." Sarvan wrote that, despite Mireille's tragic circumstances, her story is undermined because Ba's depiction of the African world is much more "vibrant and real" than that of the European culture and characters. Therefore, though Ousmane is criticized, in Sarvan's opinion "there is a strong undercurrent of sympathy for him, a sympathy trembling on the verge of vindication," and the critic viewed the conflict between Mireille and Ouleymatou "as a conflict between principle and passion, between Europe and Africa, rather than between individuals."

Bazin's evaluation of the book is different from Sarvan's. In her review of *Scarlet Song,* Bazin says that "love can only thrive in an egalitarian relationship, and egalitarian relationships are rare in a context of patriarchal customs." Bazin explained that in traditional Senegalese households the husband's mother runs and controls the household, ensuring that the daughter-in-law is powerless. "The powerlessness of the African female within her own home and within her husband's family is matched ... [in *Scarlet Song*] by the portraits of the French mother and daughter," Bazin wrote. Mireille and her mother, though part of different societies, are equally powerless, each suffering in her own world of pain and loneliness. Thus, in Bazin's opinion, like *So Long a Letter, Scarlet Song*

emphasizes the need for change to a better and more equal society.

Both of Ba's books deal with the problems women face in Senegal, a society laden with traditional values. In Bazin's opinion, the extent to which these women accept the customs of their society also determines the limitations they place on the choices available to them. Sarvan noted that in Ba's novels "the position of women is an element in a total culture." Thus, while aware of the need for change in an oppressive society, Ba also showed a concern about the effect of these changes on the uniqueness of African culture. Therefore, Sarvan stated, Ba's novels "are questioning and explorative rather than radical and imperative."

*BIOGRAPHICAL/CRITICAL SOURCES:*

*BOOKS*

Ba, Mariama, *So Long a Letter,* translated by Modupe Bode-Thomas, Heinemann, 1981.
Ba, *Scarlet Song,* translated by Dorothy S. Blair, Longman, 1986.

*PERIODICALS*

*Black Scholar,* summer/fall, 1989, pp. 8-17.
*Modern Fiction Studies,* autumn, 1988, pp. 453-64.
*Times Educational Supplement,* October 15, 1982, p. 32.

—*Sketch by Aarti D. Stephens*

\*   \*   \*

## BABB, Valerie (Melissa) 1955-

*PERSONAL:* Born May 6, 1955, in New York, NY; daughter of Lionel S. Duncan and Dorothy L. Babb. *Education:* Queen's College of City University of New York, B.A., 1977; State University of New York College at Buffalo, M.A., 1981, Ph.D., 1981.

*ADDRESSES: Office*—Department of English, Georgetown University, 338 New North, Washington, DC 20057.

*CAREER:* Georgetown University, Washington, DC, assistant professor of English, 1981—.

*AWARDS, HONORS:* Award for Academic Excellence, Seek Program, City University of New York, 1985.

*WRITINGS:*

*Ernest Gaines,* Twayne, 1991.

(With Carroll R. Gibbs and Kathleen M. Lesko) *Black Georgetown Remembered: A History of Its Black Community from the Founding of "The Town of George" in 1751 to the Present Day,* Georgetown University Press, 1991.

Contributor to *Dictionary of Literary Biography,* Gale, 1984.

\* \* \*

## BAILEY, Pearl (Mae) 1918-1990

*PERSONAL:* Born March 29, 1918, in Newport News, VA; died of a heart attack after collapsing August 17, 1990, in Philadelphia, PA; daughter of Joseph James (a minister) and Ella Mae Bailey; married John Randolph Pinkett, Jr., August 31, 1948 (divorced, March, 1952); married Louis Bellson, Jr. (a jazz drummer), November 19, 1952; children: Tony Bellson, DeeDee Bellson. *Education:* Attended public schools in Philadelphia, PA; Georgetown University, B.A., 1985.

*CAREER:* Singer, stage performer, and author, 1933-90; vocalist with various popular bands, including Count Basie and Cootie Williams bands; made Broadway stage debut in *St. Louis Woman,* 1946, followed by *Arms in the Girl,* 1950, *Bless You All,* 1950, *House of Flowers,* 1954, and *Hello, Dolly,* 1967-69; motion pictures include *Variety Girl,* 1947, *Isn't It Romantic,* 1948, *Carmen Jones,* 1954, *That Certain Feeling,* 1955, *St. Louis Blues,* 1957, *Porgy and Bess,* 1959, *All the Fine Young Cannibals,* 1960, *The Landlord,* 1970, *Norman, Is That You?,* 1976, and *Lost Generation;* television work includes the *Pearl Bailey Show,* a musical variety program on American Broadcasting Co. (ABC-TV), 1970-71, *Pearl's Kitchen,* a cooking show, and guest appearances on several variety programs; night club entertainer in New York, Boston, Hollywood, Las Vegas, Chicago, and London; contract recording artist for Coral Records, Decca Records, and Columbia Records. Special representative, United States delegation to United Nations.

*AWARDS, HONORS:* Donaldson Award for most promising new performer, 1946, for *St. Louis Woman;* Entertainer of the Year Award, *Cue* magazine, and special Tony Award, both 1967, both for *Hello, Dolly;* March of Dimes Woman of the Year, 1968; U.S.O. Woman of the Year, 1969; citation from Mayor John Lindsay of New York City, 1969; Coretta Scott King Award, American Library Association, 1976, for *Duey's Tale;* honorary degree from Georgetown University, 1978; Medal of Freedom, 1988.

*WRITINGS:*

*The Raw Pearl* (autobiography), Harcourt, 1968.
*Talking to Myself* (autobiography), Harcourt, 1971.
*Pearl's Kitchen: An Extraordinary Cookbook,* Harcourt, 1973.
*Duey's Tale* (juvenile), Harcourt, 1975.
*Hurry Up, America, and Spit,* Harcourt, 1976.
*Between You and Me: A Heartfelt Memoir on Learning, Loving and Living* (autobiography), Doubleday, 1989.

*SIDELIGHTS:* Pearl Bailey's entertainment career began in 1933 when she won first prize in an amateur night contest at the Pearl Theatre in Philadelphia. She continued in vaudeville, then moved into cabarets, eventually appearing on the stage, in movies, on television, and as one of the most popular nightclub performers in the United States. Her starring role in the long-running Broadway musical *Hello, Dolly* earned her a special Tony Award and widespread critical acclaim. "For Miss Bailey this was a Broadway triumph for the history books," wrote Clive Barnes in the *New York Times.* "She took the whole musical in her hands and swung it around her neck as easily as if it were a feather boa. Her timing was exquisite, with asides tossed away as languidly as one might tap ash from a cigarette, and her singing had that deep throaty rumble that ... is always so oddly stirring."

In 1968, Bailey published an autobiographical account of her life entitled *The Raw Pearl.* Although she expressed reservations about her skill with language in the book's foreword, writing that "this is all new to me. I don't always have the kind of words I want to express myself," many reviewers praised the book. "Pearl Bailey writes about her life the way she sings," observed a *Saturday Review* critic, "with gusto and warmth and honesty."

Following the success of *The Raw Pearl,* Bailey penned a second autobiographical account, *Talking to Myself.* According to *Publishers Weekly,* it offers "affectionate homilies laced with recollections of her life and travels during recent years." Jo Hudson acknowledged in *Black World* that the book "may be criticized from a literary standpoint as being very loosely constructed, a little off-beat, and repetitive in its message. However, if we accept Pearl as being distinctive and truly possessing a style of her own, we will accept *Talking to Myself* in like manner."

In 1978, upon accepting an honorary degree from Georgetown University in Washington, DC, Bailey surprised the audience by announcing she would enroll as a real student and work toward a college degree. After six years of attending classes, writing papers, and taking exams, the 67-year-old Bailey was awarded her bachelor's degree in theology. The event prompted the writing of her third autobiography, *Between You and Me: A Heartfelt Memoir on Learning, Loving and Living,* in which she encouraged senior citizens to pursue their lifelong dreams. She divided her book into three sections: the first describes her experiences as a college student; the second is a commentary on the breakdown of the American family; and the third recalls memorable people and experiences of her long and varied career. Praising Bailey's ability to "juggle professional and personal responsibilities," a *Publishers Weekly* reviewer commented favorably about the book and found it "buoyed by humor, compassion and a strong faith."

Bailey's 57-year musical career included volunteering her time and talents toward the goal of racial equality and harmony. She was also active in promoting research for a cure for AIDS. While in Philadelphia, visiting her two sisters and recuperating from recent knee replacement surgery, Bailey suffered a heart attack and died on August 17, 1990.

*BIOGRAPHICAL/CRITICAL SOURCES:*

*BOOKS*

Bailey, Pearl, *The Raw Pearl,* Harcourt, 1968.
Bailey, Pearl, *Talking to Myself,* Harcourt, 1971.

*PERIODICALS*

*Black World,* March, 1972.
*Booklist,* September 1, 1989.
*Cue,* January 6, 1968.
*Ebony,* January, 1968.
*Kenyon Review,* July 15, 1989.
*Maclean's,* August 27, 1990.
*Newsweek,* December 4, 1967.
*New York Times,* November 13, 1967; November 26, 1967.
*People,* September 3, 1990.
*Publishers Weekly,* August 23, 1971; July 28, 1989.
*Saturday Review,* February 22, 1969.
*Time,* November 24, 1967; August 27, 1990.

\*   \*   \*

## BAKER, Houston A., Jr. 1943-

*PERSONAL:* Born March 22, 1943, in Louisville, KY; married Charlotte Pierce; children: Mark Frederick. *Education:* Howard University, B.A. (magna cum laude), 1965; University of California, Los Angeles, M.A., 1966, Ph.D., 1968; graduate study at University of Edinburgh, 1967-68.

*ADDRESSES: Office*—Department of English, University of Pennsylvania, Philadelphia, PA 19104.

*CAREER:* Howard University, Washington, DC, instructor in English, summer, 1966; Yale University, New Haven, CT, instructor, 1968-69, assistant professor of English, 1969-70; University of Virginia, Charlottesville, associate professor, 1970-73, professor of English, 1973-74, member of Center for Advanced Studies, 1970-73; University of Pennsylvania, Philadelphia, professor of English, 1974—, director of Afro-American Studies Program, 1974-77, Albert M. Greenfield Professor of Human Relations, 1982—. Distinguished visiting professor at Cornell University, 1977; visiting professor at Haverford College, 1983-85. Member of Fulbright-Hays literature screening committee, 1973-74; member of committee on scholarly worth, Howard University Press, 1973—.

*MEMBER:* Modern Language Association of America, College Language Association, Phi Beta Kappa, Kappa Delta Pi.

*AWARDS, HONORS:* Alfred Longueil Poetry Award from University of California, Los Angeles, 1966; National Phi Beta Kappa visiting scholar, 1975-76; Center for Advanced Study in the Behavioral Sciences fellow, 1977-78; Guggenheim fellow, 1978-79; National Humanities Center fellow, 1982-83; Rockefeller Minority Group fellow, 1982-83.

*WRITINGS:*

(Contributor) John Morton Blum, general editor, *Key Issues in the Afro-American Experience,* Harcourt, 1971.
(Editor) *Black Literature in America,* McGraw, 1971.
*Long Black Song: Essays in Black American Literature and Culture,* University Press of Virginia, 1972.
(Editor) *Twentieth-Century Interpretations of Native Son,* Prentice-Hall, 1972.
*Singers of Daybreak: Studies in Black American Literature,* Howard University Press, 1974.
*A Many-Colored Coat of Dreams: The Poetry of Countee Cullen,* Broadside Press, 1974.
(Contributor) *Contemporary Poets,* St. Martin's, 1975.
(Editor) *Reading Black: Essays in the Criticism of African, Caribbean, and Black American Literature,* Africana Studies and Research Center, Cornell University, 1976.
(Editor with wife, Charlotte Pierce-Baker) *Renewal: A Volume of Black Poems,* Afro-American Studies Program, University of Pennsylvania, 1977.
(Editor) *A Dark and Sudden Beauty: Two Essays in Black American Poetry by George Kent and Stephen Henderson,* Afro-American Studies Program, University of Pennsylvania, 1977.
*No Matter Where You Travel, You Still Be Black* (poems), Lotus Press, 1979.
*The Journey Back: Issues in Black Literature and Criticism,* University of Chicago Press, 1980.
*Spirit Run,* Lotus Press, 1981.

(Editor with Leslie Fiedler) *English Literature: Opening Up the Canon, Selected Papers from the English Institute, 1979,* English Institute, Johns Hopkins University, 1981.

(Editor) *Three American Literatures: Essays in Chicano, Native American, and Asian-American Literature for Teachers of "American" Literature,* Modern Language Association of America, 1982.

(Editor and author of introduction) *Narrative of the Life of Frederick Douglass, an American Slave, Written by Himself,* Penguin Books, 1982.

*Blues, Ideology, and Afro-American Literature: A Vernacular Theory,* University of Chicago Press, 1984.

*Blues Journeys Home,* Lotus, 1985.

(Editor with Joe Weixlmann) *Belief versus Theory in Black American Literary Criticism,* Penkevill, 1985.

*Modernism and the Harlem Renaissance,* University of Chicago Press, 1987.

*Afro-American Poetics: Revisions of Harlem & the Black Aesthetic,* University of Wisconsin Press, 1988.

(Editor with Patricia Redmond) *Afro-American Literary Study in the 1990s,* University of Chicago Press, 1989.

(With Redmond and Elizabeth Alexander) *Workings of the Spirit: The Poetics of Afro-American Women's Writing,* University of Chicago Press, 1990.

Also contributor of articles and reviews to literature and black studies journals, including *Victorian Poetry, Phylon, Black World, Callaloo, Obsidian, Poetics Today, Yale Review,* and *Journal of African-Afro-American Affairs.* Advisory editor of *Columbia Literary History of the United States,* Columbia University Press. Member of advisory boards of *Maji,* 1974-76, *Black American Literature Forum,* 1976—, and *Minority Voices,* 1977—.

*BIOGRAPHICAL/CRITICAL SOURCES:*

*PERIODICALS*

*Journal of American History,* June, 1991.
*Los Angeles Times Book Review,* December 16, 1984.
*New York Times Book Review,* May 11, 1986; March, 22, 1987; October 4, 1987; January 24, 1988; April 2, 1989.
*Washington Post Book World,* January 3, 1988; February 5, 1989.

\*      \*      \*

## BAKER, Nikki  1962-

*PERSONAL:* Born in June, 1962, in Ohio. *Education:* Purdue University, B.S.; University of Chicago, M.B.A. *Politics:* "Social liberal, fiscal conservative." *Religion:* Presbyterian. *Avocational interests:* Guitar, cooking, golf, science.

*ADDRESSES: Agent*—c/o Publicity Director, Naiad Press, P. O. Box 10543, Tallahassee, FL 32302.

*CAREER:* Writer; in financial services.

*WRITINGS:*

*In the Game* (novel), Naiad Press, 1991.
*The Lavender House Murder* (novel), Naiad Press, 1992.
*Long Goodbyes* (novel), Naiad Press, 1993.

*WORK IN PROGRESS:* Research on the U.S. steel industry and the African American steel migration of the 1940s; research on probate law; research on African American history.

*SIDELIGHTS:* Nikki Baker once commented: "My primary motivation in writing *In the Game* was to create a reflection of my experience as an affluent, educated, late baby-boom, black lesbian. As I generate more novels, reflection of personal viewpoint continues to be my goal. Central to this is what I call the concept of 'free agency,' as illustrated in the work of Jean Rhys, Raymond Carver, Dashiell Hammett, and Ralph Ellison. Free agency is the sense of alienation from community that results in a 'me against the world' mentality, rather than the 'you and me against the world' identification displayed in the work of many older black writers who write from a sense of belonging predicated on racial and familial institutions. My characters are people whose belief in commonality, love, fidelity, loyalty, and fairness has been frustrated, but who do not have any traditional institutional havens to which they can turn. I don't have any special interest in genre fiction, but because I am a young writer (and not a writer by training), I like the mystery genre because it provides a ready-made structure in which I can explore these ideas. At the conclusion of this mystery series I am writing for Naiad Press, I hope to have the opportunity to write more serious fiction."

\*      \*      \*

## BAMBARA, Toni Cade  1939-
## (Toni Cade)

*PERSONAL:* Surname originally Cade, name legally changed in 1970; born March 25, 1939, in New York, NY; daughter of Helen Brent Henderson Cade. *Education:* Queens College (now Queens College of the City University of New York), B.A., 1959; attended University of Florence, 1961; attended Ecole de Mime Etienne Decroux in Paris, France, 1961, and New York, 1963; City College of the City University of New York, M.A., 1964; additional study in linguistics at New York University and New School for Social Research. Also attended Katherine Dunham Dance Studio, Syvilla Fort School of

Dance, Clark Center of Performing Arts, 1958-69, and Studio Museum of Harlem Film Institute, 1970.

*ADDRESSES: Home*—5720 Wissahickon Ave., Apt. E12, Philadelphia, PA 19144.

*CAREER:* New York State Department of Welfare, New York City, social investigator, 1959-61; Metropolitan Hospital, New York City, director of recreation in psychiatry department, 1961-62; Colony House Community Center, New York City, program director, 1962-65; City College of the City University of New York, New York City, English instructor in SEEK Program, 1965-69; New Careers Program of Newark, Newark, NJ, English instructor in SEEK Program, 1969; Rutgers University, New Brunswick, NJ, assistant professor at Livingston College, 1969-74; Stephens College, Columbia, MO, visiting professor of African American studies, 1975; Atlanta University, Atlanta, GA, visiting professor, 1977, research mentor and instructor at School of Social Work, 1977 and 1979. Production artist-in-residence for Neighborhood Arts Center, 1975-79, Stephens College, 1976, and Spelman College, 1978-79; founder and director of Pamoja Writers Collective, 1976-85; instructor at Scribe Video Center, 1986—; production consultant for WHYY-TV, Philadelphia, PA. Humanities consultant to New Jersey Department of Corrections, 1974, New York Institute for Human Services Training, 1978, and Institute of Language Arts, Emory University, 1980. Art consultant to New York State Arts Council, 1974, Georgia State Arts Council, 1976 and 1981, National Endowment for the Arts, 1980, and the Black Arts South Conference, 1981. Has conducted numerous workshops on writing, self-publishing, and community organizing for community centers, museums, prisons, libraries, and universities. Has lectured and conducted literary readings at many institutions, including the Library of Congress, Smithsonian Institution, Afro-American Museum of History and Culture. Member of board of directors of Sojourner Productions and Meridian; member of advisory boards of National Black Programming Consortium, and International Black Cinema.

*MEMBER:* National Association of Third World Writers, Screenwriters Guild of America, African American Film Society, Sisters in Support of South African Sisterhood (member of board of directors).

*AWARDS, HONORS:* Peter Pauper Press Award, 1958; John Golden Award for Fiction, Queens College (now Queens College of the City University of New York), 1959; Theatre of the Black Experience Award, 1969; Rutgers University research fellowship, 1972; *Tales and Stories for Black Folks* was named outstanding book of 1972 in juvenile literature by the *New York Times;* Child Development Institute Award for service to black children, 1973; Black Rose Award, *Encore* magazine, 1973, for *Gorilla, My Love;* Black Community

Award, Livingston College, Rutgers University, 1974; the short story "The Mama Load" was named a finalist for the Best American Short Stories of 1978; literature grant, National Endowment for the Arts, 1980; American Book Award, 1981, for *The Salt Eaters;* Langston Hughes Society Award, 1981; Best Documentary of 1986 Award from Pennsylvania Association of Broadcasters, and Documentary Award from National Black Programming Consortium, both 1986, for *The Bombing of Osage;* Langston Hughes Medallion, Langston Hughes Society of City College of the City University of New York, 1986; Zora Hurston Award, Morgan State College, 1986; Bronze Jubilee Award for Literature, WETV; honorary doctorate of letters, State University of New York at Albany, 1990; National Association of Negro Business and Professional Women's Club League Award for service to black women; George Washington Carver Distinguished African American Lecturer Award, Simpson College; Achievement in the Arts Award, *Ebony* magazine; Black Arts Award, University of Missouri.

*WRITINGS:*

*FICTION*

*Gorilla, My Love* (short stories), Random House, 1972.
*The Sea Birds Are Still Alive* (short stories), Random House, 1977.
*The Salt Eaters* (novel), Random House, 1980.
*If Blessing Comes* (novel), Random House, 1987.
*Raymond's Run,* Creative Education, 1990.

Also author of the short story "The Mama Load," published in *Redbook* magazine.

*SCREENPLAYS*

*Zora,* produced by WGBH-TV, 1971.
*The Johnson Girls,* produced by National Educational Television (NET-TV), 1972.
*Transactions,* produced by School of Social Work, Atlanta University, 1979.
*The Long Night,* produced by American Broadcasting Companies, Inc. (ABC-TV), 1981.
*Epitaph for Willie,* produced by K. Heran Productions, Inc., 1982.
*Tar Baby* (based on Toni Morrison's novel), produced by Sanger/Brooks Film Productions, 1984.
*Raymond's Run,* produced by Public Broadcasting Service (PBS-TV), 1985.
*The Bombing of Osage,* produced by WHYY-TV, 1986.
*Cecil B. Moore: Master Tactician of Direct Action,* produced by WHYY-TV, 1987.

*EDITOR*

(And contributor, both under name Toni Cade) *The Black
Woman: An Anthology* (poetry, short stories, and essays),
New American Library, 1970.

(And contributor) *Tales and Stories for Black Folks* (short
stories), Doubleday, 1971.

(With Leah Wise) *Southern Black Utterances Today,* Institute for Southern Studies, 1975.

*CONTRIBUTOR*

Addison Gayle, Jr., editor, *Black Expression: Essays by and
about Black Americans in the Creative Arts,* Weybright,
1969.

Jules Chametsky, editor, *Black and White in American Culture,* University of Massachusetts Press, 1970.

Ruth Miller, *Backgrounds to Blackamerican Literature,* Chandler Publishing, 1971.

Janet Sternburg, editor, *The Writer on Her Work,* Norton,
1980.

(Author of preface) Cecelia Smith, *Cracks,* Select Press, 1980.

(Author of foreword) Cherrie Moraga and Gloria Anzaldua,
editors, *This Bridge Called My Back: Radical Women of
Color,* Persephone Press, 1981.

Paul H. Connolly, editor, *On Essays: A Reader for Writers,*
Harper, 1981.

(Author of foreword) *The Sanctified Church: Collected Essays by Zora Neale Hurston,* Turtle Island, 1982.

Mari Evans, editor, *Black Women Writers, 1950-1980: A
Critical Evaluation,* Doubleday, 1984.

Claudia Tate, editor, *The Black Writer at Work,* Howard University Press, 1984.

*OTHER*

(With Julie Dash and Bell Hooks) *Daughters of the Dust: The
Making of an African American Woman's Film,* New
Press, 1992.

Contributor to *What's Happnin, Somethin Else,* and *Another
Eye,* all readers published by Scott, Foresman, 1969-70. Contributor of articles and book and film reviews to periodicals,
including *Massachusetts Review, Negro Digest, Liberator,
Prairie Schooner, Redbook, Audience, Black Works, Umbra,*
and *Onyx.* Guest editor of special issue of *Southern Exposure,*
summer, 1976; member of advisory board, *Essence.*

*ADAPTATIONS:* Three of Bambara's short stories, "Gorilla,
My Love," "Medley," and "Witchbird," have been adapted
for film.

*SIDELIGHTS:* Toni Cade Bambara is a well-known and respected civil rights activist, professor of English and of Afri-

can American studies, editor of anthologies of black literature,
and author of short stories as well as novels. According to Alice
A. Deck in the *Dictionary of Literary Biography,* "in many
ways Toni Cade Bambara is one of the best representatives
of the group of Afro-American writers who, during the 1960s,
became directly involved in the cultural and sociopolitical
activities in urban communities across the country." However, Deck points out that "Bambara is one of the few who continued to work within the black urban communities (filming,
lecturing, organizing, and reading from her works at rallies
and conferences), producing imaginative reenactments of
these experiences in her fiction. In addition, Bambara established herself over the years as an educator, teaching in colleges and independent community schools in various cities on
the East Coast."

Bambara's first two works of fiction, *Gorilla, My Love* and
*The Sea Birds Are Still Alive,* are collections of her short stories. Susan Lardner remarks in the *New Yorker* that the stories in these two works, "describing the lives of black people
in the North and the South, could be more exactly typed as
vignettes and significant anecdotes, although a few of them
are fairly long.... All are notable for their purposefulness, a
more or less explicit inspirational angle, and a distinctive
motion of the prose, which swings from colloquial narrative
to precarious metaphorical heights and over to street talk, at
which Bambara is unbeatable."

In a review of *Gorilla, My Love,* for example, a writer remarks
in the *Saturday Review* that the stories "are among the best
portraits of black life to have appeared in some time. [They
are] written in a breezy, engaging style that owes a good deal
to street dialect." A critic writing in *Newsweek* makes a similar observation, describing Bambara's second collection of
short stories, *The Sea Birds Are Still Alive,* in this manner:
"Bambara directs her vigorous sense and sensibility to black
neighborhoods in big cities, with occasional trips to small
Southern towns.... The stories start and stop like rapid-fire
conversations conducted in a rhythmic, black-inflected, sweet-
and-sour language." In fact, according to Anne Tyler in the
*Washington Post Book World,* Bambara's particular style of
narration is one of the most distinctive qualities of her writing. "What pulls us along is the language of [her] characters,
which is startlingly beautiful without once striking a false
note," notes Tyler. "Everything these people say, you feel,
ordinary, real-life people are saying right now on any street
corner. It's only that the rest of us didn't realize it was sheer
poetry they were speaking."

In terms of plot, Bambara tends to avoid linear development
in favor of presenting "situations that build like improvisations
of a melody," as a *Newsweek* reviewer explains. Commenting on *Gorilla, My Love,* Bell Gale Chevigny observes in the
*Village Voice* that despite the "often sketchy" plots, the sto-

ries are always "lavish in their strokes—here are elaborate illustrations, soaring asides, aggressive sub-plots. They are never didactic, but they abound in far-out common sense, exotic home truths."

Numerous reviewers have also remarked on Bambara's sensitive portrayals of her characters and the handling of their situations—her writing is marked by an affectionate warmth and pride. Laura Marcus suggests in the *Times Literary Supplement* that Bambara "presents black culture as embattled but unbowed.... Bambara depicts black communities in which ties of blood and friendship are fiercely defended." Deck expands on this idea, remarking that "the basic implication of all of Toni Cade Bambara's stories is that there is an undercurrent of caring for one's neighbors that sustains black Americans. In her view the presence of those individuals who intend to do harm to people is counterbalanced by as many if not more persons who have a genuine concern for other people."

C. D. B. Bryan admires this expression of the author's concern for other people, declaring in the *New York Times Book Review* that "Bambara tells me more about being black through her quiet, proud, silly, tender, hip, acute, loving stories than any amount of literary polemicizing could hope to do. She writes about love: a love for one's family, one's friends, one's race, one's neighborhood and it is the sort of love that comes with maturity and inner peace." According to Bryan, "all of [Bambara's] stories share the affection that their narrator feels for the subject, an affection that is sometimes terribly painful, at other times fiercely proud. But at all times it is an affection that is so genuinely *genus homo sapiens* that her stories are not only black stories."

In 1980, Bambara published her first novel, a generally well-received work titled *The Salt Eaters*. Written in an almost dream-like style, *The Salt Eaters* explores the relationship between two women with totally different backgrounds and lifestyles who are brought together by a suicide attempt by one of the women. John Leonard, who describes the book as "extraordinary," writes in the *New York Times* that *The Salt Eaters* "is almost an incantation, poem-drunk, myth-happy, mudcaked, jazz-ridden, prodigal in meanings, a kite and a mask. It astonishes because Toni Cade Bambara is so adept at switching from politics to legend, from particularities of character to prehistorical song, from LaSalle Street to voodoo. It is as if she jived the very stones to groan."

In a *Times Literary Supplement* review, Carol Rumens states that *The Salt Eaters* "is a hymn to individual courage, a sombre message of hope that has confronted the late twentieth-century pathology of racist violence and is still able to articulate its faith in 'the dream'." And John Wideman notes in the *New York Times Book Review:* "In her highly acclaimed fiction and in lectures, [Bambara] emphasizes the necessity for

black people to maintain their best traditions, to remain healthy and whole as they struggle for political power. *The Salt Eaters,* her first novel, eloquently summarizes and extends the abiding concerns of her previous work."

*BIOGRAPHICAL/CRITICAL SOURCES:*

*BOOKS*

*Authors and Artists for Young Adults,* Volume 5, Gale, 1990.
*Black Literature Criticism,* Gale, 1992, pp. 108-20.
Butler-Evans, Elliott, *Race, Gender, and Desire: Narrative Strategies in the Fiction of Toni Cade Bambara,* Temple University Press, 1989.
*Contemporary Literary Criticism,* Volume 19, Gale, 1984.
*Dictionary of Literary Biography,* Volume 38: *Afro-American Writers after 1955: Dramatists and Prose Writers,* Gale, 1985.
Parker, Bell, and Beverly Guy-Sheftall, *Sturdy Black Bridges: Visions of Black Women in Literature,* Doubleday, 1979.
Pearlman, Mickey, editor, *American Women Writing Fiction: Memory, Identity, Family, Space,* University Press of Kentucky, 1989, pp. 155-71.
Prenshaw, Peggy Whitman, editor, *Women Writers of the Contemporary South,* University Press of Mississippi, 1984.
Tate, Claudia, editor, *Black Women Writers at Work,* Continuum, 1983.

*PERIODICALS*

*Black World,* July, 1973.
*Books of the Times,* June, 1980.
*Chicago Tribune Book World,* March 23, 1980.
*Drum,* spring, 1982.
*First World,* Volume 2, number 4, 1980.
*Los Angeles Times Book Review,* May 4, 1980.
*Ms.,* July, 1977; July, 1980.
*National Observer,* May 9, 1977.
*Newsweek,* May 2, 1977.
*New Yorker,* May 5, 1980.
*New York Times,* October 11, 1972; October 15, 1972; April 4, 1980.
*New York Times Book Review,* February 21, 1971; May 2, 1971; November 7, 1971; October 15, 1972; December 3, 1972; March 27, 1977; June 1, 1980; November 1, 1981.
*Race and Class,* spring, 1985, pp. 108-10.
*Saturday Review,* November 18, 1972; December 2, 1972; April 12, 1980.
*Sewanee Review,* November 18, 1972; December 2, 1972.
*Times Literary Supplement,* June 18, 1982; September 27, 1985.

*Village Voice,* April 12, 1973.
*Washington Post Book World,* November 18, 1973; March 30, 1980, pp. 1-2.

\*    \*    \*

### BANKOLE, Timothy 1920(?)-

*PERSONAL:* Born c. 1920 in Freetown, Sierra Leone. *Education:* Received B.A. from London University.

*CAREER: London Daily Express,* staff member/journalist; *Daily Graphic* (London), assistant editor, 1951—; *London Observer* and *Ceylon Daily News,* correspondent from the Gold Coast (now Ghana).

*WRITINGS:*

*Kwame Nkrumah—His Rise to Power,* Allen & Unwin, 1955.

Also author of stories and poems, some of which have been presented on the British Broadcasting Corporation's Overseas and African "Voices" programs.

\*    \*    \*

### BARAKA, Amiri 1934-
### (LeRoi Jones)

*PERSONAL:* Original name Everett LeRoi Jones; name changed to Imamu ("spiritual leader") Ameer ("blessed") Baraka ("prince"); later modified to Amiri Baraka; born October 7, 1934, in Newark, NJ; son of Coyette Leroy (a postal worker and elevator operator) and Anna Lois (Russ) Jones; married (divorced August, 1965); married Sylvia Robinson (Bibi Amina Baraka), 1966; children: (first marriage) Kellie Elisabeth, Lisa Victoria Chapman; (second marriage) Obalaji Malik Ali, Ras Jua Al Aziz, Shani Isis, Amiri Seku, Ahi Mwenge. *Education:* Attended Rutgers University, 1951-52; Howard University, B.A., 1954; received M.A. in philosophy from Columbia University; received M.A. in German literature from New School for Social Research.

*ADDRESSES: Office*—Department of Africana Studies, State University of New York at Stony Brook, Long Island, NY 11794-4340. *Agent*—Joan Brandt, Sterling Lord Agency, 660 Madison Ave., New York, NY 10021.

*CAREER: Yugen* magazine and Totem Press, founder and editor, 1958; New School for Social Research, New York City,

instructor, 1961-64; State University of New York at Stony Brook, associate professor, 1983-85, professor of Afro-American studies, 1985—. Visiting professor, University of Buffalo, summer, 1964, Columbia University, fall, 1964, and 1966-67, Yale University, 1977-78, George Washington University, 1978-79, Rutgers University, 1988, and San Francisco State University. Founder and director, 1964-66, of Black Arts Repertory Theatre (disbanded, 1966); currently director of Spirit House (a black community theater; also known as Heckalu Community Center), and head of advisory group at Treat Elementary School, both in Newark, NJ. Member, Political Prisoners Relief Fund, and African Liberation Day Commission. Candidate, Newark community council, 1968. *Military service:* U.S. Air Force, 1954-57; weather-gunner; stationed for two and a half years in Puerto Rico with intervening trips to Europe, Africa, and the Middle East.

*MEMBER:* All African Games, Pan African Federation, Black Academy of Arts and Letters, National Black Political Assembly (secretary general; co-governor), National Black United Front, Congress of African People (co-founder; chairman), Black Writers' Union, League of Revolutionary Struggle, United Brothers (Newark), Newark Writers Collective.

*AWARDS, HONORS:* Longview Best Essay of the Year award, 1961, for *Cuba Libre;* John Whitney Foundation fellow (poetry and fiction), 1962; Obie Award, *Village Voice,* Best American Off-Broadway Play, 1964, for *Dutchman;* Guggenheim fellowship, 1965-66; Yoruba Academy fellow, 1965; second prize, International Art Festival, Dakar, 1966, for *The Slave;* National Endowment for the Arts grant, 1966; Doctorate of Humane Letters, Malcolm X College (Chicago, IL), 1972; Rockefeller Foundation fellow (drama), 1981; Poetry Award, National Endowment for the Arts, 1981; New Jersey Council for the Arts award, 1982; American Book Award, Before Columbus Foundation, 1984, for *Confirmation: An Anthology of African-American Women;* Drama Award, 1985.

*WRITINGS:*

*PLAYS UNDER NAME LEROI JONES*

*A Good Girl Is Hard to Find,* produced in Montclair, NJ, at Sterington House, 1958.
*Dante* (one-act; based on an excerpt from the novel *The System of Dante's Hell;* also see below), produced in New York at Off-Bowery Theatre, 1961; later produced as *The Eighth Ditch* at the New Bowery Theatre, 1964.
*Dutchman* (produced Off-Broadway at Village South Theatre, 1964; produced Off-Broadway at Cherry Lane Theater, 1964; produced in London, 1967; also see below), Faber & Faber, 1967.

*The Baptism: A Comedy in One Act* (produced Off-Broadway at Writers' Stage Theatre, 1964; produced in London, 1970-71; also see below), Sterling Lord, 1966.

*The Toilet* (produced with *The Slave: A Fable* Off-Broadway at St. Mark's Playhouse, 1964; produced at International Festival of Negro Arts at Dakar, Senegal, 1966; also see below), Sterling Lord, 1964.

*J-E-L-L-O* (one-act comedy; produced in New York by Black Arts Repertory Theatre, 1965; also see below), Third World Press, 1970.

*Experimental Death Unit #1* (one-act; also see below), produced Off-Broadway at St. Mark's Playhouse, 1965.

*The Death of Malcolm X* (one-act; produced in Newark at Spirit House, 1965), published in *New Plays from the Black Theatre,* edited by Ed Bullins, Bantam, 1969.

*A Black Mass* (also see below), produced in Newark at Proctor's Theatre, 1966.

### PLAYS

*Slave Ship* (produced as *Slave Ship: A Historical Pageant* at Spirit House, 1967; produced in New York City, 1969; also see below), Jihad, 1967.

*Madheart: Morality Drama* (one-act; also see below), produced at San Francisco State College, 1967.

*Arm Yourself, or Harm Yourself, A One-Act Play* (produced at Spirit House, 1967; also see below), Jihad, 1967.

*Great Goodness of Life (A Coon Show)* (one-act; also see below), produced at Spirit House, 1967; produced Off-Broadway at Tambellini's Gate Theater, 1969.

*Home on the Range* (one-act comedy; also see below), produced at Spirit House, 1968; produced in New York City at a Town Hall rally, 1968.

*Junkies Are Full of SHHH...* (produced at Spirit House, 1968; produced with *Bloodrites* Off-Broadway at Henry Street Playhouse, 1970), both published in *Black Drama Anthology,* edited by Woodie King and Ron Milner, New American Library, 1971.

*Board of Education* (children's play), produced at Spirit House, 1968.

*Resurrection in Life* (one-act pantomime), produced under the title *Insurrection* in Harlem, NY, 1969.

*Black Dada Nihilism* (one-act), produced Off-Broadway at Afro-American Studio, 1971.

*A Recent Killing* (three-act), produced Off-Broadway at the New Federal Theatre, 1973.

*Columbia the Gem of the Ocean,* produced in Washington, DC, by Howard University Spirit House Movers, 1973.

*The New Ark's A-Moverin,* produced in Newark, 1974.

*The Sidnee Poet Heroical, in Twenty-Nine Scenes,* (one-act comedy; produced Off-Broadway at the New Federal Theatre, 1975; also see below), Reed & Cannon, 1979.

*S-1: A Play with Music in 26 Scenes* (also see below), produced in New York at Washington Square Methodist Church, 1976; produced at Afro-American Studio, 1976.

(With Frank Chin and Leslie Siko) *America More or Less* (musical), produced in San Francisco at Marine's Memorial Theater, 1976.

*The Motion of History* (four-act; also see below), produced at New York City Theatre Ensemble, 1977.

*What Was the Relationship of the Lone Ranger to the Means of Production?: A Play in One Act,* (produced in New York at Ladies Fort, 1979; also see below), Anti-Imperialist Cultural Union, 1978.

*Dim Cracker Party Convention,* produced in New York at Columbia University, 1980.

*Boy and Tarzan Appear in a Clearing,* produced Off-Broadway at New Federal Theatre, 1981.

*Money: Jazz Opera* (libretto), produced in New York at Kool Jazz Festival, 1982.

*Money,* produced Off-Broadway at La Mama Experimental Theatre Club, 1982.

*Song: A One Act Play about the Relationship of Art to Real Life,* produced in Jamaica, NY, 1983.

Also author of the plays *Home on the Range* and *Police,* published in *Drama Review,* summer, 1968; *Rockgroup,* published in *Cricket,* December, 1969; *Revolt of the Moonflowers,* 1969, lost in manuscript; *The Coronation of the Black Queen,* published in *Black Scholar,* June, 1970; *Black Power Chant,* published in *Drama Review,* December, 1972; and *Vomit and the Jungle Bunnies,* unpublished. Contributor of plays to books, including *Spontaneous Combustion: Eight New American Plays,* edited by Rochelle Owens, Winter House, 1972.

### PLAY COLLECTIONS

(Under name LeRoi Jones) *Dutchman* [and] *The Slave,* Morrow, 1964.

*The Baptism* [and] *The Toilet,* Grove, 1967.

*Four Black Revolutionary Plays: All Praises to the Black Man* (contains *Experimental Death Unit #1, A Black Mass, Great Goodness of Life,* and *Madheart*), Bobbs-Merrill, 1969.

*The Motion of History and Other Plays* (contains *Slave Ship* and *S-1*), Morrow, 1978.

*Selected Plays and Prose of LeRoi Jones/Amiri Baraka,* Morrow, 1979.

### SCREENPLAYS

*Dutchman,* Gene Persson Enterprises, Ltd., 1967.

*Black Spring,* Jihad Productions, 1968.

*A Fable* (based on *The Slave*), MFR Productions, 1971.

*Supercoon,* Gene Persson Enterprises, Ltd., 1971.

*POETRY UNDER NAME LEROI JONES*

*April 13* (broadside Number 133), Penny Poems (New Haven), 1959.
*Spring & So Forth* (broadside Number 141), Penny Poems, 1960.
*Preface to a Twenty Volume Suicide Note,* Totem/Corinth, 1961.
*The Disguise* (broadside), [New Haven], 1961.
*The Dead Lecturer* (also see below), Grove, 1964.
*Black Art* (also see below), Jihad, 1966.

*POETRY*

*Black Magic* (also see below), Morrow, 1967.
*A Poem for Black Hearts,* Broadside Press, 1967.
*Black Magic: Sabotage; Target Study; Black Art; Collected Poetry, 1961-1967,* Bobbs-Merrill, 1969.
*It's Nation Time,* Third World Press, 1970.
*Spirit Reach,* Jihad, 1972.
*Afrikan Revolution: A Poem,* Jihad, 1973.
*Hard Facts: Excerpts,* People's War, 1975, second edition, Revolutionary Communist League, 1975.
*Spring Song,* Baraka, 1979.
*AM/TRAK,* Phoenix Book Shop, 1979.
*Selected Poetry of Amiri Baraka/Leroi Jones* (includes "Poetry for the Advanced"), Morrow, 1979.
*In the Tradition: For Black Arthur Blythe,* Jihad, 1980.
*Reggae or Not! Poems,* Contact Two, 1982.

*ESSAYS UNDER NAME LEROI JONES*

*Cuba Libre,* Fair Play for Cuba Committee (New York City), 1961.
*Blues People: Negro Music in White America,* Morrow, 1963, published in England as *Negro Music in White America,* MacGibbon & Kee, 1965.
*Home: Social Essays* (contains *Cuba Libre,* "The Myth of a 'Negro Literature'," "Expressive Language," "the legacy of malcolm x, and the coming of the black nation," and "state/meant"), Morrow, 1966.

*ESSAYS*

*Black Music,* Morrow, 1968.
*Raise, Race, Rays, Raze: Essays since 1965,* Random House, 1971.
*Strategy and Tactics of a Pan-African Nationalist Party,* Jihad, 1971.
*Kawaida Studies: The New Nationalism,* Third World Press, 1972.
*Crisis in Boston!,* Vita Wa Watu People's War, 1974.
*Daggers and Javelins: Essays, 1974-1979,* Morrow, 1984.

(With wife, Amina Baraka) *The Music: Reflections on Jazz and Blues,* Morrow, 1987.

*EDITOR UNDER NAME LEROI JONES*

*January 1st 1959: Fidel Castro,* Totem, 1959.
*Four Young Lady Poets,* Corinth, 1962.
(And co-author) *In-formation,* Totem, 1965.
Gilbert Sorrentino, *Black & White,* Corinth, 1965.
Edward Dorn, *Hands Up!,* Corinth, 1965.
(And contributor) *Afro-American Festival of the Arts Magazine,* Jihad, 1966, published as *Anthology of Our Black Selves,* 1969.

Also editor and author of introduction of *The Moderns: An Anthology of New Writing in America,* 1963, published as *The Moderns: New Fiction in America,* 1964.

*EDITOR*

(With Larry Neal and A. B. Spellman) *The Cricket: Black Music in Evolution,* Jihad, 1968, published as *Trippin': A Need for Change,* New Ark, 1969.
(And contributor; with Larry Neal) *Black Fire: An Anthology of Afro-American Writing,* Morrow, 1968.
*A Black Value System,* Jihad, 1970.
(With Billy Abernathy [under pseudonym Fundi]) *In Our Terribleness (Some Elements of Meaning in Black Style),* Bobbs-Merrill, 1970.
(And author of introduction) *African Congress: A Documentary of the First Modern Pan-African Congress,* Morrow, 1972.
(With Diane DiPrima) *The Floating Bear, A Newsletter, No. 1-37, 1961-1969,* McGilvery, 1974.
(With Amina Baraka) *Confirmation: An Anthology of Afro-American Women,* Morrow, 1983.

*OTHER*

(Contributor under name LeRoi Jones) Herbert Hill, editor, *Soon, One Morning,* Knopf, 1963.
(Under name LeRoi Jones) *The System of Dante's Hell* (novel; includes the play *Dante;* also see below), Grove, 1965.
(Author of introduction) David Henderson, *Felix of the Silent Forest,* Poets Press, 1967.
*Striptease,* Parallax, 1967.
*Tales* (short stories; also see below), Grove, 1967.
(Author of preface), *Black Boogaloo (Notes on Black Liberation),* Journal of Black Poetry Press, 1969.
*Focus on Amiri Baraka: Playwright LeRoi Jones Analyzes the First National Black Political Convention* (sound recording), Center for Cassette Studies, 1973.
*Three Books by Imamu Amiri Baraka (LeRoi Jones)* (contains *The System of Dante's Hell, Tales,* and *The Dead Lecturer),* Grove, 1975.

*The Autobiography of LeRoi Jones/Amiri Baraka,* Freundlich
   Books, 1984.
(Contributor of commentary) Larry Neal, *Visions of A Liber-
   ated Future: Black Arts Movement Writings,* Thunder's
   Mouth Press, 1989.
*The LeRoi Jones/Amiri Baraka Reader,* edited by William J.
   Harris, Thunder's Mouth, 1991.

Work represented in more than seventy-five anthologies, including *A Broadside Treasury, For Malcolm, The New Black
Poetry, Nommo,* and *The Trembling Lamb.* Baraka's works
have been translated into German, French, and Spanish. Contributor to periodicals, including *Evergreen Review, Poetry,
Downbeat, Metronome, Nation, Negro Digest, Saturday Review.* Editor with Diane Di Prima, *The Floating Bear,* 1961-
1963. Papers by and about Amiri Baraka/LeRoi Jones are
housed in the Dr. Martin Sukov Collection at Yale University's Beinecke Rare Book and Manuscript Library; numerous
letters to and from the author plus several of Baraka's manuscripts are collected at Indiana University's Lilly Library; the
author's letters to Charles Olson are housed at the University
of Connecticut's Special Collections Library; other manuscripts and materials are collected at Syracuse University's
George Arents Research Library.

*WORK IN PROGRESS:* "Why's/Wise," an epic poem; four
books of poetry.

*SIDELIGHTS:* Amiri Baraka (known as LeRoi Jones until
1967) is a major author whose strident social criticism and
incendiary style have made it difficult for audiences and critics to respond with objectivity to his works. His art stems from
his African American heritage. His method in poetry, drama,
fiction and essays is confrontational, calculated to shock and
awaken audiences to the political concerns of black Americans. Baraka's own political stance has changed several times,
each time finding expression in his plays, poems, and essays
so that his works can be divided into periods; a member of
the avant garde during the 1950s, Baraka became a black
nationalist, and later a Marxist with socialist ideals. Critical
opinion has been sharply divided between those who feel, with
*Dissent* contributor Stanley Kaufman, that Baraka's race and
political moment account for his fame, and those who feel that
Baraka stands among the most important writers of the age.
In *American Book Review,* Arnold Rampersad counts Baraka
with Phyllis Wheatley, Frederick Douglass, Paul Laurence
Dunbar, Langston Hughes, Zora Neale Hurston, Richard
Wright, and Ralph Ellison "as one of the eight figures ... who
have significantly affected the course of African-American
literary culture."

Baraka did not always identify with radical politics, nor did
he always train his writing to be their tool. He was born in
Newark, New Jersey, and enjoyed a middle-class education.

During the 1950s he attended Rutgers University and Howard
University. Then he spent two years in the Air Force, stationed
for most of that time in Puerto Rico. When he returned to New
York City, he attended Columbia University and the New
School of Social Research, where he took a degree in German literature. He lived in Greenwich Village's lower east side
where his friends were the Beat poets Allen Ginsberg, Frank
O'Hara, and Gilbert Sorrentino. The white avant garde—primarily Ginsberg, O'Hara, and leader of the Black Mountain
poets Charles Olson—taught Baraka that writing poetry is a
process of discovery rather than an exercise in fulfilling traditional expectations of what poems should be. Baraka learned
much from the projectivist poets who believed that a poem's
form should follow the shape determined by the poet's own
breath and intensity of feeling. In 1958 Baraka founded *Yugen*
magazine and Totem Press, important forums for new verse.
His first play, *A Good Girl Is Hard to Find,* was produced at
Sterington House in Montclair, New Jersey, that same year.

*Preface to a Twenty Volume Suicide Note,* Baraka's first published collection of poems, appeared in 1961. M. L. Rosenthal
wrote in *The New Poets: American and British Poetry* that
these poems show Baraka's "natural gift for quick, vivid imagery and spontaneous humor." The reviewer also praised the
"sardonic or sensuous or slangily knowledgeable passages"
that fill the early poems. While the cadence of blues and many
allusions to black culture are found in the poems, the subject
of blackness does not predominate. Throughout, rather, the
poet shows his integrated, Bohemian social roots. For example, the poem "Notes for a Speech" states, "African blues /
does not know me ... Does / not feel / what I am," and the
book's last line reads, "You are / as any other sad man here /
american."

With the rise of the civil rights movement, however, Baraka's
works took on a more militant tone, and he began a reluctant
separation from his Bohemian beginnings. His trip to Castro's
Cuba in July of 1960 marked an important turning point in
his life. His view of his role as a writer, the purpose of art,
and the degree to which ethnic awareness deserved to be his
subject changed dramatically. In Cuba he met writers and
artists from Third World countries whose political concerns
included the fight against poverty, famine, and oppressive
governments. They felt he was merely being self-indulgent,
"cultivating his soul" in poetry while there were social problems to solve in America. In *Home: Social Essays,* Baraka
explains how he tried to defend himself against these accusations, and was further challenged by Jaime Shelley, a Mexican poet, who had said, "You want to cultivate your soul? In
that ugliness you live in, you want to cultivate your soul? Well,
we've got millions of starving people to feed, and that moves
me enough to make poems out of." Soon Baraka began to
identify with Third World writers and to write poems and plays
that had strong ethnic and political messages.

*Dutchman,* a play of entrapment in which a white woman and a middle-class black man both express their murderous hatred on a subway, was first performed Off-Broadway in New York City in 1964. The one-act play makes many references to sex and violence and ends in the black man's murder. While other dramatists of the time were using the techniques of naturalism, Baraka used symbolism and other experimental techniques to enhance the play's emotional impact. Lula, the white woman, represents the white state, and Clay, the black man in the play, represents ethnic identity and non-white manhood. Lula kills Clay after taunting him with sexual invitations and insults such as "You ain't no nigger, you're just a dirty white man. Get up, Clay. Dance with me, Clay." The play established Baraka's reputation as a playwright and has been often anthologized and performed. Considered by many to be the best play in America, it won the *Village Voice* Obie Award in 1964. Later, Anthony Harvey adapted it for a film made in Britain, and in the 1990s it was revived for several productions in New York City. Darryl Pinckney comments in the *New York Times Book Review* that *Dutchman* has survived the test of time better than other protest plays of the 1960s due to its economical use of vivid language, its surprise ending, and its quick pacing.

The plays and poems following *Dutchman* expressed Baraka's increasing disappointment with white America and his growing need to separate from it. Baraka wrote in *Cuba Libre* that the Beat generation had become a counterculture of drop-outs, which did not amount to very meaningful politics. Baraka felt there had to be a more effective alternative to disengagement from the political, legal, and moral morass that the country had become. In *The Dead Lecturer,* Baraka explored the alternatives, finding that there is no room for compromise: if he identifies with an ethnic cause, he can find hope of meaningful action and change; but if he remains in his comfortable assimilated position, writing "quiet" poems, he will remain "a dead lecturer." The voice in these poems is more sure of itself, led by a "moral earnestness" that is wedded to action, Baraka wrote in a 1961 letter to Edward Dorn. Critics observed that as the poems became more politically intense, they left behind some of the flawless technique of the earlier poems. *Nation* review contributor Richard Howard commented, "These are the agonized poems of a man writing to save his skin, or at least to settle in it, and so urgent is their purpose that not one of them can trouble to be perfect."

To make a clean break with the Beat influence, Baraka turned to writing fiction in the mid 1960s. He wrote *The System of Dante's Hell,* a novel, and *Tales,* a collection of short stories. The novel echoes the themes and structures found in earlier poems and plays. The stories, like the poems in *Black Magic,* also published in 1967, are "fugitive narratives" that "describe the harried flight of an intensely self-conscious Afro-American artist/intellectual from neo-slavery of blinding, neutralizing whiteness, where the area of struggle is basically within

the mind," Robert Eliot Fox writes in *Conscientious Sorcerers: The Black Post-Modernist Fiction of LeRoi Jones/Baraka, Ishmael Reed, and Samuel R. Delany.* The role of violent action in achieving poilitical change is more prominent in these stories. Unlike Shakespeare's Hamlet, who deliberates at length before taking violent action, during this period Baraka sought to stand with "the straight ahead people, who think when that's called for, who don't when they don't have to," he wrote in *Tales.* The role of music in black life is seen more often in these books, also. In the story "Screamers," the screams from a jazz saxophone galvanize the people into a powerful uprising.

Baraka's classic history *Blues People: Negro Music in White America,* published in 1963, traces black music from slavery to contemporary jazz. The blues, a staple of black American music, grew out of the encounter between African and American cultures in the South to become an art form uniquely connected to both the African past and the American soil. Finding indigenous black art forms was important to Baraka at this time, for he was searching for a more authentic ethnic voice for his own poetry. In this important study, Baraka became known as an articulate jazz critic and a perceptive observer of social change. As Clyde Taylor states in *Amiri Baraka: The Kaleidoscopic Torch* by James B. Gwynne, "The connection he nailed down between the many faces of black music, the sociological sets that nurtured them, and their symbolic evolutions through socio-economic changes, in *Blues People,* is his most durable conception, as well as probably the one most indispensible thing said about black music."

Baraka will also be long remembered for his other important studies, *Black Music,* which expresses black nationalist ideals, and *The Music: Reflections on Jazz and Blues,* which expresses his Marxist views. In *Black Music,* John Coltrane emerges as the patron saint of the black arts movement, for replacing "weak Western forms" of music with more fluid forms learned from a global vision of black culture. Though some critics feel that Baraka's essay writing is not all of the same quality, Lloyd W. Brown comments in *Amiri Baraka* that his essays on music are flawless: "As historian, musicological analyst, or as a journalist covering a particular performance Baraka always commands attention because of his obvious knowledge of the subject and because of a style that is engaging and persuasive even when the sentiments are questionable and controversial."

After Black Muslim leader Malcolm X was killed in 1965, Baraka moved to Harlem and became a black nationalist. He founded the Black Arts Repertory Theatre/School in Harlem and published the collection *Black Magic.* Poems in *Black Magic* chronicle Baraka's divorce from white culture and values and display his mastery of poetic techniques. In *Amiri Baraka: The Kaleidoscopic Torch,* Taylor observed, "There are enough brilliant poems of such variety in *Black Magic* and *In Our Terribleness* to establish the unique identity and claim for respect of several poets. But it is beside the point that Baraka is probably the finest poet, black or white, writing in this country these days." There was no doubt that Baraka's political concerns superceded his just claims to literary excellence, and the challenge to critics was to respond to the political content of the works. Some critics who felt the best art must be apolitical, dismissed his new work as "a loss to literature." Kenneth Rexroth wrote in *With Eye and Ear,* "In recent years [Baraka] has succumbed to the temptation to become a professional Race Man of the most irresponsible sort.... His loss to literature is more serious than any literary casualty of the Second War." For the next ten years, Baraka hated whites and Jews, including the whites who had once been his friends. In 1966 he moved back to Newark, New Jersey, and a year later changed his name to the Bantuized Muslim appellation Imamu ("spiritual leader," later dropped) Ameer (later Amiri, "blessed") Baraka ("prince").

A new aesthetic for black art was being developed in Harlem and Baraka was its primary theorist. Black American artists should follow African, not North American standards of beauty and value, he maintained, and should stop looking to white culture for validation. The black artist's role, he wrote in *Home: Social Essays,* was to "aid in the destruction of America as he knows it." Foremost in this endeavor was the imperative to portray society and its ills faithfully so that the portrayal would move people to take necessary corrective action.

By the early 1970s Baraka was recognized as "a teacher of great talent" by Broadside Press publisher Dudley Randall and many others. Randall noted in *Black World* that younger black poets Nikki Giovanni and Don. L. Lee (now Haki R. Madhubuti) were "learning from LeRoi Jones, a man versed in German philosophy, conscious of literary tradition ... who uses the structure of Dante's *Divine Comedy* in his *System of Dante's Hell* and the punctuation, spelling and line divisions of sophisticated contemporary poets." Rampersad writes in the *American Book Review,* "More than any other black poet, however, he taught younger black poets of the generation past how to respond poetically to their lived experience, rather than to depend as artists on embalmed reputations and outmoded rhetorical strategies derived from a culture often substantially different from their own."

After coming to see black nationalism as a destructive form of racism, Baraka denounced it in 1974 and became a Third World Socialist. Hatred of non-whites, he declared in the *New York Times,* "is sickness or criminality, in fact, a form of fascism." Since 1974 he has produced a number of Marxist poetry collections and plays. His new political goal is the formation of socialist communities and a socialist state. *Daggers and Javelins* and the other books produced during this period

lack the emotional power of the works from the black nationalist period, say the American critics. However, critics who agree with his new politics such as exiled Philipino leftist intellectual E. San Juan praise his work of the late 1970s. San Juan wrote in *Amiri Baraka: The Kaleidoscopic Torch* that Baraka's 1978 play *Lone Ranger* was "the most significant theatrical achievement of 1978 in the Western hemisphere." Joe Weixlmann responds in the same source to the tendency to categorize the radical Baraka instead of analyze him: "At the very least, dismissing someone with a label does not make for very satisfactory scholarship. Initially, Baraka's reputation as a writer and thinker derived from a recognition of the talents with which he is so obviously endowed. The assaults on that reputation have, too frequently, derived from concerns which should be extrinsic to informed criticism."

Baraka's standing as a major poet is matched by his importance as a cultural and political leader. His influence on younger writers has been so significant and widespread that it would be difficult to discuss American literary history without mentioning his name. As leader of the Black Arts movement of the 1960s, Baraka did much to define and support black literature's mission into the twenty-first century. His experimental fiction of the 1960s is yet considered the most significant contribution to black fiction since that of Jean Toomer, who wrote during the Harlem Renaissance of the 1920s. Writers from other ethnic groups credit Baraka with opening "tightly guarded doors" in the white publishing establishment, notes Native American author Maurice Kenney in *Amiri Baraka: The Kaleidoscopic Torch.* Kenny adds, "We'd all still be waiting the invitation from the *New Yorker* without him. He taught us how to claim it and take it."

*BIOGRAPHICAL/CRITICAL SOURCES:*

*BOOKS*

Allen, Donald M., and Warren Tallman, editors, *Poetics of the New American Poetry,* Grove, 1973.

Baraka, Amiri, *The Autobiography of LeRoi Jones/Amiri Baraka,* Freundlich Books, 1984.

Baraka, Amiri, and Larry Neal, editors, *Black Fire: An Anthology of Afro-American Writing,* Morrow, 1968.

Baraka, Amiri, *Black Magic: Sabotage; Target Study; Black Art; Collected Poetry, 1961-1967,* Bobbs-Merrill, 1969.

Baraka, Amiri, *Tales,* Grove, 1967.

Benston, Kimberly A., editor, *Baraka: The Renegade and the Mask,* Yale University Press, 1976.

Benston, Kimberly A., editor, *Imamu Amiri Baraka (LeRoi Jones): A Collection of Critical Essays,* Prentice-Hall, 1978.

Bigsby, C. W. E., *Confrontation and Commitment: A Study of Contemporary American Drama, 1959-66,* University of Missouri Press, 1968.

Bigsby, C. W. E., *The Second Black Renaissance: Essays in Black Literature,* Greenwood Press, 1980.

Brown, Lloyd W., *Amiri Baraka,* Twayne, 1980.

*Concise Dictionary of American Literary Biography,* Volume 1: *The New Consciousness,* Gale, 1987.

*Contemporary Literary Criticism,* Gale, Volume 1, 1973; Volume 2, 1974; Volume 3, 1975; Volume 5, 1976; Volume 10, 1979; Volume 14, 1980; Volume 33, 1985.

Dace, Letitia, *LeRoi Jones (Imamu Amiri Baraka): A Checklist of Works by and about Him,* Nether Press, 1971.

*Dictionary of Literary Biography,* Gale, Volume 5: *American Poets since World War II,* 1980; Volume 7: *Twentieth Century American Dramatists,* 1981; Volume 16: *The Beats: Literary Bohemians in Postwar America,* two parts, 1983; Volume 38: *Afro-American Writers after 1955: Dramatists and Prose Writers,* 1985.

Dukore, Bernard F., *Drama and Revolution,* Holt, 1971.

Ellison, Ralph, *Shadow and Act,* New American Library, 1966.

Fox, Robert Elliot, *Conscientious Sorcerers: The Black Post-Modernist Fiction of LeRoi Jones/Baraka, Ishmael Reed and Samuel R. Delany,* Greenwood Press, 1987.

Gwynne, James B., editor, *Amiri Baraka: The Kaleidoscopic Torch,* Steppingstones Press, 1985.

Hall, Veronica, *Chicorel Theater Index to Plays in Anthologies, Periodicals, Discs and Tapes,* Chicorel Library Publishing, 1970.

Harris, William J., *The Poetry and Poetics of Amiri Baraka: The Jazz Aesthetic,* University of Missouri Press, 1985.

Henderson, Stephen E., *Understanding the New Black Poetry: Black Speech and Black Music as Poetic References,* Morrow, 1973.

Hudson, Theodore, *From LeRoi Jones to Amiri Baraka: The Literary Works,* Duke University Press, 1973.

Jones, LeRoi, *Blues People: Negro Music in White America,* Morrow, 1963.

Jones, LeRoi, *The Dead Lecturer,* Grove, 1964.

Jones, LeRoi, *Dutchman,* Faber & Faber, 1967.

Jones, LeRoi, *Home: Social Essays,* Morrow, 1966.

Jones, LeRoi, *Preface to a Twenty Volume Suicide Note,* Totem Press/Corinth Books, 1961.

Kofsky, Frank, *Black Nationalism and the Revolution in Music,* Pathfinder, 1970.

Lacey, Henry C., *To Raise, Destroy, and Create: The Poetry, Drama, and Fiction of Imamu Amiri Baraka (LeRoi Jones),* Whitson Publishing Company, 1981.

O'Brien, John, *Interviews with Black Writers,* Liveright, 1973.

Ossman, David, *The Sullen Art: Interviews with Modern American Poets,* Corinth, 1963.

Rexroth, Kenneth, *With Eye and Ear,* Herder and Herder, 1970.

Rosenthal, M. L., *The New Poets: American and British Poetry since World War II,* Oxford University Press, 1967.

Sollors, Werner, *Amiri Baraka/LeRoi Jones: The Quest for a "Populist Modernism,"* Columbia University Press, 1978.

Stepanchev, Stephen, *American Poetry since 1945,* Harper, 1965.

Weales, Gerald, *The Jumping-Off Place: American Drama in the 1960s,* Macmillan, 1969.

Whitlow, Roger, *Black American Literature: A Critical History,* Nelson Hall, 1973.

*PERIODICALS*

*American Book Review,* February, 1980; May-June, 1985.

*Atlantic,* January, 1966; May, 1966.

*Avant Garde,* September, 1968.

*Black American Literature Forum,* spring, 1980; spring, 1981; fall, 1982; spring, 1983; winter, 1985.

*Black World,* April, 1971; December, 1971; November, 1974; July, 1975.

*Book Week,* December 24, 1967.

*Book World,* October 28, 1979.

*Boundary 2,* number 6, 1978.

*Chicago Defender,* January 11, 1965.

*Chicago Tribune,* October 4, 1968.

*Contemporary Literature,* Volume 12, 1971.

*Detroit Free Press,* January 31, 1965.

*Detroit News,* January 15, 1984; August 12, 1984.

*Dissent,* spring, 1965.

*Ebony,* August, 1967; August, 1969; February, 1971.

*Educational Theatre Journal,* March, 1968; March, 1970; March, 1976.

*Esquire,* June, 1966.

*Essence,* September, 1970; May, 1984; September, 1984; May, 1985.

*Jazz Review,* June, 1959.

*Journal of Black Poetry,* fall, 1968; spring, 1969; summer, 1969; fall, 1969.

*Los Angeles Free Press,* May 3, 1968.

*Los Angeles Times,* April 20, 1990.

*Los Angeles Times Book Review,* May 15, 1983; March 29, 1987.

*Nation,* October 14, 1961; November 14, 1961; March 13, 1964; April 13, 1964; January 4, 1965; March 15, 1965; January 22, 1968; February 2, 1970.

*Negro American Literature Forum,* March, 1966; winter, 1973.

*Negro Digest,* December, 1963; February, 1964; August, 1964; March, 1965; April, 1965; March, 1966; April, 1966; June, 1966; April, 1967; April, 1968; January, 1969; April, 1969.

*Newsweek,* March 13, 1964; April 13, 1964; November 22, 1965; May 2, 1966; March 6, 1967; December 4, 1967; December 1, 1969; February 19, 1973.

*New York,* November 5, 1979.

*New Yorker,* April 4, 1964; December 26, 1964; March 4, 1967; December 30, 1972.

*New York Herald Tribune,* March 25, 1964; April 2, 1964; December 13, 1964; October 27, 1965.

*New York Post,* March 16, 1964; March 24, 1964; January 15, 1965; March 18, 1965.

*New York Review of Books,* May 22, 1964; January 20, 1966; July 2, 1970; October 17, 1974; June 11, 1984; June 14, 1984.

*New York Times,* April 28, 1966; May 8, 1966; August 10, 1966; September 14, 1966; October 5, 1966; January 20, 1967; February 28, 1967; July 15, 1967; January 5, 1968; January 6, 1968; January 9, 1968; January 10, 1968; February 7, 1968; April 14, 1968; August 16, 1968; November 27, 1968; December 24, 1968; August 26, 1969; November 23, 1969; February 6, 1970; May 11, 1972; June 11, 1972; November 11, 1972; November 14, 1972; November 23, 1972; December 5, 1972; December 27, 1974; December 29, 1974; November 19, 1979; October 15, 1981; January 23, 1984; February 9, 1991.

*New York Times Book Review,* January 31, 1965; November 28, 1965; May 8, 1966; February 4, 1968; March 17, 1968; February 14, 1971; June 6, 1971; June 27, 1971; December 5, 1971; March 12, 1972; December 16, 1979; March 11, 1984; July 5, 1987; December 20, 1987.

*New York Times Magazine,* February 5, 1984.

*Salmagundi,* spring-summer, 1973.

*Saturday Review,* April 20, 1963; January 11, 1964; January 9, 1965; December 11, 1965; December 9, 1967; October 2, 1971; July 12, 1975.

*Studies in Black Literature,* spring, 1970; Volume 1, number 2, 1970; Volume 3, number 2, 1972; Volume 3, number 3, 1972; Volume 4, number 1, 1973.

*Sunday News* (New York), January 21, 1973.

*Time,* December 25, 1964; November 19, 1965; May 6, 1966; January 12, 1968; April 26, 1968; June 28, 1968; June 28, 1971.

*Times Literary Supplement,* November 25, 1965; September 1, 1966; September 11, 1969; October 9, 1969; August 2, 1991.

*Tribune Books,* March 29, 1987.

*Washington Post,* August 15, 1968; September 12, 1968; November 27, 1968; December 5, 1980; January 23, 1981; June 29, 1987.

*Washington Post Book World,* December 24, 1967; May 22, 1983.

\*    \*    \*

## BARRAX, Gerald William 1933-

*PERSONAL:* Born June 21, 1933, in Attalla, AL; son of Aaron (a custodian) and Dorthera (Hedrick) Barrax; married Geneva Catherine Lucy, 1954 (divorced, 1971); married Joan Delli-more; children: (first marriage) Dennis Scott, Gerald William, Joshua Cameron; (second marriage) Shani Averyl, Dara Hilary. *Education:* Duquesne University, B.A., 1963; University of Pittsburgh, M.A., 1969.

*ADDRESSES: Home*—808 Cooper Rd., Raleigh, NC 27610. *Office*—Department of English, North Carolina State University, Raleigh, NC 27607.

*CAREER:* United States Post Office, Pittsburgh, PA, clerk and carrier, 1958-67; North Carolina Central University, Durham, instructor, 1969-70; North Carolina State University, Raleigh, special instructor in English department, 1970—. *Military service:* U.S. Air Force, 1953-57; became airperson first class.

*AWARDS, HONORS:* Gold Medal award, Catholic Poetry Society of America.

*WRITINGS:*

*Another Kind of Rain* (poetry), University of Pittsburgh Press, 1970.

*An Audience of One* (poetry), University of Georgia Press, 1980.

*The Deaths of Animals and Lesser Gods,* edited by Charles H. Rowell, University of Kentucky, 1984.

*Leaning against the Sun* (poetry), University of Arkansas Press, 1992.

Work represented in anthologies, including *Kaleidoscope: Poems by American Negro Poets,* edited by Robert Hayden, Harcourt, 1968, *Understanding the New Black Poetry: Black Speech and Black Music as Poetic References,* Morrow, 1973, *The Poetry of Black America: Anthology of the 20th Century,* Harper, 1973, and *Contemporary Poetry of North Carolina,* John F. Blair, 1977. Contributor of poetry to periodicals, including *Black World, Callahoo, Four Quarters, Georgia Review, Hyperion, Nimrod, Obsidian, Pembroke, Poetry Northwest, Poetry, Southern Poetry Review, Spirit,* and *World Order.*

*BIOGRAPHICAL/CRITICAL SOURCES:*

*PERIODICALS*

*Booklist,* September 15, 1980, p. 94.

*Choice,* April, 1985, p. 1156.

*Library Journal,* October 15, 1970, p. 3477.

\*    \*    \*

## BARRETT, (Eseoghene) Lindsay 1941- (Eseoghene)

*PERSONAL:* Born in 1941, in Lucea, Jamaica; married an actor.

*ADDRESSES: Agent*—c/o Publicity Director, Fourth Dimension Publishing Co. Ltd., House 16, Fifth Ave., City Layout, New Haven, PMB 01164, Eunugu, Nigeria.

*CAREER:* Jamaica Broadcasting Corporation, Jamaica, news editor, 1961; worked variously as apprentice journalist for *Daily Gleaner* and the Jamaica *Star,* free-lance worker in overseas department of British Broadcasting Corporation, lecturer for Fourah Bay College in Sierra Leone, teacher in Ghana, and worked at University of Ibadan in Ibadan, Nigeria; writer. Worked in television in Nigeria.

*AWARDS, HONORS:* Conrad Kent Rivers Memorial Award, *Black World,* c. 1971.

*WRITINGS:*

*The State of Black Desire,* illustrated by Larry Potter, Corbiere et Jugain, 1966.
*Song for Mumu: A Novel,* Longman, 1967, Howard University Press, 1974.
(Under pseudonym Eseoghene) *The Conflicting Eye* (poems), Paul Breman, 1973.
*Lipskybound,* Bladi House, 1977.
*Agbada to Khaki: Reporting a Change of Government in Nigeria,* Fourth Dimension, 1985.

Author of *Sighs of a Slave Dream* (one-act), produced in London, England; *Home Again; Blackblast; Jump Kookoo Makka;* and *After This We Heard of Fire.* Wrote radio plays for Nigerian National Radio. Work represented in anthologies, including *Black Arts,* edited by Alhamisi and Wangara, and *Black Fire,* edited by Jones and Neal. Contributor to journals, including *Black World, Black Lines,* and *Negro Digest.* Contributing editor for *Frontline* and *West Indian World.*

*BIOGRAPHICAL/CRITICAL SOURCES:*

*PERIODICALS*

*New York Times Book Review,* September 29, 1974, p. 40.

\*    \*    \*

**BART-WILLIAMS, Gaston 1938-**

*PERSONAL:* Born in 1938, in Sierra Leone.

*CAREER:* Playwright, poet, and short story and radio feature writer. Has written for the British Broadcasting Corp. (BBC), Canadian Broadcasting Corp.(CBC), and for radio stations in Sweden, Norway, and Germany. African Youth Cultural Society, West Africa, founder, 1958; World Assembly of Youth,

Mali Republic, Sierra Leone representative, 1959; Commonwealth Theatre Conference and Commonwealth Poets' Conference, London, England, 1965.

*AWARDS, HONORS:* All African Short Story Award, Congress for Cultural Freedom, 1962-63; Michael Karolyi International Award (France), 1963; German London Embassy Cultural Grant, 1964.

*WRITINGS:*

*Poems* (mimeographed volume of verse), [Cologne], 1964.
*Curse Your God and Die* (mimeographed play), [Cologne], 1965.
*Uhuru,* West German Radio, 1969.

Also author of *A Bouquet of Carnations,* BBC, and *In Praise of Madness.* Work represented in anthologies, including *Black Orpheus,* Longmans, 1964; *Young Commonwealth Poets, '65,* 1965; *New Poems,* 1966; *Commonwealth Poems of Today,* John Murray, 1967; *Pergamon Poets-2, Poetry from Africa,* Pergamon Press, 1968; *New Voices of the Commonwealth,* 1968. Contributor to periodicals, including *London Magazine, New Statesman, Outposts, Meanjin* and *Studio Du Mont.*

\*    \*    \*

**BASS, Kingsley B., Jr.**
  **See BULLINS, Ed**

\*    \*    \*

**BATES, Arthenia J.**
  **See MILLICAN, Arthenia Jackson Bates**

\*    \*    \*

**BEDIAKO, Kwabena Asare**
  **See KONADU, S(amuel) A(sare)**

\*    \*    \*

**BELL, Derrick Albert, Jr. 1930-**

*PERSONAL:* Born November 6, 1930, in Pittsburgh, PA; son of Derrick Albert and Ada Elizabeth (Childress) Bell; married Jewel Allison Hairston, June 26, 1960 (died, August, 1990); married Janet Dewart, June 28, 1992; children: (first marriage) Derrick Albert III, Douglass Dubois, Carter

Robeson. *Education:* Duquesne University, A.B., 1952; University of Pittsburgh, LL.B., 1957.

*ADDRESSES: Home*—2 Washington Square Village PH-C, New York, NY 10012-1732. *Office*—New York University, School of Law, 40 Washington Square St., New York, NY 10012.

*CAREER:* U.S. Department of Justice, Washington, DC, member of staff of conscientious objector section and civil rights division, 1957-59; National Association for the Advancement of Colored People (NAACP), New York City, staff attorney for Legal Defense and Education Fund, Inc., 1960-66; U.S. Department of Health, Education and Welfare, Washington, DC, deputy director of Office of Civil Rights, 1966-68; U.S. Office of Economic Opportunity, Western Center of Law and Poverty at University of Southern California, Los Angeles, director, 1968-69; Harvard University, Cambridge, MA, lecturer, 1969-71, professor of law, 1971-80, 1986-90; University of Oregon, Eugene, professor of law and dean of law school, 1981-85. Visiting professor, New York University, 1991-92. *Military service:* U.S. Air Force, 1952-54; became first lieutenant.

*MEMBER:* National Conference of Black Lawyers, Society of American Law Schools, American Bar Association.

*AWARDS, HONORS:* Ford Foundation grants, 1972, 1975, 1991, and 1993; National Endowment for the Humanities grant, 1980-81; honorary law degrees, Toogaloo College, 1983, Northeastern University, 1985, and Mercy College, 1988.

*WRITINGS:*

*Race, Racism, and American Law,* Little, Brown, 1973, third edition, 1992.
(Contributor) Robert J. Haws, editor, *The Age of Segregation: Race Relations in the South, 1890-1945* (essays), University Press of Mississippi, 1978.
*Shades of Brown: New Perspectives on School Desegregation,* Teachers College Press, 1980.
(Editor) *Civil Rights: Leading Cases,* Little, Brown, 1980.
*And We are Not Saved: The Elusive Quest for Racial Justice,* Basic Books, 1987.
*Faces at the Bottom of the Well: The Permanence of Racism,* Basic Books, 1992.
*Civil Rights in 2004: Where Will We Be?,* Institute for Philosophy and Public Policy, in press.

Contributor to law journals.

*SIDELIGHTS:* Though he had established himself as a talented editor and essayist more than ten years earlier, Derrick Albert

Bell, Jr. redefined his place in the literary world with his 1987 book *And We Are Not Saved: The Elusive Quest for Racial Justice.* It addresses racial issues through an intertwining of fictional parables, which the author calls "chronicles," and academic argumentation. This combination allows Bell to go "beyond the well-worn arguments, answers and accommodations about race that Americans are accustomed to reading," notes Juan Williams in the *Washington Post Book World.*

Between the often-humorous parables are dialogues between two fictional narrators: a fiery 1960's civil rights lawyer named Geneva Crenshaw and a nameless male speaker who, according to *New York Times Book Review*'s Vincent Harding, "reminds us a lot of Mr. Bell." With these two narrators acting as adversaries, moderators, and chorus, *And We Are Not Saved* allows readers to examine racial issues from a unique perspective. "Novels ... are more illuminating on racial themes [than essays] because they can convey the reality of racial discrimination," writes Williams, "the cultural biases, legal inequities, sexual rules and the struggle of children to understand so massive a sin, as well as the occasional triumph against all odds." At one point, Geneva Crenshaw is transported back in time to the Constitutional Convention, where she debates with the founding fathers as to the ramifications of drafting legal slavery into the Constitution. In the end, says Harding, Bell asks readers both black and white to "rethink our past in order to re-envision and re-create our common future." Williams observes: "The road to this conclusion is a long one.... Bell could have written a much shorter essay and made his point. But the human dimension added by his stories about the pain and psychic costs of flawed modern race relations make the trip worthwhile."

When *And We Are Not Saved* was published, it elicited in readers a kind of determined optimism; Harding placed it "near the center of our continuing discussions of the past, present and future of this nation," while Williams went so far as to say: "It has the potential to shift the national mindset as America continues to climb the mountain of racial problems." Bell, himself, grudgingly admitted to *New York Times Book Review* interviewer Rosemary L. Bray: "At some point America may actually be a land with opportunity and justice for all." During the following years, however, the face of American racial issues became even more grim, and that optimism turned slowly into indignation. Disgusted with the lack of progress, Bell once again addressed black America with his 1992 novel, *Faces at the Bottom of the Well: The Permanence of Racism.*

Where *And We Are Not Saved* was considered by critics to be melancholy, *Faces at the Bottom of the Well* is scathing and provocative; it is described by Alex Raksin of the *Los Angeles Times Book Review* as "virtually a declaration of war. Declaring that 'black people will never gain full equality in this country,' it is ... a manifesto of secession." As with his first novel, Bell combines essay with parable to illuminate the plight of the African American: that equality is, ultimately, unattainable. Notable among *Faces'* stories is a chronicle entitled "Space Traders," in which the entire population of black Americans is sold to extraterrestrials, for an unspecified purpose, in exchange for gold and other resources. "Bell spins this grim and stingingly effective tale around the thesis that 'sanctuary' is a more apt description of black citizenship in America than 'equality'," writes Lynne Duke in the *Washington Post Book World.* As with the first book, the parables are interspersed with dialogue, and Geneva Crenshaw even makes a brief return. Raksin lauds Bell's chronicles as "powerful in their eloquence," and while Duke admits that they can be "overly contrived and laborious to get through, this does not detract from Bell's profoundly engaging theme: Equality, for African-Americans, is a seductive, tranquilizing notion, but nothing more."

Bell once commented: "In my writing, there is little of craft and certainly nothing of art, but it serves as a medium of expression which, while only infrequently effectual, remains a soul-satisfying means of speaking out against racism, poverty, and this society's self-deluding conviction that happiness can be purchased, integrity feigned, and the Lord's judgment forever postponed."

*BIOGRAPHICAL/CRITICAL SOURCES:*

*PERIODICALS*

*American History Review,* December, 1988, p. 1386.
*Freedomways,* number 2, 1981, p. 123.
*Journal of American History,* September, 1988, p. 675.
*Los Angeles Times Book Review,* August 23, 1992, p. 6.
*Nation,* March 19, 1988, p. 382.
*New Republic,* November 16, 1987, p. 36.
*New York Times Book Review,* October 11, 1987, p. 7.
*Washington Post Book World,* November 1, 1987, p. 10;
    August 23, 1992, p. 1.

\*   \*   \*

## BELL, Roseann P. 1945-

*PERSONAL:* Born May 2, 1945, in Atlanta, GA; divorced; children: William David. *Education:* Howard University, B.A., 1966; Emory University, M.A. (cum laude), 1970; Ph.D. (cum laude), 1974.

*CAREER:* U.S. Civil Service Commission, Washington, DC, typist, 1964-66; Atlanta Public School System, Atlanta, GA, instructor, 1966-70; Spelman College, Atlanta, assistant professor, beginning in 1970; Cornell University, Ithaca, NY, assistant professor of Afro-American studies; free-lance edi-

tor of educational manuscripts. Producer of radio programs in St. Croix, Virgin Islands.

*AWARDS, HONORS:* National Institute of Humanities fellow, 1971-73; National Fellowships Fund fellow, Ford Foundation, 1973-74.

*WRITINGS:*

(Editor with Bettye J. Parker and Beverly Guy-Sheftall) *Sturdy Black Bridges: Visions of Black Women in Literature,* Doubleday, 1979.
(Editor with Miriam DeCosta-Willis and Reginald Martin) *Erotique Noire* (short stories and verse), Doubleday, 1992.

Also columnist for *Atlanta Voice,* 1971. Contributor to periodicals.

*SIDELIGHTS:* "My mother, religious-negro, proud of / having waded through a storm, is very obviously, / a sturdy Black bridge that I / crossed over, on." This quotation from Carolyn Rodgers' poem, entitled "It Is Deep," captures the essence of the titular *Sturdy Black Bridges,* a survey text that not only deals with black women in American, African, and Caribbean literature, but also provides information on writers of these locales. Roseann P. Bell and coeditors Miriam DeCosta-Willis and Reginald Martin spent four years meticulously gathering material for a volume which gives critical attention to African American women in literature as realistic historical reflections.

Because sufficient attention had not been given to African American female writers and texts, *Sturdy Black Bridges,* a book divided into three sections, was compiled to meet this need. Part one examines, in essay format, the theories and attitudes of black female characters and writers. Part two records interviews with a number of black female mothers, authors, and critics, including the writers Toni Morrison, Ann Petry, and critic George Kent. Part three provides samplings of the subgenres of imaginative literature (poetry, fiction, and drama) by established female writers of both traditional and contemporary literature, from the African continent and throughout the diaspora. According to Genevieve Stuttaford in *Publishers Weekly,* "This volume, clearly attesting to [black female writers'] accomplishments, should prove that this lack of attention is an inexcusable silence."

*BIOGRAPHICAL/CRITICAL SOURCES:*

*BOOKS*

Bell, Roseann P., Bettye J. Parker, and Beverly Guy-Sheftall, editors, *Sturdy Black Bridges: Visions of Black Women in Literature,* Doubleday, 1979.

*PERIODICALS*

*Booklist,* April 1, 1979.
*Freedomways,* Volume 19, number 3, 1979.
*Harvard Educational Review,* November, 1979.
*Publishers Weekly,* January 8, 1979.

\*     \*     \*

## ben-JOCHANNAN, Yosef 1918-

*PERSONAL:* Born December 31, 1918; married; wife's name, Gertrude. *Education:* "Not important to my writings."

*ADDRESSES: Home*—40 West 135th Street, New York, NY, 10037. *Office*— Alkebu-lan Books and Education Materials Associates, 209 West 125th Street, New York, NY 10027.

*CAREER:* Egyptologist, historian, and writer. Cornell University, Ithaca, NY, adjunct professor of history and African studies, 1970—; Malcolm-King College, New York City, adjunct associate professor of history; has taught or lectured at numerous colleges and universities in the United States, Europe, South America, and Africa; officer of educational trips to the Nile Valley (Ethiopia, Sudan, and Egypt) for Polo Travel. Alkebu-lan Foundation, Inc., New York City, chair of board of directors, and of Alkebu-lan Books and Education Materials Associates (a subsidiary of the Foundation); UNESCO and civilian adviser to the ambassador of Zanzibar, 1963-64.

*MEMBER:* Afro-American History Association, Society of African Historians and Anthropologists.

*WRITINGS:*

*ELEMENTARY AND SECONDARY SCHOOL TEXTBOOKS*

(With others) *Africa: Land, People, Culture,* Sadlier, 1966.
(With others) *Southern Neighbors,* Sadlier, 1966.
(With others) *Southern Lands,* Sadlier, 1966.

*ALL PUBLISHED BY ALKEBU-LAN BOOKS ASSOCIATES*

*Black Man of the Nile,* 1969.
*African Origins of the Major "Western Religions,"* 1970.
*Africa: Mother of "Western Civilization,"* 1971.
(With George E. Simmonds) *The Black Man's North and East Africa,* 1972.
*The Black Man of the Nile and His Family,* 1972, third edition, 1981.
*Cultural Genocide in the Black and African Studies Curriculum,* 1973.

*A Chronology of the Bible: Challenge to the "Standard Version,"* 1973.
*The Black Man's Religion,* three volumes, 1974.
*Influence of Great Myths of Contemporary Life; or, The Need for Black History in Mental Health: A Sociopolitical and Anthropological Student's and Researcher's Edition,* 1976.

*ALL PUBLISHED BY ALKEBU-LAN BOOKS AND EDUCATION MATERIALS ASSOCIATES*

*Our Black Seminarians and Black Clergy without a Black Theology: The Tragedy of Black People/Africans in Religion Today,* 1978.
*The Saga of the "Black Marxists" versus the "Black Nationalists": A Debate Resurrected,* 1978.
*Tutankhamon's African Roots Haley et al Overlooked,* 1978.
*In Pursuit of George G. M. James' Study of African Origins in "Western Civilization,"* 1980.
*They All Look Alike!: All of Them?,* four volumes, 1980-81.
*The Alkebu-lanians of Ta-Merry's "Mysterious System," and the Ritualization of the Late Bro. Kwesie Adebisi,* 1982.
*We the Black Jews: Witness to the "White Jewish Race" Myth,* 1983.

*OTHER*

*Axioms and Quotations of Yosef ben-Jochannan,* edited by E. Curtis Alexander, ECA Associates, 1980.
*Abu Simbel to Ghizeh: A Guide Book and Manual,* Black Classic Press, 1989.
*From Afrikan Captives to Insane Slaves: The Need for Afrikan History in Solving the "Black" Mental Health Crisis in "America" and the World,* Native Sun Publishers, 1992.

Also author of pamphlets, *We the Black Jews,* written in Spanish, 1938, and *The Rape of Africa and the Crisis in Angola,* written in Portuguese and English, 1958. Also author of recordings "Wake Up Black Man" (two records), 1973, "Egypt: The Golden Age" (one record), 1974, "The African in Ancient History before the Christian Era" (fifteen cassette tapes), 1976, "Africans of the Old Testament and Before" (fifteen cassette tapes), 1976, and "Christianity's African Roots" (one record), 1979.

*SIDELIGHTS:* Yosef ben-Jochannan is the author of numerous books, pamphlets, and recordings pertaining to African history. In much of his work, ben-Jochannan expounds on the theory of Afrocentricity, contending that the importance of Africans in history has been purposely overlooked in the classroom. Instead, he says, Europeans have been credited with providing the essential contributions to the history of the world. In books such as *Cultural Genocide in the Black and*

*African Studies Curriculum* and *Africa: Mother of Western Civilization,* he documents his case.

Dedicating much of his time to these studies, ben-Jochannan has researched such subjects for more than fifty years. Various reviewers note that the author has helped to bridge the gap in the knowledge of African history as he points out the alleged theft of a collective African legacy. "It is important for African people to read and study the works of Dr. Jochannan," asserted Roosevelt Brown in *Black World.* The critic added that Jochannan's works "demonstrate the failure of the educational system to provide the *truth* about history."

Ben-Jochannan commented that he writes because of "the fact that the major presses did not want to publish anything other than the myths about African people. More so, because my teacher in eighth grade said that 'Negroes have no history.'"

*BIOGRAPHICAL/CRITICAL SOURCES:*

*BOOKS*

Cruse, Harold, *Crisis of the Negro Intellectual,* Morrow, 1967.
Cleage, Albert, Jr., *Black Christian Nationalism: New Directions for the Black Church,* Morrow, 1972.
Henry Olela, *From Ancient Africa to Ancient Greece: An Introduction to the History of Philosophy,* Select Publishing (Atlanta), 1981.

*PERIODICALS*

*Black World,* February, 1973, p. 76.
*Journal of African Civilization,* November, 1982.
*New Republic,* February 10, 1992, p. 29.

\*   \*   \*

# BENNETT, Lerone, Jr. 1928-

*PERSONAL:* Born October 17 (one source says October 19), 1928, in Clarksdale, MS; son of Lerone and Alma (Reed) Bennett; married Gloria Sylvester, July 21, 1956; children: Alma Joy, Constance and Courtney (twins), Lerone III. *Education:* Morehouse College, A.B., 1949; Atlanta University, graduate study, 1949.

*ADDRESSES: Home*—1308 East 89th St., Chicago, IL 60619. *Office*—*Ebony* magazine, 820 South Michigan Ave., Chicago, IL 60605.

*CAREER: Atlanta Daily World,* Atlanta, GA, reporter, 1949-52, city editor, 1952-53; *Jet* (magazine), Chicago, IL, associate editor, 1953; *Ebony* (magazine), Chicago, associate edi-

tor, 1954-57, senior editor, 1958-87, executive editor, 1987—. Visiting professor of history, Northwestern University, 1968-69; Institute of the Black World, senior fellow, 1969, currently member of board of directors; member of board of directors, Chicago Public Library; member of board of trustees, Martin Luther King Memorial Center, Chicago Historical Society, Morehouse College, and Columbia College. *Military service:* U.S. Army, 1951-52; became first sergeant.

*MEMBER:* Black Academy of Arts and Letters (fellow), Phi Beta Kappa, Kappa Alpha Psi, Sigma Delta Chi.

*AWARDS, HONORS:* Book of the Year Award, Capital Press Club, 1963; D.L., Morehouse College, 1965; Patron Saints Award, Society of Midland Authors, for *What Manner of Man,* 1965; D.Hum., Wilberforce University, 1977; Academy Institute literary award, American Academy of Arts and Letters, 1978; D. Litt., Marquette University, 1979, Voorhees College, 1981, Morgan State University, 1981; L.H.D., University of Illinois, Lincoln College, and Dillard University, all 1980; honorary doctor of letters, Morris Brown University, 1985, South Carolina University, 1986, and Boston University, 1987; Humanitarian of the Year, United Negro College Fund, 1991.

*WRITINGS:*

*Before the Mayflower: A History of the Negro in America, 1619-1966,* Johnson Publishing Co. (Chicago), 1962, fifth edition, 1982.
*The Negro Mood, and Other Essays,* Johnson Publishing Co., 1964.
*What Manner of Man: A Biography of Martin Luther King, Jr., 1929-1968,* Johnson Publishing Co., 1964, third revised edition, 1968, fourth revised edition, 1976.
*Confrontation: Black and White,* Johnson Publishing Co., 1965.
*Black Power U.S.A.: The Human Side of Reconstruction, 1867-1877,* Johnson Publishing Co., 1967.
*Pioneers in Protest,* Johnson Publishing Co., 1968.
(Editor with others) *Ebony Pictorial History of Black America,* four volumes, Johnson Publishing Co., 1971.
*The Challenge of Blackness,* Johnson Publishing Co., 1972.
*The Shaping of Black America,* Johnson Publishing Co., 1975.
*Wade in the Water: Great Moments in Black History,* Johnson Publishing Co., 1979.
(With John H. Johnson) *Succeeding against the Odds,* Warner Books, 1989, reissued as *Succeeding against the Odds: The Inspiring Autobiography of One of America's Wealthiest Entrepreneurs,* Amistad, 1993.

Author of introduction to *In the Shadow of the Great White Way: Images from the Black Theatre,* Thunder's Mouth Press, 1989. Work represented in anthologies, including *The Day*

*They Marched,* edited by Doris Sanders, editor, Johnson Publishing Co., 1963; *New Negro Poets: U.S.A.,* edited by Langston Hughes, Indiana University Press, 1964; *The White Problem in America,* Johnson Publishing Co., 1966; and *Contemporary American Negro Short Stories.* Contributor of articles, short stories, and poems to popular magazines.

*SIDELIGHTS:* "Lerone Bennett, Jr., senior editor of *Ebony* magazine, has pioneered and excelled in the writing of popular black history," reports A. C. Gulliver in the *Christian Science Monitor.* From *Before the Mayflower: A History of the Negro in America, 1619-1966* to *The Shaping of Black America,* a study of black Americans in the worlds of slavery, emancipation, work and business, Bennett has produced interesting texts known for their factual accuracy and readability. Critics especially recommend *Before the Mayflower, Confrontation: Black and White,* and *Black Power, U.S.A.: The Human Side of Reconstruction.*

Pointing to the author's background in journalism (Bennett worked as a reporter for the *Atlanta Daily World* before becoming a magazine editor), Kyle Haselden of the *Christian Century* comments that, in *Before the Mayflower,* Bennett "employs a reporter's sense of what is significant and arresting.... In the main he lets the facts speak for themselves, but he selects those facts which have an emotional as well as an intellectual impact." To represent the valor of black Americans, for example, he records the victories of pre-Civil War insurrectionists and the accomplishments of black soldiers in major conflicts since then, always in the face of humiliation and opposition from their white compatriots. The highest ranking black officer at the beginning of World War I was not allowed to fight due "to high blood pressure" although his health was sound; the black commander of the all-black 369th regiment was excluded from the Rainbow Division that served in France because "he was told, he said, that black was not one of the colors of the rainbow." Nonetheless, adds Bennett, that regiment "was the first Allied unit to reach the Rhine. The regiment, which was under fire for 191 days, never lost a foot of ground, a trench or a soldier through capture." And to represent the many lynchings that took place in 1918 and 1919, Bennett writes, "More disturbing than the number [147] was the increasing sadism of the mobs.... Though pregnant, [Mary Turner] was lynched in Valdosta, Georgia. She was hanged to a tree, doused with gasoline and motor oil and burned. As she dangled from the rope, a man stepped forward with a pocketknife and ripped open her abdomen in a crude cesarean operation. 'Out tumbled the prematurely born child,' wrote Walter White. 'Two feeble cries it gave—and received for answer the heel of a stalwart man, as life was ground out of the tiny form.'" Benjamin Quarles, writing in *American History Review,* suggests that some of these materials may "seem incredible because [they are] unfamiliar.... But whether or not one is familiar with the book's content, he may well be moved by its unusual ability to evoke the tragedy and the glory of the Negro's role in the American past."

Hailed by reviewers as an objective analysis of social problems touching black Americans in the 1960s, *Confrontation* calls for better communication not only between blacks and ill-informed white Americans, but also between black leaders and the masses, which Bennett says have grown apart and need to work more closely toward meaningful change. As *New York Times Book Review* contributor Nat Hentoff sees it, the "need to stimulate masses of black Americans into cohesive action" is the book's major theme. Kenneth B. Clark, writing in the *Saturday Review,* deems the book "a valuable contribution to the understanding of America's perennial number-one domestic problem." In addition to its usefulness for civil rights leaders, writes Clark, "*Confrontation* also has much to say to the serious student of American society."

*Black Power, U.S.A.: The Human Side of Reconstruction, 1867-1877* shows Bennett's mastery "of exposition, for he makes sense out of the amazingly complex, conglomerate, and contradictory situations" found in southern cities following the Civil War, says Harry Hansen. Earlier in the *Saturday Review* article, Hansen comments, "In his remarkable assessment of the constitutional conventions, Mr. Bennett describes the black man as entering a 'desperate and bloody struggle for political survival, flanked by two white allies, one Southern-born, the other Northern-born. To remain in power the black man had to preserve the coalition. But to preserve the coalition he had to make fatal concessions on radical reform.'" Consequently, Bennett presents the growth "of black power during Reconstruction as a dream unfulfilled," Hansen relates. A. K. Randall points out in a *Library Journal* review that one need not agree with Bennett to appreciate the book's "readable synthesis of historical research" and "lively narrative."

*BIOGRAPHICAL/CRITICAL SOURCES:*

*BOOKS*

Bennett, Lerone, Jr., *Before the Mayflower: A History of the Negro in America, 1619-1966,* Johnson Publishing Co., 1962, fifth edition, 1982.

Bennett, Lerone, Jr., *Black Powers, U.S.A.: The Human Side of Reconstruction, 1867-1877,* Johnson Publishing Co., 1967.

Newquist, Roy, editor, *Conversations,* Rand McNally, 1967.

*PERIODICALS*

*American History Review,* July, 1963.
*Best Sellers,* April, 1975.
*Freedomways,* fall, 1965.
*Journal of American History,* June, 1965.

*Negro Digest,* May, 1965.
*New York Times Book Review,* February 27, 1966.
*Phylon,* June, 1977.
*Saturday Review,* January 16, 1965; October 16, 1965; April 23, 1966; March 23, 1968.
*Times Literary Supplement,* May 5, 1966.

\* \* \*

## BENNETT, Louise (Simone) 1919-
## (Miss Lou)

*PERSONAL:* Also known professionally as Louise Bennett-Coverley; born September 7, 1919, in Kingston, Jamaica; daughter of Cornelius Agustus (a baker) and Kerene (a seamstress; maiden name, Robinson) Bennett; married Eric Coverley (a draftsman and impresario), May 30, 1954; children: Fabian (stepson), Christine. *Education:* Studied journalism, late 1930s; attended Friends' College, Highgate, St. Mary, beginning c. 1943, and Royal Academy of Dramatic Art (RADA), 1945-47. *Religion:* Presbyterian.

*ADDRESSES: Home and office*—Enfield House, P.O. Box 11, Gordon Town, St. Andrew, Jamaica.

*CAREER:* Writer, poet, folklorist, and performer. British Broadcasting Corporation (BBC), West Indies Section, London, England, resident artist on "Caribbean Carnival" (variety show), 1945-46, and "West Indian Guest Night," 1950-53; high school drama teacher, Jamaica, 1947-49; actor in repertory companies in Coventry, England, Huddersfield, England, and Amersham, England; folk singer and performer in New York City, New Jersey, and Connecticut, 1953-55; Jamaica Social Welfare Commission, drama specialist and head of recreation department c. 1955-59, director, c. 1959-63; University of the West Indies, Kingston, Jamaica, lecturer and extra-mural drama officer, c. 1955-69. Director, with Eric Coverley, of *Day in Jamaica* (folk musical), c. 1953; "Miss Lou's Views," radio commentator, c. 1965-82; "Ring Ding," (children's television show), host, 1970-82. Represented Jamaica at the Royal Commonwealth Arts Festival, Britain, 1965. Member of Little Theatre Movement pantomime management committee, 1961—; member of board of directors of Radio Jamaica and Rediffusion; patron of National Dance Theatre Company, 1962—; director of Jamaica Sugar Welfare Board, 1972-76, and National Savings Committee.

*MEMBER:* Writers Union of Jamaica.

*AWARDS, HONORS:* Member of Order of the British Empire, 1960; Silver Musgrave Medal of the Institute of Jamaica, 1965; Norman Manley Award for Excellence in the Arts,

1972; Unity Award from United Manchester Association, 1972; Order of Jamaica, 1974; Gold Musgrave Medal, 1978; Institute of Jamaica Centenary Medal, 1979; D. Litt, University of West Indies, 1983.

*WRITINGS:*

*Dialect Verses,* Gleaner, 1940.
*Jamaica Dialect Verses,* compiled by George R. Bowen, Herald, 1942, enlarged edition, Pioneer Press, c. 1951.
*Jamaican Humour in Dialect,* Gleaner, 1943.
*Miss Lulu Sez: A Collection of Dialect Poems,* Gleaner, c. 1948.
(With others) *Anancy Stories and Dialect Verse,* introduced by P. M. Sherlock, Pioneer Press, 1950, new series, 1957.
*Folk Stories and Verses,* Pioneer Press, 1952.
*Laugh with Louise: A Pot-pourri of Jamaican Folklore, Stories, Songs, Verses,* foreword by Robert Verity, City Printery, c. 1961.
*Jamaica Labrish,* introduced and edited by Rex Nettleford, Sangster's Book Stores, 1966.
(Under pseudonym Miss Lou) *Anancy and Miss Lou,* Sangster's Book Stores, 1979.
(Editor) *Mother Goose/Jamaica Maddah Goose,* Friends of the Jamaica School of Art Association, 1981.
*Selected Poems,* edited by Mervyn Morris, Sangster's Book Stores, 1982, revised edition, 1983.

Also author of *Lulu Sey: Dialect Verse,* 1943. Work represented in anthologies, including *Independence Anthology of Jamaica,* Jamaican Ministry of Development; *Brightlight: An Anthology of Caribbean Poetry,* Hamish Hamilton; *Bite In: A Three-Year Secondary Course on Reading Poems,* Thomas Nelson. Contributor to *Jamaica Talk* and *Dictionary of Jamaican English.* Contributor to Jamaican periodicals; author of a column in *Sunday Gleaner.*

*RECORDINGS*

*Jamaican Folk Songs,* Folkways, 1954.
*Jamaican Singing Games,* Folkways, 1954.
*Children's Jamaican Songs & Games,* Folkways, 1957.
*West Indies Festival of Arts,* Cook, 1958.
*Miss Lou's Views,* Federal Records, 1967.
*Listen to Louise,* Federal Records, 1968.
*The Honourable Miss Lou,* Premiere Productions, 1981.
*"Yes, M'Dear": Miss Lou Live,* Imani Music, 1983.

Also recorded *Anancy Stories,* Federal Records, and *Carifesta Ring Ding,* Record Specialists.

*SIDELIGHTS:* Louise Bennett is a prominent poet, writer, and performer, internationally known for capturing the language and folklore of Jamaican culture both in print and in her oral presentations. Since the late 1930s, Bennett has been writing and reading her poems and stories in Jamaica, England, and the United States, and has earned a loyal popular following. She draws her material from Jamaica's traditional folk stories, proverbs, myths, and songs, which were preserved primarily through oral retellings, and Bennett may have saved many of these works from possible oblivion. Believing that Jamaican folklore is best expressed within the language of the people, Bennett performs and writes in the native Jamaican variant of English, which is known as Creole, "Jamaica talk," West Indian English, Jamaican dialect, or Patois. "One reason I persisted writing in dialect," explained Bennett, as cited by Carolyn Cooper in *World Literature Written in English,* "was because ... there was such rich material in the dialect that I wanted to put on paper some of the wonderful things that people say in dialect. You could never say 'look here' as vividly as 'kuyah'."

Bennett, an only child, was born on September 7, 1919, in Kingston, Jamaica. Her father, Cornelius, owned a bakery but died when Bennett was only seven years old, leaving her mother, Kerene, to provide for the family through her work as a dressmaker. From her mother, Bennett learned early to respect people, and she observed a cross-section of classes through the women her mother sewed for. As Bennett explained in an interview with Don Buckner in 1976, as quoted by Mervyn Morris in *Fifty Caribbean Writers:* "Everybody was a lady—the fish lady, the yam lady, the store lady, the teacher lady." Later, her poetry would focus on those everyday people of Jamaican life and on their thoughts and feelings. As the young Bennett matured, her interest in people grew along with her love of Jamaican folklore. Like many children, Bennett loved the folktales she had heard in her youth; unlike other children, however, her interest stayed with her into her teenage years when she traveled, on her own, to the interior of the island looking for folklore. As quoted in *Black Literature Criticism,* Bennett explained: "There I was, still a teenager, living in a society that expected respectable girls to stay home with their mother, traveling on donkeyback into the remote towns of the Maroons, the ex-slaves who had escaped and established their own free territory." This experience exposed her to a sampling of the variety of folklore in her heritage—and whetted her appetite for travel and research.

From 1936 to 1938 Bennett attended Excelsior High School, where she began writing poems in standard English, but she switched to Jamaican Creole after overhearing a vivid conversation in dialect on a Kingston tramcar. Bennett's use of dialect was long considered by many critics as a limiting factor in her art. In a 1968 *Caribbean Quarterly* interview, Bennett told Dennis Scott: "For too long, it was considered not respectable to use the dialect. Because there was a social stigma attached to the kind of person who used dialect habitually. Many people still do not accept the fact that for us there

are many things which are best said in the language of the 'common man'." It was in her high school years that Bennett began to perform, presenting renditions of her poems to audiences. Her success brought her to the attention of Eric Coverley, the organizer of a popular Christmas concert on the island. Bennett made her professional debut at that concert in 1938, and by 1940 she had published a book of poetry titled *Dialect Verses.*

Because of her evident talent as a performer, Bennett was awarded, in 1945, a British Council scholarship to attend the renowned Royal Academy of Dramatic Art in London. Within a short time after her arrival in England, Bennett also found a job at the British Broadcasting Corporation (BBC), performing in a program of her own, the "Caribbean Carnival." She was invited to remain after her schooling to pursue a career as a professional actor; however, Bennett was homesick for Jamaica and returned to her homeland in 1947. Continuing to write poetry, she taught school for a short time but returned to England two years later to continue her work with the BBC as a resident artist on the "West Indian Guest Night" program. In 1953 Bennett moved to the United States, where, for two years, she pursued a career in radio as well as drama, performing at St. Martin's Little Theater in Harlem, New York, singing folk songs at the Village Vanguard in Greenwich Village, and then directing, with Eric Coverley, a folk musical. On May 30, 1954, Bennett married Coverley in New York, and the couple returned to Jamaica the next year. Back home once more—she has not lived abroad since—Bennett resumed her travels throughout the island, gathering Jamaican folklore and oral history and giving international radio, stage, and television performances.

Characteristically, Bennett's poems focus on typical Jamaicans—their individual responses to experiences, events, topical issues, and even politics—bringing humor and insight into everyday life. Rex Nettleford, in the introduction to *Jamaica Labrish,* marvelled that in her poems she captures "all the spontaneity of the ordinary Jamaican's joys and even sorrows, his ready poignant and even wicked wit, his religion and his philosophy of life." The form that most closely describes Bennett's style is the ballad, a story typically told in song. She also uses the dramatic monologue, a poem that is delivered as a speech to the audience and often reveals the speaker's character. The persona in "Uriah Preach" from *Selected Poems,* for example, is a mother who boasts about how her son reproaches relatives through a Sunday sermon: "Him tell dem off, dem know is dem, / Dem heart full to de brim; / But as Uriah eena pulpit / Dem cyaan [can't] back-answer him." The reaction of the audience (or reader) to the son's behavior is the perception of both a subtle irony at work (through the mother's wicked approval of her son's conduct) and a recognition of the humor in the situation—distinctive trademarks of Bennett's poetry. It has been claimed by many critics that her poems are at their best in performance. A *Times Literary Supplement* reviewer asserted that without an oral presentation of the work, "not merely something, but too much, is lost." The poems lend themselves to voice, the rhythms of speaking, movement, and a punch-line delivery technique which Bennett often employs.

Believing it important to pass on the folklore and culture of her people to the children of the island, Bennett has often targeted young people through her work. For twelve years, from 1970 to 1982, she hosted a weekly television show, "Ring Ding," in which children were invited to share their pride in Jamaican culture through folk stories and songs. Bennett recorded many of the songs, games, and stories featured on the program, including the well-loved Brer Anancy narratives. The adventures of Anancy, the African spider hero-rascal of Jamaican folk tales, is the protagonist in several of Bennett's books, including *Anancy and Miss Lou,* and *Anancy Stories and Dialect Verse.*

Though long hailed as a performer and an entertainer, Bennett has only recently gained critical recognition for her written work. In her *Caribbean Quarterly* interview with Scott in 1968, Bennett commented that, although people at that time primarily thought of her as an entertainer, "I did start to write before I started to perform." Among her most popular books are *Jamaica Labrish,* published in 1966, and *Selected Poems,* published in 1982. Because of the language and the light, often comic tone of her poetry, Bennett's work, though enormously popular, had been largely dismissed for decades by literary critics, several of whom considered her work as humorous entertainment, not as serious art. Critical recognition of Bennett's art increased beginning in the mid-1960s, influenced in part by Jamaica's political independence, achieved in 1962, which created a renewed appreciation for the Jamaican heritage. In addition, linguistic specialists have recently begun to recognize Creole not as substandard English but as a language in itself, with formal rules of grammar and syntax. "That the earlier criticisms are far less applicable today is to the credit of Louise Bennett," insisted Nettleford. "[She] has never doubted the power of the language she uses to express the essential passions of her people's hearts." Bennett's loyal stand on the traditional Jamaican dialect began to be seen more as an asset than as a limitation, and her work was analyzed by many more critics as serious literature. "Her claim that dialect be taken seriously is not only valid," wrote Louis James in the introduction to *The Islands in Between: Essays on West Indian Literature,* "it is borne out by many of her own successful pieces. Through dialect she catches conversational tones that illuminate both individual and national character."

Morris's opinion of Bennett's written work is typical of other later reviews of her work: "Some of the art involved [in Bennett's poems] is unavailable to even the most alert of listeners; it is when we can linger over the page that the tightness of the organization becomes more fully apparent." By lingering, the reader may identify puns, repeated rhyme schemes, plays on words, and literary allusions to English literature, proverbs, hymns, and the Bible.

Other reviewers, such as Cooper in 1978's *World Literature Written in English,* pointed to the "comedy of manners in which those recurring rascals of Caribbean societies ... come decidedly to grief." Cooper concluded that "the strength of Bennett's poetry then is the accuracy with which it depicts and attempts to correct through laughter the absurdities of Jamaican society. Its comic vision affirms a norm of common sense and good-natured decorum." In reviewing Bennett's *Selected Poems,* Loreto Todd in *World Literature Written in English* reflected that "every poem, almost every line is worth a comment for its humour, satire, pathos, irony, insight, its love of people and life.... [Bennett's] firm opinions and keen insights are like maypoles around which the language dances."

*BIOGRAPHICAL/CRITICAL SOURCES:*

*BOOKS*

Bennett, Louise, *Jamaica Labrish,* introduced and edited by Rex Nettleford, Sangster's Book Stores, 1966.
Bennett, Louise, *Selected Poems,* edited by Mervyn Morris, Sangster's Book Stores, 1982.
*Black Literature Criticism,* Gale, 1992, pp. 180-88.
*Contemporary Literary Criticism,* Volume 28, Gale, 1984, pp 26-31.
*Contemporary Poets,* St. James Press, 1991, p. 53.
Dance, Daryl Cumber, editor, *Fifty Caribbean Writers: A Bio-Bibliographical Critical Sourcebook,* Greenwood Press, 1986. pp. 35-45.
James, Louis, editor, *The Islands in Between: Essays on West Indian Literature,* Oxford University Press, 1968, pp. 1-49.
*Twentieth-Century Caribbean and Black African Writers,* First Series, Volume 117, Gale, 1992, pp. 93-97.

*PERIODICALS*

*Caribbean Quarterly,* March-June, 1968, pp. 97-101.
*Times Literary Supplement,* December 15, 1966, p. 1173.
*World Literature Written in English,* April, 1978, pp. 317-27; spring, 1984, pp. 414-16.

—*Sketch by Linda Tidrick*

## BILLINGSLEY, Andrew 1926-

*PERSONAL:* Born March 20, 1926, in Marion, AL; son of Silas and Lucy Billingsley; married Amy Loretta Tate; children: Angela Eleanor, Bonita Rebecca. *Education:* Attended Hampton Institute, 1947-49; Grinnell College, A.B., 1951; graduate study at University of Chicago, 1954-55; Boston University, M.S., 1956; University of Michigan, M.A., 1960; Brandeis University, Ph.D., 1964.

*ADDRESSES: Office*—University of Maryland, Department of Family and Community Development, Room 1204, Marie Mount Hall, College Park, MD 20742.

*CAREER:* American Friends Service Committee (Quakers), Chicago, IL, director of Youth Services Projects, 1951-54; Wisconsin Department of Public Welfare, Mendota State Hospital, Madison, WI, psychiatric social worker, 1956-58; University of Michigan, Ann Arbor, director of Friends International Student Center, 1959-60; Massachusetts Society for the Prevention of Cruelty to Children, Boston, social worker and research assistant, 1960-63; University of California, Berkeley, assistant professor, 1964-68, associate professor of social welfare, 1968-70, assistant dean of students, 1964-65, assistant chancellor for academic affairs, 1968-70; Howard University, Washington, DC, professor of sociology and social work, 1970-74, graduate professor of the social sciences, 1975, vice president for academic affairs, 1970-74; Morgan State University, Baltimore, MD, president 1975-84; University of Maryland, College Park, professor of Afro-American studies, 1985-87, professor and chair of Department of Family and Community Development, 1988—. Visiting lecturer at educational institutions in Monrovia, Liberia; Accra, Ghana; Lagos, Nigeria; and Dar Es Salaam, Tanzania, all in 1971, and University of West Indies, 1973. Participant in International Work Camp, American Friends Service Committee, 1949; consultant, National Urban League, 1968; member of Advisory Committee on Health to Secretary of U.S. Department of Health, Education and Welfare, 1968-69; member of board of governors, Joint Center for Political Studies, 1972-75; chair, Commission of Management, Howard University Press, 1972-74. *Military service:* U.S. Army, Quartermaster Corps, 1944-46; promoted to sergeant.

*MEMBER:* American Sociological Association, National Association of Black Social Workers, Association for the Study of Afro-American Life and History, Council on Social Work Education (member of board), Child Welfare League of America (member of board).

*AWARDS, HONORS:* First biennial research award, National Association of Social Workers, 1964; grants, Children's Bureau, U.S. Department of Health, Education and Welfare, 1966-70, for research on child welfare; social science fellowship, Metropolitan Applied Research Center, 1968; Michael Schwerner Memorial Award, City of New York, 1969; D.H.L., Grinnell College, 1971; first national leadership award, Afro-American Family and Community Services, 1972; appreciation awards, National Council of Black Child Development and Howard University Science Institute, both 1974; Fros Award, Howard Institute for Arts and Humanities, 1974; Outstanding Contribution to Excellence in Education award, PUSH National Convention, 1975; Award of Excellence for Community Service and Promoting Racial Equality, India Forum, 1978; D.H.L., Mercy College, 1982.

*WRITINGS:*

*The Social Worker in a Child Protective Agency,* National Association of Social Workers, 1966.

(Assisted by Amy Tate Billingsley) *Black Families in White America,* Prentice-Hall, 1968, revised edition, Simon & Schuster, 1988.

(With Jeanne Giovannoni and Margaret Purvine) *Studies in Child Protective Services* (monograph), U.S. Department of Health, Education and Welfare, 1969.

(With Giovannoni) *Children of the Storm: Black Children and American Child Welfare,* Harcourt, 1972.

*Child Development and Family Life in the Black Community* (monograph), Office of Child Development, Department of Health, Education and Welfare, 1974.

*Black Families and the Struggle for Survival: Teaching Our Children to Walk Tall,* Friendship, 1974.

*The Evolution of the Black Family,* National Urban League, 1976.

(Editor with Julia C. Elam) *Black Colleges and Public Policy,* Follett Press, 1986.

(Editor with Elam) *Inside Black Colleges and Universities,* Follett Press, 1986.

(Editor with Elam) *Blacks on White Campuses, Whites on Black Campuses,* Follett Press, 1986.

*Climbing Jacob's Ladder: The Enduring Legacy of African-American Families,* foreword by Paula Giddings, Simon & Schuster, 1992.

Contributor to books, including *Social Work with Unmotivated Clients,* edited by Herbert Aptheker, Brandeis University Papers, 1965; *The Unwed Mother,* edited by Robert W. Roberts, Harper, 1966; *Mobilizing for Community-wide Services to Unwed Parents,* Florence Crittenden Association, 1968; *Social Service in the Model Cities,* edited by Arnold Katz, Center for Community Planning, Department of Health, Education and Welfare, 1968; *Race, Reason, and Research,* edited by Roger Miller, National Association of Social Workers, 1969; *What Black Educators Are Saying,* edited by Nathan Wright, Hawthorn, 1970; *Modern Family,* edited by Robert Winch, Holt, 1971; *Readings on the American Family System,* edited by Ira L. Reiss, Holt; *The Family, Poverty, and*

*Welfare Programs: Household Patterns and Government Policies,* U.S. Government Printing Office, 1973; *The Death of White Sociology,* edited by Joyce A. Ladner, Random House, 1973; *Mental Health Issues and the Urban Poor,* edited by Dorothy Evans, Pergamon, 1974; *The Urban Scene in the Seventies,* edited by James F. Blumstein and Eddie J. Martin, Vanderbilt University Press, 1974; *Social Research and the Black Community,* edited by Lawrence E. Gary, Institute for Urban Affairs and Research, Howard University, 1974; *Sourcebook in Marriage and the Family,* edited by Marvin B. Sussman, Houghton, 1974; *Research on African-American Families: A Holistic Approach,* Volume 2, edited by Robert B. Hill, William Monroe Trotter Institute, University of Massachusetts, 1989. Author of foreword, *The Strengths of Black Families* by Robert Hill, Emerson Hall Publishers, 1972; author of introduction, *The Survival of Black Children and Youth,* edited by Jay Chunn, National Council for Black Child Development, 1974. Contributor to periodicals, including *New Frontiers, Harvard Educational Review,* and *Black Scholar.* Member of editorial board, *Journal of Afro-American Studies,* 1969—, *Black Scholar,* 1970—, *Journal of Negro Education,* 1973—, and *Journal of Social and Behavioral Sciences,* 1973—; chair of advisory board, *Journal of Abstracts,* 1973—.

*SIDELIGHTS:* Writer and educator Andrew Billingsley has sought to provide a realistic portrayal of African Americans in both historic and contemporary terms. He is recognized and honored for his leadership in achieving academic excellence and challenging existing sociological work. While his publications are considered scholarly, critics frequently note that his formats are much livelier than many sociological works.

In 1965, the U.S. Department of Labor released a paper entitled *The Negro Family: A Case for Action.* Written by Daniel Patrick Moynihan, *The Negro Family* explored the disintegrated black family in America. It contended that centuries of racial discrimination had largely broken black family units. Many conservatives of the time embraced elements of *The Negro Family* because it was interpreted as acknowledging black stereotypes. Billingsley's *Black Families in White America* is often considered to be a response to the controversial Moynihan report. The book describes the wide range of established family patterns in the black community. *Saturday Review* contributor August Meier commented that Billingsley "offers an important corrective to the stereotypes arising from the Moynihan report." The work further illustrates the black family's adaption to circumstances in a largely hostile social climate. As a *Choice* reviewer stated: "It reflects scholarship and reason, virtues unhappily in dangerously short supply in racial discussions today."

Another work, *Orphans of the Storm: Black Children and American Child Welfare,* which Billingsley wrote with Jeanne

M. Giovannoni, traces the negative impact of racism on black children, especially through the child welfare system. In addition to a historical narrative and detailed documentation, the authors provide a summary of needed reforms in the child welfare system. *Orphans of the Storm* illustrates the effect of racism on the youngest members of society. "The book should be a stimulus for action and should have broader availability than do many academic works," stated Henry M. Kapenstein in *Library Journal.*

*BIOGRAPHICAL/CRITICAL SOURCES:*

*PERIODICALS*

*Booklist,* January 1, 1973, p. 411.
*Choice,* April, 1969, p. 281.
*Library Journal,* October 1, 1972, p. 3172.
*Saturday Review,* April 5, 1969, pp. 59-60.

\*     \*     \*

## BIRTHA, Becky 1948-

*PERSONAL:* Born in 1948.

*ADDRESSES: Home*—5116 Cedar Ave., Philadelphia, PA 19143-1510.

*CAREER:* Poet and story writer.

*WRITINGS:*

(Compiler) *Literature by Black Women: A List of Books,* privately printed, 1983.
*For Nights Like This One: Stories of Loving Women,* Frog in the Well, 1983.
*Lovers' Choice* (stories; includes "Johnieruth," "Babytown," "Past Halfway," "The Deep Heart's Core," "Ice Castle," "Her Ex-Lover," "Both Ways," "Route 23: 10th and Bigler to Bethlehem Pike," "The Saints and Sinners Run," and "In the Life"), Seal Press, 1987.
*The Forbidden Poems,* Seal Press, 1991.

Contributor to *Intricate Passions,* Banned Books, 1989.

*SIDELIGHTS:* Becky Birtha is author of *Lovers' Choice,* a volume of short stories, and *The Forbidden Poems,* her first collection of poetry. *Lovers' Choice,* published in 1987, contains many stories offering insight into the lives of black lesbians. Each of the leading characters arrives at a crossroad where her choice of direction holds the potential for momentous change. Patricia Roth Schwartz commented in *Belles*

*Lettres* that "as a Black lesbian/feminist writer, Birtha deserves praise for her courage in writing about interracial relationships, about white women from a Black woman's perspective and about Black lesbians." These elements are prevalent in "Ice Castle" and "Her Ex-Lover," each concerned with a black woman's process of coming to grips with a seemingly irrational attraction to a white woman. The adolescent Maurie's attraction to Gail in "Ice Castle" becomes for her a stepping-stone toward an awareness of her sexual orientation as well as of what it means to be black. In "Her Ex-Lover," Ernestine is eventually able to leave behind her obsession with her former lover, Lisa, allowing her to become wholeheartedly involved with her current black lover. Not all stories in *Lovers' Choice* deal with lesbian relationships. "Route 23: 10th and Bigler to Bethlehem Pike" tells of Leona May Moses, a single mother who must wrap her children in blankets and take them riding on an all-night city bus when her landlord refuses to provide heat for her apartment. "These tender, strong, enduring women," concluded Schwartz, "let us know that, as Leona May Moses insists as she takes her kids on their all-night ride, 'We ain't getting off. This trip ain't over yet.'"

Birtha followed *Lovers' Choice* with *The Forbidden Poems,* a collection of poetry in which several works are concerned with the loss of loved ones, while others praise the strength stemming from communities of women. The poems are told from the perspective of a black woman who has recently ended a long-term relationship with her white lover. Robyn Selman noted in the *Village Voice* that "*The Forbidden Poems* is honest, open, and loaded with details of lesbian life," and explained that "addressing her self is the speaker's main concern—as a woman, a black woman, and as a lesbian." *Choice* contributor L. J. Parascandola found that "despite a few overly sentimental lines," the poems possess "biting humor" and "a stark, direct quality."

*BIOGRAPHICAL/CRITICAL SOURCES:*

*PERIODICALS*

*Belles Lettres,* July-August, 1988, p. 15.
*Choice,* October, 1991, p. 276.
*Times Literary Supplement,* June 3-9, 1988, p. 623.
*Village Voice,* April 16, 1991, p. 70.

\*    \*    \*

## BLOCKSON, Charles L(eRoy) 1933-

*PERSONAL:* Born December 16, 1933, in Norristown, PA; son of Charles E. Blockson and Annie Parker Blockson; married Elizabeth Parker (divorced); children: Noelle. *Education:* Attended Pennsylvania State University during 1950s.

*ADDRESSES: Home*—P.O. Box 133, Hancock Rd., Gwynedd, PA 19436. *Office*—Sullivan Hall, Temple University, Broad and Berks Streets, Philadelphia, PA 19122.

*CAREER:* Pennsylvania Black History Committee, director, 1976—; Pennsylvania Afro-American Historical Board, director, 1976—; Governor's Heritage Affairs Commission, Afro-American commissioner, beginning in 1983; Temple University, Philadelphia, PA, member of Centennial Committee, 1983—, curator of Charles L. Blockson Afro-American Collection, c. 1984—. Director of Pennsylvania State Historical and Record Advisory Board and Black History Advisory Board; member of Pennsylvania State University Alumni Council, 1982—, Montgomery County of Pennsylvania Bicentennial Committee, 1982-83, and Underground Railroad Advisory Committee. Launched a project to erect sixty-four historical markers commemorating the contribution of African Americans to Philadelphia, 1989; served as moderator of Black Writer's Conference in Paris, France, 1992; lecturer, including tours in the West Indies and South America for the United States Information Agency; organizer of black study programs for schools and colleges; chair of the Valley Forge African-American Revolutionary Soldier Monument; co-founder of the Afro-American Historical and Cultural Museum in Philadelphia. *Military service:* U.S. Army, 1957-58.

*MEMBER:* National Association for the Advancement of Colored People, Authors Guild, Pennsylvania Abolition Society (former president), Historical Society of Pennsylvania (board member, 1976-83), Urban League of Pennsylvania.

*AWARDS, HONORS:* Alumni Fellow Award, Pennsylvania State University, 1979, for distinguished alumnus; honorary degrees from Villanova University, 1979, and Lincoln University, 1987; Pennsylvania State Quarterback Award, Pennsylvania State Quarterback Club, 1984; Lifetime Achievement Award, Before Columbus Foundation, 1987; bronze bust presented to Temple University by sculptor Antonio Salemme, 1990; Whitney Young Human Relations Award, Philadelphia Urban League, 1991; first inductee into Norristown school district's Hall of Fame and Hall of Champions.

*WRITINGS:*

*Pennsylvania's Black History,* Portfolio Associates, 1975.
(With Ron Fry) *Black Genealogy,* Prentice-Hall, 1977.
*The Underground Railroad in Pennsylvania,* Flame International, 1981.
*The Underground Railroad: First Person Narratives of Escapes to Freedom in the North,* Prentice-Hall, 1987.
*A Commented Bibliography of One Hundred and One Influential Books by and about People of African Descent, 1556-1982,* A. Gerits and Sons (Amsterdam), 1989.

*The Journey of John W. Mosley: An African-American Pictorial,* Quantum Leap Publishers, 1993.

Also author of *Handbook of Black Librarianship,* Libraries Unlimited, 1977, and *Philadelphia's Guide: African-American State Historical Markers,* Ife Designs and Associates, 1993. Contributor to *Black American Records and Research,* Greenwood Press, 1983, and *Erotique Noire/Black Erotica,* Howard University Press, 1990. Contributor to magazines and scholarly journals, including *National Geographic.*

*WORK IN PROGRESS:* An autobiography.

*SIDELIGHTS:* Charles L. Blockson is a devoted researcher and preserver of black history. Perceiving the additional difficulties blacks experience in tracing their family trees—the African and domestic American slave trade having severed entire families from their roots—Blockson and coauthor Ron Fry provide practical advice for would-be researchers in *Black Genealogy.* The authors discuss methods for locating archives and, according to Albert H. Johnston in *Publishers Weekly,* ways in which individuals can "trace family names that were changed after emancipation." A critic in *Choice* stated that the sections of the book's "chapters on public records, the directory of research sources, and the bibliography are particularly well done."

*The Underground Railroad: First Person Narratives of Escapes to Freedom in the North,* compiled and edited by Blockson, is a collection of first-hand accounts by blacks who traveled the secret routes to the North to escape slavery. Blockson, whose grandfather reached freedom by using the Underground Railroad, assembled the stories largely from sources published in the nineteenth century. The editor emphasizes "the emotion and uncertainty of escape," stated Thomas J. Davis in *Library Journal.* In *Booklist,* Denise P. Donavin found *The Underground Railroad* "a valuable addition to black history."

Drawing on his knowledge of black literature and history, Blockson presents a list of key texts in *A Commented Bibliography of One Hundred and One Influential Books by and about People of African Descent, 1556-1982.* Among Blockson's annotated selections are Alice Walker's novel *The Color Purple* and a copy of the Fugitive Slave Law of 1850, which allowed for the prosecution of anyone assisting runaway slaves. Noting that the book is of use primarily to institutions trying to assemble "a comprehensive collection on black history and culture," D. C. Dickinson adds in *Choice* that its "graphic qualities ... are excellent—type, paper, and illustrations were chosen with care."

Blockson has commented: "The preservation of black history has become my lifework. I have spent more than forty years

amassing one of the nation's largest private collections of items relating to black history and traditions.

"In 1984, I donated my collection to Temple University in Philadelphia, Pennsylvania. The Charles L. Blockson Afro-American Collection, of which I am curator, is a part of the Special Collections Department of the Temple University Libraries and is housed in Sullivan Hall. My collection now contains approximately 150,000 books, pamphlets, manuscripts, prints, drawings, sheet music, broadsides, posters, and artifacts. The collection spans nearly four centuries from Leo Africanus to the present, and geographically from Africa through Europe and the Caribbean to the United States.

"During my high school years in Norristown, Pennsylvania, I starred in football and in track, subsequently receiving offers of athletic scholarships from sixty colleges. I selected Penn State and roomed with teammates Rosey Grier and Lenny Moore. I later passed up a professional career with the New York Giants to pursue my first love, black history."

*BIOGRAPHICAL/CRITICAL SOURCES:*

*PERIODICALS*

*Booklist,* June 15, 1977, p. 1549; November 1, 1987, p. 430.
*Choice,* November, 1977, p. 1189; May, 1990, p. 1468.
*Library Journal,* June 15, 1977, p. 1374; November 15, 1987, p. 78.
*Publishers Weekly,* April 4, 1977, p. 79.

\*   \*   \*

## BOGUS, SDiane (Adams) 1946-

*PERSONAL:* First name pronounced "es-di-ann"; born January 22, 1946; daughter of Lawrence Thomas Waterhouse and Florence (Adams) Bogus; married Trilby (T.) Nelson Gilbert (divorced April 1, 1989). *Education:* Stillman College, B.A. (cum laude), 1968; Syracuse University, M.A., 1969; Miami University, Ph.D., 1988. *Politics:* "United We Stand America." *Religion:* Christian-Buddhist.

*ADDRESSES: Office*—P.O. Box 2087, Cupertino, CA 95015.

*CAREER:* Los Angeles Southwest Community College, Los Angeles, CA, English instructor, 1976-81; City College, San Francisco, CA, English instructor, 1985-86; California State University, Stanislaus, visiting lecturer, 1987-89; DeAnza College, Cupertino, CA, professor of composition and literature, 1990—. Northwestern University, Evanston, IL, student teaching supervisor of M.A. teaching program, 1972;

Compton Unified School District, English department chair, 1979-80; California State University, Stanislaus, faculty mentor, 1988-90, faculty advisor for "Umoja" (black student union), 1987-88.

*MEMBER:* International Women Writers' Guild, Modern Language Association, National Women's Studies Association, Publishing Triangle, Associated Writing Programs, Multicultural Publishers Exchange.

*AWARDS, HONORS:* Walser Fellow, Miami University, 1983; finalist, Poetry Arts Project, 1989; Lambda Literary award, 1990; Peninsula Black Writers award, 1992; Innovator of the Year, 1992-93.

*WRITINGS:*

*I'm Off to See the Goddamn Wizard, Alright!,* Whitehall, 1971.
*Woman in the Moon* (poetry), Soap Box, 1971.
*Of Hallowed Things Talked Aloud,* Woman Print Enterprises, 1981.
*Sapphire's Sampler* (anthology), W.I.M., 1982.
*Dykehands Sutras Erotic and Lyric* (poems and essays), W.I.M., 1989.
*The Chant of the Women of Magdalena,* W.I.M., 1990.
(Editor) *Who's Who in Mail: A Directory of Women & Minorities in Business,* W.I.M., 1990.
(Editor) *The Poetry Workbook: A Poet's Workbook,* W.I.M., 1991.
*For the Love of Men,* W.I.M., 1991.

Contributor to numerous anthologies, including *New Lesbian Writing,* edited by Pat Cruikshank, Grey Fox Press, 1984; *In a Different Light,* edited by Jenny Wrenn, Clothespin Fever Press, 1989; *Intricate Passions,* edited by Tee Corrine, Banned Books, 1989; *Lesbian Bedtime Stories,* edited by Terry Woodrow, 1990; *Piece of My Heart: A Lesbian of Color Anthology,* edited by Makeda Silvera, Sister Vision Press, 1991; *Double Stitch,* edited by Patricia Bell Scott, et al., Harper, 1991; *Erotique Noir/Black Erotica,* edited by Miriam DeCosta Willis, Doubleday, 1992; and *Happy Endings,* edited by Kate Brandt, Naiad Press, 1993. Contributor of stories and poems to periodicals, including *Sinister Wisdom, Sisters United, Azalea, Space and Time, Poetry Flash, Catalyst, Black American Magazine,* and *Women's Review of Books.* Contributor of articles to professional journals, including *Black Scholar, Black American,* and *Literature Forum.*

*WORK IN PROGRESS: Buddhism for My Friends* (autobiography), publication expected in December, 1993; *Hatshepsut's Horns or The Bulldagger Stories,* publication expected in August, 1994; new fiction essays for *The Studenthood Handbook,* an academic handbook.

*SIDELIGHTS:* SDiane Bogus commented: "The motivation for my career has always stemmed from my ability to be moved by important ideas in my time; I read contemporary literature to see how it relates to my own literary training and insights while, at the same time, I seek to make application of the ideas, ideals, and themes in the work of my contemporaries and predecessors. The circumstances under which I write are not always perfect. My teaching career consumes much of my available time and I must balance performance, lecture, and the operations of my publishing company, Woman in the Moon. I often find time to write in the wee hours of the morning, when all is quiet, or upon sudden inspiration. Or sometimes, when I have a surprise moment or two of free time, I create the germs of stories, drafts of poems, and theses for prose essays. Remarkably, I sometimes finish them in the same unplanned intervals. I keep a journal of my life on four principal themes: religion, love-life, writing, and teaching. My journals date back to 1962.

"My areas of interest are not only vital to my writing, they often are the subject of my writing. At present, I am interested in new age writings on spiritual topics. Also, I have continued to be strongly engaged by the gay and lesbian literature of our time, as well as the work of black writers such as Ann Allen Shockley, Alice Walker, Audre Lorde, and Toni Morrison. James Baldwin has been a major influence as have nineteenth-century American figures. Feminist writers such as Judy Grahn and Adrienne Rich are also important to my work. I also have the instruction of Gertrude Stein. Because I am a publisher, I have a strong commitment to poetry, particularly the narrative form. I accept and write books in this genre."

*BIOGRAPHICAL/CRITICAL SOURCES:*

*PERIODICALS*

*Advocate,* January 15, 1991.
*Bay Area Reporter,* June 25, 1992.
*Lambda Book Report,* March, 1991; May, 1991.
*New Directions for Women,* November, 1990.
*Small Press Review,* November, 1983; February, 1984; January, 1990.

\*    \*    \*

## BOLES, Robert (E.) 1943-

*PERSONAL:* Born in 1943.

*ADDRESSES: Home*—7 Union Park, Boston, MA 02118.

*WRITINGS:*

*The People One Knows: A Novel,* Houghton, 1964.
*Curling: A Novel,* Houghton, 1968.

Short stories published in anthologies, including *The Best Short Stories by Negro Writers: An Anthology from 1899 to the Present,* edited by Langston Hughes, Little, Brown, 1967; and *An Introduction to Black Literature in America.* Contributor to periodicals, including *Tri-Quarterly.*

*BIOGRAPHICAL/CRITICAL SOURCES:*

*PERIODICALS*

*Negro Digest,* May, 1965, p. 52; January, 1968, p. 38; August, 1968, p. 86.
*Saturday Review,* February 17, 1968, p. 38.

\*     \*     \*

**BONNER, Marita**
   **See OCCOMY, Marita Odette**

\*     \*     \*

**BORDEN, Lee**
   **See DEAL, Borden**

\*     \*     \*

**BORDEN, Leigh**
   **See DEAL, Borden**

\*     \*     \*

**BOUCOLON, Maryse**
   **See CONDE, Maryse**

\*     \*     \*

**BOYD, Candy Dawson 1946-**

*PERSONAL:* Full name is Marguerite Cecille Dawson Boyd; born August 8, 1946, in Chicago, IL; daughter of Julian Dawson and Mary Ruth Ridley. *Education:* Northeastern Illinois State University, B.A., 1967; University of California, Berkeley, M.A., 1978, Ph.D., 1982.

*ADDRESSES: Home*—1416 Madrone Way, San Pablo, CA 94806. *Office*—St. Mary's College of California, School of Education, Box 4350, Morgana, CA 94575.

*CAREER:* Overton Elementary School, Chicago, IL, teacher, 1968-71; Longfellow School, Berkeley, CA, teacher, 1971-73; University of California, Berkeley, extension instructor in the language arts, 1972-79; Berkeley Unified School District, Berkeley, district teacher trainer in reading and communication skills, 1973-76; St. Mary's College of California, Morgana, extension instructor in language arts, 1972-79, lecturer, 1975, assistant professor and director of reading leadership and teacher effectiveness programs, 1976-87, director of elementary education, 1983-88, tenured associate professor, 1983-91, professor of education, 1991—; writer.

*MEMBER:* International Reading Association, American Educational Research Association, California Reading Association.

*AWARDS, HONORS: Circle of Gold* was named a notable children's trade book in the field of social studies by the National Council for the Social Studies and the Children's Book Council in 1984, and a Coretta Scott King Award Honor Book by the American Library Association in 1985; *Breadsticks and Blessing Places* was selected for the Children's Books of the Year List by the Child Study Children's Book Committee at Bank Street College; Boyd received the Outstanding Bay Area Woman Award, 1986; Outstanding Person in Mount Diablo Unified School District, Black Educators Association, 1988; *Charlie Pippin* was nominated for the Mark Twain Award and the Dorothy Canfield Fisher Children's Book Award, 1988, and was selected by the International Reading Association and Children's Book Council for the Children's Choices for 1988 List, and by the Oklahoma Library Association for the Oklahoma Sequoyah Children's Book Award Master List, 1989; Author's Hall of Fame Certificate of Appreciation for literary and artistic contributions to the field of literature for children and adults, San Francisco Reading Association and Santa Clara Reading Association, 1989; Celebrate Literacy Award for exemplary service in the promotion of literacy, International Reading Association and the San Francisco Reading Association, 1991; Distinguished Achievement Award, National Women's Political Caucus, San Francisco Chapter, 1991; first recipient of the St. Mary's College of California Professor of the Year Award, 1992; *Chevrolet Saturday* was selected as an American Bookseller's Association "Pick of the Lists" title, 1993.

*WRITINGS:*

*Circle of Gold,* Scholastic, 1984.
*Breadsticks and Blessing Places,* Macmillan, 1985, published as *Forever Friends,* Viking, 1986.

*Charlie Pippin,* Macmillan, 1987.
*Chevrolet Saturday,* Macmillan, 1992.
*Fall Secrets,* Puffin, forthcoming.

Also contributor of articles and essays to professional journals. Reviewer of children's literature for the *Los Angeles Times* and *San Francisco Chronicle.*

*WORK IN PROGRESS: The Strategy Approach to Teaching Reading* and *Concept-Based Curriculum;* three picture books; academic research on ability-based reading groups and multiethnic children's literature.

*SIDELIGHTS:* Candy Dawson Boyd is a professor of education and an award-winning children's writer. A former teacher of children of many ethnic and cultural backgrounds, Boyd strives to provide children with the kind of rich cultural knowledge she derived from her own childhood in an African American family. In an interview, Boyd remarked that throughout her life she has been strengthened by the stories she heard as a child about the determination and fortitude of her family and ancestors. "Chicago schools were segregated," the author related, "so I got stories at school about Africa and its kingdoms. But the stories I got at home were the ones that were more powerful because they were about the things that happened to family members and how we had survived and prevailed." As a writer for children and young adults she provides the positive message she once took from those stories, the message "that you make it. It's going to be hard and tough and it's not fair," she said, "but you make it."

Among many interests, including jazz singing and acting, Boyd grew up with a deep commitment to social change. In college, she was active in the civil rights movement, and her increasing involvement in the cause eventually superseded her schoolwork. She quit school and went to work as a field staff organizer with Martin Luther King, Jr.'s, Southern Christian Leadership Conference. After working for over a year in both the North and the South, the violent deaths of movement leaders such as Medgar Evers, John and Robert Kennedy, and King, left Boyd emotionally devastated. She returned to college, this time to pursue a degree in education, continuing to participate in the civil rights movement with activist Jessie Jackson in the teacher's division of Operation PUSH (People United to Save Humanity).

After college, Boyd worked for several years as an elementary school teacher in her own predominantly black Chicago neighborhood. Although external circumstances had forced her out of the civil rights movement and into teaching, she found that she was able to pursue her social ideals in the classroom. "I was a militant teacher," Boyd commented. "I knew that being black and poor meant life was going to be a lot harder for my students, and I wanted them to have as much

opportunity as possible." Boyd demanded that the black national anthem be played in school and organized marches for beautifying the neighborhood. In her way, she "adopted" her students. "Some of my children had never seen Lake Michigan," she explained. "So we would meet by the liquor store on Saturdays and we would go downtown to the Goodman Theater and we took a Greyhound bus tour of Chicago. They became my children, and I wanted them."

Boyd moved to Berkeley, California, in 1971, where, she related, "I ended up teaching children who weren't black: Asian children and Latino children and Caucasian children and children from India and all over the world." Seeking reading material for her students, Boyd found a disturbing lack of children's books from the diverse cultural backgrounds that comprised her classroom. "I got absolutely enraged when I went out and I looked at the atrocity of the books out there. I couldn't even find decent books for some of the white ethnic groups that I had. I wanted material, good books, strong books, books that had very interesting characters and ordinary stories. But I never saw children of color in realistic fiction depicted as children whose culture—a culture embedded within them as a part of who they are—comes out in ways that are ordinary and regular. That enraged me and I decided to become a writer."

After making the decision to become a writer, Boyd went to work. "I spent the first two years reading all the books written for children in the Berkeley Public Library—from A to Z, fiction and nonfiction—because I wanted to see what was out there and what wasn't there. I also did research and took two courses at the University of California, Berkeley, on writing for children. I wrote manuscripts that my teachers thought were good, but for nine years I was rejected by publishing companies." One of the manuscripts Boyd sent to many publishers was *Breadsticks and Blessing Places,* a book that, according to Boyd, was "very, very important" to her.

*Breadsticks and Blessing Places* is the story of Toni, a twelve-year-old girl whose parents want to send her to a prestigious prep school. Toni, who has difficulties with math in her present school, fears disappointing her parents. She also struggles with two friends who are very different from one another and don't always get along. When one of them, the carefree Susan, is killed by a drunk driver, Toni is inconsolable. The novel follows her slow and painful route toward recovery from this trauma. A reviewer of *Breadsticks and Blessing Places* for the *Bulletin of the Center for Children's Books* commented: "Boyd deals fully and candidly with a child's reaction to the death of a close friend as well as to other aspects of the maturation process that are universal." The critic added that the story is presented "with insight and compassion."

Boyd commented that publishers who rejected *Breadsticks*

*and Blessing Places* said it was "relentless" on the subject of death. Boyd wrote the novel in a personal effort to work out her feelings about the death of her best friend in childhood. She also created *Breadsticks and Blessing Places* to help children who have experienced loss to work out their own emotions. To write the book, Boyd conducted two years of research on grief as experienced by children. "In that period of research," she said, "I learned that children grieve deeply over a long period of time and that the rituals that adults use at wakes and funerals don't work for children." Boyd wanted her book to respect children's emotions and give them a safe forum. "I call my books a safe place. Children are complex. They have very strong, meaningful ideas and questions about the world that they live in. They have deep emotions that persist, and I think that there should be a genre of books that they read that respect that."

Boyd's first published novel was the award-winning *Circle of Gold,* the story of Mattie Benson, a young girl on a quest to buy a gold pin for her mother. Mattie's father has died prior to the opening of the story, leaving her mother to support Mattie and her twin brother by working long hours at a factory and managing the apartment building in which they live. Mattie works hard to help out at home, but her mother is tired and unhappy and shows more irritation than love for her daughter. Mattie, already suffering the loss of her father, feels she is losing her mother as well. In school, a mean-spirited girl named Angel accuses Mattie of stealing her bracelet and, although Mattie is not punished, she is treated like a thief by her teacher and her peers. Against these harsh and daunting odds, Mattie's quest to buy the expensive pin—the circle of gold—for her mother vividly symbolizes her love of her family and her determination to make things right again.

Boyd's 1987 book, *Charlie Pippin,* again explores family relationships that have become troubled due to outside circumstances. Charlie is an energetic and curious eleven-year-old girl with unusual entrepreneurial skills. Despite her very good intentions, Charlie has difficulty following her school's disciplinary code. At home, she has difficulty with her father, a Vietnam War veteran who is embittered, isolated, and unwilling to discuss his experience except by defending the war. Charlie, trying to better understand her father, undertakes a report on the Vietnam War for her social studies class. In her research she finds a newspaper clipping about her father and two of his friends who were killed in action during the war. Asking her grandparents and her mother about the article, Charlie learns that her father was a war hero and, before his experience in Vietnam, a man of dreams and joy.

Charlie's father is not pleased with her choice of report topics, or the trouble that her extracurricular business dealings have caused at school, but Charlie's spirit is invincible. She

deceives her parents and convinces a favorite uncle to take her to Washington, DC, to see the Vietnam Veteran's War Memorial. There she acquires rubbings from the wall of the names of her father's dead friends. On her return, Charlie provokes her father to honestly confront the anguish of his past—an anguish that has broken down some of the family's lines of communication. Sybil Steinberg wrote in her *Publishers Weekly* review of *Charlie Pippin:* "A strong black protagonist makes this a rare YA book; the finesse with which Boyd ties its many themes into a very moving, unified whole turns this into a stellar offering."

In Boyd's novels, families, although loving, are besieged with real problems. Parents often inadvertently impose a cynicism—brought about by the injustice and grief they have encountered—upon children who are better able to maintain dreams and an idealistic approach to life. The young protagonists of Boyd's novels strive for a place in the world of their family as well as the world at large, despite the harshness they witness. Through youthful endeavors to set things right, the stories conclude optimistically. Boyd commented: "I refuse to have losers as characters. I hate the words 'coping' and 'adjusting.' In my families there is always a possibility of renewal."

Boyd recognizes that the family is only one aspect in children's lives. "School is a major part of what happens to the child," she related. "School is one of the places where children can have an opportunity to grow outside of the family—to find parts of themselves that they may not be able to find inside the family." Boyd's interest in what school systems have to offer children surfaces both in her novels and in her career. After completing her doctorate in education, she taught at St. Mary's College of California, where she was named the first Professor of the Year in 1992 for outstanding teaching and scholarship. She has become renowned for her devotion to training teachers and developing systems that help young people become enthusiastic readers.

Both her books and her teaching have won Boyd many distinguished awards. "My dreams of being famous were satisfied when I was still a child," Boyd commented. "Yes, I'm honored when I receive an award, but often the decision [to grant her an award] is political, and I don't know how these decisions are made. Not knowing, I take it all with less ego." The idealism that Boyd has exhibited since her own childhood now hinges on her profound belief in children. "I still have hope," she explained. "I have a lot invested in the children. Not much of my hope lies with adults. If books help children, or give them a safe place to go, then that's the biggest reward for writing."

*BIOGRAPHICAL/CRITICAL SOURCES:*

*PERIODICALS*

*Bulletin of the Center for Children's Books,* July-August, 1985; May, 1987.
*Publishers Weekly,* June 7, 1985, p. 81; April 10, 1987, p. 96.
*School Library Journal,* September, 1985, p. 142; April, 1987, p. 92; November, 1988, p. 53.
*Voice of Youth Advocates,* February, 1986, p. 382; October, 1987.

\* \* \*

## BRANCH, William (Blackwell) 1927-

*PERSONAL:* Born September 11, 1927, in New Haven, CT; son of James Matthew (a minister) and Iola (Douglas) Branch; divorced; children: Rochelle Ellen. *Education:* Northwestern University, B.S., 1949; Columbia University, M.F.A., 1958, graduate study, 1958-60; Yale University, resident fellow, 1965-66.

*ADDRESSES: Home and office*—53 Cortlandt Ave., New Rochelle, NY 10801.

*CAREER:* In early career, worked as an actor in theatre, films, radio, and television; field representative for *Ebony,* 1949-50; playwright, free-lance producer, and director of plays, films, and news documentaries, 1950—; president of William Branch Associates (development, production, and consulting firm), 1973—; professor of Africana studies, Cornell University, 1985—. Director of "The Jackie Robinson Show," NBC-Radio, 1959-60; staff producer, contributing writer of documentary films for *The City* series, Educational Broadcasting Corp., 1962-64; writer and director of "The Alma John Show," 1963-65; writer and producer of television documentary programs for NBC-TV, 1972-73; executive producer of "Black Perspectives on the News," Public Broadcasting System, 1978-79.

Visiting professor at University of Ghana, 1963, and University of Maryland, Baltimore County, 1979-82; associate in film at Columbia University, 1968-69; visiting playwright at Smith College, summer, 1970, and North Carolina Central University, spring-summer, 1971; visiting Luce Fellow at Williams College, 1983; lecturer at colleges and universities, including Harvard University, Fisk University, Howard University, and University of California, Los Angeles. Member of board of directors of American Society of African Culture, 1963-70, and National Citizens Committee for Broadcasting, 1969-71; member of national advisory board of Library of Congress Center for the Book, 1979-82; treasurer of National Confer-

ence on African American Theatre, 1987-91; member of national advisory board of W. E. B. DuBois Foundation, 1987—. *Military service:* U.S. Army, 1951-53; served as educational instructor in Germany.

*AWARDS, HONORS:* Robert E. Sherwood Television Award and National Conference of Christians and Jews citations, 1958, both for television drama *Light in the Southern Sky;* Hannah del Vecchio Award from Columbia University, 1958; John Simon Guggenheim fellowship for creative writing in drama, 1959-60; Yale University-American Broadcasting Company fellowship for creative writing in television drama, 1965-66; Emmy Award nomination from National Academy of Television Arts and Sciences and American Film Festival award, 1969, both for television documentary *Still a Brother: Inside the Negro Middle Class;* National Conference of Christians and Jews citation, 1988, for *A Letter from Booker T.;* American Book Award, 1992, for *Black Thunder: An Anthology of Contemporary African American Drama.*

*WRITINGS:*

*PLAYS*

*A Medal for Willie,* first produced in New York at Club Baron, 1951.
*In Splendid Error,* first produced in New York at Greenwich Mews Playhouse, 1955.
*To Follow the Phoenix,* first produced in Chicago at Civic Opera House, 1960.
*A Wreath for Udomo* (based on a novel by Peter Abrahams), first produced in London at Lyric Hammersmith Theater, 1961.
*Baccalaureate,* first produced in Hamilton, Bermuda, at City Hall Theatre, 1975.

*MOTION PICTURES*

*Benefit Performance,* Universal, 1969.
*Judgement!,* Belafonte Enterprises, 1969.
*Together for Days,* Olas Corp., 1971.

*STAGE DOCUMENTARIES AND DRAMAS*

*Light in the Southern Sky,* first produced in New York at Waldorf Astoria, 1958.
*Fifty Steps Toward Freedom,* National Association for the Advancement of Colored People (NAACP), 1959.
*The Man on Meeting Street,* Alpha Kappa Alpha Sorority, 1960.

*TELEVISION DOCUMENTARIES AND DRAMAS*

*The Way,* American Broadcasting Co., 1955.

*What Is Conscience?,* Columbia Broadcasting System, 1955.
*Let's Find Out* (series), National Council of Churches, 1956.
*Light in the Southern Sky,* National Broadcasting Co. (NBC-TV), 1958.
*Legacy of a Prophet,* Educational Broadcasting Corp., 1959.
*Still a Brother: Inside the Negro Middle Class,* National Educational Television, 1968.
*The Case of the Non-Working Workers,* NBC-TV, 1972.
*The 20 Billion Dollar Rip-Off,* NBC-TV, 1972.
*No Room to Run, No Place to Hide,* NBC-TV, 1972.
*The Black Church in New York,* NBC-TV, 1973.
*Afro-American Perspectives* (series), Maryland Center for Public Broadcasting, 1973-80.
*A Letter from Booker T.,* PBS-TV, 1987.

*OTHER*

(Contributor) John A. Davis, editor, *The American Negro Writer and His Roots,* American Society of African Culture, 1960.
(Editor and contributor) *Black Thunder: An Anthology of Contemporary African American Drama,* Dutton, 1992.
(Editor and contributor) *Crosswinds: An Anthology of Black Dramatists in the Diaspora,* Indiana University Press, 1993.

Also author of filmstrips, screenplay outlines, and radio scripts; author of syndicated newspaper column with Jackie Robinson, 1958-60. Work represented in anthologies, including *Black Scenes,* edited by Alice Childress, Doubleday, 1971; *Black Theater,* edited by Lindsay Patterson, Dodd, Mead, 1971; *Black Drama Anthology,* edited by Woodie King and Ron Milner, Columbia University Press, 1972; *Black Theatre U.S.A.,* edited by James V. Hatch and Ted Shine, Free Press, 1974; *Standing Room Only,* edited by Daigon and Bernier, Prentice-Hall, 1977; *Meeting Challenges,* edited by J. Nelson, American Book, 1980; and *Black Heroes, Seven Plays,* edited by Errol Hill, Applause Theatre Books, 1989. Founding member, editorial board, *African-American Theatre Journal,* 1987—. Contributor to periodicals.

*BIOGRAPHICAL/CRITICAL SOURCES:*

*BOOKS*

Abramson, Doris E., *Negro Playwrights in the American Theatre, 1925-1969,* Columbia University Press, 1969.
Aptheker, Herbert, *Toward Negro Freedom,* New Century, 1956.
Berry, Mary Frances and John W. Blassingame, *Long Memory,* Oxford University Press, 1982.
*Dictionary of Literary Biography,* Volume 76: *Afro-American Writers, 1940-1955,* Gale, 1988.

Emanuel, James and Theodore Gross, editors, *Dark Symphony,* Free Press, 1968.
Mitchell, Loften, *Black Drama: The Story of the American Negro in the Theatre,* Hawthorne, 1967.
Molette, Carlton W. and Barbara, *Black Theatre: Premise and Presentation,* Wyndham Hall Press, 1986, revised edition, 1992.

*PERIODICALS*

*Afro-American,* September 25, 1954.
*Boston Globe,* April 30, 1968.
*Boston Herald Traveler,* April 30, 1968.
*Chicago Daily News,* May 2, 1968.
*Columbia,* fall, 1992, p. 60.
*Cornell Alumni News,* March, 1991, pp. 30-33.
*Crisis,* April, 1965.
*Freedomways,* summer, 1963.
*Ithaca Journal,* April 29, 1992.
*Library Journal,* February 15, 1992, p. 166.
*Masses & Mainstream,* December, 1951, pp. 59-60; November, 1954, pp. 59-63.
*MultiCultural Review,* July, 1992, pp. 58-59.
*National Guardian,* November 3, 1954, p. 10.
*Negro Digest,* January, 1968.
*Newark Evening News,* April 30, 1968.
*New World Review,* December, 1951, p. 63.
*New York Amsterdam News,* October 6, 1951; December 26, 1992, p. 21.
*New York Herald Tribune,* July 5, 1954; August 7, 1954; October 26, 1954; October 27, 1954.
*New York Times,* October 27, 1954; November 7, 1954; October 16, 1957; April 26, 1969; April 30, 1969; December 20, 1978.
*Philadelphia Inquirer,* May 1, 1968.
*Publishers Weekly,* January 1, 1992, p. 52; January 18, 1993, p. 298.
*Seattle Post-Intelligencer,* April 29, 1968.
*Variety,* May 1, 1968.

\* \* \*

## BRAND, Dionne 1953-

*PERSONAL:* Born January 7, 1953, in Guayguayare, Trinidad; immigrated to Canada. *Education:* University of Toronto, B.A., 1975, graduate studies at Ontario Institute for Studies in Education.

*ADDRESSES: Agent*—Women's Educational Press, 517 College St., Suite 233, Toronto, Ontario, Canada M6G 4A2.

*CAREER:* Poet, writer, and journalist. Associated with Black

Education Project, Toronto, Ontario, Canada; Immigrant Women's Centre, Toronto, Caribbean women's health counselor; Agency for Rural Transformation, Grenada, Cuba, information and communications officer, 1983.

*AWARDS, HONORS:* Publisher's Grant and Artist in the Schools Award, both from Ontario Arts Council, 1978; Canada Council Arts Grant, 1980; Ontario Arts Council grant, 1982.

*WRITINGS:*

'Fore Day Morning (poems), Khoisan Artists, 1978.
*Earth Magic* (poems), illustrated by Roy Crosse, Kids Can Press, 1980.
*Primitive Offensive* (poems), Williams-Wallace, 1982.
*Winter Epigrams and Epigrams to Ernesto Cardenal in Defense of Claudia* (poems), introduction by Roger McTair, Williams-Wallace, 1983.
*Chronicles of the Hostile Sun* (poems), Williams-Wallace, 1984.
(With Krisantha Sri Bhaggiyadatta) *Rivers Have Sources, Trees Have Roots: Speaking of Racism,* Cross Cultural Communication Centre, 1986.
*Sans Souci, and Other Stories,* Firebrand Books, 1989.
*No Language Is Neutral* (poems), Coach House Press, 1990.
(With Lois De Shield) *No Burden to Carry: Narratives of Black Working Women in Ontario, 1920s-1950s,* Women's Press, 1991.

Contributor to periodicals, including *Spear* and *Contrast.*

*SIDELIGHTS:* "Dionne Brand is one of the best young poets writing in Canada today," Libby Scheier asserts in her *Books in Canada* review of Brand's collection *Primitive Offensive.* A native Trinidadian who immigrated to Canada, Brand holds a bachelor's degree in English from the University of Toronto; her published works include poetry, fiction, and nonfiction. She has also worked actively for the black community in Canada through her affiliation with the Black Education Project and as a Caribbean counselor with the Immigrant Women's Centre.

Critics note that Brand's work is highly political. "To read her poetry is to read not only about her but also about her people, her identification with their struggles both in the metropole of Canada and in the hinterland of the Caribbean," comments Himani Bannerji in *Fifty Caribbean Writers.* The poetry in *No Language Is Neutral,* says Erin Moure in *Books in Canada,* "is one of waking and attentiveness, to one's own history, one's pain as a woman, as an immigrant to the place of foreign habits, to one's own sexuality." In the title poem, Moure says, Brand explores the lives of women who know "what it means to be black and women and to struggle constantly with

that 'blood-stained blind of race and sex'." Moure feels that the collection contains some of "Brand's most engaging poetry."

*Sans Souci, and Other Stories,* a collection of short stories, "follows Brand's own cycle of growing up in Trinidad, moving to Canada as a teenager and returning to Grenada during the revolution to reconnect politically and spiritually with the Caribbean," reports Rhonda Cobham in the *Women's Review of Books.* In Cobham's opinion, Brand is a "militantly feminist and anti-imperialist writer." Cobham finds that female sexuality is a prominent theme of this collection, which contains stories of people who struggle to find a place in a world that is racist as well as sexist.

Brand's talent is not limited to poetry and fiction. *Rivers Have Sources, Trees Have Roots: Speaking of Racism,* co-authored with Krisantha Sri Bhaggiyadatta, seeks to educate readers against racism through a combination of interviews and "succinct and simply stated analysis," says *Canadian Forum* contributor Leslie Sanders. Through the testimony of the book's black, Native American, and Asian subjects, Sanders reports, the reader is led to realize that "racism is a deliberate attack on the self-image of the other." The authors also chart some of the history of the struggle against racism in Toronto, and Sanders believes that Brand and her coauthor "succeed admirably in their educative purpose." In *No Burden to Carry* Brand again uses personal recollections and interviews as the narrative support to illustrate her point. Through the accounts of fifteen black women, this book traces the role of black women in the history of Canada. Merilyn Simonds Mohr, writing in *Books in Canada,* says that reading the book "is like spending an afternoon with a roomful of charming, strong, witty women who have a lifetime of stories to share."

While Brand's work has been applauded for its thematic content, she is also recognized as an accomplished writer. Scheier says of *Primitive Offensive,* "The language is sharp and vibrant, the imagery original and evocative, the rhythmic phrasing beautifully achieved." Similarly, Cobham calls "Madame Alaird's Breasts," a short story from *Sans Souci,* "a perfect vignette of adolescent female eroticism" and declares that Brand is "*the* new Caribbean woman writer to watch." Cobham praises the whole collection, but she is especially appreciative of the technical expertise of "I Used to Like the Dallas Cowboys." The story relates the changing perception of America through the eyes of a woman facing probable death during the American invasion of Grenada in 1983. Cobham lauds it as "political art at its searing best." And while Brand has already won acclaim for both her poetry and her prose, it is Cobham's assessment that "there is more and better to come, and when Brand produces her magnum opus it's going to be out there with the big names: Toni Morrison, Toni Cade Bambara, Derek Walcott, Wilson Harris."

*BIOGRAPHICAL/CRITICAL SOURCES:*

*BOOKS*

Dance, Daryl Cumber, editor, *Fifty Caribbean Writers: A Bio-Bibliographical Critical Sourcebook,* Greenwood, 1986.

*PERIODICALS*

*Books in Canada,* December, 1983, p. 31; December, 1990, pp. 42-43; May, 1992, pp. 52-53.
*Canadian Forum,* January, 1988, pp. 39-40.
*Women's Review of Books,* July, 1990, pp. 29-31.

\*    \*    \*

## BRATHWAITE, Edward (Kamau) 1930-

*PERSONAL:* Name originally, Lawson Edward Brathwaite; born May 11, 1930, in Bridgetown, Barbados; son of Hilton Edward and Beryl (Gill) Brathwaite; married Doris Monica Welcome (a teacher and librarian), March 26, 1960; children: Michael. *Education:* Attended Harrison College, Barbados; Pembroke College, Cambridge, B.A. (honors), 1953, Diploma of Education, 1954; University of Sussex, D.Phil., 1968.

*ADDRESSES: Office*—New York University, Washington Square, New York, NY 10003.

*CAREER:* Writer, poet, playwright, and editor. Education officer with Ministry of Education of Ghana, 1955-62; University of the West Indies, Kingston, Jamaica, tutor in Department of Extra Mural Studies assigned to island of Saint Lucia, 1962-63, university lecturer, 1963-72, senior lecturer in history, 1972-76, reader, 1976-83, professor of social and cultural history, 1982-91; affiliated with New York University, New York City, 1991—. Plebiscite officer for the United Nations in the Trans-Volta Togoland, 1956-57. Visiting professor, Southern Illinois University, 1970, University of Nairobi, 1971, Boston University, 1975-76, University of Mysore (India), 1982, Holy Cross College, 1983, Yale University, 1988; visiting fellow, Harvard University, 1987.

*MEMBER:* Caribbean Artists Movement (founding secretary, 1966—).

*AWARDS, HONORS:* Arts Council of Great Britain bursary, 1967; Camden Arts Festival prize, 1967; Cholmondeley Award, 1970, for *Islands*; Guggenheim fellowship, 1972; City of Nairobi fellowship, 1972; Bussa Award, 1973; Casa de las Americas Prize for Poetry, 1976; Fulbright fellow, 1982 and 1987; Institute of Jamaica Musgrave Medal, 1983.

*WRITINGS:*

*The People Who Came* (textbooks), three volumes, Longmans, 1968-72.
*Folk Culture of the Slaves in Jamaica,* New Beacon, 1970, revised edition, 1981.
*The Development of Creole Society in Jamaica, 1770-1820,* Clarendon Press, 1971.
*Caribbean Man in Space and Time,* Savacou Publications, 1974.
*Contradictory Omens: Cultural Diversity and Integration in the Caribbean,* Savacou Publications, 1974.
*Our Ancestral Heritage: A Bibliography of the Roots of Culture in the English-Speaking Caribbean,* Literary Committee of Carifesta, 1976.
*Wars of Respect: Nanny, Sam Sharpe, and the Struggle for People's Liberation,* API, 1977.
*Jamaica Poetry: A Checklist, 1686-1978,* Jamaica Library Service, 1979.
*Barbados Poetry: A Checklist, Slavery to the Present,* Savacou Publications, 1979.
*Kumina,* Savacou Publications, 1982.
*Gods of the Middle Passage,* privately printed, 1982.
*National Language Poetry,* privately printed, 1982.
*Afternoon of the Status Crow,* Savacou Publications, 1982.
*The Colonial Encounter: Language,* University of Mysore, 1984.
*History of the Voice: The Development of Nation Language in Angolophone Caribbean Poetry,* New Beacon, 1984.
*Jah Music,* Savacou Publications, 1986.
*Roots: Literary Criticism* (essays), Casa de los Americas, 1986.
*Visibility Trigger/Le detonateur de visibilite,* Cahiers de Louvain, 1986.
*Sappho Sakyi's Meditations,* Savacou Publications, 1989.
*Shar,* Savacou Publications, 1990.
*Middle Passages,* Bloodaxe Books, 1992.

Also author of *Korabra,* 1986.

*POETRY*

*Rights of Passage* (also see below), Oxford University Press, 1967.
*Masks* (also see below), Oxford University Press, 1968.
*Islands* (also see below), Oxford University Press, 1969.
(With Alan Bold and Edwin Morgan) *Penguin Modern Poets 15,* Penguin, 1969.
*Panda No. 349,* Roy Institute for the Blind, 1969.
*The Arrivants: A New World Trilogy* (contains *Rights of Passage, Masks,* and *Islands*), Oxford University Press, 1973.
*Days and Nights,* Caldwell Press, 1975.
*Other Exiles,* Oxford University Press, 1975.
*Poetry '75 International,* Rotterdamse Kunstsichting, 1975.

*Black + Blues,* Casa de las Americas, 1976.
*Mother Poem,* Oxford University Press, 1977.
*Soweto,* Savacou Publications, 1979.
*Word Making Man: A Poem for Nicolas Guillen,* Savacou Publications, 1979.
*Sun Poem,* Oxford University Press, 1982.
*Third World Poems,* Longmans, 1983.
*X/Self,* Oxford University Press, 1987.

*PLAYS*

*Four Plays for Primary Schools* (first produced in Saltpond, Ghana, 1961), Longmans, Green, 1964.
*Odale's Choice* (first produced in Saltpond, Ghana, 1962), Evans Brothers, 1967.

*EDITOR*

*Iouanaloa: Recent Writing from St. Lucia,* Department of Extra Mural Studies, University of West Indies, 1963.
*New Poets from Jamaica* (anthology), Savacou Publications, 1979.
*Dream Rock,* Jamaica Information Service, 1987.

*RECORDINGS*

*The Poet Speaks 10,* Argo, 1968.
*Rights of Passage,* Argo, 1969.
*Masks,* Argo, 1972.
*Islands,* Argo, 1973.
*The Poetry of Edward Kamau Brathwaite,* Casa de las Americas, 1976.
*Poemas,* Casa de las Americas, 1976.
*Atumpan,* Watershed, 1989.

*OTHER*

Contributor to *Bim* and other periodicals. Editor, *Savacou* (magazine), 1970—.

*SIDELIGHTS:* Edward Brathwaite is generally regarded as one of the West Indies' most prolific and talented writers. More well known for his poetry, Brathwaite often seeks to explore in his writings his past and present self while examining his identity as a black person living in the Caribbean. Andrew Motion writes in the *Times Literary Supplement* that "throughout his career Brathwaite has been concerned to define his identity as a West Indian."

It was the publication of *Rights of Passage* in 1967, *Masks* in 1968, and *Islands* in 1969, that brought Brathwaite to the attention of a larger group of critics and readers. These three books of poetry constitute an autobiographical trilogy collectively entitled *The Arrivants: A New World Trilogy* that ex-

amines a Caribbean man's search for identity. The volumes trace Brathwaite's initial encounter with white culture, his journey to Africa in search of a racial self-image, and his eventual return to his Caribbean homeland. Laurence Lieberman writes in *Poetry:* "[Brathwaite] has been able to invent a hybrid prosody which, combining jazz/folk rhythms with English-speaking meters, captures the authenticity of primitive African rituals." "In general," writes Hayden Carruth in the *Hudson Review,* "[Brathwaite] has been remarkably successful in reproducing black speech patterns, both African and Caribbean, in English syntax, using the standard techniques of contemporary poetry, and he has been equally successful in suggesting to an international audience the cultural identities and attitudes of his own people."

In 1977 Brathwaite released *Mother Poem,* the first book in a promised second trilogy. The next book of the trilogy, *Sun Poem,* was published in 1982, and the third, *X/Self,* was released in 1987. As in Brathwaite's first trilogy, *Mother Poem, Sun Poem,* and *X/Self* continue Brathwaite's exploration of his selfhood. As Andrew Motion explains in *Times Literary Supplement:* "In *Mother Poem,* [Brathwaite] provides another detailed account of his home [in the West Indies]. But in addition to exploring his complex relationship with the place, he also recounts its own efforts to find an independent and homogeneous character." David Dorsey remarks in *World Literature Today:* "Brathwaite is particularly ingenious in achieving semantic complexity through his use of assonance, enjambment, word divisions, grammatical and lexical ambiguity, puns and neologisms. This joie d'esprit occurs within a rhythm always obedient to the emphases and feelings intended. The style paradoxically reveals the author's sober, passionate and lucid perception on the beauty and pain black Barbadians are heir to."

In a *World Literature Today* review of *Sun Poem* Andrew Salkey comments that "Brathwaite writes 'performance,' 'rituals' and 'illuminations' which result in conflated portraits of persons, places and events recalled through a filter of sequential evocative poems—no ordinary creative accomplishment."

*BIOGRAPHICAL/CRITICAL SOURCES:*

*BOOKS*

*Authors and Areas of the West Indies,* Steck-Vaughn, 1970.
Brathwaite, Doris Monica, *A Descriptive and Chronological Bibliography (1950-1982) of the Work of Edward Kamau Brathwaite,* New Beacon, 1988.
Brathwaite, Doris Monica, *Edward Kamau Brathwaite: His Published Prose and Poetry 1948-1986,* Savacou Publications, 1986.
*Caribbean Writers,* Three Continents, 1979.
*Contemporary Literary Criticism,* Volume 2, Gale, 1979.

*Contemporary Poets,* St. James, 1991, pp. 93-95.
*Dictionary of Literary Biography,* volume 125: *Twentieth-Century Caribbean and Black African Writers,* Gale, 1993, pp. 8-28.
*West Indian Literature,* Archon Books, 1979.

*PERIODICALS*

*Ariel,* April, 1990, pp. 45-57.
*Books,* January, 1970.
*Books and Bookmen,* May, 1967.
*Book World,* November 3, 1968.
*Caribbean Quarterly,* June, 1973.
*Caribbean Studies,* January, 1971.
*Choice,* June, 1976.
*Critical Quarterly,* summer, 1970.
*Hudson Review,* summer, 1974.
*Jamaica Journal,* September, 1968.
*Library Journal,* March 15, 1970.
*Nation,* April 9, 1988, pp. 504-507.
*New Statesman,* April 7, 1967.
*Partisan Review,* February, 1989, pp. 316-320.
*Poetry,* April, 1969; May, 1971.
*Saturday Review,* October 14, 1967.
*Third World Quarterly,* March, 1988, pp. 334-337.
*Times Literary Supplement,* February 16, 1967; August 15, 1968; January 28, 1972; June 30, 1972; November 14, 1975; January 20, 1978; February 18, 1983.
*Virginia Quarterly Review,* autumn, 1963, autumn, 1968, spring, 1970.
*West Africa,* March 16, 1987, pp. 514-515.
*World Literature Today,* winter, 1977; summer, 1978; summer, 1983.

\*     \*     \*

## BRAXTON, Joanne M(argaret) 1950-
(Jodi Braxton)

*PERSONAL:* Born May 25, 1950, in Washington, DC; daughter of Harry McHenry (a machinist and civic leader) and Mary Ellen (a homemaker and civil service worker; maiden name, Weems) Braxton. *Education:* Sarah Lawrence College, B.A., 1972; Yale University, M.A., 1974, Ph.D., 1984.

*ADDRESSES: Office*—American Studies Program, College of William and Mary, Williamsburg, VA 23185.

*CAREER:* University of Michigan, Ann Arbor, Michigan Society of Fellows, 1976-79; College of William and Mary, Williamsburg, VA, assistant professor, 1980-86, associate professor, 1986-89, Frances L. and Edwin L. Cummings Pro-

fessor of American Studies and English, and professor of English, 1989—.

*MEMBER:* Modern Language Association, American Studies Association, College Language Association.

*AWARDS, HONORS:* National Endowment of the Humanities fellow, 1984; American Council of Learned Societies fellow, 1986; Thomas Jefferson Teaching Award, College of William and Mary, 1986; received grant from National Endowment of the Humanities, 1986; fellow, College of William and Mary Society of the Alumni, 1988; *Wild Women in the Whirlwind: Afra-American Culture and the Contemporary Literary Renaissance* received the Koppleman Book Award in 1990; Outstanding Faculty Award, State Council of Higher Education in Virginia, 1992.

*WRITINGS:*

(As Jodi Braxton) *Sometimes I Think of Maryland,* Sunbury Press, 1977.
*Black Women Writing Autobiography: A Tradition within a Tradition,* Temple University Press, 1989.
(Editor with Andree N. McLaughlin) *Wild Women in the Whirlwind: Afra-American Culture and the Contemporary Literary Renaissance* (anthology), Rutgers University Press, 1990.
(Editor) *The Collected Poetry of Paul Laurence Dunbar,* University Press of Virginia, 1993.

Contributor of essays to books, including *The Private Self: Theory and Practice in Women's Autobiographical Writings,* edited by Shari Benstock, University of North Carolina Press, 1988; and *Modern American Women Writers,* edited by Elaine Showalter, A. Walton Litz, and Lea Baechler, Scribner's, 1990. Also contributor of poetry to anthologies, including *Equal-Time,* Equal Time Press, 1972; *Drum,* University of Massachusetts, 1975; *We Become New,* Bantam, 1975; *Synergy,* Energy Black South, 1976; *Celebrations,* Follet, 1977; and *Woman Poet: The South,* Women in Literature Press, 1988. Author of introduction to *The Work of the Afro-American Woman,* Oxford University Press, 1988. Member of editorial advisory boards, *African-American Review,* 1990—, *Autobiography Studies,* 1991—, and *Legacy,* 1992—. Contributor to periodicals, including *Massachusetts Review, Women's Review of Books, New Republic, Journal of Black Poetry, Encore, Black Creation, Presence Africaine.*

*WORK IN PROGRESS: Songs of the Southern Slave, 1755-1865,* "a documentary collection of Afro-American music."

*SIDELIGHTS:* Joanne M. Braxton is a poet and author who explores themes of black folklore and tradition, as well as loss and personal experience. Family and relationships also figure prominently in her written word. Born in 1950 in Washington, DC, Braxton grew up in the small Maryland town of Lakeland and was influenced by her tight-knit family, including her parents, three brothers, and two grandmothers. As the author relates in a biographical note in her first book, *Sometimes I Think of Maryland:* "My grandmothers taught me family history and genealogy, and told me stories they had heard about slavery; tales of horror and strength. This oral tradition constitutes the source of my artistic consciousness and my personal strength."

In *Sometimes I Think of Maryland,* Braxton reflects on topics ranging from her childhood home and love, to her late grandmother. Of the latter she writes, "No straight lines but drooping shoulders / And old hands chewed a red-brick brown / Hands that healed my bee stings / With three different kinds of leaves and loves / Offset by two skinny yellow bowed legs / Knotted with brown spots." Other verse, such as the three poems that constitute "Conversion," delves into mythological themes. The collection, written under the name Jodi Braxton, was met with praise from both critics and the public alike.

Braxton pursued her interest in black folklore and literary history in her second book, published in 1989. Titled *Black Women Writing Autobiography: A Tradition within a Tradition,* the volume was inspired by stories of the poet's ancestry. In the work's introduction Braxton explains that her "consciousness was ready shaped for the study of the slave narrative. I had learned to *listen.*" The end result is a book delineating a tradition of black women's autobiographical writing, including its various subgenres like modern autobiography, slave narrative, reminiscence, travelogue, and historical memoir. The volume, according to Braxton, "views the autobiography of black American women ... as a form of symbolic memory that evokes the black woman's deepest consciousness" and as "an occasion for viewing the individual in relation to those with whom she shares emotional, philosophical, and spiritual affinities, as well as political realities."

In 1990 Braxton returned her attention to the literature of black American women writers by coediting *Wild Women in the Whirlwind: Afra-American Culture and the Contemporary Literary Renaissance.* This collection contains essays covering the contemporary renaissance, which *New York Times Book Review*'s Eric J. Sundquist explained "includes not just the Caribbean (as a crucial part of black America) but also Africa, the Pacific Islands, or anywhere that black women have made writing an instrument of liberation." Articles explore the work of specific individuals, such as Zora Neale Hurston, Gwendolyn Brooks, Alice Walker, and Paule Marshall, and treat various aspects of black feminist literary theory as well as political topics.

*BIOGRAPHICAL/CRITICAL SOURCES:*

*BOOKS*

Braxton, Joanne M., *Black Women Writing Autobiography: A Tradition within a Tradition,* Temple University Press, 1989.

Braxton, Jodi, *Sometimes I Think of Maryland,* Sunbury Press, 1977.

*Dictionary of Literary Biography,* Volume 41: *Afro-American Poets since 1955,* edited by Trudier Harris and Thadious M. Davis, Gale, 1985, pp. 42-47.

*PERIODICALS*

*New York Times Book Review,* February 25, 1990, p. 11.

\* \* \*

## BRAXTON, Jodi
### See BRAXTON, Joanne M(argaret)

\* \* \*

## BREW, (Osborne Henry) Kwesi 1928-

*PERSONAL:* Born May 27, 1928, in Cape Coast, Ghana. *Education:* University College of the Gold Coast (now University of Ghana), B.A., 1953.

*ADDRESSES: Home*—Accra, Ghana.

*CAREER:* Assistant district commissioner, Keta, Ghana, 1953-54; district commissioner, Kete Krachi, Ghana, 1954; Public Service Commission, Ghana, assistant secretary, 1955; foreign service officer, 1957; Ghana High Commission, London, England, and Ghana Embassy, Paris, France, third secretary, 1958; Ghana High Commission, New Delhi, India, second secretary, 1959; International Atomic Energy Agency, Vienna, Austria, member of Ghana delegation, 1960-61; Ghana Embassy, Moscow, Russia, counselor, 1962; Ministry of Foreign Affairs, became director of division of the Middle East and Asia, then director of division of the United Nations and international organizations, then director of division of Western and European affairs, then director of division of protocol; State of Ghana, ambassador to Mexico, 1964, ambassador-designate to Karachi, Pakistan, 1966, ambassador to Senegal, 1966; Economic Conference, Dakar, Senegal, alternate head of delegation, 1968.

*AWARDS, HONORS:* Winner of poetry competition, The English Society, University College of the Gold Coast, 1949.

*WRITINGS:*

*The Shadows of Laughter,* Longmans, Green, 1968.
*African Panorama and Other Poems,* Greenfield, 1981.

Also author of the screenplay *The Harvest.* Contributor to various books, including *Modern Poetry from Africa,* Penguin, 1963; *A Book of African Verse,* Heinemann, 1964; and *Messages: Poems from Africa,* Heinemann, 1971. Contributor to various periodicals, including *Okyeame, Voices of Ghana, Voices of the Commonwealth, New World Writings, Schwarzer Orpheus, Ghana Review, Outpost, Presence Africaine, Times Literary Supplement,* and *Zuka: A Journal of East African Creative Writing.*

*SIDELIGHTS:* After losing both parents early in life, Ghana native Kwesi Brew was raised by K. J. Dickens, an English education officer, to whom Brew says he "owes everything," including his love for books. Brew is author of *African Panorama and Other Poems* and *The Shadows of Laughter,* both collections of poetry. In *World Literature Today,* Andrew Salkey described Brew's poems as "snapshot reports from the hinterland and urban scenes of his Ghanaian panorama" and listed essential characteristics of his work as a "crisp, clear craft, narrative persuasiveness and compassionate outlook." Much of Brew's style draws upon traditional Akan songs while largely disregarding Western prototypes, such as the didactic tone found in hymns and tracts in much of Ghanaian poetry prior to 1960. *African Authors* defines the general theme in Brew's work as "that of the value of the individual as contrasted to that of his society as a whole."

*BIOGRAPHICAL/CRITICAL SOURCES:*

*BOOKS*

*African Authors,* Volume 1, Black Orpheus Press, 1973.
*Contemporary Poets,* fifth edition, St. James Press, 1991.

*PERIODICALS*

*Times Literary Supplement,* July 24, 1969, p. 836.
*World Literature Today,* summer, 1983, p. 501.

\*    \*    \*

## BRODBER, Erna (May) 1940-

*PERSONAL:* Born April 20, 1940, in Woodside, St. Mary, Jamaica; daughter of Ernest (a farmer) and Lucy (a teacher) Brodber. *Education:* University College of the West Indies (now University of the West Indies), B.A. (honors), 1963,

M.Sc., 1968, Ph.D.; attended McGill University, and University of Washington, beginning in 1967. *Religion:* Twelve Tribes of Israel (a Rastafarian sect).

*CAREER:* Worked as civil servant; worked as a teacher in Montego Bay, Jamaica; served as head of history at St. Augustine High School for Girls, Trinidad; Ministry of Youth and Community Development, Jamaica, children's officer, beginning in 1964; University of the West Indies, lecturer in sociology, in the 1970s; Institute of Social and Economic Research, supernumary fellow, 1972-73, staff member, 1974-83; free-lance writer and researcher. Visiting scholar at University of Michigan, Ann Arbor, 1973; visiting fellow at School of African and Asian Studies of University of Sussex, 1981. Appeared in revue titled *8 O'Clock Jamaica Time,* 1972.

*AWARDS, HONORS:* Received scholarships from the University of the West Indies, and the Jamaican government, 1960; University of the West Indies postgraduate award, 1964; Ford Foundation fellowship for pre-doctoral research, 1967; National Festival award, Jamaica Festival Commission, 1975, for short story "Rosa"; Association of Commonwealth Universities staff fellowship, 1980.

*WRITINGS:*

*Abandonment of Children in Jamaica,* University of the West Indies, Institute of Social and Economic Research, 1974.
*Yards in the City of Kingston,* University of the West Indies, Institute of Social and Economic Research, 1975.
*Jane and Louisa Will Soon Come Home* (novel), New Beacon Books, 1980.
*Perceptions of Caribbean Women: Towards a Documentation of Stereotypes,* introduction by Merle Hodge, University of the West Indies, Institute of Social and Economic Research, 1982.
*Myal* (novel), New Beacon Books, 1988.
*Rural-Urban Migration and the Jamaican Child,* United Nations Educational, Scientific, and Cultural Organization (UNESCO), Regional Office for Education in Latin America and the Caribbean, 1986.

Author, with J. Edward Greene, of *Reggae and Cultural Identity in Jamaica,* 1981; author of *A History of the Second Generation of Freemen in Jamaica, 1907-1944;* author of short story, "Rosa," *Festival Commission,* 1975. Contributor to periodicals, including *Journal of Ethnic Studies* and *Jamaica Journal.*

*SIDELIGHTS:* Erna Brodber's first novel "immediately earned a place as a masterpiece within the canon of Caribbean fiction," says Rhonda Cobham in the *Women's Review of Books.* Born in Jamaica, Brodber was the child of parents actively involved in local community affairs in their hometown of Woodside. In this way, Brodber, a sociologist and researcher by vocation, was exposed to the importance of community affiliations at an early age. Brodber came to the United States on a research scholarship soon after she graduated from the University of the West Indies. It was here that she discovered the black power and women's liberation movements, two ideas that influenced her greatly. Back in Jamaica Brodber received a master's degree in sociology, also from the University of the West Indies. Since then Brodber has published numerous nonfiction works in her field, but it was with the publication of her first novel, *Jane and Louisa Will Soon Come Home,* that she established herself as a fiction writer. *Jane and Louisa Will Soon Come Home* was followed by *Myal,* her second novel, in 1988. Both books have been well received by critics and deal with issues central to Caribbean life.

*Jane and Louisa Will Soon Come Home* is set in a small rural community. In this book Brodber examines the importance and influence of traditional Jamaican society through the life of her protagonist, Nellie. Nellie, a woman who has lost her sense of self due to societal pressures, learns to use her community's strength to heal herself. Se can do this, however, only if she learns to connect with and understand the significance of the past. Nellie's family teaches her to alienate herself from her black ancestry and community because their connection with the white community has resulted in prosperity. Therefore, Nellie learns to look down at the Creole community. At the end of the book, however, she learns that it is only when she accepts this community and becomes a part of it that she will heal completely.

*Jane and Louisa Will Soon Come Home* also explores the problems facing Caribbean women through the contradictory images of womanhood that Nellie is exposed to. The fissure in Nellie's self begins at puberty, when others view her increasing sexual maturity as a change to be ashamed of, leading Nellie to view herself and her womanhood as something negative. To solve the problem, Nellie is sent to live with her Aunt Becca, a woman who advises Nellie to avoid men and repress her sexuality completely. Set against this idea is the pressure of the sexual liberation prevalent at the university Nellie attends. All these contradictions result in a breakdown of Nellie's self. Her first sexual encounter leaves her traumatized, leading her to deny her femininity altogether and therefore also her identity. This remains the case until Nellie learns to reconstruct herself as a unified being who has fused within her the many different aspects of womanhood by rejecting the traditional stereotypes she had previously accepted as models of female identity.

*Myal,* Brodber's second novel, also deals with issues of identity in Caribbean society. *Myal* is the story of Ella O Grady, a young Jamaican girl adopted by a Welsh woman, Maydene

Brassington, who rescues Ella from her poverty. Ella's connection with Maydene results in Ella's dislocation from her own culture and religion. But as Cobham explains, she finally establishes a connection with her own milieu with the help of Maydene, Brassington's Jamaican husband, and a local shaman, "who create a spiritual safety-net to pull her out of the morass of cultural alienation and spiritual violation that claims her after her white American husband betrays her." She finally becomes a teacher at the local school, where she uses her own life experiences to render new meanings in the stories of the reading primers used by her students.

According to Cobham, Brodber's narrative refers explicitly to Claude McKay's *Banana Bottom,* where the protagonist, also rescued by an Englishwoman, must break her ties with that culture completely to find self-realization. Brodber's book, unlike McKay's, acknowledges the contribution of Maydene Brassington and other white women like her who, through marriage or birth, have created connections within traditional Jamaican society. Cobham feels that *Myal* establishes Maydene Brassington "as an amazingly credible figure" who is accepted by the other village shamans at the end of the book.

Cobham's final assessment of *Myal* classifies it as a "work of unquestioned achievement" in which Brodber deals with one of the most complex issues in Caribbean society: "the place and relevance of white West Indians and the colored middle class in a predominantly black society, in which both groups have disturbing past and present histories as oppressors." In both novels, Brodber's vision is of integration. The acceptance of common Creole society is as important to Nellie's self-realization in *Jane and Louisa Will Soon Come Home* as, conversely, Maydene Brassington, a white woman who has become part of Caribbean shamanic healing, is to Ella's reclamation. For Nellie and Ella the feeling of fragmentation dissipates only when they accept all the variances that comprise their world and become part of it.

*BIOGRAPHICAL/CRITICAL SOURCES:*

*PERIODICALS*

*Women's Review of Books,* July, 1990, pp. 29-31.

\*      \*      \*

## BROOKS, Gwendolyn 1917-

*PERSONAL:* Born June 7, 1917, in Topeka, KS; daughter of David Anderson and Keziah Corinne (Wims) Brooks; married Henry Lowington Blakely, September 17, 1939; children:

Henry Lowington III, Nora. *Education:* Graduate of Wilson Junior College, 1936.

*ADDRESSES: Home*—7428 South Evans Ave., Chicago, IL 60619.

*CAREER:* Poet and novelist. Publicity director, National Association for the Advancement of Colored People (NAACP) Youth Council, Chicago, IL, 1937-38; affiliated with the David Company publishing firm. Taught poetry at numerous colleges and universities, including Columbia College, Elmhurst College, Northeastern Illinois State College (now Northwestern Illinois University), and University of Wisconsin—Madison, 1969; Distinguished Professor of the Arts, City College of the City University of New York, 1971. Member, Illinois Arts Council.

*MEMBER:* American Academy of Arts and Letters, National Institute of Arts and Letters, Society of Midland Authors (Chicago).

*AWARDS, HONORS:* Named one of ten women of the year, *Mademoiselle* magazine, 1945; National Institute of Arts and Letters grant in literature, 1946; American Academy of Arts and Letters award for creative writing, 1946; Guggenheim fellowships, 1946 and 1947; Eunice Tietjens Memorial Prize, *Poetry* magazine, 1949; Pulitzer Prize in poetry, 1950, for *Annie Allen;* Robert F. Ferguson Memorial Award, Friends of Literature, 1964, for *Selected Poems;* Thormod Monsen Literature Award, 1964; Anisfield-Wolf Award, 1968, for *In the Mecca;* named Poet Laureate of Illinois, 1968; National Book Award nomination, for *In the Mecca;* Black Academy of Arts and Letters Award, 1971, for outstanding achievement in letters; Shelley Memorial Award, 1976; Poetry Consultant to the Library of Congress, 1985-86; inducted into National Women's Hall of Fame, 1988; Lifetime Achievement Award, National Endowment for the Arts, 1989; Society for Literature Award, University of Thessoloniki (Athens), 1990; Kuumva Liberation Award; Frost Medal, Poetry Society of America; approximately fifty honorary degrees from universities and colleges, including Columbia College, 1964, Lake Forest College, 1965, and Brown University, 1974.

*WRITINGS:*

*POETRY*

*A Street in Bronzeville* (also see below), Harper, 1945.
*Annie Allen* (also see below), Harper, 1949, reprinted, Greenwood Press, 1972.
*The Bean Eaters* (also see below), Harper, 1960.
*In the Time of Detachment, In the Time of Cold,* Civil War Centennial Commission of Illinois, 1965.

*In the Mecca* (also see below), Harper, 1968.
*For Illinois 1968: A Sesquicentennial Poem,* Harper, 1968.
*Riot* (also see below), Broadside Press, 1969.
*Family Pictures* (also see below), Broadside Press, 1970.
*Aloneness,* Broadside Press, 1971.
*Aurora,* Broadside Press, 1972.
*Beckonings,* Broadside Press, 1975.
*Primer for Blacks,* Black Position Press, 1980.
*To Disembark,* Third World Press, 1981.
*Black Love,* Brooks Press, 1982.
*Mayor Harold Washington* [and] *Chicago, The I Will City,* Brooks Press, 1983.
*The Near Johannesburg Bay, and Other Poems,* David Co., 1987.
*Children Coming Home,* David Co., 1991.
*Winnie,* Third World Press, 1991.

Also author of *A Catch of Shy Fish,* 1963.

*JUVENILE*

*Bronzeville Boys and Girls* (poems), Harper, 1956.
*The Tiger Who Wore White Gloves: Or You Are What You Are,* Third World Press, 1974, reissued, 1987.

*FICTION*

*Maud Martha* (novel; also see below), Harper, 1953.

Stories included in books, including *Soon One Morning: New Writing by American Negroes, 1940-1962* (contains "The Life of Lincoln West"), edited by Herbert Hill, Knopf, 1963, published in England as *Black Voices,* Elek, 1964; and *The Best Short Stories by Negro Writers: An Anthology from 1899 to the Present,* edited by Langston Hughes, Little, Brown, 1967.

*COLLECTED WORKS*

*Selected Poems,* Harper, 1963.
*The World of Gwendolyn Brooks* (contains *A Street in Bronzeville, Annie Allen, Maud Martha, The Bean Eaters,* and *In the Mecca*), Harper, 1971.
*Blacks* (includes *A Street in Bronzeville, Annie Allen, The Bean Eaters, Maud Martha, A Catch of Shy Fish, Riot, In the Mecca,* and most of *Family Pictures*), David Co., 1987.
*The Gwendolyn Brooks Library,* Moonbeam Publications, 1991.

*OTHER*

(With others) *A Portion of That Field: The Centennial of the Burial of Lincoln,* University of Illinois Press, 1967.
(Editor) *A Broadside Treasury,* (poems), Broadside Press, 1971.

(Editor) *Jump Bad: A New Chicago Anthology,* Broadside
    Press, 1971.
*Report from Part One: An Autobiography,* Broadside Press,
    1972.
(With Keorapetse Kgositsile, Haki R. Madhubuti, and Dudley
    Randall) *A Capsule Course in Black Poetry Writing,*
    Broadside Press, 1975.
*Young Poet's Primer* (writing manual), Brooks Press, 1981.
*Very Young Poets* (writing manual), Brooks Press, 1983.

Also author of broadsides *The Wall* and *We Real Cool,* for
Broadside Press, and *I See Chicago,* 1964. Contributor to
books, including *New Negro Poets USA,* edited by Langston
Hughes, Indiana University Press, 1964; *The Poetry of Black
America: Anthology of the Twentieth Century,* edited by
Arnold Adoff, Harper, 1973; and *Celebrate the Midwest!
Poems and Stories for David D. Anderson,* edited by Marcia
Noe, Lake Shore, 1991. Contributor of poems and articles to
*Ebony, McCall's, Nation, Poetry,* and other periodicals. Con-
tributor of reviews to Chicago *Sun-Times,* Chicago Daily
News, New York Herald Tribune,* and *New York Times Book
Review.*

*WORK IN PROGRESS:* A sequel to *Maud Martha.*

*SIDELIGHTS:* In 1950 Gwendolyn Brooks, a highly regarded poet, became the first black author to win the Pulitzer Prize.
Her poems from this period, specifically *A Street in Bronzeville*
and *Annie Allen,* were "devoted to small, carefully cerebrat-
ed, terse portraits of the Black urban poor," Richard K.
Barksdale comments in *Modern Black Poets: A Collection of
Critical Essays.* Jeanne-Marie A. Miller calls this "city-folk
poetry" and describes Brooks's characters as "unheroic black
people who fled the land for the city only to discover that there
is little difference between the world of the North and the world
of the South. One learns from them," Miller continues in the
*Journal of Negro Education,* "their dismal joys and their human griefs and pain." Audiences in Chicago, inmates in prisons around the country, and students of all ages have found
her poems accessible and relevant. Haki Madhubuti, cited in
Jacqueline Trescott's *Washington Post* article on Brooks,
points out that Brooks "has, more than any other nationally
acclaimed writer, remained in touch with the community she
writes about. She lives in the core of Chicago's black community.... She is her work." In addition, notes Toni Cade
Bambara in the *New York Times Book Review,* Brooks "is
known for her technical artistry, having worked her word
sorcery in forms as disparate as Italian terza rima and the blues.
She has been applauded for revelations of the African experience in America, particularly her sensitive portraits of black
women."

Though best known for her poetry, in the 1950s Brooks published her first novel. *Maud Martha* presents vignettes from a
ghetto woman's life in short chapters, says Harry B. Shaw in
*Gwendolyn Brooks.* It is "a story of a woman with doubts about
herself and where and how she fits into the world. Maud's
concern is not so much that she is inferior but that she is perceived as being ugly." Eventually, she takes a stand for her
own dignity by turning her back on a patronizing, racist store
clerk. "The book is ... about the triumph of the lowly," comments Shaw. "[Brooks] shows what they go through and exposes the shallowness of the popular, beautiful white people
with 'good' hair. One way of looking at the book, then, is as
a war with ... people's concepts of beauty." Its other themes
include "the importance of spiritual and physical death," disillusionment with a marriage that amounts to "a step down"
in living conditions, and the discovery "that even through
disillusionment and spiritual death life will prevail," Shaw
maintains. Other reviewers feel that Brooks is more effective
when treating the same themes in her poetry, but David
Littlejohn, writing in *Black on White: A Critical Survey of
Writing by American Negroes,* feels the novel "is a striking
human experiment, as exquisitely written ... as any of Gwendolyn Brook's poetry in verse.... It is a powerful, beautiful
dagger of a book, as generous as it can possibly be. It teaches
more, more quickly, more lastingly, than a thousand pages of
protest." In a *Black World* review, Annette Oliver Shands
appreciates the way in which *Maud Martha* differs from the
works of other early black writers: "Miss Brooks does not
specify traits, niceties or assets for members of the Black community to acquire in order to attain their just rights.... So, this
is not a novel to inspire social advancement on the part of
fellow Blacks. Nor does it say *be poor, Black and happy.* The
message is to accept the challenge of being human and to assert humanness with urgency."

Although, as Martha Liebrum notes in the *Houston Post,*
Brooks "wrote about being black before being black was beautiful," in retrospect her poems have been described as sophisticated, intellectual, and European, or "conditioned" by the
established literary tradition. Like her early favorites Emily
Dickinson, John Keats, and Percy Bysshe Shelley, Brooks
expresses in poetry her love of "the wonders language can
achieve," as she told Claudia Tate in an interview for *Black
Women Writers at Work.* Barksdale states that by not directly
emphasizing any "rhetorical involvement with causes, racial
or otherwise," Brooks was merely reflecting "the literary mood
of the late 1940's." He suggests that there was little reason for
Brooks to confront the problems of racism on a large scale
since, in her work, "each character, so neatly and precisely
presented, is a racial protest in itself and a symbol of some
sharply etched human dilemma."

However, Brooks's later poems show a marked change in tone
and content. Just as her first poems reflected the mood of their
era, her later works mirror their age by displaying what *National Observer* contributor Bruce Cook calls "an intense

awareness of the problems of color and justice." Bambara comments that at the age of fifty "something happened [to Brooks], a something most certainly in evidence in 'In the Mecca' (1968) and subsequent works—a new movement and energy, intensity, richness, power of statement and a new stripped lean, compressed style. A change of style prompted by a change of mind."

"Though some of her work in the early 1960s had a terse abbreviated style, her conversion to direct political expression happened rapidly after a gathering of black writers at Fisk University in 1967," Trescott reports. Brooks told Tate, "They seemed proud and so committed to their own people.... The poets among them felt that black poets should write as blacks, about blacks, and address themselves *to* blacks." If many of her earlier poems had fulfilled this aim, it was not due to conscious intent, she said; but from this time forward, Brooks has thought of herself as an African who has determined not to compromise social comment for the sake of technical proficiency.

Although *In the Mecca* and later works are characterized as tougher and possess what a reviewer for the *Virginia Quarterly Review* describes as "raw power and roughness," critics are quick to indicate that these poems are neither bitter nor vengeful. Instead, according to Cook, they are more "about bitterness" than bitter in themselves. *Dictionary of Literary Biography* essayist Charles Israel suggests that *In the Mecca*'s title poem, for example, shows "a deepening of Brooks's concern with social problems." A mother has lost a small daughter in the block-long ghetto tenement, the Mecca; the long poem traces her steps through the building, revealing her neighbors to be indifferent or insulated by their own personal obsessions. The mother finds her little girl, who "never learned that black is not beloved," who "was royalty when poised, / sly, at the A and P's fly-open door," under a Jamaican resident's cot, murdered. The *Virginia Quarterly Review* contributor compares the poem's impact to that of Richard Wright's fiction. R. Baxter Miller, writing in *Black American Poets between Worlds, 1940-1960,* comments, "*In the Mecca* is a most complex and intriguing book; it seeks to balance the sordid realities of urban life with an imaginative process of reconciliation and redemption." Other poems in the book, occasioned by the death of Malcolm X or the dedication of a mural of black heroes painted on a Chicago slum building, express the poet's commitment to her people's awareness of themselves as a political as well as a cultural entity.

Her interest in encouraging young blacks to assist and appreciate fledgling black publishing companies led her to leave Harper & Row. In the seventies, she chose Dudley Randall's Broadside Press to publish her poetry (*Riot, Family Pictures, Aloneness, Aurora,* and *Beckonings*) and *Report from Part One,* the first volume of her autobiography. She edited two

collections of poetry—*A Broadside Treasury* and *Jump Bad: A New Chicago Anthology*—for the Detroit-based press. The Chicago-based Third World Press, run by Haki R. Madhubuti (formerly Don L. Lee, one of the young poets she had met during the sixties), has also brought two Brooks titles into print. She does not regret having given her support to small publishers who dedicated themselves to the needs of the black community. Brooks was the first writer to read in Broadside's Poet's Theatre Series when it began and was also the first poet to read in the second opening of the series when the press revived under new ownership in 1988.

*Riot, Family Pictures, Beckonings,* and other books brought out by black publishers were given brief notice by critics of the literary establishment who "did not wish to encourage Black publishers," said Brooks. Some were disturbed by the political content of these poems. *Riot,* in particular, in which Brooks is the spokesman for the "HEALTHY REBELLION" going on then, as she calls it, was accused of "celebrating violence" by L. L. Shapiro in a *School Library Journal* review. Key poems from these books, later collected in *To Disembark,* call blacks to "work together toward their own REAL emancipation," Brooks indicated. Even so, "the strength here is not in declamation but in [the poet's] genius for psychological insight," claims J. A. Lipari in the *Library Journal.* Addison Gayle points out that the softer poems of this period—the ones asking for stronger interpersonal bonds among black Americans—are no less political: "To espouse and exult in a Black identity, outside the psychic boundaries of white Americans, was to threaten.... To advocate and demand love between one Black and another was to begin a new chapter in American history. Taken together, the acknowledgment of a common racial identity among Blacks throughout the world and the suggestion of a love based upon the brotherhood and sisterhood of the oppressed were meant to transform Blacks in America from a minority to a majority, from world victims to, to use Madhubuti's phrase, 'world makers'."

In the same essay, printed in *Black Women Writers (1950-1980): A Critical Evaluation,* Gayle defends *Riot* and the later books, naming them an important source of inspiration to a rising generation: "It may well be ... that the function of poetry is not so much to save us from oppression nor from Auschwitz, but to give us the strength to face them, to help us stare down the lynch mob, walk boldly in front of the firing squad. It is just such awareness that the poetry of Gwendolyn Brooks has given us, this that she and those whom she taught/learned from have accomplished for us all. They have told us that for Black Americans there are no havens, that in the eyes of other Americans we are, each and every one of us, rioters.... These are dangerous times for Black people. The sensitive Black poet realizes that fact, but far from despairing, picks up his pen, ... and echoes Gwendolyn Brooks: 'My aim ... is to write poems that will somehow successfully "call" ... all black people ... in gutters, in schools, offices, factories, prisons, the consulate; I wish to teach black people in pulpits, black people in mines, on farms, on thrones.'" Brooks pointed out "a serious error" in this quote; she wants to "reach" people, not "teach" them. She added, "The times for Black people—when*ever* in the clutches of white *manipulation,* have ALWAYS been dangerous." She also advised young poets, "Walking in front of a firing squad is *crazy.* Your effort should be in preventing the *formation* of a firing squad."

The poet's search "for an *expression* relevant to all manner of blacks," as she described her change in focus to Tate, did not alter her mastery of her craft. "While quoting approvingly Ron Karenga's observation that 'the fact that we are black is our ultimate reality,' blackness did not, to her, require simplification of language, symbol, or moral perception," notes C. W. E. Bigsby in *The Second Black Renaissance: Essays in Black Literature.* It did include "the possibility of communicating directly to those in the black community." In the bars and on the street corners were an audience not likely to "go into a bookstore" to buy poetry by anyone, she told George Stavros in a *Contemporary Literature* interview reprinted in *Report from Part One: An Autobiography.* And in the late sixties, Brooks reported, "some of those folks DID" enter bookstores to buy poetry and read it "standing up." To better reach the street audience, Brooks's later poems use more open, less traditional poetic forms and techniques. Penelope Moffet, writing in the *Los Angeles Times,* records the poet's statement that since 1967, she has been "successfully escaping from close rhyme, because it just isn't natural.... I've written hundreds ... of sonnets, and I'll probably never write another one, because I don't feel that this is a sonnet time. It seems to me it's a wild, raw, ragged free verse time." She told Stavros, "I want to write poems that will be non-compromising. I don't want to stop a concern with words doing good jobs, which has always been a concern of mine, but I want to write poems that will be meaningful to those people I described a while ago, things that will touch them." Speaking of later works aimed for that audience, Robert F. Kiernan offers in *American Writing since 1945: A Critical Survey,* "She remains, however, a virtuoso of the lyric and an extraordinary portraitist—probably the finest black poet of the post-Harlem generation."

When *Report from Part One* came out in 1972, some reviewers complained that it did not provide the level of personal detail or the insight into black literature that they had expected. "They wanted a list of domestic spats," remarked Brooks. Bambara notes that it "is not a sustained dramatic narrative for the nosey, being neither the confessions of a private woman poet or the usual sort of mahogany-desk memoir public personages inflict upon the populace at the first sign of a cardiac.... It documents the growth of Gwen Brooks." Other reviewers value it for explaining the poet's new orientation toward

her racial heritage and her role as a poet. In a passage she has presented again in later books as a definitive statement, she writes: "I—who have 'gone the gamut' from an almost angry rejection of my dark skin by some of my brainwashed brothers and sisters to a surprised queenhood in the new Black sun—am qualified to enter at least the kindergarten of new consciousness now. New consciousness and trudge-toward-progress. I have hopes for myself.... I know now that I am essentially an essential African, in occupancy here because of an indeed 'peculiar' institution.... I know that Black fellow-feeling must be the Black man's encyclopedic Primer. I know that the Black-and-white integration concept, which in the mind of some beaming early saint was a dainty spinning dream, has wound down to farce.... I know that the Black emphasis must be not *against white* but *FOR Black....* In the Conference-That-Counts, whose date may be 1980 or 2080 (woe betide the Fabric of Man if it is 2080), there will be no looking up nor looking down." In the future, she envisions "the profound and frequent shaking of hands, which in Africa is so important. The shaking of hands in warmth and strength and union."

Brooks put some of the finishing touches on the second volume of her autobiography while serving as Poetry Consultant to the Library of Congress. Brooks was sixty-eight when she became the first black woman to be appointed to the post. Of her many duties there, the most important, in her view, were visits to local schools. "Poetry is life distilled," she told students in a Washington school, Schmich reports. "She urged them to keep journals. She read them a poem about teen suicide. She told them poetry exists where they might not recognize it," such as in John Lennon's song "Eleanor Rigby." Similar visits to colleges, universities, prisons, hospitals, and drug rehabilitation centers characterize her tenure as Poet Laureate of Illinois. In that role, she has sponsored and hosted annual literary awards ceremonies at which she presents prizes paid for "out of [her] own pocket, which, despite her modest means, is of legendary depth," Reginald Gibbons relates in Chicago *Tribune Books.* She has honored and encouraged many poets in her state through the Illinois Poets Laureate Awards and Significant Illinois Poets Awards programs. At one ceremony, says Gibbons, "poetry was, for a time, the vital center of people's lives."

Though her writing is "*to* Blacks," it is "*for* anyone who wants to open the book," she emphasized to Schmich. Brook's objectivity is perhaps the most widely acclaimed feature of her poetry. Janet Overmeyer notes in the *Christian Science Monitor* that Brooks's "particular, outstanding, genius is her unsentimental regard and respect for all human beings.... She neither foolishly pities nor condemns—she creates." Overmeyer continues, "From her poet's craft bursts a whole gallery of wholly alive persons, preening, squabbling, loving, weeping; many a novelist cannot do so well in ten times the space." Brooks achieves this effect through a high "degree of artistic control," claims Littlejohn. "The words, lines, and arrangements," he states, "have been worked and worked and worked again into poised exactness: the unexpected apt metaphor, the mock-colloquial asides amid jewelled phrases, the half-ironic repetitions—she knows it all." More importantly, Brooks's objective treatment of issues such as poverty and racism "produces genuine emotional tension," he writes.

This quality also provides her poems with universal appeal. Blyden Jackson states in *Black Poetry in America: Two Essays in Historical Interpretation* that Brooks "is one of those artists of whom it can truthfully be said that things like sex and race, important as they are, ... appear in her work to be sublimated into insights and revelations of universal application." Although Brooks's characters are primarily black and poor and live in Northern urban cities, she provides, according to Jackson, through "the close inspection of a limited domain, ... a view of life in which one may see a microscopic portion of the universe intensely and yet, through that microscopic portion see all truth for the human condition wherever it is." And although the goals and adjustments of black nationalism have been her frequent topics, Houston A. Baker, Jr., says of Brooks in the *CLA Journal:* "The critic (whether black or white) who comes to her work seeking only support for his ideology will be disappointed for, as Etheridge Knight pointed out, she has ever spoken the truth. And truth, one likes to feel, always lies beyond the boundaries of any one ideology. Perhaps Miss Brooks' most significant achievement is her endorsement of this point of view. From her hand and fertile imagination have come volumes that transcend the dogma on either side of the American veil." Baker feels that Brooks "represents a singular achievement. Beset by a double consciousness, she has kept herself from being torn asunder by crafting poems that equal the best in the black and white American literary traditions."

Proving the breadth of Brooks's appeal, poets representing a wide variety of "races and ... poetic camps" gathered at the University of Chicago to celebrate the poet's 70th birthday in 1987, reports Gibbons. Brooks brought them together, he says, "in ... a moment of good will and cheer." In recognition of her service and achievements, a junior high school in Harvey, Illinois, has been named for her. She is also honored at Western Illinois University's Gwendolyn Brooks Center for African-American Literature.

Summing up the poet's accomplishments, Gibbons writes that beginning with *A Street in Bronzeville,* Brooks has brought national attention to "a part of life that had been grossly neglected by the literary establishment.... And because Brooks has been a deeply serious artist ..., she has created works of special encouragement to black writers and of enduring importance to all readers."

*BIOGRAPHICAL/CRITICAL SOURCES:*

*BOOKS*

*Authors in the News,* Volume 1, Gale, 1976.

Baker, Houston A., Jr., *Singers of Daybreak: Studies in Black American Literature,* Howard University Press, 1974.

Bigsby, C. W. E., editor, *The Black American Writer, Volume 2: Poetry and Drama,* Deland, 1969.

Bigsby, C. W. E., *The Second Black Renaissance: Essays in Black Literature,* Greenwood Press, 1980.

*Black Literature Criticism,* Gale, 1992.

Brooks, Gwendolyn, *In the Mecca,* Harper, 1968.

Brooks, Gwendolyn, *Report from Part One: An Anthology,* Broadside Press, 1972.

Brown, Patricia L., Don L. Lee, and Francis Ward, editors, *To Gwen with Love: An Anthology Dedicated to Gwendolyn Brooks,* Johnson Publishing, 1971.

*Children's Literature Review,* Volume 27, Gale, 1992.

*Concise Dictionary of American Literary Biography: The New Consciousness, 1941-1968,* Gale, 1985.

*Contemporary Literary Criticism,* Gale, Volume 1, 1973, Volume 2, 1974, Volume 4, 1975, Volume 5, 1976, Volume 15, 1980, Volume 49, 1988.

Dembo, L. S., and C. N. Pondrom, editors, *The Contemporary Writer: Interviews with Sixteen Novelists and Poets,* University of Wisconsin Press, 1972.

*Dictionary of Literary Biography,* Gale, Volume 5: *American Poets since World War II,* 1980, Volume 75: *Afro-American Writers, 1940-1955,* 1988.

Drotning, Philip T., and Wesley W. Smith, editors, *Up from the Ghetto,* Cowles, 1970.

Emanuel and Gross, editors, *Dark Symphony: Negro Literature in America,* Free Press, 1968.

Evans, Mari, editor, *Black Women Writers (1950-1980): A Critical Evaluation,* Anchor/Doubleday, 1984.

Gates, Henry Louis, Jr., editor, *Black Literature and Literary Theory,* Methuen, 1984.

Gayle, Addison, editor, *Black Expression,* Weybright & Talley, 1969.

Gibson, Donald B., editor, *Modern Black Poets: A Collection of Critical Essays,* Prentice-Hall, 1973.

Gould, Jean, *Modern American Women Poets,* Dodd, Mead, 1985.

Jackson, Blyden, and Louis D. Rubin, Jr., *Black Poetry in America: Two Essays in Historical Interpretation,* Louisiana State University Press, 1974.

Kent, George, *Gwendolyn Brooks: A Life,* University Press of Kentucky, 1988.

Kufrin, Joan, *Uncommon Women,* New Century Publications, 1981.

Littlejohn, David, *Black on White: A Critical Survey of Writing by American Negroes,* Viking, 1966.

Madhubuti, Haki R., *Say that the River Turns: The Impact of Gwendolyn Brooks,* Third World Press, 1987.

Melhem, D. H., *Gwendolyn Brooks: Poetry and the Heroic Voice,* University Press of Kentucky, 1987.

Miller, R. Baxter, *Langston Hughes and Gwendolyn Brooks: A Reference Guide,* Hall, 1978.

Miller, R. Baxter, *Black American Poets between Worlds, 1940-1960,* University of Tennessee Press, 1986.

Mootry, Maria K., and Gary Smith, editors, *A Life Distilled: Gwendolyn Brooks, Her Poetry and Fiction,* University of Illinois Press, 1987.

Newquist, Roy, *Conversations,* Rand McNally, 1967.

Redmond, Eugene B., *Drumvoices: The Mission of Afro-American Poetry,* Doubleday, 1976.

Shaw, Harry F., *Gwendolyn Brooks,* Twayne, 1980.

Tate, Claudia, *Black Women Writers at Work,* Continuum, 1983.

*World Literature Criticism,* Gale, 1992.

*PERIODICALS*

*Atlantic Monthly,* September, 1960.

*Best Sellers,* April 1, 1973.

*Black American Literature Forum,* spring, 1977; winter, 1984; fall, 1990, p. 567.

*Black Enterprise,* June, 1985.

*Black Scholar,* March, 1981; November, 1984.

*Black World,* August, 1970; January, 1971; July, 1971; September, 1971; October, 1971; January, 1972; March, 1973; June, 1973; December, 1975.

*Book Week,* October 27, 1963.

*Book World,* November 3, 1968.

*Chicago Tribune,* January 14, 1986; June 7, 1987; June 12, 1989.

*Christian Science Monitor,* September 19, 1968.

*CLA Journal,* December, 1962; December, 1963; December, 1969; September, 1972; September, 1973; September, 1977; December, 1982.

*Contemporary Literature,* March 28, 1969; winter, 1970.

*Critique,* summer, 1984.

*Discourse,* spring, 1967.

*Ebony,* July, 1968; June, 1987, p. 154.

*Essence,* April, 1971; September, 1984.

*Explicator,* April, 1976; Volume 36, number 4, 1978.

*Houston Post,* February 11, 1974.

*Journal of Negro Education,* winter, 1970.

*Library Journal,* September 15, 1970.

*Los Angeles Times,* November 6, 1987.

*Los Angeles Times Book Review,* September 2, 1984.

*Modern Fiction Studies,* winter, 1985.

*Nation,* September, 1962; July 7, 1969; September 26, 1987, p. 308.

*National Observer,* November 9, 1968.

*Negro American Literature Forum,* fall, 1967; summer, 1974.

*Negro Digest,* December, 1961; January, 1962; August, 1962; July, 1963; June, 1964; January, 1968.

*New Statesman,* May 3, 1985.

*New Yorker,* September 22, 1945; December 17, 1949; October 10, 1953; December 3, 1979.

*New York Times,* November 4, 1945; October 5, 1953; December 9, 1956; October 6, 1963; March 2, 1969; April 30, 1990.

*New York Times Book Review,* October 23, 1960; October 6, 1963; March 2, 1969; January 2, 1972; June 4, 1972; December 3, 1972; January 7, 1973; June 10, 1973; December 2, 1973; September 23, 1984; July 5, 1987.

*Phylon,* summer, 1961; March, 1976.

*Poetry,* December, 1945; Volume 126, 1950; March, 1964.

*Publishers Weekly,* June 6, 1970.

*Ramparts,* December, 1968.

*Saturday Review,* February 1, 1964.

*Saturday Review of Literature,* January 19, 1946; September 17, 1949; May 20, 1950.

*Southern Review,* spring, 1965.

*Studies in Black Literature,* autumn, 1973; spring, 1974; summer, 1974; spring, 1977.

*Tribune Books* (Chicago), July 12, 1987.

*Virginia Quarterly Review,* winter, 1969; winter, 1971.

*Washington Post,* May 19, 1971; April 19, 1973; March 31, 1987.

*Washington Post Book World,* November 11, 1973.

*Women's Review of Books,* December, 1984.

*World Literature Today,* winter, 1985.

\* \* \*

## BROWN, Elaine 1943-

*PERSONAL:* Born March 2, 1943, in Philadelphia, PA; immigrated to France; children: a daughter.

*CAREER:* Black Panther party, Deputy Minister of Information, 1970s, became party chairperson, 1974; delegate to 1976 Democratic convention; lobbied for job-creating projects in Oakland, CA.

*WRITINGS:*

*A Taste of Power: A Black Woman's Story,* Pantheon, 1992.

Also author of *A Light Shines,* Tyndale.

*BIOGRAPHICAL/CRITICAL SOURCES:*

*PERIODICALS*

*Detroit Free Press,* March 25, 1979, p. C1; January 27, 1993, p. 3F.

*Publishers Weekly,* November 9, 1992, p. 65.
*San Francisco Review of Books,* March/April, 1993, pp. 16-
    20.
*Sepia,* September, 1977, pp. 26-28.
*Soul Illustrated,* October, 1970, pp. 50-55.

\*     \*     \*

## BROWN, Frank London   1927-1962

*PERSONAL:* Born October 7 (one source says October 17),
1927, in Kansas City, MO; died of leukemia, March 12 (one
source says March 13), 1962, in Illinois; son of Frank London Brown, Sr., and Myra Myrtle Brown; married Evelyn
Marie Jones, November 30, 1947; children: Debra, Cheryl,
Pamela, one son. *Education:* Attended Wilberforce University; Roosevelt University, B.A., 1951; attended Kent College
of Law; University of Chicago, M.A., 1960, doctoral studies
until 1962.

*CAREER:* Novelist and journalist. University of Chicago's
Union Research Center, Chicago, IL, director, until 1962.
Worked variously as a jazz singer, musician, machinist, union
organizer, and bartender. *Military service:* U.S. Army, 1946-
48.

*AWARDS, HONORS:* John Hay Whitney Foundation Award
for Creative Writing; fellow, University of Chicago Committee on Social Thought.

*WRITINGS:*

*NOVELS*

*Trumbull Park* (novel), Regnery, 1959.
*Short Stories of Frank London Brown,* privately printed, 1965.
*The Myth Makers* (novel), Path Press, 1969.

Also author of play *Short Ribs,* produced by the Penthouse
Players, Chicago, IL, in the late 1950s. Work represented in
anthologies, including *Afro-American Literature: Fiction,*
edited by Adams, Conn, and Slepian, and *The Poetry of the
Negro: 1746-1970,* edited by Hughes and Bontemps. Contributor of short stories to *Down Beat, Ebony, Negro Digest,
Chicago Review,* and *Southwest Review. Ebony,* associate
editor, 1959.

*SIDELIGHTS:* Frank London Brown wrote two novels that
document the experiences of urban black Americans. Brown
also authored numerous short stories and poems, began work
on a doctoral degree, contributed to the dawning civil rights
movement of the 1960s, and was the first writer to read his

short stories to jazz accompaniment. *Dictionary of Literary
Biography* contributor Kathleen A. Hauke quoted Brown's
widow as saying that Brown "saw and felt and lived the essential sadness of the world."

Brown's 1959 novel *Trumbull Park* is the account of a black
family that moves from Chicago's South Side to a new housing development where they are harassed—verbally and physically—by the white majority. Buggy Martin draws courage
from the strength of his wife, Helen, who, according to Hauke,
says at one point: "We got to take this foolishness of these
white folks in stride. Live in spite of them." *New York Times*
contributor R. L. Duffus wrote that Brown "probe[s] the psychology of people under fire" in *Trumbull Park.* "One of
Brown's great achievements [is] that hatred did not guide his
pen," judged Alan Paton in the *Chicago Sunday Tribune.* And
Langston Hughes, commenting in the *New York Herald Tribune Book Review,* stated: "How, in the end, determination
and decency seem about to triumph, is the theme of this story, unfolded in terms of characters who are terribly alive and
real.... [*Trumbull Park*] tells its tale well."

Brown's master's thesis evolved into his second novel, *The
Myth Makers,* which was published after Brown's death and
has been compared to nineteenth-century Russian novelist
Fyodor Dostoyevsky's *Crime and Punishment* because of its
themes of sin and redemption. The protagonist, Ernest Day,
is a drug addict who kills an elderly man merely for smiling
at him. The novel details Day's thoughts on the motivations
behind the murder. "Brown says that human behavior cannot
be prescribed by rational calculation," commented Hauke,
"that the emotional, irrational side of man's nature is far more
powerful, but that each person has his own intrinsic value
however sinful, useless, or obnoxious he may appear to be."

*BIOGRAPHICAL/CRITICAL SOURCES:*

*BOOKS*

*Dictionary of Literary Biography,* Volume 76: *Afro-American Writers, 1940-1955,* Gale, 1988, pp. 25-29.

*PERIODICALS*

*Chicago Sunday Tribune,* April 12, 1959, p. 1.
*New York Herald Tribune Book Review,* July 5, 1959, p. 5.
*New York Times,* April 12, 1959, p. 41.

\*     \*     \*

## BROWN, Lloyd L(ouis)   1913-

*PERSONAL:* Born 1913, in St. Paul, MN; married in 1937;
two children.

*ADDRESSES: Home*—156-20 Riverside Drive West, Apartment 16-I, New York, NY 10032.

*CAREER:* Writer. *Military service:* U.S. Air Force, 1942-45; became staff sergeant.

*WRITINGS:*

*Iron City* (novel), Masses and Mainstream, 1951.
(With Paul Robeson) *Here I Stand,* Othello Associates, 1958, reissued edition (with preface by Brown), Beacon Press, 1988.

Also author of pamphlets, including *Young Workers in Action: Story of the South River Strike,* Youth Publishers, 1932; *The Conspiracy Against Free Elections* (unsigned), Pittsburgh Civil Rights Committee, 1941; *Lift Every Voice for Paul Robeson,* Freedom Association, 1951; *Stand Up for Freedom: The Negro People vs. the Smith Act,* New Century Publishers, 1952; and *Paul Robeson Rediscovered,* American Institute for Marxist Studies, 1976. Contributor of articles and reviews to *New Masses,* short stories and criticism to *Masses and Mainstream,* and nonfiction to *Freedomways.*

*Iron City* has been translated into German, Japanese, Chinese, Polish, and several other languages.

*BIOGRAPHICAL/CRITICAL SOURCES:*

*PERIODICALS*

*Phylon,* Volume 12, 1951.

\*     \*     \*

## BROWN, Margery (Wheeler)

*PERSONAL:* Born in Durham, NC; daughter of John Leonidas and Margaret (Hervey) Wheeler; married Richard E. Brown, December 22, 1936 (deceased); children: Janice (Mrs. Jan E. Carden). *Education:* Spelman College, B.A., 1932; Ohio State University, art studies, 1932-34 and 1935. *Religion:* Presbyterian.

*ADDRESSES: Home*—245 Reynolds Terrace, Apt. C-1, Orange, NJ 07050.

*CAREER:* Hillside High School, Durham, NC, art teacher, 1934-35; Washington High School, Atlanta, GA, art teacher, 1935-37; Spelman College, Atlanta, instructor of art, 1943-46; Newark Public School System, Newark, NJ, art teacher, 1948-74; author and illustrator.

*WRITINGS:*

*FOR CHILDREN*

*That Ruby* (self-illustrated), Reilly & Lee, 1969.
*Animals Made by Me* (self-illustrated), Putnam, 1970.
*The Second Stone* (self-illustrated), Putnam, 1974.
*Yesterday I Climbed a Mountain* (self-illustrated), Putnam, 1976.
*No Jon, No Jon, No!* (self-illustrated), Houghton, 1981.
*Afro-Bets: Book of Shapes,* illustrated by Culverson Blair, Just Us Books, 1991.
*Afro-Bets: Book of Colors: Meet the Color Family,* illustrated by Blair, Just Us Books, 1991.

*ILLUSTRATOR*

Gordon Allred, *Old Crackfoot,* Obolensky, 1965.
Gordon Allred, *Dori the Mallard,* Astor-Honor, 1968.
*I'm Glad I'm Me,* Putnam, 1971.

*OTHER*

Contributor to *Life* and *School Arts.*

*WORK IN PROGRESS:* Stories for and about inner city children.

\*     \*     \*

## BROWN, Wesley 1945-

*PERSONAL:* Born May 23, 1945, in New York, NY. *Education:* Oswego State University, B.A., 1968.

*CAREER:* Writer.

*WRITINGS:*

*Tragic Magic* (novel), Random House, 1978.
*Early Intervention Regulation: Annotation and Analysis of Part H* (legislation), LRP Publications, 1990.
(Editor with Amy Ling) *Imagining America: Stories from the Promised Land,* Persea Books, 1991.
(Editor with Ling) *Visions of America: Personal Narratives from the Promised Land,* Persea Books, 1992.

Work represented in anthologies, including *Poetry* and *We Be Word Sorcerers.* Contributor of poems and short stories to *Essence, Harper's, Black Creation,* and other periodicals.

*SIDELIGHTS:* Wesley Brown's first novel, *Tragic Magic,* is the story of Melvin Ellington, a well-educated, young black man who returns to his Queens, New York, neighborhood after serving two years in prison as a conscientious objector to the Vietnam War. The narrative covers the events of Ellington's first day home, interspersed with recollections of prison life and college days. Trying to get all the pieces of his life back together, Melvin rejoins his family for dinner, and later in the evening he goes out with a high school friend on a nighttime excursion that turns catastrophic.

*Tragic Magic* won the attention and praise of many critics. They particularly admired Brown's ability to evoke urban black America and his sensitivity to the search for meaning and identity in life. "Wesley Brown has a careful eye for the details and nuances of urban black existence," remarked a *Choice* contributor, who then hailed Brown as "a gifted writer, capable of exploring a wide range of human emotions" and judged *Tragic Magic* "an impressive first novel." Likewise, a reviewer of the novel for *New Yorker* assessed Brown's portrait of Ellington as "effective and original" and lauded the author's recording of "the provocative, singsong slang of the street and prison." *Village Voice* contributor Lin Rosechild Harris complimented Brown for creating "a wonderful addition to the pantheon of heroic young initiates" while also observing that "the book sings with images and rhythms of urban black America," and Alan Cheuse, writing in *New York Times Book Review,* described *Tragic Magic* as a "jaunty prose version of the urban blues" that "deserves an attentive audience."

In his later work, Brown has joined forces with Amy Ling to edit two collections of short stories about coming to and living in America, *Imagining America: Stories from the Promised Land* and *Visions of America: Personal Narratives from the Promised Land.* These two collections focus on America's multiculturalism, presenting tales of twentieth-century immigrants from all over the world and include stories of the Native American experience. *Imagining America* includes "In the Land of the Free" in which a young Chinese family arriving in San Francisco is separated when a customs agent seizes their "unofficial" newborn. Other stories tell of a Jewish German refugee learning English, and a Native American denied his heritage because he lacks a Bureau of Indian Affairs registration number. Of *Imagining America, Washington Post Book World* contributor Richard Lipez notes that "in their brief, deft introduction, the editors point out that the 'Multiculturalism' of American life constitutes a whole thing that can best be known 'through its quarrelsome parts'." Lipez judges *Imagining America* to be a "vibrant book about a multiplicity of struggling people forming and re-forming a nation."

*BIOGRAPHICAL/CRITICAL SOURCES:*

*PERIODICALS*

*American Book Review,* summer, 1979.
*Choice,* February, 1979; April, 1992.
*Nation,* December 29, 1979; November 16, 1992.
*New Yorker,* October, 1978.
*New York Times Book Review,* February 11, 1979.
*New York Times Magazine,* September 10, 1989.
*Publishers Weekly,* December 20, 1991, November 23, 1992.
*Village Voice,* November 20, 1978.
*Washington Post Book World,* January 26, 1992, pp. 1, 11.

\*   \*   \*

**BRUIN, John**
  **See BRUTUS, Dennis**

\*   \*   \*

**BRUTUS, Dennis 1924-**
  **(John Bruin)**

*PERSONAL:* Born November 28, 1924, in Salisbury, Southern Rhodesia (now Harare, Zimbabwe); came to the United States, 1971, granted political asylum, 1983; son of Francis Henry (a teacher) and Margaret Winifred (a teacher; maiden name, Bloemetjie) Brutus; married May Jaggers, May 14, 1950; children: Jacinta, Marc, Julian, Antony, Justina, Cornelia, Gregory, Paula. *Education:* Fort Hare University, B.A. (with distinction), 1947; attended University of the Witwatersrand, 1963-64.

*ADDRESSES: Office*—Department of Black Community Education Research and Development, University of Pittsburgh, Pittsburgh, PA 15260.

*CAREER:* Poet and political activist. High school teacher of English and Afrikaans in Port Elizabeth, South Africa, 1948-61; journalist in South Africa, 1960-61; imprisoned for anti-apartheid activities, Robben Island Prison, 1964-65; teacher and journalist in London, England, 1966-70; Northwestern University, Evanston, IL, professor of English, 1971-85; Swarthmore College, Swarthmore, PA, Cornell Professor of English Literature, 1985-86; University of Pittsburgh, Pittsburgh, PA, professor of black studies and English, chairman of department of black community education research and development, 1986—. Visiting professor, University of Denver, 1970, University of Texas at Austin, 1974-75, Amherst College, 1981-82, Dartmouth College, 1983, and Northeastern University, 1984. Founder of Troubadour Press. South

African Sports Association (now South African Non-Racial Olympic Committee), founding secretary, 1958, president, 1963—; United Nations representative, International Defense and Aid Fund (London), 1966-71; chairman of International Campaign against Racism in Sport, 1972—; member of advisory board, ARENA: Institute for the Study of Sport and Social Analysis, 1975—; chairman, International Advisory Commission to End Apartheid in Sport, 1975—; member of board of directors, Black Arts Celebration (Chicago), 1975—; member, Emergency Committee for World government, 1978—; member of Working Committee for Action against Apartheid (Evanston), 1978—; president of Third World Energy Resources Institute; director, World Campaign for Release of South African Political Prisoners (London).


*MEMBER:* International Poetry Society (fellow), International Platform Association, Union of Writers of the African People (Ghana; vice-president, 1974—), Modern Language Association, African Literature Association (founding chairman, 1975—; member of executive committee, 1979—), United Nations Association of Illinois and Greater Chicago (member of board of directors, 1978).

*AWARDS, HONORS:* Chancellor's prize, University of South Africa, 1947; Mbari Award, CCF, 1962, for *Sirens, Knuckles, Boots;* Freedom Writers Award, Society of Writers and Editors, 1975; Kenneth Kaunda Humanism Award, 1979; awarded key to city of Sumter, SC, 1979; Langston Hughes Award, City University of New York, 1987; Paul Robeson Award for excellence, political conscience, and integrity, 1989; honorary doctorates from institutions including Worcester State College and University of Massachusetts, 1984, and Northeastern University, 1990.

*WRITINGS:*

*POETRY*

*Sirens, Knuckles, Boots,* Mbari Publications, 1963.
*Letters to Martha and Other Poems from a South African Prison,* Heinemann, 1968.
*Poems from Algiers,* African and Afro-American Research Institute, University of Texas at Austin, 1970.
(Under pseudonym John Bruin) *Thoughts Abroad,* Troubadour Press, 1970.
*A Simple Lust: Selected Poems Including "Sirens, Knuckles, Boots," "Letters to Martha," "Poems from Algiers," "Thoughts Abroad,"* Hill & Wang, 1973.
*Strains,* edited by Wayne Kamin and Chip Dameron, Troubadour Press, 1975, revised edition, 1982.
*China Poems,* translations by Ko Ching Po, African and Afro-American Studies and Research Center, University of Texas at Austin, 1975.

*Stubborn Hope: New Poems and Selections from "China Poems" and "Strains,"* Three Continents Press, 1978.
*Salutes and Censures,* Fourth Dimension Publishers (Nigeria), 1984, Africa World Press, 1985.
*Airs and Tributes,* edited by Gil Ott, Whirlwind Press, 1989.
(Editor with Hal Wylie and Juris Silenieks) *African Literature, 1988: New Masks,* Three Continents/African Literature Association, 1990.

*OTHER*

*The American-South African Connection* (sound recording), Iowa State University of Science and Technology, 1975.
*Informal Discussion in Third World Culture Class* (sound recording), Media Resources Center, Iowa State University of Science and Technology, 1975.

Work represented in anthologies, including *Seven South African Poets,* edited by Cosmo Pieterse, Heinemann, 1966, Humanities, 1973; *From South Africa: New Writing, Photographs, and Art,* edited by David Bunn and Jane Taylor, University of Chicago Press, 1988; and *Words on the Page: The World in Your Hand,* edited by Catherine Lipkin and Virginia Solotaroff, Harper, 1989. Contributor to journals. Member of editorial board, *Africa Today,* 1976—, and *South and West.* Guest editor, *The Gar,* 1978.

*WORK IN PROGRESS: Still the Sirens,* a chapbook, for Pennywhistle Press.

*SIDELIGHTS:* Describing Dennis Brutus as a "soft-spoken man of acerbic views," Kevin Klose suggests in the *Washington Post* that "he is one of English-speaking Africa's best-known poets, and also happens to be one of the most successful foes of the apartheid regime in South Africa." Born in Southern Rhodesia of racially mixed parentage, Brutus spent most of his early life in South Africa.

Dismissed from his teaching post and forbidden to write by the South African government as a result of anti-apartheid activities, he was arrested in 1963 for attending a meeting in defiance of a ban on associating with any group. Seeking refuge in Swaziland following his release on bail, Brutus was apprehended in Mozambique by Portuguese secret police, who surrendered him to South African secret police.

Fearing that he would be killed in Johannesburg, where he was subsequently taken, he again tried to escape. Pursued by police, Brutus was shot in the back, tortured, and finally sentenced to eighteen months of hard labor at Robben Island Prison—"the escape-proof concentration camp for political prisoners off the South African coast," remarks Klose in another *Washington Post* article. The time Brutus spent there, says Klose, "included five months in solitary confinement, which brought him to attempt suicide, slashing at his wrists with sharp stones."

After Brutus's release from prison, he was placed under house arrest and was prohibited from either leaving his home or receiving visitors. He was permitted to leave South Africa, however, "on the condition that he not return, according to court records, and he took his family to England," states William C. Rempel in the *Los Angeles Times.* Granted a conditional British passport because of Rhodesia's former colonial status, Brutus journeyed to the United States, where temporary visas allowed him to remain. Rempel notes, however, that Brutus's "passport became snarled in technical difficulties when Rhodesia's white supremacist government was overthrown and Zimbabwe was created." In the process of applying for a new passport, Brutus missed his application deadline for another visa; and the United States government began deportation proceedings immediately. Brutus was ultimately granted political asylum because a return to Zimbabwe, given its proximity to South Africa, would place his life in imminent danger. Klose indicates that Brutus's efforts to remain in the United States have been at the expense of his art, though: "He has written almost no poetry, which once sustained him through the years of repression and exile."

Suggesting that Brutus's "poetry draws its haunting strength from his own suffering and from the unequal struggle of 25 million blacks, 'coloreds,' Indians and Orientals to throw off the repressive rule by the 4.5 million South African whites," Klose remarks that "there is no doubt in Brutus' mind of the power and relevance of his poetry to the struggle." Brutus's works are officially banned in South Africa. When, for example, his *Thoughts Abroad,* a collection of poems concerned with exile and alienation, was published under the pseudonym of John Bruin, it was immediately successful and was even taught in South African colleges; but when the government discovered that Brutus was the author, all copies were confiscated. The effectiveness of the South African government's censorship policies is evidenced by the degree to which Brutus's writing is known there. Colin Gardner, who thinks that "it seems likely that many well-read South Africans, even some of those with a distinct interest in South African poetry, are wholly or largely unacquainted with his writing," declares in *Research in African Literatures* that "Brutus as a writer exists, as far as the Pretoria government is concerned, as a vacuum, an absence; in the firmament of South African literature, such as it is, Brutus could be described as a black hole. But it is necessary to find him and read him, to talk and write about him, to pick up the light which in fact he does emit, because he is at his best as important as any other South African who has written poetry in English."

Deeming Brutus's poetry "the reaction of one who is in mental agony whether he is at home or abroad," R. N. Egudu suggests in Christopher Heywood's *Aspects of South African Literature* that "this agony is partly caused by harassments, arrests, and imprisonment, and mainly by Brutus's concern for other suffering people." Brutus's first volume of poetry, *Sirens, Knuckles, Boots,* which earned him the Mbari Award, includes a variety of verse, including love poems as well as poems of protest against South Africa's racial policies. Much of his subsequent poetry concerns imprisonment and exile. For example, *Letters to Martha and Other Poems from a South African Prison* was written under the guise of letters—the writing of which, unlike poetry, was not prohibited—and is composed of poems about his experiences as a political prisoner. His book *A Simple Lust: Selected Poems Including "Sirens, Knuckles, Boots," "Letters to Martha," "Poems from Algiers," "Thoughts Abroad"* represents "a collection of all Brutus' poetry relating to his experience of jail and exile," notes Paul Kameen in *Best Sellers.* Similarly, *Stubborn Hope: New Poems and Selections from "China Poems" and "Strains"* "contains several poems which deal directly with the traumatic period of his life when he was imprisoned on the island," states Jane Grant in *Index on Censorship.* Discussing the "interaction between the personal and political" in Brutus's poetry, Gardner points out that "the poet is aware that he has comrades in his political campaigns and struggles, but under intense government pressure, there is no real sense of mass movement. The fight for liberation will be a long one, and a sensitive participant cannot but feel rather isolated. This isolation is an important aspect of the poet's mode and mood."

Chikwenye Okonjo Ogunyemi thinks that although Brutus's writing is inspired by his imprisonment, it is "artistic rather than overtly propagandistic"; the critic observes in *Ariel* that "he writes to connect his inner life with the outside world and those who love him.... That need to connect with posterity, a reason for the enduring, is a genuine artistic feeling." Perceiving an early "inner conflict between Brutus, the activist against *apartheid,* and Brutus, the highly literate writer of difficult, complex and lyrical poetry," Grant suggests that "the months in solitary confinement on Robben Island seem to have led him to a radical reassessment of his role as poet." Moving toward a less complex poetry, "the trend culminates in the extreme brevity and economy of the *China Poems* (the title refers both to where they were written and to the delicate nature of the poems)," says Grant. "They are seldom more than a few lines long, and are influenced by the Japanese *haiku* and its Chinese ancestor, the *chueh chu.*" These poems, according to Hans Zell's *New Reader's Guide to South African Literature,* evolved from Brutus's trip to the Republic of China and were composed "in celebration of the people and the values he met there." Calling him "learned, passionate, skeptical," Gessler Moses Nkondo says in *World Literature Today* that "Brutus is a remarkable poet, one of the most distinguished South Africa has produced." Nkondo explains that "the lucidity and precision which he is at pains to develop in his work are qualities he admires from artistic conviction, as a humanist opposed both to romantic haze and conventional trends. But they also testify to a profound cultivation of spirit, a certain wholeness and harmony of nature, as they do too to a fine independence of literary fashion."

Influenced by the seventeenth-century metaphysical poets, Brutus employs traditional poetic forms and rich language in his work; Nkondo proposes that what "Brutus fastens on is a composite sensibility made up of the passionate subtleties and the intellectual sensuousness of the metaphysical poets and the masculine, ironic force of [John] Donne." Noting that Brutus assumes the persona of a troubadour throughout his poetry, Tanure Ojaide writes in *Ariel* that while it serves to unify his work, the choice of "the persona of the troubadour to express himself is particularly significant as the moving and fighting roles of the medieval errant, though romantic, tally with his struggle for justice in South Africa, a land he loves dearly as the knight his mistress. The movement contrasts with the stasis of despair and enacts the stubborn hope that despite the suffering, there shall be freedom and justice for those *now* unfree." And Gardner believes that "Brutus's best poetry has a resonance which both articulates and generalizes his specific themes; he has found forms and formulations which dramatize an important part of the agony of South Africa and of contemporary humanity."

Brutus "has traveled widely and written and testified extensively against the Afrikaner-run government's policies," remarks Klose. "In the world of activism, where talk can easily outweigh results, his is a record of achievement." For instance, Klose states that Brutus's voice against apartheid is largely responsible for South Africa's segregated sports teams having been "barred from most international competitions, including the Olympics since 1964." Egudu observes that in Brutus's "intellectual protest without malice, in his mental agony over the apartheid situation in South Africa, in his concern for the sufferings of the others, and in his hope which has defied all despair—all of which he has portrayed through images and diction that are imbued with freshness and vision—Brutus proves himself a capable poet fully committed to his social responsibility." And according to Klose, Brutus maintains: "You have to make it a two-front fight. You have to struggle inside South Africa to unprop the regime, and struggle in the United States—to challenge the U.S. role, and if possible, inhibit it. Cut off the money, the flow of arms, the flow of political and military support. You have to educate the American people. And that is what I think I'm doing."

*BIOGRAPHICAL/CRITICAL SOURCES:*

*BOOKS*

Beier, Ulli, editor, *Introduction to African Literature,* Northwestern University Press, 1967.

*Black Literature Criticism,* Gale, 1992, pp. 307-20.
*Contemporary Authors Autobiography Series,* Volume 14, Gale, 1991, pp. 53-64.
*Contemporary Literary Criticism,* Volume 43, Gale, 1987.
*Dictionary of Literary Biography,* Volume 117: *Twentieth-Century Caribbean and Black African Writers,* Gale, 1992, pp. 98-106.
Heywood, Christopher, editor, *Aspects of South African Literature,* Africana Publishing, 1976.
*A History of Africa,* Horizon Press, 1971.
Legum, Colin, editor, *The Bitter Choice,* World Publishing, 1968.
Pieterse, Cosmo, and Dennis Duerden, editors, *African Writers Talking,* Africana Publishing, 1972.
Zell, Hans M., and others, *A New Reader's Guide to African Literature,* second revised and expanded edition, Holmes & Meier, 1983.

*PERIODICALS*

*Ariel,* October, 1982; January, 1986.
*Best Sellers,* October 1, 1973.
*Index on Censorship,* July/August, 1979.
*Los Angeles Times,* September 7, 1983.
*New York Times,* January 29, 1986.
*Research in African Literatures,* fall, 1984.
*Washington Post,* August 13, 1983; September 7, 1983.
*World Literature Today,* spring, 1979; autumn, 1979; winter, 1981.

\*   \*   \*

## BRYAN, Ashley F.  1923-

*PERSONAL:* Born July 13, 1923, in New York, NY. *Education:* Attended Cooper Union and Columbia University.

*ADDRESSES: Office*—Dartmouth College, Department of Art, Hanover, NH 03755.

*CAREER:* Author and illustrator of books for children; Dartmouth College, Hanover, NH, professor of art and visual studies, then professor emeritus.

*AWARDS, HONORS:* American Library Association, Social Responsibilities Round Table, Coretta Scott King Award, 1980, for illustrating *Beat the Story-Drum, Pum-Pum,* and 1986, for writing *Lion and the Ostrich Chicks and Other African Folk Tales;* Coretta Scott King Honor Award, 1988, for illustrating *What a Morning! The Christmas Story in Black Spirituals.*

*WRITINGS:*

*FOR CHILDREN; SELF-ILLUSTRATED, EXCEPT WHERE NOTED*

*The Ox of the Wonderful Horns and Other African Folktales,* Atheneum, 1971.

*The Adventures of Aku; or, How It Came about That We Shall Always See Okra the Cat Lying on a Velvet Cushion While Okraman the Dog Sleeps among the Ashes,* Atheneum, 1976.

*The Dancing Granny,* Macmillan, 1977.

*Beat the Story-Drum, Pum-Pum* (Nigerian folk tales), Atheneum, 1980.

*The Cat's Drum,* Atheneum, 1985.

*Lion and the Ostrich Chicks and Other African Folk Tales,* Atheneum, 1986.

*Sh-ko and His Eight Wicked Brothers,* illustrated by Fumio Yoshimura, Atheneum, 1988.

*All Night, All Day: A Child's First Book of African-American Spirituals,* Atheneum, 1988.

*Turtle Knows Your Name* (a retelling), Atheneum, 1989.

*Sing to the Sun,* HarperCollins, 1992.

Work represented in books, including *Folklore of the Antilles, French and English, Part II,* edited by Elsie Clews Parson.

*ILLUSTRATOR*

Rabindranath Tagore, *Moon, for What Do You Wait?* (poems), edited by Richard Lewis, Atheneum, 1967.

Mari Evans, *Jim Flying High* (juvenile), Doubleday, 1979.

Susan Cooper, *Jethro and the Jumbie* (juvenile), Atheneum, 1979.

John Langstaff, editor, *What a Morning! The Christmas Story in Black Spirituals,* Macmillan, 1987.

*OTHER*

(Compiler) *Black American Spirituals,* Volume 1: *Walk Together Children* (self-illustrated), Atheneum, 1974, Volume 2: *I'm Going to Sing* (self- illustrated), Macmillan, 1982.

(Compiler and author of introduction) Paul Laurence Dunbar, *I Greet the Dawn: Poems,* Atheneum, 1978.

*ADAPTATIONS:* Bryan recorded *The Dancing Granny and Other African Tales* for the Caedmon record label.

*SIDELIGHTS:* As a folklorist, Ashley F. Bryan brings Americans to an appreciation of traditions rooted in black cultures. For example, his first volume of the spirituals of American slaves, *Walk Together Children,* records "the brave and lonely cries of men and women forced to trust in heaven because they had no hope on earth," remarks Neil Millar in the *Chris-

tian Science Monitor.* The subject of bondage set to native African rhythms produced songs such as "Go Down Moses," "Deep River," "Mary Had a Baby," "Go Tell It on the Mountain," "Nobody knows the Trouble I Seen," "Walk Together Children," "O Freedom," "Little David," and "Swing Low, Sweet Chariot." "With Ashley Bryan's collection," writes Virginia Hamilton in the *New York Times Book Review,* "the tradition of preserving the spiritual through teaching the young is surely enriched."

In addition to historical spirituals, several of the folklorist's collections contain stories that explain why certain animals became natural enemies. In *The Adventures of Aku,* Bryan recounts the day that the enmity between dogs and cats began. This "is a long involved magic tale that has echoes of Aladdin's lamp and Jack and the Beanstalk to mention just two familiar stories with similar motifs," says the *New York Times Book Review*'s Jane Yolen. It utilizes a magic ring, a stupid son, a heroic quest, and Ananse, the standard trickster figure in African folklore, to capsulize the Ashanti proverb stating, "No one knows the story of tomorrow's dawn."

The Nigerian folktales in *Beat the Story-Drum, Pum-Pum* also reveal the origins of hostilities between animals, such as that between the snake and the frog or the bush cow and the elephant. These "retellings make the stories unique, offering insight into the heart of a culture," notes M.M. Burns in *Horn Book.* Each story, the reviewer adds, "has a style and beat appropriate to the subject, the overall effect being one of musical composition with dexterously designed variations and movements."

Like *The Adventures of Aku, The Dancing Granny* continues the saga of the trickster Ananse. Originally titled "He Sings to Make the Old Woman Dance," this folktale recounts the day when a little old lady, who danced continually, foiled the Spider Ananse's plan to eat all of her food. While Granny worked, Ananse sang so that she might dance. Then, when she danced away, the spider would eat up her corn. This went on four times until Granny took Ananse to be her partner and danced him away, too.

In a departure from his usual cultural interests, Bryan ventures briefly into traditional folktales from Japan with his retelling of *Sh-Ko and His Eight Wicked Brothers.* It is a story about the sibling rivalry, the nature of true beauty, and the rewards of kindness. Sh-ko, the youngest of nine brothers, is truly ugly. He accompanies his brothers on a quest to win the hand of Princess Yakami. During the journey, he helps a rabbit in distress. In return, the grateful rabbit gives Sh-ko a magic gift and, to the dismay of his brothers, Sh-ko wins the princess' hand. "The tale," says *School Library Journal* reviewer John Philbrook, is told in a straightforward manner, but it is not engaging; nor is sympathy aroused for the characters." While the art is traditional, in the style of Japanese picture scrolls, some critics feel that it may not appeal to young children.

Bryan's collection, *All Night, All Day: A Child's First Book of African-American Spirituals,* with his bright, abstract illustrations is generally considered more appealing to young readers. According to *Horn Book,* this volume offers "extraordinary gifts for all America's children." *Booklist* praised this collection in a special feature, "The African American Experience in Picture Books."

Bryan's next book, 1989's *Turtle Knows Your Name,* is a retelling of a folktale from the West Indies. An earlier version appeared in Elsie Clews Parson's *Folklore of the Antilles, French and English, Part II.* Word choice, language rhythm, and animal sounds contribute to the tale's festive mood. One *Horn Book* reviewer calls the work "a celebration of family love, traditional song and dance, and the ancient power of names." Inspired by the importance that black cultures attach to names, Bryan tells what happens when a young boy named UP-SILI-MANA TUM-PALERADO goes to the beach to sing and dance his name, in a time-honored tradition. A trickster turtle listens in on the ceremony, and records the name in shells on the sea floor. Because the boy's name is long, his peers tease him, so he befriends a group of animals. Later in the tale, his grandmother challenges him to find out her name, and, knowing how Turtle cataloged his own name, he asks the creature. "It's MAPASEEDO JACKALINDY EYE PIE TACKARINDY," Turtle announces. For convenience, the boy and his grandmother settle on the shorter names of Granny and Son. Contributor Marilyn Iarusso notes in *School Library Journal* that Bryan has "create[d] a rhythmic text which celebrates the pride of two people who learn to honor their names and their identities, and expect others to do the same."

Bryan's following work is a collection of poems written in rhythmic verse. Titled *Sing to the Sun,* the book celebrates nature, humanity, and life itself. All twenty-three poems are original and are considered appealing not only to children but to adults as well. A *Publishers Weekly* contributor comments that Bryan "artfully blends the traditions of African American culture with those of Western art.... [H]e interweaves voices that are sophisticated ... with those that are tied to folk storytelling traditions."

*BIOGRAPHICAL/CRITICAL SOURCES:*

*BOOKS*

Bryan, Ashley F., *Turtle Knows Your Name,* Atheneum, 1989.

*PERIODICALS*

*Booklist,* September 1, 1988; October 1, 1989; February 1, 1992.

*Bulletin of the Center for Children's Books,* February, 1990.
*Children's Book Review Service, Inc.,* December, 1988; December, 1989.
*Christian Science Monitor,* November 6, 1974; November 3, 1976; August 2, 1985.
*Commonweal,* November 22, 1974.
*Horn Book,* February, 1977; April, 1981; February, 1983; May, 1985; November, 1988; January, 1990; May, 1992.
*Kirkus Reviews,* August 1, 1988; August 15, 1992.
*Language Arts,* March, 1977; February, 1978; March, 1984; October, 1985.
*Ms.,* December, 1974.
*New York Times Book Review,* November 3, 1974; October 10, 1976.
*Publishers Weekly,* July 28, 1989; July 6, 1992.
*School Library Journal,* October, 1989; October, 1992.
*Scientific American,* December, 1980.
*Washington Post Book World,* November 7, 1971; December 12, 1976.
*Wilson Library Bulletin,* February, 1986.

\*    \*    \*

## BUCKLEY, Gail Lumet 1937-

*PERSONAL:* Born December 21, 1937, in Pittsburgh, PA; daughter of Louis Jones (a publisher) and Lena Horne (a singer and actress); married Sidney Lumet (a director), November 24, 1963 (divorced); married Kevin Buckley (an editor), October 1, 1983; children: (first marriage) Amy, Jenny. *Education:* Radcliffe College, B.A. (cum laude), 1959. *Politics:* Democrat. *Religion:* Roman Catholic.

*ADDRESSES: Agent*—Lynn Nesbit, International Creative Management, 40 West Fifty-seventh St., New York, NY, 10128.

*CAREER: Marie-Claire,* Paris, France, journalist, 1959-63; *Life* (magazine), New York City, journalist, 1959-62, reporter, 1962-63; National Scholarship Service and Fund for Negro Students, New York City, student counselor, 1961-62; writer. Democratic National Convention, delegate-at-large for Edward M. Kennedy, 1980. Volunteer for president John F. Kennedy, 1960.

*AWARDS, HONORS:* Honorary doctorate, University of Southern Indiana, 1987.

*WRITINGS:*

*The Hornes: An American Family,* Knopf, 1986.

Contributor to periodicals.

*SIDELIGHTS:* Daughter of singer-actress Lena Horne, Gail Lumet Buckley is descended from a long line of accomplished southern blacks, including educators, journalists, politicians, activists, and entrepreneurs. The child of a celebrity, she became what *Time* book reviewer Melvin Maddocks described as "part of a new and vibrant phase of black bourgeois life."

*The Hornes: An American Family,* Buckley's first book, traces six generations of her ancestry back to "founding mother" Sinai Reynolds, a slave living in the late eighteenth century. Her family is portrayed as industrious and respectable, with a sense of responsibility accompanying their privileged status. In spite of the disapproving attitude toward show business held by the middle-class at the time, Lena Horne, urged by her mother, began her acting career. This set the stage for Horne's own success, and for her daughter's unique childhood among the elite of Hollywood and Europe. Kim Hubbard in *People* wrote that Buckley's work "is part genealogy, part black history, part biography. In relating her family's story, Buckley also tells the history of their class."

As the descendant of a slave, great-granddaughter of a Native American suffragist, mother of two grown children, and daughter of a legend—Horne, the first black star whose allure spanned racial boundaries—Buckley wrote her family biography partially as an account of her own self-discovery. She depicts, for the first time, the obscure reality of the black American middle-class. "It took me a very long time to 'recognize' either my blackness or my *American*-ness," Buckley admitted in a *New York Times Book Review* article. "Writing this book gave me the gift of both. I was never able to find those parts of myself until I opened my grandfather's trunk and uncovered those family artifacts. What I uncovered went far beyond race and nationality, of course. I found amazing affinities of human attitudes and aspirations.... It was a happy inheritance."

Reviewers of Buckley's book emphasize that while *The Hornes* focuses largely on the author's relationship with her mother, her discretion and sense of privacy yield a work that avoids the sensationalism often associated with other works by celebrity children. "It's a measure of her gifts as a writer," commented Susan McHenry writing in *Ms.,* "that in her first book we see these puzzle-parts of her identity clearly and understand them as a whole." Nathan Irvin Huggins in the *Los Angeles Times Book Review* concluded that "Buckley is no flasher, exposing scandal. Rather, she is discreet, decent and respectful of a past she may now, only for the first time, be coming to terms with."

*BIOGRAPHICAL/CRITICAL SOURCES:*

*PERIODICALS*

*Black Enterprise,* October, 1986, p. 18.

*Book Report,* January, 1989, p. 59.
*Chicago Tribune,* July 10, 1986.
*Essence,* August, 1986, p. 38.
*Film Quarterly,* summer, 1987, p. 22.
*Los Angeles Times Book Review,* July 6, 1986, p. 3.
*Ms.,* August, 1986, p. 77.
*New York Times,* June, 20 1986, pp. 801-2; June 26, 1986.
*New York Times Book Review,* July 6, 1986, p. 5; June 21, 1987, p. 34.
*People,* July 28, 1986, p. 12.
*Time,* June 23, 1986, p. 81.
*Times Literary Supplement,* July 10, 1987, p. 749.
*Wall Street Journal,* August 5, 1986, p. 29.
*Washington Post Book World,* June 22, 1986, p. 3.

\* \* \*

## BULLINS, Ed 1935-
### (Kingsley B. Bass, Jr.)

*PERSONAL:* Born July 2, 1935, in Philadelphia, PA; son of Edward and Bertha Marie (Queen) Bullins; married; wife's name, Trixie. *Education:* Attended Los Angeles City College and San Francisco State College (now University).

*ADDRESSES: Home*—2128A Fifth St., Berkeley, CA 94710. *Agent*—Helen Merrill, 435 West 23rd St., No. 1A, New York, NY 10011.

*CAREER:* Cofounder, Black Arts/West; cofounder of the Black Arts Alliance, Black House (Black Panther party headquarters in San Francisco), cultural director until 1967, also serving briefly as Minister of Culture of the Party; joined the New Lafayette Theatre, New York City, in 1967, becoming playwright in residence, 1968, associate director, 1971-73; writers unit coordinator, New York Shakespeare Festival, 1975-82; People's School of Dramatic Arts, San Francisco, play writing teacher, 1983; City College of San Francisco, instructor in dramatic performance, play directing, and play writing, 1984—. Playwright in residence, American Place Theatre, beginning 1973; producing director, Surviving Theatre, beginning 1974; public relations director, Berkeley Black Repertory, 1982; promotion director, Magic Theatre, 1982-83; group sales coordinator, Julian Theatre, 1983; play writing teacher, Bay Area Playwrights Festival, summer, 1983. Also instructor in play writing at numerous colleges and universities, including Hofstra University, New York University, Fordham University, Columbia University, Amherst College, Dartmouth College, Antioch University, and Sonoma State University. *Military service:* U.S. Navy, 1952-55.

*MEMBER:* Dramatists Guild.

*AWARDS, HONORS:* American Place Theatre grant, 1967; Vernon Rice Drama Desk Award, 1968, for plays performed at American Place Theatre; four Rockefeller Foundation grants, including 1968, 1970, and 1973; National Endowment for the Arts play writing grant; Obie Award for distinguished play writing, and Black Arts Alliance award, both 1971, for *The Fabulous Miss Marie* and *In New England Winter;* Guggenheim fellowship, 1971 and 1976; grant from Creative Artists Public Service Program, 1973; Obie Award for distinguished play writing and New York Drama Critics Circle Award, both 1975, for *The Taking of Miss Janie;* Litt.D., Columbia College, Chicago, 1976.

*WRITINGS:*

*PUBLISHED PLAYS*

*How Do You Do? A Nonsense Drama* (one-act; first produced in San Francisco at Firehouse Repertory Theatre, 1965; produced Off-Broadway at La Mama Experimental Theatre Club, 1972), Illuminations Press, 1967.

(Editor and contributor) *New Plays from the Black Theatre* (includes *In New England Winter* [one-act; first produced Off-Broadway at New Federal Theatre of Henry Street Playhouse, 1971]), Bantam, 1969.

*Five Plays* (includes *Goin' a Buffalo* [three-act; first produced in New York City at American Place Theatre, 1968], *In the Wine Time* [three-act; first produced at New Lafayette Theatre, 1968], *A Son Come Home* [one-act; first produced Off-Broadway at American Place Theatre, 1968; originally published in *Negro Digest,* 1968], *The Electronic Nigger* [one-act; first produced at American Place Theatre, 1968], and *Clara's Ole Man* [one-act; first produced in San Francisco, 1965; produced at American Place Theatre, 1968]), Bobbs-Merrill, 1969 (published in England as *The Electronic Nigger, and Other Plays,* Faber, 1970).

*Ya Gonna Let Me Take You Out Tonight, Baby?* (first produced Off-Broadway at Public Theatre, 1972), published in *Black Arts,* Black Arts Publishing (Detroit), 1969.

*The Gentleman Caller* (one-act; first produced in Brooklyn, NY, with other plays as *A Black Quartet* by Chelsea Theatre Center at Brooklyn Academy of Music, 1969), published in *A Black Quartet,* New American Library, 1970.

*The Duplex: A Black Love Fable in Four Movements* (one-act; first produced at New Lafayette Theatre, 1970; produced at Forum Theatre of Lincoln Center, New York City, 1972), Morrow, 1971.

*The Theme Is Blackness: The Corner, and Other Plays* (includes *The Theme Is Blackness* [first produced in San Francisco by San Francisco State College, 1966], *The Corner* [one-act; first produced in Boston by Theatre Company of Boston, 1968; produced Off-Broadway at

Public Theatre, 1972], *Dialect Determinism* [one-act; first produced in San Francisco, 1965; produced at La Mama Experimental Theatre Club, 1972], *It Has No Choice* [one-act; first produced in San Francisco by Black Arts/West, 1966; produced at La Mama Experimental Theatre Club, 1972], *The Helper* [first produced in New York by New Dramatists Workshop, 1970], *A Minor Scene* [first produced in San Francisco by Black Arts/West, 1966; produced at La Mama Experimental Theatre Club, 1972], *The Man Who Dug Fish* [first produced by Theatre Company of Boston, 1970], *Black Commercial #2, The American Flag Ritual, State Office Bldg. Curse, One Minute Commercial, A Street Play, Street Sounds* [first produced at La Mama Experimental Theatre Club, 1970], *A Short Play for a Small Theatre,* and *The Play of the Play*), Morrow, 1972.

*Four Dynamite Plays* (includes: *It Bees Dat Way* [one-act; first produced in London, 1970; produced in New York at ICA, 1970], *Death List* [one-act; first produced in New York by Theatre Black at University of the Streets, 1970], *The Pig Pen* [one-act; first produced at American Place Theatre, 1970], and *Night of the Beast* [screenplay]), Morrow, 1972.

(Editor and contributor) *The New Lafayette Theatre Presents; Plays with Aesthetic Comments by Six Black Playwrights: Ed Bullins, J. E. Gaines, Clay Gross, Oyamo, Sonia Sanchez, Richard Wesley,* Anchor Press, 1974.

*The Taking of Miss Janie* (first produced in New York at New Federal Theatre, 1975), published in *Famous American Plays of the 1970s,* edited by Ted Hoffman, Dell, 1981.

Plays represented in anthologies, including *New American Plays,* Volume 3, edited by William M. Hoffman, Hill & Wang, 1970. Also author of "Malcolm: '71 or Publishing Blackness," published in *Black Scholar,* June, 1975.

*UNPUBLISHED PLAYS*

(With Shirley Tarbell) *The Game of Adam and Eve,* first produced in Los Angeles at Playwrights' Theatre, 1966.

(Under pseudonym Kingsley B. Bass, Jr.) *We Righteous Brothers* (adapted from Albert Camus's play *The Just Assassins*), first produced in New York at New Lafayette Theatre, 1969.

*A Ritual to Raise the Dead and Foretell the Future,* first produced in New York at New Lafayette Theatre, 1970.

*The Devil Catchers,* first produced at New Lafayette Theatre, 1970.

*The Fabulous Miss Marie,* first produced at New Lafayette Theatre, 1971; produced at Mitzi E. Newhouse Theatre of Lincoln Center, 1979.

*Next Time ...,* first produced in Bronx, NY, at Bronx Community College, 1972.

*The Psychic Pretenders (A Black Magic Show),* first produced at New Lafayette Theatre, 1972.

*House Party, a Soul Happening,* first produced at American Place Theatre, 1973.

*The Mystery of Phillis Wheatley,* first produced at New Federal Theatre, 1976.

*I Am Lucy Terry,* first produced at American Place Theatre, 1976.

*Home Boy,* first produced in New York at Perry Street Theatre, 1976.

*JoAnne!,* first produced in New York at Theatre of the Riverside Church, 1976.

*Storyville,* first produced in La Jolla at the Mandeville Theatre, University of California, 1977.

*DADDY!,* first produced at the New Federal Theatre, 1977.

*Sepia Star,* first produced in New York at Stage 73, 1977.

*Michael,* first produced in New York at New Heritage Repertory Theatre, 1978.

*C'mon Back to Heavenly House,* first produced in Amherst, MA, at Amherst College Theatre, 1978.

*Leavings,* first produced in New York at Syncopation, 1980.

*Steve and Velma,* first produced in Boston by New African Company, 1980.

(Author of book) *I Think It's Gonna Work out Fine* (musical), produced in New York City, 1990.

*OTHER*

*The Hungered One* (collected short fiction), Morrow, 1971.
*The Reluctant Rapist* (novel), Harper, 1973.

Editor of *Black Theatre,* 1968-73; editor of special black issue of *Drama Review,* summer, 1968. Contributor to *Negro Digest, New York Times,* and other periodicals.

*SIDELIGHTS:* Ed Bullins is one of the most powerful black voices in contemporary American theater. He began writing plays as a political activist in the mid-1960s and soon emerged as a principal figure in the black arts movement that surfaced in that decade. First as Minister of Culture for California's Black Panther party and then as associate director of Harlem's New Lafayette Theatre, Bullins helped shape a revolutionary "theater of black experience" that took drama to the streets. In over fifty dramatic works, written expressly for and about blacks, Bullins probed the disillusionment and frustration of ghetto life. At the height of his militancy, he advocated cultural separatism between races and outspokenly dismissed white aesthetic standards. Asked by *Race Relations Reporter* contributor Bernard Garnett how he felt about white critics' evaluations of his work, Bullins replied: "It doesn't matter whether they appreciate it. It's not for them." Despite his disinterest, by the late 1960s establishment critics were tracking his work, more often than not praising its lyricism and depth and commending the playwright's ability to transcend narrow

politics. As C. W. E. Bigsby points out in *The Second Black Renaissance: Essays in Black Literature,* Bullins "was one of the few black writers of the 1960s who kept a cautious distance from a black drama which defined itself solely in political terms." In the 1970s, Bullins won three Obie Awards for distinguished play writing, a Drama Critics Circle Award, and several prestigious Guggenheim and Rockefeller grants.

Bullins's acceptance into the theatrical mainstream, which accelerated as the black arts movement lost momentum, has presented some difficulty for critics trying to assess the current state of his art. The prolific output of his early years was replaced by a curious silence after 1980. One possible explanation, according to *Black American Literature Forum* contributor Richard G. Scharine, is that Bullins was facing the artistic dilemma that confronts Steve Benson, his most autobiographical protagonist: "As an artist he requires recognition. As a revolutionary he dare not be accepted. But Bullins has been accepted.... The real question is whether, severed from his roots and his hate, Bullins can continue to create effectively." In a written response published with the article, Bullins answered the charge: "I was a conscious artist before I was a conscious artist-revolutionary, which has been my salvation and disguise.... I do not feel that I am severed from my roots."

Whatever the reasons, productions of Bullins's work were absent from the New York stage for a number of years. There was no indication, however, that the author had stopped writing. Bullins remained at work on his "Twentieth Century Cycle"—a projected series of twenty plays. This dramatic cycle, which features several recurring characters at different times and in different places, is to portray various facets of black life. Bullins's hope, as he explained to Jervis Anderson in a 1973 *New Yorker* interview, is "that the stories will touch the audience in an individual way, with some fresh impressions and some fresh insights into their own lives [and] help them to consider the weight of their experience."

Bullins's desire to express the reality of ordinary black experience reflects the philosophy he developed during his six-year association with the New Lafayette Theatre, a community-based playhouse that was a showpiece of the black arts movement until it closed for lack of funds in 1973. During its halcyon days, the New Lafayette provided a sanctuary wherein the black identity could be nurtured, a crucial goal of Bullins and all the members of that theatrical family. "Our job," former New Lafayette director Robert Macbeth told Anderson, "has always been to show black people who they are, where they are, and what condition they are in.... Our function, the healing function of theatre and art, is absolutely vital."

In order to reach his black audience, Bullins has consistently ignored many accepted play writing conventions. "Bullins has never paid much attention to the niceties of formal structure, choosing instead to concentrate on black life as it very likely really is—a continuing succession of encounters and dialogues, major events and non-events, small joys and ever-present sorrows," Catharine Hughes comments in *Plays and Players*. New York theatre critic Clive Barnes calls him "a playwright with his hand on the jugular vein of people. He writes with a conviction and sensitivity, and a wonderful awareness of the way the human animal behaves in his human jungle.... Bullins writes so easily and naturally that you watch his plays and you get the impression of overhearing them rather than seeing them."

Part of the authenticity Bullins brings to his dramas may stem from his use of characters drawn from real life. Steve Benson, Cliff Dawson, and Art Garrison are but three of the recurring protagonists who have been closely identified with the author himself. In the early 1970s Steve Benson, who appears in Bullins's novel *The Reluctant Rapist* as well as in plays, including *It Has No Choice* and *In New England Winter*, became so closely associated with his creator that Bullins threatened to eliminate him. "Everybody's got him tagged as me," he told *New York Times* contributor Mel Gussow. "I'm going to kill him off." To a large extent, Steve Benson has disappeared from Bullins's recent dramas, but the link between his art and his life experiences remains a strong one. *Dictionary of Literary Biography* contributor Leslie Sanders explains: "While Bullins frequently warns against turning to his writing for factual details of his life and against identifying him with any single one of his characters, he has never denied the autobiographical quality of his writing. Thus, the tenor, if not the exact substance, of his early years emerges from several of his plays."

Bullins was born and raised in a North Philadelphia ghetto, but was given a middle-class orientation by his mother, a civil servant. He attended a largely white elementary school, where he was an excellent student, and spent his summers vacationing in Maryland farming country. As a junior high student, he was transferred to an inner-city school and joined a gang, the Jet Cobras. During a street fight, he was stabbed in the heart and momentarily lost his life (as does his fictional alter-ego Steve Benson in *The Reluctant Rapist*). The experience, as Bullins explained to *New York Times* contributor Charles M. Young, changed his attitude: "See, when I was young, I was stabbed in a fight. I died. My heart stopped. But I was brought back for a reason. I was gifted with these abilities and I was sent into the world to do what I do because that is the only thing I can do. I write."

Bullins did not immediately recognize his vocation, but spent several years at various jobs. After dropping out of high school, he served in the Navy from 1952 to 1955, where he won a shipboard lightweight boxing championship and started a program of self-education through reading. Not much is known about the years he spent in North Philadelphia after his discharge, but Sanders says "his 1958 departure for Los Angeles quite literally saved his life. When he left Philadelphia, he left behind an unsuccessful marriage and several children." In California, Bullins earned a general equivalency diploma (GED) and started writing. He turned to plays when he realized that the black audience he was trying to reach did not read much fiction and also that he was naturally suited to the dramatic form. But even after moving to San Francisco in 1964, Bullins found little encouragement for his talent. "Nobody would produce my work," he recalled of his early days in the *New Yorker*. "Some people said my language was too obscene, and others said the stuff I was writing was not theatre in the traditional sense." Bullins might have been discouraged had he not chanced upon a production of two plays by LeRoi Jones, *Dutchman* and *The Slave*, that reminded him of his own. "I could see that an experienced playwright like Jones was dealing with the same qualities and conditions of black life that moved me," Bullins explained.

Inspired by Jones's example, Bullins and a group of black revolutionaries joined forces to create a militant cultural-political organization called Black House. Among those participating were Huey Newton and Bobby Seale, two young radicals whose politics of revolution would soon coalesce into the Black Panther party. But the alliance between the violent "revolutionary nationalists," such as Seale and Newton, and the more moderate "cultural nationalists," such as Bullins, would be short-lived. As Anderson explains in the *New Yorker*: "The artists were interested solely in the idea of a cultural awakening while the revolutionaries thought, in Bullins' words, that 'culture was a gun'." Disheartened by the experience, Bullins resigned the post he had been assigned as Black Panther Minister of Culture, severed his ties with the ill-fated Black House, and accepted Robert Macbeth's invitation to work at the New Lafayette Theater in New York.

To date, Bullins's association with the New Lafayette Theatre has been one of the most productive creative periods in his life. Between 1967 and 1973 Bullins created and/or produced almost a dozen plays, some of which are still considered his finest work. He also edited the theatre magazine *Black Theatre* and compiled and edited an anthology of six New Lafayette plays. During this time, Bullins was active as a play writing teacher and director as well. Despite Bullins's close ties to the New Lafayette, his plays were also produced Off-Broadway and at other community theaters, notably the American Place Theatre where he became playwright in residence after the New Lafayette's demise.

Bullins's plays of this period share common themes. *Clara's Ole Man*, an early drama that established the playwright's reputation in New York during its 1968 production, introduces his concerns. Set in the mid-fifties, it tells the story of twenty-year-old Jack, an upwardly mobile black who goes to the ghetto to visit Clara one afternoon when her "ole man" is at work. Not realizing that Clara's lover is actually Big Girl, a lesbian bully who is home when Jack calls, he gets brutally beaten as a result of his ignorance. Leslie Sanders believes that "in *Clara's Ole Man*, Bullins's greatest work is foreshadowed. Its characters, like those in many of his later plays, emerge from brutal life experiences with tenacity and grace. While their language is often crude, it eloquently expresses their pain and anger, as well as the humor that sustains them." C. W. E. Bigsby believes that *Clara's Ole Man*, as well as *Goin' A Buffalo, In the Wine Time, In New England Winter*, and other plays that Bullins wrote in the mid- to late-1960s project the "sense of a brutalized world.... Love devolves into a violent sexuality in which communion becomes simple possession, a struggle for mental and physical dominance. Money is a dominating reality, and alcohol and drugs, like sexuality, the only relief. The tone of the plays is one of desperation and frustration. Individuals are locked together by need, trapped by their own material and biological necessities. Race is only one, and perhaps not even the dominant, reality."

By and large, Bullins's plays of this period have fared well artistically while being criticized, by both black and white critics, for their ideology. Some blacks have objected to what Bigsby calls the "reductive view of human nature" presented in these dramas, along with "their sense of the black ghetto as lacking in any redeeming sense of community or moral values." Other blacks, particularly those who have achieved material success, resent their exclusion from this art form. "I am a young black from a middle-class family and well-educated," reads a letter printed in the *New York Times Magazine* in response to a black arts article. "What sense of self will I ever have if I continue to go to the theatre and movies and never see blacks such as myself in performance?" For the white theater-going community, Bullins's exclusively black drama has raised questions of cultural elitism that seems "to reserve for black art an exclusive and, in some senses, a sacrosanct critical territory," Anderson believes.

Bullins some time ago distanced himself from the critical fray, saying that if he'd listened to what critics have told him, he would have stopped writing long ago. "I don't bother too much what anyone thinks," he told Anderson. "When I sit down in that room by myself, bringing in all that I ever saw, smelled, learned, or checked out, I am the chief determiner of the quality of my work. The only critic that I really trust is me."

*BIOGRAPHICAL/CRITICAL SOURCES:*

*BOOKS*

Bigsby, C. W. E., *The Second Black Renaissance: Essays in Black Literature*, Greenwood Press, 1980.

*Black Literature Criticism*, Gale, 1992.
*Contemporary Literary Criticism*, Gale, Volume 1, 1973, Volume 5, 1976, Volume 7, 1977.
*Dictionary of Literary Biography*, Gale, Volume 7: *Twentieth-Century American Dramatists*, 1981, Volume 38: *Afro-American Writers after 1955: Dramatists and Prose Writers*, 1985.
Gayle, Addison, editor, *The Black Aesthetic*, Doubleday, 1971.

*PERIODICALS*

*Black American Literature Forum*, fall, 1979.
*Black Creation*, winter, 1973.
*Black World*, April, 1974.
*CLA Journal*, June, 1976.
*Nation*, November 12, 1973, April 5, 1975.
*Negro Digest*, April, 1969.
*Newsweek*, May 20, 1968.
*New Yorker*, June 16, 1973.
*New York Times*, September 22, 1971, May 18, 1975, June 17, 1977, May 31, 1979, March 17, 1990.
*New York Times Book Review*, June 20, 1971, September 30, 1973.
*New York Times Magazine*, September 10, 1972.
*Plays and Players*, May, 1972, March, 1973.
*Race Relations Reporter*, February 7, 1972.

\*      \*      \*

## BUNCHE, Ralph J(ohnson)   1904-1971

*PERSONAL:* Born August 7, 1904, in Detroit, MI; died after a long series of illnesses, December 9, 1971, in New York, NY; son of Fred (a barber) and Olive Agnes (a musician; maiden name, Johnson) Bunche; married Ruth Ethel Harris, June 23, 1930; children: Ralph, Jr., Joan, Jane (Mrs. Burton Pierce; died in 1966). *Education:* University of California, Los Angeles, B.A. (summa cum laude), 1927; Harvard University, M.A., 1928, Ph.D., 1934; postdoctoral study at Northwestern University, 1936, London School of Economics and Political Science, London, 1937, and Capetown University, 1937. *Politics:* Independent. *Religion:* Nonsectarian.

*ADDRESSES: Home*—Kew Gardens, New York, NY.

*CAREER:* Howard University, Washington, DC, instructor, 1928, assistant professor and department chair, beginning in 1929, special assistant to the president of the university, 1931-32, professor of political science, 1937-42; Carnegie Corporation of New York, staff member serving as chief aide to Swedish sociologist Gunnar Myrdal, 1938-40; Office of the Coordinator of Information (later Office of Strategic Services), Washington, DC, senior social science analyst, beginning in 1941, principal research analyst in the Africa and Far East section, 1942-43, chief of the Africa Section of the Research and Analysis Branch, 1943-44; U.S. State Department, Washington, DC, divisional assistant for colonial problems in the Division of Political Studies and area specialist on Africa and dependent areas in the Division of Territorial Studies, both 1944, acting associate chief, 1945, and associate chief of the Division of Dependent Area Affairs (also serving some months as acting chief), 1945-47, assistant secretary to the U.S. delegation at Dumbarton Oaks Conference, 1944, technical expert on trusteeship for the U.S. delegation at the Conference on International Organization at San Francisco, 1945, appointed by President Harry S Truman to membership on Anglo-American Caribbean Commission, 1945, adviser to the U.S. delegation to the United Nations General Assembly in London, 1946, adviser to the U.S. delegation to International Labor conferences in Paris and Philadelphia; United Nations Secretariat, Washington, DC, director of the Trusteeship Division, 1947-55, undersecretary, 1955-57, undersecretary for special political affairs serving under Secretary-General Dag Hammarskjold, 1957-67, undersecretary-general serving under Secretary-General U Thant, 1967-71. Special assistant to the Secretary-General's Special Committee on Palestine, and appointed principal secretary of the Palestine Commission, both 1947, head of the Palestine Commission, 1948, directed peace-keeping operations in such areas as Suez, 1956, Congo, 1960, Yemen, 1962-64, Cyprus, 1964, and India and Pakistan, 1965. Founder of National Negro Congress, 1936. Co-director of Institute of Race Relations at Swarthmore College, 1936; member of faculty of Harvard University, 1950-52; became trustee of Oberlin College, 1950, and the Rockefeller Foundation, 1955; member of the Harvard University board of overseers, 1958-65.

*MEMBER:* American Political Science Association (member of executive council; president, 1953-54), National Association for the Advancement of Colored People (member of board of directors, c. 1949-71), William Allen White Committee, Phi Beta Kappa.

*AWARDS, HONORS:* New York's Town Hall Distinguished Service Award, 1949; awarded citation by the American Association for the United Nations, 1949, for "distinguished and unselfish service in advancing the ideas of the United Nations"; Spingarn Award, National Association for the Advancement of Color People, 1949, and the Nobel Peace Prize, 1950, both for negotiating the 1949 armistice between Arab and Israeli states; One World Award; Franklin D. Roosevelt Four Freedoms Award, Four Freedoms Foundation, Inc.; Medal of Freedom, 1963; Ozias Goodwin fellowship from Harvard University, Rosenwald Field fellowship, and Social Science Research Council fellowship for anthropology and colonial policy; more than fifty honorary degrees from colleges and universities.

*WRITINGS:*

*A World View of Race,* Association in Negro Folk Education, 1936, reprinted, Kennikat, 1968.
*Peace and the United Nations,* Leeds University, 1952.
*The Political Status of the Negro in the Age of FDR* (collection of interviews), edited and with an introduction by Dewey W. Grantham, University of Chicago Press, 1973.
*An African-American in South Africa: The Travel Notes of Ralph J. Bunche, 28 September 1937-1 January 1938,* edited by Robert R. Edgar, Ohio University Press, 1992.

Contributor of articles to periodicals, including *New Republic, National Municipal Review, Annals, Journal of Negro History,* and *Journal of Negro Education.* Also contributor to trusteeship sections of the United Nations Charter, 1945.

*SIDELIGHTS:* The highest ranking American official in the United Nations and the first black recipient of the Nobel Peace Prize, Ralph J. Bunche was "an ideal international civil servant, a black man of learning and experience open to men and ideas of all shades," according to Robert D. McFadden of the *New York Times.* For his leading role in negotiating peace talks between Arab and Israeli states in 1949 and his direction of numerous peace-keeping forces around the world, Bunche is considered one of the most significant American diplomats of the twentieth century.

Born in Detroit in 1904, Bunch moved to Los Angeles, California, at the age of thirteen upon the death of his parents. After graduating from the University of California at Los Angeles in 1927 and receiving his master's degree in government at Harvard University the following year, he began teaching at the all-black Howard University in Washington, D.C., soon becoming the head of the political science department there. He returned to Harvard where he obtained a doctorate in government and international relations in 1934. His later postdoctoral work in anthropology and colonial policy led to worldwide travel, field work in Africa, and completion of his 1936 book *A World View of Race.* Concerned with racial problems, Bunche went on to work with Swedish sociologist Gunnar Myrdal from 1938 to 1940 surveying the conditions of the Negro in America. Their interview work in the South—which caused them to be chased out of some Alabama towns and almost lynched by a mob of angry whites—led to the publication of Myrdal's widely acclaimed 1944 book *An American Dilemma,* a massive study of race relations.

Bunche eventually became known as an expert on colonial affairs. During World War II he served as a specialist in African and Far Eastern affairs for the Office of Strategic Services before moving to the U.S. State Department, where he soon became associate chief of its Division of Department Area Affairs. He was the first black to hold a desk job in the department. For his expertise on trusteeship, Bunche was recommended by Secretary-General Trygve Lie to direct the Trusteeship Division at the United Nations in 1947. Later that year, the diplomat was appointed special assistant to the Secretary-General's Special Committee on Palestine, and in 1948 he became head of the Palestine Commission when its original appointee, Count Folke Bernadotte of Sweden, was assassinated. Bunche consequently was faced with the great challenge of continuing cease-fire talks between the fighting Arab and Israeli nations.

"As it turned out," commented Homer Metz of *New Review*, "he was exactly suited for the difficult task of bringing Arabs and Jews together." Hailed for his endless patience, sensitivity, and optimism, Bunche, after eighty-one days of negotiations on the island of Rhodes, worked out the "Four Armistice Agreements," which resulted in an immediate cessation of the hostilities between the two combatants. "The art of his compromise," lauded McFadden, "lay in his seemingly boundless energy and the order and timing of his moves." A writer for *Time* further praised the diplomat: "It required painstaking, brilliant diplomacy to bring the Arabs and Israelis together on the island of Rhodes; Bunche's forceful personality... helped to keep them there." Garnering worldwide praise for his successful peace-keeping efforts, Bunche won the 1950 Nobel Peace Prize, becoming the first black recipient of the coveted award.

Bunche, however, did not consider his work on Rhodes his most fulfilling mission. McFadden quoted Bunche from a 1969 interview: "The Peace Prize attracted all the attention, but I've had more satisfaction in the work I've done since." For example, the statesman went on to conduct peace forces in the Congo, Yemen, Cyprus, India, and Pakistan, and he regarded his work in the Suez area of Egypt—where he organized and directed the deployment of a six-thousand-person neutral force which maintained peace there from 1956 to 1967—as his most satisfying accomplishment. About that mission, Bunche was quoted in *Time:* "For the first time ... we have found a way to use military men for peace instead of war."

Bunche's peace-keeping efforts for the United Nations soon earned the diplomat the position of undersecretary in 1955, the highest post held by an American in the world organization. And by the time he became undersecretary-general in 1967 (the post he held until his retirement in 1971), Bunche's "diplomatic skills—a masterwork in the practical application of psychology—[had] became legendary at the United Nations," noted McFadden. But the international civil servant was not only valuable to the United nations; Bunche was considered an inspiration to millions of Americans and was what *Newsweek* called "the foremost Negro of his generation—the distinguished symbol of how far a black man could rise in the

Establishment." Furthermore, concluded *Time,* "Bunche had achieved a unique status: a black without color and an American who belonged to all the nations." His book *Peace and the United Nations* appeared in 1952, and *The Political Status of the Negro in the Age of FDR*—a collection of more than five hundred interviews conducted in the American South—was published posthumously in 1973.

Bunche spent the last three months of 1937 traveling in South Africa as part of an around-the-world research trip financed by the Social Science Research Council. He took extensive research notes on what he saw there and these notes were edited and published as a book in 1992 by Robert R. Edgar. As Edgar mentions, Bunche provided one of the few "outsider" accounts of South Africa by a black person. Indeed, Bunche had considerable difficulty in securing permission to enter South Africa, though he was apparently relatively well treated during his sojourn there, probably because he was an American black. As Edgar notes, Bunche was particularly interested in the impact of segregation on black life. Hence, he devoted most of his attention to conversations with East Indians, Coloureds (persons of mixed-race ancestry), and black Africans. Bunche for the most part allowed the facts to speak for themselves but occasionally he permitted himself an unsparing conclusion. "South Africa," he wrote on December 9, 1937, "is an *entire* country ridden by race prejudice—unlike [the] U.S. in that there is absolutely no escape at all for these black and colored people." As Edgar points out, Bunche's research notes, partly because they were not intended for immediate publication, often provide significant glimpses into Bunche's own inner thoughts and emotions. The glimpses are fleeting, since Bunche was famous for his reserve and discretion. On January 1, 1938, his first day on shipboard after his departure from South Africa, Bunche noted that he was assigned to a table in the vessel's dining room with the chief engineer and a young Dutch girl. "The engineer," he observed, "didn't show up at either meal today."

*BIOGRAPHICAL/CRITICAL SOURCES:*

*BOOKS*

Kugelmass, J. Alvin, *Ralph J. Bunche: Fighter for Peace,* Messner, 1962.
Mann, Peggy, *Ralph Bunche: UN Peacemaker,* Coward, McCann & Geoghegan, 1975.

*PERIODICALS*

*American History Review,* June, 1974.
*Journal of American History,* June, 1974.
*New Review,* May 30, 1949.

OBITUARIES:

PERIODICALS

American Historical Review, June, 1974.
Boys' Life, February, 1988.
Jet, October 24, 1988; January 13, 1992; July 13, 1992.
Journal of American History, June, 1974.
Library Journal, May, 1989; July, 1992.
Nation, December 27, 1971.
New Review, May 30, 1949.
Newsweek, December 20, 1971.
New York Times, December 10, 1971.
Time, December 20, 1971.
Yale Review, spring, 1987.

\*  \*  \*

## BUSIA, Kofi Abrefa   1913(?)-1978

PERSONAL: Born July 11, 1913 (some sources say 1914), in Wenchi, Brongahafo District, Ghana; died following a heart attack, August 28, 1978, in London (one source says Oxford), England; married, 1950; children: two sons, two daughters. Education: Achimote College, B.A.; University of London, B.A.; Oxford University, M.A. and Ph.D. Avocational interests: Music, walking.

ADDRESSES: Home—Brighthampton Rd., Standlake, Oxford, England.

CAREER: Wesley College, Kumasi, Ghana, member of staff, 1932-34; Achimote College, Accra, Ghana, member of staff, 1936-39; Government of the Gold Coast, district commissioner, 1942-49, officer in charge of sociological surveys, 1947-49; University College of the Gold Coast (now University of Ghana), Accra, research lecturer in African studies, 1949-51, senior lecturer in sociology, 1952-54, professor, 1954-59; Institute of Social Studies, the Hague, Netherlands, professor of sociology, 1959-62; University of Leiden, Leiden, Netherlands, professor of sociology and culture of Africa, 1960-62; World Council of Churches, Birmingham, England, director of studies, 1962-64; Oxford University, St. Antony's College, Oxford, England, professor of sociology, 1964-66; National Liberation Advisory Council in Ghana, vice-chair, 1966-67, chair, 1967-69; founder of Progress Party in Ghana, 1969; prime minister of Ghana, 1969-72, minister of economic planning and the interior, 1971-72. Lecturer in sociology, Oxford University, 1973-78. Leader of Ghana Congress Party, 1952-57, leader of parties in opposition to Nkrumah's Convention People's Party (United Party), 1957-59; chair of Centre for Civic Education, 1967. Visiting professor at North-western University, 1954, Nuffield College, Oxford, 1955, Agricultural University of Wageningen, 1956, El Colegio de Mexico, 1962, and University of York.

MEMBER: International Sociological Association (executive member, 1953-60), International Social Science Council, International African Institute, Association of Social Anthropologists.

AWARDS, HONORS: Carnegie Foundation research fellowships, 1941-42, 1945-47; D.Litt. from University of Ghana, 1970.

WRITINGS:

Report on a Social Survey of Sekondi-Takoradi, Crown Agents for the Colonies on Behalf of the Government of the Gold Coast, 1950.
The Position of the Chief in the Modern Political System of Ashanti: A Study of the Influence of Contemporary Social Changes on Ashanti Political Institutions, Oxford University Press, for African International Institute, 1951, International Scholastic Book Service, 1968.
Education for Citizenship, Bureau of Current Affairs (London, England), 1951.
Judge for Yourself, West African Graphic Co., 1956.
Africa in Transition: A Social and Anthropological Observation, World Council of Churches, Division of Studies, 1957.
The Sociology and Culture of Africa, University of Leiden Press, 1960.
The Challenge of Africa, Praeger, 1962.
Purposeful Education for Africa, Mouton & Co., 1964, Humanities, 1969.
Urban Churches in Britain: A Question of Relevance, Lutterworth, 1966.
Ghana Will Be Truly Free and Happy, Ghana Students Association, 1966.
Africa in Search of Democracy, Praeger, 1967.
The African Consciousness: Continuity and Change in Africa, African-American Affairs Association, 1968.
The Way to Industrial Peace, Ghana Publishing Corp., 1970.
Ghana's Struggle for Democracy and Freedom: Speeches, 1957-69, compiled by H. K. Akyeampong, Danquah Memorial Publishing Co., 1970-79.
Apartheid and Its Elimination, Ghana Public Relations Department, 1971.
Dr. Busia in Singapore (speeches), Ministry of Information (Accra, Ghana), 1971.

Also author of Self-Government, 1955, and Industrialization in West Africa, 1955. Contributor to Civil Rule Returns to Ghana, edited by Akwasi A. Afrifa, Ministry of Information, 1969.

*SIDELIGHTS:* Kofi Abrefa Busia was a member of the royal family of Wenchi, of the Ashanti people. In 1957, Nkrumah's government, of which Busia was opposition leader, arrested several leaders and charged them with conspiracy to assassinate Nkrumah. At the time, Busia was lecturing abroad, and chose to remain in the Netherlands in exile. When Nkrumah was overthrown by a military coup, Busia returned to Ghana to serve as prime minister. Another military coup occurred while Busia was in office, but he chanced to be abroad again, remaining in exile until his death in 1978.

*BIOGRAPHICAL/CRITICAL SOURCES:*

*PERIODICALS*

*Ghana,* January 14, 1973.
*Listener,* November 23, 1967.
*New Statesman,* December 22, 1967.
*New York Times,* November 6, 1978.
*Time,* September 12, 1969.
*Times Literary Supplement,* November 2, 1967.

\*    \*    \*

**BUTLER,  Anna Land**
  **See BUTLER,  Anna M(abel Land)**

\*    \*    \*

**BUTLER,  Anna M(abel Land)   1901-**
  **(Anna Land Butler)**

*PERSONAL:* Born October 7, 1901, Philadelphia, PA; daughter of John Weaver Land, Sr., (a hotel doorman); married Floyd Butler; children: Maurice (deceased). *Education:* Attended Trenton State Teachers College, 1920-22 and 1936; attended Temple University, 1953; attended University of Maryland, 1942-45. *Religion:* Episcopal.

*ADDRESSES: Home*—Atlantic City, NJ.

*CAREER:* Elementary school teacher, 1922-64; Pittsburgh Courier, newspaper corespondent, 1936-65; Atlantic Public School, teacher, 1952-64; *Magazine Responsibility,* editor, 1955-59; *Philadelphia Tribune,* editor and reporter, 1965-72; *Eastern Area National Links Journal,* associate editor, 1967-70; Morris Child Care Center, head teacher and director, 1969-72. Eastern Seaboard Council Heritage House, president, beginning in 1954; New Jersey Organization for Teachers, vice president.

*MEMBER:* National Society for Literature and the Arts, Atlantic City Study Center, Phi Delta Kappa.

*AWARDS, HONORS:* Versatile Teachers Award, 1953; Teacher of the Year, New Jersey Organization of Teachers, 1961; named poet laureate of Eastern Area National Links Inc.; Northside Business and Professional Womens Achievement Award, 1963; Sach's Certificate of Recognition for Outstanding Community Services, 1963; Theta Phi Lambda Sorority Womens Showcase Award, 1964; National Association Sojourner Truth Award, 1966; Theta Kappa Omega Black Women Community Service Award, 1970; Certificate for Award of Achievement, Outstanding Negro Woman, Imperial Daughters of Isis, 1972.

*WRITINGS:*

*Album of Love Letters—Unsent,* Margent, 1952.
*Touchstone,* The Advocate Press for the Delaware Poetry Center, 1961.
*High Noon,* Prairie Press Books, 1971.

*CONTRIBUTOR*

*Spring Anthologies,* Mitre, 1963-65.
*Today's Poets,* American Poets Fellowship Society, 1965.
*American Poets Best,* Swordsman, 1962-65.

Also contributor to *Jewels on a Willow Tree,* edited by Mabelle A. Lyon, Prairie Press; contributor to the periodical *United Poets.*

*SIDELIGHTS:* Inheriting her father's inclination for writing poetry, Anna Butler has published three volumes of poetry while still active in her careers as a schoolteacher and journalist. Her work addresses a wide range of subjects including nature, love, death, and equality. A *Harlem Renaissance and Beyond* contributor described Butler's second work, *Touchstone,* as "mysterious and haunting," showing "a vivid consciousness of the importance of seeking equality with courage." Butler is quoted in *Black American Writers Past and Present* as encouraging all to "Be thankful for life, the opportunity to serve others in whatever way is possible ... Count your blessings with your woes. Be grateful always."

*BIOGRAPHICAL/CRITICAL SOURCES:*

*BOOKS*

Roses, Lorraine Elena, and Ruth Elizabeth Randolph, *Harlem Renaissance and Beyond,* G. K. Hall, 1990.
Rush, Theressa Gunnels, Carol Fairbanks Myers, and Esther Spring Arata, *Black American Writers Past and Present,* Scarecrow Press, 1975.

## BUTLER, Octavia E(stelle) 1947-

*PERSONAL:* Born June 22, 1947, in Pasadena, CA; daughter of Laurice and Octavia M. (Guy) Butler. *Education:* Pasadena City College, A.A., 1968; attended California State University, Los Angeles, 1969, and University of California, Los Angeles.

*ADDRESSES: Home*—P.O. Box 40671, Pasadena, CA 91114.

*CAREER:* Free-lance writer, 1970—.

*MEMBER:* Science Fiction Writers of America.

*AWARDS, HONORS:* Hugo Award, World Science Fiction Society, 1984, for short story "Speech Sounds"; Hugo Award and Nebula Award from Science Fiction Writers of America, Locus Award from *Locus* magazine, and award for best novelette from *Science Fiction Chronicle Reader,* all 1985, all for novelette "Bloodchild"; Nebula Award nomination, 1987, for novelette "The Evening and the Morning and the Night."

*WRITINGS:*

*SCIENCE FICTION*

*Patternmaster,* Doubleday, 1976.
*Mind of My Mind,* Doubleday, 1977.
*Survivor,* Doubleday, 1978.
*Kindred,* Doubleday, 1979, second edition, Beacon Press, 1988.
*Wild Seed,* Doubleday, 1980.
*Clay's Ark,* St. Martin's, 1984.
*Dawn: Xenogenesis* (first novel in the "Xenogenesis" trilogy), Warner Books, 1987.
*Adulthood Rites* (second novel in the "Xenogenesis" trilogy), Warner Books, 1988.
*Imago* (third novel in the "Xenogenesis" trilogy), Warner Books, 1989.
*Parable of the Sower,* Four Walls Eight Windows, 1993.

Author of novelettes "Bloodchild" and "The Evening and the Morning and the Night." Contributor to anthologies, including *Clarion,* 1970, and *Chrysalis 4,* 1979. Contributor to periodicals, including *Isaac Asimov's Science Fiction Magazine, Future Life, Omni, Essence, American Visions, Writers of the Future,* and *Transmission.*

*SIDELIGHTS:* Concerned with genetic engineering, psionic powers, advanced alien beings, and the nature and proper use of power, Octavia E. Butler's science fiction presents these themes in terms of racial and sexual awareness. "Butler consciously explores the impact of race and sex upon future society," Frances Smith Foster explains in *Extrapolation.* As one

of the few black writers in the science fiction field, and the only black woman, Butler's racial and sexual perspective is unique. This perspective, however, does not limit her fiction or turn it into mere propaganda. "Her stories," Sherley Anne Williams writes in *Ms.,* "aren't overwhelmed by politics, nor are her characters overwhelmed by racism or sexism." Speaking of how Butler's early novels deal with racial questions in particular, John R. Pfeiffer of *Fantasy Review* maintains that "nevertheless, and therefore more remarkably, these are the novels of character that critics so much want to find in science fiction—and which remain so rare. Finally, they are love stories that are mythic, bizarre, exotic and heroic and full of doom and transcendence."

Among Butler's strengths as a writer, according to some reviewers, is her creation of believable, independent female characters. "Her major characters are black women," Foster explains, and through these characters Butler explores the possibilities for a society open to true sexual equality. In such a society Butler's female characters, "powerful and purposeful in their own right, need not rely upon eroticism to gain their ends." Williams also believes that Butler posits "a multiracial society featuring strong women characters." In addition to her unique characters, critics praise Butler's controlled, economical prose style. Writing in the *Washington Post Book World,* Elizabeth A. Lynn calls the author's prose "spare and sure, and even in moments of great tension she never loses control over her pacing or over her sense of story." Dean R. Lambe of the *Science Fiction Review* similarly attests, "Butler has a fine hand with lean, well-paced prose."

Butler's stories have been well received by science fiction fans. In 1985 she won three of the field's top honors—the Nebula Award, the Hugo Award, and the Locus Award—for her novella "Bloodchild," the story of human males on another planet who bear the children of an alien race. "Bloodchild," Williams explains, "explores the paradoxes of power and inequality, and starkly portrays the experience of a class who, like women throughout most of history, are valued chiefly for their reproductive capacities."

It is through her novels, however, that Butler reaches her largest audience; and, of these, she is best known for her books set in the world of the "Patternists," including *Patternmaster, Mind of My Mind, Survivor,* and *Wild Seed.* The Patternist series tells of a society dominated by an elite, specially-bred group of telepaths who are mentally linked together into a hierarchical pattern. Originally founded by a four thousand-year-old immortal Nubian named Doro who survives by killing and then taking over younger bodies, these telepaths seek to create a race of superhumans. But Doro's plans are repeatedly thwarted in *Wild Seed* by Anyanwu, an immortal woman who does not need to kill to survive; and in *Mind of My Mind* Mary, Doro's daughter, organizes all the other telepaths to defeat him, thus giving the Patternists an alternative to Doro's selfish and murderous reign. As *Dictionary of Literary Biography* contributor Margaret Anne O'Connor says, "this novel argues for the collective power of man as opposed to individual, self-interested endeavor."

The Patternist novels cover hundreds of years of human history. *Wild Seed* takes place in the eighteenth and nineteenth centuries and *Mind of My Mind* is set in a Los Angeles of the near future, but the other books in the series are set in the distant future. *Patternmaster,* like *Mind of My Mind,* addresses the theme of the importance of compassion and empathy between people over the ambitions of the individual. In this tale Butler describes an Agrarian society now ruled by the telepaths whose communities are at constant risk of attack from humans who have been monstrously mutated by a genetic disease—just how this disease is brought to Earth by an astronaut is explained in *Clay's Ark.* During one of these raids, a Patternist ruler is wounded and becomes an invalid. His two sons vie for his position, and Butler shows how the younger son, Teray, learns from a woman healer named Amber that compassion is necessary to maintain and control the communal Pattern. By learning—as Mary did in *Mind of My Mind*—the benefits of the community over the individual, Teray defeats his brother and takes his father's place.

Although many of Butler's protagonists in the Patternist books are black women, the novelist does not display any particular favoritism towards either blacks or women. Instead, she emphasizes the need for breaking down race and gender barriers by illustrating the inability of those hindered by prejudice and narrow vision to progress and evolve. According to Foster, for "the feminist critic, Octavia Butler may present problems. Her female characters are undeniably strong and independent; but whether, as Joanna Russ insists is crucial, 'the assumptions underlying the entire narrative are feminist,' is uncertain, for 'who wins and who loses' is less clear than that a compromise has been made which unifies the best of each woman and man. For Afro-American literary critics, Butler can present problems as well, for their attention has been focused upon the assumptions and depictions about the black experience of the past and the present; yet the implications of Butler's vision should be a significant challenge."

In *Survivor,* another Patternist novel, and Butler's more recent *Xenogenesis* trilogy, the author uses alien beings to help illustrate her themes: the differences between humans and aliens magnifies the issue of cultural misunderstanding and prejudice-inspired antipathy. With *Survivor,* the character Alanna survives on a distant world by learning to understand and love one of the alien Kohn's. The *Xenogenesis* books explore the interrelationships between two peoples in greater depth by creating a race called the Oankali, nomadic aliens who interbreed with other sentient species in order to improve their gene pool. Arriving on Earth after a nuclear holocaust has wiped out almost all of humanity, the Oankali offer mankind a second chance through the combination of the best characteristics of both species. They accomplish this through a third sex called ooloi, whose function is to manipulate the two races' genes into a new species. Here, according to *Analog* reviewer Tom Easton, "we may have Butler's [main] point: The ooloi are the means for gene transfer between species, but they also come between, they are intermediaries, moderators, buffers, and Butler says that the human tragedy is the unfortunate combination of intelligence and hierarchy."

One book that Butler has written that has nothing to do with either her Patternist or her Xenogenesis series is *Kindred,* which, except for its time-travel theme, diverges enough from the science fiction genre that her publisher marketed it as a mainstream novel. *Kindred* concerns Dana, a contemporary black woman who is pulled back in time by her great-great-grandfather, a white plantation owner in the antebellum American South. To insure that he will live to father her great-grandmother, and thus insure her own birth in the twentieth century, Dana is called upon to save the slave owner's life on several occasions. "Butler makes new and eloquent use of a familiar science-fiction idea, protecting one's own past, to express the tangled interdependency of black and white in the United States," Joanna Russ writes in the *Magazine of Fantasy and Science Fiction.* Williams calls *Kindred* "a startling and engrossing commentary on the complex-actuality and continuing heritage of American slavery."

Butler enjoys a solid reputation among both readers and critics of science fiction, and Williams notes that Butler has a "cult status among many black women readers." She also notes that "Butler's work has a scope that commands a wide audience." Many of her books have been recommended by critics as examples of the best that science fiction has to offer. For example, speaking of *Kindred* and *Wild Seed,* Pfeiffer argues that with these books Butler "produced two novels of such special excellence that critical appreciation of them will take several years to assemble. To miss them will be to miss unique novels in modern fiction." And Easton asserts that with *Dawn* "Butler has gifted SF with a vision of possibility more original than anything we have seen since [Arthur C.] Clarke's *Childhood's End.*" Nevertheless, Foster believes that Butler's novels deserve more recognition because they fill a void in the science fiction genre, which often neglects to explore sexual, familial, and racial relationships. "Since Octavia Butler is a black woman who writes speculative fiction which is primarily concerned with social relationships, where rulers include women and nonwhites," Foster concludes, "the neglect of her work is startling."

*BIOGRAPHICAL/CRITICAL SOURCES:*

*BOOKS*

*Contemporary Literary Criticism,* Volume 38, Gale, 1986.
*Dictionary of Literary Biography,* Volume 33: *Afro-American Fiction Writers after 1955,* Gale, 1984.

*PERIODICALS*

*Analog: Science Fiction/Science Fact,* January 5, 1981; November, 1984; December 15, 1987; December, 1988.
*Black American Literature Forum,* summer, 1984.
*Black Scholar,* March/April, 1986.

*Equal Opportunity Forum Magazine,* Number 8, 1980.
*Essence,* April, 1979.
*Extrapolation,* spring, 1982.
*Fantasy Review,* July, 1984.
*Janus,* winter, 1978-79.
*Los Angeles Times,* January 30, 1981.
*Magazine of Fantasy and Science Fiction,* February, 1980; August, 1984.
*Ms.,* March, 1986; June, 1987.
*Salaga,* 1981.
*Science Fiction Review,* May, 1984.
*Thrust: Science Fiction in Review,* summer, 1979.
*Washington Post Book World,* September 28, 1980; June 28, 1987; July 31, 1988; June 25, 1989.

# C

## CADE, Toni
## See BAMBARA, Toni Cade

\*    \*    \*

## CAIN, George (M.) 1943-

*PERSONAL:* Born in October (some sources say November), 1943, in Harlem, NY; married in 1968; wife's name, Jo Lynne; children: Nataya. *Education:* Attended Iona College.

*WRITINGS:*

*Blueschild Baby* (novel), McGraw-Hill, 1970.

*SIDELIGHTS:* George Cain entered the literary scene with the publication of his autobiographical novel *Blueschild Baby* in 1970. Upon release from prison, the protagonist, George Cain, returns to Harlem, his loving family, and the dangerous world of drugs and addiction. He battles his drug dependency with the devoted care of Nandy, his childhood sweetheart. Nandy sustains him through his painful three day withdrawal period, during which Cain reexamines his life. The basketball scholarship to the private white school he had received had seemed to be a way for him to achieve the "American Dream" of his hard-working parents. Instead of success, Cain was introduced to the world of tokenism and painful clashes with white faculty and students. When he tried to fulfill too many people's ideal, he failed everyone, including himself. Reacting to his sense of failure, the young Cain strikes out in anger and despair at all who surround him. He uses others because he had been used. Ultimately, however, Cain realizes that in order to reclaim himself he must abandon his hatred of himself and of others. He returns to Nandy, and it is her goodness and love that bring hope to his life. In his humility before her, he reestablishes his connection to life and to himself.

"The truth of Cain's experiences and of his life is universal," Edith Blicksilver wrote in the *Dictionary of Literary Biography.* "He spent time on his craft and was attentive to his own heart's yearnings; the result is a voice resounding with the writer's unique version of the world." Although *Blueschild Baby* was well received, Cain left the literary world shortly after the publication of his novel.

*BIOGRAPHICAL/CRITICAL SOURCES:*

*BOOKS*

*Dictionary of Literary Biography,* Volume 33: *Afro-American Fiction Writers after 1955,* Gale 1984, pp. 41-43.

*PERIODICALS*

*New York Times Book Review,* January 17, 1971, p.4.

\*    \*    \*

## CAINES, Jeannette (Franklin) 1938-

*PERSONAL:* Born in 1938, in New York, NY.

*CAREER:* Writer of children's books. Works for Harper (a publishing company), New York City. Member of Coalition of 100 Black Women, Council on Adoptable Children, Negro Business and Professional Women of Nassau County, and Council of Christ Lutheran Church, Nassau County.

*MEMBER:* Salvation Army (former member of board of directors).

*AWARDS, HONORS:* National Black Child Development Institute's certificate of merit and appreciation.

*WRITINGS:*

FOR CHILDREN

*Abby,* illustrations by Steven Kellogg, Harper, 1973.
*Daddy,* Harper, 1977.
*Window Wishing,* illustrations by Kevin Brooks, Harper, 1981.
*Just Us Women,* illustrations by Pat Cummings, Harper, 1982.
*Chilly Stomach,* illustrations by P. Cummings, Harper, 1986.
*I Need a Lunch Box,* Harper, 1988.

*BIOGRAPHICAL/CRITICAL SOURCES:*

BOOKS

*Children's Literature Review,* Volume 24, Gale, 1992.
Rollock, Barbara, *Black Authors and Illustrators of Children's Books,* Garland, 1988.

PERIODICALS

*Early Years,* Vol. 13, no. 7, March, 1983, p. 24.

\*    \*    \*

## CAMPBELL, Bebe Moore 1950-

*PERSONAL:* Born in 1950; daughter of George Linwood Peter Moore and Doris Carter Moore; married; divorced; married Tiko F. Campbell (divorced); married Ellis Gordon, Jr. (a banker); children: Maia. *Education:* Received B.A. (summa cum laude) from University of Pittsburgh.

*ADDRESSES: Agent*—Lynn Nesbit, Jankow and Nesbit Associates, 598 Madison Ave., New York, NY 10022.

*CAREER:* Author and free-lance writer. Taught school in Atlanta, GA, Washington, DC, and Pittsburgh, PA. Guest on television talk shows, including *Donahue, Oprah, Sonya Live,* and *Today,* and numerous radio talk shows, including *Morning Edition,* National Public Radio (NPR).

*MEMBER:* Alpha Kappa Alpha, Delta Sigma Theta.

*AWARDS, HONORS:* Body of Work Award, National Association of Negro Business and Professional Women, 1978; National Endowment for the Arts grant, 1980; Golden Reel Award, Midwestern Radio Theatre Workshop Competition, for "Sugar on the Floor"; received Mayor's Certificate of Appreciation, Los Angeles, CA.

*WRITINGS:*

*Successful Women, Angry Men: Backlash in the Two-Career Marriage,* Random House, 1986.
*Sweet Summer: Growing Up with and without My Dad,* Putnam, 1989.
*Your Blues Ain't Like Mine* (novel), Putnam, 1992.

Also author of numerous short stories, including "Old Lady Shoes." Author of radio plays, including "Sugar on the Floor" and "Old Lady Shoes" (adapted from the author's short story). Contributor to periodicals, including *Ebony, Lear's, Ms., New York Times Book Review, New York Times Magazine, Publishers Weekly, Savvy, Seventeen, Washington Post,* and *Working Mother.* Contributing editor of *Essence.*

*ADAPTATIONS:* Motown Productions bought an option on the film rights to *Sweet Summer* in 1989; the option is now held by Aunt Jack Productions.

*SIDELIGHTS:* Bebe Moore Campbell earned widespread recognition for her 1989 book *Sweet Summer: Growing Up with and without My Dad,* her memoir as a child of divorce. Since her parents had separated when she was quite young, Campbell lived a divided existence, spending the school year in Pennsylvania with her mother and the summer in North Carolina with her father. Campbell draws a sharp contrast between the two worlds. According to *Sweet Summer,* her Philadelphia home was dominated by women—notably her mother, aunt, and grandmother—who urged her to speak well, behave properly, study hard, and generally improve herself. Life with her father, his mother, and his male friends, on the other hand, she describes as a freer one full of cigar and pipe smoke, beer, loud laughter, "roughness, gruffness, awkward gentleness," and a father's abiding love. Wheelchair-bound by a car accident, Campbell's father was nonetheless her hero, a perfect dad who loved her just for herself. When she learned that he was responsible, through speeding, not only for his own crippling accident but also for one that killed a boy, her image of him became tarnished, and Campbell had to come to terms with him as a flawed human being, no longer the dream-father she had idolized.

Critics hailed *Sweet Summer* for its poignant, positive look at a father-daughter relationship and especially for showing such a loving relationship in the black community. *Times Literary Supplement* contributor Adeola Solanke observed that in Campbell's memoir "a black father is portrayed by his daughter as a hero, instead of as the monster stalking the pages of many black American women writers." Similarly, poet Nikki Giovanni, writing in the *Washington Post Book World,* praised the book for providing "a corrective to some of the destructive images of black men that are prevalent in our society." Campbell also earned approval for her treatment of ordinary black life and for the vitality and clarity of her writing. Some reviewers expressed reservations about her work, however, suggesting that she was too hard on women; Martha Southgate of the *Village Voice* found "the absolute dichotomy Campbell perceives between men and women ... disturbing." A few critics pointed out Campbell's lack of emphasis on social context and analysis, which some deemed a drawback, others an advantage. Stated Solanke, "One of the book's main strengths is that the political and social tumult it presents never eclipses the vitality and immediacy of personal experience."

By sharing her story, Campbell gives readers "the opportunity to reflect on our own fathers," mused Melissa Pritchard in Chicago *Tribune Books*, "to appreciate their imperfect, profound impact on our lives." The importance of fathers and other men in girls' lives is in fact "perhaps the crucial message in her book," related Itabari Njeri in the *Los Angeles Times*, "one still not fully understood by society." As Campbell explained to Njeri, "Studies show that girls without that nurturing from a father or surrogate father are likely to grow up with damaged self-esteem and are more likely to have problems with their own adult relationships with men." She hoped that reading her book might inspire more divorced fathers to increase their participation in their children's lives. Reflecting on the flurry of Campbell's talk show appearances, the competition for paperback rights, and the interest shown in the book by film producers, Njeri suggested that she was indeed reaching her audience. Noted the critic, "Campbell's gentle, poignant story about her relationship with her father has struck a nerve."

Campbell also earned praise for her first novel, *Your Blues Ain't Like Mine,* which describes the interracial impact of the murder of a black youth by a Southern white. After the event makes headlines in the North, the murderer is brought to justice, but the event has disrupted both black and white lives. Writing in the *New York Times Book Review,* novelist Clyde Edgerton called it a "powerful first novel," attributing much of its power to the author's ability to convey both sides' perspectives. Campbell "wears the skin and holds in her chest the heart of each of her characters, one after another, regardless of the character's race or sex, response to fear and hate, or need for pity, grace, punishment or peace," asserted Edgerton. *Los Angeles Times Book Review* contributor Veronica Chambers similarly remarked upon Campbell's people, calling them "individuals as complicated as our country's racial history." Both critics commended the author for not oversimplifying issues, and the freshness and vividness of her writing drew additional compliments. Expressing the hope that books such as *Your Blues* could broaden understanding of the psyche and man's capacity for abusing power, Edgerton numbered Campbell among fiction writers who "pierce the shared humanness of Southern blacks *and* whites."

*BIOGRAPHICAL/CRITICAL SOURCES:*

*BOOKS*

Campbell, Bebe Moore, *Sweet Summer: Growing Up with and without My Dad,* Putnam, 1989.

*PERIODICALS*

*Los Angeles Times,* July 25, 1989; December 1, 1989.
*Los Angeles Times Book Review,* September 6, 1992, p. 3.
*New York Times Book Review,* June 11, 1989, p. 47; September 20, 1992, p. 13.
*Publishers Weekly,* June 30, 1989, pp. 82-83.
*Times Literary Supplement,* October 26, 1990, p. 1148.
*Tribune Books* (Chicago), June 18, 1989, p. 7.
*U.S. Catholic,* September, 1987, p. 48.
*Village Voice,* July 4, 1989, p. 63.
*Washington Post Book World,* June 18, 1989, pp. 1, 8.

\*      \*      \*

## CANNON, David Wadsworth, Jr.    1911(?)-1938

*PERSONAL:* Born 1911 (some sources say 1910); died December 14, 1938. *Education:* Hillside College, Michigan, B.S. 1931; University of Michigan, M.A., 1932; Columbia University, Ph.D. candidate, 1937-38.

*CAREER:* Junior State College, Cranford, NJ, instructor of psychology, 1932-36. Member of board of directors of National Council of Religious Education, 1937-38.

*AWARDS, HONORS:* Fellowship to the University of Michigan, 1932; Rosenfeld Fellowship for further study, Columbia University.

*WRITINGS:*

*POETRY*

*Black Labor Chant and Other Poems,* illustrated by John Borican, Association Press, 1940.

Contributor to anthologies, including *The Poetry of the Negro: 1746-1970,* edited by Langston Hughes and Arna Bontemps, and *Ebony Rhythm,* edited by Murphy.

*BIOGRAPHICAL/CRITICAL SOURCES:*

*BOOKS*

Rush, Theressa Gunnels, Carol Fairbanks Myers, and Esther Spring Arata, *Black American Writers Past and Present,* Scarecrow Press, 1975, pp. 136-7.

*PERIODICALS*

*Negro History Bulletin,* April 1940, p. 112.

*OBITUARIES:*

*PERIODICALS*

*New York Times,* December 16, 1938, section 4, p. 25.

\*    \*    \*

## CAREW, Jan (Rynveld)  1925-

*PERSONAL:* Born September 24, 1925 (one source says 1920), in Agricola, British Guiana (now Guyana); son of Charles Alan (a planter) and Kathleen Ethel (Robertson) Carew; married Joan Murray, June 14, 1952 (deceased); married Sylvia Wynter (a writer), c. 1960 (marriage ended July, 1971); married Joy Gleason (a university lecturer), September 28, 1975; children: Lisa St. Aubin, Christopher David, Shantoba. *Education:* Attended Howard University, 1945-46, Western Reserve University (now Case Western Reserve University), 1946-48, and Charles University, Prague, 1949-50; Sorbonne, University of Paris, M.Sc., 1952.

*ADDRESSES: Home*—1910 Orrington Ave., Evanston, IL 60201. *Office*—Department of African American Studies, Northwestern University, 2003 Sheridan Rd., Evanston, IL 60208-0002.

*CAREER:* Teacher, Berbice High School, 1939; customs officer in British Colonial Civil Service, Georgetown, British Guiana (now Guyana), 1940-43; price control officer for government of Trinidad, Port-of-Spain, 1943-44; artist and writer in Paris, France, and Amsterdam, Holland, 1950-51; toured as an actor with Laurence Olivier Company, 1952; University of London, London, England, Extra-Mural Department, lecturer in race relations, 1952-54; British Broadcasting Corp. (BBC) Overseas Service, London, broadcaster, writer and editor, 1952-65; director of culture and adviser to the prime minister of the government of British Guiana, 1962; Latin American correspondent for *London Observer,* 1962; artist and writer under contract to Associated Television (London) on island of Ibiza, Spain, 1963-64; adviser to the publicity secretariat of the government of Ghana, 1965-66; artist and writer, commissioned by Canadian Broadcasting Company (CBC) to do numerous programs in Toronto, Ontario, 1966-69; Princeton University, Princeton, NJ, senior fellow, Council of Humanities, and lecturer in Third World literature and creative writing, 1969-72; Northwestern University, Evanston, IL, professor of African American and Third World studies,

1973-87, professor emeritus, 1987—, chairman of department of African American Studies, 1973-76. Hampshire College, visiting professor, 1986-87; George Mason University, Fairfax, VA, Visiting Clarence J. Robinson Professor, 1989-91; Illinois Wesleyan University, visiting professor of international studies, 1992—. Guest lecturer at Livingston College, Douglass College, and Rutgers University, 1969-72; consultant for English language and literature programs at New York University, 1969-72; guest lecturer at University of Surinam Teacher's Training College, 1975. Exhibitions of paintings at Imperial Institute, London, 1948; Cleveland Public Library, Ohio, 1949; Commonwealth Institute, London, England, 1953. Toured Federal Republic of Germany as an official guest of the Ministry of Culture, 1963 and 1967; toured Soviet Union as a guest of the Soviet Writer's Union, 1963 and 1965. Consultant, National Council of Churches, Fifth Commission, 1975—, Pan African Skills Project, Inc., 1978—, Organization of American States, Cultural Division, 1980—, Field Museum of Natural History, Chicago, IL, 1983—, and Futures Conference Project, 1986—; director of Caribbean Foundation for Rural Development and Education in Surinam, 1975—; advisor on appropriate technology, government of Jamaica, 1976-78; co-founder and co-director, Third World Energy Institute International, 1977—, Caribbean Society for Culture and Science, 1978—, and Jamaica Support Committee, 1980; member of board of directors, Linear Alpha, Inc., 1978—; chairman of executive board, Black Press Institute, 1982—; advisor and member of board of directors, Kindred Spirits Project, 1982—; advisor, Illinois Senate Committee on Higher Education, 1984—.

*MEMBER:* Association of Caribbean Studies (president, 1982—), Caribbean Society for Culture and Science, American Association of University Professors, American Union of Writers, American Association of Retired Persons.

*AWARDS, HONORS: The Big Pride* (television play) was selected as best play of the year by the *London Daily Mirror,* 1964; Canada Arts Council grant, 1969, for significant contributions to the arts; Princeton University summer grantee, 1970-71; Rutgers University summer grantee, 1970-72; Burton International Fellowship, Harvard University Graduate School of Education, 1973 and 1974; Illinois Arts Council award for fiction, 1974, for short story "Ti-Zek"; American Institute of Graphic Arts Certificate of Excellence, 1974, for *The Third Gift;* Jan Carew Annual Lectureship Award established by Princeton University, 1975; Casa de las Americas award for poetry, 1977; Pushcart prize, 1979, for essay "The Caribbean Writer and Exile"; Walter Rodney Award, Association of Caribbean Studies, 1985; National Film Institute Award for screenplay *Black Midas,* 1985; HANSIB Publication award, London, 1990.

*WRITINGS:*

*Streets of Eternity* (poetry), privately printed, 1952.

*Black Midas* (novel), Secker & Warburg, 1958, published as *A Touch of Midas,* Coward, 1958.

*The Wild Coast* (novel), Secker & Warburg, 1958.

*The Last Barbarian* (novel), Secker & Warburg, 1960.

*Moscow Is Not My Mecca* (novel), Secker & Warburg, 1964, published as *Green Winter,* Stein & Day, 1965.

*Cry Black Power,* McClelland & Stewart, 1970.

*Sons of the Flying Wing,* McClelland & Stewart, 1970.

*Rope the Sun,* Third Press, 1973.

(Editor) *Out of Time,* illustrated by Howard Phillips, Adult Basic Education Centre (Cardiff), c. 1975.

*The Twins of Ilora,* Little, Brown, 1977.

*Sea Drums in My Blood* (poetry), New Voices (Trinidad), 1981.

*Indian and African Presence in the Americas,* Georgia State University, 1984.

*Grenada: The Hour Will Strike Again* (history), International Organization of Journalists Press (Czechoslovakia), 1985.

*The Riverman* (novella), Africa World Press, 1987.

*The Sisters* (novella), Africa World Press, 1987.

*Fulcrums of Change: Origins of Racism in the Americas and Other Essays,* Africa World Press, 1988.

*JUVENILE AND YOUNG ADULT*

*The Third Gift,* illustrated by Leo and Diane Dillon, Little, Brown, 1974.

*Stranger than Tomorrow: Three Stories of the Future,* Longman, 1976.

*Save the Last Dance for Me, and Other Stories,* Longman, 1976.

*The Lost Love, and Other Stories,* Longman, 1978.

*The Man Who Came Back,* Longman, 1979.

*The Cat People,* Longman, 1979.

*Children of the Sun,* illustrated by L. and D. Dillon, Little, Brown, 1980.

*Dark Night, Deep Water,* Longman, 1981.

*Dead Man's Creek: Two Stories,* Longman, 1981.

*House of Fear: Two Stories,* Longman, 1981.

*Don't Go Near the Water,* Longman, 1982.

*Time Loop,* Hutchinson Education, 1982.

*Death Comes to the Circus,* Hutchinson Education, 1983.

*PLAYS*

*Miracle in Lime Lane* (adaptation of a play by Coventry Taylor), produced in Spanish Town, Jamaica, 1962.

*The University of Hunger* (three-act), produced in Georgetown, Guyana, at Georgetown Theatre, 1966.

*Gentlemen Be Seated,* produced in Belgrade, Yugoslavia, 1967.

*Black Horse, Pale Rider* (two-act), University of the West Indies Extra-Mural Department, 1970.

*Behind God's Back,* Carifesta, Volume 2, 1975.

Also author of *The Peace Play,* 1987, and *Black Midas* (screenplay).

*TELEVISION PLAYS*

*The Big Pride,* Associated Television, 1963-64.

*The Day of the Fox,* Associated Television, 1963-46.

*Exile from the Sun,* Associated Television, 1963-46.

*The Baron of South Boulevard,* Associated Television, 1963-46.

*No Gown for Peter,* Associated Television, 1963-46.

*The Raiders,* Associated Television, 1963-46.

*The Smugglers,* Associated Television, 1963-46.

*A Roof of Stars,* Associated Television, 1963-46.

*The Conversion of Tiho,* Associated Television, 1963-46.

*Behind God's Back,* Canadian Broadcasting Company, 1969.

*RADIO PLAYS*

*Song of the Riverman,* British Broadcasting Corp. (BBC), 1960-69.

*The Riverman,* BBC, 1960-69.

*The University of Hunger,* BBC, 1960-69.

*The Legend of Nameless Mountain,* BBC, 1960-69.

*Ata,* BBC, 1960-69.

*Anancy and Tiger,* BBC, 1960-69.

*OTHER*

Also author of *The Origins of Racism and Resistance in the Americas,* 1976; *Rape of the Sun-people* (history), 1976; and *The Rape of Paradise,* 1992. Contributor to books, including *Breaklight* (poetry), edited by Andrew Salkey, Hamish Hamilton, 1971; and *Bite In* (poetry), edited by Cecil Gray, Thomas Nelson, 1971. Work represented in several anthologies, including *Stories from the Caribbean,* edited by Andrew Salkey, Elek, 1965; *Island Voices,* edited by Salkey, Liveright, 1970; *West Indian Stories,* edited by Salkey (London), 1971; *New Writing in the Caribbean,* edited by A. J. Seymour, Guyana Lithographic, 1972; *Carifesta Anthology,* edited by Seymour, Guyana Lithographic, 1972; *The Sun's Eye,* edited by Anna Walmsley (London), 1973; *Anthology of Writing in English,* edited by T. Nelson, 1977; and *Expressions of Power in Education: Studies of Class, Gender, and Race,* edited by Edgar B. Gumbert, Georgia State University, 1984. Reviewer for *John O'London's Weekly, Art News and Review* and British Broadcasting Corporation, 1963-64. Contributor of articles, short stories, and essays to periodicals, including *New England Review and Bread Loaf Quarterly, New York Times, Saturday Review, New Statesman, African Review,*

*Listener, Journal of African Civilizations, Black Press Review, New Deliberations, Journal of the Association of Caribbean Studies, Black American Literature Forum, Pacific Quarterly,* and *Race and Class.* Editor of *De Kim* (multi-lingual poetry magazine in Amsterdam), 1951, *Kensington Post* (London newspaper), 1953, and *African Review* (Ghana), 1965-66; publisher of *Cotopax* (a third-world literary magazine), 1969; member of the editorial boards of *Journal of African Civilizations, Obsidian, Caliban, Journal of the Association of Caribbean Studies,* and *Race and Class* (London).

Carew's works have been published in foreign languages including Japanese, Spanish, Russian, and German.

*WORK IN PROGRESS:* A biography of Maurice Bishop, to be published by the International Organization of Journalists Press; *Green Mansions of the Sun,* a novel; *An Anthology of Latin American Writing in Transition; The Destruction of Caribbean Civilization,* a historical account of the first forty years of the Columbian era; *A Study of Three Maroon Wars,* about the Black-Seminole wars in Florida, Palmares, and the Maroon wars in Surinam; *Pageant of the Gods,* a play for the stage.

*ADAPTATIONS: Black Midas* has been adapted for schools by Sylvia Wynter and illustrated by Aubrey Williams, Longman, 1969.

*SIDELIGHTS:* Writer, editor, and educator Jan Carew is a prolific and versatile writer who has lived in South and North America, the Caribbean, Africa, and Europe and whose work includes novels, poetry, plays for theater, television, and radio, screenplays, essays, and books for children and young adults. Much of his work is concerned with the search for identity by colonized peoples; the protagonists of his novels are often educated black men estranged from both the white-dominated cultures in which they have received their formal education and the indigenous cultures of their homelands. Yet Carew defies easy political labels, Kwame Dawes suggests in a discussion of the author in *Fifty Caribbean Writers,* adding that he "may be best described as an iconoclast of political systems and a propagator of unity and singleness of purpose among peoples." While critics sometimes regard the characterization in Carew's novels as weak, Dawes reports, he is noted for his perceptive and convincing evocations of physical environments and the communities that inhabit them.

When asked to comment on the aspiration of Third World peoples and on how he expressed his philosophy of life through his writing, Carew shared the following passages from his novel in progress, *Green Mansions of the Sun:* "His Carib hero, Kai, said that everyone has a place, a piece of terrain, a

spot on earth that was his very own, like the black leopard ... if a hunter tried to kill him, that leopard would find his spot in the forest, and once he found it—look out hunter—for on his turf, he was invincible!

"This was something that Atlassa understood, not just the trappings, but the power to make the lowliest believe in themselves. Atlassa succeeded where no one else had, he began with the most despised, he made us all see ourselves as we really were. After his return, he started out by listening to us. No one had ever listened since Christobal and his cutthroat sailors had been discovered by the Amer-indians on their beaches.... After that, it was a long history of colonizers shouting orders, and the colonized never talking back. After long years of listening, Atlassa showed us new images of ourselves without the distortions."

Passages from Carew's essay, "The Caribbean Writer in Exile," elaborate upon his philosophy. "The Caribbean writer today is a creature balanced between limbo and nothingness, exile abroad and homelessness at home, between the people on the one hand and the creole and the colonizer on the other.... The writer is, therefore, islanded in the midst of marginal tides of sorrow, despair, hope, whirlpools of anxiety, cataracts of rage....

"'All people have a right to share the waters of the River of Life and to drink with their own cups, but our cups have been broken,' laments the Carib poem-hymn. The writer, artist, musician, is directly involved in the creative process of reshaping the broken cups.... Therefore, while we shape exquisite new cups, we must side by side with the disinherited millions of the Third World, confront those who would deny us our fair share of the waters of the River of Life...."

*BIOGRAPHICAL/CRITICAL SOURCES:*

*BOOKS*

Dawes, Kwame, essay in *Fifty Caribbean Writers: A Bio-Bibliographic-Critical Sourcebook,* edited by Daryl Cumber Dance, Greenwood Press, 1986.
Tucker, Martin, editor, *Literary Exile in the Twentieth Century,* Greenwood Press, 1991.

*PERIODICALS*

*British Book News* (children's supplement), autumn, 1982, p. 15.
*Growing Point,* March, 1972, p. 3072.
*Kirkus Reviews,* August 1, 1974, p. 798.
*New York Times Book Review,* June 1, 1980, p. 20.
*Publishers Weekly,* August 19, 1974, p. 85; February 22, 1980, p. 109.

## CARTER, Martin (Wylde) 1927-

*PERSONAL:* Born June 7, 1927 in Georgetown, British Guiana (now Guyana). *Education:* Attended Queens College, Georgetown.

*ADDRESSES: Office*—c/o New Beacon Books, 76 Stroud Green Road, London N4 3EN, England.

*CAREER:* Secretary to superintendent of prisons, British Guiana Civil Service, until 1953; teacher, 1954-59; chief information officer, Booker Group of Companies, 1959-66; Republic of Guyana national government, Minister of Information, 1967-71, United Nations representative, 1966-67; lecturer, Essex University, England, 1975-76; University of Guyana, writer in residence, 1977-81, senior research fellow, 1981—.

*WRITINGS:*

*POETRY*

*The Hill of Fire Glows Red,* Miniature Poets, 1951.
*To a Dead Slave,* privately printed, 1951.
*The Kind Eagle,* privately printed, 1952.
*The Hidden Man,* privately printed, 1952.
*Returning,* privately printed, 1953.
*Poems of Resistance from British Guiana,* Lawrence and Gishart, 1954, republished as *Poems of Resistance,* University of Guyana Press, 1964, republished as *Poems of Resistance from Guyana,* Release, 1979.
*Poems of Succession,* New Beacon, 1977.
*Poems of Affinity, 1978-1980,* Release, 1980.
*Selected Poems,* Demerara, 1989.

Contributor to anthologies, including *Fifty Caribbean Writers,* Greenwood Press, 1986. Contributor to periodicals, including *Kyk-over-al* and *New World Fortnightly.*

*OTHER*

(Editor) *New World: Guyana Independence Issue,* New World Group Associates, Georgetown, 1966.
*Man and Making—Victim and Vehicle* (Edgar Mittelholzer Memorial Lecture), Guyanese National History and Art Council, 1971.
*Creation: Works of Art,* Cariana Press, 1977.

*SIDELIGHTS:* Writing that protests oppression is an important literary form in the developing world and Martin Carter is among the foremost practitioners of the art, particularly in the Caribbean. Born and educated in the colony of British Guiana, Carter was part of the struggles that transformed his country into an independent nation in the middle of the century. His writing, which is full of fury, righteous indignation, and the idealism of rebellion in the attempt to create a better world, reflects the birth of his country. Later in his writing career, Carter's poetry adopted a more philosophic tone, but he continues to be inspired by the problems of his society and its politics.

Carter was born in Georgetown, now the capital of Guyana, in South America. In the early 1950s, he was a clerk in the civil service that Britain created to run its colony, serving as secretary to the superintendent of prisons. He was already involved in the politics of the day; Carter's early poetry traced the development of the revolution in Guyana. In his earliest work, *The Hill of Fire Glows Red* (1951), he wrote, in the poem "The Kind Eagle," as one who sees the colonial status of his country near an end: "I dance on the wall of prison!/It is not easy to be free and bold!"

When the British deposed the legitimately elected government of Cheddi Jagan in 1953, Carter's political involvement led to a three-month jail sentence. Although Carter had previously produced several privately published poetry collections, he was "jailed into poetic eminence," as *Release* critic Paul Singh said in a review of Carter's first work brought out by a publishing house, *Poems of Resistance from British Guiana.* The poems of that work are both darker and more inspired by the turbulence of the times than his earlier pieces. *Poems of Resistance* evokes not hope and idealism but the defiance and determination of a country in the midst of wresting power from a foreign government. The titles of the poems, "This Is the Dark Time My Love," "I Come from the Nigger Yard," "I Clench My Fist," and others, reflect the actual violence of rebelling against the British.

After the Guyanese triumphed over the British and went about constructing a new society, Carter retained his role of poetic interpreter of current events. Alongside his writing, he worked in private industry during the 1960s and later went on to serve in the government. Perhaps as a member of the government, or because the Guyanese political situation grew less and less clearcut in the 1960s and 1970s, critics found Carter's work less focused on the defiance and anger that energized his earlier work. He continued to work for the government, spent the only protracted stay abroad of his life lecturing in England for a year, and joined the faculty at the University of Guyana in Georgetown upon his return in 1977. He released two collections of poetry during this time.

By 1980, the year *Poems of Affinity* was published, Carter saw Guyanese political life differently. In part the book dealt with two murders: that of Catholic priest and activist Father Drake and that of Walter Rodney, a leader in the Working People's Party political party with which Carter was affiliated. Critic Bill Carr called the poems in the book "tragic lyric poetry" in *Release,* and Professor Selwyn Cudjoe, writing in *Dictionary of Literary Biography,* said Carter had become disillusioned: "Most of the images in this collection are those of defeat and despair," Cudjoe wrote. "Carter's terse structure and intensely painful lyrics reflect the sensibilities of a disillusioned person."

Carter's colleague, fellow Guyanese writer Edward Kamau Brathwaite, provides one possible reason for such disillusionment in an essay in *Contemporary Poets:* "Carter, poet of the revolution, has really only himself and the revolution and a hope for the future to sustain his vision." While former colonies like Guyana have in many cases failed to achieve all that their liberators hoped for them, it is perceived that Carter writes to preserve the hopes of their birth into freedom. Lines from his "I Come from the Nigger Yard" demonstrate this: "O it was the heart like this tiny star near to the sorrows/straining against the whole world and the long twilight/spark of man's dream conquering the night."

*BIOGRAPHICAL/CRITICAL SOURCES:*

*BOOKS*

Carter, Martin, *The Hill of Fire Glows Red,* Miniature Poets, 1951.
Carter, *Poems of Resistance from Guyana,* Release, 1979.
*Contemporary Poets,* fifth edition, St. James Press, 1991, pp. 138-139.
Cudjoe, Selwyn R., *Dictionary of Literary Biography,* Volume 117, *Twentieth-Century Caribbean and Black African Writers, First Series,* Gale, 1992, pp. 106-11.
Markham, E. A., editor, *Hinterland: Caribbean Poetry from the West Indies and Britain,* Bloodaxe Press, 1989, pp. 66-71.
Roopnaraine, Rupert, *Web of October: Rereading Martin Carter,* Peepal Tree, 1988.

*PERIODICALS*

*Caliban,* fall-winter 1981, pp. 30-47.
*Caribbean Contact,* August 1977, p. 7.
*Caribbean Quarterly,* June-September 1977, pp. 7-23.
*Jamaica Journal,* June 1972, pp. 40-45.
*Journal of West Indian Literature,* October 1986, pp. 1-12.
*Kyk-over-al,* December 1987, pp. 59-65; December, 1988, pp. 76-81; December 1989, pp. 80-83.
*New Literature Review,* Number 7, 1979, pp. 66-72.
*New Voices,* August 1981, pp. 50-61.
*Release,* first quarter 1978; pp. 5-24; first quarter, 19, pp. 37-41.

## CARTER-HARRISON, Paul
## See HARRISON, Paul Carter

\*　　\*　　\*

## CARTEY, Wilfred (George Onslow) 1931-1992

*PERSONAL:* Born July 19, 1931, in Port-of-Spain, Trinidad, British West Indies; died after a brief illness, March 21, 1992, in New York, NY. *Education:* University of the West Indies, B.A., 1955; Columbia University, M.A., 1956, Ph.D., 1964.

*ADDRESSES: Home*—New York, NY.

*CAREER:* Columbia University, New York City, instructor in Spanish, 1957-62, associate professor of comparative literature, 1963-69, adjunct professor, 1969-92; City College of the City University of New York, New York City, professor of comparative literature, 1969-72, distinguished professor, 1973-79, distinguished professor of black studies, 1979-92; Brooklyn College of the City University of New York, Brooklyn, NY, Martin Luther King Distinguished Professor of Comparative Literature, 1972-73. University of Puerto Rico, visiting scholar and lecturer, summer, 1959; University of Vermont, visiting professor, summer, 1964; University of the West Indies, visiting professor, summer, 1965, resident professor, summer, 1973; University of Ghana, visiting professor, 1967-68; Howard University, visiting distinguished professor of Romance languages, 1976; University of California, Berkeley, visiting distinguished professor of Afro-American studies, spring, 1979.

*MEMBER:* African Studies Association, African Heritage Studies Association, American Association of University Professors, American Friends Service Committee, Association of Black and Puerto Rican Faculty, Hispanic Institute in the U.S., African American Heritage Association, Institute of Caribbean Studies, Modern Language Association of America, PEN, Black Academy of Arts and Letters.

*AWARDS, HONORS:* Bernard Van Leer Foundation Fellow, 1955-56; Fulbright travel grant, 1955-59; urban center grant, 1970; City University of New York Research Foundation fellow, 1985-86; travel and research grant from Columbia University.

*WRITINGS:*

*Some Aspects of African Literature,* University of Vermont, 1964.
*The West Indies: Islands in the Sun* (children's book), Thomas Nelson, 1967.

*Whispers from a Continent: The Literature of Contemporary Black Africa,* Random House, 1969.

(With J. G. Colmen and others) *The Human Uses of the University: Planning a Curriculum in Urban and Ethnic Affairs at Columbia University,* Praeger, 1970.

(With Marlin Kilson) *The African Reader,* Volume 1: *Colonial Africa,* Volume 2: *Independent Africa,* Random House, 1970.

*Palaver: Critical Anthology of African Literature,* Thomas Nelson, 1970.

*Black Images: The Evolution of the Image of the Black Man in the Poetry of Spanish-English-French-Speaking Caribbean, the United States, Latin America, and West Africa,* Teachers College Hall, 1970.

*The House of Blue Lightning* (poems), Emerson Hall, 1973.

*Red Rain,* Emerson Hall, 1977.

*Embryos,* illustrated by Ademola Olugebefola, W. Cartey, 1982.

*Whispers from the Caribbean: I Going Away, I Going Home,* Center for Afro-American Studies, University of California, 1991.

Also author of *Waters of My Soul,* 1975, *Suns and Shadows,* 1978, *Fires in the Wind,* 1980, *The Dawn, the Desert, the Sands, Kundiya,* 1982, *Black Velvet Time,* 1984, *Children of Lalibela,* 1985, and *Potentialities,* 1987. Co-editor of "Documents in Afro-American History" series, Random House, 1970-92. Work represented anthologies, including *The African Experience,* Northwestern University Press, 1968, and *Forum Anthology,* Columbia University Press, 1968. Contributor to *Grolier Encyclopedia, Encyclopedia Americana,* and *Standard Reference Encyclopedia.* Author of introductions for *Negritude: French African and Caribbean Poets,* edited and translated by Norman Shapiro, October House, 1970, *Ambiguous Adventure* by Cheikh Hamidou Kane, Collier Books, 1970, *Black African Voices,* Scott, Foresman, 1970, and *Tell Freedom* by Peter Abrahams, Collier Books, 1970. Contributor of articles and reviews to periodicals, including *Commonwealth, New Republic,* and *Negro Digest.* Literary editor of *African Forum,* 1967-68; member of executive board of *Pan African Journal,* 1970-92; contributing editor of *Confrontation: A Journal of Third World Literature,* 1970-92, and *SAVACOU,* 1970-92.

*SIDELIGHTS:* Wilfred Cartey was an educator, literary critic, author, and poet. Blind since young adulthood, he overcame his handicap by achieving prominence in the fields of African and Caribbean studies. He was in demand as a lecturer, speaking at universities in Puerto Rico, Vermont, Ghana, and the West Indies during his long career. In his final book, *Whispers from the Caribbean: I Going Away, I Going Home,* published the year before his death, Cartey analyzed and critiqued the themes and styles of 70 West Indian novels by 26 authors. "A welcome addition to the limited criticism on Car-

ibbean literature," wrote Joanne Snapp in *Library Journal. Choice* contributor A. L. McLeod called the book "stimulating in its fresh judgements."

*BIOGRAPHICAL/CRITICAL SOURCES:*

*PERIODICALS*

*Best Sellers,* October 1, 1970.
*Black World,* January, 1971.
*Choice,* June, 1992, p. 1539.
*Commonweal,* October 10, 1969.
*English Journal,* May, 1969.
*Journal of Black Studies,* December, 1984.
*Kenyon Review,* Volume 31, number 3, 1969.
*Library Journal,* November 15, 1991, p. 81.
*Saturday Review,* April 17, 1971.
*Times Literary Supplement,* October 1, 1971.
*Washington Post,* June 23, 1978.

*OBITUARIES:*

*PERIODICALS*

*Chicago Tribune,* March 27, 1992, section 3, p. 10.
*New York Times,* March 25, 1992, p. D22.
*Times* (London), March 24, 1992, p. 17.

\*       \*       \*

## CARTIER, Xam Wilson   1949(?)-

*PERSONAL:* Born c. 1949, in St. Louis, MO.

*ADDRESSES: Home*—San Francisco, CA.

*CAREER:* Artist, pianist, dancer, and writer.

*WRITINGS:*

*Be-Bop, Re-Bop* (novel), Available Press/Ballantine, 1987.
*Muse-Echo Blues* (novel), Harmony Books, 1991.

*SIDELIGHTS:* The unnamed black woman who narrates Xam Wilson Cartier's first novel, *Be-Bop, Re-Bop,* recalls significant moments in her childhood and young adulthood and reflects on the liberating presence of jazz in her life. Like her father before her, the narrator finds that cares surrender—at least momentarily—to the lyrics and melodies of black music. "Jazz seems to mirror key elements in black culture: spontaneity, improvisation," related Cartier, "because your situation is always in flux." Discussing *Be-Bop, Re-Bop* in the *New*

*York Times Book Review,* Valerie Smith wrote, "Jazz informs the style as well as the subject of Ms. Cartier's novel. Metaphors and rhymes resonate off one another, off alliterative phrases with all the intensity of an inspired riff." While the critic did find "minor difficulties" in the novel's singular focus ("the easy way in which music alleviates grief and fear and anxiety at times seems simplistically upbeat"), she nevertheless decided that "the power of the language ... is so compelling one can overlook these minor shortcomings." Smith added, "This marvelous first novel ... demonstrate[s] the deep connections between music and narrative."

*BIOGRAPHICAL/CRITICAL SOURCES:*

*PERIODICALS*

*New York Times Book Review,* December 13, 1987, p. 12.

\* \* \*

## CARWELL, L'Ann
### See McKISSACK, Patricia (L'Ann) C(arwell)

\* \* \*

## CARY, Lorene 1956-

*PERSONAL:* Born November 29, 1956, in Philadelphia, PA; daughter of John W. and Carole (Hamilton) Cary; married R. C. Smith, August 27, 1983; children: Laura; stepchildren: Geoffrey. *Education:* Received B.A. from University of Pennsylvania; University of Pennsylvania, M.A., 1978; University of Sussex, M.A., 1979.

*ADDRESSES: Agent*—c/o Alfred A. Knopf, 201 East 50th St., New York, NY 10022.

*CAREER:* Writer.

*WRITINGS:*

*Black Ice* (memoir), Knopf, 1991.

*WORK IN PROGRESS:* A novel about a free black Philadelphia family in 1858.

*SIDELIGHTS:* "A stunning memoir" is the accolade that *New York Times Book Review* contributor Phillp Lopate awards Lorene Cary's first book, *Black Ice.* Cary, the daughter of

African American parents living in Philadelphia, was one of the first black students to study at St. Paul's, an exclusive boarding school in New Hampshire. In *Black Ice* Cary relates the events of the two years that she spent at St. Paul's. Lopate states that Cary "analyzes her younger self's sharp impatience and shame at wanting to leave her parents for St. Paul's beautiful grounds" with "remarkable perspective." Ellen Goodman, writing in the *Los Angeles Times Book Review,* remarks that *Black Ice* is a book about "being black in a quintessentially white world, female in a male environment, scrape-by middle class in a rich world, and nontraditional newcomer in the traditional." And in this painful trip into the mainstream, says Goodman, Cary explores the changes that take place in her life, the questions and doubts that she faced within herself because of her connection with St. Paul's. Talking to Rosemary L. Bray in the *New York Times Book Review,* Cary said that the book was a result of an article she was writing for a magazine about the St. Paul's experience. In interviewing people for this story Cary realized that, as she put it, "I found I couldn't get down and dirty with anybody else's story but my own." She says that writing the book was also cathartic for herself because it "allowed her to make peace with the young girl she had been." Lopate feels that "*Black Ice* is an extraordinarily honest, lively and appealing book" and concludes, "I would be happy to follow this narrator anywhere, and hope that there will be sequels crossing into adulthood."

*BIOGRAPHICAL/CRITICAL SOURCES:*

*PERIODICALS*

*Los Angeles Times Book Review,* March 31, 1991, p. 3.
*New York Times Book Review,* March 31, 1991, p. 7.

\* \* \*

## CASELY-HAYFORD, Adelaide (Smith) 1868-1959

*PERSONAL:* Born in Sierra Leone, 1868; died in Ghana, 1959; married Joseph Ephraim Casely-Hayford (a politician and lawyer); children: Gladys May. *Education:* Attended schools in Sierra Leone, England and Germany.

*CAREER:* Girls Vocational School, Freetown, Sierra Leone, co-founder with sister and teacher, beginning 1897.

*WRITINGS:*

*Memoirs,* West African Review, 1959.

Work represented in books, including *An African Treasury,* edited by Langston Hughes, Pyramid, 1961.

## CASELY-HAYFORD, Gladys May 1904-1950 (Aquah Laluah)

*PERSONAL:* Born May 11, 1904, in Axim, Gold Coast (now Ghana); died of black water fever, October, 1950, in Freetown, Sierra Leone; daughter of Joseph Ephraim (a politician and lawyer) and Adelaide (a teacher and writer; maiden name, Smith) Casely-Hayford. *Education:* Attended schools in Sierra Leone and Wales.

*CAREER:* Girls Vocational School, Freetown, Sierra Leone, teacher. Dancer with jazz band in Berlin, Germany, during 1920s.

*WRITINGS:*

*Take 'um so* (poems), New Era Press (Freetown, Sierra Leone), 1948.

Work represented in books, including *An African Treasury,* edited by Langston Hughes, Pyramid, 1961; *Poems from Black Africa,* edited by Hughes, Indiana University Press, 1963; and *West African Verse,* edited by Donatus Ibe Nwoga, Longmans, 1967. Contributor of poems, sometimes under pseudonym Aquah Laluah, to *West African Review, Atlantic Monthly,* and *Philadelphia Tribune.*

\* \* \*

## CASELY-HAYFORD, J(oseph) E(phraim) 1866-1930

*PERSONAL:* Born in 1866, in the Gold Coast (now Ghana); died in August, 1930; son of a minister; married Adelaide Smith (a teacher and writer); children: Gladys May. *Education:* Attended Fourah Bay College, Sierra Leone; studied law at the Inner Temple, London, and at Peterhouse College, Cambridge.

*CAREER:* Worked as a high school principal in Accra, Gold Coast, as an editor of *Western Echo* and several other newspapers, and as a journalist in Sierra Leone; lawyer, beginning 1896; organizer of National Congress of British West Africa, 1920; member of Ghana Legislative Council, 1927-30.

*WRITINGS:*

*Gold Coast Native Institutions, with Thoughts upon a Healthy Imperial Policy for the Gold Coast and the Ashanti,* Sweet & Maxwell, 1903, reprinted with new introduction by W. E. Abraham, African Publishing, 1970.
*Ethiopia Unbound: Studies in Race Emancipation,* C. M. Phillips, 1911, second edition, with introduction by F. Nnabuenyi Ugonna, Frank Cass, 1969.

*United West Africa,* [London], 1919.
*West African Leadership,* edited by Magnus J. Sampson, Frank Cass, 1951.
*Public Speeches of J. E. Casely-Hayford,* edited by M. J. Sampson, Humanities Press, 1970.

Also author of *Gold Coast Land Tenure and the Forest Bill,* 1911, *The Truth about the West African Land Question,* 1913, *William Waddy Harris, the West African Reformer: The Man and His Message,* 1915, and *The Disabilities of Black Folk and Their Treatment, with an Appeal to the Labour Party,* 1929. Work represented in books, including *A Selection of African Prose,* edited by W. H. Whiteley, Clarendon Press, 1964. Contributor to periodicals, including *Gold Coast Leader.*

*SIDELIGHTS:* A leading precursor of Pan-Africanism, J. E. Casely-Hayford wrote several works which still influence African leaders with their strong arguments for preserving racial heritage. He also served as a member of the first elected legislative body in Ghana's history. Casely-Hayford's *Ethiopia Unbound,* published in 1911, remains his most influential book. Part novel, part autobiography and part political tract, *Ethiopia Unbound* examines the plight of colonized Africa in the early twentieth century and raises the possibility that, like the independent nation of Ethiopia, all African nations could become self-governing. In this and other written works, Casely-Hayford's "main concern always," wrote a reviewer for *West Africa,* "was to assert the value of African tradition and culture."

*Ethiopia Unbound,* F. Nnabuenyi Ugonna wrote in the introduction to that book's second edition, "is a veritable compendium of Casely-Hayford's thoughts on politics, native institutions, race relations, African nationalism and allied subjects." Among topics discussed are Christianity, the future of African education, and the assimilation of Africans into European society. Many of his opinions were remarkable for the time. Casely-Hayford argued strongly for traditional African religions over European Christianity, for separate African studies programs for African-American students, and for the integration of races while maintaining their distinct racial integrity. "*Ethiopia Unbound* is undoubtedly one of the most important contributions to the literature of African nationalism," Ugonna concluded.

*BIOGRAPHICAL/CRITICAL SOURCES:*

BOOKS

*Black Literature Criticism,* Gale, 1992, pp. 343-354.
Casely-Hayford, J. E., *West African Leadership,* edited by Magnus J. Sampson, Frank Cass, 1951.
Dathorne, O. R., *The Black Mind: A History of African Literature,* University of Minnesota Press, 1974, pp. 143-155.

July, Robert W., *The Origins of Modern African Thought: Its Development in West Africa during the Nineteenth and Twentieth Centuries,* Praeger, 1967, pp. 433-457.

Ofosu-Appiah, L. H., *Joseph Ephraim Casely: The Man of Vision and Faith,* Academy of Arts and Sciences, 1975.

Sampson, Magnus J., *Gold Coast Men of Affairs,* Dawsons of Pall Mall, 1969, pp. 160-173.

*Twentieth Century Literary Criticism,* Volume 24, Gale, 1987, pp. 130-139.

*PERIODICALS*

*African Times and Orient Review,* November, 1912, pp. 7-8.

*Ibadan,* Number 29, 1971, pp. 45-52.

*Journal of the Royal Society of Arts,* November, 1974, pp. 837-845.

*Pan-African Journal,* summer, 1974, pp. 111-118.

*UFAHAMU,* Volume 7, number 2, 1977, pp. 159-171.

*United Empire,* January, 1911, pp. 737-738.

*West Africa,* May 30, 1970, p. 585.

\*   \*   \*

## CASEY, Bernard Terry   1939-
### (Bernie Casey)

*PERSONAL:* Born in 1939 in Wyco, WV. *Education:* Bowling Green State University, B.A., M.F.A., 1966.

*CAREER:* Painter, screen actor, writer, and former star flanker back for Los Angeles Rams football team. Co-founder of Negro Industrial and Economic Union; president of Community Arts Foundation. Actor in films, including *The Man Who Fell to Earth,* 1976; *Never Say Never Again,* 1983; and *Steele Justice,* 1987. Has had artwork exhibited at La Jolla Museum of Art, La Jolla, CA, 1970; University of Iowa Museum of Art, 1972; Ankrum Gallery (permanent collection), Los Angeles, CA; John Bolles Gallery, San Francisco, CA.

*WRITINGS:*

*UNDER NAME BERNIE CASEY*

*Look at the People* (poetry), self-illustrated, Doubleday, 1969.

Also author of *My Point of View—Poems and Drawings,* 1971, *You Can Win the Game, if It's Your Turn, In Little Ways, Schizophrenic Moon Folly, White Bird, Some Rainy Days, Saturday's Nightscape, Shadow in the Bright Sun, Barbara,* and *An Excerpt from a Terry Trip.* Contributor to periodicals, including the *Los Angeles Herald* and *Los Angeles Times.*

*BIOGRAPHICAL/CRITICAL SOURCES:*

*BOOKS*

Atkinson, J. Edward, *Black Dimensions in Contemporary Art,* New American Library, 1971, pp. 42-43.

*PERIODICALS*

*American Artist,* February, 1970, p. 70.

*Black World,* September, 1970, pp. 51-52.

*Booklist,* December 1, 1969, p. 432.

*Ebony,* May, 1987, p. 138.

*Kirkus Reviews,* August 1, 1969, p. 813.

*Library Journal,* November 15, 1969, p. 4309; December 1, 1969, p. 4439.

\*   \*   \*

## CASEY, Bernie
### See CASEY, Bernard Terry

\*   \*   \*

## CESAIRE, Aime (Fernand)   1913-

*PERSONAL:* Born June 25, 1913, in Basse-Pointe, Martinique, West Indies; son of Fernand (a comptroller with the revenue service) and Marie (Hermine) Cesaire; married Suzanne Roussi (a teacher), July 10, 1937; children: Jacques, Jean-Paul, Francis, Ina, Marc, Michelle. *Education:* Attended Ecole Normale Superieure, Paris; Sorbonne, University of Paris, licencie es lettres.

*ADDRESSES: Office*—Assemblee Nationale, 75007 Paris, France; and La Mairie, 97200 Fort-de-France, Martinique, West Indies.

*CAREER:* Lycee of Fort-de-France, Martinique, teacher, 1940-45; member of the two French constituent assemblies, 1945-46; mayor of Fort-de-France, 1945; deputy for Martinique in the French National Assembly, 1946. Conseiller general for the fourth canton (district) of Fort-de-France; president of the Parti Progressiste Martiniquais. Founder of magazine *L'Etudiant Noir.*

*MEMBER:* Society of African Culture (Paris; president).

*AWARDS, HONORS: Aime Cesaire: The Collected Poetry* was nominated for the *Los Angeles Times* Book Award, 1984.

*WRITINGS:*

(With Gaston Monnerville and Leopold Sedar-Senghor) *Commemoration du centenaire de l'abolition de l'esclavage: Discours pronounces a la Sorbonne le 27 avril 1948* (title means "Commemoration of the Centenary of the Abolition of Slavery: Speeches Given at the Sorbonne on April 27, 1948"), Presses Universitaires de France, 1948.

*Discours sur le colonialisme,* Reclame, 1950, fifth edition, Presence Africaine (Paris), 1970, translation by Joan Pinkham published as *Discourse on Colonialism,* Monthly Review Press, 1972.

*Lettre a Maurice Thorez,* third edition, Presence Africaine, 1956, translation published as *Letter to Maurice Thorez,* 1957.

*Toussaint L'Ouverture: La revolution francaise et le probleme coloniale* (title means "Toussaint L'Ouverture: The French Revolution and the Colonial Problem"), Club Francais du Livre, 1960, revised edition, Presence Africaine, 1962.

*Ouvres completes* (title means "Complete Works"), three volumes, Editions Desormeaux, 1976.

(Contributor) *Studies in French,* William Marsh Rice University, 1977.

*Culture and Colonization,* University of Yaounde, 1978.

Also author of *Textes,* edited by R. Mercier and M. Battestini, French and European Publications.

*POEMS*

*Les armes miraculeuses* (title means "The Miracle Weapons"; also see below), Gallimard, 1946, reprinted, 1970.

*Soleil Cou-Coupe* (title means "Solar Throat Slashed"), K (Paris), 1948, reprinted (bound with *Antilles a main armee* by Charles Calixte under title *Poems from Martinique*), Kraus, 1970.

*Corps perdu,* illustrations by Pablo Picasso, 1949, translation by Clayton Eshleman and Annette Smith published as *Lost Body,* Braziller, 1986.

*Cahier d'un retour au pays natal,* Presence Africaine, 1956, second edition, 1960, translation by Emil Snyders published as *Return to My Native Land,* Presence Africaine, 1968, translation by John Berger and Anna Bostock published under same title, Penguin Books, 1969.

*Ferrements* (title means "Shackles"; also see below), Editions du Seuil, 1960.

*Cadastre* (also see below), Editions du Seuil, 1961, translation by Gregson Davis published as *Cadastre,* Third Press, 1972, translation by Snyders and Sanford Upson published under same title, Third Press, 1973.

*State of the Union,* translation by Eshleman and Dennis Kelly of selections from *Les armes miraculeuses, Ferrements,* and *Cadastre,* [Bloomington, IL], 1966.

*Aime Cesaire: The Collected Poetry,* translation and with an introduction by Eshleman and Smith, University of California Press, 1983.

*Non-Vicious Circle: Twenty Poems,* translation by Davis, Stanford University Press, 1985.

*Lyric and Dramatic Poetry, 1946-82* (includes English translations of *Et les Chiens se taisaient* and *Moi, laminaire*), translation by Eshleman and Smith, University Press of Virginia, 1990.

Also author of *Moi, laminaire.*

*PLAYS*

*Et les Chiens se Taisaient: Tragedie* (title means "And the Dogs Were Silent: A Tragedy"), Presence Africaine, 1956.

*La tragedie du roi Christophe,* Presence Africaine, 1963, revised edition, 1973, translation by Ralph Manheim published as *The Tragedy of King Christophe,* Grove, 1970.

*Une saison au Congo,* Editions du Seuil, 1966, translation by Manheim published as *A Season in the Congo* (produced in New York at the Paperback Studio Theatre, July, 1970), Grove, 1969.

*Une tempete: d'apres "le tempete" de Shakespeare. Adaptation pour un theatre negre,* Editions du Seuil, 1969, translation by Richard Miller published as *A Tempest,* Ubu Repertory, 1986.

*OTHER*

Editor of *Tropiques,* 1941-45, and of *L'Afrique.*

*SIDELIGHTS:* Because of his role in creating and promoting negritude, a cultural movement which calls for black people to renounce Western society and adopt the traditional values of black civilization, Aime Cesaire is a prominent figure among blacks in the Third World. A native of the Caribbean island of Martinique, where he has served as mayor of the city of Fort-de-France since 1945, Cesaire also enjoys an international literary reputation for his poems and plays. His 1,000-line poem *Return to My Native Land,* a powerful piece written in extravagant, surreal language and dealing with the reawakening of black racial awareness, is a major work in contemporary French-language literature. Cesaire is, Serge Gavronsky states in the *New York Times Book Review,* "one of the most powerful French poets of this century."

At the age of 18 Cesaire left his native Martinique, at that time a colony of France, to attend school in Paris. The city was the center for a number of political and cultural movements during the 1930s, several of which especially influenced the young Cesaire and his fellow black students. Marxism gave them a revolutionary perspective, while surrealism provided them with a modernist esthetic by which to express themselves. Together with Leon-Goutran Damas and Leopold Sedar Senghor, who later became president of Senegal, Cesaire founded the magazine *L'Etudiant Noir,* in which the ideology of negritude was first developed and explained. "Negritude ... proclaimed a pride in black culture and, in turning their contemporaries' gaze away from the fascination of things French, these young students began a revolution in attitudes which was to make a profound impact after the war," Clive Wake explains in the *Times Literary Supplement.* The influence of the movement on black writers in Africa and the Caribbean was so pervasive that the term negritude has come to refer to "large areas of black African and Caribbean literature in French, roughly from the 1930s to the 1960s," Christopher Miller writes in the *Washington Post Book World.*

The first use of the word negritude occurred in Cesaire's poem *Return to My Native Land* (*Cahier d'un retour au pays natal*), first published in the magazine *Volontes* in 1939. In this poem, Cesaire combines an exuberant wordplay, an encyclopedic vocabulary, and daring surreal metaphors with bits of African and Caribbean black history to create an "exorcism ... of the poet's 'civilized' instincts, his lingering shame at belonging to a country and a race so abject, servile, petty and repressed as is his," Marjorie Perloff writes in the *American Poetry Review.* Gavronsky explains that the poem "is a concerted effort to affirm [Cesaire's] stature in French letters by a sort of poetic one-upmanship but also a determination to create a new language capable of expressing his African heritage." *Return to My Native Land,* Perloff maintains, is "a paratactic catalogue poem that piles up phrase upon phrase, image upon image, in a complex network of repetitions, its thrust is to define the threshold between sleep and waking— the sleep of oppression, the blind acceptance of the status quo, that gives way to rebirth, to a new awareness of what is and may be."

Written as Cesaire himself was leaving Paris to return to Martinique, *Return to My Native Land* reverberates with both personal and racial significance. The poet's definition of his own negritude comes to symbolize the growing self-awareness of all blacks of their cultural heritage. Judith Gleason, writing in the *Negro Digest,* believes that Cesaire's poetry is "grounded in the historical sufferings of a chosen people" and so "his is an angry, authentic vision of the promised land." Jean Paul Sartre, in an article for *The Black American Writer: Poetry and Drama,* writes that "Cesaire's words do not describe negritude, they do not designate it, they do not copy it from the outside like a painter with a model: they create it; they compose it under our very eyes."

Several critics see Cesaire as a writer who embodies the larger struggles of his people in all of his poetry. Hilary Okam of *Yale French Studies,* for example, argues that "Cesaire's poetic idiosyncracies, especially his search for and use of uncommon vocabulary, are symptomatic of his own mental agony in the search for an exact definition of himself and, by extension, of his people and their common situation and destiny." Okam concludes that "it is clear from [Cesaire's] use of symbols and imagery, that despite years of alienation and acculturation he has continued to live in the concrete reality of his Negro-subjectivity." Writing in the *CLA Journal,* Ruth J. S. Simmons notes that although Cesaire's poetry is personal, he speaks from a perspective shared by many other blacks. "Poetry has been for him," Simmons explains, "an important vehicle of personal growth and self-revelation, [but] it has also been an important expression of the will and personality of a people.... [It is] impossible to consider the work of Cesaire outside of the context of the poet's personal vision and definition of his art. He defines his past as African, his present as Antillean and his condition as one of having been exploited.... To remove Cesaire from this context is to ignore what he was and still is as a man and as a poet."

The concerns found in *Return to My Native Land* ultimately transcend the personal or racial, addressing liberation and self-awareness in universal terms. Gleason calls *Return to My Native Land* "a masterpiece of cultural relevance, every bit as 'important' as 'The Wasteland,' its remarkable virtuosity will ensure its eloquence long after the struggle for human dignity has ceased to be viewed in racial terms." Andre Breton, writing in *What Is Surrealism?: Selected Writings,* also sees larger issues at stake in the poem. "What, in my eyes, renders this protest invaluable," Breton states, "is that it continually transcends the anguish which for a black man is inseparable from the lot of blacks in modern society, and unites with the protest of every poet, artist and thinker worthy of the name ... to embrace the entire intolerable though amendable condition created for *man* by this society."

Cesaire's poetic language was strongly influenced by the French surrealists of the 1930s, but he uses familiar surrealist poetic techniques in a distinctive manner. Breton claims that Cesaire "is a black man who handles the French language as no white man can handle it today." Alfred Cismaru states in *Renascence* that Cesaire's "separation from Europe makes it possible for him to break with clarity and description, and to become intimate with the fundamental essence of things. Under his powerful, poetic eye, perception knows no limits and pierces appearances without pity. Words emerge and explode like firecrackers, catching the eye and the imagination of the reader. He makes use of the entire dictionary, of artificial and vulgar words, of elegant and forgotten ones, of technical and invented vocabulary, marrying it to Antillean and African syllables, and allowing it to play freely in a sort of flaming folly that is both a challenge and a tenacious attempt at mystification."

The energy of Cesaire's poetic language is seen by some critics as a form of literary violence, with the jarring images and forceful rhythms of the poetry assaulting the reader. Perloff finds that Cesaire's "is a language so violently charged with meaning that each word falls on the ear (or hits the eye) with resounding force." Gleason explains this violence as the expression of an entire race, not just of one man: "Cesaire's is the turbulent poetry of the spiritually dislocated, of the damned. His images strike through the net.... Cesaire's is the Black Power of the imagination."

This violent energy is what first drew Cesaire to surrealism. The surrealist artists and writers of the 1930s saw themselves as rebels against a stale and outmoded culture. Their works were meant to revive and express unconscious, suppressed, and forbidden desires. Politically, they aligned themselves with the revolutionary left. As Gavronsky explains, "Cesaire's efforts to forge a verbal medium that would identify him with the opposition to existing political conditions and literary conventions [led him to] the same camp as the Surrealists, who had combined a new poetics that liberated the image from classical restraints with revolutionary politics influenced by Marx and his followers." Cesaire was to remain a surrealist for many years, but he eventually decided that his political concerns would best be served by more realistic forms of writing. "For decades," Karl Keller notes in the *Los Angeles Times Book Review*, "[Cesaire] found the surreal aesthetically revolutionary, but in the face of the torture and the suffering, he has pretty well abandoned it as a luxury."

In the late 1950s Cesaire began to write realistic plays for the theatre, hoping in this way to attract a larger audience to his work. These plays are more explicitly political than his poetry and focus on historical black nationalist leaders of the Third World. *The Tragedy of King Christophe* (*La tragedie du roi Christophe*) is a biographical drama about King Henri Christophe of Haiti, a black leader of that island nation in the early nineteenth century. After fighting in a successful revolution against the French colonists, Christophe assumed power and made himself king. But his cruelty and arbitrary use of power led to a rebellion in turn against his own rule, and Christophe committed suicide. Writing in *Studies in Black Literature*, Henry Cohen calls *The Tragedy of King Christophe* "one of French America's finest literary expressions." *A Season in the Congo* (*Une saison au Congo*) follows the political career of Patrice Lumumba, first president of the Republic of the Congo in Africa. Lumumba's career was also tragic. With the independence of the Congo in 1960, Lumumba became president of the new nation. But the resulting power struggles among black leaders led in 1961 to Lumumba's assassination by his political opponents. The reviewer for *Prairie Schoo-*

ner calls *A Season in the Congo* "a passionate and poetic drama." Wake remarks that Cesaire's plays have "greatly widened [his] audience and perhaps tempted them to read the poetry." Gavronsky claims that "in the [1960s, Cesaire] was ... the leading black dramatist writing in French."

Despite the international acclaim he has received for his poetry and plays, Cesaire is still best known on Martinique for his political career. Since 1945 he has served as mayor of Fort-de-France and as a member of the French National Assembly. For the first decade of his career Cesaire was affiliated with the Communist bloc of the assembly, then moved to the Parti du Regroupement Africain et des Federalistes for a short time, and is now president of the Parti Progressiste Martiniquais, a leftist political organization. Cesaire's often revolutionary rhetoric is in sharp contrast to his usually moderate political actions. He opposes independence for Martinique, for example, and was instrumental in having the island declared an oversea department of France—a status similar to that of Puerto Rico to the United States. And as a chief proponent of negritude, which calls for blacks to reject Western culture, Cesaire nonetheless writes his works in French, not in his native black language of creole.

But what may seem contradictory in Cesaire's life and work is usually seen by critics as the essential tension that makes his voice uniquely important. A. James Arnold, in his *Modernism and Negritude: The Poetry and Poetics of Aime Cesaire,* examines and accepts the tension between Cesaire's European literary sources and his black subject matter and between his modernist sensibility and his black nationalist concerns. Miller explains that "Arnold poses the riddle of Cesaire with admirable clarity" and "effectively defuses ... either a wholly African or a wholly European Cesaire." This uniting of the European and African is also noted by Clayton Eshleman and Annette Smith in their introduction to *Aime Cesaire: The Collected Poetry.* They describe Cesaire as "a bridge between the twain that, in principle, should never meet, Europe and Africa.... It was by borrowing European techniques that he succeeded in expressing his Africanism in its purest form." Similarly, Sartre argues that "in Cesaire, the great surrealist tradition is realized, it takes on its definitive meaning and is destroyed: surrealism—that European movement—is taken from the Europeans by a Black man who turns it against them and gives it vigorously defined function."

It is because of his poetry that Cesaire is primarily known worldwide, while in the Third World he is usually seen as an important black nationalist theoretician. Speaking of his poetry, Gavronsky explains that Cesaire is "among the major French poets of this century." Cismaru believes that Cesaire "is a poet's poet when he stays clear of political questions, a tenacious and violent propagandist when the theme requires it. His place in contemporary French letters ... is assured in spite of the fact that not many agree with his views on Whites in general, nor with his opinions on Europe, in particular." *Return to My Native Land* has been his most influential work, particularly in the Third World where, Wake notes, "by the 1960s it was widely known and quoted because of its ideological and political significance."

To European and American critics, *Return to My Native Land* is seen as a masterpiece of surrealist literature. Cesaire's coining of the term negritude and his continued promotion of a distinctly black culture separate from Western culture has made him especially respected in the emerging black nations. Eshleman and Smith report that "although Cesaire was by no means the sole exponent of negritude, the word is now inseparable from his name, and largely responsible for his prominent position in the Third World."

*BIOGRAPHICAL/CRITICAL SOURCES:*

*BOOKS*

*Aime Cesaire: Ecrivain Martiniquais,* Fernand Nathan, 1967.

Antoine, R., *Le Tragedie du roi Christophe d'Aime Cesaire,* Pedagogie Moderne, 1984.

Arnold, A. James, *Modernism and Negritude: The Poetry and Poetics of Aime Cesaire,* Harvard University Press, 1981.

Bigsby, C. W. E., editor, *The Black American Writer: Poetry and Drama,* Volume 2, Penguin Books, 1971.

Bouelet, Remy Sylvestre, *Espaces et dialectique du heros cesairien,* L'Harmattan, 1987.

Breton, Andre, *What Is Surrealism?: Selected Writings,* edited by Franklin Rosemont, Monad Press, 1978.

*Contemporary Literary Criticism,* Gale, Volume 19, 1981, Volume 32, 1985.

Eshleman, Clayton, and Annette Smith, translators and authors of introduction, *Aime Cesare: The Collected Poetry,* University of California Press, 1983.

Kesteloot, Lilyan, *Aime Cesaire,* P. Seghers, 1962, new edition, 1970.

Leiner, Jacqueline, *Soleil eclate: Melanges offerts a Aime Cesaire a l'occasion de son soixante-dixieme anniversaire par une equipe internationale d'artiste et de chercheurs,* Gunter Narr Verlag (Tubingen), 1985.

Ngal, M., editor, *Cesaire 70,* Silex, 1985.

Owusu-Sarpong, Albert, *Le Temps historique dans l'oeuvre theatrale a'Aime Cesaire,* Naaman, 1987.

Pallister, Janis L., *Aime Cesaire,* Twayne, 1991.

Scharfman, Ronnie Leah, *Engagement and the Language of the Subject in the Poetry of Aime Cesaire,* University Presses of Florida, 1980.

Songolo, Aliko, *Aime Cesaire: Une Poetique de la decouverte,* L'Harmattan, 1985.

*PERIODICALS*

*Afro-Hispanic Review,* January, 1985, p. 1.

*American Poetry Review,* January-February, 1984.

*Callaloo,* summer, 1989, p. 612.

*Choice,* March, 1991, p. 1141.

*CLA Journal,* March, 1976; September, 1984; December, 1986.

*Comparative Literature Studies,* summer, 1978.

*Concerning Poetry,* fall, 1984.

*Culture et Developpement,* Volume 15, number 1, 1983, pp. 57-63.

*Diagonales,* October 12, 1989, pp. 5-6.

*French Studies Bulletin,* 1990.

*Journal of Ethnic Studies,* spring, 1981.

*Journal of West Indian Literature,* October, 1986; June, 1987.

*La Licorne,* Number 9, 1985, pp. 153-160.

*Le Monde,* December, 1981.

*L'Esprit Createur,* spring, 1992, p. 110.

*Los Angeles Times Book Review,* December 4, 1983.

*Negro Digest,* January, 1970.

*New Scholar,* Number 8, 1982, pp. 1-2.

*New York Times Book Review,* February 19, 1984.

*Notre Librairie,* Number 74, 1984, pp. 9-13.

*Prairie Schooner,* spring, 1972.

*Quadrant,* November, 1984, pp. 50-53.

*Renascence,* winter, 1974.

*Revue de Litterature Comparee,* April/June, 1986.

*Revue Francophone de Louisiane,* spring, 1988, p. 1.

*San Francisco Review of Books,* Volume 15, number 3, 1990, p. 36.

*Studies in Black Literature,* winter, 1974.

*Studies in the Humanities,* June, 1984.

*Times Literary Supplement,* July 19, 1985.

*Twentieth Century Literature,* July, 1972.

*Washington Post Book World,* February 5, 1984.

*Yale French Studies,* Number 53, 1976.

\* \* \*

## CHASE-RIBOUD, Barbara (Dewayne Tosi) 1939-

*PERSONAL:* Surname is pronounced Chase-Ri-boo; born June 26, 1939, in Philadelphia, PA; daughter of Charles Edward (a building contractor) and Vivian May (a medical assistant; maiden name, West) Chase; married Marc Eugene Riboud (a photojournalist), December 25, 1961; divorced, 1981; married Sergio Tosi (an art expert, publisher, and historian), 1981; children: (first marriage) David Charles, Alexei Karol. *Education:* Temple University, B.F.A., 1957; Yale University, M.F.A., 1960.

*ADDRESSES: Home*—3 rue Auguste Comte, 75006 Paris, France. *Agent*—Mitch Douglas and Herb Chayette, International Creative Management, 40 West 57th St., New York, NY 10019.

*CAREER:* Sculptor, poet, and novelist. State department lecturer in Senegal, Mali, Ghana, Tunisia, and Sierra Leone, 1975. Chairman of the board, Hessmayling Corporation, Brussels, Belgium, 1983-1990; boardmember, La Napoule Art Foundation, La Napoule, France.

Personal shows at Cadran Solaire, Paris, France, 1966, Bertha Schaefer Gallery, New York City, February, 1970, Massachusetts Institute of Technology, Cambridge, MA, April 1970, Betty Parsons Gallery, New York City, March-April, 1972, University Museum, Berkeley, CA, January, 1973, Leslie Rankrow Gallery, New York City, April, 1973, Detroit Institute of Art, Detroit, MI, May, 1973, Indianapolis Art Museum, Indianapolis, IN, August, 1973, Museum of Modern Art, Paris, April-June, 1974, Kunsthalle, Baden-Baden, West Germany, September, 1974, Kunstmuseum, Dusseldorf, West Germany, October, 1974, Merian Gallery, Krefeld, West Germany, November, 1974, United States Cultural Center, Tunis, Tunisia, March, 1975, United States Cultural Center, Dakar, Senegal, April, 1975, United States Cultural Center, Tehran, Iran, December, 1975, Kunstmuseum, Freiburg, West Germany, January, 1976, and Musee Reattu, Arles, France, July-September, 1976.

Work exhibited in group shows, including "Festival of Two Worlds," Spoleto, Italy, 1957, "International Exhibition of Painting and Sculpture," Carnegie Institute, Pittsburgh, PA, 1959, "New York Architectural League Selection," Commercial Museum, Philadelphia, PA, 1965, "Premier Festival des Arts Negres," Dakar, Senegal, 1966, "Festival d'Avignon," Avignon, France, 1969, "Afro-American Artist," Boston Museum of Fine Arts, Boston, MA, 1970, "Two Generations," Newark Museum of Art, Newark, NJ, 1971, "Contemporary Black Artists," Whitney Museum of Art, New York City, 1971, "Annual Exhibition of Sculpture," Whitney Museum of Art, New York City, 1971, Salon de Mai, Paris, 1971-72, Salon des Nouvelles Realities, Paris, 1971-72, "Gold," Metropolitan Museum of Art, New York City, 1973, "Sculpture as Jewelry as Sculpture," Institute of Contemporary Art, Boston, MA, 1973, "Internationaler Markt fur Aktuelle Kunst," Dusseldorf, West Germany, 1973, "Women's Art: American Art 74," Philadelphia Civic Museum, Philadelphia, PA, 1974, "Masterworks of the 70's: Jewelers and Weavers," Albright-Knox Art Gallery, Buffalo, NY, 1974, "Documenta 77," Kessel, West Germany, 1977, and those at the Museum of Contemporary Crafts, New York City, 1977, and Renwick Gallery, Smithsonian Institution, Washington, DC, 1977.

Work represented in permanent collections including those at the Centre Pompidou, Paris, Museum of Modern Art, New York City, Metropolitan Museum of Art, New York City, University Museum, Berkeley, CA, Newark Museum, Newark, NJ, Lannon Foundation, Palm Springs, FL, Centre National des Arts Contemporains, Paris, Geigy Foundation, New York City, Philadelphia art Alliance, Philadelphia, PA, and Schoenburg Collection, New York Public Library, New York City. Has appeared in documentaries and interviews for film and television, including the television show *Sixty Minutes,* Columbia Broadcasting System (CBS), May, 1979.

*AWARDS, HONORS:* John Hay Whitney Foundation fellowship, 1957-58, for study at the American Academy in Rome; National Endowment for the Arts fellowship, 1973; first prize in the New York City Subway Competition, 1973, for architecture; U.S. State Department traveling grant, 1975; named Academic of Italy with gold medal, 1978, for sculpture and drawing; Janet Heidinger Kafka Prize, 1979, for best novel by an American woman; Carl Sandberg Poetry Prize for best poet, 1988; honorary doctorate from Temple University, 1981, and from Muhlenberg College, 1993.

*WRITINGS:*

POETRY

*From Memphis and Peking,* Random House, 1974.
*Portrait of a Nude Woman as Cleopatra,* Morrow, 1987, published as *Nu, comme Cleopatra,* Editions Felin (Paris), 1994.

NOVELS

*Sally Hemings,* Viking, 1979, revised edition, Random House, 1994.
*Valide: A Novel of the Harem,* Morrow, 1986.
*Echo of Lions,* Morrow, 1989.
*The President's Daughter,* Random House, 1994.

*Sally Hemings, Valide,* and *Echo of Lions* have all been published internationally and have been translated into eight languages.

*SIDELIGHTS:* Fascinated by Fawn Brodie's biography *Thomas Jefferson: An Intimate History,* which touches on the relationship between the U.S. president and his alleged mistress Sally Hemings, a quadroon slave, internationally known sculptress Barbara Chase-Riboud decided to research the couple herself. The result of Chase-Riboud's efforts is her 1979 best-selling historical novel, *Sally Hemings.* Although little information on Hemings's life and her relationship with Jefferson exists, Chase-Riboud's findings reaffirmed the suspicion that Jefferson was Hemings's lover and the father of her seven children. Chase-Riboud's research also allowed her to construct a rough outline of Hemings's life, beginning with the slave's employment in Jefferson's Paris household. To this, Chase-Riboud "added imagination," explained Jacqueline Trescott in the *Washington Post*. "She walked the same streets of Paris, scoured American and French libraries," trying to recreate the experiences and emotions of Hemings, continued Trescott, "and ended up with a tender story of a faithful, sometimes ambiguous woman."

In *Sally Hemings*, Chase-Riboud endeavored to present the Hemings-Jefferson relationship from various angles, exploring some of its sociological, political, and emotional implications for all races, both sexes, and the United States as a whole. Although Marcy Heidish of the *Washington Post* noted that *Sally Hemings*'s narrative thread is "uneven [and its] recurring changes in voice and chronology tend to blur the book's focus and power, disrupting the narrative flow and the reader's empathy with the characters," the consensus of reviewers was positive. The *New York Times*'s John Russell, for example, lauded Chase-Riboud's ability to portray life in Hemings's time from different points of view. "The slave world," Russell explained, "is made vivid to us in terms of physical and psychic hardship alike. The scenes of high life, whether in Monticello or in Paris, are as succinct as they are deft.... [Chase-Riboud] is everywhere on top of her material."

The Hemings-Jefferson story intrigued Chase-Riboud because of its complexity and because she saw in it a union of black and white American history. As Chase-Riboud explained to Susan McHenry of *Ms.*, "what struck me were the very complicated and convoluted relationships between those two families—the 'black' Hemingses and the 'white' Jeffersons. That's typically American." Yet, according to Chase-Riboud, "America perceives itself as a white man's country, and this has nothing to do with reality.... There *has* to be a kind of synthesis between 'black' experience and 'white' experience in America, because they are the same."

"One of the interesting things about *Sally Hemings*," Chase-Riboud commented, "was its success internationally, with 3.5 million copies sold worldwide—almost three million of which sold overseas in France, Belgium, Italy, etc. It was one of the first 'cross-over' black books of the 1980s."

In addition to garnering critical praise, *Sally Hemings* became the focus of a precedent-setting legal battle. In 1991 the playwright Granville Burgess wrote *Dusky Sally*, a dramatization of the relationship between Hemings and Jefferson. Chase-Riboud, however, felt that much of Burgess' story was based not upon history but upon her own interpretation of the story, as related in her novel. Hemings sued Burgess for copyright infringement. She explained in the *New York Times:* "When you make a big leap of imagination based on historical events,

it's not fair that this kind of imaginative effort pass into the public domain just because historical figures are involved." Though Burgess argued that he used historical sources—not Chase-Riboud's novel—as the basis for his play, a Pennsylvania judge upheld Chase-Riboud's claim that her interpretation of history was copyrighted. "The copyright laws were not enacted to inhibit creativity," the judge, as quoted in the *New York Times,* said. "But it is one thing to inhibit creativity and another thing ... to maintain that the protection of copyright law is negated by any small amount of tinkering with another writer's idea that results in a different expression."

Chase-Riboud further explored the black slave's experience in America in her historical novel *Echo of Lions.* Based on the true story of a rebellion staged by a group of Africans brought to America on a slave ship known as the *Amistad,* the novel recounts the experiences the group's leader, a Mende warrior later given the name of Joseph Cinque, who, along with several others, attempted to sail the slave ship back to Africa. Unintentionally, the crew landed the vessel in Long Island, New York, where the mutineers were captured and forced to spend the next two years imprisoned while a controversial court battle ensued; eventually the men were allowed to return to Africa. Chase-Riboud's depiction of the event received mixed reviews. While most critics found her subject matter of interest and her descriptions of the slave ships and trade vivid and convincing, some argued that the characters lack adequate development and that the narrative's structure is disjointed. Martha Southgate, in the *New York Times Book Review,* observed that Chase-Riboud "partially succeeds in conveying the unrelenting horror of the Middle Passage, but as the story proceeds [her] attempts to give the story an epic feel too often result in overblown and awkward prose." Gary Nash, on the other hand, in a review for the *Los Angeles Times Book Review,* praised Chase-Riboud for her re-creation, finding it "as personal and vividly horrific as words have been able to render this dark chapter in human history."

Calling the United States a "mulatto country," the author explained in an *International Herald Tribune* article by Flora Lewis that racial "mixing began [in the United States] when the races collided in the 17th century." According to Lewis, Chase-Riboud believes that "white, as a racial word, was invented by the colonists who wanted to distinguish themselves from the natives they found in America and the Africans they brought." And interracial mixing remains "the last taboo, which has to be faced," concluded Chase-Riboud.

The issues and concerns Chase-Riboud raises in her writings and political views are often reflected in her artwork. For instance, in her drawing and her metal and textile sculpture, Chase-Riboud is attracted to what she calls the theme of the couple, the combination of opposites. She is drawn to it, she explained to McHenry, because it is "banal and impossible, the need to join opposing forces: male/female, negative/positive, black/white." Despite the impossibility of merging these forces, Chase-Riboud feels there are harmonious ways for races, sexes, and individuals to influence each other, much as colors and materials influence one another in her art. As McHenry noted, what Chase-Riboud calls "'the metaphysics of color' gives the lie to the myth of race and to the destructive reality of racism through an essentially feminist and humanist acceptance of human diversity." "There are differences," Chase-Riboud commented to McHenry, concerning the races' experiences, "but there is no escape from the influence of one to the other, from their interrelation and interlocking," much as, in the prismatic scale, "one color relates to another, takes on its attributes as they touch." Indeed, Chase-Riboud remarked in the *International Herald Tribune* article, "white and black mean nothing by themselves, only in relation to each other."

*BIOGRAPHICAL/CRITICAL SOURCES:*

*PERIODICALS*

*Chicago Tribune,* July 3, 1979.
*Christian Science Monitor,* March 22, 1989, p. 13.
*International Herald Tribune,* October 26, 1979.
*Los Angeles Times Book Review,* June 18, 1989, p. 12.
*Ms.,* October, 1980; November, 1989, p. 40.
*National Review,* December 21, 1979.
*New Republic,* July 7, 1979.
*New York Times,* September 5, 1979; August 15, 1991.
*New York Times Book Review,* October 28, 1979: May 14, 1989, p. 22.
*People,* October 8, 1979.
*Washington Post,* June 15, 1979.
*Washington Post Book World,* February 26, 1989, p. 8.

\*   \*   \*

# CHILDRESS, Alice 1920-

*PERSONAL:* Surname is pronounced "*Chil*-dress"; born October 12, 1920, in Charleston, SC; married second husband, Nathan Woodard (a musician), July 17, 1957; children: (first marriage) Jean. *Education:* Attended public schools in New York, NY.

*ADDRESSES: Home*—New York, NY. *Office*—-Beacon Press, 25 Beacon St., Boston, MA 02108. *Agent*—-Flora Roberts, Inc., 157 West 57th St., Penthouse A, New York, NY 10019.

*CAREER:* Playwright, novelist, actress, and director. Began career in theater as an actress, with her first appearance in *On Strivers Row,* 1940; actress and director with American Negro Theatre, New York City, for eleven years; played in *Natural Man,* 1941, *Anna Lucasta,* 1944, and her own play *Florence* (which she also directed), 1949; has also performed on Broadway and television. Lecturer at universities and schools; member of panel discussions and conferences on Black American theatre at numerous institutions, including New School for Social Research, 1965, and Fisk University, 1966; visiting scholar at Radcliffe Institute for Independent Study (now Mary Ingraham Bunting Institute), Cambridge, MA, 1966-68. Member of governing board of Frances Delafield Hospital.

*MEMBER:* PEN, Dramatists Guild (member of council), American Federation of Television and Radio Artists, Writers Guild of America East (member of council), Harlem Writers Guild, Actors Equity Association, Society of Stage Directors and Choreographers, Inc., Authors Guild.

*AWARDS, HONORS:* Obie Award for best original Off-Broadway play, *Village Voice,* 1956, for *Trouble in Mind;* John Golden Fund for Playwrights grant, 1957; Rockefeller grant, 1967; *A Hero Ain't Nothin' but a Sandwich* was named one of the Outstanding Books of the Year by *New York Times Book Review,* 1973, and a Best Young Adult Book of 1975 by American Library Association; Woodward School Book Award, 1974, Jane Addams Children's Book Honor Award for young adult novel, 1974, National Book Award nomination, 1974, and Lewis Carroll Shelf Award, University of Wisconsin, 1975, all for *A Hero Ain't Nothin' but a Sandwich;* named honorary citizen of Atlanta, GA, 1975, for opening of *Wedding Band;* Sojourner Truth Award, National Association of Negro Business and Professional Women's Clubs, 1975; Virgin Islands film festival award for best screenplay, 1977, for *A Hero Ain't Nothin' but a Sandwich;* first Paul Robeson Award for Outstanding Contributions to the Performing Arts, Black Filmmakers Hall of Fame, 1977, for *A Hero Ain't Nothin' but a Sandwich;* "Alice Childress Week" officially observed in Charleston and Columbia, SC, 1977, to celebrate opening of *Sea Island Song;* Pulitzer Prize nomination, 1979, for *A Short Walk;* Paul Robeson Award, Actors Equity Association, 1980; *Rainbow Jordan* was named one of the "Best Books" by *School Library Journal,* 1981, one of the Outstanding Books of the Year by *New York Times,* 1982, and a notable children's trade book in social studies by National Council for the Social Studies and Children's Book Council, 1982; honorable mention, Coretta Scott King Award, 1982, for *Rainbow Jordan;* Achievement Award, National Association of Negro Business and Professional Women; Outstanding Pioneer Award, Audience Development Committee, Inc. (Audelco); Afrikan Poetry Theatre Award.

*WRITINGS:*

*Like One of the Family: Conversations from a Domestic's Life,* Independence Publishers, 1956, reprinted with an introduction by Trudier Harris, Beacon Press, 1986.

(Editor) *Black Scenes* (collection of scenes from plays written by Afro-Americans about the Black experience), Doubleday, 1971.

*A Hero Ain't Nothin' but a Sandwich* (novel; also see below), Coward, 1973.

*A Short Walk* (novel), Coward, 1979.

*Rainbow Jordan* (novel), Coward, 1981.

*Many Closets,* Coward, 1987.

*Those Other People,* Putnam, 1989.

*PLAYS*

*Florence* (one-act), first produced in New York City at American Negro Theatre, directed by and starring Childress, 1949.

*Just a Little Simple* (based on Langston Hughes's short story collection *Simple Speaks His Mind*), first produced in New York City at Club Baron Theatre, September, 1950.

*Gold through the Trees,* first produced at Club Baron Theatre, 1952.

*Trouble in Mind,* first produced Off-Broadway at Greenwich Mews Theatre, directed by Childress, November 3, 1955, revised version published in *Black Theatre: A Twentieth-Century Collection of the Work of Its Best Playwrights,* edited by Lindsay Patterson, Dodd, 1971.

*Wedding Band: A Love/Hate Story in Black and White* (first produced in Ann Arbor, MI, at University of Michigan, December 7, 1966; produced Off-Broadway at New York Shakespeare Festival Theatre, directed by Childress and Joseph Papp, September 26, 1972; also see below), Samuel French, 1973.

*String* (one-act; based on Guy de Maupassant's story "A Piece of String"; also see below), first produced Off-Broadway at St. Mark's Playhouse, March 25, 1969.

*Mojo: A Black Love Story* (one-act; also see below), produced in New York City at New Heritage Theatre, November, 1970.

*Mojo* [and] *String,* Dramatists Play Service, 1971.

*When the Rattlesnake Sounds: A Play* (juvenile), illustrated by Charles Lilly, Coward, 1975.

*Let's Hear It for the Queen: A Play* (juvenile), Coward, 1976.

*Sea Island Song,* produced in Charleston, SC, 1977, produced as *Gullah* in Amherst, MA, at University of Massachusetts—Amherst, 1984.

*Moms: A Praise Play for a Black Comedienne* (based on the life of Jackie "Moms" Mabley), music and lyrics by Childress and her husband, Nathan Woodard, first produced by Green Plays at Art Awareness, 1986, produced Off-Broadway at Hudson Guild Theatre, February 4, 1987.

Also author of *Martin Luther King at Montgomery, Alabama,* music by Woodard, 1969, *A Man Bearing a Pitcher,* 1969, *The African Garden,* music by Woodard, 1971, and *Vashti's Magic Mirror;* author of *The Freedom Drum,* music by Woodard, produced as *Young Man Martin Luther King,* Performing Arts Repertory Theatre (on tour), 1969-71.

*SCREENPLAYS*

*Wine in the Wilderness: A Comedy-Drama* (first produced in Boston by WGBH-TV, March 4, 1969), Dramatists Play Service, 1969.

*Wedding Band* (based on her play of the same title), American Broadcasting Companies (ABC-TV), 1973.

*A Hero Ain't Nothin' but a Sandwich* (based on her novel of the same title), New World Pictures, 1978.

*String* (based on her play of the same title), Public Broadcasting Service (PBS-TV), 1979.

*OTHER*

Contributor to *The Best Short Stories by Negro Writers: An Anthology from 1899 to the Present,* edited by Langston Hughes, Little, Brown, 1967; *Plays to Remember* (includes "The World on a Hill"), Macmillan, 1968; *The Best Short Plays of 1972,* edited by Stanley Richards, Chilton, 1972; *The Young American Basic Reading Program,* Lyons & Carnaham, 1972; *Success in Reading,* Silver Burdette, 1972; *Best Short Plays of the World Theatre, 1968-1973,* edited by Richards, Crown, 1973; *Anthology of the Afro-American in the Theatre: A Critical Approach,* edited by Patterson, Publishers Agency, 1978; *Black American Literature and Humanism,* edited by R. Baxter Miller, University of Kentucky Press, 1981; *Black Women Writers (1950-1980): A Critical Evaluation,* edited by Mari Evans, Doubleday-Anchor, 1984. Also contributor to *Keeping the Faith,* edited by Pat Exum. Author of "Here's Mildred" column in *Baltimore Afro-American,* 1956-58. Contributor of plays, articles, and reviews to *Masses and Mainstream, Black World, Freedomways, Essence, Negro Digest, New York Times,* and other publications.

*WORK IN PROGRESS:* A young adult novel about her African Great-Grandmother, enslaved until the age of twelve, and about her Scottish/Irish Great-Great-Grandmother, both of whom lived in Charleston, South Carolina.

*SIDELIGHTS:* Alice Childress's work is noted for its frank treatment of racial issues, its compassionate yet discerning characterizations, and its universal appeal. Because her books and plays often deal with such controversial subjects as miscegenation and teenage drug addiction, her work has been banned in certain locations. She recalls that some affiliate stations refused to carry the nationally televised broadcasts of *Wedding Band* and *Wine in the Wilderness,* and in the case of the latter play, the entire state of Alabama banned the telecast.

Childress notes in addition that as late as 1973 her young adult novel *A Hero Ain't Nothin' but a Sandwich* "was the first book banned in a Savannah, Georgia school library since *Catcher in the Rye,* which the same school banned in the fifties." Along with other contemporary and classical works, *A Hero Ain't Nothin' but a Sandwich* has been at the center of legal battles and court decisions over attempts to define obscenity and its alleged impact on readers. Among the most famous cases was *Board of Education, Island Trees Union Free School District v. Pico* (102 S. Ct. 2799) in which a Stephen Pico, then a high school student, and others sued the Board on the grounds that their First Amendment Rights had been denied. The case became the first ever to be heard in the U.S Supreme Court. Justice Brennan found for the plaintiffs, having determined that a school board's rights were limited to supervising curriculum, but not the general content of a library. Despite special-interest groups' growing resistance to controversial subjects in books, Childress's writing continues to win praise and respect for being, as a *Variety* reviewer terms, "powerful and poetic."

A talented writer and performer in several media, Childress has commented about the variety of genres in which she writes: "Books, plays, tele-plays, motion picture scenarios, etc., I seem caught up in a fragmentation of writing skills. But an idea comes to me in a certain form and, if it stays with me, must be written out or put in outline form before I can move on to the next event. I sometimes wonder about writing in different forms; could it be that women are used to dealing with the bits and pieces of life and do not feel as [compelled to specialize]? The play form is the one most familiar to me and so influences all of my writing—I think in scenes."

In an autobiographical sketch for Donald R. Gallo's *Speaking for Ourselves,* Childress shares how theater has influenced her fiction writing: "When I'm writing, characters seem to come alive; they move my pen to action, pushing, pulling, shoving, and intruding. I visualize each scene as if it were part of a living play.... I am pleased when readers say that my novels feel like plays, because it means they are very visual."

Alice Childress began her career in the theater, initially as an actress and later as a director and playwright. Although "theater histories make only passing mention of her,... she was in the forefront of important developments in that medium," writes *Dictionary of Literary Biography* contributor Trudier Harris. Rosemary Curb points out in another *Dictionary of Literary Biography* article that Childress's 1952 drama *Gold through the Trees* was "the first play by a black woman professionally produced on the American stage." Moreover, Curb adds, "As a result of successful performances of [her 1950s plays *Just a Little Simple* and *Gold through the Trees*], Childress initiated Harlem's first all-union Off-Broadway

contracts recognizing the Actors Equity Association and the Harlem Stage Hand Local."

Partly because of her pioneering efforts, Childress is considered a crusader by many. But she is also known as "a writer who resists compromise," says Doris E. Abramson in *Negro Playwrights in the American Theatre: 1925-1959.* "She tries to write about [black] problems as honestly as she can." The problems Childress addresses most often are racism and its effects. Her *Trouble in Mind,* for example, is a play within a play that focuses on the anger and frustration experienced by a troupe of black actors as they try to perform stereotyped roles in a play that has been written, produced, and directed by whites. As Sally R. Sommer explains in the *Village Voice,* "The plot is about an emerging rebellion begun as the heroine, Wiletta, refuses to enact a namby-Mammy, either in the play or for her director." In the *New York Times,* Arthur Gelb states that Childress "has some witty and penetrating things to say about the dearth of roles for [black] actors in the contemporary theatre, the cutthroat competition for these parts and the fact that [black] actors often find themselves playing stereotyped roles in which they cannot bring themselves to believe." And of *Wedding Band,* a play about an interracial relationship that takes place in South Carolina during World War I, Clive Barnes writes in the *New York Times,* "Childress very carefully suggests the stirrings of black consciousness, as well as the strength of white bigotry."

Critics Sommer and the *New York Times*'s Richard Eder find that Childress's treatment of the themes and issues in *Trouble in Mind* and *Wedding Band* gives these plays a timeless quality. "Writing in 1955,... Alice Childress used the concentric circles of the play-within-the-play to examine the multiple roles blacks enact in order to survive," Sommer remarks. She finds that viewing *Trouble in Mind* years later enables one to see "its double cutting edge: It predicts not only the course of social history but the course of black playwriting." Eder states: "The question [in *Wedding Band*] is whether race is a category of humanity or a division of it. The question is old by now, and was in 1965, [when the play was written,] but it takes the freshness of new life in the marvelous characters that Miss Childress has created to ask it."

The strength and insight of Childress's characterizations have been widely acknowledged; critics contend that the characters who populate her plays and novels are believable and memorable. Eder praises the "rich and lively characterization" of *Wedding Band.* Similarly impressed, Harold Clurman writes in the *Nation* that "there is an honest pathos in the telling of this simple story, and some humorous and touching thumbnail sketches reveal knowledge and understanding of the people dealt with." In the novel *A Short Walk,* Childress chronicles the life of a fictitious black woman, Cora James, from her birth in 1900 to her death in the middle of the century, illustrating, as *Washington Post* critic Joseph McLellan describes it, "a transitional generation in black American society." McLellan notes that the story "wanders considerably" and that "the reader is left with no firm conclusion that can be put into a neat sentence or two." What is more important, he asserts, is that "the wandering has been through some interesting scenery, and instead of a conclusion the reader has come to know a human being—complex, struggling valiantly and totally believable." And of Childress's novel about teenage heroin addiction, *A Hero Ain't Nothin' but a Sandwich,* the *Lion and the Unicorn*'s Miguel Ortiz states, "The portrait of whites is more realistic in this book, more compassionate, and at the same time, because it is believable, more scathing."

Some criticism has been leveled at what such reviewers as Abramson and Edith Oliver believe to be Childress's tendency to speechify, especially in her plays. "A reader of the script is very much aware of the author pulling strings, putting her own words into a number of mouths," Abramson says of *Trouble in Mind.* According to Oliver in the *New Yorker,* "The first act [of *Wedding Band*] is splendid, but after that we hit a few jarring notes, when the characters seem to be speaking as much for the benefit of us eavesdroppers out front ... as for the benefit of one another."

For the most part, however, Childress's work, particularly her novels for young adults, has been acclaimed for its honesty, insight, and compassion. When one such novel, *Those Other People,* was published in 1989, it was acknowledged by very few of the traditional children's reviewing sources. The novel deals with a teenage boy's fears about admitting to his homosexuality. Childress has created characters who confront homophobia, racism, and social taboos honestly and with dignity. In her review for *School Library Journal,* Kathryn Havris notes that *Those Other People,* skillfully and realistically addresses young people's responses to these problems. This author, says Havris, "has presented the problems and reactions with a competence that deserves reading."

In *Crisis,* Loften Mitchell notes: "Childress writes with a sharp, satiric touch. Character seems to interest her more than plot. Her characterizations are piercing, her observations devastating." In his review of *A Hero Ain't Nothin' but a Sandwich,* Ortiz writes: "The book conveys very strongly the message that we are all human, even when we are acting in ways that we are somewhat ashamed of. The structure of the book grows out of the personalities of the characters, and the author makes us aware of how much the economic and social circumstances dictate a character's actions."

In discussing how she came to write books for teenagers, Childress remarks in *Speaking for Ourselves* that she wanted to "deal with characters who feel rejected and have to painfully learn how to deal with other people, because I believe

all human beings can be magnificent once they realize their full importance." "My young years were very old in feeling," she comments elsewhere. "I was shut out of so much for so long. [I] soon began to embrace the low-profile as a way of life, which helped me to develop as a writer. Quiet living is restful when one's writing is labeled 'controversial'."

"Happily, I managed to save a bit of my youth for spending in these later years. Oh yes, there are other things to be saved [besides] money. If we hang on to that part within that was once childhood, I believe we enter into a new time dimension and every day becomes another lifetime in itself. This gift of understanding is often given to those who constantly battle against the negatives of life with determination."

*BIOGRAPHICAL/CRITICAL SOURCES:*

*BOOKS*

Abramson, Doris E., *Negro Playwrights in the American Theatre, 1925-1959,* Columbia University Press, 1969.

Betsko, Kathleen, and Rachel Koenig, *Interviews with Contemporary Women Playwrights,* Beech Tree Books, 1987.

*Children's Literature Review,* Volume 14, Gale, 1988.

*Contemporary Literary Criticism,* Gale, Volume 12, 1980, Volume 15, 1980.

*Dictionary of Literary Biography,* Gale, Volume 7: *Twentieth-Century American Dramatists,* 1981, Volume 38: *Afro-American Writers after 1955: Dramatists and Prose Writers,* 1985.

Donelson, Kenneth L., and Alleen Pace Nilson, *Literature for Today's Young Adults,* Scott, Foresman, 1980, third edition, HarperCollins, 1989.

Evans, Mari, editor, *Black Women Writers (1950-1980): A Critical Evaluation,* Doubleday-Anchor, 1984.

Gallo, Donald R., editor, *Speaking for Ourselves: Autobiographical Sketches by Notable Authors of Books for Young Adults,* National Council Teachers of English, 1990.

Hatch, James V., *Black Theater, U.S.A.: Forty-five Plays by Black Americans,* Free Press, 1974.

Mitchell, Loften, editor, *Voices of the Black Theatre,* James White, 1975.

Street, Douglas, editor, *Children's Novels and the Movies,* Ungar, 1983.

*PERIODICALS*

*Crisis,* April, 1965.

*Freedomways,* Volume 14, number 1, 1974.

*Horn Book,* May-June, 1989, p. 372.

*Interracial Books for Children Bulletin,* Volume 12, numbers 7-8, 1981.

*Lion and the Unicorn,* fall, 1978.

*Los Angeles Times,* November 13, 1978; February 25, 1983.
*Los Angeles Times Book Review,* July 25, 1982.
*Ms.,* December, 1979.
*Nation,* November 13, 1972.
*Negro Digest,* April, 1967; January, 1968.
*Newsweek,* August 31, 1987.
*New Yorker,* November 4, 1972; November 19, 1979.
*New York Times,* November 5, 1955; February 2, 1969; April 2, 1969; October 27, 1972; November 5, 1972; February 3, 1978; January 11, 1979; January 23, 1987; February 10, 1987; March 6, 1987; August 18, 1987; October 22, 1987.
*New York Times Book Review,* November 4, 1973; November 11, 1979; April 25, 1981.
*School Library Journal,* February, 1989, p. 99.
*Show Business,* April 12, 1969.
*Variety,* December 20, 1972.
*Village Voice,* January 15, 1979.
*Washington Post,* May 18, 1971; December 28, 1979.
*Wilson Library Bulletin,* September, 1989, pp. 14-15.

*       *       *

## CIEE, Grace 1961-

*PERSONAL:* Surname is pronounced "see"; born Grace Melecia Cornish, August 22, 1961, in Jamaica. *Education:* Hampshire College, B.A., 1982; attended New School for Social Research, 1990.

*ADDRESSES: Home*—New York, NY, and London, England. *Office*—c/o Fortune 27 Resources, 610 Fifth Ave., Box 4739, New York, NY 10185-0040. *Agent*—c/o Joan Ryder, CIEE Global Communications Group, 610 Fifth Ave., P.O. Box 4739, New York, NY 10185-0040.

*CAREER:* International image consultant for department stores and cosmetic companies, 1982—. Fashion designer and consultant to Jessica International and Captiva Couture, 1989.

*AWARDS, HONORS:* Certificate of Recognition for Black Women in Literature, International Public Relations Group, 1992, for *The Fortune of Being Yourself: You Can Have It All—Love, Beauty, Money, and Happiness.*

*WRITINGS:*

*The Fortune of Being Yourself: You Can Have It All—Love, Beauty, Money, and Happiness,* Fortune 27 Resources, 1991.
*Think and Grow Beautiful: A Teenage Woman's Guide to Total Beauty,* Fortune 27 Resources, 1992.

*Radiant Women of Color: Embrace, Enhance and Enjoy the Beauty of Your Natural Coloring,* Kola Publishing, 1993.

*The Fortune of Being Yourself: You Can Have It All—Love, Beauty, Money, and Happiness* was translated into Spanish.

*SIDELIGHTS:* Grace Ciee commented: "Although it is true that when you look good, you feel good, it is more important that when you think good about yourself, you'll look and feel even better. This makes you happy, and happiness is the birthright of every person on Earth."

*       *       *

## CLARKE, Cheryl 1947-

*PERSONAL:* Born May 16, 1947, in Washington, DC; daughter of James and Edna Clarke. *Education:* Howard University, B.A., 1969; Rutgers University, M.A., 1974; Rutgers University, M.S.W., 1980.

*ADDRESSES: Home*—247 Liberty Ave., Jersey City, NJ 07307.

*CAREER:* Poet and free-lance writer. Member of New York Women Against Rape, 1985-1988; member of *Collections* magazine Editorial Collective, 1981-90; co-chair of the board, Center for Gay and Lesbian Studies, City University of New York Graduate Center, 1990-1992; member of steering committee, New Jersey Women and AIDS Network; administrator, Office of the Provost, Rutgers University, New Brunswick, NJ.

*WRITINGS:*

*Narratives: Poems in the Tradition of Black Women,* illustrated by Gaia (Gay Belknap), Women of Color Press, 1983.
*Living as a Lesbian* (poems), Firebrand, 1986.
*Humid Pitch: Narrative Poetry,* Firebrand, 1989.
*Experimental Love,* Firebrand, 1993.

*SIDELIGHTS:* Cheryl Clarke is a poet with a unique perspective. As the titles of her collections make clear, her work finds its roots in her experience not only as an African American, but also as a lesbian and feminist. For Clarke, this vantage point serves not to limit, but rather to enrich her writings. Drawing upon certain long-standing traditions in black culture, particularly oral narratives, as well as jazz, blues, and gospel music, she fuses these elements with a lesbian and feminist sensibility to create poems with a voice that, in the words of *Belles*

*Lettres* reviewer Jane Campbell, "reverberate with uncompromising toughness, piercing joy, and sensual delight."

Her first collection, *Narratives: Poems in the Tradition of Black Women,* consists of fifteen poems in a style that Calvin Hernton described in *Parnassus* as "oral narratives, liberating and testimonial, written from a lesbian-feminist perspective." The poems address a variety of themes from the viewpoint of numerous narrators; as Ruthan Robson of *New Pages* noted, the speakers of the poems in this volume are "marvelous and varied," and include mothers, older women, young black girls, wives, lesbians, and sisters. Through these voices, Clarke explores what Hernton identified as her central thematic concerns: "to expose and condemn sexual repression while providing truth, honesty, and sustenance for the liberation of black women." The narratives celebrate the possibility of community among women and female sexuality, particularly lesbian sexual relations; they also expose what Hernton called "the many daily small hells of black women," including the violence directed toward women by men, and the difficulties of being a black woman in a society dominated by white men.

*Living as a Lesbian* and *Humid Pitch: Narrative Poetry,* published in 1986 and 1989, respectively, continue the themes Clarke develops in her first collection, but with a marked change in poetic direction. "Clarke, the self-proclaimed narrative poet," Dorothy Allison noted in her *Voice Literary Supplement* review of *Living as a Lesbian,* breaks out "into lyrical song, jazz melodies played in counterpoint to uncompromising political judgements." Retaining her emphasis on what Hernton labeled as "women-identified" symbolism and allusions in her earlier work, she reaches out to aspects of the larger African American culture, especially jazz, to form what Allison described as "something completely original"—poems with "raw and immediate power." This fusion of poetry, music, and sensuality is further elaborated throughout *Humid Pitch.* The poem "Epic of Song," for example, details an erotic relationship between three female singers and musicians. As Jane Campbell remarked, the poem is not simply "a celebration of women's love for women; Clarke's epic explores the connections among eroticism, creativity, and work—the power available to those who fuse art and life." Yet even with her emphasis on the sensual, Clarke does not focus on it exclusively. The volume also contains poems which address the perils of being gay in a small town, discovering one's sexual identity, and the strength of a bond between sisters. Campbell's closing comments on *Humid Pitch* might serve as both a summary of Clarke's poetry as a whole and many of her critics' responses to it. "Informing [the book]," she wrote, "are women's capacities to survive, love, and nurture; one leaves the book with new reverence for our strength, complexity, and diversity."

*BIOGRAPHICAL/CRITICAL SOURCES:*

*PERIODICALS*

*Belles Lettres,* Fall, 1990, p.53.
*New Pages,* Fall, 1984, p. 23.
*Parnassus,* Spring-Summer-Fall-Winter, 1985, p. 518-550.
*Voice Literary Supplement,* February 1987, p. 21.

\*   \*   \*

## CLARKE, John Henrik   1915-

*PERSONAL:* Born January 1, 1915, in Union Springs, AL; son of John (a farmer) and Willella (Mays) Clarke; married Eugenia Evans (a teacher), December 24, 1961; children: Nzingha Marie, Sonni Kojo. *Education:* Attended New York University, 1948-52, New School for Social Research, 1956-58; Pacific Western University, B.A.

*ADDRESSES: Home*—223 West 137th St., New York, NY 10030.

*CAREER:* New School for Social Research, New York City, occasional teacher of African and Afro-American history, 1956-58, developer of African Study Center, 1957-59, assistant to director, 1958-60; *Pittsburgh Courier,* Pittsburgh, PA, feature writer, 1957-58; *Ghana Evening News,* Accra, Ghana, feature writer, 1958; Hunter College of the City University of New York, New York City, associate professor of African and Puerto Rican studies, beginning 1970, became professor emeritus, 1985. Director, Haryou-Act (teaching program), 1964-69; lecturer in teacher training program, Columbia University, summer, 1969; Carter G. Woodson distinguished visiting professor in African history, Cornell University, 1967-70; visiting lecturer, New York University; teacher (by special license) at Malverne High School (People's College), Malverne, NY. Research director for African Heritage Exposition in New York City, 1959; coordinator and special consultant to Columbia Broadcasting System, Inc. (CBS-TV) television series, "Black Heritage," 1968; consultant to American Heritage Press and John Wiley & Sons (publishers). Member of board of directors of Langston Hughes Center for Child Development, 1967; member of advisory board of Martin Luther King Library Center, 1969. *Military service:* U.S. Army Air Forces, 1941-45; became master sergeant.

*MEMBER:* International Society of African Culture, African Studies Association, American Society of African Culture, Black Academy of Arts and Letters (founding member), Association for Study of African American Life and History (executive board member, 1949-55), American Historical Society, American Academy of Political and Social Science, African Heritage Studies Association (president, 1969-73), African Scholars Council (member of board of directors), Harlem Writers Guild (founding member).

*AWARDS, HONORS:* Carter G. Woodson Award, 1968, for creative contribution in editing, and 1971, for excellence in teaching; National Association for Television and Radio Announcers citation for meritorious achievement in educational television, 1969; L.H.D., University of Denver, 1970; Litt.D., University of District of Columbia, 1992, and Clarke-Atlanta University, 1993.

*WRITINGS:*

*Rebellion in Rhyme* (poems), Dicker Press, 1948.

(Editor) *Harlem U.S.A.: The Story of a City within a City,* Seven Seas Books (Berlin), 1964, revised edition, Collier, 1970.

(Editor) *Harlem: A Community in Transition,* Citadel, 1965, third edition, 1970.

(Editor) *American Negro Short Stories,* Hill & Wang, 1966.

(Editor) *William Styron's Nat Turner: Ten Black Writers Respond,* Beacon Press, 1968, reprinted, Greenwood Press, 1987.

(Editor and author of introduction) *Malcolm X: The Man and His Times,* Macmillan, 1969, Africa World Press, 1991.

(Editor with Vincent Harding) *Slave Trade and Slavery,* Holt, 1970.

(Editor) *Harlem: Voices from the Soul of Black America,* (short stories), New American Library, 1970.

(Editor with others) *Black Titan: W. E. B. Du Bois,* Beacon Press, 1970.

(Editor) J. A. Rogers, *World's Great Men of Color,* two volumes, Macmillan, 1972.

(Editor with Amy Jacques Garvey, and author of introduction and commentaries) *Marcus Garvey and the Vision of Africa,* Random House, 1974.

(Introduction) *Introduction to African Civilization,* Carol Publishing, 1974.

(Guest editor) *Black Families in the American Economy,* Education-Community Counselors Association (Washington, DC), 1975.

(Editor) *Dimensions of the Struggle against Apartheid: A Tribute to Paul Robeson,* African Heritage Studies Association in cooperation with United Nations Centre against Apartheid, 1979.

(Introduction) *Africa Counts,* Hill, Lawrence, 1979.

*Africans at the Crossroads: Notes for an African World Revolution,* Africa World Press, 1991.

*Christopher Columbus and the African Holocaust,* A & B Books, 1992.

*An Oral Biography of Professor John Henrik Clarke,* United Brothers and Sisters Communications Systems, 1992.

*African People in World History,* Black Classic Press, 1993.

(Editor) *Black American Short Stories,* revised edition, Hill & Wang, 1993.

Editor of *New Dimensions in African History,* Africa World Press. Contributor to books, including *Patterns of Thinking: Integrating Learning Skills in Content Teaching,* Allyn & Bacon, 1990; *Teaching Critical Thinking,* Prentice Hall, 1993. Also author of "The Lives of Great African Chiefs" published serially in *Pittsburgh Courier,* 1957-58, and of syndicated column, "African World Bookshelf." Author of numerous papers on African studies presented at international conferences. Contributor to *Negro History Bulletin, Chicago Defender, Journal of Negro Education, Phylon, Presence Africaine,* and others. Book review editor, *Negro History Bulletin,* 1947-49; co-founder and associate editor, *Harlem Quarterly,* 1949-51; editor, *African Heritage,* 1959; associate editor, *Freedomways,* 1962-83.

*WORK IN PROGRESS: The Black Woman in History;* an African curriculum for elementary school teachers.

*SIDELIGHTS:* As an editor, essayist, and educator, John Henrik Clarke has written and lectured extensively about African and Afro-American history both in the United States and West Africa. *Malcolm X: The Man and His Times,* a collection of essays about and writings by Malcolm X edited by Clarke, is described by the *New York Times*'s Christopher Lehmann-Haupt: "Malcolm is seen through different eyes at various stages of his career as Muslim, ex-Muslim, and founder of the Organization of Afro-American Unity. He is defined and redefined by friends and followers." And although Lehmann-Haupt considers the collection "overwhelmingly sympathetic," he thinks that Clarke has produced a "multifaceted picture that ... traces his development from drifter to prophet, spells out his aims (and thereby dispels his distorted image as apostle of violent separatism) and explains why his stature among so many blacks today is heroic." Similarly, in the *New York Review of Books,* Charles V. Hamilton finds that "Clarke has done an excellent job of pulling together various stimulating sources to give the reader what the title promises, a look at the man and his time—a look at a genuine folk hero of black Americans and a master of the Politics of Sportsmanship."

*BIOGRAPHICAL/CRITICAL SOURCES:*

*BOOKS*

*Authors in the News,* Volume 1, Gale, 1976.

PERIODICALS

*Atlanta Journal,* April 8, 1973.
*Black World,* February, 1971; August, 1971.
*Choice,* February, 1969; October, 1974; June, 1975.
*Essence,* September, 1989.
*New York Review of Books,* September 12, 1968.
*New York Times,* May 10, 1967; August 1-2, 1968; September 29, 1969.
*New York Times Book Review,* March 5, 1967; August 11, 1968; September 28, 1969, p. 3.
*Publishers Weekly,* July 7, 1969; July 13, 1970.
*Saturday Review,* January 14, 1967; August 12, 1968.
*Time,* October 24, 1969, p. 110; February 23, 1970, p. 88.

\*   \*   \*

## CLEAGE, Pearl (Michelle) 1948-
### (Pearl Cleage Lomax)

*PERSONAL:* Surname is pronounced "cleg"; born December 7, 1948, in Springfield, MA; daughter of Albert Buford (a minister) and Doris (a teacher; maiden name, Graham) Cleage; married Michael Lucius Lomax (an elected official of Fulton County, GA), October 31, 1969 (divorced, 1979); children: Deignan Njeri. *Education:* Attended Howard University, 1966-69, Yale University, 1969, and University of the West Indies, 1971; Spelman College, B.A., 1971; graduate study at Atlanta University, 1971.

*ADDRESSES: Home*—1665 Havilon Dr. S.W., Atlanta, GA 30311. *Office*—Just Us Theater Co., P.O. Box 42271, Atlanta, GA 30311-0271.

*CAREER:* Playwright, poet, and educator. Just Us Theater Co., Atlanta, GA, playwright-in-residence, 1983-87, artistic director, 1987—; Spelman College, Atlanta, instructor in creative writing, 1986-91, playwright-in-residence, 1991—. Martin Luther King, Jr. Archival Library, member of field collection staff, 1969-70; Southern Education Program, Inc., assistant director, 1970-71; WETV, Atlanta, hostess and interviewer, "Black Viewpoints," produced by Clark College, 1970-71; WQXI, Atlanta, staff writer and interviewer for *Ebony Beat Journal,* 1972, writer and associate producer, 1972-73; WXIA, Atlanta, executive producer, 1972-73; City of Atlanta, director of communications, beginning 1973; Brown/Gray, Ltd., writer, beginning 1976. Member of board of directors, Atlanta Center for Black Art, 1970-71.

*MEMBER:* Writers Guild of America (East).

*AWARDS, HONORS:* First prize for poetry, *Promethean Literary Magazine,* 1968; Georgia Council for the Arts residency grants, from the city of Atlanta, 1982 and 1984; National Endowment for the Arts residency grants through Just Us Theater Co., 1983-87; Audience Development Committee (AUDELCO) Recognition Awards for Best Play and Best Playwright, 1983, for *Hospice* (play won three other AUDELCO awards that year); Bronze Jubilee Award for Literature, Atlanta, Georgia, 1983; Mayor's fellowship in the arts, Atlanta Bureau of Cultural Affairs, 1986; seed grant from Coordinating Council of Literary Magazines, 1987, for *Catalyst;* AT&T New Work Development Grant, 1990; outstanding columnist award, Atlanta Association of Black Journalists, 1991; individual artist grant, Georgia Council on the Arts, 1991; grant from AT&T Onstage program, 1992, for *Flyin' West;* outstanding columnist award, Atlanta Association of Media Women, 1993; grants from the Coca-Cola Company, the Coca-Cola Foundation, and the Whitter-Bynner Foundation for Poetry.

*WRITINGS:*

*We Don't Need No Music* (poetry), Broadside Press, 1971.
(Author of essay, under name Pearl Cleage Lomax) *P. H. Polk, Photographs,* Nexus Press, 1980.
*Dear Dark Faces: Portraits of a People* (poetry), Lotus Press, 1980.
*One for the Brothers* (chapbook), privately printed, 1983.
*Mad at Miles: A Blackwoman's Guide to Truth,* Cleage Group, 1990.
*The Brass Bed and Other Stories* (young adult, short fiction and poetry), Third World Press, 1991.
*Deals with the Devil: And Other Reasons to Riot* (essays), Ballantine, 1993.

PLAYS

*Hymn for the Rebels* (one-act), first produced in Washington, DC, at Howard University, 1968.
*Duet for Three Voices* (one-act), first produced in Washington, DC, at Howard University, 1969.
*The Sale* (one-act), first produced in Atlanta, GA, at Spelman College, 1972.
*puppetplay,* first produced in Atlanta by Just Us Theater Co., 1983.
*Hospice* (first produced off-Broadway at the New Federal Theatre, New York, 1983; first international production, the MAMU Players, South Africa, 1990), published in *New Plays for the Black Theater,* edited by Woodie King, Jr., Third World Press, 1989.
*Good News,* first produced in Atlanta by Just Us Theater Co., 1984.
*Essentials,* first produced in Atlanta by Just Us Theater Co., 1985.

*Banana Bread* (two-character piece), videotaped and premiered as part of a local PBS series, "Playhouse 30," Atlanta, 1985.

(In collaboration with Walter J. Huntley) *PR: A Political Romance*, first produced by Just Us Theater Co., 1985.

*Porch Songs,* first produced by Phoenix Theater, Indianapolis, 1985.

*Come and Get These Memories,* first produced by Billie Holiday Theater, Brooklyn, NY, 1988.

*Chain* (one-act; first produced off-Broadway by the Women's Project and Productions and the New Federal Theater, 1992), published in *Playwrighting Women: Seven Plays from the Women's Project,* edited by Julia Miles, Heinemann Press, 1993.

*Late Bus to Mecca* (one-act; first produced off-Broadway by the Women's Project and Productions and the New Federal Theater, 1992), published in *Playwrighting Women: Seven Plays from the Women's Project,* edited by Julia Miles, Heinemann Press, 1993.

*Flyin' West,* produced by Atlanta's Alliance Theater Company, 1992.

*OTHER*

Also author of *Christmas, 1967* and *Christmas, 1981* (short fiction). Contributor to *The Insistent Present,* John Mahoney and John Schmittroth, editors, Houghton, 1970; *We Speak as Liberators: Young Black Poets,* Orde Coombs, editor, Dodd, 1970; *A Rock against the Wind,* Lindsay Patterson, editor, Dodd, 1973; and *The Poetry of Black America,* edited by Adoff, and *Dues,* edited by Welburn. Also author, with Zaron Burnett, of *Live at Club Zebra: The Book,* Volume 1, Just Us Theater Press. Author-performer of several performance pieces, including "The Jean Harris Reading," 1981, "The Pearl and the Brood of Vipers," 1981, "Nothin' but a Movie," 1982, "My Father Has a Son," 1986, "A Little Practice," 1986, "Love and Trouble," with Burnett, 1987, "Live at Club Zebra!" with Burnett, 1987-88, "The Final Negro Rhythm and Blues Revue," with Burnett, 1988, "Clearing the Heart," 1989, "Mad at Miles," 1990. Columnist for *Atlanta Gazette,* 1976—, *Atlanta Constitution,* 1977, and *Atlanta Tribune,* 1988—. Contributor to various periodicals and journals, including *Readers and Writers, Promethean, Afro-American Review, Journal of Black Poetry, Dues, Essence, Pride, Black World, Ms., Atlanta Magazine, New York Times Book Review, Southern Voices,* and *Black Collegian.* Founding editor, *Catalyst,* 1987—.

*WORK IN PROGRESS:* Short story collection for Third World Press.

*SIDELIGHTS:* Pearl Cleage once commented: "As a black female writer living and working in the United States, my writing of necessity reflects my blackness and my femaleness.

I am convinced that this condition of double-oppression based on race and sex gives me a unique perspective that, hopefully, adds energy and certain creative tension to my work. Here's hoping."

Cleage later added: "Amiri Baraka said that the tradition of the black writer is to write something so ba-a-a-a-d that they have to ban it. It is within the wondrous energy of that tradition that I work."

*BIOGRAPHICAL/CRITICAL SOURCES:*

*BOOKS*

*In Black and White,* third edition, two volumes, Gale, 1980, third edition, supplement, 1985.

Peterson, Bernard L., *Contemporary Black American Playwrights and Their Plays,* Greenwood Press, 1988.

\*      \*      \*

## CLIFF, Michelle   1946-

*PERSONAL:* Born November 2, 1946, in Kingston, Jamaica; naturalized United States citizen. *Education:* Wagner College, A.B., 1969; Warburg Institute, London, M.Phil., 1974.

*ADDRESSES: Home and office*—2420 Paul Minnie Ave., Santa Cruz, CA 95062. *Agent*—Faith Childs Literary Agency, 275 West 96th St., No. 31B, New York, NY 10025.

*CAREER: Life,* New York City, reporter and researcher, 1969-70; W. W. Norton & Co., Inc. (publisher), New York City, production supervisor of Norton Library, 1970-71, copy editor, 1974-75, manuscript and production editor, specializing in history, politics, and women's studies, 1975-79; *Sinister Wisdom,* Amherst, MA, copublisher and editor, 1981-83; Norwich University, Vermont College Campus, Montpelier, member of cycle faculty for adult degree program, 1983-84; Martin Luther King, Jr. Public Library, Oakland, CA, teacher of creative writing and history, 1984—; writer of Afro-Caribbean (Indian, African, European) heritage literature. Member of faculty at New School for Social Research, 1974-76, Hampshire College, 1980, 1981, University of Massachusetts at Amherst, 1980, and Vista College, 1985; visiting faculty at San Jose State, 1986, and University College of Santa Cruz, 1987; visiting lecturer at Stanford University, 1987-1991; visiting lecturer at Trinity College, 1990; Allan K. Smith Visiting Writer at Trinity College, 1992, 1993; Allan K. Smith Professor of English Language and Literature at Trinity College, 1993; speaker at workshops and symposia in United States and abroad.

*MEMBER:* Authors Guild, Authors League of America, Poets and Writers, PEN.

*AWARDS, HONORS:* MacDowell Fellow at MacDowell College, 1982; National Endowment for the Arts fellow, 1982; Massachusetts Artists Foundation fellow, 1984; Eli Kantor fellow at Yaddo, 1984; Fulbright Fellowship, New Zealand, 1988; National Endowment for the Arts fellow in fiction, 1989.

*WRITINGS:*

(Editor) *The Winner Names the Age: A Collection of Writing by Lillian Smith,* Norton, 1978.

*Claiming an Identity They Taught Me to Despise* (poems), Persephone Press, 1980, second edition, 1991.

*Abeng* (novel), Crossing Press, 1984, second edition, Penguin, 1990.

*The Land of Look Behind* (poems and prose), Firebrand Books, 1985.

*No Telephone to Heaven* (novel), Dutton, 1987, Vintage International, 1989.

*Bodies of Water* (short stories), Methuen, 1990.

*Free Enterprise* (novel), Dutton, 1993.

*Aunt Sally Hoodoo: The American Genius of Betye Saar,* University of California Press, forthcoming.

Work represented in anthologies, including *Extended Outlooks,* Macmillan, 1983; and *Home Girls,* edited by Barbara Smith, Kitchen Table Press, 1983. Author of introduction of *Macht und Sinnlichkeit,* by Audre Lorde and Adrienne Rich, Subrosa Frauenverlag, 1983. Contributor to books, including *Between Women,* edited by Carol Asher, Louise De Salvo, and Sally Ruddick, Beacon Press, 1984; *Calling the Wind,* edited by Clarence Major, Harper Collins, 1992; *To Read Literature,* Holt, 1992; *Daughters of Africa,* edited by Margaret Busby, J. Cape, 1992; and *Critical Strategies for Academic Reading and Writing,* St. Martin's Press, 1993. Also contributor of articles, reviews, short fiction, and poetry to magazines, including *American Voice, Chrysalis, Conditions, Feminary, Feminist Review, Heresies, Iowa Review, Kenyon Review, Moving Parts, Ms., Parnassus, Sojourner, Voice Literary Supplement,* and *Women: A Critical Review.* Member of editorial board of *Signs: A Journal of Women in Culture and Society,* 1980-89; contributing editor of *American Voice,* 1993—.

*WORK IN PROGRESS: Free Enterprise,* a novel about the slave trade and resistance to it; *Caliban's Daughter,* a book of essays; *The Story of a Million Items,* a second collection of short fiction.

*SIDELIGHTS:* Michelle Cliff once commented: "I received my education in the United States, Jamaica, and England. I have traveled widely in Europe and lived in London from 1971 through 1974. I am proficient in several languages, including French, Italian, and Spanish, and I have a reading knowledge of Latin. My interests, besides creative writing, are black history, especially the survival of African forms and ideas among Afro-American and Afro-Caribbean people, and visual art, particularly the art of the Italian Renaissance and the art of Afro-American women. Along with my present writing projects, I am engaged in preparing a writing course for young black writers in the Oakland, California, community.

"In my writing I am concerned most of all with social issues and political realities and how they affect the lives of people. Because I am a Jamaican by birth, heritage, and indoctrination, born during the time the island was a British Crown Colony, I have experienced colonialism as a force first-hand. Thus colonialism—and the racism upon which it is based—are subjects I address in most of my writing.

"In my novel *Abeng* I try to show the evils of colonialism, including the brutalities of slavery, the erasure of the history of a colonized people, and the rifts which occur among colonized peoples. The primary relationship in my book, around which the plot pivots, is that between a light-skinned girl named Clare Savage and a darker girl named Zoe. They have between them a past in which lighter-skinned people become the oppressors of darker people—although both groups are comprised of people of color and both groups have their origins in slavery. Generally speaking, the creoles of Jamaica, of mixed racial heritage—African and English for the most part, but also of other groups—were placed higher in the social and economic strata of the island by the colonial overlords. Zoe and Clare meet across this divide, sharing at first an idyllic friendship on the country property of Clare's grandmother, on which Zoe, her mother, and her sister are squatters. Gradually—then suddenly—through an incident of violence in which Clare's indoctrination as a member of the almost-ruling class is shown, the split between the two girls becomes obvious. The novel ends with Clare only barely aware of who she is in this society, but certain that something is wrong in her homeland and with her people.

"While most of the actual events of the book are fiction, emotionally the book is an autobiography. I was a girl similar to Clare and have spent most of my life and most of my work exploring my identity as a light-skinned Jamaican, as well as the privilege and the damage that comes from that identity. For while identification with the status of oppressor can be seen as privilege, and brings with it opportunities denied oppressed people, it also inflicts damage on the privileged person. In my sequel to *Abeng* I will take Clare Savage into her thirties through a journey in which she rejects the privilege offered her and seeks both wholeness as a person of color and a recommitment to her country.

"I am also interested in black women as visual artists, particularly in the survival of African art forms and in African philosophical and religious principles among Afro-American artists. This reflects my continuing interest in history and my growing awareness of how much of history is submerged, how much written history is distorted. I see, for example, that the leadership positions held by many Afro-American women in the abolitionist movement, the civil rights movement, and the anti-lynching movement are similar to the roles that have been assumed by women in West African societies. The book I am writing on this subject will deal with visual art but also with the larger questions of the historic role of black American women, the values they have conveyed, the social responsibility they have assumed."

\*    \*    \*

## CLIFTON, (Thelma) Lucille   1936-

*PERSONAL:* Born June 27, 1936, in Depew, NY; daughter of Samuel Louis, Sr. (a laborer) and Thelma (a laborer; maiden name, Moore) Sayles; married Fred James Clifton (an educator, writer, and artist), May 10, 1958 (died November 10, 1984); children: Sidney, Fredrica, Channing, Gillian, Graham, Alexia. *Education:* Attended Howard University, 1953-55, and Fredonia State Teachers College (now State University of New York College at Fredonia), 1955.

*ADDRESSES: Agent*—Marilyn Marlow, Curtis Brown Ltd., 10 Astor Pl., New York, NY 10003.

*CAREER:* New York State Division of Employment, Buffalo, claims clerk, 1958-60; U.S. Office of Education, Washington, DC, literature assistant for CAREL (Central Atlantic Regional Educational Laboratory), 1969-71; Coppin State College, Baltimore, MD, poet in residence, 1971-74; writer. Visiting writer, Columbia University School of the Arts; Jerry Moore Visiting Writer, George Washington University, 1982-83; University of California, Santa Cruz, professor of literature and creative writing, 1985—. Trustee, Enoch Pratt Free Library, Baltimore.

*MEMBER:* International PEN, Authors Guild, Authors League of America.

*AWARDS, HONORS:* Discovery Award, New York YW-YMHA Poetry Center, 1969; *Good Times: Poems* was cited as one of the year's ten best books by the *New York Times,* 1969; National Endowment for the Arts awards, 1969, 1970, and 1972; Poet Laureate of the State of Maryland, 1979-82; Juniper Prize, 1980; Coretta Scott King Award, 1984, for *Everett Anderson's Goodbye;* honorary degrees from University of Maryland and Towson State University.

*WRITINGS:*

*Good Times: Poems,* Random House, 1969.
*Good News about the Earth: New Poems,* Random House, 1972.
*An Ordinary Woman* (poetry), Random House, 1974.
*Generations: A Memoir* (prose), Random House, 1976.
*Two-Headed Woman* (poetry), University of Massachusetts Press, 1980.
*Good Woman: Poems and a Memoir, 1969-1980,* Boa Editions, 1987.
*Next: New Poems,* Boa Editions, 1987.
*Ten Oxherding Pictures,* Moving Parts Press, 1988.
*Quilting: Poems 1987-1990,* Boa Editions, 1991.
*Book of Light,* Copper Canyon Press, 1993.

*FOR CHILDREN*

*The Black BCs* (alphabet poems), Dutton, 1970.
*Good, Says Jerome,* illustrations by Stephanie Douglas, Dutton, 1973.
*All Us Come Cross the Water,* pictures by John Steptoe, Holt, 1973.
*Don't You Remember?,* illustrations by Evaline Ness, Dutton, 1973.
*The Boy Who Didn't Believe in Spring,* pictures by Brinton Turkle, Dutton, 1973.
*The Times They Used to Be,* illustrations by Susan Jeschke, Holt, 1974.
*My Brother Fine with Me,* illustrations by Moneta Barnett, Holt, 1975.
*Three Wishes,* illustrations by Douglas, Viking, 1976.
*Amifika,* illustrations by Thomas DiGrazia, Dutton, 1977.
*The Lucky Stone,* illustrations by Dale Payson, Delacorte, 1979.
*My Friend Jacob,* illustrations by DiGrazia, Dutton, 1980.
*Sonora Beautiful,* illustrations by Michael Garland, Dutton, 1981.

*"EVERETT ANDERSON" SERIES; FOR CHILDREN*

*Some of the Days of Everett Anderson,* Holt, 1970.
*Everett Anderson's Christmas Coming,* illustrations by Ness, Holt, 1971.
*Everett Anderson's Year,* illustrations by Ann Grifalconi, Holt, 1974.
*Everett Anderson's Friend,* illustrations by Grifalconi, Holt, 1976.
*Everett Anderson's 1 2 3,* illustrations by Grifalconi, Holt, 1977.
*Everett Anderson's Nine Month Long,* illustrations by Grifalconi, Holt, 1978.
*Everett Anderson's Goodbye,* illustrations by Grifalconi, Holt, 1983.

*OTHER*

(Contributor) Langston Hughes and Arna Bontemps, *Poetry of the Negro, 1746-1970,* Doubleday, 1970.
(Contributor) Marlo Thomas and others, *Free to Be ... You and Me,* McGraw-Hill, 1974.

Also contributor to *Free to Be a Family,* 1987, *Norton Anthology of Literature by Women, Coming into the Light,* and *Stealing the Language.* Contributor of fiction to *Negro Digest, Redbook, House and Garden,* and *Atlantic.* Contributor of nonfiction to *Ms.* and *Essence.*

*SIDELIGHTS:* Lucille Clifton "began composing and writing stories at an early age and has been much encouraged by an ever-growing reading audience and a fine critical reputation," writes Wallace R. Peppers in a *Dictionary of Literary Biography* essay. "In many ways her themes are traditional: she writes of her family because she is greatly interested in making sense of their lives and relationships; she writes of adversity and success in the ghetto community; and she writes of her role as a poet." Clifton's work emphasizes endurance and strength through adversity. Ronald Baughman suggests in his *Dictionary of Literary Biography* essay that "Clifton's pride in being black and in being a woman helps her transform difficult circumstances into a qualified affirmation about the black urban world she portrays." Writing in Mari Evans's *Black Women Writers (1950-1980): A Critical Evaluation,* Haki Madhubuti (formerly Don L. Lee) states: "She is a writer of complexity, and she makes her readers work and think. Her poetry has a quiet force without being pushy or alien. Whether she is cutting through family relationships, surviving American racial attitudes, or just simply renewing love ties, she puts something heavy on your mind. The great majority of her published poetry is significant. At the base of her work is concern for the Black family, especially the destruction of its youth. Her eye is for the uniqueness of our people, always concentrating on the small strengths that have allowed us to survive the horrors of Western life."

Clifton's first volume of poetry, *Good Times: Poems,* which was cited by the *New York Times* as one of 1969's ten best books, is described by Peppers as a "varied collection of character sketches written with third person narrative voices." Baughman notes that "these poems attain power not only through their subject matter but also through their careful techniques; among Clifton's most successful poetic devices ... are the precise evocative images that give substance to her rhetorical statements and a frequent duality of vision that lends complexity to her portraits of place and character." Calling the book's title "ironic," Baughman indicates, "Although the urban ghetto can, through its many hardships, create figures who are tough enough to survive and triumph, the overriding concern of this book is with the horrors of the location, with

the human carnage that results from such problems as poverty, unemployment, substandard housing, and inadequate education." Baughman recognizes that although "these portraits of human devastation reflect the trying circumstances of life in the ghetto ... the writer also records some joy in her world, however strained and limited that joy might be." Madhubuti thinks that although this is Clifton's first book of poetry, it "cannot be looked upon as simply a 'first effort.' The work is unusually compacted and memory-evoking." As Johari Amini (formerly Jewel C. Latimore) suggests in *Black World,* "The poetry is filled with the sensations of coming up black with the kind of love that keeps you from dying in desperation."

In Clifton's second volume of poetry, *Good News about the Earth: New Poems,* "the elusive good times seem more attainable," remarks Baughman, who summarizes the three sections into which the book is divided: the first section "focuses on the sterility and destruction of 'white ways,' newly perceived through the social upheavals of the early 1970s"; the second section "presents a series of homages to black leaders of the late 1960s and early 1970s"; and the third section "deals with biblical characters powerfully rendered in terms of the black experience." Harriet Jackson Scarupa notes in *Ms.* that after having read what Clifton says about blackness and black pride, some critics "have concluded that Clifton hates whites. [Clifton] considers this a misreading. When she equates whiteness with death, blackness with life, she says: 'What I'm talking about is a certain kind of white arrogance—and not all white people have it—that is not good. I think airs of superiority are very dangerous. I believe in justice. I try not to be about hatred.'" Writing in *Poetry,* Ralph J. Mills, Jr., says that Clifton's poetic scope transcends the black experience "to embrace the entire world, human and non-human, in the deep affirmation she makes in the teeth of negative evidence. She is a master of her style, with its spare, elliptical, idiomatic, rhythmical speech, and of prophetic warning in the same language." Angela Jackson, who thinks that it "is a book written in wisdom," concludes in *Black World* that "Clifton and *Good News about the Earth* will make you shake yo head. Ain't nothing else to say."

*An Ordinary Woman,* Clifton's third collection of poems, "abandons many of the broad racial issues examined in the two preceding books and focuses instead on the narrower but equally complex issues of the writer's roles as woman and poet," says Baughman. Peppers notes that "the poems take as their theme a historical, social, and spiritual assessment of the current generation in the genealogical line" of Clifton's great great-grandmother, who had been taken from her home in Dahomey, West Africa, and brought to America in slavery in 1830. Peppers notes that by taking an ordinary experience and personalizing it, "Clifton has elevated the experience into a public confession" which may be shared, and "it is this shared sense of situation, an easy identification between speaker and reader, that heightens the notion of ordinariness and gives ... the collection an added dimension." Helen Vendler writes in the *New York Times Book Review* that "Clifton recalls for us those bare places we have all waited as 'ordinary women,' with no choices but yes or no, no art, no grace, no words, no reprieve." "Written in the same ironic, yet cautiously optimistic spirit as her earlier published work," observes Peppers, the book is "lively, full of vigor, passion, and an all-consuming honesty."

In *Generations: A Memoir,* "it is as if [Clifton] were showing us a cherished family album and telling us the story about each person which seemed to sum him or her up best," says a *New Yorker* contributor. Calling the book an "eloquent eulogy of [Clifton's] parents," Reynolds Price writes in the *New York Times Book Review* that, "as with most elegists, her purpose is perpetuation and celebration, not judgment. There is no attempt to see either parent whole; no attempt at the recovery of history not witnessed by or told to the author. There is no sustained chronological narrative. Instead, clusters of brief anecdotes gather round two poles, the deaths of father and mother." Price, however, believes that *Generations* stands "worthily" among the other modern elegies that assert that "we may survive, some lively few, if we've troubled to *be* alive and loved." However, a contributor to *Virginia Quarterly Review* thinks that the book is "more than an elegy or a personal memoir. It is an attempt on the part of one woman to retrieve and lyrically to celebrate, her Afro-American heritage."

"Clifton is a poet of a literary tradition which includes such varied poets as Walt Whitman, Emily Dickinson, and Gwendolyn Brooks, who have inspired and informed her work," writes Audrey T. McCluskey in Evans's *Black Women Writers (1950-1980).* McCluskey finds that "Clifton's belief in her ability (and ours) to make things better and her belief in the concept of personal responsibility pervade her work. These views are especially pronounced in her books for children." Clifton's books for children are characterized by a positive view of black heritage and an urban setting peopled by nontraditional families. Critics recognize that although her works speak directly to a specific audience, they reveal the concerns of all children. In a *Language Arts* interview with Rudine Sims, Clifton was asked where she gets her ideas for stories: "Well, I had six kids in seven years, and when you have a lot of children, you tend to attract children, and you see so many kids, you get ideas from that. And I have such a good memory from my own childhood, my own time. I have great respect for young people; I like them enormously."

Clifton's books for children are designed to help them understand their world. *My Friend Jacob,* for instance, is a story "in which a black child speaks with affection and patience of his friendship with a white adolescent neighbor ... who is re-

tarded," writes Zena Sutherland in *Bulletin of the Center for Children's Books.* "Jacob is Sam's 'very very best friend' and all of his best qualities are appreciated by Sam, just as all of his limitations are accepted.... It is strong in the simplicity and warmth with which a handicapped person is loved rather than pitied, enjoyed rather than tolerated." Critics find that Clifton's characters and their relationships are accurately and positively drawn. Ismat Abdal-Haqq notes in *Interracial Books for Children Bulletin* that "the two boys have a strong relationship filled with trust and affection. The author depicts this relationship and their everyday adventures in a way that is unmarred by the mawkish sentimentality that often characterizes tales of the mentally disabled." And a contributor to *Reading Teacher* states that "in a matter-of-fact, low-keyed style, we discover how [Sam and Jacob] help one another grow and understand the world."

Clifton's children's books also facilitate an understanding of black heritage specifically, which in turn fosters an important link with the past generally. *All Us Come Cross the Water,* for example, "in a very straight-forward way ... shows the relationship of Africa to Blacks in the U.S. without getting into a heavy rap about 'Pan-Africanism'," states Judy Richardson in the *Journal of Negro Education,* adding that Clifton "seems able to get inside a little boy's head, and knows how to represent that on paper." An awareness of one's origins figures also in *The Times They Used to Be.* Called a "short and impeccable vignette—laced with idiom and humor of rural Black folk," by Rosalind K. Goddard in *School Library Journal,* it is further described by Lee A. Daniels in the *Washington Post* as a "story in which a young girl catches her first glimpse of the new technological era in a hardware store window, and learns of death and life." "Most books that awaken adult nostalgia are not as appealing to young readers," says Sutherland in *Bulletin of the Center for Children's Books,* "but this brief story has enough warmth and vitality and humor for any reader."

In addition to quickening an awareness of black heritage, Clifton's books for children frequently include an element of fantasy as well. Writing about *Three Wishes,* in which a young girl finds a lucky penny on New Year's Day and makes three wishes upon it, Christopher Lehmann-Haupt in the *New York Times Book Review* calls it "an urbanized version of the traditional tale in which the first wish reveals the power of the magic object ... the second wish is a mistake, and the third undoes the second." Lehmann-Haupt adds that "too few children's books for blacks justify their ethnicity, but this one is a winning blend of black English and bright illustration." And *The Lucky Stone,* in which a lucky stone provides good fortune for all of its owners, is described by Ruth K. MacDonald in *School Library Journal* as: "Four short stories about four generations of Black women and their dealings with a lucky stone.... Clifton uses as a frame device a grandmother telling the history of the stone to her granddaughter; by the end, the granddaughter has inherited the stone herself." A contributor to *Interracial Books for Children Bulletin* states that "the concept of past and present is usually hard for children to grasp but this book puts the passing of time in a perspective that children can understand.... This book contains information on various aspects of Black culture—slavery, religion and extended family—all conveyed in a way that is both positive and accurate." Michele Slung writes in the *Washington Post Book World* that the book "is at once talisman and anthology: over the years it has gathered unto it story after story, episodes indicating its power, both as a charm and as a unit of oral tradition. Clifton has a knack for projecting strong positive values without seeming too goody-goody; her poet's ear is one fact in this, her sense of humor another."

While Clifton's books for children emphasize an understanding of the past, they also focus on the present. Her series of books about Everett Anderson, for instance, explore the experiences of a young child's world in flux. Writing in *Language Arts* about *Everett Anderson's 1 2 3,* in which a young boy's mother considers remarriage, Ruth M. Stein notes that "previous books contained wistful references to Everett Anderson's absent daddy; the latest one tells how the worried little boy gradually became reconciled to the idea of a new father joining the family." And writing about *Everett Anderson's Nine Month Long,* which concerns the anticipated birth of the family's newest member, a contributor to *Interracial Books for Children Bulletin* considers that "this book, written in wonderful poetic style ... projects a warm, loving, understanding and supportive family." Joan W. Blos, who feels that "the establishment of an active, effective, and supportive male figure is an important part of this story," adds in *School Library Journal,* "So is its tacit acknowledgement that, for the younger child, a mother's pregnancy means disturbing changes now as well as a sibling later." However, just as the birth of a sibling can cause upheaval in a child's world, so, too, can death. In *Everett Anderson's Goodbye,* Everett has difficulty coping with the death of his father; he "misses his Daddy, as he moves through the five stages of grief: denial, anger, bargaining, depression and acceptance," writes a *Washington Post Book World* contributor.

Barbara Walker writes in *Interracial Books for Children Bulletin* that "Clifton is a gifted poet with the greater gift of being able to write poetry for children." Clifton indicates to Sims that she doesn't think of it as poetry especially for children, though. "It seems to me that if you write poetry for children, you have to keep too many things in mind other than the poem. So I'm just writing a poem." *Some of the Days of Everett Anderson* is a book of nine poems, about which Marjorie Lewis observes in *School Library Journal,* "Some of the days of six-year-old 'ebony Everett Anderson' are happy; some lonely—but all of them are special, reflecting the author's own pride in being black." In the *New York Times Book Review,*

Hoyt W. Fuller thinks that Clifton has "a profoundly simple way of saying all that is important to say, and we know that the struggle is worth it, that the all-important battle of image is being won, and that the future of all those beautiful black children out there need not be twisted and broken." *Everett Anderson's Christmas Coming* concerns Christmas preparations in which "each of the five days before Everett's Christmas is described by a verse," says Anita Silvey in *Horn Book,* observing that "the overall richness of Everett's experiences dominates the text." Jane O'Reilly suggests in the *New York Times Book Review* that "Everett Anderson, black and boyish, is glimpsed, rather than explained through poems about him." *Everett Anderson's Year* celebrates "a year in the life of a city child ... in appealing verses," says Beryl Robinson in *Horn Book,* adding that "mischief, fun, gaiety, and poignancy are a part of his days as the year progresses. The portrayals of child and mother are lively and solid, executed with both strength and tenderness."

Language is important in Clifton's writing. In answer to Sim's question about the presence of both black and white children in her work, Clifton responds specifically about *Sonora Beautiful,* which is about the insecurities and dissatisfaction of an adolescent girl and which has only white characters: "In this book, I *heard* the characters as white. I have a tendency to *hear* the language of the characters, and then I know something about who the people are." However, regarding objections to the black vernacular she often uses, Clifton tells Sims: "I do not write out of weakness. That is to say, I do not write the language I write because I don't know any other.... But I have a certain integrity about my art, and in *my* art you have to be honest and you have to have people talking the way they really talk. So all of my books are not in the same language." Asked by Sims whether or not she feels any special pressures or special opportunities as a black author, Clifton responds: "I do feel a responsibility.... First, I'm going to write books that tend to celebrate life. I'm about that. And I wish to have children see people like themselves in books.... I also take seriously the responsibility of not lying.... I'm not going to say that life is wretched if circumstance is wretched, because that's not true. So I take that responsibility, but it's a responsibility to the truth, and to my art as much as anything. I owe everybody that.... It's the truth as I see it, and that's what my responsibility is."

"Browsing through a volume of Lucille Clifton's poems or reading one of her children's books to my son," says Scarupa, "always makes me feel good: good to be black, good to be a woman, good to be alive." "I am excited about her work because she reflects me; she tells my story in a way and with an eloquence that is beyond my ability," concurs Madhubuti, who concludes: "To be original, relevant, and revolutionary in the mouth of fire is the mark of a dangerous person. Lucille Clifton is a poet of *mean* talent who has not let her gifts separate her from the work at hand. She is a teacher and an example. To read her is to give birth to bright seasons." Clifton, herself, has commented on her role as a poet in *Black Women Writers (1950-1980):* "I am interested in trying to render big ideas in a simple way ... in being understood not admired. I wish to celebrate and not be celebrated (though a little celebration is a lot of fun). I am a woman and I write from that experience. I am a Black woman and I write from that experience. I do not feel inhibited or bound by what I am." She adds: "Sometimes I think that the most anger comes from ones who were late in discovering that when the world said nigger it meant them too. I grew up knowing that the world meant me too but that was the world's insanity and not mine. I have been treated in publishing very much like other poets are treated, that is, not really very well. I continue to write since my life as a human only includes my life as a poet, it doesn't depend on it."

In Clifton's 1991 title, *Quilting: Poems 1987-1990,* the author uses a quilt as a poetic metaphor for life. Each poem is a story, bound together through the chronicles of history and figuratively sewn with the thread of experience. The result is, as Roger Mitchell in *American Book Review,* describes it, a quilt "made by and for people." Each section of the book is divided by a conventional quilt design name such as "Eight-Pointed Star" and "Tree of Life," which provides a framework within which Clifton crafts her poetic quilt. Clifton's main focus is on women's history; however, according to Mitchell her poetry has a far broader range: "Her heroes include nameless slaves buried on old plantations, Hector Peterson (the first child killed in the Soweto riot), Fannie Lou Hamer (founder of the Mississippi Peace and Freedom Party), Nelson and Winnie Mandela, W. E. B. DuBois, Huey P. Newton, and many other people who gave their lives to Black people from slavery and prejudice. Her confidence in the future wavers, however, because of the devastation now being wrought among Blacks by drugs."

Enthusiasts of *Quilting* include critic Bruce Bennett in the *New York Times Book Review,* who praises Clifton as a "passionate, mercurial writer, by turns angry, prophetic, compassionate, shrewd, sensuous, vulnerable and funny.... The movement and effect of the whole book communicate the sense of a journey" through which the poet achieves an understanding of "something new." Pat Monaghan in *Booklist* admires Clifton's "terse, uncomplicated" verse, and judges the poet "a fierce and original voice in American letters." Mitchell finds energy and hope in her poems, referring to them as "visionary." He concludes that they are "the poems of a strong woman, strong enough to ... look the impending crises of our time in the eye, as well as our customary limitations, and go ahead and hope anyway."

*BIOGRAPHICAL/CRITICAL SOURCES:*

BOOKS

Beckles, Frances N., *20 Black Women,* Gateway Press, 1978.
*Children's Literature Review,* Volume 5, Gale, 1983.
*Contemporary Literary Criticism,* Volume 9, Gale, 1981.
*Dictionary of Literary Biography,* Gale, Volume 5: *American Poets since World War II,* 1980, Volume 41: *Afro-American Poets since 1955,* 1985.
Dreyer, Sharon Spredemann, *The Bookfinder: A Guide to Children's Literature about the Needs and Problems of Youth Aged 2-15,* Volume 1, American Guidance Service, 1977.
Evans, Mari, editor, *Black Women Writers (1950-1980): A Critical Evaluation,* Doubleday-Anchor, 1984.

PERIODICALS

*America,* May 1, 1976.
*American Book Review,* June, 1992, p. 21.
*Black Scholar,* March, 1981.
*Black World,* July, 1970; February, 1973.
*Booklist,* June 15, 1991, p. 1926.
*Book World,* March 8, 1970; November 8, 1970.
*Bulletin of the Center for Children's Books,* March, 1971; November, 1974; March, 1976; September, 1980.
*Horn Book,* December, 1971; August, 1973; February, 1975; December, 1975; October, 1977.
*Interracial Books for Children Bulletin,* Volume 5, numbers 7 and 8, 1975; Volume 7, number 1, 1976; Volume 8, number 1, 1977; Volume 10, number 5, 1979; Volume 11, numbers 1 and 2, 1980; Volume 12, number 2, 1981.
*Journal of Negro Education,* summer, 1974.
*Journal of Reading,* February, 1977; December, 1986.
*Kirkus Reviews,* April 15, 1970; October 1, 1970; December 15, 1974; April 15, 1976; February 15, 1982.
*Language Arts,* January, 1978; February 2, 1982.
*Ms.,* October, 1976.
*New Yorker,* April 5, 1976.
*New York Times,* December 20, 1976.
*New York Times Book Review,* September 6, 1970; December 6, 1970; December 5, 1971; November 4, 1973; April 6, 1975; March 14, 1976; May 15, 1977; March 1, 1992; May 31, 1992; p. 28.
*Poetry,* May, 1973.
*Reading Teacher,* October, 1978; March, 1981.
*Redbook,* November, 1969.
*Saturday Review,* December 11, 1971; August 12, 1972; December 4, 1973.
*School Library Journal,* May, 1970; December, 1970; September, 1974; December, 1977; February, 1979; March, 1980.
*Tribune Books,* August 30, 1987.

*Virginia Quarterly Review,* fall, 1976.
*Voice of Youth Advocates,* April, 1982.
*Washington Post,* November 10, 1974; August 9, 1979.
*Washington Post Book World,* November 11, 1973; November 10, 1974; December 8, 1974; December 11, 1977; February 10, 1980; September 14, 1980; July 20, 1986; May 10, 1987.
*Western Humanities Review,* summer, 1970.

\*   \*   \*

## COBB, Charles E(arl), Jr. 1943-
### (Charlie Cobb)

*PERSONAL:* Born June 23, 1943, in Washington, DC; son of Charles E., Sr. (a United Church of Christ minister) and Martha (Kendrick) Cobb; married; wife's name, Ann L. Chinn; children: Kenn Blagurn (stepson), Zora Nomnikelo. *Education:* Attended Howard University, 1961-62.

*ADDRESSES: Office*—c/o *National Geographic,* 1145 17th St. NW, Washington, DC 20036.

*CAREER:* Poet, free-lance writer, 1962—. Student Nonviolent Coordinating Committee (SNCC) member, 1962-67; associated with Center for Black Education, Washington, DC, 1968-69; Drum and Spear Press, member of board of directors, 1969-74; U.S. House of Representatives, subcommittee on Africa, member of staff, 1973; WHUR radio station, reporter, 1974-75; National Public Radio, foreign affairs news reporter, 1976-79; wrote and produced documentary films on a free-lance basis for *Frontline,* Public Broadcasting Service (PBS), 1979-85; *National Geographic* magazine, writer and member of senior editorial staff, 1985—.

*MEMBER:* National Association of Black Journalists (founding member).

*WRITINGS:*

*In the Furrows of the World* (poetry), Flute, 1967.
*Everywhere Is Yours* (poetry), Third World Press, 1971.
*African Notebook: Views on Returning 'Home'* (nonfiction), Institute of Positive Education, 1971.

Also author and co-producer of documentaries, including *In the Shadow of the Capitol; Crisis in Zimbabwe; Bread, Butter, and Politics; Chasing the Basketball Dream;* and *A Class Divided,* all for Public Broadcasting Service (PBS). Contributor to *Thoughts of Young Radicals,* New Republic, 1966. Work represented in several anthologies, including *Black Fire: An Anthology of Afro-American Writing,* edited by LeRoi Jones and Larry Neal, Morrow, 1968; *Campfires of the Re-*

*sistance: Poetry from the Movement,* edited by Todd Gitlin, Bobbs-Merrill, 1971; *The Poetry of Black America,* edited by Arnold Adoff, Harper, 1973. Contributor to newspapers, magazines, and journals, including *African World Newspaper, Black Books Bulletin, Black Enterprise, Journal of Black Poetry, National Geographic,* and *Southern Exposure.*

*SIDELIGHTS:* Charles E. Cobb, Jr.'s literary career, spanning several decades and including writings in various genres, represents a clear example of a mix of the personal and political. His early work, primarily poetry and essays, explores the struggles of the civil rights movement, racial strife in the United States, and the relationship between African Americans and Africa; his more recent journalism focuses on the Third World, particularly Africa, as well as environmental issues in America. Over the years, the medium for his views has changed. But his work, notes critic Clara R. Williams in her *Dictionary of Literary Biography* profile, "continues to exemplify his love and respect for his people; there is no doubt that he is dedicated to writing the truths of the political, economic, and social problems confronting black Americans as well as citizens of the Third World."

Cobb was born in Washington, DC, in 1943. His father, the Reverend Charles E. Cobb, Sr., served as an United Church of Christ minister, and throughout his youth, the family relocated often, living at various times in Kentucky, Massachusetts, North Carolina, and other states. In 1961, Cobb entered Howard University in Washington, DC. He did not remain for long, however. The burgeoning civil rights movement held great interest for him, and in the spring of 1962 he left his studies and moved to Mississippi, where he joined the Student Nonviolent Coordinating Committee (SNCC). In an interview with Howell Raines, published in *My Soul Is Rested,* Cobb recounted how he both witnessed and himself suffered abuses during the period while registering black voters and otherwise organizing members of the community in the struggle for equality.

This political activity was significant, for it was out of these experience that Cobb's literary endeavors were born. His first volume of poetry, *In the Furrows of the World,* was published in 1967. The poems in this collection address many of the struggles in which Cobb found himself while working for the SNCC. The focus, as Clara Williams remarks, is on "the many signs of racial unrest in the United States during a time when black America was engaged in more visible means of securing equal rights." The themes and style of the poetry are mutually complimentary, and show ties to those of other African American writers. "Cobb's style of using minimal capital letters, staccato phrasing, and little or no punctuation is also seen in other black writers' compositions," notes Williams; these inversions of literary conventions, she adds, "gave these writers a way to play artistically with the established terms of language, much as their political experimentation was geared toward changing the terms of society."

As the 1960s drew to a close, Cobb began to move the focus of his writing beyond the domestic scene. In 1967 he traveled to Vietnam; during his work with the Spear and Drum Press in the late 60s and early 70s, he first visited and then lived in Tanzania for two years (1970-72). Two books, *African Notebook: Views on Returning 'Home'* and *Everywhere Is Yours,* appeared in 1971, both influenced by the wider perspective his travels offered. The first is a nonfiction work outlining Cobb's views on the relationship between Africa and African Americans. In that volume, which Williams describes as "one of his most self-revealing," Cobb encourages closer ties between the African continent and the diaspora, particularly in the United States. Williams notes that Cobb writes, "one of the most destructive elements of our condition is the separation and fragmentation that exists between us." *Everywhere Is Yours* finds Cobb again using poetry as a means to reflect on similar themes. In one poem, "Nation No. 3," the narrator speaks of Africa as his true home, and laments his being severed from it.

Cobb's recent work is in a more strictly journalistic vein. He contributes to numerous magazines, including *Black Enterprise, Africa News,* and *National Geographic.* He continues in his journalism to write about the subjects which have long interested him—Africa, the Third World, and Black Americans—while also pursuing new topics, such as environmental issues in the United States. He has, for instance, written on the dangers of radiation and on pollution in the Great Lakes for *National Geographic.* Though his work has evolved and, as Clara Williams remarks, "shown growth and maturity" over the years, Cobb's commitment to the spirit of his earliest writings endures; he remains, in Williams's words, "a dynamic personality in the literary world."

*BIOGRAPHICAL/CRITICAL SOURCES:*

*BOOKS*

*Dictionary of Literary Biography,* Volume 41: *Afro-American Poets after 1955,* Gale, 1985.
Forman, James, *The Making of Black Revolutionaries: A Personal Account,* Macmillan, 1972, pp. 297-299, 387.
Raines, Howell, *My Soul Is Rested,* Putnam, 1977, pp. 244-248.
Spradling, Mary Mace, editor, *In Black and White: A Guide to Magazine Articles, Newspaper Articles and Books,* Gale, 1980, p. 195.

*PERIODICALS*

*Black World,* February 1972, p. 91.
*Nation,* April 22, 1968, p. 547-548.

\*   \*   \*

**COBB, Charlie**
  **See COBB, Charles E., Jr.**

\*   \*   \*

**COLEMAN, Emmett**
  **See REED, Ishmael**

\*   \*   \*

**COLEMAN, Wanda 1946-**

*PERSONAL:* Born November 13, 1946, in Los Angeles, CA.

*ADDRESSES: Home*—P.O. Box 29154, Los Angeles, CA 90029.

*CAREER:* Writer and performer. Worked as production editor, proofreader, magazine editor, waitress, and assistant recruiter for Peace Corps/Vista, 1968-75; staff writer for *Days of Our Lives,* National Broadcasting Co. (NBC-TV), 1975-76; medical transcriber and insurance billing clerk, 1979-84. Writer in residence at Studio Watts, 1968-69; cohost of interview program for Pacific Radio, 1981—.

*MEMBER:* P.E.N.

*AWARDS, HONORS:* Named to Open Door Program Hall of Fame, 1975; Emmy Award, Academy of Television Arts and Sciences, best writing in a daytime drama, 1976, for *Days of Our Lives;* fellowships from National Endowment for the Arts, 1981-82, and Guggenheim Foundation, 1984.

*WRITINGS:*

*Art in the Court of the Blue Fag* (chapbook), Black Sparrow Press, 1977.
*Mad Dog Black Lady,* Black Sparrow Press, 1979.
*Imagoes,* Black Sparrow Press, 1983, reissued, 1991.
*A War of Eyes and Other Stories,* Black Sparrow Press, 1988.
(Editor) *Women for All Seasons: Poetry and Prose about the Transitions in Women's Lives,* Woman's Building, 1988.
*Dicksboro Hotel & Other Travels,* Ambrosia Press, 1989.

(Editor) Foster, Susannah, *Earthbound in Betty Grable's Shoes,* Chiron Review Press, 1990.

*African Sleeping Sickness: Stories and Poems,* Black Sparrow Press, 1990.

*Heavy Daughter Blues: Poems and Stories,* Black Sparrow Press, 1991.

*Hand Dance,* Black Sparrow Press, 1993.

Also author of "The Time Is Now" episode for *The Name of the Game,* NBC-TV, 1970. Contributor to periodicals, including *An Afro American and African Journal of Arts and Letters.*

*SIDELIGHTS:* Wanda Coleman is known in the Los Angeles area for her poetry and her poetry readings. "As a poet," she said in an interview, "I have gained a reputation, locally, as an electrifying performer/reader, and have appeared at local rock clubs, reading the same poetry that has taken me into classrooms and community centers for over five hundred public readings since 1973."

Writing in *Black American Literature Forum,* Tony Magistrale explains "Coleman frequently writes to illuminate the lives of the underclass and the disenfranchised, the invisible men and woman who populate America's downtown streets after dark, the asylums and waystations, the inner city hospitals and clinics.... Wanda Coleman, like Gwendolyn Brooks before her, has much to tell us about what it is like to be a poor black woman in America."

Coleman also commented: "Words seem inadequate in expressing the anger and outrage I feel at the persistent racism that permeates every aspect of black American life. Since words are what I am best at, I concern myself with this as an urban actuality as best I can."

Coleman's work has received considerable praise from critics. Stephen Kessler wrote in *Bachy* that Coleman "shows us scary and exciting realms of ourselves," and Holly Prado noted in the *Los Angeles Times* that Coleman's "heated and economical language and head-on sensibility take her work beyond brutality to fierce dignity." Tamar Lehrich wrote in the *Nation:* "Wanda Coleman consistently confronts her readers with images, ideas and language that threaten to offend or at least to excite." Lehrich concluded that "Wanda Coleman's poetry and prose have been inspired by her frustration and anger at her position as a black woman and by her desire to translate those feelings into action."

*BIOGRAPHICAL/CRITICAL SOURCES:*

*PERIODICALS*

*African American Review,* summer 1992, pp. 355-57.
*Bachy,* fall, 1979, spring, 1980.

*Black American Literature Forum,* fall 1989, pp. 539-54.
*Los Angeles,* April, 1983.
*Los Angeles Times,* September 15, 1969; November 26, 1973; January 31, 1982; November 13, 1983.
*Los Angeles Times Book Review,* August 14, 1988, pp. 1, 9.
*Michigan Quarterly Review,* Fall, 1991, pp. 717-31.
*Nation,* February 20, 1988, p. 242-43.
*Publishers Weekly,* July 1, 1988.
*Stern,* May 16, 1974.

\*    \*    \*

## COLLIER, Eugenia W(illiams) 1928-

*PERSONAL:* Born April 6, 1928, in Baltimore, MD; daughter of Harry Maceo (a physician) and Eugenia (an educator; maiden name, Jackson) Williams; married Charles S. Collier, July 23, 1948 (divorced); children: Charles Maceo, Robert Nelson, Philip Gilles. *Education:* Howard University, B.A. (magna cum laude), 1948; Columbia University, M.A., 1950; University of Maryland, Ph.D., 1976.

*ADDRESSES: Home*—2608 Chelsea Terrace, Baltimore, MD 21228. *Office*—Department of English and Language Arts, Morgan State University, Baltimore, MD 21229.

*CAREER:* Baltimore Department of Public Welfare, Baltimore, MD, case worker, 1950-55; Morgan State College, Baltimore, assistant instructor, 1955-56, instructor, 1956-61, assistant professor of English, 1961-66; Community College of Baltimore, assistant professor, 1966-68, associate professor, 1968-70, professor of English, 1970-74, elected to Senate Executive Committee, 1970; University of Maryland, Baltimore County, associate professor, 1974-77; Howard University, Washington, DC, associate professor 1977-87; Coppin State College, Baltimore, professor, 1987-92; Morgan State University, Baltimore, professor of English, 1992—. Visiting professor at Southern Illinois University, summer, 1970, and Atlanta University, summers, 1973 and 1974; University of Maryland, Baltimore County, lecturer, 1974-75. Consultant, Workshop of Center for African and Afro-American Studies, 1969, Call and Response Workshop at Karamu House, 1970, Pine Manor Junior College, 1970—, and Bond Humanities Fair, Atlanta, GA, 1973-74; member of Middle States Evaluation Team for Lehigh Community College, 1970.

*MEMBER:* College Language Association, Association for the Study of Negro Life and History, Middle Atlantic Writers Association, African American Writers Guild.

*AWARDS, HONORS:* Gwendolyn Brooks Award for Fiction, *Negro Digest,* 1969, for story "Marigolds"; selected for *Outstanding Educators of America,* 1972-75; Distinguished Writers Award, Middle Atlantic Writers Association, 1984.

*WRITINGS:*

(With Ruthe T. Sheffey) *Impressions in Asphalt: Images of Urban America,* Scribner, 1969.

(With Joel I. Glasser and others) *A Bridge to Saying It Well,* Norvec, 1970.

(Contributor) *Langston Hughes: Black Genius,* edited by Therman O'Daniel, Morrow, 1971.

(Editor with Richard A. Long) *Afro-American Writing: An Anthology of Prose and Poetry,* two volumes, New York University Press, 1972, enlarged edition, Pennsylvania State University Press, 1985.

(Contributor) *Modern Black Poets: A Collection of Critical Essays,* edited by Donald Gibson, Prentice-Hall, 1973.

*Ricky* (one-act play; based on her short story by the same title), produced by Kuumba Workshop, Eugene Perkins Theatre, Chicago, IL, 1976.

*Spread My Wings,* Third World Press, 1992.

*Breeder and Other Stories,* Black Classic Press, 1993.

Work represented in anthologies, including *Brothers and Sisters,* edited by Arnold Adoff, Macmillan, 1970; *Accent,* edited by James B. Phillips and others, Scott, Foresman, 1972; *Oral and Written Composition: A Unit-Lesson Approach,* edited by Albert Lavin and others, Ginn, 1972. Contributor of stories, poems, and articles to *Negro Digest, Black World, TV Guide, Phylon, College Language Association Journal,* and *New York Times.* Televised lecture included in series "The Negro in History," produced by Morgan State University.

*WORK IN PROGRESS:* A collection of autobiographical sketches.

*SIDELIGHTS:* Eugenia W. Collier commented: "The fact of my blackness is the core and center of my creativity. After a conventional Western-type education, I discovered the richness, the diversity, the beauty of my black heritage. This discovery has meant a coalescence of personal and professional goals. It has also meant a lifetime commitment."

*BIOGRAPHICAL/CRITICAL SOURCES:*

*BOOKS*

*In Black and White,* third edition, two volumes, Gale, 1980, third edition, supplement, 1985.

Peterson, Bernard L., Jr., *Contemporary Black American Playwrights and Their Plays,* Greenwood Press, 1988.

Williams, Ora, *American Black Women in the Arts and Social Sciences: A Bibliographic Survey,* Scarecrow, 1973.

# COMER, James P(ierpont) 1934-

*PERSONAL:* Born September 25, 1934, in East Chicago, IN; son of Hugh (a steelworker) and Maggie (Nichols) Comer; married Shirley Ann Arnold, June 20, 1959; children: Brian Jay, Dawn Renee. *Education:* Indiana University, B.A., 1956; Howard University, M.D., 1960, post-doctoral study, 1961-63; University of Michigan, M.P.H., 1964; Yale University, post-doctoral study, 1964-67. *Avocational interests:* Photography, travel, sports.

*ADDRESSES: Home*—North Haven, CT. *Office*—Child Study Center, Yale University, 230 South Frontage Rd., New Haven, CT 06520.

*CAREER:* St. Catherine Hospital, East Chicago, IN, intern, 1960-61; Children's Hospital of the District of Columbia, Washington, DC, fellow in child psychiatry at Hillcrest Children's Center, 1967-68; Yale University, New Haven, CT, assistant professor at Child Study Center, 1968-70, associate professor, 1970-75, professor of psychiatry, 1975-76, Maurice Falk professor of psychiatry, 1976—, director of pupil services at Baldwin-King School Program, 1968-73, associate dean of medical school, 1969—, director of Child Study Center School Unit, 1973—. National Institutes of Mental Health, member of psychiatric staff, 1967-68; Solomon Fuller Institute member, 1973—; National Council for Effective Schools, director, 1985—. Trustee or member of board of directors of Afro-American House, 1970-72; Children's Television Workshop, 1970-86; Connecticut Energy Corp., 1976—; Wesleyan University, 1978-84; Field Foundation, 1981-88; Black Family Roundtable of Greater New Haven, 1986—; Child Study Center School Unit, 1986—; Albertus Magnus College, 1989—; Carnegie Corp. and Carnegie Corp. of New York, both 1990; and Connecticut State University, 1991—. Has served on the advisory committees or boards of Macy Faculty Fellows of the Josiah Macy, Jr., Foundation, 1971-74, and National Board to Abolish Corporal Punishment in the Schools, 1974-78. Has served on numerous panels and commissions for public and private organizations. Has appeared on radio and television. Consultant to Washington, DC, Hospitality House, National Congress of Parents and Teachers, and Institute of the Black World. Licensed to practice medicine in Maryland, 1960, Indiana, 1961, and California and Connecticut, both 1965. *Military Service:* U.S. Public Health Service, Washington, DC, lecturer, planner, and clinical psychiatrist in Commission Corps, 1961-68; became lieutenant colonel.

*MEMBER:* American Medical Association, National Medical Association, American Orthopsychiatric Association, American Psychiatric Association (chair of Committee of

Black Psychiatrists, 1973-75), Institute of Medicine, Society of Health and Human Values, Associates for Renewal in Education, Black Psychiatrists of America (cofounder), American Academy of Child and Adolescent Psychiatry, National Association for the Advancement of Colored People, National Mental Health Association, Black Coalition of New Haven, Alpha Omega Alpha, Alpha Phi Alpha.

*AWARDS, HONORS:* Scholarships in academic medicine from John and Mary Markle Foundation, 1969-74; special Award from Alpha Phi Alpha, 1972, for outstanding service to mankind; award from Ebony Success Library, 1973; Howard University Distinguished Alumni Award, 1975; Child Study Association/Wel-Met Family Life Book Award, 1975, for *Black Child Care;* Rockefeller Public Service Award, 1980; Media Award, NCCJ, 1981; Community Leadership Award, Greater New Haven Council of Churches, 1983; Distinguished Fellowship Award, Connecticut chapter of Phi Delta Kappa, 1984; Distinguished Educator award, Connecticut Coalition of 100 Black Women, 1985; Distinguished Service Award, Connecticut Association of Psychologists, 1985; Elm and Ivy Award, New Haven Foundation, 1985; Outstanding Leadership Award, Children's Defense Fund, 1987; Lela Rowland Prevention award, National Mental Health Association, 1989; Whitney M. Young, Jr., Service Award, Boy Scouts of America, 1989; Harold W. McGraw, Jr., prize in Education, 1990; National Prudential Leadership award, Prudential Foundation, 1990; Agnes Purcell McGavin award, Solomon Carter Fuller award, and Special Presidential Commendation awards, all from American Psychiatric Association, all 1990; Vera S. Paster Award, American Orthopsychiatric Association, 1990; Charles A. Dana Prize in Education, 1991; James Bryant Conant award, Education Commission of the States, 1991; Distinguished Service award, Council of Chief State School Officers, 1991; honorary degrees from University of New Haven, 1977, Calumet College, 1978, Bank Street College, 1987, Albertus Magnus College, Quinnipiac College, and DePauw University, all 1989, and Indiana University, Wabash College, Amherst College, Northwestern University, Worcester Polytechnic Institute, State University of New York at Buffalo, New School for Social Research, John Jay College of Criminal Justice, Wesleyan University, Wheelock College, Rhode Island College, and Princeton University, all 1991.

*WRITINGS:*

*Beyond Black and White,* Quadrangle Press, 1972.
(With Alvin F. Poussaint) *Black Child Care: How to Bring Up a Healthy Black Child in America: A Guide to Emotional and Psychological Development,* Simon & Schuster, 1975.
*School Power: Implications of an Intervention Project,* Free Press, 1980.

*Maggie's American Dream: The Life and Times of a Black Family,* Plume, 1988.
(With Ronald Edmonds) *A Conversation between James Comer and Ronald Edmonds: Fundamentals of Effective School Improvement,* National Center for Effective Schools Research and Development Corp., 1989.
(With Poussaint) *Raising Black Children: Two Leading Psychiatrists Confront the Educational, Social, and Emotional Problems Facing Black Children,* Plume, 1992.

Contributor to books, including *Negroes for Medicine,* edited by Lee Cogan, Johns Hopkins Press, 1968; *Violence in America: Historical and Comparative Perspectives,* edited by Ted Gurr and Hugh Graham, New American Library, 1969; *The Rhetoric of Black Power,* edited by Robert Scott and Wayne Brockriede, Harper, 1969; *Boys No More: A Black Psychologist's View of Community,* edited by Charles W. Thomas, Glencoe Press, 1970; *To Improve Learning: An Evaluation of Instructional Technology,* Vol. II, edited by Sydney G. Tickton, Bowker, 1971; *Racism and Mental Health,* edited by Charles V. Willie, Bernard M. Kramer, and Bertram S. Brown, University of Pittsburgh Press, 1973; *The Child and His Family: Children at Psychiatric Risk,* Vol. III, edited by E. James Anthony and Cyrille Koupernik, Viley, 1974; *Education and Social Problems,* edited by Francis A. J. Ianni, Scott, Foresman, 1974; and *Common Decency,* edited by Alvin Schorr, Yale University Press, 1988.

Columnist for *Parents Magazine.* Contributor to periodicals, including *Ebony* and *Redbook.* Has served on the editorial boards of *American Journal of Orthopsychiatry,* 1970-76, *Youth and Adolescence,* 1971-87, and *Journal of Negro Education,* 1978-83; member of advisory board, *Renaissance Two: Journal of Afro-American Studies at Yale,* 1971—; editorial consultant, *Journal of the American Medical Association,* 1973—, and *Magazine of the National Association of Mental Hygiene,* 1975—; guest editor, *Journal of American Academy of Child Psychiatry,* 1985. *Beyond Black and White* was released as a sound recording, Center for Cassette Studies, c. 1974.

*SIDELIGHTS:* Psychiatrist and author James P. Comer theorizes that the way to improve the academic performance of children in inner-city schools is to foster a family-like atmosphere in the classroom. Comer was born into a family with strong ties of its own in East Chicago, Indiana, just south of Chicago and near the heart of the city's steel-making industry. As a young man, Comer worked in the grease pits at one of the so-called "black jobs," often the most dangerous and taxing positions. He recounts these and other memories in his book *Maggie's American Dream: The Life and Times of a Black Family,* which also features an oral history of his mother's childhood in Mississippi.

In 1966, the Baldwin-King Program of Yale's Child Study Center began a project to collaborate with two New Haven schools on improving students' performance. Comer became involved with the project and in 1980 he published a book on the experiment, *School Power: Implications of an Intervention Project,* in which he critiques ten years of attempts to reform the school. "The real value of this book," wrote a *Choice* contributor, "is in pointing out just how difficult it is to bring about change in urban schools given the complex problems of this society."

In 1972's *Beyond Black and White,* Comer meditates on the problems of race relations and discusses his experiences as a black member of the academic elite. Realizing that there wasn't a good book on black parenting, he wrote, with Alvin F. Poussaint, *Black Child Care: How to Bring Up a Healthy Black Child in America: A Guide to Emotional and Psychological Development* in 1975. *New York Times Book Review* contributor Jim Haskins noted: "The book as a whole is informative and insightful, and its bibliography is the most thorough on the subject of black emotional and psychological development I have ever found." Comer and Poussaint penned a similar title in 1992, *Raising Black Children: Two Leading Psychiatrists Confront the Educational, Social, and Emotional Problems Facing Black Children,* in which they respond to the many questions each has heard from black parents, from dealing with racism to attempting to curb violence.

*BIOGRAPHICAL/CRITICAL SOURCES:*

*PERIODICALS*

*Choice,* January, 1981, pp. 705-706.
*Christian Science Monitor,* December 9, 1988, p. D9.
*Ebony,* September, 1973.
*Newsweek,* October 2, 1989, p. 50; January 25, 1993, p. 55.
*New York Times,* May 30, 1975.
*New York Times Book Review,* July 14, 1974, p. 29; June 15, 1975, p. 28.
*New York Times Magazine,* April 18, 1971.
*Sepia,* December, 1973.
*Washington Post Book World,* November 16, 1980, p. 26; November 19, 1989.

\*   \*   \*

## CONDE, Maryse 1937-
   (Maryse Boucolon)

*PERSONAL:* Born February 11, 1937, in Guadeloupe, West Indies; daughter of Auguste and Jeanne (Quidal) Boucolon; married Mamadou Conde, 1958 (divorced, 1981); married Richard Philcox (a translator), 1982; children: (first marriage) Leila, Sylvie, Aicha. *Education:* Sorbonne, University of Paris, Ph.D., 1976.
*ADDRESSES: Home*—Montebello, 97170 Petit Bourg, Guade-loupe, French West Indies. *Agent*—Rosalie Siegel, Act III Productions, 711 Fifth St., New York, NY 10022.

*CAREER:* Ecole Normale Superieure, Conakry, Guinea, instructor, 1960-64; Ghana Institute of Languages, Accra, Ghana, 1964-66; Lycee Charles de Gaulle, Saint Louis, Senegal, instructor, 1966-68; French Services of the BBC, London, England, program producer, 1968-70; University of Paris, Paris, France, assistant at Jussieu, 1970-72, lecturer at Nanterre, 1973-80, charge de cours at Sorbonne, 1980-85; program producer, Radio France Internationale, France Culture, 1980—. Bellagio Writer in Residence, Rockefeller Foundation, 1986; visiting professor, University of Virginia and University of Maryland, 1992—; lecturer in the United States, Africa, and the West Indies. Presenter of a literary program for Africa on Radio-France.

*AWARDS, HONORS:* Fulbright Scholar, 1985-86; Prix litteraire de la Femme, Prix Alain Boucheron, 1986, for *Moi, Tituba, Sorciere Noire de Salem;* Guggenheim fellow, 1987-88; Puterbaugh fellow, University of Oklahoma, Norman, 1993.

*WRITINGS:*

(Editor) *Anthologie de la litterature africaine d'expression francaise,* Ghana Institute of Languages, 1966.
*Dieu nous l'a donne* (four-act play; title means "God Given"; first produced in Martinique, West Indies, at Fort de France, 1973), Oswald, 1972.
*Mort d'Oluwemi d'Ajumako* (four-act play; title means "Death of a King"; first produced in Haiti at Theatre d'Alliance Francaise, 1975), Oswald, 1973.
*Heremakhonon* (novel), Union Generale d'Editions, 1976, translation by husband, Richard Philcox, published under same title, Three Continents Press, 1982.
(Translator into French with Philcox) Eric Williams, *From Columbus to Castro: The History of the Caribbean,* Presence Africaine, 1977.
(Editor) *La Poesie antillaise* (also see below), Nathan (Paris), 1977.
(Editor) *Le Roman antillais* (also see below), Nathan, 1977.
*La Civilisation du bossale* (criticism), Harmattan (Paris), 1978.
*Le profil d'une oeuvre: Cahier d'un retour au pays natal* (criticism), Hatier (Paris), 1978.
*La Parole des femmes* (criticism), Harmattan, 1979.
*Tim tim? Bois sec! Bloemlezing uit de Franstalige Caribsche Literatuur* (contains revised and translated editions of *Le Roman antillais* and *La Poesie antillaise*), edited by Andries van der Wal, In de Knipscheer, 1980.

*Une Saison a Rihata* (novel), Robert Laffont (Paris), 1981, translation by Philcox published as *A Season in Rihata,* Heinemann, 1988.

*Segou: Les murailles de terre,* (novel), Robert Laffont, 1984, translation by Barbara Bray published as *Segu,* Viking, 1987.

*Segou II: La terre en miettes* (novel), Robert Laffont, 1985, translation by Linda Coverdale published as *The Children of Segu,* Viking, 1989.

*Pays Mele* (short stories), Hatier, 1985.

*Moi, Tituba, sorciere noire de Salem* (novel), Mercure de France (Paris), 1986, translation by Philcox published as *I, Tituba, Black Witch of Salem,* University Press of Virginia, 1992.

*La Vie scelerate* (novel), Seghers, 1987, translation by Victoria Reiter published as *Tree of Life,* Ballantine, 1992.

*Haiti Cherie* (juvenile), Bayard Presse, 1987.

*Pension les Alizes* (play), Mercure de France, 1988.

*Victor et les barricades* (juvenile), Bayard Presse, 1989.

*Traversee de la mangrove* (novel), Mercure de France, 1990.

*Les derniers rois mages* (novel), Mercure de France, 1992.

*La colonie du nouveau monde* (novel), Robert Laffont, 1993.

Also author of recordings for Record CLEF and Radio France Internationale. Contributor to anthologies; contributor to journals, including *Presence Africaine* and *Recherche Pedagogique.*

*SIDELIGHTS:* West Indian author Maryse Conde, "deals with characters in domestic situations and employs fictitious narratives as a means of elaborating large-scale activities," assert *World Literature Today* writers Charlotte and David Bruner. Drawing on her experiences in Paris, West Africa, and her native Guadeloupe, Conde has created several novels which "attempt to make credible on an increasingly larger scale the personal human complexities involved in holy wars, national rivalries, and migrations of peoples," the Bruners state. *Heremakhonon,* for example, relates the journey of Veronica, an Antillean student searching for her roots in a newly liberated West African country. During her stay Veronica becomes involved with both a powerful government official and a young school director opposed to the new regime; "to her dismay," David Bruner summarizes, "she is unable to stay out of the political struggle, and yet she is aware that she does not know enough to understand what is happening."

The result of Veronica's exploration, which is told with an "insinuating prose [that] has a surreal, airless quality," as Carole Bovoso relates in the *Voice Literary Supplement,* is that "there were times I longed to rush in and break the spell, to shout at this black woman and shake her. But no one can rescue Veronica," the critic continues, "least of all herself; Conde conveys the seriousness of her plight by means of a tone of

relentless irony and reproach." "Justly or not," write the Bruners, "one gains a comprehension of what a revolution is like, what new African nations are like, yet one is aware that this comprehension is nothing more than a feeling. The wise reader will go home as Veronica does," the critics conclude, "to continue more calmly to reflect, and to observe."

Conde expands her scope in *Segu,* "a wondrous novel about a period of African history few other writers have addressed," notes *New York Times Book Review* contributor Charles R. Larson. In tracing three generations of a West African family during the early and mid-1800s, "Conde has chosen for her subject ... [a] chaotic stage, when the animism (which she calls fetishism) native to the region began to yield to Islam," the critic describes. "The result is the most significant historical novel about black Africa published in many a year."

Beginning with Dousika, a Bambara nobleman caught up in court intrigue, *Segu* trails the exploits of his family, from one son's conversion to Islam to another's enslavement to a third's successful career in commerce, connected with stories of their wives and concubines and servants. In addition, Conde's "knowledge of African history is prodigious, and she is equally versed in the continent's folklore," remarks Larson. "The unseen world haunts her characters and vibrates with the spirits of the dead."

Some critics, however, fault the author for an excess of detail; *Washington Post* contributor Harold Courlander, for example, comments that "the plethora of happenings in the book does not always make for easy reading." The critic explains that "the reader is sometimes uncertain whether history and culture are being used to illuminate the fiction or the novel exists to tell us about the culture and its history." While Howard Kaplan concurs with this assessment, he adds in the *Los Angeles Times Book Review* that *Segu* "glitters with nuggets of cultural fascination.... For those willing to make their way through this dense saga, genuine rewards will be reaped." "With such an overwhelming mass of data and with so extensive a literary objective, the risks of ... producing a heavy, didactic treatise are, of course, great," the Bruners maintain. "The main reason that Conde has done neither is, perhaps, because she has written here essentially as she did in her two earlier novels: she has followed the lives of the fictional characters as individuals dominated by interests and concerns which are very personal and often selfish and petty, even when those characters are perceived by other characters as powerful leaders in significant national or religious movements." Because of this, the critics conclude, *Segu* is "a truly remarkable book.... To know [the subjects of her work] better, as well as to know Maryse Conde even better, would be a good thing."

*BIOGRAPHICAL/CRITICAL SOURCES:*

*PERIODICALS*

*Los Angeles Times Book Review,* March 8, 1987.
*New York Times Book Review,* May 31, 1987.
*Washington Post,* March 3, 1987.
*World Literature Today,* winter, 1982; winter, 1985; spring, 1985; summer, 1986; spring, 1987; summer, 1988.

\*     \*     \*

## COOPER, Clarence L(avaugn), Jr. 1942-

*PERSONAL:* Born May 5, 1942, in Decatur, GA; married, wife's name, Shirley; children: Jennae, Corey. *Education:* Clark College, B.A., 1964; Emory University School of Law, J.D., 1967; degree from the Massachusetts Institute of Technology, 1977; Harvard University John F. Kennedy School Government Public Administration, 1978.

*ADDRESSES: Office*—Judge, Fulton County Superior Court, 136 Pryor St., Atlanta, GA 30303.

*CAREER:* Atlanta Legal Service Program, Atlanta, GA, attorney, 1967-68; Fulton County, GA, assistant district attorney, 1968-76; Atlanta Municipal Court, Atlanta, GA, associate judge, 1976; currently Fulton County Superior Court, GA, judge. *Military service:* Served in United States Army, 1968-70, became staff sergeant, received Bronze Star and Certificate of Commendation.

*MEMBER:* National Bar Association, Gate City Bar Association, National Conference of Black Lawyers, State Bar of Georgia, Atlanta Bar Association, member of the executive board of the Atlanta Branch of National Alliance for the Advancement of Colored People (NAACP), member of the National Urban League, member of the board of directors of Amistrad Prod, Equal Opportunity Association Drug Program, past member of the Atlanta Judicial Commission.

*AWARDS, HONORS:* Received scholarship to Clark College, 1960-64; published "The Judiciary and It's Budget—an administrative hassle."

*WRITINGS:*

*NOVELS*

*The Scene,* Crown, 1960.
*Weed,* Regency Books, 1961.
*The Dark Messenger,* Regency Books, 1962.

*Black! Two Short Novels,* Regency Books, 1963.
*The Farm,* Crown, 1967.

Contributor to *Black Short Story Anthology.*

*BIOGRAPHICAL/CRITICAL SOURCES:*

*PERIODICALS*

*Negro Digest,* May 17, 1968, pp. 94-95.
*Publishers Weekly,* April 20, 1970, vol. 197, p. 63.

\*     \*     \*

## CORBIN, Steven 1953-

*PERSONAL:* Born October 3, 1953, in Jersey City, NJ; son of Warren Leroy Corbin (a supermarket manager) and Yvonne O'Hare (a homemaker; maiden name, Kitchens). *Education:* Attended Essex County College, c. 1973-75, and University of Southern California, c. 1975-77.

*ADDRESSES: Home*—Los Angeles, CA. *Agent*—Sherry Robb, 7551 Melrose Ave., Los Angeles, CA 90028.

*CAREER:* Held various secretarial positions and worked as a taxi driver, c. 1977-87; writer, 1981—; University of California, Los Angeles, instructor in fiction writing, 1988—.

*WRITINGS:*

*No Easy Place to Be,* Simon and Schuster, 1989.
*Fragments That Remain,* Alyson Publications, 1993.

Fiction editor for *Southern California Anthology,* Ross-Erikson, 1985.

*SIDELIGHTS:* Steven Corbin's first novel, *No Easy Place to Be,* explores such diverse issues as racism, feminism, and the significance of the arts to black culture, raising what *Los Angeles Times Book Review* critic Gail Lumet Buckley refers to as "potentially interesting" and "important questions" in these areas. The novel's use of historical figures and situations has been cited by critics, and Corbin often blends important social issues into the book's narrative story line. The author's second book, *Fragments That Remain,* also takes a historical approach, chronicling a troubled American family beginning in 1929.

*No Easy Place to Be* depicts the lives of three sisters—Velma, Miriam, and Louise—during the Harlem Renaissance of the 1920s. Corbin told *Los Angeles Times* interviewer Gary Libman that he wrote the novel because he "wanted to say something about black writers" and felt that the Harlem Renaissance had not been given its proper place in American History. "What's even more offensive," Corbin added, "is that the only thing we remember about the Harlem Renaissance is the Cotton Club, where blacks sang and danced and did buffoonery. We do not ... remember our novelists, our playwrights and our great actors."

In approaching the Harlem of the 1920s, Corbin concentrates on the historical backdrop of the era, dotting his novel with allusions to real people and places and using these as a point of reference for the issues he raises. Velma, for example, is portrayed as a writer struggling against the racism of her sponsor, a white Park Avenue patron who demands what Buckley calls "exotic primitiveness" of Velma. As the critic points out, the character of the patron is "based on the famous 'Godmother' of [black writers] Langston Hughes and Zora Neale Hurston." Corbin further uses his characters as a mode of historical exploration by making Miriam a follower of Marcus Garvey and his Universal Negro Improvement Association and having Louise work as a dancer at the Cotton Club. Louise also becomes one of Corbin's primary vehicles for exploring the issue of race, as her light complexion often allows her to pass as white. Louise eventually attempts to embrace a white identity, marrying a wealthy Italian who is unaware that she is black.

As the lives of these sisters unfold, sexuality becomes an important element of the book. Velma is involved in the lives of homosexual fellow-writers Rudy and Scott, while Miriam realizes that she is a lesbian. Buckley criticizes Corbin for this, stating that the issues raised at the outset of the novel are overshadowed by the personal entanglements of Corbin's protagonists. Julie Johnson, writing in the *New York Times Book Review,* noted a lack of "spontaneity and vitality" in the book but found several "high points" in the novel's exploration of the Harlem Renaissance.

*No Easy Place to Be* ends with the stock market crash. The three sisters are once again living together in Harlem as Velma vows, in spite of the difficulties of the Depression, to keep going. This conclusion, as Buckley notes, appears to be one of optimism, while recognizing that none of the problems faced by the characters has been truly overcome.

*BIOGRAPHICAL/CRITICAL SOURCES:*

*PERIODICALS*

*Los Angeles Times,* February 26, 1989.
*Los Angeles Times Book Review,* July 2, 1989, p. 2.
*New York Times Book Review,* May 21, 1989, p. 8.

## CORNWELL, Anita (R.) 1923-

*PERSONAL:* Born in 1923.

*ADDRESSES:Home*—3220 Powelton Ave., Philadelphia, PA 19104.

*CAREER:* Free-lance writer; novelist; Pennsylvania State Department of Public Welfare employee.

*WRITINGS:*

*Black Lesbian in White America,* Naiad Press, 1983.
*The Girls of Summer* (juvenile), illustrated by Kelly Caines, New Seed Press, 1989.

\*   \*   \*

## CORROTHERS, James D(avid)  1869-1917

*PERSONAL:* Original name, James David Carruthers; changed the spelling of his name while in grade school; born July 2, 1869, in Cass County, MI; died of a stroke, February 12, 1917, in West Chester, PA; son of James Richard and Maggie Carruthers; married Fanny Clemens (died about 1898); married and divorced a second wife; married Rosina B. Harvey (a music teacher), 1906; children: (first marriage) Willard, Richard; (third marriage) Henry. *Education:* Attended Northwestern University until 1893; studied at Bennett College.

*CAREER:* Writer, minister. Worked as a bootblack and in lumber mills, factories, hotels, and on a steamship before becoming a Methodist minister in 1898 and later a Baptist minister; published poetry, short fiction, and articles starting in the mid-1880s.

*WRITINGS:*

*The Black Cat Club,* illustrated by J. K. Bryans, Funk & Wagnalls, 1902.
*In Spite of the Handicap* (autobiography), Doran, 1916.

Contributed poetry and fiction to *Century, Colored American, Crisis, American Magazine,* and various newspapers. Published non-fiction in various periodicals, including *Chicago Daily Record.*

*SIDELIGHTS:* Although in turn-of-the-century America he was one of the most successful black poets, James D. Corrothers has since been overshadowed by the work of contemporaries such as his friend Paul Laurence Dunbar. But while his talent may not have been "of the first rank," Richard

Yarborough suggests in the *Dictionary of Literary Biography*, Corrothers nonetheless remains an important figure whose writings include short stories, sketches, magazine and newspaper articles, and an autobiography in addition to his dialect and non-dialect verse. Moreover, Yarborough points out, "his career vividly reveals how black writers striving for a broad audience in late-nineteenth- and early-twentieth-century America had to cope with the racial stereotypes which shaped the expectations of white editors and readers alike."

After his mother died in childbirth, Corrothers was raised in predominantly white South Haven, Michigan, by his grandfather, a deeply religious man of Cherokee, Irish and Scottish descent. The only black student in his class, he was harassed by classmates and teachers alike; yet he remained positive in his view of life and convinced that virtue and hard work could prevail against oppression.

In the early years of his adult life Corrothers led a peripatetic existence, living in various places in Michigan, Ohio and Indiana and supporting himself with odd jobs in lumber mills and factories, as a hotel worker and as a pantryman on a steamer. He became a voracious reader, his favorite authors including the British writers Alfred Lord Tennyson and Oliver Goldsmith and the Scottish poet Robert Burns as well as American poets Henry Wadsworth Longfellow, John Greenleaf Whittier, and James Whitcomb Riley. While living in Springfield, Ohio, where he enjoyed the support of his fellow members of the Young Men's Republican Club, Corrothers published his first poem, a nondialect verse, in the local newspaper. Soon thereafter he moved to Chicago and was working as a bootblack when befriended by the writer Henry Demarest Lloyd, who arranged publication of Corrothers's poem "The Soldier's Excuse" in the *Chicago Tribune*. Lloyd helped Corrothers obtain a job as a porter with the *Tribune,* but Corrothers was dismissed after a dispute with the editor. Corrothers's first story—an article about Chicago's black community—was rewritten by a white reporter to fit prevailing stereotypes of black behavior. After learning that the reporter had been paid fifteen dollars to ruin his story—for which Corrothers himself had not been paid—he confronted the editor and was fired.

Corrothers continued to write, however, and in 1890 was hailed at the first convention of the National Afro-American League as "the coming poet of the race." With the financial support of relatives and of prominent reformer Frances Willard, he attended Northwestern University, working at odd jobs and taking courses when he could. Following the Columbian Exposition in Chicago in 1893, at which Frederick Douglass spoke, Corrothers met Dunbar and James E. Campbell. His friendships with these poets were a source of support for him, as was his marriage to Fanny Clemens in 1894. It was his wife who sold one of his articles to the *Chi-*

*cago Daily Record* for three dollars, marking his debut as a paid journalist. He could not make a living as a writer, however, and so continued to do manual work to support his family. In 1896 the *Chicago Evening Journal* published Corrothers' comic dialect sketch "De Carvin'" and expressed an interest in receiving similar pieces. Initially Corrothers hesitated, Yarborough reports. He himself did not speak the black dialect used in such sketches and indeed had to refer to a book on dialect in composing them; he feared, he would later explain, that writing in dialect would be demeaning to him and a "slur" on his race. Yarborough attributes his eventual change of heart to the growing popularity of dialect poetry and the success in the genre of Corrothers's friend Dunbar, as well as "pressing economic considerations." Having recently entered the Methodist ministry, Corrothers "decided to give dialect verse a serious try primarily because he found it difficult to live on his preacher's salary," Yarborough asserts.

Between 1899 and 1902, Corrothers began and ended a second marriage—his first wife and younger son had succumbed to tuberculosis shortly before he received his first church assignment—and accepted a series of posts with several churches. During this time he not only wrote more poetry, but published his first book. *The Black Cat Club* was a collection of sketches based on his work for the *Chicago Evening Journal.* Caught between his desire to write authentically and the need to write what would sell, Corrothers tried to weave the comic stereotypes of blacks as superstitious bickerers into a realistic love story. The book received tepid reviews and he later expressed regret that it had been published. However, Yarborough suggests, the sketches demonstrated both Corrothers' sensitive ear for speech patterns and "his ability to incorporate aspects of the black oral poetic tradition" into his work.

The next years were difficult ones for Corrothers. Shortly after his book was published, he faced a bishop's accusation of impropriety with a young woman in the congregation, as well as charges that he had tried to destroy the bishop's reputation. Although he was acquitted of the charges, he was expelled from his ministry. He drifted for a few months in New York City, turned down an offer to perform in vaudeville, and was crushed when he lost a trunk full of mementos of his deceased wife and son, along with some of his manuscripts. Two dark years came to an end when Corrothers became a Baptist and took up a new ministry. He also remarried, to music teacher Rosina B. Harvey, in 1906.

Corrothers's work, Yarborough suggests, "reflects the demands of the editors with whom he dealt as well as the concessions he made to those demands." The white editors of mainstream journals were interested primarily in his writings in black dialect, and his depictions of simple and good-natured black folks living in an imaginary gentle South resemble the work of contemporary white Southern writers "who were busy propagating the myth of the Old South," Yarborough writes. For *Colored American* magazine, however, he penned both nondialect verses and several ingenious dialect pieces. In "Me 'N' Dunbar," Corrothers depicts the literary rivalry between himself and his poet friend as a race between two neighboring farmers: "One day when me 'n' Dunbar wuz a-hoein' in de co'n, / Bofe uv us tried an' anxious foh to heah de dinnah-ho'n, / Him in his fiel', an' me in mine, a-wo'kin' on togeddah, / A-sweatin' lak de mischief in de hottes' kine o' weddah, / A debblish notion tuck me 't Paul wuz gittin' on too fast; / But, thanks I: Wait untwel he git 'mongst all dem weeds an' grass, / 'N' I'll make him ne'ly kill his se'f, an' den come out de las'. / Tuck off ma coat, rolled up ma slebes, spit on ma han's an' say: / 'Ef God'll he'p me—'n' not he'p him—I beats ma man today!' / S'I: 'Paul, come on, le's have a race!'"

In another poem, "An Awful Problem Solved," he uses a folk narrator to make a stinging indictment of racism. These pieces appeared mostly in black publications, as did his non-dialect writing. Yarborough states that although his conventional English verse is flawed by "the saccharine, ornate style of popular magazine verse," many of these works are saved by the poet's "attempt to confront the discrepancies between the American dream and the nightmarish oppression of blacks in the United States." Even his darker poems typically end in a reaffirmation of faith in God and the future, Yarborough reports, but the critic singles out "The Snapping of the Bow" for its call for blacks to take pride in their African heritage.

By 1910, Corrothers had all but abandoned dialect poems, resolving, as he put it, to work "for my *race*, as well as for myself and my family." *Century* magazine published several nondialect poems beginning in 1912. In the following year, Corrothers apparently left the ministry for several years to devote himself exclusively to writing, and moved his family to Philadelphia. In his later poems, some of which consider the problems of being a black artist in a white-dominated world, he "protests racial prejudice with a new power and forthrightness," Yarborough finds. He also continued to publish journalistic pieces, and wrote several short stories, including "A Man They Didn't Know," published in *Crisis* in two parts, which warns that violence could result from continued oppression of the black race and calls for more contact between whites and blacks to avert catastrophe.

But Corrothers' greatest story may well have been his own. His autobiography, *In Spite of the Handicap,* was published in 1916 and was well received. In his introduction to the book, Ray Stannard Baker wrote, "Mr. Corrothers gives us, not only a real contribution to our knowledge of all those complex conditions which confront the colored man in America, but a downright interesting and well-written human document." Baker also noted that the book is "singularly without rancor."

Yarborough, however, finds the authors' depictions of other blacks to be somewhat negative, while Rebecca Chalmers Barton states that in Corrothers's account, the African American often "becomes a convenient whipping post for his negative feelings."

In 1915 Corrothers, who had now joined the Presbyterian church, once again took up the ministry at a church in West Chester, Pennsylvania, where he died of a stroke in 1917. Although shortly before his death *Crisis* magazine had cited him as one of "the greatest of living Negro American poets," his work quickly faded from view as the popularity of black dialect verse waned, and his writing has received little modern critical attention. Yarborough suggests, however, that a reassessment of his place in black literary history is in order, and that much could be learned from his work and life "about the complex, precarious situation of the black author in the United States at the turn of the century."

*BIOGRAPHICAL/CRITICAL SOURCES:*

*BOOKS*

Barton, Rebecca Chalmers, *Witnesses for Freedom: Negro Americans in Autobiography,* Harper, 1948, pp. 18-23.

Brown, Sterling, *Negro Poetry and Drama,* Associates in Negro Folk Education, 1937.

Corrothers, James D., *In Spite of the Handicap,* Doran, 1916.

*Dictionary of Literary Biography,* Volume 50: *Afro-American Writers before the Harlem Renaissance,* Gale, 1987, pp. 52-62.

Johnson, Abby Arthur and Ronald Maberry Johnson, *Propaganda and Aesthetics: The Literary Politics of Afro-American Magazines in the Twentieth Century,* University of Massachusetts Press, 1979.

Johnson, James Weldon, editor, *The Book of American Negro Poetry,* Harcourt, Brace, 1931, pp. 72-80.

Redmond, Eugene B., *Drumvoices: The Mission of Afro-American Poetry,* Anchor/Doubleday, 1976, pp. 115-18.

*PERIODICALS*

*ALA Booklist,* February, 1917, p. 199.
*Book Review Digest,* 1916, p. 127.
*Colored American,* April, 1901, p. 410.
*Dial,* November 6, 1916, p. 472.
*Explorations in Ethnic Studies,* January, 1983, pp. 1-9.
*Independent,* November 6, 1916, p. 240.
*Southern Workman,* December, 1899, pp. 508-509.
*Springfield Republican,* November 16, 1916, p. 8.

*—Sketch by Karen Withem*

## CORTEZ, Jayne 1936-

*PERSONAL:* Born May 10, 1936, in Arizona; children: Denardo Coleman.

*ADDRESSES:* Box 96, Village Station, New York, NY 10014.

*CAREER:* Poet. Has lectured and read her poetry alone and with musical accompaniment throughout the United States, Europe, Africa, Latin America, and the Caribbean.

*AWARDS, HONORS:* Creative Artists Program Service poetry awards, New York State Council on the Arts, 1973 and 1981; National Endowment for the Arts fellowship in creative writing, 1979-86; American Book Award, 1980; New York Foundation for the Arts award, 1987.

*WRITINGS:*

*POETRY*

*Pissstained Stairs and the Monkey Man's Wares,* Phrase Text, 1969.
*Festivals and Funerals,* Bola Press, 1971.
*Scarifications,* Bola Press, 1973.
*Mouth on Paper,* Bola Press, 1977.
*Firespitter,* illustrated by Mel Edwards, Bola Press, 1982.
*Coagulations: New and Selected Poems,* Thunder's Mouth Press, 1982.
*Poetic Magnetic,* illustrated by Melvin Edwards, Bola Press, 1991.

*OTHER*

*Celebrations and Solitudes: The Poetry of Jayne Cortez* (sound recording), Strata-East Records, 1975.
*Unsubmissive Blues* (sound recording), Bola Press, 1980.
*There It Is* (sound recording), Bola Press, 1982.
*War on War* (screenplay), UNESCO (Paris), 1982.
*Poetry in Motion* (screenplay), Sphinx Productions (Toronto, Ontario, Canada), 1983.
*Maintain Control* (sound recording), Bola Press, 1986.
*Everywhere Drums* (sound recording), Bola Press, 1991.
*Mandela Is Coming* (music video), Globalvision, 1991.

Contributor to anthologies, including *We Speak as Liberators,* edited by Orde Coombs, Dodd, 1970; *The Poetry of Black America,* edited by Arnold Adoff, Harper, 1972; *Homage a Leon Gontran Damas,* Presence Africaine, 1979; *Black Sister,* edited by Erlene Stedson, Indiana University Press, 1981; *Women on War,* edited by Daniela Gioseffi, Simon & Schuster, 1988; and *Daughters of Africa,* Pantheon, 1992. Contributor to numerous periodicals, including *Free Spirits, Mother Jones, UNESCO Courier, Black Scholar, Heresies,* and *Mundus Artium.*

*SIDELIGHTS:* In a review of Jayne Cortez's *Pissstained Stairs and the Monkey Man's Wares* in *Negro Digest* Nikki Giovanni remarks: "We haven't had many jazz poets who got inside the music and the people who created it. We poet about them, but not of them. And this is Cortez's strength. She can wail from Theodore Navarro and Leadbelly to Ornette and never lose a beat and never make a mistake. She's a genius and all lovers of jazz will need this book—lovers of poetry will want it." About Cortez's *Unsubmissive Blues,* Warren Woessner asserts in *Small Press Review* that the record "is the most accomplished collaboration between a poet and jazz group that I've listened to in recent years." He continues: "*Unsubmissive Blues* is an unqualified success. The sum of this collaboration is always greater than its individual pieces."

Although the influence of music is readily evident in Cortez's work, the poet also seeks to convey a message in her work. Barbara T. Christian states in *Callaloo* that "it is eminently clear from her selected edition [*Coagulations: New and Selected Poems*] that Jayne Cortez is a blatantly political poet—that her work intends to help us identify those who control our lives and the devastating effects such control has on our lives, and she rouses us to do something about it.... Like the poets and warriors whose words and actions it celebrates, Jayne Cortez's *Coagulations* is a work of resistance."

*BIOGRAPHICAL/CRITICAL SOURCES:*

*PERIODICALS*

*Callaloo,* Volume 9, number 1, 1986, pp. 235-39.
*Negro Digest,* December, 1969.
*Small Press Review,* March, 1981.

\*        \*        \*

## COSBY, Bill
## See COSBY, William Henry, Jr.

\*        \*        \*

## COSBY, William Henry, Jr. 1937-
## (Bill Cosby)

*PERSONAL:* Born July 12, 1937, in Philadelphia, PA; son of William Henry Cosby (a U.S. Navy mess steward) and Anna Cosby (a domestic worker); married Camille Hanks, January 25, 1964; children: Erika Ranee, Erinn Chalene, Ennis William, Ensa Camille, Evin Harrah. *Education:* Attended Temple University, 1961-62; University of Massachusetts, M.A., 1972, Ed. D., 1977.

*ADDRESSES: Agent*—The Brokaw Co., 9255 Sunset Blvd., Los Angeles, CA 90069.

*CAREER:* Comedian, actor, and recording artist. Performer in nightclubs, including The Cellar, Philadelphia, PA, Gaslight Cafe, New York City, Bitter End, New York City, and Hungry i, San Francisco, CA, 1962—; performer in television series including *I Spy,* National Broadcasting Co. (NBC-TV), 1965-68, *The Bill Cosby Show,* NBC-TV, 1969-71, *The New Bill Cosby Show,* Columbia Broadcasting System (CBS-TV), 1972-73, *Cos,* American Broadcasting Co. (ABC-TV), 1976, and *The Cosby Show,* NBC-TV, 1984-92; host of syndicated game show, *You Bet Your Life,* 1992-93; actor in motion pictures, including *Hickey and Boggs,* 1972, *Man and Boy,* 1972, *Uptown Saturday Night,* 1974, *Let's Do It Again,* 1975, *Mother, Jugs, and Speed,* 1976, *A Piece of the Action,* 1977, *California Suite,* 1978, *The Devil and Max Devlin,* 1981, *Bill Cosby Himself,* 1985, *Leonard Part VI,* 1987, and *Ghost Dad,* 1990; creator of animated children's programs *The Fat Albert Show* and *Fat Albert and the Cosby Kids,* CBS-TV, 1972-84. Performer on *The Bill Cosby Radio Program,* television specials *The First Bill Cosby Special* and *The Second Bill Cosby Special,* in animated feature *Aesop's Fables,* in *An Evening with Bill Cosby* at Radio City Music Hall, 1986, and in videocassette *Bill Cosby: 49,* sponsored by Kodak, 1987. Guest on Public Broadcasting Co. (PBS-TV) children's programs *Sesame Street* and *The Electric Company,* and NBC-TV's *Children's Theatre;* host of Picture Pages segment of CBS-TV's *Captain Kangaroo's Wake Up.* Commercial spokesman for Jell-O Pudding (General Foods Inc.), Coca-Cola Co., Ford Motor Co., Texas Instruments, E.F. Hutton, and Kodak Film.

President of Rhythm and Blues Hall of Fame, 1968. Member of Carnegie Commission for the Future of Public Broadcasting, board of directors of National Council on Crime and Delinquency, Mary Holmes College, and Ebony Showcase Theatre, board of trustees of Temple University, advisory board of Direction Sports, communications council at Howard University, and steering committee of American Sickle Cell foundation. *Military service:* U.S. Navy Medical Corps, 1956-60.

*AWARDS, HONORS:* Eight Grammy awards for best comedy album, National Society of Recording Arts and Sciences, including 1964, for *Bill Cosby Is a Very Funny Fellow ... Right!,* 1965, for *I Started Out as a Child,* 1966, for *Why Is There Air?,* 1967, for *Revenge,* and 1969, for *To Russell, My Brother, Whom I Slept With;* Emmy Award for best actor in a dramatic series, Academy of Television Arts and Sciences, 1965-66, 1966-67, and 1967-68, for *I Spy;* named "most promising new male star" by *Fame* magazine, 1966; Emmy Award, 1969, for *The First Bill Cosby Special;* Seal of Excellence, Children's Theatre Association, 1973; Ohio State University award, 1975, for *Fat Albert and the Cosby Kids;*

NAACP Image Award, 1976; named "Star Presenter of 1978" by *Advertising Age;* Gold Award for Outstanding Children's Program, International Film and Television Festival, 1981, for *Fat Albert and the Cosby Kids;* Emmy Award for best comedy series, 1985, for *The Cosby Show;* inducted to TV Hall of Fame, Academy of Television Arts and Sciences, 1992; Founder's Award, 19th International Emmy Awards, 1992; honorary degree, Brown University; Golden Globe Award, Hollywood Foreign Press Association; four People's Choice Awards; voted "most believable celebrity endorser" three times in surveys by Video Storyboard Tests Inc.

*WRITINGS:*

*UNDER NAME BILL COSBY*

*The Wit and Wisdom of Fat Albert,* Windmill Books, 1973.
*Bill Cosby's Personal Guide to Tennis Power; or, Don't Lower the Lob, Raise the Net,* Random House, 1975.
(Contributor) Charlie Shedd, editor, *You Are Somebody Special,* McGraw, 1978, second edition, 1982.
*Fatherhood,* Doubleday, 1986.
*Time Flies,* Doubleday, 1987.
*Love and Marriage,* Doubleday, 1989.
*Childhood,* Putnam, 1991.

Also author of *Fat Albert's Survival Kit* and *Changes: Becoming the Best You Can Be.*

*RECORDINGS*

*Bill Cosby Is a Very Funny Fellow ... Right!,* 1964, *I Started Out as a Child,* 1965, *Why Is There Air?,* 1966, *Wonderfulness,* 1967, *Revenge,* 1967, *To Russell, My Brother, Whom I Slept With,* 1969, *Bill Cosby Is Not Himself These Days, Rat Own, Rat Own, Rat Own,* 1976, *My Father Confused Me ... What Must I Do? What Must I Do?,* 1977, *Disco Bill,* 1977, *Bill's Best Friend,* 1978, *It's True, It's True, Bill Cosby Himself, 200 MPH, Silverthroat, Hooray for the Salvation Army Band, 8:15, 12:15, For Adults Only, Bill Cosby Talks to Kids about Drugs,* and *Inside the Mind of Bill Cosby.*

*SIDELIGHTS:* "When I was a kid I always used to pay attention to things that other people didn't even think about," claims Bill Cosby. "I'd remember funny happenings, just little trivial things, and then tell stories about them later. I found I could make people laugh, and I enjoyed doing it because it gave me a sense of security. I thought that if people laughed at what you said, that meant they like you." As an adult, Bill Cosby has developed his childhood behavior into a comedic talent that earns him millions of dollars annually for his work in films, television, and commercials. In 1988, Cosby was ranked the second-highest-paid entertainer in the world. "Despite his wealth," Brian D. Johnson notes in *Maclean's,* "Cosby manages to pass himself off as a clownish Everyman, treating his life as a bottomless well of folk wisdom."

What Cosby calls his "storytelling knack" may have had its roots in his mother's nightly readings of Mark Twain and the Bible to her three sons. Their father, a Navy cook, was gone for long stretches of time, but Anna Cosby did her best to provide a strong moral foundation for the family she raised in Philadelphia's housing projects. Bill Cosby helped with the family's expenses by delivering groceries and shining shoes. His sixth-grade teacher described him as "an alert boy who would rather clown than study"; nevertheless, he was placed in a class for gifted students when he reached high school. His activities as captain of the track and football teams and member of the baseball and basketball teams continued to distract him from academics, however, and when his tenth-grade year ended, Cosby was told he'd have to repeat the grade. Instead of doing so, he quit school to join the Navy. It was a decision he soon came to regret, and during his four-year hitch in the Navy, Cosby earned his high school diploma through a correspondence course. He then won an athletic scholarship to Temple University in Philadelphia, where he entered as a physical education major in 1961.

Cosby had continued to amuse his schoolmates and shipmates with his tales. He first showcased his humor professionally while a student at Temple, in a five-dollar-a-night job telling jokes and tending bar at "The Cellar," a Philadelphia coffeehouse. More engagements soon followed; before long Cosby's budding career as an entertainer was conflicting with his school schedule. Forced to choose between the two, Cosby dropped out of Temple, although the university eventually awarded him a bachelor's degree on the basis of "life experience." His reputation as a comic grew quickly as he worked in coffee-houses from San Francisco to New York City. Soon he was playing the biggest nightclubs in Las Vegas, and shortly after signing a recording contract in 1964, he became the best-selling comedian on records, with several of his recordings earning over one million dollars in sales.

His early performances consisted of about 35 percent racial jokes, but Cosby came to see this kind of humor as something that perpetuated racism rather than relieving tensions, and he dropped all such jokes from his act. "Rather than trying to bring the races together by talking about the differences, let's try to bring them together by talking about the similarities," he urges. Accordingly, he developed a universal brand of humor that revolved around everyday occurrences. A long-time jazz devotee, the comedian credits the musical improvisations of Miles Davis, Charles Mingus, and Charlie Parker with inspiring him to come up with continually fresh ways of restating a few basic themes. "The situations I talk about people can find themselves in ... it makes them glad to know

they're not the only ones who have fallen victims of life's little ironies," states Cosby.

The comedian first displayed his skill as an actor when he landed the co-starring lead in *I Spy,* a popular NBC-TV program of the late 1960s that featured suspense, action, and sometimes humor. Cosby portrayed Alexander Scott, a multilingual Rhodes scholar working as part of a spy team for the United States. Scott and his partner (played by Robert Culp) traveled undercover in the guises of a tennis pro and his trainer. The Alexander Scott role had not been created especially for a black actor, and Cosby's casting in the part was hailed as an important breakthrough for blacks in television.

*The Bill Cosby Show* followed *I Spy.* In this half-hour comedy, Cosby portrayed Chet Kincaid, a high-school gym teacher—a role closer to his real-life persona than that of Alexander Scott. In fact, at this time Cosby announced that he was considering quitting show business to become a teacher. Although he never followed through on that statement, Cosby did return to college and earned a doctorate in education in 1977. His doctoral thesis, "An Integration of the Visual Media via Fat Albert and the Cosby Kids into the Elementary School Curriculum as a Teaching Aid and Vehicle to Achieve Increased Learning," analyzed an animated Saturday-morning show that Cosby himself had created. *Fat Albert and the Cosby Kids* had its roots in the comedy routines about growing up in Philadelphia. It attempted to entertain children while encouraging them to confront moral and ethical issues, and it has been used as a teaching tool in schools.

During the 1970s, Cosby teamed with Sidney Poitier and several other black actors to make a highly successful series of comedies, including *Uptown Saturday Night, Let's Do It Again,* and *A Piece of the Action.* These comedies stood out in a time when most of the films for black audiences were oriented to violence. Critics are generous in their praise of Cosby's acting; Tom Allen notes his "free-wheeling, jiving, put-down artistry," and Alvin H. Marritt writes that, in *Let's Do It Again,* Cosby "breezes through the outrageous antics."

Concern over his family's television viewing habits led Cosby to return to prime-time in 1984. "I got tired of seeing TV shows that consist of a car crash, a gunman and a hooker talking to a black pimp," the actor states in an article by Jane Hall in *People.* "It was cheaper to do a series than to throw out my family's six TV sets." But Cosby found that network executives were resistant to his idea for a family-oriented comedy. He was turned down by both CBS and ABC on the grounds that a family comedy—particularly one featuring a black family—could never succeed on modern television. NBC accepted his proposal and *The Cosby Show* very quickly became the top-rated show on television, drawing an estimated 60 million weekly viewers.

Like most of Bill Cosby's material, *The Cosby Show* revolves around everyday occurrences and interactions between siblings and parents. Cosby plays obstetrician Cliff Huxtable, who with his lawyer wife, Claire, has four daughters and one son—just as Cosby and wife Camille do in real life. Besides entertaining audiences, Cosby aims to project a positive image of a family whose members love and respect one another. The program is hailed by some as a giant step forward in the portrayal of blacks on television. Writes Lynn Norment in *Ebony,* "This show pointedly avoids the stereotypical Blacks often seen on TV. There are no ghetto maids or butlers wisecracking about Black life. Also, there are no fast cars and helicopter chase scenes, no jokes about sex and boobs and butts. And, most unusual, both parents are present in the home, employed and are Black."

*The Cosby Show* has not been unanimously acclaimed, however. As Norment explains, "Despite its success, the show is criticized by a few for not being 'Black enough,' for not dealing with more controversial issues, such as poverty and racism and interracial dating, for focusing on a Black middle-class family when the vast majority of Black people survive on incomes far below that of the Huxtables." Cosby finds this type of criticism racist in itself. "Does it mean only white people have a lock on living together in a home where the father is a doctor and the mother is a lawyer and the children are constantly being told to study by their parents?" Hall quotes Cosby in *People:* "This is a black American family. If anybody has difficulty with that, it's their problem, not ours."

The paternal image of Cliff Huxtable led a publisher to ask Cosby for a humorous book to be called *Fatherhood.* Cosby obliged, making notes for the project with shorthand and tape recorder between his entertainment commitments. The finished book sold a record 2.6 million hardcover copies and was quite well-received by critics. *Newsweek* book reviewer Cathleen McGuigan states that it "is like a prose version of a Cosby comedy performance—informal, commiserative anecdotes delivered in a sardonic style that's as likely to prompt a smile of recognition as a belly laugh.... [But] it's not all played for laughs. There's a tough passage in which he describes the only time he hit his son, and a reference to a drinking-and-driving incident involving a daughter and her friends that calls upon him to both punish and forgive. Cosby's big strength, though, is his eye and ear for the everyday event—sibling squabbles, children's excuses." Jonathan Yardley concurs in the *Washington Post Book World:* "Cosby has an extraordinarily keen ear for everyday speech and everyday event, and knows how to put just enough of a comic spin on it so that even as we laugh we know we are getting a glimpse of the truth."

Following the huge success of *Fatherhood,* Doubleday published *Time Flies,* in which Cosby treats the subject of aging in the same style as his earlier book. Toronto *Globe & Mail* reviewer Leo Simpson comments, "Decay and the drift into entropy wouldn't get everyone's vote as a light-hearted theme, yet *Time Flies* is just as illuminating, witty and elegantly hilarious as ... *Fatherhood.*" The book sold over 1.7 million hardcover copies.

For his 1989 book, *Love and Marriage,* Cosby draws upon his own long marriage to wife Camille for an advice book on maintaining domestic tranquility. As Cosby explains to Johnson in *Maclean's,* "The book is to make people laugh, make them identify and have a good time." Some of the truths revealed by the author is that "the wife is in charge" and "even the deepest love doesn't stop a marriage from being a constant struggle for control." For any husband who believes himself to be the boss of his own house, Cosby advises that he buy some wallpaper and redecorate a room without consulting his wife first. Calling the book a "diverting but forgettable" work, Leah Rozen of *People* nonetheless finds *Love and Marriage* to be "gently amusing." Johnson finds the book "by turns tender, amusing and coy." The *New York Times Book Review* critic calls it "a scrapbook of the happier side of romance.... Cosby captures the give and take of happy marriages."

Cosby reminisces about his own youth in Philadelphia in 1991's *Childhood,* comparing that time in his life with the experiences of the present generation of children. His remembrances of childhood pranks, family advice, and schoolyard games form the bulk of the memoir. Dulcie Leimbach of the *New York Times Book Review* finds that Cosby presents a "rough-and-tumble (but never spoiled or weary) childhood." Because of his ability to reconstruct those times, she calls Cosby "a man trapped inside a child's mind."

Although Cosby complains in *Time Flies* that he is slowing down with age, his performing, directing, writing and devotion to charitable projects provide him with a very busy schedule. As he told the *Los Angeles Times,* "I think one of the most important things to understand is that my mother, as a domestic, worked 12 hours a day, and then she would do the laundry, and cook the meals and serve them and clean them up, and for this she got $7 a day. So 12 hours a day of whatever I do is as easy as eating a Jell-O Pudding Pop."

*BIOGRAPHICAL/CRITICAL SOURCES:*

*BOOKS*

Adams, Barbara Johnston, *The Picture Life of Bill Cosby,* F. Watts, 1986.

Johnson, Robert E., *Bill Cosby: In Words and Pictures,* Johnson Publishing (Chicago), 1987.

Smith, R. L., *Cosby,* St. Martin's, 1986.

Woods, H., *Bill Cosby, Making America Laugh and Learn,* Dillon, 1983.

*PERIODICALS*

*Chicago Tribune,* September 14, 1987.
*Chicago Tribune Books,* May 3, 1987.
*Ebony,* May, 1964; June, 1977; April, 1985; February, 1986; February, 1987.
*Films in Review,* November, 1975.
*Globe & Mail* (Toronto), July 5, 1986; October 24, 1987.
*Good Housekeeping,* February, 1991.
*Jet,* January 12, 1987; January 19, 1987; February 9, 1987; February 23, 1987; March 9, 1987.
*Ladies Home Journal,* June, 1985.
*Los Angeles Times,* September 25, 1987; December 20, 1987; January 24, 1988.
*Los Angeles Times Book Review,* June 15, 1986; June 18, 1989.
*Maclean's,* May 1, 1989.
*National Observer,* January 6, 1964.
*Newsweek,* November 5, 1984; September 2, 1985; May 19, 1986; September 14, 1987.
*New York Post,* February 23, 1964.
*New York Times Book Review,* September 20, 1987; May 14, 1989; October 27, 1991.
*New York Times Magazine,* March 14, 1965.
*People,* December 10, 1984; September 14, 1987; July 10, 1989.
*Playboy,* December, 1985.
*Reader's Digest,* November, 1986; November, 1987.
*Saturday Evening Post,* April, 1985; April, 1986.
*Time,* September 28, 1987.
*Village Voice,* November 3, 1975.
*Washington Post,* September 7, 1987.
*Washington Post Book World,* April 27, 1986.

\*   \*   \*

## COSE, Ellis Jonathan 1951-

*PERSONAL:* Born February 20, 1951, in Chicago, IL; son of Raney and Jetta (Cameron) Cose. *Education:* University of Illinois at Chicago Circle, B.A., 1972; George Washington University, M.A., 1978.

*ADDRESSES: Office—Newsweek Inc.,* 444 Madison Ave., New York, NY 10022.

*CAREER: Chicago Sun-Times,* Chicago, IL, columnist and reporter, 1970-77; Joint Center for Political Studies, Washington, DC, senior fellow and director of energy policy studies, 1977-79; *Detroit Free Press,* Detroit, MI, editorial writer and columnist, 1979-81; Gannett Center for Media, Colum-

bia University, New York City, fellow, 1987; *New York Daily News,* New York City, editorial page editor, 1991-93; *Newsweek,* New York City, contributing editor, 1993—. Member of environmental advisory committee of U.S. Department of Energy, 1978-79; resident fellow at National Academy of Sciences and National Research Council, 1981-82; *USA Today,* special writer, 1982-83; Institute for Journalism Education, president, 1983-86; *Time,* contributor and press critic, 1988-90.

*MEMBER:* National Association of Black Journalists.

*AWARDS, HONORS:* Newswriting award, Illinois United Press International, 1973; Stick-o-Type Award, Chicago Newspaper Guild, 1975; Lincoln University National Unity awards for Best Political Reporting, 1975 and 1977; Outstanding Young Citizen of Chicago Jaycees, 1977.

*WRITINGS:*

*Energy and the Urban Crisis,* Joint Center for Political Studies, 1978.
(Editor) *Energy and Equity: Some Social Concerns,* Joint Center for Political Studies, 1979.
*Decentralizing Energy Decisions,* Westview, 1983.
*The Quiet Crisis,* Institute for Journalism Education, 1987.
*The Press,* Morrow, 1989.
*A Nation of Strangers,* Morrow, 1992.

Also author of *Employment and Journalism,* 1986. Former columnist for periodicals, including *Chicago Sun-Times* and *Time.*

*WORK IN PROGRESS: The Rage of a Privileged Class,* for HarperCollins.

*SIDELIGHTS:* A desire to promote understanding across the color line helped lead Ellis Jonathan Cose to a career as a journalist and writer on public policy issues. Asked why he became a writer in an interview, Cose commented, "I was a sort of creature of the late 1960s." The West Side of Chicago in the late 1960s, where Cose grew up in one of the city's public housing developments, was marked by violent riots in the aftermath of the assassinations of activists Malcolm X and Martin Luther King, Jr. "Out of the riots, I saw so much destruction, so much devastation," Cose said. "At least part of it was due to the fact that people didn't understand each other well enough."

If he started writing as a way to bridge differences, Cose stayed in it because he "enjoyed writing and the process of discovery," he said. Writing was a rewarding career for Cose from early on in his life: he had his first column, writing about Chicago communities, in the *Chicago Sun-Times* when he was

19 years old. He continued working for the paper while studying psychology at the University of Illinois in Chicago. His column's subject matter began to include national politics, and the *Sun-Times* assigned Cose to cover Jimmy Carter's 1976 presidential campaign. The campaign took Cose outside Chicago and exposed him to new issues. In the wake of the energy crisis, Cose became interested in the way energy policy affected lower-class citizens. Several of his books cover the subject, including *Energy and the Urban Crisis.*

Cose continued to move back and forth between journalism and work in the public sector. After a stint in print journalism in the first years of the 1980s, he went to California to run the Institute for Journalism Education. He left the position to write *The Press,* which profiled the personalities and the companies that run major U.S. newspapers, including Katharine Graham of the *Washington Post* and Al Neuharth, head of the Gannett newspaper chain that owns *USA Today.*

Moving from journalism education to writing books and working in magazines, Cose has focused more recently on issues of race and class. In 1992's *A Nation of Strangers,* Cose discusses immigration and prejudice in U.S. history. In a work still in progress, Cose takes issue with the idea in sociology that racism most strongly affects the so-called underclass. Cose said that *The Rage of a Privileged Class,* which focuses on middle class blacks and their anger in order to show that racism continues to thrive, "deals with the growing perception that to a large extent America has overcome the growing problems of racial discrimination."

\*   \*   \*

## COUCH, William, Jr.

*PERSONAL:* Married Ola B. Criss (a gerontologist and officer in U.S. State Department), September 7, 1980; children: (previous marriage) William, another son; Gregg Antonio Jackson (stepson). *Education:* Received doctorate.

*CAREER:* North Carolina College (now North Carolina Central University), Durham, NC, 1962-78, became professor of English; Federal City College (now University of the District of Columbia), Washington, DC, academic vice-president, beginning 1968, became chair of English department, then full-time teaching faculty member, then became acting academic vice-president, until 1990; in Africa, 1991—.

*WRITINGS:*

(Editor and author of introduction) *New Black Playwrights: An Anthology,* Louisiana State University Press, 1968.

Contributor of articles and poems to periodicals, including *CLA Journal, Negro Story,* and *Phylon.*

*BIOGRAPHICAL/CRITICAL SOURCES:*

*PERIODICALS*

*Drama: The Quarterly Theatre Review,* summer, 1969, p. 66.
*Negro Digest,* September, 1969, p. 96.
*Negro History Bulletin,* March, 1969, p. 22.

\*   \*   \*

## COVIN, David L(eroy) 1940-

*PERSONAL:* Born October 3, 1940, in Chicago, IL; son of David and Lela Jane (maiden name, Clements) Covin; married Judy Bentinck Smith; children: Wendy, Holly. *Education:* University of Illinois, B.A., 1962; Colorado University, M.A., 1966; Washington State University, Ph.D., 1970.

*ADDRESSES: Office*—Director of Pan African Studies, California State University, 6000 J St., Sacramento, CA 95819.

*CAREER:* California State University, Sacramento, assistant professor of government and ethnic studies, 1970-74; associate dean of general studies, 1972-74; associate professor of government and ethnic studies, 1975-79; professor, government and ethnic studies, 1979; director of Pan African Studies. Union Graduate School, adjunct professor, 1979; State of California, consultant, 1979. Women's Civic Improvement Club, executive board member, 1987—.

*MEMBER:* National Party of Congress (delegate), National Black Independent Political Party, Black Science Resource Center (acting chairman, 1987—), Sacramento chapter of National Rainbow Coalition Organization Committee, Sacramento Area Black Caucus (chairman, 1988—).

*AWARDS, HONORS:* Community service award, Sacramento Area Black Caucus, 1976; grant, California Council for Humanities Public Policy, 1977; Sacramento community service award, Sacramento Kwanza Commission, 1978; Man of the Year, Omega Psi Phi, 1982; community service award, All African People, 1986; Meritorious Performance Award, California State University, 1988; John C. Livingston Distinguished Faculty Lecture, California State University, 1992.

*WRITINGS:*

*Brown Sky,* Path Press, 1987.

Also contributor of short stories and articles to periodicals, including the *Journal of Black Studies*. Contributing editor to *Rumble*.

\*   \*   \*

## CRUMP, Paul (Orville)   1930(?)-

*PERSONAL:* Born c. 1930. *Education:* Attended school to ninth grade. *Religion:* Catholic.

*CAREER:* Novelist. Sentenced to death and incarcerated in Cook County Jail, IL, c. 1953, for role in a robbery-murder, had sentence commuted to 199 years in prison and was transferred to Illinois State Prison in Joliet, IL, 1962; released in 1993.

*WRITINGS:*

*Burn, Killer, Burn!* (novel), Johnson Publishing, 1962.

*WORK IN PROGRESS: Walk in Fury,* a novel.

*SIDELIGHTS:* Fatherless in the Chicago ghetto from the age of six, jailed for armed robbery at sixteen and again, for murder, at twenty-three, Paul Crump went to death row in 1953. He was described as "savage" at that time, according to a 1962 *Time* article, but during his imprisonment a gradual change took place. His prison warden, Jack Johnson, believed that "men, if treated as men, would respond as men," reported an *Ebony* writer. Under Johnson's leadership, which de-emphasized punishment, prisoners like Crump were given responsibility and a chance to feel needed. Chaplain James Jones got to know Crump by joining the prisoners' card games, and eventually Crump took hold of the Christian faith that turned his life around. Again and again he strove to win clemency. His case made the newspapers, and popular support for his cause began to build. Arguing that he was truly reformed, people from his own state and beyond wrote letters, editorials, or affidavits on his behalf, including internationally known evangelist Billy Graham. In 1962, after nine years in prison and fourteen reprieves, Crump won a commutation of his sentence; forty years after his imprisonment he was finally released.

While fighting off his death sentence, Crump realized that he wanted to write about his experience, to try to prevent others from following his own criminal path. Crump, however, didn't know enough about writing. He started with an intense study of Herman Melville's classic novel *Moby Dick* under the tutelage of the assistant warden and went on to read a wide variety of other esteemed authors. A fellow inmate who was himself a writer critiqued his emerging manuscript. The publication of Crump's novel, *Burn, Killer, Burn!,* came the same year his sentence was commuted.

In the *Ebony* article Crump called his main character, Guy Morgan, Jr., "a child of action and not thought, impulsive, quick to anger, quick to be sorry, resentful of slights, real or imagined.... Fearing ideals are indications of weakness, he covers up with a facade of tough-guy sneers and violence." As the *Ebony* writer related, this description fits many urban youths, rich or poor, "whose spiritual, social, educational and emotional needs are not met, or even recognized until they have engaged in an overt act of antisocial behavior—and been caught.... The tragedy of Guy Morgan Jr. is in this sense the tragedy of urban American life."

*BIOGRAPHICAL/CRITICAL SOURCES:*

*BOOKS*

Nizer, Louis, *The Jury Returns,* Doubleday, 1966, pp. 1-137.

*PERIODICALS*

*Ebony,* July, 1962, pp. 31-34; November, 1962, pp. 88-90.
*Life,* July 27, 1962, pp. 26-31.
*Newsweek,* August 13, 1962, p. 17.
*New York Times Book Review,* June 16, 1963, p. 8.
*Time,* July 20, 1962, p. 22; August 10, 1962, p. 12.

*OTHER*

*The People versus Paul Crump,* Facets Video, 1988.

\*   \*   \*

## CRUZ, Ricardo Cortez   1964-

*PERSONAL:* Born August 10, 1964, in Decatur, IL; son of Theodore Cruz (employed in climate control) and Carol Maxine Cruz (a hospital employee; maiden name, Belue). *Education:* Richland Community College, A.A., 1985; Illinois State University, B.S., 1989, M.A., 1991. *Politics:* Democrat. *Religion:* Christian.

*ADDRESSES: Home*—712 Arcadia, Apt. 7, Bloomington, IL 61704. *Office*—Heartland Community College, 1226 Towanda Plaza, Bloomington, IL 61701. *Agent*—Faith Hampton Childs, 41 King St., New York, NY 10014.

*CAREER: Herald & Review,* Decatur, IL, sportswriter, intern, and clerk, 1982-88; *Pantagraph,* Bloomington, IL, sportswriter and clerk, 1988-89; Heartland Community College, Bloomington, instructor in English, 1992—.

*AWARDS, HONORS:* Excellence in Minority Fiction Award, Charles H. and N. Mildred Nilon, 1992, for *Straight Outta Compton.*

*WRITINGS:*

*Straight Outta Compton,* Fiction Collective Two, 1992.

Also author of *Five Days of Bleeding,* 1992. Contributor of short stories to *Fiction International, Black Ice,* and *Forthcoming in Postmodern Culture.*

*SIDELIGHTS:* Ricardo Cortez Cruz commented: "*Straight Outta Compton* is being hailed as the first major rap novel. African-American writer Clarence Major was chiefly responsible for inspiring the book. His *Dictionary of Afro-American Slang* served as a leaping-off point for the novel.

"My writing can be characterized by its use of fusion, that is, the synthesizing of a lot of brutal elements, mordant humor, and rapid fire. I feel like I'm one of the few writers who would rather write at night than in the morning.

"*Five Days of Bleeding* gets its title from a reggae song. The book literally picks up where *Straight Outta Compton* left off since its chief character is from Compton (in south central Los Angeles). My books and/or stories never have happy endings; life is a bitch in the Compton ghetto and in Central Park. One of the purposes of *Straight Outta Compton* was to tell people that they have to keep 'moving the crowd' and keep striving to better their lives, but not forget where they came from (their roots). *Five Days of Bleeding* hits on the fact that we live in a patriarchal society where women are often hated and abused. The novel focuses on the black woman specifically. In the novel, music is the key. The main character, Zu-Zu Girl, is always singing.

"In both books foreground language is used. Both are experimental and surreal. The ghettos I write about are more in the heart than actual places and are symbolic of a depressed state of mind. Both books deal exclusively with black life and culture. The action in the novels is fast-paced, and the characters are always moving. The term 'big-head' has become a trademark of my writing, as well as 'move the crowd' and 'like it was nothing'."

\* \* \*

## CRUZ, Victor Hernandez 1949-

*PERSONAL:* Born February 6, 1949, in Aguas Buenas, PR; son of Severo and Rosa Cruz; children: Ajani. *Education:* Attended high school in New York, NY.

*ADDRESSES: Office*—P.O. Box 40148, San Francisco, CA 94140.

*CAREER:* Poet. University of California, Berkeley, guest lecturer, 1969; San Francisco State University, San Francisco, CA, instructor, beginning in 1973.

*AWARDS, HONORS:* Creative Artists public service award, 1974, for *Tropicalization.*

*WRITINGS:*

*POETRY*

*Papa Got His Gun!, and Other Poems,* Calle Once Publications, 1966.
*Doing Poetry,* Other Ways, 1968.
*Snaps,* Random House, 1969.
(Editor with Herbert Kohl) *Stuff: A Collection of Poems, Visions, and Imaginative Happenings from Young Writers in Schools—Open and Closed,* Collins & World, 1970.
*Mainland,* Random House, 1973.
*Tropicalization,* Reed, Canon, 1976.
*The Low Writings,* Lee/Lucas Press, 1980.
*By Lingual Wholes,* Momo's, 1982.
*Rhythm, Content & Flavor: New and Selected Poems,* Arte Publico, 1989.
*Red Beans,* Coffee House Press, 1991.

Contributor to anthologies, including *An Anthology of Afro-American Writing,* Morrow, 1968, and *Giant Talk: An Anthology of Third World Writings,* Random House, 1975. Contributor to *Evergreen Review, New York Review of Books, Ramparts, Down Here,* and *Revista del Instituto de Estudios Puertorriquenos.* Former editor, *Umbra.*

*SIDELIGHTS:* Regarding the influences on his writing, Victor Hernandez Cruz wrote: "My family life was full of music, guitars and conga drums, maracas and songs. My mother sang songs. Even when it was five below zero in New York she sang warm tropical ballads." He continued: "My work is on the border of a new language, because I create out of a consciousness steeped in two of the important world languages, Spanish and English. A piece written totally in English could have a Spanish spirit. Another strong concern in my work is the difference between a tropical village, such as Aguas Buenas, Puerto Rico, where I was born, and an immensity such as New York City, where I was raised. I compare smells and sounds, I explore the differences, I write from the center of a culture which is not on its native soil, a culture in flight, living half the time on memories, becoming something totally new and unique, while at the same time it helps to shape and inform the new environment. I write about the city with an agonizing memory of a lush tropical silence. This contrast between landscape and language creates an intensity in my work."

Critics often remark on Cruz's unique use of language, particularly his recreation of a Hispanic dialect found in the United States, sometimes referred to as "Spanglish," or a combination of Spanish and English. In a *New York Times Book Review* article reviewing *By Lingual Wholes,* Richard Elman remarks: "Cruz writes poems about his native Puerto Rico and elsewhere which often speak to us with a forked tongue, sometimes in a highly literate Spanglish.... He's a funny, hard-edged poet, declining always into mother wit and pathos: 'So you see, all life is a holy hole. Bet hard on that.'" And Nancy Sullivan reflects in *Poetry* magazine: "Cruz allows the staccato crackle of English half-learned ... to enrich the poems through its touching dictional inadequacy. If poetry is arching toward the condition of silence as John Cage and Susan Sontag suggest, perhaps this mode of inarticulateness is a bend on the curve.... I think that Cruz is writing necessary poems in a period when many poems seem unnecessary."

Cruz's 1991 work *Red Beans,* the title of which is a play on the words "red beings," referring to Puerto Ricans, has also received critical attention. Reviewers have characterized the volume as a highly imaginative exploration of Puerto Rican history as well as the Puerto Rican's history in America. In a review for the *San Francisco Review of Books,* Jose Amaya assessed, "Cruz experiments with the vast linguistic and cultural possibilities of 'indo-afro-hispano' poetry and comes up with a strong vision of American unity." Commenting on the development of Cruz's style, Amaya noted that "Cruz is at his best in *Red Beans* when he portrays ... the distinct sounds and voices of Caribbean life which crash into his poetic consciousness like a wild ocean surf." Calling Cruz a "vigorous bilingual Latino troubadour," Frank Allen in *Library Journal* declared the book is "a dance on the edges."

*BIOGRAPHICAL/CRITICAL SOURCES:*

*PERIODICALS*

*American Book Review,* February, 1992.
*Library Journal,* October 1, 1991, p. 100.
*Melus,* spring, 1989-90.
*New York Times Book Review,* September 18, 1983.
*Poetry,* May, 1970.
*Publishers Weekly,* September 6, 1991, p. 99.
*San Francisco Review of Books,* March, 1991.
*Village Voice Literary Supplement,* November, 1991.

\*   \*   \*

# CUMMINGS, Pat (Marie) 1950-

*PERSONAL:* Born November 9, 1950, in Chicago, IL; daughter of Arthur Bernard (a management consultant) and Chris-

tine M. (a librarian; maiden name, Taylor) Cummings; married Chuku Lee (a magazine editor, lawyer, and real estate appraiser), 1975. *Education:* Attended Spelman College, 1970-71, and Atlanta School of Art, 1971-72; Pratt Institute, B.F.A., 1974. *Religion:* "Raised Catholic but practice no religion in an organized way now." *Avocational interests:* Travel and foreign languages (especially French and Italian), swimming.

*ADDRESSES: Home and office*—28 Tiffany Pl., Brooklyn, NY 11231.

*CAREER:* Free-lance author and illustrator. Exhibitions of work held at Restoration Corp., Brooklyn, NY, 1974; Black Enterprise Gallery, New York City, 1980; CRT Gallery, Hartford, CT, 1981; Master Eagle Gallery, New York City, 1984, 1985, and 1986; Akbaw Gallery, Mount Vernon, NY, 1985; Society of Illustrators group show, 1990 and 1991; Museum of Fine Arts, Grand Rapids, MI, 1991; National Museum of Women in the Arts group show, 1992.

*MEMBER:* Society of Children's Book Writers, Graphic Artists Guild, Children's Book Illustrators Guild, Black Art Directors Group of New York.

*AWARDS, HONORS:* Citation as notable children's trade book in the field of social studies, joint committee of Children's Book Council and National Council on the Social Studies, 1982, for *Just Us Women;* Coretta Scott King Honorable Mention certificate, American Library Association, 1983, for *Just Us Women,* and 1987, for *C.L.O.U.D.S.;* Coretta Scott King Award, 1984, for *My Mama Needs Me;* Black Women in Publishing Illustration Award, 1988.

*WRITINGS:*

*SELF-ILLUSTRATED BOOKS FOR JUVENILES*

*Jimmy Lee Did It,* Lothrop, 1985.
*C.L.O.U.D.S.,* Lothrop, 1986.
*Clean Your Room, Harvey Moon!,* Bradbury, 1991.
*Petey Moroni's Camp Runamok Diary,* Bradbury, 1992.

*ILLUSTRATOR*

Eloise Greenfield, *Good News,* Coward, 1977.
Trudie MacDougall, *Beyond Dreamtime: The Life and Lore of the Aboriginal Australian,* Coward, 1978.
Cynthia Jameson, *The Secret of the Royal Mounds,* Coward, 1980.
Jeanette Caines, *Just Us Women,* Harper, 1982.
Mildred Pitts Walter, *My Mama Needs Me* (Reading Rainbow book), Lothrop, 1983.
Cathy Warren, *Fred's First Day,* Lothrop, 1984.

J. Caines, *Chilly Stomach,* Harper, 1986.

C. Warren, *Springtime Bears* (also known as *Playing with Mama*), Lothrop, 1986.

J. Caines, *I Need a Lunch Box,* Harper, 1988.

Mary Stolz, *Storm in the Night,* Harper, 1988.

Barrett, Joyce Durham, *Willie's Not the Hugging Kind,* Harper, 1989.

M. P. Walter, *Two and Too Much,* Bradbury, 1990.

M. Stolz, *Go Fish,* HarperCollins, 1991.

*OTHER*

(Editor and compiler) *Talking with Artists,* Bradbury, 1991.

*WORK IN PROGRESS: The Blue Lake,* a children's book about a girl trapped underwater in the blue lake, for Harper Collins, 1995.

*SIDELIGHTS:* Pat Cummings is a children's author and illustrator whose works feature people of various races taking positive, constructive approaches to everyday problems. Her interest in diversity developed after she spent her childhood living in Germany and Japan and such U.S. states as Illinois, New York, Virginia, Kansas, and Massachusetts; her father's career with the U.S. Army involved moving to a new base every two or three years. Being immersed in different cultures as a child sensitized Cummings to the importance of including people of all races in her work as an adult. "I've chosen at times not to illustrate stories that contained what seemed to be negative stereotypes," Cummings affirmed in *Something about the Author Autobiography Series* (*SAAS*). "When the vast majority of books published for children still reflects a primarily white, middle-class reality, I've always felt it was essential to show the spectrum of skin tones that truly make up the planet. I want any child to be able to pick up one of my books and find something of value in it, even if only a laugh. The stories have truly universal themes: a jittery first day of school, the arrival of a new baby, attacking a messy room."

Born in 1950 in Chicago, Illinois, Cummings was the second of four children. Her brother and sisters were her closest friends while she was growing up, mainly because moving so often made it difficult to develop lasting friendships. She had already moved to Virginia and back to Chicago by the age of five, when she first left American soil to live in Germany. She recalled the impact of living in a foreign country in *SAAS*: "I remember exotic little details from Germany: the strange-smelling gnomelike dolls from the Black Forest, seeing my first gingerbread house one Christmas, and climbing castles that stood along the Rhine River. My mother read fairy tales to us from a book that I believe was called *Tales of the Rhine....* What I realized later, when I began illustrating children's books, was that the thin line between fantasy and reality began for me when I climbed those castle steps that seemed

fashioned right out of the fairy tales my mother had read to us."

One memorable event happened in Germany that proved to have a lasting effect on Cummings's life and career. While out one day with Linda, her older sister, Cummings decided to hop on board a school bus—uninvited—with other girls after Linda had left her alone for a moment. The bus traveled deep into Germany's Black Forest and stopped at a ballet school. Cummings got out with the other girls, pretending to belong, and spent an enchanting afternoon practicing ballet. When she finally returned home, she discovered that her distraught mother had alerted the German and army police. She was grounded for a long time after that incident. "As it turned out, I found myself with quite a bit of time on my hands to practice drawing," she recollected in *SAAS*. "I was not allowed out alone for thousands of years after that, and stuck in my room, I began drawing ballerinas. They all had pinpoint waists and enormous skirts.... As I perfected my ballerinas, I found that my classmates would pay me for them. I got a nickel for a basic ballerina, a dime for the more elaborate ones. If they had glitter, or were special requests (hearts on Valentine's Day or monsters for Halloween, for example), I might even get some M & Ms or Twinkies as payment. Candy was as good as money in those days. So, at a very early age, I made a connection between artwork being thoroughly enjoyable and good business as well."

Cummings went on creating ballerinas and other works of art throughout her school years. She never spent two years in a row at the same school, except for her junior and senior years of high school. Though many of her school experiences were positive—she used her artistic talents to help out with school projects and meet new friends—one incident at a Virginia elementary school taught her some of the harsh realities of life. "At recess I ran to the playground and hopped on a merry-go-round," she wrote in *SAAS*. "One of the nuns hastily came and led me away from the slides and see-saws, jungle gyms and sandbox I had my sights on next. She took me over to a dirt lot where there was a lone basketball hoop. My sister Linda was there. The nun told me that this was 'my' playground but that seemed ridiculous. There was nothing there. I remember that Linda was crying, having probably just found out the same on our first day. I always expected Linda to explain things, to know everything before I did, but she couldn't tell me what we had done to get kicked out of the 'real' playground. We were black and we couldn't play with the white kids we sat next to in the classroom. That wasn't clear to me then, even looking around at the other black children that had been steered to the dirt lot. It took me several years and more of such encounters to make any connection.... That non-inclusion puzzled me, troubled me, and finally, as I was growing up, led me to an awareness of America's deeply rooted racism." This experience laid the foundation to Cummings's professional goal of creating works that appeal to people of all races.

After graduating from high school in 1968, Cummings decided to attend Pratt Institute in New York City. She majored in fashion because illustration was not offered as a major at that time. Though she dropped out of Pratt, worked for a year, and traveled to Georgia to attend Spelman College and Atlanta School of Art, Cummings eventually returned to Pratt to earn her degree in fine arts in 1974. During her last year of school she began working as a free-lance commercial artist. She landed her first job after a man in a car saw her hauling her portfolio down the street after school. He informed her that a job awaited her if she would get in the car. "I sized up the situation, took a chance and went with him. That was exactly the sort of thing my parents had worried about when I went to New York. But I had developed, I thought, a fairly reliable intuition by that time and it proved to be an excellent move," Cummings related in *SAAS*. The job was drawing posters for the Billie Holiday Theatre for Little Folk, and before long Cummings had clients from other theaters as well.

Cummings's break into book illustration came after some of her artwork was featured in a publication distributed by the Council on Interracial Books for Children. Without any experience with books, Cummings was offered the chance to draw the pictures for Eloise Greenfield's *Good News.* Cummings quickly informed her editor that she knew exactly what to do, but in fact she knew nothing about book illustration. Once the job was hers, Cummings drew upon her network of friends to set up a meeting with illustrator Tom Feelings, who gave her a crash course on everything she was expected to know and do. (To this day Cummings feels a professional debt to Feelings that she tries to repay by helping other beginning artists.) After her lessons with Feelings, she still had trouble starting. "I stared at the blank paper before me," she remarked in *SAAS*. "I was convinced that this book should rival *Alice in Wonderland* and that the art should make Johnny Carson's staff call to book me. I wanted the cover of *Time* magazine. I was dizzy with panic. I finally took a pad of paper into the bedroom.... I drew all afternoon. Not artwork that would bump [*Alice in Wonderland* illustrator John] Tenniel out of place, but drawings that began to give shape to the story at hand.... I look at it today and see the hundreds of mistakes I made and remember the agony and the ecstasy it produced. When I saw the book on a shelf in Bloomingdale's it was almost like being on Carson."

Since that first book Cummings has gone on to illustrate more than a dozen works, including three of her own: *Jimmy Lee Did It, C.L.O.U.D.S.,* and *Clean Your Room, Harvey Moon!*

All three have strong ties to Cummings's family. The inspiration for *Jimmy Lee Did It* came from Cummings's brother Artie, who during childhood had his own "Jimmy Lee," an imaginary friend conveniently blamed when trouble occurred. Cummings got the idea for *C.L.O.U.D.S.* after sitting on the porch in Virginia with her mother and applauding a stunning sunset. The story's main character, Chuku—the name of Cummings's husband—is a cloud designer for Creative Lights, Opticals, and Unusual Designs in the Sky who finds himself in trouble after spelling out "Hello Down There" over New York City. A tale of the unusual things a boy keeps in his room, *Clean Your Room, Harvey Moon!* is also based on Artie and was produced while Cummings stayed with her younger sister Barbara in Jamaica.

Whether working on her own books or illustrating for others, Cummings maintains her philosophy that children's books ought to encourage optimistic, constructive approaches to life: "There is a responsibility attached to making books for young readers," she stated in *SAAS*. "A lot of stories focus on the children's emotions and scratching up those feelings is pointless unless there is a positive resolution by the book's end. I feel the best stories allow a child to discover a solution or approach to their own situation. My parents' positive outlook on life gave me and my brother and sisters the tools we needed to construct any future we envisioned. I hope to pass that feeling of capability on through the characters I write about or draw."

*BIOGRAPHICAL/CRITICAL SOURCES:*

*BOOKS*

Cummings, Pat, editor, *Talking with Artists,* Bradbury, 1991.
*Behind the Covers,* Volume 2, Libraries Unlimited, 1989, pp. 81-92.
Rollock, Barbara T., *Black Authors and Illustrators of Children's Books,* Garland, 1988, p. 36.
*Something About the Author Autobiography Series,* Volume 13, Gale, 1992, pp. 71-88.

*PERIODICALS*

*Booklist,* May 1, 1992, p. 1598.
*Bulletin of the Center for Children's Books,* October, 1985, p. 25.
*Interracial Books for Children Bulletin,* Vol. 17, no. 1, p. 8.
*Kirkus Reviews,* January 15, 1986, p. 130; February 1, 1991, p. 181; July 15, 1992, p. 919.
*Publishers Weekly,* June 27, 1986, p. 86; February 8, 1991, p. 56.
*School Library Journal,* November, 1985, p. 67.
*Voice of Youth Advocates (VOYA),* August, 1992, p. 196.

# D

## DANCE, Daryl Cumber 1938-

*PERSONAL:* Born January 17, 1938, in Richmond, VA; daughter of Allen Whitfield (in business) and Veronica (a teacher; maiden name, Bell) Cumber; married Warren C. Dance (a teacher), August 23, 1958; children: Warren C., Jr., Allen C., Daryl Lynn. *Education:* Virginia State College (now University), A.B., 1957, M.A., 1963; University of Virginia, Ph.D., 1971.

*ADDRESSES: Office*—Department of English, University of Richmond, Richmond, VA 23173.

*CAREER:* Virginia State College (now University), Petersburg, instructor in English, 1963-72; Virginia Commonwealth University, Richmond, associate professor, 1972-85, professor of English, beginning 1985; University of Richmond, Richmond, visiting scholar, 1992-93, professor of English, 1993—. Visiting professor of black studies at University of California, Santa Barbara, 1986-87.

*MEMBER:* College Language Association, Modern Language Association of America, Association of Caribbean Studies, Caribbean Studies Association, American Folklore Society, Zora Neale Hurston Society.

*AWARDS, HONORS:* Ford Foundation fellowship, 1970; Danforth associate, 1974; grants from National Endowment for the Humanities, 1974-75 and 1976; Fulbright grant for Jamaica, 1978; Robert R. Motor research grant, 1979-80.

*WRITINGS:*

*Shuckin and Jivin: Folklore from Contemporary Black Americans,* Indiana University Press, 1978.
*Folklore from Contemporary Jamaicans,* drawings by Murry N. DePillars, University of Tennessee Press, 1985.

*Fifty Caribbean Writers: A Bio-Bibliographical-Critical Sourcebook,* Greenwood Press, 1986.
*Long Gone: The Mecklenburg Six and the Theme of Escape in Black Folklore,* University of Tennessee Press, 1987.
*New World Adams: Conversations with West Indian Writers,* Peepul Tree Press, 1992.

Contributor to *Black American Writers: Bibliographic Essays,* St. Martin's, 1978. Contributor to folklore and black studies journals. Advisory editor, *Black American Literary Forum,* 1978—; editorial advisor, *Journal of West Indian Literature,* 1986—.

*BIOGRAPHICAL/CRITICAL SOURCES:*

*PERIODICALS*

*Americas,* March-April, 1986.
*New Republic,* July 29, 1978.
*Washington Post,* September 15, 1978.

\* \* \*

## DANDRIDGE, Rita B(ernice) 1940-
## (Rita Dandridge Simons)

*PERSONAL:* Born September 16, 1940, in Richmond, VA; daughter of Allen Washington Dandridge and Iva Bernice (Green) Dandridge (a homemaker); married Mills McDaniel Simons, December 22, 1962 (divorced January 25, 1971). *Education:* Virginia Union University, B.A., 1961; Howard University, M.A., 1963, Ph.D., 1970. *Religion:* Protestant. *Avocational interests:* Quilting, gardening, real estate management.

*ADDRESSES: Office*—Department of English, Norfolk State University, 2401 Corprew Ave., Norfolk, VA 23504.

*CAREER:* Morgan State University, Baltimore, MD, began as instructor, became assistant professor of English, 1964-71; University of Toledo, Toledo, OH, assistant professor of English, 1971-74; Norfolk State University, Norfolk, VA, began as associate professor, became professor of English, 1974—, member of editorial board, 1986. Fellow in residence, University of Virginia Center for the Humanities, 1987

*MEMBER:* Society for the Study of the Multi-Ethnic Literature of the United States (membership chairperson, 1992), Modern Language Association of America, College Language Association, Society for the Advancement of Good English, National Women's Studies Association.

*AWARDS, HONORS:* National Endowment for the Humanities stipend, summers, 1976 and 1977.

*WRITINGS:*

(Under name Rita Dandridge Simons; with DeLois M. Flemons) *Relevant Expository Techniques and Programmed Grammar,* Kendall/Hunt, 1971.
*Ann Allen Shockley: An Annotated Primary and Secondary Bibliography,* Greenwood Press, 1987.
*Black Women's Blues: A Literary Anthology, 1934-1988,* G.K. Hall, 1992.

Contributor to *All the Women Are White, All the Blacks Are Men, But Some of Us Are Brave,* edited by Gloria T. Hull, et al., Feminist Press, 1982; *Dictionary of Literary Biography,* Volume 33: *Afro-American Fiction Writers After 1955,* Gale, 1984; and *Black Women in America: An Historical Encyclopedia,* two volumes, edited by Darlene Clark Hine, Carlson Publishing, 1993. Also contributor of numerous critical articles and reviews to periodicals, including *CLA Journal, Black American Literature Forum, Journal of Negro Education,* and *Black Film Review.* Consultant reader for *PMLA, MELUS,* and *Signs, Journal of Women in Culture and Society.*

*SIDELIGHTS:* Rita B. Dandridge once commented: "I write with my students in mind, especially those interested in African American literature and women's studies. I use my publications in class whenever possible to convey to my students the uncharted territory in the two disciplines and the urgency in rescuing minority women writers from the borders to which traditional histories have restricted them. Sharing my work often motivates students to strive for greater self-definition, and it certainly boosts student-teacher relationships, particularly when the teacher is regarded as a role model, and not just a roll taker and grade giver."

**DARLING, T. H.**
**See HARRIS, Thomas Walter**

\*   \*   \*

**DATES, Jannette L.**

*PERSONAL:* Married to Victor Dates (an assistant professor). *Education:* Coppin State College, B.S.; Johns Hopkins University, M.Ed.; University of Maryland at College Park, Ph.D.

*ADDRESSES: Home*—2107 Carterdale Rd., Baltimore, MD 21209. *Office*—School of Communications, Howard University, Washington, DC 20059.

*CAREER:* Baltimore City Public School System, Baltimore, MD, classroom demonstration teacher, 1958-63, television demonstration teacher, 1964-69, producer and writer of elementary and secondary school telecourses, 1964-71; Goucher College, Baltimore, instructor in department of education, 1970-72; Morgan State University, Baltimore, instructor in department of education, 1970-72, instructor, 1972-77, assistant professor in department of communication and theater arts, 1977-80, coordinator of university television projects, 1973-80; Howard University, Washington, DC, assistant professor in department of radio, television, and film and sequence coordinator for broadcast management/policy, 1981-85; Coppin State College, Baltimore, associate professor in department of languages, literature, and journalism and director of video production service, 1985-87; Howard University, associate dean for educational affairs in school of communications, 1987-92, associate professor in department of radio, television and film, 1990—, member of numerous curriculum and executive committees; California State University, Dominguez Hills, Young, Gifted and Black Distinguished Resident Scholar, 1991. Executive producer of *North Star* (television series), 1971-73; Baltimore Cable Television Commission, commissioner and chairperson of education task force, 1979-81; Baltimore Cable Access Corporation, president, 1982-86, vice-president, 1986-88; Mayor's Cable Advisory Commission, member and chairperson of education task force, 1988-90; Mayor's Cable Communications Commission, member, 1990—. Speaker and panelist for numerous television programs, including *Square Off,* 1977-89; writer and narrator of various short documentaries; member of Baltimore City Cable Communication Commission.

*MEMBER:* National Communications Association, Speech Communications Association, Broadcast Education Association (chair, leadership challenge division, 1987-90; multicultural studies division, vice-chair, 1990-92, chair, 1992-93),

Association for Education in Journalism and Mass Communication, National Black Media Coalition.

*AWARDS, HONORS:* Research grant, Maryland Committee for the Humanities, 1980; co-recipient, with William Barlow, of Gustavus Meyer National Award for best book written in the U.S. in the area of human rights, 1992, for *Split Image: African Americans in the Mass Media;* Freedom Forum Media Studies Center fellow, Columbia University, 1992-93.

*WRITINGS:*

(Editor with William Barlow, and contributor) *Split Image: African Americans in the Mass Media,* Howard University Press, 1990.

Contributor to books, including *Ethnic Images in American Film and Television,* edited by Randall Miller, Balch Institute, 1978; *Mass Media and Society,* edited by Alan Wells, D. C. Heath, 1987; *The Encyclopedia of African American History and Culture,* Macmillan, in press. Contributor to periodicals, including *Film History, Crisis, Philadelphia Inquirer, Journalism Quarterly, Journal of Communication,* and *Journal of Broadcasting.*

*SIDELIGHTS:* Jannette L. Dates and coeditor William Barlow received the Gustavus Meyer award for their book, *Split Image: African Americans in the Mass Media. Washington Post Book World* reviewer Salim Muwakkil considered this book the first comprehensive examination of the treatment of black Americans in the music, film, radio, television, news, and advertising industries. Dates and Barlow explain in the introduction that the book explores the media's stereotypical and discriminatory representation of black Americans and uses "the cultural prism of race in order to assess the development of the American mass media in the twentieth century." The book also traces the limited participation of black Americans in mainstream media and their response to the stereotypes perpetuated by it. Muwakkil called *Split Image* a "virtual treasure trove of historical jewels" and an indispensable source of information for students of American history and media.

*BIOGRAPHICAL/CRITICAL SOURCES:*

*PERIODICALS*

*Washington Post Book World,* July 29, 1990, pp. 1, 10.

\*   \*   \*

# DAVENPORT, Doris 1915-1980

*PERSONAL:* Born in 1915 in Moline, IL; died June 18, 1980, in Santa Cruz, CA.

*CAREER:* Screen actress; appeared in *Kid Millions,* 1934; *The Westerner,* and *Behind the News,* 1940; writer and poet.

*WRITINGS:*

*POETRY*

*It's Like This,* D. Davenport Publisher, 1980.
*Eat Thunder and Drink Rain,* D. Davenport Publisher, 1982.
*Voodoo Chile, Slight Return,* Soque Street, 1991.

\*   \*   \*

# DAVIS, Angela (Yvonne) 1944-

*PERSONAL:* Born January 26, 1944, in Birmingham, AL; daughter of B. Frank (a teacher and businessman) and Sallye E. (a teacher) Davis. *Education:* Attended Sorbonne, University of Paris, 1963-64; Brandeis University, B.A. (magna cum laude), 1965; University of Frankfurt, graduate study, 1965-67; University of California, San Diego, M.A., 1968, graduate study, 1968-69. *Politics:* Communist.

*ADDRESSES: Office*—c/o Random House, Inc., 201 East 50th Street, New York, NY 10022.

*CAREER:* San Francisco State University professor; University of California, Los Angeles, acting assistant professor of philosophy, 1969-70; Communist Party candidate for vice-president of the United States, 1980. Currently works with National Alliance against Racist and Political Repression.

*AWARDS, HONORS:* Honorary Ph.D., Lenin University.

*WRITINGS:*

(With Ruchell Magee, the Soledad Brothers, and others) *If They Come in the Morning: Voices of Resistance,* forward by Julian Bond, Third Press, 1971.
*Angela Davis: An Autobiography,* Random House, 1974, revised edition, 1990.
*Women, Race and Class,* Random House, 1981.
*Women, Culture & Politics,* Random House, 1989.

Also author of phonodisc, "Angela Davis Speaks," Folkways, 1971. Contributor of articles to *Ebony* and other periodicals.

*SIDELIGHTS:* Long known as a political activist, Angela Davis has committed her life to the eradication of oppression and poverty, especially among blacks. Through her active involvement in the American Communist Party, she has worked tirelessly and often militantly on behalf of political freedom for repressed peoples.

From an early age, Davis was exposed to the ideas of her parents' friends, many of them radical thinkers, and she began participating in civil rights demonstrations as a teenager. She joined Advance, a Communist youth group, as a scholarship student (from the American Friends Service Committee) at Elizabeth Irwin High School in New York. As a college student, Davis studied under political philosopher Herbert Marcuse, who remarked once that she was the best student he ever taught. At the University of California, San Diego, she participated in several activist organizations, including the San Diego Black Conference and the Student Nonviolent Coordinating Committee; she also helped found the Black Students Council. Although she was only 24 when she emerged as an advocate of communism, her political perspective was complex and not optimistic: "Both the anticapitalist theory she studied and the interracial Communist community to which she was accustomed must have affected her negative analysis of the American black political scene," Elinor Langer wrote in a *New York Times Book Review.*

Davis believes that blacks have traditionally lacked the fundamental rights of whites in America. In *If They Come in the Morning: Voices of Resistance,* she states, "Needless to say, the history of the United States has been marred from its inception by an enormous quantity of unjust laws, far too many expressly bolstering the oppression of Black people." As a result, she believes, numerous minority members fall prey to the very political and economic conditions that support the upper classes. She explains in *If They Come in the Morning:* "Prisoners—especially Blacks, Chicanos, and Puerto Ricans—are increasingly advancing the proposition that they are political prisoners. They contend that they are political prisoners in the sense that they are largely the victims of an oppressive politico-economic order, swiftly becoming conscious of the causes underlying their victimization."

Davis further characterizes political prisoners as not merely "victims" but rather pioneers in a great struggle against repression. The criminal acts of which they were convicted were a form of protest against the "oppressive politico-economic order" of which she often speaks. She defines the political prisoner in *If They Come in the Morning:* "The offense of the political prisoner is his political boldness, the persistent challenging—legally or extra-legally—of fundamental social wrongs fostered and reinforced by the state. He has opposed unjust laws and exploitative, racist social conditions in general, with the ultimate aim of transforming these laws and this society into an order harmonious with the material and spiritual needs and interests of the vast majority of its members."

Davis views her work with political prisoners as an outgrowth of her personal devotion "to defend our embattled humanity," she states in *Angela Davis: An Autobiography.* She contends that she did not want to write her autobiography, but comments in it: "When I decided to write the book after all, it was because I had come to envision it as a *political* autobiography that emphasized the people, the events and the forces in my life that propelled me to my present commitment." Her autobiography details how her aims to help oppressed individuals found expression in the political ideals of communism. About her early introduction to communism, she states in her autobiography: "The *Communist Manifesto* hit me like a bolt of lightning. I read it avidly, finding in it answers to many of the seemingly unanswerable dilemmas which had plagued me.... I began to see the problems of Black people within the context of a large working-class movement. My ideas about Black liberation were imprecise, and I could not find the right concepts to articulate them; still, I was acquiring some understanding about how capitalism could be abolished." She continues, explaining the connection between communism and minority liberation, "What struck me so emphatically was the idea that once the emancipation of the proletariat became a reality, the foundation was laid for the emancipation of all oppressed groups in society."

Within the Communist Party, U.S.A., Davis allied herself primarily with the Che-Lumumba Club, a black faction of the Los Angeles party membership. The group had already declared as its goal the liberation of black peoples in the Los Angeles area through application of Marxist-Leninist philosophies when Davis officially joined the party in July, 1968. Davis' growing radicalism, expressed in speeches and protests, eroded her mainstream career; in 1969, the board of regents at the University of California dismissed her as an assistant professor, a decision reversed by court order. Nevertheless, the university declined to renew her contract in 1970, despite highly favorable reviews of her performance as a teacher. The American Association of University Professors questioned the university's action, and two years later, the institution tried but failed to win Davis back.

Davis, in the meantime, got involved in an escape attempt from the Marin County courthouse in California, along with prisoner George Jackson and others. An ensuing shoot-out left a judge dead and led to Davis's arrest on murder, kidnapping and conspiracy charges. She was subsequently acquitted of the charges, but the incident only heightened a general perception of Davis as a trouble-maker or worse, a violent radical. Davis's controversial behavior has not lessened since her prison and courtroom experiences. She adopts, however, more conventional methods for spreading ideologies than she perhaps once did. She has immersed herself within the Communist Party, lecturing around the world, and in the 1980 U.S. presidential election, Davis was the vice-presidential candidate of the Communist Party.

About *If They Come in the Morning: Voices of Resistance,* Steven V. Roberts, of *Commonweal* observes "In essence, ...

this is a book written by revolutionaries, true believers, who can justify anything in the name of their cause." Although he finds that the book "bristles with contradictions," Roberts adds, "The best parts of [the collection] are several essays by Miss Davis."

*Angela Davis: An Autobiography* "is less an autobiography than a preliminary probe of her own fiber, her humble realization that she is made of stern stuff," according to Ivan Webster of *New Republic.* "She is eloquent, tough and stubborn in her moral integrity." Yet, Webster notes a failing: "It's when she moves away from hard, stark issues that the book falters." Julius Lester of the *Progressive* commented: "One is left with the impression of a woman who lives as she thinks it necessary to live and not as she would like to, if she allowed herself to have desires. She seems to be a woman of enormous self-discipline and control, who willed herself to a total political identity. Her will is so strong that, at times, it is frightening." Davis, Lester wrote, had negated everything in herself that "would interfere with her commitment to revolutionary change."

Paula Giddings, in *Black World,* shares Lester's view of Davis's intensity and autonomous vision: "[After] reading the last page, one's immediate reaction is, but what have we learned about Angela Davis? The answer is a great deal.... She has little desire to project herself as a singularly charismatic figure ... the primary purpose of her book is to illuminate the political causes and concerns central to her life." George E. Kent, writing in *PHYLON: The Atlantic University Review of Race and Culture,* read the autobiography in much the same way: "Despite its single-minded emphasis upon proper ideological response, the passion with which this political autobiography is written enhances its educational objective."

In a review of Davis's revised *Autobiography,* Toks Williams of the *New Statesman* found Davis as bracing and pertinent as ever, praising her "single-minded dedication and hard-headed idealism," and talks about her new-found interest in the plight of women, their stake in the development of a strong political opposition, and her softened attitude toward feminism. Davis regretted that in 1974 she could not recognize the "dialectics of the personal and the political" in feminist and liberationist thinking. Davis, ever the polemicist, urges young blacks to become leaders in their own community by following the examples of civil rights leaders like Marcus Garvey.

Davis's communist world-view served as a prism for her 1981 book on the roots of the feminist movement, *Women, Race and Class.* Carolly Erickson of the *Los Angeles Times Book Review* states that the book "is as useful an exposition of the current dilemmas of the women's movement as one could hope for." She adds, "*Women, Race and Class* offers a view from the underside of 19th-century feminism, and argues that

the profound differences that estranged black and white women in the early days of the women's movement still estrange them today." Ann Jones of the *New York Times Book Review* both found the book enlightening as a perspective on the differences in black and white feminism, but Jones found the book's pedagogy an obstacle. She wrote, "I wish she had spoken to us here, as she has so movingly in the past, in a voice less tuned at times to the Communist Party, more insistently her own. But she is herself a woman of undeniable courage. She should be heard."

*Women, Culture and Politics* is a collection of essays based on 18 speeches Davis gave between 1983 and 1987. Davis's focus in these essays is the elimination of sexism, racism and poverty in university education. Lynn Wenzel in the *New York Times Book Review* chided Davis's "annoyingly glib" arguments and "persistent propagandizing for 'the eventual advent of communism'." Nevertheless, Wenzel acknowledges Davis's power as a leader with insight, stating "the sweetness of her dream cannot be denied."

Jackie Stevens, reviewing *Women, Culture and Politics* for *The Nation,* found that Davis's views hadn't changed much since *Women, Race and Class* was published; Davis attacked the Reagan Administration's policy that, as she believed, blamed black women for teenage pregnancy, and she also attacked feminism, considering it a natural outgrowth of capitalism and proposing that it sabotages the alliance between the labor Left and African American organizations. The white, middle-class women who populated the feminist movement believed feminism could transcend our racial and economic boundaries, uniting sisters under a common cause, Davis said. Stevens reports that Davis writes, "This approach leaves the existing socioeconomic system with its fundamental reliance on racism and class bias unchallenged." Still, while Davis suggested that feminism had nothing to do with the socialist revolution, that it was at odds with a proletarian struggle, these speeches were all addressed to women's organizations, Stevens pointed out: "Surely Davis had better speak to the proletariat if she intends to foment a working-class revolution, but there is not single address to a labor audience in this collection." And, Stevens added, Davis never quite pulled together a "coherent model" that would unite her thinking on the effects of sexism, racism, homophobia, consumerism and classism.

Angela Davis's political commitments keep her involved in an unending fight against oppression. Her communist beliefs alienate her from many American citizens, yet she continues to lecture and write in support of her philosophies. Although Davis's ideologies garner much opposition in the United States, Jones remarks upon her tenacity, describing Davis as one "who has never shied from impossible tasks."

*BIOGRAPHICAL/CRITICAL SOURCES:*

*BOOKS*

*The Angela Davis Trial* (microfilm), Oceana, 1974.

Ashman, Charles R., *The People vs. Angela Davis,* Pinnacle Books, 1972.

*Contemporary Issues Criticism,* Volume 1, Gale, 1982.

Davis, Angela, Ruchell Magee, the Soledad Brothers, and others, *If They Come in the Morning: Voices of Resistance,* Third Press, 1971.

Davis, Angela, *Angela Davis: An Autobiography,* Random House, 1974.

Lund, Caroline, *The Czechoslovak Frame-Up Trials,* Pathfinder Press, 1973.

Smith, Nelda J., *From Where I Sat,* Vantage, 1973.

*PERIODICALS*

*Los Angeles Times Book Review,* April 4, 1982.

*Nation,* January 27, 1989, p. 279-81.

*New Statesman,* March 16, 1990.

*New York Times Book Review,* January 10, 1982; March 26, 1989.

*PHYLON: The Atlantic University Review of Race and Culture,* March, 1976.

*Village Voice Literary Supplement,* June, 1982.

\* \* \*

## DAVIS, Arthur P(aul) 1904-

*PERSONAL:* Born November 21, 1904, in Hampton, VA; son of Andrew (a plasterer) and Frances (Nash) Davis; married Clarice Winn, October 6, 1928 (deceased); children: Arthur Paul, Jr. *Education:* Columbia University, A.B., 1927, A.M., 1929, Ph.D., 1942. *Politics:* Independent. *Religion:* Episcopalian.

*ADDRESSES: Home*—3001 Veazey Ter. N.W., Washington, DC 20008. *Office*—Graduate School, Howard University, Washington, DC 20059.

*CAREER:* North Carolina College (now North Carolina Central University), Durham, instructor in English, 1927-28; Virginia Union University, Richmond, professor of English, 1929-44; Howard University, Washington, DC, professor of English, 1944-69, university professor emeritus, 1969—. Conducted series of talks, "Ebony Harvest," on Radio WAMU-FM, Washington-Baltimore, 1972-73.

*MEMBER:* Modern Language Association of America, Col-

lege Language Association, Phi Beta Kappa, Omega Psi Phi, Sigma Pi Phi.

*AWARDS, HONORS:* Proudfit fellow, Columbia University, 1937; National Hampton alumni award, 1947; award from Howard University's Institute for the Arts and Humanities, 1973; award from College Language Association, 1975, for distinguished contribution to literary scholarship; Distinguished Critic Award, Middle Atlantic Writers Association, 1982; Litt.D., Howard University, 1984.

*WRITINGS:*

(Editor with Sterling A. Brown and Ulysses Lee) *The Negro Caravan,* Dryden, 1941, Arno, 1970.

*Isaac Watts: His Life and Works,* Dryden, 1943.

(Editor with J. Saunders Redding) *Cavalcade: Negro American Writers from 1760 to the Present,* Houghton, 1971.

*From the Dark Tower: Afro-American Writers from 1900 to 1960,* Howard University Press, 1974, reissued, 1981.

(Editor with Michael W. Peplow) *The New Negro Renaissance: An Anthology,* Holt, 1975.

(Editor with Redding and Joyce Ann Joyce) *The New Cavalcade: Negro American Writers from 1760 to the Present,* two volumes, Howard University Press, 1991, 1992.

Writer of column, "With a Grain of Salt," *Journal and Guide* newspaper, 1933-50.

*WORK IN PROGRESS: The Life and Observations of Arthur P. Davis, Middle Class Negro* (tentative title).

*SIDELIGHTS:* Davis commented: "In 1929, I taught my first course in Negro literature. Very, very few Negro and no white schools in those days had a course in this subject. Believing strongly in the importance of the Negro's contribution to American literature, I have devoted practically all of my adult working years to teaching and writing in the field of Negro letters. It has been gratifying to note the subject's growth in popularity since 1929."

Davis has co-edited several collections of African American literature, many of which are used as textbooks in college courses. *Washington Post Book World* described the 1971 anthology *Cavalcade: Negro American Writers from 1760 to the Present* as "a classic anthology of black American writing." *American Literature* called the first volume of his latest anthology, *The New Cavalcade: African American Writing from 1760 to the Present,* "a welcome resource for general survey courses as well as for courses on African American literature." *The New Cavalcade* is a two-volume collection of over 300 short stories, poems, and excerpts from essays, novels, plays, biographies and autobiographies. It includes works by such classic authors as Phillis Wheatley, Ralph Ellison, and

James Baldwin as well as selections from lesser-known and more contemporary writers.

*BIOGRAPHICAL/CRITICAL SOURCES:*

*PERIODICALS*

*American Literature,* March, 1992.
*Washington Post Book World,* January 19, 1992.

\*    \*    \*

## DAVIS, Benjamin O(liver), Jr.  1912-

*PERSONAL:* Born December 18, 1912, in Washington, DC; son of Benjamin Oliver (an army officer) and Sadie (Overton) Davis; married Agatha Scott (a homemaker), June 20, 1936. *Education:* Attended Western Reserve University (now Case Western Reserve University) and University of Chicago; U.S. Military Academy, B.S., 1936. *Politics:* Democrat. *Religion:* Protestant.

*ADDRESSES: Home*—1001 Wilson Blvd., No. 906, Arlington, VA 22209.

*CAREER:* U.S. Air Force, career officer, 1932-70, retiring as lieutenant general; commander of 99th Fighter Squadron, 332nd Fighter Group, 477th Bombardment Group, 332nd Fighter Wing, 1942-49; assigned to Air War College, 1949-50; fighter branch chief, U.S. Air Force headquarters, 1950-53; commander of 51st Fighter Interceptor Wing, Suwon, Korea; director of operations and training, Far East Air Forces headquarters, 1954-55; promoted to brigadier general, 1954; commander of Air Task Force 13, Taiwan, 1955-57; promoted to major general, 1957; deputy chief of staff, U.S. Air Force operations headquarters, Europe, 1957-61; director of manpower and organization, U.S. Air Force headquarters, 1961-65; chief of staff, United Nations Command and U.S. Forces, Korea, 1965-67; commander, 13th Air Force, Philippines, 1967-68; deputy commander-in-chief, U.S. Strike Command, McDill Air Force base, Tampa, FL, 1969-70. City of Cleveland, OH, director of public safety, 1970; U.S. Department of Transportation, Washington, DC, director of civil aviation security and assistant secretary of environment, safety, and consumer affairs, 1971-75. National Defense Transportation Association, national vice-president, 1972-74; chairman of Interagency Commission on Civilian Aviation Security, 1971-74, of board of visitors, U.S. Air Force Academy, 1973-74, and of Interagency Commission on Transportation Security; member of Campus Unrest Commission, Battle Monuments Commission, Blue Ribbon Military Pay Commission, and Citizens Advisory Committee to DC Bar; member of board of Pepperdine University.

*MEMBER:* Retired Officers Association (member of board of directors), Association of Graduates of the U.S. Military Academy (member of board of trustees, 1971-74).

*AWARDS, HONORS: Military*—Three Distinguished Service Medals; Army and Air Force Silver Star; Distinguished Flying Cross; three Legions of Merit; Air Medal with five Oak Leaf Clusters; Croix de Guerre with Palm; Star of Africa. *Other*—D.Mil.Sc., Wilberforce University, 1948; L.L.D., Tuskegee Institute, 1963; D.Sc., Morgan State University, 1963.

*WRITINGS:*

(Author of introduction) Marvin E. Fletcher, *America's First Black General: Benjamin O. Davis, Sr., 1880-1970,* University Press of Kansas, 1989.
*Benjamin O. Davis, Jr., American: An Autobiography,* Smithsonian Institution Press, 1991.

*SIDELIGHTS:* Benjamin O. Davis, Jr.'s 1991 autobiography charts the military career of the first black to graduate from the U.S. Military Academy in West Point in the twentieth century. Exposing the racial prejudice he experienced throughout his service in the U.S. Air Force, Davis discusses his struggle to rise to the rank of lieutenant general. The book also provides insight into Davis's World War II command of the Tuskegee Airmen (99th Fighter Squadron and later, 332nd Fighter Group)—an all-black fighter squadron and group that provided American black men their first opportunity to serve as fighter pilots—as well as his later duties at the Pentagon. Calling *Benjamin O. Davis, Jr., American* an "important addition to the shelf of civil rights and military literature," *New York Times* critic Herbert Mitgang noted that the book "illustrate[s] the life of a genuine hero who proved by his own example that given an equal chance at education and training, American blacks could be as effective as anybody else."

One of Davis's most vivid memories of his childhood was of a night when the Ku Klux Klan staged a march which passed right by his family's residence near the campus of Tuskegee Institute in Alabama. Officials of the Institute had recommended that black residents stay indoors with their lights out during the demonstration. However, Davis's father determined that his family would sit on their brightly lighted front porch and so they did, with the senior Davis resplendent in his full dress army uniform. This incident was symbolic of the attitude the Davis family consistently took toward racial prejudice and segregation in all their forms. Both father and son, as well as their wives, always asserted their right to full equality in a quiet but firm manner.

The senior Davis was a career member of the United States Army who had risen from private to officer status, was for many years the only black officer in the regular army, and finally achieved the rank of brigadier general in 1940. The younger Davis decided to follow his father's career and secured an appointment to the United States Military Academy at West Point in 1932. There he found himself "silenced": no one roomed with him, took meals with him, or spoke to him (except to issue an order), during his entire four years at the academy. Without telling family or friends of his ordeal, Davis grimly stuck it out to the end, graduating 35th in a class of 276 and thus becoming the first black to graduate from West Point in the twentieth century.

Davis wanted to fly airplanes in the Air Force but, since the air service at that time neither had nor wanted black pilots, he had to settle for a number of routine assignments on the ground with the then strictly segregated army. His great opportunity came in 1941 when the War Department, at the behest of the Roosevelt administration, decided to create an all-black fighter squadron, to be commanded by Davis when he completed flight training. He not only realized his dream of being a pilot but, as commander first of the black fighter squadron and then of a fighter wing during the remainder of the war in Europe, he played a key role in demonstrating that black men could be effective military pilots.

Davis's career was less dramatic after World War II, but the official ending of segregation in the armed forces in 1948 allowed him to continue his progress up the ranks as a commander of integrated Air Force units. Throughout his active service he worked quietly but tirelessly to make full equality of opportunity in the armed services a reality rather than an ideal. In his autobiography, he does not hesitate to reveal fully many of the wrongs inflicted on him and his family by the prejudice of whites. Nonetheless he is, he maintains, an optimist, and prefers to stress the progress that has been made during his lifetime rather than to dwell upon the evils of the past.

*BIOGRAPHICAL/CRITICAL SOURCES:*

*BOOKS*

*Contemporary Black Biography,* Volume 2, Gale, 1992.
Davis, Benjamin O., Jr., *Benjamin O. Davis, Jr., American: An Autobiography,* Smithsonian Institution Press, 1991.

*PERIODICALS*

*American History Illustrated,* July/August, 1991.
*American Visions,* April, 1991.
*Chicago Tribune,* January 27, 1991.
*Choice,* July, 1991.
*Foreign Affairs,* summer, 1991.
*Insight,* March 4, 1991.

*Jet,* February 11, 1991.
*Library Journal,* March 1, 1991.
*New York Times,* February 20, 1991, p. C15.
*New York Times Book Review,* January 19, 1992.
*Publishers Weekly,* January 4, 1991.
*Smithsonian,* March, 1991.
*Washington Post,* February 4, 1991.
*Washington Post Book World,* March 17, 1991, p. 9.


*       *       *


## DAVIS, Frank Marshall   1905-1987

*PERSONAL:* Born December 31, 1905, in Arkansas City, KS; died July 26, 1987, in Honolulu, HI; married; children: Lynn, Beth, Jeanne, Jill, Mark. *Education:* Attended Friends University, 1923; attended Kansas State Agricultural College (now Kansas State University of Agricultural and Applied Science), 1924-27, 1929.

*CAREER:* Worked for various newspapers in Illinois, including the *Chicago Evening Bulletin, Whip,* and *Gary American,* 1927-29; *Atlanta Daily World,* Atlanta, GA, editor and co-founder, 1931-34; Associated Negro Press, Chicago, IL, executive editor, 1935-47; *Chicago Star,* Chicago, executive editor, 1946-48; owned wholesale paper business in Honolulu, HI, beginning c. 1948. Worked as a jazz radio disc jockey in the early 1940s. Toured black colleges as a lecturer, 1973.

*MEMBER:* League of American Writers, Allied Arts Guild, Southside Chicago Writers Group.

*AWARDS, HONORS:* Julius Rosenwald Foundation grant, 1937.

*WRITINGS:*

*Black Man's Verse* (poems; includes "Giles Johnson, Ph.D.," "Lynched [Symphonic Interlude for Twenty-One Selected Instruments]," "Mojo Mike's Beer Garden," "Cabaret," and "Ebony Under Granite"), Black Cat, 1935.
*I Am the American Negro* (poems; includes "I Am the American Negro," "Flowers of Darkness," "To One Who Would Leave Me," "Awakening," "Come to Me," "Modern Man—The Superman: A Song of Praise for Hearst, Hitler, Mussolini, and the Munitions Makers," "'Mancipation Day," "Onward Christian Soldiers," "Christ Is a Dixie Nigger," "Note Left by a Suicide," "Ebony Under Granite," and "Frank Marshall Davis: Writer"), Black Cat, 1937.

*Through Sepia Eyes* (poems; includes "Chicago Skyscrapers," "To Those Who Sing America," "Life Is a Woman," and "Coincidence"), Black Cat, 1938.

*47th Street: Poems* (includes "47th Street," "Pattern for Conquest," "Egotistic Runt," "Tenement Room," "Black Weariness," "Snapshots of the Cotton South," "Peace Quiz for America," "For All Common People," "War Zone," "Nothing Can Stop the People," "Peace Is a Fragile Cup," and "Self-Portrait"), Decker, 1948.

*Awakening, and Other Poems,* Black Cat, 1978.

*Livin' the Blues: Memoirs of a Black Journalist and Poet,* edited by John Edgar Tidwell, University of Wisconsin Press, 1993.

Also author of poem, "Chicago's Congo," and of a volume of poetry entitled *Jazz Interlude,* 1985; author of the unpublished manuscript, "That Incredible Waikiki Jungle." Poems published in anthologies, including *The Negro Caravan,* Dryden, 1942; *Kaleidoscope: Poems by American Negro Poets,* Harcourt, 1967; *Black Voices: An Anthology of Afro-American Literature,* New American Library, 1968; *The Poetry of the Negro, 1746-1970,* Anchor Books, 1970; *Black Insights,* Ginn, 1971; *Understanding the New Black Poetry,* Morrow, 1973; and *The New Negro Renaissance: An Anthology,* Holt, 1975. Contributor to periodicals, including *National, Light and Heebie Jeebies,* and *Voices.* Wrote weekly column for *Honolulu Record.*

SIDELIGHTS: Frank Marshall Davis's poetry "not only questioned social ills in his own time but also inspired blacks in the politically charged 1960s," according to John Edgar Tidwell in the *Dictionary of Literary Biography.* Sometimes likened to poets such as Walt Whitman and Carl Sandburg, Davis published his first volume, *Black Man's Verse,* in 1935. The book met with much applause from critics, including Harriet Monroe, who concluded in *Poetry* that its author was "a poet of authentic inspiration, who belongs not only among the best of his race, but who need not lean upon his race for recognition as an impassioned singer with something to say." Davis concerned himself with portraying black life, protesting racial inequalities, and promoting black pride. The poet described his work thus in the poem "Frank Marshall Davis: Writer" from his *I Am the American Negro:* "When I wrote / I dipped my pen / In the crazy heart / Of mad America."

Davis grew up in Arkansas City, Kansas, surrounded by racism. Tidwell reports that when the poet was five years old he was nearly killed by some older white children who had heard stories of lynchings and wanted to try one for themselves. The result of this incident and others was that Davis hated whites in his youth. He gained some relief, according to Tidwell, when he left the prejudiced, smalltown atmosphere of Arkansas City in 1923 to attend Friends University in Wichita; he eventually transferred to Kansas State Agricultural College's

school of journalism. There, because of a class assignment, Davis received his first introduction to writing free verse—his preferred poetic form. When he left Kansas State, he travelled to Chicago, where he wrote free-lance articles for magazines and worked for several black newspapers while continuing to produce poems. After a brief return to Kansas State, Davis moved to Atlanta, Georgia, to take an editing post on a semiweekly paper. With the help of his leadership, the periodical became the *Atlanta Daily World,* the first successful black daily newspaper in America. Meanwhile, one of Davis's published poems, "Chicago's Congo," which concerns the underlying similarities between the blacks of Chicago and those still living the tribal life of the African Congo, attracted the attention of bohemian intellectual Frances Norton Manning. When Davis returned to Chicago, Manning introduced him to Norman Forgue, whose Black Cat Press subsequently published Davis's *Black Man's Verse.*

A critical success, *Black Man's Verse* "is experimental, cacophonous, yet sometimes harmonious," according to Tidwell. The volume includes poems such as "Giles Johnson, Ph.D.," in which the title character starves to death in spite of his four college degrees and knowledge of Latin and Greek because he does not wish to teach and is incapable of doing the manual labor that made up the majority of work available to blacks. Other pieces in *Black Man's Verse*— "Lynched," "Mojo Mike's Beer Garden," and "Cabaret," for example—make use of Davis's expertise on the subject of jazz to combine "the spirit of protest in jazz and free verse with ... objections to racial oppression, producing a poetry that loudly declaims against injustice," explained Tidwell. Another well-known part of the volume is entitled "Ebony Under Granite." Likened to author Edgar Lee Masters's *Spoon River Anthology,* this section discusses the lives of various black people buried in a cemetery. Characters include Reverend Joseph Williams, who used to have sex with most of the women in his congregation; Goldie Blackwell, a two-dollar prostitute; George Brown, who served life in prison for voting more than once, although in Mississippi he had seen white voters commit the same crime many times without punishment; and Roosevelt Smith, a black writer who was so frustrated by literary critics that he became a postman.

*I Am the American Negro,* Davis's second collection of poems, was published two years after his first. While drawing generally favorable reviews, it did not attract as much attention as *Black Man's Verse,* and some critics complained that it was too similar to the earlier book. For example, Tidwell quotes black critic Alain Locke's assertion that *I Am the American Negro* "has too many echoes of the author's first volume ... it is not a crescendo in the light of the achievement of [*Black Man's Verse*]." One of the obvious similarities between the two collections is that Davis also included an "Ebony Under Granite" section in the second. Members of this cast are people like the two Greeley sisters—the first's earlier promiscuous lifestyle did not prevent her from marrying respectably, while the second's lack of sexual experience caused her husband to be unfaithful; Nicodemus Perry, killed by loiterers for accidentally bumping into a white woman while, ironically, lost in memories of the sexual abuse his female relatives suffered at the hands of white men; and Mrs. Clifton Townsend, prejudiced against the darker-skinned members of her own race, who dies after giving birth to a baby much blacker than herself. Other poems featured in *I Am the American Negro* are "Modern Man—The Superman," which laments the state of modern civilization and has mock musical notations in its margins such as "Eight airplane motors, each keyed to a different pitch, are turned on and off to furnish musical accompaniment within the range of an octave"; and the title poem, which is a diatribe against Southern laws treating blacks differently from whites. Davis also placed love poems such as "Flowers of Darkness" and "Come to Me" in this book.

The poems of Davis's limited-edition third volume, *Through Sepia Eyes,* were later published along with others in his 1948 collection, *47th Street.* Though Tidwell described *47th Street* as "the culmination of Davis's thought and poetic development," Davis himself remarked on the time span between *I Am* and his fourth book in a 1973 interview for *Black World:* "I was going through a number of changes during that particular time and I had to wait for these changes to settle and jell before I produced other work which I thought would be suitable to appear in a volume. And, of course, some critics naturally have thought that I would have been better off had I just continued to jell indefinitely." *47th Street* is composed of poems such as "Coincidence," which narrates the life stories of Donald Woods, a white man, and Booker Scott, a black man, who shared their dates of birth and death—by the poem's end the reader discovers that they also shared the same white biological father. The title poem, "unlike [Davis's] previous descriptions of Southside Chicago as exclusively black," noted Tidwell, "presents a 'rainbow race' of people." Indeed, Tidwell saw the whole of *47th Street* as having more universal concerns than his earlier works. When questioned about this issue Davis declared: "I am a Black poet, definitely a Black poet, and I think that my way of seeing things is the result of the impact [of] our civilization upon what I like to think of as a sensitive Black man.... But I do not think the Black poet should confine himself exclusively to Black readership. I think poetry, if it is going to be any good, should move members of all groups, and that is what I hope for."

In the same year that *47th Street* was published, Davis left Chicago for Honolulu, Hawaii. What began as a vacation turned into permanent residency. Except for a few poems that appeared in *Voices* in 1950, Davis virtually disappeared from the literary world until going on a college lecture tour in 1973. He later published another volume of poetry, and at the time

of his death in 1987 had been working on a manuscript called "That Incredible Waikiki Jungle," about his Hawaiian experiences. When asked why he decided to remain in Hawaii, Davis cited the relative lack of racial problems and added, "I think one of the reasons why was that this [was] the first time that I began to be treated as a man instead of a Black curiosity. That was important to me, for my feeling of dignity and self-respect."

*BIOGRAPHICAL/CRITICAL SOURCES:*

*BOOKS*

Davis, Frank Marshall, *I Am the American Negro,* Black Cat, 1978.
*Dictionary of Literary Biography,* Volume 51: *Afro-American Writers from the Harlem Renaissance to 1940,* Gale, 1987.

*PERIODICALS*

*Black World,* January, 1974.
*Poetry,* August, 1936.

*OBITUARIES:*

*PERIODICALS*

*Chicago Tribune,* August 9, 1987.

\*      \*      \*

## DAVIS, Michael D. 1939-

*PERSONAL:* Born January 12, 1939; son of John P. Davis (a publisher) and Marguerite (DeMond) Davis; married Jean P. Davis, 1978 (divorced, 1988). *Education:* Morehouse College, A.B., 1963. *Avocational interests:* Chess, fishing, photography.

*ADDRESSES: Home and office*—1334 Hamlin St. N.E., Washington, DC 20017. *Agent*—Edward A. Novak III, 111 North Second St., Harrisburg, PA 17102.

*CAREER: Atlanta Constitution,* Atlanta, GA, reporter, 1964-66; *Baltimore Afro-American,* Baltimore, MD, reporter, 1966-68; Baltimore Sunpapers, Baltimore, reporter, 1968-74; *San Diego Union,* San Diego, CA, reporter, 1974-75; *Washington Star,* Washington, DC, reporter, 1975-81; WRC-TV—National Broadcasting Company (NBC) Television News, Washington, DC, metropolitan editor, 1979—, reporter, 1981-84. WETA-TV commentator.

*MEMBER:* National Association of Black Journalists.

*AWARDS, HONORS:* Award, National Association for the Advancement of Colored People (NAACP), late 1960s, for his written coverage of the Vietnam War; Front Page Award, Newspaper Guild, 1979.

*WRITINGS:*

(With Hunter R. Clark) *Thurgood Marshall: Warrior at the Bar, Rebel on the Bench,* Carol, 1992.
*Black American Women in Olympic Track and Field,* McFarland, 1992.
*Our World,* Morrow, in press.

*WORK IN PROGRESS:* Research on the Vietnam War and the American black elite.

*SIDELIGHTS:* Michael D. Davis commented: "I am a fourth-generation Washingtonian. A graduate of Morehouse College, in Atlanta, Georgia, I was one of the leaders of the Atlanta sit-ins. I worked closely with civil rights leader Martin Luther King, Jr., and in 1962 became the first black reporter on the *Atlanta Constitution.* The first suit challenging segregated schools in the nation's capital was brought in my name in 1943 by my father, John P. Davis, a Harvard Law School graduate who was publisher of *Our World* magazine and a personal friend of Thurgood Marshall, who was appointed to the U.S. Supreme Court in 1967. I have reported for the Baltimore Sunpapers, the *San Diego Union,* and the *Washington Star.*

"In 1967 I was a war correspondent in Vietnam for the Baltimore Afro-American Newspapers. I won a National Association for the Advancement of Colored People (NAACP) award for my coverage of black troops in Southeast Asia. I have also worked as metropolitan editor for WRC-TV—NBC Television News in Washington. I am the author of *Black Women in Olympic Track and Field,* the story of black women track stars who have won gold medals for America. I am coauthor, with Hunter R. Clark, of *Thurgood Marshall: Warrior at the Bar, Rebel on the Bench.* I am a frequent commentator on WETA, Washington's Public Broadcasting System station."

\*    \*    \*

## DAVIS, Ossie 1917-

*PERSONAL:* Born December 18, 1917, in Cogdell, GA; son of Kince Charles (a railway construction engineer) and Laura (Cooper) Davis; married Ruby Ann Wallace (an actress and writer under name Ruby Dee), December 9, 1948; children: Nora, Guy, La Verne. *Education:* Attended Howard University, 1935-39, and Columbia University, 1948; trained for the stage with Paul Mann and Lloyd Richards.

*ADDRESSES: Office*—Emmalyn II Productions, P.O. Box 1318, New Rochelle, NY 10802. *Agent*—Artists Agency, 10000 Santa Monica Blvd., Suite 305, Los Angeles, CA 90067.

*CAREER:* Actor, playwright, screenwriter, novelist, and director and producer of stage productions and motion pictures. Worked as janitor, shipping clerk, and stock clerk in New York City, 1938-41. Actor in numerous stage productions, including *Joy Exceeding Glory,* 1941, *Jeb,* 1946, *Anna Lucasta,* 1948, *Stevedore,* 1949, *The Green Pastures,* 1951, *No Time for Sergeants,* 1957, *A Raisin in the Sun,* 1959, *Purlie Victorious,* 1961, *Take It from the Top,* 1979, and *I'm Not Rappaport,* 1986. Actor in motion pictures and teleplays, including *The Joe Louis Story,* 1953, *The Emperor Jones,* 1955, *The Cardinal,* 1963, *Gone Are the Days,* 1963, *Man Called Adam,* 1966, "Teacher, Teacher" for *Hallmark Hall of Fame,* 1969, *Let's Do It Again,* 1976, "For Us the Living" for *American Playhouse,* 1983, *School Daze,* 1988, *Do the Right Thing,* 1989, and *Jungle Fever,* 1991; actor in television series *Evening Shade,* 1990—. Director of motion pictures, including *Cotton Comes to Harlem,* 1970, *Kongi's Harvest,* 1971, *Black Girl,* 1972, *Gordon's War,* 1973, and *Countdown at Kusini,* 1976. Cohost of radio program *Ossie Davis and Ruby Dee Story Hour,* 1974-78, and of television series *With Ossie and Ruby,* Public Broadcasting System (PBS-TV), 1981. Coproducer of stage production *Ballad for Bimshire,* 1963. Chairman of the board, Institute for New Cinema Artists; founder with wife Ruby Dee of Emmalyn II Productions. Performer on recordings for Caedmon and Folkways Records. Civil rights activist. *Military service:* U.S. Army, 1942-45; served as surgical technician in Liberia, West Africa, and with Special Services Department.

*MEMBER:* Actor's Equity Association, Screen Actors Guild, American Federation of Radio and Television Artists, Director's Guild of America, National Association for the Advancement of Colored People (advisory board), Southern Christian Leadership Conference (advisory board), Congress of Racial Equality, Masons.

*AWARDS, HONORS:* First Mississippi Freedom Democratic Party Citation, 1965; Emmy Award nomination, Academy of Television Arts and Sciences, best actor in a special, 1969, for "Teacher, Teacher," *Hallmark Hall of Fame,* and nomination, c. 1978, for *King;* Antoinette Perry Award nomination, best musical, 1970, for *Purlie;* recipient with Dee of Frederick Douglass Award, New York Urban League, for "distinguished leadership toward equal opportunity," 1970; Paul Robeson Citation, Actor's Equity Association, 1975, for "outstanding creative contributions in the performing arts and in society at large"; Coretta Scott King Book Award, American Library Association, and Jane Addams Children's Book Award, Jane Addams Peace Association, both 1979, for *Escape to Freedom;* Jury Award from Neil Simon Awards, 1983, for "For Us the Living," *American Playhouse;* National Association for the Advancement of Colored People, Image Award for best performance by a supporting actor in *Do the Right Thing,* and Hall of Fame Award for outstanding artistic achievement, both 1989.

*WRITINGS:*

*PLAYS*

(And director) *Goldbrickers of 1944,* first produced in Liberia, West Africa, 1944.

*Alice in Wonder* (one-act), first produced in New York City at Elks Community Theatre, September 15, 1952; revised and expanded version produced as *The Big Deal* in New York at New Playwrights Theatre, March 7, 1953.

*Purlie Victorious* (first produced on Broadway at Cort Theatre, 1961; also see below), French, 1961.

*Curtain Call, Mr. Aldridge, Sir* (first produced in Santa Barbara at the University of California, summer, 1968), published in *The Black Teacher and the Dramatic Arts: A Dialogue, Bibliography, and Anthology,* edited by William R. Reardon and Thomas D. Pawley, Negro Universities Press, 1970.

(With Philip Rose, Peter Udell, and Gary Geld) *Purlie* (adaptation of *Purlie Victorious;* first produced on Broadway at Broadway Theatre, March 15, 1970), French, 1971.

*Escape to Freedom: A Play about Young Frederick Douglas* (first produced in New York City at the Town Hall, March 8, 1976), Viking, 1978.

*Langston: A Play* (first produced in New York City in 1982), Delacorte, 1982.

(With Hy Gilbert, and director) *Bingo* (baseball musical based on novel *The Bingo Long Traveling All-Stars and Motor Kings* by William Brashler), first produced in New York City at AMAS Repertory Theater, November, 1985.

Also author of *Last Dance for Sybil.*

*SCREENPLAYS AND TELEPLAYS*

*Gone Are the Days* (adaptation of Davis's *Purlie Victorious;* also released as *Purlie Victorious* and *The Man from C.O.T.T.O.N.*), Trans Lux, 1963.

(With Arnold Perl, and director) *Cotton Comes to Harlem* (based on a novel by Chester Himes), United Artists, 1970.

(And director) *Kongi's Harvest* (adapted from work by Wole Soyinka), Calpenny Films Nigeria Ltd., 1970.

*Today Is Ours,* Columbia Broadcasting System (CBS-TV), 1974.

(With Ladi Ladebo and Al Freeman, Jr.) *Countdown at Kusini* (based on a story by John Storm Roberts), CBS-TV, 1976.

Also writer of television episodes of *East Side/West Side,* 1963, *The Negro People,* 1965, *Just Say the Word,* 1969, *The Eleventh Hour, Bonanza,* and *N.Y.P.D.;* and for special *Alice in Wonder,* 1987.

*OTHER*

(Contributor) *Anger, and Beyond: The Negro Writer in the United States,* edited by Herbert Hill, Harper, 1966.

(Contributor) *Soon, One Morning: New Writing by American Negroes, 1940-1962,* edited by Herbert Hill, Knopf, 1968.

(Contributor) *Glowchild, and Other Poems,* edited by Ruby Dee, Third Press, 1972.

(With others) *The Black Cinema: Foremost Representatives of the Black Film World Air Their Views* (sound recording), Center for Cassette Studies 30983, 1975.

*Just Like Martin* (novel), Simon & Schuster, 1992.

Writer of "Ain't Now But It's Going to Be" (song), for *Cotton Comes to Harlem,* 1970. Contributor to journals and periodicals, including *Negro History Bulletin, Negro Digest,* and *Freedomways.*

*SIDELIGHTS:* "Ossie Davis is best known as an actor, but his accomplishments extend well beyond the stage," writes Michael E. Greene in the *Dictionary of Literary Biography.* "In the theater, in motion pictures, and in television he has won praise both for his individual performances and those he has given with his wife, Ruby Dee. He has, however, also been a writer, director, producer, social activist, and community leader."

Davis began his career after enrolling at Howard University, where Alain Locke, a drama critic and professor of philosophy, spurred his budding interest in the theater. On Locke's counseling, Davis became involved in several facets of stage life, including maintenance and set construction, while biding time as an actor. He first appeared on the stage as a member of Harlem's Ross McClendon Players in a 1941 production of *Joy Exceeding Glory.* Few offers followed, however, and Davis was reduced to sleeping in parks and scrounging for food.

In 1942 in the midst of World War II, Davis was inducted into the U.S. Army, where he served as a medical technician in Liberia, West Africa. After his transfer to Special Services, he began writing and producing stage works to entertain military personnel. Upon discharge, though, Davis returned to his native Georgia. There he was reached by McClendon director Richard Campbell, who encouraged Davis to return to New York City and audition for Robert Ardrey's *Jeb.* Davis accepted Campbell's encouragement and eventually secured the title role in Ardrey's work. The play, which concerns a physically debilitated veteran's attempt to succeed as an adding machine operator in racist Louisiana, was poorly received, but Davis was exempted for his compelling performance.

Davis married fellow *Jeb* performer Ruby Dee in 1948 after they completed a stint with the touring company of *Anna Lucasta.* The pace of his acting career then accelerated as Davis received critical praise for his work in *Stevedore,* in which he played a servant who assumes a misplaced worldliness following a visit to Paris, and *The Green Pastures,* in which he portrayed one of several angels in a black-populated Heaven.

While acting, Davis also continued to devote attention to his writing. "As a playwright Davis was committed to creating works that would truthfully portray the black man's experience," says Jayne F. Mulvaney in a *Dictionary of Literary Biography* essay. In 1953, his play *Alice in Wonder,* which re-created McCarthy-era action, was dimly received in Harlem; however, his 1961 opus *Purlie Victorious* generated a more favorable response. Mulvaney describes the play as a comedy about the schemes of an eloquent itinerant preacher who returns to his Georgia home with hopes of buying the old barn that once served as a black church, and establishing an integrated one. To realize his plan, he must secure the inheritance of his deceased aunt, a former slave, whose daughter has also died. Because Captain Cotchipee, the play's antagonist and holder of the inheritance, is unaware of the death of Purlie's cousin, Purlie plans to have a pretty young black girl impersonate his cousin so that he can claim the inheritance to finance the church of his dreams. "The action of the play involves the hilarious efforts of Purlie, his family, and the captain's liberal son, Charlie, to outwit the captain," says Mulvaney. Many critics were especially pleased with Davis's humorous portrayal of the black preacher's efforts to swipe the $500 inheritance from the white plantation owner.

Greene calls *Purlie Victorious* a "Southern fable of right against wrong with Purlie's faith in the cause of equality triumphing over the bigotry of Ol' Cap'n Cotchipee, the local redneck aristocrat." Considering the comedy's brilliance to derive "chiefly from how cliches and stereotypes are blown out of proportion," Mulvaney suggests that *Purlie Victorious* is satire which proceeds toward reconciliation rather than bitterness. Its invective is not venomous." "Unfortunately, despite the reviews, the endorsement of the National Association for the Advancement of Colored People, and the play's seven-and-a-half month run, neither playwright nor producer made money," says Mulvaney. "The financial support of the

black community was not enough; the white audiences did not come." Greene suggests that the play would have been considerably more successful had it been written either ten years before or after it was. "Davis himself recognized that his handling of stereotypes, black and white, would have been offensive had a white writer created them," Greene noted. He added that Davis "argues that one of his purposes in the play was to present justice as an ideal, as something that is not always the same as traditional law-and-order, which allows the Ol' Cap'ns of American society to win too often."

*Purlie Victorious* was adapted by Davis as the motion picture *Gone Are the Days.* A. H. Weiler, writing in the *New York Times,* complained that the film rarely availed itself of cinematic techniques, but added that the work "is still speaking out against injustice in low, broad, comic fashion." Weiler praised the performances of Davis, who played the preacher Purlie Victorious, and Ruby Dee, the title character's lover.

In 1970 Davis collaborated with Philip Rose and the songwriting team of Peter Udell and Gary Geld on *Purlie,* a musical adaptation of the play. The *New York Times*'s Clive Barnes called the new version "so strong ... so magnificent" that audiences would respond by shouting "Hallelujah!" in praise. He deemed it "by far the most successful and richest of all black musicals" and attributed its prominence to "the depth of the characterization and the salty wit of the dialogue." For Davis, *Purlie* was not just another success—it was an experience in self-discovery. "Purlie told me," he wrote, "I would never find my manhood by asking the white man to define it for me. That I would never become a man until I stopped measuring my black self by white standards."

Race relations were at the core of Davis's novel, 1992's *Just Like Martin.* A *Kirkus Review* contributor described the story as "dramatic and simply told, with a cast of strong personalities." Set in 1963, the tale finds Isaac "Stone" and his father, Ike, struggling with their involvement in the Civil Rights movement. Ike won't let Stone, an all-A student, leave their Alabama home to go with a church youth group to a civil rights march in Washington, D.C. Ike's fear that Stone would be harmed is compounded by his wife's recent death. Ike is also opposed to his son's devotion to nonviolence and belittles the boy's admiration of Martin Luther King. Stone, who hopes to become a preacher "just like Martin," eventually organizes a children's march after two friends are killed and another is maimed when a church youth meeting room is bombed.

In *Just Like Martin,* the church's Rev. Cable asks Stone and other members in the Creative Nonviolence Workshop for Children if they have the strength to let people strike them and not strike back. Stone believes he can endure without resorting to violence, yet finds himself "fist fighting in the house of the Lord," according to Rev. Cable. Anne Scott in *Washing-*

*ton Post Book World* praised Davis's characters, despite their flaws, as they fight off "injustice ... not always knowing how to respond to the history in which they find themselves."

Other reviewers of Davis's novel commented on Ike's coming to terms with the values of his son. Watching the youth's efforts along with the shock of hearing of President John F. Kennedy's assassination, prompt Ike to resolve his inner conflict and lend his support to Stone. Lauding Davis's development of father and son, Lyn Miller-Lachmann noted in *Junior High Up* that the author "realistically portrays the boy's struggle to apply King's values in his personal life, and the ending is hopeful but not happy." Hazel Rochman of *Booklist* pointed out some minor flaws in the story, but deemed that "what is riveting here is the sense of history being made—of struggle and commitment in one community."

In addition to writing his novel, Davis has continued to work in the entertainment industry, appearing in films such as Spike Lee's *School Daze* and *Do the Right Thing*. And the careers of Dee and Davis have remained intertwined. They have performed together in stage productions, films, and recordings; shared duties as hosts/performers on the brief PBS-TV series *With Ossie and Ruby;* and cofounded Emmalyn II Productions. In the early 1990s they appeared together on an episode of *Evening Shade,* the CBS-TV series for which Davis is a regular cast member. Dee and Davis have also been active in the civil rights movement, participating in marches and hearings and sponsoring showings before hospital, church, and prison groups. *Ebony* called their marriage "a living argument against the popular notion that the theater is bound to wreck the homes of those couples who choose it as a profession."

*BIOGRAPHICAL/CRITICAL SOURCES:*

*BOOKS*

Abramson, Doris E., *Negro Playwrights in the American Theatre, 1925-1959,* Columbia University Press, 1969.
Davis, Ossie, *Just Like Martin,* Simon and Schuster, 1992.
*Dictionary of Literary Biography,* Gale, Volume 7: *Twentieth-Century American Dramatists,* 1981, Volume 38: *Afro-American Writers after 1955:* Dramatists and Prose Writers, 1985.
Funke, Lewis, *The Curtain Rises—The Story of Ossie Davis,* Grosset & Dunlap, 1971.
Patterson, Lindsay, editor, *Anthology of the American Negro in the Theatre,* Association for the Study of Life and History/Publishers Company, 1967.

*PERIODICALS*

*Booklist,* September 1, 1992.
*Detroit Free Press,* November 11, 1983.

*Ebony,* February, 1961; December, 1979.
*Freedomways,* spring, 1962; summer, 1965; summer, 1968.
*Junior High Up,* October, 1992.
*Kirkus Reviews,* September 15, 1992, p. 1185.
*Nation,* April 6, 1970.
*National Observer,* March 22, 1970.
*Negro Digest,* February, 1966; April, 1966.
*Negro History Bulletin,* April, 1967.
*Newsweek,* March 30, 1970.
*New York,* April, 1970.
*New Yorker,* October 7, 1961.
*New York Times,* September 24, 1963; May 5, 1968; October 12, 1969; March 10, 1970; November 11, 1985.
*Variety,* March 5, 1969; January 28, 1970; March 28, 1970.
*Washington Post Book World,* December 6, 1992, p. 20.

\*     \*     \*

## DAVIS, Thulani

*ADDRESSES:* c/o *Village Voice,* 842 Broadway, New York, NY 10003.

*CAREER:* Journalist, poet, and novelist. Writes for *Village Voice* weekly, New York, NY.

*WRITINGS:*

*The Renegade Ghosts Rise* (poems), Anemone, 1978.
*Playing the Changes* (poems), Wesleyan University Press, 1985.
(Author of libretto) *X: The Life and Times of Malcolm X* (opera), Nani Press, 1986.
*1959* (novel), Grove Weidenfeld, 1992.
(With Howard Chapnick) *Malcolm X: The Great Photographs,* Stewart, Tabori & Chang, 1993.

Contributor to periodicals, including *The Village Voice.*

*SIDELIGHTS:* Thulani Davis's journalism in New York City's *Village Voice* ranges widely over the black experience. While her first novel, *1959,* sees black history from a small-town perspective, her poetry shows her urban sensibility. Of her poems in the 1985 collection *Playing the Changes, Publishers Weekly* commented that Davis's work is "vibrant," with "the immediacy of spontaneous composition." Her poems contain random impressions, violence, and well-known personalities that are part of city life, as well as the mistrust and danger that are part of racial, and, most frequently, sexual relationships from a woman's point of view. "Davis' style," wrote a contributor for *Parnassus,* "may reflect the fragmented psychological attitude of the poet herself and of the impersonal, alienating, dog-eat-dog forces operating on and within people living in big cities."

In 1992, Davis wrote her first novel, *1959*, which Lucasta Miller, writing in the *Times Saturday Review*, called "more readily sympathetic" in comparison to her poetry. Though it concerns an important moment in the civil rights movement, that national phenomena is seen through the feelings of certain citizens of a small town in Virginia: a barber, for example, who has a deep relationship with his Dexter Gordon records. The protagonist, Willie Turant, is a fairly typical twelve year-old girl who changes significantly after being chosen, first to guide Martin Luther King around the local black college and, later, to be one of the first black children to integrate a white high school. Soon, college students stage sit-in protests at the lunch counter of the local Woolworth's. The characters in the novel are soon reflecting the historic events of the civil rights movement. Despite the fact that the town's black neighborhood is eventually bulldozed and its residents scattered, Davis intimates that the movement was carried on. "Ms. Davis has a masterly sense of time and place," wrote Beth Levine in the *New York Times Book Review*, "using the history of the town and Willie's aunt's diary to create a raw and moving testament to the power that rests within a community."

*BIOGRAPHICAL/CRITICAL SOURCES:*

*PERIODICALS*

*American Libraries*, February 1992, p. 192.
*Booklist*, January 1, 1992, p. 810.
*Essence*, May 1992, p. 60.
*Hungry Mind Review*, Summer 1992, p. 15.
*Kirkus Reviews*, November 1, 1991, p. 1361.
*Library Journal*, February 15, 1985, p. 171.
*Los Angeles Times Book Review*, March 1, 1992, p. 1.
*New Stateman and Society*, June 5, 1992, p. 40.
*Newsweek*, March 9, 1992, p. 60.
*New York Times* (late edition), February 11, 1992, p. C15.
*New York Times Book Review*, March 15, 1992, p. 18.
*Observer* (London), June 28, 1992, p. 66.
*Parnassus: Poetry in Review*, Spring 1985, p. 518.
*Publishers Weekly*, January 11, 1985, p. 69; December 6, 1991.
*Times Literary Supplement*, May 29, 1992, p. 21.
*Times Saturday Review*, August 1, 1992, p. 33.
*Village Voice Literary Supplement*, March 1992, p. 7.
*Washington Post Book World*, January 26, 1992, p. 12.
*Women's Review of Books*, May 1992, p. 6.

## DEAL, Borden 1922-1985
### (Lee Borden, Leigh Borden)

*PERSONAL:* Original name, Loyse Youth Deal; born October 12, 1922, in Pontotoc, MS; died of a heart attack, January 22, 1985, in Sarasota, FL; son of Borden Lee and Jimmie Anne (Smith) Deal; married second wife, Babs Hodges (a writer), 1952 (divorced, 1975); married; wife's name, Patricia; children: (second marriage) Ashley and Shane (daughters), Brett. *Education:* University of Alabama, B.A., 1949; Mexico city college, graduate study, 1950. *Politics:* Democrat. *Avocational interests:* Fishing, golf, guitar playing.

*CAREER:* U.S. Department of Labor, Washington, DC, auditor, 1941-42; Association Films, New York City, correspondent; worked variously as a skip tracer, telephone solicitor, and copywriter, 1950-55; free-lance writer. Lecturer. *Military service:* U.S. Navy, 1942-45.

*MEMBER:* Authors Guild, American PEN, Tennessee Squire Association, Sarasota Writers' Roundtable.

*AWARDS, HONORS:* Guggenheim fellow, 1957; honorable mention, American Library Association Liberty and Justice Awards, for *Walk through the Valley;* Alabama Library Association Literary Award, 1963; John H. McGinnis Memorial Award.

*WRITINGS:*

*Walk through the Valley,* Scribner, 1956.
*Dunbar's Cove,* Scribner, 1957.
*Search for Surrender,* Gold Medal, 1957.
*Killer in the House,* New American Library, 1957.
(Under pseudonym Lee Borden) *Secret of Sylvia,* Gold Medal, 1958.
*The Insolent Breed,* Scribner, 1959.
*Dragon's Wine,* Scribner, 1960.
(Under pseudonym Lee Borden) *Devil's Whispers,* Avon, 1961.
*The Spangled Road,* Scribner, 1962.
*The Tobacco Men* (based on notes by Theodore Dreiser), Holt, 1965.
*A Long Way to Go,* Doubleday, 1965.
*Interstate,* Doubleday, 1970.
*A Neo-Socratic Dialogue on the Reluctant Empire,* Outlaw Press, 1971.
*Bluegrass,* Doubleday, 1976.
(Under pseudonym Leigh Borden) *Legend of the Bluegrass,* Doubleday, 1977.
*Adventure,* Doubleday, 1978.
*Antaeus,* Learning Corp., 1982.

*There Were also Strangers; A Novel,* New Horizon Press, 1985.

*The Platinum Man; A Novel,* New Horizon Press, 1986.

*"BOOKMAN SAGA"*

*The Loser,* Doubleday, 1964.
*The Advocate,* Doubleday, 1968.
*The Winner,* Doubleday, 1973.

*"OLDEN TIMES" SERIES*

*The Least One,* introduced by Sara de Saussure Davis, Doubleday, 1967.
*... The Other Room.* Doubleday, 1974.

*OTHER*

Also author of short stories anthologized in *Best American Short Stories of 1949, Best Detective Stories of the Year, The Wonderful World of Dogs, Best American Short Stories of 1962,* and in numerous high school and college textbooks. Contributor of more than one hundred stories, poems, and reviews to *New York Times Book Review, Saturday Review,* and other periodicals. Deal's books have been translated into over twenty languages.

*ADAPTATIONS: The Insolent Breed* is the basis for the Broadway musical *A Joyful Noise.*

*SIDELIGHTS:* Borden Deal, a prolific Southern writer, recreated the South and black culture with a certainty born of experience. A Mississippi native, son of a farming family, Deal returned again and again in his fiction to places and people that he knew. The cites of farming ventures from his youth became the basis for communities written about in *The Least One* and *... The Other Room,* and the quest for land, identity, and personal ambition figure strongly in much of his work.

Deal's first novel, *Walk through the Valley,* and subsequent works such as *Dunbar's Cove* and *Interstate,* all deal in one way or another with man's attachment to the land. Deal's characters not only draw their livelihood from the land, but often appear to have an almost mystical union with the very earth. In *Walk through the Valley,* Fate Laird searches for fertile and prosperous country; in the latter two novels, the characters are dedicated to the preservation of their homes in the face of encroaching civilization, the federal government, and overzealous engineers. *Dunbar's Cove* pits protagonist Matthew Dunbar against the Tennessee Valley Authority (TVA) while *Interstate* intertwines the lives of the people attempting, respectively, to protect and to invade Blackwater Swamp, the last refuge for the ivory-billed woodpecker and the planned route for a new interstate highway.

A search for self and the celebration of life weave into Deal's writing as well. *A Long Way to Go, The Least One,* its sequel *... The Other Room,* and *There Were also Strangers* all concern themselves with youthful protagonists and their struggle with emerging selfhood. In all of these, Deal used what some critics considered provocative symbolism to represent not only the development of the young characters but also the adult world into which they were moving. *There Were also Strangers* is an autobiographical novel where a 13-year-old Borden Deal is confronted by his alter ego who leads him to view the steamy nightlife of his Southern village. In *... The Other Room,* the young protagonist explores sex with his schoolteacher, and religion with a con man. "With humor and poignance, Deal describes growing up poor in the rural South of the Depression," comments a reviewer in *Publishers Weekly.*

Adult themes of sexual infidelity, lust, greed, and socio-political ambition did not escape Deal's attention. Deal's *Bookman* series as well as the suspenseful *Adventure* and *Dragon's Wine* all address concerns of this nature. Jungian overtones, seen in many of Deal's works are, according to James R. Waddell, writing in the *Dictionary of Literary Biography,* especially strong in the latter. Deal once commented in *CA* that the theories of psychologist C. J. Jung were a major element in his work and credited Jung's idea of "ancient myths embedded so deeply in the human psyche they recur over and over again throughout the history of mankind" as being a "primary influence" in his writing. Many critics agreed that Deal succeeded not only in representing "real" characters in believable situations—in and out of history—but also managed to craft harrowing, dark tales of human fallibility.

Borden Deal once commented that he wished his books to be a "panorama of the New South." He noted that his characters "live and work in real time in real places: raising horses, building highways and TVA dams, running for public office, farming the Southern earth. The drama of their individual lives embodies the important story of the years since about 1890, when the South began gradually to emerge from the shadow of a losing war in the wrong cause, to regain at last, with the election of the first Southern president in over a hundred years, its original position as a prime mover in the destiny of the nation."

*BIOGRAPHICAL/CRITICAL SOURCES:*

*BOOKS*

*Dictionary of Literary Biography,* Volume 6: *American Novelists Since World War II, Second Series,* Gale, 1980, pp. 69-72.
*The Rising South,* Volume 2, University of Alabama Press, 1976.

*PERIODICALS*

*Best Sellers,* June 1, 1970.
*Booklist,* March 15, 1973, p. 672.
*Kirkus Reviews,* March 1, 1970, p. 270; September 15, 1978, p. 1026; October 15, 1985, p. 1096.
*National Review,* April 13, 1973.
*New Yorker,* January 4, 1969.
*New York Times Book Review,* October 27, 1974, p. 57; February 13, 1977, p. 26.
*Publishers Weekly,* November 24, 1969, p. 43; February 23, 1970, p. 150; November 20, 1972, p. 62; June 3, 1974, p. 151; November 8, 1976, p. 42; May 29, 1978, p. 50; October 16, 1978, p. 107; November 1, 1985, p. 54.
*Southwest Review,* summer, 1966.
*Washington Post Book World,* January 14, 1973, p. 15; March 24, 1974, p. 4.

\* \* \*

## DeCOSTA-WILLIS, Miriam 1934-

*PERSONAL:* Born November 1, 1934, in Florence, AL; daughter of Frank A. and Beautine (Hubert) DeCosta; married Russell B. Sugarmon, Jr., June 25, 1955; married Archie W. Willis, Jr., October 20, 1972 (deceased); children: Tarik Sugarmon, Elena S. Williams, Erika S. Echols, Monique A. Sugarmon. *Education:* Wellesley College, B.A., 1956; Johns Hopkins University, M.A., 1960, Ph.D, 1967.

*ADDRESSES: Home*—700 Seventh St., S.W., #205, Washington, DC 20024; and 585 South Greer, #703, Memphis, TN 38111. *Office*—Professor and Director of the Graduate Program in African American Studies, University of Maryland, Baltimore County, Baltimore, MD 21228.

*CAREER:* Associated with LeMoyne College, 1957-58; Owen College, instructor, 1960-65; Memphis State University, associate professor of Spanish, 1966-70; Howard University, associate professor of Spanish, 1970-74, professor and chair of department, 1974-76; LeMoyne-Owen College, professor of Spanish and director of DuBois Scholars Program, 1979-89; George Mason University, Commonwealth Professor of Spanish, 1989-91.

*MEMBER:* College Language Association, Memphis State University Center for Research on Women (member of board of directors), Federation of State Humanities Councils (member of board), National Association for the Advancement of Colored People (NAACP), Tennessee Humanities Council (chair, executive board member, 1981-87), Memphis Black Writers' Workshop (founding member; chair, 1980—), Association of Caribbean Studies.

*AWARDS, HONORS:* Johns Hopkins fellow, 1965; Outstanding Faculty Member of the Year award, LeMoyne-Owen College, 1982; Phi Beta Kappa.

*WRITINGS:*

(Editor and author of introduction) *Blacks in Hispanic Literature: Critical Essays,* National University Publications, 1977.
(Editor with Fannie P. Delk and Philip Dotson) *Homespun Images: An Anthology of Black Memphis Writers and Artists,* LeMoyne-Owen College, 1989.
(Editor with Pat Bell-Scott, Beverly Guy-Sheftall, Jacqueline Jones Royster, Janet Sims-Wood, and Lucille P. Fultz) *Double Stitch: Black Women Write about Mothers and Daughters,* Beacon Press, 1991.
(Editor with Roseann P. Bell and Reginald Martin) *Erotique Noire / Black Erotica,* Doubleday, 1992.

Contributor to books, including *Wild Women Don't Sing No Blues: Black Women Writers on Love, Men and Sex,* edited by Marita Golden, Doubleday, 1993; *Life Notes: Personal Writings by Contemporary Black Women,* edited by Patricia Bell-Scott, Norton, 1994; *Black Women's Diasporas: Writing New Worlds,* edited by Carole Boyce Davies and Omolara Ogundipe-Leslie, Pluto Press, 1994. Also contributor of articles to *Sage: A Scholarly Journal of Black Women, National Women's Studies Association Journal, Griot, West Tennessee Historical Society Papers, Journal of Caribbean Studies,* and *Afro-Hispanic Review.*

*BIOGRAPHICAL/CRITICAL SOURCES:*

*PERIODICALS*

*Choice,* October, 1977, pp. 1059-1060.
*Journal of Negro Education,* fall, 1978, p. 420.
*Library Journal,* May 1, 1977, pp. 1018-1019.
*World Literature Today,* spring, 1978, p. 264.

\* \* \*

## de GRAFT, Joe
### See de GRAFT, J(oseph) C(oleman)

\* \* \*

## de GRAFT, J(oseph) C(oleman) 1924-1978
### (Joe de Graft)

*PERSONAL:* Born April 2, 1924, in Ghana; died November 1, 1978; son of Joseph (in business) and Janet (a homemaker; maiden name, Acquaye) de Graft; married Leone Buckle (a professional accountant), 1953; children: Carol, Joseph, Dave. *Education:* Attended Mfantsipim School, 1939-43; Achimota College, 1944-46; and University College of the Gold Coast, 1950-53.

*CAREER:* Playwright, poet, novelist, and educator. Mfantsipim School, teacher of English and developer of Mfantsipim Drama Laboratory, 1955-60; University of Ghana, Legon, founder of drama and theatre studies division; Ghana Drama Studio, Accra, director, beginning in 1961; UNESCO, Nairobi, Kenya, teacher of English, 1970s; University of Ghana, associate professor and director of the School of Performing Arts, 1977-78.

*WRITINGS:*

*NOVELS*

*Sons and Daughters,* Oxford University Press, 1964.
*The Secret of Opokuwa: The Success Story of the Girl with a Big State Secret,* Anowuo Educational Publications, 1967.
*Visitor from the Past,* Anowuo, 1968.
*Muntu,* Heinemann, 1977.

*STAGE PLAYS*

*Village Investment,* first produced at Ghana Drama Studio, Accra, 1962.
*Visitor from the Past,* first produced at Ghana Drama Studio, 1962.
*Ananse and the Gum Man,* produced at Ghana Drama Studio, 1965.
*Through a Film Darkly* (adapted from *Visitor from the Past*), Oxford University Press, 1970.
*Muntu,* first produced at University of Nairobi Free Travelling Theatre, 1975.
*Mambo* (adapted from *Macbeth* by William Shakespeare), produced at School of Performing Arts, Legon, Ghana, 1978.

*SCREENPLAYS*

*No Tears for Ananse* (adapted from his stage play *Ananse and the Gum Man*), Ghana Film Production, 1965.
*Hamile* (adapted from *Hamlet* by Shakespeare), Ghana Film Production, 1965.

*OTHER*

*Beneath the Jazz and Brass* (poems), Heinemann, 1975.

Has also written under the name Joe de Graft. Contributor to anthologies, including *Messages: Poems from Ghana,* edited by Kofi Awoonor and G. Adali-Mortty, Heinemann, 1970. Contributor to periodicals, including *African Literature Today* and *Okyeame.*

*SIDELIGHTS:* After his death J. C. de Graft received the title of "elder statesman of Ghanaian letters" from a writer for *West Africa* magazine who noted that de Graft's younger colleagues "look[ed] up to him as a monumental figure, teacher and practitioner in one." In his plays, novels, and poetry, de Graft employed uniquely African themes, incorporated pieces of myth, and used aspects of Western literature. He produced numerous Shakespeare plays for radio and theatre and adapted two works with new titles. De Graft was instrumental in the development of Ghanaian theatre and spent a number of years affiliated with the Ghana Drama Studio, where several of his plays were produced. In his *West Africa* obituary, it was noted that de Graft was suited to be an elder statesman by his own background: "De Graft was a creature of the old world—in his case the settled Cape Coast oligarchy of his youth—and of the new urban jet-set."

De Graft was born into Ghana's upper class in 1932. His businessman father gave the youth a privileged education at some of the best schools of his country, including the University of the Gold Coast, from which de Graft was among the first to graduate. He then became an English teacher at the school of his childhood and helped with school theatre productions as founder of its Mfantsipim Drama Laboratory. He left Africa for a year on a fellowship that allowed him to observe the theatres of the United Kingdom and the United States.

While de Graft was pursuing his career in the 1950s, local politics in Ghana were evolving, causing the country's theatre to change as well. "De Graft appeared completely unaffected by the strong nationalist aspirations of the popular theater," writes Kofi Ermeleh Agovi in the *Dictionary of Literary Biography.* "Later, in the early 1960s, he started to develop a sympathy for the aspirations of cultural nationalism in Africa." But Agovi writes that even as de Graft warmed to the idea that African writers must concentrate on uniquely African subjects, the author balked. De Graft wrote, in a book review in *Okyeame* in 1966, of one author's "almost paranoiac search for distinctively Ghanaian forms of expression," Agovi notes.

But if de Graft had worries about the direction in which Ghana was headed, he also profited from cultural nationalism. The country's new leader, Kwame Nkrumah, opened numerous cultural institutions and sought to create a National Theatre Movement. De Graft became the first director of the Ghana Drama Studio, founded by playwright Efua Sutherland. His first play, *Village Investment,* about a boy who leaves his village to gain useful wisdom in the city never to return, appeared there in 1961.

Other plays followed soon after: A work about an African who encounters a white woman from his student days in Britain (*Visitor from the Past,* adapted and later made into a film as *Through a Film Darkly,*) and another based on a traditional folktale (*Ananse and the Gum Man*). Meanwhile, he helped to build up the country's resources for teaching drama. He carried that project from Ghana to Egypt in 1970, working for UNESCO.

Of de Graft's last two works, one was the most wholly African play he wrote, the modern classic *Muntu,* which treated African history from Creation to modern days. The other, *Mambo,* was an adaptation of Shakespeare's *Macbeth,* which was produced in 1978, the year of the playwright's death. Agovi wrote that *Muntu* was "a culmination of de Graft's consistent admiration for his roots in African culture and his desire to mold it effectively for artistic purposes." *Mambo,* on the other hand, was a political treatment of African politics as what de Graft called the "latest political murders and military coups."

Discussions of de Graft present a dichotomy in his work between old and new, Western and African influences. The writer himself was quoted in *West Africa* as saying that he was less concerned with the source of inspiration than its quality: "My imaginative life is like a fire that feeds on more than charcoal: butane gas, electricity, palm-oil, petrol as well as dry cow-dung and faggots have kept it burning."

*BIOGRAPHICAL/CRITICAL SOURCES:*

BOOKS

*Dictionary of Literary Biography:* Volume 117, *Twentieth-Century Caribbean and Black African Writers,* First Series, Gale, 1992.
Echkardt, Ulrich, editor, *Horizonte-Magazin 79,* Berliner Festspiele GmbH, 1979, pp. 28-29.
Fraser, Robert, *West African Poetry: A Critical History,* Cambridge University Press, 1986, pp. 139-146.
Ogunba, Oyin and Abiola Irele, editors, *Theatre in Africa,* Ibadan University Press, 1978, pp. 55-72.
Ogungbesan, Kolawole, editor, *New West African Literature,* Heinemann, 1989, pp. 31-44.
Zell, Hans M. and others, *A New Reader's Guide to African Literature,* Holmes & Meier, 1983, pp. 388-389.

PERIODICALS

*Cultural Events in Africa,* Number 46, 1968.
*Greenfield Review,* fall, 1972, pp. 23-30.
*Okike,* September, 1981, pp. 70-79.
*World Literature Written in English,* November, 1979, pp. 314-331.

*OBITUARIES:*

PERIODICALS

*West Africa,* January 1, 1979, pp. 16-19.

\* \* \*

## DELANY, Samuel R(ay, Jr.) 1942-
## (K. Leslie Steiner)

*PERSONAL:* Born April 1, 1942, in New York, NY; son of Samuel R. (a funeral director) and Margaret Carey (a library clerk; maiden name, Boyd) Delany; married Marilyn Hacker (a poet), August 24, 1961 (divorced, 1980); children: Iva Alyxander. *Education:* Attended City College (now of the City University of New York), 1960 and 1962-63.

*ADDRESSES: Agent*—Henry Morrison, Inc., Box 235, Bedford Hills, NY 10507.

*CAREER:* Writer. Butler Professor of English, State University of New York at Buffalo, 1975; senior fellow at the Center for Twentieth Century Studies, University of Wisconsin—Milwaukee, 1977; senior fellow at the Society for the Humanities, Cornell University, 1987; professor of comparative literature, University of Massachusetts—Amherst, 1988.

*AWARDS, HONORS:* Science Fiction Writers of America, Nebula Awards for best novel in 1966 for *Babel-17* and in 1967 for *The Einstein Intersection,* for best short story in 1967 for "Aye and Gomorrah," and for best novelette in 1969 for "Time Considered as a Helix of Semi-Precious Stones"; Hugo Award for best short story, Science Fiction Convention, 1970, for "Time Considered as a Helix of Semi-Precious Stones"; American Book Award nomination, 1980, for *Tales of Neveryon;* Pilgrim Award, Science Fiction Research Association, 1985.

*WRITINGS:*

SCIENCE FICTION

*The Jewels of Aptor* (abridged edition bound with *Second Ending* by James White), Ace Books, 1962, hardcover edition, Gollancz, 1968, complete edition published with an introduction by Don Hausdorff, Gregg Press, 1976.
*Captives of the Flame* (first novel in trilogy; bound with *The Psionic Menace* by Keith Woodcott), Ace Books, 1963, revised edition published under author's original title *Out of the Dead City* (also see below), Sphere Books, 1968.

*The Towers of Toron* (second novel in trilogy; also see below; bound with *The Lunar Eye* by Robert Moore Williams), Ace Books, 1964.

*City of a Thousand Suns* (third novel in trilogy; also see below), Ace Books, 1965.

*The Ballad of Beta-2* (also see below; bound with *Alpha Yes, Terra No!* by Emil Petaja), Ace Books, 1965, hardcover edition published with an introduction by David G. Hartwell, Gregg Press, 1977.

*Empire Star* (also see below; bound with *The Three Lords of Imeten* by Tom Purdom), Ace Books, 1966, hardcover edition published with an introduction by Hartwell, Gregg Press, 1977.

*Babel-17,* Ace Books, 1966, hardcover edition, Gollancz, 1967, published with an introduction by Robert Scholes, 1976.

*The Einstein Intersection,* slightly abridged edition, Ace Books, 1967, hardcover edition, Gollancz, 1968, complete edition, Ace Books, 1972.

*Nova,* Doubleday, 1968.

*The Fall of the Towers* (trilogy; contains *Out of the Dead City, The Towers of Toron,* and *City of a Thousand Suns*), Ace Books, 1970, hardcover edition published with introduction by Joseph Milicia, Gregg Press, 1977.

*Driftglass: Ten Tales of Speculative Fiction,* Doubleday, 1971.

*The Tides of Lust,* Lancer Books, 1973.

*Dhalgren,* Bantam, 1975, hardcover edition published with introduction by Jean Mark Gawron, Gregg Press, 1978.

*The Ballad of Beta-2* [and] *Empire Star,* Ace Books, 1975.

*Triton,* Bantam, 1976.

*Empire: A Visual Novel,* illustrations by Howard V. Chaykin, Berkley Books, 1978.

*Distant Stars,* Bantam, 1981.

*Stars in My Pocket Like Grains of Sand,* Bantam, 1984.

*The Complete Nebula Award-Winning Fiction,* Bantam, 1986.

*The Star Pits* (bound with *Tango Charlie and Foxtrot Romeo* by John Varley), Tor Books, 1989.

*They Fly at Ciron,* Incunabula, 1992.

*"RETURN TO NEVERYON" SERIES; SWORD AND SORCERY NOVELS*

*Tales of Neveryon,* Bantam, 1979.

*Neveryona; or, The Tale of Signs and Cities,* Bantam, 1983.

*Flight from Neveryon,* Bantam, 1985.

*The Bridge of Lost Desire,* Arbor House, 1987.

*OTHER*

*The Jewel-Hinged Jaw: Notes on the Language of Science Fiction,* Dragon Press, 1977, revised edition, Berkley Publishing, 1978.

*The American Shore: Meditations on a Tale of Science Fiction by Thomas M. Disch— "Angouleme"* (criticism), Dragon Press, 1978.

*Heavenly Breakfast: An Essay on the Winter of Love* (memoir), Bantam, 1979.

*Starboard Wine: More Notes on the Language of Science Fiction,* Dragon Press, 1984.

*The Motion of Light in Water: Sex and Science Fiction Writing in the East Village, 1957-1965,* Arbor House, 1988.

*Wagner/Artaud: A Play of Nineteenth and Twentieth Century Critical Fictions,* Ansatz Press, 1988.

*Straits of Messina* (essays; originally published in magazines under pseudonym K. Leslie Steiner), Serconia Press, 1989.

Also author of scripts, director, and editor for two short films, *Tiresias,* 1970, and *The Orchid,* 1971; author of two scripts for the *Wonder Woman Comic Series,* 1972, and of the radio play *The Star Pit,* based on his short story of the same title. Editor, *Quark,* 1970-71.

*SIDELIGHTS:* "Samuel R. Delany is one of today's most innovative and imaginative writers of science-fiction," comments Jane Branham Weedman in her study of the author, *Samuel R. Delany.* In his science fiction, which includes over fifteen novels and two collections of short stories, the author "has explored what happens when alien world views intersect, collide, or mesh," writes Greg Tate in the *Voice Literary Supplement.* Delany first appeared on the science fiction horizon in the early 1960s, and in the decade that followed he established himself as one of the stars of the genre. Like many of his contemporaries who entered science fiction in the 1960s, he is less concerned with the conventions of the genre, more interested in science fiction as literature, literature which offers a wide range of artistic opportunities. As a result, maintains Weedman, "Delany's works are excellent examples of modern science-fiction as it has developed from the earlier and more limited science-fiction tradition, especially because of his manipulation of cultural theories, his detailed futuristic or alternate settings, and his stylistic innovations."

"One is drawn into Delany's stories because they have a complexity," observes Sandra Y. Govan in the *Black American Literature Forum,* "an acute consciousness of language, structure, and form; a dexterous ability to weave together mythology and anthropology, linguistic theory and cultural history, gestalt psychology and sociology as well as philosophy, structuralism, and the adventure story." At the center of the complex web of personal, cultural, artistic, and intellectual concerns that provides the framework for all of his work is Delany's examination of how language and myth influence reality. "According to [the author]," writes Govan in the *Dictionary of Literary Biography,* "language identifies or negates the self. It is self-reflective; it shapes perceptions." By shaping perceptions, language in turn has the capacity to shape reality. Myths can exercise much the same power. In his science fiction, Delany "creates new myths, or inversions of old ones, by which his protagonists measure themselves and their societies against the traditional myths that Delany includes," Weedman observes. In this way, as Peter S. Alterman comments in the *Dictionary of Literary Biography,* the author confronts "the question of the extent to which myths and archetypes create reality."

In societies in which language and myth are recognized as determinants of reality, the artist—one who works in language and myth—plays a crucial part. For this reason, the protagonist of a Delany novel is often an artist of some sort. "The role which Delany defines for the artist is to observe, record, transmit, and question paradigms in society," explains Weedman. But Delany's artists do more than chronicle and critique the societies of which they are a part. His artists are always among those at the margin of society; they are outcasts and often criminals. "The criminal and the artist both operate outside the normal standards of society," observes Alterman, "according to their own self-centered value systems." The artist/criminal goes beyond observation and commentary. His actions at the margin push society's values to their limits and beyond, providing the experimentation necessary to prepare for eventual change.

Delany entered the world of science fiction in 1962 with the publication of his novel *The Jewels of Aptor.* Over the next six years, he published eight more, including *Babel-17, The Einstein Intersection,* and *Nova,* his first printed originally in hardcover. Douglas Barbour, writing in *Science Fiction Writers,* describes these early novels as "colorful, exciting, entertaining, and intellectually provocative to a degree not found in most genre science fiction." Barbour adds that although they do adhere to science fiction conventions, they "begin the exploration of those literary obsessions that define [Delany's] oeuvre: problems of communication and community; new kinds of sexual/love/family relationships; the artist as social outsider ...; cultural interactions and the exploration of human social possibilities these allow; archetypal and mythic structures in the imagination."

With the publication of *Babel-17* in 1966, Delany began to gain recognition in the science fiction world. The novel, which earned its author his first Nebula Award, is a story of galactic warfare between the forces of the Alliance, which includes the Earth, and the forces of the Invaders. The poet Rydra Wong is enlisted by Alliance intelligence to decipher communications intercepted from its enemy. When she discovers that these dispatches contain not a code but rather an unknown language, her quest becomes one of learning this mysterious tongue labeled *Babel-17.* While leading an interstellar mission in search of clues, Rydra gains insights into the nature of

language and, in the process, discovers the unique character of the enigmatic new language of the Invaders.

*Babel-17* itself becomes an exploration of language and its ability to structure experience. A central image in the novel, as George Edgar Slusser points out in his study *The Delany Intersection: Samuel R. Delany Considered as a Writer of Semi-Precious Words,* is that of "the web and its weaver or breaker." The web, continues Slusser, "stands, simultaneously, for unity and isolation, interconnectedness and entanglement." And, as Peter Alterman points out in *Science-Fiction Studies,* "the web is an image of the effect of language on the mind and of the mind as shaper of reality." Weedman elaborates in her essay on the novel: "The language one learns necessarily constrains and structures what it is that one says." In its ability to connect and constrain is the power of the language/web. "Language ... has a direct effect on how one thinks," explains Weedman, "since the structure of the language influences the processes by which one formulates ideas." At the center of the language as web "is one who joins and cuts—the artist-hero," comments Slusser. And, in *Babel-17,* the poet Rydra Wong demonstrates that only she is able to master this new language weapon and turn it against its creators.

Delany followed *Babel-17* with another Nebula winner, *The Einstein Intersection.* This novel represents a "move from a consideration of the relationship among language, thought, action and time to an analytic and imaginative investigation of the patterns of myths and archetypes and their interaction with the conscious mind," writes Alterman. Slusser sees this development in themes as part of a logical progression: "[Myths] too are seen essentially as language constructs: verbal scenarios for human action sanctioned by tradition or authority." Comparing this novel to *Babel-17,* he adds that "Delany's sense of the language act, in this novel, has a broader social valence."

*The Einstein Intersection* relates the story of a strange race of beings that occupies a post-apocalyptic Earth. This race assumes the traditions—economic, political, and religious—of the extinct humans in an attempt to make sense of the remnant world in which they find themselves. "While they try to live by the myths of man," writes Barbour in *Foundation,* "they cannot create a viable culture of their own.... Their more profound hope is to recognize that they do not have to live out the old myths at all, that the 'difference' they seek to hide or dissemble is the key to their cultural and racial salvation."

"Difference is a key word in this novel," Weedman explains, "for it designates the importance of the individual and his ability to make choices, on the basis of being different from others, which affect his life, thus enabling him to question the paradigms of his society." The artist is the embodiment of this difference and in *The Einstein Intersection* the artist is Lobey, a musician. The power of Lobey's music is its ability to create order, to destroy the old myths and usher in the new. At its core, then, "*The Einstein Intersection* is ... a novel about experiments in culture," Weedman comments.

Delany's next novel, *Nova*, "stands as the summation of [his] career up to that time," writes Barbour in *Science Fiction Writers: Critical Studies of the Major Authors from the Early Nineteenth Century to the Present Day.* "Packing his story full of color and incident, violent action and tender introspective moments, he has created one of the grandest space operas ever written." In this novel, Delany presents a galaxy divided into three camps, all embroiled in a bitter conflict caused by a shortage of the fuel illyrion on which they all depend. In chronicling one group's quest for a new source of the fuel, the author examines, according to Weedman, "how technology changes the world and philosophies for world survival. Delany also explores conflicts between and within societies, as well as the problems created by people's different perceptions and different reality models."

"In developing this tale," notes Slusser, "Delany has inverted the traditional epic relationship, in which the human subject (the quest) dominates the 'form.' Here instead is a 'subjunctive epic.' Men do not struggle against an inhuman system so much as inside an unhuman one." The system inside which these societies struggle is economic; the goal of the quester, who is driven by selfishness, is a commodity. Whether the commodity is abundant or scarce, as Jeanne Murray Walker points out in *Extrapolation,* this "is a world where groups are out of alignment, off balance, where some suffer while others prosper, where the object of exchange is used to divide rather than to unite." Walker concludes in her essay that "by ordering the action of *Nova* in the quest pattern, but assuming a value system quite different from that assumed by medieval romance writers, Delany shows that neither pattern nor action operate as they once did. Both fail." Even so, as she continues, "individuals must continue to quest. Through their quests they find meaning for themselves."

After the publication of *Nova,* Delany turned his creative urges to forms other than the novel, writing a number of short stories, editing four quarterlies of speculative fiction, and dabbling in such diverse media as film and comic books. Also at this time, he engaged himself in conceiving, writing, and polishing what would become his longest, most complex, and most controversial novel, *Dhalgren*—a work that would earn him national recognition. On its shifting surface, this novel represents the experience of a nameless amnesiac, an artist/criminal, during the period of time he spends in a temporally and spatially isolated city scarred by destruction and decay. As Alterman relates in the *Dictionary of Literary Biography,* "it begins with the genesis of a protagonist, one so unformed that he has no name, no identity, the quest for which is the

novel's central theme." The critic goes on to explain that "at the end Kid has a name and a life, both of which are the novel itself; he is a persona whose experience in *Dhalgren* defines him."

*Dhalgren*'s length and complexity provide a significant challenge to readers, but as Gerald Jonas observes in the *New York Times Book Review,* "the most important fact about Delany's novel ... is that nothing in it is clear. Nothing is meant to be clear." He adds: "An event may be described two or three times, and each recounting is slightly disconcertingly different from the one before." What is more, continues the reviewer, "the nameless narrator experiences time discontinuously; whole days seem to be excised from his memory." According to Weedman, "Delany creates disorientation in *Dhalgren* to explore the problems which occur when reality models differ from reality." And in Jonas's estimation, "If the book can be said to be *about* anything, it is about nothing less than the nature of reality."

"*Dhalgren* has drawn more widely divergent critical response than any other Delany novel," comments Govan in her *Dictionary of Literary Biography* essay. "Some reviewers deny that it is science fiction, while others praise it for its daring and experimental form." For instance, *Magazine of Fantasy and Science Fiction* book reviewer Algis Budrys contends that "this book is not science fiction, or science fantasy, but allegorical quasi-fantasy on the [James Gould] Cozzens model. Thus, although it demonstrates the breadth of Delany's education, and many of its passages are excellent prose, it presents no new literary inventions." In his *Science Fiction Writers* essay, Barbour describes the same novel as "the very stuff of science fiction but lacking the usual structural emblems of the genre." "One thing is certain," offers Jonas, "'Dhalgren' is not a conventional novel, whether considered in terms of S.F. or the mainstream."

Following the exhaustive involvement with Kid necessary to complete *Dhalgren,* Delany chose to do a novel in which he distanced himself from his protagonist, giving him a chance to look at the relationship between an individual and his society in a new light. "I wanted to do a psychological analysis of someone with whom you're just not in sympathy, someone whom you watch making all the wrong choices, even though his plight itself is sympathetic," Delany explained in an interview with Larry McCaffery and Sinda Gregory published in their book *Alive and Writing: Interviews with American Authors of the 1980s.* The novel is *Triton;* its main character is Bron.

"*Triton* is set in a sort of sexual utopia, where every form of sexual behavior is accepted, and sex-change operations (not to mention 'refixations,' to alter sexual preference) are common," observes Michael Goodwin in *Mother Jones.* In this world of freedom lives Bron, whom Govan describes in *Black American Literature Forum* as "a narrow-minded, isolated man, so self-serving that he is incapable of reaching outside himself to love another or even understand another despite his best intentions." In an attempt to solve his problems, he undergoes a sex-change operation, but finds no happiness. "Bron is finally trapped in total social and psychological stasis, lost in isolation beyond any help her society can offer its citizens," comments Barbour in *Science Fiction Writers.*

In this novel, once again Delany creates an exotic new world, having values and conventions that differ from ours. In exploring this fictional world, he can set up a critique of our present-day society. In *Triton,* he casts a critical eye, as Weedman points out, on "sexual persecution against women, ambisexuals, and homosexuals." She concludes that the work is "on the necessity of knowing one's self despite sexual identification, knowing one's sexual identity is not one's total identity."

In the 1980s, Delany continued to experiment in his fiction writing. In his "Neveryon" series, which includes *Tales of Neveryon, Neveryona; or, The Tale of Signs and Cities, Flight from Neveryon,* and *The Bridge of Lost Desire,* he chooses a different setting. "Instead of being set in some imagined future, [they] are set in some magical, distant past, just as civilization is being created," observes McCaffery in a *Science-Fiction Studies* interview of Delany. Their focus, suggests Gregory in the same interview, is "power—all kinds of power: sexual, economic, even racial power via the issue of slavery."

Throughout these tales of a world of dragons, treasures, and fabulous cities Delany weaves the story of Gorgik, a slave who rises to power and abolishes slavery. In one story, the novel-length "Tale of Plagues and Carnivals," he shifts in time from his primitive world to present-day New York and back to examine the devastating effects of a disease such as acquired immune deficiency syndrom (AIDS). And, in the appendices that accompany each of these books, he reflects on the creative process itself. Of the four, it is *Neveryona,* the story of Pryn—a girl who flees her mountain home on a journey of discovery—that has received the most attention from reviewers. *Science Fiction and Fantasy Book Review* contributor Michael R. Collings calls it "a stirring fable of adventure and education, of heroic action and even more heroic normality in a world where survival itself is constantly threatened." Faren C. Miller finds the book groundbreaking; she writes in *Locus:* "Combining differing perspectives with extraordinary talent for the *details* of a world—its smells, its shadows, workaday furnishings, and playful frills—Delany has produced a sourcebook for a new generation of fantasy writers." The book also "presents a new manifestation of Delany's continuing concern for language and the magic of fiction, whereby words become symbols for other, larger things," Collings observes.

In *Stars in My Pocket Like Grains of Sand,* Delany returns to distant worlds of the future. The book is "a densely textured, intricately worked out novelistic structure which delights and astonishes even as it forces a confrontation with a wide range of thought-provoking issues," writes McCaffery in *Fantasy Review.* Included are "an examination of interstellar politics among thousands of far flung worlds, a love story, a meandering essay on the variety of human relationships and the inexplicability of sexual attractiveness, and a hypnotic crash-course on a fascinating body of literature which does not yet exist," notes H. J. Kirchhoff in the Toronto *Globe and Mail.*

Beneath the surface features, as Jonas suggests in the *New York Times Book Review,* the reader can discover the fullness of this Delany novel. The reviewer writes: "To unpack the layers of meaning in seemingly offhand remarks or exchanges of social pleasantries, the reader must be alert to small shifts in emphasis, repeated phrases or gestures that assume new significance in new contexts, patterns of behavior that only become apparent when the author supplies a crucial piece of information at just the proper moment." Here in the words and gestures of the characters and the subtle way in which the author fashions his work is the fundamental concern of the novel. "I take the most basic subject here to be the nature of information itself," McCaffery explains, "the way it is processed, stored and decoded symbolically, the way it is distorted by the present and the past, the way it has become a commodity ... the way that the play of textualities defines our perception of the universe."

"This is an astonishing new Delany," according to Somtow Sucharitkul in the *Washington Post Book World,* "more richly textured, smoother, more colorful than ever before." Jonas commends the novel because of the interaction it encourages with the reader. "Sentence by sentence, phrase by phrase, it invites the reader to collaborate in the process of creation, in a way that few novels do," writes the reviewer. "The reader who accepts this invitation has an extraordinarily satisfying experience in store for him/her." "*Stars in My Pocket Like Grains of Sand* ... confirms that [Delany] is American SF's [science fiction's] most consistently brilliant and inventive writer," McCaffery claims.

Critics often comment on Delany's use of fiction as a forum to call for greater acceptance of women's rights and gay rights; yet, as Govan maintains in her *Dictionary of Literary Biography* contribution, "a recurring motif frequently overlooked in Delany's fiction is his subtle emphasis on race. Black and mixed-blood characters cross the spectrum of his speculative futures, both as a testimony to a future Delany believes will change to reflect human diversity honestly and as a commentary on the racial politics of the present."

In novels such as *Babel-17,* Delany demonstrates how language can be used to rob the black man of his identity. "White culture exerts a great influence because it can force stereotypic definitions on the black person," writes Weedman. She adds that "if the black person capitulates to the definition imposed on him by a force outside of his culture, then he is in danger of losing his identity." In his other novels, Govan points out, "Delany utilizes existing negative racial mythologies about blacks, but, in all his works, he twists the commonplace images and stereotypes to his own ends." In using his fiction to promote awareness of the race issue, he and other black writers like him "have mastered the dominant culture's language and turned it against its formulators in protest," writes Weedman.

"Delany is not only a gifted writer," claims Barbour in his *Foundation* article, "he is one of the most articulate theorists of sf to have emerged from the ranks of its writers." In such critical works as *The Jewel-Hinged Jaw, The American Shore,* and *Starboard Wine,* "he has done much to open up critical discussion of sf as a genre, forcefully arguing its great potential as art," adds the reviewer. In his nonfiction, Delany offers a functional description of science fiction and contrasts it with other genres such as naturalistic fiction and fantasy. He also attempts to expand "the domain of his chosen genre by claiming it the modern mode of fiction *par excellence,*" comments Slusser, "the one most suited to deal with the complexities of paradox and probability, chaos, irrationality, and the need for logic and order."

With the publication of *The Motion of Light in Water,* Delany turned to writing about himself. This memoir of his early days as a writer in New York's East Village is "an extraordinary account of life experienced by a precocious black artist of the 1960s," as E. Guereschi writes in *Choice.* The book reveals much of Delany's sexual adventures, with partners of both sexes, at the time, his nervous breakdown, and the general sense of living on the edge in an exciting and innovative period. Moreover, the book tells of Delany's realization and eventual acceptance of his homosexuality. Thomas M. Disch, writing in the *American Book Review,* finds that Delany "can't help creating legends and elaborating myths. Indeed, it is his forte, the open secret of his success as an SF writer. [Delany's] SF heroes are variations of an archetype he calls The Kid.... In his memoir, the author himself [is] finally assuming the role in which his fictive alter-egos have enjoyed their success. That is the book's strength even more than its weakness." Guereschi believes that the memoir "defines an arduous search for identity," while Disch concludes that *The Motion of Light in Water* "has the potential of being as popular, as representative of its era, as *On the Road.*"

Samuel R. Delany is not a simple man: a black man in a white society, a writer who suffers from dyslexia, an artist who is also a critic. His race, lifestyle, chosen profession, and chosen genre keep him far from the mainstream. "His own term

'multiplex' probably best describes his work (attitudes, ideas, themes, craftsmanship, all their inter-relations, as well as his relation as artist, to them all)," Barbour suggests. And, adds the reviewer, "His great perseverance in continually developing his craft and never resting on his past achievements is revealed in the steady growth in [his] artistry." In Weedman's estimation, "Few writers approach the lyricism, the command of language, the powerful combination of style and content that distinguishes Delany's works. More importantly," she concludes, "few writers, whether in science fiction or mundane fiction, so successfully create works which make us question ourselves, our actions, our beliefs, and our society as Delany has helped us do." Writing in the *Washington Post Book World,* John Clute places Delany in a central position in modern science fiction. In his best work, Clute believes, Delany "treated the interstellar venues of space opera as analogues of urban life in the decaying hearts of the great American cities. As a black gay New Yorker much too well educated for his own good, Delany ... illuminated the world the way a torch might cast light in a cellar."

*BIOGRAPHICAL/CRITICAL SOURCES:*

*BOOKS*

Bleiler, E. F., editor, *Science Fiction Writers: Critical Studies of the Major Authors from the Early Nineteenth Century to the Present Day,* Scribner, 1982.

*Contemporary Literary Criticism,* Gale, Volume 8, 1978, Volume 14, 1980, Volume 38, 1986.

Delany, Samuel R., *The Jewel-Hinged Jaw: Notes on the Language of Science Fiction,* Dragon Press, 1977, revised edition, Berkley Publishing, 1978.

Delany, Samuel R., *Heavenly Breakfast: An Essay on the Winter of Love,* Bantam, 1979.

Delany, Samuel R., *The Motion of Light in Water: Sex and Science Fiction Writing in the East Village, 1957-1965,* Arbor House, 1988.

*Dictionary of Literary Biography,* Gale, Volume 8: *Twentieth-Century American Science Fiction Writers,* 1981, Volume 33: *Afro-American Fiction Writers after 1955,* 1984.

Kostelanetz, Richard, editor, *American Writing Today,* Whitston, 1991.

McCaffery, Larry, and Sinda Gregory, editors, *Alive and Writing: Interviews with American Authors of the 1980s,* University of Illinois Press, 1987.

McEvoy, Seth, *Samuel R. Delany,* Ungar, 1984.

Peplow, Michael W., and Robert S. Bravard, *Samuel R. Delany: A Primary and Secondary Bibliography, 1962-1979,* G. K. Hall, 1980.

Platt, Charles, editor, *Dream Makers: The Uncommon People Who Write Science Fiction,* Berkley Books, 1980.

Slusser, George Edgar, *The Delany Intersection: Samuel R. Delany Considered as a Writer of Semi-Precious Words*, Borgo, 1977.

Smith, Nicholas D., editor, *Philosophers Look at Science Fiction*, Nelson-Hall, 1982.

Weedman, Jane Branham, *Samuel R. Delany*, Starmont House, 1982.

*PERIODICALS*

*American Book Review*, January, 1989.

*Analog Science Fiction/Science Fact*, April, 1985.

*Black American Literature Forum*, summer, 1984.

*Choice*, February, 1989.

*Commonweal*, December 5, 1975.

*Extrapolation*, fall, 1982; winter, 1989; fall, 1989.

*Fantasy Review*, December, 1984.

*Foundation*, March, 1975.

*Globe and Mail* (Toronto), February 9, 1985.

*Locus*, summer, 1983; October, 1989.

*Los Angeles Times Book Review*, March 13, 1988.

*Magazine of Fantasy and Science Fiction*, November, 1975; June, 1980; May, 1989.

*Mother Jones*, August, 1976.

*New York Review of Books*, January 29, 1991.

*New York Times Book Review*, February 16, 1975; March 28, 1976; October 28, 1979; February 10, 1985.

*Publishers Weekly*, January 29, 1988; October 19, 1992.

*Science Fiction and Fantasy Book Review*, July/August, 1983.

*Science Fiction Chronicle*, November, 1987; February, 1990.

*Science-Fiction Studies*, November, 1981; July, 1987; November, 1990.

*Voice Literary Supplement*, February, 1985.

*Washington Post Book World*, January 27, 1985; August 25, 1991.

\* \* \*

## De LISSER, H(erbert) G(eorge)   1878-1944

*PERSONAL:* Born December 9, 1878, in Falmouth, Jamaica; died May 18, 1944, in Kingston, Jamaica; son of H. G. De Lisser (an editor) and Miss Isaacs; married Ellen Guenther, 1909.

*CAREER:* Institute of Jamaica Library, Jamaica, assistant; *Daily Gleaner*, Jamaica, began as proofreader, became associate editor, 1903, chief editor, 1904-42. *Jamaica Times*, journalist, 1889-1903. Member of board of governors, Institute of Jamaica (also served as chair).

*MEMBER:* Jamaica Imperial Association (secretary).

*AWARDS, HONORS:* Silver Musgrave Medal, 1919; Companion of the Order of St. Michael and St. George, 1920.

*WRITINGS:*

*In Jamaica and Cuba*, Gleaner Co., 1910.

*Twentieth Century Jamaica*, The Jamaica Times Ltd., 1913.

*Jane: A Story of Jamaica*, Gleaner Co., 1913, published as *Jane's Career: A Story of Jamaica*, Methuen, 1914, Africana, 1971.

*Susan Proudleigh*, Methuen, 1915.

*Triumphant Squalitone: A Tropical Extravaganza*, Gleaner Co., 1916.

*Jamaica and the Great War*, Gleaner Co., 1917.

*Revenge: A Tale of Old Jamaica*, Gleaner Co., 1919.

*The White Witch of Rosehall*, Benn, 1929.

*Under the Sun: A Jamaica Comedy*, Benn, 1937.

*Psyche*, Benn, 1952.

*Morgan's Daughter*, Benn, 1953.

*The Cup and the Lip: A Romance*, Benn, 1956.

*The Arawak Girl*, Pioneer Press, 1958.

Contributor to periodicals, including *Planters' Punch*.

*SIDELIGHTS:* Herbert George De Lisser is well known for his novels depicting the Jamaican political arena. Frank M. Birbalsingh, writing in the *Dictionary of Literary Biography* (*DLB*), called him a "distinguished figure in Jamaican intellectual, artistic, political, and social circles." De Lisser is now remembered as one of the first important novelists of the English-speaking Caribbean.

Even though, as a result of his father's death, De Lisser could not finish a formal education, by 1904 he had become the chief editor of the *Daily Gleaner*, a post he held until his retirement in 1942 due to ill health. In Birbalsingh's opinion, it was De Lisser's association with the newspaper that provided material for his first two books, *Jamaica and Cuba* and *Twentieth Century Jamaica*. The first book contains De Lisser's impressions of Cuba after a trip he made to the country in 1909, while the second, published in 1913, is an account of Jamaican history and current affairs of the time.

With the publishing of *Jane: A Story of Jamaica*, better know as *Jane's Career*, De Lisser became a writer of fiction. *Jane's Career* is the story of Jane Burrell, a black girl who leaves the Jamaican countryside to improve herself in that country's capital of Kingston. On her arrival in the capital, Jane goes to live with Mrs. Mason and her affluent mulatto (the offspring of a union between a black and a caucasian) middle-class family. The book builds a contrast between Jane and her friends, who are black and are expected to behave in a socially unacceptable manner, and the Masons, who are supposedly genteel and virtuous because they are mulatto. Through this contrast De Lisser exposes the social inequalities based on race and color prevalent in early-twentieth century Jamaica. As Birbalsingh put it, it is Mrs. Mason's family that De Lisser describes as "hypocritical, snobbish, and venal, whereas in Jane and her friends he perceives independence, ambition, and a will to survive." According to Birbalsingh, the novel may not have been a plea for social change but it did evoke "Jamaica as it really was less than a hundred years ago, and it is because of this lifelike, realistic evocation that *Jane's Career* has proved the most enduring of de Lisser's novels." *Susan Proudleigh,* De Lisser's next novel, also describes Jamaica through the story about a woman who migrates to Panama after her lover deserts her. De Lisser next wrote *Triumphant Squalitone* in 1916. The book's plot results from a imaginary declaration of independence for Jamaica by the King of England and the events that follow it. In Birbalsingh's opinion, this book "indicates de Lisser's own faith in imperialism."

With 1929's *The White Witch of Rosehall,* De Lisser mixes the elements of history, romance, adventure, and mystery in a story set in the Jamaica of the early 1830s, when the emancipation of slaves was fast approaching. The plot is based on the life story of Annie Palmer, an actual plantation owner, who was killed by her own slaves. The real Annie Palmer had a reputation as a cruel woman who practiced necromancy and killed her husbands. Birbalsingh called De Lisser's depiction of Annie "an extraordinary portrait of unrelieved cunning, malignance, and cruelty." Birbalsingh traced, in De Lisser's portrayal of Annie, a definite influence of the Gothic romances of popular Victorian writers like Charles Reade and Wilkie Collins, and he stated that this was most likely the reason for the book's popularity.

*Under the Sun* was the last of De Lisser's novels to be published while he was alive. In this book he presents a portrait of the Jamaican upper classes in the period between the two world wars. Once again De Lisser examines the injustice of discrimination based on race and color. In this book he does this through the story of Amy Brown, an Englishwoman who is married to a colored man. Amy's husband, Christopher, is snubbed by her white friends even though he belongs to the wealthy middle-class. Eventually, because of societal pressure, Amy divorces Christopher and marries a white man while Christopher revives a relationship with an old girlfriend. Prior to his death, De Lisser wrote serialized stories for *Planters' Punch* and other periodicals. These tales were later posthumously published as novels, including *Psyche, Morgan's Daughter, The Cup and the Lip,* and *The Arawak Girl.* Throughout these novels, De Lisser continues to represent the social and historical realities of Jamaican society at the time, dramatizing the problems resulting from prejudice and social inequalities. Birbalsingh praised De Lisser's grasp of issues affecting contemporary Jamaican society and said that "De

Lisser's knowledge of history and his skill in lucid commentary are ... impressive."

Birbalsingh explained in *DLB* that besides being a successful writer, De Lisser was also an eminent public figure of Jamaica in his lifetime. And although his importance as a public figure has declined over the years, his reputation as a writer survives to this day. Birbalsingh wrote that De Lisser was the first West Indian novelist to present Jamaica from the inside and, while he was not a radical advocate of reform, his books do present an objective rendition of the problems of oppression and resistance that faced Jamaican society.

*BIOGRAPHICAL/CRITICAL SOURCES:*

*BOOKS*

*The Colonial Legacy in Caribbean Literature,* Africa World, 1987, pp. 54-58.
*Dictionary of Literary Biography,* Volume 117, *Twentieth-Century Caribbean and Black African Writers, First Series,* Gale, 1992, pp. 141-49.
*An Introduction to the Study of West Indian Literature,* Nelson, 1976, pp. 1-10.
*Six Great Jamaicans,* Pioneer, 1952, pp. 104-22.

*PERIODICALS*

*International Fiction Review,* winter, 1982, pp. 41-46.
*Jamaica Journal,* November, 1984-January, 1985, pp. 2-9.
*Journal of West Indian Literature,* November, 1990, pp. 24-45.
*Novel,* fall, 1973, pp. 93-96.
*World Literature Written in English,* April, 1973, pp. 97-105.

\* \* \*

# DERRICOTTE, Toi 1941-

*PERSONAL:* Name is pronounced "toy *dare*-i-cot"; born April 12, 1941, in Detroit, MI; daughter of Benjamin Sweeney Webster (a mortician and salesperson) and Antonia Webster Cyrus (a systems analyst; maiden name, Banquet); married Clarence Reese (an artist), July 5, 1962 (divorced, 1964); married Clarence Bruce Derricotte (a banking consultant), December 30, 1967; children: (first marriage) Anthony. *Education:* Wayne State University, B.A., 1965; New York University, M.A., 1984. *Politics:* "Anti-Nuke." *Religion:* Roman Catholic. *Avocational interests:* Cooking, "sharing good meals with good friends."

*ADDRESSES: Home*—7958 Inverness Ridge Rd., Potomac, MD 20854. *Office*—University of Pittsburgh, Department of English, Pittsburgh, PA 15260.

*CAREER:* Manpower Program, Detroit, MI, teacher, 1964-66; Farand School, Detroit, teacher of the mentally and emotionally retarded, 1966-68; Jefferson School, Teaneck, NJ, remedial reading teacher, 1969-70; New Jersey State Council on the Arts, poet in residence for Poet-in-the-Schools program, 1974-88, master teacher, 1984-88; Old Dominion University, Norfolk, VA, associate professor of creative writing and minority literature, 1988—; George Mason University, Fairfax, VA, Commonwealth Professor, 1990-91; University of Pittsburgh, Pittsburgh, PA, associate professor, 1991—. New York University, visiting professor, 1992; has served on the faculty of Squaw Valley Community of Writers, 1992, Suncoast Florida Writers' Conference, University of South Florida, 1993, and the Charleston Writers' Conference, College of Charleston, 1993. Guest poet and lecturer at numerous colleges and universities; featured poet in readings at more than one hundred theaters, museums, bookstores, and libraries. Educational consultant, Columbia University, 1979-82.

*MEMBER:* Poetry Society of America, Academy of American Poets, Associated Writing Programs.

*AWARDS, HONORS:* Pen and Brush Award, New School for Social Research, 1973, for untitled poetry manuscript; poetry teacher prizes from Academy of American Poets, 1974, for "Unburying the Bird," and 1978, for excerpts from *Natural Birth;* fellowships from MacDowell Colony, 1982, New Jersey State Council on the Arts, 1983, and New York University's graduate English creative writing program, 1984; Writer's Voice, Manhattan West Side Y, New York City, 1985; creative writing fellowships in poetry, National Endowment for the Arts, 1985 and 1990; Lucille Medmick Memorial Award, Poetry Society of America, 1985; Arts Council fellowship, State of Maryland, 1987; Poetry Committee Book Award, Folger Shakespeare Library, 1990; Distinguished Pioneering of the Arts Award, United Black Artists, Inc., 1993; Keck Fellow, Sarah Lawrence College, 1993.

*WRITINGS:*

*POETRY, EXCEPT WHERE NOTED*

*The Empress of the Death House,* Lotus Press, 1978.
*Natural Birth,* Crossing Press, 1983.
*Captivity,* University of Pittsburgh Press, 1989.

Also author of *Creative Writing: A Manual for Teachers,* 1985. Contributor to anthologies, including *Ariadne's Thread: A Collection of Contemporary Women's Journals,* edited by Lyn Lifshin, Harper, 1982; *Extended Outlooks: The Iowa Review Collection of Contemporary Women Writers,* edited by Jane Cooper and others, Macmillan, 1982; *Home Girls: A Black Feminist Anthology,* edited by Barbara Smith, Persephone, 1982. Also contributor to *An Introduction to Poetry,* edited by Louise Simpson, 1986; *Waltzing on the Water,* Dell, and *Early Ripening,* edited by Marge Piercy. Contributor of poems to numerous periodicals, including *Pequod, Iowa Review, Ironwood, Northwest Review; Poetry Northwest, American Poetry Review, Bread Loaf Quarterly, Massachusetts Review, Ploughshares,* and *Feminist Studies.* Member of editorial staff, *New York Quarterly,* 1973-77.

*WORK IN PROGRESS:* A volume of poetry and prose, *The Black Notebooks,* detailing the author's "experience being a member of one of the first black families to live in Upper Montclair, New Jersey"; another book of poetry.

*SIDELIGHTS:* Toi Derricotte is characterized by a reviewer in *Publishers Weekly* as a writer who "blends personal history, invention and reportage" in creating works that begin with a focus on the experiences of black women and ultimately discuss various themes concerning victimization. In her first book, *The Empress of the Death House,* the narrating persona seems to be at war with a world that treats her gender frivolously, if not contemptuously. Derricotte writes about female victims/survivors, develops themes of both male and female sterility or unorthodox sexual practices, and attacks white males as she paints portraits which offers insights into such black women as her grandmother and mother. Joe Weixlmann's statement in *The American Book Review,* about the female thematic in *The Empress*—that it presents a world which constantly treats African American female victims with either "indifference or contempt"—is an assessment of a theme that permeates Derricotte's works as a whole.

Derricotte commented on *The Empress of the Death House,* outlining several purposes for writing the book: *The Empress* was to confess her "sexual experience ... to confront my ambivalence as a mother, and, therefore, to examine the nature of love."

Derricotte's investigations ultimately led her to the exploration of childbearing in her second book, *Natural Birth.* Taking an otherwise socially unsanctioned topic as her inspiration, Derricotte, according to Joyce Nower in *Library Journal,* "offers a pioneering treatment of the ... experience." Sally H. Lodge writes in *Publishers Weekly,* that *Natural Birth* weaves memories of Derricotte's childhood into a frank treatment of the birth process as a painful, humiliating experience. According to critics, Derricotte distinguishes herself from male poets in the work by conveying emotions exclusive to females early in the volume and then broadening her focus. The frame ultimately depicts, as Nower asserts, the commonality of male and female experiences of "fear, pain, struggle and ecstasy."

Concerning Derricotte's third text, *Captivity,* Robyn Selman in *The Village Voice* notes that the poet's lines "alternate between long Whitmanian exhalations and short Dickinsonian gaps." Although Selman acknowledges that the poems sometimes culminate in hyperbole, the reviewer calls the work an example of "personal exploration yielding truths that apply to all of us." Her style in this text moves, as a reviewer states in *Publishers Weekly,* from the more relaxed autobiography of the first sections where she presents images of impoverished neighborhoods to a more sophisticated diction in her discussion of more troublesome portraitures of students "in ghetto schools."

Derricotte expressed her other poetical concerns as follows: "My fears of death were prominent in my early poems. In my first book, *The Empress of the Death House,* that theme persists and is embodied in 'The Grandmother Poems,' a group of poems about my early experiences at my grandparents' funeral home in Detroit. In my second book, *Natural Birth,* I am concerned again with the same themes—death, birth, and transcendence. In new manuscripts I write about our family's experiences as one of the first black families in upper Montclair, of my problems at being unrecognized because of my light complexion, and my love and rage toward my neighbors." It is true that "truthtelling as a way to self-integrity operates as a strong impulse" in Derricotte's works.

She added: "In Catholic school we learned that by confessing our sins and admitting faults and weaknesses we were forgiven, made 'whole' and acceptable, put back into a state of grace." Intrinsic to the confession itself, however, is an authorial ambivalence which seems to generate other associative and sometimes oppositional ideas. When Derricotte confided that: "As a black woman, I have been consistently confused about my 'sins,' unsure of which faults were in me and which faults were the results of others' projections." The statement casts doubt on whether or not a sin has been committed and questions the need for a confession. She added that "truthtelling in my art is also a way to separate my 'self' from what I have been taught to believe about my 'self,' the degrading stereotypes about black women."

*BIOGRAPHICAL/CRITICAL SOURCES:*

*PERIODICALS*

*American Book Review,* summer, 1979.
*Black American Literature Forum,* winter, 1983.
*Hudson Review,* winter, 1983-84.
*lammos little review,* winter, 1984.
*Library Journal,* September 15, 1983.
*Publishers Weekly,* June 10, 1983; November 17, 1989.
*13th Moon,* Volume 7, numbers 1-2, 1983.

*Village Voice,* May 15, 1990.
*Womanews,* July-August, 1983.

\* \* \*

**DIAMANO, Silmang**
**See SENGHOR, Leopold Sedar**

\* \* \*

**DIOP, Birago (Ismael) 1906-1989**
**(Max, d'Alain Provist)**

*PERSONAL:* Some sources spell middle name "Ismail"; born December 11, 1906, in Ouakam (some sources say Dakar), Senegal; died November 25, 1989, in Dakar, Senegal; son of Ismael (a master mason) and Sokhna (Diawara) Diop; married Marie-Louise Pradere (an accountant), 1934 (deceased); children: Renee, Andree. *Education:* Received doctorate from Ecole Nationale Veterinaire de Toulouse, 1933; attended Institut de Medecine Veterinaire Exotique, c. 1934, and Ecole Francaise des Cuirs et Peaux.

*ADDRESSES:* Dakar, Senegal.

*CAREER:* Head of government cattle inspection service in Senegal and French Sudan (now Mali), c. 1934-42; employed at Institut de Medecine Veterinaire Exotique in Paris, France, 1942-44; interim head of zoological technical services in Ivory Coast, 1946; head of zoological technical services in Upper Volta (now Burkina Faso), 1947-50, in Mauritania, 1950-54, and in Senegal, 1955; administrator for Societe de la Radio-diffusion d'Outre-Mer (broadcasting company), 1957; ambassador from Senegal to Tunisia during early 1960s; veterinarian in private practice in Dakar, Senegal, beginning c. 1964. Vice-president of Confederation Internationale des Societes d'Auteurs et Compositeurs, 1982; president of reading board of Nouvelles Editions Africaines (publisher); official of Institut des Hautes Etudes de Defense Nationale (French national defense institute). *Military service:* Nurse in military hospital in St.-Louis, Senegal, 1928-29.

*MEMBER:* Association des Ecrivains du Senegal (president), Bureau Senegalais des Droits d'Auteur (president of administrative council), Societe des Gens de Lettres de France, Pen-Club, Rotary-Club de Dakar, Anemon.

*AWARDS, HONORS:* Grand Prix Litteraire de l'Afrique-Occidentale Francaise, for *Les Contes d'Amadou Koumba;* Grand Prix Litteraire de l'Afrique Noire from Association des

Ecrivains d'Expression Francaise de la Mer et de l'Outre Mer (now Association des Ecrivains de Langue Francaise), 1964, for *Contes et lavanes*. Officier de la Legion d'Honneur; commandeur des Palmes Academiques; chevalier de l'Etoile Noire; chevalier du Merite Agricole; chevalier des Arts et des Lettres; grand-croix de l'Ordre National Senegalais; grand officier de l'Ordre de la Republique Tunisienne; grand officier de l'Ordre National Ivoirien.

*WRITINGS:*

*STORY COLLECTIONS*

*Les Contes d'Amadou Koumba* (includes "Maman-Caiman," "Les Mamelles," and "Sarzan"), Fasquelle, 1947, reprinted, Presence Africaine, 1978.
*Les Nouveaux Contes d'Amadou Koumba* (title means "The New Tales of Amadou Koumba"; includes "L'Os de Mor Lam"), preface by Leopold Sedar Senghor, Presence Africaine, 1958.
*Contes et lavanes* (title means "Tales and Commentaries"), Presence Africaine, 1963.
*Tales of Amadou Koumba* (includes "A Judgment"), translation and introduction by Dorothy S. Blair, Oxford University Press, 1966.
*Contes choisis,* edited with an introduction by Joyce A. Hutchinson, Cambridge University Press, 1967.
*Contes d'Awa,* illustrations by A. Diallo, Nouvelles Editions Africaines, 1977.
*Mother Crocodile: Maman-Caiman,* translation and adaptation by Rosa Guy, illustrations by John Steptoe, Delacorte Press, 1981.

*PLAYS; ADAPTED FROM HIS SHORT STORIES*

*Sarzan,* performed in Dakar, Senegal, 1955.
*L'Os de Mor Lam* (performed at Theatre National Daniel Sorano, Senegal, 1967-68), Nouvelles Editions Africaines, 1977.

Also adapted "Maman-Caiman" and "Les Mamelles."

*OTHER*

*Leurres et lueurs* (poems; title means "Lures and Lights"; includes "Viatique"), Presence Africaine, 1960.
*Birago Diop, ecrivain senegalais* (collection), commentary by Roger Mercier and M. and S. Battestini, F. Nathan, 1964.
*Memoires* (autobiography), Volume 1: *La Plume raboutee* (title means "The Piecemeal Pen"), Presence Africaine, 1978, Volume 2: *A Rebrousse-temps* (title means "Against the Grain of Time"), Presence Africaine, 1982, Volume 3: *A Rebrousse-gens: Epissures, entrelacs, et reliefs,* Presence Africaine, 1985, Volume 4: *Senegal du temps de,* L'Harmattan, c. 1989, Volume 5, *Et les yeux pour me dire,* L'Harmattan, 1989.

Work represented in anthologies, including *Anthologie de la nouvelle poesie negre et malagache de langue francaise,* edited by Leopold Sedar Senghor, Presses Universitaires de France, 1948; *A Book of African Verse,* Heinemann, 1964; and *An Anthology of African and Malagasy Poetry in French,* Oxford University Press, 1965.

Contributor to periodicals, including *L'Echo des etudiants* (sometimes under pseudonyms Max and d'Alain Provist), *L'Etudiant noir,* and *Presence africaine.*

*SIDELIGHTS:* Birago Diop was an author and poet best known for short stories inspired by the folktales of West Africa. Born and raised in Senegal, formerly a French colony, Diop wrote in French, although some of his works have been translated into English and other languages. As a young man Diop left Senegal for France, where he studied veterinary science at the Ecole Nationale Veterinaire in Toulouse. After receiving his doctorate in 1933 he went to Paris, where he encountered a community of black writers from the French colonial empire that included Aime Cesaire of Martinique and Leopold Sedar Senghor of Senegal. Senghor and Cesaire led the Negritude movement, which rejected the assimilation of black colonial peoples into French culture, asserting instead the value of the black heritage. Inspired by the movement, Diop wrote poems such as "Viatique," a vivid portrayal of the initiation ceremony of an African tribe. His work appeared in two of Senghor's groundbreaking efforts at publishing Franco-African authors: the journal *L'Etudiant noir* and the book *Anthologie de la nouvelle poesie negre et malagache de langue francaise.*

Later in the 1930s Diop returned to French West Africa, and in his work as a government veterinarian he traveled widely throughout the region, sometimes into remote areas of the interior. He turned from poetry to the short story, "the most traditional form of African literature," as Joyce A. Hutchinson observed in her introduction to *Contes choisis.* For centuries African literature was primarily spoken, and storytellers such as the *griots* of West Africa found the short story a convenient form in which to provide moral lessons or to discuss the human condition. When Diop published his first collection of stories, *Les Contes d'Amadou Koumba,* he said they were drawn verbatim from a *griot* named Amadou whom he had met during his travels. In a later interview for *Le Soleil,* however, he acknowledged that Amadou was a composite of many storytellers he had encountered, including members of his own family.

In fact many commentators, including Senghor, have suggested that Diop's stories succeed on the printed page because they are a skillful combination of African oral tradition and the author's own considerable talent as a writer. Diop "uses tradition, of which he is proud," Hutchinson wrote in 1967, "but he does not insist in an unintelligent fashion on tradition for tradition's sake. He resuscitates the spirit and the style of the traditional *conte* [tale] in beautiful French, without losing all the qualities which were in the vernacular version."

Diop's tales have often been praised for their varied and skillful observations on human nature. In "L'Os de Mor Lam," for instance, a selfish man prefers to be buried alive rather than share his supper with a neighbor. The author often drew upon traditional animal tales, which put human foibles on display by endowing animals with exaggerated forms of human characteristics. In one African story cycle, which Diop used extensively, a physically strong but foolish hyena is repeatedly bested by a hare who relies on intelligence rather than strength.

Reviewers generally note that Diop preferred laughter to melodrama in his stories, and in *The African Experience in Literature and Ideology* Abiola Irele stressed the "gentle" quality of Diop's humor. But other commentators agreed with Dorothy S. Blair, who in her foreword to *Tales of Amadou Koumba* held that some stories contain a sharper element of social satire. "Sarzan," for example, describes the comeuppance of an African villager who returns from service in the French Army and tries to impose French culture on his people. And in "A Judgment," according to John Field of *Books and Bookmen,* a couple with marital problems must endure first the "pompous legalism" of the village elders and then the "arbitrary and callous" judgment of a Muslim lord.

In adapting the oral folktale to a written form, Diop strove to maintain the spontaneity of human speech, and to do so he interspersed his prose with dialogue, songs, and poems—all part of the African storyteller's technique, as Hutchinson noted. "Diop's use of dialogue is masterly," she remarked. "He uses the whole range of human emotional expression: shouts, cries, tears, so vividly that one can without difficulty imagine and supply the accompanying gestures and the intonation of the voice." Diop adapted several of his stories for the stage, including "Sarzan" and "L'Os de Mor Lam." Writing in *World Literature Today,* Eileen Julien praised Diop's adaptation of "L'Os" for "depict[ing] in a warm and colorful style the manners of an African village," including "gatherings, prayers, communal rites and ... ubiquitous, compelling chatter." "All of these," she averred, "are the matter of which theatre is made."

Diop's adaptations of the folktale have made him one of Africa's most widely read authors, and he received numerous awards and distinctions. His first volume of tales promptly won the Grand Prix Litteraire de l'Afrique-Occidentale Francaise; for Diop's second volume, Senghor, who had be-

come one of Senegal's most prominent writers and political leaders, wrote a laudatory preface. After Senghor led Senegal to independence in 1960 he sought Diop as the country's first ambassador to Tunisia. Between 1978 and 1985 Diop produced three highly detailed volumes of memoirs, including his account of the early days of the Negritude movement in Paris. Summarizing Diop's literary achievement, Hutchinson praised the author for showing that short stories in the traditional African style are "not just children's tales, not just sociological or even historical material, but a work of art, part of Africa's cultural heritage."

*BIOGRAPHICAL/CRITICAL SOURCES:*

*BOOKS*

Diop, Birago, *Les Nouveaux Contes d'Amadou Koumba,* preface by Leopold Sedar Senghor, Presence Africaine, 1958.

Diop, Birago, *Tales of Amadou Koumba,* translation and introduction by Dorothy S. Blair, Oxford University Press, 1966.

Diop, Birago, *Contes choisis,* edited with an introduction by Joyce A. Hutchinson, Cambridge University Press, 1967.

Diop, Birago, *Memoires,* three volumes, Presence Africaine, 1978-1985.

Irele, Abiola, *The African Experience in Literature and Ideology,* Heinemann, 1981.

*PERIODICALS*

*Books and Bookmen,* October, 1986.

*Le Soleil,* December 11, 1976.

*World Literature Today,* winter, 1979, autumn, 1986.

*OBITUARIES:*

*PERIODICALS*

*New York Times,* November 29, 1989.

\*   \*   \*

## DIOP, Cheikh Anta 1923-1986

*PERSONAL:* Born in 1923 in Diourbel, Senegal; died February 7, 1986, in Dakar, Senegal. *Education:* Received a Litt.D. in France.

*CAREER:* Historian. Headed the carbon-14 dating laboratory for the Institut Fondamentale d'Afrique Noire in Senegal. Founder of two political parties in the 1960s, the Bloc des Masses Senegalaises and the Front Nationale Senegalaise.

*AWARDS, HONORS:* Honored by the World Festival of Negro Arts in 1966 as the black intellectual who had exercised the most fruitful influence in the twentieth century.

*WRITINGS:*

*Nations negres et culture,* Editions Africaines, 1955, two volume edition published as *Nations negres et culture: De L'Antiquite negre egyptienne aux problemes culturels de l'Afrique noire d'aujourd'hui,* Presence Africaine, 1979, partial translation by Mercer Cook in *The African Origin of Civilization: Myth or Reality,* Lawrence Hill, 1974 (also see below).

*L'Unite culturelle de l'Afrique noire: Domaines du patriarcat et du matriarcat dans l'antiquite classique,* Presence Africaine, 1959, translation published as *The Cultural Unity of Negro Africa: The Domains of Patriarchy and of Matriarchy in Classical Antiquity,* Presence Africaine, 1962, translation with introduction by John Henrik Clarke and afterword by James G. Spady published as *The Cultural Unity of Black Africa: The Domains of Patriarchy and of Matriarchy in Classical Antiquity,* Third World Press, 1978.

*Les Fondements culturels, techniques et industriels d'un futur etat federal d'Afrique noire,* Presence Africaine, 1960, revised edition published as *Les Fondements economiques et culturels d'un etat federal d'Afrique noire,* Presence Africaine, 1974, translation by Harold Salemson published as *Black Africa: The Economic and Cultural Basis for a Federated State,* Lawrence Hill, 1978.

*L'Afrique noire pre-coloniale: Etude comparee des systemes politiques et sociaux de l'Europe et de l'Afrique noire, de l'antiquite a la formation des etats modernes,* Presence Africaine, 1960, translation by Salemson published as *Precolonial Black Africa,* Lawrence Hill, 1987.

*Anteriorite des civilisations negres: Myth ou verite historique?,* Presence Africaine, 1967, partial translation by Cook in *The African Origin of Civilization: Myth or Reality,* Lawrence Hill, 1974 (also see below).

*Le Laboratoire de radiocarbone de l'IFAN,* Institut Fondamentale d'Afrique Noire, 1968.

*Physique nucleaire et chronologie absolue,* Institut Fondamentale d'Afrique Noire, 1974.

*The African Origin of Civilization: Myth or Reality* (translation of portions of *Anteriorite des civilisations negres* and *Nations negres et culture* by Cook), Lawrence Hill, 1974 (also see above).

*Parente genetique de l'egyptien pharaonique et des langues negro-africaines: Processus de semitisation,* Nouvelles Editions Africaines, 1977.

*Alerte sous les tropiques: Articles 1946-1960: Culture et developpement en Afrique noire,* Presence Africaine, 1990.

*Civilization or Barbarism: An Authentic Anthropology* (originally published as *Civilization ou barbarie*), translated by Yaa-Lengi Meema Ngemi, edited by Harold J. Salemson and Marjolijn de Jager, Lawrence Hill, 1991.

*SIDELIGHTS:* Cheikh Anta Diop began the first carbon-14 dating laboratory in Africa and founded two political parties in his native Senegal that were later banned, but he is best remembered for his historical works about Africa. His books attempt to prove that blacks had a larger role in the beginnings of civilization than was previously accorded them. Diop argued that the ancient Egyptians, extremely advanced in science and culture, were black; he also held that the first steps toward civilization began south of the Sahara Desert.

*BIOGRAPHICAL/CRITICAL SOURCES:*

*PERIODICALS*

*New York Times Book Review,* August 11, 1991, p. 12.
*Times Literary Supplement,* October 18, 1991, p. 3.

*OBITUARIES:*

*PERIODICALS*

*Publishers Weekly,* March 7, 1986.

*          *          *

## DIOP, David Mandessi  1927-1960

*PERSONAL:* Born July 9, 1927, in Bordeaux, France; died in a plane crash in August, 1960, near Dakar, Senegal; father was a medical doctor. *Education:* Attended Lycee Marcelin Berthelot near Paris, France in the late 1940's.

*CAREER:* Teacher at Lycee Maurice Delafosse in Dakar, 1957-58; school principal in the town of Kindia, Guinea, 1958-60.

*WRITINGS:*

*Coups de pilon: poemes,* Paris, France: Presence Africaine, 1956.

*Hammer blows and other writings [by] David Mandessi Diop,* translated and edited by Simon Mpondo and Frank Jones, Indiana University Press, 1973.

*Hammer blows: poems [by] David Mandessi Diop,* translated and edited by Simon Mpondo and Frank Jones, Heinemann, 1975.

*David Diop: 1927-1960: temoignages, etudes/Societe africaine de culture,* Presence Africaine, 1983, published in French and English.

Contributor to anthologies, including *Anthologie de la nouvelle poesie negre et malgache,* L. S. Senghor, Presence Africaine, 1947; *An Anthology of African and Malagasy Poetry in French,* Clive Wake, editor, Three Crowns Press, 1965; *Modern Poetry from Africa,* Moore and Beier, editors, Penguin, revised edition, 1968.

*BIOGRAPHICAL/CRITICAL SOURCES:*

*BOOKS*

*David Diop: 1927-1960: temoignages, etudes/Societe africaine de culture,* Presence Africaine, 1983, published in French and English.

*PERIODICALS*

*Choice,* March, 1974, p. 101; October, 1975, p. 971.

\*     \*     \*

## DIPOKO, Mbella Sonne   1936-

*PERSONAL:* Born February 28, 1936, near Douala, Cameroon; son of Paul Sonne Dipoko (a chief). *Education:* Educated in western Cameroon and eastern Nigeria, 1952-56.

*ADDRESSES: Agent*—c/o Heinemann Educational, Halley Court, Jordan Hill, Oxford OX2 8EJ, England.

*CAREER:* Development Corporation, Tiko, Cameroon, clerk, c. 1956; Nigerian Broadcasting Corporation, Lagos, reporter for Radio Nigeria, 1957-60, on assignment in Paris until 1968; later affiliated with *Presence Africaine;* writer.

*WRITINGS:*

*A Few Nights and Days* (novel), Longman, 1966.
*Overseas* (play), produced by British Broadcasting Corp., 1968.
*Because of Women* (novel), Heinemann Educational, 1969.
*Black and White in Love: Poems,* Heinemann Educational, 1972.

Work represented in anthologies, including *Modern Poetry from Africa,* Penguin, 1963; *West African Verse,* Longman, 1967; and *African Writing Today,* Penguin, 1967. Contributor to *Transition* and *United Asia.*

*BIOGRAPHICAL/CRITICAL SOURCES:*

*PERIODICALS*

*Phylon,* summer 1987, p. 204.

\*     \*     \*

## DIXON, Melvin (Winfred)   1950-1992

*PERSONAL:* Born May 29, 1950, in Stamford, CT; son of Handy and Jessie Dixon; died of complications from AIDS, October 26, 1992. *Education:* Wesleyan University, Middletown, CT, B.A., 1971; Brown University, M.A., 1973, Ph.D., 1975.

*CAREER:* Williams College, Williamstown, MA, assistant professor of English, 1976-80; Queens College of the City University of New York, Flushing, NY, associate professor, 1980-86; professor of English, 1986—.

*MEMBER:* Modern Language Association of America.

*AWARDS, HONORS:* Poetry fellow, National Endowment for the Arts, 1984; artist fellow in fiction, New York Arts Foundation, 1988; Charles H. and N. Mildred Nilon Award for Excellence in Minority Fiction, 1989, for *Trouble the Water.*

*WRITINGS:*

*Change of Territory: Poems,* University Press of Virginia, 1983.
(Translator) Genovieve Fabre, *Drumbeats, Masks, and Metaphor: Contemporary Afro-American Theatre,* Harvard University Press, 1983.
*Ride Out the Wilderness: Geography and Identity in Afro-American Literature* (criticism), University of Illinois Press, 1987.
*Trouble the Water* (novel), Fiction Collective Two/University of Colorado Press, 1989.
*Vanishing Rooms* (novel), Dutton, 1991.
(Translator) *The Collected Poetry by Leopold Sedar Senghor,* University Press of Virginia, 1991.

Contributing editor, *Callaloo.* Contributor to anthologies, including *Men on Men 2,* edited by George Stambolian, New American Library, 1988; *In the Life: A Black Gay Anthology; Brother to Brother,* edited by Essex Hemphill, Alyson Publications, 1991; and *The Southern Review.*

*SIDELIGHTS:* There were many dimensions to Melvin Dixon's identity, and these led him to create a multifaceted body of writing that included poetry, fiction, and criticism. As a gay writer, he lent an important African American perspective to the burgeoning field of gay and lesbian literature that accompanied the increasing visibility of the gay community in American society and culture since the 1970s.

In both his imaginative writing and his criticism, Dixon explored the relationship between geography and identity in the formation of the African American consciousness. As he stated in the introduction to his scholarly work *Ride Out the Wilderness: Geography and Identity in Afro-American Literature,* "I examine the ways in which Afro-American writers, often considered homeless, alienated from mainstream culture, and segregated in negative environments, have used language to create alternative landscapes where black culture and identity can flourish." Ranging over a wide literary landscape, Dixon related the historical, cultural, and political significance of real-life geographical space to the rhetorical significance of geographical imagery in slave songs and narratives. He then explored references to the underground, the wilderness, and the mountaintop as primary defining images of self and home for a number of major twentieth-century African American novelists, including Zora Neal Hurston, Alice Walker, Toni Morrison, Jean Toomer, Claude McKay, Ralph Ellison, LeRoi James, Richard Wright, Gayl Jones, and James Baldwin.

Dixon's interest in the interaction between place and identity in the African American imagination clearly informs his first novel, 1989's *Trouble the Water.* The protagonist, history professor Jordan Henry, is the only African American on the faculty of a small Massachusetts college. He and his wife feel displaced from their adopted environment when racial tensions tear the school apart. Eager to find a more accommodating location, Jordan opts to return to his hometown of Pee Dee, North Carolina, when he learns his grandmother, called Mother Harriet, has died. It was Mother Harriet who named Jordan after the Old Testament river. The protagonist's father, Jake Williams, left town before Jordan was born; his mother Chloe died in childbirth. Mother Harriet raised the lad to hate his father, and spent years urging Jordan to kill Jake in revenge of Chloe's death, until the teenaged boy finally left home, hitchhiking north. Now returning south after some twenty years, Jordan finds that Jake has come home to Pee Dee as well. Thus, he realizes he must contend with the unfinished family business he thought he had left long ago.

*Trouble the Water* is rich in mythic symbolism, and continually evokes the author's almost mystical attachment to the imagery of earth and river. Chloe's name comes from the Greek word for the first shoot of a plant in the spring. Mother Harriet had once compelled Jordan to taste the dirt from his mother's grave—an act which haunts the protagonist for years to come. Like a mythic hero, Jordan—named for the river that waters the holy land of Palestine and thus the ultimate symbol of deliverance—wanders far from home as a youth and returns to his birthplace as an adult to claim his inheritance and confront his estranged father. And while Jordan's journey is primarily one of personal discovery, Dixon's provocative juxtaposition of elements from classical mythology, the Old Testament, and African American folklore suggests a journey with much wider social, cultural, and historical significance.

Dixon's second novel *Vanishing Rooms,* set in New York City, deals explicitly with racism and homophobia (hatred and violence against homosexuals). The novel has three different narrators in alternating chapters. Each tells how his or her life is affected by the brutal gang rape and murder of Metro, a Louisiana-born, gay, white man. One of the narrators is Metro's lover, a black dancer named Jesse Duran. Another is Ruella McPhee, a fellow dancer to whom Jesse turns for comfort. The third narrator is Lonny, a white 15-year-old who has doubts about his sexuality and unwittingly contributes to the attack on Metro. Several critics noted their interest in seeing how some of Dixon's ideas about the emergence of African American identity, expressed in his criticism and his earlier fiction, relate to the issues of gay identity that he deals with in this novel. Not unlike the hypothetical African American writer to whom Dixon alludes in *Ride Out the Wilderness,* gay writers, at least historically, were often seen as estranged from their homes and families, alienated from mainstream culture, and segregated in negative environments. And they, too, have used language to create alternative landscapes where their identity—this time defined by sexuality rather than by race—could flourish.

In *Vanishing Rooms,* the various narrators use language in an attempt to find some degree of solace in a world gone tragically awry. Jesse begins to draw connections between the racially and sexually motivated violence that seem all too prevalent in the hostile urban landscape that has claimed his lover's life. Ruella learns that people's need for intimacy and emotional support can transcend differences of gender and sexuality. And Lonny, the archetypal alienated urban youth, struggles with language in the apparent hope that telling his story can help him impose some kind of sensible structure on his chaotic life.

Overall, Melvin Dixon's fiction received frequent praise for its keen development of characters and vivid detail. "He deftly probes the psyches of his characters and his tale is boosted by his use of Afro-American folklore and speech," wrote Calvin Forbes in his *Washington Post Book World* review of *Trouble the Water.* Calling *Vanishing Rooms* "powerful," Debbie

Tucker in a review for *Library Journal* lauded the book's "psychological insight, with action that is at times vividly brutal."

*BIOGRAPHICAL/CRITICAL SOURCES:*

*BOOKS*

Dixon, Melvin, *Ride Out the Wilderness: Geography and Identity in Afro-American Literature,* University of Illinois Press, 1987.

*PERIODICALS*

*Choice,* May 1988, p. 1400.
*Lambda Book Report,* March, 1992, p. 42.
*Library Journal,* January, 1991, p. 147.
*Los Angeles Times Book Review,* October 1, 1989, p. 2.
*New York Times Book Review,* September 24, 1989, pp. 48-49.
*Publishers Weekly,* January 18, 1991, p. 43; January 20, 1992, p. 60.
*Small Press,* December, 1989, pp. 39-40.
*Washington Post Book World,* March 4, 1990, p. 8.

—*Sketch by Michael Broder*

\*   \*   \*

## DJOLETO, (Solomon Alexander) Amu 1929-

*PERSONAL:* Born July 22, 1929, in Manyakpogunor, Ghana; son of Frederick Badu (a Presbyterian minister) and Victoria Shome Tetteh ("a modest trader") Djoleto; married Ann Augusta Wulff (a school administrator), May 27, 1961; children: Ofeibia Lomotey, Nii Amu, Manaa Otobia. *Education:* University of Ghana, B.A. (with honors), 1958, postgraduate degree, 1960; studied book production at University of London, 1965-66. *Politics:* "Nil." *Religion:* Presbyterian.

*ADDRESSES: Home*—128/14 Forest Ave., Dzorwulu, Accra, Ghana. *Office*—Ministry of Education, P.O. Box M.45, Accra, Ghana. *Agent*—Heinemann Publishers, Halley Court, Jordan Hill, Oxford OX2 8EJ, England.

*CAREER:* Ghana Ministry of Education, Government Secondary Technical School, Takoradi, education officer, 1958, became both senior education officer and head of the English department, 1963, assistant headmaster, 1964; affiliated with Heinemann (a publishing firm), London, England, 1965-66; Ghana Ministry of Education, editor of *Ghana Teachers Journal,* 1966, became principal education officer in charge of

information, public relations, and publications, 1967, deputy chief education officer and head of the planning division, 1973, executive director of the Ghana Book Development Council, 1975-89. Ghana Publishing Corporation, board member, 1968-74; Authorship Development Fund, vice-chair of board, 1973-89; United Nations Educational, Scientific and Cultural Organization, consultant on book development councils to several African countries, 1981-88; United Nations University, consultant, 1988-89; Ghana Ministry of Education, textbooks consultant, 1989—.

*AWARDS, HONORS:* Commonwealth Bursary Award, British Council, 1965; Amu Djoleto Award instituted by Ghana Book Publishers Association, 1989.

*WRITINGS:*

*NONFICTION*

*English Practice for the African Student* (textbook), Macmillan, 1967, revised and updated as *English Practice,* Macmillan, 1990.
(Editor with Thomas Kwami) *West African Prose Anthology,* Heinemann, 1974.
(Editor) *Ten Stories from Chaucer,* Ghana Publishing, 1979.
*Books and Reading in Ghana,* United Nations Educational, Scientific and Cultural Organization, 1985.
(Editor) *Chaucer's Prologue and Five Stories,* Sedco Publishing, 1987.

Contributor to *Publishing in the Third World: Knowledge and Development,* Heinemann, 1985.

*FICTION*

*The Strange Man,* Heinemann, 1967.
*Money Galore,* Heinemann, 1975.
*Hurricane of Dust,* Longman, 1988.

*POETRY*

*Amid the Swelling Act,* Heinemann, 1992.

*CHILDREN'S BOOKS*

*Obodai Sai* (novel), Heinemann, 1990.
*Twins in Trouble,* Heinemann, 1991.
*The Frightened Thief,* Heinemann, 1992.

*SIDELIGHTS:* Amu Djoleto commented: "I write for four principal reasons. First, I feel I should write, that's all. Second, I desperately need the money from writing. In Ghana, government salaries as I have endured are uneconomic. Third, and more important, I have always strongly held that Africans must write for Africans in the first place. Besides, Africans must write textbooks for Africans at all levels of education to begin the process of the development of the indigenous and, of course, the endogenous African intellectual. Fourth, I write both prose and poetry to record my reaction to my time and circumstance in hope that it might be useful primary source material."

\*　　\*　　\*

## DOVE, Rita (Frances) 1952-

*PERSONAL:* Born August 28, 1952, in Akron, OH; daughter of Ray (a chemist) and Elvira (Hord) Dove; married Fred Viebahn (a writer); children: Aviva Chantal Tamu Dove-Viebahn. *Education:* Miami University, Oxford, Ohio, B.A. (summa cum laude), 1973; attended Universitaet Tuebingen, West Germany, 1974-75; University of Iowa, M.F.A., 1977.

*ADDRESSES: Office*—Department of English, University of Virginia, Charlottesville, VA, 22903.

*CAREER:* Arizona State University, Tempe, assistant professor, 1981-84, associate professor, 1984-87, professor of English, 1987-89; University of Virginia, Charlottesville, professor of English 1989-93, Commonwealth Professor of English, 1993—; United States Poet Laureate, 1993—. Writer-in-residence at Tuskegee Institute, 1982. National Endowment for the Arts, member of literature panel, 1984-86, chair of poetry grants panel, 1985. Commissioner, Schomburg Center for the Preservation of Black Culture, New York Public Library, 1987—.

*MEMBER:* PEN, Associated Writing Programs (member of board of directors, 1985-88; president, 1986-87), Academy of American Poets, Poetry Society of America, Poets and Writers, Phi Beta Kappa, Phi Kappa Phi.

*AWARDS, HONORS:* Fulbright fellowship, 1974-75; grants from National Endowment for the Arts, 1978, and Ohio Arts Council, 1979; International Working Period for Authors fellowship for West Germany, 1980; Portia Pittman fellowship at Tuskegee Institute from National Endowment for the Humanities, 1982; John Simon Guggenheim fellowship, 1983; Peter I. B. Lavan Younger Poets Award, Academy of American Poets, 1986; Pulitzer Prize in poetry, 1987, for *Thomas and Beulah;* General Electric Foundation Award for Younger Writers, 1987; Honorary Doctor of Letters, Miami University, 1988; Bellagio (Italy) residency, Rockefeller Foundation, 1988; Mellon fellowship, National Humanities Center, North Carolina, 1988-89; Honorary Doctor of Humane Letters, Knox College, 1989; Literary Lion, New York Public Library, 1991; named to Ohio Women's Hall of Fame, 1991.

*WRITINGS:*

*Ten Poems* (chapbook), Penumbra Press, 1977.
*The Only Dark Spot in the Sky* (poetry chapbook), Porch Publications, 1980.
*The Yellow House on the Corner* (poems), Carnegie-Mellon University Press, 1980.
*Mandolin* (poetry chapbook), Ohio Review, 1982.
*Museum* (poems), Carnegie-Mellon University Press, 1983.
*Fifth Sunday* (short stories), Callaloo Fiction Series, 1985.
*Thomas and Beulah* (poems), Carnegie-Mellon University Press, 1986.
*The Other Side of the House* (poems), photographs by Tamarra Kaida, Pyracantha Press, 1988.
*Grace Notes* (poems), W. W. Norton & Company, Inc., 1989.
*Through the Ivory Gate* (novel), Pantheon, 1992.
*Selected Poems,* Pantheon, 1993.
*The Darker Face of the Earth* (play), Story Line Press, 1994.

Work represented in anthologies. Contributor of poems, stories, and essays to magazines, including *Agni Review, Antaeus, Georgia Review, Nation,* and *Poetry.* Member of editorial board, *National Forum,* 1984—; poetry editor, *Callaloo,* 1986—; advisory editor, *Gettysburg Review,* 1987—, and *TriQuarterly,* 1988—.

*SIDELIGHTS:* Black American writer Rita Dove has been described as a quiet leader, a poet who does not avoid race issues, but does not make them her central focus. As Dove herself explains in the *Washington Post:* "Obviously, as a black woman, I am concerned with race.... But certainly not every poem of mine mentions the fact of being black. They are poems about humanity, and sometimes humanity happens to be black. I cannot run from, I won't run from any kind of truth." As the first black poet laureate, Dove notes that, though it has less personal significance for her, "it is significant in terms of the message it sends about the diversity of our culture and our literature."

Dove is best known for her book of poems *Thomas and Beulah,* which garnered her the 1987 Pulitzer Prize in poetry. The poems in *Thomas and Beulah* are loosely based on the lives of Dove's maternal grandparents, and are arranged in two sequences: one devoted to Thomas, born in 1900 in Wartrace, Tennessee, and the other to Beulah, born in 1904 in Rockmart, Georgia. *Thomas and Beulah* is viewed as a departure from Dove's earlier works in both its accessibility and its chronological sequence that has, to use Dove's words, "the kind of sweep of a novel." On the book's cover is a snapshot of the author's grandparents, and *New York Review of Books* contributor Helen Vendler observes that "though the photograph, and the chronology of the lives of Thomas and Beulah appended to the sequence, might lead one to suspect that Dove is a poet of simple realism, this is far from the case. Dove has learned ... how to make a biographical fact the buried base of an imagined edifice."

In the *Washington Post,* Dove describes the poems this way: "The poems are about industrialization, discrimination sometimes—and sometimes not—love and babies—everything. It's not a dramatic story—nothing absolutely tragic happened in my grandparents' life.... But I think these are the people who often are ignored and lost." Peter Stitt expresses a similar view in the *Georgia Review:* "The very absence of high drama may be what makes the poems so touching—these are ordinary people with ordinary struggles, successes, and failures." He concludes: "There is a powerful sense of community, residing both in a family and in a place, lying at the heart of this book, and it is this that provides a locus to the poems. Rita Dove has taken a significant step forward in each of her three books of poems; she must be recognized as among the best young poets in the country today."

The poems in *Grace Notes,* Dove's fourth book, are largely autobiographical. Alfred Corn remarks in *Poetry* that "glimpses offered in this collection of middle-class Black life have spark and freshness to them inasmuch as this social category hasn't had poetic coverage up to now." In *Parnassus,* Helen Vendler describes Dove's poems as "rarely without drama," adding, "I admire Dove's persistent probes into ordinary language of the black proletariat." Jan Clausen notes in *The Women's Review of Books* that Dove's "images are elegant mechanisms for capturing moods and moments which defy analysis or translation." In the *Washington Post Book World,* A. L. Nielsen finds that the poems "abound in the unforgettable details of family character" and adds that Dove "is one of those rare poets who approach common experience with the same sincerity with which the objectivist poets of an earlier generation approached the things of our world."

A later work, the novel *Through the Ivory Gate,* tells the story of Virginia King, a gifted young black woman who takes a position as artist in residence at an elementary school in her hometown of Akron, Ohio. The story alternates between past and present as Virginia's return stirs up strong, sometimes painful memories of her childhood. Barbara Hoffert observes in the *Library Journal* that the "images are indelible, the emotions always heartfelt and fresh," and in the *New York Times Book Review,* Geoff Ryman notes: "*Through the Ivory Gate* is mature in its telling of little stories—Virginia's recollections of life with a troupe of puppeteers, of visiting the rubber factory where her father worked, of neighborhood boys daubing a house so that it looked as if it had measles." He concludes: "The book aims to present the richness of a life and its connections to family and friends, culture, place, seasons, and self. In this it succeeds."

*BIOGRAPHICAL/CRITICAL SOURCES:*

*PERIODICALS*

*American Book Review,* July, 1985.
*American Poetry Review,* January, 1982.
*Callaloo,* winter, 1986.
*Detroit Free Press,* July 24, 1993, pp. 5A, 7A.
*Georgia Review,* summer, 1984; winter, 1986.
*Library Journal,* August, 1992.
*New York Review of Books,* October 23, 1986.
*New York Times Book Review,* October 11, 1992.
*North American Review,* March, 1986.
*Parnassus: Poetry in Review,* Volume 16, no. 2, 1991.
*Poetry,* October, 1984; October, 1990.
*Publishers Weekly,* August 3, 1992.
*Washington Post,* April 17, 1987; May 19, 1993.
*Washington Post Book World,* April 8, 1990.
*Women's Review of Books,* July, 1990.

\*   \*   \*

# DUPLECHAN, Larry 1956-

*PERSONAL:* Surname is pronounced "*doo* pluh shahn"; born December 30, 1956, in Los Angeles, CA; son of Lawrence Duplechan, Sr. (an electronics liaison engineer), and Margie Nell Andrus Duplechan (a postal clerk, office administrator, and homemaker); became life partner of Greg Harvey (a banker), 1976. *Education:* University of California, Los Angeles, B.A., 1978. *Politics:* "Registered Democrat with feminist leanings and particular interest in the rights of gays and lesbians, women and African Americans." *Religion:* "Raised Southern Baptist. Currently vaguely Christian with a side-order of reincarnation and karma." *Avocational interests:* Reading (histories, biographies, fiction), singing, guitar playing, flute playing, drawing, bodybuilding, and twentieth-century American popular culture (music, film, theater, advertising, comic strips) pertaining particularly to African Americans and gays.

*ADDRESSES: Home*—Woodland Hills, CA. *Office*—c/o Cooper, Epstein and Hurewitz, 345 North Maple Drive, Suite 200, Beverly Hills, CA 90210.

*CAREER:* Pop/jazz vocalist (solo and with jazz vocal group String of Pearls), Los Angeles, CA, 1975-82; University of California, Los Angeles, librarian's assistant, 1976-80; word processor and secretary, various real estate-oriented companies, 1980-90; real estate legal secretary, 1990—. Taught fiction writing through the University of California at Los Angeles Continuing Education program.

*WRITINGS:*

NOVELS

*Eight Days a Week,* Alyson, 1985.
*Blackbird,* St. Martin's, 1986.
*Tangled Up in Blue,* St. Martin's, 1989.
*Captain Swing,* Alyson, 1993.

Contributor to anthologies, including *Black Men/White Men,* Gay Sunshine Press, 1983; *Revelations: A Collection of Gay Male Coming Out Stories,* Alyson, 1988; *Certain Voices: Short Stories about Gay Men,* Alyson, 1991; *Hometowns,* Dutton, 1991; *A Member of the Family,* Dutton, 1992; and *Calling the Wind: Twentieth-Century African American Short Stories,* HarperCollins, 1993. Contributor to periodicals, including *L.A. Style, Advocate, New York Native,* and *Black American Literature Forum.*

*SIDELIGHTS:* Larry Duplechan commented: "It was not my dream to become a novelist. My childhood dream was to be a singing star—sort of Johnny Mathis with a dash of Bette Midler. I'd once heard Carol Burnett advise someone to give show business five years and if it didn't look as if a viable career was in the works, give it up. So, after languishing in the extreme lower end of show business for nearly seven years without a record contract in sight, I gave it up and decided to attempt to write. It was the early 1980s and the first flowering of novels aimed at a gay readership was underway. Pleased though I was at the existence of a rapidly growing body of gay-themed literature (both serious and popular), it soon occurred to me that there were nearly no black characters in any of the gay books I found. I searched in vain for a young, black, openly gay, middle-class, college-educated protagonist with a penchant for girl group music, 1930s movie musicals and the well-placed wisecrack. Someone not unlike myself. Finding none, I decided to create one.

"Thus was born Johnnie Ray Rousseau, my literary alter ego and mouthpiece, the protagonist of three of my four published novels. When people ask me how much of Johnnie Ray Rousseau is really Larry Duplechan, my answer can vary greatly with my mood. The fact is, Johnny Ray Rousseau is almost entirely me. A bit better looking, perhaps, and a good half-inch taller, but otherwise very much me. The circumstances and events of his life are completely fictional as often as not (my own relatively happy suburban life would likely make truly soporific reading), but Johnnie's attitudes, his likes and dislikes, his borderline-bitchy sense of humor—all me.

"Blissfully ignorant of the fact that it's all but impossible to get a novel published without the benefit of an agent, I did.

*Eight Days a Week,* an interracial gay love story loosely based upon the first few years of my relationship with my life partner (and my abortive singing career), was generally treated very kindly by the gay press, utterly ignored by the mainstream press, and lambasted by a few African-American gay critics who took exception to what was perceived to be Johnnie Ray Rousseau's lack of 'Afrocentricity,' particularly concerning Johnnie's outspoken preference for white men as lovers. The field of openly gay African-American novelists writing for the gay audience remains very small and unfortunately burdens each and any book with a black gay protagonist with inordinate political importance. I had not created Johnnie Ray Rousseau as a role model, only as an interesting and amusing character. To be accused of being ashamed of my African descent by someone who'd never met me was angering and painful, both to myself and Johnnie Ray.

"But we recovered. *Blackbird,* my next book, is the story of Johnnie Ray's coming out at the age of seventeen. The people who longed for a more Afrocentric protagonist were likely not won over, but the late author, film historian and critic Vito Russo wrote 'I fell in love with Johnnie Ray,' and the late African-American writer and editor Joseph Beam wrote in the *Advocate,* 'We have all been waiting for this novel for a long time.' It is generally acknowledged as the first black, gay coming-out novel.

"In 1985, the year *Blackbird* was published, Rock Hudson died of AIDS, and a dear friend of mine tested positive for HIV— the first of many friends I was to lose to AIDS. His experiences in coping with the deadly syndrome were among the things that led to the writing of *Tangled Up in Blue,* a love triangle in which the threat of AIDS is a catalyst for emotional upheaval. Written in the third person from three different points of view—a young woman, her secretly bisexual husband and their gay friend—*Tangled Up in Blue* was in large part an attempt to answer questions I'd asked myself after the completion of *Blackbird:* Could I write in a voice other than Johnnie Ray's first-person narrative? Could I write believable Caucasian characters? Could I write from the point of view of a woman? Could I write a comic novel concerning AIDS?

"With *Captain Swing,* I returned to the first person and to Johnnie Ray (who made a brief appearance in *Tangled Up in Blue*—I couldn't get rid of him). Now in his mid-thirties, he has lost the love of his life and several friends to premature death. *Captain Swing* concerns both Johnnie's coping with the dying of his estranged father and his learning to love again.

"With the exceptions of James Baldwin (whose influence on me has more to do with subject matter than style) and Tom Robbins (whose wild flights of verbal fancy I admire but only rarely attempt to imitate, and whose *Even Cowgirls Get the Blues* is my favorite novel and the shining example toward which I ever aspire), I have no conscious literary influences. Or rather, I am influenced by everything I read—novels, biographies, magazines, cereal boxes.

"I don't make my living as a novelist—I work a forty-hour week in a law firm. As the chances of my ever making a living writing black gay novels are quite slender, I write each book purely as self-expression. When I feel like writing, I write; if not, not. If my books get published (which, so far, they have), wonderful. If not, I'll pass the manuscripts around among my friends. If I have any advice for aspiring writers, it would be the advice I give my writing students: don't write fiction for money—there very likely won't be much. If you want to make money, write for television or feature films. Only write fiction if that's how you really want to express yourself, because the work itself may be its own sole reward."

# E

## ECHERUO, Michael J(oseph) C(hukwudalu) 1937-

*PERSONAL:* Born March 14, 1937, in Umunumo, Imo State, Nigeria; son of J. M. and Martha N. Echeruo; married Rose N. Ikwueke, 1968; children: Ikechukwu, Okechukwu, Ijeoma, Chinedu, Ugonna. *Education:* Attended Stella Maris College, 1950-54; University College of Ibadan (now University of Ibadan), B.A., 1960; Cornell University, M.A., 1963, Ph.D., 1965.

*ADDRESSES: Office*—Vice-Chancellor's Office, Imo State University, Owerri, Nigeria.

*CAREER:* Nigerian College of Arts and Technology, Enugu, lecturer, 1960-61; University of Nigeria (now University of Ibadan), Nsukka, lecturer, 1961-70, senior lecturer, 1970-73, professor, 1973-74, professor of English, 1974-80, dean of postgraduate school, 1978-80; Imo State University, Owerri, Nigeria, vice-chancellor, 1981—. Founding president, Nigerian Association for African and Comparative Literature, 1977—.

*MEMBER:* Phi Beta Kappa.

*AWARDS, HONORS:* All-Africa poetry competition prize, 1963.

*WRITINGS:*

*Mortality: Poems,* Longmans, Green, 1968.
(Editor) *Igbo Traditional Life, Culture, and Literature,* Conch Magazine Ltd., 1971.
*Joyce Cary and the Novel of Africa,* Africana Publishing, 1973.
*Distanced: New Poems,* I. K. Imprints, 1976.
*Victorian Lagos: Aspects of Nineteenth-Century Lagos Life,* Macmillan, 1977, Holmes and Meier, 1978.

*The Conditioned Imagination from Shakespeare to Conrad: Studies in the Exo-Cultural Stereotype,* Macmillan, 1978.
*Joyce Cary and the Dimensions of Order,* Barnes and Noble, 1979.
(Editor) William Shakespeare, *The Tempest,* Longman, 1981.

Work represented in anthologies, including *Modern Poetry from Africa,* edited by Gerald Moore and Ulli Beier, Penguin, 1963; *West African Verse: An Anthology,* edited by Donatus I. Nwoga, Longmans, Green, 1967; and *New African Literature and the Arts,* edited by Joseph Okpaku, Crowell, 1970. Contributor of poems to periodicals, including *Black Orpheus.*

*SIDELIGHTS:* "Michael J. C. Echeruo, like his late countryman Christopher Okigbo, has forged, from the crossroads experience of an African heritage and a 'European' education, poetry which is wide-ranging, deceptively simple, and highly individual," comments Joseph Bruchac in *Contemporary Poets.* Echeruo's poetry has its roots in his African heritage, although some poems originate in and explore his experiences as a student in the United States. In his volume *Morality,* for example, the very first poem of the book, "Debut," notes that however much of the world he has seen, he still desires the palm-nuts "by which we were to live."

Besides writing poetry, Echeruo also gained critical attention for his books on Joyce Cary, who was known for his books on Africa. Echeruo's books dealing with Cary's work include *Joyce Cary and the Novel of Africa* and *Joyce Cary and the Dimensions of Order.* In the first book Echeruo discusses novels about Africa by non-African writers and then attempts to analyze Cary's fiction in this context. He also traces Cary's development as an artist. Critics have noted that Echeruo's book is unique because it evaluates Cary's African novels as a product of a European imagination. A *Times Literary Supplement* critic praised Echeruo for the accessibility of the book to readers not familiar with African fiction. "Mr. Echeruo," the critic noted, "is intelligent and often acute, and he is arguing from a passionate preoccupation with Africa and literature and not as a mere academic critic in pursuit of academic survival."

*Joyce Cary and the Dimensions of Order* is another book in which Echeruo examines Cary's writing. Brian J. Murray, writing in *Modern Fiction Studies,* judges the volume to be a "gracefully written and nicely ordered work which does much to set the record straight concerning Cary." Although Cary did not gain eminence as a writer, Echeruo feels that his ideas, because of his knowledge of philosophy, are relevant even today. In 1978 Echeruo published *The Conditioned Imagination from Shakespeare to Conrad,* a book in which he "brings together four case-studies of the racial stereotype in literature from Shylock to James Wait," describes Anne Sexton writing in the *Times Literary Supplement.* And while Sexton feels that Echeruo himself cannot escape the assumptions of his own environment while examining these works, *The Conditioned Imagination* is a book that "sends us back to Shakespeare's plays with fewer prejudices about his [Shakespeare's] prejudice."

*BIOGRAPHICAL/CRITICAL SOURCES:*

*BOOKS*

*Contemporary Poets,* fifth edition, St. Martin's, 1991.

*PERIODICALS*

*Booklist,* October 15, 1979, p. 323.
*Choice,* December, 1973, p. 1543; September, 1978, pp. 858, 955.
*Modern Fiction Studies,* summer, 1980, pp. 307-10.
*Times Literary Supplement,* August 24, 1973, p. 972; August 4, 1978, p. 895; December 7, 1979, p. 91.

\*   \*   \*

## EDELMAN, Marian Wright 1939-

*PERSONAL:* Born June 6, 1939, in Bennettsville, SC; daughter of Arthur J. and Maggie (Bowen) Wright; married Peter Benjamin Edelman, July 14, 1968; children: Joshua Robert, Jonah Martin, Ezra Benjamin. *Education:* Attended University of Paris and University of Geneva, 1958-59; Spelman College, B.A., 1960; Yale University, LL.B., 1963.

*ADDRESSES: Office*—Children's Defense Fund, 122 C St. N.W., Washington, DC 20001.

*CAREER:* National Association for the Advancement of Colored People (NAACP), Legal Defense and Education Fund, Inc., New York City, staff attorney, 1963-64, director of office in Jackson, MS, 1964-68; partner of Washington Research Project of Southern Center for Public Policy, 1968-73; Children's Defense Fund, Washington, DC, founder and president, 1973—. W. E. B. Du Bois Lecturer at Harvard University, 1986. Member of Lisle Fellowship's U.S.-U.S.S.R. Student Exchange, 1959; member of executive committee of Student Non-Violent Coordinating Committee (SNCC), 1961-63; member of Operation Crossroads Africa Project in Ivory Coast, 1962; congressional and federal agency liaison for Poor People's Campaign, summer, 1968; director of Harvard University's Center for Law and Education, 1971-73. Member of Presidential Commission on Americans Missing and Unaccounted for in Southeast Asia (Woodcock Commission), 1977, United States-South Africa leadership Exchange Program, 1977, National Commission on the International Year of the Child, 1979, and President's Commission for a National Agenda for the Eighties, 1979; member of board of directors of Carnegie Council on Children, 1972-77, Aetna Life and Casualty Foundation, Citizens for Constitutional Concerns, U.S. Committee for UNICEF, and Legal Defense and Education Fund of the NAACP; member of board of trustees of Martin Luther King, Jr., Memorial Center, and Joint Center for Political Studies.

*MEMBER:* Council on Foreign Relations, Delta Sigma Theta (honorary member).

*AWARDS, HONORS:* Merrill scholar in Paris and Geneva, 1958-59; honorary fellow of Law School at University of Pennsylvania, 1969; Louise Waterman Wise Award, 1970; Presidential Citation, American Public Health Association, 1979; Outstanding Leadership Award, National Alliance of Black School Educators, 1979; Distinguished Service Award, National Association of Black Women Attorneys, 1979; National Award of Merit, National Council on Crime and Delinquency, 1979; named Washingtonian of the Year, 1979; Whitney M. Young Memorial Award, Washington Urban League, 1980; Professional Achievement Award, Black Enterprise magazine, 1980; Outstanding Leadership Achievement Award, National Women's Political Caucus and Black Caucus, 1980; Outstanding Community Service Award, National Hookup of Black Women, 1980; Woman of the Year Award, Big Sisters of America, 1980; Award of Recognition, American Academy of Pedodontics, 1981; Rockefeller Public Service Award, 1981; Gertrude Zimand Award, National Child Labor Committee, 1982; Florina Lasker Award, New York Civil Liberties Union, 1982; Anne Roe Award, Graduate School of Education at Harvard University, 1984; Roy Wilkins Civil Rights Award, National Association for the Advancement of Colored People (NAACP), 1984; award from Women's Legal Defense Fund, 1985; Hubert H. Humphrey

Award, Leadership Conference on Civil Rights, 1985; fellow of MacArthur Foundation, 1985; Grenville Clark Prize from Dartmouth College, 1986; Compostela Award of St. James Cathedral, 1987; more than thirty honorary degrees.

*WRITINGS:*

*Families in Peril: An Agenda for Social Change,* Harvard University Press, 1987.
*The Measure of Our Success: A Letter to My Children and Yours,* Beacon Press, 1992.

Also author of *School Suspensions: Are They Helping Children?,* 1975, and *Portrait of Inequality: Black and White Children in America,* 1980. Contributor to books, including *Raising Children in Modern America: Problems and Prospective Solutions,* edited by Nathan B. Talbot, Little, Brown, 1975; *Toward New Human Rights: The Social Policies of the Kennedy and Johnson Administrations,* edited by David C. Warner, Lyndon B. Johnson School of Public Affairs, University of Texas at Austin, 1977.

*SIDELIGHTS:* Dubbed "the 101st Senator on children's issues" by Senator Edward Kennedy, Marian Wright Edelman left her law practice in 1968, just after the assassination of civil rights leader Martin Luther King, Jr., to work toward a better future for American children. She was the first black woman on the Mississippi bar and had been a civil rights lawyer with the National Association for the Advancement of Colored People (NAACP). "Convinced she could achieve more as an advocate than as a litigant for the poor," wrote Nancy Traver in *Time,* Edelman moved to Washington, DC, and began to apply her researching and rhetorical skills in Congress. She promotes her cause with facts about teen pregnancies, poverty, and infant mortality and—with her Children's Defense Fund—has managed to obtain budget increases for family and child health care and education programs. Her book, *Families in Peril: An Agenda for Social Change,* was judged "a powerful and necessary document" of the circumstances of children by *Washington Post* reviewer Jonathan Yardley, and it urges support for poor mothers and children of all races. In *Ms.* magazine Katherine Bouton described Edelman as "the nation's most effective lobbyist on behalf of children ... an unparalleled strategist and pragmatist."

Edelman once commented: "I have been an advocate for disadvantaged Americans throughout my professional career. The Children's Defense Fund, which I have been privileged to direct, has become one of the nation's most active organizations concerned with a wide range of children's and family issues, especially those which most affect America's children: our poorest Americans.

"Founded in 1968 as the Washington Research Project, the Children's Defense Fund monitors and proposes improvements in federal, state, and local budgets, legislative and administrative policies in the areas of child and maternal health, education, child care, child welfare, adolescent pregnancy prevention, youth employment, and family support systems.

"In 1983 the Children's Defense Fund initiated a major long-term national campaign to prevent teenage pregnancy and provide positive life options for youth. Since then, we have launched a multimedia campaign that includes transit advertisements, posters, and television and radio public service announcements, a national prenatal care campaign, and Child Watch coalitions in more than seventy local communities in thirty states to combat teen pregnancy.

"The Children's Defense Fund also has been a leading advocate in Congress, state legislatures, and courts for children's rights. For example, our legal actions blocked out-of-state placement of hundreds of Louisiana children in Texas institutions, guaranteed access to special education programs for tens of thousands of Mississippi's children, and represented the interests of children and their families before numerous federal administrative agencies."

*BIOGRAPHICAL/CRITICAL SOURCES:*

*PERIODICALS*

*Ebony,* July, 1987.
*Ms.,* July/August, 1987.
*New York Times Book Review,* June 7, 1987.
*School Library Journal,* September, 1992, p. 290.
*Time,* March 23, 1987.
*Washington Post,* March 4, 1987.
*Washington Post Book World,* April 19, 1992, p. 13.

\*    \*    \*

## EDWARDS, Junius 1929-

*PERSONAL:* Born 1929 in Alexandria, LA. *Education:* Attended University of Chicago and University of Oslo, Norway.

*CAREER:* Owner of advertising agency.

*AWARDS, HONORS:* First prize, *Writer's Digest* short story contest, 1958, for "Liars Don't Qualify"; Eugene F. Saxton fellowship, 1959. for creative writing.

*WRITINGS:*

*If We Must Die,* Urbanite Publishing Company, 1961, Doubleday, 1963, reprinted, Howard University Press, 1984.

Contributor to short story anthologies *Beyond the Angry Black,* edited by John A. Williams, Cooper Square, 1966; *The Best Short Stories by Negro Writers,* edited by Langston Hughes, Little, Brown, 1967; *Black Short Story Anthology,* edited by Woodie King, New American Library, 1972. Contributor to *Transatlantic Review, Urbanite,* and other publications.

*SIDELIGHTS:* Junius Edwards is known primarily for documenting the dilemmas of the black American soldier. In particular, his novel *If We Must Die* tells the story of black Korean War veteran Will Harris. The plot is spare: Harris is denied permission to register to vote in his Southern town. The next day he is fired from his job and finds that his community has blacklisted him for attempting to register. Following this discovery, Harris is attacked and beaten by a gang of whites. A samaritan attempts to save his life, but the novel ends while Harris is apparently dying. His eventual fate is ambiguous.

First printed in 1961 by a small private press before being picked up by Doubleday in 1963, *If We Must Die* was criticized by some reviewers because it seemed out of touch with the then-current civil rights movement. Faith Berry in *Crisis,* for example, had some praise, but tagged the book "anachronistic." Writing in the *New York Times Book Review,* Joseph Friedman finds that "the closing scene, turning on a melancholy mishap and rendered with pathetic irony, is affecting." Edwards received the inspiration for his novel's title from Claude McKay, who addressed blacks in one of his poems with the exhortation, "If we must die, let it not be like hogs."

The character of Will Harris made his debut in the short story "Liars Don't Qualify," for which Edwards was awarded first prize in the *Writer's Digest* short story contest in 1958. In the briefer version of Edwards' novel, Harris is denied the right to vote because he is accused of falsely claiming membership in the Army Reserve. In "Duel with the Clock," Edwards continues to focus his attention on the plight of black soldiers in the South, this time writing about a black soldier's temptation to escape his pain through drugs. The young protagonist must decide whether to use a brief pass to leave the base and get high, or remain to avoid implication in the off-base drug overdose death of a fellow soldier.

Another Edwards story illustrates the problem of intraracial prejudice of light-skinned blacks against those of darker color. "Mother Dear and Daddy" tells of two young orphans who are rejected by their mother's family because they have darker skin. Once they realize the situation, they at first strike back in anger, then laugh and sing, knowing they have relatives on their father's side who will take them in. The story, reports Australia Henderson in the *Dictionary of Literary Biography,* "has had greater longevity than [Edwards'] novel."

Henderson notes that because Edwards has published little new work since the 1960s, he has been unfairly neglected by many critics. "One may be inclined to view his repetitious style with impatience," Henderson writes, "yet it is moving and unrelenting. His realistic fiction is provocative, if dated, because it accurately reflects significant experiences in the lives of Afro-Americans, particularly the black soldier and veteran whose plight has been central to the post-World War II condition of blacks."

*BIOGRAPHICAL/CRITICAL SOURCES:*

*BOOKS*

*Dictionary of Literary Biography,* Volume 33:*Afro-American Fiction Writers after 1955,* Gale, 1984, pp. 65-67.

*PERIODICALS*

*Christian Century,* August 7, 1963, p. 983.
*Crisis,* October, 1963, pp. 508-509; December, 1963, pp. 364-365.
*Freedomways,* Number 4, 1964, pp. 173-174.
*Interracial Review,* summer, 1963, p. 177.
*New York Herald Tribune Book Review,* August 11, 1963, p. 4.
*New York Times Book Review,* August 4, 1963, p. 4.
*Pylon,* Number 25, 1963, pp. 130-131.
*Saturday Review,* August 3, 1963, p. 17.

\*   \*   \*

## EGHAREVBA, Jacob U(wadiae)   1920(?)-

*PERSONAL:* Born c. 1920 in Benin Coast, Nigeria. *Education:* Educated to university level in Nigeria; received doctorate in anthropology at a British university.

*ADDRESSES: Agent*—c/o Kraus Reprint, Route 100, Millwood, NY 10546.

*CAREER:* Edo-language poet, editor, anthropologist. Holds title of Chief.

*WRITINGS:*

*A Short History of Benin,* Church Missionary Society Bookshop, 1936, fourth edition, Ibadan University Press, 1968.

*Concise Lives of the Famous Iyases of Benin,* second edition, [Nigeria], 1947.

*Benin Law and Custom,* third edition, [Nigeria], 1949.

*Some Stories of Ancient Benin,* [Nigeria], 1950, second edition, 1951.

*Ihun-an Edo: Vbobo* (poems; title means "Edo Songs"), D. C. C. Press, 1950.

*Some Tribal Gods of Southern Nigeria,* [Nigeria], 1951.

*Benin Games and Sports,* Central Press, 1951.

*Benin Traditions and History: Some Tribal Gods of Southern Nigeria, The City of Benin, Benin Law and Custom, Some Stories of Ancient Benin,* Kraus Reprint, 1952.

*The Origin of Benin,* B. D. N. A. Museum, 1953.

*Bini Titles,* second edition, Kopin-Dogba Press, 1957.

*Concise Lives of the Famous Iyases of Benin; Benin Games and Sports; Ama z-evbo omwan tawiri—Who Does Not Speak His Native Language Is Lost; Bini Titles; The Murder of Imaguero and Tragedy of Idah War; Marriage of the Princesses of Benin; The Origin of Benin; Chronicle of Events in Benin; Fusion of Tribes; Brief Autobiography; Some Prominent Bini People; Descriptive Catalogue of Benin Museum,* Kraus Reprint, 1969.

*Itan edagbon mwen,* Ibadan University Press, 1972.


\*    \*    \*


**EGUDU, R. N.**
  **See EGUDU, Romanus N(nagbo)**


\*    \*    \*


**EGUDU, Romanus N(nagbo)   1940-**
  **(R. N. Egudu)**


*PERSONAL:* Born February 1, 1940, in Ebe, Nigeria. *Education*: University of Nigeria, B.A. (honors), 1963; Michigan State University, Ph.D., 1966.

*ADDRESSES:* Department of Modern Languages, University of Benin, Benin City, Nigeria.

*CAREER:* St. Paul's School, Eke, Enugu, Nigeria, principal, 1963; University of Nigeria, Nsukka, lecturer in English and African literature, 1966-67; University of Benin, head of Department of English. African representative of *Journal of the New African Literature and the Arts,* 1966-68.

*MEMBER:* African Literature Association, Association of African Literary Critics.

*AWARDS, HONORS:* Poetry Prize, Michigan State University, 1966; Certificate of Merit, International Biographical Center.


*WRITINGS:*

(Compiler and translator with Donatus I. Nwoga) *Poetic Heritage: Igbo Traditional Verse,* Nwankwo-Ifejika, 1971, published as *Igbo Traditional Verse,* Heinemann, 1973.

(Collector and translator) *The Calabash of Wisdom and Other Igbo Stories,* illustrated by Jennifer Lawson, NOK Publishers, 1973.

*Four Modern West African Poets,* NOK Publishers, 1977.

(Under name R. N. Egudu) *Modern African Poetry and the African Predicament,* Barnes & Noble, 1978.

*African Poetry of the Living Dead: Igbo Masquerade Poetry,* Edwin Mellen, 1992.


Also author of *The Study of Poetry,* 1977. Work represented in anthologies, including *Modern Poetry from Africa,* Penguin, 1963; *Commonwealth Poems of Today,* John Murray, 1967; and *New Voices of the Commonwealth,* Evans Brothers, 1968. Contributor to periodicals, including *Black Orpheus, Transition, Outposts,* and *Okike.* Associate editor of *Paideuma: Journal of Ezra Pound Scholarship,* editorial consultant for *Conch;* member of review staff for *Books Abroad: An International Literature Journal.*

*SIDELIGHTS:* Romanus N. Egudu is a Nigerian university professor whose internationally published work includes his own poetry, translations of poetry and tales from the Igbo language, and advanced-level critical works on African poetry and its context. His own poetry often concerns the theme of injustice. It was influenced, he once said, by a roster of English poets from John Donne to W. B. Yeats.

Of his critical works, *Four Modern West African Poets* presents the English-language verse of Christopher Okigbo and John Pepper Clark of Nigeria, Lenrie Peters of Gambia, and Kofi Awoonor of Ghana. The critical material was part of Egudu's doctoral thesis and emphasizes the special position from which these poets write, mainly, their deep roots in local cultures and fluency in European languages and culture. This situation allows them to communicate their personal, African experiences to a worldwide audience.

Egudu widened his scope to include twentieth-century English-language poetry from West, East, and South Africa in *Modern African Poetry and the African Predicament.* Egudu discusses individual poems and the poet's overall work as well as their political and social contexts. Reviewing this last work, a *Choice* writer commented that in dealing with these various issues, "Egudu is often brilliant."

*BIOGRAPHICAL/CRITICAL SOURCES:*

*PERIODICALS*

*Choice,* February, 1974, p. 1672.
*World Literature Today,* autumn, 1978, p. 679.

\* \* \*

## EKWENSI, C. O. D.
### See EKWENSI, Cyprian (Odiatu Duaka)

\* \* \*

## EKWENSI, Cyprian (Odiatu Duaka) 1921-
## (C.O.D. Ekwensi)

*PERSONAL:* Born September 26, 1921, in Minna, Nigeria; son of Ogbuefi David Duaka and Uso Agnes Ekwensi; married Eunice Anyiwo; children: five. *Education:* Attended Achimota College, Ghana, and Ibadan University; received B.A.; further study at Chelsea School of Pharmacy, London, and University of Iowa, Iowa City. *Avocational interests:* Hunting game, swimming, photography, motoring, weight-lifting.

*ADDRESSES: Home*—12 Hillview, Independence Layout, P.O. Box 317, Enugu, Nigeria.

*CAREER:* Novelist and writer of short stories and stories for children. Igbodi College, Lagos, Nigeria, lecturer in biology, chemistry, and English, 1947-49; School of Pharmacy, Lagos, lecturer in pharmacognosy and pharmaceutics, 1949-56; pharmacist superintendent for Nigerian Medical Services, 1956-57; head of features, Nigerian Broadcasting Corporation, 1957-61; Federal Ministry of Information, Lagos, director of information, 1961-66; chairman of Bureau for External Publicity during Biafran secession, 1967-69, and director of an independent Biafran radio station; chemist for plastics firm in Enugu, Nigeria; managing director of Star Printing & Publishing Co. (publishers of *Daily Star*), 1975-79; managing director of Niger Eagle Publishing Company, 1980-81. Owner of East Niger Chemists and East Niger Trading Company. Chairman of East Central State Library Board, 1972-75. Newspaper consultant to *Weekly Trumpet* and *Daily News* of Anambra State and to *Weekly Eagle* of Imo State, 1980-83; consultant on information to the executive office of the president; consultant to Federal Ministry of Information; public relations consultant.

*MEMBER:* PEN, Society of Nigerian Authors, Pharmaceutical Society of Great Britain, Institute of Public Relations (London), Institute of Public Relations (Nigeria; fellow).

*AWARDS, HONORS:* Dag Hammarskjold International Prize for Literary Merit, 1969.

*WRITINGS:*

*NOVELS*

*People of the City,* Andrew Dakers, 1954, Northwestern University Press, 1967, revised edition, Fawcett, 1969.
*Jagua Nana,* Hutchinson, 1961.
*Burning Grass,* Heinemann, 1962.
*Beautiful Feathers,* Hutchinson, 1963.
*Divided We Stand,* Fourth Dimension Publishers, 1980.

*JUVENILE*

(Under name C.O.D. Ekwensi) *Ikolo the Wrestler and Other Ibo Tales,* Thomas Nelson, 1947.
(Under name C.O.D. Ekwensi) *The Leopard's Claw,* Thomas Nelson, 1950.
*The Drummer Boy,* Cambridge University Press, 1960.
*The Passport of Mallam Ilia,* Cambridge University Press, 1960.
*An African Night's Entertainment* (folklore), African Universities Press, 1962.
*Yaba Roundabout Murder* (short novel), Tortoise Series Books (Lagos, Nigeria), 1962.
*The Great Elephant-Bird,* Thomas Nelson, 1965.
*Juju Rock,* African Universities Press, 1966.
*The Boa Suitor,* Thomas Nelson, 1966.
*Trouble in Form Six,* Cambridge University Press, 1966.
*Coal Camp Boy,* Longman, 1971.
*Samankwe in the Strange Forest,* Longman, 1973.
*The Rainbow Tinted Scarf and Other Stories* (collection), Evans Africa Library, 1975.
*Samankwe and the Highway Robbers,* Evans Africa Library, 1975.
*Masquerade Time,* Heinemann Educational Books, 1992.
*King Forever!,* Heinemann Educational Books, 1992.

*OTHER*

(Under name C.O.D. Ekwensi) *When Love Whispers* (novella), Tabansi Bookshop (Onitsha, Nigeria), 1947.
*The Rainmaker and Other Short Stories* (short story collection), African Universities Press, 1965.
*Lokotown and Other Stories* (short story collection), Heinemann, 1966.
*Iska,* Hutchinson, 1966.
*The Restless City and Christmas Gold,* Heinemann, 1975.

*Survive the Peace,* Heinemann, 1976.

(Editor) *Festac Anthology of Nigerian Writing,* Festac, 1977.

*Motherless Baby* (novella), Fourth Dimension Publishers, 1980.

*For a Roll of Parchment,* Heinemann, 1987.

*Jagua Nana's Daughter,* Spectrum, 1987.

Also author of *Behind the Convent Wall,* 1987. Writer of plays and scripts for BBC radio and television, Radio Nigeria, and other communication outlets. Contributor of stories, articles, and reviews to magazines and newspapers in Nigeria and England, including *West African Review, London Times, Black Orpheus, Flamingo,* and *Sunday Post.* Several of Ekwensi's novels have been translated into other languages, including Russian, Italian, German, Serbo-Croation, Danish, and French. His novellas have been used primarily in schools as supplementary readers.

*SIDELIGHTS:* "Cyprian Ekwensi is the earliest and most prolific of the socially realistic Nigerian novelists," according to Martin Tucker in his *Africa in Modern Literature: A Survey of Contemporary Writing in English.* "His first writings were mythological fragments and folk tales. From these African materials he turned to the city and its urban problems, which he now feels are the major issues confronting his people." Reviewing Cyprian Ekwensi's *Beautiful Feathers* in *Critique: Studies in Modern Fiction,* John F. Povey writes: "The very practice of writing, the developing professionalism of his work, makes us find in Ekwensi a new and perhaps important phenomenon in African writing.... Other Nigerian novelists have sought their material from the past, the history of missionaries and British administration as in Chinau Achebe's books, the schoolboy memoirs of Onuora Nzekwu, Ekwensi faces the difficult task of catching the present tone of Africa, changing at a speed that frighteningly destroys the old certainties. In describing this world, Ekwensi has gradually become a significant writer."

Ekwensi states that his life in government and quasi-government organizations like the Nigerian Broadcasting Corporation has prevented him from expressing any strong political opinions, but adds, "I am as much a nationalist as the heckler standing on the soap-box, with the added advantage of objectivity." During the late 1960s Biafran war, during which the eastern region of Biafra seceded temporarily from the rest of Nigeria, Ekwensi visited the United States more than once to help raise money for Biafra and to purchase radio equipment for the independent Biafran radio station of which he was director. He has also traveled in western Europe.

J.O.J. Nwachukwu-Agbada, in *World Literature Today,* describes Ekwensi as the "Nigerian Defoe;" "Ekwensi has been writing fiction since the 1940s. He is prolific and versatile, especially in the subject matter of his works, which can range

from sex to science.... The 'new' work [*For a Roll of Parchment*] also reveals considerable artistic development, particularly in language and descriptive power."

In a later edition of *World Literature Today,* Nwachukwu-Agbada talks of "Cyprian Edkwensi's Rabelaisian jeu d'esprit whose obscene flavor sparked considerable outrage among Nigerian readers of the sixties [upon the release of *Jagua Nana* in 1961]. The new novel's [*Jagua Nana's Daughter*] bawdiness twenty-five years later has not attracted similar attention, probably due to the increased permissiveness and decreased influence of tradition in modern-day Nigeria."

*BIOGRAPHICAL/CRITICAL SOURCES:*

*BOOKS*

*Contemporary Literary Criticism,* Volume 4, Gale, 1975.

Emenyonu, Ernest N., *The Essential Ekwensi: A Literary Celebration of Cyprian Ekwensi's Sixty-Fifth Birthday,* Heinemann, 1987.

*Something about the Author,* Volume 66, Gale, 1966.

Tucker, Martin, *Africa in Modern Literature: A Survey of Contemporary Writing in English,* Ungar, 1967.

*PERIODICALS*

*Books Abroad,* autumn, 1967.

*Critique: Studies in Modern Fiction,* October, 1965.

*Times Literary Supplement,* June 4, 1964.

*World Literature Today,* Volume 62, autumn, 1988; Volume 62, winter, 1989.

\* \* \*

**el-TOURE, Askia Muhammad Abu Bakr**
 **See TOURE, Askia Muhammad Abu Bakr el**

\* \* \*

**EMECHETA, (Florence Onye) Buchi 1944-**

*PERSONAL:* Born July 21, 1944, in Yaba, Lagos, Nigeria; daughter of Jeremy Nwabudike (a railway worker and molder) and Alice Ogbanje (Okwuekwu) Emecheta; married Sylvester Onwordi, 1960 (separated, 1966); children: Florence, Sylvester, Jake, Christy, Alice. *Education:* University of London, B.Sc. (with honors), 1972. *Religion:* Anglican. *Avocational interests:* Gardening, attending the theatre, listening to music, reading.

*ADDRESSES: Home*—7 Briston Grove, Crouch End, London N8 9EX, England.

*CAREER:* British Museum, London, England, library officer, 1965-69; Inner London Education Authority, London, youth worker and sociologist, 1969-76; writer and lecturer, 1972—; community worker, Camden, NJ, 1976-78. Visiting professor at several universities throughout the United States, including Pennsylvania State University, University of California, Los Angeles, and University of Illinois at Urbana-Champaign, 1979; senior president fellow and visiting professor of English, University of Calabar, Nigeria, 1980-81; lecturer, Yale University, 1982, London University, 1982—; fellow, London University, 1986. Proprietor, Ogwugwu Afor Publishing Company, 1982-83. Member of Home Secretary's Advisory Council on Race, 1979—, and of Arts Council of Great Britain, 1982-83.

*AWARDS, HONORS:* Jock Campbell Award for literature by new or unregarded talent from Africa or the Caribbean, *New Statesman*, 1978; selected as the Best Black British Writer, 1978, and one of the Best British Young Writers, 1983.

*WRITINGS:*

*NOVELS, EXCEPT WHERE INDICATED*

*In the Ditch* (diary), Barrie & Jenkins, 1972.
*Second-Class Citizen,* Allison & Busby, 1974, Braziller, 1975.
*The Bride Price* (paperback published as *The Bride Price: Young Ibo Girl's Love; Conflict of Family and Tradition*), Braziller, 1976.
*The Slave Girl,* Braziller, 1977.
*The Joys of Motherhood,* Braziller, 1979.
*Destination Biafra,* Schocken, 1982.
*Naira Power* (novella), Macmillan (London), 1982.
*Double Yoke,* Schocken, 1982.
*The Rape of Shavi,* Ogwugwu Afor, 1983, Braziller, 1985.
*Adah's Story,* Allison & Busby, 1983.
*Head Above Water* (autobiography), Ogwugwu Afor, 1984, Collins, 1986.
*A Kind of Marriage* (novella), Macmillan, 1987.
*The Family,* Braziller, 1990, published in England as *Gwendolen,* Collins, 1990.

*JUVENILE*

*Titch the Cat* (based on story by daughter Alice Emecheta), Allison & Busby, 1979.
*Nowhere to Play* (based on story by daughter Christy Emecheta), Schocken, 1980.
*The Moonlight Bride,* Oxford University Press/University Press, 1981.

*The Wrestling Match,* Oxford University Press/University Press, 1981, Braziller, 1983.
*Family Bargain* (publication for schools), British Broadcasting Corp., 1987.

*OTHER*

(Author of introduction and commentary) Maggie Murray, *Our Own Freedom* (photography), Sheba Feminist (London), 1981.
*A Kind of Marriage* (teleplay; produced by BBC-TV), Macmillan (London), 1987.

Also author of teleplays *Tanya, a Black Woman,* produced by BBC-TV, and *The Juju Landlord.* Contributor to journals, including *New Statesman, Times Literary Supplement,* and *Guardian.*

*SIDELIGHTS:* Although Buchi Emecheta has resided in London since 1962, she has become one of Nigeria's most recognizable female writers. She enjoys particular popularity in Great Britain and has gathered an appreciative audience in American as well. John Updike in the *New Yorker* calls her "Nigeria's best-known female writer" and says "Indeed, few writers of her sex ... have arisen in any part of tropical Africa." Although Emecheta has written children's books and teleplays, she is best known for her historical novels set in Nigeria, both before and after independence. Concerned with the clash of cultures and the impact of Western values upon agrarian traditions and customs, Emecheta's work is strongly autobiographical, and, as Updike observes, much of it is especially concerned with "the situation of women in a society where their role, though crucial, was firmly subordinate and where the forces of potential liberation have arrived with bewildering speed."

Born to Ibo parents in Yaba, a small village near Lagos, Nigeria, Emecheta indicates that the Ibos "don't want you to lose contact with your culture," writes Rosemary Bray in the *Voice Literary Supplement.* Bray explains that the oldest woman in the house plays an important role in that she is the "big mother" to the entire family. In Emecheta's family, her father's sister assumed this role, Bray relates: "'She was very old and almost blind,' Buchi recalls, 'And she would gather the young children around her after dinner and tell stories to us.'" The stories the children heard were about their origins and ancestors; and, according to Bray, Emecheta recalls: "I thought to myself 'No life could be more important that this.' So when people asked me what I wanted to do when I grew up I told them I wanted to be a storyteller—which is what I'm doing now."

Orphaned as a young child, Emecheta lived with foster parents who mistreated her. She attended a missionary high school for girls on a scholarship until she was sixteen and then wed a man to whom she had been betrothed since the age of eleven. A mother at seventeen, she had two sons and three daughters by the time she was twenty-two. After the birth of her second child, Emecheta followed her husband to London, where she endured poor living conditions, including one-room apartments without heat or hot water, to help finance his education. "The culture shock of London was great," notes Bray, "but even more distressing was her husband's physical abuse and his constant resistance to her attempts at independence." The marriage ended when he read and then burned the manuscript of her first book. Supporting herself and five children on public assistance and by scrubbing floors, Emecheta continued to write in the mornings before her children arose and also managed to earn an honors degree in sociology. *In the Ditch,* her first book, originally appeared as a series of columns in the *New Statesman.* Written in the form of a diary, it "is based on her own failed marriage and her experiences on the dole in London trying to rear alone her many children," states Charlotte and David Bruner in *World Literature Today.* Called a "sad, sonorous, occasionally hilarious ... extraordinary first novel," by Adrianne Blue of the *Washington Post Book World,* it details her impoverished existence in a foreign land, as well as her experience with racism, and "illuminates the similarities and differences between cultures and attitudes," remarks a *Times Literary Supplement* contributor who appraises it merits "special attention."

Similarly autobiographical, Emecheta's second novel, *Second-Class Citizen,* "recounts her early marriage years, when she was trying to support her student-husband—a man indifferent to his own studies and later indifferent to her job searches, her childbearing, and her resistance to poverty," observe the Bruners. The novel is about a young, resolute and resourceful Nigerian girl who, despite traditional tribal domination of females, manages to continue her own education; she marries a student and follows him to London, where he becomes abusive toward her. "Emecheta said people find it hard to believe that she has not exaggerated the truth in this autobiographical novel," reports Nancy Topping Bazin in *Black Scholar.* "The grimness of what is described does indeed make it painful to read." Called a "brave and angry book" by Marigold Johnson in the *Times Literary Supplement,* Emecheta's story, however, "is not accompanied by a misanthropic whine," notes Martin Levin in the *New York Times Book Review.* Author Alice Walker, who thinks it is "one of the most informative books about contemporary African life" that she has read, observes in *Ms.* that *Second Class Citizen* "raises fundamental questions about how creative and prosaic life is to be lived and to what purpose."

"Emecheta's women do not simply lie down and die," observes Bray in the *Voice Literary Supplement.* "Always there is resistance, a challenge to fate, a need to renegotiate the terms of the uneasy peace that exists between them and accepted traditions." Bray adds that "Emecheta's women know, too, that between the rock of African traditions and the hard place of encroaching Western values, it is the women who will be caught." Concerned with the clash of cultures, in *The Bride Price,* Emecheta tells the story of a young Nigerian girl "whose life is complicated by traditional attitudes toward women," writes Richard Cima in *Library Journal.* The young girl's father dies when she is thirteen, and, with her brother and mother, she becomes the property of her father's ambitious brother. She is permitted to remain in school only because it will increase her value as a potential wife. She falls in love with her teacher, who is a descendant of slaves, however, and because of familial objections, they elope, thereby depriving her uncle of the "bride price." When she dies in childbirth, she fulfills the superstition that a woman would not survive the birth of her first child if her bride price had not been paid. Susannah Clapp maintains in the *Times Literary Supplement,* that the quality of the novel "depends less on plot or characterization than on the information conveyed about a set of customs and the ideas which underlay them." Calling it "a captivating Nigerian novel lovingly but unsentimentally written, about the survival of ancient marriage customs in modern Nigeria," Valerie Cunningham adds in *New Statesman* that this book "proves Buchi Emecheta to be a considerable writer."

Emecheta's *Slave Girl* is about "a poor, gently raised Ibo girl who is sold into slavery to a rich African Marketwoman by a feckless brother at the turn of the century," writes a *New Yorker* contributor. Educated by missionaries, she joins the new church where she meets the man she eventually marries. In *Library Journal,* Cima thinks that the book provides an "interesting picture of Christianity's impact on traditional Ibo society." Perceiving parallels between marriage and slavery, Emecheta explores the issue of "freedom within marriage in a society where slavery is supposed to have been abolished," writes Cunningham in the *New Statesman,* adding that the book indicts both "pagan and Christian inhumanity to women." And although a contributor to *World Literature Today* suggests that the "historical and anthropological background" in the novel tends to destroy its "emotional complex," another contributor to the same journal believes that the sociological detail has been "unobtrusively woven into" it and that *The Slave Girl* represents Emecheta's "most accomplished work so far. It is coherent, compact and convincing."

"Emecheta's voice has been welcomed by many as helping to redress the somewhat one-sided picture of African women that has been delineated by male writers," according to Hans M. Zell in *A New Reader's Guide to African Literature.* Writing in *African Literature Today,* Eustace Palmer indicates that "The African novel has until recently been remarkable for the absense of what might be called the feminine point of view."

Because of the relatively few female African novelists, "the presentation of women in the African novel has been left almost entirely to male voices ... and their interest in African womanhood ... has had to take second place to numerous other concerns," continues Palmer. "These male novelists, who have presented the African woman largely within the traditional milieu, have generally communicated a picture of a male-dominated and male-oriented society, and the satisfaction of the women with this state of things has been ... completely taken for granted." Palmer adds that the emergence of Emecheta and other "accomplished female African novelists ... seriously challenges all these cozy assumptions. The picture of the cheerful contented female complacently accepting her lot is replaced by that of a woman who is powerfully aware of the unfairness of the system and who longs to be fulfilled in her self, to be a full human being, not merely somebody else's appendage." For instance, Palmer notes that *The Joys of Motherhood* "presents essentially the same picture of traditional society ... but the difference lies in the prominence in Emecheta's novel of the female point of view registering its disgust at male chauvinism and its dissatisfaction with what it considers an unfair and oppressive system."

*The Joys of Motherhood* is about a woman "who marries but is sent home in disgrace because she fails to bear a child quickly enough," writes Bazin. "She then is sent to the city by her father to marry a man she has never seen. She is horrified when she sees no alternative to staying with him. Poverty and repeated pregnancies wear her down; the pressure to bear male children forces her to bear child after child since the girls she has do not count." Palmer observes that "clearly, the man is the standard and the point of reference in this society. It is significant that the chorus of countrymen say, not that a woman without a child is a failed woman, but that a woman without a child for her husband is a failed woman." Bazin observes that in Emecheta's novels, "a woman must accept the double standard of sexual freedom; it permits polygamy and infidelity for both Christian and non-Christian men but only monogamy for women. These books reveal the extent to which the African woman's oppression is engrained in the African mores."

Acknowledging that "the issue of polygamy in Africa remains a controversial one," Palmer states that what Emecheta stresses in *The Joys of Motherhood* is "the resulting dominance, especially sexual, of the male, and the relegation of the female into subservience, domesticity and motherhood." Nonetheless, despite Emecheta's "angry glare," says Palmer, one can "glean from the novel the economic and social reasons that must have given rise to polygamy.... But the author concentrates on the misery and deprivation polygamy can bring." Palmer praises Emecheta's insightful psychological probing of her characters' thoughts: "Scarcely any other African novelist has succeeded in probing the female mind and displaying the female personality with such precision." Blue likewise suggests that Emecheta "tells this story in a plain style, denuding it of exoticism, displaying an impressive, embracing compassion." Calling it a "graceful, touching, ironically titled tale that bears a plain feminist message," Updike adds in the *New Yorker* that "in this compassionate but slightly distanced and stylized story of a life that comes to seem wasted, (Emecheta) sings a dirge for more than African pieties. The lives within *The Joys of Motherhood* might be, transposed into a different cultural key, those of our own rural ancestors."

Emecheta's "works reveal a great deal about the lives of African women and about the development of feminist perspectives," observes Bazin in *Black Scholar,* explaining that one moves beyond an initial perspective of "personal experience," to perceive "social or communal" oppression. This second perspective "demands an analysis of the causes of oppression within the social mores and the patriarchal power structure," adds Bazin. Finding both perspectives in Emecheta's work, Bazin thinks that through her descriptions of "what is it like to be female in patriarchal African cultures," the author provides a voice for "millions of black African women." Although her feminist perspective is anchored in her own personal life, says Bazin, Emecheta "grew to understand how son preference, bride price, polygamy, menstrual taboos, ... wife beating, early marriages, early and unlimited pregnancies, arranged marriages, and male dominance in the home functioned to keep women powerless." The Bruners write in *World Literature Today* that "obviously Emecheta is concerned about the plight of women, today and yesterday, in both technological and traditional societies, though she rejects a feminist label." Emecheta told the Bruners: "The main themes of my novels are African society and family; the historical, social, and political life in Africa as seen by a woman through events. I always try to show that the African male is oppressed and he too oppresses the African women.... I have not committed myself to the cause of African women only. I write about Africa as a whole."

Emecheta's *Destination Biafra* is a story of the "history of Nigeria from the eve of independence to the collapse of the Biafran secessionist movement," writes Robert L. Berner in *World Literature Today.* The novel has generated a mixed critical response, though. In the *Times Literary Supplement,* Chinweizu feels that it "does not convey the feel of the experience that was Biafra. All it does is leave one wondering why it falls so devastatingly below the quality of Buchi Emecheta's previous works." Noting, however, that Emecheta's publisher reduced the manuscript by half, Berner suggests that "this may account for what often seems a rather elliptical narrative and for the frequently clumsy prose which too often blunts the novel's satiric edge." Finding the novel "different from any of her others ... larger and more substantive," the Bruners state: "Here she presents neither the life story of a single character nor the delineation of one facet of a culture but the whole perplexing canvas of people from diverse ethnic groups, belief systems, levels of a society all caught in a disastrous civil war." Moreover, the Bruners feel that the "very objectivity of her reporting and her impartiality in recounting atrocities committed by all sides, military and civilian, have even greater impact because her motivation is not sadistic."

*The Rape of Shavi* represents somewhat of a departure in that "Emecheta attempts one of the most difficult tasks: that of integrating the requirements of contemporary, realistic fiction with the narrative traditions of myth and folklore," writes Somtow Sucharitkul in the *Washington Post Book World*. Roy Kerridge describes the novel's plot in the *Times Literary Supplement*: "A plane crashes among strange tribespeople, white aviators are made welcome by the local king, they find precious stones, repair their plane and escape just as they are going to be forcibly married to native girls. The king's son and heir stows away and has adventures of his own in England." Called a "wise and haunting tale" by a *New Yorker* contributor, *The Rape of Shavi* "recounts the ruination of this small African society by voracious white interlopers," says Richard Eder in the *Los Angeles Times*. A few critics suggest that in *The Rape of Shavi* Emecheta's masterful portrayal of her Shavian community is not matched by her depiction of the foreigners. Eder, for instance, calls it a "lopsided fable," and declares: "It is not that the Shavians are noble and the whites monstrous; that is what fables are for. It is that the Shavians are finely drawn and the Westerners very clumsily. It is a duet between a flute and a kitchen drain." However, Sucharitkul, writing in the *Washington Post Book World,* thinks that portraying the Shavians as "complex individuals" and the Westerners as "two dimensional, mythic types" presents a refreshing, seldom expressed, and "particularly welcome" point of view.

Although in the *New York Times* Michiko Kakutani calls *The Rape of Shavi* "an allegorical tale, filled with ponderous morals about the evils of imperialism and tired aphorisms about nature and civilization," Sucharitkul believes that "the central thesis of (the novel) is brilliantly, relentlessly argued, and Emecheta's characters and societies are depicted with a bittersweet, sometimes painful honesty." The critic also praises Emecheta's effective writing skill: "It is prose that appears unusually simple at first, for it is full of the kind of rhythms and sentence structures more often found in folk tales than in contemporary novels. Indeed, in electing to tell her multilayered and often very contemporary story within a highly mythic narrative framework, the author walks a fine line between the pitfalls of preciosity and pretentiousness. By and large, the tightrope act is a success."

*Head Above Water,* Emecheta's 1984 autobiography, "suffers from careless editing," writes Val Wilmer in *New Statesman.*

"Nevertheless, the story of her progress, sometimes blind and battered, as she drags herself out of 'the ditch', is educational material for those white feminists and others on the 'Black reality' bandwagon who cannot imagine hard times existing outside America's ghettoes and the Black Belt South." Perceiving the book's value and Emecheta's skill beyond racial awareness, Wilmer adds: "it is in the African story-telling tradition that her work should be seen."

In Emecheta's 1990 novel *The Family* (which was published in England as *Gwendolen*), a series of issues are examined through the life of Gwendolen Brillianton. As the novel begins, Gwendolen is six years old and living in a Jamaican mountain village. The story follows her through a series of tribulations that include rape and incest. She eventually stakes out an individual identity and sets out on her own at age sixteen. Reviewers again commented on Emecheta's strong storytelling ties to the African oral tradition.

"Emecheta has reaffirmed her dedication to be a full-time writer," say the Bruners. "Her culture and her education at first were obstacles to her literary inclination. She had to struggle against precedent, against reluctant publishers, and later against male-dominated audiences and readership." Her fiction is autobiographical, drawing on the difficulties she has both witnessed and experienced as a woman, and most especially as a Nigerian woman. Indicating that in Nigeria, however, "Emecheta is a prophet without honor," Bray adds that "she is frustrated at not being able to reach women—the audience she desires most. She feels a sense of isolation as she attempts to stake out the middle ground between the old and the new." Remarking that "in her art as well as in her life, Buchi Emecheta offers another alternative," Bray quotes the author: "What I am trying to do is get our profession back. Women are born storytellers. We keep the history. We are the true conservatives—we conserve things and we never forget. What I do is not clever or unusual. It is what my aunt and my grandmother did, and their mothers before them."

## BIOGRAPHICAL/CRITICAL SOURCES:

### BOOKS

*Contemporary Literary Criticism,* Gale, Volume 14, 1980, Volume 28, 1984.

Zell, Hans M., and others, *A New Reader's Guide to African Literature,* second revised and expanded edition, Holmes & Meier, 1983.

### PERIODICALS

*African Literature Today,* Number 3, 1983.
*Atlantic,* May, 1976.

*Black Scholar,* November/December, 1985; March/April, 1986.

*Booklist,* February 1, 1990.

*Library Journal,* September 1, 1975; April 1, 1976; January 15, 1978; May 1, 1979.

*Listener,* July 19, 1979.

*Los Angeles Times,* October 16, 1983; March 6, 1985; January 16, 1990.

*Ms.,* January, 1976; July, 1984; March, 1985.

*New Statesman,* June 25, 1976; October 14, 1977; June 2, 1978; April 27, 1979; February 6, 1987.

*New Yorker,* May 17, 1976; January 9, 1978; July 2, 1979; April 23, 1984; April 22, 1985.

*New York Times,* February 23, 1985; June 2, 1990.

*New York Times Book Review,* September 14, 1975; November 11, 1979; January 27, 1980; February 27, 1983; May 5, 1985; April 29, 1990.

*Publishers Weekly,* February 16, 1990.

*Times Literary Supplement,* August 11, 1972; January 31, 1975; June 11, 1976; February 26, 1982; February 3, 1984; February 27, 1987; April 20, 1990; April 30, 1990.

*Voice Literary Supplement,* June, 1982.

*Washington Post Book World,* May 13, 1979; April 12, 1981; September 5, 1982; September 25, 1983; March 30, 1985.

*World Literature Today,* spring, 1977; summer, 1977; spring, 1978; winter, 1979; spring, 1980; winter, 1983; autumn, 1984, winter, 1985.

\*   \*   \*

## ESEKI, Bruno
### See MPHAHLELE, Ezekiel

\*   \*   \*

## ESEOGHENE
### See BARRETT, (Eseoghene) Lindsay

\*   \*   \*

## EUBA, Femi 1941-

*PERSONAL:* Born April 2, 1941, in Lagos, Nigeria; son of Alphaeus Sobiyi Euba (a confectioner) and Winifred Remilekun (Dawodu) Euba (a teacher); married Addie Jane Dawson (a printmaker), August 5, 1992. *Education:* Rose Bruford College of Speech and Drama, diploma in acting, 1965; Yale University, M.F.A., 1973, M.A., 1982; University of Ife, Ph.D., 1987. *Politics:* Democrat. *Religion:* Christian/Humanist. *Avocational interests:* Scrabble, tennis, badminton, walking.

*ADDRESSES: Home*—659 Spanish Town Rd., Baton Rouge, LA 70802. *Office*—Louisiana State University, P.O. Box 16352, Baton Rouge, LA 70893.

*CAREER:* University of Ibadan, Ibadan, Nigeria, lecturer, 1975-76; University of Ife, Ile-Ife, Nigeria, senior lecturer, 1976-86; College of William and Mary, Williamsburg, VA, visiting professor, 1986-88; Louisiana State University, Baton Rouge, associate professor, 1988—. Theatre director and actor; consultant to African Theatre.

*MEMBER:* Modern Language Association, Black Theatre Network, Association for Theatre in Higher Education, Southwest Theatre Association, British Actors Equity.

*AWARDS, HONORS:* Association of Nigerian Authors Literary Award, 1988, for *The Gulf.*

*WRITINGS:*

*Archetypes, Imprecators and Victims of Fate: Origins and Developments of Satire in Black Drama,* Greenwood Press, 1989.

*The Gulf* (full-length play), Longman (Lagos, Nigeria), 1992.

Also author of the plays *Eye of Gabriel,* 1993, *A Riddle of the Palms,* and *Crocodiles;* author of the novel *Camwood at Crossroads,* 1993. Work represented in *Ten One-Act Plays,* edited by Cosmo Pieterse, Heinemann Educational Books (London, England), 1968; and *Five African Plays,* edited by Pieterse, Heinemann Educational Books, 1970. Contributor of essays to periodicals, including *Black American Literature Forum.*

*RADIO PLAYS*

*The Yam Debt,* British Broadcasting Corporation (BBC) Radio Monograph, 1964.

*The Telegram,* BBC Radio Monograph, 1965.

*Down by the Lagoon,* BBC Radio Monograph, 1965.

*The Game,* BBC Radio Monograph, 1966.

*Tortoise,* BBC Radio Monograph, 1967.

*Chameleon,* BBC Radio Monograph, 1968.

*The Devil,* BBC Radio Monograph, 1970.

*The Wig and the Honeybee,* BBC Radio Monograph, 1976.

*WORK IN PROGRESS:* Researching comparative black drama and theatre, and the ritual process in drama.

*SIDELIGHTS:* Femi Euba commented: "I began writing stories for the radio when in high school, through the encouragement of the well-known Nigerian novelist Chinua Achebe, then head of talks for Radio Nigeria. In the 1960s, when I was in England studying drama, I wrote some poems and plays for British Broadcasting Corporation (BBC) radio that were featured in its African Theatre series. This experience, along with being an actor, provided me the necessary groundwork for play writing.

"I have come to identify William Shakespeare's background with my African background, and in trying to re-create the nuances (rhythm, tone, color, characteristics, etc.) of my Yoruba culture in the English language, I see similarities in the rich, vibrant images that Shakespeare evokes with words and those commonly evoked in Yoruba language. To effect such a language in English is problematic but a challenge that I consistently strive to resolve. In this regard my mentor, and a writer I feel has explored and accomplished this re-creative process to the fullest, is Wole Soyinka, Africa's most distinguished dramatist. My own plays have turned out to be extended metaphors in which words, subjects, or ideas explore their various parallel meanings and conceptions, and these are used to dramatize the ironies of our social and human condition. Furthermore, my background in black as well as in Western cultural and theatrical traditions has richly set my artistic vision in a multicultural mode. My commitment as a playwright is to probe and dramatize evident problems underlying the inevitable interrelationships of our multicultural existence, with the view to understanding and overcoming the problems.

"As a playwright, I'm very much a classical-conservative at heart. While I appreciate the various expressions of the avant-garde/absurdists, I feel drama, if it should appeal to a wide variety of audiences (which is what most playwrights want), cannot afford to be involved with the esoteric or the abstract in an attempt to compete with pseudo-elitist critical theories like semiotics, structuralism, deconstruction, etc. At best, there seems to be a middle ground of shared expression, which consists of a focused, visible plot or idea, and style in whatever form the playwright (or the director, for that matter) wishes to express it."

*BIOGRAPHICAL/CRITICAL SOURCES:*

*PERIODICALS*

*Afro-Hispanic Review,* January, 1993, pp. 30-31.
*Callaloo,* fall, 1990, p. 931.
*Choice,* September, 1990, p. 123.

\* \* \*

## EVANZZ, Karl 1953-

*PERSONAL:* Original name, Karl E. Anderson; born January 16, 1953, in St. Louis, MO; son of Adolphus and Bernice (Leake) Anderson; married Alexandra Jane Hamilton (a registered nurse), January 1, 1977; children: Aqila, Aaron, Kanaan, Arianna, Adrian. *Education:* Attended Forest Park Community College, 1970-71; Westminster College, Fulton, MO, B.A., 1975; studied law at American University, 1975-77. *Politics:* Independent. *Religion:* None. *Avocational interests:* Photography, mysticism, history.

*ADDRESSES: Home*—P.O. Box 296, Ashton, MD 20861. *Office*—Washington Post, 1150 Fifteenth St. N.W., Washington, DC 20071.

*CAREER:* Lowe, Mark & Moffett, Alexandria, VA, law clerk, 1976-77; law clerk to Harry T. Alexander, 1977-81; *Washington Post,* Washington, DC, on-line editor, 1980—. *St. Louis Argus,* Washington correspondent, 1981-83.

*MEMBER:* National Association of Black Journalists.

*WRITINGS:*

*The Judas Factor: The Plot to Kill Malcolm X,* Thunder's Mouth Press, 1992.

Contributor of articles and poems to periodicals, including *Southern Exposure, Black Film Review,* and *Big Red News.*

*WORK IN PROGRESS: Malcolm's Son,* an autobiographical novel, publication expected in 1996; *Elijah Muhammad,* a biography, publication expected in 1997.

*SIDELIGHTS:* Karl Evanzz once commented: "The books that secure the firmest lock on our imaginations all seem to have a common theme: man overcoming events so incredible that the truth sounds like fiction. Herman Melville mesmerized us on the high seas, while Mark Twain lured us into the caverns of Hannibal. Albert Camus baked our thoughts on the desert, and Ernest Hemingway took us on a safari. In my first novel, *Malcolm's Son,* I will take the reader deep into the asphalt jungle where I spent my youth—the St. Louis ghetto. People are often amazed when I recount events from my childhood, and frequently they ask me to retell the stories to their friends or co-workers. People are uniformly startled that I could have survived so many misadventures.

"*Malcolm's Son* is a story about a boy who imagines what life would be like if Malcolm X had been his father, and who then restructures his life as though the dream was true. I wanted to write a story about young black men, who are seldom the protagonists in today's literature. If African Americans can read, enjoy, and identify with autobiographical tales written by and about whites, there is no reason that a well-told story about African Americans should not appeal to whites.

"Although my first book, *The Judas Factor,* was generally well-received, I am terribly unhappy with it. There were several problems which should have been resolved before publication. For this reason, I plan to self-publish my next book. I am a bit of a perfectionist, and I doubt that I could find a publisher who cares more deeply than I about how a book looks and reads. In days gone by, books were regarded much like works of art. In addition to reading well, they looked good. I intend to have all of my books reflect this perspective.

"I don't know for certain when I decided to become a writer, but I was toying with the idea by the age of thirteen. If all goes well, I plan to publish at least ten more books before life bids me adieu. I want to leave a body of work which will inspire other African Americans to pursue the task of telling the history of African Americans. In doing so, we will be enhancing America's glorious culture and adding missing pieces to the human puzzle as well."

Evanzz added: "The publishing industry expects every writer to promote his own books nowadays; this is really impractical. A great many gifted writers (notably J. D. Salinger) are just that: writers, not hucksters. For this reason, most of today's bestsellers reflect the writer's and publisher's showmanship, rather than the quality of the book. In January of 1993, for example, most of the top twenty bestsellers were rubbish, pure and simple. Any time that Madonna and Rush Limbaugh produce the top-selling books in America, the publishing industry, and more importantly, American culture, are in serious trouble."

\* \* \*

## EVERETT, Percival L. 1956-

*PERSONAL:* Born December 22, 1956, in Ft. Gordon, GA; son of Percival Leonard (a dentist) and Dorothy (Stinson) Everett. *Education:* University of Miami, A.B., 1977; attended University of Oregon, 1978-80; Brown University, A.M., 1982.

*ADDRESSES: Office*—Department of Creative Writing, University of California, Riverside, CA 92521. *Agent*—Candida Donadio, 231 West 22nd St., New York, NY 10011.

*CAREER:* Worked as jazz musician, ranch worker, and high school teacher. University of Kentucky, Lexington, associate professor of English, 1985-89, and director of graduate creative writing program; University of Notre Dame, Notre Dame, IN, associate professor of English, 1989-92; University of California, Riverside, professor of creative writing, 1992—.

*MEMBER:* Writers Guild of America (West), Modern Language Association.

*AWARDS, HONORS:* D. H. Lawrence fellowship, University of New Mexico, 1984; Lila Wallace-Reader's Digest fellowship.

*WRITINGS:*

*Suder,* Viking, 1983.
*Walk Me to the Distance,* Ticknor & Fields, 1985.
*Cutting Lisa,* Ticknor & Fields, 1986.
*The Weather and Women Treat Me Fair* (short story collection), August House, 1989.
*Zulus,* Permanent Press, 1989.
*For Her Dark Skin,* Owl Creek Press, 1989.
*The One That Got Away,* illustrations by Dirk Zimmer, Clarion Books, 1992.
*God's Country,* Faber, 1994.
*The Body of Martin Aguilera,* Owl Creek Press, 1994.

Contributor to *From Timberline to Tidepool: Contemporary Fiction from the Northwest,* edited by Rich Ives, Owl Creek Press, 1989. Contributor of stories to periodicals, including *Montana Review, Callaloo, Aspen Journal of the Arts, Modern Short Stories,* and *Black American Literature Forum.*

*SIDELIGHTS:* Percival L. Everett gained acclaim with his first novel, *Suder,* which tells the story of Craig Suder, a black professional baseball player. The book begins at a point in Suder's life when, due to a slump in his career, he is experiencing problems with his wife and son. As a result, Suder leaves his family and career to begin a trip across the American northwest. Carolyn See, reviewing the book in a *Los Angeles Times* article, says that Everett has created in this story of zany adventures a "mad work of comic genius." Alice Hoffman in the *New York Times Book Review* suggests that through Suder's run for freedom Everett "gives us a story of a life filled with chance events, some laughable, others tragic." The story alternates between the past and present where the reader, through Suder's recollections, is introduced to his past life and his childhood, which was filled with characters "absurd yet human," says Hoffman.

In *Walk Me to the Distance,* his second novel, Everett tells the story of David Larson, a Vietnam war veteran looking for ways to adjust to life after the war. Larson finds escape from other veterans and his sister in a small town in Wyoming called Slut's Hole. Here he lives at the ranch house of an old widow named Sixbury, an embittered old woman whose son is retarded. Sixbury, incapable of loving her own son because of his disability, becomes Larson's friend. The novel then follows Larson through his unfocused existence where he meets and tends to the town people until he and Sixbury adopt a

Vietnamese girl. When Sixbury's son kidnaps and rapes the Vietnamese girl, Larson is forced to take part in a frontier justice-style hanging. Reviewing *Walk Me to the Distance* in the *Los Angeles Times,* Don Strachan said that Everett's "ambivalence towards the lynching forces us to examine our moral positions ... he knows how to let words not said echo the loudest, how to plumb a deep emotional well with a detail."

With 1989's *Zulus* Everett enters the world of fantasy fiction. Set in a post-thermonuclear future, the book unfolds the story of Alice Achitophel, the last fertile woman on Earth. Alice, a grossly fat woman, who escaped sterilization because of an oversight becomes pregnant after she is raped. Because of this she is very valuable to rebels interested in rejuvenating the human race. Managing to escape from the rebels with her lover, Kevin Peters, Alice returns to the city where she and Kevin live until the end of the book. Reviewing *Zulus* in the *Washington Post* Clarence Major likened Everett's vision to that of Aldous Huxley's *Brave New World.* Major feels that Everett is "one of America's most promising young novelists" and says that in this book "Everett's gifts as a lyrical writer are vividly on display." He concludes that "*Zulus* is a curious, troublesome and, at times, delightful addition to the literature of the anti-heroic and the futuristic."

*BIOGRAPHICAL/CRITICAL SOURCES:*

*PERIODICALS*

*Los Angles Times,* July 31, 1983, pp. 1, 8.
*New York Times Book Review,* October 2, 1983, pp. 9, 26; March 24, 1985, p. 24.
*Washington Post,* May 20, 1990, p. 4.

# F

## FARAH, Nuruddin 1945-

*PERSONAL:* Born in 1945, in Baidoa, Somalia; son of Hassan and Aleeli. *Education:* Attended Panjab University, University of London, and University of Essex.

*ADDRESSES: Home*—P.O. Box 95, Mogadishu, Somalia. *Agent*—A. D. Peters & Co., Ltd., 10 Buckingham St., London WC2N 6BU, England.

*CAREER:* Clerk-typist for Ministry of Education in Somalia, 1964-66; teacher at secondary school in Mogadishu, Somalia, 1969-71; lecturer in comparative literature at Afgoi College of Education, 1971-74; free-lance writer translator, and broadcaster; University of Ibadan, Jos Campus, Jos, Nigeria, associate professor.

*MEMBER:* Union of Writers of the African Peoples.

*AWARDS, HONORS:* Fellow of United Nations Educational, Scientific and Cultural Organization, 1974-76; literary award, English-Speaking Union, 1980, for *Sweet and Sour Milk.*

*WRITINGS:*

*Why Die So Soon?,* Somali News, 1965.
*From a Crooked Rib,* Heinemann, 1970.
*A Naked Needle,* Heinemann, 1976.
*Sweet and Sour Milk,* Allison & Busby, 1979, Heinemann, 1980.
*Sardines,* Allison & Busby, 1981.
*Close Sesame,* Allison & Busby, 1983.
*Maps,* Pantheon, 1986.
*Gavor,* Bonniers, 1990.

*PLAYS*

*A Dagger in Vacuum,* produced in Mogadishu, Somalia, 1969.
*The Offering,* produced in Colchester, Essex, 1975.
*Yussuf and His Brothers,* produced in Jos, Nigeria, at University Theatre, 1982.
*A Spread of Butter* (radio play), BBC, 1978.

*OTHER*

Also contributor to newspapers and periodicals, including *Third World Affairs* and *Times Literary Supplement.*

*SIDELIGHTS:* An African writer best known for novels that champion the oppressed, particularly women, Nuruddin Farah sets his plots in twentieth-century Somalia, with most of the action occurring in the capital, Mogadishu.

Farah is best-known for a trilogy on an African dictatorship led by the fictional Major General Muhammad Siyad, referred to as the "General," and the subsequent demise of democracy in Somalia. The first volume, *Sweet and Sour Milk,* focuses upon a political activist who attempts to unravel the mysterious circumstances involving the death of his twin brother. The second novel, *Sardines,* depicts life under the General's repressive regime while also examining the social barriers that limit Somalian women and their quest for individuality and equality. The novel's central character is Medina, a young woman who, after losing her job as editor of a state-run newspaper, refuses to support the General's domestic policies. The final volume in the trilogy is *Close Sesame,* the story of an elderly man who spent many years in prison for opposing both colonial and postrevolutionary governments. When the man's son plots to overthrow the General's regime, the man attempts to stop the coup himself.

Farah has written two other novels that have met with high acclaim from critics. *Maps* is set during Somalia's war against Ethiopia in the late 1970s and examines the conflict between nationalism and personal commitment through the story of Askar. A Somalian orphan, Askar is raised by an Ethiopian woman. As Askar approaches adulthood, he is forced to choose between his loyalties to the ailing adoptive mother—who is suspected of being a spy—and enlisting in the army.

Farah's *A Naked Needle* is the story of a single, key day in the life of Koschin, a man on the edge of a nervous breakdown who passively accepts the arrival of an Englishwoman, a former lover, who is determined to marry him. In *A Naked Needle,* Farah explores not only Somalian politics, but the preference, at least of some elite Somalian men, for Western white women—a fact which arouses the discomfort of Koschin.

A central theme in all of Farah's unique works is the depiction of women meeting and solving challenges cast upon them by an African society which has traditionally stymied the intellectual growth of women. For example, in *From a Crooked Rib,* Ebla, the main character, sets out to extricate herself from the imprisoning women's role in traditional society. Ebla's moral and intellectual growth is detailed initially in her artful escape from an arranged marriage, then her steady progress as she searches for personal freedom and dignity.

A feature of Farah's portrayal of women is their ability to take an active part in the environment which surrounds them. Because Farah presents his women from this perspective, he is unique among African creative writers. Farah's depiction of progress made by African women in their bid for personal freedom from outdated values is typified by Medinia in *Sweet and Sour Milk.* Conscious that sacrifice is indispensable in any concerted struggle against established authority, Medinia, despite a privileged background, rises up against the General in a blow for the silent majority. As an active member of a revolutionary group, Medinia offers counsel and protection to young students who participate in protests of the General's tyrannical form of government.

Another example of Farah's portrayal of women taking an active role in the world around them is Qumman in *Sweet and Sour Milk.* A suppressed, second-class citizen of traditional Muslim culture, Qumman is the typical mother, loving, all-caring, and patient. The victim of physical abuse by her husband, Qumman lives only for her children. But despite being cast in the traditional mold, Qumman organizes the religious rituals involved with her son Soyaan's funeral while arranging for the presence of the sheikhs watching over the corpse. Though such arrangements would not be not uncommon in Western culture, this clearly exemplifies the changing role of women in African society. "Through his portrayal of educated

women like Medina, Segal, Amina and their associates, Farah presents a penetrating study of conflict between traditional Muslim culture and the encroaching Western influence," writes J. I. Okonkwo in *World Literature Today.*

Though sometimes criticized for substandard stylistic and technical writing, Farah is generally acknowledged, along with Sembene Ousmane and Ayi Kwei Armah, whose female characters also possess the same vision as Farah's women, as the African writers who have done the greatest justice in championing human rights. The political tone of his novels is evident as Farah attempts to show the pressure of the Somalian regime on individual psyches, but his writings concentrate on characters who, despite the system, slowly grow as individuals.

Critics have praised the uniqueness of Farah's writing. "The novels are, in the widest sense, political but are never simplistic or predictable," declares Angela Smith in *Contemporary Novelists.* "Farah is not politically naive or specifically anti-Soviet; his implicit theme is the imprisoning effect of outside intervention in Somalian life." Kirsten Holst Petersen, writing in *Ariel: A Review of International English Literature,* says of Farah, "Pushed by his own sympathy and sensitivity, but not pushed too far, anchored to a modified Western bourgeois ideology, he battles valiantly, not for causes but for individual freedom, for a slightly larger space round each person, to be filled as he or she chooses."

*BIOGRAPHICAL/CRITICAL SOURCES:*

*BOOKS*

*Black Literature Criticism,* Volume 2, Gale, 1992.
*Contemporary Novelists,* St. James, 1991.
*Contemporary Literary Criticism,* Volume 53, Gale, 1989.

*PERIODICALS*

*Ariel: A Review of International English Literature,* July, 1981, pp. 93-101.
*Library Journal,* May 15, 1978, p. 1079; May 15, 1992, p. 119.
*London Review of Books,* May 8, 1986, p.20.
*Observer* (London), November 6, 1983, p. 31.
*New York Times Book Review,* November 11, 1987, p.40; July 12, 1992, p. 18.
*Publishers Weekly,* April 6, 1992, p. 61.
*World Literature Today,* spring, 1984, pp. 215-221.

## FARISANI, Tshenuwani Simon 1947-

*PERSONAL:* Born August 30, 1947, in Louis Trichardt, South Africa; son of John Ratshilumela (a farmer and doctor) and Musandiwa Sarah (a homemaker) Farisani; married Mudzunga Regina (a teacher), August 16, 1978; children: Nzum Bululo, Ndamulelo, Zwovhonala. *Education:* University of South Africa, B.A., 1972, B.A. (with honors), 1982. *Politics:* "Freedom and justice." *Religion:* Lutheran.

*ADDRESSES: Home and office*—2770 Marin Ave., Berkeley, CA 94708.

*CAREER:* Church worker, 1972-74; pastor, 1975—. Evangelical Lutheran Church in Southern Africa, began as dean, became bishop's deputy, 1977—. President of Black People's Convention of South Africa, 1973-75, Bold Evangelical Christian Organization, 1974-76, Tshenuwani Christian Organization for the Handicapped, 1983-87, and Southern African through Education, 1988—.

*MEMBER:* Venda Society on Alcoholism and Drug Dependence (president, 1984-90).

*AWARDS, HONORS:* D.D., Trinity Lutheran Seminary, 1985; Confessor of Christ Award, 1987.

*WRITINGS:*

*In der Hoelle du bist auch da O Gott,* Erlangen, 1985.
*Diary from a South African Prison,* edited by John A. Evenson, Fortress, 1987.
*Justice in My Tears,* Africa World Press, 1988.
*In Transit: Between the Image of God and the Image of Man,* Eerdmans, 1990.

*WORK IN PROGRESS: When Humans Become God;* research on salvation, liberation, and justice.

*SIDELIGHTS:* Tshenuwani Simon Farisani once commented: "I have a thirst and hunger for freedom and justice and an interest in religious and international affairs."

\*    \*    \*

## FAX, Elton Clay 1909-

*PERSONAL:* Born October 9, 1909, in Baltimore, MD; son of Mark Oakland (a clerk) and Willie Estelle (Smith) Fax; married Grace Elizabeth Turner, March 12, 1929 (deceased); children: Betty Louise (Mrs. James Evans), Virginia Mae (deceased), Leon. *Education:* Attended Claflin University; Syracuse University, B.F.A., 1931. *Religion:* Protestant.

*ADDRESSES: Home*—51-28 30th Ave., Woodside, NY 11377. *Office*—P.O. Box 2188, Astoria Station, Long Island City, NY 11102-0004.

*CAREER:* Writer, illustrator, and lecturer. Claflin College, Orangeburg, SC, teacher of art, art history, and history, 1935-36; Harlem Art Center, New York City, teacher of life drawing, 1936-41; City College (now of the City University of New York), New York City, teacher of watercolor painting and art history, 1957-58. Lecturer in high schools and community centers; artist in residence at and consultant to many universities, including Purdue University, Princeton University, Fisk University, Western Michigan University, University of Hartford, and Texas Southern University. Specialist-grantee for U.S. Department of State in international cultural exchange program to South America and the Caribbean, 1955; delegate to Second International Congress of Society of African Culture in Rome, Italy, 1959; State Department lecturer in East Africa, 1963; guest writer of Soviet Writers Union to U.S.S.R., 1971, 1973; participant in Union of Bulgarian Writers Conference in Sofia, Bulgaria, 1977. Exhibitions include those at National Gallery of Art and Corcoran Gallery of Art, Washington, DC, Kerlan Collection, University of Minnesota, and National Museum, Tashkent, Uzbekistan.

*MEMBER:* Authors Guild of America, National Writers Union, P.E.N., Syracuse University Alumni Association.

*AWARDS, HONORS:* Gold medal, Women's Civic League Contest, 1932; MacDowell Colony fellow, 1968; Coretta Scott King Award, American Library Association, 1972, for *Seventeen Black Artists;* Louis E. Seley NACAL gold medal, 1972, for painting, "Machinists Board U.S.S. *Hunley,* Charleston, SC, March 1969"; Arena Players award, 1972; Rockefeller Foundation fellow, 1976; chancellor's medal, Syracuse University, 1990.

*WRITINGS:*

*West Africa Vignettes,* self-illustrated, American Society of African Culture, 1960, enlarged edition, 1963.
*Contemporary Black Leaders,* Dodd, 1970.
*Seventeen Black Artists,* Dodd, 1971.
*Garvey: The Story of a Pioneer Black Nationalist,* foreword by John Henrik Clarke, Dodd, 1972.
*Through Black Eyes: Journeys of a Black Artist in East Africa and Russia,* self-illustrated, Dodd, 1974.
*Black Artists of the New Generation,* foreword by Romare Bearden, Dodd, 1977.
*Hashar* (title means "Working Together"), self-illustrated, Progress Publishers (Moscow), 1980.

*Elyuchin* (title means "For the People"), Progress Publishers, 1983.
*Soviet People as I Knew Them,* Progress Publishers, 1988.

Also author and illustrator of *Black and Beautiful,* privately printed. Contributor to *Harlem, U.S.A.,* and *Dictionary of American Negro Biography.*

*ILLUSTRATOR*

Robert N. McClean, *Tommy Two Wheels,* Friendship Press, 1943.
Shirley Graham and George D. Lipscomb, *Dr. George Washington Carver: Scientist,* Messner, 1944.
Georgene Faulkner and John Becker, *Melindy's Medal,* Messner, 1945.
Clifford B. Upton, *Upton Arithmetic—Grade 4,* American Book Co., 1945.
Shannon Garst, *Sitting Bull: Champion of His People,* Messner, 1946.
*Story Parade Treasure Book* (includes *Susie's Story,* by Aileen Fisher, and *The Haunted Skyscraper,* by Jan Flory), John C. Winston, 1946.
Florence Hayes, *Skid,* Houghton, 1948.
Garst, *Buffalo Bill,* Messner, 1948.
Faulkner, *Melindy's Happy Summer,* Messner, 1949.
Montgomery M. Atwater, *Avalanche Patrol,* Random House, 1951.
Celeste Edell, *A Present from Rosita,* Messner, 1952.
Atwater, *Rustlers on the High Range,* Random House, 1952.
Eugene F. Moran, Sr., *Famous Harbours of the World,* Random House, 1953.
Regina Woody, *Almena's Dogs,* Farrar, Straus, 1954.
Clara Baldwin, *Cotton for Jim,* Abingdon, 1954.
Harold Lamb, *Genghis Khan and the Mongol Horde,* Random House, 1954.
Jeanette Eaton, *Trumpeter's Tale: The Story of Young Louis Armstrong,* Morrow, 1955.
James H. Robinson, editor, *Love of This Land,* Christian Education Press, 1956.
Harold Courlander, *Terrapin's Pot of Sense,* Holt, 1957.
Ella Huff Kepple, *Mateo of Mexico,* Friendship Press, 1958.
Verna Aardema, *Otwe,* Coward, 1960.
Aardema, *The Na of Wa,* Coward, 1960.
Aardema, *The Sky God Stories,* Coward, 1960.
Aardema, *Tales from the Story Hat,* Coward, 1960.
Letta Schatz, *Taiwo and Her Twin,* McGraw-Hill, 1964.
Aardema, *More Tales from the Story Hat,* Coward, 1966.
Johanna Johnston, *Paul Cuffee: America's First Black Captain,* Dodd, 1970.
Genevieve Gray, *The Seven Wishes of Joanna Peabody,* Lothrop, 1972.
Glennette Tilley Turner, *Take a Walk in Their Shoes,* Cobblehill Books, 1989.

*SIDELIGHTS:* An award-winning artist and essayist, Elton Clay Fax is well known for both his paintings and his children's book illustrations. His writing in books such as *Contemporary Black Leaders, Seventeen Black Artists,* and *Black Artists of the New Generation* profiles the diversity of black Americans while maintaining the common thread of a proud African American legacy. In each case, the author is conscious of the black experience and how it has molded the individual.

In his book *Garvey,* Fax provides a detailed narrative on the life of the charismatic black Jamaican nationalist Marcus Garvey. He explores events from the late nineteenth century, when the Panama Canal was being built with black laborers, to the 1920s, when Garvey gained prominence as a black leader with his Universal Negro Improvement Association. Fax also recounts the ambitious steamship venture, Black Star Line, which ultimately led to Garvey's imprisonment and exile. John Ralph Willis, writing in the *New York Times Book Review,* commends the author for having "succeeded in rescuing Garvey from the oblivion to which he had been consigned in the 1950's and 60's."

Fax's interest in black culture has led him to travel in black countries in East Africa as well as Soviet Central Asia. His volume *Through Black Eyes* combines text and drawings in what critics deemed a sensitive portrayal of the people and places he visited. Likewise, in *Hashar* and *Elyuchin,* Fax provides illustrations and descriptions of his journeys. Of his extensive traveling experience, Fax commented: "If I have learned anything at all from my travels and contacts with peoples whose lands and cultures seem so remote to ours it is this: as an American of African descent I find that I hold much in common with many of our overseas neighbors whose experiences with exploitation and racism parallel my own. And I am convinced that the humanity of the world's peoples (and, I fear, their inhumanity too) are of far more significance to me than are the differences of race, color, language, and custom."

*BIOGRAPHICAL/CRITICAL SOURCES:*

*BOOKS*

Driskell, David C., *Elton Fax: Drawings from Africa,* Fisk University, 1968.

*PERIODICALS*

*Best Sellers,* May 15, 1972, p. 78.
*New York Times Book Review,* August 20, 1972, pp. 5, 18.
*Saturday Review,* July 1, 1972, p. 52.

## FERDINAND, Vallery III
## See SALAAM, Kalamu ya

\* \* \*

## FIGUEROA, John J(oseph Maria) 1920-

*PERSONAL:* Born August 4, 1920, in Kingston, Jamaica; immigrated to England, 1979, dual British and Jamaican citizenship; son of Rupert Aston (in insurance sales) and Isclena (a teacher; maiden name, Palomino) Figueroa; married Dorothy Grace Murray Alexander (a teacher and author), August 3, 1944; children: Dorothy Anna Jarvis, Catherine, J. Peter, Robert P. D., Mark F. E., Esther M., Thomas Theodore (deceased). *Education:* Attended St. George's College (Kingston, Jamaica), 1931-37; College of the Holy Cross, A.B. (cum laude), 1942; London University, teachers diploma, 1947, M.A., 1950; graduate study at University of Indiana—Bloomington, 1964. *Religion:* Catholic. *Avocational interests:* Travel, Creole linguistics, cricket, Caribbean studies, music, painting, lay theology and liturgy.

*ADDRESSES: Home*—77 Station Rd., Woburn Sands, Buckinghamshire MK17 8SH, England.

*CAREER:* Water Commission, Kingston, Jamaica, clerk, 1937-38; teacher at secondary schools in Jamaica, 1942-46, and London, England, 1946-48; University of London, Institute of Education, London, lecturer in English and philosophy, 1948-53; University College of the West Indies, Kingston, senior lecturer, 1953-57, professor of education, 1957-73, dean of faculty of education, 1966-69; University of Puerto Rico, Rio Piedras and Cayey, professor of English and consultant to the president, 1971-73; El Centro Caribeno de Estudios Postgraduados, Carolina, Puerto Rico, professor of humanities and consultant in community education, 1973-76; University of Jos, Jos, Nigeria, professor of education and acting dean, 1976-80; Bradford College, Yorkshire, England, visiting professor of humanities and consultant in multicultural education, 1980; Open University, Milton Keynes, England, member of Third World studies course team, 1980-83; Manchester Education Authority, Manchester, England, adviser on multicultural studies, West Indian language and literature, and Caribbean heritage students, 1983-85; fellow at Warwick University's Center of Caribbean studies, 1988. British Broadcasting Corporation, London, sports reporter and general broadcaster for programs including "Reflections" and poetry readings, 1946-60. Consultant to Ford and Carnegie foundations; consultant to Organization of American States and to West Indian governments. External examiner, Africa and West Indies. Has lectured and read his poetry in Africa, Canada, Europe, South America, the United Kingdom, and the United States.

*MEMBER:* Linguistic Society of America, Caribbean Studies Association, Society for the Study of Caribbean Affairs, Athenaeum Club.

*AWARDS, HONORS:* British Council fellowship, 1946-47; Carnegie fellowship, 1960; Guggenheim fellowship, 1964; Lilly Foundation grant, 1973; Institute of Jamaica Medal, 1980; L.H.D. from College of the Holy Cross, 1960.

*WRITINGS:*

*POETRY*

*Blue Mountain Peak* (poetry and prose), Gleaner, 1944.
*Love Leaps Here,* [privately printed], 1962.
*Ignoring Hurts: Poems* (includes "Cosmopolitan Pig" and "The Grave Digger"), introduction by Frank Getlein, Three Continents Press, 1976.

*EDITOR*

*Caribbean Voices: An Anthology of West Indian Poetry,* Evans, Volume 1: *Dreams and Visions,* 1966, second edition, 1982, Volume 2: *The Blue Horizons,* 1970; published in one volume, Evans, 1971, Luce, 1973.
*Society, Schools, and Progress in the West Indies,* Franklin Book Co., 1971.
(And author of introduction) Sonny Oti, *Dreams and Realities: Six One-act Comedies,* J. West, 1978.
(With Donald E. Herdeck and others) *Caribbean Writers: A Bio-Bibliographical Critical Encyclopedia,* Three Continents, 1979.
*An Anthology of African and Caribbean Writing in English,* Heinemann, 1982.
*Third World Studies: Caribbean Sampler,* Open University Press, 1983.

*OTHER*

*Staffing and Examinations in British Caribbean Secondary Schools: A Report of the Conference of the Caribbean Heads,* Evans, c. 1964.
(Author of introduction) Edgar Mittelhoelzer, *A Morning at the Office,* Heinemann, 1974.
(With David Sutcliffe) *System in Black Language,* Taylor & Francis, 1992.

Author with Ed Milner of television plays, "St. Lucia: Peoples and Celebrations" series, British Broadcasting Corporation, 1983—. Translator of works by Horace. Contributor to *Poems from the West Indies,* edited by Jose A. Jarvis, Kraus Reprint, 1954; *Whose Language?,* 1985, and *The Caribbean in Europe,* Cass, 1986; contributor to periodicals, including *Commonweal, Dorenkamp, London Magazine, Universities*

*Quarterly, Caribbean Studies, Cross Currents, Caribbean Quarterly,* and *Commonwealth Essays and Studies.* General editor of "Caribbean Writers" series for Heinemann. Editor of recording, *Poets of the West Indies Reading Their Own Works,* Caedmon, 1972.

*SIDELIGHTS:* West Indian poet and scholar John J. Figueroa is known for his original verse, the anthologies he has edited, and his critical and academic writings. He draws on classical literature, such as the poetry of Virgil and Horace, as well as on the rhythms of Jamaican speech and calypso music for his poems, which at their best are regarded as sensual, spiritual, and unusually well crafted. His nonfiction writings reflect more than forty years of commitment to the academic field.

Figueroa commented: "It has been good to have grown up with and to have been part of the development and flowering of Caribbean literature, painting, and music. But it is a pity that there is so little appreciation of the *variety* as well as the achievement in these fields. People are much too quick to look for something they call identity, and to disown anyone who does not abjectly follow the tribe on the grounds that right or wrong doesn't matter—all that matters is whether it's 'one of us' who is involved.

"I have also been very lucky to have traveled and lived among various peoples in Africa, Europe, and the Americas, and to have seen the kinds of space explorations which have not, alas, made it clearer to dwellers on the Earth that caring for one's neighbor is not 'other worldly' but an imperative for life, and for living more abundantly."

*BIOGRAPHICAL/CRITICAL SOURCES:*

*PERIODICALS*

*Times Literary Supplement,* January 28, 1972.
*World Literature Today,* spring, 1977.

\*   \*   \*

# FLOURNOY, Valerie (Rose) 1952-

*PERSONAL:* Born April 17, 1952, in Camden, NJ; daughter of Payton I. Flournoy, Sr. (a chief of police), and Ivie Mae (Buchanan) Flournoy; divorced. *Education:* William Smith College, teacher's certificate and B.A., 1974. *Politics:* Independent. *Religion:* Roman Catholic.

*ADDRESSES: Office*—Vis a Vis Publishing, 505 Arch St., Palmyra, NJ 08065.

*CAREER:* Dial Books for Young Readers, New York City, assistant editor, 1977-79; Pocket Books, New York City, senior editor for Silhouette Books, 1979-82; Berkley Publishing Group, New York City, consulting editor for Second Chance at Love, 1982-83; Vis a Vis Publishing Co., Palmyra, NJ, editor in chief, 1985—.

*MEMBER:* Black Women in Publishing, Romance Writers of America.

*AWARDS, HONORS: The Patchwork Quilt* was named an American Library Association Notable Book, 1985; Christopher Award, 1985, for *The Patchwork Quilt;* Ezra Jack Keats New Writer Award, Ezra Jack Keats Foundation and New York Public Library, 1986.

*WRITINGS:*

*CHILDREN'S BOOKS, EXCEPT WHERE NOTED*

*The Best Time of Day,* illustrated by George Ford, Random House, 1978.
*The Twins Strike Back,* illustrated by Diane deGroat, Dial Press, 1980.
*The Patchwork Quilt,* illustrated by Jerry Pinkney, Dial Books for Young Readers, 1985.
*Until Summer's End* (for young adults), Doubleday, 1986.

*WORK IN PROGRESS:* A sequel to *The Patchwork Quilt;* a young-adult novel concerning inner-city kids who, along with their young hosts for the summer, are confronted with a ghostly apparition from the American Revolution who has returned to haunt a Hudson Valley town; a romance novel set on a college campus in New Hampshire.

*SIDELIGHTS:* An author of several books for children, Valerie R. Flournoy is best recognized as the award-winning author of *The Patchwork Quilt.* Released in 1985, her work tells the story of Tanya, a young black girl who is enthralled by her grandmother's sense of dedication in sewing a quilt. When the family matriarch becomes sick, Tanya and her family cooperate to continue the task for her. In addition to recognizing its merit as a story to be delivered orally, Tony Bradman of the *Times Literary Supplement* felt that *The Patchwork Quilt* "is very well written, and manages to convey ... important themes in a totally painless way." Flournoy's words are accompanied by Jerry Pinkney's illustrations, which won the Coretta Scott King Award in 1985.

*BIOGRAPHICAL/CRITICAL SOURCES:*

*PERIODICALS*

*New York Times Book Review,* October 20, 1985, p. 18
*Times Literary Supplement,* August 2, 1985, p. 862.

\*     \*     \*

## FLOYD, Samuel A(lexander), Jr.  1937-

*PERSONAL:* Born February 1, 1937, in Tallahassee, FL; son of Samuel A. and Theora (Combs) Floyd; married Barbara Jean Nealy (a retail manager), 1956; children: Wanda, Cecilia, Samuel A. III. *Education:* Florida Agricultural and Mechanical University, B.S., 1957; Southern Illinois University at Carbondale, M.M.E., 1965, Ph.D., 1969.

*ADDRESSES: Home*—901 South Plymouth Ct., #206, Chicago, IL 60605. *Office*—Center for Black Music Research, Columbia College, 600 South Michigan Ave., Chicago, IL 60605.

*CAREER:* Smith-Brown High School, Arcadia, FL, band director, 1957-62; Florida Agricultural and Mechanical University, Tallahassee, instructor in music and assistant director of bands, 1962-64; Southern Illinois University at Carbondale, 1964-78, began as instructor, became associate professor of music; Fisk University, Nashville, TN, professor of music and director of Institute for Research in Black American Music, 1978-83; Columbia College, Chicago, IL, director of Center for Black Music Research, 1983-90 and 1992, academic dean, 1990-93. Member of advisory panel on the performing arts for Illinois Arts Council, 1977; consultant and panelist for the Southern Regional Conference on the Funding of Research in the Humanities, University of Georgia, 1980. Proposal reviewer for the National Endowment for the Humanities, 1977—, and for the Fund for the Improvement of Post-Secondary Education, 1977. Field interviewer for the Smithsonian Institution's Jazz Oral History Program, 1977. Consultant to the Office for the Advancement of Public Negro Colleges, 1976-77; general consultant to the Fisk University Learning Library Program, 1981-83. Guest lecturer at a number of colleges and universities, including California State University at Los Angeles, 1980, Eastern Illinois University, 1981 and 1982, Blair School of Music at Vanderbilt University, 1982, Morgan State University, 1982 and 1983, University of Michigan, 1985, Purdue University, 1988, and University of Mississippi, 1987 and 1989; Ford Foundation Visiting Lecturer, Center for the Study of Southern Culture, University of Mississippi, 1989. Member of board of directors of Southern Illinois University Employees Credit Union, 1975-77, Nashville

Institute for the Arts, 1979-82, John W. Work Foundation, 1979-83, and member of City/Arts Panel for Chicago Office of Fine Arts, 1986—.

*MEMBER:* College Music Society (national council member, 1978-80), Sonneck Society, American Musicological Society, Pi Kappa Lambda.

*AWARDS, HONORS:* Southern Illinois University research grants, 1970-77; Newbery Library grants, 1972 and 1979; National Endowment for the Humanities research grants, 1976 and 1980; National Endowment for the Humanities grants, 1976, 1980, 1985, and 1987; National Endowment for the Arts grants, 1976 and 1989; Illinois Arts Council grant, 1976; Carbondale Bicentennial Committee grant, 1976; Justin and Valere Potter Foundation grant, 1979; Tennessee Arts Commission grant, 1979; National Endowment for the Humanities Summer Seminar for College Teachers grants, 1985 and 1990; Lloyd A. Fry Foundation grants, 1985, 1986, 1987, and 1988; Distinguished Contributions to Music Award, National Association of Negro Musicians, 1986; Borg-Warner Foundation grants, 1987 and 1988; Institute for the Humanities fellow, University of Michigan, 1988 and 1989; Robert R. McCormick Charitable Trust grant, 1988-90; Sara Lee Foundation grant, 1989; Arie and Ida Crown Foundation grant, 1989; Ruth Allen Fouche Heritage of Black Music Award, Chicago Park District, 1989, for outstanding contributions to the black cultural arts and music; Young Executives in Politics Award, Chicago, IL, 1989, for outstanding achievement in fine arts; Joyce Foundation grant, 1990; Irving Lowens Award for distinguished scholarship in American music, 1991; National Humanities Center fellow, 1992.

*WRITINGS:*

*Ninety-Nine Street Beats, Cadences, and Exercises for Percussion,* Hansen Publishing, 1961.
*One Hundred One Street Beats, Cadences, and Exercises for Percussion,* Hansen Publishing, 1965.
*Contemporary Exercises and Cadences for Marching Percussion,* University of Miami Music Publications, 1975.
(Editor) *The Great Lakes Experience: An Oral History,* Southern Illinois University, 1977.
(With Marsha J. Reisser) *Black Music in the United States: An Annotated Bibliography of Selected Reference and Research Sources,* Kraus International, 1983.
*Black Music Biography: An Annotated Bibliography,* Kraus International, 1987.
*Black Music in the Harlem Renaissance,* Greenwood Press, 1990.

Editor of *Black Music Research Newsletter,* 1977—, and *Black Music Research Journal,* 1980—; member of editorial board of *Black Perspective in Music,* 1979—, and *American Mu-*

*sic,* 1984—. Contributor to journals, including *Illinois Music Education, Music and Man, School Musician, Chronicle of Higher Education, Black Music Research Journal, Black Perspective in Music,* and *Music Educator's Journal.*

*WORK IN PROGRESS: The Power of Black Music* for Oxford University Press.

*SIDELIGHTS:* Samuel A. Floyd, Jr., commented: "My concerns are with stimulating research activity in the field of black music and the encouragement of its eventual inclusion in mainstream writing. The academic writers who have had the most influence on my work are philosopher and scholar John Dewey—especially through his *Art and Experience*—and Harvard professor Eileen Southern, author of *The Music of Black Americans* and other works. Dewey's concepts of history, continuity, and art guide my aesthetic, historical, and literary thinking; Southern's works stand as exemplars of impeccable scholarship and stimulate my scholarly activity."

\*   \*   \*

## FORREST, Leon 1937-

*PERSONAL:* Born January 8, 1937, in Chicago, IL; son of a bartender; married Marianne Duncan, September 25, 1971. *Education:* Attended Wilson Junior College, 1955-56, Roosevelt University, 1957-58, and University of Chicago, 1958-60 and 1962-64.

*ADDRESSES: Office*—Department of African American Studies, Northwestern University, Arthur Andersen Hall, 2003 Sheridan Rd., Evanston, IL 60208.

*CAREER: Woodlawn Observer,* managing editor, 1967-69; *Muhammed Speaks* (newspaper), associate director, 1969-71, managing editor, 1971-73; Northwestern University, Evanston, IL, associate professor, 1973-84, professor of African American studies, 1984—, chair of department, 1985—. Lecturer at Yale University, Rochester Institute of Technology, and Wesleyan University, 1974-79. *Military service:* U.S. Army, 1960-62.

*MEMBER:* Authors Guild, Society of Midland Authors (president, 1981).

*AWARDS, HONORS:* Grant from Northwestern University, 1975; Sandburg Medallion, Chicago Public Library, 1978; "Leon Forrest Day" celebrated in his honor in Chicago, 1985; Friends of the Chicago Public Library Carl Sandburg Award, 1985, and Society of Midland Authors Award, 1986, both for *Two Wings to Veil My Face.*

*WRITINGS:*

*There Is a Tree More Ancient Than Eden* (novel), introduction by Ralph Ellison, Random House, 1973, revised edition, Another Chicago Press, 1988.
*The Bloodworth Orphans* (novel), Random House, 1977, revised edition, introduction by John G. Cawelti, Another Chicago Press, 1987.
(Author of libretto) *Re-Creation* (musical drama; music by T. J. Anderson), produced in Chicago, IL, 1978.
(Author of libretto) *Soldier Boy, Soldier* (musical drama; music by Anderson), produced in Bloomington, IN, 1982.
*Two Wings to Veil My Face* (novel), Random House, 1983.
*Divine Days* (novel), Another Chicago Press, 1992.
*The Furious Voice for Freedom,* introduction by Willie Morris, Moyer Bell, 1992.

Contributor to periodicals, including *Callaloo, Iowa Review, Massachusetts Review, New York Times Book Review, Story Quarterly,* and *TriQuarterly.*

*SIDELIGHTS:* Leon Forrest's novels reveal his debts to the oral traditions of storytellers and songwriters and the literary traditions of writers such as James Joyce, William Faulkner, and Ralph Ellison. "Like Joyce, like Faulkner, like Ellison, Forrest focuses on a particular people in a particular time and place, and in telling their story, touches universal themes that speak to us all," writes Bernard Rodgers in the *Chicago Tribune Book World.* Like these authors too, Forrest employs a stream-of-consciousness style, and his novels are interrelated through reappearing characters and structural and stylistic similarities. Of his first three, *There Is a Tree More Ancient Than Eden* and *Two Wings to Veil My Face* received the most critical attention.

*There Is a Tree More Ancient Than Eden* is about the complex relationships between the illegitimate children of an old family who once owned slaves. The book "represents an awe-inspiring fusion of American cultural myth, Black American history, Black fundamentalist religion, the doctrine and dogma of Catholicism (stations of the Cross and the Precious Blood Cathedral), and an autobiographical recall of days of anxiety and confusion in the city," writes Houston A. Baker, Jr., in *Black World.* Another *Black World* reviewer, Jack Gilbert, notes that "Forrest has woven an hypnotic fabric with words that are part jazz, part blues, part gospel" and, likening the work to Ralph Ellison's *Invisible Man,* describes it as equally "moving and forceful in its poetic flow."

Other critics, noting the novel's stream-of-consciousness style and impending sense of doom, compare the work to Faulkner's writing. *Harvard Advocate* contributor Joel Motley calls the book "a powerful work of literature" and adds that while Forrest does use a Faulknerian style, he makes it into his own to express the "urban black experience." Baker concludes that *There Is a Tree More Ancient Than Eden* "contains insight, streaks of brilliance, and a finely-formed intelligence that promises further revelations."

In *Two Wings to Veil My Face* Nathaniel Witherspoon, a character from Forrest's first novel, records the life story of Momma Sweetie Reed, a former slave. "As she tells her story, Nathaniel is forced to redefine his own identity, to translate as well as transcribe the meaning of her memories," writes Rodgers. "In the end, the secrets Great-Momma Sweetie reveals to Nathaniel ... radically alter both their lives."

*New York Times Book Review* contributor Benjamin DeMott observes that while the novel is at times overwritten and poorly structured, these "defects somehow fail to sink it." He explains: "The reason lies in the quality and complication of the feelings breathing in Sweetie Reed as she labors to teach young black generations the uses of the souls of black folk." Rodgers concludes: "It is a novel ... that's not for everyone. Just for those who love the excitement of watching a truly unique writer practice his art; for those who can recognize the magic beneath the mundane, as Forrest does; for those who are willing to accept the challenge of a novel that really is extraordinary and unforgettable."

Forrest's fourth novel, *Divine Days,* seemed a potential "capstone" to his career to Chicago *Tribune Books* reviewer Joseph Coates. The volume is structured as the week-long journal of fictional playwright Joubert Jones, who is investigating various mythic figures from his past for material for his writing. According to Coates, the eleven-hundred-page novel manages to invoke all of black American history, from slavery to the civil rights movement, through the colorful speeches of the characters Jones meets. The critic found *Divine Days* a "wonderfully entertaining" as well as vivid and atmospheric novel by a "writer of immense talent."

*BIOGRAPHICAL/CRITICAL SOURCES:*

*BOOKS*

*Contemporary Authors Autobiography Series,* Volume 7, Gale, 1988.
*Contemporary Literary Criticism,* Volume 4, Gale, 1975.
*Dictionary of Literary Biography,* Volume 33: *Afro-American Fiction Writers after 1955,* Gale, 1984.
Lee, A. Robert, *Black Fiction: New Studies in the Afro-American Novel since 1945,* Barnes & Noble, 1980.

*PERIODICALS*

*Black World,* January, 1974.
*Chicago Tribune Book World,* February 5, 1984.
*College Language Association Journal,* December, 1978.
*Harvard Advocate,* Volume 107, number 4, 1974.
*Massachusetts Review,* winter, 1977.
*New Leader,* July 9, 1973.
*New York Times,* June 8, 1973.
*New York Times Book Review,* May 1, 1977; February 26, 1984.
*Tribune Books* (Chicago), August 2, 1992, p. 3.
*Village Voice,* October 3, 1989, p. 54.

\*    \*    \*

## FRANKLIN, John Hope   1915-

*PERSONAL:* Born January 2, 1915, in Rentiesville, OK; son of Buck Colbert (an attorney; also the first Negro judge to sit in chancery in Oklahoma district court) and Mollie (Parker) Franklin; married Aurelia E. Whittington, June 11, 1940; children: John Whittington. *Education:* Fisk University, A.B., 1935; Harvard University, A.M., 1936, Ph.D., 1941. *Avocational interests:* Fishing, growing orchids.

*ADDRESSES: Home*—208 Pineview Rd., Durham, NC 27707. *Office*—Department of History, Duke University, Durham, NC 27708.

*CAREER:* Fisk University, Nashville, TN, instructor in history, 1936-37; St. Augustine's College, Raleigh, NC, instructor in history, 1938-43; North Carolina College (now North Carolina Central University), Durham, instructor in history, 1943-47; Howard University, Washington, DC, professor of history, 1947-56; Brooklyn College of the City University of New York, Brooklyn, professor of history and chairman of department, 1956-64; University of Chicago, Chicago, IL, professor of history, 1964-82, John Matthews Manly Distinguished Service Professor, 1969-82, chairman of history department, 1967-70; Duke University, Durham, James B. Duke Professor of History, 1982-85, professor emeritus, 1985—. Visiting professor at University of California, Harvard University, University of Wisconsin, Cornell University, University of Hawaii, Australia National University, Salzburg (Austria) Seminar, and other institutions; Pitt Professor of American History and Institutions, Cambridge University, 1962-63. Board of Foreign Scholarships, member, 1962-69, chairman, 1966-69. Member of board of trustees, Fisk University, 1947-84, and De Sable Museum, Chicago.

*MEMBER:* American Historical Association (member of executive council, 1959-62; president, 1979), Organization of American Historians (president, 1975), Association for Study of Negro Life and History, NAACP (member of board of directors, Legal Defense and Education Fund), American Association of University Professors, American Philosophical Society, American Studies Association, Southern Historical Association (life member; president, 1970), Phi Beta Kappa (president, 1973-76), Phi Alpha Theta.

*AWARDS, HONORS:* Guggenheim fellowships, 1950-51, 1973-74; Jules F. Landry Award, 1975, for *A Southern Odyssey;* Clarence L. Holte Literary Award, 1986, for *George Washington Williams: A Biography.* Honorary degrees from numerous institutions, including LL.D. from Morgan State University, 1960, Lincoln University, 1961, Virginia State College, 1961, Hamline University, 1965, Lincoln College, 1965, Fisk University, 1965, Columbia University, 1969, University of Notre Dame, 1970, and Harvard University, 1981; A.M., Cambridge University, 1962; L.H.D., Long Island University, 1964, University of Massachusetts, 1964, and Yale University, 1977; Litt.D., Princeton University, 1972.

*WRITINGS:*

*The Free Negro in North Carolina,* 1790-1860, University of North Carolina Press, 1943, reprinted, Russell, 1969, Norton, 1971.

*From Slavery to Freedom: A History of Negro Americans,* Knopf, 1947, sixth edition (with Alfred A. Moss, Jr.), 1987.

*The Militant South, 1800-1860,* Belknap Press, 1956, revised edition, 1970.

*Reconstruction after the Civil War,* University of Chicago Press, 1962.

*The Emancipation Proclamation,* Doubleday, 1963.

(With John W. Caughey and Ernest R. May) *Land of the Free: A History of the United States,* Benziger, 1965, teacher's edition, 1971.

(With the editors of Time-Life Books) *Illustrated History of Black Americans,* Time-Life, 1970.

*Racial Equality in America,* University of Chicago Press, 1976.

*A Southern Odyssey: Travelers in the Antebellum North,* Louisiana State University Press, 1976.

*George Washington Williams: A Biography,* University of Chicago Press, 1985, (paper) 1987.

*Race & History: Selected Essays, 1938-1988,* Louisiana State University Press, 1990, 1992.

*The Color Line: Legacy for the Twenty-first Century,* University of Missouri Press, 1993.

*EDITOR*

*The Civil War Diary of J. T. Ayers,* Illinois State Historical Society, 1947.

Albion Tourgee, *A Fool's Errand,* Belknap Press, 1961.

T. W. Higginson, *Army Life in a Black Regiment,* Beacon Press, 1962.

*Three Negro Classics,* Avon, 1965.

(With Isadore Starr) *The Negro in Twentieth Century America: A Reader on the Struggle for Civil Rights,* Vintage Books, 1967.

*Color and Race,* Houghton, 1968.

W.E.B. Du Bois, *The Suppression of the African Slave Trade,* Louisiana State University Press, 1969.

John R. Lynch, *Reminiscences of an Active Life: The Autobiography of John R. Lynch,* University of Chicago Press, 1970.

(With August Meier) *Black Leaders of the Twentieth Century,* University of Illinois Press, 1982.

*CONTRIBUTOR*

Arthur S. Link and Richard Leopold, editors, *Problems in American History,* Prentice-Hall, 1952, second revised edition, 1966.

Rayford W. Logan, editor, *The Negro Thirty Years Afterward,* Howard University Press, 1955.

*The Americans: Ways of Life and Thought,* Cohen & West, 1956.

Charles Frankel, editor, *Issues in University Education,* Harper, 1959.

Ralph Newman, editor, *Lincoln for the Ages,* Doubleday, 1960.

Charles G. Sellars, Jr., editor, *The Southerner as American,* University of North Carolina Press, 1960.

Abraham Seldin Eisenstadt, editor, *American History: Recent Interpretations,* Crowell, 1962.

Herbert Hill, editor, *Soon One Morning,* Knopf, 1963.

H. V. Hodson, editor, *The Atlantic Future,* Longmans, Green, 1964.

John C. McKinney and Edgar T. Thompson, editors, *The South in Continuity and Change,* Duke University Press, 1965.

John P. Davis, editor, *The American Negro Reference Book,* Prentice-Hall, 1966.

Harold Hyman, editor, *New Frontiers of the American Reconstruction,* University of Illinois Press, 1966.

Kenneth Clark and Talcott Parsons, editors, *The Negro American,* Houghton, 1966.

Daniel J. Boorstin, editor, *The American Primer,* University of Chicago Press, 1966.

C. Vann Woodward, editor, *The Comparative Approach to American History,* Basic Books, 1968.

William Edward Farrison, editor, *William Wells Brown: Author and Reformer,* University of Chicago Press, 1969.

Marcia M. Mathews, *Henry Ossawa Tanner, American Artist,* University of Chicago Press, 1969.

Michael S. Harper, editor, *Chant of Saints,* University of Illinois Press, 1979.

William H. Burns, *The Voices of Negro Protest in America,* Greenwood, 1980.

Robert L. Payton, *A Melting Pot or a Nation of Minorities,* University of Texas Press, 1986.

Sidney Kaplan, Allan Austin, *American Studies in Black and White: Selected Essays, 1949-1989,* University of Massachusetts, 1991.

Eric C. Lincoln, *This Road to Freedom,* Carolina Wren Press, 1990.

Herbert Aptheker, *To Be Free,* Carol Publishing, 1992.

Also contributor to Crusade for Justice: The Autobiography of Ida B. Wells, edited by Alfreda M. Duster, 1970.

*OTHER*

Author of foreword, Scott Ellsworth, *Death in a Promised Land,* Louisiana State University Press, 1992.

Also author of pamphlets for U.S. Information Service and Anti-Defamation League of B'nai B'rith. Contributor of articles to numerous journals and periodicals. Co-editor of series in American history for Crowell and AHM Publishing, 1964—; general editor of "Zenith Book" series on secondary education, Doubleday, 1965; general editor of "Negro American Biographies and Autobiographies" series, University of Chicago Press, 1969; editor, with Eisenstadt, of "American History Series," Harlan Davidson, Inc., 1985—. Contributor of articles to numerous journals and periodicals.

*WORK IN PROGRESS:* A book on runaway slaves; a collection of essays; editing the autobiography of his father, Buck Colbert Franklin.

*SIDELIGHTS:* Author of the critically acclaimed *George Washington Williams: A Biography,* John Hope Franklin "has long been a leader in the study of Afro-American life," writes Ira Berlin in the *New York Times Book Review.* For over four decades, the distinguished Franklin has pioneered a number of historical studies; included among his books are *Reconstruction after the Civil War, The Emancipation Proclamation,* and *Racial Equality in America,* an examination of the egalitarian principles of America's founding fathers. Furthermore, his general history entitled *From Slavery to Freedom: A History of Negro Americans*—its sixth edition published in 1987—is considered by many to be the standard text on Afro-American history. Franklin's overall contributions to the field of

Afro-American history prompted Roy Wilkins in the *New Republic* to remark: "John Hope Franklin is an uncommon historian who has consistently corrected in eloquent language the misrecording of this country's rich heritage."

In 1985, Franklin won recognition for *George Washington Williams: A Biography,* which represents forty years of Franklin's research into the life and achievements of the nineteenth century black historian. "Beginning in 1945 with less than a dozen letters and a hasty reading of Williams' African diary, which has since disappeared," remarks Louis R. Harlan in the *Washington Post Book World,* "Franklin has painstakingly gathered the pieces of evidence from three continents and, like an archaeologist, reconstructed a mosaic that is astonishingly life-like." Soldier, journalist, public speaker, historian—among other roles—the multi-faceted Williams was the author in 1883 of *History of the Negro Race in America from 1619 to 1880,* a two-volume history which represents one of the first scholarly treatments of the black experience in America. "Williams's sources and methods qualify him as a pioneer in the transformation of American historical scholarship from panegyrics to professionalism," Berlin states. "One of the most significant achievements of Mr. Franklin's biography is that it restores Williams to his proper place in the development of an American historiography." Robert A. Hill likewise praises Franklin's illuminating assessment of Williams's achievements: "On the basis of the evidence here presented, it becomes clear that Williams is entitled, by his virtuosity, erudition, and contribution to the fields of history and African protest, to a place among the most notable public figures of America's Gilded Age, and this in an era truly rich in its profusion of outstanding personalities."

An aspect of *George Washington Williams* that reviewers found particularly interesting was the insight offered into Franklin's own life as an Afro-American historian. "Stalking George Washington Williams," the title of the book's opening chapter, "offers a unique view of the historian as detective as well as scholar," notes Berlin: "Beginning in 1945 when the author—who had never taken a course in Afro-American history—first considered writing a general history of black Americans, he sensed the connection between his own pioneering work and that of Williams. Through the next four decades he stalked his subject from Williams's origins in a small Pennsylvania town, across North America, to Mexico, to Europe, to central Africa, to Egypt and finally to England where Williams died. 'George Washington Williams' is thus part autobiography and part general history—a mixture that makes for fascinating and engaging reading." James Olney similarly comments in the *Southern Review:* "The major interest of the book is that the life of John Hope Franklin, is fully present in the (re)creation of the life of George Washington Williams, his predecessor, his forefather, perhaps his alter ego."

In 1975, thirty years into his study of Williams, Franklin discovered that the historian's burial place was an unmarked grave in a cemetery near the center of Blackpool, England. Accompanied by his wife, two reporters, and a photographer, Franklin laid a wreath at the site—now marked by a tablet that reads, "George Washington Williams, Afro-American Historian, 1849-1891." Onley draws a comparison to author Alice Walker's discovery of the unmarked grave of author Zora Neale Hurston, commenting on the particular importance of Franklin's work in Afro-American history: "Just as Afro-American literary history is a matter of recovering predecessors, of reviving and revising, of crossing and combining ancestral figures, so also Afro-American history, in the person and present moment of John Hope Franklin, devotes itself to recovering and resuscitating the ancestral past and to rescuing its own particular progenitors and predecessors from the obscurity that has been so often their fate in this country."

Franklin, however, didn't see himself as solely an Afro-American historian. In an interview by Mark McGurl, in the *New York Times Book Review,* Franklin said, "It's often assumed I'm a scholar of Afro-American history, but the fact is I haven't taught a course in Afro-American history in 30-some-odd years. They say I'm the author of 12 books on black history, when several of those books focus mainly on whites." In a review of his book, *Race and History: Selected Essays, 1938-1988,* in the *Washington Post Book World,* Franklin supported this notion again. "Very early," he said, "I learned that scholarship knows no national boundaries." According to Drew Gilpin Faust in the *New York Times Book Review,* "[Franklin] insists on the importance of maintaining the boundary between advocacy and scholarship. Historical work, with its established standards for evaluation of evidence, must not be 'polluted by passion'; we must not simply turn the past into a mirror of our own present-day concerns." Faust contends that Franklin's "life and work represent a commitment to learning as an important way to 'bear witness' in a society that he, perhaps better than any American scholar alive today, knows to be far from perfect."

*BIOGRAPHICAL/CRITICAL SOURCES:*

*BOOKS*

Franklin, John Hope, *George Washington Williams: A Biography,* University of Chicago Press, 1985.

*PERIODICALS*

*America,* May 12, 1990.
*American Historical Review,* April, 1962.
*Black Scholar,* Summer, 1989.

*Chicago Tribune Book World,* November 24, 1985.
*Christian Science Monitor,* September 22, 1947; February 7, 1990.
*Commonweal,* July 16, 1943; October 31, 1947; March 8, 1963.
*Ebony,* February, 1990; November, 1990.
*Journal of American History,* September, 1986; June, 1988; September, 1990.
*New Republic,* January 22, 1977; April 30, 1990.
*New York Herald Tribune Book Review,* December 14, 1947; September 23, 1956.
*New York Times,* October 12, 1947; September 23, 1956.
*New York Times Book Review,* April 7, 1963; December 10, 1967; November 17, 1985; June 3, 1990.
*Publishers Weekly,* December 22, 1989.
*Reviews in American History,* December, 1990.
*Saturday Review,* December 22, 1956.
*Saturday Review of Literature,* June 19, 1943; November 8, 1947.
*Southern Review,* spring, 1986.
*Times Literary Supplement,* July 19, 1963.
*U.S. News & World Report,* September 17, 1990.
*Washington Post Book World,* January 11, 1986; May 25, 1986; October 21, 1990.
*Yale Review,* winter, 1957.

\*    \*    \*

## FRYE, Charles A(nthony)  1946-

*PERSONAL:* Born March 18, 1946, in Washington, DC; divorced; children: Odeyo J., Sekou C., Anthony F., Lia M. *Education:* Howard University, B.A., 1968, M.A., 1970; University of Pittsburgh, Ph.D., 1976.

*ADDRESSES: Office*—Office of the Associate Dean of Students, Hampshire College, Enfield House, Amherst, MA 01002.

*CAREER:* Washington, DC, Public Library, librarian, 1968-69; Washington, DC, Public Schools, teacher, 1969-70; Howard University, Washington, DC, assistant professor, 1970-77; Fayetteville State University, director of interdisciplinary studies, 1977-78; Hampshire College, associate dean of students and associate professor of education, c. 1978—. Five College Black Studies Executive Committee, chair and journal editor, 1983-85.

*MEMBER:* National Council for Black Studies (chair and editor of council journal, 1980-82, and member of board of directors), Association for Supervision and Curriculum Development.

*AWARDS, HONORS:* Advanced Study Fellowship, Ford Foundation, 1972-73.

*WRITINGS:*

*The Impact of Black Studies on the Curricula of Three Universities,* University Press of America, 1976.

*Towards a Philosophy of Black Studies,* R & E Research Associates, 1978.

(Editor) *Level Three: A Black Philosophy Reader,* University Press of America, 1980.

(Editor) *Values in Conflict: Blacks and the American Ambivalence Toward Violence,* University Press of America, 1980.

*From Egypt to Don Juan: The Anatomy of Black Philosophy,* preface by August Coppola, University Press of America, 1988.

*The Peter Pan Chronicles* (novella), University Press of Virginia, 1989.

Contributor of reviews to *Journal of Negro History.*

*SIDELIGHTS:* A glance at Charles Frye's publications reveals his varied interests and areas of expertise. His first three books—*The Impact of Black Studies on the Curricula of Three Universities, Towards a Philosophy of Black Studies,* and *Level Three: A Black Philosophy Reader*—reflect his graduate training in both philosophy and higher education. Another of Frye's concerns is evident in his fourth text, *Blacks and the American Ambivalence Toward Violence,* which not only addresses the contemporary phenomenon of violence but also examines social values as they relate to African Americans. His fifth text, *From Egypt to Don Juan,* treats similar themes of blacks, race identity, and philosophy.

Though his mode of presentation for his sixth book, *The Peter Pan Chronicles,* shifts from analytic to creative writing, his thematic concern with contemporary black issues remains constant. The story is told through the unreliable eyes of a black patient in an insane asylum, Raynard Parker. Parker was once assigned to sabotage the efforts of black civil rights activists in the 1960s, especially those of his friend Tommy Rollins, who Parker betrayed to government authorities. Unable to deal with the guilt of his actions, Parker suffers from severe time and space disorientation. Throughout the book he transforms figures in the asylum into people from his past, yielding a disjointed recreation of his activities in the 1960s.

Some reviewers of *The Peter Pan Chronicles* complained that they found it difficult to derive meaning from the novel's unorthodox narration. Others, however, found it a refreshing deviance from traditional fictional conventions. Charles C. Nash, writing in *Library Journal,* felt that Frye's technique resulted in a "brilliant collage of images" and that the book

presented a terrifying yet convincing portrait of blacks in the United States.

*BIOGRAPHICAL/CRITICAL SOURCES:*

*PERIODICALS*

*Library Journal,* June 15, 1989.
*Publishers Weekly,* June 2, 1989, p. 78.

\*   \*   \*

## FULLER, Charles (Henry, Jr.)   1939-

*PERSONAL:* Born March 5, 1939, in Philadelphia, PA; son of Charles H. (a printer) and Lillian (Anderson) Fuller. *Education:* Attended Villanova University, 1956-58; La Salle College, B.A., 1967.

*ADDRESSES: Agent*—Esther Sherman, William Morris Agency, 1350 Avenue of the Americas, New York, NY 10019.

*CAREER:* Playwright. Cofounder and codirector of Afro-American Arts Theatre, 1967-71; writer and director of "The Black Experience," WIP-Radio, 1970-71; Temple University, Philadelphia, PA, professor of African American studies, 1988—. Lecturer.

*MEMBER:* Dramatists Guild, PEN, Writers Guild East.

*AWARDS, HONORS:* Creative Artist Public Service Award, 1974; Rockefeller Foundation fellow, 1975; National Endowment for the Arts fellow, 1976; Guggenheim fellow, 1977-78; Obie Award from *Village Voice,* 1981, for *Zooman and the Sign;* Audelco Award for best writing, 1981, for *Zooman and the Sign;* Pulitzer Prize in drama, New York Drama Critics award for best American play, Audelco Award for best play, Theatre Club Award for best play, and Outer Circle Critics award for best off-Broadway play, all 1982, all for *A Soldier's Play;* Doctor of Fine Arts (D.F.A.) from La Salle College, 1982, and Villanova University, 1983; Hazelitt Award from Pennsylvania State Council on the Arts, 1984; D.F.A. from Chestnut Hill College, 1984; Academy Award nomination for best screenplay for *A Soldier's Story,* 1985.

*WRITINGS:*

*PLAYS*

*The Village: A Party* (two-act), produced in Princeton, NJ, at McCarter Theatre, 1968, produced as *The Perfect Party,* in New York City at Tambellini's Gate Theatre, 1969.

*In My Many Names and Days* (six one-acts), produced in New York City at Henry Street Settlement, 1972.

*The Candidate* (three-act), produced at Henry Street Settlement, 1974.

*In the Deepest Part of Sleep* (two-act), produced in New York City at St. Marks Playhouse, 1974.

*First Love* (one-act), produced in New York City at Billie Holiday Theatre, 1974.

*The Lay Out Letter* (one-act), produced in Philadelphia, PA, at Freedom Theatre, 1975.

*The Brownsville Raid* (three-act), produced in New York City at the Negro Ensemble Company, 1976.

*Sparrow in Flight* (two-act), produced in New York City at the AMAS Repertory Theatre, 1978.

*Zooman and the Sign* (two-act; produced at the Negro Ensemble Company, 1979), Samuel French, 1981.

*A Soldier's Play* (two-act; produced at the Negro Ensemble Company, 1981), Samuel French, 1982.

*"WE" SERIES; PLAYS*

*Sally,* produced in Atlanta, GA, 1988; produced at the Negro Ensemble Company, 1988.

*Prince,* produced at the Negro Ensemble Company, 1988.

*Jonquil,* produced in New York City at Theater Four, 1990.

*Burner's Folic,* produced at Theater Four, 1990.

*SCREENPLAYS*

*A Soldier's Story* (adapted from the stageplay *A Soldier's Play*), Columbia Pictures, 1984.

*Paying Up,* Paramount, 1993.

*TELEPLAYS*

*Roots, Resistance, and Renaissance* (twelve-week series), WHYY-TV (Philadelphia), 1967.

*The Sky is Gray* ("American Short Story Series"), [New York], 1980.

*A Gathering of Old Men,* CBS-TV, 1987.

*OTHER*

Contributor of short stories to anthologies and periodicals, including *Black Dialogue* and *Liberator.* Also contributor of nonfiction to periodicals, including *Liberator, Negro Digest,* and *Philly Talk.*

WORK IN PROGRESS: A fifth and final play in the "We" series; new plays, *One Night...,* and *Africa,* 1993.

SIDELIGHTS: Charles Fuller is, according to Walter Kerr in the *New York Times,* "one of the contemporary American theater's most forceful and original voices." In his plays Fuller explores human relationships, particularly between blacks and whites, in what many critics find realistic, unbiased, and poignant terms. "He's not tendentious; the work isn't agitprop or anything near it," Kerr continued. "Mr. Fuller isn't really interested in special pleading, but in simply and directly—and cuttingly—observing what really does go on in this world of ours after you've brushed the stereotypes away."

Fuller first gained notice as a playwright with Princeton's McCarter Theatre production of *The Village: A Party.* The "village" is a community comprised of racially-mixed couples. Life is peaceful in the protective society until its black leader falls in love with a black woman. Fearing their image will suffer from their leader's action, the other couples murder the defector and insist that his white widow marry a black man, thus perpetuating their tradition. Fuller examines integration through his play and intimates that integration often magnifies racial tension.

"Mr. Fuller has written a not-too-fanciful fantasy about racial integration that somberly concludes that it will not at present solve anybody's racial problems," wrote Dan Sullivan in a *New York Times* review of *The Village.* "The play's originality and urgency are unquestionable and so is the talent of the playwright." A later production of *The Village,* presented as *The Perfect Party,* moved critic Lawrence Van Gelder, also writing in the *New York Times,* to applaud Fuller's "smooth, natural dialogue and deft characterization."

Another of Fuller's plays, *The Brownsville Raid,* was based on a true incident that occurred in 1906 when an entire U.S. Army regiment was dishonorably discharged because none of the 167 black soldiers comprising the unit would confess to inciting a riot in Brownsville, Texas. Witnesses of the attack gave conflicting accounts of what happened, and no evidence was supplied to indict the men, but nevertheless they were released from service. Sixty-six years later the Army cleared the men's records, calling their discharge "a gross injustice." "Though it is Fuller's intention to condemn this incident for the disgrace it was," noted Martin Gottfried in the *New York Post,* "his play is no mere tract. His white characters are not caricatures, his black soldiers are not made to be aware ahead of their times." Gottfried found the play "engrossing, unusual, and strong," while the *Village Voice* critic Julius Novick thought the story "a bit dull," but nevertheless deemed *The Brownsville Raid* "scrupulous dramatically as well as ideologically," and "clear" and "methodical."

With his play *Zooman and the Sign,* Fuller won an Obie and proved to critic Gerald Weales, writing in the *Georgia Review,* that he is "an obviously talented playwright, ambitious in his attempt to deal with difficult and complex themes." *Zooman* is set in a decaying neighborhood in Philadelphia where a young girl was shot to death while playing jacks on her front porch. The child is dead when the play opens, but the grief of her family, the ambivalence of her neighbors, and the cocky, self-justifying attitude of her teenaged murderer are demonstrated as the play progresses. "The play never quite succeeds in the ambitious terms in which it is conceived," Weales opined, "but its aspirations and its incidental strengths make it far more fascinating than many a neater, smaller play." In the *Los Angeles Times,* critic Don Shirley deemed *Zooman* "a rarity. Its story is simply but not simplistically told, and it examines vital urban issues with urgency but without hysteria."

In 1982 Fuller became the second black playwright to win the Pulitzer Prize for drama. His prizewinning *A Soldier's Play,* is set at an army base in Louisiana during World War II. The drama opens with the murder of black Technical Sergeant Vernon Waters, a tough and wrathful man who may have been killed by any one of several people or groups. For instance, Waters refused to play Uncle Tom to his white military superiors or to the white Southern community and the Ku Klux Klan surrounding the base, thus an angry Caucasian individual or group may have been responsible. But Waters was also viewed with disdain by some members of his own race; he often degraded his recruits, calling them "shiftless, lazy niggers" and other derogatory names, and chastised them for making their race look like "fools" to whites; therefore the murderer might be one of his black subordinates. Following Waters's murder, the army sends an officer to investigate, an act that is more intended to appease the other black military men than to bring about justice.

To the surprise of the white officers at Fort Neal, the investigating official who arrives is Captain Richard Davenport, the first black officer they have ever seen. As Davenport questions possible suspects, Waters's psychotic self-hatred and the damaging effects of racism on his life are revealed, as well as new episodes of racism as a result of Davenport's presence. "Here, as before," wrote Frank Rich in the *New York Times,* "the playwright has a compassion for blacks who might be driven to murder their brothers—because he sees them as victims of a world they haven't made." "Yet he doesn't let anyone off the hook," Rich continued. "Mr. Fuller demands that his black characters find the courage to break out of their suicidal, fratricidal cycle—just as he demands that whites end the injustices that have locked his black characters into the nightmare." In another *New York Times* piece on the drama, Rich wrote: "*A Soldier's Play* seems to me a rock-solid piece of architecture, briskly and economically peopled by dimensional blacks, whites, and psychological misfits caught between. The work is tough, taut and fully realized." Walter Kerr suggested in the *New York Times,* "You should make Mr. Fuller's acquaintance. Now."

Fuller eventually adapted *A Soldier's Play* into the film *A Soldier's Story,* which enjoyed substantial acclaim following

its 1984 release. Among his other noteworthy works are the plays comprising the "We" series, which presents the history of American blacks in the second half of the nineteenth century. *Sally,* the first of the series, centers on the title character, a slave who has recently been freed and who has an unsuccessful affair with Prince, an ex-slave who has become a Union soldier in the first black regiment. The second play in the series, *Prince,* examines the plight of the freed slaves, who are paid low wages to perform the same work and live in much the same style as slaves before the Civil War. *Jonquil,* features the title character of Sally from the first play in the series. Sally is raped by a member of the Ku Klux Klan, whose identity is discovered to be an esteemed judge in the community by a blind girl, Jonquil, who recognizes his voice. In the fourth play, *Burner's Frolic,* a black businessman living in Virginia in 1876 plans to run for political office and must face an opponent who is a corrupt and hateful white supremacist. Although some critics found the "We" series plays disjointed and difficult to follow, Mel Gussow in the *New York Times,* asserted that in the plays Fuller "is scrutinizing the economic entrapment of people forced to weight their pragmatic needs against their desire for complete emancipation and integration."

*BIOGRAPHICAL/CRITICAL SOURCES:*

*BOOKS*

*American Voices: Five Contemporary Playwrights in Essays and Interviews,* McFarland, 1988.
*Creating Theater: The Professionals' Approach to New Plays,* Vintage Books, 1986.
*Contemporary Literary Criticism,* Volume 25, Gale, 1983.
*Dictionary of Literary Biography,* Volume 38: *Afro-American Writers After 1955: Dramatists and Prose Writers,* Gale, 1985.
*In Their Own Words: Contemporary American Playwrights,* Theatre Communications, 1988.
*Totem Voices: Plays from the Black World Repertory,* Grove Press, 1989.
*Visions of a Liberated Future: Black Arts Movement Writings,* Thunder's Mouth Press, 1989.

*PERIODICALS*

*Black American Literature Forum,* summer, 1983.
*Clues: A Journal of Detection,* fall-winter 1986; spring-summer, 1991.
*Georgia Review,* fall, 1981.
*Los Angeles Times,* August 15, 1982; July 23, 1983; November 6, 1983.
*Nation,* January 23, 1982.
*New Leader,* July 12-26, 1982.
*Newsweek,* December 21, 1981.

*New York,* January 9, 1989.

*New Yorker,* December 20, 1976; January 9, 1989; January 29, 1990; March 19, 1990.

*New York Post,* December 6, 1976.

*New York Times,* November 13, 1968; March 21, 1969; June 5, 1974; November 8, 1978; November 17, 1981; November 27, 1981; December 6, 1981; December 27, 1981; January 10, 1982; January 11, 1982; March 24, 1982; April 13, 1982; July 31, 1988; January 15, 1990; February 26, 1990.

*Time,* January 18, 1982.

*Village Voice,* December 20, 1976.

*Washington Post,* October 26, 1983; October 28, 1983.

# G

## GABRE-MEDHIN, Tsegaye (Kawessa) 1936(?)- (Tsegaye Gabre Medhin; Gabre-Medhin Tsegaye; Gabra Madhen Sagaye)

*PERSONAL:* Born August 17, 1936 (some sources say 1935) in Ambo, Shewa, Ethiopia; son of Roba Kawessa Dabal and Feleketch Dagne Haile Amara; married Laketch Bitew (a secretary), 1961; children: (daughters) Yodit Tsegaye, Mahlet Tsegaye, Adaye Tsegaye. *Education:* Blackstone School of Law, LL.B., 1959; studied experimental theatre at Royal Court Theatre, England, and Comedie Francaise, Paris, France, and the Opera, Rome.

*ADDRESSES: Office*—Addis Ababa University, P.O. Box 1176, Addis Ababa, Ethiopia. *Home*—P.O. Box 6249, Addis Ababa, Ethiopia.

*CAREER:* Ethiopian National Theatre, Addis Ababa, director and art advisor, 1961-71; Oxford University Press, Addis Ababa, editor, 1971; Ethiopian National Theatre, general manager, 1974-1976; Addis Ababa University, Addis Ababa, assistant professor of theatre arts, 1976—. Ethiopian vice-president of Black Arts Festival, 1973-1976; permanent secretary of culture, sports, and youth affairs, 1975-1976; research fellow at University of Dakar; art adviser to Haile Selassie I National Theatre, Fine Arts Department of Ministry of Education, and Creative Arts Centre at Haile Selassie I University; secretary general of Ethiopian Peace, Solidarity, and Friendship House, 1978. Delegate to First World Negro Arts Festival, 1964, Afro-Scandinavian Cultural Conference, 1967, International Poets Night, 1968, First Pan-African Cultural Festival, 1969, Afro-European Dialogue, 1969, and African Studies Association Meeting, 1971.

*MEMBER:* Afro-Asian Writers Union, African Writers Union, African Researchers Union, Ethiopian Writers Union, Society of African Cultures, Association of Africanists.

*AWARDS, HONORS:* United Nations Educational, Scientific and Cultural Organization fellowship, 1959; Haile Selassie I National Prize from Addis Ababa International Prize Trust, 1965, for Ethiopian literature; made Commander of the Senegal National Order, 1972, in recognition of literary merit.

*WRITINGS:*

PLAYS; ALL IN AMHARIC

*Belg* (title means "Autumn"; three-act; first produced in Addis Ababa at Ethiopian National Theatre, 1957), Berhanena Selam, 1962.

*Yeshoh Aklil* (title means "Crown of Thorns"; two-act; first produced in Addis Ababa at Ethiopian National Theatre, 1958), Berhanena Selam, 1959.

*Askeyami Lijagered* (title means "The Ugly Girl"; one-act), first produced in Addis Ababa at Ethiopian National Theatre, 1959.

*Jorodegif* (title means "Mumps"; one-act), first produced in Addis Ababa at Ethiopian National Theatre, 1959.

*Listro* (title means "Shoeshine Boy"; one-act), first produced in Addis Ababa at Commercial School Theatre, 1960.

*Igni Biye Metahu* (title means "Back With a Grin"; one-act); first produced in Addis Ababa at Ethiopian National Theatre, 1961.

*Kosho Cigara* (title means "Cheap Cigarettes"; one-act), first produced in Addis Ababa at Old City Hall Theatre, 1961.

*Yemana Zetegn Melk* (title means "Mother's Nine Faces"; three-act), first produced in Addis Ababa at Ethiopian National Theatre, 1961.

*Tewodros* (in English; title means "Theodore"; two-act; first produced in Addis Ababa at Creative Arts Center, Haile Selassie I University, May 5, 1963), published in *Ethiopian Observer,* 1966.

*Othello* (five-act; translation and adaptation of the play by Shakespeare; first produced in Addis Ababa at Addis Ababa University Theatre, 1963), Oxford University Press, 1963.

*Tartuffe* (three-act; translation and adaptation of the play by Moliere), first produced in Addis Ababa at Ethiopian National Theatre, 1963.

*The Doctor in Spite of Himself* (five-act; translation and adaptation of the play by Moliere), first produced in Addis Ababa at Ethiopian National Theatre, 1963.

*Oda Oak Oracle: A Legend of Black Peoples, Told of Gods and God, Of Hope and Love, Of Fears and Sacrifices* (in English; also see below; two-act; first produced in Addis Ababa at Addis Ababa University Theatre, 1964), Oxford University Press, 1964.

*Azmari* (in English; title means "The Minstrel"; two-act; first produced in Addis Ababa at Addis Ababa University Theatre, 1964), published in *Ethiopian Observer,* 1966.

*Yekermo Sew* (title means "the Seasoned"; four-act; first produced in Addis Ababa at Ethiopian National Theatre, 1966), Berhanena Selam, 1967.

*King Lear* (five-act; translation and adaptation of the play by Shakespeare), first produced in Addis Ababa at Ethiopian National Theatre, 1968.

*Kirar Siker* (title means "Kirar Tight-Tuned"; two-act), first produced in Addis Ababa at Ethiopian National Theatre, 1969.

*The Cry of Petros at the Hour* (in English; two-act), first produced in Addis Ababa at Ethiopian National Theatre, 1969.

*Macbeth* (five-act; translation and adaptation of the play by Shakespeare; first produced in Addis Ababa at Ethiopian National Theatre), Oxford University Press, 1972.

*Hamlet* (six-act; translation and adaptation of the play by Shakespeare; first produced in Addis Ababa at Ethiopian National Theatre), Oxford University Press, 1972.

*Ha Hu Besdist Wer* (title means "A-B-C in Six Months"; five-act; first produced in Addis Ababa at Ethiopian National Theatre, 1974), Berhanena Selam, 1975.

*Enat Alem Tenu* (five-act; translation and adaptation of "Mother Courage" by Bertolt Brecht; first produced in Addis Ababa at Ethiopian National Theatre, 1974), Berhanena Selam, 1975.

*Atsim Beyegetsu* (title means "Skeleton in Pages"; six-act), first produced in Addis Ababa at Ethiopian National Theatre, 1975.

*Abugida Transform* (five-act), first produced in Addis Ababa at Ethiopian National Theatre, 1976.

*Collision of Altars* (in English; three-act; first produced in Addis Ababa at Ethiopian National Theatre), Rex Collings, 1978.

*Melikte Proletarian* (three-act), first produced in Addis Ababa at New City Hall Theatre, 1979.

*Mekdem* (title means "Preface"; three-act), first produced in Addis Ababa at New City Hall Theatre, 1980.

Also author of *Blood Harvest,* first produced at the Addis Ababa Commercial School.

*OTHER*

*Oda Oak Oracle* (novel; based on play of same title), Three-Crowns-Oxford, 1965.

Also author of poems, published in *Fire or Flower, Collection of Ethiopian Poems,* 1973, in *The African Assertion,* edited by Austin J. Shelton, Odyssey Press, 1968, and in periodicals including *Ethiopian Observer, Dialogue, Lotus, Presence Africaine, Sociology of African Culture,* and *Transition.*

*WORK IN PROGRESS: Rising Ka,* a novel on Africa's ancient cultures; a play in Amharic entitled *Gamo* (title means "warrior"), on the Ethiopian Revolution.

*SIDELIGHTS:* Tsegaye Gabre-Medhin's play *Oda Oak Oracle* is perhaps his most readily available work in English. It is a tragic story in which the village oracle dominates the lives of the southern Ethiopian characters. The play begins as the oracle decrees a marriage between Shanka and Ukutee, with their first-born child pledged as a sacrifice to the ancestral gods. The two wed, but in defiance of the oracle, the husband, Shanka, refuses to consummate the marriage. Ukutee despairs and finally beds Goaa, a friend of Shanka who has converted to the Christian faith. Ukutee conceives and near the end of the play begins her labor while the sky darkens ominously. Because Shanka and Goaa have attempted to thwart the oracle, tribal law demands that they engage in mortal combat. The battle ends when Shanka slays his opponent. Ukutee subsequently dies while giving birth not to a son, as has been prophesied, but to a daughter. The play ends with the dismal scene of Shanka holding Ukutee's newborn child while an angry mob advances to stone them.

Tsegaye Gabre-Medhin has commented: "Art and literature are commitments to the life that formed our personalities and our humanity: to the people whose dreams, aspirations, and exploits we interpret. Art is as simple as truth and as clear as good and evil. The artist mirrors and exposes these things for the people to judge. He mirrors the innocent, the weak, the ignorant, and exposes the greedy, the cunning, and the exploiting. And the people shall judge for they shall know. Through knowledge alone shall we all be transformed."

*BIOGRAPHICAL/CRITICAL SOURCES:*

BOOKS

Gerard, A. S., *Four African Literatures,* University of California Press, 1971.

PERIODICALS

*Presence Africaine,* 1966.

*      *      *

## GAINES, Ernest J(ames) 1933-

*PERSONAL:* Born January 15, 1933, in Oscar, LA (some sources cite River Lake Plantation, near New Roads, Pointe Coupee Parish, LA); son of Manuel (a laborer) and Adrienne J. (Colar) Gaines; married Diane Saulney (an attorney), May 15, 1993. *Education:* Attended Vallejo Junior College; San Francisco State College (now University), B.A., 1957; graduate study at Stanford University, 1958-59.

*ADDRESSES: Office*—Department of English, University of Southwestern Louisiana, P.O. Box 44691, Lafayette, LA 70504. *Agent*—JCA Literary Agency, Inc., 242 West 27th St., New York, NY 10001.

*CAREER:* "Writing, five hours a day, five days a week." Denison University, Granville, OH, writer in residence, 1971; Stanford University, Stanford, CA, writer in residence, 1981; University of Southwestern Louisiana, Lafayette, professor of English and writer in residence, 1983—. Whittier College, visiting professor, 1983, and writer in residence, 1986. Subject of the film, *Louisiana Stories: Ernest Gaines,* which aired on WHMM-TV in 1993. *Military service:* U.S. Army, 1953-55.

*AWARDS, HONORS:* Wallace Stegner Fellow, Stanford University, 1957; Joseph Henry Jackson Award from San Francisco Foundation, 1959, for "Comeback" (short story); award from National Endowment for the Arts, 1967; Rockefeller grant, 1970; Guggenheim fellowship, 1971; award from Black Academy of Arts and Letters, 1972; fiction gold medal from Commonwealth Club of California, 1972, for *The Autobiography of Miss Jane Pittman,* and 1984, for *A Gathering of Old Men;* award from Louisiana Library Association, 1972; honorary doctorate of letters from Denison University, 1980, Brown University, 1985, Bard College, 1985, and Louisiana State University, 1987; award for excellence of achievement in literature from San Francisco Arts Commission, 1983; D.H.L. from Whittier College, 1986; literary award from

American Academy and Institute of Arts and Letters, 1987; John D. and Catherine T. MacArthur Foundation fellowship, 1993.

*WRITINGS:*

*FICTION*

*Catherine Carmier* (novel), Atheneum, 1964.
*Of Love and Dust* (novel), Dial, 1967.
*Bloodline* (short stories; also see below), Dial, 1968.
*A Long Day in November* (story originally published in *Bloodline*), Dial, 1971.
*The Autobiography of Miss Jane Pittman* (novel), Dial, 1971.
*In My Father's House* (novel), Knopf, 1978.
*A Gathering of Old Men* (novel), Knopf, 1983.
*A Lesson Before Dying* (novel), Knopf, 1993.

Contributor of stories to anthologies and periodicals.

*ADAPTATIONS: The Autobiography of Miss Jane Pittman,* adapted from Gaines's novel, aired on the Columbia Broadcasting System (CBS-TV), January 31, 1974, starring Cicely Tyson in the title role; the special won nine Emmy Awards. "The Sky Is Gray," a short story originally published in *Bloodline,* was adapted for public television in 1980. *A Gathering of Old Men,* adapted from Gaines's novel, aired on CBS-TV, May 10, 1987, starring Lou Gossett, Jr., and Richard Widmark.

*SIDELIGHTS:* The fiction of Ernest J. Gaines, including his 1971 novel *The Autobiography of Miss Jane Pittman,* is deeply rooted in the black culture and storytelling traditions of rural Louisiana where the author was born and raised. His stories have been noted for their convincing characters and powerful themes presented within authentic—often folk-like—narratives that tap into the complex world of Southern rural life. Gaines depicts the strength and dignity of his black characters in the face of numerous struggles: the dehumanizing and destructive effects of racism; the breakdown in personal relationships as a result of social pressures; and the choice between secured traditions and the sometimes radical measures necessary to bring about social change. Although the issues presented in Gaines's fiction are serious and often disturbing, "this is not hot-and-breathless, burn-baby-burn writing," Melvin Maddocks points out in *Time;* rather, it is the work of "a patient artist, a patient man." Expounding on Gaines's rural heritage, Maddocks continues: "[Gaines] sets down a story as if he were planting, spreading the roots deep, wide and firm. His stories grow organically, at their own rhythm. When they ripen at last, they do so inevitably, arriving at a climax with the absolute rightness of a folk tale." Larry McMurtry in the *New York Times Book Review* adds that as "a swimmer cannot influence the flow of a river,... the characters of Ernest Gaines ... are propelled by a prose that is serene, considered and unexcited." Jerry H. Bryant in the *Iowa Review* writes that Gaines's fiction "contains the austere dignity and simplicity of ancient epic, a concern with man's most powerful emotions and the actions that arise from those emotions, and an artistic intuition that carefully keeps such passions and behavior under fictive control. Gaines may be one of our most naturally gifted story-tellers."

Gaines's boyhood experiences growing up on a Louisiana plantation provide many of the impressions upon which his stories are based. Particularly important, he told Paul Desruisseaux in the *New York Times Book Review,* were "working in the fields, going fishing in the swamps with the older people, and, especially, listening to the people who came to my aunt's house, the aunt who raised me." Although Gaines moved to California at the age of fifteen and subsequently went to college there, his fiction has been based in an imaginary Louisiana plantation region named Bayonne, which a number of critics have compared to William Faulkner's Yoknapatawpha County. Gaines has acknowledged looking to Faulkner, in addition to Ernest Hemingway, for language, and to French writers such as Gustave Flaubert and Guy de Maupassant for style. A perhaps greater influence, however, have been the writings of nineteenth-century Russian authors. In a profile by Beverly Beyette for the *Los Angeles Times,* Gaines explains that reading the works of authors such as Nikolai Gogol, Ivan Turgenev, and Anton Chekhov helped unlock the significance of his rural past. "I found something that I had not truly found in American writers," he told Beyette. "They [the Russian writers] dealt with peasantry differently.... I did not particularly find what I was looking for in the Southern writers. When they came to describing my own people, they did not do it the way that I knew my people to be. The Russians were not talking about my people, but about a peasantry for which they seemed to show such feeling. Reading them, I could find a way to write about my own people." That Gaines knew a different South from the one he read about in books also provided an incentive to write. "If the book you want doesn't exist, you try to make it exist," he told Joseph McLellan in the *Washington Post.* Gaines later told Beyette: "That's the book that influenced me most.... I tried to put it there on that shelf, and I'm still trying to do that."

Gaines's first novel, *Catherine Carmier,* is "an apprentice work more interesting for what it anticipates than for its accomplishments," notes William E. Grant in the *Dictionary of Literary Biography.* The novel chronicles the story of a young black man, Jackson Bradley, who returns to Bayonne after completing his education in California. Jackson falls in love with Catherine, the daughter of a Creole sharecropper who refuses to let members of his family associate with anyone darker than themselves, believing Creoles racially and socially superior. The novel portrays numerous clashes of loyalty: Catherine torn between her love for Jackson and love for her father; Jackson caught between a bond to the community he grew up in and the experience and knowledge he has gained in the outside world. "Both Catherine and Jackson are immobilized by the pressures of [the] rural community," writes Keith E. Byermann in the *Dictionary of Literary Biography,* which produces "twin themes of isolation and paralysis [that] give the novel an existential quality. Characters must face an unfriendly world without guidance and must make crucial choices about their lives." The characters in *Catherine Carmier*—as in much of Gaines's fiction—are faced with struggles that test the conviction of personal beliefs. Winifred L. Stoelting in *CLA Journal* explains that Gaines is concerned more "with how they [his characters] handle their decisions than with the rightness of their decisions—more often than not predetermined by social changes over which the single individual has little control."

Gaines sets *Catherine Carmier* in the time of the Civil Rights movement, yet avoids making it a primary force in the novel. Grant comments on this aspect: "In divorcing his tale from contemporary events, Gaines declares his independence from the political and social purposes of much contemporary black writing. Instead, he elects to concentrate upon those fundamental human passions and conflicts which transcend the merely social level of human existence." Grant finds Gaines "admirable" for doing this, yet also believes Jackson's credibility marred because he remains aloof from contemporary events. For Grant, the novel "seems to float outside time and place rather than being solidly anchored in the real world of the modern South." Byerman concurs, stating that the novel "is not entirely successful in presenting its major characters and their motivations." Nonetheless, he points out that in *Catherine Carmier,* "Gaines does begin to create a sense of the black community and its perceptions of the world around it. Shared ways of speaking, thinking, and relating to the dominant white society are shown through a number of minor characters."

Gaines's next novel, *Of Love and Dust,* is also a story of forbidden romance, and, as in *Catherine Carmier,* a "new world of expanding human relationships erodes the old world of love for the land and the acceptance of social and economic stratification," writes Stoelting. *Of Love and Dust* is the story of Marcus Payne, a young black man bonded out of prison by a white landowner and placed under the supervision of a Cajun overseer, Sidney Bonbon. Possessed of a rebellious and hostile nature, Marcus is a threat to Bonbon, who in turn does all that he can to break the young man's spirit. In an effort to strike back, Marcus pays special attention to the overseer's wife; the two fall in love and plot to run away. The novel ends with a violent confrontation between the two men, in which Marcus is killed. After the killing, Bonbon claims that to spare Marcus would have meant his own death at the hands of other Cajuns. Grant notes a similarity between *Of Love and Dust* and

*Catherine Carmier* in that the characters are "caught up in a decadent social and economic system that determines their every action and limits their possibilities." Similarly, the two novels are marked by a "social determinism [which] shapes the lives of all the characters, making them pawns in a mechanistic world order rather than free agents."

*Of Love and Dust* demonstrates Gaines's development as a novelist, offering a clearer view of the themes and characters that dominate his later work. Stoelting writes that "in a more contemporary setting, the novel ... continues Gaines's search for human dignity, and when that is lacking, acknowledges the salvation of pride," adding that "the characters themselves grow into a deeper awareness than those of [his] first novel. More sharply drawn ... [they] are more decisive in their actions." Byerman writes that the novel "more clearly condemns the economic, social, and racial system of the South for the problems faced by its characters." Likewise, the first-person narrator in the novel—a co-worker of Marcus—"both speaks in the idiom of the place and time and instinctively asserts the values of the black community."

Gaines turns to a first-person narrator again in his next novel, *The Autobiography of Miss Jane Pittman,* which many consider to be his masterwork. Miss Jane Pittman—well over one hundred years old—relates a personal history that spans the time from the Civil War and slavery up through the Civil Rights movement of the 1960s. "To travel with Miss Pittman from adolescence to old age is to embark upon a historic journey, one staked out in the format of the novel," writes Addison Gayle, Jr., in *The Way of the World: The Black Novel in America.* "Never mind that Miss Jane Pittman is fictitious, and that her 'autobiography,' offered up in the form of taped reminiscences, is artifice," adds Josh Greenfield in *Life,* "the effect is stunning." Gaines's gift for drawing convincing characters reaches a peak in *The Autobiography of Miss Jane Pittman.* "His is not ... an 'art' narrative, but an authentic narrative by an authentic ex-slave, authentic even though both are Gaines's inventions," Bryant comments. "So successful is he in *becoming* Miss Jane Pittman, that when we talk about her story, we do not think of Gaines as her creator, but as her recording editor."

The character of Jane Pittman could be called an embodiment of the black experience in America. "Though Jane is the dominant personality of the narrative—observer and commentator upon history, as well as participant—in her odyssey is symbolized the odyssey of a race of people; through her eyes is revealed the grandeur of a people's journey through history," writes Gayle. "The central metaphor of the novel concerns this journey: Jane and her people, as they come together in the historic march toward dignity and freedom in Sampson, symbolize a people's march through history, breaking old patterns, though sometimes slowly, as they do." The important histori-

cal backdrop to Jane's narrative—slavery, Reconstruction, the Civil Rights movement, segregation—does not compromise, however, the detailed account of an individual. "Jane captures the experiences of those millions of illiterate blacks who never had a chance to tell their own stories," Byerman explains. "By focusing on the particular yet typical events of a small part of Louisiana, those lives are given a concreteness and specificity not possible in more general histories."

In his fourth novel, *In My Father's House,* Gaines focuses on a theme which appears in varying degrees throughout his fiction: the alienation between fathers and sons. As the author told Desruisseaux: "In my books there always seems to be fathers and sons searching for each other. That's a theme I've worked with since I started writing. Even when the father was not in the story, I've dealt with his absence and its effects on his children. And that is the theme of this book." *In My Father's House* tells of a prominent civil rights leader and reverend (Phillip Martin) who, at the peak of his career, is confronted with a troubled young man named Robert X. Although Robert's identity is initially a mystery, eventually he is revealed to be one of three offspring from a love affair the reverend had in an earlier, wilder life. Martin hasn't seen or attempted to locate his family for more than twenty years. Robert arrives to confront and kill the father whose neglect he sees as responsible for the family's disintegration: his sister has been raped, his brother imprisoned for the murder of her attacker, and his mother reduced to poverty, living alone. Although the son's intent to kill his father is never carried out, the reverend is forced "to undergo a long and painful odyssey through his own past and the labyrinthine streets of Baton Rouge to learn what really happened to his first family," writes William Burke in the *Dictionary of Literary Biography Yearbook.* McMurtry notes that as the book traces the lost family, "we have revealed to us an individual, a marriage, a community and a region, but with such an unobtrusive marshaling of detail that we never lose sight of the book's central thematic concern: the profoundly destructive consequences of the breakdown of parentage, of a father's abandonment of his children and the terrible and irrevocable consequences of such an abandonment."

Burke writes that *In My Father's House* presents the particular problem of manhood for the black male, which he notes as a recurring theme in Gaines's fiction: "Phillip Martin's failure to keep his first family whole, to honor his and [his companion's] love by marriage, and the dissipation of the first half of his adult life—these unfortunate events are clearly a consequence of Martin's fear of accepting the responsibilities of black manhood." Burke highlights the accumulated effects of racism on black males, and cites Gaines's comments to Desruisseaux: "You must understand that the blacks who were brought here as slaves were prevented from becoming the men that they could be.... A *man* can speak up, he can do things to protect himself, his home and his family, but the slaves could never do that. If the white said the slave was wrong, he was wrong.... So eventually the blacks started stepping over the line, [saying] 'Damn what *you* think I'm supposed to be—I will be what I ought to be. And if I must die to do it, I'll die'.... Quite a few of my characters step over that line."

*A Gathering of Old Men,* Gaines's fifth novel, presents a cast of aging Southern black men who, after a life of subordination and intimidation, make a defiant stand against injustice. Seventeen of them, together with the 30-year-old white heiress of a deteriorating Louisiana plantation, plead guilty to murdering a hostile member (Beau Boutan) of a violent Cajun clan. While a confounded sheriff and vengeful family wait to lynch the black they've decided is guilty, the group members—toting recently fired shotguns—surround the dead man and "confess" their motives. "Each man tells of the accumulated frustrations of his life—raped daughters, jailed sons, public insults, economic exploitation—that serve as sufficient motive for murder," writes Byerman. "Though Beau Boutan is seldom the immediate cause of their anger, he clearly represents the entire white world that has deprived them of their dignity and manhood. The confessions serve as ritual purgings of all the hostility and self-hatred built up over the years." Fifteen or so characters—white, black, and Cajun—advance the story through individual narrations, creating "thereby a range of social values as well as different perspectives on the action," notes Byerman. Reynolds Price writes in the *New York Times Book Review* that the black narrators "are nicely distinguished from one another in rhythm and idiom, in the nature of what they see and report, especially in their specific laments for past passivity in the face of suffering." The accumulated effect, observes Elaine Kendall in the *Los Angeles Times Book Review,* is that the "individual stories coalesce into a single powerful tale of subjugation, exploitation and humiliation at the hands of landowners." Price comments that although "some of them, especially at the beginning, are a little long-winded and repetitive, in the manner of country preachers[,] ... a patient reader will sense the power of their stories through their dead-level voices, which speak not from the heart of a present fear but from lifetimes of humiliation and social impotence. They are choosing now to take a stand, on ground where they've yielded for centuries—ground that is valuable chiefly through their incessant labor."

Another theme of *A Gathering of Old Men,* according to Ben Forkner in *America,* is "the simple, natural dispossession of old age, of the traditional and well-loved values of the past, the old trades and the old manners, forced to give way to modern times." Sam Cornish writes in the *Christian Science Monitor* that the novel's "characters—both black and white—understand that, before the close of the novel, the new South must confront the old, and all will be irrevocably changed." Gaines portrays a society that will be altered by the deaths of

its 'old men,' and so presents an allegory about the passing of the old and birth of the new."

*A Lesson Before Dying,* issued ten years after *A Gathering of Old Men,* continues the author's historical reflections on the Southern world captured in all of his novels to date. The setting remains relatively the same—a plantation near and a jail in Bayonne during a six-month span in 1948. The unlikely hero is Jefferson, a scarcely literate, twenty-one-year-old manchild who works the cane fields of the Pichot Plantation. Trouble finds the protagonist when he innocently hooks up with two men, who rob a liquor store and are killed in the process along with the shop's proprietor, leaving Jefferson as an accomplice. The young man's naivete in the crime is never recognized as he is brought to trial before a jury of twelve white men and sentenced to death. Jefferson's defense attorney ineffectively attempts to save his client by presenting him as a dumb animal, as "a thing that acts on command. A thing to hold the handle of a plow, a thing to load your bales of cotton." When Jefferson's godmother learns of this analogy, she determines that her nephew will face his execution as a man, not as an animal. Thus, she enlists the help of a young teacher named Grant Wiggins, who is initially resistant but works to help Jefferson achieve manhood in his final days.

According to Sandra D. Davis in the *Detroit Free Press,* "*A Lesson Before Dying* begins much like many other stories where racial tension brews in the background." Yet, as in Gaines's other works, the racial tension in this novel is more of a catalyst for his tribute to the perseverance of the victims of injustice. Unexpectedly, pride, honor, and manhood in a dehumanizing environment emerge as the themes of this novel. Through Wiggins, the young narrator and unwilling carrier of the "burden" of the community, and his interaction with the black community, as represented by Jefferson's godmother and the town's Reverend Ambrose, Gaines "creates a compelling, intense story about heroes and the human spirit," contends Davis. Ironically, Jefferson and Reverend Ambrose ultimately emerge as the real teachers, showing Wiggins that, as Davis asserts, "education encompasses more than the lessons taught in school." Wiggins is also forced to admit, according to Jonathan Yardley in *Washington Post Book World,* "his own complicity in the system of which Jefferson is a victim."

With *A Lesson Before Dying,* Gaines remains an objective realist, alluding to all of the horrors of Jim Crowism while creating complex relationships among white power brokers, such as plantation owner Henri Pichot, and Miss Emma and other members of the black and white communities. Paul, a white jailer first introduced in *Bloodline,* is, as Yardley states, "one of the most sympathetic characters" in the novel who "befriends Grant and quietly helps Jefferson." However, *Lesson* is neither a sentimental novel in which injustice is recognized nor in which the immediate social consequences of Jefferson's negation of the "myth" of black manhood are depicted. Conversely, "the drama of the novel's final pages is psychological," Yardley concludes, and "the questions involve how Jefferson will face his final hours and what the rest of the community, Grant most particularly, can learn from them." The novel, then, is not about a single lesson but various lessons "presented in the modest but forceful terms that we have come to expect from Ernest J. Gaines," asserts Yardley.

Of that community which yields the lessons of Gaines's fiction and his relation to it, Alice Walker writes in the *New York Times Book Review* that Gaines "claims and revels in the rich heritage of Southern Black people and their customs; the community he feels with them is unmistakable and goes deeper even than pride.... Gaines is mellow with historical reflection, supple with wit, relaxed and expansive because he does not equate his people with failure." Gaines has been criticized by some, however, who feel his writing should more directly focus on problems facing blacks. Gaines responds to Desruisseaux that he feels "too many blacks have been writing to tell whites all about 'the problems,' instead of writing something that all people, including their own, could find interesting, could enjoy." Gaines has also remarked that more can be achieved than strictly writing novels of protest. In an interview for *San Francisco,* the author states: "So many of our writers have not read any farther back than [Richard Wright's] *Native Son.* So many of our novels deal only with the great city ghettos; that's all we write about, as if there's nothing else." Gaines continues: "We've only been living in these ghettos for 75 years or so, but the other 300 years—I think this is worth writing about."

*BIOGRAPHICAL/CRITICAL SOURCES:*

*BOOKS*

*Authors in the News,* Volume 1, Gale, 1976.
Babb, Valerie-Melissa, *Ernest Gaines,* Twayne, 1991.
Bruck, Peter, editor, *The Black American Short Story in the Twentieth Century: A Collection of Critical Essays,* B. R. Gruner (Amsterdam), 1977.
*Concise Dictionary of American Literary Biography: Broadening Views, 1968-1988,* Gale, 1989.
*Contemporary Literary Criticism,* Gale, Volume 3, 1975, Volume 11, 1979, Volume 18, 1981.
*Dictionary of Literary Biography,* Gale, Volume 2: *American Novelists since World War II,* 1978; Volume 33: *Afro-American Fiction Writers after 1955,* 1984.
*Dictionary of Literary Biography Yearbook: 1980,* Gale, 1981.

Gaudet, Marcia, and Carl Wooton, *Porch Talk with Ernest Gaines: Conversations on the Writer's Craft,* Louisiana State University Press, 1990.
Gayle, Addison, Jr., *The Way of the New World: The Black Novel in America,* Doubleday, 1975.
Hicks, Jack, *In the Singer's Temple: Prose Fictions of Barthelme, Gaines, Brautigan, Piercy, Kesey, and Kosinski,* University of North Carolina Press, 1981.
Hudson, Theodore R., *The History of Southern Literature,* Louisiana State University Press, 1985.
O'Brien, John, editor, *Interview with Black Writers,* Liveright, 1973.

*PERIODICALS*

*America,* June 2, 1984.
*Black American Literature Forum,* Volume 11, 1977; Volume 24, 1990.
*Callaloo,* Volume 7, 1984; Volume 11, 1988.
*Chicago Tribune Book World,* October 30, 1983.
*Christian Science Monitor,* December 2, 1983.
*CLA Journal,* March, 1971; December, 1975.
*Detroit Free Press,* June 6, 1993, p. 7J.
*Essence,* August, 1993, p. 52.
*Griot,* Volume 2, 1983; Volume 3, 1984.
*Iowa Review,* winter, 1972.
*Life,* April 30, 1971.
*Los Angeles Times,* March 2, 1983.
*Los Angeles Times Book Review,* January 1, 1984.
*Meleus,* Volume 11, 1984.
*Nation,* February 5, 1968; April 5, 1971; January 14, 1984.
*Negro Digest,* November, 1967; January, 1968; January, 1969.
*New Orleans Review,* Volume 1, 1969; Volume 3, 1972; Volume 14, 1987.
*New Republic,* December 26, 1983.
*New Statesman,* September 2, 1973; February 10, 1984.
*Newsweek,* June 16, 1969; May 3, 1971.
*New Yorker,* October 24, 1983.
*New York Times,* July 20, 1978.
*New York Times Book Review,* November 19, 1967; May 23, 1971; June 11, 1978; October 30, 1983.
*Observer,* February 5, 1984.
*San Francisco,* July, 1974.
*Southern Review,* Volume 10, 1974; Volume 21, 1985.
*Studies in Short Fiction,* summer, 1975.
*Time,* May 10, 1971, December 27, 1971.
*Times Literary Supplement,* February 10, 1966; March 16, 1973; April 6, 1984.
*Village Voice Literary Supplement,* October, 1983.
*Washington Post,* January 13, 1976.
*Washington Post Book World,* June 18, 1978; September 21, 1983; March 28, 1993, p. 3; May 23, 1993.
*Washington Times,* April 14, 1993, p. 3E.
*Xavier Review,* Volume 3, 1983.

## GATES, Henry Louis, Jr. 1950-

*PERSONAL:* Born September 16, 1950, in Keyser, WV; son of Henry Louis and Pauline Augusta (Coleman) Gates; married Sharon Adams (a potter), September 1, 1979; children: Maude, Elizabeth. *Education:* Yale University, B.A. (summa cum laude), 1973; Clare College, Cambridge, M.A., 1974, Ph.D., 1979.

*ADDRESSES: Office*—Department of Afro-American Studies, Harvard University, 1430 Massachusetts Ave., Cambridge, MA 02138. *Agent*—Carl Brandt, Brandt & Brandt Literary Agents, Inc., 1501 Broadway, New York, NY 10036.

*CAREER:* Anglican Mission Hospital, Kilimatinde, Tanzania, general anesthetist, 1970-71; John D. Rockefeller gubernatorial campaign, Charleston, WV, director of student affairs, 1971, director of research, 1972; *Time,* London Bureau, London, England, staff correspondent, 1973-75; Yale University, New Haven, CT, lecturer, 1976-79, assistant professor, 1979-84, associate professor of English, 1984-85, director of undergraduate Afro-American studies, beginning 1979; Cornell University, Ithaca, NY, professor of English, comparative literature, and African studies, 1985-88, W. E. B. DuBois Professor of Literature, 1988-90; Duke University, Durham, NC, John Spencer Bassett Professor of English and Literature, 1990-91; Harvard University, Cambridge, MA, W. E. B. DuBois Professor of the Humanities, professor of English, chair of Afro-American studies and director of W. E. B. DuBois Institute for Afro-American Research, 1991—. Created the television series *The Image of the Black in the Western Imagination,* Public Broadcasting Service (PBS), 1982. Committees include National Book Award, PBS Adult Learning Series, Ritz Paris Hemingway Prize Selection Committee, and the Schomburg Commission for the Preservation of Black Culture. Member of board of directors of African American Newspapers and Periodicals: A National Bibliography and Union List, African Labour History, American Council of Learned Societies, Center for the Study of Black Literature and Culture, Diacritics, European Institute for Literary and Cultural Studies, Everyman Library, Lincoln Center Theater Project, LIT Literature in Transition, Museum of Afro-American History, Museum of Science, New Museum of Contemporary Arts, Proceedings of the American Antiquarian Society, Studio Museum in Harlem, and UMI Research Press's "Challenging the American Canon" series.

*MEMBER:* Council on Foreign Relations; American Antiquarian Society; Union of Writers of the African Peoples; Association for Documentary Editing; African Roundtable; African Literature Association; Afro-American Academy; American Studies Association; Association for the Study of Afro-American Life and History (life); Caribbean Studies Association; College Language Association (life); Modern Language Association; Stone Trust; Zora Neale Hurston Society; Cambridge Scientific Club; American Civil Liberties Union National Advisory Council; Phi Beta Kappa.

*AWARDS, HONORS:* Carnegie Foundation Fellowship for Africa, 1970-71; Phelps Fellowship, Yale University, 1970-71; Mellon fellowships, Cambridge University, 1973-75, and National Humanities Center, 1989-90; grants from Ford Foundation, 1976-77 and 1984-85, and National Endowment for the Humanities, 1980-86; A. Whitney Griswold Fellowship, 1980; Rockefeller Foundation fellowships, 1981 and 1990; MacArthur Prize Fellowship, MacArthur Foundation, 1981-86; Yale Afro-American teaching prize, 1983; award from Whitney Humanities Center, 1983-85; Princeton University Council of the Humanities lectureship, 1985; Award for Creative Scholarship, Zora Neale Hurston Society, 1986; Virginia Commonwealth Visiting Professor, 1987; John Hope Franklin Prize honorable mention, American Studies Association, 1988; Woodrow Wilson National Fellow, 1988-89 and 1989-90; Candle Award, Morehouse College, 1989; Anisfield-Wolf Book Award for Race Relations, 1989; American Book Award, 1989; Richard Wright Lecturer, Center for the Study of Black Literature and Culture, University of Pennsylvania, 1990; Potomac State College Alumni Award, 1991; Bellagio Conference Center Fellowship, 1992; Clarendon Lecturer, Oxford University, 1992; Best New Journal of the Year award (in the humanities and the social sciences), Association of American Publishers, 1992; elected to the American Academy of Arts and Sciences, 1993; Golden Plate Achievement Award, 1993; George Polk Award for Social Commentary, 1993; recipient of honorary degrees from Dartmouth College, 1989; University of West Virginia, 1990; University of Rochester, 1990; Pratt Institute, 1990; University of Bridgeport, 1991 (declined); University of New Hampshire, 1991; Bryant College, 1992; Manhattan Community College, 1992; George Washington University, 1993; University of Massachusetts at Amherst, 1993; and Williams College, 1993.

*WRITINGS:*

*Figures in Black: Words, Signs, and the Racial Self,* Oxford University Press, 1987.
*The Signifying Monkey: Towards a Theory of Afro-American Literary Criticism,* Oxford University Press, 1988.
*Loose Canons: Notes on the Culture Wars* (essays), Oxford University Press, 1992.

*EDITOR*

(And author of introduction) *Black Is the Color of the Cosmos: Charles T. Davis's Essays on Black Literature and Culture, 1942-1981,* Garland Publishing, 1982.

(And author of introduction) Harriet E. Wilson, *Our Nig; or, Sketches from the Life of a Free Black,* Random House, 1983.

(And author of introduction) *Black Literature and Literary Theory,* Methuen, 1984.

(And author of introduction with Charles T. Davis) *The Slave's Narrative: Texts and Contexts,* Oxford University Press, 1986.

(And author of introduction) *"Race," Writing, and Difference,* University of Chicago Press, 1986.

(And author of introduction) *The Classic Slave Narratives,* New American Library, 1987.

*The Schomburg Library of Nineteenth-Century Black Women Writers,* thirty volumes, Oxford University Press, 1988.

(And author of introduction) *In the House of Oshugbo: A Collection of Essays on Wole Soyinka,* Oxford University Press, 1988.

W. E. B. DuBois, *The Souls of Black Folk,* Bantam Books, 1989.

James Weldon Johnson, *The Autobiography of an Ex-Coloured Man,* Vintage, 1989.

*Three Classic African American Novels,* Vintage, 1990.

Zora Neale Hurston, *Their Eyes Were Watching God,* Harper, 1990.

Hurston, *Jonah's Gourd Vine,* Harper, 1990.

Hurston, *Tell My Horse,* Harper, 1990.

Hurston, *Mules and Men,* Harper, 1990.

*Reading Black, Reading Feminist: A Critical Anthology,* New American Library, 1990.

(With Randall K. Burkett and Nancy Hall Burkett) *Black Biography, 1790-1950: A Cumulative Index,* Chadwyck-Healey, 1990.

(With George Bass) *Mulebone: A Comedy of Negro Life,* HarperCollins, 1991.

*The Schomburg Library of Nineteenth-Century Black Women Writers,* ten volumes, Oxford University Press, 1991.

*Bearing Witness: Selections from African American Autobiography in the Twentieth Century,* Pantheon Books, 1991.

*The Amistad Chronology of African American History from 1445-1990,* Amistad, 1993.

Editor, with Anthony Appiah, of "Amistad Critical Studies in African American Literature" series, 1993. Advisory editor of "Contributions to African and Afro-American Studies" series for Greenwood Press, "Critical Studies in Black Life and Culture" series for Garland Press, and "Perspectives on the Black World" series for G. K. Hall. General editor of *The Norton Anthology of Afro-American Literature; A Dictionary of Cultural and Critical Theory; Middle-Atlantic Writers Association Review.* Associate editor of *Journal of American Folklore.*

*CONTRIBUTOR*

Herbert Sacks, editor, *The Book of Hurdles,* Atheneum, 1978.

Robert Stepto and Dexter Fisher, editors, *Afro-American Literature: The Reconstruction of Instruction,* Modern Language Association of America, 1979. William H. Robinson, editor, *Critical Essays on Phillis Wheatley,* G. K. Hall, 1982.

Tyler Wasson, editor, *Nobel Prize Winners,* Wilson, 1987.

Harold Bloom, editor, *Zora Neale Hurston's "Their Eyes Were Watching God,"* Chelsea House, 1987.

Richard Popkin, editor, *Millenarianism and Messianism in English Literature and Thought, 1650-1800,* E. J. Brill, 1988.

James Olney, editor, *Studies in Autobiography,* Oxford University, 1988.

Betty Jean Craige, editor, *Literature, Language, and Politics,* University of Georgia, 1988.

Harold Bloom, editor, *Frederick Douglass's Narrative,* Chelsea House, 1988.

Ralph Cohen, editor, *The Future of Literary Theory,* Routledge, 1989.

Patrick O'Donnell and Robert Con Davis, editors, *Intertextuality and Contemporary American Fiction,* Johns Hopkins University, 1989.

Houston A. Baker, Jr., and Patricia Redmond, editors, *Afro-American Literary Study in the 1900s,* University of Chicago, 1989.

Linda Goss and Marian E. Barnes, editors, *Talk That Talk: An Anthology of African American Storytelling,* Simon & Schuster, 1989.

Gunter Lenz, Hartmut Keil, and Sabine Brock-Sallah, editors, *Reconstructing American Literary and Historical Studies,* CampusNerlag, 1990.

David Theo Goldberg, editor, *Anatomy of Racism,* University of Minnesota, 1990.

Guy C. McElroy, editor, *Facing History: The Black Image in American Art, 1710-1940,* Bedford Arts and the Corcoran Gallery of Art, 1990.

Christopher Ricks and Leonard Michaels, editors, *The State of the Language,* University of California, Berkeley, 1990.

Joanne M. Braxton and Andree N. McLaughlin, editors, *Wild Women in the Whirlwind,* Rutgers University, 1990.

Feroza Jussawalla, editor, *Excellent Teaching in a Changing Academy: Essays in Honor of Kenneth Eble,* Jossey-Bass, 1990.

Charles Moran and Elizabeth F. Penfield, editors, *Conversations: Contemporary Critical Theory and the Teaching of Literature,* National Council of Teachers of English, 1990.

Nicolaus Mills, editor, *Culture in an Age of Money: The Legacy of the 1980s in America,* Ivan R. Dee, 1990.

Eric J. Sundquist, editor, *Frederick Douglass: New Literary and Historical Essays,* Cambridge University, 1990.

Brian Wallis, editor, *Democracy,* Bay Press, 1990.

Susan Gubar and Jonathan Kamholtz, editors, *English Inside and Out: The Places of Literary Criticism,* Routledge, 1992.

Stephen Greenblatt and Giles Gunn, editors, *The Transformation of English and American Literary Studies,* Modern Language Association, 1992.

Michele Wallace and Gina Dent, editors, *Black Popular Culture,* Bay Press, 1992.

Mark Green, editor, *Changing America: Blueprints for the New Administration,* Newmarket Press, 1992.

Diane P. Freedman, Olivia Frey, and Frances M. Zaubar, editors, *Intimate Critique: Autobiographical Literary Criticism,* Duke University, 1993.

William L. Andrews, editor, *African American Autobiography,* Prentice Hall, 1993.

*OTHER*

(Compiler with James Gibb and Ketu H. Katrak) *Wole Soyinka: A Bibliography of Primary and Secondary Sources,* Greenwood Press, 1986.

Contributor of articles and reviews to numerous periodicals and journals, including *ALA Bulletin, American Book Review, Antioch Review, Black American Literature Forum, Black Film Review, Black Scholar, Black World, Boston Review, Cardozo Law Review, Chronicle of Higher Education, Contemporary Literature, Critical Inquiry, Dissent, Forbes, Harper's, Harvard Educational Review, Journal of Negro History, Mississippi College of Law Review, Nation, New Literary History, New Republic, New Theater Review, New York Times, New York Times Book Review, New Yorker, Newsday, Newsweek, Publication of the Modern Language Association, Representations, Research in African Literature, Saturday Review, South Atlantic Quarterly, Southern Review, Spectator, Sports Illustrated, Time, Transition, Village Voice Literary Supplement, Washington Post Book World,* and *Yale Review.* Member of the board of editors of *American Literature, Black American Literature Forum, Cultural Critique, Journal of Urban and Cultural Studies, PMLA, Proteus, Stanford Humanities Review, Studies in American Fiction,* and *Yale Journal of Law and Liberation.*

*WORK IN PROGRESS: A Dictionary of Global Literacy,* with Anthony Appiah, Knopf.

*SIDELIGHTS:* Henry Louis Gates, Jr., more casually known as Skip, grew up in West Virginia where his love of literature was nurtured by his mother and by American author and essayist James Baldwin's *Notes of a Native Son,* which he "en-gulfed" at the age of fifteen. "It fueled a love of literature like nothing I had ever experienced before," he has said, and "I began to read everything that I could order through the local newspaper store in Piedmont, West Virginia. I'd gather up bottles and get coins, then spend them all on books." Recognizing his capacious and brilliant mind, an English instructor at Potomac State Community College encouraged Gates to transfer to Yale University, from which he graduated with highest honors in 1973. While in Africa on a Carnegie Foundation Fellowship and a Phelps Fellowship during 1970-1971, he visited fifteen countries and became familiar with various aspects of African culture. His knowledge of Africa deepened when the celebrated African writer Wole Soyinka became his tutor at Cambridge University where Gates worked on his master's and doctoral degrees. According to James Olney in the *Dictionary of Literary Biography,* Gates's mission is to reorder and reinterpret "the literary and critical history of Afro-Americans in the context of a tradition that is fully modern but also continuous with Yoruba modes of interpretation that are firmly settled and at home in the world of black Americans."

In his approach to literary criticism, Gates is avowedly eclectic and defines himself as a centrist who rejects extreme positions, whether they be on the right (guardians of a Western tradition) or on the left (Afrocentricists). Gates insists that we need to transcend "ethnic absolutism" of all kinds. Like the American novelist Ralph Ellison, Gates sees the fluid, indeed porous, relationship between black and white culture in the United States. Gates argues that our conception of the literary canon needs to be enlarged accordingly.

*Black Literature and Literary Theory* is considered by many reviewers to be an important contribution to the study of black literature. Calling the book "an exciting, important volume," Reed Way Dasenbrock writes in *World Literature Today,* "It is a collection of essays ... that attempts to explore the relevance of contemporary literary theory, especially structuralism and poststructuralism, to African and Afro-American literature.... Anyone seriously interested in contemporary critical theory, in Afro-American and African literature, and in black and African studies generally will need to read and absorb this book." R. G. O'Meally writes in *Choice* that, in *Black Literature and Literary Theory,* Gates "brings together thirteen superb essays in which the most modern literary theory is applied to black literature of Africa and the U.S.... For those interested in [the] crucial issues—and for those interested in fresh and challenging readings of key texts in black literature—this book is indispensable." Finally, Terry Eagleton remarks in the *New York Times Book Review* that "the most thought-provoking contributions to [this] collection are those that not only enrich our understanding of black literary works but in doing so implicitly question the authoritarianism of a literary 'canon'."

Gates's prodigious productivity has propelled him into the limelight, leading the *Chronicle of Higher Education* to characterize him as "one of the nation's best known scholars." His reputation has allowed him to move rapidly from Cornell University to Duke University to Harvard University. In his latest assignment, "Gates faces the greatest challenge of his career," according to *U.S. News and World Report,* "as he attempts to transform Harvard's ... Afro-American studies department into a program of the first rank." Beyond the responsibilities of his current academic and administrative position, Gates has consistently sought to make a variety of texts available to the American reading public. At the same time, he has sought to sharpen the tools with which critics analyze and discuss literature. Although there are good and poor readings of texts, there is never a definitive interpretation according to Gates. In James Olney's words, "signifying" (or interpreting) "is endless, an activity generating out of itself, entirely indeterminate, and ever unfinished." As Gates's primary contribution to literary criticism, Olney identifies the "scope of [his] argument" and "the insight that it brings to reading individual texts, the matrix of the Afro-American literary tradition, and the 'signifyin[g]' practice that binds the 'American' in Afro-American writing/speaking." Olney predicts that "given his relative youth, the ambitiousness of his program, and the seemingly inexhaustible energy that he brings to it, Gates can be expected to be a central figure on the critical/cultural scene for decades to come."

*BIOGRAPHICAL/CRITICAL SOURCES:*

*BOOKS*

*Dictionary of Literary Biography,* Volume 67: *Modern American Critics since 1955,* Gale, 1988.

*PERIODICALS*

*Callaloo,* spring, 1991.
*Choice,* May, 1985.
*Emerge,* November, 1990.
*Humanities Magazine,* July/August, 1991.
*New Literary History,* autumn, 1991.
*New York Times Book Review,* December 9, 1984.
*New York Times Magazine,* April 1, 1990.
*Time,* April 22, 1991.
*Times Literary Supplement,* May 17, 1985.
*U.S. News and World Report,* March, 1992.
*Voice Literary Supplement,* June, 1985.
*Washington Post Book World,* July 3, 1983.
*World Literature Today,* summer, 1985.

# GAY, John H. 1928-

*PERSONAL:* Born December 2, 1928.

*ADDRESSES: Office*—Humanities Division, Box 277, Cuttington University College, Monrovia, Liberia.

*CAREER:* Cuttington University College, Monrovia, Liberia, chair of humanities division.

*WRITINGS:*

(With Michael Cole) *The New Mathematics and an Old Culture: A Study of Learning among the Kpelle of Liberia,* Holt, 1967.
(With William Welmers) *Mathematics and Logic in the Kpelle Language,* Institute of African Studies, 1971.
(With Michael Cole and others) *The Cultural Context of Learning and Thinking,* Basic Books, 1971.
*Red Dust on the Green Leaves: A Kpelle Twins Childhood,* introduction by Jerome Bruner, photographs by Harrison Owen, University of Ibadan Press, 1971, InterCulture Associates, 1973.
*Universals of Human Thought: Some African Evidence,* Cambridge University Press, 1981.
(With David Hall and Gerhard Deborath) *Poverty in Lesotho, a Mapping Exercise,* Lesotho Food Management Unit, 1992.

*BIOGRAPHICAL/CRITICAL SOURCES:*

*PERIODICALS*

*Choice,* April, 1974, p. 294.

\*   \*   \*

# GIBSON, P(atricia) J(oann)

*PERSONAL:* Born in Pittsburgh, PA. *Education:* Keuka College, B.A. 1973; Brandeis University, M.F.A., 1975; also studied under J. P. Miller.

*ADDRESSES:* 400 West 43rd St., No. 14L, New York, NY 10036.

*CAREER:* Voices, Inc., New York City, production stage manager, 1971-73; U.S. Department of Health, Education and Welfare, Office of Youth Development/Human Development, scriptwriter, public service announcements, 1973; Brandeis University, administrator of Summer Introductory Preparatory Program, 1974; Roxbury Children's Theatre, Dorchester, MA, creative arts director, 1974-75; Boston College, Chestnut Hill,

MA, instructor, 1975-76; WGBH-TV, Boston, MA, assistant theatrical director on "Say Brother," 1976-77; Brown University, Providence, RI, project administrator, Rites and Reason Theatre, 1976-77; Frederick Douglass Creative Arts Center, New York City, instructor, 1978-83; Project Reach Youth/Family Reception Center, Brooklyn, NY, instructor, 1979-82; CETA Arts Program, Cultural Council Foundation/Black Theatre Alliance, New York City, playwright in residence, 1979-80; Teachers and Writers Collaborative, New York City, instructor, 1980; College of New Rochelle, New Rochelle, NY, instructor, beginning 1982; currently assisistant professor of English at John Jay College of Criminal Justice, New York City.

*AWARDS, HONORS:* Shubert fellowship, 1974; National Endowment for the Arts playwriting grant, 1978; Artist Honor, Sudanese Songs and Poets Association, 1978; Key to City of Indianapolis, IN, 1980; Audelco Award for best play and playwright of the year, 1985, for *Long Time since Yesterday;* John Jay College of Criminal Justice teaching award, 1987.

*WRITINGS:*

*PLAYS*

*Shameful in Your Eyes,* produced at Keuka College, 1971.

*The Black Woman,* first produced in a one-act version at Keuka College, 1972.

*Void Passage* (one-act), first produced in a double bill with *Konvergence* in Trenton, NJ, 1973.

*Konvergence* (one-act; first produced in a double bill with *Void Passage* in Trenton, NJ, 1973), published in *Plays for Black Theatre,* Third World Press, 1989.

*The Ninth Story Window* (one-act), produced at Brandeis University, 1974.

*Spida Bug* (one-act children's play), produced at Brandeis University, 1975.

*Doing It to Death,* produced as a public reading by FSWW, 1977.

*The Zappers and the Shopping Bag Lady* (one-act), produced on summer tour, New York, 1979.

*The Androgyny* (two-act), produced in Frankfurt, Germany, 1979.

*Ain't Love Grand?* (two-act musical), first produced on U.S. tour, 1980.

*Miss Ann Don't Cry No More* (two-act), produced by the Frederick Douglass Creative Arts Center, 1980.

*My Mark, My Name* (two-act), first produced in Indianapolis, IN, 1981.

*Angel* (two-act), produced as a staged reading at the Family Theatre, 1981.

*The Unveiling of Abigail* (two-act), first produced in Torino, Italy, 1981, produced as *Unveilings* in New York City, 1982.

*Brown Silk and Magenta Sunsets* (two-act; produced as a staged reading of one act at the Frederick Douglass Creative Arts Center, 1981), published in *Nine Plays by Black Women,* Wilkerson, 1986.

*Clean Sheets Can't Soil* (two-act), produced in Providence, RI, 1983.

*Long Time since Yesterday* (two-act; produced by the New Federal Theatre, 1985), Samuel French, 1986.

Also author of plays, including *Strippa, Swing/Slide, Void Passage, Majorna and the Man Thief, A Man, Masculine and Glass Fist, Marie,* and *In Search of Me* (newly titled *Trial*).

*"PRIVATE HELLS, SKETCHES IN REALITY" PLAY TRILOGY*

*"You Must Die before My Eyes as I Have before Yours"* (one-act), produced by the Frederick Douglass Creative Arts Center, 1981.

*"But I Feed the Pigeons"/"Well, I Watch the Sun"* (one-act), produced by the Frederick Douglass Creative Arts Center, 1981.

*Can You Tell Me Who They Is?* (one-act), produced by the Frederick Douglass Creative Arts Center, 1981.

*OTHER*

Author of a one-episode television script, "The Edge of Night," televised in 1981. Work represented in anthologies, including *Long Journey Home,* 1985, and *Erotique Noire— Black Erotica,* 1992.

\*    \*    \*

## GIBSON, Richard (Thomas) 1931-

*PERSONAL:* Born May 13, 1931, in Los Angeles, CA; son of Clarence Louis and Alice (Thomas) Gibson; married Sarah Joy Kaye, March 24, 1956; children: three. *Education:* Attended Kenyon College 1950-51, University of Rome, 1951-52, Sorbonne, University of Paris, 1955-56, and Columbia University, 1961-62.

*ADDRESSES: Home*—11 Formosa St., London W9 2JS, England. *Office*—Tricontinental Development Consultants, Rue St. Georges, Bte. 4, Brussels 1050, Belgium.

*CAREER: Philadelphia Afro-American,* Philadelphia, PA, reporter, 1949-50; *Christian Science Monitor,* Rome, Italy, reporter at Mediterranean bureau, 1951-52; *Agence France-Presse,* Paris, sub-editor, 1955-58; Columbia Broadcasting System (CBS), New York City, newswriter, 1960-61; *Revolution Africaine,* Algiers, Algeria, Lausanne, Switzerland, and Paris, France, editor, 1962-64; Negro Press International,

London, England, correspondent, 1966-70; Tuesday Publications, Inc., London, international correspondent, 1970-76; International Art Associates, Ltd., overseas representative, 1976—; director, Tricontinental Development Consultants, Brussels, Belgium; Yaa Asantewaa Arts and Community Centre, London, centre director. *Military service:* U.S. Army, 1952-54.

*MEMBER:* Association of American Correspondents in London, Association de la Presse Internationale (Brussels), Foreign Press Association, American Friends of China in Europe (secretary-treasurer, 1972—), Institute of Race Relations (London).

*WRITINGS:*

*A Mirror for Magistrates* (novel), Anthony Blond, 1950.
*African Liberation Movements,* Oxford University Press, 1972.

*SIDELIGHTS:* A journalist who has traveled extensively in Africa, Richard Gibson offers an analysis of movements against Africa's white-minority rule in *African Liberation Movements.* In the book Gibson covers activity in numerous countries and territories, including South Africa, Southwest Africa, Rhodesia, Angola, Mozambique and the Comoro Islands. In addition to including information about the separate movements, Gibson comments on historical and social backgrounds of each locale covered. Although Thomas F. Hirsch of *Library Journal* felt that Gibson did not offer startling new information concerning the movements, he complimented the author for organizing the book effectively and pulling together materials from disparate and obscure sources.

*BIOGRAPHICAL/CRITICAL SOURCES:*

*BOOKS*

Gibson, Richard, *African Liberation Movements,* Oxford University Press, 1972.

*PERIODICALS*

*Library Journal,* October 15, 1972, p. 3301.
*Times Literary Supplement,* p. 598, May 26, 1972.

\* \* \*

## GILBERT, Christopher 1949-

*PERSONAL:* Born August 1, 1949, in Birmingham, AL; son of Floyd and Rosie (Walker) Gilbert. *Education:* University of Michigan, B.A., 1972; Clark University, M.A., 1975, Ph.D., 1986.

*ADDRESSES:* P.O. Box 371, West Side Station, Worcester, MA 01602.

*CAREER:* Judge Baker Guidance Center, Boston, MA, staff psychologist, 1978-84; Cambridge Family and Children's Services, Cambridge, MA, staff psychologist, 1984-85; poet, 1986—. University of Massachusetts Medical School, consultant psychologist, 1979-84; University of Pittsburgh, visiting poet, 1986; Robert Frost Center, Franconia, NH, poet in residence, 1986. Member of boards of directors of Elm Park Center for Early Education, 1980-84, Worcester Chapter Civil Liberties Union of Massachusetts, 1983-85, and Worcester Children's Friend, 1983-86.

*AWARDS, HONORS:* Fellow of Massachusetts Artists Foundation, 1981, and National Endowment for the Arts, 1986; Walt Whitman Award from Academy of American Poets, 1983, for *Across the Mutual Landscape;* Robert Frost Award, 1986.

*WRITINGS:*

*Across the Mutual Landscape* (poetry), Graywolf, 1984.
*Life and Work of Thomas Chippendale,* two volumes, Seven Hills Books, 1986.
(Editor with Neil de Marchi) *History and Methodology of Econometrics,* Oxford University Press, 1989.
*English Vernacular Furniture 1750-1900,* Yale University Press, 1991.

Also author of *World,* a collection of poems, 1987. Work represented in anthologies, including *The Morrow Anthology of Younger Poets* and *Fifty Years of American Poetry, 1934-1984.*

*WORK IN PROGRESS:* A novel.

*SIDELIGHTS:* The poems in psychologist Christopher Gilbert's award-winning first collection, *Across the Mutual Landscape,* are, according to Alan Williamson writing in the *New York Times Book Review,* influenced by black music. The poetry's "subtle, syncopated rhythms" remind one of jazz, remarked Williamson, who pointed out that this music affects Gilbert's sense of the avenues for change, struggle, and outlet afforded by art. "It is a feeling often encountered in black American literature," explained Williamson, in which people living at the urban Midwest's poverty line seek "dignity and marginally steady work, but long for the sun and culture of the black South." This theme, Williamson determined, keeps Gilbert from overindulging in protest poetry or "too simple warmth and domesticity." The reviewer concluded that *Across the Mutual Landscape* is a "very fine, very promising first book."

Gilbert wrote: "I work at both poetry and psychology. Until 1986 I had always written poems while being employed in psychology. The poems got finished at home at night, after I had finished my daytime work doing psychotherapy, or research, or teaching psychology. Sometimes I would write poetry in the early morning. Sometimes I used the weekend for writing. Sometimes I wrote between breaths. This went on for about eight years; always the poems got finished. Then I devoted a year to writing poems. I do plan to return to some kind of daytime job that involves my psychology background. Actually, I feel that my own ability to write poetry wants this; it wants its experience to be grounded in the firsthand world gained through contact with lives and people, with me—as subject—as an empathy, with a reflection toward one's deeper and longer life, with goals, with a concept of use. It is my way of making a living.

"I see the poem itself as a situation. Its formation is thought which must be musically stated. The situation is charged. The situation is sensuous. The situation is moving forward. The situation is music. Jazz pianist and composer Thelonious Monk, placing himself in the exact center of things, finding himself naked in his whole world except for his desire and his skill, could be listened to for a chart of the coming into newness that is the poem's formation.

"What I try to do is find the field in writing where I am honest, where I am determined to have a future in front of me. Once this nakedness is reached, after one has truly touched the features of 'his situation,' once one has made those parts of the usual—the regular denoted world—contextual, then there is the language that does not reach for things but poetry."

*BIOGRAPHICAL/CRITICAL SOURCES:*

*PERIODICALS*

*Boston Globe,* December 14, 1984.
*New York Times Book Review,* June 23, 1985.
*Philadelphia Inquirer,* December 2, 1984.
*Virginia Quarterly Review,* spring, 1985.

\*   \*   \*

## GILBERT, Herman Cromwell 1923-

*PERSONAL:* Born February 23, 1923, in Mariana, AR; son of Van Luther and Cora Gilbert; married Ivy McAlpine, July 19, 1949; children: Dorthea, Vincent Newton. *Education:*

Completed two years of a three-year correspondence course in law, LaSalle Extension University, 1941; attended IBM Education Center. *Politics:* Independent Democrat. *Religion:* Protestant.

*ADDRESSES: Home*—11539 South Justice St., Chicago, IL 60643. *Office*—Path Press, Inc. 53 West Jackson Blvd., Chicago, IL 60604.

*CAREER:* United Packinghouse Workers of America, Chicago, IL, program coordinator, 1955-57; Illinois Department of Labor, Bureau of Employment Security, Chicago, manager of automated systems section, 1957-70, assistant employment security administrator, 1970-81; administrative assistant and chief of staff to Congressman Gus Savage, 1981-82. Executive vice-president, Path Press, Chicago, 1968—; publicity director, Chicago League of Negro Voters and Protest at the Polls. Member of joint Federal-State Committee on Automated Systems, Interstate Conference of Employment Security Agencies. Member of International Black Writers Conference, 1992. *Military service:* U.S. Army Air Forces, 1943-46; attended Armed Forces Institute, 1944-45; became staff sergeant; received unit citation, 1944, and good conduct medal, 1945.

*MEMBER:* Society of Midland Authors.

*AWARDS, HONORS:* Congressional Commendation from U.S. Representative William L. Clay (Missouri), and Certificate of Special Congressional Recognition from U.S. Representative Mickey Leland (Texas), both 1984; Alice Browning Award for excellence in the literary arts, International Black Writers Conference, 1992.

*WRITINGS:*

*The Uncertain Sound: A Novel,* Path Press, 1969.
*The Negotiations: A Novel of Tomorrow,* Path Press, 1983.
*Sharp Blades in Tender Grass: A Play,* presented by E.T.A. Readers Theatre, 1990.

Author of column, "This Needs Saying," in Chicago's Westside Booster, 1959-60. Contributor to *Black American Literature Forum* and *Black Books Bulletin.* Managing editor of Citizen Newspapers, 1965-67.

*SIDELIGHTS:* Herman Cromwell Gilbert once commented: "As is clear from the broad range of activities in which I have been engaged over the years, writing itself has been somewhat of a sidelight. However, this does not mean that I have taken my writing lightly, only that I have placed a higher value on making a decent living for my family and sending my children through college. Now that these things have been achieved, I am free to spend the remainder of my life writing.

"I have always been clear about the types of books I wanted to write: books that helped push Black Americans along the road to full equality by spotlighting radical situations and making these situations plausible through clearly delineated characters. These things I think I have accomplished in both of my published novels, *The Uncertain Sound,* which deals with school integration, interracial love, and unionism in a southern Illinois town in 1950, and *The Negotiations,* which dramatizes the efforts of blacks to negotiate a separate state in the late 1980s. The nonfiction and autobiographical writings in which I am currently engaged are following this same intent."

*The Uncertain Sound* contains slices of both northern and southern life in this country. Whites are depicted as wanting to defend their longstanding, treasured way of life, while blacks are portrayed as trying to break out of relegation to the role of second-class citizens. As expected, confrontations break out, but the friction is not only black against white. One of the story's main characters, black activist Ralph Coleman, falls in love with Ventura, the daughter of his white boss. Coleman must struggle between that love and his support for his close associates, who are spearheading the drive for civil rights. Likewise, Ventura must also find her place in the storyline's interwoven sequence of events, especially in view of the fact that her uncle is the leader of the Klan-like gang opposing the civil rights movement.

The plot centers around the issue of school integration and of unionism among the town's skilled workers. Despite threats to his family, Robert Dennis, a committed civil rights spokesman, convinces several black families to allow their children to act as test cases in attending an all-white school. Contrary to Dennis's position is that of Dr. McGee, the town's lone black physician who is respected by the town's white community. McGee eventually collaborates with the whites by providing them with Dennis's plans of desegregation.

The novel's secondary theme—the threat of unionism—centers around John Dare, the town's wealthy construction manager who plans, to the chagrin of his employees, to hire a black foreman. Not having committed himself to anything for much of the novel, Coleman goes along with Dare up until a scheme to murder the town's Klan leader is hatched.

Jo Hudson of *Black World* said that in *The Uncertain Sound,* the "issues are not resolved," as the schools remain to be desegregated, some of the committed parents see their roles reversed and physical violence inflicted on the blacks is not blocked by police. But "in spite of this," Hudson stated, "the reader is left with the impression that the Blacks of Egypttown are somehow going to win their fight—not a fight for survival but for equality." Also writing in *Black World,* David L. Crowder said that Gilbert writes with "a fresh, bold clarity

which forms its own vibrant poetry and its own dynamics." Crowder further judged *The Uncertain Sound* as "a novel of importance which should be read not only for what it dramatically says, but also for sheer enjoyment."

Gilbert's second novel, *The Negotiations,* is set in 1987 and deals with the black community's dissatisfaction with Reaganomics in addressing their needs. The novel's plot revolves around two months of negotiations by Preston Simmons, of the Black America Council, with the federal government. The basis of their negotiations is whether to form a separate black nation within the United States. Blacks have already passed their own referendum to form their own government and now must face indifference, ridicule, and outrage not only from the federal government, but from factionalism and antiseparatist sentiment among some blacks. Among the novel's central characters are a Black tycoon, a militant, a union leader and Simmons, a prominent black novelist and columnist who was chosen by a computer to lead the committee which negotiates with the government.

Janet Boyarin Blundell, writing in *Library Journal,* found *The Negotiations* unexciting in spite of its plot, because "hairstyles, conference rooms, and even lawn furniture are described in relentless detail." However, *Booklist* contributor Martin A. Brady called *The Negotiations* "altogether a finely crafted and politically well informed work, disturbing in its realism," and asserted that "its futuristic portrait strikes at the heart of current issues central to the concerns of all Americans, regardless of race."

*BIOGRAPHICAL/CRITICAL SOURCES:*

*PERIODICALS*

*Black World,* May, 1970, p. 51; August 1970, p. 86.
*Booklist,* August, 1983, p. 1447.
*Library Journal,* July, 1983, p. 1381.

\*   \*   \*

## GILROY, Beryl (Agatha) 1924-

*PERSONAL:* Born in 1924, in British Guiana (now Guyana), South America. *Education:* Government Technical Institute, British Guyana, teacher's certificate (with first-class honors), 1945; received advanced diploma in child development psychology, 1954; London University, B.Sc. (with honors in English and Psychology), 1956, academic diplomas in education, 1958, in nutrition, 1959, in English as second language, 1965; Sussex University, M.A., 1980; Century University,

Ph.D. in counseling and psychology, 1987. *Politics:* "Pacifist." *Religion:* Society of Friends (Quakers).

*ADDRESSES: Office*—86 Messina Ave., London NW6 4LE, England.

*CAREER:* Teacher in London, England, and British Guiana, 1953-68; writer, 1962—; principal of Beckford Primary School, London, 1969-82; counseling psychologist, 1982-83; researcher, Institute of Education, London, 1982-90. Freelance journalist; book reviewer for British Broadcasting Corporation's (BBC) Caribbean Service, 1962-63; reading therapist, 1975-77; education consultant, 1980-81. Member of community race relations board, 1969-75. Writer, 1962—.

*MEMBER:* International Women Writers Guild of America, Head Teachers Association, Commonwealth Institute, Network, Society of Authors, Round Table for the Advancement of Counseling, Writers Guild of America, Black Women Writers, Hampstead Community Association.

*AWARDS, HONORS:* Inner London Ethnic Minorities Prize, 1983; award from GLC Black Literature Competition, 1985, for *Frangipani House;* Guyana Historical Fiction Prize, 1992, for *Stedman and Joanna, a Love in Bondage.*

*WRITINGS:*

*Black Teacher* (autobiography), Cassell, 1976.
*In for a Penny* (young adult fiction), Cassell, 1978.
*Frangipani House* (novel), Heinemann, 1990.
*Boy-Sandwich* (novel), Heinemann, 1990.
*Echoes and Voice* (poems), Vantage, 1991.
*Stedman and Joanna, a Love in Bondage; Dedicated Love in
   the Eighteenth Century,* Vantage, 1991.
*Sunlight and Sweet Water,* Peepul Tree Press, 1993.
*Gather the Faces,* Peepul Tree Press, forthcoming.

Also author of *Green and Blue Water* (series of three titles), 1955-62; *Green and Gold* (series of four titles), 1963-65; *Nippers and Little Nippers* (series of 13 titles), Macmillan, 1970-75; *Bubu's Street, My Dad, In Bed, Arthur Small,* and *New Shoes,* all 1972; *The Present, Rice and Peas, No More Pets,* and *Outings for All,* all 1973; *Carnival of Dreams, Knock at Mrs. Herbs, New People at 24, The Paper Bag,* and *Visitor from Home,* all 1974; *Business at Boom Farm; Grandpa's Footsteps; In Praise of Love and Children; After Columbus; Inkle and Yarico;* and "Yellow Bird" series for Macmillan. Contributor to *Caribbean Women Writers: Essays from the First International Conference,* 1990. Contributor to periodicals, including *Woman's Own, Guardian, Parents'* and *Teacher's World.*

*SIDELIGHTS:* As an elementary school teacher in London in 1953, Beryl Gilroy began writing children's books to encourage her students to read. As a child, Gilroy was an insatiable reader who disliked the regimentation of school. "The school readers bore no relationship to their lives," she wrote in a 1988 essay for the First International Conference of Caribbean Women Writers, published in *Caribbean Women Writers.* She revealed in this essay that her young pupils were from diverse cultural backgrounds, many of them non-white and non-British, but, she stated, the books available to them "bore references so disparaging to black people that one wondered why they were written." Gilroy resolved this dilemma by writing her own books based on ideas gathered during group discussions she held with the children. These early therapeutic stories reflected meaningful situations involving the children's own feelings, interests, and fears in a recognizable format. "The illustrations and language of our homemade books were naturally theirs and the narrative so sustained that their involvement was complete," Gilroy wrote in her *Caribbean Women Writers* essay. Many of the tales were later published in the "Nippers and Little Nippers" series.

Gilroy's experiences as a teacher were the focus of her next work, *Black Teacher,* an autobiography published in 1976. She explains that she wrote the book in defense of the older generation of blacks in Britain, of whom she is a part, who were being labeled "Topsies and Toms" by the younger generation. She sets the record straight, she asserts, by recounting the prejudices that she as a black woman faced in Britain in the early 1950's, and by showing how her resistance to prejudice and injustice not only affirmed her own dignity as a human being, but broke down many barriers for blacks. "I express my identity in the craft of writing," Gilroy concluded in her *Caribbean Women Writers* essay, insisting that her goal was "tolerance, which comes from a wisdom obtained from self-knowledge."

Gilroy's first full-fledged adult novel, *Frangipani House,* incorporates the author's interest in the lives of the elderly, and explores interpersonal relationships between old and young family members. Frangipani House is a Caribbean institution for elderly women, named for the hedge of brightly-colored tropical frangipani plants surrounding it. A "Dickensian rest home" is how the critic Andrew Salkey, writing in *World Literature Today,* described Frangipani House. The villagers whisper darkly about the home: "They pays plenty to die-out inside dere! Death comes to lodgers in Frangipani House!" The novel tells the story of sixty-nine-year-old Mama King, whose daughters migrate to the United States leaving their aging mother behind. They assuage their guilt with money, and plead in overseas telephone calls to the matron of Frangipani House, "[Our] mother is independent and determined. Treat her well—please treat her well." Mama King has raised her own daughters and then helped raise her grandchildren;

she views life in Frangipani House as degrading, undignified, and not to be tolerated. Mama King escapes and lives in hiding for several weeks with a group of homeless people. But after she is brutally attacked by some youths and has to be hospitalized, she is rescued by a granddaughter who welcomes her into her home even as she gives birth to twin boys.

*Frangipani House* was well received by reviewers. Salkey in *World Literature Today* stated that Gilroy's "honed, symbolic inference, together with her driving social conscience, makes of all Guyana an allegorical Frangipani House." A *Publishers Weekly* reviewer noted Gilroy's clear "lyrical" writing, and praised the author's treatment of women: "With intelligence, grace and social insight, Gilroy presents the inner lives of strong women."

The author, having experienced the trauma of cultural collision on a personal level, writes with sensitivity about cultural ambivalence in her 1990 novel, *Boy-Sandwich.* The story is told from the perspective of an eighteen year-old youth, Tyrone, who was born and raised in England but whose parents and grandparents are of Guyanese heritage. Inevitably for Tyrone, cultural loyalties and family loyalties conflict and he has to make some tough choices. The thematic concerns in *Boy-Sandwich* focus on personal and cultural problems between the generations, and the idea that ethnocentricity limits perspective. When Tyrone visits the Caribbean, the home of his ancestors, he cannot adjust and finally realizes "I don't belong here ... I am British ... I want to call myself British for the first time in my life." *Boy-Sandwich* met with favorable critical reviews. A. L. McLeod, writing in *World Literature Today,* noted Gilroy's poetic language, declaring that "figurative language abounds in the novel; in fact, the texture of the style is a delight in a time when language is not always valued and crafted in fiction."

*BIOGRAPHICAL/CRITICAL SOURCES:*

*BOOKS*

Cudjoe, Selwyn R., editor, *Caribbean Women Writers: Essays from the First International Conference,* Calaloux Publications, 1990
Gilroy, Beryl, *Black Teacher,* Cassel, 1976.
Gilroy, Beryl, *Boy-Sandwich,* Heinemann, 1990.
Gilroy, Beryl, *Frangipani House,* Heinemann, 1990.

*PERIODICALS*

*Publishers Weekly,* November 21, 1986, p. 51.
*Washington Post Book World,* March 4, 1990.
*World Literature Today,* autumn, 1987, p. 670; spring, 1990, p. 348; winter, 1993.

## GIOVANNI, Nikki 1943-

*PERSONAL:* Born Yolande Cornelia Giovanni, Jr., June 7, 1943, in Knoxville, TN; daughter of Jones (a probation officer) and Yolande Cornelia (a social worker; maiden name, Watson) Giovanni; children: Thomas Watson. *Education:* Fisk University, B.A. (with honors), 1967; postgraduate study at University of Pennsylvania and Columbia University.

*ADDRESSES: Office*—c/o William Morrow Inc., 105 Madison Ave., New York, NY 10016.

*CAREER:* Poet, writer, lecturer. Queens College, City University of New York, Flushing, NY, assistant professor of black studies, 1968-69; Rutgers University, Livingston College, New Brunswick, NJ, associate professor of English, 1969-70; Ohio State University, visiting professor of English, 1984; College of Mount St. Joseph, professor of creative writing, 1985-87; Virginia Polytechnic Institute and State University, Blacksburg, VA, professor of English, 1987—; Texas Christian University, Fort Worth, TX, Honors Week Visiting Professor of Humanities, 1991. Founder of publishing firm, Niktom Ltd., 1970; cochair of Literary Arts Festival for State of Tennessee Homecoming, 1986; Duncanson Artist-in-Residence, Taft Museum, Cincinnati, OH, 1986; appointed to Ohio Humanities Council, 1987; director of Warm Hearth Writer's Workshop, 1988—; elected to board of directors, Virginia Foundation for the Humanities and Public Policy, 1990-93; participant in Appalachian Community Fund, 1991-93, and Volunteer Action Center, 1991-94; featured poet, International Poetry Festival, Utrecht, Holland, 1991. Has given numerous poetry readings and lectures at universities in the United States and Europe, including the University of Warsaw, Poland; has made numerous television and stage appearances.

*MEMBER:* National Council of Negro Women, Society of Magazine Writers, National Black Heroines for PUSH, Winnie Mandela Children's Fund Committee, Delta Sigma Theta (honorary member).

*AWARDS, HONORS:* Grants from Ford Foundation, 1967, National Endowment for the Arts, 1968, and Harlem Cultural Council, 1969; named one of ten "Most Admired Black Women," *Amsterdam News,* 1969; "Woman of the Year" citation, *Mademoiselle,* 1971; Omega Psi Phi Fraternity Award, 1971, for outstanding contribution to arts and letters; Meritorious Plaque for Service, Cook County Jail, 1971; Prince Matchabelli Sun Shower Award, 1971; life membership and scroll, National Council of Negro Women, 1972; National Association of Radio and Television Announcers award for best spoken word album, 1972, for *Truth Is on Its Way;* Woman of the Year Youth Leadership Award, *Ladies Home Journal,* 1972; National Book Award nomination, 1973, for *Gemini;* "Best Books for Young Adults" citation, American

Library Association, 1973, for *My House;* "Woman of the Year" citation, Cincinnati chapter of YWCA, 1983; elected to Ohio Women's Hall of Fame, 1985; "Outstanding Woman of Tennessee" citation, 1985; Post-Corbett Award, 1986; Distinguished Recognition Award, Detroit City Council, 1986; Ohioana Book Award, 1988, for *Sacred Cows ... and Other Edibles*; Silver Apple Award, Oakland Museum Film Festival, 1988, for *Spirit to Spirit;* "Woman of the Year" citation, Lynchburg, VA, chapter of National Association for the Advancement of Colored People, 1989. Doctorate of Humanities, Wilberforce University, 1972, and Fisk University; Doctorate of Literature, University of Maryland (Princess Anne Campus), 1974, Ripon University, 1974, Smith College, 1975, and College of Mount St. Joseph, 1983; Doctorate of Humane Letters, Mount St. Mary College and Indiana University. Keys to numerous cities, including Dallas, TX, New York, NY, Cincinnati, OH, Savannah, GA, Miami, FL, New Orleans, LA, and Los Angeles, CA.

*WRITINGS:*

*POETRY*

*Black Feeling, Black Talk* (also see below), Broadside Press, 1968, third edition, 1970.

*Black Judgement* (also see below), Broadside Press, 1968.

*Black Feeling, Black Talk/Black Judgement* (contains *Black Feeling, Black Talk* and *Black Judgement*), Morrow, 1970.

*Re: Creation,* Broadside Press, 1970.

*Poem of Angela Yvonne Davis,* Afro Arts, 1970.

*Spin a Soft Black Song: Poems for Children,* illustrated by Charles Bible, Hill & Wang, 1971, illustrated by George Martin, Lawrence Hill, 1985, revised edition, Farrar, Straus, 1987.

*My House,* foreword by Ida Lewis, Morrow, 1972.

*Ego Tripping and Other Poems for Young People,* illustrated by George Ford, Lawrence Hill, 1973.

*The Women and the Men,* Morrow, 1975.

*Cotton Candy on a Rainy Day* (also see below), introduction by Paula Giddings, Morrow, 1978.

*Vacation Time: Poems for Children,* illustrated by Marisabina Russo, Morrow, 1980.

*Those Who Ride the Night Winds,* Morrow, 1983.

*NONFICTION*

*Gemini: An Extended Autobiographical Statement on My First Twenty-five Years of Being a Black Poet,* Bobbs-Merrill, 1971.

(With James Baldwin) *A Dialogue: James Baldwin and Nikki Giovanni,* Lippincott, 1973.

(With Margaret Walker) *A Poetic Equation: Conversations between Nikki Giovanni and Margaret Walker,* Howard University Press, 1974.

(Editor with Jessie Carney Smith) *Images of Blacks in American Culture: A Reference Guide to Information Sources,* Greenwood, 1988.

(Editor with Cathee Dennison) *Appalachian Elders: A Warm Hearth Sampler,* Pocahontas Press, 1991.

*Conversations with Nikki Giovanni,* edited by Virginia C. Fowler, University Press of Mississippi, 1992.

*SOUND RECORDINGS*

*Truth Is on Its Way,* Right-On Records, 1971.

*Like a Ripple on a Pond,* Niktom, 1973.

*The Way I Feel,* Atlantic Records, 1974.

*Legacies: The Poetry of Nikki Giovanni,* Folkways Records, 1976.

*The Reason I Like Chocolate,* Folkways Records, 1976.

*Cotton Candy on a Rainy Day,* Folkways Records, 1978.

*OTHER*

(Editor) *Night Comes Softly: An Anthology of Black Female Voices,* Medic Press, 1970.

(Author of introduction) Adele Sebastian, *Intro to Fine* (poems), Woman in the Moon, 1985.

*Sacred Cows ... and Other Edibles* (essays), Morrow, 1988.

Contributor to numerous anthologies. Author of columns "One Woman's Voice," for Anderson-Moberg Syndicate of the *New York Times,* and "The Root of the Matter," for *Encore American and Worldwide News.* Contributor to magazines, including *Black Creation, Black World, Ebony, Essence, Freedom Ways, Journal of Black Poetry, Negro Digest,* and *Umbra.* Editorial consultant, *Encore American and Worldwide News.*

A selection of Giovanni's public papers are held at Mugar Memorial Library of Boston University, Boston, Massachusetts.

*ADAPTATIONS: Spirit to Spirit: The Poetry of Nikki Giovanni,* featuring the poet reading from her published works, was produced by the the Corporation for Public Broadcasting, and the Ohio Council on the Arts and first aired in 1986.

*SIDELIGHTS:* One of the most prominent poets to emerge from the black literary movement of the late 1960s, Nikki Giovanni is famous for strongly voiced poems that testify to her own evolving awareness and experience: as a daughter and young girl, a black woman, a revolutionary in the Civil Rights Movement, and a mother. Popular for her adult poetry and essays as well as her best-selling recordings, Giovanni has also published three books of acclaimed verse for children. As a child, Giovanni gained an intense admiration and appreciation for her race from her outspoken grandmother; other members of her close-knit family influenced her in the oral tradition of poetry. "I come from a long line of storytellers," she once stated. "My grandfather was a Latin scholar and he loved the myths, and my mother is a big romanticist, so we heard a lot of stories growing up.... I appreciated the quality and the rhythm of the telling of the stories, and I know when I started to write that I wanted to retain that—I didn't want to become the kind of writer that was stilted or that used language in ways that could not be spoken."

When Giovanni was still young, she moved with her parents from Knoxville, Tennessee to a suburb of Cincinnati, Ohio, but remained close to her grandmother and spent several of her teen years with her in Knoxville. In 1960, at the age of seventeen, Giovanni enrolled in Nashville's all-black Fisk University, but eventually came into conflict with the school's dean of women and was asked to leave. She returned to Fisk in 1964, however, and became a leader in both political and literary activities. She served as editor of a campus literary magazine, *Elan,* and worked to restore Fisk's chapter of the Student Non-Violent Coordinating Committee (SNCC) at a time when the organization was pressing the concept of "black power" to bring about social and economic reform. In 1967, Giovanni graduated with an honors degree in history. As a teenager, Giovanni had been conservative in her outlook—a supporter of Republican presidential candidate Barry Goldwater and a follower of author Ayn Rand, famous for her philosophy of objectivism. In college, however, a roommate named Bertha succeeded in persuading Giovanni to adopt her revolutionary ideals. "Before I met [Bertha] I was Ayn Rand-Barry Goldwater all the way," Giovanni remarked in *Gemini: An Extended Autobiographical Statement on My First Twenty-five Years of Being a Black Poet.* "Bertha kept asking, how could Black people be conservative? What have they got to conserve? And after awhile (realizing that I had absolutely nothing, period) I came around."

Giovanni's first three books of poetry—*Black Feeling, Black Talk; Black Judgment;* and *Re: Creation*—display a strong black perspective as she recounts her growing political awareness. These early books quickly established Giovanni as a prominent new voice in black poetry; they sold numerous copies and she became an increasingly popular figure on the reading and speaking circuit. In *Dictionary of Literary Biography,* Mozella G. Mitchell described these poems, published between 1968 and 1970, as "a kind of ritualistic exorcism of former nonblack ways of thinking and an immersion in blackness. Not only are they directed at other black people whom [Giovanni] wanted to awaken to the beauty of blackness, but also at herself as a means of saturating her own consciousness." This poetic "immersion in blackness" becomes evident, Mitchell feels, in the "daring questions, interspersed with

ironic allusions to violent actions blacks have committed for the nation against their own color across the world." Giovanni's vision, however, "goes beyond ... violent change to a vision of rebuilding."

Critical reaction to Giovanni's early volumes centered upon her more revolutionary poems. "Nikki writes about the familiar: what she knows, sees, experiences," Don L. Lee observed in *Dynamite Voices I: Black Poets of the 1960s.* "It is clear why she conveys such urgency in expressing the need for Black awareness, unity, solidarity.... What is perhaps more important is that when the Black poet chooses to serve as political seer, he must display a keen sophistication. Sometimes Nikki oversimplifies and therefore sounds rather naive politically." Similarly, Mitchell remarked, "In this early stage of her commitment of her talent to the service of the black revolution, her creativity is bound by a great deal of narrowness and partiality from which her later work is freed." *Dictionary of Literary Biography* contributor Alex Batman recognized Giovanni's indebtedness to oral tradition. "The poems ... reflect elements of black culture, particularly the lyrics of rhythm-and-blues music," Batman wrote. "Indeed the rhythms of her verse correspond so directly to the syncopations of black music that her poems begin to show a potential for becoming songs without accompaniment." Lee commented, "Nikki is at her best in the short, personal poem.... Her effectiveness is in the area of the 'fast rap.' She says the right thing at the right time." Batman concluded that in reaching to create "a blues without music," Giovanni "repeats the worst mistake of the songwriter—the use of language that has little appeal of its own in order to meet the demands of the rhythm."

Critical reservations notwithstanding, Giovanni's earliest works were enormously successful, given the relatively low public demand for modern poetry. In a *Mademoiselle* article, Sheila Weller noted that *Black Judgement* sold six thousand copies in three months, making that volume five to six times more sellable than the average. Mitchell suggested that Giovanni's poems of that period brought her prominence "as one of the three leading figures of the new black poetry between 1968 and 1971."

In 1969 Giovanni took a teaching position at Rutgers University and that summer gave birth to her son, Thomas. She explained her choice in *Ebony:* "I had a baby at 25 because I *wanted* to have a baby and I could *afford* to have a baby. I did not get married because I didn't *want* to get married and I could *afford* not to get married." The author's work through the mid-1970s reflected her changing priorities after her son's birth. She remarked to *Harper's Bazaar,* "To protect Tommy there is no question I would give my life. I just cannot imagine living without him. But I can live without the revolution." Describing this period in Giovanni's career, during which she produced a collection of autobiographical essays, two books of poetry for children, and two poetry collections for adults, Mitchell wrote, "We see evidence of a more developed individualism and greater introspection, and a sharpening of her creative and moral powers, as well as of her social and political focus and understanding." Reflecting on *The Women and the Men,* published in 1975, Batman noted, "The revolution is fading from the new poems, and in its place is a growing sense of frustration and a greater concern with the nature of poetry itself. Throughout these poems is a feeling of energy reaching out toward an object that remains perpetually beyond the grasp."

The themes of family love, loneliness, frustration, and introspection explored in Giovanni's earlier works find further expression in *My House* and *The Women and the Men.* In the foreword to *My House,* Ida Lewis described the key to understanding the poet's conviction: "The central core [of Giovanni's work] is always associated with her family: the family that produced her and the family she is producing. She has reached a simple philosophy more or less to the effect that a good family spirit is what produces healthy communities, which is what should produce a strong (Black) nation." Mitchell discussed *The Women and the Men* with emphasis upon Giovanni's heightened sense of self: "In this collection of poems, ... she has permitted to flower fully portions of herself and her perception which have been evident only in subdued form or in incompletely worked-through fragments. Ideas concerning women and men, universal human relatedness, and the art of poetry are seen here as being in the process of fuller realization in the psyche of the author." Noting the aspects of personal discovery in *My House,* critic John W. Connor suggested in the *English Journal* that Giovanni "sees her world as an extension of herself ... sees problems in the world as an extension of her problems, and ... sees herself existing amidst tensions, heartache, and marvelous expressions of love.... When a reader enters *My House,* he is invited to savor the poet's ideas about a meaningful existence in today's world." "*My House* is not just poems," Kalumu Ya Salaam commented in *Black World.* "*My House* is how it is, what it is to be a young, single, intelligent Black woman with a son and no man. Is what it is to be a woman who has failed and is now sentimental about some things, bitter about some things, and generally always frustrated, always feeling frustrated on one of various levels or another."

Concurrent with her poetry for adults, Giovanni has published three volumes of poetry for children, *Spin a Soft Black Song, Ego-Tripping and Other Poems for Young People,* and *Vacation Time.* According to Mitchell, the children's poems have "essentially the same impulse" as Giovanni's adult poetry; namely, "the creation of racial pride and the communication of individual love. These are the goals of all of Giovanni's poetry, here directed toward a younger and more impression-

able audience." In a *New York Times Book Review* article on *Spin a Soft Black Song,* Nancy Klein noted, "Nikki Giovanni's poems for children, like her adult works, exhibit a combination of casual energy and sudden wit. No cheek-pinching auntie, she explores the contours of childhood with honest affection, sidestepping both nostalgia and condescension." A *Kirkus Reviews* contributor, commenting on *Ego-Tripping,* claimed: "When [Giovanni] grabs hold ... it's a rare kid, certainly a rare black kid, who could resist being picked right up." Critics of *Vacation Time* suggested that some of the rhyme is forced or guilty of "an occasional contrivance to achieve scansion," in the words of Zena Sutherland for the *Bulletin of the Center for Children's Books,* but praise is still forthcoming for the theme of Giovanni's verses. "In her singing lines, Giovanni shows she hadn't forgotten childhood adventures in ... exploring the world with a small person's sense of discovery," wrote a *Publishers Weekly* reviewer. Mitchell, too, claimed: "One may be dazzled by the smooth way [Giovanni] drops all political and personal concerns [in *Vacation Time*] and completely enters the world of the child and brings to it all the fanciful beauty, wonder, and lollipopping."

As early as 1971, Giovanni began to experiment with another medium for presenting her poetry—sound recording. Recalling how her first album, *Truth Is on Its Way,* came to be made, Giovanni told *Ebony:* "Friends had been bugging me about doing a tape but I am not too fond of the spoken word or of my voice, so I hesitated. Finally I decided to try it with gospel music, since I really dig the music." Giovanni also remarked in *Ebony* that she chose gospel music as background for her poetry because she wanted to make something her grandmother would listen to. *Truth Is on Its Way* was the best selling spoken-word album of 1971, contributing greatly to Giovanni's fame nationwide. "I have really been gratified with the response [to the album] of older people, who usually feel that black poets hate them and everything they stood for," Giovanni told *Ebony.* The popularity of *Truth Is on Its Way* encouraged Giovanni to make subsequent recordings of her poetry as well as audio- and videotapes of discussions about poetry and black issues with other prominent poets.

In 1978 Giovanni published *Cotton Candy on a Rainy Day,* which Mitchell described as "perhaps her most sobering book of verse.... It contains thoughtful and insightful lyrics on the emotions, fears, insecurities, realities, and responsibilities of living." Mitchell detected a sense of loneliness, boredom, and futility in the work, caused in part by the incompleteness of the black liberation movement. Batman, too, sensed a feeling of despair in the poems: "What distinguishes *Cotton Candy on a Rainy Day* is its poignancy. One feels throughout that here is a child of the 1960s mourning the passing of a decade of conflict, of violence, but most of all, of hope." In her introduction to the volume, Paula Giddings suggested that the emotional complacency of the 1970s is responsible for

Giovanni's apparent sense of despondency: "Inevitably, the shining innocence that comes from feeling the ideal is possible is also gone, and one must learn to live with less.... The loneliness carries no blame, no bitterness, just the realization of a void.... Taken in the context of Nikki's work [*Cotton Candy on a Rainy Day*] completes the circle: of dealing with society, others, and finally oneself."

*Those Who Ride the Night Winds,* Giovanni's 1983 publication, represents a stylistic departure from her previous works. "In this book Giovanni has adopted a new and innovative form; and the poetry reflects her heightened self-knowledge and imagination," Mitchell commented. The subject matter of *Those Who Ride the Night Winds* tends once more to drift toward a subdued but persistent political activism, as Giovanni dedicates various pieces to Phillis Wheatley, Martin Luther King, Jr., Rosa Parks, and the children of Atlanta, Georgia, who were at the time of the writing living in fear of a serial murderer. Mitchell suggests that the paragraphs punctuated with ellipses characteristic of the volume make the poems "appear to be hot off the mind of the author.... In most cases the poems are meditation pieces that begin with some special quality in the life of the subject, and with thoughtful, clever, eloquent and delightful words amplify and reconstruct salient features of her or his character." In *Sacred Cows ... and Other Edibles* Giovanni presents essays on such diverse topics as literary politics, game shows, black political leaders, termites, and national holiday celebrations, and explores them "with humor that is street and worldly wise, and with occasional insights that, in the best Giovanni style, turn a neat phrase too," Marita Golden remarked in *Washington Post Book World.* Golden described the collection as "quintessential Nikki Giovanni—sometimes funny, nervy and unnerving with flashes of wisdom." *Library Journal* reviewer Nancy R. Ives found *Sacred Cows* "both amusing and enlightening" and "a joy to read."

Over the years Giovanni's work has evolved from the "open, aggressive, and explosive revolutionary tendencies that characterized her early verses" to "expressions of universal sensitivity, artistic beauty, tenderness, warmth, and depth," Mitchell wrote. She further noted that Giovanni has a deep concern "about her own identity as a person ... and what her purpose in life should be." As Giddings noted in the introduction to *Cotton Candy on a Rainy Day,* "Nikki Giovanni is a witness. Her intelligent eye has caught the experience of a generation and dutifully recorded it. She has seen enough heroes, broken spirits, ironies, heartless minds and mindless hearts to fill several lifetimes." Giddings concluded, "I have never known anyone who cares so much and so intensely about the things she sees around her as Nikki. That speaks to her humanity and to her writing. Through the passion and the cynicism of the last two decades she has cared too much to have either a heartless mind or, just as importantly, a mindless heart."

*BIOGRAPHICAL/CRITICAL SOURCES:*

*BOOKS*

*Authors in the News,* Volume 1, Gale, 1976.
*Children's Literature Review,* Volume 6, Gale, 1984.
*Contemporary Literary Criticism,* Gale, Volume 2, 1974, Volume 4, 1975, Volume 9, 1981.
*A Dialogue: James Baldwin and Nikki Giovanni,* Lippincott, 1972.
*Dictionary of Literary Biography,* Gale, Volume 5: *American Poets Since World War II,* 1980, Volume 41: *Afro-American Poets Since 1955,* 1985.
Evans, Mari, editor, *Black Women Writers, 1950-1980: A Critical Evaluation,* Doubleday, 1984.
Fowler, Virginia C., editor, *Conversations with Nikki Giovanni,* University Press of Mississippi, 1992.
Fowler, Virginia C., editor, *Nikki Giovanni: An Introduction to Her Life and Work,* Macmillan, 1992.
Gibson, Donald B., editor, *Modern Black Poets: A Collection of Critical Essays,* Prentice-Hall, 1973.
Giovanni, Nikki, *Gemini: An Extended Autobiographical Statement on My First Twenty-five Years of Being a Black Poet,* Bobbs-Merrill, 1971.
Giovanni, Nikki, *My House,* foreword by Ida Lewis, Morrow, 1972.
Giovanni, Nikki, *Cotton Candy on a Rainy Day,* introduction by Paula Giddings, Morrow, 1978.
Henderson, Stephen, *Understanding the New Black Poetry: Black Speech and Black Music as Poetic References,* Morrow, 1973.
Lee, Don L., *Dynamite Voices I: Black Poets of the 1960s,* Broadside Press, 1971.
Noble, Jeanne, *Beautiful, Also, Are the Souls of My Black Sisters: A History of the Black Woman in America,* Prentice-Hall, 1978.
Tate, Claudia, *Black Women Writers at Work,* Crossroad Publishing, 1983.

*PERIODICALS*

*Best Sellers,* September 1, 1973; January, 1976.
*Black World,* December, 1970; January, 1971; February, 1971; April, 1971; August, 1971; August, 1972; July, 1974.
*Bulletin of the Center for Children's Books,* October, 1980.
*Choice,* May, 1972; March, 1973; September, 1974; January, 1976.
*Christian Science Monitor,* June 4, 1970; June 19, 1974.
*CLA Journal,* September, 1971.
*Ebony,* February, 1972; August, 1972.
*Encore,* spring, 1972.
*English Journal,* April, 1973; January, 1974.
*Essence,* August, 1981.

*Harper's Bazaar,* July, 1972.
*Ingenue,* February, 1973.
*Jet,* May 25, 1972.
*Kirkus Reviews,* January 1, 1974, p. 11.
*Library Journal,* February 15, 1988, p. 169.
*Los Angeles Times,* December 4, 1985.
*Los Angeles Times Book Review,* April 17, 1983.
*Mademoiselle,* May, 1973; December, 1973; September, 1975.
*Milwaukee Journal,* November 20, 1974.
*New York Times,* April 25, 1969; July 26, 1972.
*New York Times Book Review,* November 7, 1971; November 28, 1971; February 13, 1972; May 5, 1974.
*Partisan Review,* spring, 1972.
*Publishers Weekly,* November 13, 1972; May 23, 1980; December 18, 1987, p. 48.
*Saturday Review,* January 15, 1972.
*Time,* April 6, 1970; January 17, 1972.
*Washington Post,* January 30, 1987.
*Washington Post Book World,* May 19, 1974; March 8, 1981; February 14, 1988, p. 3.

*OTHER*

*The Poet Today* (sound recording), The Christophers, 1979.

\*   \*   \*

## GODOY ALCAYAGA, Lucila   1889-1957
### (Gabriela Mistral)

*PERSONAL:* Born April 7, 1889, in Vicuna, Chile; died January 10, 1957, in Hempstead, NY; daughter of Jeronimo Godoy Villanueva (a schoolteacher and minstrel) and Petronila Alcayaga de Molina; children: Juan Miguel Godoy (adopted). *Education:* Attended Pedagogical College, Santiago, Chile, 1909. *Religion:* Catholic.

*CAREER:* Poet and author. Primary and secondary school teacher and administrator in Chile, including positions with Liceo de Antofagasta, 1911-12, Liceo de los Andes, 1912-18, Liceo de Punte Arenas, 1918-20, and Liceo de Temuca, 1920-21; adviser to Mexican minister of education Jose Vasconcelos, 1922; visiting professor at Barnard and Middlebury colleges and the University of Puerto Rico. League of Nations, Chilean delegate to Institute of Intellectual Cooperation, member of Committee of Arts and Letters; consul in Italy, Spain, Portugal, Brazil, and the United States.

*AWARDS, HONORS:* Juegos Florales laurel crown and gold medal from the city of Santiago, Chile, 1914, for *Sonetos de la muerte;* Nobel Prize for literature from the Swedish Acad-

emy, 1945; Chilean National Prize, 1951; honorary degree from the University of Chile.

*WRITINGS:*

*UNDER PSEUDONYM GABRIELA MISTRAL*

*Desolacion* (poetry and prose; title means "Desolation"; also see below), preliminary notes by Instituto de las Espanas, Instituto de las Espanas en los Estados Unidos (New York), 1922, second edition augmented by Mistral, additional prologue by Pedro Prado, Nascimento, 1923, third edition, prologues by Prado and Hernan Diaz Arrieta (under pseudonym Alone), 1926, new edition with prologue by Roque Esteban Scarpa, Bello, 1979 (variations in content among these and other editions).

(Editor and contributor) *Lecturas para mujeres* (essays; also see below), introduction by Mistral, Secretaria de Educacion (Mexico), 1923, fourth edition, edited with an apology by Palma Guillen de Nicolau, Porrua (Mexico), 1967.

*Ternura: Canciones de ninos* (title means "Tenderness"; also see below), Saturnino Calleja (Madrid), 1924, enlarged edition, Espasa Calpe, 1945, eighth edition, 1965.

*Nubes blancas (poesias), y la oracion de la maestra* (poetry and prose; includes selections from *Desolacion* and *Ternura* and complete text of "Oracion de la maestra"), B. Bauza (Barcelona), 1925.

*Poesias,* Cervantes (Barcelona), c. 1936.

*Tala* (poetry; title means "Ravage"; also see below), Sur (Buenos Aires), 1938, abridged edition, Losada, 1946, reprinted with introduction by Alfonso Calderon, Bello, 1979.

*Antologia: Seleccion de la autora* (includes selections from *Desolacion, Tala,* and *Ternura*), selected by Mistral, prologue by Ismael Edwards Matte, ZigZag, 1941, third edition published as *Antologia,* prologue by Alone, 1953.

*Pequena antologia* (selected poetry and prose), Escuela Nacional de Artes Graficas, 1950.

*Poemas de las madres,* epilogue by Antonio R. Romero, illustrations by Andre Racz, Pacifico, 1950.

*Lagar* (poetry; title means "Wine Press"), Pacifico, 1954.

*Obras selectas,* Pacifico, 1954.

*Los mejores versos,* prologue by Simon Latino, Nuestra America (Buenos Aires), 1957.

*Canto a San Francisco,* El Eco Franciscano, 1957.

*Epistolario,* introduction by Raul Silva Castro, Anales de la Universidad de Chile, 1957.

*Mexico maravilloso* (essays and poetry originally published in *Lecturas para mujeres* and periodical *El Maestro*), selected with an introduction by Andres Henestrosa, Stylo (Mexico), 1957.

*Produccion de Gabriela Mistral de 1912 a 1918* (poetry, prose, and letters, most previously unpublished), edited by Silva Castro, Anales de la Universidad de Chile, 1957.

*Recados: Contando a Chile,* selected with prologue by Alfonso M. Escudero, Pacifico, 1957.

*Selected Poems of Gabriela Mistral,* translated by Langston Hughes, Indiana University Press, 1957.

*Croquis mexicanos: Gabriela Mistral en Mexico* (contains prose selections from *Lecturas para mujeres,* poetry, and a pedagogical lecture titled "Imagen y palabra en la educacion"), B. Costa-Amic (Mexico), c. 1957, reprinted, Nascimento, 1978.

*Poesias completas,* edited by Margaret Bates, prologues by Julio Saavedra Molina and Dulce Maria Loynaz, Aguilar (Madrid), 1958, third edition, introduction by Esther de Caceres, 1966.

*Poema de Chile,* revisions by Doris Dana, Pomaire, 1967.

*Antologia de Gabriela Mistral,* selected with prologue by Emma Godoy, B. Costa-Amic, 1967.

*Poesias,* edited with a prologue by Eliseo Diego, Casa de las Americas, 1967.

*Homenaje a Gabriela Mistral,* Orfeo, 1967.

*Selected Poems of Gabriela Mistral,* translated by Dana, Johns Hopkins Press, 1971.

*Todas ibamos a ser reinas,* Quimantu, 1971.

*Antologia general de Gabriela Mistral* (poems, essays, and letters; portions originally published in periodical *Orfeo,* 1969), Comite de Homenaje a Gabriela Mistral, 1973.

*Antologia poetica de Gabriela Mistral,* selected with a prologue by Calderon, Universitaria, 1974.

*Cartas de amor de Gabriela Mistral,* Bello, 1978.

*Prosa religiosa de Gabriela Mistral,* notes and introduction by Luis Vargas Saavedra, Bello, 1978.

*Gabriela presente,* selected by Ines Moreno, Literatura Americana Reunida, 1987.

Also author of *Sonetos de la muerte,* 1914, and "An Appeal to World Conscience: The Genocide Convention," 1956. Author of fables, including *Grillos y ranas,* translation by Dana published as *Crickets and Frogs,* Atheneum, 1972, and *Elefante y su secreto,* adaptation and translation by Dana published as *The Elephant and His Secret,* Atheneum, 1974. Poetry for children published as *El nino en la poesia de Gabriela Mistral,* 1978. Correspondence between Mistral and Matilde Ladron de Guevara published as *Gabriela Mistral, "rebelde magnifica,"* 1957.

Contributor to periodicals, including *Bulletin, Commonweal, Living Age,* and *Poetry.*

SIDELIGHTS: Nobel laureate Gabriela Mistral—whose actual name was Lucila Godoy Alcayaga—was a prominent Latin American poet, educator, and diplomat. A Chilean native of Spanish, Basque, and Indian descent, she was raised in a northern rural farming community. Following the example of her father, Mistral initially pursued a career in education, beginning as a primary school teacher at the age of fifteen. Over the next decade, she went on to become a secondary school professor, inspector general, and ultimately a school director. A leading authority on rural education, Mistral served as an adviser to Mexican minister of education Jose Vasconcelos in the early 1920s. Her background in teaching and value as an educational consultant led to her active service in the Chilean government. Mistral is probably best known, however, for her brand of rich but unpretentious lyrical poetry.

The tragic suicide of her fiance in the early 1900s prompted Mistral to compose her first lines of melancholy verse. Within several years she completed a small body of poetry that she would later publish under the Mistral pseudonym (which is said to be either a tribute to poets Gabriele D'Annunzio and Frederic Mistral or a combined reference to the archangel Gabriel and the brutal northerly wind, or "mistral," of southern France). Having entered her *Sonetos de la muerte* ("Sonnets on Death") in a Santiago writing contest in 1914, she earned first prize and instant fame, developing in ensuing years a reputation as one of Latin America's most gifted poets.

Critics have noted the joint influences of biblical verse and the works of Hindu poet Rabindranath Tagore and Nicaraguan poet Ruben Dario on the literary development of Mistral. She frequently expressed through her verse an urgent concern for outcasts, underprivileged or otherwise impoverished people, and ancestors—the poet donated profits from her third book to Basque children orphaned in the Spanish Civil War. Her simple, unadorned writings evoke a sense of mystery and isolation, centering on themes of love, death, childhood, maternity, and religion. Mistral had turned to religion for solace in her despair over the loss of her intended husband. Her first volume of poetry, *Desolacion* ("Desolation"), is imbued with the spirit of an individual's struggle to reconcile personal fulfillment with the will of God. In expressing her grief and anguish throughout the collection with characteristic passion and honesty, Mistral "talks to Christ as freely as to a child," commented Mildred Adams in *Nation.*

Several critics on Mistral, including Adams, have suggested that both her lover's death and her failure to bear his child inspired in the poet a fervent dedication to children. *Ternura* ("Tenderness"), her 1924 volume of children's poetry, is a celebration of the joys of birth and motherhood. While *Desolacion* reflects the pain of a lost love and an obsession with death, *Ternura* is generally considered a work of renewed hope and understanding. Infused with a decidedly Christian temper, the poems in the latter collection are among the most sentimental written by Mistral, and they evoke the poet's overriding desire to attain harmony and peace in her life.

Correlating Mistral's treatment of the love theme with her frequent depiction of mother and child, Sidonia Carmen Rosenbaum theorized in *Modern Women Poets of Spanish America:* "Her conception of love is ... profoundly religious and pure. Its purpose is not to appease desire, to satisfy carnal appetites, but soberly to give thought to the richest, the most precious, the most sacred heritage of woman: maternity." *Saturday Review* contributor Edwin Honig expressed a similar view, noting that for Mistral, "Childbearing ... approximates a mystic condition: it is like finding union with God.... The experience of gestating another life inside oneself is the supreme act of creation."

Though consistently stark, simple, and direct, Mistral's later verse is marked by a growing maturity and sense of redemption and deliverance. The 1938 collection *Tala* ("Felling"), according to Rosenbaum, possesses "a serenity that reveals an emotion more contained (whose key note is hope) and ... an expression less tortured" than the early works and therefore continues Mistral's path toward renewal. The poet achieved a greater objectivity in both this work and her final volume of poetry, *Lagar* ("Wine Press"), which was published in 1954. Through pure and succinct language, *Lagar* conveys Mistral's acceptance of death and marks her growing freedom from bitterness. Several critics have implied that this collection—the culmination of her literary career—is both a refinement of her simple and skillful writing style and a testament to her strengthened faith and ultimate understanding of God. As Fernando Alegria explained in *Las fronteras del realismo: Literatura chilena del siglo XX,* "Here we have the secret dynamism [of the poet's verse]; it contains a salvation."

In *Gabriela Mistral: The Poet and Her Work,* Margot Arce de Vazquez concluded: "[Mistral's] poetry possesses the merit of consummate originality, of a voice of its own, authentic and consciously realized. The affirmation within this poetry of the intimate 'I,' removed from everything foreign to it, makes it profoundly human, and it is this human quality that gives it its universal value."

*BIOGRAPHICAL/CRITICAL SOURCES:*

BOOKS

Alegria, Fernando, *Las fronteras del realismo: Literatura chilena del siglo XX,* ZigZag, 1962.
de Vazquez, Margot Arce, *Gabriela Mistral: The Poet and Her Work,* translated by Helene Masslo Anderson, New York University Press, 1964.
Foster, David William and Virginia Ramos Foster, editors, *Modern Latin American Literature,* Volume 2, Ungar, 1975.
Mistral, Gabriela, *Selected Poems of Gabriela Mistral,* translated by Doris Dana, Johns Hopkins Press, 1971.
Rosenbaum, Sidonia Carmen, *Modern Women Poets of Spanish America: The Precursors, Delmira Agustini, Gabriela Mistral, Alfonsina Storni, Juana de Ibarbourou,* Hispanic Institute in the United States, 1945.
Szmulewicz, Efraim, *Gabriela Mistral: Biografia emotiva,* Sol de Septiembre, 1967.
Taylor, Martin C., *Gabriela Mistral's Religious Sensibility,* University of California Press, 1968.
*Twentieth-Century Literary Criticism,* Volume 2, Gale, 1979.
Vargas Saavedra, Luis, editor, *El otro suicida de Gabriela Mistral,* Universidad Catolica de Chile, 1985.

PERIODICALS

*Cuadernos Americanos,* September-October, 1962.
*Living Age,* November 29, 1924.
*Nation,* December 29, 1945.
*Poet Lore,* winter, 1940.
*Saturday Review,* March 22, 1958, July 17, 1971.

\*     \*     \*

# GOLDEN, Marita 1950-

*PERSONAL:* Born April 28, 1950, in Washington, DC; daughter of Francis Sherman (a taxi driver) and Beatrice (a landlord; maiden name, Reid) Golden; divorced; children: Michael Kayode. *Education:* American University, B.A., 1972; Columbia University, M.Sc., 1973.

*ADDRESSES: Home*—Boston, MA. *Agent*—Carol Mann, 168 Pacific Street, Brooklyn, NY 11201.

*CAREER:* WNET-Channel 13, New York City, associate producer, 1974-75; University of Lagos, Lagos, Nigeria, assistant professor of mass communications, 1975-79; Roxbury Community College, Roxbury, MA, assistant professor of English, 1979-81; Emerson College, Boston, MA, assistant professor of journalism, 1981-83; writer. Member of nominating committee for the George K. Polk Awards; executive director of the Institute for the Preservation and Study of African American Writing, 1986-87; consultant for the Washington DC Community Humanities Council, 1986-89.

*MEMBER:* Afro-American Writer's Guild, (president, 1986—).

*WRITINGS:*

(Contributor) Beatrice Murphy, editor, *Today's Negro Voices,* Messner, 1970.

(Contributor) *Keeping the Faith: Writings by Contemporary Black American Women,* Fawcett, 1974.
*Migrations of the Heart* (autobiography), Doubleday, 1983.
*A Woman's Place* (novel), Doubleday, 1986.
*Long Distance Life* (novel), Doubleday, 1989.
*And Do Remember Me* (novel), Doubleday, 1992.

Contributor of poetry to several anthologies, and contributor to periodicals, including *Essence, Daily Times* (Nigeria), *National Observer, Black World,* and *Amsterdam News.*

*SIDELIGHTS:* Marita Golden began writing her autobiography, *Migrations of the Heart,* when she was only twenty-nine years old. When asked about her motivation for the book, Golden told *Washington Post* reporter Jacqueline Trescott that she "stumbled into" it, adding: "I wanted to meditate on what it meant to grow in the '60's, what it meant to go to Africa the first time, what it meant to be a modern black woman living in that milieu. I had to bring order to the chaos of memory.... What I wanted to do was write a book that would take my life and shape it into an artifact that could inform and possibly inspire."

The book met with generally favorable reviews and was described by Diane McWhorter in the *New York Times Book Review* as "interesting" and "told in a prose that often seems possessed by some perverse genius." Reviewer Elayne B. Byman Bass commended Golden in the *Washington Post Book World* for her account of how "the love of a girl for her father evolves through several migrations into a woman's love for her man, her child and finally herself," while in *Ms.* magazine, critic Carole Bovoso suggested that Golden has earned a place among those black women writers who share a "greater and greater commitment ... to understand self, multiplied in terms of the community, the community multiplied in terms of the nation, and the nation multiplied in terms of the world."

Golden's novel *A Woman's Place*—a "truncated *herstory*" according to Wanda Coleman in the *Los Angeles Times Book Review*—follows the lives of three black women who meet and become friends at an elite Boston university. Each of them confronts problems facing women of color in today's society. One cannot adjust to the pressures her possessive Islamic husband puts on her, another suffers from guilt related to her love of a white man, and the third tries to lose herself working in a developing African nation. "By refusing to offer easy answers to the predicaments of women, and black women in particular," says *Washington Post Book World* contributor Susan Wood, "Golden makes us believe in her characters and care about them."

*Long Distance Life,* Golden's second novel, takes the reader into the black streets of Washington, D.C., where she was raised. Beginning in the 1920s, the story follows Naomi, a southern farmer's daughter, as she moves north in search of opportunity, marries, prospers, and loses part of her spirituality along the way. The tale then turns to the family's subsequent generations, their involvement in the civil rights movement, and one grandson's drug-related death. Laura Shapiro in *Newsweek* lauded *Long Distance Life,* commenting that "[Golden] writes about the city with understanding and a sense of commitment." The critic added that within these borders the author "traces a web of determination, suffering, and renewal."

Golden's third novel, *And Do Remember Me,* charts the lives of two black women, Jesse and Macon, whose search to better themselves leads to their involvement in the civil rights movement. Jesse leaves her poor, abusive home in the south and later finds fame as an actress. And Macon, a professor at a predominantly white college, tries to help her African American students contend with the racism that has become prevalent on campus. According to Ellen Douglas in the *Washington Post Book World,* the novel "addresses the political upheavals of the '60s and '70s and the personal difficulties and tragedies of these lives with a seriousness which one must respect." Lauding *And Do Remember Me,* Douglas concluded: "We need to be reminded that young people were murdered in Mississippi in 1964 for taking black people to register to vote.... And we need to be reminded that racism is again or still a deep national problem."

Golden remarked: "I was trained to be a journalist at Columbia's graduate school of journalism, but I was born, I feel, to simply write, using whatever medium best expresses my obsession at a particular time. I have written poetry and have been included in several anthologies and want in the future to write more. I use and need journalism to explore the external world, to make sense of it. I use and need fiction to give significance to and to come to terms with the internal world of my own particular fears, fantasies, and dreams, and to weave all of that into the texture of the outer, tangible world. I write essentially to complete myself and to give my vision a significance that the world generally seeks to deny."

*BIOGRAPHICAL/CRITICAL SOURCES:*

*PERIODICALS*

*Antioch Review,* winter, 1984.
*Los Angeles Times Book Review,* April 17, 1983; September 7, 1986.
*Ms.,* June, 1983; September, 1988.
*Newsweek,* November 20, 1989, p. 79.
*New Yorker,* February 21, 1983.
*New York Times Book Review,* May 1, 1983; September 14, 1986; December 27, 1987.

*Publishers Weekly,* June 20, 1986; September 1, 1989; April 27, 1992.

*Voice Literary Supplement,* June, 1983, May, 1990.

*Washingtonian,* October, 1990; November, 1990.

*Washington Post,* May 22, 1983; December 13, 1987.

*Washington Post Book World,* June 4, 1983; July 30, 1986; December 13, 1987; September 17, 1989; December 3, 1989; May 24, 1992, p. 12; June 21, 1992.

\*   \*   \*

## GOMEZ, Jewelle 1948-

*PERSONAL:* Born September 11, 1948, in Boston, MA. *Education:* Northeastern University, B.A., 1971; Columbia University School of Journalism, M.S., 1973.

*ADDRESSES: Office*—c/o Firebrand Books, 141 The Commons, Ithaca, NY 14850. *Agent*—Frances Goldin, 305 E. 11th St., New York, NY 10003.

*CAREER:* Novelist, social activist, and teacher of creative writing. Worked in production, WGBH-TV, Boston, on *Say Brother,* 1968-71, and in New York City for Children's Television Workshop and WNET during 1970s; director, Literature Program, New York State Council on the Arts, 1989-93; Hunter College, New York City, lecturer in the departments of women's studies and English, 1989-90. Founding board member, Gay and Lesbian Alliance against Defamation (GLAAD); member of Feminist Anti-Censorship Taskforce (FACT); member of board of advisors, Cornell University Human Sexuality Archives, and National Center for Lesbian Rights; member of the board, Open Meadows Foundation and PEN American Center.

*AWARDS, HONORS:* Ford Foundation fellowship, 1973; Beards Fund award for fiction, 1986; Money for Women Fund/Barbara Deming Award for fiction, 1990; Lambda Literary awards for fiction and science fiction for *The Gilda Stories,* 1991.

*WRITINGS:*

*The Gilda Stories: A Novel,* Firebrand Books, 1991.

*Forty-three Septembers* (essays), Firebrand Books, 1993.

*VERSE*

*The Lipstick Papers,* Grace Publications, 1980.

*Flamingoes and Bears,* Grace Publications, 1986.

*SIDELIGHTS:* Since the beginning of the modern gay liberation movement in the 1970s, a steadily growing body of literature by gay and lesbian writers has explored issues of gay identity, the gay community, and the place of gay men and lesbians in mainstream society. With roots in the African American community as well as a long involvement in the feminist movement and a deep commitment to multiculturalism, Jewelle Gomez has made an important contribution to contemporary gay literature.

In *The Gilda Stories,* her first novel, Gomez combines history, romance, mystery, science fiction, and the supernatural in a story about Gilda, a vampire very different from the kind found in traditional gothic horror stories. In fact, Gilda—as well as her fellow vampires who also figure in the novel—are not horrifying at all. Indeed, they are healers, and activists for social justice. They don't sleep in coffins all day, and they don't resort to killing very easily. Moreover, they are an ethnically and culturally diverse lot, including African Americans and Native Americans, lesbians, feminists, and others. The reader follows Gilda through many incarnations, from her mortal life as a runaway slave in Louisiana around 1850, to her immortal vampire lives in the California of 1890, Missouri in 1921, Massachusetts in 1955, New York in 1981, and even into the future, including New Hampshire in the year 2020.

Although a critic for *Publishers Weekly* finds *The Gilda Stories* to be "an ultimately uninteresting romance novel," Karlyn Crowley of *Belles Lettres* calls it "one of the most imaginative novels in recent lesbian fiction" and "a rare reading experience."

*BIOGRAPHICAL/CRITICAL SOURCES:*

*PERIODICALS*

*Belles Lettres,* spring, 1992, pp. 60-61.

*MultiCultural Review,* Volume 1, number 1, pp. 549-50.

*New York Newsday,* July 28, 1992.

*Out/look,* spring, 1992, pp. 63-72.

*Outweek,* May 22, 1991, pp. 54-55.

*Publishers Weekly,* May 10, 1991, p. 277.

*Washington Blade,* November 8, 1991, pp. 42-43.

\*   \*   \*

## GOODWIN, Ruby Berkley 1903-1961

*PERSONAL:* Born October 17, 1903, in DuQuoin, IL; died May 31, 1961; daughter of a coal miner; married; children: five. *Education:* San Gabriel College (San Diego State), A.B., 1949.

*CAREER:* Syndicated columnist of "Hollywood in Bronze," 1936-52; secretary and publicist for actor Hattie McDaniel, 1936-52; actor appearing in the films *The View from Pompey's Head,* 1955, *Strange Intruder,* 1956, *The Alligator People,* 1959, and *Wild in the Country,* 1961.

*MEMBER:* Los Angeles Urban League, Chaparral Poetry Society, Screen Actors Guild, Negro Actors Guild, Fullerton Council of Churchwomen, Fullerton Young Women's Christian Association (YWCA), Actors Equity Association.

*AWARDS, HONORS:* Gold Medal, Commonwealth Award for best nonfiction by a California writer, 1953, for *It's Good to Be Black.*

*WRITINGS:*

*From My Kitchen Window* (poems), Wendell Malliet and Co., 1942.
*A Gold Star Mother Speaks* (poems), Orange County Printing Co., 1944.
*It's Good to Be Black* (autobiography), Doubleday, 1953.

Contributor to books, including *Twelve Negro Spirituals* (stories), Handy Brothers Music Co., 1937; *Negro Voices,* 1938; and *Ebony Rhythm,* 1938.

*SIDELIGHTS:* Although she started her college education late in life, Ruby Berkley Goodwin had pursued her writing career with vigor prior to beginning her undergraduate career. A wife and mother to five children, she maintained a dual career as a syndicated columnist on black Hollywood and as the publicist and secretary to the screen actor Hattie McDaniel. It was during this time that her work "Stories of Negro Life" was published in *Twelve Negro Spirituals.*

Goodwin found success with the publication of her poetry collection *From My Kitchen Window.* In her introduction, she denounced the inherent injustice in racism, but expressed hope: "love instead of hate; helpfulness and encouragement instead of arrogance and disdain." Her poetry records daily and cumulative injuries and wrongs and shows how solace can be found in God. She also affirms the integrity and pride of black Americans.

In relating her childhood as the daughter of a coal miner at the turn of the twentieth century, Goodwin provided a portrait of a strong family in *It's Good to Be Black.* A critic in *Kirkus Reviews* described the autobiography as "a personal narrative which substitutes dignity for sensationalism, a quiet strength for the more embittered and embattled attack against discrimination."

*BIOGRAPHICAL/CRITICAL SOURCES:*

*BOOKS*

Goodwin, Ruby Berkley, *From My Kitchen Window,* Wendell Malliet & Co., 1942.

*PERIODICALS*

*Kirkus Reviews,* October, 1953.

\*   \*   \*

## GORDON, Vivian V(erdell) 1934-

*PERSONAL:* Born April 15, 1934, in Washington, DC; daughter of Thomas and Susie Verdell; married Ronald Clayton Gordon (divorced); children: Ronald Clayton Jr., Susan Gordon Akkad. *Education:* Virginia State University, B.S., 1955; University of Pennsylvania, M.A., 1957; University of Virginia, Ph.D., 1974.

*ADDRESSES: Office*—Department of African American Studies, State University of New York, Albany, NY 12222.

*CAREER:* Women's Christian Alliance Child Welfare Agency, Philadelphia, PA, social worker, 1956-57; Library of Congress Legislative Reference Service, Washington, DC, research assistant, 1957, education and social analyst, 1957-63; U.S. House of Representatives Committee on Education and Labor, Washington, DC, coordinator of research, 1963; Upward Bound Project, University of California, Los Angeles, assistant director, 1966-67; California State College (now California State University, Los Angeles), director of Education Participation in Community Program, 1967-69, University of Virginia, Charlottesburg, teaching assistant, 1971-73, assistant professor and department chairperson, 1973-79, associate professor of sociology, 1979-84; State University of New York at Albany, associate professor of African and Afro-American Studies, 1987—. Black scholar in residence, Gettysburg College, 1978; visiting Black scholar, Ball State University, 1981; visiting professor, Wellesley College, 1987. Member of the editorial board of *The Negro Education Review,* 1985-86; coordinator of the National Council for Black Studies Student Contest, 1984-89; and consultant to Albany Annual Critical Black Issues Conference.

*MEMBER:* National Council for Black Studies, Association of Black Sociologists, Association of Black Women Historians.

*AWARDS, HONORS:* Outstanding Service Award, Parents Association of Jordan High School, 1968; Bethune-Roosevelt Award, The Society of Artemas of the University of Virginia, 1974, for outstanding contributions to race relations at the university; Martin Luther King Award, Alpha Phi Alpha, 1982, for service to students; Award for Distinguished Service to Students and Community, National Association for the Advancement of Colored People (NAACP) branch of the University of Virginia, 1983; Distinguished Service to Students Award, Council of Black Students Organizations at the University of Virginia, 1984; Outstanding Service to African Students, State University of New York African Students Association, 1985; Albany Black Arts and Culture Award, 1985; Outstanding Black Woman, State University of New York, 1989; Outstanding Service to Black Students, State University of New York, 1989; Martin Luther King Service Award, 1990.

*WRITINGS:*

*BOOKS*

*The Self-Concept of Black Americans,* University Press of America, 1977.
*Lectures: Black Scholars on Black Issues,* University Press of America, 1979.
*Black Women, Feminism and Black Liberation: Which Way?,* Third World Press, 1984.
*Kemet and Other Ancient African Civilizations,* Third World Press, 1991.
(With Lois Smith Owens) *Think About Prisons and the Criminal Justice System* (part of the "Think" series), Walker, 1992.

*OTHER*

Author of educational publications for the Legislative Reference Service, Council of State Governments, and United States Government Printing Office, 1958-62.

*SIDELIGHTS:* Vivian V. Gordon has produced many studies, centering on subjects from driver's education to prisons. In *Black Women, Feminism and Black Liberation: Which Way?,* she had the opportunity to unite many of her areas of knowledge, methodologies, and concerns. "The author," wrote Beverly H. Robinson in *The Black Scholar,* "conducts a systematic analysis of those issues with which Black women and Black men have grappled since the emergence of the so-called women's liberation movement." Those issues include coalition politics and how they bear upon any alliance of black and white women within the movement, the strong identification between white women and white men, and the cause and effect relationship between the Civil Rights movement and the emergence of Women's Studies.

Ironically, that latter connection resulted in the attempted erasure, in academia, of any difference between black women's and white women's problems. Gordon's historical review reveals this to be a damaging mistake. Her contemporary research with a sample of black women, moreover, shows them connecting their own liberation with the liberation of the entire African American community—male and female, upper and lower class. Unification of that community, through education and bridge-building, is and should be the black woman's priority, she concludes.

In noting that Gordon's conclusions agree with many other black feminist writings, Robinson comments that the book is still a valuable addition to those previous views. Gordon's long career has allowed her to experience social problems which affect black Americans from a wide range of perspectives—that of a social worker, researcher and analyst, and educator. "Vivian Gordon," concludes Robinson, "has analyzed all of the possible issues that must be considered for the development of a theoretical perspective on political alternatives for Black women."

*BIOGRAPHICAL/CRITICAL SOURCES:*

*PERIODICALS*

*The Black Scholar,* March, 1985.

\* \* \*

## GOSS, Clay(ton E.) 1946-

*PERSONAL:* Born May 26, 1946, in Philadelphia, PA; son of Douglas P. (a counselor) and Alfreda (a teacher; maiden name, Ivey) Jackson; married Linda McNear (a teacher and performer), March 25, 1969; children: Aisha, Uhuru (daughters). *Education:* Howard University, B.F.A., 1972.

*CAREER:* Department of Recreation, Washington, DC, drama specialist, 1969; Howard University, Washington, DC, playwright-in-residence in drama department, 1970-73, playwright-in-residence at Institute for the Arts and Humanities, 1973-75; poet, playwright, and writer. Instructor in poetry and development of Afro-American theater, Antioch College, Washington and Baltimore campuses, 1971-73.

*MEMBER:* Theatre Black, Kappa Alpha Psi.

*WRITINGS:*

JUVENILE

*Bill Pickett: Black Bulldogger* (novel), illustrated by Chico Hall, Hill and Wang, 1970.

(With wife, Linda Goss) *The Baby Leopard: An African Folktale,* illustrated by Suzanne Bailey-Jones and Michael R. Jones, Bantam Books, 1989.

(With L. Goss) *It's Kwanzaa Time!,* Philomel Books, 1993.

DRAMA

*Hip Rumpelstiltskin,* first produced in Washington, DC, by Department of Recreation, 1969.

*Andrew* (one-act), first produced in New York City at New York Shakespeare Festival Theatre, 1972.

*Mars: Monument to the Last Black Eunuch,* first produced in Washington, DC, at Howard University, 1972.

*Oursides* (one-act), first produced in New York City at New Federal Theatre, 1972.

*Spaces in Time,* produced in Washington, DC, by D. C. Black Repertory Company, 1973.

*Of Being Hit,* first produced in Brooklyn, NY, at Billie Holiday Theatre, 1973.

*Homecookin': Five Plays,* Howard University Press, 1974.

*Ornette,* first produced in Amherst, MA, at University of Massachusetts, 1974.

Also author of *Keys to the Kingdom.* Plays represented in anthologies, including *Transition,* Department of Afro-American Studies, Howard University, 1972; *Kuntu Drama,* edited by Paul Carter Harrison, Grove, 1974; and *The New Lafayette Theatre Presents: Six Black Playwrights,* edited by Ed Bullins, Anchor Press, 1974.

OTHER

Author of the television play *Billy McGhee,* for *The Place,* broadcast by WRC-TV (Washington, DC), 1974. Contributor to books, including *We Speak as Liberators: Young Black Poets,* edited by Orde Coombs, Dodd, 1970; *The Drama of Nommo,* edited by Paul Carter Harrison, Grove, 1972; and *The Sheet,* edited by Carol Kirkendall, Compared to What, Inc. (Washington, DC), 1974. Contributor of short fiction, articles, and reviews to periodicals, including *Liberator, Reflect, Black Books Bulletin, Blackstage,* and *Black World.*

*SIDELIGHTS:* Clay Goss once commented: "What we must first do is to make our goals become our models instead of models becoming our goals. Then build from there."

*BIOGRAPHICAL/CRITICAL SOURCES:*

PERIODICALS

*Choice,* January, 1976, p. 1444.
*Grade Teacher,* February, 1971, p. 147.
*Kirkus Reviews,* October 1, 1970, p. 1096.
*Library Journal,* March 15, 1971, p. 1114; June 15, 1975, p. 1236.

\*   \*   \*

## GREENFIELD, Eloise 1929-

*PERSONAL:* Born May 17, 1929, in Parmele, NC; daughter of Weston W. and Lessie (Jones) Little; married Robert J. Greenfield (a procurement specialist), April 29, 1950; children: Steven, Monica. *Education:* Attended Miner Teachers College, 1946-49.

*ADDRESSES: Office*—Honey Productions, Inc., P.O. Box 29077, Washington, DC 20017. *Agent*—Marie Brown, Marie Brown Associates, 412 West 154th St., New York, NY 10032.

*CAREER:* U.S. Patent Office, Washington, DC, clerk-typist, 1949-56, supervisory patent assistant, 1956-60; worked as a secretary, case-control technician, and an administrative assistant in Washington, DC from 1964-68. District of Columbia Black Writers' Workshop, co-director of adult fiction, 1971-73, director of children's literature, 1973-74; District of Columbia Commission on the Arts and Humanities, writer-in-residence, 1973, 1985-86. Participant in numerous school and library programs and workshops for children and adults.

*AWARDS, HONORS:* Carter G. Woodson Book Award, National Council for the Social Studies, 1974, for *Rosa Parks;* Irma Simonton Black Award, Bank Street College of Education, 1974, for *She Come Bringing Me That Little Baby Girl;* *New York Times* Outstanding Book of the Year citation, 1974, for *Sister;* Jane Addams Children's Book Award, Women's International League for Peace and Freedom, 1976, for *Paul Robeson;* American Library Association Notable Book citations, 1976, for *Me and Neesie,* 1979, for *Honey, I Love, and Other Love Poems,* 1982, for *Daydreamers;* Council on Interracial Books for Children award, 1977, for body of work; Coretta Scott King Award, 1978, for *Africa Dream;* Classroom Choice Book citation, 1978, for *Honey, I Love, and Other Love Poems;* Children's Book of the Year citation, Child Study Book Committee, 1979, for *I Can Do It by Myself;* Notable Trade Book in the Field of Social Studies citations, 1980, for *Childtimes: A Three-Generation Memoir,* 1982, for *Alesia;* New York Public Library recommended list, 1981, for

Alesia; National Black Child Development Institute award, 1981, for body of work; Mills College award, 1983, for body of work; Washington, DC Mayor's Art Award in Literature, 1983; honored at Ninth Annual Celebration of Black Writing, Philadelphia, PA, 1993, for lifetime achievement.

*WRITINGS:*

*Sister* (novel), illustrated by Moneta Barnett, Crowell, 1974.
*Honey, I Love, and Other Love Poems,* illustrated by Diane and Leo Dillon, Crowell, 1978.
*Talk about a Family* (novel), illustrated by James Calvin, Lippincott, 1978.
*Nathaniel Talking* (poems), Writers & Readers, 1988.
*Night on Neighborhood Street,* illustrated by Jan Spivey Gilchrist, Dial, 1991.
*Koya DeLaney and the Good Girl Blues,* Scholastic, 1992.
*Talk About a Family,* HarperCollins, 1993.

*PICTURE BOOKS*

*Bubbles,* illustrated by Eric Marlow, Drum & Spear, 1972, published with illustrations by Pat Cummings as *Good News,* Coward, 1977.
*She Come Bringing Me That Little Baby Girl,* illustrated by John Steptoe, Lippincott, 1974.
*Me and Neesie,* illustrated by Barnett, Crowell, 1975.
*First Pink Light,* illustrated by Barnett, Crowell, 1976.
*Africa Dream,* illustrated by Carole Byard, John Day, 1977.
(With mother, Lessie Jones Little) *I Can Do It by Myself,* illustrated by Byard, Crowell, 1978.
*Darlene,* illustrated by George Ford, Methuen, 1980.
*Grandmama's Joy,* illustrated by Byard, Collins, 1980.
*Daydreamers,* with pictures by Tom Feelings, Dial, 1981.
*Grandpa's Face,* illustrated by Floyd Cooper, Putnam, 1988.
*Under the Sunday Tree,* illustrated by Amos Ferguson, HarperCollins, 1988.
*My Doll, Keshia,* illustrated by Gilchrist, Writers & Readers, 1991.
*My Daddy and I,* illustrated by Gilchrist, Writers & Readers, 1991.
*I Make Music,* illustrated by Gilchrist, Writers & Readers, 1991.
*Big Friend, Little Friend,* illustrated by Gilchrist, Writers & Readers, 1991.
*Aaron and Gayla's Alphabet Book,* illustrated by Gilchrist, Writers & Readers, 1992.

*BIOGRAPHIES*

*Rosa Parks,* illustrated by Marlow, Crowell, 1973.
*Paul Robeson,* illustrated by Ford, Crowell, 1975.
*Mary McLeod Bethune,* illustrated by Jerry Pinkney, Crowell, 1977.

(With Little) *Childtimes: A Three-Generation Memoir* (autobiography), illustrated by Pinkney, Crowell, 1979.
(With Alesia Revis) *Alesia,* illustrated by Ford, with photographs by Sandra Turner Bond, Philomel Books, 1981.

*CONTRIBUTOR TO ANTHOLOGIES*

Alma Murray and Robert Thomas, editors, *The Journey: Scholastic Black Literature,* Scholastic Book Services, 1970.
Karen S. Kleiman and Mel Cebulash, editors, *Double Action Short Stories,* Scholastic Book Services, 1973.
*Love,* Scholastic Book Services, 1975.
*Encore* (textbook), Houghton, 1978.
*Daystreaming,* Economy Company, 1978.
*Forerunners,* Economy Company, 1978.
*Burning Bright,* Open Court, 1979.
*Friends Are Like That,* Crowell, 1979.
*Language Activity Kit: Teachers' Edition,* Harcourt, 1979.
*Building Reading Skills,* McDougal, Littell, 1980.
*New Routes to English: Book 5,* Collier Books, 1980.
*New Routes to English: Advanced Skills One,* Collier Books, 1980.
*Jumping Up,* Lippincott, 1981.
*Emblems,* Houghton, 1981.
*Listen, Children,* Bantam, 1982.
*Bonus Book, Gateways, Level K,* Houghton, 1983.
*New Treasury of Children's Poetry,* Doubleday, 1984.
*Scott, Foresman Anthology of Children's Literature,* Scott, Foresman, 1984.

*OTHER*

Contributor to *World Book Encyclopedia;* author of 1979 bookmark poem for Children's Book Council. Also contributor to magazines and newspapers, including *Black World, Cricket, Ebony, Jr.!, Horn Book, Interracial Books for Children Bulletin, Ms., Negro History Bulletin, Scholastic Scope,* and *Washington Post.*

*ADAPTATIONS: Daydreamers* was dramatized for the Public Broadcasting System (PBS) Reading Rainbow Television Series.

*SIDELIGHTS:* Eloise Greenfield stated that her goal in writing is "to give children words to love, to grow on." The author of more than a dozen prize-winning books for children, Greenfield admits that, since her own childhood, she has loved the sounds and rhythms of words. In her stories and poetry she tries to produce what she calls "word-madness," a creative, joyous response brought on by reading. As she explains in *Horn Book:* "I want to be one of those who can choose and order words that children will want to celebrate. I want to make them shout and laugh and blink back tears and care about themselves."

Greenfield also lists as a priority of her writing the communication of "a true knowledge of Black heritage, including both the African and American experiences." Through her easy-to-read biographies of famous black Americans, such as *Rosa Parks, Paul Robeson,* and *Mary McLeod Bethune,* she seeks to inform young readers about the historical contributions of blacks in this nation. "A true history must be the concern of every Black writer," she states in *Horn Book.* "It is necessary for Black children to have a true knowledge of their past and present, in order that they may develop an informed sense of direction for their future."

This concern for a personal past as well as a public one has prompted Greenfield to team with her mother for *Childtimes: A Three-Generation Memoir.* The autobiographical work describes the childhood memories of Greenfield, her mother, and her maternal grandmother. According to Rosalie Black Kiah in *Language Arts,* each experience in *Childtimes,* "though set in a different time, is rich in human feeling and strong family love." *Washington Post Book World* contributor Mary Helen Washington writes: "I recognize the significance of *Childtimes* as a document of black life because ... it unlocked personal recollections of my own past, which I do not want to lose." In the *Interracial Books for Children Bulletin,* Geraldine L. Wilson calls the book "carefully considered and thoughtful, ... moving deliberately, constructed with loving care." M. R. Singer concludes in the *School Library Journal:* "The intimate details of loving and growing up and the honesty with which they are told ... will involve all readers ... and broaden their understanding of this country's recent past."

Much of Greenfield's fiction concerns family bonding, a subject the author finds as important as black history. Noting in *Horn Book* that "love is a staple in most Black families," she writes repeatedly of the changing patterns of parental and sibling involvement, stressing the child's ability to cope with novelties both positive and negative. In her Irma Simonton Black Award-winning picture book, *She Come Bringing Me That Little Baby Girl,* for instance, a young character named Kevin must learn to share his parents' love with his new sister. A novel entitled *Sister,* which received a *New York Times* Outstanding Book of the Year citation, concerns a girl caught in the family stress following a parent's death. Greenfield explains the point of *Sister* in *Horn Book:* "Sister ... discovers that she can use her good times as stepping stones, as bridges, to get over the hard times.... My hope is that children in trouble will not view themselves as blades of wheat caught in countervailing winds but will seek solutions, even partial or temporary solutions, to their problems."

Unsatisfied with network television's portrayal of black families, which she calls "a funhouse mirror, reflecting misshapen images" in *Horn Book,* Greenfield seeks to reinforce positive and realistic aspects of black family life. While she tells *Language Arts* that she looks back on her own childhood with pleasure, she remains aware of the modern dynamics of family structure. She states: "Families come in various shapes. There is no one shape that carries with it more legitimacy than any other.... In the case of divorce and separation—the problems that parents have—the children can go on and build their own lives regardless of the problems of the parents. Children *have* to go on and build their own lives." Kiah notes that Greenfield does not construct her fiction from personal incidents but rather looks for themes from a more universal background. "She draws from those things she has experienced, observed, heard about, and read about. Then she combines them, changes them and finally develops them into her stories." The resulting work has a wide appeal, according to Betty Valdes in the *Interracial Books for Children Bulletin.* Valdes feels that Greenfield "consistently ... illuminates key aspects of the Black experience in a way that underlines both its uniqueness and its universality."

This is proven out in *Grandpa's Face,* in which Greenfield constructs a story about a young girl and her relationship with her grandfather, who she loves dearly. One day, according to Jeanne Fox-Alston in *Washington Post Book World,* little Tomika sees her grandfather, who frequently acts in community theater productions, rehearsing. "The cold, mean look on his face scares her," Fox-Alston recounts, and she worries that she might do something that will cause him to regard her with the same angry countenance. In her poetry as well as her prose, Greenfield attempts to involve children in their own worlds. In *Under the Sunday Tree* and *Night on Neighborhood Street,* Greenfield brings her young readers into the happenings around them. *Night on Neighborhood Street* examines "realistic" life an urban community, according to *Tribune Books.* The volume's seventeen poems show children in typical situations, including attending church, avoiding drug pushers, and playing games with their families.

Greenfield has resided in Washington, DC since childhood and has participated in numerous writing workshops and conferences on literature there. She explains in *Language Arts* that her work with the District of Columbia Black Writers' Workshop convinced her of the need to build a collection of "good black books" for children. "It has been inspiring to me to be a part of this struggle," she affirms. "I would like to have time to write an occasional short story, ... but I don't feel any urgency about them. It seems that I am always being pushed from inside to do children's books; those are more important." Stating another aim of hers in *Horn Book,* Greenfield claims: "Through the written word I want to give children a love for the arts that will provoke creative thought and activity.... A strong love for the arts can enhance and direct their creativity as well as provide satisfying moments throughout their lives."

*BIOGRAPHICAL/CRITICAL SOURCES:*

*BOOKS*

*Children's Literature Review,* Volume 4, Gale, 1982.

Greenfield, Eloise, and Lessie Jones Little, *Childtimes: A Three-Generation Memoir,* illustrated by Jerry Pinkney, Crowell, 1979.

Sims, Rudine, *Shadow and Substance: Afro-American Experience in Contemporary Children's Literature,* National Council of Teachers of English, 1982.

*PERIODICALS*

*Africa Woman,* March-April, 1980.

*Christian Science Monitor,* February 21, 1990, p. 13; May 1, 1992, p. 10.

*Encore,* December 6, 1976.

*Freedomways,* Volume 21, number 1, 1981; Volume 22, number 2, 1982.

*HCA Companion,* first quarter, 1984.

*Horn Book,* December, 1975; April, 1977; November-December, 1991, p. 750; January-February, 1992, p. 59.

*Instructor,* March, 1990, p. 23.

*Interracial Books for Children Bulletin,* Volume 11, number 5, 1980; Volume 11, number 8, 1980.

*Language Arts,* September, 1980.

*Metropolitan Washington,* August, 1982.

*Negro History Bulletin,* April-May, 1975; September-October, 1978.

*New York Times Book Review,* May 5, 1974; November 3, 1974; March 26, 1989.

*Parents Magazine,* December, 1991, p. 178.

*School Library Journal,* December, 1979; September, 1991, p. 245; December, 1991, p. 92; January, 1992, p. 90; March, 1992, p. 237.

*Top of the News,* winter, 1980.

*Tribune Books* (Chicago), February 26, 1989; February 9, 1992.

*Washington Post Book World,* May 1, 1977; January 13, 1980; May 10, 1981; November 5, 1989; December 9, 1990; December 1, 1991.

\*　\*　\*

**GREGORY, J. Dennis**
**See WILLIAMS, John A(lfred)**

**GROSVENOR, Verta Mae 1938-**

*PERSONAL:* Born April 4, 1938, in Fairfax, SC; married; children: Kali, Chandra. *Education:* Received high school education in Philadelphia, PA.

*ADDRESSES: Office*—c/o Penn Center, P. O. Box 126, Frogmore, SC 29920.

*CAREER:* Writer.

*MEMBER:* People United to Save Humanity (PUSH).

*WRITINGS:*

*Vibration Cooking; or, The Traveling Notes of a Geechee Girl* (autobiography), Doubleday, 1970.

*Thursday and Every Other Sunday Off: A Domestic Rap,* Doubleday, 1972.

*Plain Brown Rapper* (poems), Doubleday, 1975.

*Black Atlantic Cooking,* Prentice Hall, 1990.

Work represented in several anthologies, including *Visions of America by the Poets of Our Time.* Author of food column in *Amsterdam News* and of column in *Chicago Courier.* Contributor of articles and stories to magazines and newspapers.

\*　\*　\*

**GUILLEN (y Batista), Nicolas (Cristobal) 1902-**

*PERSONAL:* Surname pronounced "gee-*yane,*" with a hard g as in geese; born July 10, 1902, in Camaguey, Cuba; son of Nicolas (a silversmith, newspaper editor, and politician) and Argelia (Batista) Guillen. *Education:* Graduated from Camaguey Institute (high school), 1920; attended University of Havana, 1920-21.

*ADDRESSES: Home*—Calle O, No. 2, Edificio Someillan, Vedado, Havana, Cuba. *Office*—Union Nacional de Escritores y Artistas Cubanos, Calle 17, No. 351, Vedado, Havana, Cuba.

*CAREER:* Poet, 1922—. Founder and editor of *Lis* literary magazine in the early 1920s; correspondent in Spain for *Mediodia* magazine, 1937-38; candidate for political offices in Cuba on Popular Socialist (later Communist) ticket in the 1940s; lecturer and correspondent in Latin America and Europe in the 1940s and 1950s; president of Cuban National Union of Writers and Artists (UNEAC), 1961—. Served as editor in chief of *La Gaceta de Cuba* (official cultural publication of UNEAC) and as Cuban ambassador.

*AWARDS, HONORS:* Lenin Peace Prize from the Soviet Union, 1954; Cuban Order of Jose Marti from the Republic of Cuba, 1981; Order of Merit from the Republic of Haiti; Order of Cyril and Methodius (first class) from the People's Republic of Bulgaria.

*WRITINGS:*

POETRY

*Motivos de son* (title means "Motifs of Sound"), 1930, special fiftieth anniversary edition, with music by Amadeo Roldan, Editorial Letras Cubanas, 1980.

*Songoro cosongo,* 1931, published as *Songoro cosongo: Poemas mulatos,* Presencia Latinoamericana, 1981.

*West Indies Ltd.: Poemas,* Imprenta Ucar, Garcia, 1934.

*Cantos para soldados y sones para turistas,* (title means "Songs for Soldiers and Sones for Tourists"), Editorial Masas, 1937, published as *El son entero: Cantos para soldados y sones para turistas,* Editorial Losada, 1952.

*Espana: Poema en cuatro angustias y una esperanza* (title means "Spain: A Poem in Four Anguishes and a Hope"), Editorial Mexico Nuevo, 1937.

*El son entero: Suma poetica, 1929-1946* (title means "The Entire Son"; with a letter by Miguel de Unamuno and musical notation by various composers), Editorial Pleamar, 1947, Premia Editora, 1982.

*La paloma de vuelo popular* (title means "The Dove of Popular Flight"), 1958, also published, in a single volume, with *Elegias* (title means "Elegies"), Editorial Losada, 1959.

*Puedes?* (title means "Can You?"; with drawings by the author), Libreria La Tertulia, 1961.

*Elegia a Jesus Menendez,* Imprenta Nacional de Cuba, 1962.

*La rueda dentada* (title means "The Serrated Wheel"), UNEAC, 1962.

*Tengo* (title means "I Have"), prologue by Jose Antonio Portuondo, Editora del Consejo Nacional de Universidades, 1964, translation by Richard J. Carr published as *Tengo,* Broadside Press, 1974.

*Poemas de amor* (title means "Love Poems"), Ediciones La Tertulia, 1964.

*Nadie* (title means "Nobody"), Sol y Piedra, 1966.

*El gran zoo,* Instituto del Libro, 1967, translation by Robert Marquez published as *Patria o muerte! The Great Zoo and Other Poems,* Monthly Review Press, 1972.

*El diario que a diario,* UNEAC, 1972.

*Poemas Manuables,* UNEAC, 1975.

*El corazon con que vivo* (title means "The Heart with Which I Live"), UNEAC, 1975.

*Por que imperialismo?: Poemas* (title means "Why Imperialism?: Poems"), Ediciones Calarca, 1976.

*Elegias,* edited by Jose Martinez Matos, illustrations by Dario Mora, UNEAC, 1977.

*Coplas de Juan Descalzo* (title means "The Ballad of John Barefoot"), Editorial Letras Cubanas, 1979.

*Musica de camara* (title means "Chamber Music"), UNEAC, 1979.

*Sputnik 57,* [Cuba], 1980.

Also author of *Poemas para el Che* (title means "Poems for Che"), *Buenos Dias, Fidel,* for Grafica Horizonte, and *Por el Mar de las Antillas anda un barco de papel: Poemas para ninos mayores de edad* (title means "Going through the Antilles Sea in a Boat of Paper: Poems for Older Children"), with illustrations by Rapi Diego, for UNEAC. Work represented in anthologies, including *Some Modern Cuban Poems* by Nicolas Guillen and Others, translated from the Spanish by Manish Nandy, Satyabrata Pal, 1968.

POETRY COLLECTIONS

*Cuba Libre,* translated from the Spanish by Langston Hughes and Ben Frederic Carruthers, Anderson & Ritchie, 1948.

*Songoro cosongo, Motivos de Son, West Indies Ltd., Espana: Poema en cuatro angustias y una esperanza,* Editorial Losada, 1952.

*Nicolas Guillen: Sus mejores poemas,* Organizacion de los Festivales del Libro, 1959.

*Los mejores versos de Nicolas Guillen,* Editorial Nuestra America, 1961.

*Antologia mayor: El son entero y otros poemas,* UNEAC, 1964.

*Antologia mayor,* Instituto del Libro, 1969.

*Antologia clave,* prologue by Luis Inigo Madrigal, Editorial Nascimento, 1971.

*Man-Making Words: Selected Poems of Nicolas Guillen,* translated from the Spanish by Robert Marquez and David Arthur McMurray, University of Massachusetts Press, 1972.

*Cuba, amor y revolucion: Poemas,* Editorial Causachun, 1972.

*Obra poetica, 1920-1972* (two volumes), edited by Angel Augier with illustrations by the author, Editorial de Arte y Literatura, 1974.

*Latinamericason,* Quatro Editores, 1974.

*Nueva antologia mayor,* edited by Augier, Editorial Letras Cubanas, 1979.

*Paginas vueltas: Seleccion de poemas y apuntes autobiograficos* (title means "Turned Pages: Selected Poems and Autobiographical Notes"), Grupo Editor de Buenos Aires, 1980.

*Paginas vueltas: Memorias,* UNEAC, 1982.

OTHER

*Claudio Jose Domingo Brindis de Salas, el rey de las octavas* (title means "Claudio Jose Domingo Brindis de Salas, King of the Octaves"; prose), Municipio de La Habana, 1935.

*Prosa de prisa, cronicas* (title means "Hasty Prose, Chronicles"; selection of journalistic articles published from 1938 to 1961), Universidad Central de las Villas, 1962, expanded edition published as *Prosa de prisa, 1929-1972* (three volumes), edited with introduction by Augier, Editorial Arte y Literatura, 1975.

*El libro de las decimas,* UNEAC, 1980.

*El libro de los sones,* Editorial Letras Cubanas, 1982.

*Sol de domingo,* UNEAC, 1982.

*Cronista en tres epocas* (title means "Journalist in Three Epochs"; selection of journalistic articles edited by Maria Julia Guerra Avila and Pedro Rodriguez Gutierrez), Editorial Politica, 1984.

Contributor to Cuban newspapers and magazines, including *Diario de la marina.*

*ADAPTATIONS: Tengo* was made into a sound recording in the 1970s and released by Consejo Nacional de Cultura.

*SIDELIGHTS:* Nicolas Guillen, considered a master of the so-called "Afro-Cuban" style, is one of Cuba's best known and most respected poets. A mulatto from the provincial middle class, Guillen began his career as a newspaper journalist while writing poetry in his spare time. A 1930 visit to Cuba by the black American poet Langston Hughes, a leading figure in the black cultural movement known as the Harlem Renaissance, inspired Guillen to write and publish his first verse collection the same year, *Motivos de son* ("Motifs of Sound"). A group of eight poems structured rhythmically like the son, a popular Cuban song-and-dance arrangement with strong African elements, this work drew on a new international interest in primitive art and African culture and became identified with the Afro-Caribbean movement in Hispanic poetry that began in the mid-1920s. Like earlier white Afro-Caribbean poets in Cuba and Puerto Rico, Guillen treated local lower-class black life as his major theme and combined onomatopoeia—the use of words whose sounds imply their sense—and African rhythms as major stylistic devices, but he went further in both style and substance than his predecessors, who tended toward somewhat stereotypical depictions of a joyful, sensual, happy-go-lucky folk. Guillen instead wrote "from within"—as G. R. Coulthard noted in *Race and Colour in Caribbean Literature*—and subtly gave poetic voice to the lives of poverty and pathos behind the picturesque facade of Havana's black slum dwellers. Guillen was also credited with capturing the genuine dialect and speech patterns of Cuban blacks, which he blended with Yoruba African words to create a unique language that relied as much on sound and rhythm as on word sense for its meaning.

Guillen further refined his Afro-Cuban poetry in *Songoro cosongo,* a 1931 verse collection that quickly earned him a worldwide reputation and became widely regarded as the poet's masterwork. Published with Guillen's lottery winnings that year, this work evinces a deeper social consciousness and still bolder style in seeking to express the tragedy, passion, and vigor of black life in Cuba. The poet moves from an implicit criticism of slum life to direct denunciations of racism and an affirmation of the roles of black men and women in building Cuban and American culture and society. According to Guillen, he sought to create a "mulatto poetry" that would reflect Cuba's true history and racial composition.

Stylistically, Guillen's occasional use of the ballad form and reliance on naive, "nonsensical" imagery in *Songoro cosongo* shows the influence of the internationally acclaimed Spanish poet Federico Garcia Lorca, whom Guillen met in Cuba as Garcia Lorca was returning to Europe from the United States. The Cuban poet's extraordinary synthesis of traditional Spanish metric forms with Afro-Cuban words, rhythms, and folkloric symbols uniquely captures the cultural flavor of the Spanish-speaking Caribbean, critics have noted. Other poems in *Songoro cosongo* rely almost entirely on onomatopoeic effects and rhythm, becoming, in a sense, abstract word-paintings with no direct representational value at all—the title itself has no meaning other than its rhythmic and symbolic suggestions. Though seemingly spontaneous, these verses are in fact carefully crafted, with rigorous attention to rhyme, meter, and tonal nuances. Often recited publicly to a drum accompaniment, Guillen's Afro-Cuban verse has also been set to music by the Spanish composer Xavier Montsalvatge and sung by the American mezzo-soprano Marilyn Horne, among others.

The current of social protest running through *Songoro cosongo* turns deeper and swifter in *West Indies Ltd.,* published just after the 1933 revolution that deposed Cuban dictator Antonio Machado. In verse that is by turns satirical and bitter, Guillen depicts the often cruel and exploitative history of slavery, colonialism, and imperialism (particularly in its contemporary American form) in the Antilles islands of the West Indies. The poet's commitment to social change grew when he traveled to Spain in 1937 to cover the civil war for *Mediodia* magazine and participate in the anti-fascist Second International Congress of Writers for the Defense of Culture. That year he joined the Cuban Communist party (then called Popular Socialist) and wrote a long, elegiac ode to the Spanish Republic titled *Espana: Poema en cuatro angustias y una esperanza* ("Spain: A Poem in Four Anguishes and a Hope") that voiced his hope for humanity's communist future. Guillen also devoted most of his 1937 verse collection, *Cantos para soldados y sones para turistas* ("Songs for Soldiers and Sones for Tourists"), to social and political themes.

Guillen spent much of the next two decades outside of Cuba, traveling around Europe and Latin America as a lecturer and correspondent for several Cuban journals. In 1962 he published a selection of these articles under the title *Prosa de prisa* ("Hasty Prose"). Guillen's poetic output during these years was somewhat reduced, although he published a major collection titled *El son entero* ("The Entire Son") in 1947 and his first English-language selection, *Cuba-Libre* (coedited and translated by Langston Hughes), that following year. Denied permission to return to Cuba by the Fulgencio Batista dictatorship in the 1950s, Guillen spent several years in unhappy exile in Paris, France, where he wrote *La paloma de vuelo popular* ("The Dove of Popular Flight") and *Elegias* ("Elegies"), published together in one volume in 1958. These two works complement each other thematically and stylistically. The first consists mainly of broadly political—and often witty and ironical—protest poems against the Cuban dictatorship and American imperialism, while *Elegias* mourns the loss of friends and other victims of political repression in somber, lyrical tones.

The triumph of the Cuban revolution in early 1959 immediately brought Guillen back to his homeland, where he enthusiastically embraced the revolutionary cause. Already recognized as the country's greatest living poet, Guillen readily took on the role of poet laureate of the revolution. His 1964 verse collection *Tengo* ("I Have") is a joyful celebration of the revolutionary victory that reads somewhat like a historical epic, praising the insurgent heroes and depicting major battles against Batista, the dictator's flight, and the Cuban victory over the American-backed invasion at the Bay of Pigs. As the title suggests, Guillen also explores the new feelings of empowerment, possession, and comradeship that the revolution inspired in many poor Cubans.

The theme of social liberation is present as well in Guillen's 1967 collection, *El gran zoo*. Hailed as one of Guillen's outstanding later works, *El gran zoo* marked a major stylistic shift for a poet usually identified with the Afro-Cuban style. While still showing a crystalline attention to craft, these poems rely less on rhyme and strict meter than Guillen's past work and approach free verse with spare wording and fractured images. The volume is structured thematically as a visit to a metaphorical zoo, where some of the world's curious and beautiful social, natural, and metaphysical phenomena are catalogued in individual poems. Guillen's usually direct language is more allusive and enigmatic here, and his subjects range from critical jabs at imperialism to taut musings on love, the forces of nature, and the ineffable mystery of being.

Both *Tengo* and *El gran zoo,* along with another collection published in 1972, *Man-Making Words: Selected Poems of Nicolas Guillen,* are available in English translation. Guillen's poems have also been translated into many other languages, including French, German, Russian, and Hebrew. Awarded the Cuban Order of Jose Marti, the country's highest honor, in 1981, Guillen has served for many years as president of the National Union of Cuban Writers and Artists.

BIOGRAPHICAL/CRITICAL SOURCES:

*BOOKS*

Augier, Angel, *Nicolas Guillen: Notas para un estudio biografico-critico* (two volumes), Universidad de las Villas, 1963-64.

Coulthard, R. G., *Race and Colour in Caribbean Literature,* Oxford University Press, 1962.

Ellis, Keith, *Cuba's Nicolas Guillen: Poetry and Ideology,* University of Toronto Press, 1983.

Guillen, Nicolas, *Paginas vueltas: Memorias,* UNEAC, 1982.

Martinez Estrada, Ezequiel, *La Poesia de Nicolas Guillen,* Calicanto Editorial, c. 1977.

Sardinha, Dennis, *The Poetry of Nicolas Guillen: An Introduction,* New Beacon, 1976.

*PERIODICALS*

*Black Scholar,* July/August, 1985.
*Hispania,* October 25, 1942.
*Latin America Research Review,* Volume 17, number 1, 1982.
*Opportunity,* January, 1946.

\*   \*   \*

## GUY, Rosa (Cuthbert) 1928-

*PERSONAL:* Born September 1, 1928, in Trinidad; came to United States in 1932; daughter of Henry and Audrey (Gonzales) Cuthbert; married Warner Guy (deceased); children: Warner.

*CAREER:* Writer.

*MEMBER:* Harlem Writer's Guild (founder and former president).

*AWARDS, HONORS:* Best Books for Young Adults citation by American Library Association (ALA), and Outstanding Book of the Year citation by *New York Times,* 1976, both for *The Friends; The Disappearance* was named to the "Best Books for Young Adults 1979" list by the Young Adult Services Division of the American Library Association; first prize at Cabourg, France, festival, 1988, for *My Love, My Love; or the Peasant Girl.*

*WRITINGS:*

*Bird at My Window* (novel), Lippincott, 1966.
(Editor) *Children of Longing* (anthology), Holt, 1971.
*The Friends* (first book in trilogy for young adults), Holt, 1973.

*Ruby* (second book in trilogy for young adults), Viking, 1976.

*Edith Jackson* (third book in trilogy for young adults), Viking, 1978.

*The Disappearance* (novel), Delacorte, 1979.

*Mirror of Her Own* (novel), Delacorte, 1981.

(Translator and adapter) Birago Diop, *Mother Crocodile: An Uncle Amadou Tale from Senegal* (story), illustrated by John Steptoe, Delacorte, 1981.

*A Measure of Time* (novel), Holt, 1983.

*New Guys Around the Block* (novel), Delacorte, 1983.

*Paris, Pee Wee and Big Dog* (novel), Gollancz, 1984, Delacorte, 1985.

*Bird at My Window,* Schocken, 1987.

*And I Heard a Bird Sing* (novel), Delacorte, 1987.

*My Love, My Love; or, The Peasant Girl* (novel; also see below), Holt, 1985.

*The Ups and Downs of Carl Davis III* (novel), Delacorte, 1989.

*Billy the Great* (novel), illustrated by Caroline Binch, Delacorte, 1992.

*The Music of Summer* (novel), Delacorte, 1992.

Also author of one-act play, *Venetian Blinds,* 1954; author of *Time Out in Haiti* and *Summer of 1985.* Author of documentary film about her novel *The Friends* for Thames Television. Contributor to periodicals, including *Cosmopolitan* and *Freedomways.*

*ADAPTATIONS:* The 1990 Broadway musical *Once on This Island* was based on Guy's novel *My Love, My Love; or, The Peasant Girl.*

*SIDELIGHTS:* Rosa Guy often writes about black teenagers, but her topics hold universal appeal. One of Guy's publishers indicated that her "'literary themes stem from the fact that she is a black and a woman.'" About the success of her work, Katherine Paterson observes in the *Washington Post Book World* that "a great strength of Guy's work is her ability to peel back society's labels and reveal beneath them highly individual men and women."

Critics often comment on the intensity of her characters. In the *Times Literary Supplement* Brian Baumfield describes Guy's novel *Edith Jackson* as "a vigorous, uncompromising" book, with characters who "live and breathe and are totally credible. The West Indian speech may prove difficult for some, but it is a raw novel of urgency and power, which readers of sixteen and older will find a moving experience." *New York Times Book Review* critic Selma G. Lanes comments that in *New Guys around the Block,* "the reader cannot resist rooting for" the book's protagonist "with his intelligence and growing self-awareness, as he negotiates the booby traps of a difficult life." Alice Walker writes in the *New York Times Book Review* that central to Guy's novel *The Friends* is "the fight to gain perception of one's own real character; the grim struggle for self-knowledge and the almost killing internal upheaval that brings the necessary growth of compassion and humility *and courage,* so that friendship (of any kind, but especially between those of notable economic and social differences) can exist."

*A Measure of Time* is a departure from Guy's youth fiction. Stuart Schoffman of the *Los Angeles Times* states that it "is a black *Bildungsroman* in the tradition of Claude McKay, Ralph Ellison and James Baldwin, a sharp and well-written meld of storytelling and sociology. Which is to say it is hardly an Alger tale, or if anything a bitter parody." Susan Isaacs characterizes the heroine, Dorine, in the *New York Times Book Review* as "a brash and intelligent guide; her observations about people and places are funny, pointed and often moving." Isaacs further notes "the other characters in this novel do not come to life.... Only Dorine stands on her own—she and the Harlem setting are vividly described, filled with life and a pleasure to read about."

Guy returned to her stories about the young in *The Ups and Downs of Carl Davis III.* The story is a "witty, sometimes bitter romp with a very spirited boy" sent from his home in New York City to live with his grandmother in Spoonsboro, South Carolina, according to a *Washington Post Book World* reviewer. With *My Love, My Love: Or, The Peasant Girl* Guy retells the Hans Christian Andersen story of *The Little Mermaid* in a Caribbean setting. The inspiration for the Broadway musical *Once on This Island, My Love, My Love,* like all of Guy's prose, "derives much of its undeniable appeal" from the author's "ability to capture the rhythm and color of Caribbean speech," a *Los Angeles Times Book Review* critic remarked.

*BIOGRAPHICAL/CRITICAL SOURCES:*

*BOOKS*

*Contemporary Literary Criticism,* Volume 26, Gale, 1983.

*Dictionary of Literary Biography,* Volume 33: *Afro-American Fiction Writers after 1955,* Gale, 1984.

*PERIODICALS*

*Los Angeles Times,* August 24, 1983.

*New York Times Book Review,* November 4, 1973; July 2, 1978; December 2, 1979; October 4, 1981; August 28, 1983; October 9, 1983, November 2, 1986; February 17, 1991; April 21, 1991; June 7, 1992; November 8, 1992.

*Times Educational Supplement,* June 6, 1980.

*Times Literary Supplement,* September 20, 1974; December 14, 1979; July 18, 1980; August 3, 1984.

*Variety,* October 22, 1990.

*Washington Post,* January 9, 1966.

*Washington Post Book World,* November 11, 1979; May 14, 1989.

\*   \*   \*

## GUY-SHEFTALL, Beverly  1946-

*PERSONAL:* Born in 1946; grew up in Memphis, TN. *Education:* Spelman College, B.A. (with honors), 1966; attended Wellesley College, 1966-67; Atlanta University, M.A., 1968; Emory University, Ph.D.

*ADDRESSES: Office*—Women's Research and Resource Center, Spelman College, Atlanta, GA 30314.

*CAREER:* Educator and writer. Alabama State University, Montgomery, faculty member, 1968-71; Spelman College, Atlanta, GA, faculty member, 1971—, founding director of Women's Research and Resource Center, 1981—, became Anna Julia Professor of English and Women's Studies. Consultant to numerous colleges and universities with women's studies programs and programs sensitive to cultural diversity; member of numerous advisory boards for the study of race and gender. Public speaker.

*AWARDS, HONORS:* Kellogg fellowship; Woodrow Wilson fellowship for dissertations in women's studies; Spelman College Presidential Faculty Award for outstanding scholarship.

*WRITINGS:*

(Editor with Roseann P. Bell and Bettye J. Parker) *Sturdy Black Bridges: Visions of Black Women in Literature,* Anchor Books, 1979.
*Daughters of Sorrow: Attitudes toward Black Women, 1880-1920,* Carlson, 1991.

Also author of *Spelman: A Centennial Celebration,* 1981, and *Double Stitch: Black Women Write about Mothers and Daughters.* Founding coeditor with Patricia Bell-Scott of *SAGE: A Scholarly Journal on Black Women,* 1983. Contributor to journals, including *Phylon.*

# H

## HAIRSTON, William (Russell, Jr.) 1928-

*PERSONAL:* Born April 1, 1928, in Goldsboro, NC; son of William Russell Hairston and Malissa Carter Hairston; married Enid Carey; children: Ann Marie. *Education:* Received B.A. from University of Northern Colorado; attended Columbia University and New York University.

*ADDRESSES: Home*—5501 Seminary Rd, No. 511-S, Falls Church, VA 22041.

*CAREER:* Author, playwright, actor, director, producer, and public administrator. Scriptwriter for U.S. government presentations; professional actor, 1950-57, performing in New York City, on tour, in summer stock, in television shows, including *Harlem Detective* (1953), and featured in the Metro-Goldwyn-Mayer film, *Take the High Ground* (1953); Greenwich Mews Theatre, New York City, production coordinator and coproducer, 1963; New York Shakespeare Festival (NYSF), New York City theater manager, 1963-64; director of *Jerico-Jim Crow* by Langston Hughes, produced in New York City, 1964; NYSF Mobile Theatre Unit, codirector of community relations, 1965; Arena Stage, Washington, DC, assistant to executive director, 1965-66; Democratic National Committee, correspondent and radio news editor, 1968; District of Columbia, Executive Office of the Mayor, executive manager of office of personnel, 1970-90.

*MEMBER:* Authors League of America, Dramatists Guild, American Society of Public Administrators, District of Columbia Police and Firefighters Retirement and Relief Board (chair, 1979-90), Boy Scouts of America, (member of executive board of National Capitol Area Council).

*AWARDS, HONORS:* Ford Foundation Theatre Administration Grant, 1965-66; NEA Literary Study Grant, 1967; Silver Beaver Award, Boy Scouts of America, National Capitol Area, 1988; Group Theatres Multi Cultural Playwrights Festival Award, 1988, for *Ira Frederick Aldridge (The London Conflict);* Meritorious Public Service Award, District of Columbia, 1990.

*WRITINGS:*

*Swan-Song of the 11th Dawn* (three-act workshop reading), produced in New York, 1962.

*Walk in the Darkness* (three-act stage play; adapted from the novel by Hans Habe), produced at Greenwich Mews Theatre, New York City, 1963.

*Curtain Call, Mr. Aldridge, Sir!* (stage play; adapted from the radio script by Ossie Davis), produced in New York, 1966.

*Black Antigone* (one-act stage play; adapted from *Antigone* by Sophocles), produced at North Carolina Regional and State Drama Festival, 1966.

*The World of Carlos* (novel), illustrated by George Ford, Putnam, 1968.

*Ira Frederick Aldridge (The London Conflict)* (stage play), Four Workshop Productions, The Group Theatre, Seattle, WA, 1988.

*Sex and Conflict* (novel), University Editions, 1993.

Also author of scripts for the U.S. Information Agency, including *Apollo 11—Man on the Moon* (half-hour television program), *Media Hora* (half-hour television series for Latin American countries), *Festival of Heritage* (half-hour film on the "African diaspora" produced in association with the Smithsonian Institute), *Jules Verne vs. Real Flight to the Moon, Yosemite National Park* (short film), *English Training—Teaching English as a Second Language, Chicago: Portrait of a City, Masterworks of Art from Zaire,* and *Operation Money-wise ("Breadbasket)* (produced for the Social Security Administration). Also editor and publisher of the government employer's newsletter *D.C. Pipeline.*

### HALEY, Alex(ander Murray Palmer) 1921-1992

*PERSONAL:* Born August 11, 1921, in Ithaca, NY; died of cardiac arrest February 10, 1992, in Seattle, WA; buried on the grounds of the Alex Haley Museum at the site of his childhood home in Henning, TN; son of Simon Alexander (a professor) and Bertha George (a teacher; maiden name, Palmer) Haley; married Nannie Branch, 1941 (divorced, 1964); married Juliette Collins, 1964 (divorced); married Myran; children: (first marriage) Lydia Ann, William Alexander; (second marriage) Cynthia Gertrude. *Education:* Attended Alcorn Agricultural & Mechanical College (now Alcorn State University); attended Elizabeth City Teachers College, 1937-39.

*CAREER:* U.S. Coast Guard, 1939-59, retiring as chief journalist; free-lance writer, 1959-92. Founder and president of Kinte Corporation, Los Angeles, CA, 1972-92. Script consultant for television miniseries *Roots; Roots: The Next Generation;* and *Palmerstown, U.S.A.;* lectured extensively and was frequent guest on radio and television programs; adviser to African American Heritage Association, Detroit, MI.

*MEMBER:* Authors Guild, Society of Magazine Writers.

*AWARDS, HONORS:* Honorary doctorates from Simpson College, 1971, Howard University and Seaton Hill University, 1974, Williams College, 1975, and Capitol University, 1975; special citation from National Book Award committee, 1977, for *Roots;* special citation from Pulitzer Prize committee, 1977, for *Roots;* Spingarn Medal from NAACP, 1977; nominated to Black Filmmakers Hall of Fame, 1981, for producing *Palmerstown, U.S.A.,* 1981.

*WRITINGS:*

(With Malcolm X) *The Autobiography of Malcolm X,* Grove, 1965.
*Roots: The Saga of an American Family,* Doubleday, 1976.
*Alex Haley Speaks* (recording), Kinte Corporation, 1980.
(Author of preface) Dorothy Redford and Michael D'Orso, *Somerset Homecoming,* Anchor/Doubleday, 1988.
*A Different Kind of Christmas,* Doubleday, 1988.
With David Stevens, *Queen* (screenplay adapted from dictation tapes), CBS, 1993.

Initiated "Playboy Interviews" feature for *Playboy,* 1962. Contributor to periodicals, including *Reader's Digest, New York Times Magazine, Smithsonian, American History Illustrated, Harper's,* and *Atlantic.*

*ADAPTATIONS: Roots* was adapted as two television miniseries by ABC, as *Roots,* 1977, and *Roots: The Next Generation,* 1979; *Queen,* based upon the story of Haley's paternal great-grandmother and an outline and research left by Haley, was published as a novel by Morrow, 1993.

*SIDELIGHTS:* Alex Haley's reputation in the literary world rests upon his much acclaimed historical novel, *Roots: The Saga of an American Family.* Haley's tracing of his African ancestry to the Mandinka tribe in a tiny village in Juffure of the Gambia region of West Africa, spawned one of the most ambitious television productions ever undertaken and inspired a generation of ancestry-seeking Americans. Eleven years prior to the appearance of *Roots,* Haley had gained recognition for writing Malcolm X's "as-told-to" autobiography, which was released shortly after the charismatic leader was gunned down while giving a speech in New York. After Spike Lee released the movie *Malcolm X* in 1992, bookstore owners had difficulty keeping the autobiography in stock.

Haley was born in 1921 in Ithaca, New York, and reared in the small town of Henning, Tennessee. He was the eldest of three sons born to Bertha George Palmer and Simon Alexander Haley; and when he was born, both his parents were in their first year of graduate school—his mother at the Ithaca Conservatory of Music, and his father at Cornell University. After finishing school, his parents took young Alex to Henning, where he grew up under the influence of his grandmother and aunts Viney, Mathilda, and Liz, who perpetuated stories about his African ancestor Kunte Kinte. These stories became the impetus for *Roots,* with which hundreds of thousands of African Americans would identify.

Although it took Haley twelve years to research and write *Roots,* success quickly followed its publication. Recipient of numerous awards, including a citation from the judges of the 1977 National Book Awards and the Pulitzer Prizes, the book is recognized as one of the most successful bestsellers in American publishing history, having sold millions of copies worldwide in 37 languages. Combined with the impact of the televised miniseries, *Roots* has become a "literary-television phenomenon" and a "sociological event," according to *Time.* By April, 1977, almost two million people had seen all or part of the first eight-episode series; and seven of those eight episodes ranked among the top ten shows in TV ratings, attaining an average of 66% of audience share.

Although critics generally lauded Haley for his accomplishment, they seemed unsure whether to treat *Roots* as a novel or as a historical account. While it is based on factual events, the dialogue, thoughts, and emotions of the characters are fictionalized. Haley himself described the book as "faction," a mixture of fact and fiction. Most critics concurred and evaluated *Roots* as a blend of history and entertainment. And despite the fictional characterizations, Willie Lee Rose suggested in the *New York Review of Books* that Kunte Kinte's parents Omoro and Binte "could possibly become the African

proto-parents of millions of Americans who are going to admire their dignity and grace." *Newsweek* found that Haley's
decision to fictionalize was the right approach: "Instead of
writing a scholarly monograph of little social impact, Haley
has written a blockbuster in the best sense—a book that is bold
in concept and ardent in execution, one that will reach millions of people and alter the way we see ourselves."

Some concern was voiced, especially at the time of the first
television series, that racial tension in America would be aggravated by *Roots.* But while *Time* reported several incidents
of racial violence following the telecast, it commented that
"most observers thought that in the long term, *Roots* would
improve race relations, particularly because of the televised
version's profound impact on whites.... A broad consensus
seemed to be emerging that *Roots* would spur black identity,
and hence black pride, and eventually pay important divi-
dends." Some black leaders viewed *Roots* "as the most important civil rights event since the 1965 march on Selma,"
according to *Time.* Vernon Jordan, executive director of the
National Urban League, called it "the single most spectacular educational experience in race relations in America."

Haley heard only positive comments from both blacks and
whites. He told William Marmon in a *Time* interview: "The
blacks who are buying books are not buying them to go out
and fight someone, but because they want to know who they
are. *Roots* is all of our stories. It's the same for me or any black.
It's just a matter of filling in the blanks—which person, living in which village, going on what ship across the same ocean,
slavery, emancipation, the struggle for freedom.... The white
response is more complicated. But when you start talking
about family, about lineage and ancestry, you are talking about
every person on earth. We all have it; it's a great equalizer....
I think the book has touched a strong, subliminal chord."

But there was also concern, according to *Time,* that "breast-
beating about the past may turn into a kind of escapism, distracting attention from the present. Only if *Roots* turns the
anger at yesterday's slavery into anger at today's ghetto will
it really matter." And James Baldwin wrote in the *New York
Times Book Review:* "*Roots* is a study of continuities, of consequences, of how a people perpetuate themselves, how each
generation helps to doom, or helps to liberate, the coming
one—the action of love, or the effect of the absence of love,
in time. It suggests, with great power, how each of us, however unconsciously, can't but be the vehicle of the history
which has produced us. Well, we can perish in this vehicle,
children, or we can move on up the road."

*Roots* was so successful that ABC produced a sequel, *Roots:
The Next Generation,* a $16.6-million production that ran for

14 hours. The story line of *Roots II,* as it was called, begins in
1882, twelve years after the end of the *Roots I,* and it concludes
in 1967. During the 85-year span, Haley's family is depicted
against the backdrop of the Ku Klux Klan, world wars, race
riots, and the Great Depression; and the commonalities between black and white middle-class life are dramatized as well.

Haley also researched his paternal heritage; and in 1993, CBS
aired a three-episode miniseries, *Queen,* about his paternal
great-grandmother, Queen, the daughter of a mulatto slave girl
and a white slave owner. Writing in the *New York Times,* John
J. O'Connor noted that although "the scope is considerably
more limited ... the sense of unfolding history, familial and
national, is still compelling." Accusations surfaced about the
historical accuracy of *Queen,* though, which recalled the
charges of plagiarism and authenticity leveled at *Roots* by the
author of *The Africans,* Harold Courtlander, who was subsequently paid $650,000 in an out-of-court settlement. Critics
questioned whether a romance had actually existed between
Queen and her slave-owning master. According to Melinda
Henneberger in the *New York Times,* the tapes left by Haley
did not mention a romance between his paternal great-grandparents and David Stevens, who worked with Haley's research
and outline, recalled Haley's intent to soften the relationship.
Producer Mark Wolper indicated that "Haley had become
convinced by his later inquiries ... that his great-grandparents
had actually been in love," wrote Henneberger, adding that
"several scholars, all of whom said they would never contra-
dict Haley's research into his own family, added that consen-
sual, lifelong relationships between slaves and owners were
exceedingly rare." Esther B. Fein noted in the *New York Times*
that the book was published as a novel "partly because Mr.
Haley could not verify all the family folklore that inspired it
and died before the project was completed."

In 1985, Haley was working on a novel set in the Appalachian
culture that he had researched extensively. The novel was
centered around the relationships among a mountain father,
son, and grandson. Because this book was not about blacks
but primarily about whites, Haley said of the project, "I think
one of the most fascinating things you can do after you learn
about your own people is to study something about the history and culture of other people." Haley also planned to write a
book detailing the life of Madame C. J. Walker and her daughter A'Lelia. Haley had signed a three-book contract with
Ballantine for its new multicultural publishing program, for
which his first title was to be a comprehensive history of his
hometown—Henning. Those who knew Haley well say his
research on Henning predated the writing of *Roots.* Haley was
buried on the grounds of his Henning homestead, but in 1992,
his estate auctioned off virtually all his possessions to pay a
$1.5 million debt.

*BIOGRAPHICAL/CRITICAL SOURCES:*

*BOOKS*

*The Black Press U.S.A.,* Iowa State University Press, 1990.
*Contemporary Literary Criticism,* Gale, Volume 8, 1978, Volume 12, 1980.
*Dictionary of Literary Biography,* Volume 38: *Afro-American Writers After 1955: Dramatists and Prose Writers,* Gale, 1985.


*PERIODICALS*

*Black Collegian,* September/October, 1985.
*Christianity Today,* May 6, 1977.
*Ebony,* April, 1977.
*Forbes,* February 15, 1977.
*Ms.,* February, 1977.
*National Review,* March 4, 1977.
*Negro History Bulletin,* January, 1977.
*New Republic,* March 12, 1977.
*Newsweek,* June 6, 1976; September 27, 1976; February 14, 1977.
*New Yorker,* February 14, 1977.
*New York Review of Books,* November 11, 1976.
*New York Times,* October 14, 1976; February 12, 1993, p. C34; February 14, 1993, p. H1; March 3, 1993, p. C18.
*New York Times Book Review,* September 26, 1976; January 2, 1977; February 27, 1977.
*People,* March 28, 1977.
*Publishers Weekly,* September 6, 1976; March 2, 1992; October 12, 1992, p. 10
*Saturday Review,* September 18, 1976.
*Time,* October 18, 1976; February 14, 1977; February 19, 1979.
*Today's Educator,* September, 1977.

\* \* \*

## HALLIBURTON, Warren J. 1924-

*PERSONAL:* Born August 2, 1924, in New York, NY; son of Richard H. (a book shipping manager) and Blanche (maiden name, Watson) Halliburton; married Marion Jones, December 20, 1947; married second wife, Frances Fletcher (a teacher), February 11, 1971; children: (first marriage) Cheryl, Stephanie, Warren Jr., Jena. *Education:* New York University, B.S., 1949; Columbia University, M.Ed., 1975, D.Ed., 1977. *Avocational interests:* Jogging, a follow-through of his days in track and field competition.

*ADDRESSES: Home*—22 Scribner Hill Rd., Wilton, CT 06897.

*CAREER:* Prairie View Agricultural and Mechanical College (now Prairie View A & M University), Prairie View, TX, instructor in English, 1949; Bishop College, Dallas, TX, instructor in English, 1951; Institute of International Education, associate, 1952; *Recorder* (newspaper), New York City, reporter and columnist, 1953; teacher and dean in Brooklyn, NY, high school, 1958-60; New York City Board of Education, coordinator, and New York State Department of Education, associate, 1960-65; McGraw Hill, Inc., New York City, editor, 1967; Hamilton-Kirkland Colleges, Clinton, NY, visiting professor of English, 1971-72; Columbia University, Teachers College, New York City, editor, research associate, and director of scholarly journal, government program, and Ethnic Studies Center, 1972-77; currently editor and writer, *Reader's Digest,* New York City. Free-lance editor and writer. *Military service:* U.S. Army Air Forces, 1943-46.

*WRITINGS:*

(Editor with Mauri E. Pelkonen) *New Worlds of Literature,* Harcourt, 1966.
*The Heist* (novel), McGraw, 1969.
*Cry, Baby!* (novel), McGraw, 1969.
*Some Things that Glitter* (novel), illustrated by Elzia Moon, McGraw, 1969.
(With William L. Katz) *American Majorities and Minorities: A Syllabus of United States History for Secondary Schools,* Arno, 1970.
(With Laurence Swinburne and Steve Broudy) *They Had a Dream,* Pyramid Publications, 1970.
(Editor and contributor) *America's Color Caravan,* four volumes, Singer Graflex, 1971.
*The Picture Life of Jesse Jackson,* F. Watts, 1972, second edition, 1984.
(Editor) *Short Story Scene,* Globe, 1973.
*The History of Black Americans,* Harcourt, 1973.
(With Agnes A. Postva) *Composing with Sentences,* Cambridge Books, 1974.
(With Ernest Kaiser) *Harlem: A History of Broken Dreams,* Doubleday, 1974.
*Pathways to the World of English,* Globe, 1974.
*The Fighting Redtails: America's First Black Airmen,* illustrated by John Gampert, Contemporary Perspectives, 1978.
*Flight to the Stars: The Life of Daniel James, Jr.,* Contemporary Perspectives, 1979.
*The People of Connecticut: A History Textbook on Connecticut,* Connecticut Yankees, 1984.
*The Picture Life of Michael Jackson,* F. Watts, 1984.
*The Tragedy of Little Bighorn,* F. Watts, 1989.
*Clarence Thomas: Supreme Court Justice,* Enslow, 1993.

*AFRICA TODAY SERIES*

*Africa's Struggle for Independence,* Crestwood, 1992.
*African Wildlife,* Crestwood, 1992.
*Celebrations of African Heritage,* Crestwood, 1992.
*Nomads of the Sahara,* Crestwood, 1992.
*African Industries,* Crestwood, 1993.
*African Landscapes,* Crestwood, 1993.
*Africa's Struggle to Survive,* Crestwood, 1993.
*City and Village Life,* Crestwood, 1993.

*OTHER*

Also adapter of text editions of Jack London's *Call of the Wild,* Douglas Wallop's *The Year the Yankees Lost the Pennant,* and Paddy Chayefsky's *Marty* and *Printer's Measure,* all Mc-Graw, 1968.

Contributor of about one hundred short stories, adaptations, and articles to periodicals; writer of fifteen filmstrips and a motion picture, *Dig!*

*SIDELIGHTS:* Warren J. Halliburton has commented: "Writing is a sanctuary of self-realizations, affording me the opportunity for adventure and discovery of my relation with the world. This is a rare if not unique privilege in today's pigeon-holing society."

*BIOGRAPHICAL/CRITICAL SOURCES:*

*PERIODICALS*

*New Republic,* March 1, 1985.

\*   \*   \*

## HAMILTON, Charles V(ernon) 1929-

*PERSONAL:* Born October 19, 1929, in Muskogee, OK; son of Owen and Viola (Haynes) Hamilton; married Dona Louise Cooper, October 5, 1956; children: Carol, Valli. *Education:* Roosevelt University, B.A., 1951; Loyola University, Chicago, IL, J.D., 1954; University of Chicago, M.A., 1957, Ph.D., 1963.

*ADDRESSES: Office*—Department of Political Science, Columbia University, New York, NY 10027.

*CAREER:* Albany State College, Albany, GA, instructor in political science, 1957-58; Tuskegee Institute, Tuskegee, AL, assistant professor of political science, 1958-60; Rutgers University, New Brunswick, NJ, instructor in political science, 1963-64; Lincoln University, Lincoln University, PA, instruc-

tor in political science, 1964-67; Roosevelt University, Chicago, IL, professor of political science 1967-69; Columbia University, New York City, professor of political science, 1969—; Metropolitan Applied Research Center (MARC), New York, NY, head of organization, 1989—. Political Science Quarterly (board of editors, 1975—). *Military service:* U.S. Army, 1948-49.

*MEMBER:* National Association for the Advancement of Colored People (NAACP), American Political Science Association (vice-president, 1972-73 and 1989—), Twentieth Century Foundation (board of trustees, 1973—).

*AWARDS, HONORS:* John Hay Whitney fellowship, 1962; Lindback Distinguished Teaching award, Lincoln University, 1965; University of Chicago Alumni award and Roosevelt University Alumni award, both 1970; Phi Beta Kappa Visiting Lecturer Scholar, 1972-73.

*WRITINGS:*

*Minority Politics in Black Belt Alabama,* McGraw, 1962.
(With Stokely Carmichael) *Black Power: The Politics of Liberation in America,* Vintage, 1967.
(With others) *Dialogue on Violence* (edited by George Vickers, from "The Dialogue" series), Bobbs-Merrill Co., 1968.
*The Black Preacher In America,* Morrow, 1972.
(Coauthor) *The Social Scene,* Winthrop, 1972.
*The Black Experience in American Politics,* Putnam, 1973.
*The Bench and the Ballot: Southern Federal Judges and Black Voters,* Oxford University Press, 1973.
*The Struggle for Political Equality* (from "Black Perspectives on the Bicentennial" series), National Urban League, 1976.
*American Government,* Scott, Foresman, 1982.
*Adam Clayton Powell, Jr.: The Political Biography of an American Dilemma,* Atheneum, 1991.

Also author of *The Fight for Racial Justice,* a public affairs pamphlet, 1974. Contributor to scholarly journals, including *Harvard Educational Review, Black Scholar, Wisconsin Law Review,* and *Urban Violence.*

*SIDELIGHTS:* As head of New York's Metropolitan Applied Research Center (MARC), Charles V. Hamilton is concerned with social problems related to community development. His writings focus on the social and political dilemmas faced by African Americans.

*The Bench and the Ballot* chronicles one aspect of the struggle for civil rights. A reviewer in *Choice* wrote that Hamilton "has done us a service with his detailed treatment of the handling of a sampling of voting rights cases by U.S. district judges in the South." In his book, Hamilton analyzes three judicial types: the justice-seeking judge who enforces the law; the racist judge who obstructs justice outright; and the racist judge who appears willing to be educated in order that justice might be dispensed. The reviewer goes on to call *The Bench and the Ballot* "a very readable lesson on the effectiveness of using the courts to administer the law."

A writer for *Saturday Review* reports that in *Black Power: The Politics of Liberation in America,* the authors "have set down the philosophy and concept of Black Power as it has painfully emerged out of the urban and rural black ghettos these last thirteen years." The reviewer contends that the book is an important document to have come forth from the whole black-white arena of public affairs and goes on to say that the book is "perhaps the most significant single piece of writing in this area since the 1954 Supreme Court decision declaring public school segregation unconstitutional...."

*Adam Clayton Powell, Jr.: The Political Biography of an American Dilemma* examines the life of what *Nation* reviewer Peter Dailey described as "the flamboyant Congressman whose historic achievements were largely overshadowed by his controversial downfall." Hamilton's book explores the successes and foibles of Powell, from his early years as pastor of Abyssinian Baptist Church to his expulsion from the U.S. House of Representatives. The author also delves into a crucial, yet little covered period in civil rights history. According to Taylor Branch in the *New York Times Book Review* Hamilton "occasionally lapses into summary cliches, but his diligent scholarship has uncovered more than a good book's worth of Powell material."

*BIOGRAPHICAL/CRITICAL SOURCES:*

*PERIODICALS*

*American Spectator,* April, 1992, pp. 74-76.
*Choice,* March, 1974.
*Christian Science Monitor,* November 18, 1967.
*Commonweal,* April 26, 1974.
*Nation,* January 6, 1992, p. 24.
*New York Times Book Review,* October 20, 1991, p. 7.
*Political Science Quarterly,* March, 1974.
*Saturday Review,* November 11, 1967.

\* \* \*

## HAMILTON, Virginia 1936-

*PERSONAL:* Born March 12, 1936, in Yellow Springs, OH; daughter of Kenneth James (a musician) and Etta Belle (Perry) Hamilton; married Arnold Adoff (an anthologist and poet), March 19, 1960; children: Leigh Hamilton, Jaime Levi. *Education:* Studied at Antioch College, 1952-55, Ohio State University, 1957-58, and New School for Social Research, 1958-60.

*ADDRESSES: Agent*—Arnold Adoff Agency, Box 293, Yellow Springs, OH 45387.

*CAREER:* "Every source of occupation imaginable, from singer to bookkeeper."

*AWARDS, HONORS: Zeely* appeared on the American Library Association's list of notable children's books of 1967 and received the Nancy Block Memorial Award of the Downtown Community School Awards Committee, New York; Edgar Allan Poe Award for best juvenile mystery, 1969, for *The House of Dies Drear;* Ohioana Literary Award, 1969; John Newbery Honor Book Award, 1971, for *The Planet of Junior Brown;* Lewis Carroll Shelf Award, *Boston Globe-Horn Book* Award, 1974, John Newbery Medal and National Book Award, both 1975, and Gustav-Heinemann-Friedinspreis fur kinder und Lugendbucher (Dusseldorf, Germany), 1991, all for *M. C. Higgins, the Great;* John Newbery Honor Book Award, Coretta Scott King Award, *Boston Globe-Horn Book* Award, and American Book Award nomination, all 1983, all for *Sweet Whispers, Brother Rush; Horn Book* Fanfare Award in fiction, 1985, for *A Little Love;* Coretta Scott King Award, *New York Times* Best Illustrated Children's Book Award, Children's Book Bulletin Other Award, and *Horn Book* Honor List selection, all 1986, all for *The People Could Fly: American Black Folktales; Boston Globe-Horn Book* Award, 1988, and Coretta Scott King Award, 1989, both for *Anthony Burns: The Defeat and Triumph of a Fugitive Slave;* John Newbery Honor Book Award, 1989, for *In the Beginning: Creation Stories from around the World;* Honorary Doctor of Humane Letters, Bank St. College, 1990; Catholic Library Association Regina Medal, 1990; Hans Christian Andersen Award U.S., 1992, for body of work.

*WRITINGS:*

*BIOGRAPHIES FOR CHILDREN*

*W. E. B. Du Bois: A Biography,* Crowell, 1972.
*Paul Robeson: The Life and Times of a Free Black Man,* Harper, 1974.

*FICTION FOR CHILDREN*

*Zeely,* illustrated by Symeon Shimin, Macmillan, 1967.
*The House of Dies Drear,* illustrated by Eros Keith, Macmillan, 1968.
*The Time-Ago Tales of Jahdu,* Macmillan, 1969.

*The Planet of Junior Brown,* Macmillan, 1971.

*Time-Ago Lost: More Tales of Jahdu,* illustrated by Ray Prather, Macmillan, 1973.

*M. C. Higgins, the Great,* Macmillan, 1974, published with teacher's guide by Lou Stanek, Dell, 1986.

*Arilla Sun Down,* Greenwillow, 1976.

*Justice and Her Brothers* (first novel in the "Justice" trilogy), Greenwillow, 1978.

*Jahdu,* pictures by Jerry Pinkney, Greenwillow, 1980.

*Dustland* (second novel in the "Justice" trilogy), Greenwillow, 1980.

*The Gathering* (third novel in the "Justice" trilogy), Green-willow, 1981.

*Sweet Whispers, Brother Rush,* Philomel, 1982.

*The Magical Adventures of Pretty Pearl,* Harper, 1983.

*Willie Bea and the Time the Martians Landed,* Greenwillow, 1983.

*A Little Love,* Philomel, 1984.

*Junius over Far,* Harper, 1985.

*The People Could Fly: American Black Folktales,* illustrated by Leo and Diane Dillon, Knopf, 1985, published with cassette, 1987.

*The Mystery of Drear House: The Conclusion of the Dies Drear Chronicle,* Greenwillow, 1987.

*A White Romance,* Philomel, 1987.

*In the Beginning: Creation Stories from around the World,* Harcourt, 1988, 1991.

*Anthony Burns: The Defeat and Triumph of a Fugitive Slave* (an historical reconstruction based on fact), Knopf, 1988.

*The Bells of Christmas,* illustrated by Lambert Davis, Harcourt, 1989.

*The Dark Way: Stories from the Spirit World,* illustrated by Davis, Harcourt, 1990.

*Tales from the Spirit World,* illustrated by Davis, Harcourt, 1990.

*Cousins,* Putnam, 1990.

*The All Jahdu Storybook,* illustrated by Barry Moser, Harcourt, 1991.

*Many Thousand Gone: African-Americans from Slavery to Freedom,* illustrated by L. and D. Dillon, Knopf, 1992.

*Drylongso,* illustrated by Jerry Pinkney, Harcourt, 1992.

OTHER

(Editor) *The Writings of W. E. B. Du Bois,* Crowell, 1975.

Author of introduction, *The Newbery Award Reader,* edited by Martin Greenberg, Harcourt, 1984. Also editor of various publications relating to refugees. Contributor of book reviews to periodicals, including *American Historical Review.*

ADAPTATIONS: *The House of Dies Drear* was adapted for the Public Broadcasting Service series "Wonderworks" in 1984.

SIDELIGHTS: Virginia Hamilton is one of the most prolific and influential authors of children's books writing today. Not only have many of her works received awards such as the National Book Award, but her novel, *M. C. Higgins, the Great,* was the first work in history to win both the National Book Award and the Newbery Medal. Hamilton is recognized as a gifted and demanding storyteller. Ethel L. Heins, for example, writes in *Horn Book:* "Few writers of fiction for young people are as daring, inventive, and challenging to read—or to review—as Virginia Hamilton. Frankly making demands on her readers, she nevertheless expresses herself in a style essentially simple and concise." Hamilton's writing is a mix of realism, history, myth, and folklore, which, according to *Horn Book* contributor Paul Heins, "always [results in] some exterior manifestation—historical and personal—that she has examined in the light of her feelings and her intelligence."

Although Hamilton has been praised for her depiction of contemporary African American life and its historical and cultural heritage, the author does not see herself in such narrow terms. "There's nothing you can really do about being referred to as a 'minority' or 'black' writer," she once commented. "For a long time, I tried to fight it, saying I'm a writer, *period.* But in a country like ours, there really is a dominant culture. I prefer the term 'parallel culture'." Throughout her writing career, Hamilton has struggled "to find a certain form and content to express black literature as American literature and perpetuate a pedigree of American black literature for the young," she explained to Wendy Smith in the *Chicago Tribune Book World.*

Hamilton's vision has been deeply influenced by her background. Her mother's side of the family was descended from a fugitive slave, Levi Perry, who settled in the southern Ohio Miami valley town of Yellow Springs. The Perry family grew and prospered by farming the rich Ohio soil. "I grew up within the warmth of loving aunts and uncles, all reluctant farmers but great storytellers," Hamilton recalls in a *Horn Book* article by Lee Bennett Hopkins.

"When it came time for me to attempt my own telling," Hamilton writes in *Horn Book,* "I found I was good at drawing on the lapses between true memories, which had grown large with the passage of time." While attending Antioch College on a scholarship, Hamilton majored in writing and composed short stories. One of her instructors liked her stories enough to encourage the young student to leave college and test her skills in New York City. Hamilton was eager to experience the excitement of city life, and so in 1955 she began spending her summers in New York working as a book-keeper. Later, she moved to the city permanently.

Working various jobs, reading voraciously, and soaking in the artistic atmosphere of Greenwich Village, Hamilton did not place writing as a high priority. "I worked hard at my writing, but wasn't singularly fixed on it.... *The New Yorker* wrote me very encouraging letters and tried to help me. But I would never quite fit their mold. I was meeting all kinds of people and having a wonderful time. Seriousness came slowly." While in New York, Hamilton attended the New School for Social Research where one of her teachers, Atheneum cofounder Hiram Hayden, supported her efforts and tried to get her first novel, a work for adults entitled *Mayo,* published. "Unfortunately, his partners [at Atheneum] didn't agree. If they had, I might never have become a writer of children's books." Instead, at the suggestion of a friend, Hamilton expanded a children's story she had written into the novel, *Zeely.*

An important influence on the creation of *Zeely* came after Hamilton married poet and anthologist Arnold Adoff, whom she met not long after arriving in New York City. The two newlyweds traveled to Spain and then to northern Africa. "Going to Africa had been an enduring dream of Hamilton's," according to *Dictionary of Literary Biography* contributor Jane Ball, "and the land of dark-skinned people had 'a tremendous impression' on her, she said, even though her stay was brief. The impact is apparent on her first book." According to John Rowe Townsend in his *A Sounding of Storytellers: New and Revised Essays on Contemporary Writers for Children, Zeely* exemplifies the type of writing that Hamilton would produce throughout her career: there "is not taint of racism in her books.... All through her work runs an awareness of black history, and particularly of black history in America. And there is a difference in the furniture of her writing mind from that of most of her white contemporaries: dream, myth, legend and ancient story can be sensed again and again in the background of naturalistically-described present-day events."

*Zeely* is about a girl called Geeder who, fascinated by a tall, regal-looking woman she sees tending pigs on a farm, obsessively imagines her to be a Watusi queen. By the end of the tale, Zeely convinces Geeder she is nothing of the sort, "and with the aid of a parable she helps Geeder [accept herself for who she is, too]. She is not a queen; and perhaps there is an implication that for black Americans to look back towards supposed long-lost glories in Africa is unfruitful."

After living in New York City for about fifteen years, Hamilton decided to return to her home state. The city, however, did have some lingering effect on Hamilton's writing in that her books *The Time-Ago Tales of Jahdu* and *The Planet of Junior Brown* take place there.

"Most of my books have some element of fantasy," Hamilton remarked in *Children's Literature Association Quarterly,* "from little Jahdu who was born in an oven and the Night Traveller in *Zeely,* on to the dead James False Face speaking to the child, Arilla, in *Arilla Sun Down,* to the ghost in *Sweet*

*Whispers, Brother Rush* and the divine power of the gods in *The Magical Adventures of Pretty Pearl.*" Hamilton varies the degree of fantasy from book to book. With the "Justice" trilogy, which some critics have classified as science fiction, the author deals with such subjects as clairvoyance, global disaster, and time travel. Hamilton, however, does not consider these books science fiction. Rather, she feels they are fantasy books. "Science fiction is based on scientific fact; fantasy need not be," she once explained.

In books like the Jahdu tales, including *The Time-Ago Tales of Jahdu, Time-Ago Lost: More Tales of Jahdu, Jahdu,* and *The All Jahdu Storybook,* Hamilton takes an approach that mimics the style of the traditional folk tale. These works tell of the fantastic adventures of Jahdu and his "encounters [with] the allegorical figures Sweetdream, Nightmare, Trouble, Chameleon, and others...," writes Marilyn F. Apseloff in the *Dictionary of Literary Biography.* "These original tales have a timeless quality about them; in addition, they reveal racial pride, as Jahdu discovers in [*The Time-Ago Tales of Jahdu*] that he is happiest when he becomes a part of a black family in Harlem." Similarly, in the collections *The People Could Fly: American Black Folktales, In the Beginning: Creation Stories from around the World,* and *The Dark Way: Stories from the Spirit World* Hamilton retells old myths and folk tales from her own black ancestry—as well as many other cultures—in an attempt to restore pride in this diverse and rich literary heritage.

*The Dark Way: Stories from the Spirit World,* reviewed in the *New York Times* by Wendy Martin, is a "sophisticated yet accessible collection of 25 legends, fables, cautionary lore, tall tales, creation myths, parables and ghost stories...." It brings young readers stories "as divergent as Icelandic Eddas—Norse mythology and poetry—and Japanese fairy tales." Martin continued, "At the end of each story Ms. Hamilton has included incisive comments that provide historical background and literary analysis." The end of the book also has a "useful bibliography of source materials."

"Unfortunately," according to David Streitfeld in *Book World,* "the text coexists uneasily with the scholarly trappings." Streitfeld finds the footnotes "intrusive," and he wonders for "whom this book is aimed at." He describes Hamilton's writing as "serviceable, sometimes effective," and occasionally "memorable." Martin, however, admits only to some shortcomings in the book in its misleadingly negative title. The stories, she says, "probe and shape our deepest fears; read together they are a tribute to the limitless imagination common to all people."

One ethnic group in particular, American Indians, has influenced Hamilton's writing in books like the Edgar Award-winning *The House of Dies Drear.* "The references to Indians in her books," observes Apseloff, "are probably the result of two factors: Hamilton knew that many Shawnees lived in the Yellow Springs area originally, with Cherokees further south, and her grandmother claimed to be part American Indian." Despite this element in the story, however, *The House of Dies Drear* is a mystery novel centered around the history of the Underground Railroad, the route that fugitive blacks took to escape slavery in the South before the Civil War. It "is a taut mystery, one which youngsters gulp down quickly and find hard to forget," attests Hopkins. Hamilton told Hopkins, "*The House of Dies Drear* is [one of] my favorite book[s], I think, because it is so full of all the things I love: excitement, mystery, black history, the strong, black family. In it I tried to pay back all those wonderful relatives who gave me so much in the past."

Family is an important theme in all of Hamilton's books, and her strong faith and love of family, along with the fact that she has always considered herself to be a loner, has influenced the characterization in her novels. "I think I'd have to say my characters are for the most part based on me," she told Hopkins. She later added, "My characters are the way I see the artist, the *human,* isolated, out of time, in order to reveal himself more clearly. I am tremendously interested in the human as oracle and as spirit isolated." She first tackled this theme of the isolated individual head on in *The Planet of Junior Brown* in which three people, the fat but musically gifted Junior, an eccentric janitor named Mr. Pool, and the streetwise, independent Buddy Clark, find support in each other in a secret room in the school basement. The intensity of Junior's isolation from his parents and the rest of the world is so great that it finally leads to a madness induced by his piano teacher, Miss Peebs. Together, Mr. Pool and Buddy help Junior, and in so doing Buddy also matures. "He realizes that living for himself, his old belief, is not the answer," relates Apseloff: "'We have to learn to live for each other.'"

Hamilton's *M. C. Higgins, the Great* also emphasizes the importance of family. The story portrays the Higginses, a close-knit family that resides on Sarah's Mountain in southern Ohio. The mountain has special significance to the Higginses, for it has belonged to their family since M. C.'s great-grandmother Sarah, an escaped slave, settled there. The conflict in the story arises when a huge spoil heap, created by strip mining, threatens to engulf their home. M. C. is torn between his love for his home and his concern for his family's safety, and he searches diligently for a solution that will allow him to preserve both. *M. C. Higgins, the Great* was highly praised by critics, including poet Nikki Giovanni, who writes in the *New York Times Book Review:* "Once again Virginia Hamilton creates a world and invites us in. *M. C. Higgins, the Great* is not an adorable book, not a lived-happily-ever-

after kind of story. It is warm, humane and hopeful and does what every book should do—creates characters with whom we can identify and for whom we care."

The theme of family runs similarly through *Cousins.* The eleven-year-old protagonist, Cammy, "lives entirely in the world of her family: her kind and beautiful mother, her changeable but idolized older brother, and her adored Gram Tut, who lives in the Care home," notes *Los Angeles Times* reviewer Sonja Bolle. There is also an aunt as well as her two children, the "irresponsible" Richie and the "maddeningly perfect Patty Ann." When Cammy falls ill after her cousin Patty Ann's accidental death, it is through the intervention of the family members that Cammy is able to heal.

Extraordinary style is another hallmark of Hamilton which is evident in *Cousins.* Reviewer Gloria Jacobs writes in the *New York Times:* "Like the gift of perfect pitch, [Hamilton] has an ear for the cadences of everyday conversations and internal debates. She re-creates the language of African-American children in prose as smooth and liquid as poetry." *Tribune Books* contributor Mary Harris Veeder likens her style to that of Toni Morrison, which she feels is "high praise." Hamilton, however, does have an occasional detractor; Bolle notes that Hamilton's writing becomes "almost surrealistic" in the climatic chapter and may "lose readers who haven't the patience to wait for subsequent dialogue to confirm the tragedy." Still, Bolle admits "Hamilton's ambitious attempt to portray a child's grief succeeds completely."

Another family story is told in *The Bells of Christmas.* The Bell family celebrates the Christmas holidays in what *Book World* contributor Jeanne Fox-Alston describes as a "heartwarming and rich story" set in Springfield, Ohio, in 1890. Natalie Babbitt writing in the *Los Angeles Times* notes that the book reflects "careful historical research in [its] richness of detail." Hamilton created this tale from her mother's memories of Ohio Christmases near the turn of the century. Part of the book's appeal, comments Fox-Alston, is learning about what life "was like for a family 100 years ago." The book also illustrates the fact that there have always been black families in America like the Bells; "middle class, prosperous and hardworking, living free of the big-city ghettoes, with strong family ties and strong family values," notes Babbitt. Fox-Alston asserts that with its many illustrations, it is a book not only suited to its intended upper elementary grade readers, but younger children can enjoy the story, too.

A serious and dedicated writer, Hamilton has also edited numerous publications of the United States Committee for Refugees, related to the refugee crises of Uganda, Sri Lanka, and Laos. She also writes reviews of books related to the history of the American South. Today, Hamilton lives with her husband on her family's land in Ohio. Her children are now grown and pursuing careers in New York. "Virginia Hamilton has heightened the standards of children's literature as few others have," concludes Betsy Hearne in *Bookbird*. "She does not address children or the state of children so much as she explores with them, sometimes ahead of them, the full possibilities of boundless imagination."

*BIOGRAPHICAL/CRITICAL SOURCES:*

*BOOKS*

*Authors in the News,* Volume 1, Gale, 1976.
Butler, Francelia, editor, *Children's Literature: Annual of the Modern Language Association Seminar on Children's Literature and the Children's Literature Association,* Volume 4, Temple University Press, 1975.
*Children's Literature Review,* Gale, Volume 1, 1976; Volume 8, 1985; Volume 11, 1986.
*Contemporary Literary Criticism,* Volume 26, Gale, 1983.
*Dictionary of Literary Biography,* Gale, Volume 33: *Afro-American Fiction Writers after 1955,* 1984; Volume 52: *American Writers for Children since 1960: Fiction,* 1986.
Egoff, Sheila A., *Thursday's Child: Trends and Patterns in Contemporary Children's Literature,* American Library Association, 1981, pp. 31-65, 130-158.
Lystad, Mary, *From Dr. Mather to Dr. Seuss: 200 Years of American Books for Children,* Schenkman Books, pp. 179-205.
*Major 20th Century Writers,* Gale, 1991.
Rees, David, *Painted Desert, Green Shade: Essays on Contemporary Writers of Fiction for Children and Young Adults,* Horn Book, 1984, pp. 168-184.
Sims, Rudine, *Shadow and Substance: Afro-American Experience in Contemporary Children's Fiction,* National Council of Teachers of English, 1982, pp. 79-102.
Smith, J. C., editor, *Epic Lives: 100 Black Women Who Made a Difference,* Visible Ink Press, 1993, pp. 240-244.
Smith, J. C., editor, *Notable Black Women,* Gale, 1992, pp. 448-452.
*Something about the Author,* Volume 56, Gale, 1989, pp. 60-70.
Townsend, John Rowe, *A Sounding of Storytellers: New and Revised Essays on Contemporary Writers for Children,* Lippincott, 1979, pp. 97-108.

*PERIODICALS*

*Best Sellers,* January, 1983.
*Bookbird,* December 15, 1980, pp. 22-23.
*Booklist,* August, 1982, p. 1525; April 1, 1983, pp. 1034-1035; July, 1985, p. 1554; February 1, 1992, pp. 1020-1021.
*Bulletin of the Center for Children's Books,* September, 1978, p. 9; March, 1981, p. 134; July-August, 1982, p. 207; November, 1983, pp. 50-51; April, 1985, p. 148; June, 1988.
*Chicago Tribune Book World,* November 10, 1985, pp. 33-34.
*Children's Literature Association Quarterly,* fall, 1982, pp. 45-48; winter, 1983, pp. 10-14, 25-27; spring, 1983, pp. 17-20.
*Children's Literature in Education,* winter, 1983; summer, 1987, pp. 67-75.
*Christian Science Monitor,* May 4, 1972, p. B5; March 12, 1979, p. B4; May 12, 1980, p. B9; March 2, 1984, p. B7; August 3, 1984.
*Cincinnati Enquirer,* January 5, 1975.
*Growing Point,* July, 1977, pp. 3147-3148; November, 1985, pp. 4525-4526; January, 1988.
*Horn Book,* October, 1968, p. 563; February, 1970; February, 1972; October, 1972, p. 476; December, 1972, pp. 563-569; June, 1973; October, 1974, pp. 143-144; April, 1975; August, 1975, pp. 344-348; December, 1976, p. 611; December, 1978, pp. 609-619; June, 1980, p. 305; October, 1982, pp. 505-506; June, 1983; February, 1984, pp. 24-28; September-October, 1984, pp. 597-598; September-October, 1985, pp. 563-564; March-April, 1986, pp. 212-213; January-February, 1988, pp. 105-106; March-April, 1989, pp. 183-185.
*Interracial Books for Children Bulletin,* Numbers 1 and 2, 1983, p. 32; Number 5, 1984; Volume 15, number 5, 1984, pp. 17-18; Volume 16, number 4, 1985, p. 19.
*Kirkus Reviews,* July 1, 1974; October 15, 1980, pp. 1354-1355; April 1, 1983; October 1, 1985, pp. 1088-1089.
*Kliatt Young Adult Paperback Book Guide,* winter, 1982, p. 21.
*Library Journal,* September 15, 1971.
*Lion and the Unicorn,* Volume 9, 1985, pp. 50-57.
*Listener,* November 6, 1975.
*Los Angeles Times Book Review,* March 23, 1986; May 22, 1988, p. 11; December 17, 1989, p. 8; November 18, 1990, p. 8.
*New York Times Book Review,* October 13, 1968, p. 26; October 24, 1971, p. 8; September 22, 1974, p. 8; December 22, 1974, p. 8; October 31, 1976, p. 39; December 17, 1978, p. 27; May 4, 1980, pp. 26, 28; September 27, 1981, p. 36; November 14, 1982, pp. 41, 56; September 4, 1983, p. 14; March 18, 1984, p. 31; April 7, 1985, p. 20; November 10, 1985, p. 38; November 8, 1987, p. 36; October 16, 1988, p. 46; November 13, 1988, p. 52; December 17, 1989, p. 29; November 11, 1990, p. 34; August 11, 1991, p. 16.
*Publishers Weekly,* March 22, 1993, p. 26.
*School Library Journal,* December 1968, pp. 53-54; September, 1971, p. 126; December, 1978, p. 60; March, 1980, p. 140; April, 1981, p. 140; April, 1983, p. 123.

*Times* (London), November 20, 1986.

*Times Literary Supplement,* May 23, 1975; July 11, 1975, p. 766; March 25, 1977, p. 359; September 19, 1980, p. 1024; November 20, 1981, p. 1362; August 30, 1985, p. 958; February 28, 1986, p. 230; October 30, 1987, p. 1205; November 20, 1987, p. 1286; July 29, 1988, p. 841.

*Tribune Books* (Chicago), November 13, 1988, p. 6; February 26, 1989, p. 8; November 11, 1990, p. 6.

*Village Voice,* December 14, 1975.

*Voice of Youth Advocates,* August, 1980, pp. 31-32; October, 1983, p. 215.

*Washington Post Book World,* June 25, 1967, p. 12; November 10, 1974; November 7, 1976, p. G7; November 11, 1979; September 14, 1980, p. 6; November 7, 1982, p. 14; November 10, 1985; July 10, 1988, p. 11; April 8, 1990, p. 8; November 4, 1990, p. 19; December 9, 1990, p. 14.

\*　\*　\*

## HAMPTON, Henry (Eugene, Jr.)  1940-

*PERSONAL:* Born January 8, 1940, in St. Louis, MO; son of Henry E. and Veva (Guillatte) Hampton. *Education:* Washington University, B.A., 1961.

*ADDRESSES: Office*—Blackside, Inc., 486 Shawmut Ave., Boston, MA 02118.

*CAREER:* Founder of Blackside, Inc. (film production company), Boston, MA, 1968—; writer. Executive producer of television productions, including *Kinfolks,* 1979; *Voices of a Divided City,* 1983; *Eyes on the Prize,* 1987; *Eyes on the Prize II,* 1990; and *One on One.* Visiting professor of film at Tufts University. Chair of board of Museum of Afro-American History; member of board of directors, Boston Center for Arts; member of Massachusetts Film Committee. Member of board of directors for Children's Defense Fund.

*AWARDS, HONORS:* Loeb fellow at Harvard University, 1977-78; honorary degrees from various institutions, including Northeastern, Suffolk, Washington, and Boston universities.

*WRITINGS:*

(With Steve Fayer and Sarah Flynn) *Voices of Freedom: An Oral History of the Civil Rights Movement from the 1950s through the 1980s,* Bantam, 1989.

*SIDELIGHTS:* Henry Hampton has distinguished himself in production capacities with various television documentaries

on the black experience in the United States. He served as executive producer of the acclaimed documentary series *Eyes on the Prize,* which detailed the development of the black civil-rights movement after World War II. With Steve Fayer, who wrote *Eyes on the Prize,* and Sarah Flynn, Hampton later fashioned additional material—culled from more than one thousand interviews—as *Voices of Freedom,* a book that relates the black struggle for equality in America. This vast volume, numbering nearly seven hundred pages, provides first-hand testimony of the black experience. Among the incidents recalled in the book are the 1955 abduction and killing in Mississippi of young Emmett Till, who was attacked for speaking the words "Bye, baby" to a white woman, and the 1979 death in Miami of Arthur McDuffie, who was reportedly gunned down by police. (An ensuing trial, in which the accused officers were found not guilty, was followed by rioting.) In addition, the book features detailed accounts of black leaders, including Martin Luther King, Jr., Malcolm X, and Stokely Carmichael.

Like *Eyes on the Prize, Voices of Freedom* won the admiration of critics. Jonathan Kirsch, in his *Los Angeles Times* review, proclaimed the book "a stirring saga of the civil rights movement." And Henry Mayer, writing in the *New York Times Book Review,* declared that "the oral history [*Voices of Freedom*] is a vast choral pageant." Throughout the book, Mayer added, "we hear ordinary people speaking and feel the sense of empowerment that is the [civil rights] movement's continuing legacy."

*BIOGRAPHICAL/CRITICAL SOURCES:*

*PERIODICALS*

*Los Angeles Times,* January 31, 1990.

*New York,* January 15, 1990, p. 57.

*New York Times,* December 20, 1989.

*New York Times Book Review,* January 28, 1990, p. 12.

*Time,* January 15, 1990, p. 52.

\*　\*　\*

## HANSEN, Joyce (Viola)  1942-

*PERSONAL:* Born October 18, 1942, in New York, NY; daughter of Austin Victor (a photographer) and Lillian (Dancy) Hansen; married Matthew Nelson (a musician), December 18, 1982. *Education:* Pace University, B.A., 1972; New York University, M.A., 1978.

*ADDRESSES: Office*—c/o Walker and Co., 720 Fifth Ave., New York, NY 10019.

*CAREER:* Board of Education, New York City, teacher of reading and English, 1973—; Empire State College, Brooklyn, NY, mentor, 1987—.

*MEMBER:* Harlem Writers Guild, Society of Children's Book Writers, PEN.

*AWARDS, HONORS:* Parents Choice literature citation, 1986, for *Yellow Bird and Me;* honorable mention in literature, Coretta Scott King Award, 1987, for *Which Way Freedom?*

*WRITINGS:*

*CHILDREN'S FICTION*

*The Gift-Giver,* Houghton, 1980.
*Home Boy,* Houghton, 1982.
*Yellow Bird and Me* (sequel to *The Gift-Giver*), Houghton, 1986.
*Which Way Freedom?* (part of American history series for young adults), Walker, 1986.
*Out from This Place* (sequel to *Which Way Freedom?*; part of American history series for young adults), Walker, 1988.
*The Captive,* Scholastic Books, 1994.

*CHILDREN'S NONFICTION*

*Between Two Fires: Black Soldiers in the Civil War* (part of "African-American Experience" series), F. Watts, 1993.

*OTHER*

(Contributor) David E. Nelson, *Utah Education Quality Indicators,* Utah State Office of Education, 1983.

*SIDELIGHTS:* Joyce Hansen is the author of children's novels that have been praised for their convincing depiction of black children in both contemporary and historical settings. Her first three novels, *The Gift-Giver, Yellow Bird and Me,* and *Home Boy* feature the lives of inner-city children in New York, while *Which Way Freedom?* and *Out from This Place* dramatize the experiences of young blacks during the time of Civil War slavery and afterwards. An English teacher in New York City schools, Hansen strives for realistic settings in her books, in addition to authentic dialect and lively storytelling, as a way to reach out to young readers with positive messages of support and guidance. "I take writing for children very seriously," she once stated. "So many children need direction—so many are floundering. I write for all children who need and can relate to the things I write about—the importance of family, maintaining a sense of hope, and responsibility for oneself and other living things."

Hansen was born in 1942 in New York City, and grew up in a Bronx neighborhood which provides many of the experiences in her first novel, *The Gift-Giver.* During her girlhood, as she recalled, "New York City neighborhoods were thriving urban villages that children could grow and develop in." In *The Gift-Giver,* which describes a foster child who positively influences others with his caring nature, Hansen attempted to recreate the secure atmosphere of immediate and extended family that she knew as a young girl. In doing so, she also emphasized the positive forces at work within inner cities to counter such perils as poverty, violence, and drugs. "We forget that there are many people in our so-called slums or ghettos that manage to raise whole and healthy families under extreme conditions," Hansen once commented. "Not every story coming out of the black communities of New York City are horror stories."

Hansen was influenced to become a writer by both her mother and father who provided, as she once described, an atmosphere "rich in family love and caring." Her mother, who had aspirations to become a journalist at one time, passed on to Hansen an appreciation for books and reading. "My mother grew up in a large family during the depression and though she was intelligent and literate she couldn't even finish high school because she had to work...," Hansen remembered. "She was my first teacher." From her father, a photographer from the Caribbean, Hansen learned the art of storytelling. "He entertained my brothers and me with stories about his boyhood in the West Indies and his experiences as a young man in the Harlem of the 20s and 30s," she once commented. "I also learned from him to see the beauty and poetry in the everyday scenes and 'just plain folks' he captured in his photographs."

Hansen received a bachelor's degree from Pace University in 1972, followed several years later by a master's degree from New York University. In 1973, she began a career teaching in New York City schools, where she worked at one time as a special education instructor for adolescents with reading disabilities. Through her teaching work, which predominantly involves black and Hispanic students, Hansen became aware of the positive results to be gained by providing students with literature they could identify with. "Literature can be a great teacher, yet large numbers of Black and other youngsters of color never have a chance to explore themselves or their lives through the literary process," she stated in *Interracial Books for Children Bulletin.* "*All* children need sound, solid literature that relates to their own experiences and interests," she added, especially those "children who, for whatever reason, have learning difficulties."

Hansen's own work as a children's novelist has been greatly influenced by her students. "Though I often complain that I don't have enough time to write because I teach, if I didn't teach, I wouldn't have been moved to write some of the stories I've created thus far," she stated in *Horn Book.* Describing her students as her "muse," Hansen commented in *Horn Book* that, as is the case with the innovative nicknames derived by her students, she is "influenced by their creativity— the way they twist, bend, enliven, deconstruct, and sometimes even destroy language; their loves, hates, fears, feelings, and needs filter into my writing." While Hansen's objectives as a reading teacher propel a major part of her writing, she maintains the necessity of relating stories that students like her own would respond to. Hansen tests her writing by asking, as she recounted in *Horn Book,* "what I am going to do ... to make a reluctant reader want to read [a story].... I imagine I hear Tatoo whispering in my ear, 'Miss Hansen, you know I'm not going to read all of that description'; or Milk Crate muttering, 'Boring, boring, boring'; or Skeletal yelling, 'This ain't like us.'"

As a result, Hansen's novels have been praised by critics for their convincingly-drawn characters and accurate depictions of atmosphere and black dialect. Regarding *The Gift-Giver,* which is told through the language and observations of a fifth-grade girl (Doris), Hansen "paints an effective, inside picture of childhood in a New York ghetto," commented Judith Goldberger in *Booklist.* The novel tells the story of Doris's friendship with Amir, her shy and quiet classmate, from whom she learns valuable lessons in friendship and caring for others. According to Zena Sutherland in the *Bulletin of the Center for Children's Books,* the novel's strengths are "well-developed plot threads that are nicely knit, a memorable depiction of a person whose understanding and compassion are gifts to his friends, and a poignantly realistic ending." In *Yellow Bird and Me,* the sequel to *The Gift-Giver,* Hansen relates the story of Doris as she, in turn, helps a troubled classmate overcome a learning disability and discover his talents as a theatrical performer. "Smoothly written and easy to read," according to a contributor to *Kirkus Reviews,* the novel utilizes colloquial black English with "strength and vitality." Furthermore, the contributor continues, the novel is "rich with the distinctive personalities in Doris's world ... [and] is particularly valuable for its emphasis on friendship, generosity of spirit, and seeing what's below the surface."

In her novel *Home Boy,* likewise set in New York's inner city, Hansen relates the life of a troubled teenaged boy (Marcus) from the Caribbean who stabs another boy in a fight. Alternating between scenes of New York and Marcus's native Caribbean, the novel reveals the damaging influences of the boy's family, his involvement with selling drugs, and the pressures of adjusting to life in a foreign city. Inspired by an actual newspaper account of a Jamaican boy who stabbed and killed another youth in a New York City high school, Hansen modeled Marcus as "a composite of the many young men I've met through teaching," she once commented. Despite its tragic

overtones, the novel finds positives in the efforts of Marcus's girlfriend to get him on track, in addition to the affirming support of his reconciled parents and Marcus's own will to reform. The novel "revolves around Blacks and inner city life," wrote Kevin Kenny in *Voice of Youth Advocates,* yet holds appeal for many readers in its exploration of such universal themes as "quests for dignity, pursuits of familial and personal love, and the search for individual understanding."

After writing three works set in New York City, Hansen made a notable departure with two historical novels that take place during the American Civil War and postwar Reconstruction period. Again influenced by her students, Hansen evolved into historical fiction after she "began to think about how much drama there is in the black experience that is unknown to our youth and how historical fiction is a good way to make history come alive for young people," she wrote in *Horn Book.* Although vastly different in location and time period than her previous fiction, Hansen's historical novels similarly offer strong characterizations, in addition to authentic depictions of atmosphere and dialect. *Which Way Freedom?* tells the story of a young slave (Obi) who escapes from South Carolina and joins a black Union regiment during the Civil War, while the sequel, *Out from This Place,* tells the story of Obi's female friend (Easter) as she moves forward with her life after the Civil War. In both books, Hansen intersperses authentic black Gullah Island dialect with documented and little-known details of everyday life for slaves in their struggles before and after freedom.

Initially, Hansen had some difficulty making the transition to this type of writing: "Not being an historian, and deciding to write an historical novel, I felt like a trespasser on someone else's property who was tampering with a story that was not my own," she explained in the *New Advocate.* "I was an explorer in a strange land without a map or compass." Hansen did extensive research and read numerous histories of the period, including a collection of interviews with former slaves, for over a year before she began to write. She was surprised to find that the facts she uncovered during this period reshaped her view of history and her ideas about the way history should be presented to young readers: "My problem was that not all [the historic facts discovered through research] were compatible with the images that I wanted to create—images of a people bravely struggling to be free," she remembered in the *New Advocate.* "As I continued my reading and research, I came across still more conflicting and contradictory information. As a result, I had to reassess my purposes. Was I trying merely to confirm my own beliefs, or was I attempting to understand what those times might have been like? What I was, in fact, learning was that history is made up of individual stories shaded by individual perceptions and experiences ... I was beginning to understand just how complex history is and that it defies any grand, simplistic interpretations."

Hansen also commented in the *New Advocate* on the responsibility involved in writing books for a young audience. "As [children] seek to understand an increasingly confusing world, their minds are malleable and vulnerable. Because of this, the responsibility of writers is enormous. Our job is to arrest the spread of ignorance, to inform, to provide insight and perspective, to entertain. Our words are powerful and those of us who are fortunate enough to have our words read must not abuse that power and privilege." Hansen added comments which give insight into the motivation behind her work: "I think the ultimate aim in any book we write for young people should be to show the heights to which humanity can reach even as we expose the depths to which we can sink. The word is powerful. We must use our words to help our children acquire a richness of soul and spirit so that maybe one fine day we will learn to live with ourselves and each other in love and harmony."

*BIOGRAPHICAL/CRITICAL SOURCES:*

*BOOKS*

*Children's Literature Review,* Volume 21, Gale, 1990.
*Something about the Author,* Volume 46, Gale, 1987, pp. 83-84.
*Twentieth-Century Children's Writers,* third edition, St. James Press, 1989.

*PERIODICALS*

*Booklist,* January 1, 1981, p. 624; January 15, 1989, p. 871.
*Bulletin of the Center for Children's Books,* January, 1981, p. 94; April, 1986; July-August, 1986.
*Horn Book,* December, 1980, p. 641; November, 1986, p.745; September/October, 1987, pp. 644-646.
*Interracial Books for Children Bulletin,* Volume 15, number 4, 1984, pp. 9-11.
*Kirkus Reviews,* April 1, 1986, p. 545.
*Language Arts,* December, 1986, p. 823.
*Los Angeles Times Book Review,* July 13, 1986, p. 6.
*New Advocate,* Volume 3, number 3, summer 1990, pp. 167-173.
*Publishers Weekly,* October 24, 1980, p. 49.
*Voice of Youth Advocates,* February, 1983, p. 36; February, 1989, p. 285.

\*     \*     \*

## HARE, Nathan 1934-

*PERSONAL:* Born April 9, 1934, in Slick, OK; son of Seddie Henry (a farmer) and Tishia (Davis) Hare; married Julie Reed (a public relations specialist), December 27, 1956. *Education:* Langston University, A.B., 1954; University of Chicago, M.A., 1957, Ph.D. (sociology), 1962; California School of Professional Psychology, Ph.D., 1975; also studied at Northwestern University, 1959.

*ADDRESSES: Office*—1801 Bush St., San Francisco, CA 94109.

*CAREER:* Worked briefly as a professional boxer; Virginia State College, Petersburg, instructor in sociology, 1957-58; National Opinion Research Center, Chicago, IL, interviewer, 1959-61; Howard University, Washington, DC, instructor, 1961-63, assistant professor of sociology, 1964-67; San Francisco State College (now University), director of Black Studies Curriculum, 1968, chairman of department of Black Studies, 1968-69, director, Center for Educational Innovation, summer, 1968; *Black Scholar,* Sausalito, CA, founding publisher, 1969-75; Child Development Services, Oakland, CA, clinical psychologist, 1975-76; psychologist in private practice, 1977—; San Francisco State University, lecturer, 1984—. Part-time visiting professor, Lone Mountain College, 1972-73. Chairman of task force on demographic and communal characteristics, Teachers College, Columbia University, 1966-67; chairman of workshop on education, National Conference on Black Power, 1968; founding president, Black World Foundation, 1970. Member of board of advisors, San Francisco Black Exposition, 1972; member of board of directors, North American Committee, Second World Black and African Festival of Arts and Culture, Lagos, Nigeria, 1974, and San Francisco Local Development Corporation; affiliated with Complete Help and Assistance Necessary for College Education (CHANCE) project, 1976. President and chairman of the board, Black Think Tank, 1982—. *Military service:* U.S. Army Reserve, 1958-64, active duty, 1958.

*MEMBER:* American Sociological Association, Association of Behavioral and Social Sciences, American Psychological Association, Association of Orthopsychiatry, American Association of University Professors, Eastern Sociological Association, New York Academy of Sciences, Sigma Gamma Rho.

*AWARDS, HONORS:* Danforth fellow, 1954-57; "Black Is Beautiful" citation from United Black Artists, 1968; Distinguished Alumni Award, Langston University, 1975; community-clinical psychology award, Southern Regional Education Board, Atlanta, 1978; Professional Person of the Year, San Francisco chapter of the National Association of Negro Business and Professional Women's Clubs, 1980; presidential citation, National Association for Equal Opportunity in Higher Education, 1982; national award, National Council on Black Studies, 1983.

*WRITINGS:*

*The Black Anglo-Saxons,* Marzani & Munsell, 1965, second
   edition, Third World Press, 1991.
(Editor, with Robert Chrisman) *Contemporary Black Thought:
   The Best from the Black Scholar,* Bobbs-Merrill, 1973.
(Editor, with Chrisman) *Pan-Africanism,* Bobbs-Merrill,
   1974.
(With wife, Julia Hare) *The Endangered Black Family: Cop-
   ing with the Unisexualization and Coming Extinction of
   the Black Race,* Black Think Tank, 1984.
*Bringing the Black Boy to Manhood: The Passage,* Black
   Think Tank, 1987.
(Editor, with Julia Hare) *Crisis in Black Sexual Politics,* fore-
   word by Gus Savage, Black Think Tank, 1989.
(With Julia Hare) *The Hare Plan to Overhaul the Public
   Schools and Educate Every Black Man, Woman, and
   Child,* Black Think Tank, 1991.

Contributor to books, including *American Education: A Sociological View,* edited by David W. Swift, Houghton, 1976;
author of introduction, *The Souls of Black Folk,* by W. E. B.
DuBois, Signet, 1969, and *Black Political Life in the United
States,* edited by Lenneal Henderson, Chandler Publishing,
1972. Contributor of numerous articles to periodicals, including *Newsweek, Ramparts, Saturday Review,* and *U.S. News
and World Report.* Contributing editor, *Journal of Black Studies, Ebony, Black Scholar, Journal of Black Education,* and
*Black Law Journal.*

*SIDELIGHTS:* Nathan Hare is considered "a major leader of
the Black Studies movement" according to Richard Barksdale
and Keneth Kinnamon in *Black Writers of America: A Comprehensive Anthology.* Characterized as "an unorthodox aca-
demician," Hare sparked controversy while serving on the
faculty of Howard University in the 1960s through his opposition to the war in Vietnam and the draft, his advocacy of
"black power," his stint as a professional boxer, and his criticism of the university administration. In 1968 he launched a
Black Studies program at San Francisco State College. The
following year, Hare began the *Black Scholar,* a publication
which Barksdale and Kinnamon call an "important 'Journal
of Black Studies and Research'."

Hare's work centers on the necessity for African Americans
everywhere to recognize the power of traditional Black mores and ideas. For instance, in Hare's opinion, the mission of
the African American scholar is to rethink European modes
of thought, replacing them with new insights and solutions to
old problems. In an article published in Barksdale's and

Kinnamon's *Black Writers of America,* he states, "[The black
scholar must] de-colonize his mind so that he may effectively guide other intellectuals and students in their search for liberation." Because of the legacy of miseducation and abuse of
learning, he continues, white society is "increasingly corrupt
and bloody with no clear future. The air is filled with pollution and the land and forests are being destroyed as human
alienation and conflict remain on the rise." The cure to this
problem, according to Hare, lies in the removal of "icons of
objectivity, amoral knowledge and its methodology, and the
total demolition of the anti-social attitudes of Ivory-
Towerism."

Similar views are expressed in Hare's book *The Black Anglo-
Saxons* and the volume, co-edited with Robert Chrisman,
called *Pan-Africanism. The Black Anglo-Saxons* is a critique
of the African American middle class, a group Hare perceives
as having shed black values and mores in favor of assimilated ethics and standards from white culture. *Pan-Africanism*
is a collection of essays by both Africans and African Americans which promotes traditional black political concepts of
communalism, as opposed to European socialism, in an attempt to chart Africa's future. Both works encourage a return
to pre-colonial black ideals as a solution to problems in modern life.

Hare continues to advance ideals and mores drawn from African American tradition. He writes in *Ebony* magazine: "The
Black middle class could begin now to solve the problems of
juvenile delinquency, of in-group violence, school drop-outs,
low academic performance, and many another ailments—
maybe even racism—if we could come together, return to our
own people, live with them, love them, learn from the wisdom of a long-suffering and creative race. But it will first be
necessary to abandon the unbridled pursuit of materialism and
the all-engulfing frenzy for White approval and acceptance."

*BIOGRAPHICAL/CRITICAL SOURCES:*

*BOOKS*

Barksdale, Richard, and Keneth Kinnamon, editors, *Black
   Writers of America: A Comprehensive Anthology,* Macmillan, 1972.

*PERIODICALS*

*American Sociological Review,* December, 1965.
*Annals of the American Academy,* November, 1965.
*Choice,* June, 1974.
*Ebony,* August, 1987.
*New York Times Book Review,* February 21, 1971.

## HARRIS, Thomas Walter 1930-
### (Tom Harris; T. H. Darling, a pseudonym)

*PERSONAL:* Born April 30, 1930, in the Bronx, NY; son of Melvin (owner of a transport-taxi) and Mary (a homemaker) Harris; married Joyce Carter (a teacher), December, 1956. *Education:* Howard University, B.A., 1957; University of California, Los Angeles, M.A., 1959; University of Southern California, M.L.S., 1962. *Politics:* Democrat. *Religion:* "Methodist—leans toward Quaker."

*ADDRESSES: Home*—1786 South Fairfax Ave., Los Angeles, CA 90019. *Office*—630 West Fifth St., Los Angeles, CA 90013.

*CAREER:* Affiliated with Appeal Printing Company, New York, 1948-49; affiliated with Bureau of Internal Revenue, Washington, DC, 1956-57; Los Angeles Public Library, Los Angeles, CA, librarian in literature and fiction department, 1961—; University of California, Los Angeles, teacher of playwriting, 1966—; teacher of mass communications at Inner City Cultural Center, 1968. Board member of Actors Studio West Playwrights Unit; director of Studio West; executive producer and director of Los Angeles Citizens Co. Actor, appearing in productions including the radio play *Hometown U.S.A. Military service:* U.S. Army, 1951-53, served in army ordnance in Korea.

*MEMBER:* Dramatists Guild, National Playwrights Co., Black Theatre Network, National Association for the Advancement of Colored People, American Association of Retired People, American Federation of State, County, and Municipal Employees, Los Angeles Black Playwrights, Alliance of Los Angeles Playwrights.

*AWARDS, HONORS:* All C.I.A.A. (basketball), Howard University, 1956-57; received honorarium from University of California, Los Angeles, 1966; received City Council citation from Los Angeles Mayor Bradley, for distinguished contribution to Los Angeles Theatre; grant from Audrey Skirball-Kenis Theatre Foundation.

*WRITINGS:*

PLAYS

*Daddy Hugs and Kisses,* Theatre West, 1960.
*The Relic,* Studio West and Actor's Studio, 1961.
*The Selma Maid,* Studio West, 1967.
*The Solution,* Actor's Studio, 1970, revised as *Model City,* 1991.
*Mary Queen of Crackers,* Actor's Studio, 1971.
*Suds,* Actor's Studio, 1973.
*A Streetcar Salad,* Los Angeles Citizen's Co., 1979.

Also author of *Fall of an Iron Horse; All Tigers Are Tame; City Beneath the Skin; Who Killed Sweetie; Beverly Hills Olympics; At Wits End; The Man Handlers;* and the musical *Clothespins and Dreams.*

OTHER

*Always with Love,* Hill & Wang, 1970.
*No Time to Play,* Acrobat Books, 1977.

Also author of the fiction works *When I Grow Up* and *The Little Dude,* both in press. Writer for television shows, including *M Squad, I Spy, Rin Tin Tin,* and *The Junkyard.* Script doctor for numerous films, including *When I Grow Up, Man Made Angry, Desert Killing, The Ally, The Guardian, Street Heat, Then Came the Winter, The Brothers,* and *The Voice.* Writer for the radio show *Voice of America.* Also author of works under the name Tom Harris and under the pseudonym T. H. Darling.

*SIDELIGHTS:* Thomas Walter Harris commented: "I was born in the old Bronx, New York—that is the civilized Bronx full of Old World European culture and New World ambition. My Bronx was cobblestone streets, horse-drawn wagons that carried dairy and other food products, elevated trains, street safety at night, radio and music everywhere. My mother, having died when I was six months old, left the rearing of her four children to my grandparents. This was a blessing in disguise, for my grandparents were 'readers' from my earliest recollection. I remember lessons from 'THE' books of God, then from every and all books at hand. We sat around the pot-bellied stove and experienced wondrous tales written by fertile imaginations. I could dream before I could write.

"During the Depression my grandfather worked the Broadway theatre circuit as a night watchman and caretaker. I saw my first play when I was five. My grandfather and I placed dust covers on the theatre seats after the performances and removed them the next evening. It was a hooking experience.

"My first active participation came through the church—Epworth Methodist in the Bronx. I began my first novel when I was fifteen. It was called *Under the El.* It was to chronicle life under and around the Third Avenue elevated trains. I actually finished three chapters. Then basketball season started and the novel disappeared into the attic, never to be seen again. The same with my flirtation with the world of dance. There were highlights—like being onstage at club 'Sugar Hill with Larry Steeles Smart Affairs' and meeting Ava Gardner, James Mason, and Pamela Kelino.

"The early 1950s found me in Korea lying around in the mud trying to figure out what I was born to do, if I survived. Home again, back to Howard University in 1953 to complete my education with a revived interest in writing. Joined the 'Howard Players' and began writing plays about local political strife. These early plays were short, hardened political tracts which few cared about. Then came the more generic, non-biased, people-driven works with wider points of view. These bore fruit. I shall always aim high with a conscience in my work that bypasses the mundane non-social. I believe every work should expose and enlighten without the preachiness of dogma.

"Had a brief career as an actor. Spent hours in front of the mirror rehearsing my live 'Bwana, you come.' When told by the director and a fellow actor to add more bug-eyed hysteria to it, I put away my spear and loincloth. Thus, the jungles and plantations of the world lost a budding Laurence Olivier.

"At present I have a grant from the Audrey Skirball-Kenis Theatre Foundation to create a history of theatre in Southern California at the Los Angeles Public Library. I am collecting all produced work which has not been published, binding the scripts, and creating a database. The resultant catalog of such scripts will be housed as a special collection in the library."

*   *   *

## HARRIS, Tom
## See HARRIS, Thomas Walter

*   *   *

## HARRIS, (Theodore) Wilson 1921-
## (Kona Waruk)

*PERSONAL:* Born March 24, 1921, in New Amsterdam, British Guiana (now Guyana); immigrated to England, 1959; son of Theodore Wilson (an insurer and underwriter) and Millicent Josephine (Glasford) Harris; married Cecily Carew, 1945; married Margaret Nimmo Burns (a writer), April 2, 1959. *Education:* Queen's College, Georgetown, British Guiana, 1934-39; studied land surveying and geomorphology under government auspices, 1939-42.

*ADDRESSES: Home*—London, England. *Office*—c/o Faber & Faber, 3 Queen Sq., London WC1N 3AU, England.

*CAREER:* British Guiana Government, assistant government surveyor, 1942-44, government surveyor, 1944-54, senior surveyor, 1955-58; full-time writer in London, England, 1958—. Visiting lecturer, State University of New York at Buffalo, 1970, Yale University, 1970; guest lecturer, Mysore

University (India), 1978; regents' lecturer, University of California, 1983. Writer in residence, University of West Indies, 1970, University of Toronto, 1970, Newcastle University, Australia, 1979, University of Queensland, Australia, 1986. Visiting professor, University of Texas at Austin, 1972, 1981-82 and 1983, University of Aarhus, Denmark, 1973, and in Cuba. Delegate for United Nations Educational, Scientific, and Cultural Organization (UNESCO) symposium on Caribbean Literature in Cuba, 1968, and National Identity Conference in Brisbane, Australia, 1968.

*AWARDS, HONORS:* English Arts Council grants, 1968 and 1970; Commonwealth fellow at University of Leeds, 1971; Guggenheim fellow, 1972-73; Henfield writing fellow at University of East Anglis, 1974; Southern Arts fellow, Salisbury, 1976; D.Litt., University of West Indies, 1984; Guyana Prize for Fiction, 1985-87; D.Litt., University of Kent at Canterbury, 1988.

*WRITINGS:*

FICTION

*Palace of the Peacock* (first novel in "Guyana Quartet"), Faber, 1960.
*The Far Journey of Oudin* (second novel in "Guyana Quartet"), Faber, 1961.
*The Whole Armour* (third novel in "Guyana Quartet"), Faber, 1962.
*The Secret Ladder* (fourth novel in "Guyana Quartet"), Faber, 1963.
*The Whole Armour* [and] *The Secret Ladder,* Faber, 1963.
*Heartland,* Faber, 1964.
*The Eye of the Scarecrow,* Faber, 1965.
*The Waiting Room,* Faber, 1967.
*Tamatumari,* Faber, 1968.
*Ascent to Omai,* Faber, 1970.
*The Sleepers of Roraima* (short stories), Faber, 1970.
*The Age of the Rainmakers* (short stories), Faber, 1971.
*Black Marsden: A Tabula Rasa Comedy,* Faber, 1972.
*Companions of the Day and Night,* Faber, 1975.
*Da Silva da Silva's Cultivated Wilderness* [and] *Genesis of the Clowns* (also see below), Faber, 1977.
*Genesis of the Clowns,* Faber, 1978.
*The Tree of the Sun,* Faber, 1978.
*The Angel at the Gate,* Faber, 1982.
*The Guyana Quartet* (boxed set), Faber, 1985.
*Carnival* (first novel in trilogy), Faber, 1985.
*The Infinite Rehearsal* (second novel in trilogy), Faber, 1987.
*The Four Banks of the River of Space* (third novel in trilogy), Faber, 1990.
*Resurrection at Sorrow Hill,* Faber, 1993.

*POETRY*

(Under pseudonym Kona Waruk) *Fetish*, privately printed (Georgetown, British Guiana), 1951.

*The Well and the Land,* [British Guiana], 1952.

*Eternity to Season,* privately printed (Georgetown, British Guiana), 1954, second edition, New Beacon, 1978.

*OTHER*

*Tradition and the West Indian Novel* (lecture), New Beacon, 1965.

*Tradition, the Writer and Society: Critical Essays,* New Beacon, 1967.

*History, Fable and Myth in the Caribbean and Guianas* (booklet), National History and Arts Council (Georgetown, Guyana), 1970.

*Fossil and Psyche* (criticism), African and American Studies and Research Center, University of Texas, 1974.

*Explorations: A Series of Talks and Articles, 1966-1981,* edited with an introduction by Hena Maes-Jelinek, Dangaroo Press, 1981.

*The Womb of Space: The Cross-Cultural Imagination* (criticism), Greenwood Press, 1983.

*The Radical Imagination* (essays, lectures, and interview), edited by Alan Riach and Mark Williams, University of Liege, 1991.

Contributor to anthologies, including *Caribbean Rhythms,* 1974, and *Critics on Caribbean Literature,* 1978; contributor to periodicals, including *Literary Half-Yearly, Kyk-over-al,* and *New Letters.*

*SIDELIGHTS:* The novels of Wilson Harris incorporate philosophy, poetic imagery, symbolism, and myth, creating new and unique visions of reality. His fiction shows the reader a world where the borders between physical and spiritual reality, life and death, have become indistinguishable. In *World Literature Today,* Richard Sander states that Harris has "realized a new, original form of the novel that in almost all respects constitutes a radical departure from the conventional novel." Reed Way Dasenbrock, also writing in *World Literature Today,* claims that Harris "has always operated at a very high level of abstraction, higher than any of his fellow West Indian novelists, higher perhaps than any other contemporary novelist in English.... And whether one regards Harris's evolution as a rich and exciting development of a one-way trip down an abstractionist cul-de-sac, there is no denying his unique vision or dedication to that vision." The use of abstraction has brought Harris both praise and criticism; while some regard his work as challenging and rewarding, others find his unorthodox methods alienate the reader.

Harris is perhaps best known for the four novels in the "Guyana Quartet." Important to all four works of the quartet is the landscape of Guyana, which Harris came to know well during his years as a government surveyor. Hena Maes-Jelinek writes in *West Indian Literature,* "Two major elements seem to have shaped Harris's approach to art and his philosophy of existence: the impressive contrasts of the Guyanese landscapes ... and the successive waves of conquest which gave Guyana its heterogeneous population polarised for centuries into oppressors and their victims." Furthermore, she comments, "The two, landscape and history, merge in his work into single metaphors symbolising man's inner space saturated with the effects of historical—that is, temporal—experiences."

The plots of Harris's works are frequently difficult for critics to summarize since they are comprised of events, dreams, hallucinations, and psychic experiences, which are frequently not clearly distinguished from one another. In addition, time in Harris's works is often nonlinear. Such works move so far from the accepted definition of a novel that critics are often compelled to invent a genre in order to discuss them. Michael Thorpe in *World Literature Today* calls the author's more recent books "psychical 'expeditions'." And an *Encounter* contributor describes Harris's work as "a metaphysical shorthand on the surface of a narrative whose point cannot readily be grasped by any but those thoroughly versed in his previous work and able at once to recognise the recurrent complex metaphors."

Many reviewers note that to fully appreciate Harris's work the reader must be familiar with his metaphors, since the elaborately written passages and complex symbolism can make the writing nearly impenetrable for readers accustomed to more traditional fiction. A *Times Literary Supplement* contributor warns, "no reader should attempt Mr. Harris's novels unless he is willing to work at them." But according to J. P. Durix, also a *Times Literary Supplement* contributor, the reader who stays with Harris is rewarded by his "dense style and meticulous construction, his attention to visual and rhythmic effects, [which] are matched by an inventiveness which few contemporary novelists can equal."

Another Harris achievement is his 1990 novel *The Four Banks of the River of Space,* which is part of a trilogy containing *Carnival* and *The Infinite Rehearsal.* In this volume, Anselm, a Guyanese land surveyor who functions as Harris's alter ego, searches for God through a series of dreams. Characteristically complex and demanding, the entire trilogy has been praised for its poetic prose style and has been compared to Homer's *Odyssey.* Brian Morton concludes in his essay for *Listener* that Harris is "difficult, often maddeningly so, but he is also funny and humane, and he really must be read."

Harris has also written several studies in literary criticism. In *The Womb of Space,* he expands upon many of the ideas expressed in his novels. Harris's goal in the work is to establish parallels between writers of various cultural backgrounds. He observes in *The Womb of Space* that "literature is still constrained by regional and other conventional but suffocating categories." His vision is of a new world community, based on cultural heterogeneity, not homogeneity, which, "as a cultural model, exercised by a ruling ethnic group, tends to become an organ of conquest and division because of imposed unity that actually subsists on the suppression of others." Sander believes that *The Womb of Space* is "an attack on the traditional critical establishment." A *Choice* contributor agrees, claiming, "*The Womb of Space* issues a direct challenge to the intellectual provincialism that often characterises literary study in the U.S."

In his literary theory as well as in his fictional works, some critics find Harris's ideas difficult to discern. For instance, Steven G. Kellman writes in *Modern Fiction Studies,* "I take it that Wilson Harris' theme is the ability of consciousness to transcend a particular culture. But his articulation of that theme is so turgid, so beset by mixed and obscure metaphors and by syntactical convolutions that much of the book simply remains unintelligible even to a sympathetic reader." However, *Choice* elected *The Womb of Space* as the best critical study published in 1983.

Despite their degree of difficulty, Harris's works are praised by many critics who believe he has made a significant contribution to our understanding of art and consciousness. John Hearne writes in *The Islands in Between,* "No other British Caribbean novelist has made quite such an explicitly and conscious effort as Harris to reduce the material reckonings of everyday life to the significance of myth." And speaking of the breadth of Harris's work, Louis James states in the *Times Literary Supplement,* "The novels of Wilson Harris ... form one ongoing whole. Each work is individual; yet the whole sequence can be seen as a continuous, ever-widening exploration of civilization and creative art."

Wilson remarked that he has "moved away from the framework of the conventional novel and sought a different architecture of the Imagination and of space within an endangered, biased world, that is still susceptible to cross-cultural capacities and to subtle, dramatic, far-reaching, testing changes within a civilisation in dialogue with changes in reality reflected in quantum physics, quantum mechanics, and chaos theory." Recent important studies that present Wilson's work from various approaches are *Wilson Harris: The Uncompromising Imagination* and *The Literate Imagination.*

*BIOGRAPHICAL/CRITICAL SOURCES:*

BOOKS

Baugh, Edward, editor, *Critics on Caribbean Literature: Readings in Literary Criticism,* St. Martin's, 1978.
*Contemporary Literary Criticism,* Volume 25, Gale, 1983.
Drake, Sandra E., *Wilson Harris and the Modern Tradition: A New Architecture of the World,* Greenwood Press, 1986.
Gilkes, Michael, *The Literate Imagination,* Macmillan, 1989.
Gilkes, Michael, *The West Indian Novel,* Twayne, 1981.
Gilkes, Michael, *Wilson Harris and the Caribbean Novel,* Longman, 1975.
Harris, Wilson, *The Tree of the Sun,* Faber, 1978.
Harris, Wilson, *The Womb of Space: The Cross-Cultural Imagination,* Greenwood Press, 1983.
James, Louis, editor, *The Islands in Between,* Oxford University Press, 1968.
Maes-Jelinek, Hena, *The Naked Design,* Dangaroo Press, 1976.
Maes-Jelinek, Hena, *Wilson Harris,* Twayne, 1982.
Munro, Ian, and Reinhard Sander, editors, *Kas-Kas: Interviews with Three Caribbean Writers in Texas,* African and Afro-American Research Institute, University of Texas at Austin, 1972.
*Wilson Harris: The Uncompromising Imagination,* Dangaroo Press, 1991.

PERIODICALS

*Canadian Literature,* summer, 1992.
*Choice,* March, 1984.
*Encounter,* May, 1987.
*Listener,* September, 1990.
*Modern Fiction Studies,* summer, 1984.
*New Statesman,* September 7, 1990.
*Observer,* July 7, 1985.
*Quill and Quire,* October, 1985.
*Spectator,* March 25, 1978.
*Times Literary Supplement,* December 9, 1965; July 4, 1968; May 21, 1970; October 10, 1975; May 25, 1977; May 19, 1978; October 15, 1982; July 12, 1985; September 25-October 1, 1987.
*World Literature Today,* winter, 1984; summer, 1985; spring, 1986.

\*   \*   \*

## HARRISON, Paul Carter 1936-
### (Paul Carter-Harrison)

*PERSONAL:* Born March 1, 1936, in New York, NY. *Education:* Attended New York University, 1953-55; Indiana University, B.A., 1957; graduate study at Ohio University, summers, 1959 and 1960; New School for Social Research, M.A., 1962.

*ADDRESSES:* Home—P.O. Box 143, Leeds, MA 01053. Office—Department of Theater/Music, Columbia College, 600 South Michigan Ave., Chicago, IL 60605.

*CAREER:* Howard University, Washington, DC, assistant professor of theater arts, 1968-70; Kent State University, Kent, Ohio, associate professor of Afro-American literature, 1969; California State University, Sacramento, professor of theater arts, 1970-72; University of Massachusetts at Amherst, professor of theater arts and Afro-American studies, 1972-76; Columbia College, Chicago, IL, artistic producer and chairman of theater/music department, 1976-80, writer in residence, 1980—. Visiting artist in residence at State University of New York at Buffalo, summer, 1965; Institute of Pan-African Culture, resident fellow at the University of Massachusetts at Amherst, consultant to the New England Regional Committee in Lagos, Nigeria, 1973-74; adjunct professor of theater communications at University of Illinois at Chicago Circle, 1978-82; visiting professor of Afro-American studies at Smith College and Wesleyan University, spring, 1984. Dramaturgical consultant to the Mickery Theater, Loenesloat, Netherlands, 1967; resource advisor to Colloquium on Black Education, Pajaro Dunes, CA, 1970-71; touring symposium member of the African Continuum Forum, 1970-72; literary adviser to Lincoln Center Repertory Company, 1972-73; consultant to Theater Communications Group, 1972-74; theater panelist of Illinois Arts Council, 1976-79. Associate producer of the Association for the Advancement of Creative Musicians concert series, Columbia College, 1983-85.

Director of plays, including *Junebug Graduates Tonight,* 1967, *Tabernacle,* 1969, *Ain't Supposed to Die a Natural Death,* 1970, *Tophat,* 1971, *Homecookin',* 1971, *Lady Day: A Musical Tragedy,* 1972; *Freeman,* 1978; *Ceremonies in Dark Old Men,* 1979; *The Owl Answers,* 1980, *In an Upstate Motel,* 1981, *My Sister, My Sister,* 1981, *No Place to be Somebody,* 1983, *The River Niger,* 1987, and *Anchorman,* 1988. Producer of plays, including *Black Recollections,* 1972; artistic producer of new American plays at Columbia College Performance Company, 1976-80. Developer and associate producer of television film *Leave 'Em Laughin',* Columbia Broadcasting System (CBS-TV), 1981.

*MEMBER:* American Theater Association, Dramatists Guild, Society for Directors and Choreographers, Actors Studio (playwrights and directors units).

*AWARDS, HONORS:* National Science Foundation fellow-

ship; Obie Award for Best Play from the *Village Voice,* 1974, for *The Great MacDaddy;* Audelco (Audience Development Committee) Recognition Award for outstanding musical creator, 1981, for *Tabernacle;* Humanitas Prize from the Human Family Educational and Cultural Institute, 1981, for *Leave 'Em Laughin';* Illinois Art Council grant for playwriting, 1984; Rockefeller Foundation fellowship for American playwriting, 1985-86; Meet the Composer/Reader's Digest Commission, 1992.

*WRITINGS:*

(Editor, under name Paul Carter-Harrison) *Voetnoten bij modern toneel* (essays; title means "The Modern Drama Footnote"), Bezige, 1965.
*Dialog van het verzet* (essays; title means "Dialogue From the Opposition"), Bezige, 1966.
(Under name Paul Carter-Harrison) *The Drama of Nommo: Black Theater in the African Continuum* (essays), Grove, 1972.
(Editor, contributor, and author of introduction) *Kuntu Drama: Plays of the African Continuum,* preface by Oliver Jackson, Grove, 1974.
*Chuck Stewart's Jazz Files* (photographs by Charles Stewart), New York Graphic Society/Little, Brown, 1985.
(Editor, contributor, and author of introduction) *Totem Voices: Plays from the Black World Repertory* (plays), Grove, 1988.
(With Bert Andrews) *In the Shadow of the Great White Way: Images from the Black Theater* (photo documentary), Thunder's Mouth Press, 1989.
*Black Light: The African American Hero* (includes photographs from Schomburg Center for Research in Black Culture), Thunder's Mouth, 1993.

*PLAYS*

*The Postclerks* (one-act), first produced in New York at Actor's Studio, 1963.
*Pavane for a Dead-Pan Minstrel* (one-act; first produced in New York at Actor's Studio, 1964), published in *Podium* (Amsterdam), November, 1965.
*Tophat* (one-act), first produced at Buffalo University Summer Theater, 1965; produced in New York by Negro Ensemble Co., 1972.
*Pawns* (one-act), first produced in New York by 2nd Story Players, 1966.
*The Experimental Leader* (one-act; first produced in New York by Dore Co., 1968), published in *Podium,* 1965.
*Folly for Two* (one-act; first produced in New York at Actor's Studio, 1968), published in *Podium,* 1967, revised as *Interface.*

*Tabernacle* (first produced in Washington, DC, at Howard University, 1969; produced in New York at Afro-American Studio, 1976), published in *New Black Playwrights,* Avon, 1970.

*Ain't Supposed to Die a Natural Death* (adapted from Melvin Van Peebles's recordings *Ain't Supposed to Die a Natural Death* and *Brer Soul*), first produced at University of California, Sacramento, 1970.

*The Great MacDaddy* (first produced at University of California, Sacramento, 1972; produced in New York at St. Mark's Playhouse, February 12, 1974), published in *Kuntu Drama: Plays of the African Continuum,* Grove, 1974.

*Dr. Jazz* (two-act), first produced on Broadway, 1975.

*The Death of Boogie Woogie* (two-act; first produced in Northampton, MA, at Smith College, 1976; produced in New York at Richard Allen Center, 1979), published in *Callaloo,* 1985.

*Ameri/cain Gothic* (two-act), first produced in Chicago at Columbia College, 1980; produced in New York at New Federal Theater, 1985.

*Abercrombie Apocalypse* (two-act), first produced in Chicago at Columbia College, 1981; produced Off-Broadway at Westside Arts Theater, June 22, 1982.

*SCREENPLAYS*

*Impressions of American Negro Society,* VPRO-TV (Hilversum, Netherlands), c. 1963.

*Stranger on a Square,* VPRO-TV, 1964.

*Intrusion,* (Belgium), 1965.

*Lord Shango,* Bryanstone Pictures, 1974.

*Youngblood,* Aion, 1978.

*Gettin' to Know Me,* Children's Television International, 1980.

*OTHER*

(With Julius Hemphill) *Anchorman* (two-act operetta; with music by Hemphill), first produced in Chicago at Columbia College, 1982; produced in New York at Theater Four, 1988.

Contributor to American and Dutch periodicals, including *American Rag, Black Review, Black World, Choice, Nommo,* and *Players.* Critical consultant to *Choice,* 1973—; theater and contributing editor to *Elan,* 1981-83.

*WORK IN PROGRESS:* Goree Crossing, an operetta; and *Doxology,* an opera.

*SIDELIGHTS:* The playwright Paul Carter Harrison, best known for integrating modern American thought and African tradition in his works, sums up his theories on drama and the philosophy behind his play writing in his 1972 collection of critical essays, *The Drama of Nommo.* In this book, as in his plays, Harrison stresses the importance of combining traditional African values, rituals, and philosophy—including the belief in a holistic universe, where all elements are connected—with contemporary American points of view to reflect the total black experience on stage. The author feels that the theater should attempt to create a ritual out of the collective spiritual energy of black actors and audience. Furthermore, Harrison maintains, a play should utilize black vernacular experience for linguistic idiom, character, music, literature, and folklore, in order to reveal the traditional mythologies at work in contemporary black experience. Critics deemed *The Drama of Nommo* valuable and thought-provoking, praising Harrison for stimulating African culture, for advancing black dramatic criticism, and for establishing black drama, like black music, as an ascetic entity separate from the conventional body of writing for the theater.

Harrison graduated from Indiana University and then the New School for Social Research before setting out for Europe in 1961. He eventually settled in Amsterdam, Netherlands, and lived there for seven years, staging readings by black poets and writing and producing television programs and plays for the theater. He began composing one-act plays during this period, with characters ranging from blue-collar workers unhappy with their lives to a Jew living in Nazi Germany unsure of his future. Harrison also experimented with reversing traditional roles based on gender or race. For example, *Tophat* features a female dominating a submissive male, and in *Pavane for a Dead-Pan Minstrel* a white man and black man switch identities by marking their faces with clown-white and minstrel cork, with each assuming the other's behavior.

While visiting the United States in 1964 Harrison witnessed the Harlem riots. When he returned to Europe he began writing his first full-length play, *Tabernacle,* about the events leading up to the racial unrest. The main character, the Reverend, has been compared to an African ceremonial leader as he guides his congregation (the audience) in a church service (ritual) toward the illumination of the victimization of black youths by the police. Throughout the play Harrison mixes jazz and African music—thereby symbolically integrating American innovation with African tradition—and uses a number of devices to remove the barrier between actor and audience, such as giving the audience an active role in the drama. Although Harrison completed the play in 1965, he felt that because of its content *Tabernacle* should be performed only by Afro-Americans, so it was not presented until 1969 at Howard University in Washington, D.C., where he directed the production.

Harrison also utilized techniques to lessen the distance between actor and audience in his adaptation of work by Melvin Van Peebles. He saw Van Peebles's work as an exploration of city life, so he created an urban atmosphere in the theater, filling it—on stage and in the audience—with actors playing derelicts, drunks, prostitutes, and other lowlife, who interacted with the theatergoers. Because the productions of *Ain't Supposed to Die* were improvisational, with Van Peebles's works acting only as the tying thread, each of the performances presented at California State University in Sacramento in November, 1970, provoked a unique audience response.

Four years later Harrison won an Obie Award for the Off-Broadway production of his play *The Great MacDaddy*. In a review for the *New York Times* Clayton Riley declared the play a "brilliant ritual drama" and admired its "metaphorical richness and visual imagery." *The Great MacDaddy* features mythic figures from black American folklore, all of whom MacDaddy encounters on his spiritual trek across Depression-era America in search of, according to Riley, "the knowledge needed for blacks to retain their soul in the soulless technology of America." This play, in which many of Harrison's dramatic principles are winningly combined, is considered his masterpiece. In it the playwright introduced African cultural elements in an American setting, placed emphasis on the Afro-American's spirituality and place in society, and utilized black street slang and dialect and African rhythmic music in the drama. Harrison published *The Great MacDaddy* in a collection of critically acclaimed works that he edited, *Kuntu Drama: Plays of the African Continuum*. The anthology contains plays by black writers—including Aime Cesaire, Amiri Baraka, Adrienne Kennedy, and Lennox Brown—who agreed with Harrison's dramatic tenets and drew extensively on African speech rhythms, rituals, traditions, values, and myths in their works featured.

Harrison has also written on black themes for television and film. During the early 1960s he penned and produced two films for television in the Netherlands, *Impressions of American Negro Poetry* and *Stranger on a Square*. His writing for American television includes four segments of a children's folklore series produced in 1980, *Gettin' to Know Me*. In addition, Harrison wrote the screenplays for an American short feature filmed in Belgium and for the motion picture *Youngblood*, an American commercial release about a teenager who joins a ghetto street gang.

Harrison provides a historical framework in his preface and later interview with photographer Bert Andrews in *In the Shadow of the Great White Way: Images from the Black Theater*. It contains 150 photos by Andrews and is, according to Ebony magazine, "an important record of Black accomplishment on the New York stage during Broadway's reign as the center of American theater."

In an interview, Harrison said an interest in poetry first led him to the theater, especially "listening to poets in Greenwich Village in New York as a kid, and being fascinated with the language of the new poets of that time, the Beat Generation Poets: LeRoi Jones, Ted Jones, Frank O'Hara, (Allen) Ginsberg, and that crowd." His interest leaned toward European theater rather than American theater, which, he said, "doesn't seem to have a collective world view that I can identify with." Of his philosophy, he said, "if you understand the world to be made up of forces, then your characters must all be forces as opposed to being personalized, individualized characters. They have to be archetypes, in my sense."

Harrison said a lot of new plays written for and about blacks don't often get to the production stage because the audience is too limited. "They must clearly count on the black population seeing these plays," he said, "but that's not enough. It's harder to sustain them without the whites coming to see them.... So many of these plays are seen in the provinces, in community theaters and/or the university theaters, but might not necessarily get back to New York or to the mainstream public or be witnessed by mainstream critics."

In advice to a young black student who wanted to write plays with white characters, Harrison told him there are enough whites doing that. "There must be, in the heart of your plays," Harrison said, "a life, something that produces a pulse we can feel. If you cannot bring a pulse to these characters, your play will have no resonance. It will be a hollow experience." He said the young student's plays were well written, but had no "pulse." "The only way you can have that pulse is by having at least one black character that you recognize and identify with," Harrison said.

*BIOGRAPHICAL/CRITICAL SOURCES:*

*BOOKS*

Arata, Esther Spring, *More Black American Playwrights*, Scarecrow Press, 1978.
*Dictionary of Literary Biography*, Volume 38: *Afro-American Writers After 1955: Dramatists and Prose Writers*, Gale, 1985.
Fabre, Genevieve, *Drumbeats, Masks, and Metaphors: Contemporary Afro-American Theater*, translated by Melvin Dixon, Harvard University Press, 1983.
Hill, Errol, editor, *The Theater of Black Americans*, two volumes, Prentice-Hall, 1980.

*PERIODICALS*

*Ebony*, December, 1989.
*Essence*, February, 1990.
*Library Journal*, February 15, 1990.

*Los Angeles Times Book Review,* January 5, 1986.
*New York Times,* March 3, 1974, May 25, 1978, June 27, 1982.

\* \* \*

## HASKINS, James S. 1941-
### (Jim Haskins)

*PERSONAL:* Born September 19, 1941, in Montgomery, AL; son of Henry and Julia (Brown) Haskins. *Education:* Georgetown University, B.A., 1960; Alabama State University, B.S., 1962; University of New Mexico, M.A., 1963; graduate study at New School for Social Research, 1965-67, and Queens College of the City University of New York, 1967-68.

*ADDRESSES: Home*—325 West End Ave., Apt. 7D, New York, NY 10013. *Office*—Department of English, University of Florida, Gainesville, FL 32611.

*CAREER:* Smith Barney & Co., New York City, stock trader, 1963-65; *New York Daily News,* New York City, production, 1963-64; New York City Board of Education, teacher, 1966-68; New School for Social Research, New York City, visiting lecturer, 1970-72; Staten Island Community College of the City University of New York, Staten Island, NY, associate professor, 1970-77; University of Florida, Gainesville, professor of English, 1977—. Visiting lecturer, Elisabeth Irwin High School, New York City, 1971-73; visiting professor, Indiana University/Purdue University-Indianapolis, 1973-76; visiting professor, College of New Rochelle, New York City campus, 1977. Director, Union Mutual Life, Health, and Accident Insurance Co., Philadelphia, PA, 1970-73; member of board of advisers, Psi Systems, 1971-72; member of board of directors, Speedwell Services for Children, 1974-76. Consultant, Education Development Center, Newton, MA, 1975—, Department of Health, Education, and Welfare, 1977-79, National Research Council, 1979-80, and Grolier, Inc., 1979-82. Member, Manhattan Community Board No. 9, 1972-73; academic council for the State University of New York, 1972-74; New York Urban League Manhattan Advisory Board, 1973-75; vice-director of Southeast Region of Statue of Liberty—Ellis Island Foundation, 1986. Member of National Education Advisory Committee, Commission on the Bicentennial of the Constitution.

*MEMBER:* National Book Critics Circle, Authors League of America, Authors Guild, 100 Black Men, Phi Beta Kappa, Kappa Alpha Psi.

*AWARDS, HONORS:* Notable children's book in the field of social studies citations, from *Social Education,* 1971, for *Rev-* olutionaries: Agents of Change, from *Social Studies,* 1972, for *Resistance: Profiles in Nonviolence, The War and the Protest: Viet Nam,* and *Profiles in Black Power,* and 1973, for *A Piece of the Power: Four Black Mayors,* from National Council for the Social Studies-Children's Book Council Book Review Committee, 1975, for *Fighting Shirley Chisholm,* and 1976, for *The Creoles of Color of New Orleans* and *The Picture Life of Malcolm X,* and from Children's Book Council, 1978, for *The Life and Death of Martin Luther King, Jr.;* World Book Year Book literature for children citation, 1973, for *From Lew Alcindor to Kareem Abdul-Jabbar;* Books of the Year citations, Child Study Association of America, 1974, for *Adam Clayton Powell: Portrait of a Marching Black* and *Street Gangs: Yesterday and Today;* Books for Brotherhood bibliography citation, National Council of Christians and Jews book review committee, 1975, for *Adam Clayton Powell: Portrait of a Marching Black;* Spur Award finalist, Western Writers of America, 1975, for *The Creoles of Color of New Orleans;* Eighth Annual Coretta Scott King Award, and Books Chosen by Children citation, Children's Book Council, both 1977, both for *The Story of Stevie Wonder;* Deems Taylor Award, American Society of Composers, Authors, and Publishers, 1979, for *Scott Joplin: The Man Who Made Ragtime;* Merit Award, National Council for Social Studies, 1980, for *James Van DerZee: The Picture Takin' Man;* Ambassador of Honor book, English-Speaking Union Books-Across-the-Sea, 1983, for *Bricktop;* American Library Association best book for young adults citation, 1987, for *Black Music in America;* Alabama Library Association best juvenile work citation, 1987, for "Count Your Way" series; "Bicentennial Reading, Viewing, Listening for Young Americans" citations, American Library Association and National Endowment for the Humanities, for *Street Gangs: Yesterday and Today, Ralph Bunche: A Most Reluctant Hero,* and *A Piece of the Power: Four Black Mayors;* certificate of appreciation, Joseph P. Kennedy Foundation, for work with the Special Olympics program.

*WRITINGS:*

*Pinckney Benton Stewart Pitchback: A Biography,* Macmillan, 1973.
*A New King of Joy: The Story of the Special Olympics,* Doubleday, 1976.
(With Kathleen Benson) *Scott Joplin: The Man Who Made Ragtime,* Doubleday, 1978.
(With Bricktop) *Bricktop,* Atheneum, 1983.
(With Benson) *Lena: A Personal and Professional Biography,* Stein & Day, 1984.
(With Benson) *Nat King Cole,* Stein & Day, 1984.
(With David A. Walker) *Double Dutch,* Enslow, 1986.
*Mabel Mercer: A Life,* Atheneum, 1988.
(As told to James S. Haskins) *The Autobiography of Rosa Parks,* Dial, 1990.

*The Methodists,* Hippocrene Books, 1992.

(With Hugh F. Butts) *Psychology of Black Language,* enlarged edition, Hippocrene Books, 1992.

*JUVENILE*

*Resistance: Profiles in Nonviolence,* Doubleday, 1970.

*Revolutionaries: Agents of Change,* Lippincott, 1971.

*The War and the Protest: Viet Nam,* Doubleday, 1971.

*Religions,* Lippincott, 1973.

*Witchcraft, Mysticism and Magic in the Black World,* Doubleday, 1974.

*Street Gangs: Yesterday and Today,* Hastings House, 1974.

*Jobs in Business and Office,* Lothrop, 1974.

*The Creoles of Color of New Orleans,* Crowell, 1975.

*The Consumer Movement,* F. Watts, 1975.

*Who Are the Handicapped?,* Doubleday, 1978.

(With J. M. Stifle) *The Quiet Revolution: The Struggle for the Rights of Disabled Americans,* Crowell, 1979.

*The New Americans: Vietnamese Boat People,* Enslow, 1980.

*Black Theater in American,* Crowell, 1982.

*The New Americans: Cuban Boat People,* Enslow, 1982.

*The Guardian Angels,* Enslow, 1983.

*Black Music in America: A History through Its People,* Crowell, 1987.

(With Benson) *A Sixties Reader,* Viking Children's Books, 1988.

*Black Dance in America: A History through Its People,* HarperCollins, 1990.

*The March on Washington,* HarperCollins, 1993.

*JUVENILE BIOGRAPHIES*

*From Lew Alcindor to Kareem Abdul Jabbar,* Lothrop, 1972.

*A Piece of the Power: Four Black Mayors,* Dial, 1972.

*Profiles in Black Power,* Doubleday, 1972.

*Deep Like the Rivers: A Biography of Langston Hughes, 1902-1967,* Holt, 1973.

*Adam Clayton Powell: Portrait of a Marching Black,* Dial, 1974; updated, Africa World Press, 1992.

*Babe Ruth and Hank Aaron: The Home Run Kings,* Lothrop, 1974.

*Fighting Shirley Chisholm,* Dial, 1975.

*The Picture Life of Malcolm X,* F. Watts, 1975.

*Dr. J: A Biography of Julius Erving,* Doubleday, 1975.

*Pele: A Biography,* Doubleday, 1976.

*The Story of Stevie Wonder,* Doubleday, 1976.

*Always Movin' On: The Life of Langston Hughes,* F. Watts, 1976; updated, Africa World Press, 1992.

*Barbara Jordan,* Dial, 1977.

*The Life and Death of Martin Luther King, Jr.,* Lothrop, 1977.

*George McGinnis: Basketball Superstar,* Hastings, 1978.

*Bob McAdoo: Superstar,* Lothrop, 1978.

*Andrew Young: Man with a Mission,* Lothrop, 1979.

*I'm Gonna Make You Love Me: The Story of Diana Ross,* Dial, 1980.

*"Magic": A Biography of Earvin Johnson,* Enslow, 1981.

*Katherine Dunham,* Coward-McCann, 1982.

*Donna Summer,* Atlantic Monthly Press, 1983.

*Lena Horne,* Coward-McCann, 1983.

*About Michael Jackson,* Enslow, 1985.

*Diana Ross: Star Supreme,* Viking, 1985.

*Leaders of the Middle East,* Enslow, 1985.

*Corazon Aquino: Leader of the Philippines,* Enslow, 1988.

*The Magic Johnson Story,* Enslow, 1988.

*Shirley Temple Black: Actress to Ambassador,* Viking Children's Books, 1988.

(With Lionel Hampton) *Hamp: An Autobiography,* Warner Books, 1989, revised edition, Amistad Press, 1993.

*India under Indira and Rajiv Gandhi,* Enslow, 1989.

*Nat King Cole,* Madison Books, 1991.

*Colin Powell: A Biography,* Scholastic, 1992.

*I Am Somebody!: A Biography of Jesse Jackson,* Enslow, 1992.

*Thurgood Marshall: A Life of Justice,* Henry Holt, 1992.

*Sports Great Magic Johnson,* revised and expanded edition, Enslow, 1992.

*UNDER NAME JIM HASKINS*

*Diary of a Harlem Schoolteacher,* Grove, 1969.

(Editor) *Black Manifesto for Education,* Morrow, 1973.

(With Hugh F. Butts) *The Psychology of Black Language,* Barnes & Noble, 1973.

*Snow Sculpture and Ice Carving,* Macmillan, 1974.

*The Cotton Club,* Random House, 1977.

(With Benson and Ellen Inkelis) *The Great American Crazies,* Condor, 1977.

*Voodoo and Hoodoo: Their Tradition and Craft as Revealed by Actual Practitioners,* Stein & Day, 1978.

(With Benson) *The Stevie Wonder Scrapbook,* Grosset & Dunlap, 1978.

*Richard Pryor, a Man and His Madness: A Biography,* Beaufort Books, 1984.

*Queen of the Blues: A Biography of Dinah Washington,* Morrow, 1987.

*Bill Cosby: America's Most Famous Father,* Walker & Co., 1988.

(With Helen Crothers) *Scatman: An Authorized Biography of Scatman Crothers,* Morrow, 1991.

*I Have a Dream: The Life and Words of Martin Luther King, Jr.,* Millbrook Press, 1992.

*UNDER NAME JIM HASKINS; JUVENILE*

*Jokes from Black Folks,* Doubleday, 1973.

*Ralph Bunche: A Most Reluctant Hero,* Hawthorne, 1974.

*Your Rights, Past and Present: A Guide for Young People,* Hawthorne, 1975.

*Teen-age Alcoholism,* Hawthorne, 1976.

*The Long Struggle: The Story of American Labor,* Westminster, 1976.

*Real Estate Careers,* F. Watts, 1978.

*Gambling—Who Really Wins?,* F. Watts, 1978.

*James Van DerZee: The Picture Takin' Man,* Dodd, Mead, 1979; updated, Africa World Press, 1991.

(With Pat Connolly) *The Child Abuse Help Book,* Addison Wesley, 1981.

*Werewolves,* Lothrop, 1982.

*Sugar Ray Leonard,* Lothrop, 1982.

(With Stifle) *Donna Summer: An Unauthorized Biography,* Little, Brown, 1983.

(With Benson) *Space Challenge: The Story of Guion Bluford, an Authorized Biography,* Carolrhoda Books, 1984.

*Break Dancing,* Lerner, 1985.

*The Statue of Liberty: America's Proud Lady,* Lerner, 1986.

*Christopher Columbus: Admiral of the Ocean Sea,* Scholastic, 1991

*Outward Dreams: Black Inventors and Their Inventions,* Walker & Co., 1991.

*Amazing Grace: The Story Behind the Song,* Millbrook, 1992.

*The Day Martin Luther King, Jr., Was Shot: A Photo History of the Civil Rights Movement,* Scholastic, 1992.

*Against All Opposition: Black Explorers in America,* Walker & Co., 1992.

*One More River to Cross: Twelve Black Americans,* Scholastic, 1992.

*Get on Board: The Story of the Underground Railroad,* Scholastic, 1993.

*UNDER NAME JIM HASKINS; JUVENILE; "COUNT YOUR WAY" SERIES*

*Count Your Way through China,* Carolrhoda Books, 1987.

*Count Your Way through Japan,* Carolrhoda Books, 1987.

*Count Your Way through Russia,* Carolrhoda Books, 1987.

*Count Your Way through the Arab World,* Carolrhoda Books, 1987.

*Count Your Way through Korea,* Carolrhoda Books, 1989.

*Count Your Way through Mexico,* Carolrhoda Books, 1989.

*Count Your Way through Africa,* Carolrhoda Books, 1989.

*Count Your Way through Canada,* Carolrhoda Books, 1989.

*Count Your Way through Germany,* Carolrhoda Books, 1990.

*Count Your Way through Israel,* Carolrhoda Books, 1990.

*Count Your Way through Italy,* Carolrhoda Books, 1990.

*Count Your Way through India,* Carolrhoda Books, 1990.

*OTHER*

(Contributor) Emily Mumford, *Understanding Human Behavior in Health and Illness,* Williams & Wilkins, 1977.

(Contributor) *New York Kid's Catalog,* Doubleday, 1979.

(Contributor) *Notable American Women Supplement,* Radcliffe College, 1979.

(Contributor) Jerry Brown, *Clearings in the Thicket: An Alabama Humanities Reader,* Mercer University Press, 1985.

(Editor) David C. Gross, *Judaism,* Hippocrene Books, 1991.

(Editor) Barrie R. Strauss, *The Catholic Church,* Hippocrene Books, 1992.

Also contributor to *Author in the Kitchen* and *Children and Books,* fourth edition, 1976. General editor, under name Jim Haskins, of *The Filipino Nation,* three volumes, Grolier International, 1982. Series editor for "Hippocrene Great Religions of the World." Contributor of articles and reviews to periodicals, including *American Visions, Now, Applause, Arizona, English Bulletin, Rolling Stone, Children's Book Review Service, Western Journal of Black Studies, Elementary English, Amsterdam News, New York Times Book Review, Afro-Hawaii News,* and *Gainesville Sun.*

*ADAPTATIONS: Diary of a Harlem Schoolteacher* has been recorded by Recordings for the Blind. *The Cotton Club* was the inspiration for the 1984 film of the same title.

*SIDELIGHTS:* In his essay in *Something about the Author Autobiography Series,* James S. Haskins writes: "It has always seemed to me that truth is not just 'stranger than fiction,' but also more interesting. Also, it seems to me that the more you know about the real world the better off you are, and since there is so much in the real world to learn about, you are better off concentrating on fact rather than fiction." Haskins supports this idea in his many biographies of important black people, many of them politicians, performers, or sports figures, as well as in his other writings, ranging from discussions of ice sculpture to forms of rope jumping to histories of gang violence and the Harlem night life of the Cotton Club.

Haskins's first book grew out of his experiences teaching a Special Education class at Public School 92 in New York. A social worker, he relates, "gave me a diary and suggested that I write down my thoughts about my students and teaching disadvantaged children in Harlem. *Diary of a Harlem Schoolteacher* was the result." Ronald Gross of the *New York Times Book Review* describes the book as "plain, concrete, unemotional and unliterary.... By its truthfulness alone does it command our concern." The episodes Haskins relates are not about "education with a big E," the critic continues; "Rather, the entries catalog the unremitting series of catastrophes, irritations and frustrations which make teaching and learning virtually impossible in most ghetto schools."

Once *Diary* was published, Haskins continues, "major publishing companies actually approached me about writing books for young people. I knew exactly the kinds of books I wanted to do—books about current events and books about important black people so that students could understand the larger world around them through books written on a level that they could understand." Soon he produced volumes on the nonviolent civil rights movement, the Black Power movement, and the war in Vietnam—attempting to put these events in historical perspective. He also penned biographies of important black people in politics and international affairs, including Barbara Jordan, Adam Clayton Powell, Ralph Bunche, Shirley Chisholm, and Jesse Jackson. Haskins originally steered away from sports figures, he says, because "it seemed to me that young blacks should have other role models besides successful athletes," but gradually "I realized that it doesn't matter so much what kids read as it does that they read. You can use new words and put sentences together properly just as easily when you are writing about a sports hero as when you are writing about a politician. The same goes for show-business stars like Stevie Wonder." Biographies of people ranging from black astronaut Guion Bluford to superstar Michael Jackson followed.

While many of Haskins's biographies are intended for a young audience, others are meant for adults. Some of his biographies of famous black performers and artists, such as Nat King Cole, Dinah Washington, Richard Pryor, and Scott Joplin, have attracted critical attention because of their illumination of the stars' black experience. For instance, *Scott Joplin: The Man Who Made Ragtime,* states Joseph McLellan in the *Washington Post Book World,* focuses "special attention on his origins and plac[es] his life and his music in the black-American context without which it can be only incompletely understood." A biography of Nat King Cole "really points out the racial contradictions in American society [and] reveals the conflicts that exist between upper-class and lower-class African-Americans," according to Norman Richmond in the Toronto *Globe and Mail.* Another *Globe and Mail* contributor, Paul Washington, declares that *Queen of the Blues: A Biography of Dinah Washington* "ties Washington's story to the history of black Americans."

"Most of my books and articles are about black subjects—black history, black people," Haskins states. The reasons for this are partly due to "a certain segregation in the publishing industry," but also "because I remember being a child and not having many books about black people to read. I want children today, black and white, to be able to find books about black people and black history in case they want to read them."

*BIOGRAPHICAL/CRITICAL SOURCES:*

BOOKS

Brown, Jerry, *Clearings in the Thicket: An Alabama Humanities Reader,* Mercer University Press, 1985.

*Children's Literature Review,* Volume 3, Gale, 1978.
*Something about the Author Autobiography Series,* Volume 4, Gale, 1987.

PERIODICALS

*Bloomsbury Review,* June, 1991.
*Chicago Tribune Book World,* April 13, 1986.
*Children's Book Review Service,* August, 1991.
*Christian Science Monitor,* March 12, 1970.
*Down Beat,* May, 1990.
*Ebony,* April, 1992.
*Globe and Mail* (Toronto), July 6, 1985; September 12, 1987.
*Los Angeles Times Book Review,* July 24, 1983; March 11, 1984; January 20, 1985.
*Manhattan Tribune,* March 7, 1970.
*New Leader,* April 16, 1970.
*New York Post,* February 7, 1970.
*New York Times Book Review,* February 8, 1970; December 6, 1970; May 7, 1972; May 5, 1974; August 4, 1974; November 20, 1977; September 23, 1979; October 7, 1979; January 20, 1980; March 4, 1984; January 19, 1986; March 2, 1986; June 15, 1986; August 24, 1986; September 7, 1986; October 19, 1986; January 25, 1987; March 1, 1987; April 26, 1987; May 17, 1987; September 13, 1987; June 26, 1988; December 3, 1989; February 2, 1992.
*Parenting Magazine,* September, 1992.
*Publishers Weekly,* April 10, 1987; October 23, 1987; March 11, 1988; March 25, 1988; October 6, 1989; March 30, 1990; July 25, 1991; November 29, 1991; January 6, 1992; April 27, 1992; July 20, 1992.
*Saturday Evening Post,* March, 1990.
*School Library Journal,* January, 1986; April, 1986; September, 1986; June-July, 1987; September, 1987; June-July, 1988; July, 1989; September, 1989; June, 1990; August, 1990; February, 1991; June, 1991; February, 1992; April, 1992; May, 1992; June, 1992; August, 1992.
*Times Literary Supplement,* May 24, 1985.
*U.S. News and World Report,* June 16, 1986.
*Variety,* March 2, 1988; March 9, 1988.
*Washington Post Book World,* November 15, 1973; November 10, 1974; September 11, 1977; February 5, 1978; July 24, 1978; August 17, 1983; January 16, 1985; May 10, 1987; September 1, 1991.
*Wilson Library Bulletin,* September, 1988; January, 1989.

*      *      *

**HASKINS, Jim**
**See HASKINS, James S.**

## HAYGOOD, Wil 1954-

*PERSONAL:* Born September 19, 1954 in Columbus, OH. *Education:* Miami University, Oxford, OH, B.A., 1976.

*ADDRESSES: Office*—Feature Reporter, the *Boston Globe,* 135 Morrissey Blvd, Boston, MA 02107.

*CAREER:* Author, journalist. *Call & Post,* Columbus, OH, reporter, 1977-78; Community Information and Referral, hotline operator, 1978-79; Macy's department store, New York City, executive, 1980-81; *The Charleston Gazette,* copyeditor, 1981-83; *Post Gazette,* Pittsburgh, PA, reporter, 1984-85; *The Boston Globe,* feature reporter.

*AWARDS, HONORS:* National Headliner Award, Outstanding Feature Writing, 1986.

*WRITINGS:*

*Two on the River,* photographs by Stan Grossfield, Atlantic Monthly Press, 1986.
*King of the Cats: The Life and Times of Adam Clayton Powell, Jr.* (biography), Houghton Mifflin, 1993.

Contributor of articles to periodicals.

\* \* \*

## HEAD, Bessie 1937-1986

*PERSONAL:* Original name Bessie Amelia Emery; born July 6, 1937, in Pietermaritzburg, South Africa; died of hepatitis, April 17, 1986, in Botswana; married Harold Head (a journalist), September 1, 1961 (divorced); children: Howard. *Education:* Educated in South Africa as a primary school teacher. *Politics:* None ("dislike politics"). *Religion:* None ("dislike formal religion").

*ADDRESSES: Home*—P.O. Box 15, Serowe, Botswana, Africa. *Agent*—John Johnson, Clerkenwell House, 45/47 Clerkenwell Green, London EC1R 0HT, England.

*CAREER:* Teacher in primary schools in South Africa and Botswana for four years; journalist at Drum Publications in Johannesburg for two years; writer. Represented Botswana at international writers conference at University of Iowa, 1977-78, and in Denmark, 1980.

*AWARDS, HONORS: The Collector of Treasures and Other Botswana Village Tales* was nominated for the Jock Campbell Award for literature by new or unregarded talent from Africa or the Caribbean, *New Statesman,* 1978.

*WRITINGS:*

*When Rain Clouds Gather* (novel), Simon & Schuster, 1969.
*Maru* (novel), McCall, 1971.
*A Question of Power* (novel), Davis Poynter, 1973, Pantheon, 1974.
*The Collector of Treasures and Other Botswana Village Tales* (short stories), Heinemann, 1977.
*Serowe: Village of the Rain Wind* (historical chronicle), Heinemann, 1981.
*A Bewitched Crossroad: An African Saga* (historical chronicle), Donker (Craighall), 1984, Paragon House, 1986.
*Tales of Tenderness and Power,* introduction by Gillian Stead Eilersen, Donker, 1989, Heinemann, 1990.
*A Woman Alone: Autobiographical Writings,* selected and edited by Craig MacKenzie, Heinemann, 1990.
*A Gesture of Belonging: Letters from Bessie Head, 1965-1979,* edited by Randolph Vigne, Heinemann, 1991.

Contributor to periodicals, including the London *Times, Presence Africaine, New African,* and *Transition.*

Head's work has been translated into several European languages, including Danish, Dutch, and German.

*SIDELIGHTS:* "Unlike many exiled South African writers," said a London *Times* contributor, "[Bessie Head] was able to root her life and her work anew in a country close to her tormented motherland." Born of racially mixed parentage in South Africa, Head lived and died in her adopted Botswana, the subject of much of her writing; in 1979, after fifteen years as part of a refugee community located at Bamangwato Development Farm, she was granted Botswanan citizenship. In *World Literature Written in English,* Betty McGinnis Fradkin described Head's meager existence after a particularly lean year: "There is no electricity yet. At night Bessie types by the light of six candles. Fruit trees and vegetables surround the house. Bessie makes guava jam to sell, and will sell vegetables when the garden is enlarged." Despite her impoverished circumstances, Head acknowledged to Fradkin that the regularity of her life in the refugee community brought her the peace of mind she sought: "In South Africa, all my life I lived in shattered little bits. All those shattered bits began to grow together here.... I have a peace against which all the turmoil is worked out!"

"Her novels strike a special chord for the South African diaspora, though this does not imply that it is the only level at which they work or produce an impact as novels," observed Arthur Ravenscroft in *Aspects of South African Literature.* "They are strange, ambiguous, deeply personal books which initially do not seem to be 'political' in any ordinary sense of the word." Head's racially mixed heritage profoundly influenced both her work and her life, for an element of exile as well as an abiding concern with discrimination, whatever its guise, permeate her writing. Noting in *Black Scholar* that Head has "probably received more acclaim than any other black African woman novelist writing in English," Nancy Topping Bazin added that Head's works "reveal a great deal about the lives of African women and about the development of feminist perspectives." According to Bazin, Head's analysis of Africa's "patriarchal system and attitudes" enabled her to make connections between the discrimination she experienced personally from racism and sexism, and the root of oppression generally in the insecurity that compels one to feel superior to another.

Head is "especially moving on the position of women, emerging painfully from the chrysalis of tribalist attitudes into a new evaluation of their relationship to men and their position in society," stated Mary Borg in a *New Statesman* review of Head's first novel, *When Rain Clouds Gather.* Considered "intelligent and moving" by one *Times Literary Supplement* contributor, it is described by another as combining "a vivid account of village life in Botswana with the relationship between an Englishman and an embittered black South African who try to change the traditional farming methods of the community." The black male flees South African apartheid only to experience discrimination from other blacks as a refugee in Botswana. For this novel, Head drew upon her own experience as part of a refugee community, which she indicated in *World Literature Written in English* had been "initially, extremely brutal and harsh." Head explained that she had not experienced oppression by the Botswanan government itself in any way, but because South African blacks had been "stripped bare of every human right," she was unaccustomed to witnessing "human ambition and greed ... in a black form." Calling *When Rain Clouds Gather* "a tale of innocence and experience," Ravenscroft acknowledged that "there are moments of melodrama and excessive romanticism, but the real life of the novel is of creativity, resilience, reconstruction, fulfilment." Most of the major characters "are in one sense or another handicapped exiles, learning how to mend their lives," said Ravenscroft, adding that "it is the vision behind their effortful embracing of exile that gives Bessie Head's first novel an unusual maturity."

Head's second novel, *Maru,* is also set in a Botswanan village. According to Ravenscroft, though, in this book, "workaday affairs form the framework for the real novel, which is a drama about inner conflict and peace of mind and soul." *Maru* is about the problems that accompany the arrival of the well-educated new teacher with whom two young chiefs fall in love. It is "about interior experience, about thinking, feeling, sensing, about control over rebellious lusts of the spirit," said Ravenscroft, who questioned whether or not "the two chief male characters ... who are close, intimate friends until they become bitter antagonists, are indeed two separate fictional

characters, or ... symbolic extensions of contending character-traits within the same man?" Although the new teacher has been raised and educated by a missionary's wife, she belongs to the "lowliest and most despised group in Botswana, the bushmen," explained the London *Times* contributor. "Problems of caste and identity among black Africans are explored with sensitivity," remarked Martin Levin in the *New York Times Book Review.* Ravenscroft suggested that while the novel is a more personal one than Head's first, it is also a more political one, and he was "much impressed and moved by the power ... in the vitality of the enterprise, which projects the personal and the political implications in such vivid, authentic parallels that one feels they are being closely held together."

Head's critically well-received third novel, *A Question of Power,* relates the story of a young woman who experiences a mental breakdown. In a *Listener* review, Elaine Feinstein observed that "the girl moves through a world dominated by strange figures of supernatural good and evil, in which she suffers torment and enchantment in turn: at last she reaches the point where she can reject the clamorous visions which beset her and assert that there is 'only one God and his name is Man'." According to Bazin, Head acknowledged in an interview with Lee Nichols in her *Conversations with African Writers: Interviews with Twenty-six African Authors* that *A Question of Power* is largely autobiographical. "Like Elizabeth, the protagonist in *A Question of Power,* Bessie Head was born in a South African mental hospital," explained Bazin. "Her mother, a wealthy, upperclass, white woman, was to spend the rest of her life there, because in an apartheid society, she had allowed herself to be made pregnant by a black stableman. Until age thirteen, Bessie Head, like Elizabeth, was raised by foster parents and then put in a mission orphanage." Paddy Kitchen pointed out in the *New Statesman,* though, that the novel merely "contains parallels and winnowings from life, not journalist records," adding that "the incredible part is the clarity of the terror that has been rescued from such private, muddled nightmares." Similarly, Ravenscroft discerned no "confusion of identity" between the character and her creator: "Head makes one realize often how close is the similarity between the most fevered creations of a deranged mind and the insanities of deranged societies."

Gillian Stead Eilersen, in her introduction to *Tales of Tenderness and Power,* wrote, "Today most critics agree that *A Question of Power* is [Head's] greatest work." Lauded for the skill with which she recreated the hellish world of madness, Head was also credited by critics such as Jean Marquard in *London Magazine* with having written "the first metaphysical novel on the subject of nation and a national identity to come out of Southern Africa." In his *The Novel in the Third World,* Charles R. Larson credits the importance of *A Question of Power* not just to the introspection of its author but to her exploration of subjects hitherto "foreign to African fiction as a sub-division of the novel in the Third World: madness, sexuality, guilt." Noting that the protagonist's "Coloured classification, her orphan status at the mission, and her short-lived marriage" represent the origin of most of her guilt, Larson attributed these factors directly to "the South African policy of apartheid which treats people as something other than human beings." Further, Larson felt that Head intended the reader to consider all the "variations of power as the evils that thwart each individual's desire to be part of the human race, part of the brotherhood of man."

Critics have analyzed Head's first three novels, *When Rain Clouds Gather, Maru,* and *A Question of Power,* collectively in terms of their thematic concerns and progression. Suggesting that the three novels "deal in different ways with exile and oppression," Marquard noted that "the protagonists are outsiders, new arrivals who try to forge a life for themselves in a poor, under-populated third world country, where traditional and modern attitudes to soil and society are in conflict." Unlike other African writers who are also concerned with such familiar themes, said Marquard, Head "does not idealize the African past and ... she resists facile polarities, emphasizing personal rather than political motives for tensions between victim and oppressor." Ravenscroft recognized "a steady progression from the first novel to the third into ever murkier depths of alienation from the currents of South African, and African, matters of politics and power." Similarly, Marquard detected an inward movement "from a social to a metaphysical treatment of human insecurities and in the last novel the problem of adaptation to a new world, or new schemes of values, is located in the mind of a single character." Ravenscroft posited that "it is precisely this journeying into the various characters' most secret interior recesses of mind and (we must not fight shy of the word) of soul, that gives the three novels a quite remarkable cohesion and makes them a sort of trilogy." Considering *When Rain Clouds Gather, Maru,* and *A Question of Power* to be "progressive in their philosophical conclusion about the nature and source of racism," Cecil A. Abrahams suggested in *World Literature Written in English* that "ultimately, Head examines ... sources of evil and, conversely, of potential goodness. The most obvious source is the sphere of political power and authority; it is clear that if the political institutions which decree and regulate the lives of the society are reformed or abolished a better or new society can be established."

Head's collection of short stories, *The Collector of Treasures and Other Botswana Village Tales,* which was considered for the *New Statesman*'s Jock Campbell Award, explores several aspects of African life, especially the position of women. Eilersen has written that Head "could be regarded as a genuine teller of tales, part of an ancient African tradition, and she liked to refer to her short stories as tales." In the *Listener,* John

Mellors related Head's statement that "she has 'romanticised and fictionalized' data provided by old men of the tribe whose memories are unreliable." In its yoking of present to past, the collection also reveals the inevitable friction between old ways and new. The world of Head's work "is not a simply modernizing world but one that seeks, come what may, to keep women in traditionally imprisoning holes and corners," said Valerie Cunningham in the *New Statesman.* "It's a world where whites not only force all blacks into an exile apart from humanity but where women are pushed further still into sexist exile." In *The Collector of Treasures and Other Botswana Village Tales,* added Cunningham, "Head puts a woman's as well as a black case in tales that both reach back into tribal legend and cut deep into modern Africa."

Head's last two books published in her lifetime, *Serowe: Village of the Rain Wind* and *A Bewitched Crossroad: An African Saga,* are categorized as historical chronicles and combine historical accounts with the folklore of the region. The collected interviews in *Serowe* focus on a time frame that spans the eras of Khama the Great (1875-1923) and Tshekedi Khama (1926-1959) through the Swaneng Project beginning in 1963 under Patrick Van Rensburg, "a South African exile who, like Head herself, has devoted his life in a present-day Botswana to make some restitution for white rapacity," wrote Thorpe. Larson, who considers "reading any book by Bessie Head ... always a pleasure," added that *Serowe* "falls in a special category." Calling it a "quasi-sociological account," Larson described it as "part history, part anthology and folklore." "Its citizens give their testimonies, both personal and practical, in an unselfconscious way," said Paddy Kitchen in the *Listener,* "and Bessie Head—in true African style—orders the information so that, above all, it tells a story." *Serowe* is "a vivid portrait of a remarkable place ... one wishes there were many more studies of its kind," remarked a *British Book News* contributor. Kitchen believed it to be "a story which readers will find themselves using as a text from which to meditate on many aspects of society." And discussing her last book, *A Bewitched Crossroad,* which examines on a broader scope the African tribal wars in the early nineteenth century, Thorpe found that "in her moral history humane ideals displace ancestor-worship, and peace-loving strength displaces naked force." *A Bewitched Crossroad* presents a historical view of Africa from a black point of view and "focuses especially on the Bamangwato tribe and its famous chieftain, Khama III, who lived in Serowe and lies buried there with his successors, including his grandson, Seretse Khama," wrote Eilersen.

Three pieces of Head's writing which have been published posthumously are *Tales of Tenderness and Power, A Woman Alone,* and *A Gesture of Belonging.* A. A. Elder wrote in *Choice* that the publication of these additional works "provide[s] rich contexts for the work of Bessie Head." *Tales of Tenderness and Power* is a collection of stories dating from the early 1960s to the 1980s. Eilersen stated that not all of the pieces can accurately be called stories. She explained that "some are short descriptive observations, some are fictional or semi-fictional, some historical stories. But most of them have one thing in common. They are closely-rooted in actual events." The pieces are organized both chronologically, then, and with an eye to their type. The first four historical tales date from Head's earliest writings in Cape Town; the next seven pieces were written during a particularly difficult time, her early days in Serowe when she was a stateless refugee; these are then followed by historical tales more directly related to the events of the last years of her life. Of these last stories Eilersen wrote, "Bessie Head's own lack of a family, her many years of historical research, her life in a rural area of a free African state clearly play their part in focusing her attention on the soil as a symbol of a person's roots and identity." One story in particular which has caught the attention of several critics is called "The Prisoner Who Wore Glasses." In *Washington Post Book World* Larson praised Head's story this way: "In six terse pages, she brilliantly describes the subtle and shifting relationship between a political prisoner and a warden in a South African jail.... The story is also one of Bessie Head's few overt presentations of conditions in South Africa under the apartheid she had experienced until her flight into exile." "The Prisoner Who Wore Glasses" has been anthologized in several other places and translated into Danish, Dutch, and German.

Some of the pieces from *Tales of Tenderness and Power* reappear in *A Woman Alone* and themes of exile and identity are continued. The pieces in this volume are arranged chronologically, divided into three sections meant to reflect the three major phases of Head's life: her years in South Africa (1937-1964), early Botswanan exile and statelessness (1964-1979), and her later life as a citizen of Botswana (1979-1986). The pieces themselves are a mix of journalism, novel-writing, stories, interviews, histories, and autobiography. In his introduction Craig MacKenzie explained that "The writings that make up this collection ... are intended as a 'piece-meal' portrait of [Head's] life, a mosaic of sketches, essays and personal notes—making the present work primarily a biographical (as opposed to critical) study." Carole Boyce Davies found the volume helpful in that it allows one to see "in one place many of the themes with which [Head] worked, many of her positions on a variety of issues and, importantly, some of her creative reflections on the writing process" she stated in *Belles Lettres.*

*A Gesture of Belonging* is a collection of letters written from Head to Randolph Vigne, a former editor of *The New African* who worked with Head in South Africa, both in journalism and political activism. The letters reveal many of the themes of her fiction. According to Elder, "of significant literary interest is the light the letters shed on the composition and re-

ception of her works." The editor, Vigne, has added brief summaries in several places to clarify how the letters which follow relate to Head's particular situation at the time, such as what book she was working on, and where she was residing. The letters span the time period from October, 1965, to January, 1977.

Questioned by Fradkin about the manner in which she worked, Head explained: "Every story or book starts with something just for myself. Then from that small me it becomes a panorama—the big view that has something for everyone." Head "stresses in her novels the ideals of humility, love, truthfulness, freedom, and, of course, equality," wrote Bazin. At the time of her death, she had achieved an international reputation and had begun to write her autobiography. Davies wrote that "Head's untimely death in 1986 left a void in the African female literary world. Her works, like *Maru, The Collector of Treasures,* and *A Question of Power,* identified her as one of the most important critical thinkers and creative writers in the field." Her writings have been translated into several European languages, and she was invited on numerous all-expense-paid trips abroad. Despite these clear indications of success, however, Head lived in relative poverty throughout her life. Visiting her in 1985 MacKenzie found Head to be "a woman alone with her son, living in a two-roomed dwelling without the convenience of electricity or plumbing." Head obviously endured much difficulty during her life; despite her rejection of and by South Africa as well as the hardships of her exiled existence, however, she emerged from the racist and sexist discrimination that she both witnessed and experienced, to the affirmation she told Fradkin represented the only two themes present in her writing—"that love is really good ... and ... that it is important to be an ordinary person." She added, "More than anything I want to be noble." Eilersen wrote that Head "always retained her individualism. Though feeling strongly about racism and sexual discrimination—and having gained by the bitterest experience a considerable knowledge of both problems—she would never allow herself to be totally identified with either African nationalism or feminism. Her visions included whites and blacks, men and women. What she feared was the misuse of power, what she strove towards was human goodness and love."

*BIOGRAPHICAL/CRITICAL SOURCES:*

*BOOKS*

Abrahams, Cecil, editor, *The Tragic Life: Bessie Head and Literature in Southern Africa,* Africa World Press, 1990.
*Contemporary Literary Criticism,* Volume 25, Gale, 1983.
Gardner, Susan and Patricia E. Scott, compilers, *Bessie Head: A Bibliography,* National English Literary Museum, 1986.

Heywood, Christopher, editor, *Aspects of South African Literature,* Heinemann, 1976.

Larson, Charles R., *The Novel in the Third World,* Inscape Publishers, 1976.

MacKenzie, Craig and Cherry Clayton, editors, *Between the Lines: Interviews with Bessie Head, Sheila Roberts, Ellen Kuzwayo, Miriam Tlali,* National English Literary Museum, 1989.

Nichols, Lee, editor, *Conversations with African Writers: Interviews with Twenty-six African Authors,* Voice of America (Washington, DC), 1981.

Zell, Hans M., and others, *A New Reader's Guide to African Literature,* second edition, Holmes & Meier, 1983.


PERIODICALS


*Belles Lettres,* summer, 1991, pp. 52-53.
*Best Sellers,* March 15, 1969.
*Black Scholar,* March/April, 1986.
*Books Abroad,* winter, 1975.
*British Book News,* November, 1981.
*Choice,* December, 1991, p. 592.
*Essence,* October, 1987, p. 28.
*Listener,* February 4, 1971; November 22, 1973; April 20, 1978; July 2, 1981.
*London Magazine,* December/January, 1978-79.
*New Republic,* April 27, 1974.
*New Statesman,* May 16, 1969; November 2, 1973; June 2, 1978.
*New York Times Book Review,* September 26, 1971.
*Research in African Literatures,* fall, 1990, pp. 115-124; summer, 1988, pp. 170-181.
*Sage,* fall, 1986, pp. 44-47.
*Times Literary Supplement,* May 2, 1969; February 5, 1971; December 7, 1990, p. 1326.
*Washington Post Book World,* February 17, 1991, p. 4.
*Women's Review of Books,* January, 1991, pp. 1-4.
*World Literature Today,* winter, 1982; summer, 1983; winter, 1983; winter, 1986.
*World Literature Written in English,* Volume 17, number 1, 1978; Volume 17, number 2, 1978; Volume 18, number 1, 1979.


OBITUARIES:


PERIODICALS


*Journal of Commonwealth Literature,* Volume 21, number 1, 1986.
*Ms.,* January, 1987.
*Times* (London), May 1, 1986.

—*Sketch by Wendy W. Walters*


## HEATH, Roy A(ubrey) K(elvin) 1926-

*PERSONAL:* Born August 13, 1926, in Georgetown, British Guiana (now Guyana); son of Melrose A. (a teacher) and Jessie R. (a teacher) Heath; married Aemilia Oberli; children: three. *Education:* University of London, B.A., 1956.

*ADDRESSES: Agent*—Bill Hamilton, A. M. Heath and Company. Ltd., 40-42 William IV St., London WC2N 4DD, England.

*CAREER:* Called to the Bar, Lincoln's Inn, 1964. Worked in civil service in British Guiana, 1942-50; held various clerical jobs in London, England, 1951-58; teacher of French and German in London, 1959—.

*AWARDS, HONORS:* Drama award, Theatre Guild of Guyana, 1971, for *Inez Combray;* fiction prize, London *Guardian,* 1978, for *The Murderer;* Guyana Award for Literature, 1989, for *The Shadow Bride.*

*WRITINGS:*

NOVELS

*A Man Come Home,* Longman, 1974.
*The Murderer,* Allison & Busby, 1978.
*From the Heat of the Day* (part one of the "Georgetown" trilogy), Allison & Busby, 1979.
*One Generation* (part two of the "Georgetown" trilogy), Allison & Busby, 1980.
*Genetha* (part three of the "Georgetown" trilogy), Allison & Busby, 1981.
*Kwaku; or, The Man Who Could Not Keep His Mouth Shut,* Allison & Busby, 1982.
*Orealla,* Allison & Busby, 1984.
*The Shadow Bride,* Collins, 1988.

OTHER

*The Reasonable Adventurer,* University of Pittsburgh Press, 1964.
*Inez Combray* (stage play), produced in Georgetown, Guyana, 1972.
*Princeton Retrospectives: Twenty-Fifth-Year Reflections on a College Education,* Darwin Press, 1979.
*Art and History* (lectures), Ministry of Education (Georgetown, Guyana), 1983.
*Shadows Round the Moon* (memoir), Collins, 1990.

Contributor of short stories to anthologies, including *Firebird 2,* edited by T. J. Binding, Penguin, 1983; *Colours of a New Day: New Writing for South Africa,* edited by Sarah Lefanu and Stephen Hayward, Pantheon, 1990; and *So Very English,* edited by Marsha Rowe, Serpent's Tail, 1991. Contributor of short stories to periodicals, including *London, Savacou,* and *Kaie.*

*SIDELIGHTS:* A resident of London since 1951, Roy A. K. Heath sets his fiction in Georgetown, British Guiana (now Guyana), where he was born in 1926. "My work is intended to be a chronicle of twentieth-century Guyana," he told *CA.* By providing detailed descriptions of Georgetown streets, slums, brothels, and suburbs, combined with insights on local colonial roots, Heath not only provides information on contemporary Guyana but also reveals a deeper, more historical concern. "His reference to ancestors illustrates a vital aspect of Heath's vision as a novelist," comments Ian H. Munro in the *Dictionary of Literary Biography,* "for though the surface of his work is naturalistic, his narrative technique relentlessly probes the hidden realities of Guyanese life, the complex web of myths, dreams, customs, and prejudices arising from the aboriginal, African, and East Indian legacies." Recognizable are "the familiar landmarks of his fiction—the narrowness of colonial life, the fractured relationships between the sexes, and, above all," writes Clive Davis in *New Statesman and Society,* "ambiguous status of the 'respectable' classes."

Published in 1974, Heath's first novel, *A Man Come Home,* is a tale "pungent with the sex, sweat and wit of Georgetown's 'yard' society," as noted by Sally Emerson in *Books and Bookmen.* The main character, Bird Foster, is a slouch of a man, living off his mistress, Stephanie. Inspired suddenly to acquire money and independence, he leaves the community and eventually returns a rich man. Legend credits his new fortune to the powers of Fair Maid, a local spirit from Guyanese folklore. But Bird's happiness is short-lived. Stephanie casts off a gold chain given to Bird by Fair Maid, and the enraged supernatural being brings death to the hapless hero. Mixing modern story with myth, Heath's "allusions to Guyana's tormented history are reminders that the explosive, unexamined emotions ... have counterparts in the larger world," observes Munro.

A winner of the *Guardian* Fiction Prize, Heath's 1978 novel, *The Murderer,* is an in-depth examination of the thoughts and motivations of Galton Flood, who murders his wife, Gemma, after learning she had sexual relations with someone else— prior to their marriage. Flood struggles against "the web of domination and subservience lying at the heart of Guyanese society as Heath perceives it," says Munro, concluding that "the flood of repressed emotion he feels when he kills her is his one moment of emotional truth." The strength of the ethnic soul in this plot emanating from Georgetown is further support for the author's dedication to his natural homeland. "It is the geography of Guyana, states one of Heath's characters, that determines the disposition of her people," writes Shena

Mackay in the *Times Educational Supplement.* "Trapped between the oceans and the forest, they move like degagee silhouettes against the landscape.... In the main, people are isolated and frustrated; friendships founder, resentments and misunderstandings smoulder, good intentions explode into violence; love and regrets cannot be expressed."

Heath's "Georgetown" trilogy began with his 1979 novel, *From the Heat of the Day,* which follows the saga of the Armstrong family from the wedding of Sonny Armstrong and Gladys Davis and continues with discussions of their children's lives in subsequent volumes. *One Generation,* released in 1980, focuses on the life of their son, Rohan; *Genetha,* published in 1981, charts the life of their daughter. Tracing Guyanese culture from the 1920s to the 1950s, the trilogy is partly autobiographical. "Its common theme is social prejudice in all its uniquely Guyanese dimensions," Munro writes. *From the Heat of the Day* presents a foredoomed marriage. Gladys comes from an upper crust of society, and her family scorns Sonny, who is a mere civil servant. He reacts to their prejudice by being abusive to Gladys and is constantly torn between natural feelings of compassion and the drive to belittle her, as a result of his feeling inferior. The story takes place in the 1930s, and John Naughton in *Listener* comments that "the book is nicely evocative of the mood of that paralysed decade, and nicely evocative also of the sultry hopelessness of a society where few people have anything, and where the men have the lion's share of what little is going."

*One Generation* continues the history of Sonny Armstrong and his two children after his wife's death, focusing on his son, Rohan, who becomes an aimless civil servant who frequents pool halls with "a disreputable acquaintance known as Fingers," explains a reviewer in *Publishers Weekly.* After Fingers gets involved with Rohan's sister, Genetha, Rohan hurls himself into a tragic affair in another part of Guyana with an East Indian woman named Indrani. Although *One Generation* extends the reach of Heath's novel writing outside the Georgetown society, Munro feels that "the strange, exotic world of the East Indians tilts the novel toward the melodramatic. The murder of Rohan and Indrani at the hands of one of Rohan's underlings in the civil service, is unsatisfactorily motivated, with the novel thereafter taking on some of the qualities of a detective thriller."

In *Genetha* Heath focuses on the destructive relationship between Rohan's sister and Fingers, which results in a life of poverty and degradation for the title character. Taken in by a former family servant who is now a prostitute, Genetha becomes further enslaved by a world of sex-for-money. Ironically, Genetha is aware of the depravity she has fallen into— but also finds it strangely satisfying. "Heath's compassion for his ill-fated characters is impressive," comments a reviewer for *Publishers Weekly.*

Heath's 1982 novel, *Kwaku; or, The Man Who Could Not Keep His Mouth Shut,* is about a shoemaker who lives in a small Guyanese village with eight children to support and dreams of one day becoming successful. He travels to the Guyanese town of New Amsterdam and passes himself off as a medicine man. When some patients are accidentally made well by using his prescribed garlic purgatives, Kwaku becomes instantly successful. "No matter what impossible circumstances he boxes himself into, Kwaku manages to escape by sheer impudence and buoyancy," says Charles R. Larson in the *New York Times Book Review.* Kwaku's newfound social status and financial success take him to new heights. But when, in his prime of achievement, he returns to his old village, his world starts to come apart. His wife is seized by an illness that his remedies cannot cure, and a new medicine man begins to challenge Kwaku's monopoly of the business. At its compassionate close, the novel shows Kwaku and his wife depending upon one another for support. Alan Bold in the *Times Literary Supplement* concludes that "Heath puts all of his considerable skills—of narration, characterization and description—on display in a book that conveys its comic vision with wisdom as well as wit."

Heath's 1984 work, *Orealla,* takes place in 1920 Georgetown, where "the aura of gas lamps, shadows, burning sun, and horses passing on rain-sodden streets provides a haunting background to this most disturbing of Heath's novels," comments Munro. *Orealla* is the story of Ben, a free-lance writer and begrudging private chauffeur, who moonlights as a burglar. Robbing houses is his way of retaliating against class and racial prejudice in Guyanese society. He craves freedom but is saddled with a job as driver for a civil servant, Schwartz. Although he dreams of escaping to freedom by traveling to the village of Orealla, he instead kills the overbearing Schwartz which affords him a measure of freedom that does not require a physical journey.

Heath's 1988 novel about East Indians living in Guyana, *The Shadow Bride,* focuses on the well-to-do Singh family. One of the children, Betta, dedicates his life to healing the poor and sickly. In the course of the novel, Betta's widowed mother emerges as a destructive force. She has been brought from India by Betta's father, but rages against her exile. Additionally, she works to influence the hapless Betta to consider himself more an Indian than a citizen of Guyana. Although torn by conflict, Betta ultimately comes to accept the contradictions in his life, avoiding ultimate despair. Calling the novel a tale of "the tragic isolation of this Indian version of Medea," John Spurling in the London *Observer* noted that the mother character "is as fully explored and credible as that of the place, time and people amongst which he sets her."

Of Heath's general appeal to readers in countries other than Guyana, Reed Way Dasenbrock in *World Literature Today*

comments that "Heath's portrait of a society undergoing but resisting creolization is as relevant to the Britain in which he writes and lives as to the Guyana about which he writes." By conveying in his eight novels his compassion for the land of his birth, Heath has enriched the world's consciousness of Guyana. He has, in Munro's opinion, "added a new dimension to the literary map of Guyana."

*BIOGRAPHICAL/CRITICAL SOURCES:*

*BOOKS*

*Dictionary of Literary Biography:* Volume 117, *Twentieth-Century Caribbean and Black African Writers, First Series,* Gale, 1992.

*PERIODICALS*

*Booklist,* September, 1982.
*Books and Bookmen,* April, 1975.
*Listener,* December 13, 1979.
*Los Angeles Times Book Review,* April 12, 1992.
*New Statesman and Society,* December 7, 1979; May 11, 1990.
*New York Times Book Review,* January 15, 1984.
*Observer* (London), April 17, 1988.
*Publishers Weekly,* June 25, 1982; January 6, 1992.
*Times Educational Supplement,* February 22, 1985.
*Times Literary Supplement,* December 27, 1974; November 12, 1982; July 27, 1984.
*World Literature Today,* winter, 1989; autumn, 1991.

—*Sketch by John Arthur Shanks*

\*     \*     \*

## HEMPHILL, Essex

*CAREER:* Editor, poet, and essayist.

*WRITINGS:*

(Editor) *Brother to Brother* (anthology of writings by black gay men), Alyson Publications, 1991.
*Ceremonies: Prose and Poetry,* New American Library, 1992.

Also author of two self-published chapbooks of poetry, *Earth Life* and *Conditions,* both 1985; contributed to the films *Looking for Langston,* by Isaac Julien, and *Tongues Untied,* by Marlon Riggs.

*SIDELIGHTS:* Since the beginning of the modern gay liberation movement in the 1970s, a steadily growing body of literature by gay and lesbian writers has explored issues of gay identity, the gay community, and the place of gay men and lesbians in mainstream society. As the movement gained an even greater momentum in the 1980s, the contributions of black gay and lesbian writers assumed increasing importance. As an editor, poet, and essayist, Essex Hemphill has been a key figure in the emergence of a distinctive African American perspective in the overall field of gay literature.

Although Essex Hemphill grew up in a comfortable working-class neighborhood in Washington, D.C., he still had to contend with the racism that he observed around him. And as he entered adolescence and became increasingly aware of his own homosexuality, he had to contend with yet another kind of oppression, although he might have been a few years shy of learning that the word for that oppression was "homophobia." As Hemphill writes in his book *Ceremonies,* "My sexual curiosity would have blossomed in any context, but in Southeast Washington, where I grew up, I had to carefully allow my petals to unfold. If I had revealed them too soon they would have been snatched away, brutalized, and scattered down alleys. I was already alert enough to know what happened to the flamboyant boys at the school who were called 'sissies' and 'faggots.' I could not have endured then the violence and indignities they often suffered."

In his twenties, Hemphill was attracted to the ideas embodied in the black nationalist movement that flourished in the 1960s and 1970s. But as he got older, he began to question the rhetoric that had previously inspired him. "I moved away from black nationalism," Hemphill writes in *Ceremonies,* "as being too narrow a politic for the interests that reside in me." But he also found that a narrowly defined lesbian and gay political ideology could not adequately accommodate his personal vision, and went on to seek his own unique creative voice.

That literary voice had to accommodate the numerous conflicts and contradictions that Hemphill faced, both as an African American male in a predominantly white society afflicted by racism, and as a gay man in a predominantly heterosexual society afflicted by homophobia. And as many black gay writers, including Hemphill, have expressed repeatedly in recent years, being both black and gay carries a special burden, because the homophobia that characterizes the black community in contemporary American society is qualitatively different, and in some ways more intense, than that of the predominantly white mainstream. Throughout American history, the culture of slavery and racism often encouraged white men to bolster their own sense of masculinity by asserting their dominance over black men. In response to this violent and abusive history, the black community placed a high premium on strong male images. Homosexuality, understood only through stereotypes of effeminacy and submissiveness, was

particularly repugnant in this context. Thus, where many in white American were reluctant to tolerate homosexuals, many in black America were reluctant even to acknowledge that homosexuals existed in their community. Moreover, the racism that prevailed in mainstream American society could also be found in the newly emerging and predominantly white gay community, an especially frustrating and disheartening fact for the many black gay men and lesbians seeking to participate in the newfound gay liberation of the past 25 years.

Given these multiple layers of oppression and rejection, black gay and lesbian writers were truly courageous in staking out a new literary terrain for themselves. The writings of 35 such black gay men were gathered by Hemphill in *Brother to Brother,* an anthology of poetry and prose. The pieces in this collection are primarily autobiographical, and lend a personal immediacy to discussions of racism, religious intolerance, homophobia, and life in the age of AIDS. Given the sensitivity of these topics, *Brother to Brother* could not help but be controversial. The book is divided into four sections, each with a distinct theme. The first section, called "When I Think of Home," focuses on varying notions of home and family, from those we grow up in to those we choose and create for ourselves as adults. The second section, called "Baby, I'm for Real," explores the false identities that black gay men create for themselves and hide behind, identities that often represent what they wish they could truly be or could truly have, including white skin or heterosexuality. The third section, called "Hold Tight, Gently," considers life in the age of AIDS, and includes personal accounts of dealing with the epidemic, or at times of choosing not to deal with it. The final section, "The Absence of Fear," contrasts the way black men are represented in mainstream culture with the way black men represent themselves. It includes discussions of homoerotic images of black men by the gay white photographer Robert Mapplethorpe, as well as recent films by and about black gay men, like Isaac Julien's *Looking for Langston* and Marlon Riggs's *Tongues Untied.* Hemphill himself contributes a selection of poetry which, according to Donald Suggs in his *Village Voice* review of the book, "effectively brackets and enlarges many of the conflicts in the anthology."

*Ceremonies,* an anthology of poetry and prose written entirely by Hemphill, spans the author's entire writing career, and includes pieces from his self-published 1985 chapbooks *Earth Life* and *Conditions* as well as previously unpublished work. As did the writings by Hemphill and others in *Brother to Brother,* the poems and essays in *Ceremonies* continue to explore the double burden of being a minority within a minority. "One of Hemphill's most persistent themes [is] the outsider confronting the dominant culture," wrote David Trinidad in his *Village Voice Literary Supplement* review of the book. Hemphill "has forged—with few role models to emulate, and with little or no support from the white gay literary establishment—an identity and a style characterized by anger and point-blank honesty," according to Trinidad. In addition to overtly political pieces, Hemphill includes love poems, celebrations of sexuality, and affirmations of gay identity, along with heartfelt and moving accounts of the fears and dangers of growing up black and gay. "He makes passionate common sense," wrote Thomas Tavis in his *Library Journal* review, concluding that "this is urgent, fiercely telling work." According to Craig Allen Seymour II, writing in the *Advocate,* Hemphill "is poised to become the most widely known black gay writer since James Baldwin."

*BIOGRAPHICAL/CRITICAL SOURCES:*

*PERIODICALS*

*Advocate,* June 2, 1992, p. 38.
*Library Journal,* October 1, 1992, p. 88.
*Los Angeles Times Book Review,* September 8, 1991, p. 18.
*The Village Voice,* October 1, 1991, p. 74.
*Village Voice Literary Supplement,* June 1992, pp. 7-8.

—*Sketch by Michael Broder*

\* \* \*

## HENSHAW, James Ene 1924-

*PERSONAL:* Born August 29, 1924 in Calabar, Nigeria; son of Richard (a political agent) and Susana (Antigha Cobham Ene) Henshaw; married Caroline Nchelem Amadi (a dress designer), February 15, 1958; children: James Ewa, Caroline Iyi-Afo, Emmanuel Ekeng, Susan Ene, Joseph Antigha Ene, Helen Bassey, Paul Itiaba, John Peter Etebong. *Education:* Christ the King College, Onitsha, Nigeria, 1938-41; National University of Ireland, Dublin, M.D. 1949; University of Wales, Cardiff, T.D.D., 1954. *Religion:* Roman Catholic.

*ADDRESSES: Home*—Itiaba House, Calabar Rd., Calabar, Nigeria.

*CAREER:* Physician, playwright, writer. Medical consultant to Government of Eastern Nigeria, 1955-78; Controller of medical services in South Eastern State of Nigeria (now Cross River State of Nigeria), 1968-72; senior consultant on tuberculosis control to Rivers State of Nigeria, 1973-78.

*MEMBER:* National Council on Health, Nigerian Medical Council, Chairman, South Eastern State branch of St. John's Ambulance Association of Nigeria (chair, 1973), Cultural Centre Board of Arts Council of the Cross River State of Nigeria, Association of Nigerian Authors, Nigerian Medical Association, African Club, Port Harcourt Sports Club.

*AWARDS, HONORS:* Henry Carr Memorial Cup, First Prize, playwriting, All Nigerian Festival of the Arts, 1952 for *The Jewel of the Shrine;* named Knight of the Order of St. Gregory the Great by Pope Paul VI, 1965; appointed editor, *Eastern Nigeria Medical Circular,* special publication *Nigerian Independence,* 1960-61; Officer, Order of the Niger for medical services and literary contributions, 1978.

*WRITINGS:*

*PLAYS*

*This Is Our Chance: Plays from West Africa* (includes *The Jewel of the Shrine, A Man of Character,* and *This Is Our Chance*), University of London Press, London, UK, 1957.
*Children of the Goddess and Other Plays* (includes *Companion for a Chief, Magic in the Blood,* and *Children of the Goddess*), University of London Press, London, UK, 1964.
*Medicine for Love,* University of London Press, London, UK, 1964.
*Dinner for Promotion,* (includes *The African Writer, the Audience,* and *The English Language*), University of London Press, London, UK, 1967.
*The Jewel of the Shrine,* in *Plays from Black Africa,* edited by Fredric M. Litto, Hill and Wang, 1968.
*Enough is Enough: A Play of the Nigerian Civil War* (first produced in Benin City, Nigeria, 1975), Ethiope Publishing House, 1976.
*A Song to Mary Charles, Irish Sister of Charity* (produced Owerri, 1981), [Calabar, Nigeria], 1985.

Contributor to medical journals in Africa and United Kingdom. Contributor of short stories to periodicals, including "Matron's Darling" in *Eastern Nigerian Medical Journal.*

*SIDELIGHTS:* James Ene Henshaw commented: "Writing plays has been a long-time hobby and comes as a welcome intrusion whenever opportunity occurs in the course of medical practice. It is a great relaxation for which I am always grateful. I do not know how it happened, but I am sure I just strayed into it. The profession itself gives one a lot of opportunity to observe and to interpret all kinds of human behavior and attitudes.

"My books are almost exclusively directed to the young African audience. The matters treated are common, and not so common, situations of contradictions, conflicts, and agreements. The themes are varied and the introductory essays cover my views on many areas of interest to the African reader in particular. The young African should carry with them their praiseworthy traditions in the course of rapid social progress. These good traditions, such as the respect for the older person (even of the same 'age group') and the obligatory sharing of the other person's burdens, should not merely make the young African distinct, but should continue to be the 'earth he walks on, and the air he breathes' (from *This Is Our Chance*).

"Nigerian theatre is very lively. The plays range from Greek-style tragedies and African folklore to something like what may be called 'realism.' I run away from realism that preaches defeat and pessimism. I prefer a blending of the natural and the ideal, which are beautifully represented in the ordinary lives and traditions of the people of Nigeria.

"Perhaps if I have to state the one single factor which urges me to write, I shall come back to say simply that it is the need to influence younger people through the dramatic medium, which is natural to their environment and which delights as well as informs them. To the young African, especially the young Nigerian, I try in my books to remain basic, communicative, personal, and, by different methods, to keep a dialogue of understanding between them and me. My criterion for a suitable play for the young African is that in which anybody in the audience should be able to feel that he or she could easily have written that play and that what is being shown on the stage or the television screen is what happened or could have happened to them just that day."

\*   \*   \*

## HERRON, Carolivia 1947-

*PERSONAL:* Born July 22, 1947, in Washington, DC; daughter of Oscar Smith and Georgia Carol (Johnson) Herron. *Education:* Eastern Baptist College, A.B., 1969; Villanova University, M.A., 1973; University of Pennsylvania, M.A., Ph.D., 1985.

*ADDRESSES: Home*—34 Rockport Rd., Unit 1, Gloucester, MA 01930.

*CAREER:* Harvard University, Cambridge, MA, assistant professor of Afro-American studies and comparative literature, 1986-90; Mount Holyoke College, South Hadley, MA, director of Epicenter for the Study of Epic Literature, 1988—, associate professor of English, 1990-92. National Endowment for the Humanities, member of board of directors of curriculum development program, 1988-90; Carleton College, visiting professor, 1989.

*MEMBER:* Modern Language Association, Renaissance Society of America, Classical Association of New England, African Literature Association, Latin American Studies Association.

*AWARDS, HONORS:* Fulbright scholarship, 1985-86; Beinecke Library of Yale University, visiting fellow, 1988; Bunting fellow, Radcliffe College, 1988-89; Folger Shakespeare Library, visiting fellow, 1989.

*WRITINGS:*

*Thereafter Johnnie* (novel), Random House, 1991.
(Editor) *Selected Works of Angelina Weld Grimke,* Oxford University Press, 1991.

Contributor of articles to professional journals.

*WORK IN PROGRESS: Early African-American Poetry,* an anthology to be published by Vintage Press; *Asenath,* a novel to be published by Random House; *African-American Epic Tradition,* a three-volume literary history; *Nappy Hair,* an illustrated children's book.

*SIDELIGHTS:* Carolivia Herron published her first novel, *Thereafter Johnnie,* in 1991. Written over a period of eighteen years, *Thereafter Johnnie* is a mythic family saga set against the backdrop of a worldwide race war in the year 2000. The novel chronicles the decline and ultimate redemption of a black middle-class family while exploring the historical and psychological roots of ongoing racial tension in contemporary American life. One character in the novel calls it "a mythological narration of incest and national identity."

At the center of *Thereafter Johnnie* is the Snowdon family. John Christopher Snowdon is a successful Washington, D.C., heart surgeon with three daughters. Snowdon is estranged from his wife, Camille, and out of loneliness he commits incest with his seductive middle daughter, Patricia. The daughter gives birth to his child, a girl with blue eyes whom she names Johnnie. Exiled by her family, Patricia raises Johnnie alone in a Georgetown house until her growing despair leads her to commit suicide. Seventeen-year-old Johnnie—who was mute until she was fourteen—then leaves Georgetown for the first time and walks into Washington on an quest for identity. There she discovers Patricia's two sisters and, eventually, her long-suffering grandmother, Camille. Camille's welcome begins a process of healing for the family.

Herron's novel is one of mythic complexity; it sweeps into the past to explore the corrosive effects of America's history of slavery and miscegenation in modern black-white relations. And it inches into a future in which Washington, D.C., has been devastated in a racial war, but where Johnnie assumes the heroic proportions of a messiah who will be a source of light and renewal. The result is a dense, demanding book that draws heavily on the language and themes of the Old and New

Testaments, the ancient Greek epics, the legend of the Holy Grail, and African American folk legend.

*Thereafter Johnnie* is intensely autobiographical. In an interview with *Newsweek,* Herron stated that writing the book unleashed long-forgotten memories of sexual abuse she endured as a child in Washington, D.C.: "Two or three times a week I was taken from nursery school to a house of prostitution on 14th Street, where I became the partner of a man I called Big White Daddy.... I was 4 years old." Herron also stated that as an infant she was raped by an uncle. Although most of Herron's family support her in her allegations, some of her relatives deny that this incident occurred. Some of the most vividly realized scenes in *Thereafter Johnnie* confront the taboos of rape and incest that Herron herself says she confronted as a child.

*Thereafter Johnnie* was widely reviewed when it was published, inviting comparison with the work of other African American women writers such as Toni Morrison and Alice Walker. Though *New Statesman and Society* contributor Andrea Stuart considered Herron's style to be "overblown and opaque" at times, the reviewer also noted that "her incandescent and visionary prose-poetry is capable, like a divinely wrought gospel song, of raising hairs on the back of your neck or moving you to tears." Herron, according to Richard Eder in the *Los Angeles Times Book Review,* "has written a swirling and terrifying epic." The critic went on to comment that the author's "vision is as harsh and fulminating as a prophet's." In the *New York Times Book Review,* John Bierhorst deemed *Thereafter Johnnie* "an accomplished, lyrical piece of writing that is also passionately intellectual." Bierhorst added, "Like myth itself, *Thereafter Johnnie* does not provide a neat ending. Rather it offers possibilities; the struggle goes on.... it is more than a saga of black revitalization. Part vision, part parable, it is a story for all America."

Carolivia Herron once commented: "As the director of the Epicenter for the Study and Promotion of Epic Literature, I am currently working along with computer professionals to develop interactive computer books based on epic literature such as *The Illiad, Chaka the Great,* and *Beowulf.* This project includes the computer programming of my own faerie tale, *The Gazelle of the Stars,* which fictionalizes and fantasizes the heroics of recovering from severe childhood sexual abuse. A third aspect of the Epicenter program is the development of a computer program for young people, *Mayfair Mansions,* in conjunction with natural and anthropological scientists at the Simthsonian Institutes in Washington, D.C. Mayfair Mansions is an actual African American community in Washington and the computer software bearing its name is a cluster of educational and entertaining experiences focusing on Washington, D.C."

*BIOGRAPHICAL/CRITICAL SOURCES:*

*BOOKS*

Herron, Carolivia, *Thereafter Johnnie,* Random House, 1991.

*PERIODICALS*

*Los Angeles Times Book Review,* April 28, 1991, p. 3.
*New Statesman and Society,* June 5, 1992, pp. 40-41.
*Newsweek,* July 15, 1991, p. 53.
*New York Times Book Review,* June 23, 1991, p. 16.
*Publishers Weekly,* March 1, 1991, p. 58.
*Times* (London), July 4, 1992.
*Washington Post Book World,* June 9, 1991, p. 11.

\*   \*   \*

## HILL, Errol Gaston  1921-

*PERSONAL:* Born August 5, 1921, in Trinidad, Trinidad and Tobago; son of Thomas David (an accountant) and Lydia (Gibson) Hill; married Grace Hope (a teacher), August 12, 1956; children: Da'aga, Claudia, Melina, Aaron. *Education:* University of London, diploma in drama, 1951; Royal Academy of Dramatic art (England), graduate diploma, 1951; Yale University, B.A., 1962, M.F.A., 1962, D.F.A., 1966.

*ADDRESSES: Home*—3 Haskins Road, Hanover, NH 03755.

*CAREER:* British Broadcasting Corporation, London, England, announcer and actor, 1951-52; University of the West Indies, Kingston, Jamaica, and Port-of-Spain, Trinidad, creative arts tutor, 1953-58, 1962-65; University of Ibadan, Ibadan, Nigeria, teaching fellow in drama, 1965-67; Richmond College of the City University of New York, New York City, associate professor of drama, 1967-68; Dartmouth College, Hanover, NH, associate professor, 1968-69, professor of drama, 1969-76, John D. Willard Professor of Drama and Oratory, 1976-89, head of department, 1970-73, 1976-79, director of theatre for summer repertory programs, 1979-82, 1984, and 1987. Guest lecutrer and director of Graduate Theatre Workshop, Leeds University, 1978; scholar-in-residence at Bullagio Study and conference center, 1981 and 1991; visiting professor at University of California, San Diego, 1982; Chancellor's Distinguished Professor at University of California, Berkeley, 1983. Evaluator, National Association of Schools Theatre; consultant, National Humanities Faculty, 1971-80. Producer and director of numerous plays and pageants. *Military service:* U.S. military engineer, Trinidad, 1941-43.

*MEMBER:* American Society for Theatre Research, Association for Commonwealth Language and Literature Studies.

*AWARDS, HONORS:* British Council Scholar, 1949-51; Rockefeller Foundation fellow, 1958-60 and 1965; Theatre Guild of America playwriting fellow, 1961-62; Hummingbird Gold Medal, government of Trinidad and Tobago, 1973; Barnard Hewitt Award for outstanding research in theater history research, American Theatre Association, 1985; Bertram Joseph Award for Shakespeare studies, Queens College of the City University of New York, 1985; Guggenheim fellow, 1985-86; Fulbright fellow, 1988; Presidential Medal for outstanding leadership and achievement, Dartmouth College, 1991.

*WRITINGS:*

*EDITOR*

*Caribbean Plays,* Extramural Department, University of the West Indies, Volume 1, 1958, Volume 2, 1965.
(And contributor) *The Artist in West Indian Society,* Extramural Department, University of the West Indies, 1964.
*A Time ... and a Season: Eight Caribbean Plays,* Extramural Department, University of the West Indies, 1976.
*Three Caribbean Plays for Secondary Schools,* Longman, 1979.
*The Theatre of Black Americans: A Collection of Critical Essays,* two volumes, Prentice-Hall, 1980.
*Plays for Today,* Longman, 1985.
*Black Heroes: Seven Plays,* Applause Theatre Book Publishers, 1989.
*The Jamaican Stage, 1655-1900: Profile of a Colonial Theatre,* University of Massachusetts Press, 1992.

*CRITICAL STUDIES*

*The Trinidad Carnival: Mandate for a National Theatre,* University of Texas Press, 1972.
(With Peter Greer) *Why Pretend?* (a dialogue on the arts in education), Chandler, 1973.
*Shakespeare in Sable: A History of Black Shakespearean Actors,* foreword by John Houseman, University of Massachusetts Press, 1984.
*The Jamaican Stage, 1655-1900: Profile of a Colonial Theatre,* University of Massachusetts Press, 1992.

*PLAYS*

*The Ping-Pong* (one-act), Extramural Department, University of the West Indies, 1958.

*Man Better Man* (three-act folk musical; first produced on Broadway at St. Mark's Playhouse, July 2, 1969), in *Three Plays from the Yale School of Drama,* edited by John Gassner, Dutton, 1964.
*Dance Bongo* (one-act), Extramural Department, University of the West Indies, 1965.
*Oily Portraits* (one-act), Extramural Department, University of the West Indies, 1966.
*Square Peg* (one-act), Extramural Department, University of the West Indies, 1966.
*Dilemma* (one-act), Extramural Department, University of the West Indies, 1966.
*Strictly Matrimony* (one-act), Extramural Department, University of the West Indies, 1966.
*Wey-Wey* (one-act), Extramural Department, University of the West Indies, 1966.

Also author of *Broken Melody,* 1954. Plays anthologized in *Caribbean Literature,* edited by G. R. Coulthard, University of London Press, 1966; and *Black Drama Anthology,* edited by Woody King and Ron Milner, Signet, 1971.

*OTHER*

Contributor to books, including *Resource Development in the Caribbean,* McGill University, 1972. Contributor to periodicals, including *West Indian Review, Caribbean, Trinidad Guardian, Ethnomusicology, Cutures, Caribbean Quarterly, Theatre Survey, Black American Literature Forum,* and *Theatre Journal.* Editor, *Bulletin of Black Theatre* (of the American Theatre Association), 1971-78.

*SIDELIGHTS:* Errol Gaston Hill is an educator, an editor of anthologies, and a playwright. His drama collections and critical studies focus on making the reader aware of the many contributions black dramatists and actors have made to the theater in the United States, Jamaica, and the Caribbean countries. His book *Shakespeare in Sable: A History of Black Shakespearean Actors* documents "a long and often distinguished history of black actors who, while struggling against great adversity, made their mark on classical theatre," writes Robin Breon in the Toronto *Globe and Mail.* Covering the years from the 1820s through the 1970s, *Shakespeare in Sable* is the first book to describe how difficult it was, and sometimes still is, for even the most highly skilled black actors and actresses to secure roles in Shakespearean productions. *Shakespeare in Sable* is, therefore, "a story of courage to the point of heroism, persistence on to madness, and dreaming without hope," concludes James V. Hatch in *Black American Literature Forum.*

Hill's *Black Heroes: Seven Plays* was described by Joel Berkowitz in *Black American Literature Forum* as providing "a theatrical chronicle of episodes in the black struggle for freedom and equality over the last two centuries." The collection features plays telling the stories of such notable African Americans as Paul Robeson, Nat Turner, and Harriet Tubman as well as Jamaican and Haitian activists Jean Jacques Dessalines and Marcus Garvey. In his introduction to the anthology, Hill maintains that his purpose is "identifying black heroes and ensuring that they are appropriately memorialized for present and future generations."

*BIOGRAPHICAL/CRITICAL SOURCES:*

*PERIODICALS*

*American Anthropologist,* August, 1973.
*American Historical Review,* June, 1985.
*Black American Literature Forum,* summer, 1985, spring, 1991, pp. 209-11.
*Comparative Drama,* spring, 1986.
*Globe and Mail* (Toronto), February 9, 1985.
*Journal of American Folklore,* April, 1975.
*Shakespeare Quarterly,* summer, 1986.
*Spotlight* (Jamaica), October, 1958.
*Theatre Journal,* October, 1985.
*Urbanite,* March, 1961.

\*    \*    \*

## HILLIARD, Asa G(rant) III 1933-

*PERSONAL:* Born August 22, 1933, in Galveston, TX; married; wife's name, Patsy Jo; children: Asa IV, Robi Nsenga Bailey, Patricia Nefertari, Hakim Sequenenre. *Education:* University of Denver, B.A., 1955, M.A., 1961, Ed.D., 1963.

*ADDRESSES: Office*—Georgia State University, P.O. Box 243, Atlanta, GA 30303.

*CAREER:* Denver Public Schools, Denver, CO, teacher, 1955-60; University of Denver, teaching fellow, 1960-63; San Francisco State University, San Francisco, CA, professor, and dean of education, 1963-83; Georgia State University, Atlanta, distinguished professor of education, 1980—. Automated Services Inc., director of research, 1970-72; National Black Child Development Institute, member of board of directors, 1973-75; American Psychology Association, member of Board of Ethnic and Minority Affairs, 1982-84.

*MEMBER:* National Association for the Education of Young Children.

*AWARDS, HONORS:* Fellow, National Defense Education Act (University of Denver), 1960-63; Knight Commander of

the Human Order of African Redemption, 1972; Distinguished Leadership Award, Association of Teacher Educators, 1983; award for outstanding scholarship, Association of Black Psychologists, 1984.

*WRITINGS:*

*An Exploratory Study of Relationships Between Student Teachers' Personality, Ability, Lower Division Grades, and the Student Teachers' Evaluation of Pupils,* University Microfilms, 1963.
(Editor with Larry Williams and Nia Damali) *The Teachings of Ptahhotep: The Oldest Book in the World,* illustrated by Babatunde K. S. Abdullah, Blackwood Press, 1987.

Also author of *Strengths: African American Children and Families,* 1982; and, with Betty M. Caldwell, *What Is Quality Child Care?,* 1985.

\*    \*    \*

## HILLIARD, David 1942-

*PERSONAL:* Born May 15, 1942, in Alabama; son of Lee and Lelar (Williams) Hilliard; married Patricia Parks (divorced); children: Darryl, Patrice, Dorian. *Politics:* Democrat. *Religion:* Baptist.

*ADDRESSES: Home*—Berkeley, CA. *Office*—United Public Employees Local 790, 522 Grand Ave., Oakland, CA 94612.

*CAREER:* Black Panther party, Oakland, CA, program administrator, 1966-74; Campaign for Economic Democracy, Los Angeles, CA, community liaison representative, 1979-83; People's Organized Response Inc., Oakland, executive director, 1989—; United Public Employees Local 790, Oakland, field representative, 1990—. Participant in documentaries, including *The Rise and Fall of the Black Panther Party,* Public Broadcasting System, 1990. Member of International Longshoreman's and Warehouseman's Union.

*AWARDS, HONORS:* Honored by the City Council of Oakland, CA, 1993; John George Award for Social Change, 1993.

*WRITINGS:*

(With Lewis Cole) *This Side of Glory: The Autobiography of David Hilliard and the Story of the Black Panther Party,* Little, Brown, 1993.

*WORK IN PROGRESS: Genet' in America* with Robert Sandbarg.

*SIDELIGHTS:* David Hilliard first gained fame for his involvement with the Black Panther party, a militant, revolutionary black organization founded in 1966 in Oakland, California. The party was founded by Huey Newton, a childhood friend of Hilliard's, and Bobby Seale, who visualized it as a forum through which black Americans could demand equal rights. The Panthers opposed Martin Luther King, Jr.'s philosophy of peaceful change and believed in armed struggle to gain power for black Americans. Because of their aggressive philosophy, the Panthers were perceived as a threat to internal security by the then Federal Bureau of Investigation (FBI) director, J. Edgar Hoover. As a result, the party was closely watched. Following the arrest of Newton, who was charged with murder after an encounter with the police in the late 1960s, party members initiated a "Free Huey" campaign to free their leader and became the focus of national attention. During these years Hilliard, along with Newton and Eldridge Cleaver, was one of the highest officials of the party, which began to disintegrate in the mid-1970s.

*This Side of Glory,* Hilliard's first book, is an autobiographical account of the years he spent as part of the Panthers, including the rise and fall of the party and the effect it has had on his own life. Reviewing the book in the *Stamford Sun,* Emily Laber states that Hilliard "depicts with bare honesty and a vivid sense of immediacy every facet of this compelling and ultimately tragic story." *Washington Post Book World* reviewer Scott McLemee remarks that *This Side of Glory* presents "a vivid, at times insightful record of the party's heyday, as recalled by a participant who witnessed important events from his vantage point near the top of the group's hierarchy." Critics largely agree that the book, besides being a history of the party, is also, as McLemee puts it, "a series of tributes to friends and comrades who died in violent confrontations with the law." The narrative of the book begins with Newton's death in 1989 and goes back to reveal instances of Hilliard's own childhood, his friendship with Newton and decision to join the Panthers because of his own dissatisfaction with life, and, finally, the decline of the organization and his and Newton's addictions to alcohol and drugs.

Hilliard commented: "I began my writing career basically to correct the misinformation that had been constantly put out by the FBI. My primary purpose for writing *This Side of Glory* was to set the record straight about the true meaning of the Black Panther party and to demonstrate to the youth that it is possible to bring about change if they're willing to sacrifice and commit themselves to long arduous struggle for the things they believe in. This book will act as a historical reference for people who are willing to commit themselves to social change. This is a 'how to' book, showing it is possible to make changes in the system."

"My writing habits mainly consist of ingesting a lot of historical material to jog my memory, talking with former party members, and doing a lot of research. Writers who have influenced my work are Franz Fanon, Malcolm X, Huey P. Newton, Eldridge Cleaver, Bobby Seale, George Jackson, and Ralph Ellison. We share a lot in common, and they were the foundation for my memoirs. It's a continuation of their writings.

"To aspiring writers: Be prepared to do extensive research into the subject, and don't give up because it can become a very disappointing and tiring process. Definitely find a good agent to market your work."

*BIOGRAPHICAL/CRITICAL SOURCES:*

*PERIODICALS*

*New York Post,* January 25, 1993, p. 6.
*New York Times,* May 5, 1993, p. A17.
*San Jose Mercury News,* March 14, 1993.
*Stamford Sun,* February 1, 1993.
*Washington Post Book World,* March 28, 1993.

\*　　\*　　\*

## HIMES, Chester (Bomar) 1909-1984

*PERSONAL:* Born July 29, 1909, in Jefferson City, MO; died November 12, 1984, of Parkinson's disease, in Moraira, Spain; son of Joseph Sandy (a teacher) and Estelle (a teacher; maiden name, Bomar) Himes; married Jean Lucinda Johnson, August 13, 1937 (divorced); married wife Lesley. *Education:* Attended Ohio State University, 1926-28.

*CAREER:* Writer. Convicted of armed robbery of $53,000 at the age of nineteen and sentenced to twenty years in Ohio State Penitentiary; while in prison, began to write and contribute prison stories to magazines; released from prison about 1935, after serving six years; worked for Federal Writer's Project, subsequently completing a history of Cleveland (never published); worked briefly as a journalist for the *Cleveland Daily News,* as a writer for the labor movement and the Communist party, and at odd jobs; during World War II, worked in shipyards and for aircraft companies in Los Angeles and San Francisco; left the United States to travel and live abroad in 1953; lived in Paris for many years; suffered a stroke in Mexico, 1965, and was temporarily inactive; made a film in Harlem for French television, 1967; lived in Spain for the last fifteen years of his life.

*AWARDS, HONORS:* Julius Rosenwald fellowship in creative writing, 1944-45; Yaddo fellowship, 1948; Grand Prix Policier, 1958, for *For Love of Imabelle.*

*WRITINGS:*

*NOVELS*

*If He Hollers, Let Him Go,* Doubleday, 1945, new edition, Berkley Publishing, 1964, reprinted, Thunder's Mouth, 1986.

*Lonely Crusade,* Knopf, 1947, reprinted, Thunder's Mouth, 1987.

*Cast the First Stone,* Coward, 1952, reprinted, New American Library, 1975.

*The Third Generation,* World Publishing, 1954, reprinted, Thunder's Mouth, 1989.

*The Primitive,* New American Library, 1955, reprinted, 1971.

*Pinktoes,* Olympia Press (Paris), 1961, Putnam, 1965.

*Ne nous enervons pas!* (title means "Be Calm"), translation by J. Fillon, Gallimard, 1961.

*Mamie Mason; ou, Un Exercise de la bonne volonte,* translation by Andre Mathieu, Editions Les Yeux Ouverts, 1963.

*Une Affaire de viol,* translation by Mathieu, Editions Les Yeux Ouverts, 1963, published in the original English as *A Case of Rape,* Howard University Press, 1984.

*"SERIE NOIR"/"HARLEM DOMESTIC" SERIES; TRANSLATED INTO FRENCH FROM ORIGINAL ENGLISH MANUSCRIPTS*

*For Love of Imabelle,* Fawcett, 1957, revised edition published as *A Rage in Harlem,* Avon, 1965, reprinted, Vintage, 1989.

*Il pleut des coups durs,* translation by C. Wourgaft, Gallimard, 1958, published as *The Real Cool Killers,* Avon, 1959.

*The Crazy Kill* (originally published in French by Gallimard, 1958), Avon, 1959, reprinted, Vintage, 1989.

*Couche dans le pain* (title means "A Jealous Man Can't Win"), translation by J. Herisson and H. Robillot, Gallimard, 1959.

*Tout pour plaire,* translation by Yves Malartic, Gallimard, 1959, published as *The Big Gold Dream,* Avon, 1960.

*Dare-dare,* translation by Pierre Verrier, Gallimard, 1959, published as *Run Man, Run,* Putnam, 1966.

*Imbroglio negro,* translation by Fillon, Gallimard, 1960, published as *All Shot Up,* Avon, 1960.

*Retour en Afrique,* translation by Pierre Sergent, Plon, 1964, published as *Cotton Comes to Harlem,* Putnam, 1965, reprinted, Vintage, 1988.

*The Heat's On* (originally published in French by Gallimard, 1960), Putnam, 1966, published as *Come Back, Charleston Blue,* Dell, 1967.

*Blind Man with a Pistol,* Morrow, 1969, published as *Hot Day Hot Night,* Dell, 1970, reprinted, Vintage, 1989.

*OTHER*

*The Autobiography of Chester Himes,* Doubleday, Volume 1: *The Quality of Hurt,* 1972, reprinted, Paragon Book Reprint, 1990, Volume 2: *My Life of Absurdity,* 1977, reprinted, Paragon Book Reprint, 1990.

*Black on Black: Baby Sister and Selected Writings* (stories), Doubleday, 1973.

*The Collected Stories of Chester Himes,* Thunder's Mouth, 1991.

Work represented in many anthologies, including *Black Writers of America, Negro Caravan, Right On!, American Negro Short Stories,* and *The Best Short Stories by Negro Writers.* Contributor of articles and stories to periodicals, including *Atlanta Daily World, Ebony, Coronet, Esquire,* and *Pittsburgh Courier.* Yale University has a major collection of Himes's literary manuscripts and letters.

*ADAPTATIONS: Cotton Comes to Harlem* was produced as a film, starring Godfrey Cambridge and Raymond St. Jacques, by United Artists, 1970; *The Heat's On* was produced as *Come Back, Charleston Blue,* starring the same actors, by Warner Bros., 1972.

*SIDELIGHTS:* Chester Himes, whose work has been been published in France, Germany, Denmark, Sweden, Italy, Holland, Portugal, Norway, and Japan, wrote successfully in many genres, including novels of social protest, autobiographies, and popular crime thrillers. But whatever form his writing took, it was always dedicated to one subject—"racism, the hurt it inflicts, and all the tangled hates," according to Stephen F. Milliken's book *Chester Himes: A Critical Appraisal.* Himes wrote about racial oppression with a bitter, unrelenting anger that earned him comparisons to Richard Wright and James Baldwin. "He writes with the same intense ferocity with which he might knock a man down," declared *Virginia Quarterly Review* writer Raymond Nelson. This sense of rage and the unforgiving strokes with which Himes painted both black and white characters alienated many readers of both races; as a result, Himes was for years almost unknown in this country, though he was highly respected in Europe even during his lifetime.

Himes was born to socially successful parents, but his early life was troubled due to the constant fighting between his light-skinned mother and his dark-skinned father. The racial tension between the couple was to form one of the recurring themes in Himes's fiction, that of discrimination by light-skinned blacks against those of darker color. He attended Ohio State University for two years before being expelled for leading his fraternity on a romp through Columbus's red light district that ended in a speakeasy brawl. Drifting into a life of petty crime, he was arrested for armed robbery in less than a year and sentenced to twenty years in Ohio State Penitentiary. There, Himes witnessed beatings, killings, riots, and a fire that took the lives of over three hundred convicts. He began to write short stories based on these experiences; they were soon accepted for publication in *Esquire* magazine, where they appeared signed with Himes's name and prison identification number.

Released from prison after serving six years of his sentence, Himes worked variously for the Federal Writers Project, the labor movement, the Communist party and the *Cleveland Daily News* over the next few years. In 1941 he set out for California, lured by the prospect of profitable work in wartime industry. The government shipyards had a reputation for fair hiring and employment practices, but Himes found discriminatory "Jim Crow" policies as prevalent there as anywhere else. He later wrote in his autobiography that the hypocrisy of Los Angeles sickened him more than the outright hostility of the South. He expressed his bitter reaction to his Los Angeles experiences in *If He Hollers, Let Him Go,* his first novel.

In this work, the author used a naturalistic style to describe five days of steadily mounting tension in the life of Bob Jones, a black foreman in a wartime shipyard. Madge, his antagonist, is a bigoted Texan who pretends to fear Bob while secretly desiring him. Bob finds his hatred and disgust for her tinged with an inexplicable sexual attraction. Tension mounts between the two, culminating in Madge's attempted seduction of Bob; when he rejects her advances, she cries rape and he is nearly lynched.

Himes followed *If He Hollers, Let Him Go* with *Lonely Crusade,* a novel similar in plot and theme to his first. *Lonely Crusade* is less powerful than its predecessor, however, due to "Himes's tendency toward melodrama and overstatement," in Campenni's opinion. Next came a trio of novels that were largely autobiographical: *Cast the First Stone, The Third Generation* and *The Primitive. Cast the First Stone* is regarded by many critics as the classic prison novel. It relates the harrowing events of Himes's term in Ohio State Penitentiary. In *The Third Generation,* the author skillfully reduced "the traumas generated within the black American Community itself by the pressures of racism to the story of a single black family, rent by the conflict between a black-hating mother and a black-accepting father, and the sons caught in between—Himes's own story," explained Milliken.

At the time of their publication, these early novels received scant critical attention and sold very few copies. Unable to support himself by writing, Himes was also barred from all but the most menial jobs because of his prison record. Completely disillusioned with what American society had to offer him, Himes left the country permanently in 1953. For many

years he lived in Paris in the company of other black American expatriates, including Himes's literary model, Richard Wright. But while Wright lived as something of a Parisian celebrity, Himes was penniless and unknown when he arrived in France.

In his autobiography, Himes states that he was leading a "desperate" life in "a little crummy hotel" when he was contacted by French publisher Marcel Duhamel in 1956. Duhamel was familiar with Himes's work and wanted the author to produce a novel set in Harlem for his popular series of crime thrillers, "Serie Noir." Himes responded by locking himself in his room with two or three bottles of wine each day and within three weeks handed Duhamel a finished manuscript entitled *For Love of Imabelle.* Translated into French and published as *La Reine des Pommes,* the book was a tremendous success, winning the Grand Prix Policier in 1958. Himes went on to produce a total of ten novels for "Serie Noir"; he called the books his "Harlem Domestic" series.

All ten novels followed the same formula: a violent and inexplicable crime, enacted in private, touches off a wave of equally violent reactions in anarchy-ridden Harlem. Black detectives "Coffin" Ed Jones and "Grave Digger" Johnson try to bring order to the scene, usually by methods as illegal and deadly as those of the criminals. More often than not, they are only partially successful. French readers loved the irony and mordant humor which marked these fast-paced novels. Several of the books were eventually published in English under such titles as *A Rage in Harlem, The Real Cool Killers,* and *The Heat's On.* American critics at first voiced many objections to the graphic excesses of Himes's stories, but the books sold well, and it was through the "Harlem Domestic" series that the author first received some measure of recognition in the United States.

"Seven years after his death," according to Luc Sante in *New York Review of Books,* "a majority of [Himes's] books are again available in America" after being out of print in English during the last years of his life. Sixteen volumes, novels, autobiographies, and a short story collection have been reissued.

*The Collected Stories of Chester Himes* is the most recent publication of Himes's work. It is a collection of 60 stories with themes, according to a *Publishers Weekly* reviewer, of "racism, poverty and bad luck." Some of the stories were written in the 1930s while Himes was in prison; others were written as recently as 1979. According to Ishmael Reed, writing in the *Los Angeles Times Book Review,* the writing "often falls flat, especially the love stories in which, typically, a man is involved with a woman of a higher class than his own." The characters range from black males acting out their rage against

American society or else suppressing it in order to survive, to racist or bigoted white men and women who deliberately or inadvertently bring pain or calamity to the black (usually male) characters. Reed contends that though many of these stories were written in the 1930s and 1940s, they address contemporary issues; "Himes' America is alive and well, and racism, that ugly social parasite, has found a host in parts other than the South." Still, Himes's hallmark humor and humanity are evident in the "carnage" of his plots. The *Publishers Weekly* reviewer says, "these stories ... survive as history, as powerful fiction, and unfortunately, as commentary on the current situation of the Afro-American."

*BIOGRAPHICAL/CRITICAL SOURCES:*

*BOOKS*

*Amistad I,* Knopf, 1970.
*Black Literature Criticism,* Gale, 1992.
*Contemporary Literary Criticism,* Gale, Volume 2, 1974, Volume 4, 1975, Volume 7, 1977, Volume 18, 1981, Volume 58, 1990.
*Dictionary of Literary Biography,* Gale, Volume 2: *American Novelists since World War II,* 1978, Volume 76: *Afro-American Writers, 1940-1955,* 1988.
Fabre, M., *Chester Himes: An Annotated Primary and Secondary Bibliography,* Greenwood Press, 1992.
*From Harlem to Paris, Black American Writers in France, 1840-1980,* University of Illinois Press, 1991.
Himes, Chester, *The Autobiography of Chester Himes,* Doubleday, Volume 1: *The Quality of Hurt,* 1972, Volume 2: *My Life of Absurdity,* 1977.
Hughes, Carl Milton, *The Negro Novelist, 1940-1950,* Citadel, 1970.
Littlejohn, David, *Black on White: A Critical Survey of Writing by American Negroes,* Viking, 1966.
Lundquist, James, *Chester Himes,* Ungar, 1976.
Margolies, Edward, *Native Sons: A Critical Study of Twentieth-Century Negro American Authors,* Lippincott, 1968, pp. 87-101.
Margolies, Edward, *Which Way Did He Go?: The Private Eye in Dashiell Hammett, Raymond Chandler, Chester Himes, and Ross Macdonald,* Holmes & Meier, 1982, pp. 53-70.
Milliken, Stephen, *Chester Himes: A Critical Appraisal,* University of Missouri Press, 1976.
Skinner, Robert E., *Two Guns from Harlem: The Detective Fiction of Chester Himes,* Bowling Green State University Press, 1989.
Symons, Julian, *Mortal Consequences: A History—From the Detective Story to the Crime Novel,* Harper, 1972.

*PERIODICALS*

*America,* April 15, 1972; July 21, 1973.
*American Film,* March, 1991.
*American Libraries,* October, 1972.
*American Visions,* August, 1988, pp. 43-44.
*Best Sellers,* July 15, 1965; December 1, 1966; March 15, 1969.
*Black World,* July, 1970; March, 1972; July, 1972.
*Booklist,* July 15, 1972.
*Books and Bookmen,* September, 1967; August, 1968; October, 1971.
*Book Week,* March 28, 1965; August 8, 1965.
*Book World,* February 22, 1970; March 26, 1972.
*Chicago Review,* Volume 25, number 3, 1973.
*College Language Association Journal,* Number 15, 1972.
*Commonweal,* December 1, 1972.
*Critique: Studies in Modern Fiction,* Volume 16, number 1, 1974.
*Esquire,* May, 1972.
*Journal of American Studies,* April, 1978, pp. 99-114.
*Journal of Eastern African Research and Development,* Volume 1, number 1, 1981, pp. 3-18.
*Journal of Popular Culture,* spring, 1976, pp. 935-947.
*L'Express,* April 5-11, 1971.
*Los Angeles Times,* December 11, 1988; June 30, 1991.
*Melus,* winter, 1981, pp. 33-59.
*Nation,* December 20, 1971; November 15, 1986.
*Negro American Literature Forum,* spring, 1976, pp. 13-22.
*Negro Digest,* July, 1967.
*New Statesman,* April 11, 1975.
*New York Review of Books,* January 16, 1992.
*New York Times,* March 6, 1972; March 8, 1972.
*New York Times Book Review,* February 7, 1965; August 15, 1965; November 27, 1966; February 23, 1969; March 12, 1972; April 30, 1972; June 4, 1972; February 13, 1977; October 15, 1989.
*Observer Review,* June 18, 1967; June 29, 1969.
*Prairie Schooner,* winter, 1974-75.
*Publishers Weekly,* January 17, 1972; January 31, 1972; April 3, 1972; June 23, 1975; April 5, 1991.
*Punch,* July 23, 1969.
*Saturday Review,* March 22, 1969; April 15, 1972.
*Spectator,* July 12, 1969.
*Studies in Black Literature,* summer, 1970.
*Studies in Short Fiction,* summer, 1975.
*Times* (London), June 28, 1969; August 11, 1985.
*Times Literary Supplement,* April 25, 1975.
*Variety,* April 9, 1969; March 15, 1972; July 5, 1972.
*Virginia Quarterly Review,* spring, 1972, pp. 260-276; summer, 1972; summer, 1973.
*Washington Post Book World,* January 21, 1990; November 11, 1990.
*Western Humanities Review,* autumn, 1983, pp. 191-206.

*OBITUARIES:*

*PERIODICALS*

*Detroit Free Press,* November 14, 1984.
*Los Angeles Times,* November 15, 1984.
*Newsweek,* November 16, 1984.
*New York Times,* November 14, 1984.
*Publishers Weekly,* November 30, 1984.
*Times* (London), November 14, 1984.
*Washington Post,* November 16, 1984.


\*   \*   \*


**HOOKS, Bell**
  **See WATKINS, Gloria**


\*   \*   \*


**HOPKINS, Pauline Elizabeth   1859-1930**
  **(Sarah A. Allen)**


*PERSONAL:* Born in 1859, in Portland, ME; died in a fire, August 13, 1930, in Boston, MA.

*CAREER:* Novelist, dramatist, journalist, and editor. Worked throughout much of her life as a stenographer; performed her own musicals and those of others with family troupe, The Hopkins' Colored Troubadours, 1880-92; *Colored American* magazine, Boston, MA, editorial staff member and frequent contributor, 1900-04.

*AWARDS, HONORS:* First Prize, Congregational Publishing Society of Boston essay contest, 1874, for "Evils of Intemperance and Their Remedies."

*WRITINGS:*

*Slaves' Escape: or the Underground Railroad* (play), produced in Boston, MA, at Oakland Garden, July 5, 1880, revised as *Peculiar Same, or the Underground Railroad.*
*Contending Forces: A Romance Illustrative of Negro Life North and South* (novel), Colored Co-operative Publishing Company, 1900.
*A Primer of Facts Pertaining to the Greatness of Africa* (nonfiction), P.E. Hopkins, 1905.

*The Magazine Novels of Pauline Hopkins* (includes *Hagar's Daughter: A Story of Southern Caste Prejudice* [originally serialized under pseudonym Sarah A. Allen, in *Colored American* magazine, 1901-02], *Winona: A Tale of Negro Life in the South and Southwest* [originally serialized in *Colored American* magazine, 1902]; and *Of One Blood; or, The Hidden Self* [originally serialized in *Colored American* magazine, 1902-03), Oxford University Press, 1988.

Also author of the short story "The Mystery Within Us," published in *Colored American* magazine, 1900. Author of the novella *Topsy Templeton,* published in *New Era* magazine, 1916. Author of the biographical sketches *Famous Men of the Negro Race* and *Famous Women of the Negro Race,* both published in *Colored American* magazine, 1901-02. Author of the essay "Evils of Intemperance and Their Remedies." Contributor of additional articles, editorials, and short stories to *Colored American* magazine, 1900-04, and *Voice of the Negro,* 1904-05.

*SIDELIGHTS:* Pauline Elizabeth Hopkins dedicated her entire output—of fiction, dramas, and editorial writing—to exploring the plight of enslaved and post-slavery African Americans up to her era, which rounded the turn of the century. She has often been pointed to as the first black woman writer to use the popular romance genre to depict that situation. Her fiction and editorial writing also presented her own views on advancement, which were not unlike those of American educator and author W. E. B. Du Bois, but were augmented by her feminine perspective. One of the most prolific black female intellectuals of her time, "Hopkins was virtually ignored in the first few decades following her death," wrote Jane Campbell in *Dictionary of Literary Biography.* But, "truly a 'literary foremother' to the development of black American literature," Campbell continued, "Pauline Elizabeth Hopkins will perhaps one day be more widely recognized by her descendants."

Hopkins's best-known work is her first novel, *Contending Forces: A Romance Illustrative of Negro Life North and South.* Here, complex subplots and historical lead-ups anticipate later concern for origins in African American literature. The novel traces the fortunes of a racially-mixed family from 1790 Bermuda to late nineteenth-century Boston, where the central drama takes place. Characters include Will Smith, a descendant of the aforementioned family, who studies philosophy at Harvard; his sister, Dora, who helps their mother run a boarding house; and Sappho Clark, a beautiful "octoroon"—an individual of one-eighth black descent—who holds a dark secret in her personal, Southern past. Through the machinations of John Langley, a mulatto of white appearance who is affianced to Dora, Sappho is wrenched away from her lover Will, and her secret—of rape and forced prostitution in her youth—surfaces. The characters eventually separate from one another as Will continues his studies in England and John pursues western financial ventures and dies in a mining accident. A joyous reunification in Louisiana then brings the romance full circle: There, Dora's newly-wed husband heads a large industrial school for Negroes, and Will, visiting the couple, refinds Sappho and marries her.

Although *Contending Forces* was Hopkins's first novel, she was forty by the time she wrote it and had previously written dramas and short stories, each containing, in the more fragmentary forms of those genres, themes similar to *Contending Forces*. The wide-ranging context of the novel allowed Hopkins the opportunity to impart her life-long rumination on the best routes for the advancement of African Americans, and she often used her characters to expound at length, embracing ideas of black economic advancement coupled with increased political power and liberal education. She also devoted an entire chapter to praising newly-formed black women's clubs and espousing education, enfranchisement, and power for black women within the traditional family structure. This strongly-stated content has earned her much praise from contemporary black critics.

However, other aspects of the novel have kept critics from applauding the work in its entirety. There are widespread aesthetic reservations: "Most commentators agree that *Contending Forces* is overplotted and confusingly constructed," according to *Black Literature Criticism*. In addition, many reviewers pointed out that, while her virtuous characters all embrace their African identity, Hopkins's ideals of physical beauty, educational content, and culture in general, are all those of European civilization. She also seems to advocate advancement through a morally and genetically advantageous marriage. But this is only part of a program for progress that runs throughout her all books: "In each work," wrote Claudia Tate in *Conjuring: Black Women, Fiction, and Literary Tradition,* "we find that she habitually insisted that black men and women be responsible for the course of their own advancement and that duty, virtue, carefully controlled emotions, and the institution of marriage are the key components for directing social progress."

Hopkins's flurry of magazine fiction, which followed close on the heels of *Contending Forces,* retains the black identity of the main characters, but loses any overt program for improvement of the situation of African Americans, other than the general outline summed up by Tate in *Conjuring.* Instead there is a utilization of many of the devices of the nineteenth-century romance novel, including heroism, picaresque adventure, extraordinary coincidences, secret civilizations, and occasional magic, threaded along an idealized love story. Sur-

mised to be an effort at reaching a wide reading public, Hopkins' use of the genre in, especially, the serialized novels *Winona: A Tale of Negro Life in the South and Southwest, Hagar's Daughter: A Story of Southern Caste Prejudice,* and *Of One Blood; or, The Hidden Self,* often provides effective surprises, not the least of which is, frequently, that a character previously thought to be white finds out he or she is of African descent.

But this kind of plot twist serves a major goal of Hopkins, who wanted the humanity of her characters to shine through their racial categorization. As stated in her preface to *Contending Forces,* she sought to create characters "who will faithfully portray the inmost thoughts and feelings of the Negro with all the fire and romance which lie dormant in our history, and, as yet, unrecognized by writers of the Anglo-Saxon race."

*BIOGRAPHICAL/CRITICAL SOURCES:*

*BOOKS*

Berzon, Judith R., *Neither White nor Black: The Mulatto Character in American Fiction,* New York University Press, 1978.
*Black Literature Criticism,* Gale, 1992, pp. 1023-1037.
Bone, Robert, *The Negro Novel in America,* Yale University Press, 1965.
Carby, Hazel V., *Reconstructing Womanhood: The Emergence of the Afro-American Woman Novelist,* Oxford University Press, 1987, pp. 121-44.
*Dictionary of Literary Biography,* Volume 50: *Afro-American Writers Before the Harlem Renaissance,* Gale, 1987, pp. 182-189.
Gloster, Hugh M., *Negro Voices in American Fiction,* University of North Carolina Press, 1948.
Hopkins, Pauline Elizabeth, *Contending Forces: A Romance Illustrative of Negro Life North and South,* Colored Cooperative Publishing Company, 1900.
Loggins, Vernon, *The Negro Author: His Development in America to 1900,* Columbia University Press, 1931.
Pryse, Marjorie, and Hortense J. Spillers, editors, *Conjuring: Black Women, Fiction, and Literary Tradition,* Indiana University Press, 1985, pp. 53-66.
Rush, Theressa Gunnels, Carol Fairbanks Myers, and Esther Spring Arata, *Black American Writers Past and Present: A Biographical and Bibliographical Dictionary,* Scarecrow Press, 1975, Volume 1, pp. 389-90.

*PERIODICALS*

*Choice,* January, 1979, p. 1518.
*Kliatt,* September, 1980, p. 7.

## HORD, Frederick (Lee) 1941-
## (Mzee Lasana Okpara)

*PERSONAL:* Born November 7, 1941, in Kokomo, IN; son of Noel E. and Jessie (maiden name, Tyler) Hord; divorced; children: Teresa D. Hord-Owens, F. Mark, Laurel E. *Education:* Indiana State University, B.S., 1963, M.S., 1965; Union Graduate School, Ph.D., 1987.

*ADDRESSES: Office*—Director of Black Studies, Knox College, Box 13, Galesburg, IL 61401.

*CAREER:* Wabash College, Crawfordsville, IN, professor of black studies, 1972-76; Indiana University, guest lecturer in black studies, 1976; Community Service Administration, research director, 1977-80; Frostburg State University, Frostburg, MD, assistant director of minority affairs, 1980-84; Howard University, Washington, DC, professor of Afro-American studies, 1984-87; West Virginia University, Morgantown, WV, Center for Black Culture, director, 1987-88; Knox College, Galesburg, IL, director of black studies, 1988—. Performer/lecturer with PANFRE, 1981—; regional consultant for NAMSE; consultant on black studies for Aframeric Enterprises.

*MEMBER:* Association for Black Culture Centers (founder).

*AWARDS, HONORS:* Governor's Award, 1963, for Outstanding Black Male Scholar in Indiana Colleges and Universities.

*WRITINGS:*

*After(h)ours* (poems), Third World Press, 1974.
*Into Africa, the Color Black* (poems), Third World Press, 1987.
*Reconstructing Memory: Black Literary Criticism* (essays), Third World Press, 1991.

Contributor of poems and articles to journals, including *Black Books Bulletin, Western Journal of Black Studies, Black American Literature Forum, West Virginia Law Review,* and *Obsidian II.* Consulting editor of *Nightsun.*

*BIOGRAPHICAL/CRITICAL SOURCES:*

*PERIODICALS*

*Choice,* April, 1992, p. 1225.
*Reference and Research Book News,* October, 1991, p. 34.
*Small Press Book Review,* November, 1991, p. 14.

## HORNE, Aaron 1940-

*PERSONAL:* Born December 3, 1940, in Chipley, FL; son of Albert and Laura (Brown) Horne; married Myrtle Griffen (a social worker); children: Ericka, Aaron, Jr. *Education:* Tennessee State University, B.S., 1968; Roosevelt University, M.Mus., 1972; University of Iowa, M.F.A., 1973, D.M.A., 1976. *Politics:* Democrat. *Religion:* Baptist.

*ADDRESSES: Home*—8848 Bennett, Evanston, IL 60203. *Office*—Northeastern Illinois University, 5500 North St. Louis, Chicago, IL 60625.

*CAREER:* Northeastern Illinois University, Chicago, professor of music, 1977—. Member of Illinois Art Council and Evanston Art Council. *Military service:* U.S. Army, 1958-61.

*MEMBER:* American Association for Higher Education, Music Educators National Conference.

*WRITINGS:*

*Woodwind Music of Black Composers,* Greenwood Press, 1990.
*String Music of Black Composers,* Greenwood Press, 1991.
*Keyboard Music of Black Composers,* Greenwood Press, 1992.

*WORK IN PROGRESS: Brass Music of Black Composers,* publication expected in 1994; a chronological survey of jazz saxophone styles.

*SIDELIGHTS:* Aaron Horne commented: "The series of books about the music of black composers was a necessary pioneering effort. The attempt was to provide complete data about all known black composers. The scholar, performer, student, and listener will now have the opportunity to learn more about the black composer."

\* \* \*

## HORNE, Gerald (C.) 1949-

*PERSONAL:* Born January 3, 1949, in St. Louis, MO; son of Jerry (a truck driver) and Flora (a maid) Horne. *Education:* Princeton University, B.A., 1970; University of California, Berkeley, J.D., 1973; Columbia University, M.Phil. and Ph.D., both 1982. *Politics:* Peace and Freedom Party.

*ADDRESSES: Home*—972 West Campus Point Ln., Goleta, CA 93117. *Office*—c/o Black Studies, University of California, Santa Barbara, Santa Barbara, CA 93106.

*CAREER:* Writer, lawyer, journalist. Sarah Lawrence College, Bronxville, NY, professor of history and law, beginning 1982. Former executive director of National Conference of Black Lawyers; conducted human rights investigations in West Bank/Gaza and Philippines. American Civil Liberties Union, vice chair of equality committee, beginning 1981; Free South Africa Movement, member of steering committee, beginning 1984; chair of Peace and Freedom Party.

*AWARDS, HONORS:* McConnell fellow, Princeton University, 1969; Revson fellow, City College of New York, 1980-81; Nellon fellow, Sarah Lawrence College, 1983; Hope Stevens Award, National Conference of Black Lawyers, 1983.

*WRITINGS:*

*Black and Red: W. E. B. Du Bois and the Afro-American Response to the Cold War, 1944-1963,* State University of New York Press, 1985.
*Communist Front?: The Civil Rights Congress, 1946-1956,* Fairleigh Dickinson University Press, 1988.
*Studies in Black: Progressive Views and Reviews of the African American Experience,* Kendall/Hunt, 1992.
*Reversing Discrimination: The Case for Affirmative Action,* International Publishers, 1992.

Also contributor to *Thinking and Rethinking U.S. History,* Council on Interracial Books for Children, 1988. *National Lawyers,* member of editorial board, beginning 1982.

\*   \*   \*

## HOUSE, Gloria 1941-
### (Aneb Kgositsile)

*PERSONAL:* Born February 14, 1941, in Tampa, FL; daughter of Fred and Rubye (Robinson) Larry; married William Stuart House, 1966 (divorced, 1974); children: Uri Stuart. *Education:* American River College, A.A. (with highest honors), 1959; Monterey Institute of Foreign Studies (now Monterey Institute of International Studies), diploma in French Studies, 1959; University of California, Berkeley, B.A., 1961, M.A., 1969; University of Michigan, Ph.D., 1986. *Avocational interests:* Travel (France, the Netherlands, Sweden, Denmark, Mexico, England, Italy, Egypt, Kenya, Tanzania, Ethiopia, Algeria, Bermuda, Cuba, Grenada, and Barbados), the arts, modern dance, architecture, politics, and international affairs.

*ADDRESSES: Home*—2822 Ewald Circle, Detroit, MI 48238. *Office*—Weekend College Program, Wayne State University, 5950 Cass Ave., Detroit, MI 48202.

*CAREER:* French teacher at school in Cambridge, England, 1961; San Francisco State College (now University), San Francisco, CA, instructor in French, spring, 1965; Cass Technical High School, Detroit, MI, high school teacher of French and English, 1967-68; free-lance television broadcaster in Detroit, 1969; *Detroit Free Press,* Detroit, news and editorial copy editor, 1969-71; Wayne State University, Detroit, instructor in Afro-American literature, spring, 1969, instructor, 1971-74, associate professor of humanities, 1974—, coproducer and instructor of record for university-produced television series *An American Mosaic,* 1977, curriculum developer of Module at Jackson Prison Program, 1974-77. Coproducer and interviewer for television series *Take the Black,* 1970. Field secretary for Lowndes County, AL, Student Non-Violent Coordinating Committee, 1965-67; member of board of directors of Interfaith Centers for Racial Justice, 1973-74, and Detroit Council of the Arts, 1980-88; member of Michigan Alliance Against Political and Racist Repression, 1973-74, and Michigan Council for the Humanities, 1974-75. Volunteer editor and coordinator of cultural presentations for Broadside/Crummell Press, 1977—; guest on radio and television programs; featured poet at poetry series and other cultural events; lecturer and consultant; poet-in-residence at Detroit public high schools, spring, 1980, and Richard Branch, Detroit Public Library, summer, 1992.

*MEMBER:* Progressive Artist and Educators Association (member of board of directors), Weekend Alumni Association (faculty founder).

*AWARDS, HONORS:* Rackham graduate fellow at University of Michigan, 1978-79, 1980-86; Center for Continuing Education of Women scholar, 1979-80; grant from Detroit Council of the Arts, 1981, for *Cinders Smoldering: Detroit since '67;* National Endowment for the Humanities fellowship, 1983; award for community service, Black Medical Association, 1984; award from the Michigan Labor Committee for Democracy and Human Rights in Central America, 1987; Distinguished Award for Pioneering in the Arts, United Black Artists, 1988.

*WRITINGS:*

(Under name Aneb Kgositsile) *Blood River: Poems, 1964-1983,* Broadside Press, 1983.
(Editor) *Cinders Smoldering: Detroit since '67* (anthology), Broadside Press, 1986.
*Three Who Believed in Freedom: The Historical Contributions of Ella Baker, Septima Clark, and Fannie Lou Hamer* (video documentary), Council on Interracial Books for Children, 1989.
(Under name Aneb Kgositsile) *Rainrituals,* Broadside Press, 1990.

*Tower and Dungeon: A Study of Place and Power in American Culture,* Casade Unidad, 1991.

Work represented in anthologies, including *Black Arts Anthology,* edited by Ahmed Alhanuisi, Broadside Press, 1969; *The Black Aesthetic,* edited by Addison Gayle, Doubleday, 1971; *Moving to Antarctica,* edited by Margaret Kaminski, Dustbooks, 1975. Contributor of poems to periodicals, including *Negro Digest, Essence, Metro Times, Against the Current, Michigan Poetry Sampler, Moving Out,* and *Solid Ground: A New World Journal.* Contributor of articles and book reviews to numerous periodicals, including *History Teacher, City Arts Quarterly,* and *Detroit News.* Poetry editor, *The Witness.*

\* \* \*

## HOWARD, Elizabeth Fitzgerald 1927-

*PERSONAL:* Born December 28, 1927, in Baltimore, MD; daughter of John MacFarland (a teacher and in real estate) and Bertha McKinley (a teacher and clerk; maiden name, James) Fitzgerald; married Lawrence Cabot Howard (a professor), February 14, 1953; children: Jane Elizabeth, Susan Carol, Laura Ligaya. *Education:* Radcliffe College, A.B., 1948; University of Pittsburgh, M.L.S., 1971, Ph.D., 1977. *Politics:* Democrat. *Religion:* Episcopalian. *Hobbies and other interests:* African folklore, French conversation, symphony concerts, grandchildren, family history.

*ADDRESSES: Home*—919 College Ave., Pittsburgh, PA 15232. *Office*—Library Science Program, West Virginia University, Morgantown, WV 26506. *Agent*—Kendra Marcus, Book Stop Literary Agency, 67 Meadow View Rd., Orinda, CA 94563.

*CAREER:* Boston Public Library, Boston, MA, cataloging assistant, 1948-51, children's librarian, 1951-56; Hofstra College (now Hofstra University), Hempstead, NY, research assistant in political science, 1956-57; Episcopal Diocese of Pittsburgh, Pittsburgh, PA, resource director, 1972-74; Pittsburgh Theological Seminary, Pittsburgh, reference librarian, 1974-77; University of Pittsburgh, Pittsburgh, visiting lecturer in library science, 1977-78; West Virginia University, Morgantown, assistant professor, 1978-81 and 1982-85, associate professor, 1985-91, professor of library science, 1991—. Member of Radcliffe Alumnae Association Board of Management, 1969-72, Ellis School Board of Trustees, 1969-75, Magee-Women's Hospital Board of Directors, 1980—, QED Communications Board of Directors, 1987—, and Beginning with Books Board of Directors, 1987—; member of vestry, Calvary Church, 1991—.

*MEMBER:* American Library Association (member of Caldecott committee, 1984), Association for Library Services to Children (board member), Society of Children's Book Writers and Illustrators, National Council of Teachers of English, Beta Phi Mu.

*AWARDS, HONORS: Booklist* Picture Books of the '80s, American Library Association (ALA) notable book citation, 1990, and Hedda Seisler Mason honor book, Enoch Pratt Library, 1991, all for *Chita's Christmas Tree;* Parents' Choice Award, and Teachers' Choice Award, International Reading Association, both 1992, both for *Aunt Flossie's Hats (and Crab Cakes Later).*

*WRITINGS:*

*America as Story: Historical Fiction for Secondary Schools,* American Library Association, 1988.
*The Train to Lulu's,* Bradbury, 1988.
*Chita's Christmas Tree,* Bradbury, 1989.
*Aunt Flossie's Hats (and Crab Cakes Later),* Clarion, 1991.
*Mac and Marie and the Train Toss Surprise,* Four Winds, 1993.
*Papa Tells Chita a Story,* Four Winds, in press.

*SIDELIGHTS:* Elizabeth Fitzgerald Howard commented: "Although I have always been writing something—fat letters from the Philippines Peace Corps days or from Nigeria during a year's leave, newsletters for the Brandeis Faculty Women's Organization and for the Episcopal Society for Cultural Racial Unity, articles for library periodicals, book reviews—it is still new for me to believe that I can be thought of as a writer. It's wonderful! It's really exciting! Why didn't I try writing books for children long ago?

"It was inevitable that I would think back to my own childhood when I began to write stories for children. My sister Babs and I really did take *The Train to Lulu's.* This book was my first effort to try to capture for today's young readers some of the unique and yet universal experiences of children in one African American family mid-century. I hope to write about growing up in Mrs. Ella Ford's rooming house, our quarters in the attic, and sharing the one bathroom with the several black graduate students on the second floor. *Chita's Christmas Tree* tells of old time Christmas as celebrated in my father's family. Chita, my father's first cousin, now age eighty-four, was the daughter of one of Baltimore's first African American doctors. This is a glimpse of a little known facet of African American life. *Aunt Flossie's Hats (and Crab Cakes Later)* celebrates my mother's sister, Aunt Flossie. A teacher in Baltimore schools, she lived to be almost 101, in the same house for sixty-five years, and never threw anything away. There are more stories about Aunt Flossie. And there are stories to be told about my father's father, and his five brothers, who came to Baltimore from Tennessee, and practiced law, medicine, pharmacy and real estate. And great grandfather John Henry Smith and his drydock at Baltimore Harbor. And my mother's uncle Jimmy who owned a grocery store with— to quote Aunt Flossie—'fine terrapins and the best peaches anywhere.'

"This is a time of great richness in children's books. Publishers are interested now in stories that portray the variety of American life so that all children can share in the multicolored experience. Today there are many works by truly distinguished and prolific African American children's authors. But there is so much still to be told. I would like to write more about black American life at the turn of the century, through stories culled from my family's history. I also hope to convey some of the experiences of my sister and me, and of my daughters. There is still a need for more and more books so that children of all colors may discover more and more about growing up black in America—what is different and what is familiar, and how we are all connected."

\* \* \*

## HOWARD, Vanessa 1955-

*PERSONAL:* Born in 1955, in Brooklyn, NY.

*CAREER:* Poet and fiction writer. Participant in the Fort Greene Writing Workshop.

*WRITINGS:*

*A Screaming Whisper* (poetry), photographs by J. Pinderhughes, Holt, 1972.

Work represented in anthologies, including *Soulscript, Voice of the Children,* and *Tales and Stories.*

*SIDELIGHTS:* Vanessa Howard was still a teenager when *A Screaming Whisper,* a book of forty-four poems, was published. Among the works collected in the volume is "Observations of a Subway Train," in which Howard perceives both the projected images and the true personalities of other passengers on the train. Despite Howard's youth, Margaret A. Dorsey, critic for the *Library Journal,* commended the author for her "maturity of understanding." In the *English Journal* John W. Conner found that Howard's "observations are poignant and real. She is restless and impatient with the age-old restlessness and impatience of youth."

*BIOGRAPHICAL/CRITICAL SOURCES:*

*PERIODICALS*

*English Journal,* May, 1973, p. 829.
*Library Journal,* December 15, 1972, p. 4078.

\* \* \*

## HUDSON, Wade 1946-

*PERSONAL:* Born October 23, 1946, in Mansfield, LA; son of Wade and Lurline (Jones) Hudson; married Cheryl Willis (a publisher and writer), June 24, 1972; children: Katura, Stephan. *Education:* Attended Southern University and Agricultural and Mechanical College, 1964-68. *Politics:* Democrat. *Religion:* Baptist.

*ADDRESSES: Home*—202 Dodd St., East Orange, NJ 07017. *Office*—Just Us Books, 301 Main St., Suite 22-24, Orange, NJ 07050.

*CAREER:* Just Us Books, Orange, NJ, co-owner, 1987—; writer.

*MEMBER:* Multicultural Publishers Exchange (board member), African American Publishers, Writers and Booksellers Association.

*WRITINGS:*

(With Valerie Wilson Wesley) *Afro-Bets Book of Black Heroes from A to Z: An Introduction to Important Black Achievers,* illustrated by Cheryl W. Hudson, Just Us Books, 1988.
*Afro-Bets Alphabet Rap Song,* Just Us Books, 1990.
*Jamal's Busy Day,* illustrated by George Ford, Just Us Books, 1991.
*Afro-Bets Kids: I'm Gonna Be!,* illustrated by Culverson Blair, Just Us Books, 1992.
(With Debbi Chocolate) *NEATE: To the Rescue,* Just Us Books, 1992.
*I Love My Family,* illustrated by Cal Massey, Scholastic, 1993.
(Editor) *Pass It On: African-American Poetry for Children,* illustrated by Floyd Cooper, Scholastic, 1993.

Also author of the children's book *Beebe's Lonely Saturday,* New Dimension Publishing, and the stage plays *Freedom Star,* Macmillan, *Sam Carter Belongs Here, The Return, A House Divided..., Black Love Story,* and *Dead End.*

*SIDELIGHTS:* Wade Hudson's children's books present uplifting portraits of African American family life and historical black figures. Co-owner with his wife, Cheryl, of Just Us Books, Hudson is committed to publishing positive books for a young black audience.

Hudson's stories provide subtle self-affirmation for his readers. His first story, for example, *Jamal's Busy Day,* has been praised for its use of a clever conceit that draws parallels between the daily activities of a young boy, Jamal, and those of his accountant mother and architect father. Like them, he gets himself ready for his "work," takes a crowded bus, works with numbers, attends meetings, does drawings, and so on. "The upbeat message," according to *Publishers Weekly,* "is that both parents and children can 'work hard' and accomplish much in their respective arenas: all have something to contribute and all work has value."

In 1988 Wade Hudson and Valerie Wilson Wesley collaborated on *Afro-Bets Book of Black Heroes from A to Z,* which presents profiles of 49 black men and women who have achieved success in the face of adversity and have made important contributions to society. Although the "information is uneven," *Afro-Bets* has been called "a useful item for black history collections," by a *Booklist* critic. Included in the book are entries on such diverse people as Shaka, the Zulu king, to Thurgood Marshall, the Supreme Court justice, boxer Muhammad Ali, activist Martin Luther King, and writer Zora Neal Hurston. Some reviewers noted that the work offers hard-to-find information on individuals such as sculptress Edmonia Lewis and educator Fanny Coppin, who are often overlooked in reference works.

In all his books, Hudson hopes to fill a shortage in black-oriented children's books. Speaking of his Just Us Books publishing house to Claire Serant of *Black Enterprise,* Hudson states: "There's an age-old belief in publishing that blacks don't read. But it's actually the mainstream market that hasn't devised a strategy to reach that audience."

Wade Hudson also commented: "One can never take any image for granted. Images, whether in print, film, television, or on stage, are constantly shaping the way we feel and what we think and believe. This is particularly crucial to the African-American community which has been deliberately given negative images of its history and culture. I find it rewarding to help reshape and change those negative images to reflect truth. I think the struggle to present the correct images, the truth, is the most crucial one facing us all."

*BIOGRAPHICAL/CRITICAL SOURCES:*

*PERIODICALS*

*Black Enterprise,* March, 1991, p. 21.
*Booklist,* January 1, 1989, p. 788.

*Bookwatch,* January, 1989, p. 7.
*Publishers Weekly,* December 6, 1991, p. 71.
*School Library Journal,* December, 1988, p. 117; February, 1992, p. 74.
*Social Education,* April, 1992, p. 262.

\* \* \*

## HULL, Gloria T(heresa Thompson) 1944-

*PERSONAL:* Born December 6, 1944, in Shreveport, LA; daughter of Robert T. (a laborer) and Jimmie (a domestic worker; maiden name, Williams) Thompson; married Prentice R. Hull, June 12, 1966 (divorced, 1983); children: Adrian Prentice. *Education:* Southern University, B.A. (summa cum laude), 1966; graduate study at University of Illinois, 1966; Purdue University, M.A., 1968, Ph.D., 1972.

*ADDRESSES: Office*—Department of English, University of Delaware, Newark, DE 19716.

*CAREER:* University of Delaware, Newark, instructor, 1971, assistant professor, 1972-77, associate professor, 1977-86, professor of English, 1986—. Visiting scholar, Stanford University, 1987-88. Has given poetry readings, conducted poetry workshops, and guest lectured at various institutions nationwide, including Lincoln University, 1974, Wilmington College, 1977, Yale University, 1977, and University of Alabama, 1979.

*MEMBER:* College Language Association, Modern Language Association of America, National Association for the Advancement of Colored People (NAACP), Alpha Kappa Alpha.

*AWARDS, HONORS:* Outstanding Service Award, University of Delaware Black Student Union, 1975-76; University of Delaware research grant, summer, 1976; National Endowment for the Humanities stipend, summer, 1979; Rockefeller Foundation fellowship, 1979-80; Outstanding Contribution and Service to University of Delaware Minority Students Award, 1980-81; National Institute of Women of Color Award, 1982, for *All the Women Are White, All the Blacks Are Men, but Some of Us Are Brave: Black Women's Studies;* Mellon National fellowship to University of West Indies, Jamaica, 1984-86; Ford Foundation fellowship, 1987-88.

*WRITINGS:*

(Editor with Patricia Bell Scott and Barbara Smith, and contributor) *All the Women Are White, All the Blacks Are Men, but Some of Us Are Brave: Black Women's Studies,* Feminist Press, 1982.

(Editor and author of introduction) *Give Us Each Day: The Diary of Alice Dunbar-Nelson,* Norton, 1984.

*Color, Sex and Poetry: Three Women Writers of the Harlem Renaissance,* Indiana University Press, 1987.

(Editor and author of introduction) *The Works of Alice Dunbar-Nelson,* three volumes, Oxford University Press, 1988.

*Healing Heart, Poems 1973-1988,* Kitchen Table: Women of Color Press, 1989.

*OTHER*

*A Day with Alice Dunbar-Nelson* (videotape), Instructional Resource Center, University of Delaware, 1976.

Contributor to books, including *The Princeton Encyclopedia of Poetry and Poetics,* edited by Alex Preminger, Princeton University Press, 1974; *Sturdy Black Bridges: Visions of Black Women in Literature,* edited by Roseann Bell, Parker, and Sheftall, Doubleday, 1979; *Home Girls: A Black Feminist Anthology,* edited by Smith, Kitchen Table Press, 1983; *Conjuring: Black Women, Literary Tradition, and Fiction,* edited by Marjorie Pryse and Hortense Spillers, Indiana University Press, 1985; *Changing Our Own Words: Essays on Criticism, Theory, and Writing by Black Women,* edited by A. Cheryl, Rutgers University Press, 1989. Contributor of articles, reviews, and poetry to periodicals, including *Black American Literature Forum, Radical Teacher, Ariel: A Review of International English Literature, Obsidian: Black Literature in Review, Feminist Studies, Black Scholar, Ms., New Orleans Review,* and *Mississippi Quarterly.* Advisory editor, *Black American Literature Forum,* 1978-86; editorial consultant, *Feminist Studies,* 1981—.

*SIDELIGHTS:* A poet with a powerful voice, Gloria T. Hull is perhaps best known as an eminent black studies scholar. In her work entitled *All the Women Are White, All the Blacks Are Men, But Some of Us Are Brave: Black Women's Studies,* Gloria T. Hull wrote: "Everything that I have been saying ... illustrates the Black feminist critical approach which I used in researching [Alice] Dunbar-Nelson....

"It goes without saying that I approached her as an important writer and her work as genuine literature. Probably as an (over?)reaction to the condescending, witty but empty, British urbanity of tone which is the hallmark of traditional white male literary scholarship (and which I dislike intensely), I usually discuss Dunbar-Nelson with level high seriousness—and always with caring. Related to this are my slowly-evolving attempts at being so far unfettered by conventional style as to write creatively, even poetically, if that is the way the feeling flows. Here, the question of audience is key. Having painfully developed these convictions and a modicum of courage to buttress them, I now include, visualize everybody (my

department chair, the promotion and tenure committee, my mother and brother, my Black feminist sisters, the chair of Afro-American Studies, lovers, colleagues, friends) for each organic article, rather than write sneaky, schizophrenic essays from under two or three different hats."

Hull once commented: "*But Some of Us Are Brave* is the first published interdisciplinary work on Afro-American women compiled/written from a conscious and avowed anti-racist, anti-sexist perspective. It was sorely needed because the black studies and women's studies movements were not adequately incorporating the untapped wealth of material on the lives and experiences of black women—despite the fact that an audience of students, teachers, and general readers was eager for this information."

Hull later added: "I am still urged by my need to heal, to communicate through and around deceptive splits (within myself, in critical language-practice, between 'politics' and writing, etc.) in order to produce ever more transformative work which will change consciousness and reverberate in manifest ways."

*Color, Sex, and Poetry: Three Women Writers of the Harlem Renaissance* is such a work. In this volume, Hull examines the Harlem Renaissance through the lives and work of three influential women—Alice Dunbar-Nelson, Georgia Douglas Johnson, and Angelina Weld Grimke. She discusses gender issues and sexuality and their effects on female black writers. Hull also notes that due to the lesbian orientation of much of Grimke's work, the author remained largely unpublished at the time. As book reviewer Jewelle Gomez writes in the *Nation,* "With her study of Grimke and her book as a whole, Hull opens up a very important discussion about the part sexuality plays in the growth and appreciation of black women's writing. It is an issue frequently discussed in lesbian journals, and it certainly deserves attention when looking at all black women's work. Hull's candor about these women's lives indicates that the mountainous terrain of sexuality must be tackled in order to make a place for a full, realized body of literature by Afro-American women."

In *Healing Heart, Poems 1973-1988,* Hull contemplates one's evolving identity as experience and cultural influences shape one's life. She writes, "We love in circles / touching round— / faces in a ritual ring / echoing blood and color / nappy girlheads in a summer porch swing / belligerent decisions to live / and be ourselves." Leonard D. Moore, writing in the *Library Journal,* called the book "richly passionate ... deeply rooted in a feminist vision." Pat Monaghan, in a *Booklist* review, noted: "She is raw and gritty, sometimes mean and sometimes weak," as she writes about the "difficult changes," love, and pain, a black woman experiences in a society that prefers her silence.

*BIOGRAPHICAL/CRITICAL SOURCES:*

PERIODICALS

*Booklist,* May 15, 1989.
*Choice,* May, 1988.
*Compass,* April 2, 1981.
*Evening Journal* (Wilmington, Delaware), June 6, 1977.
*Library Journal,* June 15, 1989.
*Ms.,* January, 1982.
*Nation,* April 30, 1988, pp. 615-18.
*New York Times Book Review,* April 14, 1985.
*off our backs: a women's newsjournal,* May, 1985.
*University of Delaware Review,* October 8, 1976.
*Washington Post,* March 15, 1982.

\* \* \*

## HUNT, Marsha 1946-

*PERSONAL:* Born in 1946, in Europe; children: Karis.

*CAREER:* Model, actress, singer, and writer.

*WRITINGS:*

*Real Life* (autobiography), Chatto & Windus, 1986.
*Joy* (novel), Dutton, 1990.
*Free* (novel), Dutton, 1993.

*SIDELIGHTS:* Both of Marsha Hunt's published novels are, in a sense, voyages of self-discovery—voyages during which, with both humorous and tragic effect, blinders are lifted from the eyes of the main characters. The main characters of the books are African Americans who have for some time failed to notice changes in the world around them, at the same time ignoring terrible truths concerning the people to whom they have been closest.

The earlier novel, *Joy,* gains much of its inside knowledge of the entertainment industry and those who have been swept up into its limelight from Hunt's own experiences as a singer, songwriter and actress, most famous for her starring role in the London production of *Hair.* The central character and narrator is Baby Palatine, an elderly, church-going woman, who is travelling from California to New York to assist in the funeral of Joy Bang, one of three sisters she helped raise. The three had gained brief stardom in the sixties as a girl group calling itself Bang Bang Bang. The group crashed as quickly

as it had become famous, leaving the sisters free to pursue the excesses of their respective personalities. Joy was Baby's favorite, her "God-sent child;" Baby ignored Joy's corruption while she was alive and continues to do so as she recollects Joy's life during the trip eastward. It is not until the very end of the novel that Baby realizes the unpleasant truth and her own part in creating it. At that point a bloodfest ends the novel, leaving many critics agreeing with Jewelle Gomez, who wrote in *The Women's Review of Books* that "the additional deaths in the final pages seem gratuitous and completely at odds with the humorous bantering style of Baby P.'s narrative."

Teenotchy, the protagonist of *Free,* Hunt's second novel, carries a weightier repression: that of the rape and murder of his mother. As a teenager in turn of the century Germantown, Pennsylvania, he is "a slave to habit," working as a servant for the same man his mother had worked for—a man who had a role in her murder and afterward had become his kindly protector. Teenotchy's journey of self-discovery comes when an upper-class Englishman visits and takes him to England. He falls in love with his benefactor and also learns a great deal about himself, though the novel ends tragically.

Marsha Hunt has conducted her own voyages of discovery through her many careers that have led her from Germantown to Europe. Her widely praised writing talent has allowed her to use her own personal illuminations to explore the possibilities and dangers of black self-knowledge in a world dominated by whites.

*BIOGRAPHICAL/CRITICAL SOURCES:*

BOOKS

Hunt, Marsha, *Real Life,* Chatto & Windus, 1986.

PERIODICALS

*Booklist,* December 1, 1990, p. 717.
*Books,* May, 1991, p. 16; July, 1992, p. 11.
*Essence,* July, 1991, p. 36.
*Kirkus Reviews,* November 15, 1990, p. 1559.
*Lambda Book Report,* May, 1991, p. 40.
*Library Journal,* January, 1991, p. 152.
*Listener,* April 12, 1990, p. 25.
*New Statesman and Society,* April 13, 1990, p. 36.
*Publishers Weekly,* December 7, 1990, p. 69.
*Punch,* June 8, 1990, p. 37.
*Spectator,* May 12, 1990, p. 38.
*Times Literary Supplement,* August 7, 1992, p. 18.
*Women's Review of Books,* June, 1991, p. 20.

## HUNTER-GAULT, Charlayne 1942-

*PERSONAL:* Born February 27, 1942, in Due West, SC; daughter of Charles S. H. Hunter, Jr. (a minister and chaplain), and Althea Brown Hunter; married Walter Stovall (marriage ended); married Ronald T. Gault (an investment banker), September 17, 1973; children: Susan Stovall, Chuma Hunter-Gault. *Education:* University of Georgia, A.B., 1963.

*ADDRESSES: Home*—356 West 58th St., New York, NY 10019. *Office*—Sterling Lord Literistic Inc., One Madison Ave., New York, NY 10010.

*CAREER: New Yorker,* New York City, "Talk of the Town" reporter, beginning in 1963; *Trans-Action* (magazine), staff member; WRC-TV, Washington, DC, investigative reporter and news anchor; *New York Times,* New York City, began as metropolitan reporter, later became Harlem bureau chief; *The MacNeil/Lehrer Report* (became *The MacNeil/Lehrer NewsHour,* 1983), PBS-TV, correspondent, 1978—. Correspondent for *Learning in America,* MacNeil/Lehrer Productions, 1989. Columbia University, adjunct professor of journalism.

*AWARDS, HONORS:* Journalist of the Year, National Association of Black Journalists, 1986; Russell Sage Fellowship; Distinguished Urban Reporting Award, National Urban Coalition; George Foster Peabody Award for Excellence in Broadcast Journalism, University of Georgia; Broadcast Personality of the Year Award, *Good Housekeeping;* American Women in Radio and Television Award; awards for excellence in local programming, Corporation for Public Broadcasting; National News and Documentary Emmy Awards, Academy of Television Arts and Sciences, for Outstanding Coverage of a Single Breaking News Story, and for outstanding background/analysis of a single current story. Recipient of more than one dozen honorary degrees from colleges and universities, including the University of Massachusetts and Morehouse College.

*WRITINGS:*

*In My Place* (memoir), Farrar, Straus, 1992.

Contributor of articles to publications, including *New York Times Magazine, Essence,* and *Vogue.*

*SIDELIGHTS:* Charlayne Hunter-Gault, the first black female to attend the University of Georgia in 1961, recalls what it was like to be on the front lines of desegregation in the memoir *In My Place.* The author begins with a pleasant account of her childhood in the Deep South (and, for a brief period, Alaska), describing school and church activities. A gifted student, Hunter-Gault decided in high school she was going to be a

journalist and applied to a number of colleges. Although she was accepted at Wayne State University in Detroit, Hunter-Gault was "encouraged by local civil rights leaders to apply ... to the University of Georgia," according to a critic for *Kirkus Reviews.* The same reviewer commented that Hunter-Gault's account of facing racial prejudice there is "remarkably generous." Indeed, Hunter-Gault told *Publishers Weekly* that "the people who attacked me didn't know me ... they stood outside my dormitory and threw rocks, but it was the idea, not the person they were against." *In My Place* concludes with Hunter-Gault's graduation from college and presents her "stirring" 1988 University of Georgia commencement speech "as a sort of epilog," commented Gwen Gregory in *Library Journal.* A critic in *Publishers Weekly* considered the work a "warmhearted, well-observed memoir" and believed "that Hunter-Gault could write a rich sequel."

*BIOGRAPHICAL/CRITICAL SOURCES:*

*PERIODICALS*

*Kirkus Reviews,* September 1, 1992, pp. 1106-07.
*Library Journal,* October 15, 1992, p. 74.
*Publishers Weekly,* August 17, 1992, pp. 36, 40; September 7, 1992, pp. 83-84.

\*   \*   \*

## HUTCHINSON, Earl Ofari 1945-

*PERSONAL:* Born October 8, 1945, in Chicago, IL; son of Earl (in real estate) and Nina (Brown) Hutchinson; married Barbara Bramwell (in real estate), March 5, 1988; children: Fanon, Sikivu. *Education:* California State University, Los Angeles, B.S., in the 1970s; California State University, Dominguez Hills, M.Hum., 1989; Pacific Western University, Ph.D., 1991.

*ADDRESSES: Home and office*—5517 Secrest Dr., Los Angeles, CA 90043.

*CAREER:* Writer and public speaker; lecturer at colleges and universities; guest on radio stations. Paul Robeson Community Center, member of board of directors.

*MEMBER:* Black Journalists Association.

*WRITINGS:*

*The Myth of Black Capitalism,* Monthly Review Press, 1970.
*Let Your Motto Be Resistance,* Beacon Press, 1974.
*Crime: Why It Exists, What Can Be Done,* Impact! Publications (Inglewood, CA), 1987.

*Crime, Drugs, and African Americans,* Impact! Publications, 1990.

*The Mugging of Black America,* African American Images, 1991.

*Black Fatherhood: Guide to Male Parenting,* Impact! Publications, 1992.

Author of the book *From Black Fathers With Love,* 1986. Contributor to periodicals, including *Ebony, Black World, Newsday, Nation, Harper's,* and *Black Scholar.* Author and publisher of *Ofari's Bi-Monthly,* 1982—.

*WORK IN PROGRESS: Blacks and Reds: Blacks in the Communist Party, 1930-1970; Under Assault: Police and the African American Community;* revising *The Myth of Black Capitalism.*

*SIDELIGHTS:* Earl Ofari Hutchinson commented: "To me, writing is more than a career, or even an art. It is a medium through which to promote the advocacy of issues and ideas that can impact and change or influence opinion. My prime focus is on the African-American experience and the role it has played in shaping part of American society."

# I-J

**IONE**
See IONE, Carole

*   *   *

**IONE, Carole   1937-**
    **(Ione)**

*PERSONAL:* Born May 28, 1937, in Washington, DC; daughter of Hylan Lewis (a sociologist) and Lela Ford (a writer; maiden name, Whipper); married Salvatore J. Bovoso, 1971 (divorced, 1982); children: Alessandro, Santiago, Antonio. *Education:* Attended Bennington College, New York University, New School for Social Research, Helix Institute for Psychotherapy and Healing, and Chinese Healing Arts Center. *Religion:* "Buddhist-Episcopalian."

*ADDRESSES: Home*—156 Hunter St., Kingston, NY 12401. *Agent*—Melanie Jackson Literary Agency, 250 West 57th St., Suite 1110, New York, NY 10107.

*CAREER:* Author. *Letters* (now *Live Letters*), founder, 1974, and editor; *Essence,* contributing editor, 1981-83; *Village Voice,* poetry editor; Manhattan Theatre Club, director of Writers in Performance; producer of plays and performances. Pauline Oliveros Foundation, co-artistic director; Renaissance House, Inc., artistic director; Unison Learning Center, poetry curator; Live Letters (literary program) artistic director. Poet in residence, Jazzmobile, Inc., and Teachers and Writers Collaborative; gives readings and presentations on television and radio programs and at colleges and universities.

*MEMBER:* International Women's Writing Guild, National Writers Union, Poets and Writers.

*AWARDS, HONORS: Pride of Family: Four Generations of American Women of Color* was selected as a *New York Times* notable book of the year, 1991, and one of the New York Public Library's twenty-five books to remember; grants from South Carolina Commission for the Humanities, Rockefeller Foundation, and National Endowment for the Arts; fellow of MacDowell Colony, Yaddo, Edward Albee Foundation, and Writers Room.

*WRITINGS:*

*The Coffee Table Lover,* Country Press, 1973.
*Private Pages,* Ballantine, 1987.
*Unsealedlips,* Capra, 1990.
*Piramida Negro: Selected Poetry, 1973-1991,* Live Letters Press, 1991.
*Pride of Family: Four Generations of American Women of Color,* Summit Books, 1991.

Some writings published under the name Ione. Scripts include *Evidence,* a work for five voices; *A Friend,* a multimedia performance work, Cycle Arts Foundation; *Mirage* (with Hugues Lavergne); and *A Diary of Reconstruction,* South Carolina Commission for the Humanities. Work represented in anthologies, including *Contemporary Literary Criticism,* 1989. Contributor to periodicals, including *New Dawn, Oui, Ms., American Film Ambassador, Working Woman,* and *Vogue.*

*WORK IN PROGRESS:* A play, *Nzinga the Queen-King;* research on Nzinga, a seventeenth-century queen of Angola.

*SIDELIGHTS:* Carole Ione is the author of *Pride of Family: Four Generations of American Women of Color,* which *New York Times Book Review* contributor Maggie Scarf called a "remarkable, beautifully written memoir." In this work the author explores the relationships among the women in her family. Because both Ione's mother and grandmother had only short-term relationships with men, the stable influences in the author's childhood were female. Ione rebelled against her mother because she sent her to live with relatives and later learned that this issue fueled similar conflicts between mothers and daughters in her family for generations. Ione notes in *Pride of Family* that her journalist mother, her physician great-aunt, and her chorus-girl grandmother all imparted the same wisdom to her: "always have some money of your own"; "you can't trust a man"; "always put cold cream on your face at night"; "a woman never tells her age." But the author adds, "I started to realize that there was something essential they weren't telling me; some reason why it was so difficult for us to feel at home with one another and with our lives." Ione then attempted to uncover her earlier maternal roots, hoping to find someone with whom she could feel more at home. She discovered a positive role model in Frances Anne Rollin, her nineteenth-century paternal great-grandmother who was the first Southern black woman diarist. Scarf commented, "*Pride of Family* introduces us to a vital black patrician world with which many of us are relatively unacquainted. But what I loved most were the women.... Carole Ione, their loyal descendant, has captured them here and, in her own way, immortalized them."

Ione commented: "I have always encouraged others to heal through creativity. 'The personal' has always been my instrument. I have spent years facilitating journalism and notebook classes, dream circles, and Women's Mysteries, a training program in the intuitive arts."

*BIOGRAPHICAL/CRITICAL SOURCES:*

*BOOKS*

Ione, Carole, *Pride of Family: Four Generations of American Women of Color*, Summit Books, 1991.

*PERIODICALS*

*New York Times Book Review,* October 13, 1991, p. 12.

\* \* \*

## JABAVU, Davidson Don Tengo 1885-1959

*PERSONAL:* Born October 20, 1885, in Healdtown, South Africa; died of cancer, 1959; buried in Middlerift, Cape Province, South Africa; son of John Tengo and Elda (Sakuba) Jabavu; married Florence Nolwandle Tandiswa, September 2, 1916 (died 1951); children: Helen Nontan-o, Alexandra Nothemba, Tengo Max. *Education:* University of London, B.A. (with honors), 1912; Birmingham University (England),

teacher's degree, 1916. *Religion:* Wesleyan Methodist. *Advocational interests:* Playing the piano and violin, singing.

*CAREER:* Native College at Fort Hare (now Fort Hare University College), South Africa, lecturer, 1916-42, professor of Bantu languages, Latin, English, and history, 1942-46, secretary of College Senate. *Imvo zabantsundu* ("Opinion of the Blacks," a newspaper founded by his father), co-editor and co-publisher, beginning in 1921. Organized the Cape African Teachers' Association, South African Federation of Native Teachers, Native Farmers' Association, and Cape Native Voters' Association; member of the Native Conferences sponsored by the Government, 1920-30; called the first All-African Convention, 1935, president, 1935-48; worked with Joint Councils of Europeans and Natives. South African Institute of Race Relations, vice-president, 1932-59. Established All-African Insurance Company, 1959.

*AWARDS, HONORS:* Ph.D., Rhodes University, 1946; medal created in his honor, Royal African Society, 1946; Freedom of New Brighton award, May, 1954; a memorial stone was placed on Jabavu's grave, 1961.

*WRITINGS:*

*POETRY*

*Izithuko* (title means "Abuses"), Lovedale Press, 1954.
*Izidungulwana* (title means "Twigs"), Maskew Miller, c. 1960.

*NONFICTION*

*The Black Problem,* Lovedale Press, 1920, second edition, 1921.
*Bantu Literature,* Lovedale Press, 1921.
*The Life of John Tengo Jabavu,* Lovedale Press, 1922.
*What Methodism Has Done for the Natives,* Lovedale Press, 1923.
*Incwadi Yaba Limi* (title means "On Agriculture"), Lovedale Press, 1923.
*The Segregation Fallacy,* Lovedale Press, 1928.
*E-Jerusalem* (title means "To Jerusalem"), Lovedale Press, 1928.
(Editor) Richard Tainton Kawa, *I-bali lama Mfengu* (title means "The Story of the Mfengu People"), Lovedale Press, 1929.
(Editor) Chief Shadrach Fuba Zibi, *U'Kayakhulu,* Lovedale Press, 1930.
*"Native Disabilities" in South Africa,* Lovedale Press, 1932.
*E-Amerika* (title means "To America"), Lovedale Press, 1932.
*The Influence of English on Bantu Literature:* Lovedale Press, 1943.
*E-Indiya nase-East Africa* (title means "To India and East Africa"), Lovedale Press, 1951.

*OTHER*

Contributor to *International Review of Missions* (London).

*BIOGRAPHICAL/CRITICAL SOURCES:*

*BOOKS*

Herdeck, Donald E., *African Authors: A Companion to Black African Writing,* Volume 1: *1300-1973,* Black Orpheus Press, 1973.

\* \* \*

**JABBAR, Kareem Abdul**
**See ABDUL-JABBAR, Kareem**

\* \* \*

**JAMES, C(yril) L(ionel) R(obert)   1901-1989**
**(J. R. Johnson)**

*PERSONAL:* Born January 4, 1901, in Chaguanas, Trinidad and Tobago; died of a chest infection, May 31, 1989, in London, England; son of a schoolteacher; divorced from first wife; married Constance Webb (marriage ended); married Selma Weinstein, 1955; children: (first marriage) one. *Education:* Graduated from Queen's Royal College secondary school, Port of Spain, 1918.

*ADDRESSES: Home*—Brixton, London, England. *Agent*—c/o Allison & Busby, 6-A Noel St., London W1V 3RB, England.

*CAREER:* Member of the Maple cricket team, Port of Spain, Trinidad and Tobago; *Trinidad* (literary magazine), Port of Spain, editor, 1929-30; Queen's Royal College, Port of Spain, teacher, until 1932; *Manchester Guardian,* London, England, correspondent, 1932-38; *Fight* (later *Workers' Fight;* Marxist publication), London, editor, until 1938; trade union organizer and political activist in the United States, 1938-53; West Indian Federal Labor Party, Port of Spain, secretary, 1958-60; *Nation,* Port of Spain, editor, 1958-60. Lecturer at colleges and universities, including Federal City College, Washington, DC; commentator for the British Broadcasting Corporation (BBC); cricket columnist for *Race Today.*

*AWARDS, HONORS:* Honorary Doctor of Literature, University of the West Indies.

*WRITINGS:*

*The Life of Captain Cipriani: An Account of British Government in the West Indies,* Nelson, Lancashire, Coulton, 1932, abridged edition published as *The Case for West-Indian Self-Government,* Hogarth, 1933, University Place Book Shop, 1967.
(With L. R. Constantine) *Cricket and I,* Allan, 1933.
*Minty Alley* (novel), Secker & Warburg, 1936, New Beacon, 1971.
*Toussaint L'Ouverture* (play; first produced in London, 1936; revised version titled *The Black Jacobins* and produced in Ibadan, Nigeria, 1967), published in *A Time and a Season: Eight Caribbean Plays,* edited by Errol Hill, University of the West Indies (Port of Spain), 1976.
*World Revolution, 1917-1936: The Rise and Fall of the Communist International,* Pioneer, 1937, Hyperion Press, 1973.
*A History of Negro Revolt,* Fact, 1938, Haskell House, 1967, revised and expanded edition published as *A History of Pan-African Revolt,* Drum and Spear Press, 1969.
*The Black Jacobins: Toussaint L'Ouverture and the San Domingo Revolution,* Dial, 1938, Random House, 1963.
(Translator from the French) Boris Souvarine, *Stalin: A Critical Survey of Socialism,* Longman, 1939.
*State Capitalism and World Revolution* (published anonymously), privately printed, 1950, Facing Reality, 1969.
*Mariners, Renegades, and Castaways: The Story of Herman Melville and the World We Live In,* privately printed, 1953, Bewick Editions, 1978.
*Modern Politics* (lectures), PNM (Port of Spain), 1960.
*Beyond a Boundary,* Hutchinson, 1963, Pantheon, 1984.
*The Hegelian Dialectic and Modern Politics,* Facing Reality, 1970, revised edition published as *Notes on Dialectics: Hegel, Marx, Lenin,* Lawrence Hill, 1980.
*The Future in the Present: Selected Writings of C. L. R. James,* Lawrence Hill, 1977.
(Under pseudonym J. R. Johnson) *The Books of American Negro Spirituals,* edited by James Weldon Johnson, Da Capo Press, 1977.
*Nkrumah and the Ghana Revolution,* Lawrence Hill, 1977, revised edition, Allison & Busby, 1982.
(With Tony Bogues and Kim Gordon) *Black Nationalism and Socialism,* Socialists Unlimited, 1979.
(With George Breitman, Edgar Keemer, and others) *Fighting Racism in World War II,* Monad, 1980.
*Spheres of Existence: Selected Writings,* Lawrence Hill, 1981.
*Eightieth Birthday Lectures,* Race Today, 1983.
*At the Rendezvous of Victory: Selected Writings,* Lawrence Hill, 1985.
*Cricket,* Allison & Busby, 1986.
*The C L R James Reader,* edited by Anna Grimshaw, Blackwell, 1992.

Contributor of short stories to the collections *The Best Short Stories of 1928,* Cape, 1928, and *Island Voices,* Liveright, 1970; author, sometimes under pseudonym J. R. Johnson, of numerous political pamphlets; contributor of articles to newspapers and magazines.

*WORK IN PROGRESS:* An autobiography.

*SIDELIGHTS:* C. L. R. James was a leading political and literary figure of Trinidad and Tobago whose interests and values were profoundly shaped by his experience growing up in the British West Indian colony at the beginning of the century. The son of a schoolteacher father, James was raised in the capital of Port of Spain in a highly respectable—indeed, rather puritanical—middle-class black family suffused in British manners and culture. The James family home faced the back of a cricket field, and young Cyril developed a lifelong passion for the baseball-like sport watching matches from his living room window. The boy also grew up with an intense love for English literature—at age ten he had memorized long passages of William Makepeace Thackeray's *Vanity Fair*—and both his reading and his cricket playing often distracted him from his studies at the elite Queen's Royal College in Port of Spain. Dashing his parents' hopes that he would pursue a political career with the colonial administration, James chose instead to play professional cricket and teach at the Queen's Royal College in the 1920s. At the same time, he set about chronicling the lives of his nation's lower class in a series of naturalistic short stories that shocked his peers and foreshadowed his future Marxism. James's firsthand study of the Port of Spain slums also furnished background for his only novel, *Minty Alley,* an affecting but unsentimental look at the complex personal relationships and humble aspirations of the denizens of a rundown boarding house.

In 1932, chafing under the placid routines of a life in a colonial backwater, James accepted an invitation to go to London to help the great black cricketer Learie Constantine of Trinidad and Tobago write his autobiography. With Constantine's help, James secured a job as a cricket correspondent with the *Manchester Guardian* and published his first nonfiction book, *The Life of Captain Cipriani: An Account of British Government in the West Indies* (later abridged and published as *The Case for West-Indian Self-Government*). This influential treatise—one of the first to urge full self-determination for West Indians—introduced James to leading figures in the two political movements that were to profoundly shape his thinking in the years to come: Pan Africanism and Marxism.

James first developed his Pan Africanist ideas in leftist activist George Padmore's London-based African Bureau, where he joined future African independence leaders Jomo Kenyatta and Kwame Nkrumah as a political propagandist in the mid-1930s. James emphasized the importance of West Indians' coming to terms with their African heritage in order to help forge a sense of national identity in their racially and culturally polyglot society. He also came to regard the struggle to liberate and politically unify colonial Africa as a way of inspiring and mobilizing oppressed people of color around the world to seize control of their destinies. James later examined Pan Africanist theory and practice in two historical works, *A History of Negro Revolt* (later revised and published as *A History of Pan-African Revolt*), which surveys nearly two centuries of the black liberation struggle against European colonialism, and *Nkrumah and the Ghana Revolution,* an analysis of the first successful independence movement in modern Africa.

While participating in the vanguard of the African liberation movement, James also became a committed Marxist during his sojourn in London in the 1930s. He took the Trotskyist position in the great dispute over Stalinism that split the world communist movement during those years and wrote a history from that perspective in 1937 titled *World Revolution, 1917-1936: The Rise and Fall of the Communist International.* James's Marxism also informed his 1938 historical study *The Black Jacobins: Toussaint L'Ouverture and the San Domingo Revolution.* In this book, generally regarded as his masterwork, James analyzes the socioeconomic roots and leading personalities of the Haitian revolution of 1791 to 1804, the first and only slave revolt to achieve political independence in world history.

At the center of the revolution and the book stands Toussaint L'Ouverture. The self-taught black slave turned charismatic political leader and redoubtable military commander organized and led a disciplined army of former slaves, who defeated crack French and British expeditionary forces mustered to crush the insurgency. Of particular interest in *The Black Jacobins,* critics noted, is the author's success in relating the Haitian events to the course of the French Revolution, whose ideals inspired Toussaint even as he fought first Maximilien Robespierre and then Napoleon Bonaparte to free France's most important Caribbean sugar colony, then known as Saint Domingue. The democratic ideals of the Haitian revolution, which culminated in full political independence a year after Toussaint's death in 1803, touched off a wave of slave revolts throughout the Caribbean and helped inspire anti-slavery forces in the southern United States. *New York Herald Tribune Books* reviewer Clara Gruening Stillman judged *The Black Jacobins* as gripping as the events it recounted: "Brilliantly conceived and executed, throwing upon the historical screen a mass of dramatic figures, lurid scenes, fantastic happenings, the absorbing narrative never departs from its rigid faithfulness to method and documentation." A stage version of the book was first performed in 1936, with renowned actor Paul Robeson cast as Toussaint. In the mid-1980s, the play was revived by Yvonne Brewster's Talawa company.

Shortly after publishing *The Black Jacobins* James moved to the United States, where he joined the Trotskyist Socialist Workers Party (SWP) and became a full-time political activist, organizing auto workers in Detroit, Michigan, and tenant farmers in the South. He broke with the SWP in the late 1940s over the question of the nature of the Soviet Union, which he dubbed "state capitalist," and co-founded a new Detroit-based Trotskyist political organization with Leon Trotsky's former secretary Raya Dunayevskaya. James's political activities eventually provoked the wrath of the McCarthy-era U.S. government, which denied him American citizenship and deported him to Great Britain in 1953. While awaiting his expulsion on Ellis Island, the ever-resourceful James managed to write a short study of Herman Melville titled *Mariners, Renegades, and Castaways: The Story of Herman Melville and the World We Live In* that drew a parallel between Ahab's pursuit of the great white whale in Melville's classic, *Moby Dick,* and left-wing intellectuals' infatuation with Soviet political leader Joseph Stalin.

After five years in London, James returned to Trinidad and Tobago in 1958 to join the movement for political independence there. In Port of Spain he edited *Nation* magazine and served as secretary of the West Indian Federal Labor Party, whose leader, Eric Williams, became the island nation's first premier in 1960. Like the United States authorities, however, Williams found James's outspoken Marxism politically threatening and soon compelled James, who had once been Williams's schoolmaster, to go back to England. James left Trinidad and Tobago aggrieved that the emerging Caribbean nations had failed to achieve a lasting formula for political federation, which he believed necessary to further their social and economic development.

Back in London, James returned to political writing and lecturing, particularly on the Pan Africanist movement, West Indian politics, and the black question in the United States. He also rekindled his passion for cricket after leading a successful campaign to have Frank Worrell of Trinidad and Tobago named the first black captain of the West Indian international cricket team. Worrell's spectacular playing at the Australian championship competition in 1961 galvanized a sense of national pride and identity among the emerging West Indian nations and partly inspired James to write *Beyond a Boundary,* his much-praised 1963 survey of cricket's social and cultural significance in Great Britain and the Caribbean. The book's title refers both to the game's objective of driving a ball beyond a marked boundary and James's thesis that this gentleman's sport can help overcome certain false cultural, racial, and political boundaries within society. On a purely

aesthetic level, James argues, cricket has "the perfect flow of motion" that defines the essence of all great art; he holds that a good cricket match is the visual and dramatic equivalent of so-called "high art" and that the sport should be recognized as a genuinely democratic art form. Cricket's high standards of fairness and sportsmanship, on the other hand, illustrate "all the decencies required for a culture" and even played a historic role by showing West Indian blacks that they could excel in a forum where the rules were equal for everyone. The integrated Caribbean cricket teams, James believes, helped forge a new black self-confidence that carried the West Indian colonies to independence. The author renders these observations in an anecdotal style that includes both biographical sketches of great cricketers and personal reminiscences from his own lifelong love affair with the sport. *"Beyond a Boundary* is one of the finest and most finished books to come out of the West Indies," remarked novelist V. S. Naipaul in *Encounter.* "There is no more eloquent brief for the cultural and artistic importance of sport," added *Newsweek*'s Jim Miller.

Before his death in 1989, James published two well-received collections of essays and articles that display his broad literary, cultural, and political interests. *The Future in the Present: Selected Writings of C.L.R. James* contains the author's short story "Triumph," about women tenants in a Port of Spain slum, along with essays ranging from critical interpretations of Pablo Picasso's painting "Guernica" and Melville's *Moby Dick* to a political analysis of workers' councils in Hungary and a personal account of organizing a sharecroppers' strike in Missouri in 1942. "The writings are profound, sometimes; cranky, occasionally; stimulating, always," remarked *Village Voice* critic Paul Berman, and *Times Literary Supplement* reviewer Thomas Hodgkin found the book "a mine of richness and variety." *At the Rendezvous of Victory: Selected Writings,* whose title James took from a verse by the great West Indian poet Aime Cesaire, includes an essay on the Solidarity union movement in Poland and critical discussions of the work of black American novelists Toni Morrison and Alice Walker. The more than eighty-year-old James "show(ed) no diminution of his intellectual energies," wrote Alastair Niven in his review of the collection for *British Books News.* "Throughout this book James's elegant but unmannered style, witty and relaxed when lecturing, reflective and analytical when writing for publication, always conveys a sense of his own robust, humane, and giving personality. Was there ever a less polemical or more persuasive radical?"

In 1992, James's secretary, Anna Grimshaw, published *The C L R James Reader,* a 450-page anthology of James's numerous unpublished letters and documents. The book includes letters to James's wife Constance during his 1940s residence in the United States, and a stage version of his play *The Black Jacobins.* Clive Davis in *New Statesman & Society,* observed that "the book is broadly divided between political, literary and cultural analysis."

*BIOGRAPHICAL/CRITICAL SOURCES:*

BOOKS

*Contemporary Literary Criticism,* Volume 33, Gale, 1983.
Grimshaw, Anna, editor, *The C L R James Reader,* Blackwell, 1992.
James, C. L. R., *The Future in the Present: Selected Writings of C. L. R. James,* Lawrence Hill, 1977.
James, C. L. R., *Beyond a Boundary,* Pantheon, 1984.
Mackenzine, Alan and Paul Gilroy, *Visions of History,* Pantheon, 1983.

PERIODICALS

*American Scholar,* summer, 1985.
*British Books News,* May, 1984.
*CLA Journal,* December, 1977.
*Encounter,* September, 1963.
*Nation,* May 4, 1985.
*Newsweek,* March 26, 1984.
*New Statesman & Society,* June 26, 1992, p. 40.
*New Yorker,* June 25, 1984.
*New York Herald Tribune Books,* November 27, 1938.
*New York Times Book Review,* March 25, 1984; November 15, 1992, p. 28.
*Radical America,* May, 1970.
*Times Literary Supplement,* December 2, 1977; January 20, 1978; September 25, 1987.
*Village Voice,* February 11, 1981; July 10, 1984.
*Washington Post Book World,* April 22, 1984.

*OBITUARIES:*

PERIODICALS

*Los Angeles Times,* June 3, 1989.
*New York Times,* June 2, 1989.
*Times* (London), June 2, 1989.
*Washington Post,* June 3, 1989.
*Village Voice,* February 11, 1981, July 10, 1984.
*Washington Post Book World,* April 22, 1984.

\*   \*   \*

## JAMES, Luther 1928-

*PERSONAL:* Born August 8, 1928, in New York, NY; son of Joseph and Alice James; married Thelma (divorced); married Marguerite Brisby; children: (first marriage) Robin, Julian. *Education:* Attended Dramatic Workshop of the New School for Social Research, 1951.

*ADDRESSES: Home*—1308 South New Hampshire, Los Angeles, CA 90006. *Office*—Department of Theatre, University of California, San Diego, 9500 Gilman Rd., La Jolla, CA 92093.

*CAREER:* Affiliated with Comet Productions, 1950s; Luther James Theatre Workshop, New York City, teacher, 1958-68; Arena Productions, MGM, Culver City, CA, assistant to supervising producer, 1965-66; CBS-TV, Los Angeles, CA, executive producer, 1966-68; Negro Ensemble Company, New York City, instructor, 1968-69; WGBH-TV, Boston, MA, producer of *On Being Black,* 1968-70; TV writer and director, 1970-75. Teacher of drama, Portland State University, California State University, Los Angeles, and California State University, Northridge, 1971-73; University of California San Diego Department of Theatre, associate professor, 1975—. Director of plays, Oregon Shakespeare Festival, 1980—; theatre editor, *Crisis* magazine, 1986—.

*MEMBER:* Directors Guild of America, Writers Guild of America.

*AWARDS, HONORS:* John Hay Whitney fellowship, 1959-60; Ford Foundation fellowship, 1962.

*WRITINGS:*

*Liberty* (one-act play; telecast early 1970s), published in *Interactions,* Altshuler, 1972.

*BIOGRAPHICAL/CRITICAL SOURCES:*

BOOKS

*Contemporary Black American Playwrights and Their Plays,* Greenwood Press, 1988.

\*   \*   \*

## JEFFERSON, Roland S(pratlin) 1939-

*PERSONAL:* Born May 16, 1939, in Washington, DC; son of Bernard S. (a judge) and Devonia (a professor of drama; maiden name, Spratlin) Jefferson; married Melanie L. Moore (a teacher), 1966; children: Roland Jr., Rodney, Shannon, Royce. *Education:* University of Southern California, B.A., 1961; Howard University, M.D., 1965.

*ADDRESSES: Home*—3870 Crenshaw Blvd., No. 215, Los Angeles, CA 90008.

*CAREER:* Physician in Los Angeles, CA, 1965—; writer and filmmaker. Films include *Disco 9000, Pacific Inferno, Angel Dust: The Wack Attack,* and *Perfume. Military service:* U.S. Air Force, 1969-71; became captain.

*MEMBER:* Writers Guild of America, Association of Black Motion Picture and Television Producers, National Medical Association.

*AWARDS, HONORS:* Admitted to Black Filmmakers Hall of Fame, 1979.

*WRITINGS:*

*The School on 103rd Street* (novel), Vantage Press, 1976, published as *The Secret below 103rd Street,* Holloway, 1983.
*A Card for the Players* (novel), edited by Saul Burnstein, New Bedford Press, 1978.
*559 to Damascus* (novel), edited by Marian O'Farrell, New Bedford Press, 1986.

Also writer and director of film *Perfume,* 1989.

*SIDELIGHTS:* Roland S. Jefferson once commented: "Most of my writing (with the exception of *A Card for the Players*) covers subject matter that I consider to be socially relevant. I particularly like political background conflicts against the development of my characters. *The School on 103rd Street* was conceived because of the prevailing belief at the time by black America that it was not inconceivable to feel threatened by government attempts to incarcerate the entire population. Certainly I was influenced by Sam Greenlee's *The Spook Who Sat by the Door* and John Williams's *The Man Who Cried I Am,* as well as Sam Yette's *The Choice*—all novels of the sixties and seventies that reflected a similar viewpoint.

"My views and feelings come from the people I've known in life. As a psychiatrist, I have the unique opportunity to observe and to listen to people express themselves, so I borrow a little from this person and a little from that person, add my own interpretation to the mixture, and thus my characters are born.

"I became involved in filmmaking quite by accident. I had always wanted to be a writer of sorts. In college I was frustrated in this pursuit because my family was very traditional and felt that writers could not support themselves; thus, I had to study medicine. I have no regrets except that I waited longer than I would have liked to begin writing again. So, while in the Air Force, I became a film critic. This evolved into writing fiction in the form of novels, and eventually this moved me into film.

"Film is the most creative and the most expensive art form there is, but its influence is unfathomable. I discovered that what I really wanted was to be able to move or to touch, if you will, masses of people in some capacity. But the film industry is a closed shop, and breaking in is very difficult. To do so you must find one who thinks, feels, and is willing to gamble as much as you will on a project. I've been lucky on four occasions. *Disco 9000* was my first film and preceded *Saturday Night Fever* by over a year. *Pacific Inferno,* my second film, is a World War II adventure set in the Philippines and has racial overtones not normally found in films of the genre. *Angel Dust: The Wack Attack,* my only film made for television (ABC-TV) ... was a powerful drama about the evils of drug abuse. All of the films had subtle, unconscious meanings attached to them that, in some respects, made them quite controversial for their times." Jefferson added that his fourth film, *Perfume,* which he both wrote and directed, "is about people and their emotions and their reactions and interactions with one another."

He concluded: "I practice medicine now as infrequently as I can manage. Some of my writing in the past has been for academic journals, but my real interest is in writing fiction with universal themes that people can all identify with. My aspirations are much like those of Michael Crichton [*Jurassic Park*], Somerset Maugham, and George Miller [director of the film *The Witches of Eastwick*]; they were all physicians who gave up medicine because they discovered the beauty and satisfaction that lay within the arts."

\*   \*   \*

## JOHNSON, Charles (Richard) 1948-

*PERSONAL:* Born April 23, 1948, in Evanston, IL; son of Benjamin Lee and Ruby Elizabeth (Jackson) Johnson; married Joan New (an elementary school teacher), June, 1970; children: Malik, Elizabeth. *Education:* Southern Illinois University, B.A., 1971, M.A., 1973; post-graduate work at State University of New York at Stony Brook, 1973-76.

*ADDRESSES: Office*—Department of English, University of Washington, Seattle, WA 98105.

*CAREER: Chicago Tribune,* Chicago, IL, cartoonist and reporter, 1969-70; *St. Louis Proud,* St. Louis, MO, member of art staff, 1971-72; University of Washington, Seattle, assistant professor, 1976-79, associate professor, 1979-82, professor of English, 1982—, director of creative writing program.

Writer and cartoonist. Fiction editor of *Seattle Review,* 1978—. Director of Associated Writing Programs Awards Series in Short Fiction, 1979-81, member of board of directors, 1983—.

*AWARDS, HONORS:* Named journalism alumnus of the year by Southern Illinois University, 1981; Governors Award for Literature from State of Washington, 1983, for *Oxherding Tale; Callaloo* Creative Writing Award, 1983, for short story "Popper's Disease"; citation in *Pushcart Prize*'s Outstanding Writers section, 1984, for story "China"; Writers Guild Award for best children's show, 1986, for "Booker"; nomination for the PEN/Faulkner Award from the PEN American Center, 1987, for *The Sorcerer's Apprentice;* National Book Award for *Middle Passage,* 1990.

*WRITINGS:*

*NOVELS*

*Faith and the Good Thing,* Viking, 1974.
*Oxherding Tale,* Indiana University Press, 1982.
*Middle Passage,* Atheneum, 1990.

*CARTOON COLLECTIONS*

*Black Humor* (self-illustrated), Johnson Publishing, 1970.
*Half-Past Nation Time* (self-illustrated), Aware Press, 1972.

Contributor of cartoons to periodicals, including *Ebony, Chicago Tribune, Jet, Black World,* and *Players.*

*TELEVISION SCRIPTS*

*Charlie's Pad* (fifty-two-part series on cartooning), PBS, 1970.
*Charlie Smith and the Fritter Tree,* PBS "Visions" series, 1978.
(With John Alman) *Booker,* PBS, 1983.

Contributor of scripts to numerous television series, including *Up and Coming,* PBS, 1981, and *Y.E.S., Inc.,* PBS, 1983.

*OTHER*

*The Sorcerer's Apprentice: Tales and Conjurations* (short stories), Atheneum, 1986.
(Contributor) Jeff Henderson, editor, *Thor's Hammer: Essays on John Gardner,* Arkansas Philological Association, 1986.

*Being and Race: Black Writing since 1970,* Indiana University Press, 1988.
*All This and Moonlight* (play), Samuel French, 1990.
(With Ron Chernow) *In Search of a Voice,* Library of Congress, 1991.

Work represented in anthologies, including *Best American Short Stories, 1982,* edited by John Gardner and Shannon Ravenel, Houghton, 1982. Contributor of short stories and essays to periodicals, including *Mother Jones, Callaloo, Choice, Indiana Review, Nimrod, Intro 10, Obsidian, Playboy,* and *North American Review.*

*SIDELIGHTS:* "Charles Johnson has enriched contemporary American fiction as few young writers can," observed *Village Voice* critic Stanley Crouch, adding that "it is difficult to imagine that such a talented artist will forever miss the big time." A graduate of Southern Illinois University, Johnson studied with the late author John Gardner, under whose direction he wrote *Faith and the Good Thing.* Though Johnson had written six "apprentice" novels prior to his association with Gardner, *Faith* was the first to be accepted for publication. Johnson professes to "share Gardner's concern with 'moral fiction'" and believes in the "necessity of young (and old) writers working toward becoming technicians of language and literary form."

*Faith and the Good Thing* met with an enthusiastic response from critics such as Garrett Epps of *Washington Post Book World,* who judged it "a brilliant first novel" and commended its author as "one of this country's most interesting and inventive younger writers." Roger Sale, writing in the *Sewanee Review,* had similar praise for the novel. He commented: "Johnson, it is clear, is a writer, and if he works too hard at it at times, or if he seems a little too pleased with it at other times, he is twenty-six, and with prose and confidence like his, he can do anything."

The book is a complex, often humorous, folktale account of Faith Cross, a Southern black girl traveling to Chicago in search of life's "Good Thing," which she has learned of from her dying mother. In her quest, noted *Time*'s John Skrow, Faith "seeks guidance from a swamp witch, a withered and warty old necromancer with one green and one yellow eye," who nonetheless "spouts philosophy as if she were Hegel." Skrow deemed the work a "wry comment on the tension felt by a black intellectual," and Annie Gottlieb of *New York Times Book Review* called *Faith and the Good Thing* a "strange and often wonderful hybrid—an ebullient philosophical novel in the form of a folktale-cum-black-girl's odyssey." She noted that the novel's "magic falls flat" on occasion, "when the mix ... is too thick with academic in-jokes and erudite references," but she added that "fortunately, such moments are overwhelmed by the poetry and wisdom of the book." In conclusion, Gottleib found the novel "flawed yet still fabulous."

Johnson described his second novel, *Oxherding Tale,* as "a modern, comic, philosophical slave narrative—a kind of dramatization of the famous 'Ten Oxherding Pictures' of Zen artist Kakuan-Shien," which represent the progressive search of a young herdsman for his rebellious ox, a symbol for himself. The author added that the novel's style "blends the eighteenth-century English novel with the Eastern parable."

Like his first novel, Johnson's *Oxherding Tale* received widespread critical acclaim. It details the coming of age of Andrew Hawkins, a young mulatto slave in the pre-Civil War South. Andrew is conceived when, after much drinking, plantation owner Jonathan Polkinghorne convinces his black servant, George Hawkins, to swap wives with him for the evening. Unaware that the man sharing her bed is not her husband, Anna Polkinghorne makes love with George and consequentially becomes pregnant with Andrew. After the child is born Anna rejects him as a constant reminder of her humiliation, and he is taken in by George's wife, Mattie. Though he is raised in slave quarters Andrew receives many privileges, including an education from an eccentric tutor who teaches him about Eastern mysticism, socialism, and the philosophies of Plato, Schopenhauer, and Hegel.

Writing in *Literature, Fiction, and the Arts Review,* Florella Orowan called Andrew "a man with no social place, caught between the slave world and free white society but, like the hapless hero Tom Jones, he gains from his ambiguous existence the timeless advantage of the Outsider's omniscience and chimerism: he can assume whatever identity is appropriate to the situation." *Oxherding Tale* accompanies its hero on a series of adventures that include an exotic sexual initiation, an encounter with the pleasures of opium, escape from the plantation, "passing" as white, and eluding a telepathic bounty hunter called the Soulcatcher. As Michael S. Weaver observed in *Gargoyle,* Andrew "lives his way to freedom through a succession of sudden enlightenments.... Each experience is another layer of insight into human nature" that has "a touch of Johnson's ripe capacity for laughter." The book's climax, noted Crouch, is "remarkable for its brutality and humble tenderness; Andrew must dive into the briar patch of his identity and risk destruction in order to express his humanity."

Weaver admitted that "at times *Oxherding Tale* reads like a philosophical tract, and may have been more adequately billed as Thus Spake Andrew Hawkins." But he concluded that the novel "is nonetheless an entertaining display of Johnson's working knowledge of the opportunities for wisdom afforded by the interplay between West and East, Black and White, man and woman, feeling and knowing—all of them seeming con-

tradictions." According to Crouch, the novel is successful "because Johnson skillfully avoids melodramatic platitudes while creating suspense and comedy, pathos and nostalgia. In the process, he invents a fresh set of variations on questions about race, sex, and freedom."

*The Sorcerer's Apprentice,* Johnson's collection of short stories, met with highly favorable reviews and garnered him a nomination for the PEN/Faulkner Award for fiction. "These tales," reported Michael Ventura in the *New York Times Book Review,* "are realistic without strictly adhering to realism, fantastic without getting lost in fantasy." The title story concerns a young black man, Allan, who is the son of a former slave and wishes to become a sorcerer. He is taken under wing by Rubin, an African-born member of the Allmuseri, a tribe of wizards, and must accept his heritage before winning the ability to make true magic. The book also contains "Alethia," about a black professor, seemingly well-assimilated to academia, who must deal with his past in the slums of Chicago. "The Education of Mingo" again focuses attention on the Allmuseri, and "Popper's Disease" discusses the issues of assimilation and alienation through an encounter between a black doctor and the sick extraterrestrial he is called in to treat. "It is one of the achievements of these stories," lauded Michiko Kakutani of the *New York Times,* "that, while concerned at heart with questions of prejudice and cultural assimilation, they are never parochial and only rarely didactic. Rather, Mr. Johnson has used his generous storytelling gifts and his easy familiarity with a variety of literary genres to conjure up eight moral fables that limn the fabulous even as they remain grounded in the language and social idioms of black American communities." Kakutani did not, however, extend this praise to the volume's "Moving Pictures," calling it "a tired one-liner about escapism and the movies." Ventura concurred, lamenting that Johnson's "magic wears thin" in the case of "Moving Pictures," but he asserted that "there's no risk in predicting that 'The Education of Mingo,'... 'Alethia' and 'The Sorcerer's Apprentice' will be anthologized for a very long time."

Johnson's fiction reached a pinnacle of success with the awarding of the National Book Award for his novel, *Middle Passage.* Arend Flick, in the *Los Angeles Times Book Review* commented, "In his highly readable though densely philosophical fiction, Johnson gives us characters forced to chart a middle passage between competing ways of ordering reality: sensual or ascetic, Marxist or Freudian, Christian or pagan. They quest for a unity of being beyond all polarities, for what the heroine of his first novel calls 'the one thing all ... things have in common.' And happily for them and for us, they usually find it." *New York Review of Books*'s Garry Wills stated, "In the novel as in his critical writing, Johnson resists the idea of expressing 'black experience' as opposed to a black's experience of his or her inevitably multicultural world."

Like his mentor, John Gardner, Johnson's belief is, according to Flick, "that all true art is moral, not the promulgating of doctrine (which inevitably distorts morality) but the exploration and testing of values," a formula consistent with *Middle Passage*. As Flick surmised, "It's informed by a remarkably generous thesis: that racism generally, and the institution of slavery in particular, might best be seen as having arisen from political or sociological or economic causes, not ... from pigment envy, but from a deep fissure that characterizes Western thought in general, our tendency to split the world into competing categories: matter and spirit, subject and object, good and evil, black and white." Flick concluded, "What always saves the novel from the intellectual scheme that would otherwise kill it is the sheer beauty of its language.... Philosophy and art are not simply joined here. They are one."

Johnson commented: "As a writer I am committed to the development of what one might call a genuinely systematic philosophical black American literature, a body of work that explores classical problems and metaphysical questions against the background of black American life. Specifically, my philosophical style is phenomenology, the discipline of Edmund Husserl, but I also have a deep personal interest in the entire continuum of Asian philosophy from the Vedas to Zen, and this perspective inevitably colors my fiction to some degree.

"I have been a martial artist since the age of nineteen and a practicing Buddhist since about 1980. So one might also say that in fiction I attempt to interface Eastern and Western philosophical traditions, always with the hope that some new perception of experience—especially 'black experience'—will emerge from these meditations."

Johnson and two fellow writers, Frank Chin and Colleen McElroy, are the subjects of a documentary film profile titled "Spirit of Place." Written by filmmaker Jean Walkinshaw, the film was first broadcast by KCTS-TV in Seattle, Washington, and has been submitted for national broadcast by the Public Broadcasting Service.

*BIOGRAPHICAL/CRITICAL SOURCES:*

BOOKS

*Contemporary Literary Criticism,* Volume 7, Gale, 1977.
*Dictionary of Literary Biography,* Volume 33: *Afro-American Fiction Writers After 1955,* Gale, 1984.

PERIODICALS

*Atlantic,* April, 1986, p. 130.
*Callaloo,* October, 1978; summer, 1989.
*CLA Journal,* June, 1978.

*Forbes,* March 16, 1992.
*Gargoyle,* June, 1978.
*Literature, Fiction, and the Arts Review,* June 30, 1983.
*Los Angeles Times Book Review,* November 21, 1982; June 24, 1990, pp. 1, 7.
*Nation,* September 13, 1986.
*New Statesman,* April 22, 1988.
*New Statesman and Society,* June 14, 1991.
*New Yorker,* December 20, 1982.
*New York Review of Books,* January 17, 1991.
*New York Times,* February 5, 1986.
*New York Times Book Review,* January 12, 1975; January 9, 1983; March 30, 1986; July 1, 1990; November 3, 1991.
*Sewanee Review,* January, 1975.
*Time,* January 6, 1975.
*Times Literary Supplement,* January 6, 1984.
*Tribune Books* (Chicago), July 8, 1990.
*Village Voice,* July 19, 1983.
*Washington Post Book World,* December 15, 1982.


*   *   *


**JOHNSON, J. R.**
**See JAMES, C(yril) L(ionel) R(obert)**


*   *   *


**JOHNSON, Lemuel A. 1941-**

*PERSONAL:* Born December 15, 1941, in Northern Nigeria; son of Thomas Ishelu and Daisy (a teacher; maiden name, Williams) Johnson; married Marian Yankson (a dental hygienist), August 28, 1965; children: Yma, Yshely. *Education:* Oberlin College, B.A., 1965; Pennsylvania State University, M.A., 1966; University of Michigan, Ph.D., 1969; also studied at Middlebury College, Universite d'Aix-Marseille II, and University of Paris.

*ADDRESSES: Home*—415 Ventura Court, Ann Arbor, MI 48163. *Office*—Department of English, University of Michigan, Ann Arbor, MI 48164.

*CAREER:* Pennsylvania State University, University Park, faculty member in department of Spanish, Italian, and Portuguese, 1966; University of Michigan, Ann Arbor, faculty member in department of Romance languages and literature, 1967-68, faculty member in department of English, 1968-70; University of Sierra Leone, Fourah Bay College, Freetown, faculty member in department of English, 1970-72; University of Michigan, associate professor of English, 1972—.

Peace Corps, training program instructor, 1964; West African Examinations Council, examiner in English oral literature, 1970-72; Sierra Leone Broadcasting Service, host for "Radio Forum Series," 1971-72; has given poetry readings at University of Michigan, 1973 and 1974.

*MEMBER:* African Studies Association, Midwest Modern Language Association, African Literature Association (president, 1977-78).

*AWARDS, HONORS:* Avery Hopwood Awards, University of Michigan, 1967, for essay "Piano and Drum" and short story collection *The Voice of the Turtle;* Bredvold-Thorpe prize for scholarly publication, University of Michigan, 1972, for *The Devil, the Gargoyle and the Buffoon: The Negro as Metaphor in Western Literature.*

*WRITINGS:*

(Contributor of translation) *Modern Spanish Theatre,* Dutton, 1968.
*The Devil, the Gargoyle and the Buffoon: The Negro as Metaphor in Western Literature* (revision of the author's thesis), Kennikat, 1971.
*Highlife for Caliban* (poetry), Ardis, 1973.
*Hand on the Navel* (poetry), Ardis, 1978.
*Toward Defining the African Aesthetic* (selected papers of the African Literature Association), Three Continents Press, 1983.

Also author of the short story collection *The Voice of the Turtle* and the essay "Piano and Drum." Contributor to anthologies, including *African Writing Today,* Manyland Books, 1970; *New African Literature and the Arts,* edited by Joseph Okpaku, Crowell, 1970; and *Blacks in Hispanic Literature,* edited by Miriam DeCosta. Contributor to *Literary Review* and *Journal of New African Literature and the Arts.*

*BIOGRAPHICAL/CRITICAL SOURCES:*

*BOOKS*

*African Authors: A Companion to Black African Writing:* Volume 1, *1300-1973,* Black Orpheus Press, 1973, p. 167.

*PERIODICALS*

*Choice,* September, 1972, p. 806; June, 1974, p. 609; December, 1978, p. 1379.
*Library Journal,* May 1, 1974, p. 1307; September 1, 1978, p. 1641.

## JONES, Edward P. 1950-

*PERSONAL:* Born October 5, 1950. *Education:* Attended College of the Holy Cross, Worcester, MA, and University of Virginia.

*ADDRESSES: Home*—Arlington, VA.

*CAREER:* Columnist for *Tax Notes.*

*AWARDS, HONORS:* National Book Award finalist, National Book Foundation, 1992, for *Lost in the City.*

*WRITINGS:*

*Lost in the City* (short stories), photographs by Amos Chan, Morrow, 1992.

*SIDELIGHTS:* Called "a poignant and promising first effort" by *Publishers Weekly,* Edward P. Jones' first book, *Lost in the City,* was greeted with both critical and popular acclaim. The work was nominated for the 1992 National Book Award, the first short story collection to achieve this honor in six years, and its first printing sold out.

The appeal of the fourteen stories collected in *Lost in the City* lies in the realness of the people and the experiences that Edward P. Jones presents. Each of the stories profiles African American life in Washington, D.C., through characters that evoke sympathy. According to Mary Ann French, a staff writer for the *Washington Post,* Jones "writes seemingly simple stories about people and situations that were so commonly found that they won't seem at all remarkable to the average city dweller. Other readers say he creates sympathy through understanding—a sadly needed service that is too seldom performed."

The characters in Jones's stories are all lost in the nation's capital—some literally, some figuratively. They are black working-class heroes who struggle to preserve their families, communities and neighborhoods, and themselves amid drugs, violence, divorce, and other crises. Jones tells the characters' stories frankly—especially regarding social ills—but also intelligently and compassionately. The assortment of people he portrays includes a mother whose son buys her a new home with drug money; a husband who repeatedly stabs his wife as their children sleep; and a girl who watches her pigeons fly from her home after their cages are destroyed by rats. "Jones has near-perfect pitch for people," remarked Michael Harris in the *Los Angeles Times Book Review.* "Whoever they are, he reveals them to us from the inside out."

BIOGRAPHICAL/CRITICAL SOURCES:

PERIODICALS

Los Angeles Times Book Review, July 12, 1992, p. 6.
New York Times, June 11, 1992, p. C18; August 23, 1992,
    section 7, p. 16.
Publishers Weekly, March 23, 1992, p. 59.
Washington Post, July 22, 1992, p. G1; October 6, 1992, p.
    B4.

\*   \*   \*

## JONES, Gayl 1949-

PERSONAL: Born November 23, 1949, in Lexington, KY;
daughter of Franklin (a cook) and Lucille (Wilson) Jones.
Education: Connecticut College, B.A., 1971; Brown University, M.A., 1973, D.A., 1975.

ADDRESSES: c/o Lotus Press, P.O. Box 21607, Detroit, MI
48221.

CAREER: University of Michigan, Ann Arbor, 1975-83, began as assistant professor, became professor of English; writer.

MEMBER: Authors Guild, Authors League of America.

AWARDS, HONORS: Award for best original production in
the New England region, American College Theatre Festival,
1973, for Chile Woman; grants from Shubert Foundation,
1973-74, Southern Fellowship Foundation, 1973-75, and
Rhode Island Council on the Arts, 1974-75; fellowships from
Yaddo, 1974, National Endowment of the Arts, 1976, and
Michigan Society of Fellows, 1977-79; award from Howard
Foundation, 1975; fiction award from Mademoiselle, 1975;
Henry Russell Award, University of Michigan, 1981.

WRITINGS:

FICTION

Corregidora, Random House, 1975.
Eva's Man, Random House, 1976.
White Rat: Short Stories, Random House, 1977, reissued,
    Northern University Press, 1991.

POETRY

Song for Anninho, Lotus Press, 1981.
The Hermit-Woman, Lotus Press, 1983.
Xarque and Other Poems, Lotus Press, 1985.

OTHER

Chile Woman (play), Shubert Foundation, 1974.
Liberating Voices: Oral Tradition in African American Literature, Harvard University Press, 1991.

Contributor to anthologies, including Confirmation, 1983,
Chants of Saints, Keeping the Faith, Midnight Birds, and
Soulscript. Contributor to periodicals, including Massachusetts Review and Presence-Africane.

SIDELIGHTS: "Though not one of the best-known of contemporary black writers, Gayl Jones can claim distinction as
the teller of the most intense tales," Keith E. Byerman writes
in the Dictionary of Literary Biography. Jones's novels
Corregidora and Eva's Man, in addition to many of the stories in her collection White Rat, offer stark, often brutal accounts of black women whose psyches reflect the ravages of
accumulated sexual and racial exploitation. In Corregidora
Jones reveals the tormented life of a woman whose female
forebears—at the hands of one man—endured a cycle of slavery, prostitution, and incest over three generations. Eva's
Man explores the deranged mind of a woman institutionalized for poisoning and sexually mutilating a male acquaintance. And in "Asylum," a story from White Rat, a young
woman is confined to a mental hospital for a series of bizarre
behaviors that protest a society she sees bent on personal violation. "The abuse of women and its psychological results
fascinate Gayl Jones, who uses these recurring themes to
magnify the absurdity and the obscenity of racism and sexism in everyday life," comments Jerry W. Ward, Jr., in Black
Women Writers (1950-1980): A Critical Evaluation. "Her
novels and short fictions invite readers to explore the interior
of caged personalities, men and women driven to extremes."
Byerman elaborates: "Jones creates worlds radically different from those of 'normal' experience and of storytelling convention. Her tales are gothic in the sense of dealing with madness, sexuality, and violence, but they do not follow in the
Edgar Allan Poe tradition of focusing on private obsession and
irrationality. Though her narrators are close to if not over the
boundaries of sanity, the experiences they record reveal clearly
that society acts out its own obsessions, often violently."

Corregidora, Jones's first novel, explores the psychological
effects of slavery and sexual abuse on a modern black woman.
Ursa Corregidora, a blues singer from Kentucky, descends
from a line of women who are the progeny, by incest, of a
Portuguese slaveholder named Corregidora—the father of
both Ursa's mother and grandmother. "All of the women,
including the great-granddaughter Ursa, keep the name
Corregidora as a reminder of the depredations of the slave

system and of the rapacious natures of men," explains Byerman. "The story is passed from generation to generation of women, along with the admonition to 'produce generations' to keep alive the tale of evil." Partly as a result of this history, Ursa becomes involved in abusive relationships with men. The novel itself springs from an incident of violence; after being thrown down a flight of stairs by her first husband and physically injured so that she cannot bear children, Ursa "discharges her obligation to the memory of Corregidora by speaking [the] book," notes John Updike in the *New Yorker.* The novel emerges as Ursa's struggle to reconcile her heritage with her present life. *Corregidora* "persuasively fuses black history, or the mythic consciousness that must do for black history, with the emotional nuances of contemporary black life," Updike continues. "The book's innermost action ... is Ursa's attempt to transcend a nightmare black consciousness and waken to her own female, maimed humanity."

*Corregidora* was acclaimed as a novel of unusual power and impact. "No black American novel since Richard Wright's *Native Son* (1940)," writes Ivan Webster in *Time,* "has so skillfully traced psychic wounds to a sexual source." Darryl Pinckney in *New Republic* calls *Corregidora* "a small, fiercely concentrated story, harsh and perfectly told.... Original, superbly imagined, nothing about the book was simple or easily digested. Out of the worn themes of miscegenation and diminishment, Gayl Jones *excavated* the disturbingly buried damage of racism." Critics particularly praised Jones's treatment of sexual detail and its illumination of the central character. "One of the book's merits," according to Updike, "is the ease with which it assumes the writer's right to sexual specifics, and its willingness to explore exactly how our sexual and emotional behavior is warped within the matrix of family and race." In the book's final scene, Ursa comes to a reconciliation with her first husband, Mutt, by envisioning an ambivalent sexual relationship between her great-grandmother and the slavemaster Corregidora. *Corregidora* is a novel "filled with sexual and spiritual pain," writes Margo Jefferson in *Newsweek:* "hatred, love and desire wear the same face, and humor is blues-bitter.... Jones's language is subtle and sinewy, and her imagination sure."

Jones second novel, *Eva's Man,* continues her exploration into the psychological effects of brutality, yet presents a character who suffers greater devastation. Eva Medina Canada, incarcerated for the murder and mutilation of a male acquaintance, narrates a personal history which depicts the damaging influences of a society that is sexually aggressive and hostile. Updike describes the exploitative world that has shaped the mentally deranged Eva: "Evil permeates the erotic education of Eva Canada, as it progresses from Popsicle-stick violations to the witnessing of her mother's adultery and a growing awareness of the whores and 'queen bees' in the slum world around her, and on to her own reluctant initiation through

encounters in buses and in bars, where a man with no thumb monotonously propositions her. The evil that emanates from men becomes hers." In a narrative that is fragmented and disjointed, Eva gives no concrete motive for the crime committed; furthermore, she neither shows remorse nor any signs of rehabilitation. More experimental than *Corregidora, Eva's Man* displays "a sharpened starkness, a power of ellipsis that leaves ever darker gaps between its flashes of rhythmic, sensuously exact dialogue and visible symbol," according to Updike. John Leonard adds in the *New York Times* that "not a word is wasted" in Eva's narrative. "It seems, in fact, as if Eva doesn't have enough words, as if she were trying to use the words she has to make a poem, a semblance of order, and fails of insufficiency." Leonard concludes: "'Eva's Man' may be one of the most unpleasant novels of the season. It is also one of the most accomplished."

*Eva's Man* was praised for its emotional impact, yet some reviewers found the character of Eva extreme or inaccessible. June Jordan in the *New York Times Book Review* calls *Eva's Man* "the blues that lost control. This is the rhythmic, monotone lamentation of one woman, Eva Medina, who is nobody I have ever known." Jordan explains: "Jones delivers her story in a strictly controlled, circular form that is wrapped, around and around, with ambivalence. Unerringly, her writing creates the tension of a problem unresolved." In the end, however, Jordan finds that the fragmented details of Eva's story "do not mesh into illumination." On the other hand, some reviewers regard the gaps in *Eva's Man* as appropriate and integral to its meaning. Pinckney calls the novel "a tale of madness; one exacerbated if not caused by frustration, accumulated grievances" and comments on aspects that contribute to this effect: "Structurally unsettled, more scattered than *Corregidora, Eva's Man* is extremely remote, more troubling in its hallucinations.... The personal exploitation that causes Eva's desperation is hard to appreciate. Her rage seems never to find its proper object, except, possibly, in her last extreme act." Updike likewise holds that the novel accurately portrays Eva's deranged state, yet points out that Jones's characterization skills are not at their peak: "Jones apparently wishes to show us a female heart frozen into rage by deprivation, but the worry arises, as it did not in 'Corregidora,' that the characters are dehumanized as much by her artistic vision as by their circumstances."

Jordan raises a concern that the inconclusiveness of *Eva's Man* harbors a potentially damaging feature. "There is the very real, upsetting accomplishment of Gayl Jones in this, her second novel: sinister misinformation about women—about women, in general, about black women in particular." Jones comments in *Black Women Writers (1950-1980)* on the predicament faced in portraying negative characters: "To deal with such a character as Eva becomes problematic in the way that 'Trueblood' becomes problematic in [Ralph Ellison's] *Invisible*

*Man.* It raises the questions of possibility. Should a Black writer ignore such characters, refuse to enter 'such territory' because of the 'negative image' and because such characters can be misused politically by others, or should one try to reclaim such complex, contradictory characters as well as try to reclaim the idea of the 'heroic image'?" In an interview with Claudia Tate for *Black Women Writers at Work,* Jones elaborates: "'Positive race images' are fine as long as they're very complex and interesting personalities. Right now I'm not sure how to reconcile the various things that interest me with 'positive race images.' It's important to be able to work with a range of personalities, as well as with a range within one personality. For instance, how would one reconcile an interest in neurosis or insanity with positive race image?"

Although Jones's subject matter is often charged and intense, a number of critics have praised a particular restraint she manages in her narratives. Regarding *Corregidora,* Updike remarks: "Our retrospective impression of 'Corregidora' is of a big territory—the Afro-American psyche—rather thinly and stabbingly populated by ideas, personae, hints. Yet that such a small book could seem so big speaks well for the generous spirit of the author, unpolemical where there has been much polemic, exploratory where rhetoric and outrage tend to block the path." Similarly, Jones maintains an authorial distance in her fiction which, in turn, makes for believable and gripping characters. Byerman comments: "The authority of [Jones's] depictions of the world is enhanced by [her] refusal to intrude upon or judge her narrators. She remains outside the story, leaving the reader with none of the usual markers of a narrator's reliability. She gives these characters the speech of their religion, which, by locating them in time and space, makes it even more difficult to easily dismiss them; the way they speak has authenticity, which carries over to what they tell. The results are profoundly disturbing tales of repression, manipulation, and suffering."

Reviewers have also noted Jones's ability to innovatively incorporate Afro-American speech patterns into her work. In *Black Women Writers (1950-1980),* Melvin Dixon contends that "Gayl Jones has figured among the best of contemporary Afro-American writers who have used Black speech as a major aesthetic device in their works. Like Alice Walker, Toni Morrison, Sherley Williams, Toni Cade Bambara, and such male writers as Ernest Gaines and Ishmael Reed, Jones uses the rhythm and structure of spoken language to develop authentic characters and to establish new possibilities for dramatic conflict within the text and between readers and the text itself." In her interview with Tate, Jones remarks on the importance of storytelling traditions to her work: "At the time I was writing *Corregidora* and *Eva's Man* I was particularly interested—and continue to be interested—in oral traditions of storytelling—Afro-American and others, in which there is always the consciousness and importance of the hearer, even

in the interior monologues where the storyteller becomes her own hearer. That consciousness or self-consciousness actually determines my selection of significant events."

Jones's 1977 collection of short stories, *White Rat,* received mixed reviews. A number of critics noted the presence of Jones's typical thematic concerns, yet also felt that her shorter fiction did not allow enough room for character development. Diane Johnson comments in the *New York Review of Books* that the stories in *White Rat* "were written in some cases earlier than her novels, so they confirm one's sense of her direction and preoccupations: sex is violation, and violence is the principal dynamic of human relationships." Mel Watkins remarks in the *New York Times,* however, on a drawback to Jones's short fiction: "The focus throughout is on desolate, forsaken characters struggling to exact some snippet of gratification from their lives.... Although her prose here is as starkly arresting and indelible as in her novels, except for the longer stories such as 'Jeveta' and 'The Women,' these tales are simply doleful vignettes—slices of life so beveled that they seem distorted."

*White Rat* was reissued in 1991, meeting with more favorable estimations. In a review in *Belles Lettres,* Marilyn Sanders Mobley comments that to reread *White Rat* "is to bear witness to a writer who knows the power of the word and of the stories we tell. She also knows the expressive power of the African American vernacular to communicate the depths of interpersonal relations ... [and] we gasp in awe at the gift of language she has at her command."

Also in 1991, Jones published *Liberating Voices: Oral Tradition in African American Literature,* her first full-length literary study. The book discusses the writing of a variety of twentieth-century black authors, including Zora Neale Hurston and Amiri Baraka, many of whom have adapted various aspects of oral traditions in their own writing. In the words of J. A. Miller in *Choice,* the author is concerned with "the movement from restrictive literary forms towards the liberating possibilities of African American oral traditions."

While Jones's fiction writing often emphasizes a tormented side of life—especially regarding male-female relationships—it also raises the possibility for more positive interactions. Jones points out in the Tate interview that "there seems to be a growing understanding—working itself out especially in *Corregidora*—of what is required in order to be genuinely tender. Perhaps brutality enables one to recognize what tenderness is." Some critics have found ambivalence at the core of Jones's fiction. Dixon remarks: "Redemption ... is most likely to occur when the resolution of conflict is forged in the same vocabulary as the tensions which precipitated it. This dual nature of language makes it appear brutally indifferent, for it contains the source and the resolution of conflicts.... What

Jones is after is the words and deeds that finally break the sexual bondage men and women impose upon each other."

*BIOGRAPHICAL/CRITICAL SOURCES:*

*BOOKS*

*Black Literature Criticism,* Gale, 1992.
*Contemporary Literary Criticism,* Gale, Volume 6, 1976, Volume 9, 1978.
*Dictionary of Literary Biography,* Volume 33: *Afro-American Fiction Writers after 1955,* Gale, 1984.
Evans, Mari, editor, *Black Women Writers (1950-1980): A Critical Evaluation,* Anchor Books, 1984.
Tate, Claudia, editor, *Black Women Writers at Work,* Continuum, 1986.

*PERIODICALS*

*Belles Lettres,* summer, 1992, p. 4.
*Black World,* February, 1976.
*Callaloo,* October, 1982, pp. 31-111, winter, 1984, pp. 119-31.
*Choice,* November, 1991, p. 445.
*College Language Association Journal,* June, 1982, pp. 447-57, June 1986, pp. 400-13.
*Esquire,* December, 1976.
*Frontiers,* fall, 1980, pp. 1-5.
*Kliatt,* spring, 1986.
*Literary Quarterly,* May 15, 1975.
*Massachusetts Review,* winter, 1977.
*National Review,* April 14, 1978.
*New Republic,* June 28, 1975, June 19, 1976.
*Newsweek,* May 19, 1975, April 12, 1976.
*New Yorker,* August 18, 1975, August 9, 1976.
*New York Review of Books,* November 10, 1977.
*New York Times,* April 30, 1976, December 28, 1978.
*New York Times Book Review,* May 25, 1975, May 16, 1976.
*Time,* June 16, 1975.
*Washington Post,* October 21, 1977.
*Yale Review,* autumn, 1976.

\*   \*   \*

## JONES, LeRoi
## See BARAKA, Amiri

\*   \*   \*

## JONES, Nettie (Pearl) 1941-

*PERSONAL:* Born January 1, 1941, in Arlington, GA; daughter of Benjamin (a farmer) and Delonia (a homemaker; maiden name, Mears) Jones; married Frank Stafford, June, 1958 (divorced 1961); married Frank W. Harris, November 23, 1963 (divorced May 29, 1975); children: Lynne Cheryl Stafford Harris. *Education:* Wayne State University, B.S., 1962; Marygrove College, M.E., 1971; postgraduate study at New School of Social Research, 1971; attended Fashion Institute of Technology, 1973-76, and University of Chicago Divinity School, 1990-92.

*ADDRESSES: Home*—Detroit, MI. *Agent*—Julian Bach Literary Agency, 747 Third Ave., New York, NY 10017.

*CAREER:* Teacher of secondary social studies, English, and reading in Detroit, MI, 1963-72; Royal George School, Greenfield Park, Quebec, Canada, teacher of secondary English, 1966-68; Martin Luther King School, New York City, teacher of reading, 1971-72; Wayne State University, Detroit, lecturer, visiting writer, 1986-87; Wayne County Commission, Detroit, writer, 1988; Wayne County Community College, Detroit, teacher of developmental reading, 1988; Michigan Technological University, Houghton, assistant professor and writer in residence, 1988-89, minority affairs assistant to the vice president, 1989—. King-Chevis-Parks Scholar, 1988-90; Benjamin Mays Scholar, University of Chicago Divinity School, 1991-92.

*AWARDS, HONORS:* Yaddo fellowship, 1985; awards from Michigan Council of the Arts, 1986 and 1989; second runner-up, D. H. Lawrence competition, 1987; grant from National Endowment for the Arts, 1989.

*WRITINGS:*

*Fish Tales* (novel), Random, 1984.
*Mischief Makers* (novel), Weidenfeld & Nicholson, 1989.

Contributor to *Detroit Free Press Magazine* and *Detroit Monthly.*

*SIDELIGHTS:* Nettie Jones is known for her provocative, sexually explicit novels about life in contemporary America. Her first book, the episodic *Fish Tales,* was described by *Chicago Tribune* contributor William O'Rourke as "a story of one woman's contradictory oppression and satisfaction through sex, drugs, and alcohol, rendered in graphic, uncompromising prose." The novel's narrator is Lewis Jones, a black woman obsessed with sex. Lewis relates, in frank detail, her encounters with such partners as Peter, a twenty-four-year-old social studies teacher who seduces her when she is only twelve; her husband, Woody, a pharmacist who continues to support her even after their marriage degenerates; and Brook, a manipulative quadriplegic. Lewis eventually becomes obsessed with possessing Brook's body and soul, and when frustration and jealousy undermine her efforts, she resorts to violence.

Upon publication in 1984, *Fish Tales* readily gained recognition as an unsettling, dramatically charged work. Margo Jefferson, in her *Village Voice Literary Supplement* appraisal, affirmed that Jones's novel strides "a highwire between sex and sentiment" and she described the work as "bawdy, funny, and desperate." And Carolyn Gaiser, writing in the *New York Times Book Review,* noted that *Fish Tales* "often reads like a case study in psychopathology." She declared that Jones's prose "generates a great deal of power" and observed that the entire work serves to blur "the boundaries between the literary and the pornographic." Similarly, Ann Snitow wrote in *Ms.,* "Pornography and the fantasies of romance keep widening their borders here." Jones, Snitow stated, "knows the sexual pain women feel, both the dependency and the exploitation." *Los Angeles Times Book Review* contributor Don Strachan was among those critics impressed with Jones's economical prose, which he deemed "exquisite." And although the reviewer found *Fish Tales* "a trifle undersize," he added that it constituted an "impressive" first work.

Jones followed *Fish Tales* with *Mischief Makers,* a relatively short novel that nonetheless documents three generations and spans from the 1920s to the 1950s. Among the book's characters is Raphael, a light-skinned woman of European, African, Caribbean, and Native American ancestry who leaves Detroit and her black lover to go to northern Michigan. Raphael, who never discusses her ethnic background, marries Mishe, a Chippewa Indian. They eventually have three daughters—Blossom Rose, Lilly, and Puma—before Raphael dies in childbirth. These daughters are reared in the traditions of both their Native American family and their predominantly European-American environment. Race does not become an issue until Lilly travels to Detroit to visit her grandparents. Caught in a brutal confrontation between blacks and whites during the Detroit race riot of 1943, Lilly is fatally struck by a brick. Blossom Rose also encounters violence in *Mischief Makers,* as she is shot while protecting her Aunt Suk from the woman's abusive husband. Jones explained that the America she reveals in *Mischief Makers* is "a true ethnic melting pot whose temperature is perpetually near the boiling point because most Americans refuse to recognize this beauty in the beast."

*Mischief Makers,* which matched *Fish Tales* in its graphic depictions of sex and violence, won Jones further attention as an author of bold, forthright fiction. O'Rourke, for instance, wrote in his *Chicago Tribune* review that the novel served as a "daring ... portrait of color and class in America." Jones, O'Rourke added, "has managed to tell a very complicated story with calculated simplicity, and the characters ... are never

stereotypes." *New York Times* contributor Caryn James was also particularly impressed with Jones's skills of characterization; she lauded the novelist for "daring to create people who are intriguing and intricate."

Jones once commented: "I am interested in focusing upon some aspects of American culture—Western culture, Detroit culture—that I feel competent to comment upon as a storyteller. I am committed to extolling good and exorcising evil in our world. I am very much concerned with American mythology and cultural anthropology, believing in the cyclical theory of human history. God is at the center of this universe, and human beings are the links in this spiritual chain."

*BIOGRAPHICAL/CRITICAL SOURCES:*

*BOOKS*

*Contemporary Literary Criticism,* Volume 34, Gale, 1985, pp. 67-69.

*PERIODICALS*

*Chicago Tribune,* May 15, 1989.
*Detroit Free Press Magazine,* February 5, 1989.
*Detroit Monthly,* January, 1989.
*Detroit News,* March 1, 1987.
*Interview,* December, 1989.
*Library Journal,* March 15, 1984.
*Los Angeles Times Book Review,* July 8, 1984, p. 6; February 5, 1989, p. 1.
*Ms.,* April, 1984, p. 30.
*New York Review of Books,* December 8, 1984, pp. 12-14.
*New York Times,* March 1, 1989.
*New York Times Book Review,* April 29, 1984, p. 42; March 17, 1985, p.40; July 16, 1989, p. 24.
*Publishers Weekly,* February 10, 1984, p. 189.
*Village Voice Literary Supplement,* May, 1984, pp. 3-4.
*Washington Post Book World,* February 5, 1989, p. 6.

*        *        *

## JORDAN, June 1936-
## (June Meyer)

*PERSONAL:* Born July 9, 1936, in Harlem, NY; daughter of Granville Ivanhoe (a postal clerk) and Mildred Maude (Fisher) Jordan; married Michael Meyer, 1955 (divorced, 1965); children: Christopher David. *Education:* Attended Barnard College, 1953-55 and 1956-57, and University of Chicago, 1955-65. *Politics:* "Politics of survival and change." *Religion:* "Humanitarian."

*ADDRESSES: Home*—New York, NY. *Office*—Department of English, State University of New York, Stony Brook, NY 11794. *Agent*—Joan Daves, 59 East 54th St., New York, NY 10022.

*CAREER:* Poet, novelist, essayist, and writer of children's books. Assistant to producer for motion picture *The Cool World,* New York City, 1963-64; Mobilization for Youth, Inc., New York City, associate research writer in technical housing department, 1965-66; City College of the City University of New York, New York City, instructor in English and literature, 1966-68; Connecticut College, New London, teacher of English and director of Search for Education, Elevation and Knowledge (SEEK Program), 1967-69; Sarah Lawrence College, Bronxville, NY, instructor in literature, 1969-74; City College of the City University of New York, assistant professor of English, 1975-76; State University of New York at Stony Brook, professor of English, 1982—.

Visiting poet in residence at MacAlester College, 1980; writer in residence at City College of the City University of New York; playwright in residence, New Dramatists, New York City, 1987—. Visiting lecturer in English and Afro-American studies, Yale University, 1974-75; chancellor's distinguished lecturer, University of California, Berkeley, 1986. Has given poetry readings in schools and colleges around the country and at the Guggenheim Museum. Founder and co-director, Voice of the Children, Inc.; co-founder, Afro-Americans against the Famine, 1973—. Director of Poetry Center, 1986—, and Poets and Writers, Inc. Member of board of directors, Teachers and Writers Collaborative, Inc., 1978—, and Center for Constitutional Rights, 1984—; member of board of governors, New York Foundation for the Arts, 1986—.

*MEMBER:* American Writers Congress (member of executive board), PEN American Center (member of executive board).

*AWARDS, HONORS:* Rockefeller grant for creative writing, 1969-70; Prix de Rome in Environmental Design, 1970-71; Nancy Bloch Award, 1971, for *The Voice of the Children; New York Times* selection as one of the year's outstanding young adult novels, 1971, and nomination for National Book Award, 1971, for *His Own Where;* New York Council of the Humanities award, 1977; Creative Artists Public Service Program poetry grant, 1978; Yaddo fellowship, 1979; National Endowment for the Arts fellowship, 1982; achievement award for international reporting from National Association of Black Journalists, 1984; New York Foundation for the Arts fellow in poetry, 1985.

*WRITINGS:*

*Who Look at Me,* Crowell, 1969.
(Editor) *Soulscript: Afro-American Poetry,* Doubleday, 1970.

(Editor with Terri Bush) *The Voice of the Children* (a reader), Holt, 1970.
*Some Changes* (poems), Dutton, 1971.
*His Own Where* (young adult novel), Crowell, 1971.
*Dry Victories* (juvenile and young adult), Holt, 1972.
*Fannie Lou Hamer* (biography), Crowell, 1972.
*New Days: Poems of Exile and Return,* Emerson Hall, 1973.
*New Room: New Life* (juvenile), Crowell, 1975.
*Things That I Do in the Dark: Selected Poetry,* Random House, 1977.
*Okay Now,* Simon & Schuster, 1977.
*Passion: New Poems, 1977-1980,* Beacon Press, 1980.
*Civil Wars* (essays, articles, and lectures), Beacon Press, 1981.
*Kimako's Story* (juvenile), illustrated by Kay Burford, Houghton, 1981.
*Living Room: New Poems, 1980-84,* Thunder's Mouth Press, 1985.
*On Call: New Political Essays, 1981-1985,* South End Press, 1985.
*High Tide—Marea Alta,* Curbstone, 1987.
*Naming Our Destiny: New and Selected Poems,* Thunder's Mouth Press, 1989.
*Moving Towards Home: Political Essays,* Virago, 1989.
*Lyrical Campaigns: Selected Poems,* Virago, 1989.
*Technical Difficulties: African-American Notes on the State of the Union,* Pantheon, 1992.

*PLAYS*

*In the Spirit of Sojourner Truth,* produced in New York City at the Public Theatre, May, 1979.
*For the Arrow that Flies by Day* (staged reading), produced in New York City at the Shakespeare Festival, April, 1981.

*OTHER*

Contributor to *Double Stitch: Black Women Write About Mothers and Daughters,* edited by Patricia Bell-Scott, HarperPerennial, 1992. Composer of lyrics and libretto, "Bang Bang Ueber Alles," 1985. Contributor of stories and poems, prior to 1969 under name June Meyer, to periodicals, including *Esquire, Nation, Evergreen, Partisan Review, Black World, Black Creation, Essence, Village Voice, New York Times,* and *New York Times Magazine.*

*SIDELIGHTS:* June Jordan is considered one of the more significant black women writers publishing today. Although better known for her poetry, Jordan writes for a variety of audiences from young children to adults and in a number of genres from essays to plays. However, in all of her writings, Jordan powerfully and skillfully explores the black experience in America. "The reader coming to June Jordan's work for the first time can be overwhelmed by the breadth and diversity of her concern, and by the wide variety of literary forms in which she expresses them," writes Peter B. Erickson in the *Dictionary of Literary Biography*. "But the unifying element in all her activities is her fervent dedication to the survival of black people."

Chad Walsh writes of Jordan in *Washington Post Book World*, "Exploring and expressing black consciousness, [Jordan] speaks to everyman, for in his heart of hearts every man is at times an outsider in whatever society he inhabits." Susan Mernit writes in the *Library Journal* that "Jordan is a poet for many people, speaking in a voice they cannot fail to understand about things they will want to know." In a *Publishers Weekly* interview with Stella Dong, Jordan explains: "I write for as many different people as I can, acknowledging that in any problem situation you have at least two viewpoints to be reached. I'm also interested in telling the truth as I know it, and in telling people, 'Here's something new that I've just found out about.' I want to share discoveries because other people might never know the thing, and also to get feedback. That's critical."

Reviewers have generally praised Jordan for uniquely and effectively uniting in poetic form the personal everyday struggle and the political oppression of blacks. For example, Mernit believes that Jordan "elucidates those moments when personal life and political struggle, two discrete elements, suddenly entwine.... [Jordan] produces intelligent, warm poetry that is exciting as literature." Honor Moore comments in *Ms.* that Jordan "writes ragalike pieces of word-music that serve her politics, both personal and public." And Peter B. Erickson remarks: "Given her total commitment to writing about a life beset on all sides, Jordan is forced to address the whole of experience in all its facets and can afford to settle for nothing less. Jordan accepts, rises to, the challenge."

Jordan sees poetry as a valid and useful vehicle to express her personal and political ideas while at the same time masterfully creating art. "Jordan is an accomplished poet, who knows how to express her political views while at the same time practicing her art; hence these poems make for engaging reading by virtue of their rhythm and poignant imagery." And Moore states in *Ms.* that Jordan "never sacrifices poetry for politics. In fact, her craft, the patterning of sound, rhythm, and image, make her art inseparable from political statement, form inseparable from content. [She] uses images contrapuntally to interweave disparate emotions."

Jordan is also noted for the intense passion with which she writes about the struggles against racism. Susan McHenry remarks in *Nation* that "Jordan's characteristic stance is combative. She is exhilarated by a good fight, by taking on her antagonists against the odds.... However, Jordan [succeeds] in effectively uniting her impulse to fight with her need and

'I' desire to love." Jascha Kessler comments in *Poetry* that Jordan's literary "expression is developed out of, or through, a fine irony that manages to control her bitterness, even to dominate her rage against the intolerable, so that she can laugh and cry, be melancholic and scornful and so on, presenting always the familiar faces of human personality, integral personality." Kessler adds that Jordan "adapts her poems to the occasions that they are properly, using different voices, and levels of thought and diction that are humanly germane and not disembodied rages or vengeful shadows; thus she can create her world, that is, people it for us, for she has the singer's sense of the dramatic and projects herself into a poem to express its special subject, its individuality. Of course it's always her voice, because she has the skill to use it so variously: but the imagination it needs to run through all her changes is her talent."

Faith and optimism are perhaps the two common threads that weave through all of Jordan's work, whether it be prose or poetry, for juvenile readers or for a more mature audience. For example, in a *Ms.* review of Jordan's *Civil Wars,* Toni Cade Bambara comments that Jordan has written a "chilling but profoundly hopeful vision of living in the USA. Jordan's vibrant spirit manifests itself throughout this collection of articles, letters, journal entries, and essays. What is fundamental to that spirit is caring, commitment, a deep-rooted belief in the sanctity of life.... 'We are not powerless,' she reminds us. 'We are indispensable despite all atrocities of state and corporate power to the contrary.'" And as Patricia Jones points out in the *Village Voice:* "Whether speaking on the lives of children, or the victory in Nicaragua, or the development of her poetry, or the consequences of racism in film Jordan brings her faithfulness to bear; faith in her ability to make change.... You respect June Jordan's quest and her faith. She is a knowing woman."

*BIOGRAPHICAL/CRITICAL SOURCES:*

*BOOKS*

*Children's Literature Review,* Volume 10, Gale, 1986.
*Contemporary Literary Criticism,* Gale, Volume 5, 1976, Volume 11, 1979, Volume 23, 1983.
*Dictionary of Literary Biography,* Volume 38: *Afro-American Writers after 1955: Dramatists and Prose Writers,* Gale, 1985.

*PERIODICALS*

*Black Scholar,* January-February, 1981.
*Choice,* October, 1985.
*Christian Science Monitor,* November 11, 1971.
*Library Journal,* December 1, 1980.
*Ms.,* April, 1975, April, 1981.

*Nation,* April 11, 1981.
*Negro Digest,* February, 1970.
*New York Times,* April 25, 1969.
*New York Times Book Review,* November 7, 1971.
*Poetry,* February, 1973.
*San Francisco Examiner,* December 7, 1977.
*Saturday Review,* April 17, 1971.
*Washington Post,* October 13, 1977.
*Washington Post Book World,* July 4, 1971.


\* \* \*


## JOSEY, E(lonnie) J(unius) 1924-

*PERSONAL:* Born January 20, 1924, in Norfolk, VA; son of Willie J. and Frances (Bailey) Josey; married Dorothy Johnson, September 11, 1954 (divorced); children: Elaine Jacqueline. *Education:* Howard University, A.B., 1949; Columbia University, M.A., 1950; State University of New York at Albany, M.S.L.S., 1953; Shaw University, L.H.D., 1973; University of Wisconsin-Milwaukee, D.P.S., 1987; North Carolina Central University, Ph.D., 1989. *Politics:* Democrat. *Religion:* Protestant.

*ADDRESSES: Home*—5 Bayard Rd., Unit 505, Pittsburgh, PA 15213. *Office*—School of Library and Information Science, University of Pittsburgh, Pittsburgh, PA 15260.

*CAREER:* Columbia University Libraries, New York City, desk assistant, 1950-52; New York Public Library, New York City, technical assistant, 1952; Free Library of Philadelphia, Philadelphia, PA, librarian, 1953-54; Savannah State College, Savannah, GA, instructor in social science, 1954-55; Delaware State College, Dover, librarian and assistant professor of library science, 1955-59; Savannah State College, librarian and associate professor of library science, 1959-66; New York State Education Department, Division of Library Development, Albany, associate in academic and research libraries, 1966-68; chief of Bureau of Academic and Research Libraries, 1968-76; chief of Bureau of Specialist Library Services, 1976-86; professor at University of Pittsburgh, School of Library and Information Science, 1986—. Savannah Public Library, member of board of managers, 1962-66. Member of the board of directors, Coretta Scott King Award, 1970—. *Military service:* U.S. Army, 1943-46.

*MEMBER:* American Library Association (member of council, 1970-74; founder and present chair of Black Caucus; member of board of directors), Association of College and Research Libraries (chair of committee on community use of academic libraries, 1965-69; president, 1984-85; chair of international relations committee, 1987-90; chair of committee

on legislation, 1990-92, 1993-94), Association for the Study of African American Life and History, American Academy of Political and Social Science, National Association for the Advancement of Colored People (Georgia State youth adviser, 1960-66; life member, and president of Albany, NY, branch, 1982-86), American Civil Liberties Union, New York Library Association, Pennsylvania Library Association, Kappa Phi Kappa, Alpha Phi Omega.

*AWARDS, HONORS:* American Library Association John Cotton Dana Award, 1962, 1964; Savannah State College Chapter, National Association for the Advancement of Colored People (NAACP) Award, 1964; award from national office of NAACP, 1965, and from Georgia Conference, 1966, for service to youth; Savannah Chatham county merit Award for Work on Economic Opportunity Task Force, 1966; Savannah State College Award for distinguished service to librarianship, 1967; award from *Journal of Library History,* 1970, for best piece of historical research to appear in the *Journal* in 1969; L.H.D., Shaw University, 1973; ALA Black Caucus Award for Distinguished Service to Librarianship, 1979; New York Black Librarians Caucus Award for Excellence 1979; ALA Joseph W. Lippincott Award, 1980; Distinguished Alumni Award for Contributions to Librarianship from School of Library and Information Science, State University of New York, 1981; Distinguished Service Award, Library Association of City University New York, 1982; D.C. Association of School Librarians Award, 1984; Africa Librarianship Award, Kenya Library Association, 1984; Afro-Caribbean Library Association Award, 1984; New York Library Association Award, 1985; Presidents Award, NAACP, 1986; Honorary Doctor of Public Service, University of Wisconsin-Milwaukee, 1987; Honorary Doctor of Humanities, North Carolina Central University, 1989; ALA Black Caucus Trailblazer Award, 1990; Equality Award, ALA, 1991.

*WRITINGS:*

(Editor) *The Black Librarian in America,* Scarecrow, 1970.
(Contributor) *Teaching for Better Use of Libraries,* edited by Charles Trinker, Shoe String, 1970.
(Editor) *What Black Librarians Are Saying,* Scarecrow, 1972.
(Editor) *New Dimensions for Academic Library Service,* Scarecrow, 1975.
(Editor with Sidney L. Jackson and Eleanor B. Herling) *A Century of Service: Librarianship in the United States and Canada,* American Library Association, 1976.
(Editor with Kenneth E. Peoples) *Opportunities for Minorities in Librarianship,* Scarecrow, 1977.
(Editor with Ann Allen Shockley) *Handbook of Black Librarianship,* Libraries Unlimited Inc., 1977.
(Editor) *The Information Society: Issues and Answers,* Oryx Press, 1978.
(Editor) *Libraries in the Political Process,* Oryx Press, 1980.

(Editor with Marva L. DeLoach) *Ethnic Collections in Librar-ies,* Neal-Schuman, 1983.

(Editor) *Libraries, Coalitions, and the Public Good,* Neal-Schuman, 1987.

(Editor with Kenneth D. Shearer) *Politics and the Support of Libraries,* Neal-Schuman, 1990.

(Editor) *The Black Librarian in America Revisited,* Scarecrow, 1993.

*Directory of Ethnic Professionals in LIS,* edited by George C. Grant, Four G, 1991.

Publications include library directories and surveys. Contributor of numerous articles and reviews to *Savannah Tribune, Savannah Herald,* and to library, history, and education journals. Editor of *Bookmark,* 1976-86, co-editor, 1986—. Contributing editor, *Afro-Americans in New York Life.*

*SIDELIGHTS:* E. J. Josey's writings focus on the special needs, problems, and circumstances surrounding libraries and librarians in both the academic and specialized categories. Strategies for funding, public relations, and other forms of support for libraries are all of concern to him, and he conveys information and ideas with what critics find to be sound, practical advice.

Special attention is paid to minority librarians and library needs in such works as *The Black Librarian in America,* a volume of 25 essays profiling two dozen black librarians. Their varying personal experiences provide an overview of differing opinions while concentrating on what Edsel Ford McCoy in *Library Journal* called "their shared collage of 'the black experience'." He concluded that *The Black Librarian in America* is "an indispensable volume for college, large public and high school libraries." Further observations by black librarians are presented in *What Black Librarians Are Saying.* Josey's co-edited volume *Handbook of Black Librarianship* presents 37 essays by 24 contributors speaking to topics such as resources for African and African American studies and the Black Caucus of the American Library Association (ALA). A writer for *Booklist* called *Handbook of Black Librarianship* "a compilation of interesting, useful and valuable data on the distinguished history of black librarianship" and suggested that the statistical data revealed within would prove useful to a variety of persons from students and educators to writers and publishers.

Development of ethnic archives and library programs are covered in *Ethnic Collections in Libraries.* A variety of ethnic groups including Asian Americans, Hispanic Americans, Native Americans, and African Americans are addressed. Another work centered on the special needs of minority groups is *Opportunities for Minorities in Librarianship.* As the title

suggests, this 20-essay collection stimulates thought on the part of young minority group members seeking a career in librarianship.

Josey has also spent time focusing on the needs of libraries in the face of economic and political difficulties. *Politics and the Support of Libraries* is another collection of essays, this time addressing such topics as private fund raising, public relations, and local political issues that affect academic and special libraries. Another 27 essays appear in *Libraries in the Political Process.* Here, the discussion turns to the library legislative histories of various regions of the United States and the role of the State Association and the State Library Agency. Critics find it a useful tool for private citizens who wish to support their libraries; featured in Josey's work is Miriam Braverman's essay which states that "to increase access to resources and services, libraries' real strength and hope lie in the mobilization of local citizens concern for their own library."

Other volumes which critics reviewed are *Libraries, Coalitions, and the Public Good,* containing sixteen papers originally presented during Josey's ALA presidency at the ALA Annual Conference in 1985; *The Information Society: Issues and Answers;* and *New Dimensions for Academic Library Service.* All three volumes are concerned with the past, present, and future of libraries in the face of economic, political, and technological changes. Josey's work is library-specific, but numerous reviewers find the volumes well-researched and highly relevant to anyone interested in the history, preservation, and future of the library system in the United States.

*BIOGRAPHICAL/CRITICAL SOURCES:*

*BOOKS*

*E. J. Josey: An Activist Librarian,* edited by Ismail Abdullahi, Scarecrow Press, 1992.

Josey, E. J., *Libraries in the Political Process,* Oryx Press, 1980.

*PERIODICALS*

*Booklist,* July 1, 1971, p. 879; May 15, 1973, p. 872; May 15, 1978, p. 1519; January 15, 1981, p. 669; April 1, 1988, p. 1310; April 1, 1991, p. 1542.

*Library Journal,* March 15, 1971, p. 937; December 15, 1975, p. 2308; October 1, 1977, p. 2017; January 1, 1979, p. 85; February 1, 1981, p. 315; July, 1983, p. 1345; July, 1987, p. 56.

*Reference Quarterly,* spring, 1978, pp. 263-64.

*Wilson Library Bulletin,* October, 1983, p. 142; May, 1991, p. 119-20.

## JOYCE, Donald Franklin 1938-

*PERSONAL:* Born November 4, 1938, in Chicago, IL; son of Raleigh and Pearl (Jackson) Joyce. *Education:* Fisk University, B.A., 1957; University of Illinois at Urbana-Champaign, M.S., 1960; University of Chicago, Ph.D., 1978. *Politics:* Democrat. *Religion:* Baptist. *Avocational interests:* Collecting paintings, jazz recordings, gospel recordings.

*ADDRESSES: Home*—2503 Independence Dr., Clarksville, TN 37043. *Office*—Felix G. Woodward Library, Austin Peay State University, Sixth and College Sts., Clarksville, TN 37044.

*CAREER:* Chicago Public Library, Chicago, IL, began as cataloger, became branch librarian, division chief, and curator of Vivian G. Harsh Collection of Afro-American History and Literature, 1960-81; Tennessee State University, Nashville, administrative assistant to director of libraries, head of reference, and coordinator of Downtown Campus Library, 1981-87, chair of Library Institute, 1984-85; Austin Peay State University, Clarksville, TN, director of Felix G. Woodward Library, 1987—. Producer of the television program *Harambee,* 1971-73. Member of Illinois Minority Manpower Committee; consultant to National Endowment for the Humanities.

*MEMBER:* American Library Association (and its Black Caucus), Association for the Study of Afro-American Life and History, Southeastern Library Association, Tennessee Library Association, Mensa.

*WRITINGS:*

(Editor) *The Chicago Afro-American Union Analytic Catalog: An Index to Materials on the Afro-American in the Principal Libraries of Chicago,* four volumes, G. K. Hall, 1972.
(Editor) *The Dictionary Catalog of the Vivian G. Harsh Collection of Afro-American History and Literature,* four volumes, G. K. Hall, 1978.
*Gatekeepers of Black Culture: Black-Owned Book Publishing in the United States, 1817-1981,* Greenwood Press, 1983.
*Blacks in the Humanities, 1750-1984: A Selected Annotated Bibliography,* Greenwood Press, 1986.
*Black Book Publishers in the United States: A Historical Dictionary of the Presses, 1817-1990,* Greenwood Press, 1991.

Work represented in anthologies, including *We Wish to Plead Our Own Cause: Black-Owned Book Publishing in the United States, 1817-1987,* New York Public Library, 1988; and *Reading in America: Social and Historical Essays,* edited by Cathy Davidson, Johns Hopkins University Press, 1989. Contributor of articles and reviews to professional journals.

*WORK IN PROGRESS:* A collection of short stories; a work on Afro-American cultural history; entries for the *African American Almanac,* sixth edition.

*SIDELIGHTS:* Donald Franklin Joyce commented: "My interest in reading, writing, and books was rooted in my early childhood. My maternal grandfather, a former schoolteacher who had become blind, was my babysitter. He often read to me from braille books which he received by mail from the local regional library for the blind. I liked the stories he read to me as well as I liked story hour at our local public library. At Fisk University, I took several creative writing courses with the noted poet Robert Hayden, and I was happiest when I was working in the university library with books. Hence, I was won to the world of libraries, books, and writing for life.

"As my career in librarianship developed, I discovered black writers like Richard Wright, Chester Himes, and James Baldwin. I became fascinated with the portrayal of black people's lives—my own life—staring up at me from the printed page. This fascination stirred in me an insatiable desire to read every book that I could find on the black experience.

"During my years as the curator of the Vivian G. Harsh Collection of Afro-American History and Literature, I had the intellectually invigorating experience of expanding the collection from two thousand to about fifteen thousand titles. In my search for books and manuscripts on the black experience, I discovered a number of books which black Americans had written and published themselves. My interest in black book publishing followed me into the doctoral program at the University of Chicago. My dissertation, after several revisions, was published as *Gatekeepers of Black Culture.* This work made me aware of the many intellectual and artistic contributions that blacks have made to knowledge in Western civilization. Consequently, my quest has become to document and write about these contributions."

# K

**KAYMOR, Patrice Maguilene**
**See SENGHOR, Leopold Sedar**

\*   \*   \*

## KENAN, Randall (G.) 1963-

*PERSONAL:* Born March 12, 1963, in Brooklyn, NY. *Education:* University of North Carolina, B.A., 1985.

*ADDRESSES: Office*—Lecturer in Writing, Sarah Lawrence College, Bronxville, NY 10708.

*CAREER:* Alfred A. Knopf, New York City, editor, 1985-89; lecturer at Sarah Lawrence College, Bronxville, NY, 1989—, Vassar College, Poughkeepsie, NY, 1989—, and Columbia University, New York City, 1990—.

*AWARDS, HONORS:* Grant, New York Foundation of the Arts, 1989; MacDowell Colony Fellowship, 1990.

*WRITINGS:*

*A Visitation of Spirits* (novel), Grove Press, 1989.
*Let the Dead Bury Their Dead and Other Stories,* Harcourt, 1992.

*SIDELIGHTS:* Randall Kenan's first two fictional publications have drawn much attention for their stylistic virtuosity and thematic richness. They work together, as well as singly, in bringing to life a small African American community in North Carolina called Tims Creek. Critics have been impressed by Kenan's skill in filling that community with magical as well as realistic imagery and complex individuals within racial and sexual types.

Readers were first introduced to Tims Creek in the novel, *A Visitation of Spirits.* Horace Thomas Cross, a brilliant student, is led to relive much of his life, and generations of his family's history, through a long night in April, 1984, which ends in tragedy. Taking him on this tour towards doom are demons which may be real or figurative—for Cross is full of confusion and guilt, and disgusted by his own homosexuality. Interspersed with this narrative is one in which Cross's older cousin, the Reverend James Malachai Green, takes his aunt and uncle to visit a dying relative in December, 1985. On the way, the trio provide perspective on Cross and the town's history. Besides these time leaps, the narrative also shifts between various third and first-person narrations, including discourses on subjects from chicken plucking to contemporary music. "Truth is," George Garrett wrote in the Chicago *Tribune Books,* "Kenan tries pretty much of everything and pretty much gets away with all of it, too."

Kenan continues to explore Tims Creek, and the human condition, from an even greater variety of perspectives in *Let the Dead Bury the Dead and Other Stories.* "Each of these stories," said Valerie Miner in *The Nation,* "builds on and resonates with the others, giving readers a textured appreciation for Tims Creek, pious and witty, poor and affluent, black and white." In the title novella, Horace Cross's surname turns out to be that of the plantation owner whose slaves escaped and founded the town in a then-isolated swamp. A history of the founding and development of the town—from which myth and chronicle are hard to separate—is related in the novella through a variety of prisms: oral history, diary entries, and letters, all recorded by Reverend Green, whose unfinished opus is incorporated into a heavily annotated academic treatise by the narrator "RK" in the late 1990's. "The result," commented Jean Hanff Korelitz in the *Washington Post Book World,* "is a conjuring at once specific to one imaginary corner of the south and yet somehow evocative of the entire region and period." The conjuring, as well as sensuality—lost, recovered, genuine, manipulative, hetero- and homo-erotic—runs throughout the remaining stories in the collection, as do humourous and enlightening (but non-didactic) encounters, such as that between Booker T. Washington and two former schoolmates in 1909.

The liveliness, variety, and dexterity of the writer has been impressive to many. Miner concluded, "Kenan explores the territories in between the living and the dead, between the fantastic and mundane in an energetic, inventive prose that never descends to contrivance or sentimentality."

*BIOGRAPHICAL/CRITICAL SOURCES:*

*PERIODICALS*

*Booklist,* March 15, 1992, p. 1336.
*Callaloo,* fall, 1990, p. 913.
*Essence,* September, 1989, p. 28; August, 1992, p. 44.
*Kirkus Reviews,* May 1, 1989, p. 650; January 15, 1992, p. 67.
*Lambda Book Report,* January, 1991, p. 37.
*Library Journal,* February 15, 1992, p. 199.
*Los Angeles Times Book Review,* October 28, 1990, p. 14; September 13, 1992, p. 14.
*Nation,* July 6, 1992, p. 28.
*New York Times Book Review,* June 14, 1992.
*Publishers Weekly,* May 12, 1989, p. 283; January 13, 1992, p. 45.
*Tribune Books* (Chicago), August 13, 1989, p. 6; May 3, 1992, p. 6.
*Virginia Quarterly Review,* winter, 1990, p. 14.
*Washington Post Book World,* August 2, 1992, pp. 1, 11.

\*   \*   \*

## KENNEDY, Adrienne (Lita) 1931-

*PERSONAL:* Born September 13, 1931, in Pittsburgh, PA; daughter of Cornell Wallace and Etta (Haugabook) Hawkins; married Joseph C. Kennedy, May 15, 1953; children: Joseph C., Adam. *Education:* Ohio State University, B.A., 1952; graduate study at Columbia University, 1954-56; also studied at New School for Social Research, American Theater Wing, Circle in the Square Theatre School, and Edward Albee's workshop.

*ADDRESSES: Office*—Department of Afro-American Studies, Princeton University, Princeton, NJ 08544. *Agent*—Bridget Aschenberg, 40 West 57th St., New York, NY 10019.

*CAREER:* Playwright. Lecturer, Yale University, 1972-74, and Princeton University, 1977; visiting associate professor, Brown University, 1979-80. International Theatre Institute representative, Budapest, 1978. Member of playwriting unit, Actors Studio, New York City, 1962-65.

*MEMBER:* PEN (member of board of directors, 1976-77).

*AWARDS, HONORS:* Obie Award from Village Voice, 1964, for *Funnyhouse of a Negro;* Guggenheim memorial fellowship, 1967; Rockefeller grants, 1967-69, 1974, 1976; National Endowment for the Arts grant, 1973; CBS fellow, School of Drama, 1973; Creative Artists Public Service grant, 1974; Yale fellow, 1974-75; Stanley award for play writing; New England Theatre Conference grant.

*WRITINGS:*

*People Who Led to My Plays* (memoir), Knopf, 1987.
*In One Act,* University of Minnesota Press, 1988.
*Deadly Triplets: A Theatre Mystery and Journal,* University of Minnesota Press, 1990.
*The Alexander Plays,* University of Minnesota Press, 1992.

*PLAYS*

*Funnyhouse of a Negro* (one-act; first produced Off-Broadway at Circle in the Square Theatre, 1962), Samuel French, 1969.
*The Owl Answers* (one-act; also see below), first produced in Westport, CT, at White Barn Theatre, 1963, produced Off-Broadway at Public Theatre, January 12, 1969.
*A Lesson in a Dead Language* (also see below), first produced in 1964.
*A Rat's Mass* (also see below), first produced in Boston, MA, by the Theatre Company, April, 1966, produced Off-Broadway at La Mama Experimental Theatre Club, November, 1969.
*A Beast's Story* (one-act, also see below), first produced in 1966, produced Off-Broadway at Public Theatre, January 12, 1969.
(With John Lennon and Victor Spinetti) *The Lennon Play: In His Own Write* (adapted from Lennon's books *In His Own Write* and *A Spaniard in the Works;* first produced in London by National Theatre, 1967; produced in Albany, NY, at Arena Summer Theatre, August, 1969), Simon & Schuster, 1969.
*Sun: A Poem for Malcolm X Inspired by His Murder* (also see below), first produced on the West End, London, at Royal Court Theatre, 1968, produced in New York at La Mama Experimental Theatre Club, 1970.
*Cities In Bezique* (contains *The Owl Answers* and *A Beast Story;* first produced in New York at Shakespeare Festival, 1969), Samuel French, 1969.
*Boats,* first produced in Los Angeles at the Forum, 1969.

*An Evening With Dead Essex,* first produced in New York by American Place Theatre Workshop, 1973.

*A Movie Star Has to Star in Black and White* (also see below), first produced in New York by Public Theatre Workshop, 1976.

*A Lancashire Lad* (for children), first produced in Albany, NY, at Governor Nelson A. Rockefeller Empire State Plaza Performing Arts Center, May, 1980.

*Black Children's Day,* first produced in Providence, RI, at Brown University, November, 1980.

*Solo Voyages* (contains excerpts from *The Owl Answers, A Rat's Mass,* and *A Movie Star Has to Star in Black and White*), first produced in New York at Interart Center, 1985.

*OTHER*

Also contributor of plays to books and periodicals, including *New American Plays,* edited by William M. Hoffman, Hill & Wang, 1968; *Collision Courses* (includes *A Lesson in a Dead Language*), edited by Edward Parone, Random House, 1968; *New Black Playwrights* (includes *A Rat's Mass*), edited by William Couch, Jr., Louisiana State University Press, 1968; *Spontaneous Combustion* (includes *Sun: A Poem for Malcolm X Inspired by His Murder*), edited by Rochelle Owens, Winter House, 1972; *Kuntu Drama* (includes *A Beast's Story* and *The Owl Answers*), edited by Paul C. Harris, Grove Press, 1974; *Wordplay 3* (includes *A Movie Star Has to Star in Black and White*), Performing Arts Journal Publications, 1984; and *Scripts.*

*SIDELIGHTS:* "While almost every black playwright in the country is fundamentally concerned with realism ... Miss [Adrienne] Kennedy is weaving some kind of dramatic fabric of poetry," Clive Barnes comments in the *New York Times.* "What she writes is a mosaic of feeling, with each tiny stone stained with the blood of gray experience. Of all our black writers, Miss Kennedy is most concerned with white, with white relationships, with white blood. She thinks black, but she remembers white. It gives her work an uneddying ambiguity."

"Adrienne Kennedy is one of America's most important black playwrights," commented Philip C. Kolin in *World Literature Today.* "Although *Funnyhouse of a Negro* (1964) won an Obie, her innovative plays have not received the critical attention they deserve. Not employing the naturalism of social protest found in Bullins or Baraka, her surrealistic dramas confess the torments of her own nightmare world. 'The characters are myself,' she has said."

In her complex and introspective plays, Martin Duberman remarks in *Partisan Review,* Kennedy is "absorbed by her private fantasies, her interior world. She disdains the narra-

tive, 'everyday' language and human interaction; the dream, the myth, the poem and her domain." James Hatch and Ted Shine also note that "in a tradition in which the major style has long been realism, Adrienne Kennedy has done what few black playwrights have attempted; used form to project an interior reality and thereby created a rich and demanding theatrical style."

Kennedy's first play, *Funnyhouse of a Negro,* examines the psychological problems of Sarah, a young mulatto woman who lives with a Jewish poet in a boarding house run by a white landlady. Dealing with the last moments before Sarah's suicide, the play consists of scenes of the young woman's struggle with herself. Tortured by an identity crisis, Sarah is "lost in a nightmare world where black is evil and white is good, where various personages, including Queen Victoria, Patrice Lumumba and Jesus Himself, materialize to mock her," says *New Yorker*'s Edith Oliver. *Funnyhouse of a Negro* earned Kennedy an Obie Award, and, notes a *Variety* reviewer, a reputation as a "gifted writer with a distinctive dramatic imagination."

Oliver described *The Owl Answers* as another fantasy of "a forbidden and glorious white world, viewed with a passion and frustration that shed the spirit and nerves and mind of the dispossessed heroine." The illegitimate child of a black cook and the wealthiest white man in Georgia, the heroine is riding on a New York subway. The subway doors become the doors to a chapel of the Tower of London through which appear masked historical characters, including Chaucer, Shakespeare, Anne Boleyn, and the Virgin Mary, who at times unmask to become other characters, such as the heroine's mother and father.

In *American Literature,* Kennedy cites a passage from Aristotle to explain why she stresses the metaphor: "The greatest thing by far is to be a master of metaphor. It is the one thing that cannot be [learned from others] and it is also a sign of genius since a good metaphor implies an intuitive perception of the similarity in dissimilars."

*A Beast's Story,* produced with *The Owl Answers* under the title *Cities in Bezique,* was described as more elaborate, hallucinatory and obscure than the first play. It draws analogies, says Steve Tennen in *Show Business,* "between inhuman beings and man's bestial tendencies." Kennedy's later play *A Rat's Mass,* staged as a parody mass, is also abstract, centering around the relationship between a black brother and sister and their childhood involvement with the white girl next door.

In all of these plays, Kennedy's writing is poetic and symbolic; plot and dialogue are secondary to effect. Her reliance on such devices as masks, characters who become other characters,

characters played by more than one actor, and Christian symbolism make her work difficult to understand, and her plays have been seen as both nightmarish rituals and poetic dances. Marilyn Stasio explains in *Cue:* "Kennedy is a poet working with disjoined time sequences, evocative images, internalized half-thoughts and incantatory language to create a netherworld of submerged emotions surfacing only in fragments. Events are crucial only for the articulated feelings they evoke."

During 1971, Kennedy joined five other women playwrights to found the Women's Theatre Council, a theatre cooperative devoted to producing the works of women playwrights and providing opportunities for women in other aspects of the theatre, such as directing and acting. Mel Gussow of the *New York Times* notes that the council's "founding sisters all come from Off-Off-Broadway, are exceeding prolific, have had their plays staged throughout the United States and in many foreign countries and feel neglected by the New York commercial theatre. Each has a distinctive voice, but their work is related in being largely non-realistic and experimental. The women feel unified as innovators and by their artistic consciousness."

Kennedy branched out into juvenile theater in 1980 after being commissioned by the Empire State Youth Theatre Institute. *A Lancashire Lad,* her first play for children, is a fictionalized version of Charles Chaplin's childhood. Narrated by the hero, the play traces his life growing up in Dickensian England and beginning his career in the British music halls. Although an entertaining musical, the show confronts the poverty and pain of Chaplin's youth. Praising Kennedy's language for achieving "powerful emotional effects with the sparest of mean," *New York Times* reviewer Frank Rich concludes: "The difference between *The Lancashire Lad* and an adult play is, perhaps, the intellectual simplicity of its ambitions. Yet that simplicity can also be theater magic in its purest and most eloquent form."

In *Deadly Triplets, New York Times* reviewer Michael Bloom says, "It seems that she [Kennedy] had adapted John Lennon's 'nonsense books' into a play that was eventually given a tryout at the National Theatre. Laurence Olivier held her hand throughout the performance, then decided that Lennon, not she, should do the adaptation when the project was resumed a few months later. It is in these sharp sketches and telling anecdotes that Ms. Kennedy's considerable talents are most evident."

In reviewing Kennedy's autobiography, *People Who Led to My Plays, Theatre Journal 43* critic Katherine E. Kelly says, "It is—ironically—impossible to determine whether the black or white influences were more important to Kennedy. The rich texture and imagination of her plays emerged from the intermixture and interdependence of these people in her life. I found

myself wishing, however, that Kennedy had revealed a bit more about her reaction to certain black figures such as Paul Roberson or Nkrumah or Billie Holiday. Too often they were summarized in a short sentence, passage or word which leaves the reader wondering about their importance. Nevertheless, *People Who Led to My Plays* is a fascinating journey into the mind and creative genius of a major American playwright."

*BIOGRAPHICAL/CRITICAL SOURCES:*

*BOOKS*

Ambramson, Doris E., *Negro Playwrights in the American Theatre, 1925-1959,* Columbia University Press, 1969.
Betsko, Kathleen, and Rachel Koenig, *Interviews with Contemporary Women Playwrights,* Beech Tree Books, 1987.
Cohn, Ruby, *New American Dramatists: 1960-1980,* Grove Press, 1982.
*Dictionary of Literary Biography,* Volume 38: *Afro-American Writers after 1955; Dramatists and Prose Writers,* Gale, 1985.
Harrison, Paul Carter, *The Drama of Nommo,* Grove Press, 1972.
Hatch, James V., and Ted Shine, editors, *Black Theatre U.S.A.,* Free Press, 1974.
Kelly, Katherine E., editor, *Theatre Journal 43,* The Johns Hopkins University Press, 1991.
Mitchell, Loften, *Black Drama,* Hawthorne Books, 1967.
Oliver, Clinton, and Stephanie Sills, *Contemporary Black Drama,* Scribners, 1971.

*PERIODICALS*

*American Literature,* September, 1991.
*Belles Letters,* Spring, 1989.
*City Arts Monthly,* February, 1982.
*CLA Journal,* December, 1976.
*Cue,* January 18, 1969; October 4, 1969.
*Drama Review,* December, 1977.
*International Times,* September 22, 1968.
*Library Journal,* May 1, 1987; August, 1992.
*Los Angeles Times Book Review,* July 12, 1987.
*Ms.,* June, 1987.
*New Yorker,* January 25, 1964; January 25, 1969.
*New York Times,* January 15, 1964; June 20, 1968; July 9, 1968; January 13, 1969; January 19, 1969; November 1, 1969; February 22, 1972; May 21, 1980; February 15, 1981; September 11, 1985; September 20, 1985.
*New York Times Book Review,* October 14, 1990.
*Observer Review,* June 23, 1968.
*Partisan Review,* number 3, 1969.
*Publishers Weekly,* May 1, 1987.
*Show Business,* January 25, 1969; October 4, 1969.
*Studies in Black Literature,* summer, 1975.

*Variety,* January 29, 1969; March 16, 1992.
*Village Voice,* August 14, 1969; September 25, 1969.
*World Literature Today,* winter, 1989.

\*    \*    \*

## KERSEY, Tanya-Monique 1961-

*PERSONAL:* Born March 22, 1961, in New York, NY; daughter of Al Smith and Cynthia (Wallace) Kersey; married Clif Love (an account executive), August 29, 1987 (divorced); children: Monique, Brittany. *Education:* Rutgers University, B.A., 1983.

*ADDRESSES: Home*—5724 Irvine Ave., North Hollywood, CA 91601. *Office*—Love Child Publishing, 6565 Sunset Blvd., Suite 318, Hollywood, CA 90028.

*CAREER:* Actress in New York City and Los Angeles, CA, 1983—; Love Child Publishing, Hollywood, CA, founder and chief executive officer, 1990—; writer. Computer consultant, 1984-92.

*MEMBER:* Screen Actors Guild, American Federation of Television and Radio Artists, Entertainment Networking Association, Multicultural Publishers Exchange, National Association of Female Executives, Black Actors Network, American Black Book Writers Association, AUDELCO.

*WRITINGS:*

(With Bruce Hawkins) *Black State of the Arts: A Guide to Developing a Successful Career as a Black Performing Artist,* Love Child Publishing, 1991.
*The Performer's Plan: A Career Plan for Performers,* second edition, Love Child Publishing, 1992.
(Editor) *The 1992-93 Black Talent Resource Guide,* Love Child Publishing, 1992.
(Editor) *The Black Players Directory,* Love Child Publishing, 1992.

Columnist for *Showcase World.* Contributor to periodicals. Editor of *Black Talent News: The Newsletter for Creative Black Talent* and *ENA News.*

*WORK IN PROGRESS: Marketing Your Books in the Afrocentric Marketplace.*

*SIDELIGHTS:* Tanya-Monique Kersey studied acting at the Mason Gross School of the Arts at Rutgers University. She has appeared on television programs, including *All My Children, Search for Tomorrow,* and *The Guiding Light,* and in radio and television commercials and print advertisements.

Kersey also worked as the director of a California modeling agency. The author commented: "I hope someday to form a talent guild to further the careers, recognition, awareness, and contributions of black performers, writers, directors, and producers."

\*    \*    \*

## KGOSITSILE, Aneb
## See HOUSE, Gloria

\*    \*    \*

## KGOSITSILE, Keorapetse (William) 1938-

*PERSONAL:* Born September 19, 1938, in Johannesburg, South Africa; married, wife's name, Melba. *Education:* Educated in Africa; additional study at Lincoln University, University of New Hampshire, New School for Social Research, and Columbia University.

*ADDRESSES: Office*—University of Botswana, Private Bag, 0022, Gabarone, Botswana.

*CAREER:* Poet, essayist, and critic. North Carolina Agricultural and Technical State University, Greensboro, poet-in-residence, beginning 1971; University of Nairobi, lecturer in literature. Visiting professor at Sarah Lawrence College, Queens College of the City University of New York, Bennett College, North Carolina Central University, and University of Denver. Member of staff, *Black Dialogue* and *Spearhead.*

*AWARDS, HONORS:* Conrad Kent Rivers memorial Award, 1969; National Endowment for the Arts grant, 1970.

*WRITINGS:*

*Spirits Unchained* (poems), Broadside Press, 1969.
*For Melba* (poems), Third World Press, 1970.
*My Name Is Afrika* (poems), introduction by Gwendolyn Brooks, Doubleday, 1971.
(Editor) *The Word Is Here: Poetry from Modern Africa,* Doubleday, 1973.
*The Present Is a Dangerous Place to Live,* Third World Press, 1974.
(With others) *A Capsule Course in Black Poetry Writing,* Broadside Press, 1975.
*Place and Bloodstains: Notes for Ipelang,* Achebe Publications, 1975.
*When the Clouds are Clear,* introduction by Ari Sitas, Congress of South African Writers, 1990.

Also author of introduction, *Steps to Break the Circle*, by Sterling Plumpp, Third World Press, 1974. Contributor to periodicals, including *Transition and Guerrilla*. African editor-at-large, *Black Dialogue*.

SIDELIGHTS: Although Keorapetse Kgositsile lived in the United States for several years, his poetry has always been considered "African" in its treatment of the themes of black unification and liberation. In *My Name Is Afrika*, according to *Booklist*, "passionate poems of the horror of black slavery in Africa and America symbolize universal suffering of the oppressed. Rhythmic and rhetorical calls to action, contemplations on black leaders, and acute observations couched in authentic dialogue are preceded by a characteristically penetrating and artistic introduction by Gwendolyn Brooks." Diane Ackerman writes in the *Library Journal* that in *My Name Is Afrika*, "Kgositsile demands militancy—if he ignites his reader, his poems are successful. [However,] when the furor subsides, Kgositsile can be passionate, perceptive, even delicate, producing an articulate record of black protest."

In *For Melba*, writes Christopher Scott in *Books Abroad*, "Kgositsile employs the medium of his love for his wife Melba to make a rather political statement. Revolutionary nationalism, as the poet sees it, has its foundation in the (concrete of) the family unit, both nuclear and extended. it would seem that for revolutionary nationalism the health of the personal and familial building blocks of society is causally related to the health of the nation. Kgositsile's message to his black brothers and sisters is, finally, 'Let us stop playing games.'" The poems of *For Melba*, Scott adds, trace the "physical and spiritual movement of the poet (and, by extension, all black people) in his personal and consequently political struggle for dignity."

A *Choice* reviewer calls Kgositsile's *The Word Is Here: Poetry from Modern Africa* an "attractive, original, and highly recommended collection of recent poetry from Africa."

*BIOGRAPHICAL/CRITICAL SOURCES:*

*PERIODICALS*

*Booklist*, September 1, 1971.
*Books Abroad*, spring, 1971.
*Choice*, October, 1973.
*Christian Century*, March 14, 1973.
*Library Journal*, March 15, 1971.

\*   \*   \*

## KIBERA, Leonard  1940(?)-

*PERSONAL:* Born in Kenya c. 1940.

*AWARDS, HONORS:* Third prize, British Broadcasting Corporation African drama contest, 1967, for play, *Potent Ash*.

*WRITINGS:*

*Potent Ash* (play; produced in London on the British Broadcasting Corporation's African Service, June, 1967), published in *New African Literature and the Arts*, Volume 2, edited by Joseph Okpaku, Thomas Y. Crowell, 1968.
(With Samuel Kahiga) *Potent Ash* (short stories), East African Publishing House, 1968.
*Voices in the Dark* (novel), East African Publishing House, 1970.

Also author of short story, "The Spider Web," published in *Presence Africaine*, second trimester, 1970.

*BIOGRAPHICAL/CRITICAL SOURCES:*

*BOOKS*

*African Authors: A Companion to Black African Writing*, Volume 1: *1300-1973*, Black Orpheus Press, 1973.

\*   \*   \*

## KILLENS, John Oliver  1916-1987

*PERSONAL:* Born January 14, 1916, in Macon, GA; died of cancer, October 27, 1987, in Brooklyn, NY; son of Charles Myles, Sr., and Willie Lee (Coleman) Killens; married Grace Ward Jones; children: Jon Charles, Barbara Ellen Rivera. *Education:* Attended Edward Waters College, Morris Brown College, Atlanta University, Howard University, Robert H. Terrell Law School, Columbia University, and New York University.

*ADDRESSES: Home*—1392 Union St., Brooklyn, NY 11212.

*CAREER:* Member of staff, National Labor Relations Board, 1936-42, and 1946; free-lance writer, 1954-87. Writer in residence, Fisk University, 1965-68, Columbia University, 1970-73, Howard University, 1971-72, Bronx Community College, 1979-81, and Medgar Evers College of the City University of New York, 1981-87. Former lecturer and teacher of creative writing at New School for Social Research, and lecturer at several other colleges and universities, including Southern University, Cornell University, Rutgers University, University of California, Los Angeles, Tufts University, Brandeis College (now Bradeis University), Springfield College, Western Michigan University, Savannah State College, and Trinity College. Co-founder and past chairperson, Harlem Writers Guild, 1952. *Military service:* U.S. Army, Pacific Amphibian Forces, 1942-45.

*MEMBER:* PEN, American Poets, Playwrights, Editors, Essayists, and Novelists (former member of executive board), Black Academy of Arts and Letters (former vice-president), National Center of Afro-American Artists (former member of executive board).

*AWARDS, HONORS:* Afro Art Theatre Cultural Award, 1955; Literary Arts Award, National Association for the Advancement of Colored People (Brooklyn), 1957; Culture, Human Relations Award, Climbers Business Club; citation from Empire State Federation of Women; cultural award, New York State Fraternal Order of Elks; Charles Chesnut Award, Brooklyn Association for the Study of Negro Life and History; *And Then We Heard the Thunder* was nominated for a Pulitzer Prize, 1962; Rabinowitz Foundation grant, 1964; *The Cotillion; or, One Good Bull Is Half the Herd* was nominated for a Pulitzer Prize, 1971; Harlem Writers Guild award, 1978; National Endowment for the Arts fellowship, 1980; Lifetime Achievement Award, Before Columbus Foundation, 1986; elected to Black Filmmaker's Hall of Fame.

*WRITINGS:*

FICTION

*Youngblood,* Dial, 1954, published with foreword by Addison Gayle, University of Georgia Press, 1982.
*And Then We Heard the Thunder,* Knopf, 1962.
*'Sippi,* Trident Press, 1967.
*Slaves,* Pyramid, 1969.
*The Cotillion; or, One Good Bull Is Half the Herd,* Trident Press, 1971.
*Great Gittin' Up Morning: A Biography of Denmark Vesey* (young adult), Doubleday, 1972.
*A Man Ain't Nothin' but a Man: The Adventures of John Henry* (young adult), Little, Brown, 1975.
*The Great Black Russian: A Novel on the Life and Times of Alexander Pushkin,* Wayne State University Press, 1989.

Also author of *The Minister Primarily.*

PLAYS

(With Loften Mitchell) *Ballad of the Winter Soldier,* first produced in Washington, DC, at Philharmonic Hall, Lincoln Center, September 28, 1964.
*Lower Than the Angels,* first produced in New York City, at American Place Theatre, January, 1965.
*Cotillion* (based on Killens's novel of same title, with music by Smokey Robinson and Willie Hutch), first produced in New York City, at New Federal Theatre, July, 1975.

SCREENPLAYS

(With Nelson Gidding) *Odds Against Tomorrow,* Belafonte Productions/United Artists, 1959.
(With Herbert J. Biberman and Alida Sherman) *Slaves,* Theatre Guild-Walter Reade/Continental, 1969.

WORK REPRESENTED IN ANTHOLOGIES

David Boroff, *The State of the Nation,* Prentice-Hall, 1966.
John Henrik Clarke, editor, *American Negro Short Stories,* Hill & Wang, 1966.
Langston Hughes, editor, *The Best Short Stories by Negro Writers: An Anthology from 1899 to the Present,* Little, Brown, 1967.
*Harlem,* New American Library, 1970.
Raman K. Singh and Peter Fellowes, editors, *Voices from the Soul of Black America,* Crowell, 1970.
Nick Aaron, editor, *Black Insights: Significant Literature by Black Americans, 1760 to the Present,* Ginn, 1971.
Patricia L. Brown, Don L. Lee, and Francis Ward, editors, *To Gwen with Love: An Anthology Dedicated to Gwendolyn Brooks,* Johnson, 1971.
Addison Gayle, Jr., editor, *The Black Aesthetic,* Doubleday, 1971.
John A. Williams and Charles F. Harris, editors, *Amistad 2,* Vintage Books, 1971.
William H. Robinson, editor, *Nommo: An Anthology of Modern African and Black American Literature,* Macmillan, 1972.

OTHER

*Black Man's Burden* (essays), Trident Press, 1965.
(Author of prologue) Fred Halstead, *Harlem Stirs,* photographs by Don Hogan Charles and Anthony Aviles, Marzani & Munsell, 1966.
(Contributor) John Henrik Clarke, editor, *William Styron's Nat Turner: Ten Black Writers Respond,* Beacon, 1968.
(Editor and author of foreword) *Trial Record of Denmark Vesey,* Beacon, 1970.
(Author of introduction) Woodie King, editor, *Black Short Story Anthology,* Columbia University Press, 1972.
*John O. Killens on Alexander Pushkin* (audio cassette), Institute of Afro-American Affairs (New York), 1976.
*John Oliver Killens* (audio cassette), Tapes for Readers (Washington, DC), 1978.
(Editor with Jerry W. Ward) *Black Southern Voices: An Anthology of Fiction, Poetry, Drama, Nonfiction, and Critical Essays,* NAL/Meridian, 1992.

Also author of *Write On!: Notes from a Writers Workshop.* Contributor to periodicals, including *Ebony, Black World, Black Aesthetic, African Forum, Library Journal, Nation,*

*Saturday Evening Post, Black Scholar, Freedomways, Redbook,* and *Arts in Society.*

*SIDELIGHTS:* "Ever since I can remember, I have always been a sucker for a well-told tale, and the more outlandish and outrageous, the better, as far as I was concerned," John Oliver Killens wrote in his autobiographical essay "The Half Ain't Never Been Told" in *Contemporary Authors Autobiography Series.* Killens credited his beloved paternal great-grandmother for his decision to become a writer. Seven years old when slavery was abolished, she had regaled Killens in his youth with memorable stories about those days: "Puffing on her corncob pipe, speaking in the mellifluous voice, enriched by age.... She seemed to encompass within herself all the wisdom of the ages. Sometimes at the end of each tale, she would shake her head, all white with age, the skin of her face unwrinkled and tight as a newborn baby's backside, stretched tautly over high cheekbones. And she'd say, 'Aaah Lord, Honey, THE HALF AIN'T NEVER BEEN TOLD!'" And challenged to tell at least part of that untold half, Killens remarked, "I felt I owed that much to Granny."

Killens also indicated in his autobiographical essay that he had been a voracious reader as a child, taking his cherished library books to bed with him to read by flashlight. During his teen-age years, his early dreams of becoming a physician were replaced with those of becoming a lawyer. Despite years of studying law by night and working by day at the National Labor Relations Board, he decided during a stint with the U.S. Army in the South Pacific that he would not return to law school, but would become a writer instead. "One evening in the early fifties or late forties, I gathered with seven others up above a store front on 125th Street in Harlem and, in a very trembly voice, read the first chapter of *Youngblood,*" wrote Killens in his autobiographical essay. This early group of young, black, and soon-to-be prominent writers, formed the nucleus of the distinguished and prolific Harlem Writers Guild, and Killens's first book, *Youngblood,* was the first novel to be published from it.

*Youngblood* is about a Southern black family's struggle for survival. Through the characters of the parents and their two children, Killens "exposes his readers to what life was like for Afro-Americans living in the American South during the first third of this century," wrote William H. Wiggins, Jr., in the *Dictionary of Literary Biography.* "The novel demonstrates how these four characters band together to overcome the economic, educational, social, and religious manifestations of Jim Crow life in their hometown of Crossroads, Georgia." Called a "fine novel, vivid, readable," by Ann Petry in the *New York Herald Tribune Book Review, Youngblood* is described by Granville Hicks in the *New York Times* as "a record of petty, mean-spirited, wanton discrimination." And although Hicks found it "didactic" at times, he also found it to have "the power

of the author's passion" and declared that "the novel of social protest, which survives precariously today, justifies itself when it is as moving as *Youngblood* and deals with so gross an evil."

Killens's second novel, *And Then We Heard the Thunder,* is based on his own experience with segregation and racism in the military during the Second World War. According to Martin Levin in the *New York Times Book Review,* the novel's black protagonist, who wishes only to be "the best damn soldier," is forced instead "to make common cause with his race rather than with his army." Although critics tended to fault the style of the novel, they nonetheless responded well to its message. While Nelson Algren suggested in the *New York Herald Tribune Book Review* that the book "lacked the passion of men at war," J. H. Griffin in the *Saturday Review* found the battle scenes, in particular, filled with "hallucinatory power," and declared that the reader who has not experienced racial discrimination, "living all the indignities of the Negro soldier, sees clearly how it looked from the other side of the color line." Griffin concludes that "this novel magnificently illumines the reasons why" the wounds remain despite discrimination having been eliminated from the armed forces.

Killens's *'Sippi* "reflects his new militancy," wrote Wiggins, indicating that the title originates from a "civil rights protest joke" in which a black man informs his white landlord that he will no longer include mister or miss when addressing others, including the state of Mississippi. "It's just plain 'Sippi from now on!," he says. The novel concerns the struggles over voting rights during the 1960s, and Wiggins added that Killens "recounts in vivid detail the bombings, shootings, and other acts of terror and intimidation endured by the courageous students and local blacks who dare stand up and push for voter registration." Wiggins reported that there was a lack of a critical middle ground regarding the novel—critics either did or did not like it. Acknowledging in his autobiographical essay that the novel "was a critical bust," Killens added, "I heartily disagreed with the critics, naturally. Or else why would I have written it?"

Killens's *The Cotillion; or One Good Bull Is Half the Herd* is a satire about an annual ball held by an exclusive black women's club in Brooklyn. "Through hyperbole and cutting social and political commentary, Killens's novel becomes a biting didactic piece of Afro-American literature, written in the tradition of verbal contests known as the dozens to many Afro-Americans," explained Wiggins. "The object of the game is to unsettle one's verbal opponent with exaggerated statements of personal insults." Noting that "this is precisely the plot" of *The Cotillion,* Wiggins wrote that by the end of the novel, "Killens has reduced this sedate group of society matrons to a confused and disorganized group of babbling black women who have been verbally stripped of their veneer of white middle-class values and exposed for what they truly are:

comically tragic Afro-Americans who are out of touch with their cultural heritage." Calling its language "Afro-Americanese," George Davis commented in *Black World* that *The Cotillion* "signifies and lies and intrudes on itself whenever it sees fit. It dances around while it is talking and comes all out of itself to make sure you get the point that it is making. It starts to exaggerate and keeps on exaggerating even though it knows that you know that the truth is being stretched out of shape." Leonard Fleischer observed in *Saturday Review* that "in a prose often buoyantly evocative and musical, Killens caricatures some of the more egregious foibles of black and white society." Moreover, continued Fleischer, while making use of stereotyped blacks to satirically reveal a "willing acceptance of the standards of white culture," Killens is simultaneously "mocking the rage for instant blackness."

"Killens's major themes evolve around social protest and cultural affirmation," wrote Wiggins, who felt that Killens "fashioned his career in the protest mold of Richard Wright. For both of these writers the primary purpose of art is to attack and ultimately change society for the better." Although recognized and praised for his novels, Killens also achieved distinction for his essays on the quality of black life in America. Wiggins wrote that Killens's collection of political essays, *Black Man's Burden*, "demonstrates the shift in Killens's philosophy" away from the nonviolence espoused by Martin Luther King, Jr., and toward the more militant views of his friend, Malcolm X: "In the series of essays on such subjects as white paternalism, black manhood, unions, sit-ins, boycotts, religion, black nationalism, Africa, nonviolence, and the right of self-defense, Killens argued that passive acceptance of racial oppression only encourages more racial violence. Killens believed that the only way blacks could break the vicious cycle of racial violence would be to respond to white violence with black violence." In the *Saturday Review*, Frank M. Cordasco observed that Killens had assembled "a pastiche of perceptive, sharply delineated vignettes animated by the twin engines of hate and despair."

Killens's work is internationally known, having been translated into more than a dozen languages. In his autobiographical essay, he wrote that when he travelled to Africa in 1961 to do research for a British Broadcasting Corporation script, he viewed a screening of his own motion picture, *Odds Against Tomorrow*, with French subtitles. And when the author journeyed to China in 1973 with a group of writers and teachers, he learned that he and Ernest Hemingway were "two of the most widely read writers there." Killens's travels also took him to the Soviet Union. In 1968 and 1970, he attended a festival in the Soviet Union where "writers and artists [were] invited ... from all over the world to celebrate the life of Alexander Sergeievich Pushkin," the subject of a novel on which he had worked since the middle 1960s. That novel, *The Great Black Russian: A Novel on the Life and Times of Alexander Pushkin,*

was published posthumously in 1989. The result of twelve years of research and writing, Killens's biography of the poet was one of the first to give weight to Pushkin's black lineage. Killens details Pushkin's history, tracing his descent from his grandfather, an African known as "the Negro of Peter the Great," through the emergence of the revolutionary writer and poet who, though much loved by the Russian people, was exiled by the Czar. Reviewer Zofia Smardz lauded Killens's "wildly erratic but somehow mesmerizing prose," and proclaimed in the *New York Times Book Review* that the work "capture[d] the essence of Pushkin's greatness." D. H. Stewart, commenting in *Choice*, noted: "Despite the racist emphasis on Pushkin's fractional blackness, Killens's narrative is informative and lively." Calvin Forbes stated in a review in the *Washington Post Book World* that the author "tells his story with suitable flair. Pushkin's adventures and troubled life ... are served up like a feast for us to enjoy."

Killens indicated in his autobiographical essay that he had also completed a comedic novel entitled *The Minister Primarily*, and a book about the art and craft of creative writing entitled *Write On!: Notes from a Writers Workshop*. As a prominent novelist, playwright, essayist, and teacher, Killens "strove in all his work to distill and express the black experience in this country," wrote Richard Pearson in the *Washington Post*. "In doing so he reached an audience that transcended boundaries of race or color to express common denominators in human nature."

*BIOGRAPHICAL/CRITICAL SOURCES:*

*BOOKS*

*Contemporary Authors Autobiography Series,* Volume 2, Gale, 1985.
*Contemporary Literary Criticism,* Volume 10, Gale, 1979.
*Dictionary of Literary Biography,* Volume 33: *Afro-American Fiction Writers after 1955,* Gale, 1984.
Gayle, Addison, Jr., *The Way of the World: The Black Novel in America,* Anchord Press/Doubleday, 1975.
Killens, John Oliver, *'Sippi,* Trident Press, 1967.
Littlejohn, David, *Black on White: A Critical Survey of Writing by American Negroes,* Viking Penguin, 1966.
Williams, John A., and Charles F. Harris, editors, *Amistad 2,* Random House, 1971.

*PERIODICALS*

*Atlantic,* February, 1971.
*Best Sellers,* February 1, 1963; October 1, 1965; March 15, 1972.
*Black Scholar,* November, 1971.
*Black World,* June, 1971.
*Booklist,* October 15, 1992, p. 393.

*Callaloo,*, fall, 1990, p. 914.
*Choice,* March, 1990, p. 1134.
*Christian Science Monitor,* May 4, 1972.
*Crisis,* October 1954; April, 1965.
*Keystone Folklore Quarterly,* fall, 1972.
*Midwest Journal,* summer, 1954.
*Nation,* August 21, 1954.
*National Observer,* July 15, 1968.
*Negro Digest,* November, 1967.
*Newsweek,* May 26, 1969.
*New York Herald Tribune Book Review,* July 11, 1954; April 14, 1963.
*New York Review of Books,* April 20, 1972.
*New York Times,* June 6, 1954; March 2, 1969; March 28, 1969; March 27, 1970; May 29, 1972; February 18, 1990, p. 20.
*New York Times Book Review,* February 27, 1966; January 17, 1971; April 30, 1972; August 10, 1975, February 18, 1990, p. 20.
*Publishers Weekly,* May 6, 1988, p. 103; September 15, 1989, p. 108.
*Saturday Review,* January 26, 1963; March 12, 1966; March 6, 1971.
*Small Press,* August, 1989, p. 43.
*Time,* October 26, 1959.
*University Press Book News,* June, 1990, p. 35.
*Washington Post,* November 3, 1987.
*Washington Post Book World,* May 29, 1988; March 4, 1990, p. 8.

OBITUARIES:

PERIODICALS

*Jet,* November 16, 1987, p. 16.
*Los Angeles Times,* October 31, 1987.
*New York Times,* October 30, 1987.
*Washington Post,* November 3, 1987.

\* \* \*

## KINCAID, Jamaica 1949-

*PERSONAL:* Born May 25, 1949, in St. John's, Antigua, West Indies; immigrated to United States; naturalized U.S. citizen; daughter of a carpenter and Annie Richardson; married Allen Shawn (a composer); children: one daughter. *Religion:* Methodist.

*ADDRESSES: Home*—284 Hudson, New York, NY. *Office*—*New Yorker,* 25 West 43rd St., New York, NY 10036.

*CAREER:* Writer. *New Yorker,* New York, NY, staff writer, 1976—.

*AWARDS, HONORS:* Morton Dauwen Zabel Award, American Academy and Institute of Arts and Letters, 1983, for *At the Bottom of the River.*

*WRITINGS:*

*At the Bottom of the River* (short stories), Farrar, Straus, 1983.
*Annie John* (short story cycle), Farrar, Straus, 1985.
*A Small Place* (essay), Farrar, Straus, 1988.
*Annie, Gwen, Lilly, Pam and Tulip,* illustrations by Eric Fischl, Knopf and Whitney Museum of American Art, 1989.
*Lucy* (novel), Farrar, Straus, 1990.

Contributor to periodicals, including *New Yorker.*

*SIDELIGHTS:* Jamaica Kincaid's first three books, *At the Bottom of the River, Annie John,* and *A Small Place* are about life on the Caribbean island of Antigua, where she was born. In *Lucy,* Kincaid writes of a young Antiguan girl who moves to the United States. Kincaid employs a highly poetic literary style, one celebrated for its rhythms and imagery, and shows herself a master of characterization and elliptic narration. As Ike Onwordi wrote in *Times Literary Supplement:* "Jamaica Kincaid uses language that is poetic without affection. She has a deft eye for salient detail while avoiding heavy symbolism and diverting exotica. The result captures powerfully the essence of vulnerability."

In her first book, *At the Bottom of the River,* Kincaid showed an imposing capacity for detailing life's mundane aspects. This characteristic of her writing is readily evident in the often cited tale, "Girl," which consists almost entirely of a mother's orders to her daughter: "Wash the white clothes on Monday and put them on the stone heap; wash the color clothes on Tuesday and put them on the clothesline to dry; don't walk barehead in the hot sun; cook pumpkin fritters in very hot sweet oil ... ; On Sunday try to walk like a lady, and not like the slut you are so bent on becoming." Anne Tyler, in her review for *New Republic,* declared that this passage provides "the clearest idea of the book's general tone; for Jamaica Kincaid scrutinizes various particles of our world so closely and so solemnly that they begin to take on a nearly mystical importance."

"The Letter from Home," another story from *At the Bottom of the River,* serves as further illustration of Kincaid's style of repetition and her penchant for the mundane. In this tale a character recounts her daily chores in such a manner that the entire tale resembles an incantation: "I milked the cows, I churned the butter, I stored the cheese, I baked the bread, I brewed the tea," the tale begins, and it continues in this manner for several pages before ending as one long sentence. In *Ms.,* Suzanne Freeman cited this tale as evidence that Kincaid's style "is ... akin to hymn-singing or maybe even chanting." Freeman added that Kincaid's "singsong style" produces "images that are as sweet and mysterious as the secrets that children whisper in your ear."

Upon publication in 1983, *At the Bottom of the River* marked Kincaid's arrival as an important new voice in American fiction. Edith Milton wrote in the *New York Times Book Review* that Kincaid's tales "have all the force of illumination, and even prophetic power," and David Leavitt noted in the *Village Voice* that they move "with grace and ease from the mundane to the enormous." Leavitt also stated that "Kincaid's particular skill lies in her ability to articulate the internal workings of a potent imagination without sacrificing the rich details of the external world on which that imagination thrives." Doris Grumbach expressed similar praise in her review for the *Washington Post Book World.* She declared that the world of Kincaid's narrators "hovers between fantasy and reality" and asserted that Kincaid's prose "results not so much in stories as in states of consciousness." Grumbach also wrote that Kincaid's style, particularly its emphasis on repetition, intensifies "the feelings of poetic jubilation Kincaid has ... for all life."

That exuberance for life is also evident in Kincaid's second book, *Annie John,* which contains interrelated stories about a girl's maturation in Antigua. In *Annie John,* the title character evolves from young girl to aspiring nurse and from innocent to realist: she experiences her first menstruation, buries a friend, gradually establishes a life independent of her mother, and overcomes a serious illness. After recovering her health Annie John decides to depart from Antigua to become a nurse in England, though this decision results in a painful, and necessary, separation from her mother. "No I am not you," Annie John eventually informs her mother in one tale; "I am not what you made me." By book's end Annie John has left her mother to pursue a nursing career. She is ultimately torn by her pursuit of a career outside her life in Antigua, and Kincaid renders that feeling so incisively that, as Elaine Kendall noted in her review for the *Los Angeles Times,* "You can almost believe Kincaid invented ambivalence."

Like *At the Bottom of the River,* Kincaid's *Annie John* earned widespread acclaim. Susan Kenney, writing in the *New York Times Book Review,* observed that "Kincaid ... has packed a lot of valuable insight about the complex relationship between mothers and daughters into this slender novel." Kenney noted Annie John's ambivalence about leaving behind her life in Antigua and declared that such ambivalence was "an inevitable and unavoidable result of growing up." Furthermore, Kenney stated that she couldn't "remember reading a book that illustrates this [ambivalence] more poignantly than" *Annie John.* Kendall, who called *Annie John* a "fully fledged novel," seconded Kenney's assessment and confirmed Kincaid's status as a major writer. According to Kendall, *Annie John* pos-

sessed "a timeless quality, adding substance and weight to the smallest incident and detail."

Many critics focused particular praise on Kincaid's poetic style and artistic sensitivity. An *Atlantic* reviewer noted the "cool, precise style" of *Annie John,* and *Nation* reviewer Barbara Fisher Williamson noted that the volume's first-person narrative—*Annie John*'s "tone flat, her language modest"— "works best when it is undercut by ironic detachment or overburdened by intense feeling." Comparing *Annie John* favorably to the earlier *At the Bottom of the River, Washington Post* critic Susan Wood noted that the later work "retains the shimmering, strange beauty of the earlier stories, but its poetry is grounded in detail, in the lovingly rendered life of its adolescent heroine." And Kendall wrote in the *Los Angeles Times* that "Kincaid's imagery is so neon-bright that the traditional story of a young girl's passage into adolescence takes on a shimmering strangeness, the familiar outlines continually forming surprising patterns."

Kincaid's third book, *A Small Place,* continues her focus on Antigua, but in a dramatically different tone. It is written as an essay about the ills of tourism on this small island, but one reviewer, Isabel Fonseca commented in the *Times Literary Supplement* that the book's "style owes more to the manifesto than the essay." Fonseca added that in this book "Kincaid condemns her native Antigua's tragic development, from its colonial past to the new tourism which has replaced it and which she sees, alarmingly, as identical." Kincaid's essay is addressed to a generic, white, or European tourist, and it coldly shows this tourist not only what the tourist thinks he sees, but what he doesn't see as well. She condemns Antigua's bureaucratic corruptions as holdovers from British colonialism, as well as the unequal relationship between island dweller and visiting tourist. Several reviewers have been put off by what they see as a harsh or anger-filled tone in Kincaid's writing in this book. Adewale Maja-Pearce, a reviewer for the *New Statesman,* for example, found that the "embarrassing tone of self-pity ... damages the structure of the essay as a whole." Fonseca, however, found the anger appropriate, but felt that "her savage tone is ... diffused by the shapelessness of the essay." Writing in the *New York Times Book Review,* Alison Friesinger Hill had a mixture of praise and criticism for the book: "*A Small Place* is strongest when Ms. Kincaid is concrete in her grievances, or when she indulges in her wily, wonderful descriptions. Often, however, the writing is distorted by her anger, which backs the reader into a corner ... Consequently, both writer and reader are left unsatisfied."

Kincaid's novel *Lucy* is a first-person narrative which contains some of the same forms of rage so apparent in *A Small Place.* Lucy, the narrator, is a 19-year-old woman who has just moved from her home in Antigua to an unnamed northeastern United States city to work as an *au pair.* Thulani Davis writes in the *New York Times Book Review* that Lucy's "story is not about the shock of emigrating from one culture to another; it dwells in the psychological space between leaving and arriving. In sparse prose punctuated with the most economical yet precise description, Ms. Kincaid's Lucy makes an accounting of her first year abroad—a year in which she never quite arrives where she expected to be." Lucy cares for the four daughters of an upper-middle-class white family. Though the husband and wife, Lewis and Mariah, encourage her to think of herself as a member of their family, Lucy remains somewhat detached and cannot help but observe the contradictions between Mariah's "socially progressive" attitudes and her obvious economic privilege. Richard Eder writes in the *Los Angeles Times* that "The anger of Lucy ... is an instrument of discovery, not destruction. It is lucid and cold, but by no means unsparing." Eder calls Mariah "a romantic environmentalist." Lucy notes that she "couldn't bring myself to point out to her that if all the things she wanted to save in the world were saved, she might find herself in reduced circumstances." As Carol Anshaw states in the *Tribune Books*, "Kincaid's brilliant stroke in this book ... is to make its narrator-observer also its most interesting character." Coupled with her critical eye to her present surroundings Lucy also possesses a fraught sense of longing for and rejection of her island past. She reveals that her one true love has been her mother in Antigua, and yet throughout the book she refuses to read or even open her mother's letters. Thus Eder wrote that the anger of the book is "in delicate and painful dialogue with longing," and he called this "the energy that propels her journey between distant places: between the Caribbean and the United States, childhood and growing up, the hunger for love and the hunger for autonomy."

A unity of theme can be seen between Kincaid's three fiction works, *At the Bottom of the River, Annie John,* and *Lucy.* Davis commented that "The manner of telling varies, but the seminal events and the narrow, internal focus are the same in all three books." Davis added that "whereas the images in [*At the Bottom of the River*] are luminous and disjointed, as if refracted through a pool of water, they return as singular, sparkling pictures in the more orderly, representational narrative of *Annie John.* In *Lucy,* they recur as slightly misshapen by memory and distance." Susanna Moore praised Kincaid's work, stating in *Washington Post Book World* that, "The toughness and elegance of Kincaid's writing is all that one could want. It is both poetic and matter-of-fact in its precision and spareness."

Kincaid has become a prominent figure in American literature, and even though most of her books are set in the West Indies, she credits the United States as the place where "I did find myself and did find my voice." In the *New York Times Book Review,* where she made the aforementioned comment, she added: "What I really feel about America is that it's given me a place to be myself—but myself as I was formed somewhere else."

## BIOGRAPHICAL/CRITICAL SOURCES:

### BOOKS

*Contemporary Literary Criticism,* Volume 43, Gale, 1987.
Cudjoe, Selwyn, editor, *Caribbean Women Writers: Essays from the First International Conference.* Calaloux, 1990.

### PERIODICALS

*American Book Review,* September, 1989, p. 19.
*Antioch Review,* winter, 1991, p. 156.
*Atlantic,* May, 1985.
*Belles Lettres,* winter, 1991, p. 15.
*Books in Canada,* March, 1989, p. 32.
*Boston Herald,* March 31, 1985.
*Callaloo,* spring, 1989, pp. 396-411; spring, 1990, pp. 325-340.
*Canadian Literature,* spring, 1991, p. 141.
*Chicago Tribune Books,* October 28, 1990, p. 6.
*Christian Science Monitor,* April 5, 1985; November 26, 1990, p. 13.
*Commonweal,* November 4, 1988, p. 602.
*English Journal,* April, 1992, p. 37.
*Essence,* January, 1991, p. 32; May, 1991, p. 86.
*Harper's Bazaar,* October, 1990, p. 82.
*Hudson Review,* summer, 1991, p. 323.
*Library Journal,* December 1, 1989, p. 118.
*Listener,* January 10, 1985.
*London Review of Books,* July 11, 1991, p. 20.
*Los Angeles Times,* April 25, 1985.
*Los Angeles Times Book Review,* October 21, 1990, p. 3; October 27, 1991, p. 10; January 12, 1992, p. 10.
*Maclean's,* May 20, 1985.
*Mississippi Review,* Number 20, 1991.
*Ms.,* January, 1984.
*Nation,* June 15, 1985; February 18, 1991, p. 207.
*New Republic,* December 31, 1983.
*New Statesman & Society,* September 7, 1984; October 7, 1988, p. 40.
*Newsweek,* October 1, 1990, p. 68.
*New Yorker,* December 17, 1990, p. 122.
*New York Times Book Review,* January 15, 1984; May 25, 1986, p. 24; July 10, 1988, p. 19; October 28, 1990, p. 11; October 6, 1991, p. 32.
*New York Times Magazine,* October 7, 1990, p. 42.
*People,* September 26, 1988, p. 37; November 5, 1990, p. 40.
*Sulfur,* spring, 1990, p. 241.
*Times Literary Supplement,* November 29, 1985; January 13, 1989, p. 30.

*Tribune Books* (Chicago), October 28, 1990, p. 6; November 3, 1991, p. 8.

*Village Voice,* January 17, 1984.

*Virginia Quarterly Review,* summer, 1985; spring, 1991, p. 58.

*Voice Literary Supplement,* April, 1985; October, 1989; October, 1990, p. 21; December, 1990, p. 12.

*Wall Street Journal,* October 16, 1990, p. A24.

*Washington Post,* April 2, 1985.

*Washington Post Book World,* February 5, 1984; October 7, 1990, p. 7.

*West Coast Review of Books,* Volume 15, number 6, 1990, p. 16.

*Women's Review of Books,* February, 1991, p. 5.

*World Literature Today,* autumn, 1985; summer, 1989; winter, 1992.

*World Literature Written in English,* autumn, 1988.

*    *    *

## KING, Martin Luther, Jr.   1929-1968

*PERSONAL:* Given name, Michael, changed to Martin; born January 15, 1929, in Atlanta, GA; assassinated April 4, 1968, in Memphis, TN; originally buried in South View Cemetery, Atlanta; reinterred at Martin Luther King, Jr., Center for Nonviolent Social Change, Atlanta; son of Martin Luther (a minister) and Alberta Christine (a teacher; maiden name, Williams) King; married Coretta Scott (a concert singer), June 18, 1953; children: Yolanda Denise, Martin Luther III, Dexter Scott, Bernice Albertine. *Education:* Morehouse College, B.A., 1948; Crozer Theological Seminary, B.D., 1951; Boston University, Ph.D., 1955, D.D., 1959; Chicago Theological Seminary, D.D., 1957; attended classes at University of Pennsylvania and Harvard University.

*CAREER:* Ordained Baptist minister, 1948; Dexter Avenue Baptist Church, Montgomery, AL, pastor, 1954-60; Southern Christian Leadership Conference (S.C.L.C.), Atlanta, founder, 1957, and president, 1957-68; Ebenezer Baptist Church, Atlanta, co-pastor with his father, 1960-68. Vice-president, National Sunday School and Baptist Teaching Union Congress of National Baptist Convention; president, Montgomery Improvement Association.

*MEMBER:* National Association for the Advancement of Colored People (NAACP), Alpha Phi Alpha, Sigma Pi Phi, Elks.

*AWARDS, HONORS:* Selected one of ten outstanding personalities of 1956 by *Time,* 1957; Spingarn Medal, National As-

sociation for the Advancement of Colored People, 1957; L.H.D., Morehouse College, 1957, and Central State College, 1958; L.L.D., Howard University, 1957, and Morgan State College, 1958; Anisfield-Wolf Award, 1958, for *Stride toward Freedom; Time* Man of the Year, 1963; Nobel Prize for Peace, 1964; Judaism and World Peace Award, Synagogue Council of America, 1965; Brotherhood Award, 1967, for *Where Do We Go from Here: Chaos or Community?;* Nehru Award for International Understanding, 1968; Presidential Medal of Freedom, 1977; received numerous awards for leadership of Montgomery Movement; two literary prizes were named in his honor by National Book Committee and Harper & Row.

*WRITINGS:*

*Stride toward Freedom: The Montgomery Story,* Harper, 1958, reprinted, 1987.

*The Measure of a Man,* Christian Education Press (Philadelphia), 1959, memorial edition, Pilgrim Press, 1968, reprinted, Fortress, 1988.

*Letter from Birmingham City Jail,* American Friends Service Committee, 1963, published as *Letter from Birmingham Jail* (also see below), Overbrook Press, 1968.

*Why We Can't Wait* (includes "Letter from Birmingham Jail"), Harper, 1964, reprinted, New American Library, 1987.

*Where Do We Go from Here: Chaos or Community?,* Harper, 1967, memorial edition with an introduction by wife, Coretta Scott King, Bantam, 1968, published in England as *Chaos or Community?,* Hodder & Stoughton, 1968.

*SPEECHES*

*The Montgomery Story,* [San Francisco, CA], 1956.

*I Have a Dream,* John Henry and Mary Louise Dunn Bryant Foundation (Los Angeles), 1963.

*Nobel Lecture,* Harper, 1965.

*Address at Valedictory Service,* University of the West Indies (Mona, Jamaica), 1965.

*The Ware Lecture,* Unitarian Universalist Association (Boston), 1966.

*Conscience for Change,* Canadian Broadcasting Co., 1967.

*Beyond Vietnam,* Altoan Press, 1967.

*Declaration of Independence from the War in Vietnam,* [New York], 1967.

*A Drum Major for Justice,* Taurus Press, 1969.

*A Testament of Hope* (originally published in *Playboy,* January, 1969), Fellowship of Reconciliation, 1969.

*OMNIBUS VOLUMES*

*"Unwise and Untimely?"* (letters; originally published in *Liberation,* June, 1963), Fellowship of Reconciliation, 1963.

*Strength to Love* (sermons), Harper, 1963, reprinted, Walker, 1985.

*A Martin Luther King Treasury,* Educational Heritage (New York), 1964.

*The Wisdom of Martin Luther King in His Own Words,* edited by staff of Bill Alder Books, Lancer Books, 1968.

*"I Have a Dream": The Quotations of Martin Luther King, Jr.,* edited and compiled by Lotte Hoskins, Grosset, 1968.

*The Trumpet of Conscience* (transcripts of radio broadcasts), introduction by C. S. King, Harper, 1968.

*We Shall Live in Peace: The Teachings of Martin Luther King, Jr.,* edited by Deloris Harrison, Hawthorn, 1968.

*Speeches about Vietnam,* Clergy and Laymen Concerned about Vietnam (New York), 1969.

*A Martin Luther King Reader,* edited by Nissim Ezekiel, Popular Prakashan (Bombay), 1969.

*Words and Wisdom of Martin Luther King,* Taurus Press, 1970.

*Speeches of Martin Luther King, Jr.,* commemorative edition, Martin Luther King, Jr., Memorial Center (Atlanta), 1972.

*Loving Your Enemies, Letter from Birmingham Jail* [and] *Declaration of Independence from the War in Vietnam* (also see below), A. J. Muste Memorial Institute, 1981.

*The Words of Martin Luther King, Jr.,* edited and with an introduction by C. S. King, Newmarket Press, 1983.

*A Testament of Hope: The Essential Writings of Martin Luther King, Jr.,* edited by James Melvin Washington, Harper, 1986.

*I Have a Dream: Writings and Speeches that Changed the World,* edited by James Melvin Washington, foreword by Coretta Scott King, Harper, 1992.

*The Papers of Martin Luther King, Jr., Volume 1: Called to Serve, January 1929-June 1951,* edited by Clayborne Carson, Ralph E. Luker, Penny A. Russell, and Louis R. Harlan, University Press, 1992.

OTHER

*Pilgrimage to Nonviolence* (monograph; originally published in *Christian Century*), Fellowship of Reconciliation, 1960.

Author of introduction for *Three Lives for Mississippi,* by William Bradford Huie, New American Library, 1968; contributor to *Black Titan: W. E. B. Du Bois,* edited by John Henrik Clarke and others, Beacon Press, 1970. Works represented in anthologies, including *Crisis in Modern America,* edited by H. John Heinz III, Yale University, 1959; *Shall Not Perish: Nine Speeches by Three Great Americans,* edited by William B. Thomas, Gyldendalske Boghandel, 1969; *Black Writers of America: A Comprehensive Anthology,* edited by Richard K. Barksdale and Kenneth Kinnamon, Macmillan, 1972. Contributor to periodicals, including *Harper's, Nation,* and *Christian Century.*

*WORK IN PROGRESS:* King's papers are being edited by Clayborne Carson to be published in a projected 14-volume set over a 15-year period.

*SIDELIGHTS:* "We've got some difficult days ahead," civil rights activist Martin Luther King, Jr., told a crowd gathered at Memphis's Clayborn Temple on April 3, 1968, in a speech now collected in *The Words of Martin Luther King, Jr.* "But it really doesn't matter to me now," he continued, "because I've been to the mountaintop.... And I've seen the promised land. I may not get there with you. But I want you to know tonight that we as a people will get to the promised land." Uttered the day before his assassination, King's words were prophetic of his death. They were also a challenge to those he left behind to see that his "promised land" of racial equality became a reality; a reality to which King devoted the last twelve years of his life.

Just as important as King's dream was the way he chose to achieve it: through nonviolent resistance. He embraced nonviolence as a method for social reform after being introduced to the nonviolent philosophy of Mahatma Gandhi while doing graduate work at Pennsylvania's Crozer Seminary. Gandhi had led a bloodless revolution against British colonial rule in India. According to Stephen B. Oates in *Let the Trumpet Sound: The Life of Martin Luther King, Jr.,* King became "convinced that Gandhi's was the only moral and practical way for oppressed people to struggle against social injustice."

What King achieved during the little over a decade that he worked in civil rights was remarkable. "Rarely has one individual," noted Flip Schulke and Penelope O. McPhee in *King Remembered,* "espousing so difficult a philosophy, served as a catalyst for so much significant social change.... There are few men of whom it can be said their lives changed the world. But at his death the American South hardly resembled the land where King was born. In the twelve years between the Montgomery bus boycott and King's assassination, Jim Crow was legally eradicated in the South."

The first public test of King's adherence to the nonviolent philosophy came in December, 1955, when he was elected president of the Montgomery [Alabama] Improvement Association (M.I.A.), a group formed to protest the arrest of Rosa Parks, a black woman who refused to give up her bus seat to a white. Planning to end the humiliating treatment of blacks on city bus lines, King organized a bus boycott that was to last more than a year. Despite receiving numerous threatening phone calls, being arrested, and having his home bombed, King and his boycott prevailed. Eventually, the U.S. Supreme Court declared Montgomery's bus segregation laws illegal and, in December, 1956, King rode on Montgomery's first integrated bus.

"Montgomery was the soil," wrote King's widow in her autobiography, *My Life with Martin Luther King, Jr.,* "in which the seed of a new theory of social action took root. Black people found in nonviolent, direct action a militant method that avoided violence but achieved dramatic confrontation which electrified and educated the whole nation."

King was soon selected president of an organization of much wider scope than the M.I.A., the Southern Christian Leadership Conference (S.C.L.C.). The members of this group were black leaders from throughout the South, many of them ministers like King. Their immediate goal was for increased black voter registration in the South with an eventual elimination of segregation.

1957 found King drawn more and more into the role of national and even international spokesman for civil rights. In February a *Time* cover story on King called him "a scholarly ... Baptist minister ... who in little more than a year has risen from nowhere to become one of the nation's remarkable leaders of men." In March, he was invited to speak at the ceremonies marking the independence from Great Britain of the new African republic of Ghana.

The following year, King's first book, *Stride toward Freedom: The Montgomery Story,* which told the history of the boycott, was published. *New York Times* contributor Abel Plenn called the work "a document of far-reaching importance for present and future chroniclings of the struggle for civil rights in this country." A *Times Literary Supplement* writer quoted U.S. Episcopalian Bishop James Pike's reaction to the book: *Stride toward Freedom* "may well become a Christian classic. It is a rare combination: sound theology and ethics, and the autobiography of one of the greatest men of our time."

In 1959, two important events happened. First, King and his wife were able to make their long-awaited trip to India where they visited the sites of Gandhi's struggle against the British and met with people who had been acquainted with the Indian leader. Second, King resigned as pastor of Dexter Avenue Baptist Church in Montgomery so he could be closer to S.C.L.C.'s headquarters in Atlanta and devote more of his time to the civil rights effort.

King's trip to India seemed to help make up his mind to move to Atlanta. The trip greatly inspired King, as Oates observed: "He came home with a deeper understanding of nonviolence and a deep commitment as well. For him, nonviolence was no longer just a philosophy and a technique of social change; it was now a whole way of life."

Despite his adherence to the nonviolent philosophy, King was unable to avoid the bloodshed that was to follow. Near the end of 1962, he decided to focus his energies on the desegrega-tion of Birmingham, Alabama. Alabama's capital was at that time what King called in his book *Why We Can't Wait,* "the most segregated city in America," but that was precisely why he had chosen it as his target.

In *Why We Can't Wait* King detailed the advance planning that was the key to the success of the Birmingham campaign. Most important was the training in nonviolent techniques given by the S.C.L.C.'s Leadership Training Committee to those who volunteered to participate in the demonstrations. "The focus of these training sessions," King noted in his book, "was the socio-dramas designed to prepare the demonstrators for some of the challenges they could expect to face. The harsh language and physical abuse of the police and self-appointed guardians of the law were frankly presented, along with the non-violent creed in action: to resist without bitterness; to be cursed and not reply; to be beaten and not hit back."

One of the unusual aspects of the Birmingham campaign was King's decision to use children in the demonstrations. When the protests came to a head on May 3, 1963, it was after nearly one thousand young people had been arrested the previous day. As another wave of protestors, mostly children and teenagers, took to the streets, they were hit with jets of water from fire hoses. Police dogs were then released on the youngsters.

The photographs circulated by the media of children being beaten down by jets of water and bitten by dogs brought cries of outrage from throughout the country and the world. U.S. president John F. Kennedy sent a Justice Department representative to Birmingham to work for a peaceful solution to the problem. Within a week negotiators produced an agreement that met King's major demands, including desegregation of lunch counters, restrooms, fitting rooms, and drinking fountains in the city and the hiring of blacks in positions previously closed to them.

Although the Birmingham campaign ended in triumph for King, at the outset he was criticized for his efforts. Imprisoned at the beginning of the protest for disobeying a court injunction forbidding him from leading any demonstrations in Birmingham, King spent some of his time in jail composing an open letter answering his critics. This document, called "Letter from Birmingham Jail," appeared later in his book *Why We Can't Wait.* Oates viewed the letter as "a classic in protest literature, the most elegant and learned expression of the goals and philosophy of the nonviolent movement ever written."

In the letter King addressed those who said that as an outsider he had no business in Birmingham. King reasoned: "I am in Birmingham because injustice is here.... I cannot sit idly by in Atlanta and not be concerned about what happens in Birmingham. Injustice anywhere is a threat to justice everywhere. We are caught in an inescapable network of mutuality, tied in a single garment of destiny."

Another important event of 1963 was a massive march on Washington, D.C., which King planned together with leaders of other civil rights organizations. When the day of the march came, an estimated 250 thousand people were on hand to hear King and other dignitaries speak at the march's end point, the Lincoln Memorial.

While King's biographers noted that the young minister struggled all night writing words to inspire his people on this historic occasion, when his turn came to speak, he deviated from his prepared text and gave a speech that Schulke and McPhee called "the most eloquent of his career." In the speech, which contained the rhythmic repetition of the phrase "I have a dream," King painted a vision of the "promised land" of racial equality and justice for all, which he would return to often in speeches and sermons in the years to come, including his final speech in Memphis. Schulke and McPhee explained the impact of the day: "The orderly conduct of the massive march was an active tribute to [King's] philosophy of non-violence. Equally significant, his speech made his voice familiar to the world and lives today as one of the most moving orations of our time."

On January 3, 1964, King was proclaimed "Man of the Year" by *Time* magazine, the first black to be so honored. Later that same year, King's book, *Why We Can't Wait,* was published. In the book King gave his explanation of why 1963 was such a critical year for the civil rights movement. He believed that celebrations commemorating the one-hundredth anniversary of Lincoln's Emancipation Proclamation reminded American blacks of the irony that while Lincoln made the slaves free in the nineteenth century, their twentieth-century grandchildren still did not feel free.

Reviewers generally hailed the work as an important document in the history of the civil rights movement. In *Book Week*, J. B. Donovan called it "a basic handbook on non-violent direct action." *Critic* contributor C. S. Stone praised the book's "logic and eloquence" and observed that it aimed a death blow "at two American dogmas—racial discrimination, and the even more insidious doctrine that nourishes it, gradualism."

In December of 1964, King received the Nobel Peace Prize, becoming the twelfth American, the third black, and the youngest—he was 35—person ever to receive the award. He donated the $54,600 prize to the S.C.L.C. and other civil rights groups. The Nobel Prize gave King even wider recognition as a world leader. "Overnight," commented Schulke and McPhee, "King became ... a symbol of world peace. He knew that if the Nobel Prize was to mean anything, he must commit himself more than ever to attaining the goals of the black movement through peace."

The next two years were marked by both triumph and despair. First came King's campaign for voting rights, concentrating on a voters registration drive in Selma, Alabama. Selma would be, according to Oates, "King's finest hour."

Voting rights had been a major concern of King's since as early as 1957 but, unfortunately, little progress had been made. In the country surrounding Selma, for example, only 335 of 32,700 blacks were registered voters. Various impediments to black registration, including poll taxes and complicated literacy tests, were common throughout the South.

Demonstrations continued through February and on into early March, 1965, in Selma. One day nearly 500 school children were arrested and charged with juvenile delinquency after they cut classes to show their support for King. In another incident, more than 100 adults were arrested when they picketed the county courthouse. On March 7, state troopers beat nonviolent demonstrators who were trying to march from Selma to Montgomery to present their demands to Alabama governor George Wallace.

Angered by such confrontations, King sent telegrams to religious leaders throughout the nation calling for them to meet in Selma for a "ministers' march" to Montgomery. Although some 1,500 marchers assembled, they were again turned back by a line of state troopers, but this time violence was avoided.

King was elated by the show of support he received from the religious leaders from around the country who joined him in the march, but his joy soon turned to sorrow when he learned later that same day that several of the white ministers who had marched with him had been beaten by club-wielding whites. One of them died two days later.

The brutal murder of a clergyman seemed to focus the attention of the nation on Selma. Within a few days, President Lyndon B. Johnson made a televised appearance before a joint session of Congress in which he demanded passage of a voting rights bill. In the speech Johnson compared the sites of revolutionary war battles such as Concord and Lexington with their modern-day counterpart, Selma, Alabama.

Although Johnson had invited King to be his special guest in the Senate gallery during the address, King declined the honor, staying instead in Selma to complete plans to again march on Montgomery. A federal judge had given his approval to the proposed Selma-to-Montgomery march and had ordered Alabama officials not to interfere. The five-day march finally took place as hundreds of federal troops stood by overseeing the safety of the marchers.

Later that year, Johnson signed the 1965 Voting Rights Act into law, this time with King looking on. The act made literacy tests as a requirement for voting illegal, gave the Attorney General the power to supervise federal elections in seven southern states, and urged the Attorney General to challenge the legality of poll taxes in state and local elections in four Southern states. "Political analysts," Oates observed, "almost unanimously attributed the voting act to King's Selma campaign.... Now, thanks to his own political sagacity, his understanding of how nonviolent, direct-action protest could stimulate corrective federal legislation, King's long crusade to gain southern Negroes the right to vote ... was about to be realized."

By this time, King was ready to embark on his next project, moving his nonviolent campaign to the black ghettoes of the North. Chicago was chosen as his first target, but the campaign did not go the way King had planned. Rioting broke out in the city just two days after King initiated his program. He did sign an open-housing agreement with Chicago mayor Richard Daley but, according to Oates, many blacks felt it accomplished little.

Discord was beginning to be felt within the civil rights movement. King was afraid that advocates of "black power" would doom his dream of a nonviolent black revolution. In his next book, *Where Do We Go from Here: Chaos or Community?,* published in 1967, he explored his differences with those using the "black power" slogan.

According to *New York Times Book Review* contributor Gene Roberts, while King admitted in the volume that black power leaders "foster[ed] racial pride and self-help programs," he also expressed regret that the slogan itself produced "fear among whites and [made] it more difficult to fashion a meaningful interracial political coalition. But above all, he [deplored] ... an acceptance of violence by many in the movement."

In *Saturday Review* Milton R. Knovitz noted other criticisms of the movement which King voiced in the book. King saw black power as "negative, even nihilistic in its direction," "rooted in hopelessness and pessimism," and "committed to racial—and ethical—separatism." In *America,* R. F. Drinan wrote, "Dr. King's analysis of the implications of the black power movement is possibly the most reasoned rejection of the concept by any major civil rights leader in the country."

*Where Do We Go from Here* touched on several issues that became King's major concerns during the last two years of his life. He expressed the desire to continue nonviolent demonstrations in the North, to stop the war in Vietnam, and to join underprivileged persons of all races in a coalition against poverty.

His first wish never materialized. Instead of nonviolent protest, riots broke out in Boston, Detroit, Milwaukee and more than thirty other U.S. cities between the time King finished the manuscript for the book and when it was published in late summer.

By that time, King had already spoken out several times on Vietnam. His first speech to be entirely devoted to the topic was given on April 15, 1967, at a huge antiwar rally held at the United Nations Building in New York City. Even though some of King's followers begged him not to participate in antiwar activities, fearful that King's actions would antagonize the Johnson administration which had been so supportive in civil rights matters, King could not be dissuaded.

In *The Trumpet of Conscience,* a collection of radio addresses published posthumously, King explained why speaking out on Vietnam was so important to him. He wrote: "I cannot forget that the Nobel Prize for Peace was also a commission— a commission to work harder than I ever worked before for the 'brotherhood of man.' This is a calling which takes me beyond national allegiances."

Commenting on King's opposition to the war, Coretta Scott King observed that her husband's "peace activity marked incontestably a major turning point in the thinking of the nation.... I think history will mark his boldness in speaking out so early and eloquently—despite singularly virulent opposition—as one of his major contributions."

When King was assassinated in Memphis on April 4, 1968, he was in the midst of planning his Poor People's Campaign. Plans called for recruitment and training in nonviolent techniques of three thousand poor people from each of fifteen different parts of the country. The campaign would culminate when they were brought to Washington, D.C., to disrupt government operations until effective antipoverty legislation was enacted.

On hearing of King's death, angry blacks in 125 cities across the nation rioted. As a result, 30 people died, hundreds suffered injuries, and more than 30 million dollars worth of property damage was incurred. But, fortunately, rioting was not the only response to his death. Accolades came from around the world as one by one world leaders paid their respects to the martyred man of peace. Eventually, King's widow and other close associates saw to it that a permanent memorial— the establishment of Martin Luther King, Jr.'s birthday as a national holiday in the United States—would assure that his memory would live on forever.

In her introduction to *The Trumpet of Conscience,* Coretta Scott King quoted from one of King's most famous speeches as she gave her thoughts on how she hoped future generations would remember her husband. "Remember him," she wrote, "as a man who tried to be 'a drum major for justice, a drum major for peace, a drum major for righteousness.' Remem-

ber him as a man who refused to lose faith in the ultimate redemption of mankind."

King's Christian optimism is evident in *The Papers of Martin Luther King, Jr., Volume 1: Called to Serve, January 1929-
June 1951.* The first of a projected 14 volumes includes essays collected from King as a boy and young man through
his graduation, as valedictorian, from Crozer Theological
Seminary in 1951. John Carleton Hayden in a *Washington
Post Book Review* says "the belief that, in spite of civil and
human suffering God's will would ultimately triumph in the
world and bring liberation and salvation to all people, was
sounded early in King's writings." Anthony O. Edmonds
points out in *Library Journal* that the essays "reveal his attempts to form an eclectic synthesis among liberal, neocon-
servative, and deeply personal Christianity."

Most of the essays were written by King at Crozer and were
at the center of a controversy concerning the originality of his
writings. Hayden says the essays allow the reader "to trace
King's theological development, show that King was not an
original thinker but possessed great skill in taking theological arguments and adapting them to the faith with which he
entered the seminary." The editors of *The Papers of Martin
Luther King, Jr., Volume 1,* Hayden says, point to King's
methodology in writing, "especially his alleged tendency to
plagiarize.... It is clearly not intended plagiarism, for in most
instances, sources are cited in his bibliography; however, the
fact that they are not footnoted does obscure the extent of
derivation in his essays."

Brad Hooper, in a *Booklist* review, describes Kings essays as
full of energy. "The passion that drove him is observable in
nearly every document, and his way with words is obvious
and enviable." Hayden focuses on King's genius: "Although
he struggled with the theological antinomies of liberalism and
neo-orthodoxy, spirituality and activism, personal salvation
and social gospel, King fused them into an ideology that would
make the black religious tradition accessible and understandable to whites. That process can be seen at work in most of
these documents."

King's early work shows how much he was influenced by "the
black family, the black church and the larger black community, to all of which he added the western intellectual tradition," Hayden notes. "In one statement, King writes, 'In the
quiet recesses of my heart, I am fundamentally a clergyman,
a Baptist preacher. This is my being and my heritage, for I
am also the son of a Baptist preacher, the grandson of a Baptist preacher, and the great grandson of a Baptist preacher.'"

*BIOGRAPHICAL/CRITICAL SOURCES:*

*BOOKS*

Bennett, Lerone, Jr., *What Manner of Man,* Johnson Publishing (Chicago, IL), 1964.

Bishop, Jim, *The Days of Martin Luther King, Jr.,* Putnam,
1971.

Bleiweiss, Robert M., editor, *Marching to Freedom: The Life
of Martin Luther King, Jr.,* New American Library, 1971.

Clayton, Edward T., *Martin Luther King, Jr.: The Peaceful
Warrior,* Prentice-Hall, 1968.

Collins, David R., *Not Only Dreamers: The Story of Martin
Luther King, Sr., and Martin Luther King, Jr.,* Brethren
Press, 1986.

Davis, Lenwood G., *I Have a Dream: The Life and Times of
Martin Luther King, Jr.,* Adams Book Co., 1969.

Frank, Gerold, *An American Death: The True Story of the
Assassination of Dr. Martin Luther King, Jr., and the
Greatest Manhunt of Our Time,* Doubleday, 1972.

Garrow, David J., *Bearing the Cross: Martin Luther King, Jr.,
and the Southern Christian Leadership Conference,*
Morrow, 1986.

Harrison, Deloris, editor, *We Shall Live in Peace: The Teachings of Martin Luther King, Jr.,* Hawthorn, 1968.

Haskins, Jim, *I Have a Dream: The Life and Words of Martin
Luther King, Jr.,* Millbrook Press, 1992.

King, Coretta Scott, *My Life with Martin Luther King, Jr.,* Holt,
1969.

King, Martin Luther, Jr., *The Trumpet of Conscience,* with an
introduction by Coretta Scott King, Harper, 1968.

King, Martin Luther, Jr., *The Words of Martin Luther King,
Jr.,* edited and with an introduction by Coretta Scott King,
Newmarket Press, 1983.

Lewis, David L., *King: A Critical Biography,* Praeger, 1970.

Lincoln, Eric C., editor, *Martin Luther King, Jr.: A Profile,*
Hill & Wang, 1970, revised edition, 1984.

Lokos, Lionel, *House Divided: The Life and Legacy of Martin Luther King,* Arlington House, 1968.

Lomax, Louis E., *To Kill a Black Man,* Holloway, 1968.

*Martin Luther King, Jr.: The Journey of a Martyr,* Universal
Publishing & Distributing, 1968.

*Martin Luther King, Jr., 1929-1968,* Johnson Publishing,
1968.

*Martin Luther King, Jr.,* Norton, 1976.

Miller, William Robert, *Martin Luther King, Jr.: His Life,
Martyrdom, and Meaning for the World,* Weybright,
1968.

Oates, Stephen B., *Let the Trumpet Sound: The Life of Martin Luther King, Jr.,* Harper, 1982.

Paulsen, Gary and Dan Theis, *The Man Who Climbed the
Mountain: Martin Luther King,* Raintree, 1976.

*Playboy Interviews,* Playboy Press, 1967.

Schulke, Flip, editor, *Martin Luther King, Jr.: A Documentary ... Montgomery to Memphis,* with an introduction by Coretta Scott King, Norton, 1976.

Schulke, Flip and Penelope O. McPhee, *King Remembered,* with a foreword by Jesse Jackson, Norton, 1986.

Small, Mary Luins, *Creative Encounters with "Dear Dr. King": A Handbook of Discussions, Activities, and Engagements on Racial Injustice, Poverty, and War,* edited by Saunders Redding, Buckingham Enterprises, 1969.

Smith, Kenneth L. and Ira G. Zepp, Jr., *Search for the Beloved Community: The Thinking of Martin Luther King, Jr.,* Judson, 1974.

Westin, Alan, and Barry Mahoney, *The Trial of Martin Luther King,* Crowell, 1975.

Witherspoon, William Roger, *Martin Luther King, Jr.: To the Mountaintop,* Doubleday, 1985.

*PERIODICALS*

*AB Bookman's Weekly,* April 22, 1968.

*America,* August 17, 1963; October 31, 1964; July 22, 1967; April 20, 1968.

*American Vision,* January/February, 1986.

*Antioch Review,* spring, 1968; summer, 1991, p. 470.

*Booklist,* February 1, 1992, p. 994.

*Books Abroad,* autumn, 1970.

*Book World,* July 9, 1967; September 28, 1969.

*Choice,* February, 1968.

*Christian Century,* August 23, 1967; January 14, 1970; August 26, 1970.

*Christian Science Monitor,* July 6, 1967.

*Commonweal,* November 17, 1967; May 3, 1968.

*Critic,* August, 1964.

*Ebony,* April, 1961; May, 1968; July, 1968; April, 1984; January, 1986; January, 1987; April, 1988.

*Economist,* April 6, 1968.

*Esquire,* August, 1968.

*Harper's,* February, 1961.

*Library Journal,* February 15, 1992, p. 182.

*Life,* April 19, 1968; January 10, 1969; September 12, 1969; September 19, 1969.

*Listener,* April 11, 1968; April 25, 1968.

*Los Angeles Times Book Review,* December 11, 1983.

*National Review,* February 13, 1987; February 27, 1987.

*Negro Digest,* August, 1968.

*Negro History Bulletin,* October, 1956; November, 1956; May, 1968.

*New Republic,* February 3, 1986; January 5, 1987; May 11, 1992, p. 33.

*New Statesman,* March 22, 1968.

*Newsweek,* January 27, 1986.

*New Yorker,* June 22, 1967; July 22, 1967; April 13, 1968; February 24, 1986; April 6, 1987, pp. 102, 105-12.

*New York Herald Tribune,* October 16, 1964.

*New York Post,* October 15, 1964.

*New York Review of Books,* August 24, 1967; January 15, 1987.

*New York Times,* October 12, 1958; October 15, 1964; July 12, 1967; April 12, 1968; April 13, 1968.

*New York Times Book Review,* September 3, 1967; February 16, 1969; February 16, 1986; November 30, 1986; March 15, 1992, pp. 13-14.

*Punch,* April 3, 1968.

*Ramparts,* May, 1968.

*Saturday Review,* July 8, 1967; April 20, 1968.

*Time,* February 18, 1957; January 3, 1964; February 5, 1965; February 12, 1965; April 19, 1968; October 3, 1969; January 27, 1986; January 19, 1987.

*Times* (London), April 6, 1968.

*Times Literary Supplement,* April 18, 1968.

*Virginia Quarterly Review,* autumn, 1968.

*Washington Post,* January 14, 1970.

*Washington Post Book World,* January 19, 1986; January 18, 1987; February 3, 1991, p. 12; July 26, 1992, p. 10.

*OBITUARIES:*

*PERIODICALS*

*New York Times,* April 5, 1968.

*Time,* April 12, 1968.

*Times* (London), April 5, 1968.

\* \* \*

## KING, Woodie, Jr.  1937-

*PERSONAL:* Born July 27, 1937, in Mobile, AL; son of Woodie and Ruby (Johnson) King; married Willie Mae Washington; children: Michelle, Woodie Geoffrey, Michael. *Education:* Attended Will-o-Way School of Theatre, 1958-62, Wayne State University, 1961, and Detroit School of Arts and Crafts.

*ADDRESSES: Office*—Woodie King Associates, Inc., 417 Convent Ave., New York, NY 10031.

*CAREER:* Professional model, 1955-68; Mobilization for Youth, New York City, cultural arts director, 1965-70; New Federal Theatre, New York City, founder and artistic director, 1970—. Co-founder and manager of Concept East Theatre, Detroit, MI, 1960-63; founder of National Black Touring Circuit, 1980; president of Woodie King Associates. Actor in touring production of *Study in Color* at Union Theological Seminary in New York City, 1964; actor, *Serpico* and

*Together for Days.* Directed five plays at American Place Theatre, 1965. Associate producer at Lincoln Center; producer of plays, including *A Black Quartet,* 1969, *Black Girl,* 1971, *Prodigal Sister,* 1974, *Medal of Honor Rag,* 1976, *Slaveship, In New England Winters, What the Wine Sellers Buy,* and *For Colored Girls Who have Considered Suicide/When the Rainbow Is Enuf;* executive producer of Broadway musical *Reggae,* 1980. Producer of films, including *Right On!,* 1970, and of short films with Mobilization for Youth; producer and director of *The Long Night,* 1975, *The Black Theatre Movement: 'A Raisin in the Sun' to the Present,* 1978, and *The Torture of Mothers,* 1980. Director of plays, including *Splendid Mummer,* 1988 and *Checkmate,* 1989. Producer of record albums "New Black Poets in America" and "Nation Time" for Motown, 1972. Arts and humanities consultant to Rockefeller Foundation, 1968-70.

*AWARDS, HONORS:* John Hay Whitney fellowship, American Place Theatre, 1965-66; award from Venice Festival, 1968, for *The Game;* Oberhausen Award, 1968, for *The Game;* International Film Critics Award, 1970, for *Right On!;* A. Phillip Randolph Award, New York Film Festival, 1971, for *Epitaph.*

*WRITINGS:*

(Editor with Ron Milner) *Black Drama Anthology,* Columbia University Press, 1971.
(Editor) *A Black Quartet: Four One-Act Plays,* New American Library, 1971.
(Editor) *Black Spirits: A Festival of New Black Poets in America,* Random House, 1972.
(Editor with Earl Anthony, and contributor) *Black Poets and Prophets: The Theory, Practice, and Esthetics of the Pan-Africanist Revolution,* New American Library, 1972.
(Editor and contributor) *Black Short Story Anthology,* Columbia University Press, 1972.
(Editor) *The Forerunners: Black Poets in America,* preface by Dudley Randall, Howard University Press, 1975.
*Black Theatre, Present Condition,* Publishing Center for Cultural Resources, 1981.
(Editor) *New Plays for the Black Theatre,* Third World Press, 1989.

*SCRIPTS*

*The Weary Blues* (two-act play; adaptation of work by Langston Hughes), first produced in New York City at Lincoln Center Library, 1966.
*Simple Blues* (one-act play; adaptation of work by Hughes), first produced in New York City at Clark Center of Performing Arts, 1967.

(Coauthor) *The Long Night* (film), released by Mahler Films of New York, 1976.

*OTHER*

Work represented in books, including *The Best Short Stories by Negro Writers,* edited by Langston Hughes, Little, Brown, 1967, and *We Be Word Sorcerers,* edited by Sonia Sanchez, Bantam, 1973. Also author of screenplays, including *The Black Theatre Movement: 'A Raisin in the Sun' to the Present,* 1978, *The Torture of Mothers,* 1980, and *Death of a Prophet,* 1982. Writer for television series, including "Sanford and Son" and "Hot 1 Baltimore." Contributor to periodicals, including *Black Creation, Black Scholar, Black American Literature Forum, Drama Review, Liberator, Negro Digest,* and *Negro History Bulletin.* Drama critic for Detroit *Tribune,* 1959-62.

*SIDELIGHTS:* "Woodie King, Jr., has been called the renaissance man of black theater," comments Stephen M. Vallillo in the *Dictionary of Literary Biography.* Vallillo continues that while King has adapted plays and written short stories, "his real importance to black literature is his support for black theater. Through his essays and his productions, he has tried to bring about a vital theater for black audiences." From his experience as an actor and director, King found that popular productions contained little to spark a black audience. Vallillo relates that King "was not interested in continuing the traditions that he saw in the white educational and commercial theaters of the time, but wanted blacks to address their theater to their needs." While King had been arguing for such a change through essays and articles, in 1970 he was able to pursue it concretely by taking the position of artistic director of Henry Street Settlement's New Federal Theatre, located on the lower east side of New York City. According to Mel Gussow in the *New York Times,* "Under Mr. King's leadership, Henry Street has become a prime generator of new black plays. In common, many of these plays have been naturalistic and socially conscious (though not polemical). A number of them have dealt with, as Mr. King describes it, 'split black families.' Occasionally the plays are roughhewn and unpolished, but they are charged with energy, conviction and passion."

The plays King selects must match his audience. He told Gussow, "I stay away from plays that have a European setting. I turn down plays dealing with senseless black-white conflict, plays that make fun of people just for the sake of making fun, or plays where the writer has not yet made a commitment to be a writer." Ticket prices at the New Federal Theatre are low and audiences tend to represent the community, instead of an artistic elite. "It takes away the image of the man in the suit-and-tie watching some heavy intellectual thing on stage," King remarked to Gussow. "We give the audience a lot of fun—and let the message sneak up on them."

*BIOGRAPHICAL/CRITICAL SOURCES:*

*BOOKS*

*Dictionary of Literary Biography,* Volume 38, *Afro-American Writers after 1955: Dramatists and Prose Writers,* Gale, 1985.

*PERIODICALS*

*Negro Digest,* January, 1968.
*New York Times,* October 31, 1976; October 16, 1981.

\*   \*   \*

**KITUOMBA**
   See ODAGA,   Asenath (Bole)

\*   \*   \*

**KONADU,  Asare**
   See KONADU,  S(amuel) A(sare)

\*   \*   \*

**KONADU,  S(amuel) A(sare)  1932-**
   **(Asare Konadu; pseudonyms: Bediako Asare, Kwabena Asare Bediako)**

*PERSONAL:* Born January 18, 1932, in Asamang, Ghana; son of Kofi (a farmer) and Abena (Anowuo) Konadu; married Alice Dede, February 26, 1958; children: Samuel Asare, Jr., Cecilia, Lucy, Frederick, Birago, Yamoah. *Education:* Attended Abuakwa State College, Kibi, Ghana, 1948-51, Polytechnic, London, England, 1956-58, and University of Strasbourg, 1958. *Religion:* Seventh-day Adventist.

*ADDRESSES: Home*—100 Aburaso St., Asamang, Ashanti, Ghana. *Office*—2R McCarthy Hill, Box 3918, Accra, Ghana.

*CAREER:* Ghana Information Services, Accra, junior reporter, 1952-56, journalist, 1956-58; Ghana News Agency, Accra, editor, 1958-60, chief editor, 1961-63; full-time writer, 1963— . Worked for Gold Coast Broadcasting Service; publisher and director of Anowuo Educational Publications.

*MEMBER:* Ghana Writers Club, Ghana Journalists Association.

*AWARDS, HONORS:* University of Strasbourg fellowship for research in history of the Ghanaian press, 1959.

*WRITINGS:*

*Wizard of Asamang* (novel), Waterville Publishing, 1962.
*The Lawyer Who Bungled His Life* (novel), Waterville Publishing, 1965.
*Night Watchers of Korlebu* (novel), Anowuo Educational Publications, 1967, Humanities Press, 1969.
*Come Back Dora* (novel), Humanities Press, 1969.

Also author of short stories.

*UNDER NAME ASARE KONADU*

*Shadow of Wealth* (novel), Anowuo Educational Publications, 1966.
*A Woman in Her Prime* (novel), Heinemann, 1967, Humanities Press, 1969.
*Ordained by the Oracle* (novel), Heinemann, 1968, Humanities Press, 1969.
*Vanishing Shadows,* Anowuo Educational Publications, 1987.
*Reconciliation,* Anowuo Educational Publications, 1988.
*Devils in Waiting,* Anowuo Educational Publications, 1989.

*UNDER PSEUDONYM BEDIAKO ASARE*

*Rebel,* Heinemann Educational, 1969.
*Majuto,* East African Literature Bureau, 1975.
*The Stubborn,* East African Literature Bureau, 1976.

*UNDER PSEUDONYM KWABENA ASARE BEDIAKO*

*Don't Leave Me Mercy* (novel), Anowuo Educational Publications, 1966.
*A Husband for Esi Ellua* (novel), Anowuo Educational Publications, 1967, Humanities Press, 1969.
*Return of Mercy,* Anowuo Educational Publications, 1987.
*The Koala Called Too Late,* Anowuo Educational Publications, 1988.

*WORK IN PROGRESS:* Research into traditional healing and Ghanaian customs.

*SIDELIGHTS:* In 1961 S. A. Konadu toured the Soviet Union with Kwame Nkrumah, ex-president of Ghana, visiting all of its states. He traveled in Europe in 1958 and 1962 and in the Congo, Rwanda, and Burundi in 1963. In 1968 Konadu was the guest of the U.S. State Department and spent ninety days on a publishing tour of eleven states.

\*   \*   \*

**KOUROUMA,  Ahmadou  1940-**

*PERSONAL:* Born in 1940, in the Ivory Coast.

*CAREER:* Writer. Living in exile.

*WRITINGS:*

*Les Soleils des Independences,* Seuil, 1968, translation by
    Adrian Adams published as *The Suns of Independence,*
    Africana, 1981.
*Monne, Outrages et Defis,* Seuil, 1990, translation by Nidra
    Poller published as *Monnew,* Mercury House, 1993.

*SIDELIGHTS:* Using degraded African princes as the focal
points of his two novels, Ahmadou Kourouma has written
angry satires about the disasters wrought in black Africa by
both colonialism and post-independence black African governments. Critics have found exceptional both this unflinch-
ing anger and its modes of expression.

Kourouma's stylistic innovations were evident in his first
novel, *The Suns of Independence,* both in the French original
and the subsequent English translation. "The first novel of
Ahmadou Kourouma...," remarked Suzanne Gasster in the
*French Review,* "marked the beginning of the adaptation of
French deliberately opened to African language. From the
African folk narration came a headlong rhythm, syntax reversals, and exclamations from different narrative sources." In
*The Suns of Independence,* much of the material for this language play is given by the fallen prince himself, Fama, who,
discarded by the post-colonial dictatorship and slightly daft,
makes a bare living by giving ritual orations. Prey to the seemingly arbitrary forces in power, his situation worsens until he
is fatally wounded crossing a newly established territorial
border.

The title of Kourouma's second novel, *Monnew,* means
"shame." It describes the fate of another prince, Djigui. In his
own interest he cooperates with the French conquest of the
Malinke peoples at the end of the nineteenth century, resulting in much slaughter and ruination of the kingdom. Kourouma uses a series of eyewitness narrators to relate the downfall. There are frequent comments on these recitations, anonymous voices responding with proverbial words from Malinke
folklore or Islam; another verbal layer is provided by the mis-
interpretations given to Djigui—and, possibly to the reader—
by French translators and local soothsayers.

But despite the continual verbal interest of the novel, it ends
in much the same contemporary mood as *The Suns of Independence,* revealing the same priorities of that novel noted by
John F. Povey in the *World Literature Today:* "the disaster of
modern Africa must be exposed in words that burn with the
bitterness of their despair. As the author concludes, colonized
or independent, Africans will keep on suffering 'until such
times as God unpeels the curse stuck fast in their black back-
sides.'"

*BIOGRAPHICAL/CRITICAL SOURCES:*

*BOOKS*

Zell, Hans M., and others, *A New Reader's Guide to African
    Literature,* Holmes & Meier, 1983.

*PERIODICALS*

*African Today,* v.31, no. 1, 1984, p.71.
*Booklist,* June 1, 1974, p. 1084.
*French Review,* October, 1991, p. 171.
*Times Literary Supplement,* October 18, 1985, p. 1180.
*World Literature Today,* winter, 1983, p. 159.

# L

## LADNER, Joyce A(nn) 1943-

*PERSONAL:* Born October 12, 1943, in Waynesboro, MS; married Walter Carrington. *Education:* Tougaloo College, B.A., 1964; Washington University, Ph.D., 1968; postdoctoral research at University of Dar es Salaam, Tanzania.

*ADDRESSES: Office*—Department of Sociology, Hunter College of the City University of New York, 695 Park Ave., New York, NY 10021.

*CAREER:* Southern Illinois University, Edwardsville, assistant professor and curriculum specialist, 1968-69; affiliated with Wesleyan University, Middletown, CT, 1969-70; University of Dar es Salaam, Dar es Salaam, Tanzania, research associate, 1970-71; Howard University, Washington, DC, associate professor of sociology, 1971-76; Hunter College of the City University of New York, New York City, member of faculty of sociology, beginning in 1976.

*MEMBER:* American Sociological Association (member of board of directors), National Institute of Mental Health (review committee member of Minority Center), Social Science Research Council (fellow), Society for the Study of Social Problems, Caucus of Black Sociologists (member of board of directors), Association for the Study of Afro-American Life and History, Institute of the Black World (senior research fellow, 1969-71), Twenty-first Century Foundation (member of board of directors).

*AWARDS, HONORS:* Recipient of first fellowship from Black Women's Community Development Foundation, 1970-71, for study "Involvement of Tanzanian Women in Nation Building"; Russell Sage Foundation grant, 1972-73; Cummins Engine Foundation grant, 1972-73.

*WRITINGS:*

*Tomorrow's Tomorrow: The Black Woman,* Doubleday, 1971.
(Editor) *The Death of White Sociology* (collection of essays), Random House, 1973.
*Mixed Families: Adopting Across Racial Boundaries,* Doubleday, 1977.
(Editor with Peter B. Edelman) *Adolescence and Poverty: Challenge for the 1990s,* Center for National Policy Press, 1991.

Contributor to anthologies and to newspapers and periodicals. Contributing editor to *Black Scholar* and *Journal of Black Studies and Research.*

*SIDELIGHTS:* Sociologist Joyce A. Ladner has centered her twenty years of research and teachings on intergroup relations and minority issues in America. In her first work, *Tomorrow's Tomorrow: The Black Woman,* Ladner examines the lives of black women and the forces that mold their self-perceptions. Her findings are the result of interviews with more than thirty black adolescent girls from a St. Louis, Missouri, ghetto. The girls, in the words of Toni Cade Bambara in *Black World,* "speak on and live out what it means to grow up Black and female in a country that regards neither with any special fondness." Analyzing her observations in the context of the black people's troubled history in America ("a society infamous for the lack of understanding and sympathy between the races," commented Susan E. Burke in *Best Sellers*), Ladner found the girls' aspirations refreshingly optimistic and their self-images surprisingly positive. Consequently, stated Bambara, *Tomorrow's Tomorrow* focuses not on "the weakness of the Black community ... or on the crippling effects of racism ... but rather on the intricate network of influences (familial, peer, societal, etc.) that bombard the young girl [and on] the counters and stratagems she devises to get over from day to day—her inner strength." Dispelling the popular notion of low self-esteem among poor black women, noted Burke, Ladner found that "most of the girls [she interviewed] have the determination to 'make something' of themselves, and self-hatred is practically non-existent."

Ladner relates the inner strength of black women to their position in a society that holds different values from those of the white middle class. Because of differing cultural views of sexual morality, for example, an unmarried, pregnant black woman is less likely to be shunned or chastised than is an unmarried, pregnant white woman. Carol L. Adams, writing in the *American Journal of Sociology,* cited illegitimacy as a "concept viewed as inappropriate when studying the black community." Adams explained Ladner's perception "that the low-income black community holds an inherent value that no child can be 'illegal.' The child is seen as having the right to exist and [as] representing the fulfillment of womanhood, thus neither the mother nor the child is degraded and stigmatized." Adams praised Ladner's "notion that black women are now serving as role models for white women who are beginning to question such things as the institution of marriage, the concept of illegitimacy, and the general moral code traditionally associated with this society." Although some critics accused Ladner's survey as being unscientific and thus inconclusive, Burke affirmed that "her observations are both valid and important," and Bambara called the study "a solid piece of scholarship ... moving and vital and eminently sensible."

Ladner's 1977 *Mixed Families: Adopting Across Racial Boundaries* is "an interesting, well-balanced study" of transracial adoption, according to Diane A. Parente in *Best Sellers.* Transracial adoption became a popular trend in America during the late 1960s when white couples, eager to adopt but discouraged by a shortage of white infants available, were strongly encouraged by adoption agencies to take in "hard to place" minority children. During an era of civil rights activity, such an undertaking was also considered an important step in promoting interracial harmony. In the early 1970s, however, the trend slowed when an opposing philosophy arose, strongly supported by the National Association of Black Social Workers, maintaining that black children needed to grow up in black families to develop a positive self-image and a strong sense of identity. Attempting to resolve the debate, Ladner interviewed 136 adoptive families to find out how they were coping with the personal and societal pressures they encountered. "Both sides of the controversy are objectively presented" in *Mixed Families,* determined Parente, adding that the "truth, apparently, lies somewhere in the middle." Some black adoptees—children and adults alike—and their white parents agree that it would have been better to have placed the black children with black parents, while other families maintain that the adoption helped them gain an irreplaceable understanding of racial differences and similarities. The author herself concludes that although efforts should be made

to avoid unnecessary trauma by placing children with families of their own ancestry, transracial adoptions are preferable to institutional or foster care. Ladner emphasizes the importance of parental understanding and patience, whatever the race of the adoptive parents and their adopted children. As David C. Anderson concluded in *New York Times Book Review*: "Relations between parent and child aren't supposed to be perfect; instead, they are richly complicated, molded by imponderable forces great and small. Our task, as parents, is only to manage the complexity as best we can." For mixed families, Ladner points out in her book this involves maintaining "a balanced view and not [erring] too much in either direction"—neither denying the child's blackness nor attempting, as a white parent, to become black by rejecting whiteness. Marti Wilson of *Black Scholar* remarked that "the strength of *Mixed Families* is in the fact that it approaches the question of integration from a new perspective, and heightens the level of dialogue on the subject of cross racial adoptions." And Parente asserted that in *Mixed Families* "the author provides a realistic glimpse of American racial attitudes and their day-to-day effects on all concerned."

*BIOGRAPHICAL/CRITICAL SOURCES:*

*BOOKS*

*Contemporary Issues Criticism,* Volume 1, Gale, 1982.
Ladner, Joyce A., *Mixed Families: Adopting Across Racial Boundaries,* Doubleday, 1977.

*PERIODICALS*

*American Journal of Sociology,* September, 1972.
*Best Sellers,* August, 1971, October, 1977.
*Black Scholar,* November/December, 1979.
*Black World,* October, 1971.
*New York Times Book Review,* August 14, 1977.

\* \* \*

**LALUAH, Aquah**
**See CASELY-HAYFORD, Gladys May**

\* \* \*

**LAMMING, George (William) 1927-**

*PERSONAL:* Born June 8, 1927, in Barbados; immigrated to England, 1950. *Education:* Attended Combermere High School in Barbados.

*ADDRESSES: Home*—14-A Highbury Place, London N 5, England.

*CAREER:* Writer. Worked as schoolmaster in Trinidad, 1946-50; factory worker in England, 1950; broadcaster for British Broadcasting Corp. (BBC) Colonial Service, 1951. Writer-in-residence and lecturer in Creative Arts Centre and Department of Education, University of West Indies, Mona, Jamaica, 1967-68; visiting professor at University of Texas at Austin, 1977, and at University of Pennsylvania. Lecturer in Denmark, Tanzania, and Australia.

*AWARDS, HONORS: Kenyon Review* fellowship, 1954; Guggenheim Fellowship, 1955; Somerset Maugham Award, 1957; Canada Council fellowship, 1962; Commonwealth Foundation grant, 1976; Association of Commonwealth Literature Writers Award; D.Litt., University of West Indies.

*WRITINGS:*

NOVELS

*In the Castle of My Skin,* with introduction by Richard Wright, McGraw, 1953, with a new introduction by the author, Schocken, 1983.
*The Emigrants,* M. Joseph, 1954, McGraw, 1955, reprinted, Allison & Busby, 1980.
*Of Age and Innocence,* M. Joseph, 1958, reprinted, Allison & Busby, 1981.
*Season of Adventure,* M. Joseph, 1960, reprinted, Allison & Busby, 1979.
*Water With Berries,* Holt, 1972.
*Natives of My Person,* Holt, 1972.

OTHER

*The Pleasures of Exile* (essays and autobiographical observations), M. Joseph, 1960, reprinted, Allison & Busby, 1984.
(With Henry Bangou and Rene Depestre) *Influencia del Africa en las literaturas antillanas* (title means "*The Influence of Africa on the Antillian Literatures*"), I. L. A. C. (Montevideo, Uruguay), 1972.
(Editor) *Cannon Shot and Glass Beads: Modern Black Writing,* Pan Books, 1974.

Also contributor to poetry anthologies, including *Young Commonwealth Poets '65,* edited by Peter Brent, Heinemann, 1965; *Caribbean Voices,* two volumes, edited by John Figueroa, Evans, 1966; and *Caribbean Verse,* edited by O. R. Dathorne, Heinemann, 1968. Contributor to short fiction anthologies, including *West Indian Stories,* edited by Andrew Salkey, Faber, 1960; *Stories from the Caribbean,* edited by Andrew Salkey, Dufour, 1965, published as *Island Voices,* Liveright, 1970; *Caribbean Narrative,* edited by O. R. Dathorne, Heinemann, 1966; *From the Green Antilles,* edited by Barbara Howes, Macmillan, 1966; *Caribbean Prose,* edited by Andrew Salkey, Evans, 1967; and *Caribbean Rhythms,* edited by James T. Livingston, Pocket Books, 1974.

Co-editor of Barbados and Guyana independence issues of *New World Quarterly* (Kingston), 1965 and 1967. Contributor to journals, including *Bim* (Barbados), *Savacou, New World Quarterly, Caribbean Quarterly,* and *Casa de las Americas* (Cuba).

*SIDELIGHTS:* Barbadian writer "George Lamming is not so much a novelist," asserts *New York Times Book Review* contributor Jan Carew, "as a chronicler of secret journeys to the innermost regions of the West Indian psyche." George Davis, however, believes Carew's assessment does not go far enough. Davis notes in his own *New York Times Book Review* critique, "I can think of very few writers who make better use of the fictional moments of their stories to explore the souls of any of us—West Indian or not."

In Lamming's essay, "The Negro Writer in His World," the West Indian explains the universality on which Davis comments. In the essay Lamming maintains that black writers are the same as all other writers who use writing as a method of self-discovery. According to Carolyn T. Brown in *World Literature Today,* in Lamming's opinion, "the contemporary human condition ... involves a 'universal sense of separation and abandonment, frustration and loss, and above all, of man's direct inner experience of something missing.'"

In Lamming's work the "something missing" is a true cultural identity for the West Indian. This lack of identity is, according to Lamming, a direct result of the long history of colonial rule in the region. Caribbean-born writer V. S. Naipaul explains the importance of this idea in his *New Statesman* review of Lamming's novel, *Of Age and Innocence:* "Unless one understands the West Indian's search for identity, [the novel] is almost meaningless. It is not fully realised how completely the West Indian Negro identifies himself with England.... For the West Indian intellectual, speaking no language but English, educated in an English way, the experience of England is really traumatic. The foundations of his life are removed." James Ngugi makes a similar observation in his *Pan-Africanist* review of the same novel. "For Lamming," Ngugi writes, "a sense of exile must lead to action and through action to identity. The West Indian's alienation springs ... from his colonial relationship to England."

Lamming's first four novels explore the West Indian search for identity, a search which often leads to a flight to England followed by, for some, a return to their Caribbean roots. His first novel, *In the Castle of My Skin,* which is nearly universally acclaimed by critics, is a quasi-autobiographical look at childhood and adolescence on Lamming's fictional Caribbean island, San Cristobal. The book "is generally regarded," notes Michael Gilkes in *The West Indian Novel,* "as a 'classic' of West Indian fiction. It is one of the earliest novels of any substance to convey, with real assurance, the life of ordinary village folk within a genuinely realized, native landscape: a 'peasant novel' ... written with deep insight and considerable technical skill."

Several reviewers compare Lamming's prose style in the book to poetry. In *New Statesman and Nation* Pritchett describes Lamming's prose as "something between garrulous realism and popular poetry, and ... quite delightful," while in the *San Francisco Chronicle* J. H. Jackson says Lamming "is a poet and a human being who approaches a question vital to him, humanly and poetically." A *Time* contributor finds the book "a curious mixture of autobiography and a poetic evocation of a native life.... It is one of the few authentically rich and constantly readable books produced [thus far] by a West Indian."

Lamming's next novel, *The Emigrants,* follows a group of West Indians who—like Lamming himself—leave their native islands for exile in England, while the two novels that follow, *Of Age and Innocence* and *Season of Adventure,* feature a return to San Cristobal. According to Carew, these last two novels also have a bit of autobiography in them because through their action it seems "as though Lamming [is] attempting to rediscover a history of himself by himself."

In Lamming's novels, as critics note, self-discovery is often achieved through an inquiry into his characters' pasts. For example, while *Yale Review* contributor Michael Cook quotes Lamming's *Of Age and Innocence* description of San Cristobal—"an old land inhabiting new forms of men who can never resurrect their roots and do not know their nature," the reviewer comments that "it is obvious" that in "*Season of Adventure* ... [Lamming] is committed to his characters' at least trying to discover their roots and their natures." Details of the plot seem to verify Cook's assessment for the novel traces Fola Piggott's quest to discover whether her father was European or African.

According to Kenneth Ramchand in *The West Indian Novel and Its Background,* "*Season of Adventure* is the most significant of the West Indian novels invoking Africa." In the novel, Ramchand maintains, Lamming invokes "the African heritage not to make statements about Africa but to explore the troubled components of West Indian culture and nationhood." Lamming accomplishes "this without preventing us from seeing that Fola's special circumstances ... are only a manifestation ... of every man's need to take the past into account with humility, fearlessness, and receptivity."

After a silence of over a decade Lamming published two new novels almost simultaneously: *Water with Berries* and *Natives of My Person.* Again, his fiction focuses on the effects of history on the present. In both books Lamming uses symbolism to tell his story. In *Water with Berries* Lamming uses a theme previously dealt with in his nonfiction work *The Pleasures of Exile.* A *Times Literary Supplement* reviewer quotes from Lamming's collection of essays: "My subject is the migration of the West Indian writer, as colonial and exile, from his native kingdom, once inhabited by Caliban, to the tempestuous island of Prospero's and his language." Caliban and Prospero are both characters from Shakespeare's *The Tempest,* Caliban being the deformed slave of Prospero, ruler of an enchanted island. According to the *Times Literary Supplement* contributor, Lamming also refers to himself in the same book as an "exiled descendent of Caliban."

In *Water with Berries* Lamming uses the plot of *The Tempest* to symbolize the various ills of West Indian society, but critics are divided on the success of the novel. In *World Literature in English* Anthony Boxill notes that Lamming uses *The Tempest* to "help put across his points about disintegration of personality ..., especially in people who are products of a colonial past.... However, the *Tempest* pattern which might have been the strength of this novel proves its undoing.... In his unrelenting faithfulness to this ... pattern Lamming loses touch with the characters he is creating; they cease to be credible." A *Times Literary Supplement* contributor similarly states, "Lamming writes very well, but *Water with Berries* does not entirely convince either as a study of the pains of exile, or as an allegory of colonialism.... [And,] as for the melodrama of ... Lamming's *Tempest* myth, it tells us nothing new."

Other critics praise Lamming's novel and disregard its connections to *The Tempest.* Paul Theroux and George Davis, for instance, find the work a very compelling statement on the effects of colonialism. In *Encounter* Theroux claims, "the poetic prose of the narrative has a perfect dazzle.... When expatriation is defined and dramatised ... *Water with Berries* takes on a life of its own, for ... Lamming is meticulous in diagnosing the condition of estrangement." *New York Times Book Review* contributor Davis writes: "This is an effectively written fictional work. Lamming brings his characters ... into the same nightmare of arson, perversity, suicide and murder, which, we are forced to feel, is the legacy of the colonial experience."

*Natives of My Person,* according to Gilkes, "is an exceedingly complex work, full of allegorical and historical meanings and echoes. It is an embodiment of all [Lamming's] themes: a kind of *reviewing* process in which he appears to take stock of things." Boxill notes that the novel "provides richly complex insights into human personality and the history of colonialism." It tells the story of the sixteenth-century voyage of the ship *Reconnaissance* from Europe to America by way of Africa. The chief goal of the ship's Commandant is the establishment of a slave-free settlement on the island of San Cristobal, but he is killed by two of the ship's officers before he can accomplish his mission.

Some critics find that Lamming's prose detracts from the novel. In *Book World* Theroux calls Lamming "a marvelously skillful writer" but also refers to the novel's "shadowy action and vaguely poetical momentousness." A *Times Literary Supplement* reviewer complains that Lamming writes "a prose of discovery which is effortful, uncolloquial, and almost always mannered." While Thomas R. Edwards and Carew also regret the complexity of Lamming's prose they are able to find redeeming qualities in the novel. "Lamming's prose is portentous," Edwards notes in the *New York Review of Books,* "hooked on simile, and anxious to suggest more than it says, inviting questions the story never answers.... Yet if reading *Natives of My Person* is a voyage into frustration and annoyance, Lamming's story survives and grows in the mind afterward.... This imagined history reveals itself as a version of significances that 'real' history is itself only a version of."

Carew similarly comments on the book's difficult prose but calls the work "undoubtedly ... Lamming's finest novel." In the book, according to Carew's assessment, Lamming expresses better than in any of his other novels his concerns about the effects of colonization on the West Indies and its people. In *Natives of My Person,* Carew maintains, Lamming "succeeds in illuminating new areas of darkness in the colonial past that the colonizer has so far not dealt with; and in this sense it is a profoundly revolutionary and original work."

*BIOGRAPHICAL/CRITICAL SOURCES:*

*BOOKS*

Baugh, Edward, editor, *Homecoming: Essays on African and Caribbean Literature, Culture and Politics,* Laurence Hill, 1972.
*Contemporary Literary Criticism,* Gale, Volume 2, 1974, Volume 4, 1975.
Cooke, Michael G., editor, *Modern Black Novelists: A Collection of Critical Essays,* Prentice-Hall, 1971.
Gilkes, Michael, *The West Indian Novel,* Twayne, 1981.
Lamming, George, *In the Castle of My Skin,* McGraw, 1954.
Lamming, George, *Of Age and Innocence,* M. Joseph, 1958.
Lamming, George, *The Pleasures of Exile,* M. Joseph, 1960.
Massa, Daniel, editor, *Individual and Community in Commonwealth Literature,* University Press (Malta), 1979.
Paquet, Sandra Pouchet, *The Novels of George Lamming,* Heinemann, 1982.
Ramchand, Kenneth, *The West Indian Novel and Its Background,* Faber, 1970.

*PERIODICALS*

*Book World,* January 23, 1972.
*Canadian Literature,* winter, 1982.
*Caribbean Quarterly,* February, 1958.
*Encounter,* May, 1972.
*New Statesman,* December 6, 1958; January 28, 1972; December 19, 1980.
*New Statesman and Nation,* April 18, 1953.
*New Yorker,* December 5, 1953; May 28, 1955; April 29, 1972.
*New York Herald Tribune Book Review,* July 17, 1955.
*New York Review of Books,* March 9, 1972.
*New York Times,* November 1, 1953; July 24, 1955; January 15, 1972.
*New York Times Book Review,* February 27, 1972; June 4, 1972; October 15, 1972; December 3, 1972.
*Observer,* October 8, 1972.
*Pan-Africanist,* March, 1971.
*Punch,* August 19, 1981.
*San Francisco Chronicle,* November 17, 1953; June 24, 1955.
*Saturday Review,* December 5, 1953; May 28, 1955.
*Studies in Black Literature,* spring, 1973.
*Time,* November 9, 1953; April 25, 1955.
*Times Literary Supplement,* March 27, 1953; February 11, 1972; December 15, 1972; September 4, 1981; October 24, 1986.
*World Literature Today,* winter, 1983; spring, 1985.
*World Literature Written in English,* November, 1971; April, 1973; November, 1979.
*Yale Review,* autumn, 1953; summer, 1973.

\*    \*    \*

## LANE, Pinkie Gordon   1923-

*PERSONAL:* Born January 13, 1923, in Philadelphia, PA; daughter of William Alexander (a longshoreperson) and Inez Addie West Gordon (a domestic worker); married Ulysses Simpson Lane (a teacher), May, 1948 (died, 1971); children: Gordon Edward. *Education:* Spelman College, B.A. (magna cum laude), 1949; Atlanta University, M.A., 1956; Louisiana State University, Ph.D., 1967. *Avocational interests:* Oil painting, sewing, listening to jazz music, taking care of pets.

*ADDRESSES: Home*—2738 77th Ave., Baton Rouge, LA 70807.

*CAREER:* High school English teacher in Florida and Georgia, 1949-55; Southern University, Baton Rouge, LA, instructor, 1959-60, assistant professor, 1960-62, associate professor, 1963-67, professor of English, 1967-86, professor emerita,

1986—, chairperson of the department, 1974-86. Visiting distinguished professor at University of Northern Iowa, 1993-94; du Pont Scholar, Bridgewater College, 1994. Charter member, Mayor—President's Commission on the Needs of Women; Melvin A. Butler Poetry Festival, director, 1974-80. Has given readings from her works in Arkansas, Tennessee, Oklahoma, New York, Mississippi, and Louisiana, as well as in the African nations of Ghana, Cameroon, Zambia, and South Africa, and in Paris, France.

*MEMBER:* Modern Language Association of America, National Council of Teachers of English, Poetry Society of America, National Organization for Women, College Language Association, Young Women's Christian Association, Capital Area Network of Executive and Professional Women, Delta Sigma Theta.

*AWARDS, HONORS:* Awards from National Writer's Club, 1970, and Tulsa Poets, 1970; nominated for Pulitzer Prize, 1978, for *Mystic Female;* national award from Washington chapter of Spelman College Alumnae Association, 1983, for outstanding achievement in the arts and humanities; Woman of Achievement award, Baton Rouge Young Women's Christian Association (YWCA), 1984; honored as one of fifty-eight outstanding women in Louisiana, 1984; Tribute to Black Women Writers, Inaugural Celebration of Johnetta Cole, Spelman College, 1988; National Award for Achievement in Poetry, College Language Association, 1988; named Louisiana State Poet Laureate, 1989-92; Arts Council of Greater Baton Rouge multicultural award, 1990; Louisiana State Conference of National Association for the Advancement of Colored People award, 1990; Black Caucus of National Council of Teachers of English tribute, 1990; WomenElect 2000 award, 1991; inducted into Louisiana Black History Hall of Fame, 1991; Delta Pearl Award, Delta Sigma Theta (Baton Rouge chapter), 1991.

*WRITINGS:*

*Wind Thoughts* (poems), South & West, 1972.
(Editor and contributor) *Discourses on Poetry* (anthology of prose and poetry by black authors), South & West, 1972.
(Editor and contributor) *Poems by Blacks,* Volume 3, South & West, 1973.
*Mystic Female* (poems), introduction by Jerry W. Ward, South & West, 1978.
*I Never Scream: New and Selected Poems,* Lotus Press, 1985.
*Girl at the Window* (poems), Louisiana State University Press, 1991.

Contributor to anthologies, including *To Gwen with Love,* edited by Patricia L. Brown, Don L. Lee, and Francis Ward, Johnson Publishing Co., 1971; *Poems by Blacks,* volumes one and two, edited by Sue Abbott Boyd, South & West, 1972;

*Griefs of Joy,* edited by Eugene B. Redmond, Black River Writers, 1977; *A Milestone Sampler: 15th Anniversary Anthology,* edited by Naomi Long Madgett, Lotus Press, 1988; *Wordsmiths: Choices,* edited by Andrew Kaplan, Millbrook Press, 1991; *Adam of Ife: Black Women in Praise of Black Men,* edited by Madgett, Lotus Press, 1991; *Literatures of the World,* edited by Freddy L. Thomas, Ginn Press, 1992; and *Double Stitch: Black Women Write about Mothers and Daughters,* edited by Patricia Bell-Scott and others, Beacon Press. Contributor to literary journals, including *Phylon, Southern Review, Ms., Negro American Literature Forum, Journal of Black Poetry, Bardic Echoes, Confrontation, New Orleans Review, Personalist, Voices International, Energy West, Jeopardy, Poet: India, African American Review, Louisiana Review, Last Cookie,* and *Hoo Doo.* Member of editorial board, South & West, Inc. Advisory editor, *Black Box,* 1976-79; editor-in-chief, *South and West: An International Literary Quarterly,* 1979-81; contributing and advisory editor, *Callaloo,* 1979-84, and *Black Scholar,* 1979-86; poetry editor, *Black American Literature Forum.*

Lane's works are included in the Beinecke Rare Book and Manuscript Library at Yale University in the James Weldon Johnson Collection of Negro Arts and Letters.

*SIDELIGHTS:* Pinkie Gordon Lane frequently writes poems to mark important events in her life and in the lives of family and friends. In this respect, her poetry has been favorably compared to that of Phillis Wheatley, one of the first black American poets published in modern times. Lane's most acclaimed book of poetry, *The Mystic Female,* was nominated for a Pulitzer Prize in 1979. Alluding to Lane's title, *Black Scholar* contributor S. Diane Bogus comments: "That [Lane] is great ripples through the low tide of her poetry like a moccasin through its Bayou waters—natural, deadly on contact, to be regarded with respect. Is this not mystic and female?" In a review of Lane's 1985 book *I Never Scream: New and Selected Poems,* which contains several poems from *The Mystic Female,* Lillian D. Roland writes in *Black American Literature Forum,* "Lane's poetic presence and power, arising from a great sub-conscious reservoir of knowledge, communicate, soul to soul, the deepest impulses of the human heart and mind."

*BIOGRAPHICAL/CRITICAL SOURCES:*

*BOOKS*

Brown, Dorothy H. and Barbara C. Ewell, editors, *Louisiana Women Writers,* Louisiana State University Press, 1992.
*Dictionary of Literary Biography,* Volume 41: *Afro-American Poets since 1955,* Gale, 1985.
Salaam, Kalumu ya, editor, *Word Up: Black Poetry of the 80s from the Deep South,* Beans and Brown Rice Publishers, 1990.

*PERIODICALS*

*American Book Review,* April-May, 1993.
*Baton Rouge Magazine,* January 24, 1992.
*Black American Literature Forum,* fall, 1986, pp. 294-298.
*Black Books Bulletin,* May 4, 1992.
*Black Scholar,* May/June, 1980.
*Callaloo,* February, 1979, pp. 153-155.
*CLA Journal,* March, 1980.
*Greater Baton Rouge METRO,* January, 1986.
*Jackson Advocate,* February 25, 1993, p. B14.
*Louisiana Literature,* fall, 1987, pp. 49-60; spring, 1989; fall,
    1990; spring, 1992.
*LSU Today,* May 7, 1993.
*New Orleans Tribune,* September, 1989.
*Platinum Record,* August, 1993, pp. 4, 12.
*Shreveport Journal,* August 6, 1990.
*South and West,* fall, 1978.
*States Times* (Baton Rouge), February 27, 1984.
*Sunday Advocate* (Baton Rouge), February 4, 1979; August
    31, 1986; July 2, 1989; January 12, 1992.
*Times-Picayune,* November 3, 1991, p. D18.
*Zora Neale Hurston Forum,* spring, 1987, p. 30.

\* \* \*

## LAUNKO, Okinba
### See OSOFISAN, Femi

\* \* \*

## LAWRENCE, Paul Frederic 1912-

*PERSONAL:* Born March 20, 1912, in Paterson, NJ; son of
Joshua Lawrence and Louise Lawrence; married Vivian Ann
Hall; children: Katherine Louise, Robin Ann. *Education:*
Newark State Teachers College, B.S., 1935; Stanford University, M.A., 1946, Ed.D., 1947; Kean College, D.H.L., 1965.

*ADDRESSES: Home*—4837 Crestwood Way, Sacramento,
CA 95822.

*CAREER:* Princeton, NJ schools, classroom teacher and art
supervisor, 1935-41; Howard University, associate director of
counseling, 1948-56; Willowbrook School District, superintendent of schools, 1956-60; California State College, associate dean of counseling, 1960-63; California State Department of Education, associate state superintendent, 1963-67;
U.S. Office of Education, regional commissioner of education, 1967-73, deputy assistant commissioner at regional of-

fice, 1973-79, director, postsecondary liaison, 1979-82;
Consultants in Educational Policy and Administration, chief
executive officer, 1985-. Fair Play Council, Palo Alto, CA,
board member, 1946-48; Southern Field Project National
Scholarship Service Foundation, director, 1949-54; National
Conference of Christians and Jews, Los Angeles region, board
member, 1956-60; *Scholastic Magazine* Advisory Board
member, 1964-68; College Placement Bureau, board member, 1966-70; National Academy of Sciences Engineering
Council, pre-college council, chairman, 1975-80; Stanford
University Alumni Association, board member, 1984-. Settlement team member and federal court monitor in case of National Association for the Advancement of Colored People vs.
San Francisco School District and California State Department
of Education. Private consultant. *Military service:* United
States Air Force, 22 years; became lieutenant colonel.

*MEMBER:* Phi Delta Kappa.

*AWARDS, HONORS:* Numerous military decorations; honorary doctorate, New Jersey State University, 1965; Keys to
City, Riverside, CA, 1966-70; two citations, California State
Legislature (Senate and Assembly), 1967-68; service award,
U.S. Office of Education, 1970; Distinguished Educator,
National Alliance of Black School Educators, 1974.

*WRITINGS:*

Author of *College Primer for Negro Youth,* 1946, and *Primer
for Compliance Monitoring,* 1989; co-author of *Negro American Heritage* (textbook), 1964.

\* \* \*

## LEE, Don L.
### See MADHUBUTI, Haki R.

\* \* \*

## LEE, Shelton Jackson 1957-
### (Spike Lee)

*PERSONAL:* Born March 20, 1957, in Atlanta, GA; son of
William (a musician and composer) and Jacqueline (a teacher;
maiden name, Shelton) Lee. *Education:* Morehouse College,
B.A., 1979; graduate study at New York University, 1982.

*ADDRESSES: Home*—Brooklyn, NY. *Office*—40 Acres & a
Mule Filmworks, 124 DeKalb Ave., Brooklyn, NY, 11217.

*CAREER:* Screenwriter, actor, director, and producer of motion pictures, commercials, and music videos. Founder and director, 40 Acres & a Mule Filmworks, Brooklyn, NY, 1986—.

*MEMBER:* Screen Actors Guild.

*AWARDS, HONORS:* Student Director's Award from Academy of Motion Picture Arts and Sciences, 1982, for *Joe's Bed-Stuy Barber Shop: We Cut Heads;* Prix de Jeunesse from Cannes Film Festival and New Generation Award from the Los Angeles Film Critics, both 1986, for *She's Gotta Have It.*

*WRITINGS:*

*Spike Lee's "Gotta Have It": Inside Guerilla Filmmaking* (includes interviews and a journal), illustrated with photographs by brother, David Lee, foreword by Nelson George, Simon & Schuster, 1987.
(With Lisa Jones) *Uplift the Race: The Construction of "School Daze,"* Simon & Schuster, 1988.
(With Jones) *"Do the Right Thing": The New Spike Lee Joint,* Fireside Press, 1989.
(With Jones) *"Mo' Better Blues,"* Simon & Schuster, 1990.
*Five for Five: The Films of Spike Lee,* photographs by David Lee, Stewart, Tabori, 1991.
(With Ralph Wiley) *By Any Means Necessary: The Trials and Tribulations of the Making of "Malcolm X,"* Hyperion Adult, 1992.

*SCREENPLAYS; AND DIRECTOR*

*She's Gotta Have It,* Island, 1986.
*School Daze,* Columbia, 1988.
*Do the Right Thing,* Universal, 1989.
*Mo' Better Blues,* Universal, 1990.
*Jungle Fever,* Universal, 1991.
*Malcolm X,* Warner Bros., 1992.

Also writer and director of short films, including *The Answer,* 1980; *Sarah,* 1981; and *Joe's Bed-Stuy Barbershop: We Cut Heads,* 1982. Contributor of short films to *Saturday Night Live* and to the Music Television network (MTV).

*WORK IN PROGRESS: Crooklyn,* a film for Universal.

*SIDELIGHTS:* The son of a musician, Spike Lee has become the equivalent of a composer, conductor, lead cellist and symphony T-shirt salesman in the industry of filmmaking. Since *She's Gotta Have It* was released in 1986 on a small budget, Lee has proven himself as a screenwriter, director/producer, actor, and merchandiser of films. "I truly believe I was put here to make films, it's as simple as that," Lee wrote in his

book *Spike Lee's "Gotta Have It": Inside Guerilla Filmmaking.* "I'm doin' what I'm 'posed to be doin'. It's not for me to say whether [*She's Gotta Have It*] is a landmark film (I make 'em, that's all) but I do want people to be inspired by it, in particular, black people. Now there is a present example of how we can produce. We can do the things we want to do, there are no mo' excuses. We're tired of that alibi, 'White man this, white man that.' ... It's on us. So let's all do the work that needs to be done by us *all.* And to y'all who aren't down for the cause, move out of the way, step aside."

Lee was born in Atlanta, Georgia, where he earned his nickname, Spike. "A lot of people think it's made up—one of those stage names," he explained in *Spike Lee's "Gotta Have It."* "My mother ... said I was a very tough baby.... I was like three or four months old when I got the nickname." Lee's father, a jazz musician, Bill Lee, soon moved his family to the jazz mecca, Chicago. "Then there was an exodus of jazz musicians from Chicago to New York," Lee related, "and my father went with that. I think we came to New York in '59, '60." During his youth Lee's leadership ability began to emerge. For neighborhood sports, he said, he "was always the captain of the team, the spark plug. Not the best athlete, though."

A jazz purist, Lee's father placed strains on the family by adhering to his artistic principles. As Lee reported in *Spike Lee's "Gotta Have It":* "In the early sixties [my father] was the top folk/jazz bassist. If you look on the albums of Peter, Paul and Mary, Bob Dylan, Judy Collins, Odetta, Theodore Bikel, Leon Bibbs and Josh White, you'll see that my father was playing with all of them. He also played with Simon and Garfunkel. He got tired of playing that music, though, and then the electric bass became popular and he refused to play it. To this day, he's never played Fender bass. With that kind of stance, you don't work.... I got some of my stubbornness from him, if the word is stubbornness.... [It's] nonconformist, to a degree."

Following a long family tradition, Lee went to college at Morehouse, an all-black college in Atlanta. "I'm a third-generation Morehouse graduate," he said. "My father and grandfather went to Morehouse.... The Lee family has always been like that." Majoring in mass communications, he decided by his sophomore year to become a filmmaker—though he still did a bit of everything else, including hosting his own radio show on jazz station WCLK and writing for the school newspaper. More importantly, he began making films. Of the first film he wrote, *Black College: The Talented Tenth,* Lee said: "I do not like that film at all.... It's a corny love story at a black campus. Real corny.... I'm glad there's only one copy in existence."

After graduation from Morehouse, Lee enrolled at the New York University (NYU) Film School. "There's no way I could have made the films I made if I lived in [Los Angeles] 'cause I didn't know anybody," he explained in his book. "I couldn't have called people for locations. Also you had to have an astronomical score on the [Graduate Record Exams] to get in. Plus at USC and UCLA [University of Southern California and University of California, Los Angeles], not everybody makes a film. The teachers assign by committee who gets to make a film."

Filmed in his senior year, *Joe's Bed-Stuy Barbershop* earned Lee a student academy award. Monty Ross starred in the film about a local barber who gets caught up in the numbers racket and organized crime. "That summer before my final year in school I was in Atlanta writing a script," he wrote. "I let Monty read it and he suggested that he act in it. I never thought of Monty ... coming up to New York, dropping what he was doing, to act in it. But he did. I think Monty gave a very fine performance. What people don't realize is that Monty—a very unselfish person—was not only acting in the film, he was driving the van, he was crewing, he was doing a lot of other things that no doubt affected his performance. But we got the film made."

Winning the student academy award didn't really surprise Lee. "Because I know that NYU is one of the best film schools, and I saw a lot of films that came out of the school. I know that this was as good or better than anything that was in USC or UCLA.... I never went to NYU expecting teachers to teach me. I just wanted equipment, so I could make films, and learn filmmaking by making films.... That's the only way to learn. People call me now wanting to know what the secret to successful filmmaking is. I get so mad. There *is* no secret formula let's say, for the success of *She's Gotta Have It.* I'm not gonna tell them anything that will help them. We just killed ourselves to get it made. That's how we did it."

After he won the student academy award, some of the larger talent agencies approached Lee and, although they represented him for a year-and-a-half, nothing much materialized, as he reported in his book. "I had the first draft of what is now *School Daze,* but then it was called 'Homecoming.' The script was a lot different but I had the third draft of it. It was an all-black film. They said nah. Forget it. Nothing. Not even an 'Afterschool Special.' And there were a lot of my classmates who didn't even win Academy Awards who did get 'Afterschool Specials'." Since then, Lee hasn't had an agent. "You've got to make your own personal choice," he asserted. "I will not have an agent, though I have a good lawyer and a good accountant.... That's all I need ... you still have to find a job like everybody else."

Lee's first post-NYU production, *The Messenger,* was a failed venture by a businessman's yardstick. Started in 1984, *The Messenger* was about a Brooklyn bike messenger and his fam-

ily. After spending forty thousand dollars, Lee decided to terminate the project. "It just never really came together with all the money and stuff," he said in a *Film Comment* article. One of the project's obstacles that Lee was not able to hurdle was the Screen Actors Guild (SAG). Lee applied for experimental film rates so that he would be able to afford an actor like Larry Fishburne. The Guild refused Lee's application for waiver of the standard rates. "There are too many black actors out of work for them to nix it," he wrote in *Spike Lee's "Gotta Have It."* But "they said no. So I had to recast the entire picture in four days with non-SAG people. And it never came together so we were all devastated. I got a list of ten films that had been given a waiver within the [previous] year. All of them were done by white independent filmmakers. All of them worked with a whole lot more money than I had. Yet they said my film was too commercial.... That was a definite case of racism."

By the next year, 1985, Lee was immersed in his next project, *She's Gotta Have It.* The screenplay, written by Lee, explores black female sexuality through its main character, Nola Darling, played by Tracy Camilla Johns. Nola dates three different men, Jamie Overstreet, Greer Childs and Mars Blackmon (played by Lee). One offers stability; another, physical attraction; the third, humor. "Everybody's character was reflected in how they perceived Nola. That's the whole film, how everybody perceives Nola," Lee wrote in *Spike Lee's "Gotta Have It."* Eventually Nola leaves all three of her suitors. "It's about control," she explains in the film. "My body. My mind. Whose gonna own it, them or me?"

With the failure of *The Messenger,* the American Film Institute withdrew the twenty thousand dollars it had granted Lee. "There were times when I didn't know where the next nickel was coming from," Lee related in his book, "but it would come. Sure enough, the money came whenever we needed it." With eighteen thousand dollars from the New York arts council as his most-sizable funding, Lee assembled a small cast and crew that included family members and directed *She's Gotta Have It* in only twelve days.

The release of *She's Gotta Have It* in 1986 made Spike Lee an international celebrity. The film was a financial success, grossing more than eight million dollars, and critically it was an even bigger success. *Washington Post* reviewer Paul Attanasio deemed it an "impressive first feature" and added that it was "discursive, jazzy, vibrant with sex and funny as heck." Michael Wilmington wrote in the *Los Angeles Times* that Lee's film was "a joyfully idiosyncratic little jazz-burst of a film, full of sensuous melody, witty chops and hot licks." Wilmington was particularly impressed with the film's non-stereotypical perspective and characters, declaring that it "gives you as non-standard a peek at black American life as you'll get: engaging, seductive and happily off-kilter.... These characters aren't the radiant winners or sad victims you usually see, and there's not a normal citizen ... in the bunch." The film's appeal was evident at the Cannes Film Festival. When the power failed during the film's screening, the audience refused to leave until they saw the ending.

That success led to Lee securing approximately six million dollars from Columbia Pictures to film *School Daze,* a musical comedy about rival factions at a black college. Lee discussed his subject in *Spike Lee's "Gotta Have It":* "I'm not going to say there are not a lot of ills on black college campuses. We [hoped] to address some of those things in the film *School Daze.* But I still love Morehouse, regardless. The thing that amazed me about being there was how some guys couldn't get no play from women, but the minute they pledged to a fraternity the women were all over them. It was amazing."

Much of the humor in *School Daze* derives from the antics of Lee's character. Here he plays Half Pint, a Gamma Phi Gamma hopeful preoccupied with losing his virginity. The factional conflicts at the college are underscored by Half Pint, a Wannabee (as in want-to-be-white), and his relationship with his cousin, Dap, a dark-skinned Jigaboo (a member of the black underclass) and the key figure in a campus campaign to force the university divestiture from South Africa. Dap's rival is Julian, leader of the Gamma Phi Gammas. The characters' conflicts allow Lee to explore bigotry as well as elitism.

The major obstacle placed in Lee's path in filming *School Daze* was reluctance from his alma mater, Morehouse, as well as other Atlanta black colleges (Spelman College, Clark College, Morris Brown College and Atlanta University) to allow the use of their facilities. "There were so many rumors circulating around the [Atlanta University Center] about the movie," he wrote in his second book, *Uplift the Race: The Construction of "School Daze."* "The students were influenced by the propaganda being pushed out by the administrations. When I was at Morehouse the atmosphere was different. The student body was more vocal and certainly more political. We didn't take what the administration told us at face value. I think we would have been really upset if a young Black filmmaker came to our campus to shoot a film and got kicked off by the school. But there wasn't a whimper from any of the students at Morehouse, Spelman, Clark or Morris Brown." As it turned out, after three weeks of shooting, Lee was forced to use just Atlanta University's facilities and reshoot all of the footage shot on other campuses.

*School Daze* earned commendations from many critics, but it also brought Lee notoriety as a provocateur within the African American community. Prominent African Americans protested that Lee had produced an unfavorable depiction of their race and others, while conceding that he offered a valid

perspective, nonetheless argued that his perception of black college campus life was one best withheld from a white society. In his third book, *"Do the Right Thing": The New Spike Lee Joint,* Lee wrote that he "did an interview with Bryant Gumbel on the *Today* show" in which they discussed the film. "Bryant Gumbel jumped all over me, but I kept my composure. He disapproved of *School Daze* because I aired Black folks' dirty laundry."

After the release of *School Daze,* Lee shifted from internal prejudice to external when he began work on *Do the Right Thing.* Occurring on the hottest day of the year, *Do the Right Thing* takes place in Bedford-Stuyvesant, a largely black neighborhood of New York City. It evokes real interracial incidents, like one he mentioned in his book *"Do the Right Thing":* "I heard a radio newscast that two Black youths had been beaten up by a gang of white youths," Lee wrote. "The two Black kids were hospitalized. They were collecting bottles and cans when they got jumped. This happened on Christmas night.... Can you imagine if [this incident] had taken place in the summer, on the hottest day of the year? I'd be a fool not to work the subject of racism into *Do the Right Thing.*"

*Do the Right Thing* centers on a pizzeria owned and run by Italians and headed by Sal, ostensibly a non-racist who is comfortable with his black clientele and employees. Trouble begins when Buggin' Out, a black patron, asks Sal to add some black people to his pizzeria's "Wall of Fame," which consists of only Italian-Americans. Sal refuses, and as tempers rise, a racial slur triggers violence. The climax occurs when the police wind up choking one of the blacks to death in front of the whole neighborhood. Sal's delivery boy, Mookie (played by Lee), then incites a riot by throwing a garbage can through the pizzeria window. In a sequence preceding the fight, Lee had stopped the story to have his characters spout racial slurs into the camera. It "was meant to rouse emotions," Lee explained in *"Do the Right Thing."* "It's funny the way people react to it. They laugh at every slur except the one directed at their ethnic group." The honesty with which Lee treated his subject earned *Do the Right Thing* substantial praise from some critics and many laughs of self-recognition from audiences. David Chute, reviewing Lee's book about the film in the *Los Angeles Times Book Review,* called *Do the Right Thing* Lee's "most controlled and effective picture" to date and noted that his vision is that of an artist, not a journalist. "A personal frame of reference like this would not seem startling in an Italian-American or WASP director," Chute noted, "but to the great discredit of the American film biz the black version is still a novelty. Not for long."

Lee's next venture, *Mo' Better Blues,* paired him for the first time with Denzel Washington, who would later star in another Lee film, *Malcolm X. Mo' Better Blues* also brought Lee back to his father's work—music—a profession that Spike Lee had avoided. "Being the first born, not becoming a musician was a part of my rebelliousness," he wrote in *Spike Lee's "Gotta Have It."* But jazz was still close to his heart, and when filmmakers such as Clint Eastwood and Woody Allen started making films about it, Lee felt he had to get involved himself. As he said in his book about the making of *Mo' Better Blues:* "I couldn't let Woody Allen do a jazz film before I did. I was on a mission." *Mo' Better Blues* follows the life of a modern-day trumpeter and shows the conflicts he faces between his music and his love life.

*Mo' Better Blues* was the first film produced by Lee's own company, 40 Acres & a Mule, named for what every black person in America had been promised at the end of slavery. He commented on his intention to make films in his own way in *Spike Lee's "Gotta Have It":* "You really carry a burden as a black filmmaker. There are so few black films that when you do one it has to represent every black person in the world. If you're white, you're not going to protest in front of a theater because the film is about this or that because it is one of two hundred white Hollywood films that might have been released that year."

Lee's next release, *Jungle Fever,* was his fifth film in six years. "I know for sure I cannot keep up this pace," he said in a 1991 book about his career, *Five for Five: The Films of Spike Lee.* "It could kill me.... Historically, black filmmakers have found it extremely hard to go from film to film. I didn't want a long layoff between films. When things are clicking, ya gotta stay with it."

Critics characterized *Jungle Fever* variously as a film about interracial sex, a cry from the heart about the tragedies of the drug culture, and a collection of vignettes on a wide range of current issues. The film features a married black architect named Flipper and his Italian-American secretary, Angie, who have an affair. The repercussions from their liaison ripple through their relationships with a host of others, including Flipper's crack-addicted brother and Angie's racist family. Calling *Jungle Fever* Lee's "best movie" in his *Newsweek* review of the film, Jack Kroll commented on how the filmmaker "uses the theme of interracial sex to explore the mythology of race, sex and class in an America where both blacks and whites are reassessing the legacy of integration and the concept of separatism from every point on the political spectrum." Lee's treatment of the issue of skin color, which is sometimes a point of contention even among blacks, was of particular interest to *Times Literary Supplement* writer Gerald Early, who noted that Lee shows both dark-skinned Flipper and his lighter-complexioned wife as being "obsessed with the insults they endured as children about their colour. What is racial identity if someone can be attacked from outside a group for pretensions of purity, and from inside because of a 'mongrelized' appearance?" Other critics pointed to the pow-

erful drug theme that grows in importance as the film progresses. In his *Time* article on black filmmaking, Richard Corliss summed up *Jungle Fever* as an "assured" film about "the ghetto epidemic of drugs.... Who is sleeping with whom matters less here, as it should anywhere, than the people who die and the things that kill them."

The fall of 1992 saw the release of Lee's biggest film, *Malcolm X.* Nearly three and a half hours long, it cost more than thirty million dollars and grossed nearly two and a half million the day it was released. The film chronicles the life of the controversial and multifaceted black leader who in a single lifetime was a street hustler, black-separatist preacher, and eloquent humanist. A number of reviewers acknowledged the challenge of portraying such a complex life on film, of pleasing the various factions in black society that each focused on their favorite aspects of the man. Lee himself felt that many blacks have "a very limited view of Malcolm" and fail to understand that "the man evolved, was constantly evolving, even at the time of [his] assassination," he said in a *Time* interview with Janice C. Simpson.

Lee embarked on the film amid a storm of controversy. Black cultural figures such as poet Amiri Baraka, a vocal critic of Lee's movies, warned the filmmaker not to "trash" Malcolm's legacy. Some worried that he would overemphasize certain aspects of Malcolm's life, like his street years or his split from the militant, separatist Black Muslim organization, which some say prompted Malcolm's assassination. Lee caused a stir of his own before winning the opportunity to make the film, when he questioned why a white director—Norman Jewison—had been selected to film a black story. He also wrestled with the Warner Brothers film studio over the movie's length and cost. When he exceeded his budget, financial—but not creative—control of the project was taken from Lee's hands.

Upon its release, late in 1992, Lee's treatment of Malcolm's life earned a mixed critical response. Assessing the film in the *New Yorker,* Terrence Rafferty acknowledged the dedication Lee showed in the making of the film but regretted what he saw as its impersonal feel. Still, Rafferty felt that "viewers who know nothing about Malcolm, or who know him only by his formidable reputation as a black-pride firebrand, might find everything in the film fascinating, revelatory." Opining that of all Lee's films it is "the least Spikey," *Time*'s Corliss judged it "the movie equivalent of an authorized biography." Several critics questioned the necessity of the film's length, a concern Lee addressed in his *Time* interview. "There was so much to tell," he asserted. "This was not going to be an abbreviated, abridged version of Malcolm X." Vincent Canby, writing for the *New York Times,* largely applauded Lee's efforts, calling the movie "an ambitious, tough, seriously considered biographical film that, with honor, eludes easy characterization."

He did not find it entirely successful, but as he put it, Lee had "attempted the impossible and almost brought it off." One measure of *Malcolm X*'s impact was that soon after the film's release, the book upon which it was partly based, *The Autobiography of Malcolm X,* reached the top of the *New York Times* nonfiction best-seller list—nearly thirty years after its original 1965 publication.

*BIOGRAPHICAL/CRITICAL SOURCES:*

*BOOKS*

*Authors and Artists for Children and Young Adults,* Volume 4, Gale, 1990, pp. 165-79.

Lee, Spike, *Five for Five: The Films of Spike Lee,* Stewart, Tabori, 1991.

Lee, Spike, *Spike Lee's "Gotta Have It": Inside Guerilla Filmmaking,* Simon and Schuster, 1987.

Lee, Spike, and Lisa Jones, *Uplift the Race: The Construction of "School Daze,"* Simon & Schuster, 1988.

Lee, Spike, and Lisa Jones, *"Do the Right Thing": The New Spike Lee Joint,* Fireside Press, 1989.

*PERIODICALS*

*Advertising Age,* August 9, 1993, pp. 1, 29.

*American Film,* September, 1986; January-February, 1988; July-August, 1989.

*Chicago Tribune,* August 13, 1986; August 20, 1986; October 5, 1986; February 25, 1988; March 3, 1988.

*Ebony,* January, 1987; September, 1987.

*Essence,* September, 1986; February, 1988; July 1988.

*Film Comment,* October, 1986.

*Film Quarterly,* winter, 1986-87.

*Jet,* November 10, 1986; February 2, 1988; May 2, 1988.

*Los Angeles Times,* August 21, 1986; February 11, 1988; February 12, 1988.

*Los Angeles Times Book Review,* June 30, 1989, p. 6.

*Ms.,* September-October, 1991, p. 78.

*Newsweek,* September 8, 1986, p. 65; February 15, 1988, p. 62; July 3, 1989, pp. 64-66; October 2, 1989, p. 37; August 6, 1990, p. 62; June 10, 1991, pp. 44-47; August 26, 1991, pp. 52-54; November 16, 1992, pp. 66, 71, 74.

*New Yorker,* October 6, 1986, pp. 128-30; July 24, 1989, pp. 78-81; August 13, 1990, pp. 82-84; June 17, 1991, p. 99; November 30, 1992, pp. 160-62.

*New York Review of Books,* September 28, 1989, p. 37.

*New York Times,* March 27, 1983; April 10, 1986; August 8, 1986; September 7, 1986; November 14, 1986; August 9, 1987; February 12, 1988; February 20, 1989; October 29, 1992, p. C22; November 15, 1992, p. H1, H23; November 18, 1992, pp. C19, C23; November 19, 1992, p. B4.

*New York Times Book Review,* December 13, 1987, p. 14.

*New York Times Magazine,* August 9, 1987, pp. 26, 29, 39, 41.

*People,* October 13, 1986, p. 67; July 10, 1989, p. 67; March 5, 1990, pp. 97, 99.

*Rolling Stone,* December 1980; April 21, 1988, p. 32; June 30, 1988, p. 21; December 1, 1988, p. 31; June 29, 1989, p. 27; July 13, 1989, pp. 104, 107, 109, 174; June 27, 1991, p. 75; July 11, 1991, p. 63.

*Time,* October 6, 1986, p. 94; July 3, 1989, p. 62; July 17, 1989, p. 92; August 20, 1990, p. 62; June 17, 1991, pp. 64-66, 68; March 16, 1992, p. 71; November 23, 1992, pp. 64-65; November 30, 1992.

*Times Literary Supplement,* September, 6, 1991, p. 18.

*Village Voice,* February 16, 1988; March 22, 1988.

*Wall Street Journal,* November 16, 1992.

*Washington Post,* August 22, 1986; August 24, 1986; August 29, 1986; March 20, 1987; February 19, 1988.

\*    \*    \*

**LEE, Spike**
**See LEE, Shelton Jackson**

\*    \*    \*

**LESHOAI, Benjamin Letholoa   1920-**

*PERSONAL:* Born July 1, 1920, in Bloemfontein, Orange Free State, South Africa. *Education:* Healdtown Missionary Institution, Teacher's Certificate, 1944; Fort Hare, B.A., 1947; University of Illinois, M.A., 1964.

*ADDRESSES: Office*—University College, Department of Theatre Arts, Dar es Salaam, Tanzania.

*CAREER:* High school in Pretoria, South Africa, English teacher, 1947-57, headmaster, 1957-60; Union Artists (Bantu players), Johannesburg, South Africa, assistant manager; English teacher, Ndola (while in exile in Zambia in 1963); Mufulira Teachers' College, Zambia, English teacher, 1965-68; University College, Department of Theatre Arts, Dar es Salaam, Tanzania, teacher, 1968—.

*WRITINGS:*

*Masilo's Adventures and Other Stories,* Longmans, 1968.

Also author of play, *The Wake,* published in *New Writing from Zambia,* number 2, Lusaka, 1968.

*BIOGRAPHICAL/CRITICAL SOURCES:*

*BOOKS*

Gerard, Albert S., *Four African Literatures*, University of California Press, 1971.

\* \* \*

## LESTER, Julius (Bernard) 1939-

*PERSONAL:* Born January 27, 1939, in St. Louis, MO; son of W. D. (a minister) and Julia (Smith) Lester; married Joan Steinau (a researcher), 1962 (divorced, 1970); married Alida Carolyn Fechner, March 21, 1979; children: (first marriage) Jody Simone, Malcolm Coltrane; (second marriage) Elena Milad (stepdaughter), David Julius. *Education:* Fisk University, B.A., 1960.

*ADDRESSES: Office*—University of Massachusetts—Amherst, Amherst, MA 01002.

*CAREER:* Newport Folk Festival, Newport, RI, director, 1966-68; New School for Social Research, New York City, lecturer, 1968-70; WBAI-FM, New York City, producer and host of live radio show "The Great Proletarian Cultural Revolution," 1968-75; University of Massachusetts—Amherst, professor of Afro-American studies, 1971-88, professor of Near Eastern and Judaic Studies, 1982—, acting director and associate director of Institute for Advanced Studies in Humanities, 1982-84; Vanderbilt University, Nashville, TN, writer-in-residence, 1985. Professional musician and singer. Host of live television show "Free Time," WNET-TV, New York City, 1971-73. Lester's photographs of the 1960s civil rights movement have been exhibited at the Smithsonian Institution and are on permanent display at Howard University.

*AWARDS, HONORS:* Distinguished Teacher's Award, 1983-84; Faculty Fellowship Award for Distinguished Research and Scholarship, 1985; National Professor of the Year Silver Medal Award, from Council for Advancement and Support of Education, 1985; Massachusetts State Professor of the Year and Gold Medal Award for National Professor of the Year, both from Council for Advancement and Support of Education, both 1986; chosen distinguished faculty lecturer, 1986-87; *To Be a Slave* was nominated for the Newbery Award; *The Long Journey Home: Stories from Black History* was a National Book Award finalist.

*WRITINGS:*

(With Pete Seeger) *The 12-String Guitar as Played by Leadbelly,* Oak, 1965.

*Look Out Whitey! Black Power's Gon' Get Your Mama!,* Dial, 1968.
*To Be a Slave,* Dial, 1969.
*Black Folktales,* Baron, 1969.
*Search for the New Land: History as Subjective Experience,* Dial, 1969.
*Revolutionary Notes,* Baron, 1969.
(Editor) *The Seventh Son: The Thoughts and Writings of W. E. B. Du Bois,* two volumes, Random House, 1971.
(Compiler with Rae Pace Alexander) *Young and Black in America,* Random House, 1971.
*The Long Journey Home: Stories from Black History,* Dial, 1972.
*The Knee-High Man and Other Tales,* Dial, 1972.
*Two Love Stories,* Dial, 1972.
(Editor) Stanley Couch, *Ain't No Ambulances for No Nigguhs Tonight* (poems), Baron, 1972.
*Who I Am* (poems), Dial, 1974.
*All Is Well: An Autobiography,* Morrow, 1976.
*This Strange New Feeling,* Dial, 1982.
*Do Lord Remember Me* (novel), Holt, 1984.
*The Tales of Uncle Remus: The Adventures of Brer Rabbit,* Dial, 1987.
*More Tales of Uncle Remus: The Further Adventures of Brer Rabbit, His Friends, Enemies, and Others,* Dial, 1988.
*Lovesong: Becoming a Jew* (autobiography), Holt, 1988.
*How Many Spots Does a Leopard Have? and Other Tales,* illustrations by David Shannon, Scholastic, Inc., 1989.
*Falling Pieces of the Broken Sky* (essays), Arcade, 1990.
*Further Tales of Uncle Remus: The Misadventures of Brer Rabbit, Brer Fox, Brer Wolf, the Doodang, and Other Creatures,* illustrations by Jerry Pinkney, Dial, 1990.

Contributor of essays and reviews to numerous magazines and newspapers, including *New York Times Book Review, New York Times, Nation, Katallagete, Democracy,* and *Village Voice.* Associate editor, *Sing Out,* 1964-70; contributing editor, *Broadside of New York,* 1964-70. Lester's books have been translated into seven languages.

*SIDELIGHTS:* Julius Lester is "foremost among young black writers who produce their work from a position of historical strength," writes critic John A. Williams in the *New York Times Book Review.* Drawing on old documents and folktales, Lester fashions stories that proclaim the heritage of black Americans and "attempt to recreate the social life of the past," note Eric and Naomi Foner in the *New York Review of Books.* Lester's tales are more than simple reportage. Their purpose, as the Foners point out, is "not merely to impart historical information, but to teach moral and political lessons." Because he feels that the history of minority groups has been largely ignored, Lester intends to furnish his young readers with what he calls "a usable past" and with what the Foners call "a sense of history which will help shape their lives and politics." Lester has also retold the traditional Uncle Remus tales for children, while in *How Many Spots Does a Leopard Have?* he combines folktales from the African and Jewish cultures.

Lester's characters fall into two categories: those drawn from Afro-American folklore and those drawn from black history. The former are imaginary creatures, or sometimes animals, such as *The Knee-High Man's* Mr. Bear and Mr. Rabbit; the latter are real people, "ordinary men and women who might appear only in ... a neglected manuscript at the Library of Congress," according to William Loren Katz in the *Washington Post Book World.* Critics find that Lester uses both types of characters to reveal the black individual's struggle against slavery.

*Black Folktales,* Lester's first collection of folk stories, features larger-than-life heroes (including a cigar-smoking black God), shrewd animals, and cunning human beings. While some of the characters are taken from African legends and others from American slave tales, they all demonstrate that "black resistance to white oppression is as old as the confrontation between the two groups," says Williams. Most reviewers applaud Lester's view of Afro-American folklore and praise his storytelling skills, but a few object to what they perceive as the anti-white tone of the book. Zena Sutherland, writing in *Bulletin of the Center for Children's Books,* calls *Black Folktales* "a vehicle for hostility.... There is no story that concerns white people in which they are not pictured as venal or stupid or both."

Lester also deals with white oppression in his second collection of folktales, *The Knee-High Man and Other Tales.* Although these six animal stories are funny, *New York Times Book Review* critic Ethel Richards suggests that "powerfully important lessons ride the humor. In 'The Farmer and the Snake,' the lesson is that kindness will not change the nature of a thing—in this case, the nature of a poisonous snake to bite." A *Junior Bookshelf* reviewer points out that this story— as well as others in the book—reflects the relationship between owner and slave. While pursuing the same theme, Lester moves into the realm of nonfiction with *The Long Journey Home: Stories from Black History,* a documentary collection of slave narratives, and *To Be a Slave,* a collection of six stories based on historical fact. Both books showcase ordinary people in adverse circumstances and provide the reader with a look at what Lester calls "history from the bottom up." *Black Like Me* author John Howard Griffin, writing in the *New York Times Book Review,* commends Lester's approach, saying that the stories "help destroy the delusion that black men did not suffer as another man would in similar circumstances," and the Foners applaud the fact that "Lester does not feel it is necessary to make every black man and woman a super-hero." *New York Times Book Review* contributor Rosalind K. Goddard recommends Lester's writing as both lesson and en-

tertainment: "These stories point the way for young blacks to find their roots, so important to the realization of their identities, as well as offer a stimulating and informative experience for all."

In *Lovesong: Becoming a Jew* Lester presents the autobiographical story of his conversion to the Jewish faith. Beginning with his southern childhood as the son of a Methodist minister, following his years of atheism and civil rights activity, and ending with his exploration of many faiths, *Lovesong* concludes with Lester's embrace of Judaism in 1983. Discussing the book in a *Partisan Review* article, David Lehman remarked that the author relates his experiences with "conviction and passion."

With *How Many Spots Does a Leopard Have?* Lester drew from folktales of both the African and Jewish traditions to write new stories in a modern language. "Although I am of African and Jewish ancestry," Lester writes in his introduction to the collection, "I am also an American.... I have fitted the story to my mouth and tongue." Assessing the collection in the *Los Angeles Times Book Review,* Sonja Bolle called the stories "so lively they positively dance."

*BIOGRAPHICAL/CRITICAL SOURCES:*

*BOOKS*

*Children's Literature Review,* Volume 2, Gale, 1976.
Krim, Seymour, *You and Me,* Holt, 1972.
Lester, Julius, *All Is Well: An Autobiography,* Morrow, 1976.
Lester, Julius, *Lovesong: Becoming a Jew,* Holt, 1988.
Lester, Julius, *How Many Spots Does a Leopard Have? and Other Stories,* Scholastic, Inc., 1989.

*PERIODICALS*

*Bulletin of the Center for Children's Books,* February, 1970.
*Dissent,* winter, 1989, p. 116.
*Essence,* August, 1989, p. 98; July, 1991, p. 100.
*Junior Bookshelf,* February, 1975.
*Los Angeles Times Book Review,* January 31, 1988; January 27, 1991, p. 8.
*Nation,* June 22, 1970.
*New Advocate,* summer, 1990, p. 206.
*New York Review of Books,* April 20, 1972.
*New York Times Book Review,* November 3, 1968; November 9, 1969; July 23, 1972; February 4, 1973; September 5, 1982; February 17, 1985; May 17, 1987, p. 32; January 14, 1990, p. 17; August 12, 1990, p. 29.
*Partisan Review,* Volume 57, number 2, 1990, pp. 321-25.
*Publishers Weekly,* February 12, 1988.
*Quill and Quire,* December, 1989, p. 24.
*Times Literary Supplement,* April 3, 1987.

*Tribune Books* (Chicago), February 26, 1989, p. 8; February
    11, 1990, p. 6.
*Washington Post,* March 12, 1985.
*Washington Post Book World,* September 3, 1972; February
    14, 1988.

\*   \*   \*

## LIGHTFOOT, Sara Lawrence

*PERSONAL:* Daughter of Charles Radford (a sociologist) and
Margaret (a child psychiatrist; maiden name, Morgan)
Lawrence. *Education:* Attended Swarthmore University.

*ADDRESSES: Office*—Harvard Graduate School of Education, Dept. of Educational Administration, Harvard University, Cambridge, MA 02138.

*CAREER:* Nonfiction writer, academic. Harvard Graduate
School of Education, Cambridge, MA, professor.

*AWARDS, HONORS:* Candace Award, National Coalition of
100 Black Women; MacArthur Prize; Christopher Award for
*Balm in Gilead.*

*WRITINGS:*

*NONFICTION*

*Worlds Apart: Relationships between Families and Schools,*
    Basic Books, 1978.
(Coauthor with Jean V. Carew) *Beyond Bias: Perspectives on
    Classrooms,* Harvard University Press, 1979.
*The Good High School: Portraits of Character and Culture,*
    Basic Books, 1983.
*Balm in Gilead: Journey of a Healer* (biography), Addison-
    Wesley, 1988.

Also author of several articles on American schools and education, including "A Question of Perspective: Toward a More
Complex View of Classrooms" which was part of the Urban
Diversity Series published by Columbia University, 1978;
contributor to *Daedulus.*

*SIDELIGHTS:* Sociologist Sara Lawrence Lightfoot's writings examine the issues of race and class and the experience
of the American school system, focusing closely on that experience of education which is particular to minorities. With
several extensive works published, Lightfoot has produced
studies that one critic, writing in *Choice,* describes as "particularly insightful ... analytic and descriptive."

In *Worlds Apart,* her first book, Lightfoot challenges the generally held notion that the competitive relationship between
parents and teachers for the child is a necessary and socially
valuable one. Criticizing this analysis, Lightfoot draws on her
own observations as well as existing literature to reach conclusions about the negative impact of this struggle between
family and school and to make recommendations for a more
integrative, and therefore beneficial, approach to education.
Lightfoot also places the relationship between family and
school in a socio-historical context, holding the lack of educational resources available to slave parents in America prior
to emancipation responsible for the current negative feelings
of black parents towards urban schools.

Continuing her examination of American schools, Lightfoot
chose in *The Good High School: Portraits of Character and
Culture* to follow the negative appraisal given in *Worlds Apart*
with a look at the positive qualities of six schools. Described
in the *Los Angeles Times Book Review* by Myra Glazer as a
"refreshing antidote to our anger at our schools," *The Good
High School* offers "penetrating portraits" of two urban public schools, two suburban public schools, and two elite private schools, in what Lightfoot characterizes as an attempt to
portray "their positive struggles and their strengths, the dynamic ways in which they cope with problems." David Owen
in *The New Republic* refers to the book as an occasionally
"enlightening" attempt at "something grander" than mere
sociology, "a kind of intimate portraiture." In this context,
Lightfoot interviews teachers and examines such aspects of
the six schools as the unique curriculum offered by some (New
York's John F. Kennedy High School, for example, offers
courses as diverse as yoga and roller disco), as well as the
dedication of the various schools' faculty members. Lightfoot
concludes by offering *The Good High School* as a potential
"catalyst for change within an institution," setting forth her
examples of what aspects of education in America work in
an attempt to add to the solutions offered previously in *World's
Apart.*

Although primarily an academic writer, Lightfoot's next work
is the biography *Balm in Gilead: Journey of a Healer.* The
biography is viewed as an alternative perspective on her al-
ready-established preferred themes of race, class, and education. Lightfoot completed the work aided by her winnings
from the MacArthur Prize. *Balm in Gilead* relates the life of
Lightfoot's mother, a topic that Phyllis Crockett, writing for
the *Los Angeles Times Book Review,* sees as encompassing
facets of the issues of race, class, and education. Crockett notes
that the lives of Lightfoot's mother and father "would be an
exceptional story, even if the couple were white," pointing out
that Lightfoot's mother, Margaret Morgan Lightfoot, represents a woman whose "love and desire to help the race" pushed
her to fight against the racism she encountered and fight for
an education so that she could help others both by being an

example and, more tangibly, by becoming a child psychologist. The reader is shown that Lightfoot's mother had to overcome many of the obstacles examined by Lightfoot in her previous works.

Occasionally criticized for approaching her subjects with an overly pedagogical writing style, in *Balm in Gilead* Lightfoot writes with little of what critic Suzanne Fox of *Parnassus Poetry in Review* refers to as "the familiar academic biographical apparatus." In keeping with the less academic, more personal subject matter, Lightfoot's prose style is, according to Fox, "reflective, patient and tender." It is also made all the more personal by the fact that, over the course of the book, Lightfoot reveals almost as much about herself through what she writes as she reveals about her mother. Taking on the aspect of a dual biography or dialogue, *Balm in Gilead* offers the reader insight into Lightfoot's background that helps explain some of her own choices and interests. The reader discovers, for example, that father, like daughter, was a sociologist. And when she describes the struggle of her mother to gain acceptance into medical school in the face of racism (after being rejected, Margaret is told by the dean that "twenty-five years ago there was a Negro man admitted to Cornell Medical School and he didn't work out ... he got tuberculosis"), Lightfoot's preoccupation with the subjects of race, class, and education and the ways in which they relate becomes illuminated.

Currently a professor in the department of Education at Harvard University, Lightfoot is still concerned with the state of education in America, once again viewing her subject, as she did in *Balm in Gilead,* from an insider's perspective. This perspective informs her work as a whole as she seeks to display the problems brought about by racism and the impact it has on society, particularly schools as a microcosm of society, while at the same time offering recommendations for solutions. This ability to achieve "tremendous balance" in her work, states Fox, is one of "the best of her gifts." Commenting in *Balm in Gilead,* Lightfoot herself aptly summarizes her work as "books that [try] to get beyond surface and stereotypes."

*BIOGRAPHICAL/CRITICAL SOURCES:*

*BOOKS*

Lightfoot, Barbara Lawrence, *Balm in Gilead: Journey of a Healer,* Addison-Wesley, 1988.
Lightfoot, Barbara Lawrence, *The Good High School: Portraits of Character and Culture,* Basic Books, 1983.

*PERIODICALS*

*Chicago Tribune,* November 28, 1988; August 19, 1990.

*Choice,* May, 1979, p. 431.
*Los Angeles Times Book Review,* October 23, 1983, p. 3; January 29, 1989, p. 1.
*New Republic,* January 23, 1984, p. 40.
*New York Times Book Review,* January 1, 1988, p. 7.
*Parnassus Poetry in Review,* Volume 17, number 1, p. 132.
*Publishers Weekly,* July 24, 1978, p. 88.

\*   \*   \*

## LINCOLN, C(harles) Eric   1924-

*PERSONAL:* Born June 23, 1924, in Athens, AL; son of Less and Mattie (Sowell) Lincoln; married second wife, Lucy Cook (a teacher), July 1, 1961; children: (first marriage) Cecil Eric, Joyce Elaine; (second marriage) Hilary Anne, Less Charles II. *Education:* LeMoyne College, A.B., 1947; Fisk University, M.A., 1954; University of Chicago Divinity School, B.D., 1956; Boston University, M.Ed., 1960, Ph.D., 1960.

*ADDRESSES: Office*—Department of Religion, Duke University, Durham, NC 27706.

*CAREER:* LeMoyne College, Memphis, TN, director of public relations, 1950-51; Fisk University, Nashville, TN, associate personnel dean, 1953-54; Clark College, Atlanta, GA, assistant professor of religion and philosophy, 1954-57, associate professor of social philosophy, 1960-61, professor of social relations, 1961-64, administrative assistant to president, 1961-63, director of Institute for Social Relations, 1963-65, assistant personnel dean; Portland State College (now University), Portland, OR, professor of sociology, 1965-67; Union Theological Seminary, New York City, professor of sociology of religion, 1967-73; Fisk University, Nashville, TN, professor of religion and sociology and chairman of department of religious and philosophical studies, 1973-76; Duke University, Durham, NC, professor of religion and culture, 1976-93, William R. Kenan, Jr. distinguished professor emeritus, 1991-93. Boston University, Human Relations Center, director of Panel of Americans, 1958-60, adjunct professor, 1963-65; Dartmouth College, lecturer-in-residence, 1962, visiting professor, 1962-63; visiting professor, Spelman College, 1966; adjunct professor, Vassar College, 1969-70; visiting professor at State University of New York at Albany, 1970-72, and Queens College of the City University of New York, 1972; adjunct professor of ethics and society, Vanderbilt University, 1973-76. Lecturer; has made numerous appearances on local and national television and on radio. Member of boards of directors or boards of trustees of several institutions, including Boston University, Jewish Theological Seminary, Institute for Religious and Social Studies, Clark Atlanta University, and Association of Theological Schools. Consultant in human relations. *Military service:* U.S. Navy hospital corps, 1944-45.

*MEMBER:* American Academy of Arts and Sciences (fellow), American Sociological Association, Society for the Psychological Study of Social Issues, American Academy of Political and Social Science, Society for the Scientific Study of Religion, National Association of University Professors, National Education Association, Association for the Study of Negro Life and History, Black Academy of Arts and Letters (founding president; member of board of directors), Society for the Study of Black Religion, American Association of Intergroup Relations Officials, Authors Guild, Authors League of America, National Association for the Advancement of Colored People (life member), National Geographic Society, Southern Sociological Society, Southern Fellowship of Writers, New York Academy of Arts and Sciences, New York Academy of Sciences, Kappa Alpha Psi, Sigma Pi Phi, Free and Accepted Masons, International Frontiers Club.

*AWARDS, HONORS:* John Hay Whitney fellow, 1957; Crusade fellow, Methodist Church, 1958; Lilly Endowment fellow, 1959; human relations fellow, Boston University, 1959-60; L.L.D. from Carleton College, 1968, Lane College, 1982, and Clark College, 1983; Creative Communications Award, Art Institute of Boston, 1970; L.H.D. from St. Michael's College, 1972, and Clark University, 1993; D.C.L. from Shaw University, 1988; D.D. from Interdenominational Theological Center, 1990, and Emory University, 1993; research grants from Society for the Psychological Study of Social Issues, Anti-Defamation League of B'nai B'rith, Fund for the Advancement of Education, Lilly Endowment, and Ford Foundation.

*WRITINGS:*

*The Black Muslims in America,* Beacon Press, 1961, second revised edition, 1982.
*My Face Is Black,* Beacon Press, 1964.
*Sounds of the Struggle,* Morrow, 1967.
*The Negro Pilgrimage in America: The Coming of Age of the Blackamericans,* Bantam, 1967.
*Is Anybody Listening?,* Seabury, 1968.
(With Langston Hughes and Milton Meltzer) *A Pictorial History of the Negro in America,* Crown, 1968, fifth revised edition, 1983.
*A Profile of Martin Luther King, Jr.,* Hill & Wang, 1969, revised edition, 1984.
*The Blackamericans,* Bantam, 1969.
*The Black Church since Frazier* (also see below), Schocken, 1974.
(With E. Franklin Frazier) *The Negro Church in America* (bound with *The Black Church since Frazier*), Schocken, 1974.
(Editor) *The Black Experience in Religion: A Book of Readings,* Doubleday, 1974.

*Race, Religion, and the Continuing American Dilemma,* Hill & Wang, 1984.
*The Avenue: Clayton City,* Morrow, 1988.
(With Lawrence H. Mamiya) *The Black Church in the African-American Experience,* Duke University Press, 1990.
*This Road since Freedom: Collected Poems,* Carolina Wren Press, 1990.

*EDITOR; "C. ERIC LINCOLN SERIES IN BLACK RELIGION"*

James H. Cone, *A Theology of Black Liberation,* Lippincott, 1970.
Henry Mitchell, *Black Preaching,* Lippincott, 1970.
Gayraud Wilmore, *Black Religion and Black Radicalism,* Doubleday, 1972.
Joseph R. Washington, Jr., *Black Sects and Cults,* Doubleday, 1972.
William R. Jones, *Is God a White Racist?,* Doubleday, 1973.
Leonard E. Barrett, *Soul-Force,* Doubleday, 1973.

*CONTRIBUTOR*

Alice Horowitz, editor, *The Outlook for Youth,* H.W. Wilson, 1962.
Earl Raab, editor, *New Frontiers in Race Relations,* Doubleday, 1962.
Mulford Sibley, editor, *The Quiet Battle,* Doubleday, 1963.
Louis Lomax, editor, *When the Word Is Given,* New American Library, 1963.
Arnold Rose, editor, *Assuring Freedom to the Free,* Wayne State University Press, 1963.
Rolf Italiaander, editor, *Die Herasforderung des Islam,* Muster-Schmidt-Verlag (Gottingen), 1965.
Arnold Rose and Caroline Rose, editors, *Minority Problems,* Harper, 1965.
Gerald H. Anderson, editor, *Sermons to Men of Other Faiths,* Abingdon, 1966.
John P. Davis, editor, *The American Negro Reference Book,* Prentice-Hall, 1966.
Nils Petter Gleditsch, editor, *Kamp Uten Vapen,* Eides Boktrykkeri (Bergen), 1966.
Edgar A. Shuler and others, editors, *Readings in Sociology,* Crowell, 1967.
William C. Kvaraceus and others, editors, *Poverty, Education and Race Relations,* Allen & Bacon, 1967.
Milgon L. Barron, editor, *Minorities in a Changing World,* Knopf, 1967.
Bradford Chambers, editor, *Chronicles of Negro Protest,* New American Library, 1968.
Peter T. Rose, editor, *Old Memories, New Moods,* Atherton Press, 1970.
David Reimers, editor, *The Black Man in America since Reconstruction,* Crowell, 1970.

Benjamin Brawley, editor, *A Social History of the American Negro,* Macmillan, 1970.

George Ducas, editor, *Great Documents in Black American History,* Praeger, 1970.

Robert Weisbard and Arthur Stein, editors, *The Bittersweet Encounter,* Negro Universities Press, 1970.

Scott G. McNall, editor, *The Sociological Perspective,* Little, Brown, 1971.

Michael V. Namorato, editor, *Have We Overcome?: Race Relations since Brown,* University Press of Mississippi, 1979.

*OTHER*

Contributor to *Encyclopaedia Britannica, Encyclopedia Americana, Encyclopedia of Southern Religion, World Book Encyclopedia,* and *Encyclopedia of World Biography.* Contributor of articles, poetry, and reviews to numerous journals and popular periodicals. Consultant for *Change* magazine; associate editor for scientific study of religion, *Review of the Religious Research Society.*

*SIDELIGHTS:* C. Eric Lincoln has long been considered an important and respected sociologist studying such topics as race relations in the United States, the historical development of black protest and black nationalism, the growth and importance of the Black church, the Black Muslim movement, and the backgrounds and influence of Black leaders on the civil rights cause. Many reviewers feel that through his lectures, his appearances on national television and radio programs, and his writings, Lincoln has examined the various elements of black life in America in an intelligent, insightful, and thorough manner. As Herbert Mitgang remarks in the *Saturday Review,* "[Lincoln] writes dispassionately and from the inside about where the Negro stands and what he hopes for today."

The publication of his first book, *The Black Muslims in America,* gained Lincoln and his work national attention. As one of the first sociological accounts of the Black Muslim movement in the United States, this book explores the movement's beginnings, doctrines, goals, strengths, leaders, and the powerful influence the group has had on the black American. P.J. Gleason writes in the *San Francisco Chronicle* that "Lincoln's study of the pseudo-Islamic sect of Black Muslims is timely, fascinating ... to read." Gleason adds that "the story of the rise of this sect is logically and deftly told by Dr. Lincoln.... This is the first survey in depth on one of the most important, as well as one of the most significant, movements in contemporary America and it is well done."

"As an objective study of a social phenomenon [*The Black Muslims in America*] is outstanding," remarks K. B. Clark in the *Saturday Review.* "The author is at his best when he is describing the ideas, manner, ambiguities—intentional or un-

intentional—of the leaders and the appeals to and techniques of control of their followers.... [Lincoln] writes with clarity, with compassion, and with some evidence of deep personal conflict." And M. E. Burgess states in *Social Forces* that "whatever course the Movement takes in years ahead, it bears close watching. Dr. Lincoln's insightful analysis of the rationale, the appeal, and the implications of such a movement is a valuable contribution to the literature."

*BIOGRAPHICAL/CRITICAL SOURCES:*

*PERIODICALS*

*Atlanta Journal/Constitution,* March 13, 1988.
*Best Sellers,* February 15, 1970.
*Commonweal,* August 9, 1985.
*Fayetteville Observer,* April 3, 1988.
*Greensboro News and Record,* April 22, 1988.
*Library Journal,* January 15, 1970.
*New York Review of Books,* February 11, 1965.
*New York Times Book Review,* April 23, 1961.
*San Francisco Chronicle,* May 7, 1961.
*Saturday Review,* May 13, 1961; January 16, 1965; January 27, 1968; February 14, 1970.
*Social Forces,* December, 1961.

\*    \*    \*

## LIYONG, Taban lo 1938(?)-

*PERSONAL:* Born in 1938 (some sources say 1939) in Uganda (some sources indicate the Sudan). *Education:* Attended Government Teacher Training College, Kyambogo, Uganda, Knoxville College, University of North Carolina, and Georgetown University; National Teachers College, Kampala, Uganda, B.A.; Howard University, B.A., 1966; University of Iowa, M.F.A., 1968.

*ADDRESSES: Office*—Department of English, University of Nairobi, P.O. Box 30197, Nairobi, Kenya.

*CAREER:* University of Nairobi, Nairobi, Kenya, lecturer in English, 1968—, member of Institute for Development Studies Cultural Division, 1968—.

*WRITINGS:*

*Fixions and Other Stories by a Ugandan Writer,* Humanities, 1968 (published in England as *Fixions and Other Stories,* Heinemann, 1969).

*The Last Word: Cultural Synthesism,* East African Publishing House, 1969.

*The Uniformed Man* (short stories), East African Literature Bureau, 1971.

*Popular Culture of East Africa: Oral Literature,* Longmans, 1972.

*Thirteen Offensives Against Our Enemies,* East African Literature Bureau, 1973.

(Editor of reprint) Ham Mukasa, *Sir Apolo Kagwa Discovers Britain,* Heinemann, 1975.

*Ballads of Underdevelopment: Poems and Thoughts,* East African Literature Bureau, 1976.

*Another Last Word,* Heinemann, 1990.

*Culture Is Rutan,* Longmans, 1991.

*NOVELS*

*Meditations in Limbo,* Equatorial Publishers, 1970, revised edition published as *Meditations of Taban lo Liyong,* Collings, 1978.

*POEMS*

(Editor) *Eating Chiefs: Lwo Culture from Lolwe to Malkal,* Heinemann, 1970.

*Frantz Fanon's Uneven Ribs, with Poems, More and More,* Heinemann, 1971.

*Another Nigger Dead: Poems,* Heinemann, 1972.

*Ballads of Underdevelopment: Poems and Thoughts,* East African Literature Bureau, 1976.

Also author of *To Still a Passion* (poems), 1977. Editor of *Mila.*

*EDITOR*

*Popular Culture of East Africa: Oral Culture,* Longmans, 1972.

*WORK IN PROGRESS: A Calendar of Wisdom,* proverbs in verse; *The African Tourist,* culture criticism; *The American Education of Taban lo Liyong; The Lubumbashi Lectures;* editing *East African Anthology: Literature from Zinjanthropus to Extelcom.*

*SIDELIGHTS:* Taban lo Liyong is the author of stories, essays, poems, and folktales created using unconventional and extravagant forms and styles. Deemed a highly original writer, he has received much critical attention, both positive and negative. He has delved into numerous genres, often exploring a variety of ideological positions. His themes range from East Africa's literary barrenness to meditations on his own life and experiences. "Taban conforms to no expectations, not even

his own," according to K. L. Goodwin in *Understanding African Poetry.* "He never loses the sense of being a jester, an entertainer." Pointing out the author's provocative writing style, Peter Nazareth in *Dictionary of Literary Biography* declared "he has brought fresh perspectives to African literature and has inspired and helped younger writers."

*BIOGRAPHICAL/CRITICAL SOURCES:*

*BOOKS*

*Dictionary of Literary Biography,* Volume 125: *Twentieth-Century Caribbean and Black African Writers,* edited by Bernth Lindfors and Reinhard Sander, Gale, 1993, pp. 327-331.

Goodwin, K. L., *Understanding African Poetry,* Heinemann, 1972.

*PERIODICALS*

*African Literature Today,* Volume 12, 1982, pp. 104-117.

*African Studies Review,* Volume 27, 1984, pp. 41-55.

*Presence Africaine,* Volume 140, 1986, pp. 10-24.

\*   \*   \*

## LOCKETT, Reginald (Franklin) 1947-

*PERSONAL:* Born November 5, 1947, in Berkeley, CA; son of Jewell and Alyce Irene (Matthis) Lockett; married Faye Arvis West, January 23, 1983 (divorced September 1, 1987); children: Maya Lomasi Lauren Aimee. *Education:* San Francisco State University, B.A., 1971, M.A., 1972.

*ADDRESSES: Home*—3717 Market St., Oakland, CA 94608. *Office*—Department of Language Arts, San Jose City College, 2100 Moorpark Ave., San Jose, CA 95128-2723.

*CAREER:* North Peralta Community College, Oakland, CA, instructor in English, 1973-75; Laney College, Oakland, instructor in English, 1975-76; San Francisco State University, San Francisco, CA, lecturer in creative writing, 1976-78; City College of San Francisco, San Francisco, reading lab instructor, beginning in 1982; San Jose City College, San Jose, CA, member of department of language arts.

*WRITINGS:*

*Good Times and No Bread* (poetry), Jukebox Press, 1978.

Contributor of numerous poems to literary magazines and anthologies; editor, *Folio,* 1977.

\* \* \*

**LOMAX, Pearl Cleage**
  See CLEAGE, Pearl (Michelle)

\* \* \*

**LONG, Naomi Cornelia**
  See MADGETT, Naomi Long

\* \* \*

**LONG, Richard A(lexander) 1927-**
  **(Ric Alexander)**

*PERSONAL:* Born February 9, 1927, in Philadelphia, PA; son of Thaddeus B. and Leila (Washington) Long. *Education:* Temple University, A.B., 1947, M.A., 1948; further study at University of Pennsylvania and University of Paris; University of Poitiers, D.es L., 1965.

*ADDRESSES: Office*—Graduate Institute of the Liberal Arts, Emory University, Atlanta, GA 30322.

*CAREER:* West Virginia State College, Institute, WV, instructor in English, 1949-50; Morgan State College (now University), Baltimore, MD, assistant professor, 1951-64, associate professor of English, 1964-66; Hampton Institute, Hampton, VA, professor of English and French, 1966-68; Atlanta University, Atlanta, GA, professor of English and Afro-American studies, 1968-87; currently faculty member of Graduate Institute of the Liberal Arts, Emory University, Atlanta. Visiting lecturer in Afro-American Studies, Harvard University, 1970-72. *Military service:* U.S. Army, 1944-45.

*MEMBER:* American Dialect Society, American Studies Association, South Atlantic Modern Language Association, Modern Language Association of America, College Language Association (president, 1971-72), Modern Humanities Research Association, Linguistics Society of America, Southeastern Conference on Linguistics.

*AWARDS, HONORS:* Fulbright scholar, University of Paris, 1957-58.

*WRITINGS:*

(Editor with Albert H. Berrian) *Negritude: Essays and Studies,* Hampton Institute Press, 1967, revised edition, 1987.

(Editor with Eugenia W. Collier) *Afro-American Writing: An Anthology of Prose and Poetry,* two volumes, Pennsylvania State University Press, 1972, enlarged edition, 1985, second enlarged edition, 1990.
*Ascending and Other Poems,* Du Sable Museum, 1975.
*Black Americana,* Chartwell, 1985.
*Black Writers and the American Civil War,* Blue and Gray Press, 1988.
*The Black Tradition in American Dance,* Rizzoli, 1989.
*Black Americans: A Portrait,* Crescent, 1993.

*OTHER*

Also author, under name Ric Alexander, of dramatic works, including *The Pilgrim's Pride* (sketches), 1963; *Stairway to Heaven* (gospel opera), 1964; *Joan of Arc* (folk opera), 1964; *Reasons of State* (play), 1966; and *Black Is Many Hues* (play), 1969. Contributor to anthologies of essays, including *The Harlem Renaissance Re-Examined,* edited by Victor A. Kramer, AMS, 1987, and *Swords upon This Hill: Preserving the Literary Tradition of Black Colleges and Universities,* edited by Burney J. Hollis, Morgan State University Press, 1984. Former member of editorial board of *Black Books Bulletin.*

*BIOGRAPHICAL/CRITICAL SOURCES:*

*PERIODICALS*

*American Visions,* April, 1990.
*Booklist,* January 1, 1990.
*Choice,* September, 1990.
*Dance Magazine,* March, 1991.
*Ebony,* March, 1990.
*Essence,* March, 1990.
*Journal of American Studies,* April, 1987.
*Library Journal,* February 1, 1973; January, 1990.
*Reference & Research Book News,* February, 1990.
*Washington Post Book World,* December 3, 1989.

\* \* \*

**LOPES, Henri (Marie-Joseph) 1937-**

*PERSONAL:* Born September 12, 1937, in Leopoldville, Belgian Congo (now Kinshasa, Zaire); son of Jean-Marie Lopes and Elie Micheline Vulturi; married Nirva Pasbeau, May 13, 1961; children: one son, three daughters. *Education:* University of Paris, Sorbonne, B.A., 1962, M.A., 1963.

*ADDRESSES: Home*—Paris, France. *Office*—Assistant Director-General for Culture, UNESCO, 7 place de Fontenoy, F75700 Paris, France.

*CAREER:* Higher Teachers Training College of Central Africa, Brazzaville, Congo, professor, 1965-66; People's Republic of the Congo, director-general of education, 1966-68, minister of education, 1969-71, minister of foreign affairs, 1971-73, prime minister and minister of planning, 1973-75, minister of finance, 1977-80; United Nations Educational, Scientific, and Cultural Organization (UNESCO), Paris, France, assistant director-general for program support, 1982-85, assistant director-general for culture and communication, 1986-90, assistant director-general for culture, 1990—. Chairperson of the jury for the Concours de la Meilleure Nouvelle de la Langue Francaise (best French-language short story), awarded by Radio-France Internationale and L'Agence de Cooperation Culturelle et Technique.

*MEMBER:* Haut Conseil de la Francophonie (High Council for French Speaking Communities).

*AWARDS, HONORS:* Grand Prix Litteraire de L'Afrique Noire, 1972, for *Tribaliques;* Prix SIMBA de Litterature, 1978; Prix de Litterature du President (Congo); Prix Jules Verne de L'Academie de Bretagne et des Pays de la Loire, 1990; commander of the Orders of the Congo and Chad; grand officer of the National Order of Senegal; honorary doctorate, University of Paris.

*WRITINGS:*

*Tribaliques,* preface by Guy Tirolien, Cle (Yaounde, Cameroon), 1971, translation by Andrea Leskes published as *Tribaliks: Contemporary Congolese Stories,* Heinemann, 1987.
(With Edgar Faure, Felipe Herrera, Abdul-Razzak Kaddoura, and Arthur V. Petrovsky) *Learning to Be: The World of Education Today and Tomorrow,* UNESCO, 1972.
*La Nouvelle Romance* (novel), Cle, 1976.
*Sans tam-tam,* Cle, 1977.
*Le Pleurer-Rire* (novel), Presence Africaine, 1982, translation by Gerald Moore published as *The Laughing Cry: An African Cock and Bull Story,* Readers International, 1987.
*Le Chercheur d'Afriques* (novel), Seuil, 1990.
*Sur l'autre rive* (novel), Seuil, 1992.

Contributor of poems to anthologies, including *La Nouvelle Somme de poesie noire* and *L'Anthologie de la litterature congolaise,* edited by J. B. Tati-Loutard. Contributor of articles on Black African literature to periodicals.

*SIDELIGHTS:* An assistant director-general for culture for UNESCO and a former prime minister of the West African nation of the People's Republic of the Congo, Henri Lopes writes novels and short stories that comment on the disparity between developing and traditional Africa. Schooled in France, Lopes returned to Africa in the mid-1960s where a career in education swiftly led to the highest level of government service. His first book of eight short stories, 1971's *Tribaliques,* won the Grand Prix Litteraire de L'Afrique Noire and was translated from French into English as *Tribaliks: Contemporary Congolese Stories* in 1987. The tales of the volume center on modern Africa's sophisticated urban elite and their perpetuation of the colonial structures—particularly tribalism and the subjugation of women—that retard social and political development in many African states.

Lopes's works have been published in Spanish, Portuguese, Dutch, Bulgarian, Ukrainian, Russian, German, Slovenian, Danish, and Italian. In *Le Pleurer-Rire (The Laughing Cry)*—the first of his novels to be translated into English—Lopes conjures a mythical contemporary African republic beset by a megalomaniacal dictator. Lopes's imaginary state is governed by a paranoid bully reminiscent of notorious Ugandan president Idi Amin. Maitre, the tale's narrator, is palace administrator and valet to "Daddy," as the resident tyrant insists on being called. Portrayed as a simple man of earthy human appetites with little concern for politics, Maitre describes without artifice the degenerative effect Daddy's alleged reforms have on the country. As Lopes satirizes the archetypal African despot and his court in conversational style, he vividly illustrates the tribalism endemic to African politics and the symbiotic alliance of African politicians and the white Europeans on whom they depend to keep their so-called independent governments viable. Noting the author's unique perspective, *New York Times Book Review* contributor Donald E. Westlake commented, "Lopes has both the experience to give his work its grounding in reality and sufficient civilized distance to give his contempt its cutting edge." Similarly, Alan Ryan observed in the *Washington Post,* "He sees the life and the complex ways of West Africa realistically and honestly from a European point of view. But he still sees them through African eyes. Somewhere in the middle, in that conflict of views, is the truth about Africa, and Lopes has captured it in *The Laughing Cry.*"

*BIOGRAPHICAL/CRITICAL SOURCES:*

*PERIODICALS*

*Le Figaro,* March 26, 1990; July 7, 1992.
*Jeune Afrique,* June 11-17, 1992, pp. 51-52; July 1-7, 1992, pp. 70-71.
*New Statesman,* November 6, 1987, p. 30.
*New York Times Book Review,* May 3, 1987.
*Publishers Weekly,* March 27, 1987, p. 43.
*Le Quotidien de Paris,* January 3, 1990; June 17, 1992.
*Le Soleil* (Quebec), June 22, 1992.

*Washington Post,* August 13, 1987.
*World Literature Today,* autumn, 1988, pp. 713-714.

\* \* \*

## LOVELACE, Earl 1935-

*PERSONAL:* Born July 13, 1935, in Toco, Trinidad; grew up in Tobago and Port of Spain; came to United States, 1966; returned to West Indies, 1977. Wife's name, Jean; children: Walt and Che. *Education:* Eastern Caribbean Institute of Agriculture and Forestry, 1961-62; Howard University, 1966-67; Johns Hopkins University, M.A., 1974.

*ADDRESSES: Home*—Matura, West Indies.

*CAREER:* Proofreader for *Trinidad Guardian,* 1953-54; field assistant for the Department of Forestry and then agricultural assistant for Department of Agriculture, 1956-66; editorial writer, columnist, and reviewer for daily *Trinidad and Tobago Express,* 1967; teacher at Virginia Union University, Richmond, VA, 1967; lecturer in English at University of the District of Columbia, 1971-73; lecturer at University of the West Indies at Saint Augustine, 1977—; visiting novelist in residence at Johns Hopkins University, middle 1970s; writer in residence at University of Iowa, 1980-81; writer in residence at Harwick College, Oneonta, NY, 1986; writer.

*AWARDS, HONORS:* Independence Award, British Petroleum, 1964, for *While Gods Are Falling;* Pegasus Literary Award for outstanding contributions to the arts in Trinidad and Tobago, 1965; Best Play Award and Best Music Award, 1976, for *My Name Is Village;* Guggenheim fellowship, 1980; National Endowment for the Humanities grant, 1986.

*WRITINGS:*

*FICTION*

*While Gods are Falling,* Collins, 1965, Regnery 1966.
*The Schoolmaster,* Regnery, 1968.
*The Dragon Can't Dance,* Deutsch, 1979, Three Continents, 1981.
*The Wine of Astonishment,* Deutsch, 1982, Vintage, 1984.
*A Brief Conversion and Other Stories,* Heinemann, 1988.

*PLAYS*

*The New Boss,* first produced Matura, Trinidad, 1962.
*My Name Is Village,* first produced Port of Spain, 1976.
*Pierrot Ginnard* (musical), first produced Port of Spain, 1977.
*Jestina's Calypso* (first produced Saint Augustine, Trinidad, 1978), included in *Jestina's Calypso, and Other Plays,* Heinemann, 1984.

*The New Hardware Store,* first produced Saint Augustine, Trinidad, 1980; produced West End, 1985.
*The Wine of Astonishment* (based upon his novel; first produced Port of Spain, 1987), Deutsch, 1982, Vintage, 1984.
*The Dragon Can't Dance* (adapted from his novel; first produced in London, 1990), included in *Black Plays 2,* edited by Yvonne Brewster, Methuen, 1989.

*OTHER*

Contributor to *El Caribe y America Latina,* edited by Ulrich Fleischmann and Ineke Phaf, Berlin, 1987. Contributor to periodicals, including *Voices, Wasafiri,* and *South Magazine.* Lovelace's papers are collected in the Lovelace Archives in Port of Spain, Trinidad.

*SIDELIGHTS:* Earl Lovelace writes about Trinidad and the problems of displaced cultures, lost roots and living struggles, polyglot speech and poetry. "Lovelace writes eloquently of a culture of resistance that has sprung up within black communities in Trinidad," states Cezia Thompson-Cager in the *Dictionary of Literary Biography.* "However, his definition of this culture embraces all New World communities that utilize resistance as a survival strategy."

His first novel, *While Gods Are Falling,* winner of the British Petroleum Independence Award in 1965, chronicles decolonized Trinidadian life in ways that a *Times Literary Supplement* contributor describes as "sharply observed and excitingly alive." *The Schoolmaster,* a parable compared in elegance by one reviewer to Steinbeck's *The Pearl,* explores the residual darkness at the heart of the post-colonial situation as a town in the island's interior establishes a school. The sexually violent plot accelerates into what A. S. Byatt, in *New Statesman,* calls a "delicately ambivalent climax." *The Dragon Can't Dance* refines Lovelace's use of dialect, which Ian Thomson describes in *Books and Bookmen* as "vigorous and at times almost hallucinatory." In his fourth novel, *The Wine of Astonishment,* Lovelace takes up the history of the Spiritual Baptists, a creole sect banned on the island from 1917 to 1951. Again reviewers found his language impressive: In the *Washington Post Book World,* Donald McCaig called it a "patois, a musical dialect, full of sweet metaphors," while in the *New York Times Book Review,* Julius Lester describes the work as "a poetic wonder ... a sustained prose poem molded from the lyricism of everyday speech and life." Miniatures of this same style fill *A Brief Conversion and Other Stories* with small revelations and daily ironies.

Lovelace's drama shares with his fiction the preoccupation with the search for a viable sense of identity under the shadow of colonialism's strangling cultural legacy. *Jestina's Calypso,* darkly comic and at once full of personal pathos and allegorical suggestion, introduces an unattractive Trinidadian woman, Jestina, preparing to go the airport to meet her romantic pen pal, also Trinidadian but a resident in the U.S. Jestina agonizes over the fact that she substituted a photo of a lighter-skinned, more attractive woman for her own in her correspondence. *The New Hardware Store* sketches a brutal caricature of a soulless petit-bourgeois shopkeeper. *My Name Is Village,* a didactic stage musical, presents an old carnival stickman and his son lightly struggling with all the perennial problems of contemporary Trinidadian culture: generational tension, conflict between rural and urban, fame and failure, originality and mediocrity. As Thompson-Cager points out, "All of Lovelace's writing and work displays an uncommon love for himself as a black man, for his language, for his people, and for their potential greatness."

*BIOGRAPHICAL/CRITICAL SOURCES:*

*BOOKS*

*Contemporary Literary Criticism,* Volume 51, Gale, 1989.
*Contemporary Novelists,* St. James Press, 1991.
*Critical Issues in West Indian Literature,* Caribbean, 1984.
*Dictionary of Literary Biography,* Volume 125: *Twentieth-Century Caribbean and Black African Writers,* Gale, 1993.
*Fifty Caribbean Writers,* Greenwood Press, 1986.
*West Indian Literature and Its Social Context,* University of the West Indies Department of English, 1985.

*PERIODICALS*

*American Book Review,* January, 1988, p. 9.
*Americas: A Quarterly Review of Inter-American History,* January, 1970, p. 343.
*Artrage,* summer, 1986, pp. 4-5.
*Booklist,* November 1, 1984, p. 2080.
*Books,* September, 1987, p. 24.
*Books and Bookmen,* July, 1986, p. 33.
*British Book News,* September, 1982, p. 577; November, 1986, p. 621.
*Caribbean Contact,* June, 1977, pp. 15-16.
*Contributions in Black Studies,* Number 8, 1986-87, pp. 101-105.
*Journal of Commonwealth Literature,* July, 1969, pp. 117-122.
*Kirkus Reviews,* September 1, 1984, p. 818.
*Library Journal,* November 1, 1984, p. 343.
*New Statesman,* January 5, 1968; October 24, 1986, p. 30.
*New Yorker,* April 8, 1985, p. 126.
*New York Times Book Review,* October 30, 1966; November 24, 1968; January 6, 1985, p. 9.
*Observer* (London), November 4, 1979, p. 39
*Publishers Weekly,* September 14, 1984, p. 139.

*Times* (London), March 12, 1985.
*Times Educational Supplement,* January 27, 1984, p. 29.
*Wasafiri,* autumn, 1990, pp. 25-27.
*Washington Post Book World,* March 6, 1988, p. 7.
*World Literature Today,* spring, 1982, p. 394; autumn, 1984, pp. 405-13; summer, 1985, p. 480; spring, 1989, p. 357.
*World Literature Written in English,* spring, 1984, pp. 405-413; spring, 1988, pp. 103-114; spring, 1991, pp. 8-20.

\*   \*   \*

## LUTHULI, Albert John  1898(?)-1967

*PERSONAL:* Born c. 1898, in Groutville, Natal, South Africa (one source says Rhodesia); died of injuries from being hit by a train while crossing tracks near his home, July 21, 1967 (one source says 1964), in Groutville, South Africa; son of John and Mtonya Gumede Luthuli, and grandson of Zulu chief; married Nokukhanya Bhengu in 1927; children: two sons, five daughters. *Education:* Attended Groutville Mission School; Adams College; Methodist Institute, teacher training. *Politics:* African National Congress. *Religion:* Congregationalist.

*CAREER:* Adam's Mission Station College, South Africa, teacher, 1921-1936; Abasemakholweni Tribe, South Africa, Chief, 1936-1953; African National Congress, Natal Provincial Division, President-General, 1953-1967. International Missionary Council, India, delegate, 1938; Christian Council of South Africa, representative and executive member; Congregational Churches of America, chairmen of the board; Natal Mission Conference, president.

*AWARDS, HONORS:* Nobel Prize for Peace, 1960; United National Human Rights Prize, 1968.

*WRITINGS:*

*BOOKS*

*Let My People Go* (autobiography), McGraw-Hill, 1962.
(With others) *Africa's Freedom,* Allen & Unwin, 1964, Barnes & Noble, 1964.

*OTHER*

*Fifty Years of Union* (political review), South African Institute of Race Relations, 1960.
*Freedom is the Apex* (speech), South African Congress of Democrats, 1960.
*The Road to Oslo, and Beyond!,* (contains Luthuli's Nobel lecture and other speeches given in connection with the presentation to him of the Nobel Peace Prize in 1961), [London], 1962.

*BIOGRAPHICAL/CRITICAL SOURCES:*

*BOOKS*

Benson, Mary, *Chief Albert Luthuli of South Africa,* Oxford
    University Press, 1963.
Luthuli, A.J., *Let My People Go* (autobiography), McGraw-
    Hill, 1962.

*PERIODICALS*

*New York Times,* October 24, 1961, p. 22.


*OBITUARIES:*

*BOOKS*

*Contemporary Authors,* Volume 113, Gale, 1985.

*PERIODICALS*

*New York Times,* July 22, 1967.

# M

## MADGETT, Naomi Long 1923-
### (Naomi Cornelia Long, Naomi Long Witherspoon)

*PERSONAL:* Born July 5, 1923, in Norfolk, VA; daughter of Clarence Marcellus (a member of the clergy) and Maude (a teacher; maiden name, Hilton) Long; married Julian F. Witherspoon, March 31, 1946 (divorced April 27, 1949); married William Harold Madgett, July 29, 1954 (divorced December 21, 1960); married Leonard Patton Andrews (an elementary school principal), March 31, 1972; children: (first marriage) Jill Witherspoon Boyer. *Education:* Virginia State College, B.A. (with honors), 1945; Wayne State University, M.Ed., 1956; International Institute for Advanced Studies (now of Greenwich University), Ph.D., 1980. *Politics:* Independent, but usually Democratic Party. *Religion:* Protestant (Congregational).

*ADDRESSES: Home*—16886 Inverness St., Detroit, MI 48221. *Office*—18080 Santa Barbara Dr., Detroit, MI 48221.

*CAREER: Michigan Chronicle,* Detroit, MI, reporter and copy reader, 1945-46; Michigan Bell Telephone Co., Detroit, service representative, 1948-54; English teacher in public high schools, Detroit, 1955-65, 1966-68; Oakland University, Rochester, MI, research associate, 1965-66; Eastern Michigan University, Ypsilanti, MI, associate professor, 1968-73, professor of English, 1973-84, professor emeritus, 1984—. Visiting lecturer in English, University of Michigan, 1970-71; lecturer on Afro-American literature at colleges and universities. Conducts poetry readings and writing workshops. Member, trustee board, Plymouth Congregational United Church of Christ.

*MEMBER:* College Language Association, National Association for the Advancement of Colored People, Langston Hughes Society, Zora Neale Hurston Society, Howard University Stylus Society, Metropolitan Detroit Poetry Resource Center, Detroit Women Writers, Alpha Kappa Alpha (Alpha Rho Omega chapter), Fred Hart Williams Genealogical Society.

*AWARDS, HONORS:* Mott fellowship in English, Oakland University, 1965-66; Esther R. Beer poetry award, National Writers Club, 1957, for poem, "Native"; Josephine Nevins Keal Development Fund Award, 1979; Distinguished Service Award, Chesapeake/Virginia Beach Links, Inc., 1981; testimonial resolutions, Michigan State Legislature, 1982, 1984; testimonial resolutions, Detroit City Council, 1982, 1985; citation, Afro-American Museum of Detroit, 1983; citation, National Coalition of Black Women, 1984; citation, Black Caucus, National Council of Teachers of English, 1984; Robert Hayden Runagate Award, Heritage House, 1985; Arts Achievement Award, Wayne State University, 1985; Creative Artist Award, Michigan Council for the Arts, 1987; Creative Achievement Award, College Language Association, 1988, for *Octavia and Other Poems;* "In Her Lifetime" tribute, Afrikan Poets Theatre, 1989; Arts Foundation of Michigan Award, 1990; D.H.L from Siena Heights College, 1991; Award of Excellence, *Black Scholar* magazine, 1992; American Book Award, 1993; D.H.L., Loyola University, 1993; Ninth Annual Governor's Arts Award, Concerned Citizens for the Arts in Michigan, 1993. Madgett has also been honored by the Hilton-Long Poetry Foundation with an annual award named after her, the Naomi Long Madgett Poetry Award, beginning in 1993.

*WRITINGS:*

*POETRY*

(Under name Naomi Cornelia Long) *Songs to a Phantom Nightingale,* Fortuny's, 1941.
*One and the Many,* Exposition, 1956.

*Star by Star,* Harlo, 1965, revised edition, 1970.

*Pink Ladies in the Afternoon,* Lotus Press, 1972, enlarged edition, 1990.

*Exits and Entrances,* Lotus Press, 1978.

*Deep Rivers, A Portfolio: Twenty Contemporary Black American Poets* (with teacher's guide), Lotus Press, 1978.

*Phantom Nightingale: Juvenilia,* Lotus Press, 1981.

*Octavia and Other Poems,* Third World Press, 1988.

(Editor) *A Milestone Sampler: Fifteenth Anniversary Anthology,* Lotus Press, 1988.

(Editor and author of introduction) *Adam of Ife: Black Women in Praise of Black Men,* Lotus Press, 1992.

*Remembrance of Spring,* Michigan State University Press, 1993.

*NONFICTION*

(With Ethel Tincher and Henry B. Maloney) *Success in Language and Literature—B,* Follett, 1967.

*A Student's Guide to Creative Writing,* Penway Books, 1980.

*OTHER*

Lotus Press, editor, 1974-93, director 1993—, and senior editor of Michigan State University Lotus Poetry Series, 1993—. Contributor to more than 100 anthologies, including *The Third Woman,* edited by Dexter Fischer, Houghton, 1980, *Refugees: An Anthology of Poems and Songs,* edited by Brian Coleman, Ottowa, 1988, and *Contemporary Michigan Poetry,* edited by Conrad Hilberry, Michael Delp, and Herbert Scott, Wayne State University Press, 1988. Contributor of poetry to numerous periodicals, including *Michigan Quarterly Review, Argo, World Order, Zora Neale Hurston Forum, Great Lakes Review,* and, some under the name Naomi Long Witherspoon, *Michigan Chronicle.* Madgett's papers are being collected in the Special Collections Library at Fisk University.

*SIDELIGHTS:* Naomi Long Madgett, a poet and educator active in Detroit, Michigan, area schools, once commented: "As a child I was motivated by my father's library and the interests and inspiration of literary parents. I discovered Alfred Lord Tennyson and Langston Hughes at about the same time, [while] sitting on the floor of my father's study when I was about seven or eight. I think my poetry represents something of the variety of interest and style that these two widely divergent poets demonstrate."

In addition to her many esteemed volumes of poetry and numerous contributions to anthologies, Madgett provided an introductory essay to a collection entitled *Adam of Ife: Black Women in Praise of Black Men,* noted for its unique perspective on a central issue in African American studies. According to a publisher's release, "At a time when jail cells are bulging with disproportionate numbers of black men, and the breakdown of family values would seem to validate the negative literary characters as the norm, it is convenient to conclude that the black male in America is indeed a lost cause. Here to refute such a conclusion is the first anthology of its kind by African American women poets about black men who have had a positive impact on their lives." Madgett also commented: "It is my hope that a few of my poems will continue to have meaning for others after my voice is still."

*BIOGRAPHICAL/CRITICAL SOURCES:*

*BOOKS*

Arata, Esther Spring, and others, *Black Writers Past and Present,* Morrow, 1975.

*Dictionary of Literary Biography,* Volume 76: *Afro-American Writers, 1940-1955,* Gale, 1988.

Redmond, Eugene B., editor, *Drumvoices: The Mission of Afro-American Poetry,* Doubleday, 1976.

*PERIODICALS*

*Black American Literature Forum,* summer, 1980.

*Black Books Bulletin,* spring, 1974.

*Black Scholar,* March-April, 1980.

*Black World,* September, 1974.

*City Arts Quarterly,* Volume 3, number 4, 1988.

*Ebony,* March, 1974.

*English Journal,* April, 1957.

*First World,* Volume 2, number 4, 1980.

*Michigan Chronicle,* January 15, 1966.

*Negro Digest,* September, 1966.

*New Orleans Review,* September, 1976.

*Phylon,* winter, 1956.

*Richmond News Leader* (Virginia), March 28, 1979.

\*    \*    \*

## MADHUBUTI, Haki R. 1942-
## (Don L. Lee)

*PERSONAL:* Born February 23, 1942, in Little Rock, AR; son of Jimmy L. and Maxine (Graves) Lee; married Safisha L.; children: five. *Education:* Attended Wilson Junior College, Roosevelt University, and University of Illinois, Chicago Circle; University of Iowa, M.F.A., 1984.

*ADDRESSES: Office*—Third World Press, P.O. Box 19730, Chicago, IL 60619; Department of English, Speech, and Theatre, Chicago State University, 95th St. at King Dr., Chicago, IL 60628.

*CAREER:* DuSable Museum of African American History, Chicago, IL, apprentice curator, 1963-67; Montgomery Ward, Chicago, stock department clerk, 1963-64; post office clerk in Chicago, 1964-65; Spiegels, Chicago, junior executive, 1965-66; Cornell University, Ithaca, NY, writer-in-residence, 1968-69; Northeastern Illinois State College, Chicago, poet-in-residence, 1969-70; University of Illinois, Chicago, lecturer, 1969-71; Howard University, Washington, DC, writer-in-residence, 1970-78; Morgan State College, Baltimore, MD, 1972-73; Chicago State University, Chicago, professor of English, 1984—. Publisher and editor, Third World Press, 1967—. Director of Institute of Positive Education, Chicago, 1969-91. *Military service:* U.S. Army, 1960-63.

*MEMBER:* African Liberation Day Support Committee (vice-chairperson, 1971-73), Congress of African People (member of executive council, 1970-74), Organization of Black American Culture, Writers Workshop (founding member, 1967-75).

*WRITINGS:*

UNDER NAME DON L. LEE

*Think Black,* Broadside Press, 1967, revised edition, 1968, enlarged edition, 1969.

*Black Pride,* Broadside Press, 1967.

*For Black People (and Negroes Too),* Third World Press, 1968.

*Don't Cry, Scream* (poems), Broadside Press, 1969.

*We Walk the Way of the New World* (poems), Broadside Press, 1970.

(Author of introduction) *To Blackness: A Definition in Thought,* Kansas City Black Writers Workshop, 1970.

*Dynamite Voices I: Black Poets of the 1960s* (essays), Broadside Press, 1971.

(Editor with P. L. Brown and F. Ward) *To Gwen with Love,* Johnson Publishing, 1971.

*Directionscore: Selected and New Poems,* Broadside Press, 1971.

(Author of introduction) Marion Nicholas, *Life Styles,* Broadside Press, 1971.

*The Need for an African Education* (pamphlet), Institute of Positive Education, 1972.

UNDER NAME HAKI R. MADHUBUTI

*Book of Life* (poems), Broadside Press, 1973.

*From Plan to Planet—Life Studies: The Need for Afrikan Minds and Institutions,* Broadside Press, 1973.

(With Jawanza Kunjufu) *Black People and the Coming Depression* (pamphlet), Institute of Positive Education, 1975.

(Contributor) *A Capsule Course in Black Poetry Writing,* Broadside Press, 1975.

*Enemies: The Clash of Races* (essays), Third World Press, 1978.

*Earthquakes and Sunrise Missions: Poetry and Essays of Black Renewal, 1973-1983* (poems), Third World Press, 1984.

*Killing Memory, Seeking Ancestors* (poems), Lotus, 1987.

*Say That the River Turns: The Impact of Gwendolyn Brooks* (poetry and prose), Third World Press, 1987.

*Kwanzaa: A Progressive and Uplifting African American Holiday,* Third World Press, 1987.

*Black Men: Obsolete, Single, Dangerous?; Afrikan American Families in Transition: Essays in Discovery, Solution, and Hope,* Third World Press, 1990.

(Editor) *Confusion by Any Other Name: Essays Exploring the Negative Impact of the Blackman's Guide to Understanding the Blackwoman,* Third World Press, 1992.

OTHER

Also author of *Back Again, Home,* 1968, and *One Sided Shootout,* 1968; editor of *Why L.A. Happened: Implications of the 1992 Los Angeles Rebellion,* 1993. Contributor to more than one hundred anthologies, including *Black Women Writers (1950-1980): A Critical Evaluation,* edited by Mari Evans, Anchor-Doubleday, 1984, and *Tapping Potential: English and Language Arts for the Black Learner,* edited by Charlotte K. Brooks and others, Black Caucus of National Council of Teachers of English, 1985. Contributor to numerous magazines and literary journals, including *Black World, Negro Digest, Journal of Black Poetry, Essence, Journal of Black History, Chicago Defender,* and *Black American Literature Forum.* Founder and editor of *Black Books Bulletin,* 1972—; contributing editor, *Black Scholar* and *First World.*

*SIDELIGHTS:* "Poetry in my home was almost as strange as money," Don L. Lee, also known by his Swahili name Haki R. Madhubuti, relates in *Dynamite Voices I: Black Poets of the 1960s.* Abandoned by his father, then bereaved of his mother at the age of sixteen, Madhubuti made his living by maintaining two paper routes and cleaning a nearby bar. Poetry was scarce in his early life, he explains in the same source, because "what wasn't taught, but was consciously learned, in our early educational experience was that writing of any kind was something that Black people just didn't do." Nonetheless, he has become one of the best known poets of the black arts movement of the 1960s, a respected and influential critic of Black poetry, and an activist dedicated to the cultural unity of his people. "In many ways," writes Catherine Daniels Hurst in *Dictionary of Literary Biography,* Madhubuti "is one of the most representative voices of his time. Although most significant as a poet, his work as an essayist, critic, publisher, social activist, and educator has enabled him to go beyond the confines of poetry to the establishment of a black press and a school for black children."

The literature of the Harlem Renaissance—a literary movement of the 1920s and 1930s in which the works of many black artists became popular—was not deeply felt by the majority of America's black population, he writes. "In the Sixties, however, Black Art in all its various forms began to flourish as never before: music, theater, art (painting, sculpture), films, prose (novel[s], essays), and poetry. The new and powerful voices of the Sixties came to light mainly because of the temper of the times." The writers of this turbulent generation who worked to preserve a cultural heritage distinct from white culture did not look to previous literary traditions—black or white—for inspiration. Says Madhubuti, "The major influences on the new Black poets were/are Black music, Black life style, Black churches, and their own Black contemporaries."

An *Ebony* article on the poet by David Llorens hails him as "a lion of a poet who splits syllables, invents phrases, makes letters work as words, and gives rhythmic quality to verse that is never savage but often vicious and always reflecting a revolutionary black consciousness." As a result, his "lines rumble like a street gang on the page," remarks Liz Gant in a *Black World* review. Though Madhubuti believes, as he declares in *Don't Cry, Scream,* that "most, if not all blackpoetry will be *political,*" he explains in *Dynamite Voices I* that it must do more than protest, since "mere 'protest' writing is generally a weak reaction to persons or events and often lacks the substance necessary to motivate and move people." Black poetry will be powerful, he says, if it is "a genuine reflection of [the poet] and his people," presenting "the beauty and joy" of the black experience as well as outrage against social and economic oppression.

However, some critics hear only the voice of protest in Madhubuti's work. Paul Breman's piece in C. W. E. Bigsby's *The Black American Writer, Volume 1: Poetry and Drama,* calls him a poet whose "all-out ranting ... has become outdated more rapidly than one could have hoped." And Jascha Kessler, writing in a *Poetry* review, sees no poetry in Madhubuti's books. "Anger, bombast, raw hatred, strident, aggrieved, perhaps charismatically crude religious and political canting, propaganda and racist nonsense, yes.... [Madhubuti] is outside poetry somewhere, exhorting, hectoring, cursing, making a lot of noise." But the same elements that grate against the sensibilities of such critics stem from the poet's cultural objectives and are much better received by the poet's intended audience, say others. "He is not interested in modes of writing that aspire to elegance," writes Gwendolyn Brooks in the introduction of *Don't Cry, Scream.* Madhubuti writes for and to Blacks, and "the last thing these people crave is elegance. It is very hard to enchant, with elegant song, the ears of a fellow whose stomach is growling," she notes. Explains Hurst, "often he uses street language and the dialect of the uneducated Black community.... He uses unconventional abbreviations

and strung-together words ... in a visually rendered dialect designed to convey the stress, pitch, volume, texture, resonance, and the intensity of the black speaking voice. By these and other means, Madhubuti intends to engage the active participation of a black audience accustomed to the oral tradition of storytelling and song."

Poems in *Don't Cry, Scream* and *We Walk the Way of the New World* show the activist-poet's "increasing concern for incorporating jazz rhythms"; more and more, the poet styled the poems "for performance, the text lapsing into exultant screams and jazz scats," writes Bigsby in *The Second Black Renaissance.* The title poem of *Don't Cry, Scream,* believes Hurst, "should be dedicated to that consummate musician, John Coltrane, whose untimely death left many of his admirers in deep mourning. In this poem (which begs to be read out loud as only the poet himself can do it), Madhubuti strains to duplicate the virtuoso high notes of Coltrane's instrumental sound." Critic Sherley Anne Williams, speaking to interviewer Claudia Tate in *Black Women Writers at Work,* explains why this link to music is significant for the black writer. Whereas white Americans preserve themselves or their legacy through literature, black Americans have done so in music, in the blues form: "The blues records of each decade explain something about the philosophical basis of historical continuity for black people. It is a ritualized way of talking about ourselves and passing it on. This was true until the late sixties." Madhubuti elaborates in *Dynamite Voices I:* "Black music is our most advanced form of Black art. In spite of the debilitating conditions of slavery and its aftermath, Black music endured and grew as a communicative language, as a sustaining spiritual force, as entertainment, and as a creative extension of our African selves. It was one of the few mediums of expression open to Black people that was virtually free of interferences.... To understand ... art ... which is uniquely Black, we must start with the art form that has been least distorted, a form that has so far resisted being molded into a *pure* product of European-American culture." Numerous references to Black musicians and lines that imitate the sounds of Black music connect Madhubuti's poetry to that tradition and extend its life as well.

Hurst claims that the poet's "unique delivery has given him a popular appeal which is tantamount to stardom." In 1969, the poet averaged three appearances a week, reading his poetry and carrying on dialogs at institutions across the country. Phenomenal sales in excess of 100,000 by then alerted Helen Vendler that "something [was] happening." Writing in the *New York Times Book Review,* she attributed the sales to Madhubuti's "nerve, stamina, and satire. In him the sardonic and savage turn-of-phrase long present in black speech as a survival tactic finds its best poet." Daniel Greene suggested in the *National Observer* that a general concern about black militance and possible urban rioting accounted for sales, but went on to say that "people in the publishing industry are convinced that untold numbers of older and ill-educated Negroes, whose reading up till now might have been limited to comic and pulp fiction, are being lured to book shops and paperback stands by volumes exploring the 'black experience' in language they can understand."

Madhubuti's poetic voice softened somewhat during the 1970s, during which time he directed his energies to the writing of political essays (*From Plan to Planet—Life Studies: The Need for Afrikan Minds and Institutions* and *Enemies: The Clash of Races*). In addition, he contributed to the establishment of a black aesthetic for new writers through critical essays and reviews. *Dynamite Voices I,* for instance, "has become one of the major contemporary scholarly resources for black poetry," notes Hurst. Fulfilling the role of "cultural stabilizer," he also gave himself to the construction of institutions that promote the cultural independence and education of his people. In a fight against "brain mismanagement" in America, he founded the Third World Press in 1967 to encourage literacy and the Institute of Positive Education in 1969 "to provide educational and communication services to a community struggling to assert its identity amidst powerful, negative forces," he told Donnarae MacCann for an interview published in *Interracial Books for Children Bulletin.*

Students at the Institute in Chicago are schooled in the works of black writers because he feels black children need a better education than the one he received: "My education was ... acculturation, that process in which one is brought into another's culture, regardless of the damage. For the most part, my generation did not question this acculturation process.... In school I read Hawthorne, Twain, Hemingway, Fitzgerald—the major Western writers. My generation learned from that Western tradition, but we were not given the tradition that spoke best to our insides." Black authors such as Langston Hughes, Margaret Walker, Gwendolyn Brooks and Richard Wright (discovered "by accident" when he was thirteen), helped him to become "complete."

In the same interview, he defines the publishing goals of the Third World Press: "We look for writers who continue to critically assess the ambivalence of being Black in America.... What we are trying to do is to service the great majority of Black people, those who do not have a voice, who have not made it. Black themes over the past years have moved from reaction and rage to contemplative assessments of today's problems to a kind of visionary look at the world," a vision that includes not only blacks, but all people. But the development of the black community remains its main focus, he told David Streitfeld for a *Washington Post* article. "There's just so much negative material out there, and so little that helps. That's not to say we don't publish material that is critical, but it has to be constructive." As Streitfeld reports, "Third World's greatest success has been with ... Chancellor Williams' De-

struction of Black Civilization, which has gone through 16 printings." Other articles as well commended the press for breaking even for the first time in nineteen years in 1987.

Summing up Madhubuti's accomplishment as a writer, Williams comments in *Give Birth to Brightness: A Thematic Study in Neo-Black Literature* that as one of "the vocal exponents of Neo-Black literature," he has "come to symbolize most of what is strong and beautiful and vital in Black Experience and Black Art." Hurst's summary states, "His books have sold more than a million copies, without benefit of a national distributor. Perhaps Madhubuti will even succeed in helping to establish some lasting institutions in education and in the publishing world. Whether he does or not, he has already secured a place for himself in American literature. He is among the foremost anthologized contemporary revolutionary poets, and he has played a significant role in stimulating other young black talent. As Stephen Henderson has observed, he is 'more widely imitated than any other Black poet with the exception of Imamu Baraka (LeRoi Jones).... His influence is enormous, and is still growing.'"

*BIOGRAPHICAL/CRITICAL SOURCES:*

*BOOKS*

Bigsby, C. W. E., *The Black American Writer, Volume 1: Poetry & Drama,* Penguin, 1969.
Bigsby, C. W. E., *The Second Black Renaissance: Essays in Black Literature,* Greenwood Press, 1980.
*Contemporary Literary Criticism,* Gale, Volume 2, 1974, Volume 6, 1976.
*Dictionary of Literary Biography,* Gale, Volume 5: *American Poets since World War II,* 1980, Volume 41: *Afro-American Poets since 1955,* 1985.
Gibson, Donald B., editor, *Modern Black Poets: A Collection of Critical Essays,* Prentice-Hall, 1973.
Henderson, Stephen, *Understanding the New Black Poetry: Black Speech and Black Music as Poetic References,* Morrow, 1973.
Lee, Don L., *Don't Cry, Scream,* Broadside Press, 1969.
Lee, Don L., *Dynamite Voices I: Black Poets of the 1960s,* Broadside Press, 1971.
Mosher, Marlene, *New Directions from Don L. Lee,* Exposition, 1975.
Tate, Claudia, editor, *Black Women Writers at Work,* Continuum, 1983.
Vendler, Helen, *Part of Nature, Part of Us,* Howard University Press, 1980.
Williams, John A., and Charles F. Harris, editors, *Amistad 2,* Random House, 1971.
Williams, Sherley Anne, *Give Birth to Brightness: A Thematic Study in Neo-Black Literature,* Dial, 1972.

*PERIODICALS*

*Black Collegian,* February/March, 1971; September/October, 1974.

*Black World,* April, 1971; June, 1972; January, 1974.

*Chicago Sun Times,* December 11, 1987.

*Chicago Sun Times Showcase,* July 18, 1971.

*Chicago Tribune,* December 23, 1987.

*College Literature Association Journal,* September, 1971.

*Ebony,* March, 1969.

*Interracial Books for Children Bulletin,* Volume 17, number 2, 1986.

*Jet,* June 27, 1974.

*Journal of Negro History,* April, 1971.

*Los Angeles Times Book Review,* March 25, 1990, p. 6.

*National Observer,* July 14, 1969.

*Negro Digest,* December, 1969.

*New Lady,* July/August, 1971.

*New York Times,* December 13, 1987.

*New York Times Book Review,* September 29, 1974.

*Poetry,* February, 1973.

*Washington Post,* June 6, 1971; January 17, 1988.

\* \* \*

## MAJOR, Clarence 1936-

*PERSONAL:* Born December 31, 1936, in Atlanta, GA; son of Clarence and Inez (Huff) Major; married Joyce Sparrow, 1958 (divorced, 1964); married Pamela Jane Ritter, May 8, 1980. *Education:* Attended Art Institute of Chicago, 1953, Armed Forces Institute, 1956, and New School for Social Research, 1972; State University of New York at Albany, B.S.; Union for Experimenting Colleges and Universities, Ph.D.

*ADDRESSES: Office*—Department of English, University of California at Davis, Davis, CA 95616. *Agent*—Susan Bergholz, 340 West 72nd St., New York, NY 10023.

*CAREER:* Writer. Harlem Education Program, The New Lincoln School, New York City, director of creative writing program, 1967-68; Sarah Lawrence College, Bronxville, NY, lecturer, 1972-75; Howard University, Washington, DC, assistant professor, 1974-76; University of Washington, Seattle, assistant professor, 1976-77; University of Colorado, Boulder, associate professor, 1977-81, professor of English, 1981-89; University of California at Davis, professor of English, 1989—. Visiting professor, University of Nice, France, 1981-82 and 1983; visiting assistant professor, University of Maryland at College Park and State University of New York at Binghamton, 1987. Writer-in-residence at colleges and universities. Research analyst for Simulmatics Corp., New York City, 1967; newspaper reporter, 1968. Lecturer and guest lecturer at colleges, universities, libraries, and other institutions in the United States, Europe, and Africa; has given readings of his work at various institutions around the world and has recorded his work on tapes, videotapes, and records; has been interviewed radio and television. Judge, Creative Artists Public Service Program, 1972; Whiteside Poetry Contest, Brooklyn College, 1975; Massachusetts Foundation for the Arts and Humanities, 1976; Academy of American Poets, University of Washington, 1976; Ohio Arts Consortium, 1979; Consuelo Ford Award, Poetry Society of America, 1979; Arts Symposium, Colorado State University, 1981; Henfield Foundation Fiction Prize, 1983; National Endowment for the Arts, 1987; National Book Awards, 1991. Artist; has exhibited and published his photographs and paintings. Editorial consultant, University of Pittsburgh Press, 1974, Wesleyan University Press, 1984, and University of Georgia Press, 1987; consultant, Pennsylvania Advancement School, 1967-68, University of Colorado Writers Conference, 1977, and Liberian Association of Writers, 1982; member of advisory board, Reading Program, New York Public School District 5, 1970. *Military service:* U.S. Air Force, 1955-57; served as record specialist.

*AWARDS, HONORS:* Recipient of numerous grants; National Council on the Arts Award, Association of American University Presses, 1970; National Council on the Arts Award, 1970, for *Swallow the Lake;* Pushcart Prize certificate, 1976, for poem "Funeral," from *The Syncopated Cakewalk;* Fulbright-Hays Inter-University Exchange Award, Franco-American Commission for Education Exchange, Paris, France, 1981-83; Western States Book Award for fiction, 1986, for *My Amputations; New York Times Book Review* notable book of the year citation, 1988, for *Painted Turtle: Woman with Guitar; Los Angeles Times* Book Critic Award nomination, 1990, for *Fun and Games.*

*WRITINGS:*

*POETRY*

*Love Poems of a Black Man,* Coercion, 1965.
*Human Juices,* Coercion, 1966.
*Swallow the Lake,* Wesleyan University Press, 1970.
*Symptoms and Madness,* Corinth Books, 1971.
*Private Line,* Paul Breman Ltd., 1971.
*The Cotton Club,* Broadside Press, 1972.
*The Syncopated Cakewalk,* Barlenmir, 1974.
*Inside Diameter: The France Poems,* Permanent Press, 1985.
*Surfaces and Masks,* Coffee House Press, 1987.
*Some Observations of a Stranger in the Latter Part of the Century,* Sun and Moon, 1988.
*Parking Lots,* Perishable Press, 1992.

Also author of *Un Poco Loco: New and Selected Poems,* forthcoming. Contributor of poetry to numerous periodicals, including *American Poetry Review, Kenyon Review, Michigan Quarterly Review, Folger Poetry Broadside, Poetry Miscellany, Unmuzzled Ox, Yardbird Reader,* and *Black Orpheus* (Nigeria).

### NOVELS

*All-Night Visitors,* Olympia, 1969.
*No,* Emerson Hall, 1973.
*Reflex and Bone Structure,* Fiction Collective, 1975.
*Emergency Exit,* Fiction Collective, 1979.
*My Amputations,* Fiction Collective, 1986.
*Such Was the Season* (Literary Guild selection), Mercury House, 1987.
*Painted Turtle: Woman with Guitar,* Sun & Moon, 1988.

### SHORT STORIES

*Fun & Games,* Holy Cow! Press, 1990.

Also author of *Scat and Other Stories,* 1993. Contributor of short fiction to periodicals, including *Massachusetts Review, Essence, Zyzzyva, Witness, Boulevard, Fiction, Chelsea, Baltimore Sun, Black Scholar, Black American Literature Forum, Agni Review, Seattle Review, Hambone,* and *Callaloo.*

### CONTRIBUTOR TO ANTHOLOGIES

*19 Necromancers from Now* (fiction), Doubleday, 1970.
*Black on Black* (fiction), Bantam, 1972.
*Penguin Book of Black Verse,* Penguin, 1972.
*Black Spirits* (poetry), Random House, 1972.
*From the Belly of the Shark* (nonfiction), Random House, 1973.
*The Pushcart Prize: The Best of the Small Presses,* Pushcart Press, 1976.

Work also represented in *Ten Times Black; Writing under Fire: Stories of the Vietnam War; Norton Anthology of Postmodern Poetry in America: 1950s to the Present; Norton Anthology: Men of Our Time, Male Poetry in Contemporary America; Dynamics of Violence; Mirrors; Words on the Page,* and more than thirty other anthologies.

### NONFICTION

*Dictionary of Afro-American Slang,* International Publications, 1970 (published in England as *Black Slang: A Dictionary of Afro-American Talk,* Routledge & Kegan Paul, 1971).
*The Dark and Feeling: Black American Writers and Their Work* (essays), Third Press, 1974.
*Juba to Jive: Dictionary of African American Slang,* Viking Penguin, forthcoming.

Also author of *Afterthoughts: Selected Essays and Reviews,* forthcoming. Contributor of articles, essays, reviews, and other nonfiction prose to numerous periodicals, including *New York Times Book Review, Washington Post Book World, Los Angeles Times Book Review, American Poetry Review, Epoch, American Book Review, John O'Hara Journal, Essence, Negro Digest, Black Scholar, Journal of Black Studies and Research,* and *Black Orpheus* (Nigeria).

### EDITOR

*Writers Workshop Anthology,* Harlem Education Program, 1967.
*Man Is like a Child: An Anthology of Creative Writing by Students,* Macomb Junior High School, 1968.
(And author of introduction) *The New Black Poetry,* International Publications, 1969.
Jerry Bumpus, *Things in Place* (short stories), Fiction Collective, 1975.
*Calling the Wind: Twentieth-Century African-American Short Stories* (Book-of-the-Month Club selection), HarperCollins/Burlingame, 1992.

### OTHER

Also author of *The Fires That Burn in Heaven,* 1954. Columnist, *American Poetry Review,* 1973-76. Distinguished Contributing Editor, *The Pushcart Prize: The Best of the Small Presses,* 1977—. Author of television script, "Africa Speaks to New York," 1970. Contributor of fiction, nonfiction, and poetry to numerous periodicals in the United States, Mexico, Africa, India, Canada, Europe, Russia, and Australia; staff writer, *Proof,* 1960-61. Editor, *Coercion Review,* 1958-66; *American Book Review,* editor, 1977-78, associate editor, 1978—; associate editor, *Caw,* 1967-70, *Journal of Black Poetry,* 1967-70, *Bopp,* 1977-78, *Gumbo,* 1978, *Departures,* 1979, and *par rapport,* 1979—; contributing editor, *American Poetry Review,* 1976—, and *Dark Waters,* 1977. Member of board of directors, *What's Happening* magazine, Columbia University, 1969; member of editorial board, *Umojo: A Scholarly Journal of Black Studies,* 1979; committee member, *Signes,* 1983—; fiction editor, *High Plains Literary Review,* 1986—.

*All-Night Visitors* has been translated into Italian and German; *Reflex and Bone Structure* has been translated into French; *Such Was the Season* has been translated into German.

*SIDELIGHTS:* American writer Clarence Major "has been in the forefront of experimental poetry and prose," Eugene B. Redmond writes in *Parnassus.* "In prose he fits 'loosely' into a category with William Melvin Kelley and Ishmael Reed. But his influences and antecedents are not so easy to identify." Best known for his novels—like *All-Night Visitors, Reflex and Bone Structure, No,* and *Emergency Exit*—the author draws on his experience as a Southern Black American to "[defy] the white-imposed 'traditions' of black literature [and] to develop a brilliant lyricism in new forms of fiction," states Jerome Klinkowitz in his book *The Life of Fiction.* But Major's art, continues Klinkowitz, "inevitably turns back to the basic social and personal concerns which must remain at the heart of any literary experience." Noting the high incidence of violent scenes in Major's work, *Black Creation* critic Jim Walker comments, "Major has filled *No* with the violence we expect of Southern life; violence of whites against Blacks, and more unfortunately, violence of Blacks against Blacks.... But the point Major is obviously trying to make with these kinds of scenes is that violence is an integral part of life for Southern Blacks and moreover, that it helps shape their lives and attitudes."

But it is the writer's innovative use of language that has brought him the most critical attention. As Klinkowitz notes, "By focusing on language, Major has found a way to treat a recognizable subject matter without having it turn into a stereotyped notion of the documentary world. He creates the flavor and tone of everyday black speech not by mimicking dialect, but by using his syntax to suggest the rhythm of the spoken word. He is less interested in external characters than in the imaginations he creates for them, which we are never allowed to forget are projections of the author's own mind. In his novels, the fictional experience is often suspended on images rather than dependent upon narrative drive."

In *Reflex and Bone Structure,* for example, "Major slips deliberately surreal images into otherwise realistic scenes (a rubber plant dries the dishes, the TV slushes back and forth), reminding the reader that for all the comfortable associations with reality this is still an artificially constructed work," Klinkowitz notes in *The Practice of Fiction in America: Writers from Hawthorne to the Present.* Similarly, although the novel *Emergency Exit* presents a conventional story line, "Major has found several ways to keep the story from turning into social realism," Klinkowitz observes. "As in *Reflex,* images are culled from American popular culture—movies, records, and folk mores.... A mood emerges from them quite independently of the narrative story line, and as a result that story line becomes less important to the reader. Attention has been focused on the writing and the words."

Critics again praise Major's unique use of language in *My Amputations: A Novel,* the winner of the Western States Book Award in 1986. On the narrative level, it shows how easily the well-read parolee Mason Ellis impersonates a black novelist named Clarence McKay, whom he has taken hostage. McKay's literary agent plays along, and almost no one who meets the imposter on his world-wide lecture tour can tell the difference between Mason and the author whose identity he has usurped. "Major has fashioned a parable of the black writer as the most invisible and misrepresented of us all," notes Greg Tate in a *Washington Post* review. *New York Times Book Review* contributor Richard Perry finds *My Amputations* "a book in which the question of identity throbs like an infected tooth, ... a picaresque novel that comes wailing out of the blues tradition: it is ironic, irreverent, sexy, on a first-name basis with the human condition, and defined in part by exaggeration and laughter." In a *Nation* review, Stuart Klawans writes, "Mere description cannot convey the wild humor and audacity to be found here, nor the anxiety and cunning.... The novel is supersaturated with names, allusions, quotations.... When a writer loads a book with so many references, the reader is entitled to ask whether he knows what he's doing. Believe me, Clarence Major knows. He has fashioned a novel that is simultaneously a deception and one great, roaring self-revelation." Tate comments, "Major feels particular ardor for mixing the rhythms of American slang with those of historical, scientific, mythological and occult texts. He turns these combinations into marvelously florid passages, creating a homemade mythos full of mirth and mystery.... The integration of such alchemical language into the mundane human affairs of its subjects is part of what makes *My Amputations* such a provocative advance in contemporary American writing. This novel should do much to make the name of Clarence Major a byword among aficionados of adventurous fiction everywhere."

*Such Was the Season* is "more structured and accessible" than Major's earlier novels, writes David Nicholson in the *Washington Post Book World.* To Nicholson, it "seems rooted in Major's experience, and much of the book's success has to do with the warmth of the central character.... Annie Eliza ... speaks to us for more than 200 pages of things past and present in a voice that is always uniquely hers." In this matriarch of a black middle-class Atlanta family who speaks an authentic vernacular, "Major has created a delightfully lifelike, storytelling woman whose candor is matched only by her devotion to truth and her down-to-earth yea-saying to life," Al Young writes in the *New York Times Book Review.* "It is as if Clarence Major, the avid *avant-gardiste,* has himself come home to touch base with the blues and spirituals that continue to nourish and express the lives of those people he writes about so knowingly, and with contagious affection."

*Such Was the Season,* Young summarizes, is a "straight-ahead narrative crammed with action, a dramatic storyline and meaty characterization." In the one week described by Annie Eliza, several scandals touching family members erupt in the wake of her daughter-in-law's candidacy for the State Senate. Even so, "the book's pleasures have less to do with what happens and more with Annie Eliza and her tale," Nicholson maintains; details that belong more to fantasy than to reality, and the matriarch's frequent digressions from the story line, draw attention to the storyteller's craft and away from the plot. Therefore, he writes, "Though at first glance Major seems to have abandoned his postmodern explorations, *Such Was the Season* actually has much in common with those earlier works."

In *Fun & Games*, Major's 1990 collection of short "fictions," the author continues to bend and twist social realism around experimental narratives and prose. Writing in the *New York Times Book Review*, Karen Brailsford takes note of Major's "eloquent" prose, but finds that his "plots are frequently pointless, and ultimately disappointing." But while commenting that some of the stories in *Fun & Games* lack "the thematic and technical complexities that are Major's trademark," Maurice Bennett asserts in *Washington Post Book World* that Major "is still here doing what he has done for the past 25 years: producing some of the very best experimental fiction." He adds, "Major remains at heart the poet he was at the beginning of his career, importing into his fictions a poetic fascination with the 'word' and its power to create realities, whether they be realities of identity, relationship, or phenomena." Merle Rubin, writing in *Los Angeles Times Book Review*, suggests that Major uses the "realist mode" to comment on the way we construct reality. "In Major's hands, straightforward realism has a way of wandering off into the labyrinths of literary self-awareness.... Major's 'short fictions' remind us that reality is not simply something out there: Ours, as he puts it, is a 'man-made world,' influenced by our ability to reflect, re-imagine, re-interpret and reform it."

"When he is at his best," Doug Bolling remarks in the *Black American Literature Forum*, "Major helps us to see that fiction created within an aesthetic of fluidity and denial of 'closure' and verbal freedom can generate an excitement and awareness of great value; that the rigidities of plot, characterization, and illusioned depth can be softened and, finally, dropped in favor of new and valid rhythms. Spaces and times need no longer conform to the abstract demands either of plot or symbolic urgency, for example, but can be free to float in their own energies." Commenting on the author's place in the history of fiction, Klinkowitz concludes in *The Practice of Fiction in America,* "Major's innovations have made a fully nonrepresentational fiction possible. Such a radical aesthetic makes for an entirely new kind of fiction, much as visual art was reinvented by the cubists in the first decade of this century." It also asks for more alert and active readers, Bolling thinks. "His way and that of other postmodern writers can help us realize all over again that the activity of 'reading' is a highly conditioned one, too often a matter of the learned response rather than an engagement of the free and open mind. Thus, time spent with the fictions can be both a trip into the richness and surprise of words and their relationships and a way of redefining the self."

*BIOGRAPHICAL/CRITICAL SOURCES:*

*BOOKS*

Bell, Bernard W., *The Afro-American Novel and Its Tradition,* University of Massachusetts Press, 1987.

*Blacks in America: Bibliographical Essays,* Doubleday, 1971.

Byerman, Keith E., *Fingering the Jogged Grain: Tradition and Form in Recent Black Fiction,* University of Georgia Press, 1985.

Chapman, A., editor, *New Black Voices: An Anthology of Contemporary Afro-American Literature,* New American Library, 1972.

*Contemporary Authors Autobiography Series,* Volume 6, Gale, 1988.

*Contemporary Literary Criticism,* Gale, Volume 3, 1975, Volume 19, 1981.

*Critical Survey of Short Fiction: Current Writers,* Salem Press, 1981.

*Dictionary of Literary Biography,* Volume 33: *Afro-American Writers since 1955,* Gale, 1984.

Dillard, J. L., *Lexicon of Black English,* Seabury Press, 1977.

*Finding the Words: Conversations with Writers Who Teach,* Ohio University Press, 1984.

Henderson, Bill, editor, *Pushcart Prize: The Best of the Small Presses, 1976-77,* Pushcart Press, 1976.

Hoffman, Daniel, editor, *The Harvard Guide to Contemporary American Writing,* Harvard University Press, 1979.

Johnson, Charles, *Being and Race,* Indiana University Press, 1988.

Kiernan, Robert F., *American Writing since 1945: A Critical Survey,* Ungar, 1983.

Klinkowitz, Jerome, *The Life of Fiction,* University of Illinois Press, 1977.

Klinkowitz, Jerome, *The Practice of Fiction in America: Writers from Hawthorne to the Present,* Iowa State University Press, 1980.

Klinkowitz, Jerome, *Literary Disruptions: The Making of a Post-Contemporary American Fiction,* revised edition, University of Illinois, 1980.

Major, Clarence, *The Dark and Feeling: Black American Writers and Their Work,* Third Press, 1974.

O'Brien, John, *Interviews with Black Writers,* Liveright, 1973.

Redmond, Eugene B., *Drumvoices: The Mission of Afro-American Poetry—A Critical History,* Anchor/Doubleday, 1976.

Shapiro, Nancy and Ron Padgett, editors, *The Point: Where Teaching and Writing Intersect,* Teachers and Writers, 1983.

Wepman, Dennis, and others, *The Life: The Lore and Folk Poetry of the Black Hustler,* University of Pennsylvania Press, 1976.

Williams, Sherley Anne, *Give Birth to Brightness: A Thematic Study in Neo-Black Literature,* Dial, 1972.

*World Literature since 1945: Critical Surveys of the Contemporary Literatures of Europe and the Americas,* Ungar, 1973.

PERIODICALS

*American Anthropologist,* June, 1975.
*American Book Review,* September/October, 1982; September, 1986.
*Best Sellers,* June 1, 1973.
*Black American Literature Forum,* Number 12, 1978; Volume 12, number 2, 1979; fall, 1983.
*Black Creation,* summer, 1973.
*Black Scholar,* January, 1971.
*Chicago Sun-Times,* April 28, 1974.
*Chicago Tribune,* October 6, 1986.
*Cleveland Plain Dealer,* December 3, 1987.
*Essence,* November, 1970.
*Greenfield Review,* winter, 1971.
*Los Angeles Times Book Review,* February 18, 1990.
*Ms.,* July, 1977.
*Nation,* January 24, 1987.
*Negro Digest,* December, 1969.
*Newsday,* November 1, 1987.
*New York Times,* April 7, 1969.
*New York Times Book Review,* February 13, 1972; July 1, 1973; November 30, 1975; September 28, 1986; December 13, 1987; May 20, 1990.
*Obsidian,* Volume 4, number 2, 1978.
*Parnassus,* spring/summer, 1975.
*par rapport,* Volume 2, number 1, 1979.
*Penthouse,* February, 1971.
*Phylon,* winter, 1972.
*Poetry,* August, 1971.
*Publishers Weekly,* March 24, 1969; March 19, 1973; May 9, 1986; July 4, 1986; July 31, 1987.
*Quarterly Journal of Speech,* April, 1977.
*San Francisco Review of Books,* Volume 1, number 12, 1976; Volume 7, number 3, 1982.
*Saturday Review,* December 5, 1970; April 3, 1971.
*Tribune Books* (Chicago), October 6, 1986.
*Virginia Quarterly Review,* winter, 1971.
*Voice Literary Supplement,* February, 1987.
*Washington Post Book World,* September, 13, 1986; January 10, 1988; February 18, 1990.

\*   \*   \*

## MAKUMI, Joel 1945(?)-

*PERSONAL:* Born c. 1945 in Kenya; educated in local schools.

*WRITINGS:*

*The Children of the Forest* (novelette), Macmillan, 1961.
*The Feather in the Lake and Other Stories* (includes "The Feather in the Lake," "The Greedy Lover," "Mburumbu the Monster," and "Muriria and Wamwitha"), illustrated by Beryl Moore, East African Publishing House, 1969.
*End of the Beginning* (novel), East African Publishing House, 1970.

\*   \*   \*

## MANAKA, Matsemela 1956-

*PERSONAL:* Born, June 20, 1956, in Alexandra Township, South Africa; son of Gilbert and Nelly Manaka; married in 1984; wife's name, Nomsa; children: Maakomela, Mthutezeli.

*ADDRESSES: Home*—Soweto, South Africa. *Office*—Ekhaya Soweto Museum, 973 Phase 3, Diepkloof 1864, Soweto, South Africa. *Agent*—c/o PEN, 568 Broadway, fourth floor, New York, NY 10012.

*CAREER:* Writer, artist, director, producer, and performer. Worked as a teacher at Madibane High School, Ithuteng Commercial College, Madibane Adult Education, Masisizane Community College for Secretarial Practice; Soyikwa Institute of African Theatre, Soweto, South Africa, founder and teacher; Funda Arts Centre, Soweto, acting and directing teacher. Director of stage productions, including *Shaka: An Excerpt from Ogun Abibman,* written by Wole Soyinka, 1980, *Dark Voices,* written by Zakes Mda, 1984, *Buwa,* written by Caiphus Semenya, 1986-88, and *Nkosi: The Healing Song,* written by Mothobi Mutloatse, 1992; producer of stage productions, including *eGoli* and *Blues Afrika Cafe.* Artwork presented in numerous exhibitions in South Africa and Europe, 1978-1992, including shows at Commonwealth Institute, London, England, 1981, Alliance Francaise, Cape Town, South Africa, 1984, and Berman Gallery, Johannesburg, South Africa, 1992. Ekhaya Soweto Neighborhood Museum, Soweto, founder and curator. Affiliated with Raven Press.

*AWARDS, HONORS:* Freedom-to-Write Award, PEN, 1987; Edinburgh Fringe First Award for productions of *Pula* and *Imbumba.*

*WRITINGS:*

*PLAYS*

(Coauthor with members of Creative Youth Association) *The Horn,* produced in South Africa, 1977.

*eGoli* (title means "City of Gold"), produced in South Africa, 1978.

*Blues Afrika,* produced in West Germany, 1980.

*Pula* (title means "Rain"), produced in South Africa, 1982, produced in London, 1984.

*Imbumba,* produced in London, 1984.

*Children of Asazi* (one-act), produced Off-Broadway, 1986.

(And director) *Domba, the Last Dance,* produced in South Africa, 1986.

(With Motsumi Makhene and Peter Boroko) *Goree* (musical; book by Manaka; music by Manaka, Makhene, and Boroko), produced in New York City, 1989.

Also author and director of *Vuka,* 1981, *Toro the African Dream,* 1987, *Blues Afrika Cafe,* 1990, *Ekhaya Museum of Soweto,* 1991, and *Yamina,* 1993.

OTHER

Coauthor, with Ratshaka Ratshitanga, Mark Newman, and Eddie Wes, of the film screenplay *Two Rivers;* author of the screenplay *Kiba: The Beat Between.* Editor of *Staffrider,* 1979-82.

*SIDELIGHTS:* Matsemela Manaka is a leading black playwright in South Africa. Long associated with the Soyikwa Institute of African Theatre in Soweto, Manaka is known for his Afrocentric—and sometimes controversial—works, which he has successfully presented at home despite South Africa's racist apartheid policy. Manaka began as a playwright in the late 1970s with such productions as *The Horn, Imbumba,* and *eGoli* (which means "City of Gold," a reference to Johannesburg). He discussed his creative philosophy in an interview with T. Philemon Wakashe in *Drama Review:* "Serious theatre in South Africa has to have an effect on black people. It has to stop simply describing. People say I'm changing, that my plays are no longer as radical as before. No, I say, my plays are now focusing on human experience.... I am examining the conflict of the South African experience, a human experience that is not limited to me as a black South African."

In 1984 the Soyikwa company presented *Imbumba* with another Manaka play, *Pula* (the title means "Rain"), as a double bill in London. *Imbumba* concerns life on a prison farm. *Pula* uses song, dance, and mime to tell the story of a young black and his experiences in Johannesburg. Anthony Masters, writing in the London *Times,* found himself in "awe at the pain and anger" expressed by the performers in the production.

Manaka's *Children of Asazi* was presented in New York City in 1986 as part of a festival called "Woza Africa!" (which means "Arise Africa!"). Like many of Manaka's plays, *Children of Asazi* incorporates chanting and other ethnic devices. This play, a love story set against the South African govern-

ment's destruction of a black community, is written, according to the *New York Times*'s Mel Gussow, "with a kind of homely poetry." Gussow found the festival production was "performed with a forthright sincerity."

Among Manaka's other plays produced in the United States is *Goree,* which was presented in New York City in 1989. This work, a musical, concerns a girl who embarks to find a women renowned as Africa's finest singer and dancer. When the girl becomes stranded on Goree, an island, she befriends a woman who, in turn, teaches her to sing and dance. *New York Times* reviewer Wilborn Hampton found the work juvenile but "entertaining."

Manaka commented: "For me, theatre as a totality of the arts has become a way of life. It is a ritual without which my life would be empty. It is a ritual from which we derive the comfort and hope that one day the wounds of our people will be healed. As a writer, I see myself as a custodian of the past for the future. We are historians, educators, and liberators. As the saying goes—'a book is a universe.' We are engaged in the universal dialogue to bring an end to human suffering and let peace prevail."

*BIOGRAPHICAL/CRITICAL SOURCES:*

*PERIODICALS*

*Drama Review,* winter, 1986, pp. 48-50.
*New York Times,* August 31, 1986; September 26, 1986; October 5, 1986.
*Times* (London), March 15, 1984; September 24, 1989.

\*    \*    \*

## MANDELA, Nelson R(olihlahla) 1918-

*PERSONAL:* Born 1918 in Umtata, Transkei, South Africa; son of Henry Mandela (a Tembu tribal chief); married Edith Ntoko (a nurse; divorced); married Nomzamo Winnie Madikileza (a social worker and political activist), June 14, 1958; children: (first marriage) Makgatho, Thembi (deceased), Makaziwe Phumla Mandela; (second marriage) Zenani (married to Prince Thumbumuzi Dhlamini of Swaziland), Zindziswa. *Education:* Attended University College of Fort Hare and Witwatersrand University; University of South Africa, law degree, 1942.

*ADDRESSES: Office*—c/o African National Congress of South Africa, 801 Second Avenue, New York, NY 10017.

*CAREER:* Mandela and Tambo law firm, Johannesburg, South Africa, partner, 1952- c. 1960; political organizer and leader of the African National Congress (ANC), Johannesburg, South Africa, 1944—, held successive posts as secretary and president of the Congress Youth League, deputy national president of the ANC, and commander of the Umkonto we Sizwe ("Spear of the Nation") paramilitary organization; sentenced to five years in prison for inciting Africans to strike and for leaving South Africa without a valid travel document, 1962; sentenced to life imprisonment for sabotage and treason, 1964; incarcerated in various penal institutions, including Robben Island and Pollsmoor prisons, South Africa, 1962-90. President of African National Congress, 1991—.

*AWARDS, HONORS:* Honorary doctor of laws degrees from the National University of Lesotho, 1979, and City College of the City University of New York, 1983; Jawaharlal Nehru Award for International Understanding from the government of India, 1980; Bruno Kreisky Prize for Human Rights from the government of Austria, 1981; named honorary citizen of Glasgow, 1981, and Rome, 1983; Simon Bolivar International Prize from UNESCO, 1983; nominated for 1987 Nobel Peace Prize; human rights award, American Jewish Committee, 1993.

*WRITINGS:*

NONFICTION

*No Easy Walk to Freedom,* Basic Books, 1965.
*Nelson Mandela Speaks,* African National Congress Publicity and Information Bureau (London), c. 1970.
*The Struggle Is My Life,* International Defence and Aid Fund (London), 1978, revised and updated edition, Pathfinder Press, 1986, further revised and updated edition published as *Nelson Mandela: The Struggle Is My Life: His Speeches and Writings Brought Together with Historical Documents and Accounts of Mandela in Prison by Fellow-prisoners,* International Defence and Aid Fund, 1990.
*Nelson Mandela, Symbol of Resistance and Hope for a Free South Africa: Selected Speeches Since His Release,* edited by E. S. Reddy, Sterling, 1990.
*Nelson Mandela, Speeches 1990: "Intensify the Struggle to Abolish Apartheid,"* edited by Greg McCartan, photographs by Margrethe Siem, Pathfinder Press, 1990.
(With Fidel Castro) *How Far We Slaves Have Come! South Africa and Cuba in Today's World,* Pathfinder Press, 1991.

OTHER

Contributor of articles to the South African political journal *Liberation,* 1953-59; author of introduction to *Oliver Tambo Speaks: Preparing for Power,* Braziller, 1988.

*SIDELIGHTS:* Nelson Mandela has been called both "the world's most famous political prisoner" and "South Africa's Great Black Hope" by journalist Tom Mathews in *Newsweek.* A leader of the banned African National Congress insurgent movement during the 1950s and 1960s, Mandela had been jailed by white governments for a quarter of a century for his efforts to enfranchise his fellow blacks. Through his leadership and personal sacrifices, Mandela has come to symbolize the struggle against apartheid, the system of enforced racial inequality that denied political rights to the country's black majority. Mandela's release from prison in February of 1990, was followed by a triumphant world tour that included eight major cities in the United States. Strong admiration for the former political prisoner provided a common bond for many Americans who were at odds over how to defeat racial injustice. "No leader since the Rev. Martin Luther King, Jr., has brought together such a diverse coalition in the fight against racial injustice," noted a writer for *Time.*

Upon his release, Mandela commended his wife, Winnie, for her steadfast support during his long confinement. Carrying her husband's political torch, she endured repeated jailings, banishment and house arrest to emerge as a formidable leader in her own right. Although Winnie's disputed involvement with the kidnappings, assaults and murder perpetrated by her bodyguards has tarnished her image as "Mother of the Nation," her husband has lost none of his political charisma. Since his release from prison, Mandela has been engaged in negotiations on behalf of the ANC with South African president F. W. de Klerk over a settlement of power that would result in democratic-styled elections. Among the challenges endangering Mandela's efforts, however, are a bloody feud between the Zulu organization Inkatha and the ANC over who speaks for black South Africans, and threats from the South African right wing, which vows to take up arms if the ANC comes to power.

Both Nelson and Winnie Mandela are descended from Xhosa-speaking tribal chieftains from the Transkei region of South Africa. Mandela left his ancestral home at a young age to avoid an arranged marriage and pursue a professional career in the commercial capital of Johannesburg. Obtaining his law degree from the University of South Africa in 1942, Mandela joined the ANC two years later at the age of twenty-six and helped found the Congress Youth League (CYL) with Walter Sisulu, Oliver Tambo, and others. With Mandela as its secretary, the CYL urged its parent organization, the ANC, to abandon the strictly constitutional approach to reform that it had fruitlessly pursued with successive white minority governments since its founding in 1912 in favor of a more militant and confrontational strategy.

Under strong youth pressure, the ANC adopted a new program of action in 1949 that recognized such nonviolent—but sometimes illegal—tactics as electoral boycotts, "stay-at-homes" (general strikes), student demonstrations, and civil disobedience. In June of 1952, Mandela mounted the first major test of the new ANC program by organizing the Defiance Against Unjust Laws campaign, a coordinated civil disobedience of six selected apartheid laws by a multiracial group of some 8,600 volunteers. The government's violent response to the Defiance Campaign generated a backlash of popular support for the ANC that helped thrust Mandela to national prominence; it also brought him a nine-month suspended jail sentence, a two-year government "banning" order that confined him to Johannesburg and prohibited him from attending public gatherings, and an order to resign his ANC leadership posts as deputy president of the national organization, president of the Transvaal branch, and president of the CYL. Mandela refused to do so, and as a result he was obliged to conduct most of his political organizing work under the cover of his Johannesburg law partnership with Oliver Tambo and to limit his public profile to writing articles for the pro-ANC journal *Liberation.*

In December of 1956, following a year of ANC-led mass protests against the Nationalists' proposal to create seven tiny tribal "homelands" in which to segregate South Africa's black population, the government brought charges against Mandela and 155 other anti-apartheid leaders under anti-Communist and treason statutes. During most of the four-and-one-half years that the "Treason Trial" lasted, Mandela remained free on bail, continuing to work at his law office during the evenings and discreetly engage in political activities within the limitations of a new five-year banning order leveled on him in February of 1956.

In March of 1960, an action occurred that marked a historical watershed in the struggle for black rights in South Africa. Responding to a demonstration against "pass laws," which required black South Africans to carry government identification documents, the police in the Johannesburg suburb of Sharpeville turned their weapons on a group of unarmed protesters, killing 69 people. The massacre sparked a wave of angry new protests and public pass-book burnings, to which Pretoria responded by declaring a state of national emergency. The government banned the ANC and PAC, and detained some 1,800 political activists without charges, including Mandela and the other "Treason Trial" defendants. This crackdown prompted the trial lawyers to withdraw from the case, declaring that the emergency restrictions prevented them from mounting an effective defense, and left Mandela, Duma Nokwe, Walter Sisulu, and several others to represent their sizable group of ANC leaders.

As an advocate for his group, Mandela distinguished himself with his legal ability and eloquent statements of the ANC's political and social philosophy. He defended the 1949 Programme of Action and the Defiance Campaign as necessary disruptive tactics when the government was indifferent to legal pressure; he also sought to assuage white fears of a black political takeover by insisting that the ANC's form of nationalism recognized the right of all South African racial groups to enjoy political freedom and nondiscrimination together in the same country. In a unique legal victory for South African black activists, the trial judge acquitted all the defendants for insufficient evidence in March of 1961, finding that the ANC did not have a policy of violence.

Immediately after his release, Mandela went underground to avoid new government banning orders. He surfaced in late March to deliver the keynote speech at the All-In African Conference held in Pietermaritzburg, which had been organized by the ANC and other opposition political organizations to address the Nationalists' plan to declare a racialist South African republic in May of that year. The All-In Conference opposed this proposal with a demand that the government hold elections for a fully representative national convention empowered to draft a new and democratic constitution for all South Africans. Meeting no response to the assembly's demands from the H. F. Verwoerd government, Mandela helped organize a three-day general strike for the end of May to press for the convention. Verwoerd's security forces mobilized heavily against the strike by suspending civil liberties, making massive preemptive arrests, and deploying heavy military equipment, which succeeded in limiting public support for the action, although hundreds of thousands of Africans nationwide still stayed away from work.

Facing arrest, Mandela once again disappeared underground, this time for 17 months, assuming numerous disguises in a cat-and-mouse game with the police during which he became popularly known as the "Black Pimpernel." The ANC leader was finally captured disguised as a chauffeur in the province of Natal by police acting on an informer's tip in August, 1962. Brought to trial in October on charges of inciting Africans to strike and on leaving the country without a valid travel document, Mandela turned his defense into an indictment of the apartheid system. In an eloquent statement to the presiding judge, the ANC leader rejected the right of the court to hear the case on the grounds that—as a black man—he could not be given a fair trial under a judicial system intended to enforce white domination, and furthermore, he considered himself neither legally nor morally bound to obey laws created by a parliament in which he had no representation. Despite his impressive courtroom performance, Mandela was convicted of both charges and sentenced to five years in prison.

Unknown to the authorities at the time of his trial, Mandela and other ANC leaders had reluctantly decided to launch an underground paramilitary movement in 1961 for the first time in the ANC's history. In November of 1961, Mandela helped organize and assumed command of the Umkonto we Sizwe ("Spear of the Nation") guerrilla organization and began planning a sabotage campaign directed against government installations and the economic infrastructure. Umkonto's first military action occurred on December 16, 1961, when the organization simultaneously attacked government buildings in Johannesburg, Port Elizabeth, and Durban. The group went on to engage in many more acts of sabotage over the next year while Mandela traveled surreptitiously to England, Ethiopia, Algeria, and other African countries to meet political leaders, seek arms for the movement, and undergo military training.

Mandela's role in leading Umkonto came to light in June, 1963, when police raided the ANC's underground headquarters in the Johannesburg suburb of Rivonia and discovered documents relating to the armed movement. Nine top ANC leaders, including Mandela, were arrested and brought to trial in early 1964 on charges of committing sabotage and conspiring to overthrow the government by revolution with the help of foreign troops. Mandela once again conducted his own defense, using the courtroom as a platform to explain and justify the ANC's turn to armed struggle and to condemn the apartheid regime. Mandela declared at the trial, "It would be unrealistic and wrong for African leaders to continue preaching peace and non-violence at a time when the Government met our peaceful demands with force." He fully acknowledged helping to found Umkonto and planning acts of sabotage, but denied the government's contention that the ANC and Umkonto intended to subject the antiapartheid struggle to revolutionary control, either foreign or domestic.

While he acknowledged being strongly influenced by Marxist thought, Mandela denied ever having been a member of the Communist party, insisting that he held a deep and abiding admiration for Western legal and political institutions and wished to "borrow the best from both East and West" to reshape South African society. As elaborated in the ANC's Freedom Charter (a 1955 manifesto that Mandela helped to draft which remains the basic statement of the group's political purpose), the ANC looked forward to a democratic, pluralist society with certain mildly socialistic reforms—including land redistribution, nationalization of the country's mines, and a progressive tax and incomes policy—intended to dilute the economic power of the white race and raise the country's majority out of poverty.

Mandela's trial ended in June of 1964, when he and eight other defendants were convicted of sabotage and treason and sentenced to life imprisonment. Confined to the Robben Island fortress for political prisoners seven miles offshore from Cape Town, the ANC leaders were kept rigidly isolated from the outside world. They were denied access to radio, television, and newspapers, and prohibited from publishing articles, giving public interviews, or even discussing politics with visitors. All Mandela's past speeches and published works were banned, and merely possessing his writings in South Africa was made a criminal offense. Despite these restrictions, two book-length collections of Mandela's best known political statements were published abroad and have since circulated widely among South African anti-apartheid activists. *No Easy Walk to Freedom,* published in 1965, includes Mandela's 1953 presidential address to the Transvaal province ANC (in which he discusses the Defiance Campaign), his speech at the 1961 All-In African Conference, and excerpts from his testimony at his three political trials. A second collection, *The Struggle Is My Life,* contains material from 1944 to 1985, including four prison statements from Mandela; a revised 1986 edition of the title incorporates the memoirs of two of Mandela's fellow prisoners from Robben Island prison who had been released. Six speeches made by Mandela between February and May of 1990, during his first months of freedom, are collected in *Nelson Mandela, Speeches 1990: "Intensify the Struggle to Abolish Apartheid."* Published in 1990, the volume also includes Mandela's 1989 letter to South African president P. W. Botha stressing the need for negotiations between the government and the ANC.

Shortly after her husband's 1962 conviction, Winnie Mandela received her first government banning order restricting her to Johannesburg and preventing her from attending public or private meetings of any kind. In 1965, the government forced her out of her job with the Child Welfare Society by further restricting her to her home township of Orlando West and preventing her from engaging in essential fieldwork elsewhere in the Soweto district. She was then fired from a succession of low-paying jobs in the white commercial district after the security police pressured her employers, and she finally found herself reduced to supporting her two young daughters on the charity of friends and political associates. Despite this hardship, Winnie Mandela continued to work surreptitiously with the ANC during the 1960s by helping produce banned political pamphlets and newsletters in her home. During this period, the suspicious police ransacked the Mandela house repeatedly, but prosecutors could never find enough evidence to bring a court case against her. In May, 1969, however, Winnie Mandela was arrested with other suspected ANC sympathizers under a new law that allowed the government to detain "terrorist" suspects indefinitely without charges. Taken to Pretoria Prison, she was interrogated virtually nonstop for five days and nights about her supposed links to ANC saboteurs. She was then jailed without charges for 17 months, spending the first 200 days of this period incommunicado and in solitary confinement. Finally, under pressure from Nelson Mandela's lawyers, the authorities improved Winnie's confinement conditions and brought her to trial on 21 political charges in September of 1970. The trial judge dismissed the case against her and all but one of her co-defendants for in- sufficient evidence, and Winnie Mandela was released that month.

Though freed from prison, Winnie Mandela was still subjected to close police vigilance in the early 1970s as South Africa's white minority government reacted to new challenges from a growing world anti-apartheid movement and the anti-colonial wars in nearby Mozambique and Angola. Immediately upon her release, she was placed under a new five-year banning order that confined her to her home during the evenings and on weekends. She was subjected to frequent police home searches in ensuing years and was arrested and sentenced to six months in prison for talking to another banned person in 1974. The authorities eventually allowed her banning order to expire in October of 1975, and over the next ten months she was able to enjoy the rights of free association and move- ment for the first time in many years.

This period of relative freedom for Winnie Mandela coincided with the birth of a militant "Black Consciousness" youth movement led by Stephen Biko and other students in Soweto. The student revolt had as its immediate aim the annulment of the Bantu Education Act, which consigned blacks to inferior education and obliged them to learn Afrikaans, the language of South African whites of Dutch descent, instead of English. When police shot down a number of unarmed demonstrators in Soweto in June of 1976, however, the township's youth erupted in a fury of uncontrolled rioting and clashes with the security forces that left at least six hundred people dead. Many of the participants in the Soweto uprising who escaped being killed or imprisoned fled the country and made contact with ANC exile headquarters in Lusaka, Zambia. This militant young cadre helped to radicalize the Congress and substan- tially strengthen its military wing, allowing the ANC to rees- tablish both a political and military presence inside South Africa by the end of the decade.

The ebb in the popular struggle after the Soweto uprising lasted until 1984, when the townships exploded again over the adop- tion of a new South African constitution that gave parliamen- tary representation to "Coloureds" and Indians but not to blacks. The townships remained in a state of near-continuous political turmoil in succeeding years as anti-government youth clashed violently with the security forces and other blacks accused of collaborating with the regime. But, unlike the situ- ation a decade earlier, when the township civilians stood un- organized and alone against the apartheid government, a num- ber of powerful social and political forces joined the fray in the mid-1980s to mount the greatest challenge to white mi- nority rule in South African history. The United Democratic Front (UDF), a coalition of some 680 anti-apartheid organi- zations that supports the political line of the ANC, organized

large street demonstrations and protests by township squat- ters facing eviction that were harshly repressed by the gov- ernment in 1985. Meanwhile, the ANC itself stepped up its guerrilla campaign in South Africa and began targeting white residential areas and causing civilian casualties for the first time. The Nationalist government of P. W. Botha also came under mounting attack from abroad as the United States and other Western countries imposed limited trade and investment sanctions on South Africa in a bid to force reform. Finally, in 1987, the one-million-strong black trade union movement began to flex its powerful muscles with strikes by workers in the strategic transport and mining sectors.

A common demand voiced throughout the previous decade by the diverse forces seeking to change the apartheid system was that Mandela be released immediately. In 1985, Winnie Mandela managed to break her government restrictions and return to Soweto to join the fight for her husband's freedom (this turn of events occurred after her Brandfort house was firebombed and burned to the ground in August of that year while she was in Johannesburg for medical treatment). Ac- cusing the security police of the attack and saying that she feared for her life, Winnie Mandela insisted on moving back to her Soweto house; amid much local and international pub- licity, the Botha government permitted her to do so. In suc- ceeding months, she took advantage of the government's weakened position to openly flout her banning orders by giv- ing press interviews and speaking out militantly at public demonstrations and at the funerals of young township victims of government repression. Speaking at a funeral on a return visit to Brandfort in April of 1986, for example, she denounced the authorities as "terrorists" and called on blacks to take "di- rect action" against the government to free the imprisoned nationalist leaders. "The time has come where we must show that we are disciplined and trained warriors," she added in what some observers interpreted as a call to insurrection. In a bid to improve its international image and deflect criticism of a new state of emergency it had imposed the previous month, the Botha regime, in July of 1986, chose not to prosecute Winnie Mandela and instead lifted all banning restrictions on her. Among her first public actions once her right to free speech had been restored was to call for international economic sanctions against the apartheid government.

The Botha government met the current crisis with a "divide and rule" strategy combining harsh repression and isolated reforms that did not fundamentally alter the structure of apart- heid. While repealing such symbols of apartheid as pass laws and long-standing bans on interracial sex and marriage, the government violently crushed the township uprisings and detained tens of thousands of antiapartheid protestors with- out trial under sweeping state-of-emergency powers. Fearing the popular reaction if Mandela were to die in prison, previous South African governments sought to find a way to free him as early as 1973, but the confined ANC leader had always rejected conditions that he accept exile abroad or in the Transkei "homeland" and that he renounce violence by the insurgent organization. In late 1987, the Botha regime began hinting at the possibility that it might finally release Mandela unconditionally in an attempt to mollify domestic and international public opinion. The advisability of releasing the ANC leader in terms of domestic politics reportedly stimulated a heated debate in the Botha cabinet, with those in favor of the move arguing that Mandela was now more conservative than much of the current ANC leadership and could therefore effect a split in the organization. Detractors contended that freeing South Africa's best-known political prisoner could further alienate hard-line whites and possibly stimulate a black insurrection. Reform-minded South Africans, on the other hand, believed Mandela was the only political leader prestigious enough to win the confidence of both liberal whites and the increasingly alienated black township youth, thereby delivering the country from the specter of race war.

In November of 1987, the authorities unconditionally freed Mandela's long-time comrade-in-arms Govan Mbeki (a top ANC and South African Communist party leader who was convicted at the Rivonia Trial and served 24 years on Robben Island), as a way of testing the political waters for Mandela's possible release. In August of 1988, Mandela was diagnosed with tuberculosis, and the announcement prompted a new round of demands from the international community that he should be set free. The next year brought the release of Walter Sisulu—considered by some to be the second most important figure in South Africa's fight against apartheid—along with the rest of the Rivonia prisoners with the exception of Mandela himself. South African president F. W. de Klerk, who succeeded Botha in 1989, came into power on a reform platform; with these amnesties, de Klerk initiated the first conciliatory measures which soon included unconditional freedom for Mandela and the lifting of the ban on the ANC (the government had delayed Mandela's pardon with the stipulation that he formally renounce violence, but finally relented, granting his freedom February 11, 1990). De Klerk was quoted in *Time* as saying, "I came to the conclusion that [Mandela] is committed to a peaceful solution and a peaceful process." Bruce W. Nelan of *Time* suggested that de Klerk intended to demystify Mandela and the antiapartheid movement by setting its "spiritual leader" free: "By legalizing the ANC, [de Klerk] removes its cloak of underground heroism and turns it into an ordinary political party. Both Mandela and his organization will then be forced by circumstance and expectation to make compromises. And compromises are expected to anger and disillusion segments of the black majority, giving the government opportunities to divide the opposition." Nelan further conjectured that the South African president looked for the end of international sanctions against South Africa by

beginning talks with black leaders—and the longer the government dragged out negotiations, the more likely momentum behind the antiapartheid movement would falter.

Embarking on a 13-country tour in June and July of 1990, Mandela was received in the United States as, in the words of Nelan, a "heroic superstar." His mission, however, was political; he wanted both assurances from governments that sanctions would remain in place until South Africa was committed to peaceful change, and donations to revitalize the ANC. In New York City, people jammed the streets to catch a glimpse of Mandela passing by in a ticker-tape parade. Speaking at a crossroads in Harlem, Mandela told a crowd nearing 100,000, "I am here to claim you because ... you have claimed our struggle." Mandela also appeared at rallies in seven other American cities, including Boston, Miami, Detroit, and Los Angeles. In Washington, D.C., President George Bush—who, as vice-president under Ronald Reagan, fought against the Comprehensive Anti-Apartheid Act of 1986—agreed to keep economic sanctions in place, at least for the short term. "I want to find a way to show our appreciation to de Klerk, and yet I don't want to pull the rug out from under Mr. Mandela," Bush was reported as saying in *Time*.

Upon his return to South Africa, Mandela was faced with serious obstacles which threatened to disrupt any progress he made negotiating with the government. Bloody clashes between the ANC and its backers, and Inkatha, a Zulu organization of about 1.5 million members, had been flaring up since 1987 in Natal Province. Led by Chief Mangosuthu Buthelezi, who "opposes strikes, armed struggle and foreign sanctions against the country's white government," according to Jeffrey Bartholet in *Newsweek*, Inkatha had been targeting the United Democratic Front, an organization comprised of Zulus who support the ANC. While still in prison, Mandela had hoped for a reconciliation with Buthelezi, but his very release sparked two days of violence in Natal that killed fifty people. In March of 1990, Mandela agreed to hold a joint rally with Buthelezi in Durban, but cancelled out when the venue appeared too potentially explosive. Two weeks after the ANC announced an end to armed struggle against apartheid in August of 1990, a raid by Inkatha supporters on train passengers at Soweto's Inhlazane Station resulted in a wave of violence that spread to other townships around Johannesburg, leaving more than 200 people dead. Right-wing politicians exploited the turmoil, attempting to use the ethnic strife as proof of the unviability of a black South African government. "The rivalry plays on white fears that tribalism could rip apart a post-apartheid South Africa. While de Klerk's National Party ties its future to the ANC, the right-wing Conservative Party has seized on Buthelezi's demands for a role equal to Mandela's," commented Joseph Contreras in *Newsweek*. While de Klerk pressed Mandela to help quell the violence by meeting with Buthelezi, Mandela blamed Pretoria. "Under the noses of the police, Inkatha *impis* go places fully armed and attack and kill people," Mandela reportedly said.

Black-on-black violence continued unabated, with the ANC withdrawing from talks in May of 1991, after the government refused to outlaw tribal weapons carried by Inkatha party members. In the same month, Winnie Mandela was convicted of kidnapping and being an accessory to assault, and sentenced to six years in prison. The conviction stemmed from the actions of her bodyguards, who called themselves the Mandela United Football Club; although, as John Bierman reported in *Maclean's,* "they never played a single organized game of soccer." In 1988, members of the club kidnapped four black youths from a hostel. According to Bierman, "Evidence showed that [Winnie] Mandela's bodyguards took the victims to her Soweto home, where they tied them up and savagely beat them. One of the youths, 14-year-old James (Stompie) Moeketsi Seipei, was later found dead." Winnie Mandela denied any involvement in the crime, stating in court that she was in the Orange Free State—300 kilometers away—when it occurred; she has since appealed the decision. Mandela supported his wife throughout her trial. He appeared to observers to be devoted to the woman who supported him through the many years of his imprisonment with her visits and letters, who endured jail and police mistreatment on his behalf. "There have been moments when conscience and a sense of guilt have ravaged every part of my being," Mandela once wrote his wife, agonized by separation from his family.

Mandela insisted that the negative publicity surrounding his wife's court case had no effect on his negotiations with Pretoria. Although far from fully enfranchising the black population, the government did institute further reforms, including the repeal of the Population Registration Act in June of 1991, which required every South African baby to be documented by race. Although international response was positive, the South African government was far from eradicating apartheid; blacks still did not have the right to vote. Mandela, whom political experts considered outmaneuvered by de Klerk, had become increasingly cynical of the president, stating, "What he has done is merely to bring about changes which maintain the status quo."

The ANC addressed their setbacks at a national conference in Durban during July of 1991—the first such gathering in South Africa in thirty years. The party had been splitting between young radicals who favored a more militant approach toward immediate change, and older, conservative leaders who recommended negotiating gradually with the government. The Durban conference reaffirmed the moderate philosophy within the ANC by electing Mandela president, Walter Sisulu deputy president, and Cyril Ramaphosa secretary general. "This is an overwhelming victory for the moderates and a crushing blow

to the militants who were outpolled two-to-one," commented South African political expert Donald Simpson in *Maclean's.*

Mandela struggled to balance his group's objectives with assurances to white South Africans that the ANC did not wish to turn the country into a socialist state. "We would nationalize the mines, the banks and other monopolies, but the rest of the economy is based on private enterprise," Mandela informed *Newsweek* in an interview. "Not even the land is nationalized, which is normally the first sector of the economy which socialist [governments] nationalize."

A growing distrust of de Klerk among blacks soured into seething resentment in June of 1992, when about 200 Inkatha supporters rampaged through the township of Boipatong with guns, machetes and spears, killing at least 40 people. Witnesses claimed the Zulu attackers had been assisted by the police. Rejecting calls among militant members to reengage in armed struggle, ANC leaders instead displayed their frustration with the government's inability to control the violence—and the seeming insincerity within de Klerk's National Party in negotiating a new, nonracial constitution—by withdrawing from the talks. A campaign of mass-action (boycotts, strikes and sit-ins) was instituted while the ANC pressed Pretoria with a list of demands, including a full investigation of the Boipatong massacre.

Addressing a Pretoria rally of 70,000 peaceful marchers in August of 1992, Mandela responded to the crowd's calls of "De Klerk must go!" with a statement indicating the true purpose of the march: not to overthrow de Klerk, but to prompt him into faster action towards creating a democratic government. Mandela and de Klerk finally met on September 26, 1992, for the first time since May, agreeing to resume negotiations on the constitution and to accelerate efforts in forging an interim government. Several conditions laid down by the ANC for the resumption of talks were met by de Klerk, namely the erection of fences around single-sex workers' hostels (often the origination point of Inkatha-inspired violence), a ban on carrying tribal weapons in public, and the release of close to 500 blacks, deemed political prisoners by the ANC. In exchange for the amnesty, the ANC agreed to a general amnesty for white governmental officials accused of crimes during the years of apartheid. One day after Mandela's summit with de Klerk, Buthelezi walked out of negotiations, angered over the deals struck between the two leaders. Buthelezi made it clear that Inkatha would not participate in postapartheid elections, even though political experts suggested de Klerk's Nationalist Party was counting on Buthelezi's (and Inkatha's) support to bolster their showings at the polls against the ANC. De Klerk denied Buthelezi's charges of striking "illegitimate" deals and claimed the real impediment to progress was due to factionalism between the blacks. Addressing this setback on television, de Klerk said, "It appears to me more and more that we won't have peace until Mr. Mandela and Chief Buthelezi make their peace."

Despite his long imprisonment and personal suffering, political setbacks and the unrelenting strife between Inkatha and the ANC, Mandela's efforts to end institutional apartheid were finally realized in June of 1993, when South Africa's first free elections were announced. Scheduled for April 27, 1994, the election was agreed upon by a majority of the country's 26 parties as a measure to reassure blacks that change is coming. "And the voters will almost certainly reward Mandela's stoic struggle by conferring on him the leadership of his country," declared Scott MacLeod in *Time.* The populace is expected to elect a bicameral legislature, with the party winning the most seats selecting the next president of South Africa. During the transition period, the legislature will serve a term of five years and also be given the duty of drafting a new constitution. De Klerk is insisting, on behalf of his party, on a power-sharing clause in the constitution which will prevent the ANC from assuming absolute control of the government. "We must ensure that there will never be domination again in South Africa. I'm not talking about minority vetoes but about preventing the misuse of power to the detriment of minorities," de Klerk told *Time.* However, Mandela commented to interviewers in *Time* that the National Party's definition of power sharing "means the party that loses the elections should continue to govern," adding, "we have moved them away from that."

Apartheid's official demise signals a turbulent period of adjustment for South Africa; for Mandela, it means a difficult role at the forefront of the healing process. While the announcement of elections will result in the lifting of remaining sanctions against South Africa, the economy has been in recession, staggered by millions of dollars in lost investments. Educational opportunities among black children are poor, and the country's black majority—who have had so little for so long—are now beginning to expect an immediate redistribution of resources. Bloodshed continues to rip apart the black community, despite Buthelezi's pledge to join Mandela in quelling the violence (more than 100 people were killed in factional fighting in July of 1993, in the townships of Tokoza and Katlehong, which observers linked to the ongoing feud between Inkatha and ANC supporters). And a Mandela-led government faces the additional threat from white rightists who have declared they will take up arms in insurrection.

Mandela looks forward to the future, however. He has stated that he will be looking to Western nations, led by the United States, to provide substantial assistance to South Africa along the lines of the Marshall Plan (the blueprint for the rebuilding of Europe at the end of World War II). While Mandela does not discount the threats from the right-wing, he believes that a reorganized police force will protect the new society from those who wish to sabotage it. Despite the many hardships

Mandela has endured at the behest of the state—most notably his bleak confinement in Robben Island and Pollsmoor Prisons, and the forced estrangement from his family—he has remained remarkably free of bitterness. In an interview with *Time,* Mandela described his struggle for racial equality as just one among many: "There are countless people who went to jail and aren't bitter at all, because they can see that their sacrifices were not in vain, and the ideas for which we lived and sacrificed are about to come to fruition. And that removes the bitterness from their hearts."

*BIOGRAPHICAL/CRITICAL SOURCES:*

*BOOKS*

Benson, Mary, *Nelson Mandela: The Man and the Movement,* Norton, 1986.
Harrison, Nancy, *Winnie Mandela* (biography), Braziller, 1986.
Mandela, Nelson R., *No Easy Walk to Freedom,* Basic Books, 1965.
Mandela, Nelson R., *The Struggle Is My Life,* Pathfinder Press, 1986.
Mandela, Winnie, *Part of My Soul Went with Him* (autobiography), edited by Anne Benjamin and Mary Benson, Norton, 1985.
*Newsmakers: 1990,* Gale, 1990.


*PERIODICALS*

*Crisis,* February, 1983.
*Detroit News,* July 6, 1993, p. 2A.
*Ebony,* December, 1985; September, 1986.
*Globe and Mail* (Toronto), December 14, 1985.
*Library Journal,* December, 1986, p. 117; September 15, 1990, p. 61.
*Maclean's,* May 27, 1991, pp. 22-23; July 15, 1991, p. 23.
*Ms.,* November, 1985; January, 1987.
*Nation,* July 1, 1991, pp. 15-18.
*National Review,* April 30, 1990, pp. 37-39.
*New Republic,* October 19, 1992, pp. 16-19.
*New Statesman,* June 7, 1985; September 25, 1992, pp. 26-27.
*Newsweek,* September 9, 1985; February 24, 1986; February 19, 1990, pp. 44-51; March 5, 1990, p. 31; July 2, 1990, pp. 16-20; August 27, 1990, pp. 41-42; May 27, 1991, p. 33; July 1, 1991, p. 37; March 2, 1992, p. 42; July 6, 1992, p. 47.
*New York Review of Books,* May 8, 1986.
*New York Times,* July 19, 1978; July 7, 1985; July 29, 1986; June 21, 1992, sec. 1, pp. 1, 14; October 25, 1992, p. E5; July 7, 1993, p. A3.
*New York Times Book Review,* December 8, 1985.
*People,* February 26, 1990, p. 77-79.

*Time,* January 5, 1987; August 29, 1988, p. 43; May 29, 1989, p. 77; October 23, 1989, p. 49; December 25, 1989, p. 28; January 29, 1990, p. 49; February 19, 1990, p. 42-44; June 25, 1990, pp. 20-21; December 17, 1990, p. 25; July 1, 1991, pp. 38-39; August 17, 1992, p. 15; June 14, 1993, pp. 34-38.

*U.S. News & World Report,* February 27, 1989, p. 13; April 9, 1990, p. 15.

—*Sketch by Scot Peacock*

\* \* \*

## MARSHALL, Paule 1929-

*PERSONAL:* Born April 9, 1929, in Brooklyn, NY; daughter of Samuel and Ada (Clement) Burke; married Kenneth E. Marshall, 1950 (divorced, 1963); married Nourry Menard, July 30, 1970; children (first marriage): Evan. *Education:* Brooklyn College (now of the City University of New York), B.A. (cum laude), 1953; attended Hunter College (now of the City University of New York), 1955.

*ADDRESSES: Home*—407 Central Park West, New York, NY 10025.

*CAREER:* Free-lance writer. Worked as librarian in New York Public Libraries; *Our World* magazine, New York City, staff writer, 1953-56. Lecturer on creative writing at Yale University, New Haven, CT, 1970—; lecturer on Black literature at colleges and universities including Oxford University, Columbia University, Michigan State University, Lake Forrest College, and Cornell University. Professor of English, Virginia Commonwealth University.

*MEMBER:* Harlem Writers Guild, Zora Neale Hurston Forum, Phi Beta Kappa.

*AWARDS, HONORS:* Guggenheim fellow, 1960; Rosenthal Award, National Institute of Arts and Letters, 1962, for *Soul Clap Hands and Sing;* Ford Foundation grant, 1964-65; National Endowment for the Arts grant, 1967-68; Before Columbus Foundation American Book Award, 1984, for *Praisesong for the Widow.*

*WRITINGS:*

*Brown Girl, Brownstones* (novel), Random House, 1959, reprinted with an afterword by Mary Helen Washington, Feminist Press, 1981.
*Soul Clap Hands and Sing* (short stories), Atheneum, 1961, reprinted, Howard University Press, 1988.

*The Chosen Place, The Timeless People,* Harcourt, 1969, reprinted, Vintage Books, 1984.
*Praisesong for the Widow* (novel), Putnam, 1983.
*Reena, and Other Stories* (includes novella *Merle,* and stories "The Valley Between," "Brooklyn," "Barbados," and "To Da-duh, in Memoriam"), with commentary by the author, Feminist Press, 1983, reprinted as *Merle: A Novella, and Other Stories,* Virago Press, 1985.
*Daughters,* (novel), Athenum, 1991.

Also author of a teleplay based on *Brown Girl, Brownstones,* 1960. Contributor of articles and short stories to periodicals.

*ADAPTATIONS:* A television version of *Brown Girl, Brownstones* was produced as a CBS-TV Workshop Production, 1980.

*SIDELIGHTS:* "My work asks that you become involved, that you think," writer Paule Marshall once commented in the *Los Angeles Times.* "On the other hand,... I'm first trying to tell a story, because I'm always about telling a good story." Marshall received her first training in storytelling from her mother, a native of Barbados, and her mother's West Indian friends, all of whom gathered for daily talks in Marshall's home after a hard day of "scrubbing floor." Marshall pays tribute to these "poets in the kitchen" in a *New York Times Book Review* essay where she describes the women's gatherings as a form of inexpensive therapy and an outlet for their enormous creative energy. She writes: "They taught me my first lessons in the narrative art. They trained my ear. They set a standard of excellence. This is why the best of my work must be attributed to them; it stands as testimony to the rich legacy of language and culture they so freely passed on to me in the wordshop of the kitchen."

The standard of excellence set by these women has served Marshall well in her career as a writer. Her novels and stories have been lauded for their skillful rendering of West Indian/Afro-American dialogue and colorful Barbadian expressions. *Dictionary of Literary Biography* contributor Barbara T. Christian believes that Marshall's works "form a unique contribution to Afro-American literature because they capture in a lyrical, powerful language a culturally distinct and expansive world." This pursuit of excellence makes writing a time-consuming effort, according to Marshall. "One of the reasons it takes me such a long time to get a book done," she explained in the *Los Angeles Times,* "is that I'm not only struggling with my sense of reality, but I'm also struggling to find the style, the language, the tone that is in keeping with the material. It's in the process of writing that things get illuminated."

Marshall indicates, however, that her first novel *Brown Girl, Brownstones* was written at a faster pace. "I was so caught up in the need to get down on paper before it was lost the whole sense of a special kind of community, what I call Bajan (Barbardian) Brooklyn, because even as a child I sensed there was something special and powerful about it," she stated in the *Los Angeles Times*. When the novel was published in 1959, it was deemed an impressive literary debut, but because of the novel's frank depiction of a young black girl's search for identity and increasing sexual awareness, *Brown Girl, Brownstones* was largely ignored by readers. The novel was reprinted in 1981, and is now considered a classic in the female *bildungsroman* genre, along with Zora Neale Hurston's *Their Eyes Were Watching God* and Gwendolyn Brooks's *Maud Martha*.

The story has autobiographical overtones, for it concerns a young black Brooklyn girl, Selina, the daughter of Barbadian immigrants Silla and Deighton. Silla, her ambitious mother, desires most of all to save enough money to purchase the family's rented brownstone. Her father Deighton, on the other hand, is a charming spendthrift who'd like nothing better than to return to his homeland. When Deighton unexpectedly inherits some island land, he makes plans to return there and build a home. Silla meanwhile schemes to sell his inheritance and fulfill her own dream.

Selina is deeply affected by this marital conflict, but "emerges from it self-assured, in spite of her scars," writes Susan McHenry in *Ms*. Selina eventually leaves Brooklyn to attend college; later, realizing her need to become acquainted with her parents' homeland, she resolves to go to Barbados. McHenry writes: "*Brown Girl, Brownstones* is meticulously crafted and peopled with an array of characters, and the writing combines authority with grace.... Paule Marshall ... should be more widely read and celebrated." Carol Field comments in the *New York Herald Tribune Book Review:* "[*Brown Girl, Brownstones*] is an unforgettable novel written with pride and anger, with rebellion and tears. Rich in content and in cadences of the King's and 'Bajan' English, it is the work of a highly gifted writer."

*Praisesong for the Widow,* winner of the Before Columbus American Book Award, is thematically similar to *Brown Girl, Brownstones* in that it also involves a black woman's search for identity. This book, though, concerns an affluent widow in her sixties, Avatar "Avey" Johnson, who has lost touch with her West Indian-Afro-American roots. In the process of struggling to make their way in the white man's world, Avey and her husband Jay lost all of the qualities that made them unique. Novelist Anne Tyler remarks in the *New York Times Book Review*, "Secure in her middle class life, her civil service job, her house full of crystal and silver, Avey has become sealed away from her true self."

While on her annual luxury cruise through the West Indies however, Avey has several disturbing dreams about her father's great aunt whom she visited every summer on a South Carolina island. She remembers the spot on the island where the Ibo slaves, upon landing in America, supposedly took one look around at their new life and walked across the water back to Africa. Avey decides to try to escape the uneasiness by flying back to the security of her home. While in her hotel on Grenada awaiting the next flight to New York, Avey reminisces about the early years of her and Jay's marriage, when they used to dance to jazz records in their living room, and on Sundays listen to gospel music and recite poetry. Gradually though, in their drive for success they lost "the little private rituals and pleasures, the playfulness and wit of those early years, the host of feelings and passions that had defined them in a special way back then, and the music which had been their nourishment," writes Marshall in the novel. In the morning, Avey becomes acquainted with a shopkeeper who urges her to accompany him and the other islanders on their annual excursion to Carriacou, the island of their ancestors. Still confused from the past day's events, she agrees. During the island celebration, Avey undergoes a spiritual rebirth and resolves to keep in close contact with the island and its people and to tell others about her experience.

Reviewers question if Avey's resolution is truly enough to compensate for all that she and Jay have lost, if "the changes she envisions in the flush of conversion commensurate with the awesome message of the resisting Ibos," to use *Village Voice Literary Supplement* reviewer Carol Ascher's words. "Her search for roots seems in a way the modern, acceptable equivalent of the straightened hair and white ways she is renouncing," writes *Times Literary Supplement* contributor Mary Kathleen Benet, who adds: "On the other hand there is not much else she can do, just as there was not much else Jerome Johnson could do. Paule Marshall respects herself enough as a writer to keep from overplaying her hand; her strength is that she raises questions that have no answers." *Los Angeles Times Book Review* contributor Sharon Dirlam offers this view: "[Avey] has learned to stay her anger and to swallow her grief, making her day of reckoning all the more poignant. She has already missed the chance to apply what she belatedly learns, except for the most important lesson: What matters is today and tomorrow, and, oh yes, yesterday—life, at age 30, age 60, the lesson is to live." Jonathan Yardley concludes in the *Washington Post Book World:* "*Praisesong for the Widow* ... is a work of quiet passion—a book all the more powerful precisely because it is so quiet. It is also a work of exceptional wisdom, maturity and generosity, one in which the palpable humanity of its characters transcends any considerations of race or sex; that Avey Johnson is black and a woman is certainly important, but Paule Marshall understands that what really counts is the universality of her predicament."

*Reena, and Other Stories,* although a collection of short stories, contains the title story, "Reena" and the novella, *Merle,* adapted from the novel, *The Chosen Place, The Timeless*

*People.* The title is based on a protagonist of the novel. "Reena" is frequently anthologized, particularly in collections of writings by African American women writers. In her introductory comments to a reissued version of *Black-eyed Susans/Midnight Birds,* Mary Helen Washington refers to "Reena"'s theme of cultural identity and the role of the African American female. Dr. Washington's commentary and analysis bolster Paule Marshall's accompanying sketch for "Reena." Reena is autobiographical and is a continuation of *Brown-Girl, Brownstones.* Marshall describes Reena as "like herself from a West Indian- American background who had attended the free New York City colleges during the forties and fifties. The theme would be our efforts to realize whatever talents we had and to be our own persons in the face of the triple-headed hydra of racism, sexism, and class bias we confronted each day."

*Daughters* is widely reviewed and has won critical acclaim. According to Marshall herself, the novel explores significant personal themes. "Ursa is a young urban woman trying to come to terms with the two worlds that shaped her.... Her mother is American, her father West Indian. [Marshall] wanted to write something that was symbolic of the two wings of the black diaspora in this part of the world." Defining the role of the role of the female—upwardly mobile, well-educated—in the black diaspora is the cog around which *Daughters* turns. In a *New York Times Book Review,* Susan Fromberg Schaeffer sees the key for Ursa is in what she learns from those most important in her life. Ursa learns that "to be human one must be of use. To be of use, men and women must work together— and that the relationship between the sexes is far more complicated than Ursa has ever imagined." Working together involves a struggle—sometimes erupting in conflict between men and women. Ursa discovers by novel's end that she must not evade struggle/conflict toward a common goal. She learns to stop allowing love for another to becloud her judgment, as in the case of ignoring the corruption that her father, Primus, confused with success. Ursa learns that she is "hobbled by love of her father ... and so complete is his possession of her that she needs to *abort* him." Ursa must break free to define herself, continue to be "useful," continue to love all humans, yet not be bogged down by that love and get off course. "Marshall shows us how ... *women* can—-and perhaps should—find themselves becoming men's consciences."

*BIOGRAPHICAL/CRITICAL SOURCES:*

*BOOKS*

Bruck, Peter, and Wolfgang Karrer, editor, *The Afro-American Novel since 1960,* B. R. Gruener, 1982.

Christian, Barbara, *Black Women Novelists,* Greenwood Press, 1980.

*Contemporary Literary Criticism,* Volume 27, Gale, 1984.

*Dictionary of Literary Biography,* Volume 33: *Afro-American Fiction Writers after 1955,* Gale, 1984.

Evans, Mari, editor, *Black Women Writers, 1950-1980,* Anchor Press, 1984.

Marshall, Paule, *Brown Girl, Brownstones,* Random House, 1959, reprinted with an afterword by Mary Helen Washington, Feminist Press, 1981.

Marshall, Paule, *Praisesong for the Widow,* Putnam, 1983.

Morgan, Janice, Collette Hall, Carol L. Snyder, eds., *Redefining Autobiography in Twentieth-Century Women's Fiction: An Essay Collection,* Garland, 1991.

Wall, Cheryl, editor, *Changing Our Own Words—Essays on Criticism, Theory, and Writing by Black Women,* Rutgers University Press, 1989.

Washington, Mary Helen, editor, *Black-Eyed Susans/Midnight Birds,* 1990.

*PERIODICALS*

*Black American Literature Forum,* winter, 1986; spring/summer, 1987.

*Black World,* August, 1974.

*Book World,* December 28, 1969.

*Callaloo,* spring/summer, 1983.

*Chicago Tribune,* December 8, 1991.

*Chicago Tribune Book World,* May 15, 1983.

*Christian Science Monitor,* January 22, 1970; March 23, 1984.

*CLA Journal,* March, 1961; September, 1972.

*Critical Quarterly,* summer, 1971.

*Essence,* May, 1980; October, 1991.

*Freedom Ways,* 1970.

*Journal of Black Studies,* December, 1970.

*Kirkus Reviews,* July 15, 1991.

*London Review of Books,* March 7, 1985.

*Los Angeles Times,* May 18, 1983.

*Los Angeles Times Book Review,* February 27, 1983; September 13, 1992.

*Ms.,* November, 1981.

*Nation,* April 2, 1983.

*Negro American Literature Forum,* fall, 1975.

*Negro Digest,* January, 1970.

*New Letters,* autumn, 1973.

*New Yorker,* September 19, 1959.

*New York Herald Tribune Book Review,* August 16, 1959.

*New York Review of Books,* April 28, 1983.

*New York Times,* November 8, 1969; February 1, 1983.

*New York Times Book Review,* November 30, 1969; January 9, 1983; February 20, 1983; October 27, 1991.

*Novel: A Forum on Fiction,* winter, 1974.

*Saturday Review,* September 16, 1961.

*Southern Review,* winter, 1992.

*Times Literary Supplement,* September 16, 1983; April 5, 1985.

*Village Voice,* October 8, 1970; March 22, 1983; May 15, 1984.
*Village Voice Literary Supplement,* April, 1982.
*Washington Post,* February 17, 1984.
*Washington Post Book World,* January 30, 1983.

\*   \*   \*

## MARTIN, Reginald 1956-

*PERSONAL:* Born May 15, 1956, in Memphis, TN; son of Lester (a janitor) and Carrie Lee (a maid; maiden name, Jones) Jackson. *Education:* Boston University, B.S., 1977; Memphis State University, M.A., 1979; University of Tulsa, Ph.D., 1985; Vermont College, M.F.A., 1993; State Technical Institute at Memphis, A.S., 1993.

*ADDRESSES: Home*—P.O. Box 111306, Memphis, TN 38111-1306.

*CAREER: News,* Boston, MA, feature editor and reporter, 1974-77; Memphis State University, Memphis, TN, instructor in English, 1979-80; Tulsa Center for the Study of Women's Literature, Tulsa, OK, research fellow, 1980-81; Tulsa Junior College, Tulsa, instructor in English, 1982; University of Tulsa, Tulsa, assistant instructor in English, 1982-83; Memphis State University, began as assistant professor, became an associate professor and then professor of composition, 1983-91. Visiting lecturer at Mary Washington College, 1984; lecturer in literary criticism at University of Wisconsin-Eau Claire, Wellesley College, Harvard University, University of Pennsylvania, University of Mississippi, 1988-92. Filer and clerk at Boston Public Library, 1976-77; editor at Continental Heritage Press, 1981; director of professional writing programs, 1987-89, and special assistant to president, Memphis State University, 1991—; dean of students, Georgia State University, 1993.

*MEMBER:* National Council of Teachers of English, National Council of Black Studies, National Honors Association, Modern Language Association, Popular Culture Association, Philological Association (Tennessee, Arkansas, Mississippi, and Louisiana), Society for Technical Communicators, Southeastern Society for Nineteenth-Century Studies, Conference of College Composition and Communication, Southern Conference on Afro-American Studies.

*AWARDS, HONORS:* Mark Allen Everett Poetry Contest winner, 1981; Friends of the Library Contest winner in fiction, 1982, and in poetry, 1983; Award in Service for Education, Alpha Kappa, 1984; award for best novel, Deep South Writers Competition, 1987; award for best critical article, South Atlantic Modern Language Association, 1987; award

for best critical/article, College English Association, 1988; Ford Foundation post-doctoral fellowship, 1989; American Council on Education fellowship, 1992; National Foundation for the Improvement of Education Award, 1993.

*WRITINGS:*

*Ntozake Shange's First Novel: In the Beginning Was the Word,* Mary Washington College Press, 1984.
*Ishmael Reed and the New Black Aesthetic Critics,* Macmillan, 1985, St. Martin's Press, 1988.
(Coeditor with Roseann P. Bell and Miriam DeCosta-Willis) *Erotique Noire/Black Erotica,* Doubleday, 1992.
*Black Aesthetic Criticism: An Annotated Bibliography,* Garland Publishing, 1992.

Also author of *The Failure to Interface: "Mainstream" Criticism and Black Aesthetic Criticism,* St. Martin's Press; and *The Writing Circle* (rhetorical reader), Macmillan. Contributor of stories, poems, articles, and reviews to anthologies, including *HomeSpun Images,* and to periodicals, including *Calamus, Callaloo, Explicator, Griot, Obsidian, South Atlantic Review, South Central Review,* and *Yellow Silk.* Contributing editor of *Next Move,* 1977; editor of *Phoenix,* 1978, and *Interpretations,* 1980.

*WORK IN PROGRESS: Secrets,* a book of poems; *Technical Exchanges,* a book on intra-company business and technical writing texts; *Everybody Knows What Time It Is,* a novel.

*SIDELIGHTS:* Reginald Martin once commented: "I write because I must, to get it out. While I do enjoy writing, it has to be done even when I don't feel like it, otherwise I'll explode—like the singers who must sing because it's in them and has to get out, whether they have an audience or not. In my personal life, singing, weightlifting, and running seem to help round out and make pleasant the awesome and unspeakable things I encounter each day.

"My desire to study Ishmael Reed came from my initial and still debilitatingly persistent weakness for reading criticism. It became apparent to my nineteen-year-old lizard brain that I had better start reading this guy who seemed to both fascinate and repel so many people. I believe I read his poetry first, and it both intrigued and clued me to the fact that I should read the fiction also. Usually, I try to encounter an author's works chronologically, but the first novel of Reed's that I read (luckily for me) was his 1972 *Mumbo Jumbo.* I have yet to recover from the cleansing and mind-expanding experience, and the book opened up my knowledge of my and my family's past and our relationship to Voodoo.

"Doing research on Reed introduced me to the new black aesthetic critics, a powerful group of academics in the late

1960s and early 1970s who had concrete notions on what writing by black authors should and should not do. Their movement fascinated me so much that they are currently the subjects of my second literary-critical book, which will principally concern Amiri Baraka, Houston Baker, and Addison Gayle.

"As is true of Reed's work, I find that all of my writings turn back upon themselves to explain themselves and make a part of 'the big picture.' My poetry is, I think, especially relevant in this respect as I think it is the most concise and clear of my works, completely unencumbered by publishing houses who think that my novels, short stories, and scholarly books must be of a certain length to fit into a genre. Sometimes, when you change the length of a work just to fit into an arbitrary genre, you hurt the force of the work immensely. Brevity, excitement, and clarity are the three gods I constantly seek to evoke when I write."

*BIOGRAPHICAL/CRITICAL SOURCES:*

*PERIODICALS*

*Choice,* February, 1989, p. 941.
*Times Literary Supplement,* July 15-21, 1988, p. 786.

\* \* \*

## MARTIN, Tony 1942-

*PERSONAL:* Born February 21, 1942, in Port-of-Spain, Trinidad and Tobago; son of Claude G. and Vida (Scope) Martin. *Education:* Honourable Society of Gray's Inn, Barrister-at-Law, 1965; University of Hull, B.Sc. (with honors), 1968; Michigan State University, M.A., 1970, Ph.D., 1973.

*ADDRESSES: Office*—Department of Africana Studies, Wellesley College, Wellesley, MA 02181.

*CAREER:* Called to English Bar, 1966, and to Trinidad Bar, 1969; accounts clerk in Water Department, Trinidad Public Service, 1961; accounts clerk, Office of the Prime Minister, Federal Government of the West Indies, Trinidad and Tobago, 1961-62; master of Latin, French, Spanish, English, history, and geography, St. Mary's College, Trinidad and Tobago, 1962-63; lecturer in economics and politics, Cipriani Labour College, Trinidad and Tobago, 1968-69; Michigan State University, East Lansing, instructor in history, 1970-71; University of Michigan—Flint, assistant professor of history and coordinator of African-Afro-American studies program, 1971-73; Wellesley College, Wellesley, MA, associate professor, 1973-79, professor of Africana studies, 1979—, chairman of department, 1976-78, 1981-84, and 1985—. Visiting profes-

sor at Brandeis University, fall, 1974 and 1981; University of Minnesota, fall, 1975; Colorado College, 1985 and 1986; and Brown University, 1991 and 1992.

*MEMBER:* Association of the Study of Afro-American Life and History, African Heritage Studies Association (member of executive board, 1982-88), Association of Caribbean Historians (member of executive board, 1985-86, 1986-87), National Council for Black Studies (vice-president of New England region, 1984-86), Organization of American Historians, Negro Historical Association of Colorado Springs, Association for the Study of Classical African Civilizations.

*WRITINGS:*

*Race First: The Ideological and Organizational Struggles of Marcus Garvey and the Universal Negro Improvement Association,* Greenwood Press, 1976.
(Co-author) *Rare Afro-Americana: A Reconstruction of the Adger Library,* G.K. Hall, 1981.
(Editor and compiler) *The Poetical Works of Marcus Garvey,* Majority Press, 1983.
*Literary Garveyism: Garvey, Black Arts, and the Harlem Renaissance,* Majority Press, 1983.
*Marcus Garvey, Hero,* Majority Press, 1983.
*The Pan-African Connection: From Slavery to Garvey and Beyond,* Majority Press, 1984.
(Editor) *In Nobody's Backyard: The Grenada Revolution in Its Own Words,* Majority Press, Volume 1: *The Revolution at Home,* 1984, Volume 2: *Facing the World,* 1985.
(Editor) *Marcus Garvey, Message to the People: The Course of African Philosophy,* Majority Press, 1986.
(Editor and compiler) *African Fundamentalism: A Literary and Cultural Anthology of Garvey's Harlem Renaissance,* Majority Press, 1991.
*Amy Ashwood Garvey: Pan-Africanist, Feminist, and Wife Number One,* Majority Press, forthcoming.

Also author of pamphlets. Contributor of numerous articles and reviews to professional journals, including *Negro History Bulletin, American Historical Review, Journal of Modern African Studies, African Studies Review, Journal of Negro History, Mazungumzo, Race, Journal of American History,* and *Journal of Human Relations.* Guest editor, *Pan-African Journal,* 1974.

*WORK IN PROGRESS: Audrey Jeffers,* a biography; *Auntie Kay,* a biography.

*SIDELIGHTS:* A *Choice* magazine reviewer calls Tony Martin "perhaps the leading academic defender" of the "Pan-Africanist vision" of black-nationalist leader Marcus Garvey, who founded the Universal Negro Improvement Association in 1914. In his study *Literary Garveyism,* the reviewer suggests, "Martin performs a valuable service to Afro-American-ists by drawing attention to the extent of Garveyite literary activity, particularly in the *Negro World* newspaper." In a 1976 critique, *Choice* terms Martin's *Race First* "the most thoroughly researched book on Garvey's ideas by a historian of black nationalism."

*BIOGRAPHICAL/CRITICAL SOURCES:*

*PERIODICALS*

*Choice,* November, 1976; March, 1984; April, 1984.

\* \* \*

**MASTER OF LIFE, The**
    **See OLISAH, Sunday Okenwa**

\* \* \*

**MATHABANE, Mark 1960-**

*PERSONAL:* First name originally Johannes; name changed, 1976; born in Alexandra, South Africa; son of Jackson (a laborer) and Magdelene (a washerwoman; maiden name, Mabaso) Mathabane; married Gail Ernsberger (a writer), 1987. *Education:* Attended Limestone College, 1978, St. Louis University, 1979, and Quincy College, 1981; Dowling College, B.A., 1983; attended Columbia University, 1984. *Religion:* "Believes in God."

*ADDRESSES: Home*—341 Barrington Park Ln., Kernersville, NC 27284

*CAREER:* Free-lance lecturer and writer, 1985—.

*MEMBER:* Authors Guild.

*AWARDS, HONORS:* Christopher Award, 1986.

*WRITINGS:*

*Kaffir Boy: The True Story of a Black Youth's Coming of Age in Apartheid South Africa,* Macmillan, 1986, published as *Kaffir Boy: Growing out of Apartheid,* Bodley Head, 1987.
*Kaffir Boy in America: An Encounter with Apartheid,* Macmillan, 1989.
*Love in Black and White: The Triumph of Love over Prejudice and Taboo,* HarperCollins, 1992.

*SIDELIGHTS:* "What television newscasts did to expose the horrors of the Vietnam War in the 1960s, books like *Kaffir Boy* may well do for the horrors of apartheid in the '80s," Diane Manuel determined in a *Chicago Tribune Book World* review of Mark Mathabane's first novel. In his 1986 *Kaffir Boy: The True Story of a Black Youth's Coming of Age in Apartheid South Africa,* Mathabane recounts his life in the squalid black township of Alexandra, outside of Johannesburg, where he lived in dire poverty and constant fear until he seemingly miraculously received a scholarship to play tennis at an American college. *Washington Post Book World* critic Charles R. Larson called *Kaffir Boy* "violent and hard-hitting," while Peter Dreyer in the *Los Angeles Times Book Review* found Mathabane's autobiography "a book full of a young man's clumsy pride and sorrow, full of rage at the hideousness of circumstances, the unending destruction of human beings, [and] the systematic degradation of an entire society (and not only black South African society) in the name of a fantastic idea."

The Alexandra of *Kaffir Boy* is one of overwhelming poverty and deprivation, of incessant hunger, of horrific crimes committed by the government and citizen gangs, and of fear and humiliation. It is a township where one either spends hours at garbage dumps in search of scraps of food discarded by Johannesburg whites or prostitutes himself for a meal, and where "children grow up accepting violence and death as the norm," reflected Larson. One of Mathabane's childhood memories is of his being startled from sleep, terrified to find police breaking into his family's shanty in search of persons who emigrated illegally, as his parents had, from the "homelands," or tribal reserves. His father was imprisoned following one of these raids, and was repeatedly jailed after that. Mathabane recalls in *Kaffir Boy* that his parents "lived the lives of perpetual fugitives, fleeing by day and fleeing by night, making sure that they were never caught together under the same roof as husband and wife" because they lacked the paperwork that allowed them to live with their lawful spouses. His father was also imprisoned—at one time for more than a year with no contact with his family—for being unemployed, losing jobs as a laborer because he once again lacked the proper documents.

"Born and bred in a tribal reserve and nearly twice my mother's age," Mathabane wrote in his memoir, "my father existed under the illusion, formed as much by a strange innate pride as by a blindness to everything but his own will, that someday all white people would disappear from South Africa, and black people would revert to their old ways of living." Mathabane's father, who impressed upon his son tribal laws and customs, was constantly at odds with his wife, who was determined to see her son get an education. Mathabane's mother waited in lines at government offices for a year in order to obtain his birth certificate so that he could attend school, then worked as a washerwoman for a family of seventeen so that he could continue to study and, with luck, escape the hardships of life in Alexandra. The father burned his son's schoolbooks and ferociously beat his wife in response to her efforts, claiming that an education would only teach Mathabane to be subservient.

Yet those living in the urban ghettos near Johannesburg are more fortunate than people in the outlying "homelands," where black Africans are sent to resettle. "Nothing is more pathetic in this book than the author's description of a trip he takes with his father to the tribal reserve, ostensibly so that the boy will identify with the homelands," judged Larson. "The son, however, sees the land for what it really is—barren, burned out, empty of any meaning for his generation." In *Kaffir Boy* Mathabane depicts the desolation of the Venda tribal reserve as "mountainous, rugged and bone-dry, like a wasteland.... Everywhere I went nothing grew except near lavatories.... Occasionally I sighted a handful of scrawny cattle, goats and pigs grazing on the stubbles of dry bush. The scrawny animals, it turned out, were seldom slaughtered for food because they were being held as the people's wealth. Malnutrition was rampant, especially among the children." Larson continued to note that "the episode backfires. The boy is determined give up his father's tribal ways and acquire the white man's education."

Although Mathabane had the opportunity to get at least a primary education, he still contemplated suicide when he was only ten years old. "I found the burden of living in a ghetto, poverty-stricken and without hope, too heavy to shoulder," he confesses in his memoir. "I was weary of being hungry all the time, weary of being beaten all the time: at school, at home and in the streets.... I felt that life could never, would never, change from how it was for me." But his first encounter with apartheid sparked his determination to overcome the adversities.

His grandmother was a gardener for an English-speaking liberal white family, the Smiths, in an affluent suburb of Johannesburg. One day she took her grandson to work where he met Clyde Smith, an eleven-year-old schoolboy. "My teachers tell us that Kaffirs [blacks] can't read, speak or write English like white people because they have smaller brains, which are already full of tribal things," Smith told Mathabane, the author recalled in his autobiography. "My teachers say you're not people like us, because you belong to a jungle civilization. That's why you can't live or go to school with us, but can only be our servants." He resolved to excel in school, and even taught himself English—blacks were allowed to learn only tribal languages at the time—through the comic books that his grandmother brought home from the Smith household. "I had to believe in myself and not allow apartheid to define my humanity," Mathabane points out.

Mrs. Smith also gave Mathabane an old wooden tennis racket. He taught himself to play then obtained coaching. As he improved and fared well at tournaments he gained recognition as a promising young athlete. In 1973 Mathabane attended a tennis tournament in South Africa where the American tennis pro Arthur Ashe publicly condemned apartheid. Ashe became Mathabane's hero, "because he was the first free black man I had ever seen," the author was quoted as saying in the *New York Times.* After watching the pro play, he strove to do as well as Ashe. Mathabane eventually became one of the best players in his country and made contacts with influential white tennis players who did not support apartheid. Stan Smith, another American tennis professional, befriended Mathabane, and urged him to apply for tennis scholarships to American schools. Mathabane won one, and *Kaffir Boy* ends with the author boarding a plane headed for South Carolina.

Mathabane could have easily left his troubles behind in South Africa, escaping into the religion of American consumerism and TV. And while he married Gail Ernsberger, a white American journalist and writer, after a two-year courtship, he did so with profound awareness of the struggle they were taking on as an interracial couple. Their early days are memorialized in *Love in Black and White,* a book they wrote together and published in 1992. "The Mathabanes write well of the sweet, nervous, first days of their love, and they don't flinch from the bad stuff," noted Hettie Jones in the *Washington Post Book World,* concluding: "As Mark and Gail Mathabane show, all it takes is love, and defending yourself at nearly every turn."

Mathabane took on American racism, too, in his 1990 sequel to *Kaffir Boy. Kaffir Boy in America: An Encounter with Apartheid* contains his reflections on the racial divisions in his adopted country, his own evolution as a writer and his reunion with his family. Clarence Peterson, in a *Chicago Tribune Book World* review, calls it a book "with a big heart." A critic in the *New York Times Book Review* praises *Kaffir Boy in America* as providing "a better understanding of South Africa, of America—and of being human."

"For me to deny my anger and bitterness would be to deny the reality of apartheid," Mathabane told David Grogan in *People* magazine. The author resides in the United States and maintains that he would have been jailed for speaking out against apartheid if he had returned to South Africa in the 1980s. "If I can turn that anger into something positive, I really am in a very good position to go on with my life," he commented in the *New York Times.* Now he lectures, taking the memoir of his early life "as a springboard to talk about apartheid in human terms." But he does want to return to a new South Africa, with hopes of inspiring "other boys and girls into believing that you can still grow up to be as much of an individual as you have the capacity to be," Mathabane was quoted in another article in the *New York Times.* "That is my dream."

*BIOGRAPHICAL/CRITICAL SOURCES:*

BOOKS

Mathabane, Mark, *Kaffir Boy,* Macmillan, 1986.
Mathabane, Mark, *Kaffir Boy in America: An Encounter with Apartheid,* Macmillan, 1989.
Mathabane, Mark, and Gail Mathabane, *Love in Black and White: The Triumph of Love over Prejudice and Taboo,* HarperCollins, 1992.

PERIODICALS

*Chicago Tribune Book World,* April 13, 1986; August 19, 1990, p. 8.
*Christian Science Monitor,* May 2, 1986.
*Los Angeles Times Book Review,* March 30, 1986.
*New York Times,* March 2, 1987; September 24, 1987.
*New York Times Book Review,* April 27, 1986; July 29, 1990, p. 32; February 16, 1992, p. 18.
*Newsweek,* March 9, 1992.
*People,* July 7, 1986.
*Times Literary Supplement,* August 21, 1987.
*Washington Post Book World,* April 20, 1986; August 19, 1990, p.12; February 16, 1992, pp. 1, 10.

\* \* \*

## MATHIS, Sharon Bell 1937-

*PERSONAL:* Born February 26, 1937, in Atlantic City, NJ; daughter of John Willie and Alice Mary (Frazier) Bell; married Leroy Franklin Mathis, July 11, 1957 (divorced January 24, 1979); children: Sherie, Stacy, Stephanie. *Education:* Morgan State College, B.A. (magna cum laude), 1958; Catholic University of America, M.L.S., 1975. *Religion:* Roman Catholic.

*ADDRESSES: Home*—Fort Washington, MD. *Agent*—Marilyn Marlow, Curtis Brown Ltd., 10 Astor Place, New York, NY 10003.

*CAREER:* Children's Hospital of District of Columbia, Washington, DC, interviewer, 1958-59; Holy Redeemer Elementary School, Washington, DC, teacher, 1959-65; Stuart Junior High School, Washington, DC, special education teacher, 1965-75; Benning Elementary School, Washington, DC, librarian, 1975-76; Patricia Roberts Harris Educational Center, Washington, DC, librarian, 1976—. Writer-in-residence,

Howard University, 1972-74. Writer in charge of children's literature division, Washington, D.C. Black Writers Workshop, 1970-73. Member of board of advisers of lawyers committee of District of Columbia Commission on the Arts, 1972-76; member of Black Women's Community Development Foundation, 1973-74.

*AWARDS, HONORS:* Award from Council on Interracial Books for Children, 1970, for *Sidewalk Story;* awards from *New York Times* and American Library Association, 1972, for *Teacup Full of Roses;* fellowship from Wesleyan University and Weekly Readers Book Club, awarded at Bread Loaf Writer's Conference, 1970; Coretta Scott King Award, 1974, for *The Hundred Penny Box;* Arts and Humanities Award from Club Twenty, 1975; Arts and Humanities award from Archdiocese of Washington Black Secretariat, 1978; fellowship, MacDowell Colony, 1978; Wallace Johnson Memorial Award, 1984, for "Outstanding Contributions to the Literary Arts"; arts and letters award from the Boys and Girls Clubs of Greater Washington, 1984; arts and letters award from Delta Sigma Theta sorority, 1985; outstanding writer award from the Writing-to-Read Program, Washington, DC, Public Schools, 1986.

*WRITINGS:*

JUVENILE

*Brooklyn Story,* Hill & Wang, 1970.
*Sidewalk Story,* Viking, 1971, reprinted, Penguin, 1986.
*Teacup Full of Roses,* Viking, 1972, reprinted, Penguin, 1987.
*Ray Charles,* Crowell, 1973.
*Listen for the Fig Tree,* Viking, 1973.
*The Hundred Penny Box,* Viking, 1975.
*Cartwheels,* Scholastic Book Services, 1977.
*Red Dog, Blue Fly: Football Poems,* illustrated by Jan Spivey Gilchrist, Viking, 1991.

Author of "Ebony Juniors Speak!," a monthly column in *Ebony, Jr!* 1972-85, and "Society and Youth," a bi-weekly column in the now defunct *Liteside.* Articles and stories appear in *Negro History Bulletin, Black America, Essence, Encore, Black World, Black Books Bulletin, Acorn,* and *Horn Book.*

*WORK IN PROGRESS: Sammy's Baby,* a children's book; a book on voter registration.

*SIDELIGHTS:* With the publication of her books *Brooklyn Story, Sidewalk Story, Teacup Full of Roses, Listen for the Fig Tree,* and *The Hundred Penny Box,* Sharon Bell Mathis established herself as a leader of the trend in children's literature that advocates portraying people and events in a starkly realistic light. "There are people in [Mathis's books]," writes

Eloise Greenfield in *Black World*, "real, live people that every black reader will recognize. With every word, [the author] reveals ... a profound knowledge of people and an infinite love and respect for black children.... [However,] these books will not be a comfort to those escapist adults who refuse to acknowledge that our children do not live carefree, Dick and Jane lives."

The basis of the latter observation becomes clear after scanning the contents of the books, for the predominant themes include drug addiction, alcoholism, senility, and death. Nevertheless, continues Greenfield, "every young person trying to grow up and survive physically, emotionally, mentally and spiritually will recognize them as truth."

Carol T. Gallagher also applauds Mathis's willingness to break the "last taboo" in children's books by realistically discussing such subjects as aging, senility, and death (specifically in *The Hundred Penny Box*), but she questions the ability of young children to understand what they are reading in the way in which the author intended (at least without the benefit of adult guidance). In general, though, she praises Mathis for illustrating the strong bond of affection and respect that can exist between the very young and the very old and also for her attempts to explore the "day-to-day effects of an older person living with a young family ... very different from the 'holiday visit from grandma' syndrome."

Annie Gottlieb, writing in *New York Times Book Review* about *The Hundred Penny Box* notes: "The story makes you think of whoever has been old and dear in your life.... The experience is universal.... What is so fine about this book is that it does not set out in that kind, condescending, nervous way to acquaint its young readers with the concepts of Old Age and Death.... It is a quiet work of art, not an educational project."

Hazel Copeland, however, feels that *The Hundred Penny Box* successfully blends both artistic and educational elements. She explains in *Black Books Bulletin*: "[It] is an excellent story of the family life and love that transcends generations and paints a very warm picture of human interactions.... [It] is definitely a step in the right direction toward literature that entertains and provides some positive direction for our children."

However "negative" the theme, though, Mathis never allows it to overwhelm the reader. For at the base of each story is a wellspring of hope, pride, love, and a will to survive. Although she is speaking primarily of *Teacup Full of Roses*, Greenfield's observation holds true for Mathis's other books as well: "Black strength is what this book is all about.... The story is told in words and symbols that confirm, without slogans, the strength and beauty of Blackness.... [It is] a book to grow on."

*BIOGRAPHICAL/CRITICAL SOURCES:*

*BOOKS*

*Children's Literature Review*, Volume 3, Gale, 1978.
*Dictionary of Literary Biography*, Volume 33: *Afro-American Fiction Writers After 1955*, Gale, 1984.
*Something About the Author Autobiography Series*, Volume 3, Gale, 1987.

*PERIODICALS*

*American Visions*, December, 1991.
*Black Books Bulletin*, winter, 1975.
*Black World*, August, 1971; May, 1973; August, 1973; May, 1974.
*Catholic Library World*, October, 1977.
*Children's Literature Association Quarterly*, summer, 1988.
*Ebony*, December, 1972.
*Essence*, April, 1973.
*Jet*, April 23, 1970; May 2, 1974.
*Journal of Negro Education*, summer, 1974.
*New York Times*, March 27, 1970.
*New York Times Book Review*, September 10, 1972; May 4, 1975.
*Redbook*, August, 1972.
*Washington Post*, March 21, 1971.

\*    \*    \*

# MAX
## See DIOP, Birago (Ismael)

\*    \*    \*

# MAZRUI, Ali A(l'Amin) 1933-

*PERSONAL:* Surname is accented on the second syllable; born February 24, 1933, in Mombasa, Kenya; son of Al'Amin Ali (a judge of Islamic law) and Safia (Suleiman) Mazrui; married Molly Vickerman (a teacher), October 27, 1962 (marriage dissolved); children: (with Vickerman) Jamal, Al'Amin Ali, Kim Abubakar (all sons); one son with Pauline Uti. *Education:* University of Manchester, B.A. (with distinction), 1960; Columbia University, M.A., 1961; Oxford University, D.Phil., 1966. *Religion:* Islam.

*ADDRESSES: Home*—38-42 Front Street, Apt. 3E, Binghamton, NY 13905. *Office*—Department of Political Science, 5601 Haven Hall, University of Michigan, Ann Arbor, MI 48109. *CAREER:* Makerere University, Kampala, Uganda, lecturer, 1963-65, professor and head of political science, 1965-69, dean of Faculty of Social Sciences, 1967-73; University of Michigan, Ann Arbor, professor of political science, 1973—, director of Center for Afroamerican and African Studies, 1979—; University of Jos, Nigeria, Albert Luthuli Professor-at-Large, 1981-86; Cornell University, Andrew D. White Professor-at-Large, 1986-92; State University of New York, Binghamton, Albert Schweitzer Professor of Humanities, 1989-91. Visiting research scholar, University of California, Los Angeles, summer, 1965; research associate, Center for International Affairs, Harvard University, 1965-66; visiting professor, University of Chicago, 1965, Northwestern University, 1969, and University of Denver, 1969; Commonwealth visiting professor, University of London and University of Manchester, 1971; Dyason lecturer, Australian Institute of International Affairs, 1972; British Broadcasting Corporation Reith Lecturer, 1979. Guest lecturer in more than twenty countries since 1964, including United States, Canada, India, Sweden, England, Iraq, Australia, Singapore, and many countries in his home continent of Africa. Associate political analyst for British Broadcasting Corporation, 1962-65, and Radio Uganda, 1964-65; special correspondent for Radio Tanzania, 1964-65. Expert advisor to World Bank, 1988—, and United Nations Commission on Transnational Corporations, 1987—. Member of advisory committee, Trans-Africa Run for Wildlife Foundation, Inc., 1987—; member of advisory board of directors, AFRICARE (Detroit chapter), 1987—, and Pan-African Advisory Council to UNICEF, 1988—.

*MEMBER:* World Congress of Black Intellectuals (vice-president, 1988—), International Political Science Association (member of executive committee, 1967-76; vice-president, 1970-73), International Sociological Association (member of steering committee of military sociology group, 1967-74), International Congress of Africanists (vice-president, 1967-73), International Congress of African Studies (vice-president, 1978—), International African Institute (member of executive committee, 1968—; vice-president, 1987—), African Studies Association (president, 1978-79), African Association of Political Science (member of executive committee, 1973-76), World Order Models Project (director of African section, 1968—).

*AWARDS, HONORS:* Rockefeller Foundation fellowship in United States, 1960-61, and research grant, 1965-66; National Unity Book prize, Northwestern University, 1969; Center for Advanced Study in Behavioral Sciences fellowship, Stanford University, 1972-74; Hoover Institution on War, Revolution, and Peace fellowship, Stanford University, 1973-74; International Development Research Center research grant, 1975.

*WRITINGS:*

*Towards a Pax Africana: A Study of Ideology and Ambition,* University of Chicago Press, 1967.

*The Anglo-African Commonwealth: Political Friction and Cultural Fusion,* Pergamon, 1967.
*On Heroes and Uhuru-Worship,* Longmans, Green, 1967.
*Ancient Greece in African Political Thought* (inaugural lecture), East African Publishing House, 1967.
*Violence and Thought: Essays on Social Tensions in Africa,* Humanities, 1969.
*The Trial of Christopher Okigbo,* (novel), Heinemann, 1971.
*Cultural Engineering and Nation-Building in East Africa,* Northwestern University Press, 1972.
*World Culture and the Black Experience,* University of Washington Press, 1974.
*The Political Sociology of the English Language: An African Perspective,* Mouton, 1975.
*Soldiers and Kinsmen in Uganda: The Making of a Military Ethnocracy,* Sage Publications, 1975.
*A World Federation of Cultures: An African Perspective,* Free Press, 1976.
*Africa's International Relations: The Diplomacy of Dependency and Change,* Westview, 1977.
*Political Values and the Educated Class in Africa,* University of California Press, 1978.
*The Barrel of the Gun and the Barrel of Oil in the North-South Equation,* Transaction, 1978.
*Sex in Politics and Modern History,* Julian Friedmann, 1979.
*The African Condition: A Political Diagnosis,* Cambridge University Press, 1980.
*The Moving Cultural Frontier of World Order: From Monotheism to North-South Relations,* World Policy, 1982.
(With Michael Tidy) *Nationalism and the New States in Africa: From about 1935 to the Present,* Heinemann, 1984.
*The Africans: A Triple Heritage,* Little, Brown, 1986.
*Cultural Forces in World Politics,* Heinemann, 1990.

*EDITOR*

(With Robert I. Rothberg) *Protest and Power in Black Africa,* Oxford University Press, 1970.
(With Hasu H. Patel) *Africa in World Affairs: The Next Thirty Years,* Third Press, 1973, published in England as *Africa: The Next Thirty Years,* Julian Friedmann, 1974.
*The Warrior Tradition in Modern Africa* (essays), E. J. Brill, 1978.
(With Toby Kleban) *The Africans: A Reader,* Greenwood, 1986.

*OTHER*

Also author of poetry, short stories, and literary criticism. Contributor of articles to *International Affairs* (London), *American Political Science Review, Africa Quarterly* (New Delhi), *Ethics,* and numerous other journals in Africa, Europe, the United States, and Asia. Associate editor, *Transition,* 1965-73; editor, *UNESCO General History of Africa,* Volume 8.

Member of editorial board of *Encyclopaedia Africana,* 1964—, *Makerere Journal,* 1964-67, *Journal of African and Asian Studies,* 1966—, *Mawazo,* 1967-73, *Comparative Political Studies,* 1967—, and *East African Law Journal,* 1967—.

*ADAPTATIONS: The Africans: A Triple Heritage* was broadcast by British Broadcasting Corporation.

*SIDELIGHTS:* Political scientist Ali A. Mazrui's scholarly writing is recognized as an integral part of the body of literature on modern Africa. His topics include disunity among African nations, violence and its impact on African society, the problems associated with Africa's multilingualism, the role of the West in African politics, and Africa's place in the modern world. *The Trial of Christopher Okigbo,* Mazrui's only work of fiction, addresses the issue of African unity as it follows the trial of the title character on charges of putting his Ibo tribe before both his poetry and the interests of Nigeria. The trial takes place after Okigbo's death in the Nigerian Civil War, and features testimony from living and dead witnesses. George Davis, writing in the *New York Times Book Review,* found the novel a "fine and unusual piece of fiction" and found that the book "becomes its own best proof that important political questioning and art are not mutually exclusive."

"Adept at thinking quickly and synthesizing ideas, Mazrui is a witty, articulate, and dangerous intellectual adversary, especially in public exchanges," *Dictionary of Literary Biography* contributor Omari H. Kokole noted. "His most potent intellectual weapon is his capacity to see though ideas and arguments and to point out quickly any internal contradictions or irrationality. He reminds one of what German sociologist Max Weber once termed an 'exposer of nonsense'."

*BIOGRAPHICAL/CRITICAL SOURCES:*

*BOOKS*

*Dictionary of Literary Biography,* Volume 125: *Twentieth-Century Caribbean and Black African Writers,* Gale, 1993, pp. 82-88.
Herdeck, Donald E., *African Authors: A Companion to Black African Writing,* Volume 1: 1300-1973, Black Orpheus Press, 1973.

*PERIODICALS*

*Black World,* January, 1971, p. 98.
*Books and Bookmen,* June, 1974, pp. 45-46.
*Choice,* June, 1970, p. 586; May, 1973, p. 500; June, 1976, p. 512; January, 1977, p. 1468; July/August, 1978, p. 753; March, 1979, p. 117; June, 1979, p. 571; April, 1980, p. 193; December, 1984, p. 602.

*Library Journal,* August, 1972, p. 2646; June 15, 1973, p. 1924; December 1, 1974, p. 3140; May 1, 1978, p. 982.
*New Republic,* July 5, 1980, pp. 31-32.
*New York Times Book Review,* September 17, 1972, p. 48; November 16, 1986, p. 24.
*Times Literary Supplement,* March 3, 1972, p. 247; September 22, 1978, p. 1059; December 1, 1978, p. 1390; September 5, 1980, p. 970; November 14, 1986, p. 1285; February 8, 1990, p. 8.
*Wilson Library Bulletin,* February, 1973, p. 492.

\* \* \*

## McELROY, Colleen J(ohnson)  1935-

*PERSONAL:* Born October 30, 1935, in St. Louis, MO; daughter of Jesse O. (an army officer) and Ruth (Long) Johnson; married David F. McElroy (a writer), November 28, 1968 (divorced); children: Kevin D., Vanessa C. *Education:* Attended University of Maryland, 1953-55; Harris Teachers College, A.A., 1956; Kansas State University, B.S., 1958, M.S., 1963; graduate study at University of Pittsburgh, 1958-59, and Western Washington State College (now Western Washington University), 1970-71; University of Washington, Ph.D., 1973.

*ADDRESSES: Home*—Seattle, WA. *Office*—Department of English, University of Washington, Seattle, WA 98105.

*CAREER:* Rehabilitation Institute, Kansas City, MO, chief speech clinician, 1963-66; Western Washington State College (now Western Washington University), Bellingham, assistant professor of English, 1966-73; University of Washington, Seattle, 1973—, began as assistant professor, currently professor of English. Affiliate member of speech faculty, University of Missouri—Kansas City, 1965-66; summer instructor, Project Head Start and Project New Careers. Moderator of "Outlook," KVOS-TV, 1968-72. Artist; watercolors and pen-ink sketches displayed at gallery exhibit, 1978. Member of board, Washington State Commission for the Humanities.

*MEMBER:* American Speech and Hearing Association, National Council of Teachers of English, Conference on College Composition and Communication, Writers Guild of America East, Writers Union, Author's Guild, Dramatist Guild, United Black Artists Guild (Seattle).

*AWARDS, HONORS:* Carnation teaching incentive award, 1973; Breadloaf scholarship for fiction, 1974; Best of Small Presses award for poetry, Pushcart Book Press, 1976; National Endowment for the Arts fellowship in creating writing, 1978 and 1991; Matrix Women of Achievement Award, 1985; Before Columbus American Book Award, 1985, for *Queen of the Ebony Isles;* Fulbright Creative Writing fellowship, 1990; Rockefeller fellowship, 1991; Jessie Ball DuPont Distinguished Black Scholar Residency, 1992.

*WRITINGS:*

*Speech and Language Development of the Preschool Child: A Survey,* C. C. Thomas, 1972.
*The Mules Done Long Since Gone* (poems), Harrison-Madronna Press, 1973.
*Music from Home: Selected Poems,* Southern Illinois University Press, 1976.
(Contributor) *Iron Country* (anthology), Copper Canyon Press, 1978.
(Contributor) Dexter Fisher, editor, *The Third Woman* (anthology), Houghton, 1980.
(Contributor) *Backbone 2* (anthology), Seal Press, 1980.
*Winters without Snow* (poems), I. Reed, 1980.
*Looking for a Country under Its Original Name* (poems), Blue Begonia Press, 1985.
*Queen of the Ebony Isles* (poems), Wesleyan University Press, 1985.
*Jesus and Fat Tuesday and Other Short Stories,* Creative Arts Book Company, 1987.
*Bone Flames* (poems), Wesleyan University Press, 1987.
*Lie and Say You Love Me* (poems), Circinatum Press, 1988.
*Blue Flames* (poems), Wesleyan University Press, 1989.
*What Madness Brought Me Here: New and Selected Poems, 1968-1988,* University Press of New England, 1990.

Also author of *Driving under the Cardboard Pines.* Contributor to anthology *Black Sister: Poems by Black American Women, 1946-1980,* 1981. Contributor of essays, poems, and short fiction to numerous literary reviews and magazines, including *Wormwood Review, Poetry Northwest, Choice, Seneca Review, Southern Poetry Review, Confrontation, Massachusetts Review, Georgia Review, Manhattan Review, Kenyon Review, Southern Poetry Review,* and *Black Warrior Review.*

*WORK IN PROGRESS: Study War No More,* a novel; *Halfway to Nosybe,* a collection of essays.

\*   \*   \*

## McGIRT, James E(phraim)   1874-1930

*PERSONAL:* Born September 1874; died June 13, 1930; son of Madison (a farmer) and Ellen Townsend McGirt. *Education:* private and public schools; Bennett College, North Carolina, B.A., 1895.

*CAREER:* Poet, songwriter, and publisher of *McGirt's Magazine.* Founder of the Constitutional Brotherhood of America.

*WRITINGS:*

*Avenging the Maine, A Drunken A.B., and Other Poems,* Edwards & Broughton, 1899, revised and enlarged edition, 1900, second revised edition, Lasher, 1901.
*Some Simple Songs and a Few More Ambitious Attempts,* Lasher, 1901.
*For Your Sweet Sake: Poems,* Winston, 1906, enlarged edition, 1909.
*The Triumphs of Ephraim,* McGirt, 1907.

*SIDELIGHTS:* James E. McGirt's most notable contribution to black literature is generally considered to be his publication, *McGirt's Magazine,* and not his own writings. Through this periodical, he reprinted the work of major black writers, and he gave voice to political activism, encouraging blacks to gain autonomy through voting and education.

Immediately following his college career, McGirt made a modest but comfortable career as in business, working as a launderer and drayman. His first collection of poems, *Avenging the Maine, A Drunken A.B., and Other Poems,* was published by Edwards and Broughton in 1899. The work received generally unfavorable reviews, which McGirt was not to better even with two expanded editions of the same book in 1900 and 1901.

His poetry follows the folk dialect style popularized by Paul Laurence Dunbar and James D. Corrothers. But according to Walter C. Daniel in the *Dictionary of Literary Biography,* in at least one poem, "Memory of Lincoln and the Yankees," McGirt "fails to achieve the unity in structure or the high level of poetic skill that characterize Dunbar's work."

McGirt sought a mentor from among the prominent poets and scholars of his day, both black and white. Lacking a patron, he featured his own work in *McGirt's Magazine,* which was published first from Greensboro, North Carolina, then from Philadelphia, where he moved in 1903. He also printed the work of Dunbar, W. E. B. Du Bois, Benjamin T. Tanner, Frances E. W. Harper, and other prominent black writers. Although McGirt never found sustaining support from among the literary circle of his day, he was encouraged by Du Bois, whose political orientation was in alignment with his own.

*McGirt's Magazine* served as the official voice of the Constitutional Brotherhood of America, which McGirt founded in an effort to increase the power of blacks within the Republican Party. Through his periodical, he also supported the National Afro-American Council and the Niagara Movement, the latter cause being led by Du Bois.

In 1906, while McGirt was in Philadelphia, his second collection of poems was published. Some poems were written in the sentimental style which reached its zenith in the mid-nine-teenth century; others were in dialect form. But McGirt's work was deemed uneven by critics. In 1909 his publishing company failed, and he returned to his home in Greensboro the following year. Upon returning home, McGirt turned around a fledgling family cosmetics business, building it into one of the pre-eminent black-owned businesses in North Carolina. He also met with success as a realtor. Even with his business obligations, however, he continued to be a prolific writer. But he shifted from poetry to short stories, perhaps hoping to receive more favorable reviews. In 1907, he self-published *The Triumphs of Ephraim,* a collection of his prose pieces. The stories centered around plantation blacks and soldiers of the Civil and Spanish-American wars.

The landscape for black Americans was changing, and McGirt was never to develop a literary artistry as profound as that of his contemporaries. His contribution to the cause of the Negro at the turn of the century was his activism and the expression of a strong editorial voice in *McGirt's Magazine.* Selected copies of the magazine can be found at Howard University in Washington, D.C.

*BIOGRAPHICAL/CRITICAL SOURCES:*

*BOOKS*

*Dictionary of Literary Biography,* Volume 50, *Afro-American Writers before the Harlem Renaissance,* Gale, 1987, pp. 212-17.

*PERIODICALS*

*Crisis,* May, 1953, pp. 287-89.
*Negro History Bulletin,* March, 1953, pp. 123-26.

\*   \*   \*

## McKISSACK, Patricia (L'Ann) C(arwell) 1944- (L'Ann Carwell)

*PERSONAL:* Born August 9, 1944, in Nashville, TN; daughter of Robert (a civil servant) and Erma (a civil servant) Carwell; married Fredrick L. McKissack (a writer), December 12, 1965; children: Fredrick L., Jr., Robert and John (twins). *Education:* Tennessee Agricultural and Industrial State University (now Tennessee State University), B.A., 1964; Webster University, M.A., 1975. *Avocational interests:* World travel, entertaining, and touring old houses.

*ADDRESSES: Home*—5900 Pershing Ave., St. Louis, MO 63112. *Office*—All-Writing Services, 225 South Meramec, No. 506, St. Louis, MO 63105.

*CAREER:* Junior high school English teacher in Kirkwood, MO, 1968-75; Forest Park College, St. Louis, MO, part-time instructor in English, 1975—. Children's book editor at Concordia Publishing House, 1976-81, and Institute of Children's Literature, 1984—; instructor at University of Missouri—St. Louis, 1978—; co-owner of All-Writing Services. Educational consultant on minority literature.

*MEMBER:* Society of Children's Book Writers.

*AWARDS, HONORS:* Helen Keating Ott Award, National Church and Synagogue Librarians Association, 1980, for editorial work at Concordia Publishing House; C. S. Lewis Silver Medal awards, *Christian School* magazine, 1984, for *It's the Truth, Christopher* and *Abram, Abram, Where Are We Going?;* Coretta Scott King Award, and Jane Addams Peace Award, both 1990, both for *Long Hard Journey: Story of the Pullman Car Porter;* Parent's Choice Award, 1990, for *Nettie Jo's Friends.*

*WRITINGS:*

*FOR CHILDREN*

(Under name L'Ann Carwell) *Good Shepherd Prayer,* Concordia, 1978.
(Under name L'Ann Carwell) *God Gives New Life,* Concordia, 1979.
*Ask the Kids,* Concordia, 1979.
*Who Is Who?,* Children's Press, 1983.
*Martin Luther King, Jr.: A Man to Remember,* Children's Press, 1984.
*Paul Laurence Dunbar: A Poet to Remember,* Children's Press, 1984.
*Michael Jackson, Superstar,* Children's Press, 1984.
*Lights Out, Christopher,* illustrated by Bartholomew, Augsburg, 1984.
*It's the Truth, Christopher,* illustrated by Bartholomew, Augsburg, 1984.
*The Apache,* Children's Press, 1984.
*Mary McLeod Bethune: A Great American Educator,* Children's Press, 1985.
*Aztec Indians,* Children's Press, 1985.
*The Inca,* Children's Press, 1985.
*The Maya,* Children's Press, 1985.
*Flossie and the Fox,* illustrated by Rachel Isadora, Dial, 1986.
*Our Martin Luther King Book,* illustrated by Isadora, Child's World, 1986.
*Who Is Coming?,* illustrated by Clovis Martin, Children's Press, 1986.
*Give It with Love, Christopher: Christopher Learns about Gifts and Giving,* illustrated by Bartholomew, Augsburg, 1988.
*Speak Up, Christopher: Christopher Learns the Difference between Right and Wrong,* illustrated by Bartholomew, Augsburg, 1988.

*A Troll in a Hole,* Milliken, 1988.

*Nettie Jo's Friends,* illustrated by Scott Cook, Knopf, 1988.

*Mirandy and Brother Wind,* illustrated by Jerry Pinkney, Knopf, 1988.

*Monkey-Monkey's Trick: Based on an African Folk-Tale,* illustrated by Paul Meisel, Random House, 1989.

*Jesse Jackson: A Biography,* Scholastic, 1989.

(With Ruthilde Kronberg) *A Piece of the Wind and Other Stories to Tell,* Harper, 1990.

*No Need for Alarm,* Milliken, 1990.

*A Million Fish—More or Less,* illustrated by Dena Schutzer, Knopf, 1992.

*The Dark Thirty: Southern Tales of the Supernatural,* illustrated by Brian Pinkney, 1992.

*Christmas in the Big House—Christmas in the Quarters,* Scholastic, 1992.

*Sojourner Truth: "Ain't I a Woman?,"* Scholastic, 1992.

*WITH HUSBAND, FREDRICK L. MCKISSACK*

*Look What You've Done Now, Moses,* illustrated by Joe Boddy, David Cook, 1984.

*Abram, Abram, Where Are We Going?,* illustrated by Boddy, David Cook, 1984.

*Cinderella,* illustrated by Tom Dunnington, Children's Press, 1985.

*Country Mouse and City Mouse,* illustrated by Anne Sikorski, Children's Press, 1985.

*The Little Red Hen,* illustrated by Dennis Hockerman, Children's Press, 1985.

*The Three Bears,* illustrated by Virginia Bala, Children's Press, 1985.

*The Ugly Little Duck,* illustrated by Peggy Perry Anderson, Children's Press, 1986.

*When Do You Talk to God? Prayers for Small Children,* illustrated by Gary Gumble, Augsburg, 1986.

*King Midas and His Gold,* illustrated by Dunnington, Children's Press, 1986.

*Frederick Douglass: The Black Lion,* Children's Press, 1987.

*A Real Winner,* illustrated by Quentin Thompson and Ken Jones, Milliken, 1987.

*The King's New Clothes,* illustrated by Gwen Connelly, Children's Press, 1987.

*Tall Phil and Small Bill,* illustrated by Kathy Mitter, Milliken, 1987.

*Three Billy Goats Gruff,* illustrated by Dunnington, Children's Press, 1987.

*My Bible ABC Book,* illustrated by Reed Merrill, Augsburg, 1987.

*The Civil Rights Movement in America from 1865 to the Present,* Children's Press, 1987, second edition, 1991.

*All Paths Lead to Bethlehem,* illustrated by Kathryn E. Shoemaker, Augsburg, 1987.

*Messy Bessey,* illustrated by Richard Hackney, Children's Press, 1987.

*The Big Bug Book of Counting,* illustrated by Bartholomew, Milliken, 1987.

*The Big Bug Book of Opposites,* illustrated by Bartholomew, Milliken, 1987.

*The Big Bug Book of Places to Go,* illustrated by Bartholomew, Milliken, 1987.

*The Big Bug Book of the Alphabet,* illustrated by Bartholomew, Milliken, 1987.

*The Big Bug Book of Things to Do,* illustrated by Bartholomew, Milliken, 1987.

*Bugs!,* illustrated by Martin, Children's Press, 1988.

*The Children's ABC Christmas,* illustrated by Kathy Rogers, Augsburg, 1988.

*Constance Stumbles,* illustrated by Dunnington, Children's Press, 1988.

*Oh, Happy, Happy Day! A Child's Easter in Story, Song, and Prayer,* illustrated by Elizabeth Swisher, Augsburg, 1989.

*God Made Something Wonderful,* illustrated by Ching, Augsburg, 1989.

*Messy Bessey's Closet,* illustrated by Hackney, Children's Press, 1989.

*James Weldon Johnson: "Lift Every Voice and Sing,"* Children's Press, 1990.

*A Long Hard Journey: The Story of the Pullman Porter,* Walker & Co., 1990.

*Taking a Stand against Racism and Racial Discrimination,* F. Watts, 1990.

*W. E. B. DuBois,* F. Watts, 1990.

*The Story of Booker T. Washington,* Children's Press, 1991.

*Messy Bessy's Garden,* illustrated by Martin, Children's Press, 1991.

*"GREAT AFRICAN AMERICANS" SERIES; JUVENILES; WITH FREDRICK L. MCKISSACK*

*Carter G. Woodson: The Father of Black History,* illustrated by Ned O, Enslow Publishers, 1991.

*Frederick Douglass: Leader against Slavery,* illustrated by Ned O, Enslow Publishers, 1991.

*George Washington Carver: The Peanut Scientist,* illustrated by Ned O, Enslow Publishers, 1991.

*Ida B. Wells-Barnett: A Voice against Violence,* Enslow Publishers, 1991.

*Louis Armstrong: Jazz Musician,* illustrated by Ned O, Enslow Publishers, 1991.

*Marian Anderson: A Great Singer,* Enslow Publishers, 1991.

*Martin Luther King, Jr.: Man of Peace,* Enslow Publishers, 1991.

*Mary Church Terrell: Leader for Equality,* illustrated by Ned O, Enslow Publishers, 1991.

*Mary McLeod Bethune: A Great Teacher,* illustrated by Ned O, Enslow Publishers, 1991.

*Ralph J. Bunche: Peacemaker,* illustrated by Ned O, Enslow
    Publishers, 1991.
*Jesse Owens,* illustrated by Ned O, Enslow Publishers, 1992.
*Langston Hughes,* illustrated by Ned O, Enslow Publishers,
    1992.
*Sojourner Truth,* illustrated by Ned O, Enslow Publishers,
    1992.
*Zora Neale Hurston,* illustrated by Ned O, Enslow Publish-
    ers, 1992.
*Satchel Paige,* illustrated by Ned O, Enslow Publishers, 1992.

OTHER

(With Mavis Jukes) *Who Owns the Sun?* (film script), Disney
    Educational Productions, 1991.

Also author, with Fredrick L. McKissack, of "Start Up" series (for beginning readers), four volumes, Children's Press,
1985; editor, with McKissack, of "Reading Well" series, and
"Big Bug Books" series, both for Milliken. Writer for preschool series "L Is for Listening," broadcast by KWMU-Ra-
dio, 1975-77. Author of radio and television scripts. Contributor of articles and short stories to magazines, including *Friend,
Happy Times,* and *Evangelizing Today's Child.*

*WORK IN PROGRESS:* A book about the McKissack family
and several biographies about great African Americans.

*SIDELIGHTS:* Patricia C. McKissack's books for children
cover a range of topics, including religious stories and biographies of black historical figures. *Flossie and the Fox,* which
*Kirkus Reviews* called "a perfect picture book," is based on a
folktale McKissack's grandfather told her as a child. The action surrounds little Flossie Finley as she delivers a basket of
eggs to a neighbor and outsmarts the fox who wants the eggs
for himself. *Abram, Abram, Where Are We Going?* is a retelling of the biblical stories about Abraham as father to many
nations.

McKissack's title *Jesse Jackson: A Biography* was reviewed
in the *New York Times* by Rosemary Bray, who wrote: "The
complex story [McKissack] tells may seem at odds with the
simplicity of the languages she uses.... But Patricia McKissack
is excellent at conveying sophisticated themes and ideas, so
that *Jesse Jackson: A Biography* can be read with pleasure by
both children and young adults." In 1991, she wrote her first
movie script with award-winning author Mavis Jukes. The
movie, titled *Who Owns the Sun?,* won several major film
awards and was up for consideration as an Academy Award
nominee for short subject.

McKissack commented: "Teaching and writing are compatible careers. My teaching experiences help me identify materials kids like to read and also target what they need to read. I

understand the resistance teachers and parents get from the
reluctant reader. So, my writing goals are twofold. First, I
choose subjects kids need to know about. Second, I try to make
the material as interesting as possible. Nothing is more satisfying than a letter from a reader saying, for example, 'Thank
you for writing about Paul Laurence Dunbar. I'd never heard
of him until I read your book. Now I read his poems.' On days
like that the rejection slips seem unimportant. The writer in
me pats the teacher in me on the back."

*BIOGRAPHICAL/CRITICAL SOURCES:*

PERIODICALS

*Horn Book,* March, 1989, p. 201; September, 1989, p. 613;
    January, 1990, pp. 87, 125.
*Kirkus Reviews,* July 15, 1986, p. 1120; November 1, 1988,
    p. 1607.
*New York Times Book Review,* November 20, 1988, p. 48;
    February 25, 1990, p. 32.
*School Library Journal,* February, 1989, p. 74; May, 1989,
    p. 88; November, 1989, p. 78; December, 1989, p. 114;
    January, 1990, p. 125.
*Voice of Youth Advocates,* December, 1989, pp. 303, 304.

\*    \*    \*

## McMILLAN, Terry (L.) 1951-

*PERSONAL:* Born October 18, 1951, in Port Huron, MI;
daughter of Edward McMillan and Madeline Washington
Tillman; children: Solomon Welch. *Education:* University of
California, Berkeley, B.S., 1979; Columbia University,
M.F.A., 1979.

*ADDRESSES: Home*—Free at Last, P.O. Box 2408, Danville,
CA 94526. *Agent*—Molly Friedrich, Aaron Priest Literary
Agency, 122 East 42nd St., Suite 3902, New York, NY 10168.

*CAREER:* University of Wyoming, Laramie, instructor, 1987-
90; University of Arizona, Tucson, professor, 1990-92; writer.

*MEMBER:* PEN, Author's League.

*AWARDS, HONORS:* National Endowment for the Arts fellowship, 1988; American Book Award, Before Columbus
Foundation, 1988, for *Mama;* Matrix Award for Books, New
York Women in Communications, 1993, for *Waiting to Exhale.*

*WRITINGS:*

*Mama* (novel), Houghton, 1987.

*Disappearing Acts* (novel), Viking, 1989.
(Editor) *Breaking Ice: An Anthology of Contemporary African-American Fiction,* Viking, 1990.
*Waiting to Exhale* (novel), Viking, 1992.

Adapted *Disappearing Acts* for a screenplay. Work represented in *Touching Fire: Erotic Writings by Women,* Carroll and Graf, 1989; and *Five for Five: The Films of Spike Lee,* Stewart, Tabori, 1991. Contributor to periodicals, including *Callaloo, Esquire,* and *Other Voices.*

SIDELIGHTS: "Terry McMillan has the power to be an important contemporary novelist," stated Valerie Sayers reviewing *Disappearing Acts* in the *New York Times Book Review* back in 1989. "Watch Terry McMillan. She's going to be a major writer," predicted a short but positive review of the same novel in *Cosmopolitan.* McMillan had already garnered attention and critical praise for her first novel, *Mama,* which was published in 1987. Over the next five years, these predictions began to come true. In 1992 McMillan saw the publication of *Waiting to Exhale,* her third novel. Her publisher sent her on a twenty-city, six-week tour, and McMillan appeared on several popular television programs including the *Oprah Winfrey Show,* the *Arsenio Hall Show,* and *Today.*

"Seriously, I just don't get it; I really don't," the author mused during an interview with Audrey Edwards for *Essence.* But McMillan's honest, unaffected writings have clearly struck a chord with the book-buying public. Paperback rights for *Waiting to Exhale* fetched a hefty $2.64 million, making the deal with Pocket Books the second largest of its kind in publishing history. The book has also been adapted for a screenplay.

McMillan grew up in Port Huron, Michigan, a city approximately 60 miles northeast of Detroit. Her working-class parents did not make a point of reading to their five children, but McMillan discovered the pleasure of reading as a teenager shelving books in a local library. Prior to working in the library, she had no exposure to books by black writers. McMillan recalled feeling embarrassed when she saw a book by James Baldwin with his picture on the cover. In a *Washington Post* article, she was quoted as saying, "I ... did not read his book because I was too afraid. I couldn't imagine that he'd have anything better or different to say than [German essayist and novelist] Thomas Mann, [American writer] Henry Thoreau, [American essayist and poet] Ralph Waldo Emerson.... Needless to say, I was not just naive, but had not yet acquired an ounce of black pride."

Later, as a student at a community college in Los Angeles, McMillan immersed herself in most of the classics of African American literature. After reading Alex Haley's *Autobiography of Malcolm X,* McMillan realized that she had no reason to be ashamed of a people who had such a proud history. At age 25, she published her first short story; and 11 years after that, her first novel, *Mama,* was released by Houghton Mifflin.

McMillan was determined not to let her debut novel go unnoticed. Typically, first novels receive little publicity other than the press releases and galleys sent out by the publisher. When McMillan's publisher told her that they could not do more for her, McMillan decided to promote the book on her own. She wrote over 3,000 letters to chain bookstores, independent booksellers, universities, and colleges. Although what she was doing seemed logical in her own mind, the recipients of her letters were not used to such efforts by an author. They found her approach hard to resist, so by the end of the summer of 1987 she had several offers for readings. McMillan then scheduled her own book publicity tour and let her publicist know where she was going instead of it being the other way around.

By the time *Waiting to Exhale* was published, it was the other way around. The scene at a reading from the novel was described in the *Los Angeles Times* this way: "Several hundred fans, mostly black and female, are shoehorned into Marcus Bookstore on a recent Saturday night. Several hundred more form a line down the block and around the corner. The reading ... hasn't begun because McMillan is greeting those who couldn't squeeze inside.... Finally, the writer ... steps through the throng."

McMillan has come a long way since the publication of her first novel, which started out as a short story. "I really love the short story as a form," stated McMillan in an interview with *Writer's Digest.* "Mama" was just one of several short stories that McMillan had tried with limited success to get into print. Then the Harlem Writer's Guild accepted her into their group and told her that "Mama" really should be a novel and not a short story. After four weeks at the MacDowell artists colony and two weeks at the Yaddo colony, McMillan had expanded her short story into over 400 pages. When her agent suggested certain revisions to the book, McMillan questioned whether the woman truly understood what the book was about.

Frustrated by this and by certain events taking place in her personal life, McMillan took things into her own hands and sent her collection of short stories to Houghton Mifflin. Hoping that she would at least get some free editorial advice, McMillan was surprised when the publisher contacted her about the novel she had mentioned briefly in her letter to them. She sent them pages from *Mama* and approximately four days later got word from Houghton Mifflin that they loved it.

*Mama* tells the story of the struggle Mildred Peacock has raising her five children after she throws her drunkard husband out of the house. The novel begins: "Mildred hid the ax beneath the mattress of the cot in the dining room." With those words, McMillan's novel becomes "a runaway narrative pulling a crowded cast of funny, earthy characters," stated Sayers in the *New York Times Book Review*. Because of McMillan's promotional efforts, the novel received numerous reviews—the overwhelming majority of which were positive—and McMillan gave 39 readings. Six weeks after *Mama* was published, it went into its third printing.

*Disappearing Acts,* her second novel, proved to be quite different from *Mama.* For *Disappearing Acts,* McMillan chose to tell the story of star-crossed lovers by alternating the narrative between the main characters. Zora Banks and Franklin Swift fall in love "at first sight" when they meet at Zora's new apartment, where Franklin works as part of the renovating crew. Zora is an educated black woman working as a junior high school music teacher; Franklin is a high-school dropout working in construction. In spite of the differences in their backgrounds, the two become involved, move in together, and try to overcome the fear they both feel because of past failures in love.

Writing in the *Washington Post Book World,* David Nicholson pointed out that although this difference in backgrounds is an old literary device, it is one that is particularly relevant to black Americans: "Professional black women complain of an ever-shrinking pool of eligible men, citing statistics that show the number of black men in prison is increasing, while the number of black men in college is decreasing. Articles on alternatives for women, from celibacy to 'man-sharing' to relationships with blue-collar workers like Franklin have long been a staple of black general interest and women's magazines."

McMillan expressed her thoughts on this issue in an article she wrote entitled "Looking for Mr. Right" for the February, 1990, issue of *Essence.* "Maybe it's just me, but I'm finding it harder and harder to meet men.... I grew up and became what my mama prayed out loud I'd become: educated, strong, smart, independent and reliable.... Now it seems as if carving a place for myself in the world is backfiring. Never in a million years would I have dreamed that I'd be 38 years old and still single."

Throughout the rest of the article, McMillan discusses how she had planned to be married by age twenty-four but found herself attending graduate school instead. She ended up loving and living with men who did not, as she puts it, "take life as seriously as I did." When she was 32 years old, she gave birth to her son, Solomon. Shortly after that she ended a three-year relationship with her son's father. After that McMillan was involved in what she called "two powerful but short-lived relationships," both of which ended when, without any explanation, the man stopped calling.

McMillan believes that "even though a lot of 'professional' men claim to want a smart, independent woman, they're kidding themselves." She thinks that these men do not feel secure unless they are with passive women or with women who will "back down, back off or just acquiesce" until they appear to be tamed. "I'm not tamable," declared McMillan in *Essence.* In response to a former boyfriend who told her that it is lonely at the top, McMillan replied, "It is lonely 'out here.' But I wouldn't for a minute give up all that I've earned just to have a man. I just wish it were easier to meet men and get to know them."

Reviewers commended McMillan on her ability to give such a true voice to the character of Franklin in *Disappearing Acts.* One reviewer for the *Washington Post Book World* called the novel "one of the few ... to contain rounded, sympathetic portraits of black men and to depict relationships between black men and black women as something more than the relationship between victimizer and victim, oppressor and oppressed." In the *New York Times Book Review,* another reviewer stated: "The miracle is that Ms. McMillan takes the reader so deep into this man's head—and makes what goes on there so complicated—that [the] story becomes not only comprehensible but affecting." Not only did McMillan's second novel win critical acclaim, it also was optioned for a film; McMillan eventually wrote the screenplay for Metro-Goldwyn-Mayer.

Leonard Welch, McMillan's former lover and the father of their son, also found that portions of *Disappearing Acts* rung true—so true, in fact, that in August of 1990 he filed a $4.75 million defamation suit against McMillan. Welch claimed that McMillan used him as the model for the novel's main male character, and therefore the book defamed him. The suit also named Penguin USA (parent company of Viking, the publisher of the book) and Simon & Schuster (publisher of the book in paperback) as defendants. The suit alleged that McMillan had acted maliciously in writing the novel and that she had written it mainly out of vindictiveness and a sense of revenge toward Welch and that he had suffered emotional stress. McMillan had dedicated the book to their son, and Welch feared that Solomon would believe the defamatory parts of the novel when he was old enough to read it. Martin Garbus, the lawyer for Penguin USA, maintained that if McMillan had been an obscure writer who had written an obscure book, then there would not have been a lawsuit at all. One of McMillan's writing peers was quoted in the *Los Angeles Times* as saying, "I think it's just part of the general nastiness of the time, that people see someone doing well and they want part of it."

The suit raised the issue of the delicate balance fiction writers must maintain. Many novelists draw on their experiences when writing, and most feel that they have an obligation to protect the privacy of an individual. In the *Los Angeles Times,*

Garbus explained: "What Terry McMillan has done is no different than what other writers have done. It has to be permissible to draw on your real-life experiences. Otherwise, you can't write fiction." Most people involved in the suit, including Welch's lawyer, agreed that a victory for Welch could set an unfortunate precedent that would inhibit the creativity of fiction writers. In April of 1991, the New York Supreme Court ruled in McMillan's favor. As reported in the *Wall Street Journal,* the judge in the case wrote that although "the fictional character and the real man share the same occupation and educational background and even like the same breakfast cereal ... the man in the novel is a lazy, emotionally disturbed alcoholic who uses drugs and sometimes beats his girlfriend." The judge declared that "Leonard Welch is none of these things."

In 1990 Viking published *Breaking Ice: An Anthology of Contemporary African-American Fiction.* Edited by McMillan, the anthology came into being as a result of the anger she experienced after reading a collection of short stories that did not include any black or Third World writers. Her research and book proposal were the first steps in correcting what McMillan felt was the publishing industry's neglect of black writers. She received almost three hundred submissions for the anthology and chose 57 seasoned, emerging, or unpublished writers. In reviewing *Breaking Ice* for the *Washington Post Book World,* author Joyce Carol Oates characterized the book as "a wonderfully generous and diverse collection of prose fiction by our most gifted African-American writers." Oates credited McMillan's judgment for selecting such "high quality of writing ... that one could hardly distinguish between the categories [of writers] in terms of originality, depth of vision and command of the language."

McMillan's third novel, *Waiting to Exhale,* tells the stories of four professional black women who have everything except for the love of a good man. The overall theme of the book is men's fear of commitment; a subtheme is the fear of growing old alone. The novel has hit a nerve with its readers—both male and female. Many women seem to identify with McMillan's characters; so do some men. According to the *Los Angeles Times,* one black male from an audience of over 2,000 proclaimed: "I think I speak for a lot of brothers. I know I'm all over the book.... All I can say is, I'm willing to learn. Being defensive is not the answer." This is precisely the response to the book that McMillan was hoping to get. She wants people to understand that she is not trying to offend or insult black males. She just wants men to be aware of the things they do that make it difficult for women to love them.

One issue that emerged from many reviews of McMillan's earlier books is the amount of profanity she uses. *Waiting to Exhale* met with the same criticism. One critic called her characters male-bashing, stand-up comedians who use foul language. For McMillan, reproducing her characters' profane language is her way of staying close to them. She believes that basically the language she uses is accurate. She told *Publishers Weekly:* "That's the way we talk. And I want to know why I've never read a review where they complain about the language that male writers use!"

For her portrayal of feisty, tough, black heroines, McMillan has been compared to acclaimed black women writers Alice Walker, Gloria Naylor, and Zora Neale Hurston. McMillan acknowledges the compliment but asserts in the introduction to *Breaking Ice* that her generation of black writers is "a new breed, free to write as we please ... because of the way life has changed." Life has changed for her generation but it has also stayed the same for many women in one fundamental way: the search for happiness and fulfillment continues. In an article in the *Los Angeles Times,* McMillan maintained: "A house and a car and all the money in the bank won't make you happy. People need people. People crave intimacy."

Ever mindful of the fleeting nature of fame, McMillan views her celebrity status with a clear eye and remains focused on her mission as a writer. "This won't last," she stated in *Essence.* "Today it's me. Tomorrow it will be somebody else. I always remember that."

*BIOGRAPHICAL/CRITICAL SOURCES:*

*BOOKS*

*Contemporary Literary Criticism,* Gale, Volume 50, 1988, Volume 61, 1991.
McMillan, Terry, *Mama,* Houghton, 1987.
McMillan, Terry, editor, *Breaking Ice: An Anthology of Contemporary African-American Fiction,* Viking, 1990.

*PERIODICALS*

*Callaloo,* summer, 1988, pp. 649-50.
*Cosmopolitan,* August, 1989.
*Detroit Free Press,* June 29, 1992, pp. 1E-2E.
*Detroit News,* September 7, 1992.
*Emerge,* September, 1992.
*Esquire,* July, 1988, pp. 100, 102, 104.
*Essence,* February, 1990; October, 1992.
*Los Angeles Times,* February 23, 1987; October 29, 1990, section E, p. 1; June 19, 1992.
*New York Times Book Review,* February 22, 1987, p. 11; August 6, 1989, p. 8; May 31, 1992, p. 12.
*New York Times Magazine,* August 9, 1992, p. 20.
*People,* July 20, 1992.
*Publishers Weekly,* May 11, 1992, pp. 50-51; July 13, 1992; September 21, 1992.
*Tribune Books* (Chicago), September 23, 1990, p. 1; May 31, 1992, p. 6.

*Village Voice,* March 24, 1987, p. 46.
*Wall Street Journal,* April 11, 1991.
*Washington Post,* November 17, 1990, section D, p. 1.
*Washington Post Book World,* August 27, 1989, p. 6; September 16, 1990, pp. 1, 7; May 24, 1992, p. 11.
*Writer's Digest,* October, 1987.

\*   \*   \*

## McNEILL, Anthony 1941-

*PERSONAL:* Born December 17, 1941, in Kingston, Jamaica; married Olive Samuel, 1971; children: one. *Education:* Attended Excelsior College, 1952; St. George's College, 1953-59; Nassau Community College, 1964-65; Johns Hopkins University, M.A., 1971; University of Massachusetts, Amherst, M.A., 1976.

*ADDRESSES: Agent*—L. Wint, Camperdown, Linstead P.O., Jamaica, West Indies.

*CAREER:* Civil service clerk, Port Maria, Jamaica, and Kingston, Jamaica, 1960-64; Gleaner Co., Kingston, journalist, 1965-66; JIS-Radio, St. Andrew, producer and scriptwriter, 1966-68; Jamaica Playboy Club Hotel, Ocho Rios, trainee manager, 1968-69; *Jamaica Journal,* Kingston, editorial assistant, 1970; Johns Hopkins University, Baltimore, MD, teaching fellow, 1970-71; University of Massachusetts, Amherst, teaching assistant, 1971-75; Institute of Jamaica, Kingston, assistant director of publications, 1976-81; *The Gleaner,* columnist, 1981-82; Excelsior Community College, Kingston, lecturer, 1982-83.

*AWARDS, HONORS:* Jamaica Festival Literary Competition, First Prize and Silver Medal, 1966, First Prize and Gold Medal, 1971; Silver Musgrave Medal, 1972, for poetry.

*WRITINGS:*

*POETRY*

*Hello Ungod,* Peacewood Press, 1971.
*Reel From "The Life-Movie,"* Savacou Publications, 1972.
(Editor and author of introduction with Neville Dawes) *The Caribbean Poem: An Anthology of Fifty Caribbean Voices,* Institute of Jamaica, 1976.
*Credences at The Altar of Cloud,* Institute of Jamaica, 1979.

*BIOGRAPHICAL/CRITICAL SOURCES:*

*BOOKS*

Dance, Daryl C., editor, *Fifty Caribbean Writers: A Bio-Bibliographical Sourcebook,* Greenwood Press, 1986.

*PERIODICALS*

*Caribbean Quarterly,* March, 1984.
*Contraband,* May 1, 1972.
*Jamaica Daily News,* June 29, 1975.
*Jamaica Journal,* March-June, 1973.
*Sunday Gleaner,* January 28, 1973; October 21, 1979; January, 1980.
*Trinidad Express,* March 26, 1979.

\*   \*   \*

## MEDHIN, Tsegaye Gabre
### See GABRE-MEDHIN, Tsegaye (Kawessa)

\*   \*   \*

## MEYER, June
### See JORDAN, June

\*   \*   \*

## MILLER, E(ugene) Ethelbert 1950-

*PERSONAL:* American. Born November 20, 1950, in New York, NY. Married Denise King, 1982; children: Jasmine-Simone, Nyere-Gibran. *Education:* Howard University, B.A., 1972.

*ADDRESSES: Office*—Department of Afro-American Studies, P.O. Box 441, Howard University, Washington, DC 20059.

*CAREER:* African-American Resource Center, Howard University, director, 1974—; Ascension Poetry Reading Series, Washington, DC, founder and organizer, 1974—. University of Nevada—Las Vegas, visiting professor of English, 1993.

*MEMBER:* D.C. Community Humanities Council, PEN American Center, Cultural Alliance of Greater Washington, PEN/Faulkner Foundation, Associated Writing Programs, Institute for Policy Studies, National Writers Union.

*AWARDS, HONORS:* Achievement Award, Institute for Arts and Humanities, Howard University, 1978; E. Ethelbert Miller Day proclaimed by Mayor of Washington, D.C., September 28, 1979; Washington, D.C., Mayor's Art Award, 1982; Washington, DC, Arts Commission fellowship, 1989; Columbia Merit Award, 1993.

*WRITINGS:*

*POETRY*

*The Land of Smiles and the Land of No Smiles,* privately
printed, 1974.
*Andromeda,* [Chiva], 1974.
*The Migrant Worker,* Washington Writers Publishing House,
1978.
*Season of Hunger/Cry of Rain: Poems 1975-1980,* Lotus
Press, 1982.
*Where Are the Love Poems for Dictators?,* Open Hand, 1986.
*First Light: New and Selected Poems,* Black Classic Press,
1993.

*EDITOR*

(With Ahmos Zu-Bolton) *Synergy D.C. Anthology,* Energy
Blacksouth Press, 1975.
*Women Surviving Massacres and Men,* Anemone Press, 1977.
*In Search of Color Everywhere,* Stewart Tabori and Chang,
forthcoming.

*OTHER*

Also author with Amma Khalil of *Interface,* 1972. Author of
introduction, *Fast Talk, Full Volume,* Gut Punch Press, 1993.
Contributor to periodicals, including *Essence, Greenfield
Review, Washingtonian, Caliban, Obsidian, Black American
Literature Forum, Praxis, Black Scholar, Yardbird Reader,*
and *Unrealist.*

*SIDELIGHTS:* A self-proclaimed "literary activist" described
by others as an "aesthetic entrepreneur," prolific poet, editor,
and organiser E. Ethelbert Miller is descended from a line of
proselytizers of new writing that includes Ezra Pound,
Langston Hughes, Lawrence Ferlinghetti, and Ishmael Reed.
Particularly noteworthy is Miller's dedication to the mission
of bringing poetry into the lives of as many people as possible.
In an article in the *Washington Review,* Miller commented,
"I tried from the beginning to make my work accessible to
both language and Ideas. In some ways I modeled myself after Langston Hughes—he was the writer who best embodied
and articulated the hopes and dreams of our people." As a poet
interested in moving society toward the utopian and idealistic goals of moving "beyond race and color" and seeking ways
to "eliminate the divisions of class," Miller has confronted the
fact that there are two literary cultures operating at the present
time: "There are two traditions operating within African
American culture," he remarked, "one oral, the other literary.
At times they intersect and influence each other. Some writers borrow readily from the oral tradition and attempt to
'stretch' their text into being more responsive to sound, music, and mobility. How you sound is still important within the

African American community." Miller's poetry—with influences from "Paul Simon, Donovan, and other 1960s American folk-rock artists" combined with "some of the concerns
and techniques which predominate in the poetry of the 1960s
black arts movement" blends and balances oral techniques
with the modernist experiments of William Carlos Williams'
poetic minimalism and American idiom and Ishmael Reed's
conversational narrative idiom and pervasive irony.

Miller's career as a poet began at Howard University, where
he enrolled as a history major in 1968, intending to eventually study law. Influenced by the Black Arts Movement, Miller
went against the wishes of his family, changed his major to
Afro-American Studies and began to develop his style of
poetry. A decisive influence on Miller at the beginning of his
career as a poet was his partnership with fellow poet Ahmos
Zu-Bolton II, with whom he founded *Hoo-Doo Magazine,* a
poetry journal, and edited *Synergy: An Anthology of Washington D.C. Blackpoetry.* Miller's first volume of poems,
*Andromeda,* is described by Theodore R. Hudson in *Contemporary Poets* as "that of a young poet predictably concerned
with values, introspection, and love." *Dictionary of Literary
Biography* contributor Priscilla R. Ramsey observed that
*Andromeda* already showed characteristics which were to
become fixtures in Miller's poetry, including the absence of
punctuation, the exploration of feelings, the narrator's grasp
of "the ironic significance of his condition," and the premium
the poet places on his emotional life. Themes explored in
*Andromeda* include "the quest toward religious self-definition,
love, and isolation," Ramsey commented. "From *Andromeda*
through Miller's later work, we can watch his development
of an ironic, self-aware, psychological distancing that is centered on his increasing social and political experience."
Miller's next volume came the same year. *The Land of Smiles
and the Land of No Smiles,* a single long poem, according to
Ramsey "chronicles Africa's colonial history and the western exploitation of human beings as it separated African people
from a cultural identity and sense of place.... The poem identifies the failure of both Africa and the West to create a new
black civilization."

In *Migrant Worker* Miller brought together a collection of
poems that directly confronted present conditions in Washington, D.C. Miller speaks of his own experiences in the 1960s
and 1970s, and what the *Small Press Review* calls "irreverent
satires of the human condition." Ramsey sees Miller's chief
distinction in *Migrant Worker* as being "lowering the barriers between street people and intellectuals." This feature is
most clearly manifested in the poems featuring Bo Willie,
Miller's streetwise alter ego. In the title poem he speaks as
himself, betraying the weariness that comes from living in a
time of struggle: "i want to yell / join hands demonstrate / free
my brothers around the world / free the world around my
brothers / but the thrill is gone." *Season of Hunger/Cry of Rain,*

*Poems: 1975-1980* was introduced by June Jordan, a poet known for her political activism. Miller's poems in that volume are characterized by a deepening understanding of complex social and human issues. The direction toward political concerns culminated in Miller's experiments with writing poems openly concerned with Latin American politics. In an essay in the *Washington Review* he stated that he began to recognize his own roots when he recalled that his father was born in Panama and spoke only Spanish when he reached the United States. Miller commented, "The opportunity to recite my poetry to people from Central America was a challenge. I responded by writing a series of poems in the voices of people living in the region." These poems made up much of Miller's next volume, *Where Are the Love Poems for Dictators?* Miller was also "attracted to how women held up during the [Nicaraguan] war and revolution." His interest in women also had a large influence on the poems in *Where Are the Love Poems for Dictators?,* and Hudson commented that "sensitive to feminist concerns and attitudes, he is adept at using a female persona."

Miller's style has clarified and simplified over the years. Hudson sees Miller's poetry in terms of lines that are characteristically conversational, "sometimes idiomatic, pithy, as if they are quiet spurts of thought fragments or little whispers," adding that "Miller has a noticeable talent for the conceit" ... and is "especially good at revelatory, pointed closure that can reverberate for the reader."

Miller has brought work from his previous volumes together in *First Light: Selected and New Poems.* This volume is divided into eight sections, thematically grouping the poems so that while it is possible to read poems related by subject, it is impossible to identify the order in which they were written and published or to tell the previously published poems from the new poems. Miller's concerns are demonstrated by the way the poems are distributed in the volume, with the longest sections bringing together political poems on Latin America ("El Salvador") and often quizzical and ironic poems about love affairs ("Chinatown"). One evocative section, "A Death in the Family," groups together poems on the deaths of W. E. B. DuBois, Malcolm X, James Baldwin, C. L. R. James, and others.

Miller's reputation as a poet and advocate of a politics of inclusion is increasingly bringing him a wider exposure. While serving as vice-president of the PEN/Faulkner Foundation he came to the attention of Richard Wiley of the University of Nevada at Las Vegas and was invited to the campus for a semester as a visiting professor. Increasingly Miller is being recognized as an important poet; he was deemed by poet Gwendolyn Brooks to be "one of the most significant and influential poets of our time." Miller's reputation as a poet is based equally on the accessibility and honesty of his poetry

and his political statements. Miller sees no separation between the roles of art and conscience; he writes in the introduction to *Fast Talk/Full Volume* that "there is now a need for all of us to become more involved.... With so many changes occurring in Africa, and throughout the world, it is critical that we keep writing and dreaming."

*BIOGRAPHICAL/CRITICAL SOURCES:*

*BOOKS*

*Contemporary Poets,* fifth edition, St. James Press, 1991, pp. 655-656.
*Dictionary of Literary Biography,* Volume 41: *Afro-American Poets since 1955,* Gale, 1985, pp. 233-240.
*Fast Talk, Full Volume,* Gut Punch Press, 1993.

*PERIODICALS*

*Las Vegas Accent,* May 17, 1993.
*New York Times,* June 5, 1988.
*Small Press Review,* April, 1988.
*Washington Post,* March 11, 1987.
*Washington Review,* February/March, 1991.

\*   \*   \*

## MILLER, May 1899-

*PERSONAL:* Born January 26, 1899, in Washington, DC; daughter of Kelly Miller (a scholar, writer, and university dean) and Annie May Butler (a teacher); married John Sullivan (a U.S. postal supervisor). *Education:* Received bachelor's degree from Howard University; attended American University and Columbia University.

*ADDRESSES:* c/o Miller Newman, 1208 Girard St., NW, Washington, DC 20009.

*CAREER:* Poet, educator, and playwright. Leader in Negro Little Theatre Movement; teacher of speech and drama at Frederick Douglass High School, Baltimore, MD; panelist, reader, lecturer, and poet-in-residence at Monmouth College, University of Wisconsin, Milwaukee, and Phillips Exeter Academy. Coordinator of performing poets for Friends of the Arts, Washington, DC, Public Schools. Chair of literature division and member of Commission on the Arts of the District of Columbia; member of Folger Library Advisory Committee.

*AWARDS, HONORS:* Third prize award, *Opportunity* magazine, 1925, for *The Bog Guide.*

*WRITINGS:*

*POETRY*

*Into the Clearing,* Charioteer Press, 1959.

*Poems,* Cricket Press, 1962.

(With K. L. Lyle and M. Rubin) *Lyrics of Three Women,* Linden Press, 1964.

*The Clearing and Beyond,* Charioteer Press, 1973.

*Not That Far,* Solo Press, 1973.

*Dust of an Uncertain Journey,* Lotus Press, 1975.

*Halfway to the Sun* (includes "The Great Gem"), Washington Writers' Publishing House, 1981.

*The Ransomed Wait,* Lotus Press, 1983.

*Collected Poems,* Lotus Press, 1989.

*OTHER*

(Editor with Willis Richardson; and contributor) *Plays and Pageants from the Life of the Negro* (includes *Riding the Goat* and *Graven Images*), Associated Publishers, 1930.

(Editor with Richardson; and contributor) *Negro History in Thirteen Plays* (includes *Christophe's Daughters, Samory, Harriet Tubman,* and *Sojourner Truth*), Associated Publishers, 1935.

(Editor) *Green Wind,* Commission of Arts and Humanities, 1978.

(Editor) *My World,* Fine Arts Commission, 1979.

Author of the one-act plays *Scratches,* published in *Carolina* magazine, April, 1929, *The Bog Guide,* and *The Cuss'd Thing.* Contributor of poems, articles, and short stories to periodicals, including *Phylon, Antioch Review, Arts Quarterly, Carolina, Cafe Solo, Common Ground, Crisis, Energy West, Nation, New York Times, Poetry,* and *Writer.*

*SIDELIGHTS:* Inspired by writers including Edgar Allan Poe and Walt Whitman, fictional characters such as Brer Rabbit and Uncle Remus, and ancient myths penned in Greek and Latin, May Miller remembers growing up as the well-nourished and amused daughter of Annie May Butler, a teacher for Baltimore schools, and Kelly Miller, a celebrated scholar, writer, and dean at Howard University. Miller's childhood memories are filled with encouragement and anecdotes from the famed artists, writers, composers, and intellectuals who once visited her parent's campus house, among them W. E. B. Du Bois, William Stanley Braithwaite, and Paul Laurence Dunbar.

Inspired to write from an early age, Miller joined the Howard University Players in her undergraduate years, garnering social attention. Befriended by Georgia Douglas Johnson, Miller joined her early literary salon "The Saturday Nighters" and turned her attention for the next twenty years to teaching

speech and drama. In 1972 she declared to interviewer Cassandra Williams that "we would have no [dramatist] Lorraine Hansberry if there had not been behind her those people who were slowly leading up to her great productions," as quoted in *Dictionary of Literary Biography.* As a teacher, Miller nurtured the dreams of young, aspiring black playwrights (she energized Baltimore's junior high schools with the Negro Little Theatre Movement), emphasizing later in an interview that "we started to dramatize Negro history because it is a treasure trove and greatness has no [racial] boundaries," as cited in *Harlem Renaissance and Beyond.*

This period, too, marks Miller's own incursions into the world of the avant-garde New Negro literary movement in Washington and New York City. Du Bois's Krigwa Players welcomed her into their circle in the late 1920s, with the production of Johnson's *Blue Blood* at the 135th Street Library in New York City. Miller also produced many dramatic works of her own during this duration, and many of her one-acts often take on overtones of racial anger and anti-colonialist sentiment. *The Bog Guide,* written in 1925, describes the sordid and swampy vengeance exacted by an exiled woman on her white English cousin, when she learns of his role in destroying her father's health and chances for success. *The Cuss'd Thing* journeys into a small Harlem apartment, where a pregnant woman and her musician husband argue over the religious and aesthetic factors which accompany an offer to work on a black folk musical in a white Broadway industry. During this time, Miller also forged a long-time theatrical and editorial collaboration with Washington playwright Willis Richardson (their drama collections only sometimes name Miller for her role). *Riding the Goat,* included in the collection *Plays and Pageants from the Life of the Negro,* is a comical and often satirical exploration of the black fraternity lodge and community pressure. The work follows a novice physician through the extraordinary and absurd measures he takes in order to blend into his Baltimore community and ingratiate himself to prospective clients.

The 1930s saw Miller move distinctly toward a more symbolic view of both ancient and modern Western civilization, as well as of the black historical figures (often women) her works either denigrate or monumentalize. Among the characters featured are Henry Christophe, the ill-fated nineteenth-century Haitian King, in *Christophe and His Daughters;* Samory, a late-nineteenth-century Sudanese conqueror, in *Samory;* Zipporah, Moses's debased Ethiopian wife, in *Graven Images;* Harriet Tubman, renowned freedom fighter and founder of the Underground Railroad, in *Harriet Tubman;* and Sojourner Truth, feminist, former slave, and human rights preacher, in *Sojourner Truth.* Miller's attention to black history and black memory mirrors those of her friends, colleagues, and literary counterparts: Langston Hughes, Jean Toomer, Marita Bonner, Zora Neale Hurston, and Gertrude

427

Parthenia McBrown. Her interest in black and American motifs—struggles for success, African mythologies, fables, and nature stories—suggests that she wants her dramatic works to be accessible to a broad readership.

This sense of obligation to the community has been a persistent theme and motivator for Miller in her career both as an artist and social worker. When Miller married John Sullivan and retired from dramatic circles in 1943, she turned full time to her second love: poetry. Her collections to date share among them a simple and straightforward style, designed for a reader's personal reflection without the intensity of modernist abstractionism. In 1985, as quoted in *Harlem Renaissance and Beyond,* literary critic Claudia Tate pointed out that Miller's poetry is contemplative: Each "poem creates a dramatic setting and places the actor, who is the meditative speaker, within it."

Since the time Miller wrote these volumes and edited a number of collections of her work, she has served in a variety of academic and administrative posts. Her pen has often led her to humanitarian causes: she has resided as a poet-in-residence at Monmouth College; served as poetry coordinator for the Friends of Art, a District of Columbia-based program in which she mentored children's poetry and arranged for its publication; delivered her works at the Smithsonian and Martin Luther King, Jr., Library; and participated on the Folger Library Poetry Advisory Committee. In the words of writer and editor Robert E. Hayden, as cited in the *Dictionary of Literary Biography,* Miller is a "poet of humane vision." Her gifts to her Washington black community and the world beyond come from her enduring commitment to place the beauty of folk language and performance arts within reach of all audiences. In "The Great Gem," a children's poem that is collected in her 1981 volume *Halfway to the Sun,* she writes: "It's a picture / of our earth I'm sending / back to you. / It's your world you're / too close to see."

*BIOGRAPHICAL/CRITICAL SOURCES:*

*BOOKS*

*Dictionary of Literary Biography,* Volume 41: *Afro-American Poets Since 1955,* Gale, 1985, pp. 241-47.
Miller, May, *Halfway to the Sun,* Washington Writers' Publishing House, 1981.
Roses, Lorraine Elena, and Ruth Elizabeth Randolph, *Harlem Renaissance and Beyond,* G. K. Hall, 1990, pp. 236-40.

*PERIODICALS*

*Booklist,* April, 1936, p. 228.
*Callaloo,* fall, 1990, p. 912.
*Catholic World,* summer, 1936, p. 765.

*Kliatt Young Adult Paperback Book Guide,* April, 1989, p. 30.
*Survey Guide,* November, 1936, p. 632.

—*Sketch by Marcy J. Epstein*

\* \* \*

## MILLER, Warren 1921-1966
## (Amanda Vail)

*PERSONAL:* Born August 31, 1921, in Stowe, PA; died of lung cancer, April 20, 1966, in New York, NY; son of Carl Miller and Rose Singer; married; children: Scott, Eve. *Education:* University of Iowa, B.A. and M.A., 1948.

*CAREER:* Writer. University of Iowa, Iowa City, instructor of literature, during 1950s; also worked in public relations and sales in New York City. *Military service:* Served during World War II.

*AWARDS, HONORS:* National Institute of Arts and Letters grant, 1961.

*WRITINGS:*

*NOVELS*

*The Sleep of Reason,* Secker & Warburg, 1956, Little, Brown, 1960.
*The Way We Live Now,* Little, Brown, 1958.
*The Cool World,* Little, Brown, 1959.
*Flush Times,* Little, Brown, 1962.
*Looking for the General,* McGraw-Hill, 1964.
*The Siege of Harlem,* McGraw-Hill, 1965.

*ROMANTIC NOVELS; UNDER PSEUDONYM AMANDA VAIL*

*Love Me Little,* McGraw-Hill, 1957.
*The Bright Young Things,* Little, Brown, 1958.

*CHILDREN'S BOOKS*

*King Carlo of Capri,* illustrations by Edward Sorel, Harcourt, 1958.
*Pablo Paints a Picture,* illustrations by Edward Sorel, Little, Brown, 1959.
*The Goings-On at Little Wishful,* illustrations by Edward Sorel, Little, Brown, 1959.

*OTHER*

*Ninety Miles from Home: The Face of Cuba Today* (nonfiction), Little, Brown, 1961, (published in England as *The Lost Plantation: The Face of Cuba Today,* Secker & Warburg, 1961.)

Literary editor for the *Nation,* 1965-66; contributor to *New Yorker, Saturday Evening Post,* and *Esquire.*

*BIOGRAPHICAL/CRITICAL SOURCES:*

*PERIODICALS*

*New York Times,* February 13, 1972, p. 5.

*OBITUARIES:*

*PERIODICALS*

*Antiquarian Bookman,* May 2, 1966.
*Newsweek,* May 9, 1966.
*New York Herald Tribune,* April 21, 1966.
*New York Times,* April 21, 1966, p. 39.
*Publishers Weekly,* May 2, 1966, p. 36.


*        *        *


## MILLICAN, Arthenia Jackson Bates 1920-
## (Arthenia J. Bates)

*PERSONAL:* Born June 1, 1920, in Sumter, SC; daughter of Calvin Shepard (an educator) and Susan Emma (a crafter; maiden name, David) Jackson; married Noah Bates, June 11, 1950 (divorced, 1956); married Wilbert Millican, August 14, 1969 (died April 10, 1982); children: (second marriage) Wilbert James (stepson). *Education:* Morris College, B.A. (magna cum laude), 1941; Atlanta University, M.A., 1948; graduate study at North Carolina Central University, 1953; University of Michigan 1955, 1958; Louisiana State University, Ph.D., 1972. *Politics:* Democrat. *Religion:* Roman Catholic.


*ADDRESSES: Home*—16571 Charlton Rd., Baker, LA 70714-5132. *Office*—P.O. Box 335, Baker, LA 70704-0335.


*CAREER:* High school English teacher in Kershaw, SC, 1942-46; high school teacher of English and civics in Harsville, SC, 1945-46; Morris College, Sumter, SC, chair of English department, 1947-49; Halifax Training School, Halifax, VA, instructor in English, 1949-55; Mississippi Vocational College (now Mississippi Valley State University), Itta Bena, instructor in English, 1955-56; Southern University, Baton Rouge, LA, instructor, 1956-59, assistant professor, 1959-63, associate professor, 1963-72, professor of English, 1972-74; Norfolk State College, Norfolk, VA, professor of English, 1974-77; Southern University, professor of English and creative writ-

ing, 1977-80. Instructor in creative writing, Camp Miniwanca, Stony Lake, MI, summers, 1962, 1963; American Youth Foundation, official scholarship recruiter, 1964-67; Community Advancement Incorporation for East Baton Rouge Parish, member of board of directors, 1967-70; reviewer for National Endowment for the Humanities, 1978-82. Researcher for State of Louisiana's first "Black Culture Registry" project, 1985; panelist and reader, Carolina Correction (an international group of all writers born in South Carolina), Charleston, SC, 1989; honorary writer-in-residence, Scenic High School, Louisiana Training School, Baker, LA, 1989—.


*MEMBER:* Modern Language Association, College Language Association (life member; chair of creative writing committee, 1974-75), National Council of Teachers of English, Conference on College Composition and Communication, Society for the Study of Southern Literature, Conference on Black South Literature and the Arts, Louisiana Folklore Society, Phillis Wheatley Club, Gamma Sigma Sigma (chair of advisory committee, 1959-64), Delta Sigma Theta.


*AWARDS, HONORS:* First prize from College Language Association creative writing contest, 1960, for "The Entertainers"; award of merit and second prize from McKendree Writers Association, 1962, for short story, "Dear Sis"; bronze medal from American Youth Foundation, 1963; fiction award from National Endowment for the Arts, 1976, for "Where You Belong"; award and presidential citation from National Association for Equal Opportunity in Higher Education, 1981; first Delta Pearl Award in Literature from Delta Sigma Theta, 1989; award from Societas Docta (international organization for women of color who have earned doctorates and offer proof of exceptional service in their field), 1991.


*WRITINGS:*


(Under name Arthenia J. Bates) *Seeds Beneath the Snow* (short stories; includes "The Entertainers"), Greenwich Book Publishers, 1969, published as *Seeds Beneath the Snow: Vignettes from the South,* Howard University Press, 1975.
(Under name Arthenia J. Bates) *The Deity Nodded* (novel), Harlo, 1973.
*Such Things from the Valley* (short stories), Millican, 1977.

Also author of *Hand on the Throttle: Touchstones in the Life of Lionel Lee, Sr.,* Volume 1: *Holding On* (biography), 1993. Work represented in anthologies, including *Poetry Broadcast: An Anthology Compiled for Radio Programs,* 1946; *National Poetry Anthology,* 1958, 1962, 1963, and 1973; *James Baldwin: A Critical Evaluation,* 1977; *Rhetoric and Readings for Writing,* 1975, 1977, 1979, and 1981; *Sturdy Black Bridges: Visions of Black Women in Literature,* 1979; *The*

*Heath Anthology of American Literature,* 1990; *Black Women's Blues,* 1992; *Black Southern Voices,* 1992; *Louisiana Women Writers,* 1992; and *Literature of the World,* 1992. Contributor to periodicals, including *African American Review, Baptist Advocate of Baton Rouge, Black World, CLA Journal, English Newsletter, Essence, Le Monde, Mahogany, Negro American Literature Forum, Negro Digest, New Orleans Review,* and *Southern University Digest.* Contributing editor, *Obsidian: Black Literature in Review,* 1974-76, and *Callaloo,* 1976-84.

*WORK IN PROGRESS:* A sequel to *The Deity Nodded;* collecting humorous material "peculiar to a local area in southern Louisiana"; short stories on mother-daughter relationships in the South from 1900 to the present.

*SIDELIGHTS:* Arthenia Bates Millican commented: "One of the most difficult lessons for me to learn as a student of creative writing is the advice about slanting. An essay delivered as a speech eulogizing Langston Hughes soon after his death, entitled 'The Sun Legend: A Tribute to Langston Hughes,' seemed to me to be a masterpiece of slanting. It would be of interest to blacks because Hughes is the subject, and of interest to scholars because it is a research article with the rich allusions in Greek mythology, and of interest to everyone else because the theme is death.

"You know the audacity of young blacks during the sixties. A young black poet said, 'Your idea of finding what you call sun-sense in Hughes is alright. You try to explain his warmth in terms of the folk quality, the African ethos and the humane factor in general; but you messed it up by alluding to Greek mythology. Hughes would have appreciated your using Egyptian mythology.'

"What he did not understand, from my point of view, was that I was a student (anthology-read) of Greek literature. I had the right to allude to Phaeton, the son of Apollo, and the nymph Clymene. Had he asked me, 'What does Africa mean to you?,' I would have said, 'Nothing,' because I had not come to know the joy of riding on the communal wave of the mother spirit that matured with the *Roots* phenomenon.

"Almost twenty years have passed, and I am just coming into the knowledge of what I hope he also understands.

"The oil rigs are being constructed here and there in the Baker community of East Baton Rouge Parish where I used to live. A court case of slant-drilling against a driller seeking to cash in on this Tuscaloose Trend opened my eyes. How rich are your unmined resources? Mine? How will you know unless you drill? Slant-drilling is illegally mining the resources of another. You may have the rig on your territory but the gold, that black splatter, comes from the other man's territory.

"I know what the young poet was trying to tell me about the tradition and the individual talent."

*BIOGRAPHICAL/CRITICAL SOURCES:*

*BOOKS*

Bell, Roseann P., Bettye J. Parker and Beverley Guy-Sheftall, editors, *Sturdy Black Bridges: Visions of Black Women in Literature,* Anchor Press, 1979, pp. 201-9.
Dandridge, Rita B., *Black Women's Blues: A Literary Anthology, 1934-1988,* G. K. Hall, 1992, pp. 225-31.
*Dictionary of Literary Biography,* Volume 38: *Afro-American Writers after 1955: Dramatists and Prose Writers,* Gale, 1985, pp. 195-201.
Thomas, Freddy L., editor, *Literatures of the World,* Ginn, 1990, p. 951.

*PERIODICALS*

*African American Review,* spring, 1993, pp. 25-28.
*Baton Rouge Morning Advocate,* March 13, 1970.
*Baton Rouge News Leader,* February 9, 1959; March 15, 1970; June 14, 1970; August 13, 1973; December 23, 1973; January 13, 1974; January 20, 1974, p. 6A; May 19, 1974.
*Chantaqua Daily,* July 24, 1962.
*CLA Journal,* March, 1970, pp. 325-327; December, 1973, pp. 279-86.
*College Language Association Journal,* June, 1970; December, 1973.
*Delta,* summer, 1970.
*Essence,* July, 1980.
*Freedom Ways,* November 11, 1975.
*MELUS,* fall, 1985, pp. 13-22.
*Negro Digest,* August, 1969, p. 94.
*Norfolk Journal and Guide,* November 9, 1974.
*Norfolk-Portsmouth Ledger Star,* November 18, 1974.
*Nuance,* March, 1982, pp. 14-16.
*Observer* (Baker, LA), January 26, 1984, p. 2B.
*Obsidian: Black American Literature in Review,* spring, 1977, 14-34.
*Publishers Weekly,* November 11, 1974.
*Southern University Digest,* May 4, 1973, p. 4.
*Sunday Advocate* (Baton Rouge), September 9, 1973, p. 2F.
*Virginian Pilot,* July 4, 1976.
*Washington Afro-American,* June 2, 1970.

*Washington Post,* June 11, 1970; July 11, 1970, section B, p. 2.

\* \* \*

**MISS LOU**
See BENNETT, Louise (Simone)

\* \* \*

**MISTRAL, Gabriela**
See GODOY ALCAYAGA, Lucila

\* \* \*

**MORNINGHOUSE, Sundaira**
See WILSON, Carletta

\* \* \*

**MORRISON, Toni 1931-**

*PERSONAL:* Born Chloe Anthony Wofford, February 18, 1931, in Lorain, OH; daughter of George and Ramah (Willis) Wofford; married Harold Morrison, 1958 (divorced, 1964); children: Harold Ford, Slade Kevin. *Education:* Howard University, B.A., 1953; Cornell University, M.A., 1955.

*ADDRESSES: Office*—Department of Creative Writing, Princeton University, Princeton, NJ 08544-1099. *Agent*—Amanda Urban, International Creative Management, 40 West 57th St., New York, NY 10019.

*CAREER:* Texas Southern University, Houston, instructor in English, 1955-57; Howard University, Washington, DC, instructor in English, 1957-64; Random House, New York, NY, senior editor, 1965-85; State University of New York at Albany, Albert Schweitzer Chair in the Humanities, 1984-89; Princeton University, Princeton, NJ, Robert F. Goheen Professor in the Council of the Humanities, 1989—. State University of New York at Purchase, associate professor of English, 1971-72; visiting lecturer, Yale University, 1976-77, and Bard College, 1986-88; Clark Lecturer at Trinity College, Cambridge, and Massey Lecturer at Harvard University, both 1990. Trustee of the National Humanities Center; co-chair of the Schomburg Commission for the Preservation of Black Culture.

*MEMBER:* American Academy and Institute of Arts and Letters, American Academy of Arts and Sciences, National Council on the Arts, Authors Guild (member of council), Authors League of America.

*AWARDS, HONORS:* National Book Award nomination and Ohioana Book Award, both 1975, for *Sula;* National Book Critics Circle Award and American Academy and Institute of Arts and Letters Award, both 1977, for *Song of Solomon;* New York State Governor's Arts Award, 1986; first recipient of the Washington College Literary award, 1987; National Book Award nomination and National Book Critics Circle Award nomination, both 1987, and Pulitzer Prize for fiction and Robert F. Kennedy Award, both 1988, all for *Beloved;* Elizabeth Cady Stanton Award from National Organization for Women.

*WRITINGS:*

*The Bluest Eye* (novel), Holt, 1969.
*Sula* (novel), Knopf, 1973.
(Editor) *The Black Book* (anthology), Random House, 1974.
*Song of Solomon* (novel; Book-of-the-Month Club selection), Knopf, 1977.
*Tar Baby* (novel), Knopf, 1981.
*Dreaming Emmett* (play), first produced in Albany, NY, 1986.
*Beloved* (novel), Knopf, 1987.
*Jazz* (novel), Knopf, 1992.
*Playing in the Dark: Whiteness and the Literary Imagination* (lectures), Harvard University Press, 1992.
(Editor) *Race-ing Justice, En-Gendering Power: Essays on Anita Hill, Clarence Thomas, and the Construction of Social Reality,* Pantheon, 1992.

Author of lyrics for "Honey and Rue," commissioned by Carnegie Hall for Kathleen Battle, with music by Andre Previn, 1992. Contributor of essays and reviews to numerous periodicals, including *New York Times Magazine.*

*WORK IN PROGRESS:* A journal; a revision of *The Bluest Eye;* a novel tentatively titled *Paradise,* third in a series chronicling the African American experience.

*SIDELIGHTS:* Through novels such as *The Bluest Eye, Song of Solomon, Beloved,* and *Jazz,* Toni Morrison has earned a reputation as a gifted storyteller whose troubled characters seek to find themselves and their cultural riches in a society that warps or impedes such essential growth. According to Charles Larson in the *Chicago Tribune Book World,* each of Morrison's novels "is as original as anything that has appeared in our literature in the last 20 years. The contemporaneity that unites them—the troubling persistence of racism in America—is infused with an urgency that only a black writer can have about our society."

Morrison's artistry has attracted critical acclaim as well as commercial success; *Dictionary of Literary Biography* contributor Susan L. Blake calls the author "an anomaly in two respects" because "she is a black writer who has achieved national prominence and popularity, and she is a popular writer who is taken seriously." Indeed, Morrison has won two of modern literature's most prestigious citations, the 1977 National Book Critics Circle Award for *Song of Solomon* and the 1988 Pulitzer Prize for *Beloved. Atlantic* correspondent Wilfrid Sheed notes: "Most black writers are privy, like the rest of us, to bits and pieces of the secret, the dark side of their group experience, but Toni Morrison uniquely seems to have all the keys on her chain, like a house detective.... She [uses] the run of the whole place, from ghetto to small town to ramshackle farmhouse, to bring back a panorama of black myth and reality that [dazzles] the senses." *Newsweek* contributor Jean Strouse observes: "Like all the best stories, [Morrison's] are driven by an abiding moral vision. Implicit in all her characters' grapplings with who they are is a large sense of human nature and love—and a reach for understanding of something larger than the moment."

"It seems somehow both constricting and inadequate to describe Toni Morrison as the country's preeminent black novelist, since in both gifts and accomplishments she transcends categorization," writes Jonathan Yardley in the *Washington Post Book World,* "yet the characterization is inescapable not merely because it is true but because the very nature of Morrison's work dictates it. Not merely has black American life been the central preoccupation of her ... novels ... but as she has matured she has concentrated on distilling all of black experience into her books; quite purposefully, it seems, she is striving not for the particular but for the universal." In her work Morrison strives to lay bare the injustice inherent in the black condition and blacks' efforts, individually and collectively, to transcend society's unjust boundaries. Blake notes that Morrison's novels explore "the difference between black humanity and white cultural values. This opposition produces the negative theme of the seduction and betrayal of black people by white culture ... and the positive theme of the quest for cultural identity."

Quest for self is a motivating and organizing device in Morrison's writing, as is the role of family and community in nurturing or challenging the individual. In the *Times Literary Supplement,* Jennifer Uglow suggests that Morrison's novels "explore in particular the process of growing up black, female and poor. Avoiding generalities, Toni Morrison concentrates on the relation between the pressures of the community, patterns established within families, ... and the developing sense of self." According to Dorothy H. Lee in *Black Women Writers (1950-1980): A Critical Evaluation,* Morrison is preoccupied "with the effect of the community on the individual's achievement and retention of an integrated, acceptable self.

In treating this subject, she draws recurrently on myth and legend for story pattern and characters, returning repeatedly to the theory of *quest....* The goals her characters seek to achieve are similar in their deepest implications, and yet the degree to which they attain them varies radically because each novel is cast in unique human terms." In Morrison's books, blacks must confront the notion that all understanding is accompanied by pain, just as all comprehension of national history must include the humiliations of slavery. She tempers this hard lesson by preserving "the richness of communal life against an outer world that denies its value" and by turning to "a heritage of folklore, not only to disclose patterns of living but also to close wounds," in the words of *Nation* contributor Brina Caplan.

Although Morrison herself told the *Chicago Tribune* that there is "epiphany and triumph" in every book she writes, some critics find her work nihilistic and her vision bleak. "The picture given by ... Morrison of the plight of the decent, aspiring individual in the black family and community is more painful than the gloomiest impressions encouraged by either stereotype or sociology," observes Diane Johnson in the *New York Review of Books.* Johnson continues, "Undoubtedly white society is the ultimate oppressor, and not just of blacks; but, as Morrison [shows,] ... the black person must first deal with the oppressor in the next room, or in the same bed, or no farther away than across the street." Morrison is a pioneer in the depiction of the hurt inflicted by blacks on blacks; for instance, her characters rarely achieve harmonious heterosexual relationships but are instead divided by futurelessness and the anguish of stifled existence. Uglow writes: "We have become attuned to novels ... which locate oppression in the conflicts of blacks (usually men) trying to make it in a white world. By concentrating on the sense of violation experienced within black neighborhoods, even within families, Toni Morrison deprives us of stock responses and creates a more demanding and uncomfortable literature." *Village Voice* correspondent Vivian Gornick contends that the world Morrison creates "is thick with an atmosphere through which her characters move slowly, in pain, ignorance, and hunger. And to a very large degree Morrison has the compelling ability to make one believe that all of us (Morrison, the characters, the reader) are penetrating that dark and hurtful terrain—the feel of a human life—simultaneously." Uglow concludes that even the laughter of Morrison's characters "disguises pain, deprivation and violation. It is laughter at a series of bad, cruel jokes.... Nothing is what it seems; no appearance, no relationship can be trusted to endure."

Other critics detect a deeper undercurrent to Morrison's work that contains just the sort of epiphany for which she strives. "From book to book, Morrison's larger project grows clear," declares Ann Snitow in the *Voice Literary Supplement.* "First, she insists that every character bear the weight of responsibility for his or her own life. After she's measured out each one's private pain, she adds on to that the shared burden of what the whites did. Then, at last, she tries to find the place where her stories can lighten her readers' load, lift them up from their own and others' guilt, carry them to glory.... Her characters suffer—from their own limitations and the world's —but their inner life miraculously expands beyond the narrow law of cause and effect." *Harvard Advocate* essayist Faith Davis writes that despite the mundane boundaries of Morrison's characters' lives, the author "illuminates the complexity of their attitudes toward life. Having reached a quiet and extensive understanding of their situation, they can endure life's calamities.... Morrison never allows us to become indifferent to these people.... Her citizens ... jump up from the pages vital and strong because she has made us care about the pain in their lives." In *Ms.,* Margo Jefferson concludes that Morrison's books "are filled with loss—lost friendship, lost love, lost customs, lost possibilities. And yet there is so much life in the smallest acts and gestures ... that they are as much celebrations as elegies."

Morrison sees language as an expression of black experience, and her novels are characterized by vivid narration and dialogue. She acknowledges the powerful influences of her community and family on how she writes. In a PBS interview with Charlie Rose, Morrison said: "I'm completely informed by that community, by my extended family, the language particularly. Not just the survival, but the way they spoke, you know. The language of average, of poor African-Americans is always discredited as though it was impossible for them to speak, or they were stupid. But there was this incredible merging of new language and Biblical language and sermonic language and street language and standard that created a third thing for me.... A third kind of way of expressing myself. They pulled from all the places, and that's what I tried to incorporate in my books."

*Village Voice* essayist Susan Lydon observes that the author "works her magic charm above all with a love of language. Her soaring ... style carries you like a river, sweeping doubt and disbelief away, and it is only gradually that one realizes her deadly serious intent." In the *Spectator,* Caroline Moorehead likewise notes that Morrison "writes energetically and richly, using words in a way very much her own. The effect is one of exoticism, an exciting curiousness in the language, a balanced sense of the possible that stops, always, short of the absurd." Although Morrison does not like to be called a poetic writer, critics often comment on the lyrical quality of her prose. "Morrison's style has always moved fluidly between tough-minded realism and lyric descriptiveness," notes Margo Jefferson in *Newsweek.* "Vivid dialogue, capturing the drama and extravagance of black speech, gives way to an impressionistic evocation of physical pain or an ironic, essay-like analysis of the varieties of religious hypocrisy." Uglow writes:

"The word 'elegant' is often applied to Toni Morrison's writing; it employs sophisticated narrative devices, shifting perspectives and resonant images and displays an obvious delight in the potential of language." *Nation* contributor Earl Frederick concludes that Morrison, "with an ear as sharp as glass ... has listened to the music of black talk and deftly uses it as the palette knife to create black lives and to provide some of the best fictional dialogue around today."

According to Jean Strouse, Morrison "comes from a long line of people who did what they had to do to survive. It is their stories she tells in her novels tales of the suffering and richness, the eloquence and tragedies of the black American experience." Morrison was born Chloe Anthony Wofford in Lorain, Ohio, a small town near the shores of Lake Erie. *New York Review of Books* correspondent Darryl Pinckney describes her particular community as "close enough to the Ohio River for the people who lived [there] to feel the torpor of the South, the nostalgia for its folkways, to sense the old Underground Railroad underfoot like a hidden stream." While never explicitly autobiographical, Morrison's fictions draw upon her youthful experiences in Ohio. In an essay for *Black Women Writers at Work* she claims: "I am from the Midwest so I have a special affection for it. My beginnings are always there.... No matter what I write, I begin there.... It's the matrix for me.... Ohio also offers an escape from stereotyped black settings. It is neither plantation nor ghetto."

Two important aspects of Chloe Wofford's childhood—community spirit and the supernatural—inform Toni Morrison's mature writing. In a *Publishers Weekly* interview, Morrison suggests ways in which her community influenced her. "There is this town which is both a support system and a hammer at the same time," she notes. "Approval was not the acquisition of things; approval was given for the maturity and the dignity with which one handled oneself. Most black people in particular were, and still are, very fastidious about manners, very careful about behavior and the rules that operate within the community. The sense of organized activity, what I thought at that time was burdensome, turns out now to have within it a gift—which is, I never had to be taught how to hold a job, how to make it work, how to handle my time."

On several levels a unique and sometimes eccentric individual figures in Morrison's fictional reconstruction of black community life. "There is always an elder there," she notes of her work in *Black Women Writers: A Critical Evaluation.* "And these ancestors are not just parents, they are sort of timeless people whose relationships to the characters are benevolent, instructive, and protective, and they provide a certain kind of wisdom." Sometimes this figure imparts his or her wisdom from beyond the grave; from an early age Morrison absorbed the folklore and beliefs of a culture for which the supernatural holds power and portent. Strouse notes that Morrison's world, both within and outside her fiction, is "filled with signs, visitations, ways of knowing that [reach] beyond the five senses."

Morrison's birthplace of Lorain, Ohio, is in fact the setting of *The Bluest Eye,* published in 1969. Morrison's first novel portrays "in poignant terms the tragic condition of blacks in a racist America," to quote Chikwenye Okonjo Ogunyemi in *Critique: Studies in Modern Fiction.* In *The Bluest Eye,* Morrison depicts the onset of black self-hatred as occasioned by white American ideals such as "Dick and Jane" primers and Shirley Temple movies. The principal character, Pecola Breedlove, is literally maddened by the disparity between her existence and the pictures of beauty and gentility disseminated by the dominant white culture. As Phyllis R. Klotman notes in the *Black American Literature Forum,* Morrison "uses the contrast between Shirley Temple and Pecola ... to underscore the irony of black experience. Whether one learns acceptability from the formal educational experience or from cultural symbols, the effect is the same: self-hatred." Darwin T. Turner discusses the novel's intentions in *Black Women Writers: A Critical Evaluation.* Morrison's fictional milieu, writes Turner, is "a world of grotesques—individuals whose psyches have been deformed by their efforts to assume false identities, their failures to achieve meaningful identities, or simply their inability to retain and communicate love."

Morrison elaborated on the theme of self-esteem in *The Bluest Eye* during the PBS interview. "I was really writing a book I wanted to read.... I hadn't seen a book in which black girls were center stage.... And I had a major, major question in my mind at that time, which was, How does a child learn self-loathing, for racial purposes? Who enables it? How is it infectious? And what might be the consequences?" Self-loathing can be learned, she says, from a society that lies about what is attractive. "It's interior death. You never have an opportunity to develop what's really valuable, which is grace, balance, health, virtue—all those good things that each of us can be."

Blake characterizes *The Bluest Eye* as a novel of initiation, exploring that common theme in American literature from a minority viewpoint. Ogunyemi likewise contends that, in essence, Morrison presents "old problems in a fresh language and with a fresh perspective. A central force of the work derives from her power to draw vignettes and her ability to portray emotions, seeing the world through the eyes of adolescent girls." Klotman, who calls the book "a novel of growing up, of growing up young and black and female in America," concludes her review with the comment that the "rite of passage, initiating the young into womanhood at first tenuous and uncertain, is sensitively depicted.... *The Bluest Eye* is an extraordinarily passionate yet gentle work, the language lyrical yet precise—it is a novel for all seasons."

In *Sula,* Morrison's 1973 novel, the author once again presents a pair of black women who must come to terms with their lives. Set in a Midwestern black community called The Bottom, the story follows two friends, Sula and Nel, from childhood to old age and death. Snitow claims that through *Sula,* Morrison has discovered "a way to offer her people an insight and sense of recovered self so dignified and glowing that no worldly pain could dull the final light." Indeed, *Sula* is a tale of rebel and conformist in which the conformity is dictated by the solid inhabitants of The Bottom and even the rebellion gains strength from the community's disapproval. *New York Times Book Review* contributor Sara Blackburn contends, however, that the book is "too vital and rich" to be consigned to the category of allegory. Morrison's "extravagantly beautiful, doomed characters are locked in a world where hope for the future is a foreign commodity, yet they are enormously, achingly alive," writes Blackburn. "And this book about them—and about how their beauty is drained back and frozen—is a howl of love and rage, playful and funny as well as hard and bitter." In the words of *American Literature* essayist Jane S. Bakerman, Morrison "uses the maturation story of Sula and Nel as the core of a host of other stories, but it is the chief unification device for the novel and achieves its own unity, again, through the clever manipulation of the themes of sex, race, and love. Morrison has undertaken a ... difficult task in *Sula.* Unquestionably, she has succeeded."

Other critics have echoed Bakerman's sentiments about *Sula.* Yardley declares: "What gives this terse, imaginative novel its genuine distinction is the quality of Toni Morrison's prose. *Sula* is admirable enough as a study of its title character, ... but its real strength lies in Morrison's writing, which at times has the resonance of poetry and is precise, vivid and controlled throughout." Turner also claims that in *Sula* "Morrison evokes her verbal magic occasionally by lyric descriptions that carry the reader deep into the soul of the character.... Equally effective, however, is her art of narrating action in a lean prose that uses adjectives cautiously while creating memorable vivid images." In her review, Davis concludes that a "beautiful and haunting atmosphere emerges out of the wreck of these folks' lives, a quality that is absolutely convincing and absolutely precise." *Sula* was nominated for a National Book Award in 1974.

From the insular lives she depicted in her first two novels, Morrison moved, in *Song of Solomon,* to a national and historical perspective on black American life. During the PBS interview, she explained how she made this happen. "*Song of Solomon* was about this sort of political problem that young adults have, which is trying to combine upward mobility—middle-class, bourgeois, upward mobility—with some kind of respect and reverence for their ancestors. There's always this conflict, as though if you go to college, you can't go back to Lorain, Ohio; or if you stay in Lorain, Ohio, you have to despise everybody who went on. Not quite that simple, but you understand what that tension is. So I was trying to figure out how somebody who's in his late 20s or 30s got educated ... and what would help inform him to learn how to be a complete human being, without these conflicts, without these self-destructive impulses for material things.... I try to figure out what kinds of people can manifest that for me ... and set that up. Then I have to fully realize the characters and sort of love them, without approving of them necessarily, but really love them, and my earnest desire is whomever they are ... to do them justice."

"Here the depths of the younger work are still evident," contends Reynolds Price in the *New York Times Book Review,* "but now they thrust outward, into wider fields, for longer intervals, encompassing many more lives. The result is a long prose tale that surveys nearly a century of American history as it impinges upon a single family." With an intermixture of the fantastic and the realistic, *Song of Solomon* relates the journey of a character named Milkman Dead into an understanding of his family heritage and hence, himself. Lee writes: "Figuratively, [Milkman] travels from innocence to awareness, i.e., from ignorance of origins, heritage, identity, and communal responsibility to knowledge and acceptance. He moves from selfish and materialistic dilettantism to an understanding of brotherhood. With his release of personal ego, he is able to find a place in the whole. There is, then, a universal—indeed mythic—pattern here. He journeys from spiritual death to rebirth, a direction symbolized by his discovery of the secret power of flight. Mythically, liberation and transcendence follow the discovery of self." Blake suggests that the connection Milkman discovers with his family's past helps him to connect meaningfully with his contemporaries; *Song of Solomon,* Blake notes, "dramatizes dialectical approaches to the challenges of black life." According to Anne Z. Mickelson in *Reaching Out: Sensitivity and Order in Recent American Fiction by Women,* history itself "becomes a choral symphony to Milkman, in which each individual voice has a chance to speak and contribute to his growing sense of well-being."

Mickelson also observes that *Song of Solomon* represents for blacks "a break out of the confining life into the realm of possibility." Charles Larson comments on this theme in a *Washington Post Book World* review. The novel's subject matter, Larson explains, is "the origins of black consciousness in America, and the individual's relationship to that heritage." However, Larson adds, "skilled writer that she is, Morrison has transcended this theme so that the reader rarely feels that this is simply another novel about ethnic identity. So marvelously orchestrated is Morrison's narrative that it not only excels on all of its respective levels, not only works for all of its interlocking components, but also—in the end—says something about life (and death) for all of us. Milkman's epic jour-

ney ... is a profound examination of the individual's understanding of, and, perhaps, even transcendence of the inevitable fate of his life." Gornick concludes: "There are so many individual moments of power and beauty in *Song of Solomon* that, ultimately, one closes the book warmed through by the richness of its sympathy, and by its breathtaking feel for the nature of sexual sorrow."

*Song of Solomon* won the National Book Critics Circle Award in 1977. It was also the first novel by a black writer to become a Book-of-the-Month Club selection since Richard Wright's *Native Son* was published in 1940. *World Literature Today* reviewer Richard K. Barksdale calls the work "a book that will not only withstand the test of time but endure a second and third reading by those conscientious readers who love a well-wrought piece of fiction." Describing the novel as "a stunningly beautiful book" in her *Washington Post Book World* piece, Anne Tyler adds: "I would call the book poetry, but that would seem to be denying its considerable power as a story. Whatever name you give it, it's full of magnificent people, each of them complex and multilayered, even the narrowest of them narrow in extravagant ways." Price deems *Song of Solomon* "a long story,... and better than good. Toni Morrison has earned attention and praise. Few Americans know, and can say, more than she has in this wise and spacious novel."

Morrison's 1981 book, *Tar Baby,* remained on best-seller lists for four months. A novel of ideas, the work dramatizes the fact that complexion is a far more subtle issue than the simple polarization of black and white. Set on a lush Caribbean Island, *Tar Baby* explores the passionate love affair of Jadine, a Sorbonne-educated black model, and Son, a handsome knockabout with a strong aversion to white culture. According to Caplan, Morrison's concerns "are race, class, culture and the effects of late capitalism—heavy freight for any narrative.... She is attempting to stabilize complex visions of society—that is, to examine competitive ideas.... Because the primary function of Morrison's characters is to voice representative opinions, they arrive on stage vocal and highly conscious, their histories symbolically indicated or merely sketched. Her brief sketches, however, are clearly the work of an artist who can, when she chooses, model the mind in depth and detail." In a *Dictionary of Literary Biography Yearbook* essay, Elizabeth B. House outlines *Tar Baby*'s major themes; namely, "the difficulty of settling conflicting claims between one's past and present and the destruction which abuse of power can bring. As Morrison examines these problems in *Tar Baby,* she suggests no easy way to understand what one's link to a heritage should be, nor does she offer infallible methods for dealing with power. Rather, with an astonishing insight and grace, she demonstrates the pervasiveness of such dilemmas and the degree to which they affect human beings, both black and white."

*Tar Baby* uncovers racial and sexual conflicts without offering solutions, but most critics agree that Morrison indicts all of her characters—black and white—for their thoughtless devaluations of others. *New York Times Book Review* correspondent John Irving claims: "What's so powerful, and subtle, about Miss Morrison's presentation of the tension between blacks and whites is that she conveys it almost entirely through the suspicions and prejudices of her black characters.... Miss Morrison uncovers all the stereotypical racial fears felt by whites and blacks alike. Like any ambitious writer, she's unafraid to employ these stereotypes—she embraces the representative qualities of her characters without embarrassment, then proceeds to make them individuals too." *New Yorker* essayist Susan Lardner praises Morrison for her "power to be absolutely persuasive against her own preferences, suspicions, and convictions, implied or plainly expressed," and Strouse likewise contends that the author "has produced that rare commodity, a truly public novel about the condition of society, examining the relations between blacks and whites, men and women, civilization and nature.... It wraps its messages in a highly potent love story." Irving suggests that Morrison's greatest accomplishment "is that she has raised her novel above the social realism that too many black novels and women's novels are trapped in. She has succeeded in writing about race and women symbolically."

Reviewers have praised *Tar Baby* for its provocative themes and for its evocative narration. *Los Angeles Times* contributor Elaine Kendall calls the book "an intricate and sophisticated novel, moving from a realistic and orderly beginning to a mystical and ambiguous end. Morrison has taken classically simple story elements and realigned them so artfully that we perceive the old pattern in a startlingly different way. Although this territory has been explored by dozens of novelists, Morrison depicts it with such vitality that it seems newly discovered." In the *Washington Post Book World*, Webster Schott claims: "There is so much that is good, sometimes dazzling, about *Tar Baby*—poetic language, ... arresting images, fierce intelligence—that ... one becomes entranced by Toni Morrison's story. The settings are so vivid the characters must be alive. The emotions they feel are so intense they must be real people." Maureen Howard states in *New Republic* that the work "is as carefully patterned as a well-written poem.... *Tar Baby* is a good American novel in which we can discern a new lightness and brilliance in Toni Morrison's enchantment with language and in her curiously polyphonic stories that echo life." Schott concludes: "One of fiction's pleasures is to have your mind scratched and your intellectual habits challenged. While *Tar Baby* has shortcomings, lack of provocation isn't one of them. Morrison owns a powerful intelligence. It's run by courage. She calls to account conventional wisdom and accepted attitude at nearly every turn."

In addition to her own writing, Morrison has served as an editor at Random House and has helped to publish the work of other noted black Americans, including Toni Cade Bambara, Gayle Jones, Angela Davis, and Muhammad Ali. Discussing her aims as an editor in a quotation printed in the *Dictionary of Literary Biography*, Morrison said: "I look very hard for black fiction because I want to participate in developing a canon of black work. We've had the first rush of black entertainment, where blacks were writing for whites, and whites were encouraging this kind of self-flagellation. Now we can get down to the craft of writing, where black people are talking to black people." One of Morrison's important projects for Random House was *The Black Book*, an anthology of items that illustrate the history of black Americans. *Ms.* magazine correspondent Dorothy Eugenia Robinson describes the work: "*The Black Book* is the pain and pride of rediscovering the collective black experience. It is finding the essence of ourselves and holding on. *The Black Book* is a kind of scrapbook of patiently assembled samplings of black history and culture. What has evolved is a pictorial folk journey of black people, places, events, handcrafts, inventions, songs, and folklore.... *The Black Book* informs, disturbs, maybe even shocks. It unsettles complacency and demands confrontation with raw reality. It is by no means an easy book to experience, but it's a necessary one."

While preparing *The Black Book* for publication, Morrison uncovered the true and shocking story of a runaway slave who, at the point of recapture, murdered her infant child so it would not be doomed to a lifetime of slavery. For Morrison the story encapsulated the fierce psychic cruelty of an institutionalized system that sought to destroy the basic emotional bonds between men and women, and worse, between parent and child. "I certainly thought I knew as much about slavery as anybody," Morrison told the *Los Angeles Times*. "But it was the interior life I needed to find out about." It is this "interior life" in the throes of slavery that constitutes the theme of Morrison's Pulitzer Prize-winning novel, *Beloved*. Set in Reconstruction-era Cincinnati, the book centers on characters who struggle fruitlessly to keep their painful recollections of the past at bay. They are haunted, both physically and spiritually, by the legacies slavery has bequeathed to them. The question in this novel, Morrison told PBS host Charlie Rose, was "Who is the beloved? Who is the person who lives inside us that is the one you can trust, who is the best thing you are. And in that instant, for that segment, because I had planned books around that theme, it was the effort of a woman to love her children, to raise her children, to be responsible for her children. And the fact that it was during slavery made all those things impossible for her."

According to Snitow, *Beloved* "staggers under the terror of its material—as so much holocaust writing does and must." In *People* magazine, V. R. Peterson describes *Beloved* as "a brutally powerful, mesmerizing story about the inescapable, excruciating legacy of slavery. Behind each new event and each new character lies another event and another story until finally the reader meets a community of proud, daring people, inextricably bound by culture and experience." Through the lives of ex-slaves Sethe and her would-be lover Paul D., readers "experience American slavery as it was lived by those who were its objects of exchange, both at its best—which wasn't very good—and at its worst, which was as bad as can be imagined," writes Margaret Atwood in the *New York Times Book Review.* "Above all, it is seen as one of the most viciously antifamily institutions human beings have ever devised. The slaves are motherless, fatherless, deprived of their mates, their children, their kin. It is a world in which people suddenly vanish and are never seen again, not through accident or covert operation or terrorism, but as a matter of everyday legal policy." *New York Times* columnist Michiko Kakutani contends that *Beloved* "possesses the heightened power and resonance of myth—its characters, like those in opera or Greek drama, seem larger than life and their actions, too, tend to strike us as enactments of ancient rituals and passions. To describe 'Beloved' only in these terms, however, is to diminish its immediacy, for the novel also remains precisely grounded in American reality—the reality of Black history as experienced in the wake of the Civil War."

Acclaim for *Beloved* has come from both sides of the Atlantic. In his *Chicago Tribune* piece, Larson claims that the work "is the context out of which all of Morrison's earlier novels were written. In her darkest and most probing novel, Toni Morrison has demonstrated once again the stunning powers that place her in the first ranks of our living novelists." *Los Angeles Times Book Review* contributor John Leonard likewise expresses the opinion that the novel "belongs on the highest shelf of American literature, even if half a dozen canonized white boys have to be elbowed off.... Without *Beloved* our imagination of the nation's self has a hole in it big enough to die from." Atwood states: "Ms. Morrison's versatility and technical and emotional range appear to know no bounds. If there were any doubts about her stature as a pre-eminent American novelist, of her own or any other generation, *Beloved* will put them to rest." London *Times* reviewer Nicholas Shakespeare concludes that *Beloved* "is a novel propelled by the cadences of ... songs—the first singing of a people hardened by their suffering, people who have been hanged and whipped and mortgaged at the hands of white people—the men without skin. From Toni Morrison's pen it is a sound that breaks the back of words, making *Beloved* a great novel."

*Jazz,* the second in Morrison's suite of novels about black life from the 1800s to the present, continues many themes set out in *Beloved:* the individual's struggle to establish and sustain a personal identity, the clash between individual interests and community interests, and which takes priority. "Here," says Andrea Stuart, "the desire for individuation and rebirth collides with another of the author's favourite themes: the futil-

ity, even the danger, of jettisoning one's history." As Morrison noted in her PBS interview, the question, Who is the beloved? also repeats itself. The answer in *Jazz* has to do with "real passion," Morrison said, "the sort of thing where you say, 'I can't live without you,' and you really mean it." The inspiration came from a photo of a young girl in a coffin by the Harlem Renaissance photographer James VanderZee. Her boyfriend had shot her, and she kept his identity secret so that he could escape. Morrison explained, "And I thought, now if that isn't the most romantic teenage passion! And to put it right in the jazz age, which is full of passion, romance, music, license—you know, black people in the city, empowered now.... I wanted the book to really be about the people who didn't know they were living in an era."

*Jazz* is about a middle-aged couple—Joe Trace, waiter and door-to-door cosmetics salesman, and his wife, Violet, a home hairdresser—who migrated to Harlem from the rural South in the early 1900s. As background, Morrison offers some scenes of the brutal Virginia country life blacks endured as sharecroppers at the end of the nineteenth century. By contrast, Joe and Violet are initially dazzled by the prospect of life in New York. But novelist Edna O'Brien's critique in *The New York Times Book Review* describes the main characters as "people enthralled, then deceived by 'the music the world makes'." Reality sets in.

Despite Joe's attachment to Violet, he falls in love with Dorcas, who is a teenager, then kills her when she tries to leave him. No one wants to turn Joe in. At the funeral parlor, Violet attempts to slash Dorcas's face but is thrown out, running home and freeing her treasured birds. Later she establishes a relationship with Dorcas's mother. Critic Richard Eder of *The Los Angeles Times Book Review* notes the grief and humor of the story, writing that *Jazz* "could have been either a tragedy or a melodrama with appropriate climactic endings. But Morrison has written a book that ruminates and discourses, ... that follows its riffs through pain and celebration, ... that is, in her word, jazz." In Chicago *Tribune Books,* acclaimed author Michael Dorris calls it a "brilliant, daring new novel" and observes that *Jazz* "is much more than 'story.' ... It is the blues song of people who understand suffering and survival."

In another 1992 book, the nonfiction work *Playing in the Dark: Whiteness and the Literary Imagination,* Morrison examines how black people, often portrayed in stereotypical ways or ignored by white writers, nonetheless shaped white literature. It is a "revolutionary little monograph," in the opinion of *Los Angeles Times Book Review* contributor Diane Middlebrook, "a major work by a major American author." Morrison examines the writings of literary masters such as Saul Bellow, Willa Cather, Ernest Hemingway, Herman Melville, Edgar Allan Poe, and Mark Twain, exploring how their characters and symbolism reflected the African presence. Writing in the *New York Times Book Review,* Wendy Steiner relates how in literature blacks and blackness have been used variously to ward off whites' fears of powerlessness and to explore sexuality, for instance. But Morrison also explores a more positive side of stories of slavery, that of illuminating human nature. Morrison's study, the critic suggests, "is meant to teach a black author about white motivation. It should also teach whites about how they have constructed not only black but white identity, and how they have contemplated their own humanity by observing the dehumanization of others." Through her subtle and perceptive analysis, asserts Chicago *Tribune Books* contributor Michael Eric Dyson, Morrison shows that "an Africanist presence was essential in forming and extending an American national literature."

Morrison has no objection to being called a black woman writer. As she told the *New York Times:* "I really think the range of emotions and perceptions I have had access to as a black person and a female person are greater than those of people who are neither.... My world did not shrink because I was a black female writer. It just got bigger." Nor does she strive for that much-vaunted universality that purports to be a hallmark of fine fiction. "I never asked Tolstoy to write for me, a little colored girl in Lorain, Ohio," she told the *New Republic.* "I never asked [James] Joyce not to mention Catholicism or the world of Dublin. Never. And I don't know why I should be asked to explain your life to you. We have splendid writers to do that, but I am not one of them. It is that business of being universal, a word hopelessly stripped of meaning for me. [William] Faulkner wrote what I suppose could be called regional literature and had it published all over the world. That's what I wish to do. If I tried to write a universal novel, it would be water. Behind this question is the suggestion that to write for black people is somehow to diminish the writing. From my perspective there are only black people. When I say 'people,' that's what I mean."

Black woman writer or simply American novelist, Toni Morrison is a prominent and respected figure in modern letters. In the *Detroit News,* Larson suggests that hers has been "among the most exciting literary careers of the last decade" and that each of her books "has made a quantum jump forward." Ironically, Elizabeth House commends Morrison for the universal nature of her work. "Unquestionably," House writes, "Toni Morrison is an important novelist who continues to develop her talent. Part of her appeal, of course, lies in her extraordinary ability to create beautiful language and striking characters. However, Morrison's most important gift, the one which gives her a major author's universality, is the insight with which she writes of problems all humans face.... At the core of all her novels is a penetrating view of the unyielding, heartbreaking dilemmas which torment people of all races." Snitow notes that the author "wants to tend the imagination, search for an expansion of the possible, nurture

a spiritual richness in the black tradition even after 300 years in the white desert." Dorothy Lee concludes of Morrison's accomplishments: "Though there are unifying aspects in her novels, there is not a dully repetitive sameness. Each casts the problems in specific, imaginative terms, and the exquisite, poetic language awakens our senses as she communicates an often ironic vision with moving imagery. Each novel reveals the acuity of her perception of psychological motivation of the female especially, of the Black particularly, and of the human generally."

"The problem I face as a writer is to make my stories mean something," Morrison states in *Black Women Writers at Work.* "You can have wonderful, interesting people, a fascinating story, but it's not about anything. It has no real substance. I want my books to always be about something that is important to me, and the subjects that are important in the world are the same ones that have always been important." In *Black Women Writers: A Critical Evaluation,* she elaborates on this idea. Fiction, she writes, "should be beautiful, and powerful, but it should also work. It should have something in it that enlightens; something in it that opens the door and points the way. Something in it that suggests what the conflicts are, what the problems are. But it need not solve those problems because it is not a case study, it is not a recipe." The author who has said that writing "is discovery; it's talking deep within myself" told the *New York Times Book Review* that the essential theme in her growing body of fiction is "how and why we learn to live this life intensely and well."

*BIOGRAPHICAL/CRITICAL SOURCES:*

*BOOKS*

*Authors and Artists for Children and Young Adults,* Volume 1, Gale, 1989.

Bell, Roseann P., editor, *Sturdy Black Bridges: Visions of Black Women in Literature,* Doubleday, 1979.

*Black Literature Criticism,* Gale, 1992.

Christian, Barbara, *Black Women Novelists: The Development of a Tradition, 1892-1976,* Greenwood Press, 1980.

*Concise Dictionary of American Literary Biography: Broadening Views, 1968-1988,* Gale, 1989.

*Contemporary Literary Criticism,* Gale, Volume 4, 1975, Volume 10, 1979, Volume 22, 1982, Volume 55, 1989.

Cooper-Clark, Diana, *Interviews with Contemporary Novelists,* St. Martin's, 1986.

*Dictionary of Literary Biography,* Gale, Volume 6: *American Novelists since World War II,* 1980, Volume 33: *Afro-American Fiction Writers after 1955,* 1984.

*Dictionary of Literary Biography Yearbook: 1981,* Gale, 1982.

Evans, Mari, editor, *Black Women Writers (1950-1980): A Critical Evaluation,* Doubleday, 1984.

Mekkawi, Mod, *Toni Morrison: A Bibliography*, Howard University Library, 1986.

Mickelson, Anne Z., *Reaching Out: Sensitivity and Order in Recent American Fiction by Women*, Scarecrow Press, 1979.

Ruas, Charles, *Conversations with American Writers*, Knopf, 1985.

Tate, Claudia, editor, *Black Women Writers at Work*, Continuum, 1986.

*PERIODICALS*

*American Literature*, January, 1981.

*Atlantic*, April, 1981.

*Black American Literature Forum*, summer, 1978; winter, 1979.

*Black Scholar*, March, 1978.

*Black World*, June, 1974.

*Callaloo*, October-February, 1981.

*Chicago Tribune*, October 27, 1987.

*Chicago Tribune Book World*, March 8, 1981.

*CLA Journal*, June, 1979; June, 1981.

*Commentary*, August, 1981.

*Contemporary Literature*, winter, 1983.

*Critique: Studies in Modern Fiction*, Volume 19, number 1, 1977.

*Detroit News*, March 29, 1981.

*Essence*, July, 1981; June, 1983; October, 1987.

*First World*, winter, 1977.

*Harper's Bazaar*, March, 1983.

*Harvard Advocate*, Volume 107, number 4, 1974.

*Hudson Review*, spring, 1978.

*Kirkus Reviews*, September 1, 1992.

*Los Angeles Times*, March 31, 1981; October 14, 1987.

*Los Angeles Times Book Review*, August 30, 1987; April 19, 1992, pp. 3, 5; May 24, 1992, pp. 2, 7.

*Massachusetts Review*, autumn, 1977.

*MELUS*, fall, 1980.

*Ms.*, June, 1974; December, 1974; August, 1987.

*Nation*, July 6, 1974; November 19, 1977; May 2, 1981.

*New Republic*, December 3, 1977; March 21, 1981.

*New Statesman*, May 1, 1992, p. 39.

*Newsweek*, November 30, 1970; January 7, 1974; September 12, 1977; March 30, 1981; April 27, 1992, p. 66.

*New York*, April 13, 1981.

*New Yorker*, November 7, 1977; June 15, 1981.

*New York Post*, January 26, 1974.

*New York Review of Books*, November 10, 1977; April 30, 1981.

*New York Times*, November 13, 1970; September 6, 1977; March 21, 1981; August 26, 1987; September 2, 1987.

*New York Times Book Review*, November 1, 1970; December 30, 1973; June 2, 1974; September 11, 1977; March 29, 1981; September 13, 1987; April 5, 1992, pp. 1, 25, 29.

*New York Times Magazine*, August 22, 1971; August 11, 1974; July 4, 1976; May 20, 1979.

*Obsidian*, spring/summer, 1979.

*People*, July 29, 1974; November 30, 1987.

*Philadelphia Inquirer*, April 1, 1988.

*Publishers Weekly*, August 21, 1987; August 17, 1992.

*Saturday Review*, September 17, 1977.

*Spectator*, December 9, 1978; February 2, 1980; December 19, 1981.

*Studies in Black Literature*, Volume 6, 1976.

*Time*, September 12, 1977; March 16, 1981; September 21, 1987; April 27, 1992, p. 70.

*Times* (London), October 15, 1987.

*Times Literary Supplement*, October 4, 1974; November 24, 1978; February 8, 1980; December 19, 1980; October 30, 1981; October 16-22, 1987; May 8, 1992, p. 21.

*Tribune Books* (Chicago), August 30, 1988; April 19, 1992, pp. 1, 5; May 3, 1992, pp. 7, 11.

*U.S. News and World Report*, October 19, 1987.

*Village Voice*, August 29, 1977; July 1-7, 1981.

*Vogue*, April, 1981; January, 1986.

*Voice Literary Supplement*, September, 1987.

*Washington Post*, February 3, 1974; March 6, 1974; September 30, 1977; April 8, 1981; February 9, 1983; October 5, 1987.

*Washington Post Book World*, February 3, 1974; September 4, 1977; December 4, 1977; March 22, 1981; September 6, 1987; April 19, 1992, pp. 1-2.

*World Literature Today*, summer, 1978.

*OTHER*

Interview on *Charlie Rose*, PBS, May 7, 1993.

\* \* \*

## MOSLEY, Walter 1952-

*PERSONAL:* Born 1952, in Los Angeles, CA; married Joy Kellman (a dancer and choreographer). *Education:* Attended City College of New York.

*ADDRESSES: Home*—New York, NY. *Agent*—c/o W. W. Norton, 500 Fifth Ave., New York, NY 10110.

*CAREER:* Mystery novelist. Former computer programmer.

*AWARDS, HONORS:* Shamus Award, Private Eye Writers of America, 1990, and Edgar Award nomination, Mystery Writers of America, 1990, both for *Devil in a Blue Dress*.

*WRITINGS:*

*MYSTERY NOVELS*

*Devil in a Blue Dress,* Norton, 1990.
*A Red Death,* Norton, 1991.
*White Butterfly,* Norton, 1992.

*ADAPTATIONS: Devil in a Blue Dress* is being filmed.

*SIDELIGHTS:* "A good private-eye novel ... is not really about violence; it's about the fallibility of people, about the grotesqueries of modern life, and not least it is about one man, the detective, who defines the moral order." This statement, from *Washington Post* reviewer Arthur Krystal, captures the essence of Walter Mosley's three widely praised detective stories. The author's novels are the start of an ongoing series of hard-boiled detective tales featuring Ezekiel "Easy" Rawlins, who reluctantly gets drawn into investigations that lead him through the tough streets of black Los Angeles. There, Easy operates in a kind of gray area, where moral and ethical certainties are hard to decipher.

Ironically, Mosley had ambitions other than writing early in his career. Born in Los Angeles, he made his way to the East Coast, where he began his professional life as a computer programmer. Then one day in New York, he told D. J. R. Bruckner of the *New York Times,* "I wrote out a sentence about people on a back porch in Louisiana. I don't know where it came from. I liked it. It spoke to me." From that moment, he defined himself as a writer and fulfilled the dream of many would-be authors bound to an office: He quit to devote his full attention to his craft. He continues to write the way he began: "First there is a sentence. Then characters start coming in."

In 1990, readers first met Mosley's Rawlins—and his short-tempered sidekick, Mouse—in *Devil in a Blue Dress.* The novel is set in 1948, when many black World War II veterans, like Easy, found jobs in the area's booming aircraft industry. When Easy loses his job, he grows concerned about the source of his next mortgage payment, until he is introduced to a wealthy white man who offers him a way to make some quick cash: He will pay Easy one hundred dollars to locate a beautiful blonde woman named Daphne Monet, who is known to frequent jazz clubs in the area. Easy takes the job, but soon realizes that the task is far more dangerous then he imagined.

Mosley followed *Devil in a Blue Dress* with *A Red Death,* set five years later. In the sequel, Easy has used stolen money to buy a couple of apartment buildings and is enjoying the life of a property owner. But he gets into a jam with the Internal Revenue Service, and his only way out is to cooperate with the FBI by spying on a union organizer suspected of being a Communist. Again, he gets mired in complications as he tries to make sense out of a dark underworld of extortion and murder.

Mosley's third novel, *White Butterfly,* fast-forwards to 1956. Easy is married and has a new baby, and his businesses are going well. When three young black women—"good-time girls"—are brutally slain, the crimes are barely reported. But when a white UCLA student meets a similar death, the serial killings finally make headlines. In the meantime Easy is hired by the police to help investigate. His inquiries take him through bars, rib joints, and flophouses until he makes the startling discovery that the latest victim, the daughter of a city official, was a stripper, known to her fans as the "White Butterfly." In fact, nothing in the novel is as it appears, but Easy sorts through the corruption and deception to solve the mystery—at a terrible price to his personal life.

According to biographical notes appearing in *Devil in a Blue Dress,* Mosley's successful novels incorporate narrative skills that he learned from his father and from "thousands of his 'cousins'" who, like Easy, had moved to Los Angeles in the years after the war and passed the time by telling stories. As a result of this oral heritage, Mosley presents "a black world of slang and code words that haven't been delivered with such authority since Chester Himes created his Harlem detective stories," Herbert Mitgang wrote in the *New York Times.* Commenting on Mosley's strength as a writer, Gary Dretzka of *Tribune Books* surmised that the author demonstrates "his ability to tell an interesting period story in an entertaining and suspenseful manner and to create dead-on believable characters whose mouths are filled with snappy dialogue." Clarence Petersen of the *Chicago Tribune* praised "the rhythm of his prose" and the "startling originality of his imagery," presented with an "unselfconscious ease." Beyond capturing both the music and the nuances of his characters' language, Mosley uses his stories to explore issues of race and class. Commented Digby Diehl in the *Los Angeles Times Book Review,* "The insightful scenes of black life ... provide a sort of social history that doesn't exist in other detective fiction." The critic added, "He re-creates the era convincingly, with all of its racial tensions, evoking the uneasy combination of freedom and disillusion in the post-war black community."

Mosley's aim is less to create a memorable gumshoe than it is to explore the ethical dilemmas that the character constantly faces. He summed up his achievement for Bruckner: "Mysteries, stories about crime, about detectives, are the ones that really ask the existentialist questions such as 'How do I act in an imperfect world when I want to be perfect?' I'm not really into clues and that sort of thing, although I do put them in my stories. I like the moral questions." In Easy Rawlins, Mosley has created the character to ask those questions.

*BIOGRAPHICAL/CRITICAL SOURCES:*

*PERIODICALS*

*Armchair Detective,* spring, 1991, p. 228; winter, 1992, p. 123.

*Bloomsbury Review,* November, 1990, p. 32.

*Chicago Tribune,* July 1, 1990; June 19, 1991; July 21, 1991; June 28, 1992.

*Essence,* January, 1991, p. 32.

*Globe and Mail* (Toronto), July 18, 1992, p. C7.

*Los Angeles Times,* May 5, 1992.

*Los Angeles Times Book Review,* July 29, 1990, p. 3; July 12, 1992, pp. 2, 12.

*Newsweek,* July 9, 1990, p. 65.

*New York,* September 3, 1990, p. 18.

*New Yorker,* September 17, 1990, p. 110.

*New York Times,* August 15, 1990; September 4, 1990, pp. C13, C16; August 7, 1991; August 7, 1992.

*New York Times Book Review,* September 6, 1992, p. 25.

*San Francisco Review of Books,* February, 1991.

*Tribune Books* (Chicago), June 16, 1991, pp. 1, 7; June 28, 1992, p. 1.

*USA Weekend,* June 11, 1993.

*Village Voice,* September 18, 1990, p. 74.

*Wall Street Journal,* July 24, 1991, p. A8.

*Washington Post,* June 22, 1990.

*Washington Post Book World,* August 16, 1992.

*West Coast Review of Books,* May, 1990, p. 26.

\*   \*   \*

## MPHAHLELE, Es'kia
### See MPHAHLELE, Ezekiel

\*   \*   \*

## MPHAHLELE, Ezekiel 1919-
### (Es'kia Mphahlele; Bruno Eseki, a pseudonym)

*PERSONAL:* Born December 17, 1919, in Pretoria, South Africa; son of Moses (a messenger) and Eva (a domestic; maiden name, Mogale) Mphahlele; married Rebecca Mochadibane (a social worker), August 29, 1945; children: Anthony, Teresa Kefilwe, Motswiri, Chabi Robert, Puso. *Education:* Adams Teachers Training College, teaching diploma, 1940; University of South Africa, B.A. (with honors), 1949, M.A., 1956; University of Denver, Ph.D., 1968.

*ADDRESSES: Home*—P.O. Box 303, Chuenesport 0745, South Africa.

*CAREER:* Clerk for an institute for the blind, 1941-45; Or-

lando High School, Johannesburg, South Africa, teacher of English and Afrikaans, 1945-52; *Drum* magazine, Johannesburg, fiction editor, 1955-57; University of Ibadan, Ibadan, Nigeria, lecturer in English literature, 1957-61; Congress for Cultural Freedom, Paris, France, director of African program, 1961-63; Chemchemi Creative Centre, Nairobi, Kenya, director, 1963-65; University College, Nairobi, lecturer, 1965-66; University of Denver, Denver, Co, teaching fellow, 1966-68; University of Zambia, Lusaka, senior lecturer in English, 1968-70; University of Denver, associate professor in English department, 1970-74; University of Pennsylvania, Philadelphia, professor of English, 1974-77; inspector of schools, Lebowa, South Africa, 1977-78; University of the Witwatersrand, Johannesburg, senior research fellow at African Studies Institute, 1979-82, professor of African literature, 1983-87, professor emeritus, 1987—. Founding director of Council for Black Education and Research (COBERT), 1980-92.

*MEMBER:* Mbari Writers Club (cofounder), Phi Beta Kappa.

*AWARDS, HONORS: African Arts* magazine prize, 1972, for *The Wanderers;* Carnegie Foundation grant, 1980; Claude Harris Leon Foundation Prize, 1985, for outstanding community service; honorary doctorates from University of Pennsylvania, 1982, and University of Natal at Pietermaritzburg, 1983.

*WRITINGS:*

*Man Must Live, and Other Stories,* African Bookman, 1946.

(Contributor) Prudence Smith, editor, *Africa in Transition,* Reinhardt, 1958.

*Down Second Avenue* (autobiography), Faber, 1959, Anchor, 1971.

*The Living and the Dead and Other Stories,* Black Orpheus, 1961.

*The African Image,* Praeger, 1962, revised edition, Faber & Faber, 1974.

(Editor with Ellis Ayitey Komey) *Modern African Stories,* Faber, 1964.

*The Role of Education and Culture in Developing African Countries,* Afro-Asian Institute for Labor Studies in Israel, 1965.

*A Guide to Creative Writing,* East African Literature Bureau, 1966.

*In Corner B and Other Stories,* Northwestern University Press, 1967.

(Editor and contributor)*African Writing Today,* Penguin, 1967.

*The Wanderers* (novel) Macmillan, 1971.

*Voices in the Whirlwind, and Other Essays,* Hill & Wang, 1972.

(Under name Es'kia Mphahlele) *Chirundu* (novel), Ravan Press, 1979, Lawrence Hill, 1981.

*Let's Write a Novel,* Miller, 1981.

(Under name Es'kia Mphahlele) *The Unbroken Song: Selected Writings,* Ravan Press, 1981.

(Under name Es'kia Mphahlele) *Afrika My Music: An Autobiography, 1957-1983,* Ravan Press, 1984.

*Father Come Home* (juvenile), Ravan Press, 1984.

(Under name Es'kia Mphahlele) *Bury Me at the Marketplace: Selected Letters of Es'kia Mphahlele, 1943-1980,* edited by N. Chabani Manganyi, Skotaville, 1984.

*Let's Talk Writing: Prose,* Skotaville, 1985.

*Let's Talk Writing: Poetry,* Skotaville, 1985.

*Poetry and Humanism,* Witwatersrand University Press, 1986.

*Echoes of African Art,* Skotaville, 1987.

*Renewal Time* (stories), Readers International, 1988.

(Author of text) Alf Kumalo, *Mandela: Echoes of an Era,* Penguin, 1990.

Contributor to numerous books, including *An African Treasury: Articles, Essays, Stories, Poems by Black Africans,* edited by Langston Hughes, Crown, 1960; *Drum Beats: An Anthology of African Writing,* compiled by Ime Ikiddeh, E. J. Arnold, 1968; and *New African Literature and the Arts I,* edited by Joseph Okpaku, Crowell, 1987. Contributor, sometimes under pseudonym Bruno Eseki, to periodicals, including *Drum, Africa South, Denver Quarterly, Journal of Modern African Studies, Black World,* and *New Statesman.* Editor, *Black Orpheus,* 1960-66; member of staff, *Presence Africaine,* 1961-63; member of editorial staff, *Journal of New African Literature and the Arts.*

Unpublished correspondence between Mphahlele and Ursula A. Barnett is housed in the National English Literary Museum, Grahamstown, South Africa. Mphahlele's works have been translated into several languages.

*WORK IN PROGRESS: A Critical Anthology of African Poetry.*

*SIDELIGHTS:* "A writer who has been regarded as the most balanced literary critic of African literature," Ezekiel Mphahlele can also "be acknowledged as one of its most significant creators," writes Emile Snyder in the *Saturday Review.* Mphahlele's transition from life in the slums of South Africa to life as one of Africa's foremost writers was an odyssey of struggle both intellectually and politically. He trained as a teacher in South Africa but was banned from the classroom in 1952 as a result of his protest of the segregationist Bantu Education Act. Although he later returned to teaching, Mphahlele first turned to journalism, criticism, fiction, and essay writing. Mphahlele is acknowledged as one of the leading scholars on African literature.

During an exile that took him to France and the United States, Mphahlele was away from Africa for over a decade. Never-

theless, "no other author has ever earned the right to so much of Africa as has Ezekiel Mphahlele," says John Thompson in the *New York Review of Books.* "In the English language, he established the strength of African literature in our time." Some critics, however, feel that Mphahlele's absence from his homeland has harmed his work by separating him from its subject. Ursula A. Barnett, writing in the conclusion of her 1976 biography *Ezekiel Mphahlele,* asserts that Mphahlele's "creative talent can probably gain its full potential only if he returns to South Africa and resumes his function of teaching his discipline in his own setting, and of encouraging the different elements in South Africa to combine and interchange in producing a modern indigenous literature."

Mphahlele himself has agreed with this assessment, for after being officially silenced by the government of his homeland and living in self-imposed exile for twenty years, Mphahlele returned to South Africa in 1977. "I want to be part of the renaissance that is happening in the thinking of my people," he commented. "I see education as playing a vital role in personal growth and in institutionalizing a way of life that a people chooses as its highest ideal. For the older people, it is a way of reestablishing the values they had to suspend along the way because of the force of political conditions. Another reason for returning, connected with the first, is that this is my ancestral home. An African cares very much where he dies and is buried. But I have not come to die. I want to reconnect with my ancestors while I am still active. I am also a captive of place, of setting. As long as I was abroad I continued to write on the South African scene. There is a force I call the tyranny of place; the kind of unrelenting hold a place has on a person that gives him the motivation to write and a style. The American setting in which I lived for nine years was too fragmented to give me these. I could only identify emotionally and intellectually with the African-American segment, which was not enough. Here I can feel the ancestral Presence. I know now what Vinoba Bhave of India meant when he said: 'Though action rages without, the heart can be tuned to produce unbroken music,' at this very hour when pain is raging and throbbing everywhere in African communities living in this country."

His 1988 publication, *Renewal Time,* contains stories he published previously as well as an autobiographical afterword on his return to South Africa and a section from *Afrika My Music,* his 1984 autobiography. Stories like "Mrs. Plum" and "The Living and the Dead" have received praise by critics reviewing Mphahlele's work. Charles R. Larson, reviewing the work in the *Washington Post Book World,* says that the stories in the book present "almost ironic images of racial tension under apartheid." He cites "Mrs. Plum" as "the gem of this volume." The story is a first-person narrative by a black South African servant girl, and through her words, says

Larson, "Mphahlele creates the most devastating picture of a liberal South African white."

*Chirundu,* Mphahlele's first novel since his return to South Africa, "tells with quiet assurance this story of a man divided," says Rose Moss in a *World Literature Today* review. The novel "is clearly this writer's major work of fiction and, I suppose, in one sense, an oblique commentary on his own years of exile," observes Larson in an article for *World Literature Today.* Moss finds that in his story of a man torn between African tradition and English law, "the timbre of Mphahlele's own vision is not always clear"; nevertheless, the critic admits that "in the main his story presents the confused and wordless heart of his character with unpretentious mastery." "*Chirundu* is that rare breed of fiction—a novel of ideas, and a moving one at that," says Larson. "It has the capacity to involve the reader both intellectually and emotionally." The critic concludes by calling the work "the most satisfying African novel of the past several years."

On the subject of writing, Mphahlele commented: "In Southern Africa, the black writer talks best about the ghetto life he knows; the white writer about his own ghetto life. We see each other, black and white, as it were through a keyhole. Race relations are a major experience and concern for the writer. They are his constant beat. It is unfortunate no one can ever think it is healthy both mentally and physically to keep hacking at the social structure in overcharged language. A language that burns and brands, scorches and scalds. Language that is as a machete with a double edge—the one sharp, the other blunt, the one cutting, the other breaking. And yet there are levels of specifically black drama in the ghettoes that I cannot afford to ignore. I have got to stay with it. I bleed inside. My people bleed. But I must stay with it."

*BIOGRAPHICAL/CRITICAL SOURCES:*

*BOOKS*

Barnett, Ursula A., *Ezekiel Mphahlele,* Twayne, 1976.
*Black Literature Criticism,* Gale 1992.
*Contemporary Literary Criticism,* Volume 25, Gale, 1983.
*Dictionary of Literary Biography,* Volume 125: *Twentieth-Century Caribbean and Black African Writers, Second Series,* Gale, 1993.
Durden, Dennis, editor, *African Writers Talking,* Heinemann, 1972.
Herdeck, Donald E., *African Writers: A Companion to Black African Writing, 1300-1973,* Black Orpheus, 1973.
Lindfors, Bernth, editor, *South African Voices,* African and Afro-American Studies Center, 1975.
Manganyi, N. Chabani, *Exiles and Homecomings: A Biography of Es'kia Mphahlele,* Ravan Press, 1983.

Moore, Gerald, *Seven African Writers,* Oxford University Press, 1962.
Moore, Gerald, *The Chosen Tongue,* Longmans, Green, 1969.
Mphahlele, Es'kia, *Afrika My Music: An Autobiography, 1957-1983,* Ravan Press, 1984, Ohio University Press, 1986.
Mphahlele, Ezekiel, *Down Second Avenue,* Faber, 1959.
Woeber, Catherine, and John Read, *Es'kia Mphahlele: A Bibliogrpahy,* National English Literary Museum, 1989.

*PERIODICALS*

*Modern African Studies,* March, 1963.
*Nation,* March 20, 1972.
*New Statesman,* April 25, 1959.
*New York Review of Books,* September 23, 1971.
*New York Times Book Review,* October 22, 1972; June 28, 1987; p. 9, April 30, 1989, p. 38.
*Saturday Review,* June 19, 1971.
*Times Literary Supplement,* August 11, 1961; March 23, 1967; March 10, 1972; June 16, 1989, p. 670.
*Washington Post Book World,* February 5, 1989, p. 8.
*World Literature Today,* summer, 1983; winter, 1983; winter, 1987; summer 1989.

\*   \*   \*

## MTSHALI, Oswald Mbuyiseni 1940-

*PERSONAL:* Former name, Oswald Joseph Mtshali; born January 17, 1940, in Kwa-Bhanya, Natal, South Africa; son of Joseph Josiaih (a teacher) and Florence (a teacher; maiden name, Matobi) Mtshali; married Peggy Margaret Mntambo, December 12, 1968 (divorced, November 11, 1975); married Glaudinah Jacoba (a medical doctor), April 13, 1983; children: Celiwe, Michael, Michelle, and Zanefa. *Education:* New York School of Social Research, B.A.; Columbia University, M.F.A. and M.J., 1979; Rhodes University, doctoral studies. *Politics:* Supported Freedom Charter of African National Congress, United Democratic front. *Religion:* Anglican.

*ADDRESSES: Home and office*—3 Washington Square Village, Bleeker St., New York, NY 10012.

*CAREER:* Driver for engineering firm, 1963-1965; short imprisonment then acquitted; after 1965, messenger and general deliveryman, National Growth fund investment company, Johannesburg, South Africa; *Rand Daily Mail,* columnist, Johannesburg, 1972; Pace Community College, Juhilani, Soweto, deputy headmaster, 1981-86. South African Council of Churches, director of communications, 1986—. Fairleigh Dickenson University, assistant professor of black literature. Art critic, *The Star,* 1979—.

*MEMBER:* Congress of South African Writers (general secretary, 1987).

*AWARDS, HONORS:* Olive Schreiner Poetry Prize, English Academy of South Africa, 1974.

*WRITINGS:*

*Sounds of a Cowhide Drum* (poetry collection), Renoster (Johannesburg), 1971, Third Press, 1972.
*Fireflames* (poetry collection), Shuter and Shooter (Natal), 1980, Chicago Review, 1983.
(Editor) *Give Us a Break: Diaries of a Group of Soweto Children,* Skotaville (Johannesburg), 1988.

Also translator of William Shakespeare's *Romeo and Juliet* into Zulu.

*PLAYS*

(With Barney Simon and others) *Honey Makes Madness* (adapted from *Volpone* by Ben Johnson), produced in Johannesburg, 1972.

Also author of *Black Dawn—White Twilight,* a one-act play.

*OTHER*

Work represented in anthologies, including *A Century of South African Poetry,* edited by Michael Chapman; *Voices From Within,* edited by Chapman and Achmat Dango; *Voices of the Land,* edited by Marcia Levenson and Jonathan Paton; contributor to *Aspects of South African Literature,* edited by Christopher Heywood, Africana, 1976.

*WORK IN PROGRESS: The Belly of Nanana Boselesele,* an autobiographical novel; *The Arrival of the Phantom Foetus,* a nonfiction work.

*SIDELIGHTS:* Oswald Mbuyiseni Mtshali has been hailed as an outspoken black voice in South African English poetry as well as a Zulu "scooter messenger" with an extraordinary gift for poetic writing. His first published collection of poems, *Sounds of a Cowhide Drum,* met rapid success primarily among a white, liberal audience. His readers found him to be sensitive to the plight of the black man in the midst of apartheid. Mtshali's writing stems from his own life experiences, he told *Contemporary Poets,* giving him a view of "humanity as a whole, as reflected in my environment, ... my community, ... [and] my society." Ernest Pereiru, writing in *Contemporary Poets,* contends that much of Mtshali's sensi-

tivity was brought about by his own brief imprisonment, which "gave his work direction and purpose; yet compassion, irony, and ... control, rather than bitterness and anger."

*Fireflames* was not as well-received as *Sounds of a Cowhide Drum.* Critics felt the radical and revolutionary tone of the collection made it more of a political statement, representing the anger of blacks towards their oppressors, rather than a literary work. *Fireflames* was dedicated "to the ... brave schoolchildren of Soweto," many who had died or had been imprisoned during the uprising in Soweto in 1976. Shortly after the uprising, the book was banned, probably due to its resistant demeanor.

Mtshali uses vivid imagery of urban existence in free-verse form, rather than rhyme and meter, claiming it is less restrictive and allows him to freely express his thoughts. He feels his messages are more powerful without the "loftiness" of style, which permits him to more effectively question the actions of those who would support apartheid. Mtshali once commented: "My main motivation for writing is to share my experiences by commenting to all my readers who want to know [how] I feel about living in an apartheid society where the white minority is oppressing the black majority."

*BIOGRAPHICAL/CRITICAL SOURCES:*

*BOOKS*

*Contemporary Poets,* St. James Press, 1991.
*Dictionary of Literary Biography,* Volume 125: *Twentieth-Century Caribbean and Black African Writers, Second Series,* Gale, 1993.

\* \* \*

## MUDIMBE, V. Y. 1941-

*PERSONAL:* Born December 8, 1941, in Likasi (formerly Jadotville), Zaire; son of Gustave and Victorine Mudimbe; married Elizabeth Mbulamuanza Boyi, December 31, 1966; children: Daniel, Claude. *Education:* Lovanium University, Kinshasa, Zaire, B.A., 1966; Lovain University, Belgium, D. Phil Let., 1970; attended University of Paris, France. *Religion:* Agnostic.

*ADDRESSES: Office*—The Literature Program, Art Museum 115, Duke University, Durham, NC 27708.

*CAREER:* Lovanium University, Kinshasa, Zaire, assistant in department of Romance languages, 1966-68, assistant professor, 1970-71; National School of Law and Public Administration, Kinshasa, Zaire, lecturer, 1967-68; University of Paris—Nanterre, France, lecturer, 1969-71; National University of Zaire, Lubumbashi, associate professor, 1971-74, dean of the faculty of philosophy and letters, 1972-74, professor, 1974-80; Haverford College, Haverford, PA, professor, 1981-87; Duke University, Durham, NC, professor, 1988—. International Congress of African Studies, vice-president, 1978-85; Duke University Press, member of editorial board, 1988—; Society for African Philosophy in North America, general secretary, 1988—.

*AWARDS, HONORS:* Grand Prize, International Catholic Literature, 1975, for novel *Entre les Eaux;* Senghor Grand Prize, French-language Writers' Association, 1977; Chevalier de la Pleiade, Order of the French-speaking World and Dialogue of Cultures, 1977; senior scholar fellowship, Foundation of Japan, 1979; Gold Medal of Scientific and Civil Merit, Republic of Zaire, 1980; Senior Fulbright Scholar, University of Pittsburgh, 1980; Margaret Gest Professor, Haverford College, 1981-82; Ira Reid Professor, Haverford College, 1984-87; Herskovits Award, U.S. African Studies Association, for *The Invention of Africa,* 1989; Ruth F. DeVarney Professor, Duke University, 1991; juror, Neustadt International Prize for Literature, 1992.

*WRITINGS:*

*Dechirures* (poetry), Editions du Mont Moir, 1971.
*Initiation au Francais,* two volumes, Celta, 1971.
*Autour de la nation* (essay), Editions du Mont Noir, 1972.
*Francais: Les Structure Fondamentales I,* Centre de Recherches Pedagogiques, 1972.
*Francais: Les Structures Fondamentales II,* Centre de Recherches Pedagogiques, 1972.
*Reflexions sur la vie quotidienne* (essay), Editions du Mont Noir, 1972.
*Entre les eaux* (novel), Presence Africaine, 1973, translation by Stephen Becker, published as *Between Tides,* Simon & Schuster, 1991.
*Entretailles [and] Fulgurances d'une lezarde* (poetry), Saint-Germain-des-Pres, 1973.
*L'Autre Face du royaume: Une introduction a la critique des languages en folie* (essay), L'Age d'homme, 1973.
(With P. Detienne) *Francais: Les Structures Fondamentales,* Centre de Recherches Pedagogiques, 1973.
(With A. Tashdjian, M. Le Boul, and M. Pierre) *Francais: Les Structures Fondamentales IV,* Celta, 1974.
(With J. L. Vincke) *Le Prix du peche: Essai de psychanalyse existentielle des traditions Europeenes et Africaines,* Editions du Mont Noir, 1974.
*Les Fuseaux parfois...* (poetry), Saint-Germain-des-Pres, 1974.

*Carnets d'Amerique* (essay), Saint-Germain-des-Pres, 1976.
*Contributions a l'etude des variations du genre grammatical des Mots francais d'Origine latine: I. Mots a initiale vocalique,* Celta, 1976.
(With Mombo Lutece, Kilanga M., and Lupukisa Wasamba) *Procedes d'enrichissement et creation de termes nouveaux dans un groupe de langues de l'Afrique Centrale,* UNESCO, 1976.
(With Eloko a N.O., Losso Gazi, Matumele M., et al.) *La Vocabulaire Politique Zairois,* Celta, 1976.
*Le Bel Immonde* (novel), Presence Africaine, 1976, translation by M. de Jager, published as *Before the Birth of the Moon,* Simon & Schuster, 1989.
*Air: etude semantique,* Acta Ethnologica et Linguistica, 1979.
*L'Ecart* (novel), Presence Africaine, 1979.
*La Culture et la science au Zaire 1960-1975: Essai sur les sciences sociales et humaines* (essay), Brussels, 1980.
(Editor) *Africa's Dependence: La Dependance de l'Afrique,* Berger-Levrault, 1980.
(With A. Huybrechts, L. Peeters, J. Vanderlinden, et al.) *Du Congo au Zaire 1960-1980: Essai de bilan,* Centre de Recherche et d'Information socio-politiques—CRISP, 1980.
*Visage de la philosophie et de la theologie comtemporaines au Zaire* (essay), Cedaf Cahiers du CEDAF, 1981.
*L'Odeur du pere* (essay), Presence Africaine, 1982.
*The Invention of Africa,* Indiana University Press, 1988.
*Shaba Deux* (novel), Presence Africaine, 1989.
*Fables and Parables,* University of Wisconsin Press, 1991.
(Editor) *The Surreptitious Speech: Presence Africaine 1947-1987,* University of Chicago Press, 1992.
(Editor with Robert Bates and Jean O'Barr) *Africa and the Disciplines,* University of Chicago Press, 1993.
*The Idea of Africa,* Indiana University Press, in press.
*Tales of Faith,* London University, in press.
(Editor) *The Encyclopedia of African Religions and Philosophy,* Garland Publishing, in press.

Also contributor to *Africa and the West: The Legacies of Empire,* edited by I. J. Mowoe and R. Bjornson, Greenwood Press, 1986, and *Africa Explores: Twentieth Century African Art,* edited by S. Vogel, Center for African Art, 1991. Author of more than seventy articles for scholarly journals.

*WORK IN PROGRESS: Les Corps glorieux des mots et des etres,* 1994.

*SIDELIGHTS: Before the Birth of the Moon* is a novel about love and political rebellion set in the author's homeland of Zaire; it is Mudimbe's first novel published in the United States.

*BIOGRAPHICAL/CRITICAL SOURCES:*

*BOOKS*

Mouralis, Bernard, *V. Y. Mudimbe ou le Discours, l'Ecart et l'Ecriture,* Presence Africaine, 1988.

*PERIODICALS*

*Callaloo,* Volume 14, number 4.
*New York Times Book Review,* April 30, 1989.
*Voice Literary Supplement,* February, 1990.

\*   \*   \*

## MURPHY, Beatrice M. 1908-1992

*PERSONAL:* Born June 25, 1908, in Monessen, Pennsylvania; died of heart disease, May 12, 1992, in Washington, DC; daughter of Benjamin Murphy and Maud Harris Murphy; divorced; children: Alvin H.; *Education:* Dunbar High School, Washington, DC, 1928. *Politics:* Democrat. *Religion:* Roman Catholic.

*CAREER:* Catholic University of America Department of Sociology, secretary to head, 1935-41; U.S. Government Office of Price Administration & Veteran's Administration, correspondence reviewer, editorial clerk, 1942-59; Minority Research Center, Inc. (known as Negro Bibliographic & Research Center, Inc., 1965-71), founder & managing editor/director, 1965-1977; Beatrice M. Murphy Foundation, Martin Luther King Library, founder & executive director, 1977-1992.

*MEMBER:* Center City Community Development Corp.(served on board of directors), Emery Community Center Senior Citizens (president), D.C. Committee on the Aging, Blind Action Forum (publicity chair), American Foundation for the Blind, Pen and Brush Club (former president), Women's National Book Association, D.C. Press Club—Political Study Club.

*AWARDS, HONORS:* First Prize, *Easterner* magazine, for "Something to Remember"; Special Citation, Emery Community Center, for donating library; Meritorious Public Service Award, Mayor of Washington, DC, 1981; Meritorious Service Award, State Health and Development Agency, 1984; Super Senior Award, Iona House Senior Service Center, 1986; Certificate of Appreciation, American Foundation for the Blind, 1988; nomination for D.C. Commission Women's Hall of Fame, 1988, 1989, 1990.

*WRITINGS:*

*POETRY*

*Love Is a Terrible Thing,* Hobson Book Press, 1945.
(With Nancy L. Arnez) *The Rocks Cry Out,* Broadside Press, 1969.
*Get with It Lord: New & Selected Poems,* The Wineberry Press, 1977.

*OTHER*

(Editor) *Ebony Rhythm: An Anthology of Contemporary Negro Verse,* Exposition Press, 1938, Books for Libraries, 1968.
(Editor) *Negro Voices: An Anthology of Contemporary Voices,* Harrison, 1938, University Microfilms, 1971.
*Catching the Editor's Eye* (publishing advice), Hobson, 1949.
(Editor) *Today's Negro Voices: An Anthology by Young Negro Poets,* Messner, 1970.

Also author, with Nancy L. Arnez, of *Home Is Where the Heart Is.* Contributor of columns to *Washington Tribune,* and for *Associated Negro Press.* Contributor to periodicals, including *Afro-American, Christian Herald, Crisis, Interracial Review, New York Times, Our Colored Missions, San Antonio Register,* and *Tan Confessions.* Contributor to anthologies, including *The Light of Day, Contemporary American Women Poets: 1937, Crown Anthology of Verse,* and *Poetry of the Negro.*

*SIDELIGHTS:* Beatrice Murphy devoted herself to advocacy as a writer, an editor, a bibliographer, and an organizer. Always an advocate for African American writing, after beginning to lose her sight in 1967—eventually becoming legally blind—she dedicated herself to disability issues. Murphy first published poetry in *Crisis.* Her first book of poems, *Love Is a Terrible Thing,* a study of a woman's love for a man, is seen as a mild departure from conventional restrictions on eroticism and final disillusionment. *The Rocks Cry Out,* her second book of poems, is a collaboration with Nancy L. Arnez that was published in 1969. The collection responds to the mood of upheaval in the black community with dismay. Murphy's third volume, *Get with It, Lord,* published in 1977, gathers her inspirational verses on African American inflected Christian themes. She also collaborated with Arnez on another book of poems, titled *Home Is Where the Heart Is.*

Throughout her life, Murphy wrote reviews and features for periodicals, beginning with the *Washington Tribune* and ultimately including the *New York Times.* She also served as an editor of other poets' work, editing three anthologies of poetry by African Americans. All three volumes sought to give exposure to work by new writers of college and even high school age side by side with contributions by such luminaries as Langston Hughes. To further aid struggling writers, Murphy wrote *Catching the Editor's Eye,* an advice volume explaining how to submit poems to anthologies and journals for publication.

In 1965 Murphy helped found the Negro Bibliographic and Research Center, rechristened in 1971 as the Minority Research Center. The organization published the *Bibliographic Survey: The Negro in Print* and contributed three thousand books to the Martin Luther King Library in 1968. In 1977 Murphy organized the Beatrice M. Murphy Foundation, which sought to collect, distribute, and preserve literature by and about African Americans and to encourage the growth of such literature. The Foundation initially donated 1700 books to the King Library, hoping to supplement holdings included at other libraries thereafter.

*BIOGRAPHICAL/CRITICAL SOURCES:*

*BOOKS*

*Dictionary of Literary Biography,* Volume 76: *Afro-American Writers, 1940-1955,* Gale, 1988.
*Harlem Renaissance and Beyond,* G. K. Hall, 1990, pp. 247-48.

*PERIODICALS*

*Best Sellers,* April 1, 1970, p. 18.
*Negro Digest,* August 1969, p.97.
*New York Times Book Review,* September 6, 1970, p.16.

*OBITUARIES:*

*PERIODICALS*

*Washington Post,* May 14, 1992, p. 36.

\*　　\*　　\*

## MURRAY, Albert L. 1916-

*PERSONAL:* Born June 12, 1916, in Nokomis, AL; son of John Lee and Sudie (Graham) Young; married Mozelle Menefee, May 31, 1941; children: Michele. *Education:* Tuskegee Institute, B.S., 1939; New York University, M.A., 1948; postgraduate work at University of Michigan, 1940, Northwestern University 1941, and University of Paris, 1950. *Avocational interests:* Recordings, photography, gourmet cooking.

*ADDRESSES: Home and office*—45 West 132nd St., New York, NY 10037.

*CAREER:* U.S. Air Force, 1943-62, retired as major. Instructor, Tuskegee Institute, 1940-43, 1946-51, director of College Little Theatre; lecturer, Graduate School of Journalism, Columbia University, 1968; Colgate University, O'Connor Professor of Literature, 1970, O'Connor Lecturer, 1973, professor of humanities, 1982; visiting professor of literature, University of Massachusetts, Boston, 1971; Paul Anthony Brick lecturer, University of Missouri, 1972; writer in residence, Emory University, 1978; adjunct associate professor of creative writing, Barnard College, 1981-83; lecturer and participant in symposia.

*MEMBER:* PEN International, Authors League of America, Authors Guild, Alpha Phi Alpha.

*AWARDS, HONORS:* Lillian Smith Award for fiction, 1974, for *Train Whistle Guitar;* Litt.D., Colgate University, 1975; American Society of Composers, Authors, and Publishers (ASCAP) Deems Taylor Award for music criticism, 1976, for *Stomping the Blues.*

*WRITINGS:*

*The Omni-Americans: New Perspectives on Black Experience and American Culture* (essays), Outerbridge & Dientsfrey, 1970, published as *The Omni-Americans: Some Alternatives to the Folklore of White Supremacy,* Vintage Books, 1983, Da Capo, 1989.
*South to a Very Old Place,* McGraw, 1972.
*The Hero and the Blues,* University of Missouri Press, 1973.
*Train Whistle Guitar* (novel), McGraw, 1974, Northeastern University Press, 1988.
*Stomping the Blues,* McGraw, 1976, Da Capo, 1989.
(With Count Basie) *Good Morning Blues: The Autobiography of Count Basie,* Random House, 1985.
*The Spyglass Tree* (novel), Pantheon, 1992.

*SIDELIGHTS:* "As a writer, [Albert L. Murray] implicitly perceives himself as proceeding in the same fashion as he maintains legendary heroes, early Americans, and black Americans have always proceeded: by conceptualizing their lives out of chaos and against hostile forces," wrote *Dictionary of Literary Biography* contributor Elizabeth Schultz. She declared that the "abiding concern of [Murray's] writing is the triumph of Afro-American people who, despite and indeed, in Murray's view, because of centuries of difficulties, created a courageous, complex, life-sustaining, and life-enhancing culture—apparent in their language, religion, sports, fashions, food, dance, and above all in their music." Murray articulates these views in his collection of essays *The Omni-Americans: New Perspectives on Black Experience and American Culture,* in which he argues that black Americans have a distinctive identity of their own, developing a unique culture "which allows them to see themselves 'not as the substandard, abnormal *non-white* people of American social science surveys and the news media, but rather as if they were, so to speak, fundamental *extensions* of contemporary possibilities,'" says Schultz. "Like jam session musicians and blues singers," she continues, "they have learned the skills of improvisation, not only translating white models of excellence into their own terms, but also transforming degrading conditions into culture."

Murray expresses an interest in jazz in other works, especially in *The Hero and the Blues* and *Stomping the Blues. Stomping the Blues* is Murray's history, aesthetics and values of the blues, an attempt to redefine "the music and its connotations for American culture," Jason Berry wrote in *The Nation.* S. M. Fry, writing in *Library Journal,* points out that Murray "views the music not as a primitive musical expression of black suffering but as an antidote to the bad times—active good-time music, music to be danced to, music that because of its substance and talented exponents has emerged as the most significant American music." Murray, the reviewer says, also emphasizes the importance of the performance, "the performing style and the music itself over the lyrics and social or political connotations of the blues as significant factors in its expression as an art." These books have made him "one of the foremost literary interpreters of blues, jazz and improvisation," states Brent Staples in the *New York Times Book Review.*

But Murray is much more than a music writer or social critic at large; he "is our premier writer about jazz and the blues, an incisive literary critic, a social commentator of wide-ranging vision, and a fictional tale spinner in the grand Southern tradition of William Faulkner, Joel Chandler Harris, Walker Percy, Reynolds Price, Eudora Welty and Flannery O'Connor," Charles Monaghan declares in a *Washington Post Book World* review of *The Spyglass Tree,* Murray's second novel. *The Spyglass Tree* is a sequel to Murray's earlier work, *Train Whistle Guitar,* which introduced the character of Scooter, a child growing up in 1920s Alabama. In *The Spyglass Tree,* Scooter returns as a college student at Tuskegee Institute, Murray's alma mater. Again, the novel is populated by a dizzy array of characters and riveting tales from a bygone era, all set in the cadences of music—the up-tempo of jazz and the sultriness of the blues. In the first part of the book the scene is set, the characters introduced. In the second half, Scooter tells of a hapless man caught in a gambling debt and the beating of a black man by a redneck store owner over a few coins. Yet, the tales are buoyed by the joys of recollection and growing up, and "the delights of bluesology and jazzology," wrote Reginald McKnight in a *New York Times Book Review* critique of *The Spyglass Tree.* "Reading this novel will be, for

some, like sitting in a room with your father or grandfather and letting him take you so fully into his past that after a while it occurs to you that his world is more palpable, in many respects, than the one in which you live. But it isn't simply the distilling effect of time that makes the novel so vital; it is also the indelible quality of its voices," he added.

In *Newsweek,* Malcolm Jones Jr. calls Murray's prose in *The Spyglass Tree* "loosy goosy" and "shimmering." He quotes a passage in the novel wherein Scooter reflects on the savage, racist beating he has witnessed, recognizing that as a black man in Alabama he must always wear a mask lest he do "anything that's going to make somebody realize how scared they are of you." Yet, Jones found *The Spyglass Tree* as joyful as McKnight did. "One does not have to ignore the hard realities it sets forth to call this novel warm and joyful," he wrote. Monaghan opined that the book "displays Murray's prose style at its best—rolling cadences of Faulkner and Joyce, but soaked in jazz rhythms and electrified by a terrifically keen ear for Southern black speech."

*BIOGRAPHICAL/CRITICAL SOURCES:*

*BOOKS*

*Dictionary of Literary Biography,* Volume 38: *Afro-American Writers since 1955: Dramatists and Prose Writers,* Gale, 1985.
Murray, Albert L., *The Omni-Americans: New Perspectives on Black Experience and American Culture,* Outerbridge & Dientsfrey, 1970.

*PERIODICALS*

*Book World,* March 22, 1970; December 26, 1971.
*Chicago Tribune Book World,* January 19, 1986.
*Library Journal,* February 1, 1977.
*Los Angeles Times Book Review,* March 26, 1986.
*Nations,* January 15, 1977.
*Newsweek,* March 23, 1970; January 31, 1972; December 20, 1976; December 9, 1991, p. 71.
*New Yorker,* October 17, 1970; January 8, 1972, July 22, 1974.
*New York Review of Books,* February 24, 1972; June 18, 1974; January 16, 1986.
*New York Times,* April 4, 1972; December 11, 1976.
*New York Times Book Review,* May 3, 1970; January 2 ,1972; June 4, 1972; December 3, 1972; May 12, 1974; December 1, 1974; December 26, 1976; December 26, 1982; February 2, 1986; March 1, 1992, p. 23.
*Rolling Stone,* January 13, 1977.
*Saturday Review,* January 22, 1972.
*Time,* January 10, 1972.
*Times Literary Supplement,* July 28, 1978; July 11, 1986.
*Tribune Books* (Chicago), October 6, 1991, p. 8.

*Voice Literary Supplement,* February, 1982.
*Washington Post Book World,* December 8, 1974; January 8, 1986; May 27, 1990, p. 12; October 6, 1991, p. 8; November 3, 1991, pp. 7, 11.

\* \* \*

## MURRAY, (Anna) Pauli(ne) 1910-1985

*PERSONAL:* Born November 20, 1910, in Baltimore, MD (one source says Durham, NC); died of cancer, July 1, 1985, in Pittsburgh, PA; daughter of William Henry (a school principal) and Agnes Georgianna (a nurse; maiden name, Fitzgerald) Murray; divorced. *Education:* Hunter College (now of the City University of New York), A.B., 1933; Howard University, LL.B. (cum laude), 1944; University of California (now University of California, Berkeley), LL.M., 1945; Yale University, J.S.D., 1965; General Theological Seminary, M.Div. (cum laude), 1976.

*ADDRESSES: Home*—Pittsburgh, PA.

*CAREER:* Worked at a number of odd jobs, including four years in U.S. Government work relief program Work Projects Administration. Admitted to the Bar of California State, 1945, the Bar of New York State, 1948, and the Bar of the U.S. Supreme Court, 1960; deputy attorney general of California, 1946; American Jewish Congress, New York, NY, attorney for commission on law and social action, 1946-47; worked for a time at private practice of law in New York City; Paul, Weiss, Rifkind, Wharton & Garrison (law firm), New York City, associate attorney in litigation department, 1956-60. University of Ghana, near Accra, senior lecturer, 1960-61; Benedict College, Columbia, SC, vice-president, 1967-68, also served as professor of political science; Brandeis University, Waltham, MA, professor of American studies, 1968-73, Louis Stulberg Professor of Law and Politics, 1972-73; Boston University, Boston, MA, lecturer at school of law, 1972. Ordained Episcopal priest, 1977, served churches in Washington, DC, Baltimore, MD, and Pittsburgh, PA, retired in 1984; fourth assembly of World Council of Churches in Uppsala, Sweden, consultant, 1968; member of Commission on Ordained and Licensed Ministries, 1969-70. Beacon Press, director, 1968-69. Affiliated with a number of government agencies and civil rights groups, including Presidential Commission on the Status of Women, 1962-63; American Civil Liberties Union, 1965-73; Equal Employment Opportunity Commission, 1966-67; and Martin Luther King, Jr., Center for Non-Violent Social Change, 1970-84.

*MEMBER:* National Bar Association, American Bar Association (vice-chairperson of committee on women's rights, 1971-73), National Association for the Advancement of Colored People (NAACP; life member), National Association of Women Lawyers, National Council of Negro Women, National Organization for Women (co-founder and member, 1970-84), New York County Bar Association, Hunter College Alumni Association.

*AWARDS, HONORS:* Recipient of honorary degrees, including LL.D. from Dartmouth College, 1976, D.H.L. from Radcliffe College, 1978, and D.D. from Yale University, 1979; named Woman of the Year by National Council of Negro Women, 1946, and by *Mademoiselle* magazine, 1947; alumni award for distinguished postgraduate achievement in law and public service from Howard University, 1970; Eleanor Roosevelt award from Professional Women's Caucus, 1971; recipient of first Whitney M. Young, Jr., Memorial Award, 1972; named to Hunter College Hall of Fame, 1973; award for "Exemplary Christian Ministry" from National Institute for Women of Color, 1982; Robert F. Kennedy Book Award and Christopher Award, both 1988, both for *Song in a Weary Throat: An American Pilgrimage.*

*WRITINGS:*

(Editor) *States' Laws on Race and Color,* Woman's Division of Christian Service, Board of Missions and Church Extension, Methodist Church, 1951, supplement (with Verge Lake), 1955.
*Proud Shoes: The Story of an American Family* (biography), Harper, 1956, new edition, 1978.
(With Leslie Rubin) *The Constitution and Government of Ghana,* Sweet & Maxwell, 1961.
*Human Rights U.S.A., 1948-1966,* Service Center, Board of Missions, Methodist Church, 1967.
*Dark Testament, and Other Poems* (collection), Silvermine, 1970.
(Contributor) *Voices of the New Feminism,* edited by Mary Lou Thompson, Beacon Press, 1970.
*Song in a Weary Throat: An American Pilgrimage* (autobiography), Harper, 1987.
*Pauli Murray: The Autobiography of a Black Activist, Feminist, Lawyer, Priest, and Poet,* University of Tennessee Press, 1989.

Also author of speeches and addresses, including *The Negro Woman in the Quest for Equality,* 1964. Poetry represented in anthologies, including *The Poetry of Black America,* edited by Arnold Adoff, Macmillan, 1968; *The Poetry of the Negro, 1746-1970,* edited by Langston Hughes and Arna Bontemps, Doubleday, 1970; and *A Rock Against the Wind: Black Love Poems,* edited by Lindsay Patterson, Dodd, 1973. Contributor to journals and other publications, including *Crisis* magazine.

*SIDELIGHTS:* For her pioneering efforts in a number of different areas, Pauli Murray is remembered as a woman ahead of her time. As an activist for the civil rights and feminist movements, beginning in the late 1930s, she became a forerunner in the subsequent struggle for racial and sexual equality in the United States. During a period when blacks and women were still restricted from certain educational and professional opportunities, she achieved consecutive goals as an attorney and educator, and in 1977 Murray became the first black woman to be ordained an Episcopal priest. An aspiring writer, she also published a number of books on law as well as a collection of poetry, *Dark Testament, and Other Poems,* and two critically acclaimed personal histories, *Proud Shoes* and *Song in a Weary Throat.* Described as a versatile and determined woman, Murray allegedly maintained that her successive careers followed a logical progression toward eliminating racial and sexist discrimination. Along the way, Murray earned a dual reputation as a "freedom fighter" and a "firebrand." Each of her prodigious achievements "represented a calculated attack on some boundary—of sex, of race—that society had placed in her way," remarked Pat Williams in the *New York Times Book Review.* Similarly, *Detroit News* writer Frances A. Koestler commented that Murray's diverse accomplishments "were dictated by a burning sense that social inequities had to be challenged and overcome."

To some extent Murray's childhood both shaped her character and influenced her ambitions as an adult. Orphaned at the age of three, when her mother died and her father subsequently entered a mental hospital, she grew up in the care of her mother's relatives in Durham, North Carolina. Though sources disagree on whether it was Murray's maternal grandparents or aunts who actually reared her, there is a consensus of opinion attributing Murray's independent nature and strong sense of pride to that of her appointed guardians. From them she learned of her heterogeneous ancestry that included not only blacks and whites, slaves and slave owners, but Cherokee Indians as well. Like most black Americans of her day who descended from a blend of cultures and races, Murray experienced alienation—feelings of not belonging to any specific group of people. Her mulatto background both prevented her from identifying solely with her African heritage and excluded her from white society. Though proud of her individuality, Murray—who preferred the term "Negro" to the word "black"—sought to discover the origins of her being and thus establish her roots.

In an attempt to recreate her past, Murray wrote *Proud Shoes: The Story of an American Family.* Due to a general lack of interest in its subject matter, however, the book "sank with scarcely a trace" after its initial publication in 1956, reflected *Los Angeles Times* reviewer Robert Kirsch. But with the appearance of an expanded edition in 1978, Murray's biography captured public attention and critical acclaim, eliciting comparisons to Alex Haley's best-selling novel *Roots.* Despite some similarities between the two works, Kirsch observed that Murray's "marvelous and moving family memoir ... is a very different story." Describing what he thought distinguished Murray's story from Haley's, Jack Hicks wrote in *Nation* that "*Proud Shoes* traps the beast of American slavery" while *Roots* "dwells on African continuations in the black American family." Essentially, Murray's book focuses on the multiple conflicts affecting the progeny of interracial unions, those "unwilling agents of love and animosity" who were trapped between black and white, Hicks commented. According to Nellie McKay in the *Dictionary of Literary Biography,* Murray's *Proud Shoes* represents more than an individual's search for identity; it "embodies the most important elements in the evolution of the contemporary black family" and serves as a microcosm of the total black experience in white America. As such, McKay noted, *Proud Shoes* also qualifies as a slice of U.S. history.

During the course of her personal search for identity, Murray was confronted by questions of equality on the basis of sex and skin color. In particular, she "was awakened to the universal dimensions of the struggle for human dignity by sustained contact with the labor movement," reported Sherley Anne Williams in the *Los Angeles Times Book Review.* With characteristic defiance she challenged various institutions of government, business, education, and finally religion, opposing practices of discrimination and segregation that historically excluded blacks and women. In 1938, for example, Murray "waged a highly publicized battle for admission to" the University of North Carolina at Chapel Hill, related Susan McHenry in *Ms.* Though school officials rejected her application, her efforts forged the path leading to a federal court ruling that ordered the school's integration in 1951. Similarly, Murray was jailed for refusing to sit in the back of a Virginia bus in 1940. She also organized and/or participated in a number of rallies and demonstrations, among them a series of sit-ins aimed at desegregating restaurants and other public places in Washington, D.C., Murray's activism recurrently led to confrontations with the law. In view of this fact, she chose to become an attorney, convinced "that the law was the fastest route to racial equality," wrote Koestler.

Murray's ongoing crusade against racial and sexual barriers eventually took issue with the U.S. Supreme Court and later with the Episcopal church. Though she proved unsuccessful in her appeal to fill the traditionally male-occupied position of Supreme Court Justice, Murray's initiative again prepared the way for others of her sex. Amid controversy she resolved in 1974 to enter the priesthood, a station the Episcopal church hitherto reserved only for men. In an article for the *New York Times,* Eleanor Blau quoted Murray on her objective: "I want to be a positive force for reconciliation both in terms of race and ... sex." Three years later Murray became the first woman ordained an Episcopal priest.

*Dark Testament, and Other Poems,* Murray's 1970 collection, serves as a reflection of her personal and professional encounters. In the words of McKay in *Dictionary of Literary Biography,* the volume is "a poetic mirror of Murray's life and career," and also documents the broad expanse of her personal interests. Utilizing her imagination and an array of emotions, Murray features a melange of topics that range from philosophic musings and the concerns of racial oppression to themes of love and friendship. Several critics found the title poem especially noteworthy, citing Murray's use of symbolism to address specific characteristics of the human mind and will.

Like her volume of poetry, Murray's posthumously published autobiography, *Song in a Weary Throat: An American Pilgrimage,* documents her multifaceted career and exists as a testament to her lifelong quest for personal identity. Furthermore, according to McHenry in *Ms.,* the book "distinctively recounts the kind of sustained commitment and often unheralded effort that fed into the great civil rights victories." Numerous critics viewed Murray's highly acclaimed book as a unique, eloquent, and inspiring piece of work. Reviewing the book in *Washington Post Book World,* Jonathan Yardley added that *Song in a Weary Throat* is "a splendid book ... smoothly written, good-humored, passionate, thoughtful.... One comes to its powerfully moving final pages utterly convinced that Murray was one of the great Americans of her time."

*BIOGRAPHICAL/CRITICAL SOURCES:*

BOOKS

Diamonstein, Barbaralee, *Open Secrets: Ninety-four Women in Touch with Our Time,* Viking, 1972.
*Dictionary of Literary Biography,* Volume 41: *Afro-American Poets since 1955,* Gale, 1985.
Roses, Lorraine Elena, and Ruth Elizabeth Randolph, *Harlem Renaissance and Beyond,* G. K. Hall, 1990.

PERIODICALS

*American Visions,* August, 1989.
*Detroit News,* April 26, 1987.
*Ebony,* June, 1987.
*Los Angeles Times Book Review,* October 6, 1978; May 24, 1987.
*Ms.,* May, 1987.
*Nation,* December 16, 1978; May 23, 1987.
*New York Times,* February 11, 1974.

*New York Times Book Review,* March 29, 1987; May 24, 1987.
*Washington Post Book World,* April 5, 1987.

*OBITUARIES:*

PERIODICALS

*New York Times,* July 4, 1985.
*Washington Post,* July 4, 1985.

\*   \*   \*

## MWANGI, Meja   1948-

*PERSONAL:* Born in December, 1948, in Nyeri, Kenya; son of a domestic worker. *Education:* Attended Kenyatta College; attended the University of Iowa, 1975.

*CAREER:* Writer. Served as assistant director on the film *Out of Africa,* 1985; was a member of the film production team that adapted James Fox's *White Mischief,* 1988.

*AWARDS, HONORS:* Jomo Kenyatta Prize, 1974, for *Kill Me Quick;* Commonwealth Writers Prize nomination, 1990, for *Striving for the Wind.*

*WRITINGS:*

FICTION

*Kill Me Quick,* Heinemann Educational, 1973.
*Carcase for Hounds,* Heinemann Educational, 1974.
*Taste of Death,* East African Publishing House (Kenya, Nairobi), 1975.
*Going down River Road,* Heinemann Educational, 1976.
*The Bushtrackers* (adapted from a screenplay by Gary Strieker), Longman Drumbeat (Nairobi), 1979.
*The Cockroach Dance,* Longman Kenya (Nairobi), 1979.
*Bread of Sorrow,* Longman Kenya, 1987.
*The Return of Shaka,* Longman Kenya, 1989.
*Weapon of Hunger,* Longman Kenya, 1989.
*Striving for the Wind,* Heinemann Kenya, 1990; Heinemann, 1992.

*SIDELIGHTS:* Kenyan Meja Mwangi describes the current African social and political situation in his writings, which employ the suspense, violence, and pacing that typify the modern thriller genre. The son of a maid who worked for white families in the British town of Nyeri, Kenya, Mwangi grew up during the Mau Mau massacres and Kenya's tumultuous independence movement. While violence raged on the outskirts of town, Mwangi spent his childhood absorbing much of the white settlers' culture from both his mother's contact with the settlers in their homes and from his reading of European children's books, which were gifts from his mother's employers.

Mwangi has remained in Kenya and bases his work upon the sufferings of his people, drawing upon his experiences with the Anglo-African society and childhood memories of the Mau Mau uprising and combining them with a sense of place in order to dramatize his characters' lives and their struggle for survival in contemporary Africa. Several members of Mwangi's family were sent to detention camps because they had been active in the revolution. According to Simon Gikandi, writing in the *Dictionary of Literary Biography,* Mwangi recalled being held captive in a detention camp with his mother for a short time. Mwangi was so affected by what he had witnessed and the stories he had heard of the Mau Mau uprising that he wrote about it in his first book, *Taste of Death,* when he was seventeen years old (it was not published until Mwangi was twenty-four). In this novel, the young hero, Kariuki, is swept along by the passion and excitement of the Mau Mau insurrection and Kenya's fight for independence even though he does not understand the basis of the conflict and is not ready to sacrifice his own life for the rebellion. Mwangi glorifies the conflict in the novel, telling of the freedom fighters' futile attempt to avoid death at the hands of colonial forces.

Mwangi's realistic novel *Kill Me Quick* takes place after Kenya had established its independence. The protagonists, two boys who are life-long friends, try to improve their lives by attending school. They move to Nairobi in order to find work, but they discover that their classroom education is worthless in the city. They become stranded in the urban jungle, without hope for improving their situation or the ability to return to their rural homes. Desperate for money, the boys turn to crime and are apprehended, and only after they are incarcerated does the quality of their lives improve. Gikandi explained that *Kill Me Quick* is considered significant "because of Mwangi's ... journalistic style; he renders scenes with the hard and sharp ear of a reporter on the beat." A *Choice* contributor called the novel "an incisive look at the way crime is created by poverty rather than by innate evil."

In his third book, *Carcase for Hounds,* Mwangi returns to the themes of pessimism, futility, and hopelessness. A Mau Mau soldier and his mortally wounded revolutionary commander are trapped and surrounded by hostile British forces in a forest, a situation that Mwangi uses as a metaphor for the hopelessness both the revolutionaries and the British colonial forces feel in this stand-off. "Mwangi has usurped the language of the American thriller, of Raymond Chandler, Mickey Spillane, and Chester Himes," Gikandi wrote. "His characters speak in an American idiom that is incongruous with their situation, and the authorial descriptions also seems more appropriate for the 'jungles' of Harlem or the Bronx than for those of Kenya."

In *Going down River Road,* which is considered to be his greatest achievement, Mwangi returns to the horrors of the urban jungle. According to *World Literature Today* contributor Charles R. Larson, Mwangi paints a culture "composed ... of young bar girls, urban thugs or youths." In 1979's *The Cockroach Dance,* Mwangi attempts to realize a balance between entertaining the reader and criticizing society. His main character, a water meter reader, is driven to despair and violence by the hopelessness and injustice he witnesses every day on his job. Mwangi's novelization of Gary Strieker's screenplay *The Bushtrackers* was also published in 1979. *Black Scholar* contributor Roland S. Jefferson called it "the first indigenous novel/film to come out of Africa with an eye toward appealing to the U.S./westernized culture." The main character reacts to every situation with anger and rage. Jefferson wrote that the novel "highlights a character who views the political and justice system around him as virtually impotent and unable to extract retribution."

In 1987's *Bread of Sorrow,* Mwangi uses the thriller genre to address the problems of apartheid and racial oppression, while his 1989 Americana-packed novel *The Return of Shaka* focuses on an African prince touring the United States on a Greyhound bus, chased across the continent by hired killers. In *Weapon of Hunger,* the worst of Africa's horrors—famine, drought, civil war, the atrocities of revolution—are played against an American pop star's efforts to save the starving. Mwangi returns to African concerns with *Striving for the Wind,* a novel of contemporary rural despair and loneliness. Mwangi's depiction of the depleted Kenyan landscape and the exhausted humans who till it earned the volume a nomination for the Commonwealth Writers Prize.

*BIOGRAPHICAL/CRITICAL SOURCES:*

*BOOKS*

*Dictionary of Literary Biography,* Volume 125: *Twentieth-Century Caribbean and Black African Writers: Second Series,* Gale, 1993.
Zell, Hans M., and others, *A New Reader's Guide to African Literature,* Holmes and Meier, 1983.

*PERIODICALS*

*Black Scholar,* November/December, 1984, pp. 61-63.
*Choice,* March 1976, p. 78; June, 1976, p. 528.

*World Literature Today,* autumn, 1977, p. 565.

—*Sketch by Mel Wathen*

\* \* \*

## MYERS, Walter Dean 1937-
### (Walter M. Myers)

*PERSONAL:* Given name Walter Milton Myers; born August 12, 1937, in Martinsburg, WV; son of George Ambrose and Mary (Green) Myers; raised from age three by Herbert Julius (a shipping clerk) and Florence (a factory worker) Dean; married second wife, Constance Brendel, June 19, 1973; children: (first marriage) Karen, Michael Dean; (second marriage) Christopher. *Education:* Attended State College of the City University of New York; Empire State College, B.A.

*ADDRESSES: Home*—2543 Kennedy Blvd., Jersey City, NJ 07304.

*CAREER:* New York State Department of Labor, Brooklyn, employment supervisor, 1966-69; Bobbs-Merrill Co., Inc. (publisher), New York City, senior trade book editor, 1970-77; writer, 1977—. Has also taught creative writing and black history on a part-time basis in New York City, 1974-75. *Military service:* U.S. Army, 1954-57.

*MEMBER:* PEN, Harlem Writers Guild.

*AWARDS, HONORS:* Council on Interracial Books for Children Award, 1968, for the manuscript of *Where Does the Day Go?;* Woodward Park School Annual Book Award, 1976, for *Fast Sam, Cool Clyde, and Stuff;* American Library Association "Best Books for Young Adults" citations, 1978, for *It Ain't All for Nothin',* 1979, for *The Young Landlords,* and 1982, for *Hoops;* Coretta Scott King Awards, 1980, for *The Young Landlords,* and 1984, for *Motown and Didi: A Love Story;* Notable Children's Trade Book in Social Studies citation, 1982, for *The Legend of Tarik; Scorpions* was named a Newbery Honor Book, 1989; Coretta Scott King Award, 1991, for *Now is Your Time!: The African-American Struggle for Freedom.*

*WRITINGS:*

*FOR CHILDREN*

(Under name Walter M. Myers) *Where Does the Day Go?,* illustrated by Leo Carty, Parents' Magazine Press, 1969.

*The Dragon Takes a Wife,* illustrated by Ann Grifalconi, Bobbs-Merrill, 1972.
*The Dancers,* illustrated by Anne Rockwell, Parents' Magazine Press, 1972.
*Fly, Jimmy, Fly!,* illustrated by Moneta Barnett, Putnam, 1974.
*The World of Work: A Guide to Choosing a Career,* Bobbs-Merrill, 1975.
*Fast Sam, Cool Clyde, and Stuff,* Viking, 1975.
*Social Welfare,* F. Watts, 1976.
*Brainstorm,* with photographs by Chuck Freedman, F. Watts, 1977.
*Mojo and the Russians,* Viking, 1977.
*Victory for Jamie,* Scholastic Book Services, 1977.
*It Ain't All for Nothin',* Viking, 1978.
*The Young Landlords,* Viking, 1979.
*The Black Pearl and the Ghost; or, One Mystery after Another,* illustrated by Robert Quackenbush, Viking, 1980.
*The Golden Serpent,* illustrated by Alice Provensen and Martin Provensen, Viking, 1980.
*Hoops,* Delacorte, 1981.
*The Legend of Tarik,* Viking, 1981.
*Won't Know Till I Get There,* Viking, 1982.
*The Nicholas Factor,* Viking, 1983.
*Tales of a Dead King,* Morrow, 1983.
*Mr. Monkey and the Gotcha Bird,* illustrated by Leslie Morrill, Delacorte, 1984.
*Motown and Didi: A Love Story,* Viking, 1984.
*The Outside Shot,* Delacorte, 1984.
*Sweet Illusions,* Teachers & Writers Collaborative, 1986.
*Crystal,* Viking, 1987.
*Shadow of the Red Moon,* Harper, 1987.
*Fallen Angels,* Scholastic, Inc., 1988.
*Scorpions,* Harper, 1988.
*Me, Mop, and the Moondance Kid,* Delacorte, 1988.
*The Mouse Rap,* Harper & Row, 1990.
*Now Is Your Time!: The African American Struggle for Freedom,* HarperCollins, 1991.
*Somewhere in the Darkness,* Scholastic, 1992.
*A Place Called Heartbreak: A Story of Vietnam,* illustrated by Frederick Porter, Raintree Steck-Vaughn, 1992.
*The Righteous Revenge of Artemis Bonner,* HarperCollins, 1992.
*Mop, Moondance, and the Nagasaki Knights,* Delacorte Press, 1992.
*Young Martin's Promise,* Raintree Steck-Vaughn, 1992.
*Malcolm X: By Any Means Necessary,* Scholastic, 1993.

*"THE ARROW" SERIES; FOR CHILDREN*

*Adventure in Granada,* Viking, 1985.
*The Hidden Shrine,* Viking, 1985.
*Duel in the Desert,* Viking, 1986.
*Ambush in the Amazon,* Viking, 1986.

*CONTRIBUTOR TO ANTHOLOGIES*

Orde Coombs, editor, *What We Must See: Young Black Sto-
     rytellers,* Dodd, 1971.
Sonia Sanchez, editor, *We Be Word Sorcerers: Twenty-five
     Stories by Black Americans,* Bantam, 1973.

*OTHER*

Contributor of articles and fiction to periodicals, including
*Black Creation, Black World, McCall's, Espionage, Alfred
Hitchcock Mystery Magazine, Essence, Ebony Jr.!,* and *Boy's
Life.*

*ADAPTATIONS: The Young Landlords* was filmed by Topol
Productions.

*SIDELIGHTS:* Walter Dean Myers is commonly recognized
as one of modern literature's premier authors of fiction for
young black people. Two of his novels for teens, *The Young
Landlords* and *Motown and Didi: A Love Story,* have won the
prestigious Coretta Scott King Award, and his text for the
picture book *Where Does the Day Go?* received the Council
on Interracial Books for Children Award in 1969. As Carmen
Subryan notes in the *Dictionary of Literary Biography,*
"Whether he is writing about the ghettos of New York, the
remote countries of Africa, or social institutions, Myers captures the essence of the developing experiences of youth."

While Myers is perhaps best known for his novels that explore
the lives of young Harlem blacks, he is equally adept at producing modern fairy tales, ghost stories, and adventure sagas.
Subryan finds a common theme throughout Myers's far-rang-
ing works. "He is concerned with the development of youths,"
she writes, "and his message is always the same: young people
must face the reality of growing up and must persevere, knowing that they can succeed despite any odds they face.... This
positive message enables youths to discover what is important in life and to reject influences which could destroy them."

In the *Interracial Books for Children Bulletin,* Myers describes
his priorities as an author. He tries, he says, to provide good
literature for black children, "literature that includes them and
the way they live" and that "celebrates their life and their person. It upholds and gives special place to their humanity." He
elaborates on this point in an essay for *Something about the
Author Autobiography Series:* "I realized how few resources
are available for Black youngsters to open the world to them.
I feel the need to show them the possibilities that exist for them
that were never revealed to me as a youngster; possibilities
that did not even exist for me then."

One possibility Myers never foresaw as a youth was that of
supporting himself as a writer. He was born into an impoverished family in Martinsburg, West Virginia, and at age three
was adopted by Herbert and Florence Dean, who settled in
New York City's Harlem district. Although he wrote poems
and stories from his early teens onward and won awards for
them, his parents did not encourage his literary talents. "I was
from a family of laborers," he remembers in his autobiographical essay, "and the idea of writing stories or essays was far
removed from their experience. Writing had no practical value
for a Black child. These minor victories [and prizes] did not
bolster my ego. Instead, they convinced me that even though
I was bright, even though I might have some talent, I was still
defined by factors other than my ability." The dawning realization that his possibilities were limited by race and economic
status embittered Myers as a teen. "A youngster is not trained
to want to be a gasoline station attendant or a clerk in some
obscure office," he states. "We are taught to want to be lawyers and doctors and accountants—these professions that are
given value. When the compromise comes, as it does early in
Harlem to many children, it comes hard."

Myers admits he was not ready to accept that compromise.
Through high school and a three-year enlistment in the Army,
he read avidly and wrote short stories. After his discharge from
the service, he worked in a variety of positions, including mail
clerk at the post office, interoffice messenger, and interviewer
in a factory. None of these tasks pleased him, and when he
began to publish poetry, stories and articles in magazines, he
cautiously started to consider a writing profession. "When I
entered a contest for picture book writers," he claims, "it was
more because I wanted to write *anything* than because I wanted
to write a picture book."

Myers won the contest, sponsored by the Council on Interracial Books for Children, for his text of *Where Does the Day
Go?* In that story, a group of children from several ethnic
backgrounds discuss their ideas about night and day with a
sensitive and wise black father during a long walk. Inspired
by the success of his first attempt to write for young people,
Myers turned his attention to producing more picture books.
Between 1972 and 1975, he published three: *The Dancers, The
Dragon Takes a Wife,* and *Fly, Jimmy, Fly!* More recent releases include *The Golden Serpent,* a fable set in India, and
an animal adventure, *Mr. Monkey and the Gotcha Bird.*

Myers accepted an editorial position with the Bobbs-Merrill
publishing company in 1970 and worked there until 1977. His
seven-year tenure taught him "the book business from another
viewpoint," as he puts it in his autobiographical essay. "Publishing is a business," he writes. "It is not a cultural institution.... It is *talked* about as if it were a large cultural organization with several branches. One hears pronouncements like

'anything worthwhile will eventually be published.' Nonsense, of course. Books are published for many reasons, the chief of which is profit." In retrospect, however, Myers feels that he has benefitted from his experiences at Bobbs-Merrill, even though he was laid off during a restructuring program. "After the initial disillusionment about the artistic aspects of the job, I realized how foolish I had been in not learning, as a writer, more about the business aspects of my craft," he concludes. Armed with the pragmatic knowledge of how the publishing industry works, Myers has supported himself by his writing alone since 1977.

By the time he left Bobbs-Merrill, Myers had already established a reputation as an able author of fiction for black children, based largely upon his highly successful novels for teens such as *Fast Sam, Cool Clyde, and Stuff* and *Mojo and the Russians.* Both tales feature, in Subryan's words, adventures depicting "the learning experiences of most youths growing up in a big city where negative influences abound." Central to the stories is the concept of close friendships, portrayed as a positive, nurturing influence. Subryan states: "Because of the bonding which occurs among the members of the group, the reader realizes that each individual's potential for survival has increased." Myers followed the two upbeat novels with a serious one, *It Ain't All for Nothin',* that Subryan feels "reflects much of the pain and anguish of ghetto life." The account of a boy caught in a web of parental abuse, conflicting values, and solitary self-assessment, *It Ain't All for Nothin'* "pretties up nothing; not the language, not the circumstances, not the despair," according to Jane Pennington in the *Interracial Books for Children Bulletin.* The story has a positive resolution, however, based on the care and support the central character receives from fellow community members.

Myers strives to present characters for whom urban life is an uplifting experience despite the potentially dangerous influences. In his first Coretta Scott King Award-winner, *The Young Landlords,* several teens learn responsibility when they are given a ghetto apartment building to manage. Lonnie Jackson, the protagonist of *Hoops,* profits from the example of an older friend who has become involved with gamblers. Concerned with stereotyping of a sexual as well as a racial sort, Myers creates plausible female characters and features platonic friendships between the sexes in his works. "The love in *Fast Sam, Cool Clyde, and Stuff* is not between any one couple," writes Alleen Pace Nilsen in the *English Journal.* "Instead it is a sort of a general feeling of good will and concern that exists among a group of inner city kids." Nilsen, among others, also notes that Myers's fiction can appeal to readers of any race. She concludes that he "makes the reader feel so close to the characters that ethnic group identification is secondary." Subryan expresses a similar opinion: "By appealing to the consciousness of young adults, Myers is touching perhaps the most important element of our society. Myers's books demonstrate that writers can not only challenge the minds of black youths but also emphasize the black experience in a nonracist way that benefits all young readers."

With *Scorpions,* Myers tells the story of Jamal, a seventh grader whose life is forever changed when he accepts a gun from an older teen. For this provocative story Myers received the Newbery Honor Book award in 1989. In *Fallen Angels,* a Harlem teenager volunteers for service in the Vietnam War. Mel Watkins in the *New York Times Book Review* writes, "*Fallen Angels* is a candid young adult novel that engages the Vietnam experience squarely. It deals with violence and death as well as compassion and love, with deception and hypocrisy as well as honesty and virtue. It is a tale that is as thought-provoking as it is entertaining, touching and, on occasion, humorous." Jim Naughton, reviewing *Me, Mop, and the Moondance Kid* in the *Washington Post Book World,* calls Myers "one of the best writers of children's and young adult fiction in the country and *Me, Mop, and the Moondance Kid* shows why" in relating the schemes of two recently adopted orphans to find a home for their friend, left behind in the orphanage. In the Coretta Scott King Award-winning *Now Is Your Time! The African-American Struggle for Freedom,* a *Washington Post Book World* contributor finds that Myers "writes with the vividness of a novelist, the balance of an historian and the passion of an advocate. He tells a familiar story and shocks us with it all over again." Focusing on the black experience in America, Myers relates tales of Malcolm X, Coretta Scott King, Frederick Douglass, businessman James Forten, rebels Nat Turner and John Brown, journalist Ida B. Wells, inventor Lewis Latimer, and sculptor Meta Vaux Warrick, and even the Dandridges of Virginia, the "owners" of Myers's great-grandmother. The *Washington Post Book World* critic calls *Now Is Your Time!* a "thrilling portrait gallery, expertly delineated.... Quite a story, quite a book."

Myers writes in *Something About the Author Autobiography Series* that the reception of his novels gave him a new role as an author. "As my books for teenagers gained in popularity I sensed that my soul-searching for my place in the artistic world was taking on added dimension. As a Black writer I had not only the personal desire to find myself, but the obligation to use my abilities to fill a void." Children and adults, he suggests, "must have role models with which they can identify," and he feels he must "deliver images upon which [they] could build and expand their own worlds." Noting that in his own life he has "acquired the strengths to turn away from disaster," Myers concludes: "As a Black writer, I want to talk about my people.... The books come. They pour from me at a great rate. I can't see how any writer can ever stop. There is always one more story to tell, one more person whose life needs to be held up to the sun."

*BIOGRAPHICAL/CRITICAL SOURCES:*

*BOOKS*

*Children's Literature Review,* Volume 4, Gale, 1982.
*Contemporary Literary Criticism,* Volume 35, Gale, 1985.
*Dictionary of Literary Biography,* Volume 33: *Afro-American Fiction Writers after 1955,* Gale, 1984.
Rush, Theressa G., editor, *Black American Writers: Past and Present,* Scarecrow Press, 1975.
*Something about the Author Autobiography Series,* Volume 2, Gale, 1986.

*PERIODICALS*

*Christian Science Monitor,* May 1, 1992, p. 10.
*Ebony,* September, 1975.
*Interracial Books for Children Bulletin,* Volume 10, number 4, 1979; Volume 10, number 6, 1979.

*New York Times Book Review,* April 9, 1972; May 4, 1975; January 6, 1980; November 9, 1980; July 12, 1981; June 13, 1982; April 19, 1987, p. 21; September 13, 1987, p. 48; January 22, 1989, p. 29; May 20, 1990, p. 44; February 16, 1992, p. 26.
*Tribune Books* (Chicago), February 26, 1989, p. 8.
*Washington Post Book World,* July 9, 1989, p. 10; March 8, 1992, p. 11.


*       *       *


**MYERS, Walter M.**
**See MYERS, Walter Dean**

# N

## NAGENDA, John 1938-

*PERSONAL:* Born in 1938 in Gahini, Uganda. *Education:* Received B.A. from Makerere University, Kampala, Uganda. *Avocational interests:* Member of Uganda's national cricket team.

*CAREER:* Poet, story writer, playwright, and scholar.

*WRITINGS:*

*Mukasa* (children's book), illustrated by Charles Lilly, Macmillan, 1973.
*The Seasons of Thomas Tebo,* Heinemann Educational Books, 1986.

Author of story "And This, At Last," which appeared originally in *Penpoint and Transition,* Kampala; also in *Pan African Short Stories,* edited by Neville Denny, London, Nelson, 1965. Contributor of stories and/or poems to *Origin East Africa,* edited by David Cook, Heinemann, 1965; and *New Voices from the Commonwealth,* edited by Howard Sergeant, Evans, 1968. A speech delivered at the African-Scandinavian Writers' Conference in Stockholm in 1967 appeared in *The Writer in Modern Africa,* edited by Per Wastberg, Scandinavian Institute of African Studies (Uppsala, Sweden), 1968. Author of the essay "Generations in Conflict," which appeared in *Protest and Conflict in African Literature,* edited by Pieterse and Munro, New York, 1969.

*BIOGRAPHICAL/CRITICAL SOURCES:*

*PERIODICALS*

*Booklist,* September 15, 1973, p. 124.
*British Book News,* November 1986, p. 621.
*Bulletin of the Center for Children's Books,* November 1973, p. 48.

*Childhood Education,* January 1974, p. 165.
*Horn Book Magazine,* August 1973, p. 380.
*Kirkus Reviews,* December 15, 1972, p. 1429.
*Top of the News,* April 1974, p. 309.

\* \* \*

## NAYLOR, Gloria 1950-

*PERSONAL:* Born January 25, 1950, in New York, NY; daughter of Roosevelt (a transit worker) and Alberta (a telephone operator; maiden name, McAlpin) Naylor. *Education:* Brooklyn College of the City University of New York, B.A., 1981; Yale University, M.A., 1983.

*CAREER:* Missionary for Jehovah's Witnesses in New York, North Carolina, and Florida, 1968-75; worked for various hotels in New York City, including Sheraton City Squire, and as telephone operator, 1975-81; writer, 1981—. Writer in residence, Cummington Community of the Arts, 1983; visiting lecturer, George Washington University, 1983-84, and Princeton University, 1986-87; cultural exchange lecturer, United States Information Agency, India, 1985; scholar in residence, University of Pennsylvania, 1986; visiting professor, New York University, 1986, and Boston University, 1987; Fannie Hurst Visiting Professor, Brandeis University, 1988. Senior fellow, Society for the Humanities, Cornell University, 1988; President of One Way Productions, New York, 1990.

*AWARDS, HONORS:* American Book Award for best first novel, 1983, for *The Women of Brewster Place;* Distinguished Writer Award, Mid-Atlantic Writers Association, 1983; National Endowment for the Arts fellowship, 1985; Candace Award, National Coalition of 100 Black Women, 1986; Guggenheim fellowship, 1988; Lillian Smith Award, 1989.

*WRITINGS:*

*FICTION*

*The Women of Brewster Place,* Viking, 1982.
*Linden Hills,* Ticknor & Fields, 1985.
*Mama Day,* Ticknor & Fields, 1988.
*Bailey's Cafe,* Harcourt, 1992.

*NONFICTION*

(Contributor) *Centennial,* Pindar Press, 1986.

Also author of an unproduced original screenplay for Public Broadcasting System's "In Our Own Words," 1985. Contributor of essays and articles to periodicals, including *Southern Review, Essence, Ms., Life, Ontario Review,* and *People.* Contributing editor, *Callaloo,* 1984—. Author of column, "Hers," *New York Times,* 1986.

*ADAPTATIONS:* "Gloria Naylor: Reading and Interview" (cassette), American Audio Prose, 1988; "Mama Day" (cassette), Brilliance, 1989. *The Women of Brewster Place* was adapted into a miniseries, produced by Oprah Winfrey and Carole Isenberg, and broadcast by American Broadcasting Co. (ABC-TV) in 1989; it became a weekly ABC series in 1990, produced by Winfrey, Earl Hamner, and Donald Sipes.

*WORK IN PROGRESS:* A screenplay for Zenith Productions, London; a film adaptation of *Mama Day,* to be produced by Naylor's company, One Way Productions, Inc.

*SIDELIGHTS:* "I wanted to become a writer because I felt that my presence as a black woman and my perspective as a woman in general had been underrepresented in American literature," Gloria Naylor once commented. Her first novel, *The Women of Brewster Place,* which features a cast of seven strong-willed black women, won the American Book Award for best first fiction in 1983. Naylor has continued her exploration of the black female experience while also expanding her fictional realm in her subsequent three novels. In *Linden Hills,* for example, Naylor uses the structure of Dante Alighieri's *Inferno* to create a contemporary allegory about the perils of black materialism and the ways in which denying one's heritage can endanger the soul. Naylor's third novel, *Mama Day,* draws on another literary masterpiece—William Shakespeare's play *The Tempest*—and artfully combines Shakespearean elements with black folkloric strains. Her fourth novel, *Bailey's Cafe,* echoes both the narrative voice and earthiness of Chaucer's *The Canterbury Tales* and the hellish dislocation of Sartre's *No Exit.* By drawing on traditional western sources, Naylor places herself firmly in the literary mainstream, broadening her base from ethnic to American writing. Unhappy with what she calls the "historical ten-

dency to look upon the output of black writers as not really American literature," Naylor told *Publishers Weekly* interviewer William Goldstein that her work attempts to "articulate experiences that want articulating—for those readers who reflect the subject matter, black readers, and for those who don't—basically white middle class readers." In an interview with Dieter Miller for *Authors and Artists for Young Adults,* Naylor revealed her fictional plan: "In the beginning, I visualized these books as a quartet upon which to build my career. Once I complete that foundation I can truly say, 'Hey, I'm a writer.'"

Naylor's first novel grew out of a desire to reflect the diversity of the black experience—a diversity that she feels neither the black nor the white critical establishment has recognized. "There has been a tendency on the part of both," she has said, "to assume that a black writer's work should be 'definitive' of black experience. This type of critical stance denies the vast complexity of black existence, even if we were to limit that existence solely to America. While *The Women of Brewster Place* is about the black woman's condition in America, I had to deal with the fact that one composite picture couldn't do justice to the complexity of the black female experience. So I tried to solve this problem by creating a microcosm on a dead-end street and devoting each chapter to a different woman's life. These women vary in age, personal background, political consciousness, and sexual preference. What they do share is a common oppression and, more importantly, a spiritual strength and sense of female communion that I believe all women have employed historically for their psychic health and survival."

Reviewing *The Women of Brewster Place* in the *Washington Post,* Deirdre Donahue writes: "Naylor is not afraid to grapple with life's big subjects: sex, birth, love, death, grief. Her women feel deeply, and she unflinchingly transcribes their emotions.... Naylor's potency wells up from her language. With prose as rich as poetry, a passage will suddenly take off and sing like a spiritual.... Vibrating with undisguised emotion, *The Women of Brewster Place* springs from the same roots that produced the blues. Like them, her book sings of sorrows proudly borne by black women in America."

To date, Naylor has linked her novels by carrying over characters from one narrative to another. In *The Women of Brewster Place,* one of the young residents is a refugee from Linden Hills, an exclusive black suburb. Naylor's second novel spotlights that affluent community, revealing the material corruption and moral decay that would prompt an idealistic young woman to abandon her home for a derelict urban neighborhood. Though *Linden Hills,* as the book is called, approaches the African American experience from the upper end of the socioeconomic spectrum, it also creates a black microcosm. This book "forms the second panel of that picture of contemporary urban black life which Naylor started with in *Women of Brewster Place*," writes *Times Literary Supplement* contributor Roz Kaveney. "Where that book described the faults, passions, and culture of the good poor, this shows the nullity of black lives that are led in imitation of suburban whites."

In addition to shifting her focus, Naylor has also raised her literary sights in her second novel. *Linden Hills,* which has been described as a contemporary allegory with gothic overtones, is an ambitious undertaking structurally modeled after Dante's *Inferno,* a complex fourteenth-century Italian masterpiece that describes the nine circles of hell, Satan's imprisonment in their depths, and the lost souls condemned to suffer with him. In Naylor's modern version, "souls are damned not because they have offended God or have violated a religious system but because they have offended themselves. In their single-minded pursuit of upward mobility, the inhabitants of Linden Hill, a black, middle-class suburb, have turned away from their past and from their deepest sense of who they are," writes Catherine C. Ward in *Contemporary Literature.* To correspond to Dante's circles, Naylor uses a series of crescent-shaped drives that ring the suburban development. Her heroes are two young street poets—outsiders from a neighboring community who hire themselves out to do odd jobs so they can earn Christmas money. "As they move down the hill, what they encounter are people who have 'moved up' in American society ... until eventually they will hit the center of their community and the home of my equivalent of Satan," Naylor told Goldstein. Naylor's Satan is one Luther Needed, a combination mortician and real estate tycoon, who preys on the residents' baser ambitions to keep them in his sway.

Though *Women's Review of Books* contributor Jewelle Gomez argues that "the Inferno motif ... often feels like a literary exercise rather than a groundbreaking adaptation," most critics commend Naylor's bold experiment. *San Francisco Review of Books* contributor Claudia Tate, for instance, praises "Naylor's skill in linking together complicated stories in a highly structured but unobtrusive narrative form. In combining elements of realism and fantasy with a sequence of ironic reversals, she sets into motion a series of symbols which become interlinked, producing complex social commentary. For example, the single ambition for residents of Linden Hills is to advance economically, but in order to achieve this end they must sacrifice the possibility of emotional and personal fulfillment. When the goal is attained, they measure their success by reversing the expected movement in social climbing."

Even those who find the execution flawed endorse Naylor's daring. Says *New York Times Book Review* contributor Mel Watkins: "Although Miss Naylor has not been completely successful in adapting the *Inferno* to the world of the black

middle class, in *Linden Hills* she has shown a willingness to expand her fictional realm and to take risks. Its flaws notwithstanding, the novel's ominous atmosphere and inspired set pieces ... make it a fascinating departure for Miss Naylor, as well as a provocative, iconoclastic novel about a seldom-addressed subject." Concludes a reviewer for *Ms.,* "In this second novel, Naylor serves notice that she is a mature literary talent of formidable skill."

The title character of Naylor's third novel, *Mama Day,* is "Mama" or Miranda Day, a wise old woman with magical powers. This ninety-year-old conjurer makes a walk-on appearance in *Linden Hills* as the illiterate, toothless aunt who hauls about cheap cardboard suitcases and leaky jars of preserves. But it is in *Mama Day* that this "caster of hoodoo spells ... comes into her own," according to *New York Times Book Review* contributor Bharati Mukherjee. "The portrait of Mama Day is magnificent," she declares.

Mama Day lives on Willow Springs, a wondrous island off the coast of Georgia and South Carolina that has been owned by her family since before the Civil War. The portrayal of slaves as property owners is just one of the ways that Naylor turns the world upside down, according to Rita Mae Brown. Another, continues Brown in the *Los Angeles Times Book Review,* is "that the women possess the real power, and are acknowledged as having it." When Mama Day's grandniece Cocoa brings George, her citified new husband, to Willow Springs, he learns the importance of accepting mystery. "George is the linchpin of *Mama Day,*" Brown says. "His rational mind allows the reader to experience the island as George experiences it. Mama Day and Cocoa are of the island and therefore less immediately accessible to the reader. The turning point comes when George is asked not only to believe in Mama Day's power but to act on it. Cocoa is desperately ill. A hurricane has washed out the bridge so that no mainland doctor can be summoned." Only Mama Day has the power to help George save Cocoa's life. She gives him a task, which he bungles because he is still limited by purely rational thinking. Ultimately, George is able to save Cocoa, but only by great personal sacrifice.

Several reviewers find echoes of works by Shakespeare in the plot twists and thematic concerns of *Mama Day.* "Whereas *Linden Hills* was Dantesque, *Mama Day* is Shakespearean, with allusions, however oblique and tangential, to *Hamlet, King Lear,* and, especially, *The Tempest,*" writes *Chicago Tribune Books* critic John Blades. "Like Shakespeare's fantasy, Naylor's book takes place on an enchanted island.... Naylor reinforces her Shakespearean connection by naming her heroine Miranda." Mukherjee also believes that *Mama Day* "has its roots in *The Tempest.* The theme is reconciliation, the title character is Miranda (also the name of Prospero's daughter), and Willow Springs is an isolated island where, as on Prospero's isle, magical and mysterious events come to pass."

Naylor's ambitious attempt to elevate a modern love story to Shakespearean heights "is more bewildering than bewitching," according to Blades. "Naylor has populated her magic kingdom with some appealingly offbeat characters, Mama Day foremost among them. But she's failed to give them anything very original or interesting to do." Mukherjee also acknowledges the shortcomings of Naylor's mythical love story, but asserts, "I'd rather dwell on *Mama Day*'s strengths. Gloria Naylor has written a big, strong, dense, admirable novel; spacious, sometimes a little drafty like all public monuments, designed to last and intended for many levels of use."

Naylor continues to deal with what Donahue calls "life's big subjects" in her fourth novel, *Bailey's Cafe.* This is another novel in stories, modeled on a musical composition with minor and major melodies. The melodies are refracted from the ostensibly magical world of Bailey's Cafe, a "partly grounded and partly moving cafe," as Richard Eder notes in the *Los Angeles Time Book Review,* located nowhere and everywhere in urban America. The present of the novel is from 1948 to 1949, although the "melodies" within the orchestration provide fragments of earlier historical periods in the lives of Naylor's "blues people."

The novel's epigram ("hush now can you hear it can't be far away/needing the blues to get there...") foreshadows what Dan Wakefield, in the *New York Times Book Review,* calls the "virtuoso orchestration of survival, suffering, courage and humor" that bonds the singers and creators of Bailey's Cafe. Naylor, Wakefield observes, "takes us many keys down, and sometimes back up," via the dark improvisations played out by a number of different singers. Sadie, a real lady, is a dreamer whose dream is realized only through Five Star wine—for which she sells her body, but only for the precise amount she needs at the moment. Jesse Bell, of a strong stock of Longshoremen women, turns to heroin as a means of coping with her destruction by the self-hating bourgeois blacks symbolized by Uncle Eli. Mary (Take One)/Peaches is fragmented by the external mirrors which define her only as a sexual object and ultimately disfigures that whorish image by slicing her face with a beer opener. Miss Maple is, in fact, a man— "a formidably powerful and intelligent black man," Eder comments, who in his long and futile search for professional employment "eventually ... calculates that his chances would be no worse if he wore dresses to his interviews." The characters who frequent Bailey's Cafe make up a chorus whose "emotional outbursts make them universal," contends Roz Kaveney in the *Times Literary Supplement.*

Some critics find Naylor's magical realism less than effective. Kaveney feels "it was a mistake" to set the novel "not in a

mundane diner in a particular location, but in a magic diner which is there, in whatever city, for the people who need to find it." Additionally, she argues that the novel lacks the "unifying commitment which kept [*The Women of Brewster Place*] so tightly structured under its apparently loose and flowing surface," for the characters' lives "hardly impinge on each other, yet they share the same grief." Nevertheless, the critical reception also suggests that Naylor has written a powerful and universal book, one in which, as Wakefield observes, "the pain that is a natural component of these lives is seared into our consciousness." In some of the novel's episodes, asserts Eder, "the sheer strength and color of the story more than make up for a spot of undigested uplift here and there."

*Bailey's Cafe,* rounding out Naylor's proposed "quartet," continues the interconnecting of Naylor's fictional world, this time with a character and a place from *Mama Day.* Immediately after George tells Cocoa that he does not like being called a "son of a bitch" because his mother was a whore, but not, he believes, a bitch, they pass by Bailey's Cafe, near "the edge of the pier." While the novel was in progress, Naylor revealed to Dieter Miller that it would have a tie-in with George and his mother: "I expand upon her and the other whores who were with her and deal with the Madonna complex we have in the Western mind when thinking about female sexuality." This and much more Naylor has attempted in what the proprietor of Bailey's Cafe calls "snatches of a few melodies to make you feel."

## BIOGRAPHICAL/CRITICAL SOURCES:

### BOOKS

*Authors and Artists for Young Adults*, Volume 6, Gale, 1991.
Christian, Barbara, editor, *Black Feminist Criticism,* Pergamon Press, 1985.
*Contemporary Literary Criticism,* Gale, Volume 28, 1984, Volume 52, 1989.
Evans, Mari, editor, *Black Women Writers: 1950-1980,* Doubleday, 1984.

### PERIODICALS

*Chicago Tribune Book World,* February 23, 1983.
*Christian Science Monitor,* March 1, 1985.
*Commonweal,* May 3, 1985.
*Contemporary Literature,* Volume 28, number 1, 1987.
*Detroit News,* March 3, 1985; February 21, 1988.
*Ebony,* July 1989, pp. 76-78.
*Essence,* December, 1989, pp. 48-51; May 1990, Volume 21.
*Life,* spring, 1988, p. 65.
*Literary Review,* spring, 1990, Volume 5, number 2, pp. 98-107.
*Los Angeles Times,* December 2, 1982.

*Los Angeles Times Book Review,* February 24, 1985; March 6, 1988; August 30, 1992, pp. 3, 7.

*London Review of Books,* August 1, 1985.

*Ms.,* June, 1985; May 1986, pp. 56-58.

*New Republic,* September 6, 1982.

*New York Times,* February 9, 1985; May 1, 1990.

*New York Times Book Review,* August 22, 1982; March 3, 1985; November 16, 1986; February 21, 1988; May 14, 1989; October 4, 1992, pp. 11-12.

*Publishers Weekly,* September 9, 1983.

*San Francisco Review of Books,* May, 1985.

*Southern Review,* summer, 1985, Volume 21, number 3, pp. 567-593.

*Times* (London), April 21, 1983.

*Times Literary Supplement,* May 24, 1985; July 17, 1992, p. 20.

*Tribune Books* (Chicago), January 31, 1988.

*Washington Post,* October 21, 1983; May 1, 1990.

*Washington Post Book World,* March 24, 1985; February 28, 1988.

*Women's Review of Books,* August, 1985.

*Yale Review,* autumn, 1988; autumn, 1989, pp. 19-31.

\* \* \*

## NGEMA, Mbongeni 1955-

*PERSONAL:* Born in 1955, in a township outside Durban, South Africa. *Education:* high school graduate.

*CAREER:* Worked as a laborer; musician and actor, 1976-78; performed with Gibson Kente's theater company, South Africa, 1979-c. 1981; Committed Artists theater company, South Africa, founder, playwright and director, 1982—.

*AWARDS, HONORS:* Tony Award nomination, best director, 1987, for *Asinamali!*

*WRITINGS:*

*PLAYS*

(With Percy Mtwa) *Woza Albert!* (produced in South Africa, 1981, produced in United States, 1984), Methuen, 1983, reprinted, Heinemann, 1988.

*Asinamali!,* produced in Lamontville, South Africa, 1983, produced in Harlem, NY, September, 1986.

(With Hugh Masekela) *Sarafina!* (musical; produced in Johannesburg, South Africa, then in New York City, June, 1987) cast recording, Shanachie and RCA Victor Records, 1988 (also see below).

Also author and director of a play produced in Durban, South Africa, c. 1978.

*OTHER*

(With William Nicholson) *Sarafina!* (feature film based on the musical), directed by Darrell James Roodt, Buena Vista, 1992.

*SIDELIGHTS:* Despite the variety of Mbongeni Ngema's theatrical productions—ranging from a satirical fantasy, to a dramatic ensemble piece combining elements of agitprop and street theater, to an exuberant musical—his works are united by their frenetic energy, their humor in the face of oppression, their defiance of apartheid, and their celebration of life and of black South African culture. While his plays are relentlessly political in protesting apartheid—the South African system of racial segregation and discrimination against non-whites—Ngema is also committed to the production of quality theater. "I wanted technique as well as the truth," he told *Africa Report* interviewers Margaret A. Novicki and Ameen Akhalwaya in discussing his play *Asinamali!* "What was the key for me was a play that we could do for people in [the black tent cities near Durban, South Africa] but that could also be performed on a Broadway stage.... They should go and see it because it's good theatre. At the same time, it should be about the spirit of our people."

Born and raised in the black townships around Durban, South Africa, Ngema worked as a laborer and a guitarist before becoming involved in local theatrical productions as a musician and actor. During a tour of the western United States in 1982, he was inspired by the work of the Mexican-American company El Teatro Campesino, which was producing theater for and by farm workers. On his return to South Africa, he brought together a number of artists, actors, writers, and musicians in the Durban area to form Committed Artists, a theater company intended to serve the cultural needs of the black townships and tent cities. He also began collaborating with Percy Mtwa, a fellow South African actor and playwright, on a satirical play in which Christ's Second Coming takes place in South Africa, the Afrikaaner government attempts to exploit the Messiah for political gain, and Christ is ultimately banished to a high-risk black penitentiary on Robben Island. First produced in South Africa in 1981 and presented in the United States in 1984, *Woza Albert!* won international acclaim.

Ngema's next production, *Asinamali!,* presented a view of black life in South Africa through the eyes of five black prisoners, who re-enacted the events that led to their arrests. The five men, noted Frank Rich in the *New York Times,* had "been variously victimized by racist laws, unemployment, forced separation from their families, violent police tactics and a seeming infinity of daily humiliations." The actors themselves were people from the townships who had taken part in Ngema's drama workshops, and the play was based on actual events surrounding the concurrent protests against rent increases in Lamontville, a black township near Durban. The play's title, *Asinamali!,*—meaning, "We have no money!"—was the slogan of the Lamontville protesters, whose leader, Msizi Dube, was murdered at the instigation of the South African authorities. Four days after the play opened, police raided a performance and arrested several of the actors, one of whom received an eight-year sentence.

In 1986, in collaboration with Duma Ndlovu, a black South African emigre writer, Ngema brought *Asinamali!* to the United States, where it premiered in Harlem. Rich described the play as a "stunningly performed tapestry of satire, tragedy and reportage from the land of apartheid.... Ngema's staging eschews realism for a tightly choreographed melding of indigenous ritual, storytelling and musical theater." Despite its tragic themes and serious political message, reported Humm in *Variety,* "*Asinamali!* is a joyous expression of human individuality and the life force that oppression can't extinguish.... Ngema ... has a sly fondness for low comedy which lightens what is essentially somber material." Reviewing the play in *Maclean's,* Mark Abley quoted a Zulu saying cited in the play itself: "We laugh even though there is death."

The 1987 musical *Sarafina!* was inspired by the 1976 student uprisings in Soweto protesting the government's attempt to impose classroom instruction in Afrikaans, the language of the ruling white South African minority. Hundreds of black schoolchildren were killed by South African police and soldiers during the uprising. In the play, a group of students is putting together a show to celebrate the imagined release of Nelson Mandela, a black anti-apartheid leader who had been imprisoned by the South African authorities since 1962. (Mandela's actual release would not occur until 1990.) One of the students—the title character, Sarafina—is briefly detained by the authorities, interrogated and tortured. Produced in collaboration with South African emigre jazz trumpeter Hugh Masekela, the play makes use of the black South African pop music known as "Mbaqanga," which taps into the indigenous African musical tradition as well as black American jazz and gospel, white missionary hymns, Motown rhythm-and-blues and contemporary rock. "I decided the show had to celebrate the spirit of the students and the power of Mbaqanga, which I call the music of liberation," Ngema told *New York Times* contributor Robert Palmer. The director held auditions throughout the country to choose a cast of 24 young people, most of them in their teens, whom he then trained for the production.

The show opened in Johannesburg, South Africa early in 1987 and in New York City later that year. In *Sarafina!,* Clive Barnes wrote in the *New York Post,* "you will encounter per-

haps the most joyous music to be heard in New York City.... Ngema's achievement simply in forging this troupe into a cutting-edge theater force is almost incredible." The production suffered somewhat from a "rudimentary book" and a tendency toward "cliche," wrote John Simon in *New York.* Nonetheless, he added, it also possessed "the strength, spirit, and savvy with which to overcome [its flaws]." "Spontaneously performed and precisely choreographed, the musical numbers provide a running commentary on the children's experiences—the acts of protest, troops and police in the classroom, imprisonment and torture, and the funerals of the victims," reported John Beaufort in the *Christian Science Monitor.* "The score of *Sarafina!*—whether driven by timeless drums or jazzy horns or electric guitar—evokes the cacophony of life in a black society both oppressed and defiant, at once sentenced to hard labor and ignited by dreams of social justice," wrote Frank Rich in the *New York Times.* Concluded Clive Barnes, "*Sarafina!* lives—and celebrates man, while dramatizing man's injustice."

A movie version of *Sarafina!,* directed by Darrell James Roodt and starring Whoopi Goldberg and Leleti Khumalo, was released by Buena Vista in 1992. *Voices of Sarafina!,* a film documentary by Nigel Noble about the American production of the musical, appeared in 1988.

*BIOGRAPHICAL/CRITICAL SOURCES:*

*BOOKS*

*Contemporary Literary Criticism,* Volume 57, Gale, 1990, pp. 339-347.

*PERIODICALS*

*Africa Report,* July/August, 1987, pp. 36-39.
*Christian Science Monitor,* October 28, 1987.
*Maclean's,* November 10, 1996, p. 79.
*New Statesman,* January 15, 1993.
*Newsweek,* September 22, 1986, p. 85.
*New York,* September 29, 1986, pp. 98, 100; November 9, 1987, pp. 124, 128.
*New York Post,* October 26, 1987.
*New York Times,* September 12, 1986, p. C3; October 25, 1987, pp. H5, H15; October 26, 1987, p. C15.
*Variety,* September 17, 1986, p. 112.

*   *   *

**NGUGI, James T(hiong'o)**
**See NGUGI wa Thiong'o**

## NGUGI wa Thiong'o 1938-
## (James T[hiong'o] Ngugi)

*PERSONAL:* Original name, James Thiong'o Ngugi; born January 5, 1938, in Limuru, Kenya; son of peasant farmers; married; children: six. *Education:* Makerere University, B.A. (with honors), 1963.

*ADDRESSES: Office*—New York University, 19 University Place, New York, NY 10003. *Agent*—c/o Heinemann International, Halley Court, Jordan Hill, Oxford OX2 8EJ, England.

*CAREER:* University of Nairobi, Kenya, lecturer in English literature, 1967-69, senior lecturer and chairperson of literature department, 1972-77; visiting professor of English and comparative literature at Yale University, New Haven, CT, 1989-92; presently professor of comparative literature and performance studies at New York University, New York City. Creative writing fellow, Makerere University, 1969-70; visiting associate professor, Northwestern University, 1970-71; guest professor, Bayreuth University, 1982; guest lecturer, Auckland University; visiting distinguished professor of comparative literature at Amherst College, 1991. Worked variously as columnist for Nairobi's *Sunday Nation* and as a reporter for the *Daily Nation,* 1962-65.

*AWARDS, HONORS:* East Africa Novel Prize, 1962, for *The River Between;* UNESCO first prize from the 1965 Dakar Festival of Negro Arts and the East African Literature Bureau, both for *Weep Not, Child;* Lotus Prize for Literature, 1973; Paul Robeson Award, 1991; Zora Neale Hurston-Paul Robeson Award, 1993.

*WRITINGS:*

*This Time Tomorrow: Three Plays* (includes "This Time Tomorrow," "The Reels," and "The Wound in the Heart"; produced and broadcast in 1966), East African Literature Bureau, 1970.
*Homecoming: Essays on African and Caribbean Literature, Culture, and Politics,* Heinemann, 1972, Lawrence Hill, 1973.
*Secret Lives, and Other Stories,* Heinemann, 1974, Lawrence Hill, 1975.
(With Micere Githae Mugo) *The Trial of Dedan Kimathi* (produced as a play in Nairobi, 1974), Heinemann, 1976, Swahili translation by the authors published as *Mzalendo kimathi,* c. 1978.
*Petals of Blood* (novel), Heinemann, 1977, Dutton, 1978.
*Mtawa Mweusi,* Heinemann, 1978.
*Caitaani mutharaba-ini,* Heinemann, 1980, translation by the author published as *Devil on the Cross,* Heinemann, 1982, Zimbabwe Publishing, 1983.

(With Ngugi wa Mirii) *Ngaahika Ndeenda: Ithaako ria Ngerekano* (play; produced in Kamiriithu, Kenya, 1977), Heinemann, 1980, translated by the authors as *I Will Marry When I Want,* Heinemann, 1982.
*Detained: A Writer's Prison Diary,* Heinemann, 1981.
*Writers in Politics: Essays,* Heinemann, 1981.
*Education for a National Culture,* Zimbabwe Publishing, 1981.
*Njamba Nene na mbaathi i mathagu* (juvenile), Heinemann, 1982, translation by Wangui wa Goro published as *Njamba Nene and the Flying Bus,* Heinemann, 1986.
*Barrel of a Pen: Resistance to Repression in Neo-Colonial Kenya,* Africa World, 1983.
*Bathitoora ya Njamba Nene* (juvenile), Heinemann, 1984, translation by Wangui published as *Njamba Nene's Pistol,* Heinemann, 1986.
*Decolonising the Mind: The Politics of Language in African Literature,* Heinemann, 1986.
*Writing against Neocolonialism,* Vita, 1986.
*Njamba Nene na Chibu King'ang'i,* Heinemann, 1986.
*Matigari ma Njiruungi,* Heinemann, 1986, translation by Wangui published as *Matigari,* Heinemann, 1989.
*The First Walter Rodney Memorial Lecture, 1985,* Friends of Bogle, 1987.
*Moving the Centre: The Struggle for Cultural Freedoms,* Heinemann, 1993.

*This Time Tomorrow* also aired on BBC Africa Service in 1967.

*ORIGINALLY UNDER NAME JAMES T. NGUGI*

*The Black Hermit* (play; first produced in Uganda National Theatre, November, 1962), Makerere University Press, 1963, Humanities, 1968.
*Weep Not, Child* (novel), introduction and notes by Ime Ikeddeh, Heinemann, 1964, Northwestern University Press, 1967.
*The River Between* (novel), Humanities, 1965, Northwestern University Press, 1967, Swahili translation published as *Njia Panda,* East African Publishing House, 1974.
*A Grain of Wheat* (novel), Heinemann, 1967, second edition, Humanities, 1968.

*CONTRIBUTOR TO ANTHOLOGIES*

E. A. Komey and Ezekiel Mphahlele, editors, *Modern African Short Stories,* Faber, 1964.
W. H. Whiteley, editor, *A Selection of African Prose,* Oxford University Press, 1964.
Neville Denny, editor, *Pan African Short Stories,* Nelson, 1965.
Oscar Ronald Dathorne and Willfried Feuser, editors, *Africa in Prose,* Penguin, 1969.

*OTHER*

Contributor of stories to *Transition* and *Kenya Weekly News.*
Editor of *Zuka* and *Sunday Nation* (Nairobi).

*SIDELIGHTS:* Novelist, dramatist, essayist, and literary critic Ngugi wa Thiong'o is one of East Africa's most prominent
writers. Known to many simply as Ngugi, he has been described by Shatto Arthur Gakwandi in *The Novel and Contemporary Experience in Africa* as a "novelist of the people,"
for his works show his concern for the inhabitants of his native country, Kenya, who have been oppressed and exploited
by colonialism, Christianity, and in recent years, by black
politicians and businesspeople. As *Africa Today* contributor
D. Salituma Wamalwa observes: "Ngugi's approach to literature is one firmly rooted in the historical experience of the
writer and his or her people, in an understanding of society as
it is and a vision of society as it might be."

Throughout his career as a writer and professor, Ngugi has
worked to free himself and his compatriots from the effects
of colonialism, Christianity, and other non-African influences. In the late 1960s, for example, Ngugi and several colleagues
at the University of Nairobi successfully convinced school
officials to transform the English Department into the Department of Literature. Shortly thereafter Ngugi renounced his
Christian name, James, citing the religion's ties to colonialism. He took in its place his name in Gikuyu (or Kikuyu), one
of several languages of Kenya. Ngugi strengthened his commitment to the Kenyan culture in 1977, when he declared his
intention to write only in Gikuyu or Swahili, not English. In
response to a query posed in an interview for *Journal of Commonwealth Literature* concerning this decision, Ngugi stated:
"Language is a carrier of a people's culture, culture is a carrier of a people's values; values are the basis of a people's self-
definition—the basis of their consciousness. And when you
destroy a people's language, you are destroying that very
important aspect of their heritage ... you are in fact destroying that which helps them to define themselves ... that which
embodies their collective memory as a people."

Ngugi's determination to write in Gikuyu, combined with his
outspoken criticisms of both British and Kenyan rule, have
posed threats to his security. In 1977 Ngugi's home was
searched by Kenyan police, who confiscated nearly one hundred books then arrested and imprisoned Ngugi without a trial. At the time of his arrest, Ngugi's play *Ngaahika Ndeenda*
(translated as *I Will Marry When I Want*), co-authored with
Ngugi wa Mirii, had recently been banned on the grounds of
being "too provocative," according to *American Book Review*
contributor Henry Indangasi; in addition, Ngugi's novel *Petals of Blood,* a searing indictment of the Kenyan government,
had just been published in England. Although Ngugi was released from prison a year later, his incarceration cost him his

professorship at the University of Nairobi. When his theater
group was banned by Kenyan officials in 1982, Ngugi, fearing further reprisals, left his country for London.

Ngugi chronicles his prison experience in *Detained: A Writer's Prison Diary,* and expresses his political views in other
nonfiction works such as *Barrel of a Pen: Resistance to Repression in Neo-Colonial Kenya.* He has received the most
critical attention, however, for his fiction, particularly his
novels. Ngugi's first novel *Weep Not, Child* deals with the Mau
Mau rebellion against the British administration in the 1950s,
and his third novel *A Grain of Wheat* concerns the aftermath
of the war and its effects on Kenya's people. Although some
critics describe the first novel as somewhat stylistically im-
mature, many comment favorably on the universality of its
theme of the reactions of people to the stresses and horrors of
war and to the inevitable changes brought to bear on their lives.

In contrast, several reviewers believe that *A Grain of Wheat*
fulfills the promise of Ngugi's first novel. *A Grain of Wheat*
portrays four characters who reflect upon the events of the Mau
Mau uprising and its consequences as they await the day of
Kenyan independence, December 12, 1963. G. D. Killam
explains in his book *An Introduction to the Writings of Ngugi:*
"Uhuru Day, the day when independence from the colonial
power is achieved, has been the dream of each of these figures from their schooldays. But there is little joyousness in their
lives as they recall over the four days their experiences of the
war and its aftermath."

In their book *Ngugi wa Thiong'o: An Exploration of His
Writings,* David Cook and Michael Okenimkpe praise the
"almost perfectly controlled form and texture" of *A Grain of
Wheat.* Killam comments: "*A Grain of Wheat* is the work of
a writer more mature than when he wrote his first two books....
In *A Grain of Wheat* [Ngugi] takes us into the minds of his
characters, sensibilities resonant with ambiguities and contradictions, and causes us to feel what they feel, to share in significant measure their hopes and fears and pain." Shatto Arthur
Gakwandi similarly observes in *The Novel and Contemporary
Experience in Africa:* "The general tone of *A Grain of Wheat*
is one of bitterness and anger. The painful memories of Mau
Mau violence still overhang the Kikuyu villages as the attain-
ment of independence fails to bring the cherished social
dreams." Gakwandi adds: "While the novel speaks against the
harshness of colonial oppression, it is equally bitter against
the new leaders of Kenya who are neglecting the interests of
the peasant masses who were the people who made the greatest sacrifices during the war of liberation. Ngugi speaks on
behalf of those who, in his view, have been neglected by the
new government."

*Petals of Blood,* Ngugi's fourth novel, is considered his most
ambitious and representative work. Like *A Grain of Wheat,*

*Petals of Blood* describes the disillusionment of the common people in post-independence Kenya. Killam notes, however, that in *Petals of Blood* Ngugi "widens and deepens his treatment of themes which he has narrated and dramatized before—themes related to education, both formal and informal; religion, both Christian and customary; the alienation of the land viewed from the historical point of view and as a process which continues in the present; the struggle for independence and the price paid to achieve it." *Petals of Blood* is also described as Ngugi's most overtly political novel. A *West Africa* contributor notes an ideological shift in the novel "from the earlier emphasis on nationalism and race questions to a class analysis of society." Critics cite in particular the influence of both Karl Marx and Frantz Fanon, the latter of whom, according to Killam, "places the thinking of Marx in the African context." In *World Literature Written in English* Govind Narian Sharma comments: "Whereas traditional religious and moral thought has attributed exploitation and injustice in the world to human wickedness and folly, Ngugi, analyzing the situation in Marxist terms, explains these as 'the effect of laws of social development which make it inevitable that at a certain stage of history one class, pursuing its interests with varying degrees of rationality, should dispossess and exploit another.'"

*Petals of Blood* concerns four principle characters, all being held on suspicion of murder: Karega, a teacher and labor organizer; Munira, headmaster of a public school in the town of Ilmorog; Abdulla, a half-Indian shopkeeper who was once a guerrilla fighter during the war for independence; and Wanja, a barmaid and former prostitute. "Through these four [characters]," writes Civia Tamarkin in *Chicago Tribune Book World,* "Ngugi tells a haunting tale of lost hopes and soured dreams, raising the simple voice of humanity against the perversity of its condition." *American Book Review* contributor Henry Indangasi describes *Petals of Blood* this way: "Through numerous flashbacks, and flashbacks within flashbacks, and lengthy confessions, a psychologically credible picture of the characters, and a vast canvas of Kenya's history is unfolded."

Several reviewers note that Ngugi's emphasis on the economic and political conditions in Kenya at times overshadows his narrative. The *West Africa* contributor explains: "*Petals of Blood* is not so much a novel as an attempt to think aloud about the problems of modern Kenya: the sharp contrast between the city and the countryside, between the 'ill-gotten' wealth of the new African middle-class and the worsening plight of the unemployed workers and peasants." Charles R. Larson expresses a like opinion in *World Literature Today:* "*Petals of Blood* is not so much about these four characters (as fascinating and as skillfully drawn as they are) as it is about political unrest in post-independence Kenya, and what Ngugi considers the failures of the new black elite (politicians and businessmen) to live up to the pre-independence expectations."

Foreshadowing Ngugi's 1977 arrest, Larson concludes, "In this sense *Petals of Blood* is a bold venture—perhaps a risky one—since it is obvious that the author's criticisms of his country's new ruling class will not go unnoticed."

Critics also maintain that this emphasis lends a didactic tone to the novel. Larson, for instance, comments in the *New York Times Book Review:* "The weakness of Ngugi's novel as a work of the creative imagination ultimately lies in the author's somewhat dated Marxism: revolt of the masses, elimination of the black bourgeois; capitalism to be replaced with African socialism. The author's didacticism weakens what would otherwise have been his finest work." *New Yorker* contributor John Updike similarly observes that "the characters ... stagger and sink under the politico-symbolical message they are made to carry." *World Literature Today* contributor Andrew Salkey, on the other hand, offers this view: "It's a willfully diagrammatic and didactic novel which also succeeds artistically because of its resonant characterization and deadly irony. It satisfies both the novelist's political intent and the obligation I know he feels toward his art."

Despite these reservations, the majority of critics concur that *Petals of Blood* is an important literary contribution. Sharma, for example, writes that "Ngugi's *Petals of Blood* is a complex and powerful work. It is a statement of his social and political philosophy and an embodiment of his prophetic vision. Ngugi provides a masterly analysis of the social and economic situation in modern Kenya, a scene of unprincipled and ruthless exploitation of man by man, and gives us a picture of the social and moral consequences of this exploitation." Cook and Ikenimkpe state that *Petals of Blood* "stands as a rare literary achievement: with all its faults upon it, [it is still] a skillfully articulated work which in no degree compromises the author's fully fledged radical political viewpoint." Indangasis concludes: "In many senses, literary and nonliterary, *Petals of Blood* will remain a major but controversial contribution to African literature, and the literature of colonised peoples."

Controversy was also prevalent following the 1986 publication of Ngugi's second novel in Gikuyu, entitled *Matigari ma Njiruungi.* Set in an unspecified location, although critics are quick to point out the area's similarities to Kenya, the story centers around the title character, whose name translates as "the patriots who survived the bullets." The tale finds Matigari, who once used violence in the fight for his people's liberation, leaving the forest to reclaim his home and reunite his family through peaceful means. After discovering that the heirs of his oppressors have gained control of the house, he is soon arrested. He escapes, embarking on a quest for truth and justice that ends as he is confined to a mental hospital. He again eludes his captors, resolving that "armed power of the people" is needed for justice to prevail. The novel concludes on an ominous note as Matigari burns the house and is attacked by police dogs.

"The publication of *Matigari* in Kenya fired the imagination of peasants and workers in a way that closely paralleled the hero's effect on their fictional counterparts," reported David Maughan-Brown in *Dictionary of Literary Biography: Twentieth-Century Caribbean and Black African Writers.* "Kenya's rulers understood the message only too well," explained *Times Literary Supplement*'s Richard Gibson, adding "at first the police actually searched for the mythical Matigari. Failing to lay hands on him, they seized all the copies they could find of the book." Maughan-Brown concluded: "The 'arrest' of his book effectively consigns Ngugi to a double exile: with Ngugi physically cut off from the peasants and workers in Kenya, who are the source of his inspiration, the banning of his book means that he cannot, through his fiction, communicate with those for whom he writes."

*BIOGRAPHICAL/CRITICAL SOURCES:*

*BOOKS*

Bailey, Diana, *Ngugi wo Thiong'o: The River Between, a Critical View,* edited by Yolande Cantu, Collins, 1986.

Bjorkman, Ingrid, *Mother, Sing for Me: People's Theatre in Kenya,* Zed Books, 1989.

*Contemporary Literary Criticism,* Gale, Volume 3, 1975, Volume 7, 1977, Volume 13, 1980, Volume 36, 1986.

Cook, David and Michael Okenimkpe, *Ngugi wa Thiong'o: An Exploration of His Writings,* Heinemann, 1983.

*Dictionary of Literary Biography,* Volume 125: *Twentieth-Century Caribbean and Black African Writers,* edited by Bernth Lindfors and Reinhard Sander, Gale, 1993, pp. 145-169.

Gakwandi, Shatto Arthur, *The Novel and Contemporary Experience in Africa,* Africana Publishing, 1977.

Killam, G. D., *An Introduction to the Writings of Ngugi,* Heinemann, 1980.

Ngugi wa Thiong'o, *Detained: A Writer's Prison Diary,* Heinemann, 1981.

Ngugi wa Thiong'o, *Matigari,* Heinemann, 1989.

Larson, Charles R., *The Emergence of African Fiction,* Indiana University Press, 1972.

Palmer, Eustace, *An Introduction to the African Novel,* Africana Publishing, 1972.

Palmer, Eustace, *The Growth of the African Novel,* Heinemann, 1979.

Robson, Clifford B., *Ngugi wa Thiong'o,* Macmillan (London), 1979.

Roscoe, Adrian, *Uhuru's Fire: African Literature East to South,* Cambridge University Press, 1977.

Sicherman, Carol, *Ngugi wa Thiong'o, the Making of a Rebel: A Source Book in Kenyan Literature and Resistance,* Zell, 1990.

Tibble, Ann, *African/English Literature,* Peter Owen (London), 1965.

Tucker, Martin, *Africa in Modern Literature: A Survey of Contemporary Writing in English,* Ungar, 1967.

*PERIODICALS*

*African Literature Today,* Number 5, 1971; Number 10, 1979.

*Africa Today,* Volume 33, number 1, 1986.

*American Book Review,* summer, 1979.

*Books Abroad,* autumn, 1967; spring, 1968.

*Books in Canada,* October, 1982.

*Chicago Tribune Book World,* October 22, 1978.

*Christian Science Monitor,* October 11, 1978; September 5, 1986.

*Iowa Review,* spring/summer, 1976.

*Journal of Commonwealth Literature,* September, 1965; Number 1, 1986.

*Listener,* August 26, 1982.

*Michigan Quarterly Review,* fall, 1970.

*New Republic,* January 20, 1979.

*New Statesman,* October 20, 1972; July 24, 1981; June 18, 1982; August 8, 1986.

*New Yorker,* July 2, 1979.

*New York Times,* May 10, 1978; November 9, 1986.

*New York Times Book Review,* February 19, 1978.

*Observer,* June 20, 1982.

*Research-in-African Literatures,* fall, 1989, pp. 347-370; winter, 1991, pp. 53-61; spring, 1991, pp. 5-15.

*Times Literary Supplement,* January 28, 1965; November 3, 1972; August 12, 1977; October 16, 1981; June 18, 1982; May 8, 1987; June 16, 1989, p. 670.

*Washington Post,* October 9, 1978.

*West Africa,* February 20, 1978.

*World Literature Today,* spring, 1978; fall, 1978; spring, 1981; autumn, 1982; summer, 1983; winter, 1984; fall, 1987.

*World Literature Written in English,* November, 1979; autumn, 1982.

\* \* \*

**NJAU, Rebecca**
**See NJAU, Rebeka**

## NJAU, Rebeka 1932-
### (Rebecca Njau)

*PERSONAL:* Born in Kanyariri, Kenya. *Education:* Makerere University College, diploma in education.

*CAREER:* Alliance Girls' School, teacher, 1958-59; Makerere College School, teacher, 1960-62; Nairobi Girls' School, headmistress, 1964—. University College Council, Kenyan representative, 1965-66.

*AWARDS, HONORS:* East African Writing Committee Prize, for unpublished novel, *Alone with the Fig Tree.*

*WRITINGS:*

*The Scar: A Tragedy in One Act* (play), *Transition,* March, 1963, Kibo Art Gallery, 1965.
*The Round Chain* (play), *Transition,* March, 1963.
*Ripples in the Pool* (novel), Transafrica, 1975, Heinemann, 1978.
(With Gideon Mulaki) *Kenya Women Heroes and Their Mystical Power,* Risk Publications, 1984.

Also author of unpublished novel, *Alone with the Fig Tree.*

*BIOGRAPHICAL/CRITICAL SOURCES:*

*BOOKS*

Herdeck, Donald E. *African Authors: A Companion to Black African Writing,* Volume 1: *1300-1973,* Black Orpheus Press, 1973.

*PERIODICALS*

*World Literature Today,* winter, 1980.

\*   \*   \*

## NJERI, Itabari (Lord)

*PERSONAL:* Originally named Jill Stacey Moreland, name changed to Itabari, 1971, legally changed to Itabari Njeri, 1975, later changed to Itabari Lord Njeri; born in Brooklyn, NY; daughter of Marc Marion Moreland (a historian) and Yvonne Delcinia Lord Moreland Williams (a registered nurse and hospital administrator). *Education:* Studied voice at High School of Music and Art, New York City; received B.S. from Boston University School of Public Communications, and M.S. from Columbia University Graduate School of Journalism. *Politics:* Independent. *Religion:* "No religious affiliation."

*Avocational interests:* Music and community organizing involving education issues and conflict resolution.

*ADDRESSES: Office*—*Los Angeles Times Magazine,* Times Mirror Square, Los Angeles, CA 90053. *Agent*—Russell & Volkening, Inc., Literary Agents, 50 West 29th St., New York, NY 10001.

*CAREER:* Journalist and author. Professional singer and actress, performing in summer stock, in concerts, at nightclubs, and as a studio musician, 1965-78; Spirit House Movers Theatre Company, actress and singer, 1970-73; affiliated with Blakluv (music and theatre ensemble), 1970-74; National Public Radio (NPR), WBUR-Radio, Boston, MA, reporter, 1972-73, reporter and coproducer of "The Drum" (a weekly program), and rotating host of "Multiversity" (a weekly program), 1973-75; reporter and producer for several radio documentaries, including *The War in Angola,* for NPR and Pacifica Radio; host and producer of the syndicated *Pan African News Report; Greenville News,* Greenville, SC, reporter, feature writer, and arts critic, 1978-81; *Miami Herald,* Miami, FL, feature writer for "Living Today" section, 1981-84, arts writer, essayist, and critic for "Lively Arts" section, 1984-86; *Los Angeles Times,* Los Angeles, CA, staff writer for "View" section, 1986-92; *Los Angeles Times Magazine,* Los Angeles, contributing editor, 1992—. Frequent university lecturer and television and radio talk-show guest on topics including the philosophy of multiculturalism, reporting on inter-ethnic issues, and the art of the memoir and the autobiographical African American tradition.

*MEMBER:* Authors Guild, National Association of Black Journalists.

*AWARDS, HONORS:* Njeri was named "Best New Pop Vocalist" by MGM Records; Hovey Distinguished Lecture Award from University of Michigan; South Carolina Associated Press Award, feature writing, 1980; Lincoln University UNITY Media Award, education reporting, 1982; Penney-University of Missouri Journalism Prize, feature writing, 1983; National Endowment for the Humanities fellowship, 1983-84; Los Angeles Press Club award, excellence in entertainment reporting, 1989; National Association of Black Journalists Award, feature writing, 1990, for year-long *Los Angeles Times* series, "The Challenge of Diversity"; *Every Good-bye Ain't Gone: Family Portraits and Personal Escapades* was selected as a notable book of 1990 by the *New York Times Book Review;* American Book Award, Before Columbus Foundation, 1990, for *Every Good-bye Ain't Gone.*

*WRITINGS:*

*Every Good-bye Ain't Gone: Family Portraits and Personal Escapades,* Times Books, 1990.

*The Last Plantation,* Random House, 1993.
*Sushi & Grits: The Challenge of Diversity,* Random House, 1993.

Work has appeared in anthologies, including *Bearing Witness: Selections from African-American Autobiography in the Twentieth Century,* edited by Henry Louis Gates, Jr., Pantheon, 1991; *Life Studies: A Thematic Reader,* edited by David Cavitch, St. Martin's, 1992; *Voices in Black & White: Writings on Race in America from Harper's Magazine,* edited by Katherine Whittemore and Gerald Marzorati, Franklin Square Press, 1992; and *Lure and Loathing: Race, Identity and the Ambivalence of Assimilation,* edited by Gerald Early, Viking, 1993. Contributor to periodicals, including *Essence, Emerge, Harper's,* and *Boston Globe Magazine.*

*WORK IN PROGRESS:* A screenplay adaptation of *Every Good-bye Ain't Gone; The Secret Life of Fred Astaire,* a novel.

*SIDELIGHTS:* In 1990, Itabari Njeri received the American Book Award for her memoir *Every Good-bye Ain't Gone: Family Portraits and Personal Escapades.* Njeri—African, East Indian, English, Amer-Indian and French—described herself as "a typical descendant of the African diaspora." Her memoir evokes the life of middle-class African Americans and West Indians in Brooklyn and Harlem during the 1950s, 1960s, and 1970s. Her book, in great part, attempts to challenge racist conceptions of identity in America through an examination of her own family and of her life. "Nobody really knows us," she writes of African Americans. "So institutionalized is the ignorance of our history, our culture, our everyday existence that, often, we do not even know ourselves."

As a child, Njeri lived with her family in New York City and was encouraged to develop a singing talent and pursue a career in opera. Her father, who also had a beautiful voice, admired her when she sang, but had a difficult time showing affection otherwise. He was an alcoholic who often displayed violent behavior, and his problem was compounded because Njeri's mother refused to acknowledge that substance abuse contributed to his strained relations with his family.

Njeri also notes that her father suffered psychologically because his work as a historian, according to Njeri, was overlooked by dominant white culture. Njeri writes: "Since my father at once critiqued the society that denied him and longed for its approbation, he lived with the pain-filled consciousness of one who knows he is a joke. I think, sometimes, he laughed hardest, so often did I stumble upon him alone, chuckling into his balled fist at some silent, invisible, comedian." According to Meg Wolitzer of the *New York Times Book Review,* "the most persuasive piece in the book is Ms. Njeri's portrait of

her father, whom she depicts as a brilliant, tormented Marxist historian who would sit for hours in his boxer shorts reading and writing, an applesauce jar of Teacher's Scotch beside him. Despite her father's repeated episodes of violence and neglect, she is charitable toward him—more charitable, even, than a dispassionate author might have been."

During her teenage years, Njeri became a member of the Congress of African People (CAP), a Pan-African nationalist group headed by writer Amiri Baraka. While associated with the organization, Njeri was named Itabari by Baraka—she was originally named Jill Moreland—and abandoned a college major in music to study journalism. After a three-year association with the organization, Njeri became dismayed by cultural and sexual chauvinism and anti-Semitic attitudes held by some members of the CAP, however, and left the group. In the early 1970s she began singing and acting with ensembles which included the Spirit House Movers Theatre Company and Blakluv. She eventually abandoned a career in the performing arts, however, for other pursuits. She commented: "I left music not because I couldn't make a living singing modern music (at least if it was jazz or musical theatre) but because I was not willing to endure what one must—sexism, racism, etc.—on the way up."

Though Njeri details many aspects of her professional and personal life in her book, many reviewers found such insights less compelling than the stories that Njeri shares about her family. In addition to commenting on herself and her parents in *Every Good-bye Ain't Gone* Njeri remarks on members of her extended family, including a cousin who was killed by drug dealers and an aunt who earned a living as a "Moll" during the 1940s and 1950s, involved in activities such as prostitution. Also notable in the memoir, according to several critics, is "Granddaddy," the story of Njeri's trip to Georgia to find out about the death of her grandfather E. A. R. Lord, which occurred in 1960. While growing up, Njeri had been told that white men who had been drag racing while drinking alcohol collided with her grandfather's automobile and then tried to keep the authorities from finding out about the accident. After repeated attempts at unraveling the mystery in a community where people are reluctant to speak about the incident, Njeri eventually discovers that the person driving the other car had not been drag racing and that there had been no attempt to divert local officials. Unbeknownst to the family, Lord's second wife received a court settlement after the accident. In addition to finding out the truth about her grandfather's death, Njeri discovers that the people living in the Georgia community hold racist attitudes that were prevalent in the early 1960s. Njeri writes that shortly after the accident, when Lord's light-skinned wife ran to tell a white officer about the incident, she was told, "Don't worry yourself ma'am. It's just a nigger."

Of Njeri's accomplishment in writing *Every Good-bye Ain't Gone* Gail Lumet Buckley remarked in the *Los Angeles Times Book Review* that she "is a gifted and generous writer who rarely hides her feelings. These explorations of family myths and revelations of family conflict are a tumble of colliding emotions—love, hate, anger, regret—and are often very funny." And looking toward the future of Njeri's career as an author, Sherley Anne Williams in the *Washington Post* acknowledged that "Njeri's wit and style reveal a complex, independent character that many readers will want to know more about."

In *Bearing Witness: Selections from African-American Autobiography in the Twentieth Century,* Henry Louis Gates, Jr., one of the most influential contemporary scholars of African American history and culture, placed *Every Good-bye Ain't Gone* in the following literary and social context: "The African-American literary tradition is distinctive in that an author typically publishes as a first book her or his autobiography." He continued, saying that this is "true for many of the most prominent figures in the African-American tradition, from Frederick Douglass to Itabari Njeri. Through autobiography, these writers could, at once, shape a public 'self' in language, and protest the degradation of their ethnic group by the multiple forms of American racism. Njeri's contribution[s] to [this] tradition are considerable. [Her text] has played a role for our generation of black intellectuals that Claude Brown's *Man-child in the Promised Land* played at the cusp of the civil rights era."

Njeri commented: "I was not thinking of the great African-American autobiographical tradition when I first started my memoir, but I knew instinctively that by telling key aspects of my family's story, I would be illuminating important aspects of Black life. And I'm always thinking about the larger political picture when I write.

"To impose order on the chaos of memory is a universal impulse fueling the desire to write autobiography. But first and foremost, I hoped to create a work of art out of my experience as a woman of color in the New World at the end of the twentieth century. I wanted to illuminate the beauty, pain and complexity of a particular piece of the African diaspora, a piece central to the American experience. I wanted to tell the truth and make it sing.

"I consider myself a typical New World Black. And I understand that the substance of Black identity is complex. Please note that I consider Black a proper noun, referring not to color, but to culture and history. It is not the narrowly defined notion that obtains in the United States—a notion concocted by slave masters to perpetuate their chattel population, even if many were their own offspring. That notion is commonly known as the one-drop-in-the-bucket theory of descent, or what I think of as the little-dab'll-do-you school of genetics.

In other words, one drop of African blood makes you Black in America and erases any other ancestry. Black identity in the New World is composite. I conceive of it no differently than the generally accepted notion of Latino or Hispanic identity, a generic ethnic label for people who are to varying degrees a mixture of Indian, European and African ancestry.

"Americans do not think of Black identity in this way. Therefore, that I acknowledge and embrace the complex substance of Black identity in the New World has led some reviewers to disproportionately emphasize this aspect of my memoir, even to suggest that one of the book's major themes is my attempts to come to terms with my miscegenated background. I've never met a Negro in America who doesn't have a mixed background—they've just been conditioned not to acknowledge it.

"What I write about in *Every Good-bye* is that some of my relatives, who were phenotypically at the extreme ends of the color spectrum and looked White, suffered because American society has perpetuated by custom and law (and Blacks have accepted) a narrow definition of Black identity, one that exoticizes light-skinned Blacks (and penalizes dark-skinned Blacks). I explore the issue of color oppression thoroughly in several works: 'Sushi & Grits,' an essay published in *Lure and Loathing: Race, Identity and the Ambivalence of Assimilation;* my own collection of essays on diversity, *Sushi & Grits: The Challenge of Diversity;* and *The Last Plantation.*"

*BIOGRAPHICAL/CRITICAL SOURCES:*

*BOOKS*

Gates, Henry Louis, Jr., editor, *Bearing Witness: Selections from African-American Autobiography in the Twentieth Century,* Pantheon, 1991.
Njeri, Itabari, *Every Good-bye Ain't Gone: Family Portraits and Personal Escapades,* Times Books, 1990.

*PERIODICALS*

*Los Angeles Times Book Review,* February 25, 1990, p. 1.
*New York Times Book Review,* February 4, 1990, p. 9.
*Washington Post,* March 2, 1990.

\*    \*    \*

## NJOROGE, J(ames) K(ingangi) 1933-

*PERSONAL:* Born May 18, 1933, in Kangemi, Kenya; son of John Kingagi and Phylis (maiden name, Wanjiru) Thiongo; married Lizzie Nyambura, January 3, 1959; children: John, Jane, Mary, Patrick. *Education:* Makerere University College,

B.A., 1958; Royal College, Nairobi, diploma in education, 1962, and public administration.

*ADDRESSES: Home*—P.O. Box 48525, Nairobi, Kenya.

*CAREER:* Fiction writer and poet, 1966—. Njiris High School, 1958-61; Kenyan Government, assistant secretary, 1961, member of the ministry of state for constitutional affairs and administration, 1962, under secretary, ministry of commerce and industry, 1962, permanent secretary, ministries of commerce and industry, education, information, and defense, 1963-70; East African Rys. Corporation, Nairobi, resident director; Industrial Development Corporation, vice-chairman, 1963-64. Member of finance and general purpose committees, University of Dar-es-Salaam, 1965-70; member of the board of directors, Pan-Foods Co., Kenya.

*MEMBER:* Kenya National Union of Teachers, (treasurer and general secretary, 1958-61), Table Tennis and Gardening Club.

*WRITINGS:*

FICTION

*Tit for Tat and Other Stories,* East African Publishing House, 1966.
*The Proud Ostrich and Other Stories,* East African Publishing House, 1967.
*Pestle and Mortar,* East African Publishing House, 1969.

POETRY

*Spectrum: A Book of Poems,* Equatorial Publishers, 1970.

\*   \*   \*

## NKRUMAH, Kwame 1909-1972

*PERSONAL:* Name originally Francis Nwia Nkrumah (some sources say Francis Nwia Kofi or Kofie); born September 21, 1909, in Nkroful, Gold Coast, British West Africa (now Ghana); died April 27, 1972, in Bucharest, Romania (some sources say Conakry, Guinea); son of a goldsmith and a market trader; married Fathia Halim Ritzk, December 30, 1957; children: Gamal, Samia, Sekou. *Education:* Graduated from the Government Training College (now Achimota College), 1930; Lincoln University, Pennsylvania, B.A., 1939; University of Pennsylvania, B. Theol., M. Sci. in Education; attended London School of Economics and studied law in London, 1945-47, received M.A. and J.D.

*CAREER:* Worked as a schoolteacher in the Gold Coast, West Africa (now Ghana), c. 1931-35; Lincoln University, Lincoln University, PA, lecturer in political science; African Students Organization of America and Canada, founder and president; *New African,* London, England, editor, c. 1945-47; Fifth Pan-African Congress, Manchester, England, co-chairman, 1945; West African National Secretariat, general secretary, c. 1945-47; West African Students' Union, London, vice-president, c. 1945-47; United Gold Coast Convention, Accra, Gold Coast, organizing secretary, 1947-49; Convention Peoples' Party, Accra, founder and general secretary, 1949-66, became life chairman; elected to the colonial Legislative Assembly, 1951; Leader of Government Business, 1951-52; prime minister of the Gold Coast, 1952-56; prime minister of Ghana, 1956-60; president of Ghana, 1960-66; overthrown by a military coup, 1966, and lived in exile in Conakry, Guinea, 1966-72, as titular co-president. Chancellor, University of Ghana, Legon, and Kwame Nkrumah University of Science and Technology.

*AWARDS, HONORS:* Ph.D., Lincoln University, 1951; Lenin Peace Prize from the U.S.S.R., 1962.

*WRITINGS:*

NONFICTION

*Ghana: The Autobiography of Kwame Nkrumah,* Nelson, 1957, International Publishers, 1971.
*Speeches by the Prime Minister of Ghana at the Opening and Closing Sessions on 7th and 10th April, 1960,* Government Printer (Ghana), 1960.
*Selected Speeches of Osagyefo Dr. Kwame Nkrumah, First President of the Republic of Ghana,* compiled by Samuel Obeng, Afram Publications (Accra), 1961.
*I Speak of Freedom: A Statement of African Ideology,* Praeger, 1961, Greenwood, 1976.
*Statement by the President Concerning Properties and Business Connections of Ministers and Ministerial Secretaries,* Government Printer, 1961.
*Towards Colonial Freedom: Africa in the Struggle against World Imperialism,* Panaf, 1962, reissued 1973.
*Africa Must Unite,* Praeger, 1963, new edition, International Publishers, 1970.
*Consciencism: Philosophy and Ideology for Decolonization and Development with Particular Reference to the African Revolution,* Heinemann, 1964, Monthly Review Press, 1970.
*Neo-Colonialism: The Last Stage of Imperialism,* Nelson, 1965, International Publishers, 1966, Heinemann Educational, 1968.
*Axioms of Kwame Nkrumah,* Nelson, 1967, enlarged edition published as *Axioms of Kwame Nkrumah: Freedom Fighters' Edition,* International Publishers, 1969.

*Challenge of the Congo,* International Publishers, 1967.
*Handbook of Revolutionary Warfare: A Guide to the Armed
    Phase of the African Revolution,* Panaf Books (London),
    1968, International Publications, 1969.
*The Struggle Continues,* Panaf Books, 1968.
*Dark Days in Ghana,* International Publishers, 1968.
*Class Struggle in Africa,* International Publishers, 1970.
*Revolutionary Path,* International Publishers, 1973.
*Rhodesia File,* Panaf Books, 1976.
*Kwame Nkrumah: The Conakry Years, His Life and Letters,*
    compiled by June Milne, Panaf, 1990.

Author of numerous pamphlets on political and social issues;
contributor of articles to newspapers and magazines.

*SIDELIGHTS:* Ghanian independence leader Kwame Nkrumah rose from humble roots to international political prominence. Born the son of a goldsmith and a market trader from
the Nzima tribe in what was then known as the Gold Coast of
British West Africa, Nkrumah received his education from
Catholic missionaries and worked as a rural schoolteacher
during the 1930s. In 1935 he traveled to the United States to
further his education at Lincoln University and the University of Pennsylvania, where he studied economics, sociology,
theology, philosophy, and education. He also met left-lean-
ing black intellectuals who introduced him to socialist literature and the pan-Africanist ideas of Jamaican political thinker and activist Marcus Garvey. Already a gifted orator with a
charismatic presence, Nkrumah served as president of the
African Students' Association of America and Canada before
moving to London in 1945 to complete his studies.

In postwar London, home to many young intellectuals from
Britain's colonial possessions and a center of pan-Africanist
activism, Nkrumah quickly made a political name for himself. He edited a leading pan-Africanist journal called *The New
African,* served as vice-president of the West African Students'
Union, and helped organize the Fifth Pan-African Conference
in Manchester. Nkrumah's political reputation reached back
to the Gold Coast and prompted James B. Danquah, founder
of the nationalist United Gold Coast Convention (UCGC), to
invite him to become organizing secretary for the newly
formed party. Nkrumah accepted the post and returned in 1947
to his native land, where he immediately set about organizing mass support for a program of decolonization and self-
government.

But Nkrumah soon broke with Danquah and the UCGC over
the questions of when and how to achieve political independence. When Danquah's conservative and largely middle-class
organization agreed to a compromise settlement with the British that kept much of the colonial power intact, Nkrumah
denounced the deal and formed his own Convention Peoples'

Party (CPP) to demand immediate self-government. He urged
this militant program forward with a "positive action" campaign of mass strikes and civil disobedience that culminated
in his arrest and imprisonment on charges of sedition in 1950.
But even as he condemned the electoral compromise with the
British, the politically astute Nkrumah used it for his own
purposes, leading his party from prison to an overwhelming
victory in the 1951 Legislative Assembly elections. Nkrumah
himself won 98 percent of the vote cast for the seat he con-
tested in Accra, persuading the colonial authorities to release
him from prison and offer him the post of leader of government business, a position equivalent to prime minister.

After sharing power amicably with the British during a four-
year transition period, Nkrumah led the Gold Coast, now
named Ghana, to complete independence in April, 1956. As
the first sub-Saharan colonial territory to achieve its political
emancipation, Ghana captured the world's imagination and
was widely seen as a proving ground for Africans' ability to
govern themselves democratically. But Ghana, like other
emerging African nations, faced daunting obstacles to building a stable and representative national political culture. Widespread poverty and illiteracy, tribal rivalries, linguistic barriers, and the absence of any democratic tradition all worked
against successfully transplanting Western-style representative government. Even before independence, Nkrumah confronted a powerful opposition movement of Ashanti tribespeople whose fears of domination by the CPP's coastal popular base were only partly assuaged by a constitutional provi-
sion for regional government consultative assemblies. Nkrumah discussed the independence movement and the enormous
challenges of leading a new nation in *Ghana,* his widely read
political autobiography published in 1957.

As Ghana's founding father, or Osagyefo ("Emancipator"),
as he called himself, Nkrumah enjoyed immense prestige both
at home and abroad during the first few years of his term in
office. Almost immediately, though, he began to take measures to strengthen his authority and undermine his fractious
political opposition. In 1958 he used the CPP's legislative
majority to dilute the power of the regional assemblies and to
pass a Preventive Detention Act allowing him to imprison
without trial for a term of up to five years any individual
deemed a danger to state security. Nkrumah used this power
as a bludgeon against his political enemies, including his
former mentor Danquah, who eventually died in a Ghanian
prison cell. Still a popular figure in 1960, when he overwhelmingly defeated Danquah in Ghana's first presidential election,
Nkrumah lost public support as he stepped up repression amid
charges of government corruption and mismanagement. A
1964 referendum to establish the CPP as Ghana's state party
and to give the president control over the judiciary returned a
clearly fraudulent 99.9 percent "yes" vote and underscored
Nkrumah's political weakness. Several assassination attempts

against the Ghanian leader reinforced his suspicion, isolation, and authoritarianism.

Nkrumah sought to cover his dictatorial course with socialist rhetoric, although Ghana remained essentially a capitalist country throughout his tenure. Still, the Ghanian leader appeared genuinely committed to promoting social welfare, raising popular living standards, and developing the national economy, and he accomplished much in these areas. He developed a national road system, modernized harbor facilities, built elementary schools and universities, improved health, housing, and primary education, and constructed a huge dam on the Volta River to supply electric power to consumers and a new aluminum smelter. Nkrumah described some of these achievements and his vision for developing Ghana and greater Africa in his books *I Speak of Freedom* and *Africa Must Unite.* The author took a more theoretical approach to the same subject in *Consciencism,* which attempts to demonstrate the political and economic necessity for an independent, united, and socialist Africa.

This pan-Africanist ideal remained central to Nkrumah's political identity, and its failure to materialize during his lifetime was perhaps his greatest disappointment. Nkrumah believed that the economic and political unification of the emerging African nation-states would greatly accelerate development and help make the continent a world power. In *Africa Must Unite* and other works, he urged the new West and East African nations to throw off their arbitrarily defined borders fixed by the former colonial powers and pronounced Ghana willing to surrender its national sovereignty to a Union of African States when this became possible. To this end, Nkrumah organized several continental conferences to explore the possibility of African unification and succeeded in persuading the West African countries of Guinea and Mali to join Ghana in founding the Union of African States in 1961. But Nkrumah seemed to underestimate the immense barriers to unification posed by widely differing cultures and languages, not to mention political rivalries, and the pan-Africanist ideal was never realized. The Organization of African States, founded in 1963, explicitly recognized the inviolability of the national borders inherited from colonialism, and the Ghana-Guinea-Mali alliance itself never achieved political unification.

With his prestige undermined at home and abroad, Nkrumah was ousted from office by a military coup in 1966, and he and his ministers were accused of treason and corruption. He took refuge in Guinea, where President Sekou Toure, an old political ally, named him honorary "co-president" of the country. From exile, Nkrumah tried unsuccessfully to organize a Ghanian popular movement to regain power and penned *Dark*

*Days in Ghana,* a bitter diatribe against his political enemies. Nkrumah also wrote several books about revolutionary struggle in Africa and a volume of axioms that outlines his basic political principles.

Nkrumah died of cancer in 1972 while undergoing medical treatment in Bucharest, Romania. A sadly powerless figure in his final years, Nkrumah is still honored as a brilliant and inspiring independence leader who helped awaken national pride and political confidence throughout the African continent.

*BIOGRAPHICAL/CRITICAL SOURCES:*

BOOKS

Ames, Sophia Ripley, *Nkrumah of Ghana,* Rand McNally, 1961.

Bankole, Timothy, *Kwame Nkrumah: His Rise to Power,* Macmillan, 1956.

Barker, Peter, *Operation Cold Chop: The Coup That Toppled Nkrumah,* Ghana Publishing Corp., 1969.

Botchway, Francis, *Political Development and Social Change in Ghana: Ghana under Nkrumah,* Black Academy Press (Buffalo, NY), 1972.

Bretton, Henry L., *Rise and Fall of Kwame Nkrumah: A Study of Personal Rule in Africa,* Praeger, 1966.

Davidson, Basil, *Black Star: A View of the Life and Times of Kwame Nkrumah,* Praeger, 1974.

Donkoh, C., *Mother Africa Mourns Kwame Nkrumah, the Emancipator,* [Ghana], 1978.

Fitch, Bob, and Mary Oppenheimer, *Ghana: End of Illusion,* Monthly Review Press, 1966.

Harvey, William Burnett, *Law and Social Change in Ghana,* Princeton University Press, 1966.

James, Cyril Lionel Robert, *Nkrumah and the Ghana Revolution,* Allison Busby, 1977.

Jones, Peter Walter Handley, *Kwame Nkrumah and Africa,* Hamilton, 1965.

Marais, Genoveva, *Kwame Nkrumah As I Knew Him,* Janay Publishing Co., 1972.

McKenzie-Rennie, Rhoda, *Nkrumah, Greatest of Modern Philosophers,* Vantage, 1977.

McKown, Robin, *Nkrumah: A Biography,* Doubleday, 1973.

Milne, June, compiler, *Kwame Nkrumah: The Conakry Years, His Life and Letters,* Panaf, 1990.

Nkrumah, Kwame, *Ghana: The Autobiography of Kwame Nkrumah,* Nelson, 1957.

Omari, Thompson Peter, *Kwame Nkrumah: The Anatomy of an African Dictatorship,* C. Hurst & Co., 1970.

Phillips, John Frederick Vicars, *Kwame Nkrumah and the Future of Africa,* Praeger, 1961.

Segal, Ronald, *African Profiles,* Penguin, 1963.

Taylor, Sidney, editor, *The New Africans,* Putnam's, 1967.

*OBITUARIES:*

*PERIODICALS*

*New York Times,* April 28, 1972.
*Times* (London), April 28, 1972.
*Time,* May 8, 1972.

\*   \*   \*

## NORTJE, (Kenneth) Arthur  1942-1970

*PERSONAL:* Born December 16, 1942, in Oudtshoorn, Cape Province, South Africa; committed suicide by overdose of prescription drugs, c. December 10, 1970; son of Cecilia Potgieter. *Education:* Belleville College of the Western Cape, B.A., 1963; Oxford University, 1965, B.Phil., 1970. *Politics:* None.

*CAREER:* Teacher in Hope, British Columbia, 1967, and in Toronto, Ontario, 1969; also taught at South End High School, Post Elizabeth, South Africa.

*AWARDS, HONORS:* Mbari Poetry Prize, Ibadan University, 1962.

*WRITINGS:*

*Dead Roots* (poetry), Heinemann, 1973.

Work represented in anthologies, including *Seven South African Poets,* edited by Cosmo Pieterse, Heinemann, 1971, and *Arthur Nortje and Other Poets,* COSAW, 1988; contributor to periodicals.

*SIDELIGHTS:* Arthur Nortje was symbolic of anti-apartheid among South Africans. He struggled with intense feelings of being a "marginal" person, which is reflected in a number of his poems. Of mixed descent, he suffered a life of constant self-examination in an attempt to find his identity while living in a society that practiced discrimination.

Labeled a "coloured" by the South African government, which identified Nortje as a product of mixed heritage—part native South African, part European-Asian—Nortje used haunting and pervasive themes to face the realism of what was one of the most repressive eras in South African history. In *Dead Roots,* not only was his lack of personal identity a primary motivation, but also his self-imposed exile to London and his lack of political commitment. It was his independent nature that placed him in conflict with those who opposed apartheid. His critics felt he was misusing his talent as a writer by not utilizing it to "speak out" against apartheid.

Exile to London in 1965 helped Nortje find a more objective approach to his writing. In England, he felt that he had more freedom to express himself than he did in his native South Africa. Nortje soon discovered, however, that it was difficult to relate the aspects of apartheid to a culture which had no experience of it. Within a short time, he departed for Canada, which inspired some of his more haunting works, incorporating political insight that had been missing in some of his earlier poems.

Shortly before his death, Nortje returned to London, beginning a downward spiral of self-doubt and despair. It is believed that Nortje was pressured by anti-apartheid groups to read some of his poems at Human Rights Day, in December of 1970. The thought of opposing contemporary political powers was a task which Nortje met with anxiety. It is only through Nortje's feelings of inadequacy and his own inner exile that he touches those who would read his work, drawing attention to the tragedy of his death.

*BIOGRAPHICAL/CRITICAL SOURCES:*

*BOOKS*

*Dictionary of Literary Biography,* Volume 125: *Twentieth-Century Caribbean and Black African Writers, Second Series,* Gale, 1993.
*Literary Exiles in the Twentieth Century,* Gale, 1991.

\*   \*   \*

## NWANKWO, Nkem  1936-

*PERSONAL:* Born June 12, 1936, in Nigeria; immigrated to the United States, 1972; married Ifeoma Azuka Ejindu (a nurse); children: Ikenna (son), Adora (daughter). *Education:* University of Ibadan, B.A. (honors), 1962; Indiana University, M.A., 1976, Ph.D., 1982. *Religion:* Roman Catholic.

*ADDRESSES: Office*—Department of English, Tennessee State University, 3500 John Merritt Blvd., Nashville, TN 37203.

*CAREER:* High school English teacher in Ibadan, Nigeria, 1962-64; Nigeria Broadcasting Corp., Lagos, writer and producer of radio programs, 1964-70; *Daily Times,* Lagos, deputy editor, 1970-71; *African Impact* (weekly news magazine), Benin, Nigeria, editor in chief, 1971-72; Michigan State University, East Lansing, writer in residence and specialist at African Studies Center, 1972-73; San Diego State University, San Diego, CA, visiting professor, 1976; Ohio State University, Columbus, assistant professor, 1977-85; currently associate professor at Tennessee State University, Nashville. Founder, Niger House Publishers, 1993.

*MEMBER:* National Society of Literature and the Arts (United States).

*AWARDS, HONORS:* National short story prize from Nigerian Arts Council, 1960, for "The Gambler"; international drama prize from *Encounter,* 1960, for *The Two Sisters.*

*WRITINGS:*

*Danda* (novel), Deutsch, 1964.
*Tales Out of School,* illustrated by Adebayo Ajayi, African Universities Press, 1965.
*More Tales Out of School,* illustrated by Ajayi, African Universities Press, 1966.
(With Samuel X. Ufejika) *Biafra: The Making of a Nation,* Praeger, 1968.
*My Mercedes Is Bigger than Yours,* Harper, 1975.
*The Scapegoat* (novel), Fourth Dimension, 1984 (unauthorized), authorized version, Niger House, 1993.
*A Song for Fela and Other Poems,* Niger House, 1993.
*The Shadow of the Masquerade* (memoir), Niger House, 1993.

Contributor of stories, such as "The Gambler," and poems to magazines, including *Black Orpheus* and *Nigeria.*

*STAGE PLAYS*

*Eroya,* first produced at the Arts Theatre of University of Ibadan, Ibadan, Nigeria, 1964.
*Danda* (dramatized version of his novel by the same title), produced at First World Festival of Negro Arts, Dakar, Senegal, 1966.

*RADIO PLAYS; ALL PRODUCED BY THE NIGERIA*
*BROADCASTING CORPORATION*

*The Inheritors,* 1964.
*Fire and Brimstone,* 1965.
*In My Father's House,* 1965.
*Full Circle,* 1965.
*The Two Sisters,* 1966.
*Who Gave Monkey Banana?* (satire), 1966.
*The Serpent in the Garden,* 1966.

*SIDELIGHTS:* Nkem Nwankwo, a novelist and playwright from the Ibo ethnic group in Nigeria, grew up during a tumultuous period in the development of his country. Nigerian nationalism, which eventually led to the freeing of the country from the British and to ensuring self-government, left vivid impressions that would not only remain fixed in his memory

but also influence his thought and writings. Nwankwo commented that his first book, *Danda,* published in 1964, is permeated with a postcolonial feeling of euphoria, of "inheritors of a brave new world rescued from the West."

D. A. N. Jones noted in the *Times Literary Supplement* that soon after his country's independence Nwankwo experienced the shattering of this pristine view of his world and a brutal return to reality when the antagonism between the three major groups—the Ibo in the East, the Hausa-Fulani in the North and the Yoruba in the West—escalated progressively and rapidly. At times, the conflict was exacerbated by the arrest of other minorities who felt discriminated against by these three. The violent elections of 1964, a revolt by the Ibos and other military officers, and reforms of short duration followed by more turbulence and murder caused more than two million Ibos, from 1967 to 1970, to flee to the East. When Colonel Ojukwu declared eastern Nigeria independent and renamed it Biafra, Nwankwo commented that he had fought in the civil war on the Biafran side. Nwankwo stated that this action "caused a three year gap in my literary activities." Their side lost the war, and a few years hence Nwankwo immigrated to the United States as a "spiritual exile."

In Nwankwo's own words, "My subsequent books have reflected the inevitable disillusionment with the gap between idyll and reality." It is the uneasy coexistence between the ideal and the real and between the traditional and the Western that not only inform his work via the influences of both biography and history, but that also surface in such creations as the title character of the novel *Danda.* Although expected to adhere to traditional Ibo expectations of being a productive and respectful member of society, Danda indulges in drinking, dancing, and making cuckolds of the village elders.

In *Long Drums and Cannons* Margaret Lawrence noted that Nwankwo's *Tales Out of School,* a volume of stories concerning a young African boy about to enter school to become Westernized, is spicy, vibrant, and full of Ibo words and phrases, and, though broad in scope, it nonetheless has a clear focus on Afrocentric values, with a Eurocentric influence which manifests itself mainly through the "aggressive puritanical Christians in the village." Nwankwo's 1965 book, *More Tales Out of School,* concerns itself with two thirteen-year-old boys, Iko and Bayo, who skip school so that they can investigate a mystery. They enjoy the status of heroes after they are captured, manage to escape, then aid the police in apprehending the villains.

Nwankwo's style, though reminiscent of Ibo oral storytelling, is mocking according to Lawrence. In his works, readers see an authorial lack of resolve as Nwankwo oscillates between a past, traditional world that is disappearing and a more contemporary one, replete with cars and plush jobs. This theme is particularly evident in *My Mercedes Is Better than Yours.* Jones noted in *Times Literary Supplement* that, though "motorized transport developed gradually in Britain ... in Nigeria, it came with a bang, and was immediately a fit subject for poetry and drama." The satirical novel plays upon a number of bittersweet themes which reflect upon the author's breadth of experience. Nwankwo's remarks summed up the course and trajectory of his works: "My writing from now [on] is going to be progressively picaresque; it is the point of view of the rogue. It is my way of paying life back for having conspired with events to alienate me from most of the human race."

*BIOGRAPHICAL/CRITICAL SOURCES:*

*BOOKS*

Lawrence, Margaret, *Long Drums and Cannons,* Macmillan, 1968.
Nwankwo, Nkem, and Samuel X. Ufejika, *Biafra: The Making of a Nation,* Praeger, 1968.
Rubin, Leslie and Brian Weinstein, *Introduction to African Politics: A Continental Approach,* Praeger, 1974, pp. 169-171.

*PERIODICALS*

*Booklist,* Volume 73, July 15, 1977, p. 1734.
*Times Literary Supplement,* October 17, 1975, p. 1238.

—*Sketch by Lillian D. Roland*

\* \* \*

# NWAPA, Flora 1931-

*PERSONAL:* Full name, Florence Nwanzuruahu Nkiru Nwapa; born January 18, 1931, in Oguta, East Central State, Nigeria; married Gogo Nwakuche (an industrialist), 1967; children: Amede, Uzoma, Ejine. *Education:* Queen's College, Lagos, 1951; University College of Ibadan, B.A., 1957; University of Edinburgh, Diploma in Education, 1958.

*ADDRESSES: Office*—c/o Tana Press Ltd., 2-A Menkiti Lane, Ogui, Enugu, Nigeria. *Agent:* David Bolt Associates, 12 Heath Dr., Send, Surrey GU23 7EP, England.

*CAREER:* Novelist, short story writer, writer of children's literature; managing director, Tana Press Ltd. and Flora Nwapa and Company, Enugu, 1978—. Woman education officer, Calabar, Nigeria, 1958; Queen's School, Enugu, Nigeria, teacher, 1959-62; University of Lagos, assistant registrar (public relations), 1962-67; East Central State, commissioner and

member of the Executive Council, 1970-75, served variously as commissioner for Health and Social Welfare, commissioner for Lands, Survey and Urban Development, and commissioner for Establishments. Visiting professor of creative writing, department of English, University of Maiduguri, 1989-90.

*AWARDS, HONORS:* Nigerian national honor of Officer of the Order of the Niger (O.O.N.) for literature.

*WRITINGS:*

*NOVELS, EXCEPT WHERE NOTED*

*Efuru,* Heinemann, 1966.
*Idu,* Heinemann, 1970.
*Never Again* (autobiography), Nwamife, 1975.
*One Is Enough,* Tana Press, 1981.
*Women Are Different,* Tana Press, 1986.
*Cassava Song and Rice Song* (poetry), Tana Press, 1986.

*SHORT STORIES*

*This Is Lagos and Other Stories,* Nwankwo-Ifejika, 1971.
*Wives at War and Other Stories,* Tana Press, 1980.

*CHILDREN'S LITERATURE*

*Emeka, Driver's Guard* (fiction), illustrated by Roslyn Isaacs, University of London Press, 1972.
*Mammywater* (fiction), illustrated by Obiora Udechukwu, Tana Press, 1979.
*My Tana Colouring Book* (educational), illustrated by P. S. C. Igboanugo, Tana Press, 1979.
*Journey to Space* (fiction), illustrated by Chinwe Orieke, Tana Press, 1980.
*The Miracle Kittens* (fiction), illustrated by Emeka Onwudinjo, Tana Press, 1980.
*The Adventures of Deke* (fiction), illustrated by Obiora Udechukwu, Tana Press, 1980.
*My Animal Number Book* (educational), illustrated by Emeka Onwudinjo, Tana Press, 1981.

*SIDELIGHTS:* As a teacher, former government official, businesswoman and writer, Flora Nwapa expresses an avid interest in the traditions and momentous changes taking place in Nigeria. Such interests are a focus of her writing, whether she is educating children about the myths and spiritual beliefs of the Igbo in *Mammywater* and *Cassava Song and Rice Song* or depicting the impact of change on the women characters in her novels and short stories. All of Nwapa's works are grounded in Igbo life and culture. Her characters are drawn, like many in the African literary tradition, from the outside in, so that the orality, or the richness of African dialogue emerges. For her talent in dramatizing the special nature of Igbo women's talk, she is praised by such critics as Lloyd Brown in *Women Writers of Black Africa* and Gay Wilentz in *Binding Cultures, Black Women Writers in Africa and the Diaspora.*

Nwapa's adult fiction comprises a transformational whole, as her women characters begin by operating within the accepted traditions of Igbo society, but move outside its codes when their social, economic and spiritual needs grow beyond the Igbo ideal of how a woman should behave. Hence, as the women protagonists in *Efuru* and *Idu* maintain individual will, they "demonstrate the ability of women to transform both motherhood and childlessness into positive, self-defined and powerful experiences," says Jane Bryce-Okunla in *Motherlands.* Greater movement outside these traditions is depicted in *Wives at War.* This new direction is signaled first by the title, which when related to some of the stories, means not only women's participation in the Nigerian Civil War between Igbos and opposing tribal groups (also called the Biafran War), but also women's direct confrontation with men for political rights; their private bonding against paternalism and the male who cannot think realistically; and their determination to avoid being used solely as sexual objects.

*Wives at War* is indeed an apt prelude to the novels, *One Is Enough* and *Women Are Different.* In *One Is Enough,* Amaku, the protagonist, relinquishes the pre-determined role of wife against the wishes of her mother, the father of her children and her community. In short, Amaku's transformation embodies a number of Nwapa's previous women characters because she begins by endorsing her community's belittlement of her childless status but ends by questioning any standards which she feels may demean her self-image. *Women Are Different* follows the development of three women who begin as schoolmates, each looking to the future for husbands and family. Like Amaku, they find that, as adults, their dreams of a stable family life are unfulfilled and they must work hard to achieve financial independence, without their errant husbands' help.

Transformation and transition of women characters lie at the center of Nwapa's themes. The struggle of women as wives and mothers is interwoven with their change and emergence. In *Efuru* and *Idu* the theme of the relationship between women and their communities is essential to understanding Nwapa's portraits of the traditional wife whose status is achieved through childbirth; of the women who achieve rank and power in seeing to it that traditions are maintained, no matter how restrictive; and of aggressive women who are the protectors of other women as they openly and brazenly challenge the men for fair treatment. In *One Is Enough* and *Women Are Different* Nwapa celebrates the strength, imagination and energy of the woman who becomes economically and spiritually independent in Nigeria's fast-paced urban centers.

One underlying theme in both *This Is Lagos and Other Stories* and *Women Are Different* is the loss of some traditions brought about by westernization and changes in economics and political structure. In *Kunapipi* Kirsten Holst Petersen also observes that in *This Is Lagos, Never Again* and *Wives at War* the shift in environments causes women to lose "the secure moral universe of the village" and instead be confronted by "problems of individual survival in a city jungle with no guide lines except those provided by success, modern life and wealth, exemplified by cars, drink, wigs, etc."

Nwapa's themes clearly have a feminine slant. The power of feminine bonding is a theme she presents in *Women Are Different, Wives at War and Other Stories* and *One Is Enough.* Nwapa does not dehumanize or reject her male characters, but as upholders of paternalistic values, they are sometimes blind or indifferent to women's needs; they impede women's progress and exploit them economically or sexually. Commenting on Nwapa's feminism in *Efuru,* critic Adewale Maja-Pearce concludes in *World Literature Written in English* that Nwapa's feminism "isn't of the strident kind. Far from hating men, she doesn't even dislike them. The women in the novel [*Efuru*] possess some extra quality that the men lack: her women are 'good' in a way that her men never are." Underscoring this theme of feminine power Brenda Berrian in the *College Language Association Journal* (*CLAJ*) says that "Nwapa insists that although the African woman may be vulnerable to men, she does not play a subordinate role."

While women are still at the center of these texts, *This Is Lagos, Never Again* and *Wives at War* depict the Biafran War in terms of how it affects soldiers, women, families, villages and towns in Biafra. Biafra, so called by the Igbos of Nigeria's Eastern Region, seceded from Nigeria May 30, 1967, as a result of massacres of thousands of Igbos by two other tribal groups, the Yorubas and Hausas, who believed the rumor that Igbos were attempting to control all of Nigeria. In *This Is Lagos,* the story, "My Soldier Brother," is one of the few told from a male perspective. An adoring youth joins his Igbo militia unit to avenge his brother's death. The irony in the story captures Nwapa's sense of tragedy in all of her war stories: those Igbos most enthusiastic about an Igbo victory seem to lose sight of the fact that they were not only losing the war but also suffering the loss of entire generations of Igbos. It is this irony of fanatic patriotism amid tremendous loss and suffering that Nwapa's heroine, Kate, observes in *Never Again.* "In Nwapa's novel, the refrain 'never again' becomes the expressed resolve that such suffering, the dehumanization, and the fragmentation would no longer be tolerated," explains Maxine Sample in *Modern Fiction Studies.* In "Wives at War," and "A Certain Death" Nwapa depicts the vital role of women in the war. They organized kitchens for starving soldiers, and they were the main force behind the Biafran Red Cross. In the case of the woman character in "A Certain Death," they saved the lives of the remaining men in their families by paying substitutes to go to war. Nwapa notes in *Never Again* and *One Is Enough* that women participated in the "attack trade." Using their acquired skills in market trade, these women bargained with the enemy, the Nigerians, for items of which the starving Biafrans were in dire need.

Often referred to as Africa's first woman novelist to publish in English, Flora Nwapa is highly credited for being a literary voice of the African woman during a period when African literature was dominated by men. She enriches the English language with Igbo folk idioms spoken largely by and about women. In her early novels Nwapa offers a view of women's lives in precolonial times; through Nwapa the African woman is no longer silent. As Elleke Boehmer observes in *Motherlands,* Nwapa gives voice to texts which challenge the conventional literary image of women created by the African male writer and which depict the evolution of female characters who define their own lives, whether or not they are mothers or wives.

*BIOGRAPHICAL/CRITICAL SOURCES:*

*BOOKS*

Brown, Lloyd, *Women Writers of Black Africa,* Greenwood, 1981.
*Dictionary of Literary Biography,* Volume 125: *Twentieth-Century Caribbean and Black African Writers, Second Series,* Gale, 1993.
James, Adeola, editor, *In Their Own Voices, African Women Writers Talk,* Heinemann, 1990.
Nasta, Susheila, editor, *Motherlands: Black Women's Writing from Africa, the Caribbean and South Asia,* Rutgers, 1992.
Wilentz, Gay, *Binding Cultures, Black Women Writers in Africa and the Diaspora,* Indiana, 1992.

*PERIODICALS*

*Africa Woman,* July/August, 1977.
*African Literature Today,* Number 7, 1975.
*College Language Association Journal,* Volume 25, number 3, 1982.
*Kunapipi,* Volume 7, number 2-3, 1985.
*Modern Fiction Studies,* autumn, 1991.
*Nigeria Magazine,* June, 1966.
*Presence Africaine,* volume 82, 1972.
*World Literature Written in English,* spring, 1985.

—*Sketch by Australia Tarver*

## NYERERE, Julius K(ambarage) 1922-

*PERSONAL:* Born in March, 1922, in Butiama-Musoma, Tanganyika (now Tanzania); son of Mtemi Nyerere Burito and Mugaya Nyang'ombe; married Maria Magige (a shopkeeper), 1953; children: five sons, two daughters. *Education:* Makerere University, teacher's diploma, 1945; received M.A., Edinburgh University. *Religion:* Roman Catholic. *Avocational interests:* Reading.

*ADDRESSES: Office*—P.O. Box 9120, Dar es Salaam, Tanzania.

*CAREER:* St. Mary's Roman Catholic School, Tabora, Tanganyika, teacher, 1946-49; St. Francis's Roman Catholic College, Pugu, Tanganyika, teacher, 1953-55; Tanganyika Government, member of legislative council, 1957, leader of Elected Members Organization, 1958-60, member for Easter Province, 1958, member for Dar es Salaam, 1960; Republic of Tanganyika (now Tanzania), Dar es Salaam, chief minister, 1960-61, prime minister, 1961-62, president, 1962-64, minister of external affairs, 1962-63; United Republic of Tanzania, Dar es Salaam, president, 1964-85, minister of external affairs, 1965-72, commander in chief of the armed forces, beginning in 1973, founder and chairman of Chama Cha Mapinduzi (Revolutionary Party), beginning in 1977, chairman of Defense and Security Committee of Tanzania. Chancellor of University of East Africa, 1963-70, and of University of Dar es Salaam, 1970-85. President of Pan-African Freedom Movement of Eastern and Central Africa.

*MEMBER:* Organization for African Unity (chairman, 1984-85), African Association of Dar es Salaam (president, 1953), Tanganyika African Association (now Tanganyika African National Union; president, 1953-77).

*AWARDS, HONORS:* Third World Award, 1981; LL.D. from Edinburgh University and Duquesne University.

*WRITINGS:*

(Translator into Swahili) William Shakespeare, *Julius Caesar,* Oxford University Press, 1963.
(With Joshua Nkomo) *Rhodesia: The Case for Majority Rule,* Indian Council for Africa, 1966.
*Freedom and Unity—Uhuru na Umoja: A Selection from Writings and Speeches, 1952-1965,* Oxford University Press, 1967.
*Freedom and Socialism—Uhuru na Ujamaa: A Selection from Writings and Speeches, 1965-1967,* Oxford University Press, 1968.
*Ujamaa: Essays on Socialism,* Oxford University Press, 1968.
*Nyerere on Socialism,* Oxford University Press, 1969.

(Translator into Swahili) Shakespeare, *The Merchant of Venice,* Oxford University Press, 1969.

*Quotations from President Julius K. Nyerere, Collected from Speeches and Writings,* edited and published by Morogoro College of National Education, 1970.

*Tanzania Ten Years after Independence: Report,* Ministry of Information and Broadcasting, 1971.

*Freedom and Development—Uhuru na Maendeleo: A Selection from Writings and Speeches, 1968-1973,* Oxford University Press, 1973.

*Moyo kabla ya silaha,* EAPH, 1973.

*Man and Development—Binadamu na Maendeleo,* Oxford University Press, 1974.

*The Arusha Declaration Ten Years After,* Government Printer, 1977.

*Wafanyakazi na ujamaa Tanzania,* Makao Makuu ya NUTA, 1977.

*Crusade for Liberation,* Oxford University Press, 1978.

(With Samir Amin and Daniel Perren) *Le Dialogue inegal: Ecueils du nouvel ordre economique international,* Centre Europe-Tiers Monde, 1979.

*Awamu ya pili ya mradi wa kuimarisha chama,* Ofisi ya Katibu Mkuu wa CCM, 1987-91.

Also author of booklet "Barriers to Democracy."

*SIDELIGHTS:* When the African nation of Tanganyika became independent in 1961, after decades of foreign rule, Julius K. Nyerere was its first prime minister. After the 1964 union of Tanganyika and Zanzibar under the name Tanzania, Nyerere governed the new country as well. Rising out of a tribal background to become teacher, political leader, and writer, he is "the father of homespun African socialism" and "one of the Third World's most prominent statesmen," according to *Time* writer Hunter R. Clark. Assessed John Darnton in the *New York Times,* "No other African head of state has set such high standards for his countrymen, for Africa or, for that matter, for all mankind as the intense, scholarly ... President of Tanzania."

Originally a teacher, Nyerere turned increasingly to politics in the early 1950s, ultimately giving up academia to lead his country to independence and improved socioeconomic conditions. As president he socialized farming and industry—although eighty-five percent of the farmers returned to subsistence farming as a result of inefficient pricing and distribution—and promoted national pride, a national language, and improved health care and education. Noted Clark, "Although he has failed ... to create the prosperous, egalitarian society that he once envisioned, his policies will continue to shape the country—and the continent—for decades." Several of his policies were at least partially successful: Tanzania has achieved eighty-three percent literacy and enjoys "perhaps the lowest level of tribal strife of any country on the continent," observed

Clark, and it has demonstrated concern for civil and human rights—helping to overthrow neighboring Uganda's brutal dictator Idi Amin in 1979.

Nyerere's numerous speeches, essays, and other writings detail his policies and viewpoints, emphasizing central themes such as the importance of human beings and of allowing a country to develop in its own way, considering useful ideas from without and within. *Freedom and Socialism—Uhuru na Ujamaa: A Selection from Writings and Speeches, 1965-1967* "sets out guidelines for new policies which are among the most exciting, and encouraging, in Africa," judged a *Times Literary Supplement* reviewer, who considered Nyerere's prescription "entirely realistic and rational." The author highlights racial equality and African unity in *Freedom and Unity—Uhuru na Umoja: A Selection from Writings and Speeches, 1952-1965.*

Throughout his political career, asserted a *Times Literary Supplement* critic, "Tanzania's President has dwelt on the deep underlying principles of statecraft." He has earned a reputation for consistency and integrity, for supporting human rights and democratic institutions such as free elections and independent courts of law. In 1976 U.S. Secretary of State Henry Kissinger "made it clear that he regards Mr. Nyerere as the prime link to black Africa," remarked Darnton. Upon Nyerere's resignation in 1985 a political opponent, quoted in *Time,* characterized the former president as "a real man of the people."

*BIOGRAPHICAL/CRITICAL SOURCES:*

*BOOKS*

Hatch, John, *Two African Statesmen: Kaunda of Zambia and Nyerere of Tanzania,* Regnery, 1976.

*PERIODICALS*

*New York Times,* September 16, 1976.
*Time,* November 4, 1985.
*Times Literary Supplement,* March 30, 1967; August 28, 1969.

\* \* \*

## NZEKWU, Onuora 1928-

*PERSONAL:* Born in 1928, in Kafanchan, Nigeria. *Education:* St. Anthony's E.T.C., 1943; attended St. Charles' Higher Elementary Teacher Training College.

*CAREER:* Fiction writer, editor, and teacher; *Nigeria Maga-*

*zine,* editorial assistant, 1956, editor-in-chief, 1962—; teacher, Oturkpo, Onitsha, and Lagos, 1947-56.

*AWARDS, HONORS:* Rockefeller Foundation fellowship; U.N.E.S.C.O. fellowship.

*WRITINGS:*

*FICTION*

*Wand of Noble Wood,* Hutchinson, 1961, Signet, 1963.
*Blade Among the Boys,* Hutchinson, 1962.
*Highlife for Lizards,* Hutchinson, 1965.

*CHILDREN'S STORIES*

(With Michael Crowder) *Eze Goes to School,* African University Press, 1963.

*BIOGRAPHICAL/CRITICAL SOURCES:*

*BOOKS*

*A New Reader's Guide to African Literature,* edited by Hans M. Zell and others, Holmes & Meier, 1983.

# O

## OCCOMY, Marita (Odette) Bonner 1899-1971
### (Marita Bonner; Joseph Maree Andrew)

*PERSONAL:* Born June 16, 1899 (some sources say 1898), in Boston, MA (some sources say Brookline); died 1971, in Chicago, IL; daughter of Joseph Andrew (a machinist) and Mary Anne (a homemaker; maiden name, Nowell) Bonner; married William Almay Occomy; children: Warwick Gale, William, and Marita Joyce. *Education:* Radcliffe College, B.A., 1922. *Religion:* Church of Christ Scientist.

*CAREER:* English teacher, Bluefield Colored Institute, Bluefield, VA, 1922-24, Armstrong High School, Washington, DC, 1925-30, and Phillips High School, Chicago, IL, 1950-63. Author and playwright.

*MEMBER:* "Round Table," a literary salon (also known as "The Saturday Nighters," 1925-30), Krigwa Players.

*AWARDS, HONORS: Crisis* award winner, *Crisis,* 1925, for "On Being Young—a Woman—and Colored"; honorable mention citation, *Opportunity,* 1925, for "The Hands"; first prize in *Crisis* Contest Awards, *Crisis,* 1927, for "Drab Rambles," "The Young Blood Hungers," *The Purple Flower,* and *Exit—An Illusion;* literary prize for fiction, *Opportunity,* 1933, for "Tin Can."

*WRITINGS:*

*Frye Street and Environs: The Collected Works of Marita Bonner Occomy* (includes "On the Altar," "One True Love," *Exit—An Illusion,* and *The Pot-Maker*), Beacon Press, 1987.

*PLAYS*

*Exit—An Illusion* (one-act), *Crisis,* 1923.

*The Pot-Maker* (one-act), *Opportunity,* 1927.
*The Purple Flower* (one-act), *Crisis,* 1928.

*OTHER*

Contributor to *Ebony and Topaz,* edited by Charles S. Johnson, 1927, under pseudonym Joseph Maree Andrew. Work has been anthologized in *Black Theater USA,* edited by James Hatch and Ted Shine, Free Press, 1974. Also, under name Marita Bonner, contributor of short stories, essays, and plays to periodicals, including *Opportunity, A Journal of Negro Life, Black Life,* and *The Crisis: A Record of the Darker Races.*

Occomy's extant manuscripts and letters can be found at the Arthur and Elizabeth Schlesinger Library on History of Women in America, Radcliffe College, Harvard University, Cambridge, Massachusetts.

*SIDELIGHTS:* Marita Bonner Occomy's published works span nearly three decades. She launched her writing career in 1925, at the height of the Harlem Renaissance Movement, with an essay, "On Being Young—a Woman—and Colored." This piece heralds the popular Harlem Renaissance theme of race pride, even though Occomy was not among the Harlem coterie. Her plays *Exit—An Illusion* and *The Pot-Maker,* as well as her short story "Nothing New," also treat popular Harlem Renaissance themes of interracial prejudice, romantic intrigue, and generational conflicts. These pieces, together with her affiliation with the "Round Table," a literary salon held at the Washington, DC, home of poet Georgia Douglas Johnson, entitle Occomy to a place among better-known Harlem Renaissance figures such as Jessie Fauset, Zora Neale Hurston, and Nella Larsen.

Occomy published most of her fiction in the 1930s, after a three-year respite following her marriage to William Occomy. These short stories do not dwell on blacks' economic failure, a theme common to the literature of the Depression years. Instead, the stories relate the ordeals of black American women who encounter familial and communal stress. "On the Altar," for instance, depicts a manipulative grandmother who separates her newly married, light-complexioned granddaughter from her dark-skinned husband. Enmeshed in a web of entanglements from intraracial prejudice to unrelenting violence, the women foreshadow Dorothy West's Cleo in *The Living Is Easy* and Alice Walker's Sophia in *The Color Purple.* According to *Black American Literature Forum*'s Lorraine Elena Roses and Ruth Elizabeth Randolph, "the issues raised transcend time" and depict "a cry for freedom of choice."

Occomy's last short story, "One True Love," heralds the direction of her fiction in the early 1940s—toward the black woman's difficult struggle for independence and self-definition. The protagonist, Nora, a kitchen maid, shuns her male lover's overtures of marriage and enrolls in law school at night, because she believes education, not love, will bring her happiness. Naively, Nora does not realize the barriers that her race, class, and sex create in obtaining her goal. Her failure to pass her exams and the beginning stages of a terminal illness keep Nora from accomplishing her dreams. "One True Love," note Roses and Randolph, "is a comment on the American Dream that upholds the myth of unlimited opportunity and advancement.... Bonner ... recognized the systemic biases that must be countered before black women may be free."

*BIOGRAPHICAL/CRITICAL SOURCES:*

*BOOKS*

*Dictionary of Literary Biography,* Volume 51: *Afro-American Writers from the Harlem Renaissance to 1940,* Gale, 1987.
Kellner, Bruce, editor, *The Harlem Renaissance: A Historical Dictionary for the Era,* Greenwood Press, 1984.

*PERIODICALS*

*Black American Literature Forum,* spring/summer, 1987, pp. 165-183.

\*   \*   \*

## OCULI, Okello 1942-

*PERSONAL:* Born in 1942 in Dokolo County, Lang'o, Uganda. *Education:* Attended Soroti College, St. Peter's College, Tororo, and St. Mary's College, Kisubi; received B.A. from Makerere University, Kampala, Uganda.

*CAREER:* Poet, novelist, editor, and journalist. Reporter and columnist for *People* (Uganda); news editor for *Makererean.*

*WRITINGS:*

*Prostitute* (fiction), Modern African Library, 1968.
*Orphan* (fiction), East African Publishing House, 1968.
*Malak: An African Political Poem,* illustrated by V. Murray Ngoima, East African Publishing House, 1976.
*Kookolem,* Kenya Literature Bureau, 1978.
(Editor) *Health Problems in Rural and Urban Africa: A Nigerian Political Economy Health Science, Ahmadu Bello University, Department of Political Science Project, 1981,* The Department (Zaria, Nigeria), 1981.
*Food and Revolution in Africa,* Vanguard, 1986.
(Editor) *Nigerian Alternatives,* Ahmadu Bello University, Department of Political Science (Zaria), 1987.
*Political Economy of Malnutrition,* Ahmadu Bello University Press, 1987.

Also author and/or editor of other government and academic papers on health, nutrition, and economic conditions in Nigeria, beginning c. 1978.

\*   \*   \*

## ODAGA, Asenath (Bole) 1937- (Kituomba)

*PERSONAL:* Born July 5, 1937, in Rarieda, Kenya; daughter of Blasto Akumu Aum (a farmer and catechist) and Patricia Abuya Abok (a farmer); married James Charles Odaga (a manager), January 27, 1957; children: Odhiambo Odongo, Akelo, Adhiambo, Awnor. *Education:* Attended Kikuyu Teacher Training College, 1955-56; University of Nairobi, B.A. (with honors), 1974, Dip.Ed., 1974, M.A., 1981. *Religion:* Protestant. *Avocational interests:* Reading, photography, music, cooking, walking, painting, collecting traditional costumes and other artifacts of Kenyan people.

*ADDRESSES: Home*—P.O. Box 1743, Kisumu, Kenya.

*CAREER:* Church Missionary Society's Teacher Training College, Ngiya, Kenya, teacher, 1957-58; teacher at Kambare School, 1957-58; Butere Girls School, Kahamega, Kenya, teacher, 1959-60; Nyakach Girls School, Kisumu district, Kenya, headmistress, 1961-63; Kenya Railways, Nairobi, Kenya, assistant secretary, 1964; Kenya Dairy Board, Nairobi, assistant secretary, 1965-68; Kenya Library Services, Nairobi, secretary, 1968; *East African Standard,* Nairobi, advertising assistant, 1969-70; Kerr Downey and Selby Safaris, Nairobi, advertising and office manager, 1969-70; Christian Churches Educational Association, Nairobi, assistant director of curriculum and development program, 1974-75; Institute of African Studies, University of Nairobi, Nairobi, research fellow,

1976-81; free-lance researcher, writer, and editor, 1982—. Manager of Thu Tinda Bookshop, 1982—, and Lake Publishers and Enterprises, 1982—; affiliated with Odaga & Associates (consulting firm), 1984—. Chair of the board of governors of Nyakach Girls High School; member of Museum Management Committee, Kisumu, 1984—, and vice chair, 1984—.

*MEMBER:* Writers' Association of Kenya (founding member and secretary, 1978-87), Kenya Association of University Women (chair of Kisumu chapter, 1983-87), Kenya Business and Professional Women's Club (past chair), Rarieda Women's Group, Akala Women's Group (patron).

*AWARDS, HONORS:* Best Story award from *Voice of Women* magazine, 1967, for short story, "The Suitor," and unpublished play, "Three Brides in an Hour."

*WRITINGS:*

*JUVENILE*

*The Secret of Monkey the Rock,* illustrated by William Agutu, Thomas Nelson, 1966.

*Jande's Ambition,* illustrated by Adrienne Moore, East African Publishing, 1966.

*The Diamond Ring,* illustrated by A. Moore, East African Publishing, 1967.

*The Hare's Blanket and Other Tales,* illustrated by A. Moore, East African Publishing, 1967.

*The Angry Flames,* illustrated by A. Moore, East African Publishing, 1968.

*Sweets and Sugar Cane,* illustrated by Beryl Moore, East African Publishing, 1969.

*The Villager's Son,* illustrated by Shyam Varma, Heinemann Educational (London), 1971.

*Kip on the Farm,* illustrated by B. Moore, East African Publishing, 1972.

(Editor, with David Kirui and David Crippen) *God, Myself, and Others,* Evangel, 1976.

*Kip at the Coast,* illustrated by Gay Galsworthy, Evans, 1977.

*Kip Goes to the City,* illustrated by Galsworthy, Evans, 1977.

*Poko Nyar Mugumba* (title means "*Poko Mugumba's Daughter*"), illustrated by Sophia Ojienda, Foundation, 1978.

*Thu Tinda: Stories from Kenya,* Uzima, 1980.

*The Two Friends* (folktales), illustrated by Barrack Omondi, Bookwise (Nairobi), 1981.

*Kenyan Folk Tales,* illustrated by Margaret Humphries, Humphries (Caithness, Scotland), 1981.

(With Kenneth Cripwell) *Look and Write Book One,* Thomas Nelson, 1982.

(With Cripwell) *Look and Learn Book Two,* Thomas Nelson, 1982.

*My Home Book One,* Lake Publishers (Kisumu), 1983.

*Odilo Nungo Piny Kirom* (title means "Ogilo, the Arms Can't Embrace the Earth's Waist"), illustrated by H. Kiruikoske, Heinemann Educational (London), 1983.

*Nyamgondho Whod Ombare* (title means "'Nyamgondho, the Son of Ombare' and Other Stories"), illustrated by Joseph Odaga, Lake Publishers, 1986.

*Munde and His Friends,* illustrated by Peter Odaga, Lake Publishers, 1987.

*The Rag Ball,* illustrated by J. Odaga, Lake Publishers, 1987.

*Munde Goes to the Market,* illustrated by P. Odaga, Lake Publishers, 1987.

*Weche Sigendi gi Timbe Luo Moko* (title means "Stories and Some Customs of the Luo"), Lake Publishers, 1987.

*Story Time* (folktales), Lake Publishers, 1987.

*OTHER*

*Nyathini Koa e Nyuolne Nyaka Higni Adek* (title means "Your Child from Birth to Age Three"), Evangel, 1976.

"*Miaha*" (five-act play; title means "The Bride"), first produced in Nairobi, 1981.

(With S. Kichamu Akivaga) *Oral Literature: A School Certificate Course,* Heinemann Educational (Nairobi), 1982.

*Simbi Nyaima* (four-act play; title means "The Sunken Village"; first produced in Kisumu, 1982), Lake Publishers, 1983.

*Nyamgondho* (four-act play), first produced in Kisumu, 1983.

*Yesterday's Today: The Study of Oral Literature,* Lake Publishers, 1984.

*The Shade Changes* (fiction), Lake Publishers, 1984.

*The Storm,* Lake Publishers, 1985.

*Literature for Children and Young People in Kenya,* Kenya Literature Bureau (Nairobi), 1985.

*Between the Years* (fiction), Lake Publishers, 1987.

*A Bridge in Time* (fiction), Lake Publishers, 1987.

*The Silver Cup* (fiction), Lake Publishers, 1987.

*Riana's Choice* (short stories), Lake Publishers, 1987.

*A Taste of Life,* Lake Publishers, 1988.

*Love Potion and Other Stories,* Lake Publishers, 1988.

*A Reed on the Roof, Block Ten, with Other Stories,* Lake Publishers, 1988.

Member of editorial committee of Western Kenya branch of Wildlife Society. Contributor, sometimes under the name Kituomba, to periodicals, including *Women's Mirror* and *Viva.*

*WORK IN PROGRESS:* A Luo-English, English-Luo dictionary; a book on Juogi beliefs among the Abasuba of Rusinga Island; a book on Luo oral literature.

*SIDELIGHTS:* Asenath Odaga commented: "I'm basically a storyteller to both children and adults. And like any other artist, I strive to attain perfection through deeper perception and clear insights into the experiences of life and daily events that go on around me, because it's from some of these common banalities that I draw and fashion some of my writing. I realize that together with all those who possess this creative ability, we have in a small way, in all humility, become cocreators with our gods. In the foregoing realization lies my sensitivity (akin to religion) and profound feelings against injustices meted on others through negation of some of the universal human values on account of race (as in the case in South Africa): creed, gender, and culture.

"What I'm driving at is that art (literature) has several functions apart from providing entertainment. At least this has always been the case in most African societies where art, including literature, was never indulged in just for art's sake—or purely for its aesthetic and entertainment values—but always had several other functions in society."

*   *   *

## ODEKU, Emmanuel Latunde   1927-

*PERSONAL:* Born June 29, 1927, in Awe, Nigeria; son of Daniel Lapido and Regina Eyinade Folowiyo (Adensina) Odeku; married Katherine Jille Adcock, 1971; children: Lenora Folawiyo, Peter Glenn, Alan John Lapapo. *Education:* Howard University, B.S. (summa cum laude), 1950, M.D., 1954; University of Michigan, proficiency certificate neurosurgery, 1960.

*ADDRESSES: Home*—University of Ibadan Campus, Ibadan, Nigeria.

*CAREER:* Howard University College of Medicine, Washington, DC, instructor in neuroanatomy and neurosurgery, 1961-62; University of Ibadan, Ibadan, Nigeria, member of faculty, 1962—, professor of neurosurgery and dean of the Faculty of Medicine, 1968-70, head of surgery department, 1969-71. University College Hospital, Ibadan, member of board of management, 1968-70. Western State, Nigeria, member of medical advisory board, 1970—.

*MEMBER:* Kappa Pi.

*AWARDS, HONORS:* Fellow A.C.S., Association of Surgeons of West Africa, International College of Surgeons, Medical Council in Surgery, Nigeria.

*WRITINGS:*

*POETRY*

*Twilight Out of the Night,* 1964.
*Whispers from the Night,* 1969.

## OFFORD, Carl Ruthven   1910-

*PERSONAL:* Born April 10, 1910, in Trinidad, West Indies; immigrated to United States in 1929; son of George (a machinist) and Ottie Simmonds (a socialite) Offord. *Education:* Studied writing, drama, and painting at the New School for Social Research, New York.

*CAREER:* Novelist, newspaper publisher, businessman, painter. Staff writer, *Crusader News,* late 1930s; founder of *Black American,* New York City, 1961. Directed Black American Film Festival, 1977. *Military service:* U.S. Army, 1943-45, first sergeant.

*WRITINGS:*

*BOOKS*

*The White Face,* McBride, 1943.
*The Naked Fear,* Ace Books, 1954.

Also contributor to anthologies, including *Cross Section: A Collection of New American Writing,* edited by Edwin Seaver, Fischer, 1944; and *Black Hands on a White Face,* edited by Whit Burnett, Mead, 1971. Contributor to periodicals, including *Story* and *Masses and Mainstream.*

*SIDELIGHTS:* In his two novels and numerous short stories, Carl Ruthven Offord created dramatic accounts of characters caught up in violence and turmoil. Perhaps best known for his novel, *The White Face,* Offord also wrote short stories and worked as a newspaper editor and publisher.

Knowing he wanted to be a writer by age 11, Offord left school in his native Trinidad and read all he could while working at various jobs. At age 19, he left the West Indies to pursue his dream in New York. He dabbled in theater, intending first to be a playwright. But he found some of the characters he had to play demeaning, and he left the small acting company disillusioned.

Offord studied drama and writing, along with painting, at the School for Social Research, and he began writing for *Crusader News,* a weekly news digest for black audiences. In his spare time he completed his first novel, *The White Face,* which was published in 1943.

*The White Face* is the story of Chris and Nella Woods, a black couple who leave their Georgia home for New York after Chris beats his cruel white employer. Instead of relief, the couple finds danger in Fascist agitators who exploit the oppressed black community in Harlem and foment hatred of Jews. While Nella finds employment with a Jewish family, Chris is taken by the ideas of a charismatic black Fascist. Chris succumbs to the pressures all around him and severely beats the son of Nella's employers. Chris is arrested, and while he is in prison, he learns that his employer in Georgia has died. Nella is able to obtain some legal help for her husband, but with "his hate piled up into a crunching volcano," she cannot prevent his tragic end.

Critics gave qualified praise to *The White Face.* Rose Field, reviewing the work in the *New York Times,* stated that "in spite of its weaknesses, Offord's story in its exploration of racial psychology, with its serious national implications, makes a profound impression." *Book Week* critic Josephine Herbst observed, "Carl Offord has written a powerful story of one Negro's fate. It is a challenging document, enriched by a genuine understanding of all the vital issues involved."

Offord's background in journalism may have lent credibility to the plot intricacies of *The White Face.* But his second novel, *The Naked Fear,* went without critical review. It is the story of a destructive white couple, who steals and harbors, and eventually tries to kill, a baby.

Between his two novels, Offord had served in the Army during the Second World War, started and lost several businesses, and sold freelance articles and short stories. He ultimately returned to journalism, founding the weekly newspaper *Black American* in 1961. He has worked for black causes, including the United Black Appeal, a relief agency for troubled African nations. Offord also directed, in 1977, the first Black American Film Festival. Although his success as a novelist was limited, a distinguished and multifaceted career marks Offord's life.

*BIOGRAPHICAL/CRITICAL SOURCES:*

*BOOKS*

*Dictionary of Literary Biography,* Volume 76: *Afro-American Writers, 1940-1955,* 1988, pp. 130-133.

*PERIODICALS*

*Book Week,* May 9, 1943, p. 4.
*Library Journal,* May 1, 1943, p. 363.
*Nation,* June 15, 1943, p. 816.
*New Republic,* May 31, 1943, p. 741.
*New York Times,* May 23, 1943, p. 12.

\*     \*     \*

## OGALI, Ogali A(gu)   1931-

*PERSONAL:* Born in 1931 in Umuafia, Iboland, Nigeria.

*CAREER:* Playwright and fiction writer, 1956—. Worked at United Africa Company, Ltd., and Nigerian Railway Corporation.

*WRITINGS:*

*PLAYS*

*Veronica, My Daughter,* Zik Enterprises, 1956.
*Adelabu,* 1958.
*Mr. Rabbit Is Dead,* 1958.
*Patrice Lumumba,* 1961.
*The Ghost of Lumumba,* 1961.
*Veronica, My Daughter and Other Onitsha Plays and Stories,* Three Continents Press, 1980.

*FICTION*

*Long, Long Ago,* Omaliko and Sons, 1957.
*Smile Awhile,* Zike Enterprises Ltd., 1957.
*Okeke the Magician,* 1958.
*Eddy, the Coal-city Boy,* 1959.
*Caroline the One Guinea Girl,* (no publisher), 1960, Goodwill Press and Bookshop, 1965.
*Coal City,* Fourth Dimension Publishers, 1977.

*BIOGRAPHICAL/CRITICAL SOURCES:*

*PERIODICALS*

*World Literature Today,* winter, 1981, p. 166.

\*     \*     \*

## OGBAA, Kalu   1945-

*PERSONAL:* Born August 21, 1945, in Umuchiakuma, Nigeria; son of Stephen Ogbaa and Ogonnaya Ogbaa (a farmer); married Clara Nwankwo (a librarian), April 5, 1975; children: Ikenna, Ndubuisi, Emeka, Nneka, Enyinna, Kelechi. *Education:* University of Nigeria, Nsukka, B.A. (with honors), 1973; Ohio State University, M.A., 1977; University of Texas, Ph.D., 1981. *Politics:* None. *Religion:* Christian.

*ADDRESSES: Home*—1816 Ella T. Grasso Blvd., New Haven, CT 06515. *Office*—Department of English, Southern Connecticut State University, 501 Crescent St., New Haven, CT 06515.

*CAREER:* Alvan Ikoku College of Education, Nigeria, assistant lecturer, 1974-76; University of Texas, Austin, assistant instructor of English, 1978-81, lecturer in English, 1981; Imo

State University, Nigeria, assistant professor, 1982-85, associate professor of English, 1985-89, acting director, Division of General Studies, 1986-89; Oral Roberts University, visiting associate professor of English, 1989-90; Clark Atlanta University, visiting associate professor of English, 1990-92; Southern Connecticut State University, New Haven, associate professor of English, 1992—.

*AWARDS, HONORS:* Scholars Honor Society of *Phi Kappa Phi,* Ohio State University Chapter, nominated member, 1978; Postgraduate Scholarship Award, from Imo State University of Nigeria and from Federal Government of Nigeria, both 1980; nominated Fellow of the International Biographical Association and International Man of the Year, both 1993, by International Biographical Centre (England).

*WRITINGS:*

*Gods, Oracles and Divination: Folkways in Chinua Achebe's Novels,* Africa World Press, 1992.
(Editor) *The Gong and the Flute: Essays in Honour of Michael Echeruo,* in press.

Contributor to books, including *English and the Nigerian Situation,* Department of English and Literary Studies Publication, 1986; and *African Literature: Links and Challenges,* edited by Emenyonu and Vivekananda, [Stockholm, Sweden].

Contributor of articles and reviews to numerous scholarly journals, including *Canadian Journal of African Studies, Caribbean Quarterly, College Language Association Journal, Commonwealth Quarterly, Nigeria Magazine,* and *World Literature Today.*

*WORK IN PROGRESS:* Researching literary feminism in Africa, and the effects of racism, colonialism, and imperialism in Africana literature; monograph entitled *The Igbo of Nigeria* for the Rosen Publishing group's new multi-volume reference project, "The Library of African Peoples."

*SIDELIGHTS:* Kalu Ogbaa commented: "I am an associate professor of English, which implies that I teach literary criticism of African, African American, and American literature. I began writing critical essays and books when I noticed that there were misreadings of African and African American writings by readers who were unfamiliar with the black cultures and folklore that the texts explored. My intention was to provide such 'uninformed' readers with the information that they needed to appreciate Africana culture through its literatures. From the reviews and general critical comments on my writing, I think I am succeeding.

"My first book, *Gods, Oracles and Divination: Folkways in Chinua Achebe's Novels,* was written to explain the 'lgbo

folkways' in Achebe's novels, which are read all over the world. Each of his first four novels that my book examines has sold over three million copies; and my book is now being used by many universities in Africa, America, and Europe. This is because Achebe is Africa's foremost novelist. I have a forthcoming book titled *The Gong and the Flute,* which is about African literature and language.

"Achebe himself influenced me, for when other African writers were imitating European writers, he wrote about Africa and her culture and civilization. So, I am his critical interpreter. Also, I am doing critical interpreting in the area of African American literature.

"I am essentially a teacher. Writing of critical essays and books is, therefore, a secondary career—evidence of the research I do in order to teach effectively and maintain currency in my field.

"My advice to aspirant writers is that they should think of the contributions they want to make towards human culture and civilization in a particular area of knowledge before they start writing. Also, they have to have a means of financial support before they begin writing, for writing costs a lot of money and time."

*BIOGRAPHICAL/CRITICAL SOURCES:*

*PERIODICALS*

*Choice,* November, 1992, p. 191.

\* \* \*

## OGOT, Grace 1930-

*PERSONAL:* Birthname, Grace Emily Akinyi; born May 15, 1930, in Butere, Central Nyanza, Kenya; married Bethwell Allan Ogot (a historian), 1959. *Education:* Attended Nursing Training Hospital, 1949-53; additional training at Saint Thomas' Hospital and the British Hospital for Mothers and Babies, 1955-58. *Religion:* Christian.

*CAREER:* British Broadcasting Company Africa Service, London, England, broadcaster, scriptwriter, and editor, 1959-61; Makerere University College, Uganda, nursing sister in charge of student health services, 1963-64; delegate, United Nations General Assembly, 1975; appointed member of parliament, 1983 (resigned position to successfully become an elected member, 1985). Broadcaster for weekly radio program, Voice of Kenya, Nairobi; public relations officer, Air India Corporation of East Africa.

*MEMBER:* Writers' Association of Kenya (founding chairperson).

*WRITINGS:*

*The Promised Land* (novel), East African Publishing House, 1966.
*Land without Thunder* (short story collection), East African Publishing House, 1968.
*The Other Woman: Selected Short Stories,* Transafrica, 1976.
*The Island of Tears* (short story collection), Uzima, 1980.
*The Graduate* (novella), Uzima, 1980.
*Miaha* (Luo myth) Heinemann, 1983, translation published as *The Strange Bride,* Heinemann Kenya, 1989.

Also contributor to periodicals, including *Black Orpheus, Transition,* and *East African Journal.*

*ADAPTATIONS: Simbi Nyaima* was adapted as a play by Asenath B. Odaga, and produced at the Reunion Cultural Group Theatre, in Kisumu, Kenya, 1982; *In the Beginning* was adapted as a play by Ms. Ogot's son, Michael Ogot, in Nairobi, 1983.

*SIDELIGHTS:* Influenced by the folktales of her heritage, biblical readings, and various storybooks, Grace Ogot's writing is mainly devoted to relating the native Luo folklore to the younger generations of Kenya. She uses the day-to-day life experiences of both herself and those whom she has known to retell the stories she remembers from her childhood. Although she is quite aware of the changes in society, Ogot continues to show a strong appreciation for the Luo traditions and beliefs.

Ogot's marriage to historian Bethwell Allan Ogot granted her an "extra benefit" as she was privy to his historical knowledge of the people of Kenya. It is with his assistance that she acquired enough facts to write her book and manuscript, *In the Beginning* and *Simbi Nyaima,* respectively. The adaptation of these works as plays allowed the Luo folktales to be heard and seen by a wider audience.

Ogot's fascination with the tragic aspects of Kenyan history gives her stories a poignant view of the rural and urban society of Kenya. Her belief is that there are typically more tragic elements than comic ones in the lives of all people, regardless of their social standing, thus allowing her works to relate to all classes of people in her native land. This belief is evident in an array of short stories published in *Land without Thunder, The Other Woman,* and *The Island of Tears.* Several of Ogot's stories in *The Promised Land* and *Land without Thunder* were strongly influenced by her brief career as a nurse; Brenda F. Berrian reports in the *Dictionary of Literary Biography* that Ogot once told Bernth Lindfors, "Stories of

African traditional medicine and of the medicine man against the background of modern science and medicine fascinated me."

Through her vast and varied career and close connections to the customs, superstitions, and history of her Kenyan heritage, Ogot has created a name for herself as an African writer. According to Berrian, "one must admire her energy, persistence, and pioneering spirit. She has made her distinctive mark on Kenyan literature and politics."

*BIOGRAPHICAL/CRITICAL SOURCES:*

BOOKS

*Dictionary of Literary Biography,* Volume 125: *Twentieth-Century Caribbean and Black African Writers, Second Series,* Gale, 1993.

\*   \*   \*

## OGUNYEMI, Wale   1939-

*PERSONAL:* Born 1939 (some sources say 1932), in Yoruba country, Western Nigeria.

*CAREER:* Playwright and scholar.

*AWARDS, HONORS:* Top prize for new work, *African Arts,* 1971, for the screenplay *The Vow.*

*WRITINGS:*

PLAYS

*Be Mighty, Be Mine, Nigeria Magazine,* 1968.
*Aare Akogun* (adaptation of *Macbeth*), *Nigeria Magazine,* 1969.
*Ijaye War, A Historic Drama,* Orison Acting Editions, 1970.
*Eshu Elegbara* (based on the Yoruba creation myth "The coming to the world of the gods and goddesses"), Orison Acting Editions, 1970.
*Kiriji* (historic drama based on Ekita Parapo War in the nineteenth century), 1976.
*The Divorce,* Onibonoje Press, 1977.

OTHER

Also author of unpublished screenplay *The Vow.* Contributor to *Three Nigerian Plays,* with introduction and notes by Ulli Beier, Longmans, 1967.

## OKPARA, Mzee Lasana
### See HORD, Frederick (Lee)

\*   \*   \*

## OKRI, Ben 1959-

*PERSONAL:* Born in 1959 in Minna, Nigeria. *Education:* Attended Urhobo College, Warri, Nigeria, and the University of Essex, England.

*ADDRESSES:* c/o Jonathan Cape, 20 Vauxhall Bridge Rd., London SW1V 25A, England.

*CAREER:* Writer. Visiting Fellow at Trinity College, Cambridge, England. Has worked as a journalist and as a poetry editor for *West Africa* magazine.

*AWARDS, HONORS:* Commonwealth Writers' Prize for Africa; *Paris Review* Aga Khan prize for fiction; Booker Prize for fiction, 1991, for *The Famished Road.*

*WRITINGS:*

*Flowers and Shadows* (novel), Longman, 1980.
*The Landscapes Within* (novel), Longman, 1981.
*Incidents at the Shrine* (short stories), Heinemann, 1986.
*Stars of the New Curfew* (short stories), Secker & Warburg, 1988, Viking, 1989.
*The Famished Road* (novel), Cape, 1991, Doubleday, 1992.
(Contributor) *The Heinemann Book of Contemporary African Short Stories,* edited by Chinua Achebe, Heinemann, 1992.
(Contributor) *So Very English,* edited by Marsha Rowe, Consortium, 1992.

*WORK IN PROGRESS: An African Elegy,* a volume of poems.

*SIDELIGHTS:* Novelist and short story writer Ben Okri uses nightmarish imagery and surrealist contortions of reality to portray the bizarre social and political conditions inside his native Nigeria. Critics have associated Okri's techniques with those practiced by magic realists, a school of writers who incorporate supernatural elements into otherwise realistic settings. Michiko Kakutani, reviewing *Stars of the New Curfew* for the *New York Times,* commented that Okri's Africa "seems like a continent dreamed up, in tandem, by Hieronymus Bosch and Jorge Luis Borges—a land where history has quite literally become a nightmare." However, Okri insists that the supernatural elements in works such as *Incidents at the Shrine, Stars of the New Curfew,* and *The Famished Road* are realistic representations of the Nigerian experience, demonstrating the continuity between the realistic and mystical realms of experience that exists for Nigerians.

Much of Okri's work is devoted to describing the political and social chaos inside Nigeria, a country that has not had a stable government for nearly thirty years. The pictures he creates are dark and often violent. In his review of *Incidents at the Shrine* for the London *Observer,* Anthony Thwaite called Okri "an obsessive cataloguer of sweat, phlegm, ordure and vomit," and Kakutani noted that the author's characters "live in a state of suspended animation, their private lives overshadowed by political atrocities, whatever ideals they might have had eroded by the demands of day-to-day survival." The narrator of the title story of *Stars of the New Curfew* is a vagabond medicine salesman whose cures often backfire, sending people to violent, grisly deaths. He is constantly on the run from his victims, but can not outrun his visions. An unnamed character in the story "Worlds That Flourish," also in *Stars of the New Curfew,* flees a hellish city only to find himself in a more literal hell, where some people have wings but can not fly, others have feet that face backward, and an old neighbor appears with three eyes. Susan Cronje, who called the book "an important comment on Nigerian society" in her review for *New Statesman & Society,* said that "Okri's writing is suffused with helpless anger at the alienation of Nigerian society, the corruption not only of the rulers but also of the ruled who seem to connive at their own oppression."

Okri's 1991 novel, *The Famished Road,* which received England's prestigious Booker Prize, further explores the Nigerian dilemma. Charles R. Larson, writing in *World & I,* remarked that "the power of Ben Okri's magnificent novel is that it encapsulates a critical stage in the history of a nation ... by chronicling one character's quest for freedom and individuation." *The Famished Road's* main character is Azaro, an *abiku* child torn between the spirit and natural world. His struggle to free himself from the spirit realm is paralleled by his father's immersion into politics to fight the oppression of the poor. By the novel's end, Azaro recognizes the similarities between the nation and the *abiku;* each is forced to make sacrifices to reach maturity and a new state of being. *Detroit Free Press* contributor John Gallagher deemed the work "a majestically difficult novel that may join the ranks of greatness." In her appraisal for the London *Observer,* Linda Grant commented, "Okri's gift is to present a world view from inside a belief system."

Okri explores the tensions between hope and despair in language that is spare and simple. Of his writing in *Incidents at the Shrine,* Sara Maitland said in *New Statesman & Society* that "sentence by sentence he turns in beautiful, strong prose, dense with lyricism and metaphor, skipping elegantly along the edge of surrealism and never collapsing into it." Maureen Freely, who reviewed *Stars of the New Curfew* for the London *Observer,* commented: "There are many novelists who write as well as Okri, many who share his gift for recreating the texture of everyday life, many who can cut through the surface to expose, as he does, the myths our elders and betters use to keep us in our place. There are very few novelists who can do all three. The fact that Ben Okri has done so in short stories, without ever losing his balance, his humour, or his edge, makes his accomplishment all the more exceptional."

*BIOGRAPHICAL/CRITICAL SOURCES:*

*PERIODICALS*

*Christian Science Monitor,* November 23, 1987.
*Detroit Free Press,* August 30, 1992, p. 9P.
*London Times,* July 24, 1986.
*Los Angeles Times Book Review,* September 24, 1989, pp. 3, 13.
*New Statesman & Society,* May 9, 1986, p. 35; July 13, 1986, p. 27; July 25, 1986, p. 30; October 17, 1986, p. 36; July 29, 1988, pp. 43-44; March 22, 1991, p. 44.
*New York Times,* July 28, 1989.
*New York Times Book Review,* August 13, 1989, p. 12.
*Observer* (London), July 10, 1988, p. 42; October 27, 1991, p. 61.
*Time,* June 19, 1989.
*Times Literary Supplement,* August 8, 1986, p. 863; August 5-11, 1988, p. 857; April 19, 1991, p. 22.
*Tribune Books* (Chicago), July 16, 1989, p. 6.
*Washington Post,* August 7, 1989.
*World & I,* March 1992, pp. 383-387.
*World Literature Today,* spring, 1990, p. 349.

\* \* \*

## OLISAH, Sunday Okenwa 1936-1964
### (The Strong Man of the Pen, The Master of Life)

*PERSONAL:* Born 1936 in Ibo country, eastern Nigeria.

*CAREER:* Fiction writer, playwright, biographer, and pamphleteer. Principal of Lisabi Grammar School in Aeokuta, Western Nigeria.

*WRITINGS:*

Author of numerous novelettes or "chapbooks" and pamphlets published in and around Onitsha, Nigeria, in the 1950s and 1960s, including *The World Is Hard,* 1957; *Drunkards Believe Bar as Heaven,* Chinyelu Printing Press; (under pseud-

onym The Strong Man of the Pen) *How to Live Bachelor's Life and Girl's Life without Much Mistakes,* New Era Printers; *How to Live Better Life and Help Yourself,* Okenwa Publications; *Money Palaver,* 1960; *The Story about Mammy-Water, Dangerous Man Vagabond versus Princess,* 1960; *Half-Educated Messenger,* 1960; *Elizabeth My Lover,* early 1960s, reprinted by Kraus Reprint; *Money Hard to Get But Easy to Spend,* J.O. Nnadozie, 1965(?); *Life Turns Man Up and Down, Money and Girls Turn Man Up and Down,* 1963(?); (under pseudonym The Master of Life) *My Wife: No Condition Is Permanent,* N. Njoku, 1964(?); *The Ibo Native Law and Custom,* New Era Press; *The Life of the Prison Yard,* 1966.

Also author of a play, *My Seven Daughters Are after Young Boys,* and biographies, *The Life Story and the Death of Mr. Lumumba,* 1964, and *Mr. Lumumba and President Kasavubu in Congo Politics.*

*BIOGRAPHICAL/CRITICAL SOURCES:*

*BOOKS*

Herdeck, Donald E., *African Authors: A Companion to Black African Writing,* Volume 1: *1300-1973,* Black Orpheus Press, 1973.

\* \* \*

## OMOTOSO, Kole 1943-

*PERSONAL:* Born April 21, 1943, in Akure, Nigeria; married; children: three. *Education:* Attended King's College, Lagos; University of Ibadan, B.A., 1968; University of Edinburgh, Ph.D., 1972.

*CAREER:* Ibadan University, Ibadan, Oye, Nigeria, lecturer, 1972-76; University of Ife, Ife, Nigeria, professor, beginning c. 1976.

*MEMBER:* Association of Nigerian Authors (founder; national secretary, 1981-84; president, 1986-87).

*WRITINGS:*

*Notes, Q & A on Peter Edwards' West African Narrative,* Onibonoje, 1968.
*Pitched against the Gods* (stage play), first produced at Deen Playhouse, Ikare, Nigeria, 1969.
*The Edifice,* Heinemann, 1971.
*The Combat,* Heinemann, 1972.
*Miracles and Other Stories,* Onibonoje, 1973, revised, 1978.

*Fella's Choice,* Ethiope, 1974.

*Sacrifice,* Onibonoje, 1974, revised, 1978.

*The Curse,* New Horn, 1976.

*The Scales,* Onibonoje, 1976.

(Coeditor) *The Indigenous for National Development,* Onibonoje, 1976.

*Shadows in the Horizon,* Omotoso/Sketch, 1977.

*Kole Omotoso of Nigeria* (recording), Voice of America, 1978.

*To Borrow a Wandering Leaf,* Olaiya Fagbamigbe, 1979.

*The Form of the African Novel,* Olaiya Fagbamigbe, 1979, revised edition, McQuick, 1986.

*Memories of Our Recent Boom,* Longman, 1982.

*The Theatrical into Theatre: A Study of the Drama and Theatre of the English-Speaking Caribbean,* New Beacon, 1982.

*A Feast in the Time of Plague,* Dramatic Arts/Unife, 1983.

*The Girl Sunshine,* Dramatic Arts/Unife, 1983.

*The Last Competition* (stage play), first produced at National Theatre, Lagos, 1983.

*All This Must Be Seen,* Progress, 1986.

*Just before Dawn,* Spectrum, 1988.

Contributor to periodicals and newspapers, including Lagos *Sunday Times, Top Life,* Lagos *Sunday Concord Okike,* and *Index on Censorship.*

*SIDELIGHTS:* Kole Omotoso is a prominent Nigerian writer who writes both to offer answers to Nigeria's problems as well as to entertain. Omotoso's belief that the artist must help lead the way to a better life for the common people is reflected in his writing. "Art for art's sake is intellectual crap," Omotoso told J. B. Alston in *Yoruba Drama in English,* "Whereas if you are committed to communicating with everyone who reads your works, that's a very basic and responsible kind of commitment."

Omotoso, the nephew of Yoruba author Olaiya Fagbamigbe, began writing in primary school. His first influences were family folktales, and his first audience his schoolmates. By the time he was in secondary school, Omotoso began to be published, but in English, rather than his native Yoruba. Later, when he went to Great Britain to study Arabic, the racism he experienced there provided the inspiration for his first novel. With the publication of *The Edifice,* Omotoso's career blossomed.

He wrote essays, plays, short stories, and novels. Among them was *Miracles and Other Stories,* a collection that focused on the plight of poor children in Nigeria. During his career, the author's work has become increasingly politicized. The content of his novels reflects Omotoso's concern with the future

of his homeland. He was strongly influenced by the shaky political climate of Nigeria, a country where military rule predominates. Omotoso struggled against the limitations of that situation.

In 1977, the author released his play *Shadows in the Horizon* privately after publishers deemed it too controversial. The piece was successful; ultimately, it was translated into Russian. Like other authors, including the well-known playwright Wole Soyinka, whom Omotoso calls his major influence, African themes are important in his work. F. Odun Balogun points out in the *Dictionary of Literary Biography* that in *Fella's Choice* and another mystery-adventure work, the 1976 book *The Scales,* Omotoso makes communalism the basis for heroism, rather than Western individualism.

Omotoso's fiction reflects a preoccupation with the future of the common folk of one's country. In *Yoruba Drama in English* Omotoso is quoted as saying that "the conscious artist can contribute towards building a new mode of life. Anything he does—the way he presents his characters, the way he lives his own life—is likely to influence what other people are going to do."

*BIOGRAPHICAL/CRITICAL SOURCES:*

*BOOKS*

Agetua, John, *Interviews with Six Nigerian Writers,* Bendel Newspapers Corporation, 1974, pp. 9-16.

Alston, J. B., *Yoruba Drama in English,* Edwin Mellen, 1989, pp. 107-115.

*Dictionary of Literary Biography:* Volume 125, *Twentieth Century Caribbean and Black-African Writers, Second Series,* Gale, 1993.

Nazareth, Peter, *The Third World Writer,* Kenya Literature Bureau, 1978, pp. 71-86.

Nichols, Lee, *Conversations with African Writers,* Voice of America, 1981, pp. 218-229.

*PERIODICALS*

*African Book Publishing Record,* Number 2, 1976, pp. 12-14.

*Commonwealth Essays and Studies,* autumn, 1984, pp. 36-50.

*Cultural Events in Africa,* Number 103, 1973, pp. 2-12.

*Daily Times* (Lagos), March 12, 1974, p. 12.

*Guardian* (Lagos), June 9, 1986, p. 10.

*Journal of Commonwealth Literature,* Volume 25, number 1, 1990, pp. 98-108.

*Notre Librairie,* Volume 98, July-September, 1989, pp. 68-70.

*Theatre Research International,* autumn, 1982, pp. 235-244.

*World Literature Written in English,* April, 1977, pp. 39-53.

## OPITZ, May
### See AYIM, May

\* \* \*

## OSOFISAN, Femi 1946-
### (Okinba Launko)

*PERSONAL:* Original name, Babafemi Adeyemi Osofisan; born June 16, 1946, in Erunwon, Nigeria. *Education:* Attended Government College, Ibadan, c. 1960s; University of Dakar, D.E.S., 1968; University of Ibadan, B.A., 1969, Ph.D., 1974. Also attended University of Paris III, c. 1973.

*CAREER:* Teacher in a secondary school, c. 1969; University of Ibadan, Ibadan, Nigeria, faculty member, became senior lecturer in theater arts, 1973—; University of Benin, Benin, Nigeria, chairman of the theater arts department, beginning in 1980s. *The Guardian,* Lagos, Nigeria, founding member of editorial board, c. 1980s. Visiting professor at institutions, including University of Pennsylvania, Philadelphia, 1983, and University of Ife, Nigeria, 1985-86.

*MEMBER:* Association of Nigerian Authors (president, 1989-90).

*AWARDS, HONORS:* Association of Nigerian Authors, literature prize, 1983, for *Morountodun,* and poetry prize, 1987, for *Minted Coins.*

*WRITINGS:*

*Kolera Kolej* (novel), New Horn, 1975.
*Beyond Translation: A Comparatist Look at Tragic Paradigms and the Dramaturgy of Ola Rotimi and Wole Soyinka,* UniversityoF Ife, 1986.
*Wonderland and Orality of Prose: A Comparative Study of Rabelais, Joyce and Tutuola,* University of Ife, 1986.
(As Okinba Launko) *Minted Coins* (poetry), Heinemann, 1987.
(As Launko) *Cordelia* (novella), Malthouse, 1989.

*PLAYS, AND DIRECTOR*

*Odudwa, Don't Go!,* produced in Ibadan, Nigeria, 1967.
*You Have Lost Your Fine Face,* produced at University of Ibadan Theatre, 1969.
*A Restless Run of Locusts* (produced in Akure, Nigeria, 1970), Onibonoje, 1975.
*The Chattering and the Song* (produced at University of Ibadan Theatre, 1976), Ibadan University Press, 1977.
*Who's Afraid of Solarin* (produced at University of Ibadan Theatre, 1977), Scholars Press, 1978.

*Once upon Four Robbers* (produced at University of Ibadan Theatre, 1978), BIO Educational Services, 1980.
*Farewell to a Cannibal Rage* (produced at University of Ibadan Theatre, 1978, revised version produced at University of Benin Theatre, Benin City, Nigeria, 1984), Evans, 1986.
*Morountodun,* produced at University of Ibadan Theatre, 1979, revised version produced by Kakaun Sela Kompany, Ibadan, 1980.
*Birthdays Are Not for Dying* (produced at University of Ibadan Theatre, 1980), Evans, 1987.
*The Oriki of a Grasshopper,* produced at University of Ibadan Theatre, 1981, revised version produced at University of Benin Theatre, 1985.
*No More the Wasted Breed,* produced in Ibadan, 1982.
*Midnight Hotel* (produced by Kakaun Sela Kompany, 1982), Evans, 1986.
*Altine's Wrath,* produced at University of Benin Theatre, 1984.
*Esu and the Vagabond Minstrels* (produced at University of Benin Theatre, 1984, revised version produced at University of Ife Theatre, Ife, Nigeria, 1986), New Horn, 1987.
*Another Raft* (produced at University of Ibadan Theatre, 1987), Malthouse, 1988.
*Aringindin and the Night Watchmen* (produced at University of Ibadan Theatre, 1988), Heinemann, 1991.
*Yungba-Yungba and the Dance Concert,* produced at University of Ibadan Theatre, 1990.
*The Engagement,* produced at African Studies Association, 1991.

*COLLECTIONS OF PLAYS*

*Morountodun and Other Plays* (contains *Morountodun, No More the Wasted Breed,* and *Red Is the Freedom Road*), Longman, 1982.
*Two One-Act Plays* (contains *The Oriki of a Grasshopper* and *Altine's Wrath*), New Horn, 1986.
*Birthdays Are Not for Dying and Other Plays* (contains *Birthdays Are Not for Dying, Fires Burn and Die Hard,* and *The Inspector and the Hero*), Malthouse, 1990.

*SCREENPLAYS*

*The Visitors* (television series), BCOS-TV, Ibadan, 1982.
*No More the Wasted Breed,* BCOS-TV, 1982.

*OTHER*

Contributor of poetry to anthologies, including *Don't Let Him Die,* edited by Chinua Achebe and Dubem Okafor, Fourth Dimension, 1978; contributor of poetry to periodicals, including *Opon Ifa;* contributor of articles to anthologies, including *Theatre in Africa,* edited by Oyin Ogunba, and Abiola Irele,

University of Ibadan Press, 1978, and *West African Studies in Modern Language Teaching and Research,* edited by Ayo Banjo, Conrad-Benedict Brann, and Henri Evans, National Language Center, 1981; contributor of articles to journals, including *Afriscope, Ch'indaba,* and *African Theatre Review;* contributor or articles and columns to the Lagos *Guardian.*

*SIDELIGHTS:* The writings of Femi Osofisan are devoted to exposing to audiences the various social and political problems facing the author's native Nigeria. Osofisan has achieved renown for fusing a populist critique of Nigerian society with avant-garde theater, combining contemporary themes with traditional African performance techniques. Osofisan is primarily concerned with freedom—not just political, but religious and cultural liberties, as well—and the contradictions that exist within a former colonial society torn by strife and corruption.

Early struggles with poverty helped to define Osofisan's ideological sympathy with Nigeria's poor and downtrodden. Three months after Osofisan was born in Erunwon, a Yoruba farming village, his father died, and he became dependent upon numerous relatives for his upbringing and the payment of his school fees. Overshadowing his youth was Nigeria's Biafran civil war and the military coups that shook the Nigerian government during its first decade of independence. Osofisan started writing stories and poems years before attending the University of Ibadan on a scholarship, where he also studied acting and directing for the theater and television. Strongly influenced by the chaotic political climate in Nigeria, Osofisan completed his first published play, *A Restless Run of Locusts,* at the University of Ibadan.

*A Restless Run of Locusts* pits a young reformer against a corrupt tribal chief in Yorubaland. Both die at the end of the play, leaving women to mourn them. The theme of a positive force canceling out a negative one but being destroyed in the process became increasingly common in Osofisan's work. Another early play—*Red is the Freedom Road*—depicts the rise of Akanji, a Yoruba warrior who must give the appearance of betraying his own people to restore their liberty. Although Akanji ultimately launches a successful counterattack against the oppressors, the resulting violence dashes any hopes for the future.

In *Kolera Kolej,* a surrealistic novel Osofisan finished in Paris (where he briefly attended graduate school), a poet stands accused by his muse for refusing to live up to the vitality of his beautiful verses. Like Osofisan's earlier plays, the book deals with the challenge—and in the first version of the text, the futility—of creating a good society. The plot is set at a college that has been granted independence from the state after a quarantine; when the poet, inspired to action by the muse figure, attempts to speak out against the charismatic leader of

the new realm, he is killed in a coup. "At the conclusion an illusionary hope is rekindled, and the people can 'begin to die again with renewed fervor'," remarked Sandra L. Richards in the *Dictionary of Literary Biography.* In response to the perceived pessimism in the dramatized version of *Kolera Kolej* by audiences, Osofisan added a second ending to the novel in which a plot to enslave the dissenting group fails, and the muse figure, according to Richards, "is heard welcoming the imprisoned back to freedom."

Osofisan continued to write plays, and his subsequent work showed even further influences of surrealism. Nonetheless, the struggle between good and evil remains an important theme in his work. His 1978 play *Once upon Four Robbers,* for example, focuses on the controversy surrounding public executions. In this drama a band of thieves are given a magic charm which will ease their victims' suspicions; however, they must steal from the rich (in public places) and not kill anyone. Eventually, the thieves are caught when they start to argue amongst themselves. Just before they are to be executed, the play's narrator stops the action—the audience must decide if the thieves are to be executed or to receive freedom. If the audience chooses death, it is forced to watch the criminals dying in agony. On the other hand, a verdict of freedom will cause the audience themselves to become victims of the liberated robbers.

Plays like *Once upon Four Robbers* characterize Osofisan's interest in social critique. In 1982, however, Osofisan was able to contribute to a medium other than the stage and the novel when he became a founding member of the board of the Lagos *Guardian.* As a columnist for the independent newspaper, Osofisan wrote about cultural and political matters for the general public. During the late 1980s he also wrote a column under the pseudonym Okinba Launko called "Tales the Country Told Me," which was anthologized into the novella *Cordelia.*

Osofisan's work in television includes thirteen episodes of the television series *The Visitors,* a murder mystery with a social subtext. His 1982 script, *No More the Wasted Breed,* was also performed for television, and served as a public vehicle for the author's disagreement with playwright Wole Soyinka's *The Strong Breed. No More the Wasted Breed* "renders in dramatic form Osofisan's long-standing objections to metaphysical solutions," pointed out Richards in the *Dictionary of Literary Biography.* The play is concerned with Biokun, who decides to renounce worldly possessions and devote himself to the gods in a desperate attempt to save his sick and dying son. Two gods arrive incognito as a married couple to judge the entire town (which had long disregarded the gods), and Biokun argues with them over matters relating to worship and divinity. Ultimately, the god posing as a man decides they are no longer arbiters of the town's fate, dismisses his "wife," and leaves the townsfolk to get along on their own.

Osofisan's literary output has not shown a tendency to mellow as the playwright ages—his 1988 play *Aringindin and the Night Watchmen* is a grim study on the effects of a fascist state. In the drama a duplicitous guardian, Aringindin, is hired by the merchants of a town to protect their businesses. Although Aringindin restores order, he is eventually revealed to be negotiating with the town's criminals and elected officials. The only person to stand up to Aringidin is a young woman, but, at the end of the play, she kills herself to avoid arrest.

Although Osofisan's work tends to end bleakly, he is nonetheless committed to improving the social order. "His plays ... speak to those outsiders who cherish the potential of men and women to both dream and struggle," commented Richards in the *Dictionary of Literary Biography*. She also noted that Osofisan's technique of confrontation is a positive force. "Within Nigeria he is often viewed as a radical intent upon completely destroying the past, but his radicalism actually builds on the best of tradition while seeking to encourage pervasive change."

*BIOGRAPHICAL/CRITICAL SOURCES:*

*BOOKS*

*Contemporary Dramatists,* St. James Press, 1988.

*Dictionary of Literary Biography,* Volume 125: *Twentieth-Century Caribbean and Black African Writers, Second Series,* Gale, 1993.

Jeyifo, Biodun, *The Truthful Lie: Essays in a Sociology of African Drama,* New Beacon, 1985, pp. 51-54 and 82-87.

Ogunbiyi, Yemi, *Drama and Theatre in Nigeria: A Critical Source Book,* Nigeria Magazine, 1981, pp. 3-53.

Ogunbiyi, Yemi, *Perspective on Nigerian Literature, 1700 to the Present,* Guardian, 1988, pp. 223-232.

Vanamali, R., Emelia Oko and Azubike Iloeje, *Critical Theory and African Literature,* Heinemann, 1987, pp. 25-36, 81-98, 121-131.

*PERIODICALS*

*African Literature Today,* Volume 12, 1982, pp. 118-136.

*Africana Journal,* October-December, 1981, pp. 323-332.

*Afriscope,* July 1977, pp. 31-32; July 1979, pp. 19, 21-22, and 25.

*Brecht Yearbook,* 1989, pp. 168-183.

*Canadian Journal of African Studies,* Volume 25, number 1, 1991, pp. 58-69.

*Commonwealth Essays and Studies,* autumn, 1989, pp. 108-116.

*Greenfield Review,* spring, 1979, pp. 76-80.

*Le Monde Diplomatique,* September 12, 1982, p. 23.

*Nigerian Theatre Journal,* Volume 1, number 1, 1984, pp. 9-15.

*Neohelicon,* Volume 17, number 2, 1990 pp. 157-168.

*New Literature Review,* January, 1986, pp. 82-90.

*New Theatre Quarterly,* August, 1987, pp. 280-288.

*Notre Librairie,* July-September, 1989, pp. 94-97.

*Okike,* March, 1988, pp. 43-55.

*Sage: A Scholarly Journal on Black Women,* summer, 1988, pp. 25-28.

*Theatre Journal,* May, 1987, pp. 215-227.

*Theatre Research International,* autumn, 1982, pp. 235-244.

*West Africa,* January 28, 1980, pp. 147-150; September 20, 1982, pp. 2406-2410.

*—Sketch by Gordon Mayer*

\*    \*    \*

## OTTLEY, Roi (Vincent)  1906-1960

*PERSONAL:* Born August 2, 1906, in New York City; died October 1, 1960; buried in Burr Oak Cemetery, Chicago, IL; son of Jerome P. and Beatrice (Brisbane) Ottley; married Gladys Tarr, April 27, 1941 (marriage ended); married Alice L. Dungey, February 14, 1951; children: Lynne. *Education:* Attended St. Bonaventure College, 1926-27, University of Michigan, two years, Columbia University, 1934-35, New York University, 1935-36, and St. John's University School of Law. *Religion:* Roman Catholic.

*CAREER: Amsterdam Star News,* New York City, reporter, beginning 1930, columnist, 1932-37, became an editor by 1935, columnist and theatrical and sports editor, 1937-38; editor with New York City Writers Project, 1937; free-lance writer, 1937-41; National C.I.O. War Relief Committee, director of public relations, 1943; war correspondent for *Liberty* and *P.M.,* 1944, and *Pittsburgh Courier* and Overseas News Agency, 1945; *Chicago Tribune,* columnist, 1945-60. Social worker, 1932-37; director, Drexel National Bank, Chicago, and Victory Mutual Life Insurance Company.

*MEMBER:* National Geographic Society, War Correspondents' Association, P.E.N., Chicago Press Club.

*AWARDS, HONORS:* Houghton Life in America Award and Rosenwald fellowship, both 1944, for *"New World A-Coming";* Ainsworth Award, 1944; Peabody Award, 1945; *New World A-Coming* radio series won Schomburg Award, 1945; Brotherhood Award from Chicago Conference for Brotherhood, Inc.

*WRITINGS:*

*"New World A-Coming": Inside Black America,* Houghton, 1943.
*Black Odyssey: The Story of the Negro in America,* Scribner, 1948.
*No Green Pastures,* Scribner, 1951.
*The Lonely Warrior: The Life and Times of Robert S. Abbott,* Regnery, 1955.
*White Marble Lady* (novel), Farrar, Straus, 1965.
(Editor with William J. Weatherby) *The Negro in New York: An Informal Social History,* New York Public Library, 1967, published as *The Negro in New York: An Informal Social History, 1626-1940,* Praeger, 1969.

Also coauthor of scripts for radio series *New World A-Coming,* WMCA (New York), 1944-46. Work represented in anthologies, including *Radio Drama in Action,* 1945. Contributor to periodicals, including *Pittsburgh Courier, Baltimore Afro-American, Herald-Tribune,* and *New York Times.*

*OBITUARIES:*

*PERIODICALS*

*New York Times,* October 2, 1960.
*Publishers Weekly,* October 17, 1960.

# P-Q

## PARKER, Pat 1944-1989

*PERSONAL:* Born January 20, 1944, in Houston, TX; died of cancer, June 4, 1989; daughter of Ernest Nathaniel (a tire retreader) and Marie Louise (a domestic; maiden name, Anderson) Cooks; married Ed Bullins, June 20, 1962 (divorced, January 17, 1966); married Robert F. Parker, January 20, 1966 (divorced); children: Cassidy Brown, Anastasia Dunham-Parker. *Education:* Attended Los Angeles City College and San Francisco State College (now University). *Politics:* "Black Feminist Lesbian."

*ADDRESSES: Home*—Oakland, CA. *Office*—Aya Enterprises, 1547 Palos Verdes Mall, Walnut Creek, CA 94569.

*CAREER:* Worked variously as a proofreader, proof operator, waitress, maid, clerk, and creative writing instructor. Director, Feminist Women's Health Center, Oakland, California, 1978-89; founder, Black Women's Revolutionary Council, Oakland, 1980.

*AWARDS, HONORS:* WIM Publications Memorial Poetry Award established in her name.

*MEMBER:* Gente.

*WRITINGS:*

*VERSE*

*Child of Myself,* Women's Press Collective, 1972.
*Pit Stop: Words,* Women's Press Collective, 1974.
*Movement in Black: The Collected Poetry of Pat Parker, 1961-1978* (includes work from *Child of Myself* and *Pit Stop*), foreword by Audre Lorde, introduction by Judy Grahn, Diana Press, 1978.
*WomanSlaughter,* Diana Press, 1978.
*Jonestown and Other Madness,* Firebrand Books, 1985.

*OTHER*

*Where Would I Be without You: The Poetry of Pat Parker and Judy Grahn* (audio recording), Olivia Records, c. 1976.
(Contributor) *This Bridge Called My Back: Writings by Radical Women of Color,* edited by Cherrie Moraga and Gloria Anzaldua, Women of Color Press, 1981.

Contributor to *Plexus, Amazon Poetry, I Never Told Anyone, Home Girls,* other anthologies, magazines and newspapers.

*SIDELIGHTS:* "This loud and rich-mouthed poet," Lyndie Brimstone writes of Pat Parker in *Feminist Review,* "who planted her feet firmly on platforms all over America and demanded that her audiences, whoever they may be, pay attention, was not only working class, she was Black and lesbian: the very first to refuse to compromise and speak openly from all her undiluted experience." Until her death from cancer in 1989, Parker was not only a highly visible black Lesbian poet—Adrian Oktenberg, writing in the *Women's Review of Books,* calls her "the poet laureate of the Black and Lesbian peoples"—but a committed activist in radical politics and community issues. In addition to urgent, angry poems against racism, sexism, and homophobia, Parker wrote "exquisitely sensual love poems," Brimstone reports.

In a *Callaloo* review of the 1978 collection *Movement in Black,* which includes poems from her earlier books, Gerald Barrax commends Parker's qualities of "wit, humor, and irony" but suggests that her work often falls into "rhetoric, sentimentality and didacticism." He particularly praises the autobiographical poem "Goat Child" for its "ease, speed and charm." Brimstone terms the same poem "a courageous, sinewy work" and "a fine example of Pat Parker's skill." In her review of Parker's final book, *Jonestown and Other Madness,* Oktenberg suggests that if Parker's poetry is "simple," it is "deceptively so." "She gets down on paper complicated states of feeling, lightning-quick changes of thought, and she deals with complex issues in language and imagery that any bar dyke can understand," Oktenberg says, adding, "You don't have to have an education in poetry to read [Parker's work], though the more you have, the better the work becomes." Parker's "standpoint as a black lesbian mother," Rochelle Ratner comments in *Library Journal,* "imbues her poetry with a highly political consciousness." The feeling and vision behind Pat Parker's poetry may perhaps be summed up in the closing lines of the first poem in *Jonestown and Other Madness:* " I care for you / I care for our world / if I stop / caring about one / it would be only / a matter of time / before I stop / loving / the other."

*BIOGRAPHICAL/CRITICAL SOURCES:*

*BOOKS*

McEwen, Christian, editor, *Naming the Waves: Contemporary Lesbian Poetry,* Virago, 1988.
Moraga, Cherrie, and Gloria Anzaldua, *This Bridge Called My Back: Writings by Radical Women of Color,* Women of Color Press, 1981.
Parker, Pat, *Jonestown and Other Madness,* Firebrand Books, 1985.

*PERIODICALS*

*Callaloo,* winter, 1986, pp. 259-62.
*Colby Library Quarterly* (Waterville, Maine), March 1982, pp. 9-25.
*Conditions: Six,* 1980, p. 217.
*Feminist Review,* No. 34, spring 1990, pp. 4-7.
*Library Journal,* July 1985, p. 77.
*Margins,* Vol. 23, 1987, pp. 60-61.
*Women's Review of Books,* April 1986, pp. 17-19.

\*   \*   \*

## PARKER, Percy Spurlark 1940-

*PERSONAL:* Born April 6, 1940, in Chicago, IL; son of Percy S. and Ponce (a high school teacher; maiden name, Jones) Parker; married Shirley Davis, August 2, 1958; children: Sheila, Sherri, Percy III. *Politics:* "Democrat, mostly." *Religion:* Baptist.

*ADDRESSES: Home*—11351 South Lowe, Chicago, IL 60628.

*CAREER:* Apprentice pharmacist with independent drugstore in Chicago, IL, 1958-65; Osco Drug, Chicago, store manag-

er, 1965-72; Jewel Family Center, Chicago, general merchandise manager, 1972-77; manager of Perry Drug Store, 1977-87; appliance salesman for Highland Superstore, 1987-92; appliance salesman for Montgomery Ward, 1992—.

*MEMBER:* Mystery Writers of America (director of Midwest chapter), Private Eye Writers of America.

*WRITINGS:*

*FICTION*

*Good Girls Don't Get Murdered,* Scribner, 1974.

Work represented in *Mirror, Mirror, Fatal Mirror* (anthology), edited by Hans Stefan Santesson, Doubleday, 1973. Contributor to *Ellery Queen Mystery Magazine, Alfred Hitchcock Mystery Magazine, Woman's World, Espionage,* and *Hardboiled.*

*BIOGRAPHICAL/CRITICAL SOURCES:*

*PERIODICALS*

*Best Sellers,* November 15, 1974, p. 376.
*New York Times Book Review,* December 15, 1974, p. 10.

\*   \*   \*

## PARKERSON, Michelle (Denise) 1953-

*PERSONAL:* Born January 11, 1953, in Washington, DC. *Education:* Temple University, B.A., 1974.

*ADDRESSES: Home*—1716 Florida Ave. N.W., No. 2, Washington, DC 20009.

*CAREER:* WRC-TV, Washington, DC, television engineer, 1975; WTTG-TV Metromedia Inc., Washington, DC, television engineer, 1976-83; Eye of the Storm Productions Inc., Washington, DC, director and producer, 1982—. Director and producer of films, including *Sojourn,* 1973, and *But Then, She's Betty Carter,* 1980; producer of video *Gotta Make This Journey,* 1983; affiliated with Robert Flaherty Film Seminar, Cornell University, 1984. University of Delaware, visiting instructor, 1985; Temple University, assistant professor, 1986; lecturer.

*MEMBER:* American Film Institute, Association of Independent Video and Filmmakers.

*AWARDS, HONORS: Sojourn* won the Judges Prize, American Women in Radio and Television, 1975; grand prize, New

York Black Film Festival, 1976; National Endowment for the Arts fellow, 1980; grants from District of Columbia Commission on Arts and Humanities, 1980-81 and 1984-85, Corporation for Public Broadcasting, 1983, and Gay Education Fund, 1983; Edith Blum Lecture Performance Series Award, Washington Women's Arts Center, 1983; ENIK Arts Society Award, 1984; Community Recognition Award, University of the District of Columbia, 1984; Jerry Heil Memorial Award, Gertrude Stein Democratic Club, 1985; *Gotta Make This Journey* won the Leigh Whipper Award, Philadelphia International Film Festival, 1985.

*WRITINGS:*

*Waiting Rooms* (poetry), illustrated by Jean Vallon, Common Ground Press, 1983.

Contributor of essays, reviews, poetry, and fiction to periodicals.

\* \* \*

## PARKS, Gordon (Alexander Buchanan) 1912-

*PERSONAL:* Born November 30, 1912, in Fort Scott, KS; son of Andrew Jackson and Sarah (Ross) Parks; married Sally Alvis, 1933 (divorced, 1961); married Elizabeth Campbell, December, 1962 (divorced, 1973); married Genevieve Young (a book editor), August 26, 1973; children: (first marriage) Gordon (deceased), Toni (Mrs. Jean-Luc Brouillaud), David; (second marriage) Leslie. *Education:* Attended high school in St. Paul, MN. *Politics:* Democrat. *Religion:* Methodist.

*ADDRESSES: Home*—860 United Nations Plaza, New York, NY 10017. *Agent*—(Film) Creative Management Associates, 9255 Sunset Blvd., Los Angeles, CA 90069.

*MEMBER:* Authors Guild (member of council, 1973-74), Authors League of America, Black Academy of Arts and Letters (fellow), Directors Guild of America (member of national council, 1973-76), Newspaper Guild, American Society of Magazine Photographers, Association of Composers and Directors, American Society of Composers, Authors, and Publishers, American Federation of Television and Radio Artists, National Association for the Advancement of Colored People, Directors Guild of New York (member of council), Urban League, Players Club (New York), Kappa Alpha Mu.

*CAREER:* Photographer, writer, film director, and composer. Worked at various jobs prior to 1937; free-lance fashion photographer in Minneapolis, 1937-42; photographer with Farm Security Administration, 1942-43, with Office of War Information, 1944, and with Standard Oil Co. of New Jersey, 1945-48; *Life,* New York City, photo-journalist, 1948-72; *Essence* (magazine), New York City, editorial director, 1970-73. President of Winger Corp. Film director, 1968—, directing motion pictures for Warner Brothers-Seven Arts, Metro-Goldwyn-Mayer (M.G.M.), and Paramount Pictures, including "The Learning Tree," Warner Brothers, 1968, "Shaft," M.G.M., 1972, "Shaft's Big Score," M.G.M., 1972, "The Super Cops," M.G.M., 1974, and "Leadbelly," Paramount, 1975, as well as several documentaries. Composer of concertos and sonatas performed by symphony orchestras in the United States and Europe.

*AWARDS, HONORS:* Rosenwald Foundation fellow, 1942; once chosen Photographer of the Year, Association of Magazine Photographers; Frederic W. Brehm award, 1962; Mass Media Award, National Conference of Christians and Jews, for outstanding contributions to better human relations, 1964; Carr Van Adna Journalism Award, University of Miami, 1964; Ohio University, 1970; named photographer-writer who had done the most to promote understanding among nations of the world in an international vote conducted by the makers of Nikon photographic equipment, 1967; A.F.D., Maryland Institute of Fine Arts, 1968; Litt.D., University of Connecticut, 1969, and Kansas State University, 1970; Spingarn Medal from National Association for the Advancement of Colored People, 1972; H.H.D., St. Olaf College, 1973, Rutgers University, 1980, and Pratt Institute, 1981; Christopher Award, 1980, for *Flavio;* President's Fellow award, Rhode Island School of Design, 1984; named Kansan of the Year, Native Sons and Daughters of Kansas, 1986; National Medal of Arts, 1988; National Film Register (Library of Congress) named "The Learning Tree" one of 25 most significant movies in America, 1989; additional awards include 24 honorary degrees from, among others, Fairfield University, 1969, Boston University, 1969, Macalaster College, 1974, Colby College, 1974, Lincoln University, 1975, and awards from Syracuse University School of Journalism, 1963, University of Miami, 1964, Philadelphia Museum of Art, 1964, and Art Directors Club, 1964, 1968.

*WRITINGS:*

*Flash Photography,* [New York], 1947.
*Camera Portraits: The Techniques and Principles of Documentary Portraiture,* F. Watts, 1948.
*The Learning Tree* (novel; also see below), Harper, 1963.
*A Choice of Weapons* (autobiography), Harper, 1966, reprinted, Minnesota Historical Society, 1986.
*A Poet and His Camera,* self-illustrated with photographs, Viking, 1968.
(And composer of musical score) *The Learning Tree* (screenplay; based on novel of same title), Warner Brothers-Seven Arts, 1968.

*Gordon Parks: Whispers of Intimate Things* (poems), self-illustrated with photographs, Viking, 1971.

*Born Black* (essays), self-illustrated with photographs, Lippincott, 1971.

*In Love* (poems), self-illustrated with photographs, Lippincott, 1971.

*Moments without Proper Names* (poems), self-illustrated with photographs, Viking, 1975.

*Flavio,* Norton, 1978.

*To Smile in Autumn: A Memoir,* Norton, 1979.

*Shannon* (novel), Little, Brown, 1981.

*Voices in the Mirror: An Autobiography,* Doubleday, 1990.

Also author of several television documentaries produced by National Educational Television, including "Flavio" and "Mean Streets." Contributor to *Show, Vogue, Venture,* and other periodicals.

*SIDELIGHTS:* Gordon Parks's "life constitutes an American success story of almost mythic proportions," Andy Grundberg once commented in the *New York Times.* A high school dropout who had to fend for himself at the age of sixteen, Parks overcame the difficulties of being black, uneducated, and poor to become a *Life* magazine photographer; a writer of fiction, nonfiction, and poetry; a composer; and a film director and producer. The wide scope of Parks's expertise is all the more impressive when viewed in its historical context, for many of the fields he succeeded in formerly had been closed to blacks. Parks was the first black to work at *Life* magazine, *Vogue,* the Office of War Information, and the Federal Security Administration. He was also the first black to write, direct, produce, and score a film, *The Learning Tree,* based on his 1963 novel. Parks maintains that his drive to succeed in such a variety of professions was motivated by fear. "I was so frightened I might fail that I figured if one thing didn't work out I could fall back on another," Parks stated in the *Detroit News.*

Parks's first professional endeavor was photography, a craft he practiced as a free-lance fashion photographer in Minneapolis and later as a Rosenwald Foundation fellow in 1942. In 1948 he was hired as a *Life* magazine photographer, and throughout his more than twenty-year affiliation with that publication, Parks photographed world events, celebrities, musicians, artists, and politicians. In addition to his work for *Life,* Parks has exhibited his photography and illustrated his books with photos. In a *New York Times* review of one of Parks's photography exhibitions, Hilton Kramer notes that while Parks is a versatile photographer, "it is in the pictures where his 'black childhood of confusion and poverty' still makes itself felt that he moves us most deeply." Grundberg similarly notes that Parks's "most memorable pictures, and the most vividly felt sections of the exhibition, deal specifically with the conditions and social fabric of black Americans."

Parks found, however, that despite his love of and expertise in photography, he needed to express in words the intense feelings about his childhood. This need resulted in his first novel, *The Learning Tree,* which in some ways parallels Parks's youth. The novel concerns the Wingers, a black family living in a small town in Kansas during the 1920s, and focuses in particular on Newt, the Wingers' adolescent son. "On one level, it is the story of a particular Negro family who manages to maintain its dignity and self-respect as citizens and decent human beings in a border Southern town," writes *Dictionary of Literary Biography* contributor Jane Ball. "On another, it is a symbolic tale of the black man's struggle against social, economic, and natural forces, sometimes winning, sometimes losing." A *Time* reviewer comments: "[Parks's] unabashed nostalgia for what was good there, blended with sharp recollections of staggering violence and fear, makes an immensely readable, sometimes unsettling book." In 1990, *The Learning Tree* was in its 47th printing, a success that Parks attributes to the novel's balanced treatment of blacks and whites, and its positive and negative themes.

Parks explores his life further in three autobiographical volumes, *A Choice of Weapons, To Smile in Autumn,* and *Voices in the Mirror.* The first volume begins when Parks is sixteen and describes how, after his mother's death and an unsuccessful stint living with relatives in Minneapolis, Parks found himself out on the street. For a decade, Parks struggled to feed and clothe himself, all the while cultivating his ambition to be a photographer. The book's theme, according to *Washington Post* contributor Christopher Schemering, is that "one's choice of weapons must be dignity and hard work over the self-destructive, if perhaps understandable, emotions of hate and violence." Alluding to the unfortunate circumstances of his youth, Parks expressed a similar view in the *Detroit News.* "I have a right to be bitter, but I would not let bitterness destroy me. As I tell young black people, you can fight back, but do it in a way to help yourself and not destroy yourself."

*Saturday Review* contributor Edwin M. Yoder, Jr., writes: "[*A Choice of Weapons*] is an excellent introduction to what it must have been like to be black and ambitious—and poor—in the America of a generation ago, when nearly every door was sealed to Negroes as never before or since in American history." Observing that "what [Parks] has refused to accept is the popular definition of what being black is and the limitations that the definition automatically imposes," Saunders Redding concludes in the *New York Times Book Review:* "*A Choice of Weapons* is ... a perceptive narrative of one man's struggle to realize the values (defined as democratic and especially American) he has been taught to respect."

*To Smile in Autumn,* Parks's second autobiographical volume, covers the years from 1943 to 1979. Here Parks celebrates "the triumph of achievement, the abundance and glamour of a productive life," writes *New York Times Book Review* contributor Mel Watkins. Parks also acknowledges, however, that his success was not without a price. Ralph Tyler comments in the *Chicago Tribune Book World:* "Although this ... memoir doesn't have the drama inherent in a fight for survival, it has a drama of its own: the conflict confronting a black American who succeeds in the white world." As Parks writes in *To Smile in Autumn:* "In escaping the mire, I had lost friends along the way.... In one world I was a social oddity. In the other world I was almost a stranger."

Schemering notes that the book contains material "recast" from Parks's earlier work, *Born Black,* and is in this respect somewhat disappointing. He writes: "It's unfortunate to see a major talent and cultural force coast on former successes. Yet, even at half-mast, Parks manages a sporadic eloquence, as in the last few pages when he pays tribute to his son Gordon Parks Jr., who died in a plane crash." Watkins offers this view: "Gordon Parks emerges here as a Renaissance man who has resolutely pursued success in several fields. His memoir is sustained and enlivened by his urbanity and generosity."

Parks's third autobiographical volume, *Voices in the Mirror,* was published in 1990. "More memoir than thorough account," according to *Washington Post Book World* reviewer Hettie Jones, the book "conveys the feelings as well as the facts." It is "a flesh-and-blood family story, with wives, children, and grandchildren included." Categorized as a children's or young adult book, *Voices in the Mirror* begins with Park's birth into a Kansas family of fifteen children and follows him through adolescence and adulthood. The book details his triumphs and disappointments, chronicling his career and the many prominent and news-making people he encountered. Mary Ann Grossman in a *St. Paul Pioneer Press-Dispatch* review quotes Parks's description of the work: "I think this book deals more with the highs and lows of my life from my point of view.... In this one, I become more assertive about myself and what I feel about myself and what I've done." According to Grossman, Parks sees this autobiographical volume as the one that will "clear the air," which is why he originally planned to title it "Explaining Myself."

His second novel, *Shannon,* is an adult novel that tells the story of an Irish family in New York in the early years of the twentieth century. Though a black couple figures significantly in the story, it is the romance of Irish couple Kevin and Shannon O'Farrell, with its elements of tragedy and revenge, that Parks develops. *Shannon* is a very different novel from *The Learning Tree* and offers further evidence of Parks's desire to continually challenge his own talents.

*BIOGRAPHICAL/CRITICAL SOURCES:*

*BOOKS*

*Authors in the News,* Volume 2, Gale, 1976.
Buchsteiner, Thomas, and Karl Steinorth, *Gordon Parks,* Kodak Aktiengesellschaft, 1989.
*Contemporary Literary Criticism,* Gale, Volume 1, 1973, Volume 16, 1981.
*Dictionary of Literary Biography,* Volume 33: *Afro-American Fiction Writers after 1955,* Gale, 1984.
Harnan, Terry, *Gordon Parks: Black Photographer and Film Maker,* Garrard, 1972.
Monaco, James, *American Film Now: The People, the Power, the Money, the Movies,* New American Library, 1979.
Parks, Gordon, *A Choice of Weapons,* Harper, 1966, reprinted, Minnesota Historical Society, 1986.
Parks, Gordon, *To Smile in Autumn: A Memoir,* Norton, 1979.
Parks, Gordon, *Voices in the Mirror: An Autobiography,* Doubleday, 1991.
Rolansky, John D., editor, *Creativity,* North-Holland Publishing, 1970.
Turk, Midge, *Gordon Parks,* Crowell, 1971.

*PERIODICALS*

*Atlantic,* December, 1990.
*Best Sellers,* April 1, 1971.
*Black Enterprise,* January, 1992.
*Black World,* August, 1973.
*Boston Globe,* March 10, 1991.
*Chicago Tribune Book World,* December 30, 1979.
*Commonweal,* September 5, 1969.
*Cue,* August 9, 1969.
*Detroit News,* February 1, 1976.
*Films in Review,* October, 1972.
*Horn Book,* April, 1971; August, 1971.
*Modern Maturity,* June-July, 1989.
*Newsweek,* April, 29, 1968; August 11, 1969; April 19, 1976.
*New York,* June 14, 1976.
*New Yorker,* November 2, 1963; February 13, 1966.
*New York Times,* October 4, 1975; December 3, 1975; March 1, 1986.
*New York Times Book Review,* September 15, 1963; February 13, 1966; December 23, 1979; February 2, 1992.
*Saturday Review,* February 12, 1966; August 9, 1969.
*Show Business,* August 2, 1969.
*Smithsonian,* April, 1989.
*St. Paul Pioneer Press-Dispatch,* December 16, 1990.
*Time,* September 6, 1963; September 29, 1969; May 24, 1976.
*Variety,* November 6, 1968; June 25, 1969.
*Vogue,* October 1, 1968.
*Washington Post,* October 20, 1978; January 24, 1980.
*Washington Post Book World,* November 18, 1990, p. 4.

## p'BITEK, Okot 1931-1982

*PERSONAL:* Born in 1931 in Gulu, Uganda; died c. July 19, 1982; son of a schoolteacher; married twice. *Education:* Attended King's College, Budo; Government Training College, Mbarara, teaching certificate; Bristol University, certificate of education; University College of Wales, LL.B.; Institute of Social Anthropology, Oxford, B.Litt., 1963.

*CAREER:* Taught school in the area of Gulu, Uganda, and played on the Ugandan national soccer team in the mid-1950s; Makerere University, Kampala, Uganda, lecturer in sociology, 1964; Uganda National Theater and Uganda National Cultural Center, Kampala, director, 1966-68; University of Iowa, Iowa City, fellow of international writing program, 1969-70, writer in residence, 1971; University of Nairobi, Nairobi, Kenya, senior research fellow at Institute of African Studies and lecturer in sociology and literature, 1971-78; University of Ife, Ife, Nigeria, professor, 1978-82; Makerere University, professor of creative writing, 1982; writer. Visiting lecturer at University of Texas, 1969. Founder of the Gulu Arts Festival, 1966, and the Kisumu Arts Festival, 1968.

*AWARDS, HONORS:* Jomo Kenyatta Prize for Literature, Kenya Publishers Association, for *Two Songs,* 1972.

*WRITINGS:*

*POETIC NOVELS*

*Song of Lawino: A Lament,* East African Publishing, 1966, Meridian Books, 1969.
*Song of Ocol,* East African Publishing, 1970.
*Song of a Prisoner,* Third Press, 1971.
*Two Songs: Song of Prisoner* [and] *Song of Malaya,* East African Publishing, 1971.
*Song of Lawino and Song of Ocol,* introduction by G. A. Heron, East African Publishing, 1972, Heinemann (London), 1984.

*OTHER*

*Lak tar miyo kinyero wi lobo?* (novel), Eagle Press, 1953, translation published as *White Teeth,* Heinemann (Kenya), 1989 .
*African Religions in Western Scholarship,* East African Literature Bureau, c. 1970.
*Religion of the Central Luo,* East African Literature, 1971.
*Africa's Cultural Revolution* (essays), introduction by Ngugi wa Thiong'o, Macmillan Books for Africa, 1973.
(Compiler and translator) *The Horn of My Love* (folk songs), Heinemann Educational Books, 1974.
(Compiler and translator) *Hare and Hornbill* (folktales), Heinemann Educational Books, 1978.

*Okot p'Bitek of Uganda* (recording), Voice of America, 1978.
(Compiler and translator) *Acholi Proverbs,* Heinemann (Kenya), 1985.
*Artist, the Ruler: Essays on Art, Culture and Values,* Heinemann (Kenya), 1986.

Contributor to periodicals, including *Transition.*

*ADAPTATIONS: Song of Lawino* was adapted as a ballet by the Bessie Schonberg Theater, performed in New York, 1988.

*SIDELIGHTS:* Eulogized as "Uganda's best known poet" in his London *Times* obituary, Okot p'Bitek had a distinguished career in the fields of sports, education, and the arts. While serving as a teacher in his native Uganda during the 1950s, he played on the country's national soccer team, going to the 1956 Summer Olympic Games in London, England. P'Bitek stayed in Great Britain to obtain degrees from several universities before returning to Uganda to teach at the college level. He published his first book, *Lak tar miyo kinyero wi lobo?* (later translated as *White Teeth*), in 1953, but it was the 1966 publication of his *Song of Lawino: A Lament* that brought p'Bitek his first real acclaim. In the same year, p'Bitek was named director of the Uganda National Theater and Cultural Center. In this post he founded the successful Gulu Arts Festival, a celebration of the traditional oral history, dance, and other arts of his ancestral Acholi people. Due to political pressures, however, p'Bitek was forced from his directorship after two years. He moved to Kenya, where, with the exception of visits to universities in the United States, he remained throughout the reign of Ugandan dictator Idi Amin. After founding the Kisumu Arts Festival in Kenya and later serving as a professor in Nigeria, p'Bitek eventually returned to Makerere University in Kampala, Uganda. He was a professor of creative writing there when he died in 1982.

P'Bitek sought, in his role as cultural director and author, to prevent native African culture from being swallowed up by the influences of Western ideas and arts. He was particularly interested in preserving the customs of his native Acholi. While serving as director for the Uganda National Theater and Cultural Center, p'Bitek proclaimed in an interview with Robert Serumaga which appeared in *African Writers Talking:* "The major challenge I think is to find what might be Uganda's contribution to world culture.... [W]e should, I think, look into the village and see what the Ugandans—the proper Ugandans—not the people who have been to school, have read—and see what they do in the village, and see if we cannot find some root there, and build on this." He further explained to Serumaga his feelings about the influence of Western culture on his own: "I am not against having plays from England, from other parts of the world, we should have this, but I'm very concerned that whatever we do should have a basic starting point, and this should be Uganda, and then, of course, Africa, and then we can expand afterwards."

*Song of Lawino,* p'Bitek's most famous work, takes as its central issue the defense of Acholi tradition against the encroachment of Western cultural influences. P'Bitek originally composed *Song of Lawino* in the Acholi (sometimes known as Lwo or Luo) language, and translated it into English before its publication. He put the English words to traditional Acholi verse patterns, however, and the result was pleasing to many critics. A reviewer in the *Times Literary Supplement* lauded p'Bitek's creation thus: "In rewriting his poem in English he has chosen a strong, simple idiom which preserves the sharpness and frankness of [its] imagery, a structure of short, free verses which flow swiftly and easily, and an uncondescending offer of all that is local and specific in the original." Writing in the *Dictionary of Literary Biography,* Bernth Lindfors believes that with *Song of Lawino* p'Bitek created something unique: "No European echoes could be heard in the background. His *Song of Lawino* was the first long poem in English to achieve a totally African identity."

Categorized as a poetic novel, *Song of Lawino* is narrated by an Acholi woman named Lawino who tells an audience her life story in the form of an Acholi song. Her main complaint is against her husband Ocol, who neglects her because of her adherence to Acholi ways. Ocol, in contrast, tries to become as westernized as possible, rejecting his culture as backward and crude. His negative feelings toward his background are further symbolized by his preference of his mistress, Clementina, over Lawino. Clementina is thoroughly westernized, from her name to her high-heeled shoes. Lawino tells us that her rival straightens her hair, uses lipstick, and "dusts powder on her face / And it looks so pale; / She resembles the wizard / Getting ready for the midnight dance." Lawino speaks disdainfully of what she perceives as unnatural behavior on the part of her husband and his mistress; in favorable opposition to this she praises the life of her village. Most critics agree that Lawino's loving descriptions of the simple Acholi rural activities and rituals leave the reader with no doubt as to whose side the author takes. As reported in the *Times Literary Supplement,* "It is Lawino's voice that we need to hear, reminding us of the human reality behind glib rejections of the backward, the primitive, the 'bush people'." P'Bitek later wrote *Song of Ocol,* which purports to offer Lawino's husband's defense, but most reviewers concurred in believing that Ocol's words merely confirm Lawino's condemnation of him. Another *Times Literary Supplement* critic judged that *Song of Ocol* "savo[rs] too much of a conscientious attempt to give a voice to an essentially dull, pompous, and vindictive husband."

P'Bitek's next poetic novels, published as *Two Songs: Song of Prisoner* [and] *Song of Malaya,* together won him the Kenya

Publishers Association's Jomo Kenyatta Prize in 1972. *Song of Prisoner* relates the thoughts, both hopeful and despairing, of a political prisoner, and, according to the *Times Literary Supplement,* "its imagery has much of the freshness and inventive energy of Okot's best work." The narrator describes his cell as a cold, imprisoning woman and relates his feelings of betrayal, his fears of his lover's unfaithfulness, and his daydreams of merrymaking. *Song of Malaya* is written in the persona of a prostitute and tells of the abuses she suffers. Judged slightly sentimental by some critics, the prose poem discusses, among other things, the irony in the fact that prostitutes are often rounded up and jailed by men who were their patrons the previous evening.

In his later years, p'Bitek turned his literary efforts primarily to translation. He published *The Horn of My Love,* a collection of Acholi folk songs in both Acholi and English translation, in 1974, and *Hare and Hornbill,* a collection of African folktales, in 1978. In *The Horn of My Love,* declared reviewer Gerald Moore in the *Times Literary Supplement,* "p'Bitek argues the case for African poetry as poetry, as an art to be enjoyed, rather than as ethnographic material to be eviscerated." The book contains ceremonial songs about death, ancient Acholi chiefs, and love and courtship. *Hare and Hornbill,* according to Robert L. Berner critiquing in *World Literature Today,* is divided roughly in half between tales of humans and tales of animals, including one about a hare seducing his mother-in-law. "P'Bitek is particularly qualified to deal with these tales," Berner proclaimed, and "reveals a thorough understanding of African folk materials."

*BIOGRAPHICAL/CRITICAL SOURCES:*

*BOOKS*

Chinweizu, Onwuchekwa Jemie, and Ihechukwu Madubuike, *Toward the Decolonization of African Literature,* Fourth Dimension, 1980.

*Dictionary of Literary Biography,* Volume 125: *Twentieth-Century Caribbean and Black African Writers,* second series, Gale, 1993.

Goodwin, Ken, *Understanding African Poetry: A Study of Ten Poets,* Heinemann, 1982.

Gurr, Andrew, *Writers in Exile: The Creative Use of Home in Modern Literature,* Humanities Press, 1981.

Heron, George A., *The Poetry of Okot p'Bitek,* Africana Press, 1976.

Killam, G. D., editor, *The Writing of East and Central Africa,* Heinemann, 1984, pp. 144-158.

King, Bruce and Kolawole Ogungbesan, editors, *A Celebration of Black and African Writing,* Oxford University Press, 1975, pp. 217-231.

Liyong, Taban lo, *The Last Word: Cultural Synthesis,* East African Publishing House, 1969, pp. 135-156.

Moore, Gerald, *Twelve African Writers,* Indiana University Press, 1980.

Ngara, Emmanuel, and Andrew Morrison, editors, *Literature, Language and the Nation,* Atoll & Baobab, 1989, pp. 83-97.

Nichols, Lee, editor, *Conversations with African Writers: Interviews with Twenty-Six African Authors,* Voice of America, 1981, pp. 242-252.

Nichols, Lee, *African Writers at the Microphone,* Three Continents Press, 1984.

p'Bitek, Okot, *Song of Lawino: A Lament,* East African Publishing, 1966.

Pieterse, Cosmo, and Dennis Duerden, editors, *African Writers Talking,* Africana Publishing, 1972.

Roscoe, Adrian, *Uhuru's Fire: African Literature East to South,* Cambridge University Press, 1977, pp. 32-66.

Schild, Ulla, *The East African Experience: Essays on English and Swahili Literature,* Reimer (Berlin), 1980, pp. 9-24.

Thiong'o, Ngugi wa, *Homecoming: Essays on African and Caribbean Literature, Culture and Politics,* Heinemann, 1972, Hill, 1973, pp. 67-77.

Wanambisi, Monica Nalyaka, *Thought and Technique in the Poetry of Okot p'Bitek,* Vantage, 1984.

Wanjala, Chris, editor, *Standpoints in African Literature: A Critical Anthology,* East African Literature Bureau, 1973, pp. 52-61.

Wanjala, Chris, *The Season of Harvest: Some Notes on East African Literature,* Kenya Literature Bureau, 1978.

Wanjala, Chris, *For Home and Freedom,* Kenya Literature Bureau, 1980.


*PERIODICALS*

*Afer,* Number 17, 1975, pp. 280-289.

*Africa Now,* October, 1982, pp. 100-102.

*African Studies Association of the West Indies Bulletin,* Number 8, 1977, pp. 18-31.

*African Studies Review,* Volume 28, number 4, 1985, pp. 87-99.

*Busara,* Volume 3, number 4, 1971, pp. 51-65.

*Callaloo,* spring, 1986, pp. 371-383.

*Commonwealth Essays and Studies,* autumn, 1989, pp. 95-107.

*Commonwealth Newsletter,* Number 10, 1976, pp. 27-32.

*Contemporary Poetry,* Volume 4, number 1, 1981, pp. 19-39.

*Dance Magazine,* May, 1988, p. 84.

*East African Journal,* Volume 4, number 6, 1967, pp. 31-36.

*Griot,* winter, 1984, pp. 17-26.

*Ife Studies in African Literature and the Arts,* Number 1, 1982, pp. 18-36.

*Jolan: Journal of the Linguistics Association of Nigeria,* Number 2, 1983-1984, pp. 133-131.

*Kola,* spring, 1988, pp. 29-36.

*Kunapipi,* Volume 1, number 1, 1979, pp. 89-93; Volume 8, number 3, 1986, pp. 100-114.

*Literary Criterion,* Volume 23, numbers 1-2, 1988, pp. 13-29.

*Literary Half-Yearly,* January, 1978, pp. 66-93.

*Meta,* Number 31, 1986, pp. 300-313.

*Occasional Papers,* Volume 1, number 1, 1975, pp. 22-53.

*Pan African Book World,* Volume 2, number 2, 1982, pp. 3-4, 6-9.

*Papua New Guinea Writing,* Number 23, 1976, pp. 12-13.

*Presence Africaine,* Number 113, 1980, pp. 235-257; Number 125, 1983, pp. 379-381; Number 135, 1985, pp. 102-112.

*Quaderni di Lingue e Letterature,* Number 6, 1981, pp. 67-82.

*Research in African Literatures,* Number 16, 1985, pp. 370-383; fall, 1988, pp. 312-340.

*Saiwa,* Number 3, 1985, pp. 59-70.

*Sunday Nation* (Nairobi), December 18, 1977, p. 8, 9.

*Sunday Standard* (Nairobi), August 1, 1982, p. 11.

*Times Literary Supplement,* February 16, 1967; November 5, 1971; February 21, 1975.

*UNESCO Courier,* January, 1986, p. 16.

*World Literature Today,* summer, 1979.

*World Literature Written in English,* April, 1977, pp. 7-24; November, 1977, pp. 281-299; autumn, 1986, pp. 243-244.


*OBITUARIES:*

*PERIODICALS*

*Times* (London), July 23, 1982.

\* \* \*

## PEMBERTON, Gayle Renee 1948-

*PERSONAL:* Born June 29, 1948, in St. Paul, MN; daughter of Lounneer (executive with Urban League) and Muriel E. (homemaker and board of education worker; maiden name, Wigington) Pemberton. *Education:* University of Michigan, B.A., 1969; Harvard University, M.A., 1971, Ph.D., 1981. *Avocational interests:* Family biography, secondary and advanced education for minority students.

*ADDRESSES: Office*—Princeton University, 112 Dickinson Hall, Princeton, NJ 08544-1017.

*CAREER:* Biographer, teacher, academic administrator, and anti-racism activist. Has held academic posts at Smith College, Columbia University, Middlebury College, Northwestern University, Reed College, and Bowdoin College; currently associate director of Afro-American Studies at Princeton University, Princeton, NJ.

*AWARDS, HONORS:* Ford Foundation doctoral fellowship; W.E.B. DuBois doctoral fellowship; John Simon Guggenheim Memorial Foundation fellowship.

*WRITINGS:*

*On Teaching the Minority Student: Problems and Strategies,* Bowdoin College, 1988.

*The Hottest Water in Chicago: On Family, Race, Time, and American Culture,* Faber & Faber, 1992, reprinted as *The Hottest Water in Chicago: Notes of a Native Daughter,* Anchor Books, 1993.

Contributor, *Race-ing Justice/En-gendering Power: Essays on Anita Hill, Clarence Thomas and the Construction of Social Reality,* edited by Toni Morrison, Pantheon, 1992.

Contributor, *American Visions* (travel book), Holt, 1994.

Also contributor to periodicals, including *Women's Review of Books, Publishers Weekly, Chicago Tribune, Los Angeles Tiomes, Mirabella,* and *Chicago Sun-Times.*

*WORK IN PROGRESS:* A book on black women and American cinema, and a book of short stories.

*SIDELIGHTS:* When Gayle Pemberton first published *The Hottest Water in Chicago: On Family, Race, Time, and American Culture* in 1992, she barely anticipated the events which would mark that year as well as the consciousness of most of America. In that year, however, the riots that followed the trial of four Los Angeles, California, police officers accused of beating motorist Rodney King violently reflected the pent-up frustration of many African Americans regarding their status in a white-dominated society. Pemberton's study portrays a struggling and celebratory American black middle-class and its relation to white academic, social, and political structures. In her comparison, Pemberton details the inequalities inherent in the current social system. Associate Director of Afro American Studies at Princeton University, and seasoned thoroughly with academic posts at Bowdoin, Columbia, Middlebury, Northwestern, and Smith, Pemberton provides a detailed dialogue between images of Black inner city life and her memories as a black woman at predominately white universities.

*New York Times Book Review* contributor Nancy Mairs emphasizes Pemberton's return to a "'double consciousness,' voiced by W. E. B. Du Bois, wherein black identity is shaped not purely by the self but only in relation to white demands or dreams of blackness." On one hand, Pemberton's subject matter and critical position suggest an indelible African American identity: black, female, midwestern, socially conscious, and politically active, much like her parents and their parents before them. Intermingled with memories of Paul Laurence Dunbar, Langston Hughes, Du Bois, Richard Wright, and Ralph Ellison, however, are the more mundane traces of her Midwest upbringing: Saturday morning cartoons, *Porgy and Bess,* the University of Michigan, fifties game shows, and a formidable Episcopalian presence in family and community. The hottest waters of childhood identity, however, are often also the most clear: Pemberton rejoins these memories with a critique of how American normalcy can stifle a realistic understanding of an African American self or a black culture. "There are the white images that reinforce what I am not, writes Pemberton in *The Hottest Water,* "and the black ones that are supposed to define blackness, and that are in some ways naturalistic, always symbolic of the whole, designed to elicit pity, fear, or cheap sentiment. They are always there to diffuse and displace the potential meanings of black life."

Pemberton clarifies the anger and weariness of the black middle class from which she emerges in her book: "surviving in black skin saps the energies; not only does it keep real political and social power in the hands of the whites, but it makes the self no more than a sociological fact, dancing, marionette-style, to a degrading tune." An earlier 1988 monograph issue by Pemberton, *On Teaching the Minority Student; Problems and Strategies,* addresses both the burdens placed on minorities and possibilities for intercultural exchange within the American educational system. This earlier publication, more practical rather than biographical in nature than *The Hottest Waters,* nonetheless precipitated Pemberton's anger on determining the nature of Black people by a name given to them from outside their communities: "Minority is a word for statisticians, not a self-identifier for their victims."

Language provides one of the greatest barriers to real change, Pemberton's work contends, coming between family members, intervening in productive academic conversations about race and cultural identity, or healing the wounds on each side of the color line over the latter half of the twentieth century. The couching of the meanings, illusions, and rules of an exclusive white civilization challenges the African American critic of the eighties and early nineties and obscures even the most recent past, so Pemberton argues. Reacting against the American impulse to "put it behind us," Pemberton relates in *The Hottest Waters* memories of racial conflict with an immediate need to find a language which tells both where African Americans come from and what needs to be done for the future: "It is important to know the path, the process, through which the present is made. Inducing cultural amnesia runs the risk of reproducing the medical scenario of 'the operation was a success but the patient died.'"

*BIOGRAPHICAL/CRITICAL SOURCES:*

BOOKS

Pemberton, Gayle, *The Hottest Water in Chicago: On Family, Race, Time, and American Culture,* Faber & Faber, 1992.
Pemberton, Gayle, *On Teaching the Minority Student: Problems and Strategies,* Bowdoin College, 1988.

PERIODICALS

*New York Times Book Review,* August 2, 1992, p.17.
*Washington Post Book World,* May 10, 1992, p. 8.

\*   \*   \*

# PERKINS, (Useni) Eugene 1932-
## (Useni)

*PERSONAL:* Born September 13, 1932, in Chicago, IL; son of Marion Perkins (a sculptor) and Eva Perkins; married, 1969; wife's name, Janis; children: Julia, Russell, Jamila Saran. *Education:* George Williams College, B.S., 1961, M.S., c. 1964; graduate work at DePaul University.

*ADDRESSES: Home*—6800 S. Jeffrey, Chicago, IL 60649. *Office*—1512 S. Polaski, Chicago, IL 60623.

*CAREER:* Ada S. McKinley House, group worker, 1959-60; Fiaman House, group worker, 1960s; Henry Horner Boys Club, Chicago, IL, program director, 1960s; Chicago Boys Club, Youth Development Project, extension worker, 1963; Chicago Better Boys Foundation, Chicago, executive director, 1965-82. Instructor at Central YMCA College, 1968-69, Malcolm X College, c. 1968-72, Roosevelt University, 1969, Lewis University, 1970-73, Triton College, 1974, and Chicago State College (now Chicago State University), 1974—. Southside Community Art Center, workshop instructor, 1967-71; creative writing teacher at Helen Robinson Library, 1968-70, Farragut High School, 1969-70, Cook County Jail, 1970-71, Pontiac Prison, 1970—, and DuSable Museum of African American History, 1973—. Consultant for various organizations, including YMCA National Outreach Program, Chicago Public Schools, and Museum of Afro-American History. Affiliated with Contemporary Speakers Forum and Ebony Talent Inc. *Free Black Press,* editor and publisher. *Military service:* Served in U.S. Air Force.

*MEMBER:* National Association of Black Social Workers, Association for the Development of Black Children (founder), National Black Educators, Catalysts, Union of Black United Artists.

*AWARDS, HONORS:* Malcolm X Black Manhood Award, 1968; Concerned Parents of Lawndale Award, 1970; Special Award, Council on Interracial Books for Children, 1972, for *Ghetto Fairy;* community service fellowship, 1985.

*WRITINGS:*

PLAYS

*Turn a Black Cheek* (three-act), produced in Chicago, IL, 1965.
*Assassination of a Dream* (two-act), produced in Chicago, 1967.
*Nothing but a Nigger* (one-act), produced in Chicago, 1969.
*Black Is So Beautiful* (one-act), produced in Chicago, 1970.
*Cry of the Black Ghetto* (one-act), produced in Chicago, 1970.
*Ghetto Fairy* (two-act, produced in Chicago, c. 1974; also known as *Black Fairy*), Third World Press, 1972.
*Fred Hampton* (one-act), produced in Chicago, 1972.
*The Image Makers* (two-act), produced in Chicago, c. 1972.
*Professor J. B.* (three-act), produced in Chicago, 1973.
*God Is Black, but He's Dead* (one-act), produced in Chicago, 1974.
*Our Street* (one-act), produced in Chicago, 1975.
*Pride of Race,* produced in Chicago, 1984.

Also author of plays *Quinn Chapel* (three-act), 1974, *The Legacy of Leadbelly* (one-act), *Thunder Is Not Yet Rain* (three-act), *It Can Never Be in Vain* (one-act), *Brothers* (three-act), *Cinque* (three-act) and *Maternity Ward.*

POETRY

*An Apology to My African Brother, and Other Poems* (includes "Who'll Sound the Requiem"), Adams Press, 1965.
(Editor) *Black Expressions: An Anthology of New Black Poets,* YMCA, 1967.
*Black Is Beautiful,* Free Black Press, 1968.
*West Wall,* photographs by Roy Lewis, Free Black Press, 1969.
*Silhouette,* Free Black Press, 1970.
(Editor) *Dark Meditations: A Collection of Poems,* Free Black Press, 1971.
(Editor) *Poetry of Prison: Poems by Black Prisoners,* DuSable Museum of African American History, 1972.
(Under name Useni) *When You Grow Up: Poems for Children,* Black Child Journal, 1982.
(Under name Useni) *Midnight Blues in the Afternoon and Other Poems,* INESCU Production, 1984.

Work represented in anthologies, including *Port Chicago Poets: A New Voice in Anthology,* edited by Don Arthur Torgersen, Chicago International Manuscripts, 1966; *Black Arts: An Anthology of Black Creations,* edited by Ahmed Alhamisi and Harun Kofi Wangara, Black Arts Publications,

1969; and *To Gwen with Love,* edited by Patricia L. Brown and others, Johnson, 1971.

*UNDER NAME USENI EUGENE PERKINS*

*Harvesting New Generations: The Positive Development of Black Youth,* Third World, 1986.
*Explosion of Chicago Black Street Gangs,* Third World, 1987.
*The Afrocentric Self-Inventory and Discovery Workbook,* Third World, 1990.

*OTHER*

*Home Is a Dirty Street: The Social Oppression of Black Children,* Third World, 1975.

Contributor to periodicals, including *Chicago Sun-Times, Inner City Studies Journal, Black World, Freedomways,* and Illinois *English Bulletin. Black Expression, A Journal of Literature and Art,* founder and editor.

*SIDELIGHTS:* A prolific playwright and poet, Eugene Perkins is also a professional sociologist. Says Michael Greene in the *Dictionary of Literary Biography:* "Had Eugene Perkins never published a volume of poetry, or staged a single play, his contribution as a sociologist ... would still have given him stature." After graduating with a degree in group work from George Williams College in Chicago, Perkins worked as the executive director of the Better Boys Foundation Family Center for many years. His book *Home Is a Dirty Street: The Social Oppression of Black Children* is a "major contribution to urban sociology," says Greene, who also feels that Perkins's concerns as a sociologist affect his creative writing, which is concerned with themes rooted in his African American heritage.

In Greene's opinion, *An Apology to My African Brother,* Perkins's first collection of poems, addresses "aspects of what blackness means in America" through such poems as "An Apology to My African Brother," where the poet attempts to reconcile his Americanized lifestyle with his African heritage. Another dimension Perkins explores in this collection, opines Greene, is the political concerns of black people in America, and he cites "Who'll Sound the Requiem," a poem dedicated to three murdered civil rights activists of Mississippi, as an example. Going on to discuss *Silhouette,* Perkins's 1970 publication, Greene states that the "ambitious" poems in the book "present a wide-ranging political and social canvas." In several poems Perkins presents the idea that white culture has attempted to duplicate black culture in many ways, the most obvious being music. This attempt, however, has not been successful. For Perkins, preserving black music is integral to the preservation of black culture, says Greene. In a poem from *Midnight Blues in the Afternoon and Other Poems,* a collec-

tion he published in 1984, Perkins expresses a concern about the "rapid paces of feet keeping / in time with the quick / inventions of ibm machines." Greene says that the poems in the collection are "innovative and experimental" and that "tonally, thematically, and stylistically, this volume is Perkins's best poetry to date."

Perkins's concern with raising consciousness about black culture is also integral to his plays. Although most of his plays have never been published, they have been performed in the Chicago area and have been received well by local audiences, reports Greene. *The Black Fairy* is a musical and tells the story of a fairy who acquires self-confidence and pride in her own culture through a series of encounters with vital African American characters.

Although Perkins has written numerous plays, Greene relates that Perkins himself considers poetry his "first love" because, in Perkins's opinion, the language of poetry is fundamental to other writing. In Greene's assessment, it is in his poetry that Perkins combines the impulses of his work and concerns as a sociologist: "[That] same compassion, the same strong sense of social commitment, of having a responsibility to the urban ghetto, appears in his poetry." He feels that because of books like *Midnight Blues,* "Perkins's stature as an important poetic voice should increase as his work becomes better known."

*BIOGRAPHICAL/CRITICAL SOURCES:*

*BOOKS*

*Dictionary of Literary Biography,* Volume 41: *Afro-American Poets since 1955,* Gale, 1985, pp. 251-257.
Useni, *Midnight Blues in the Afternoon and Other Poems,* INESCU Production, 1984.

\*     \*     \*

## PETERSON, Louis (Stamford, Jr.) 1922-

*PERSONAL:* Born June 17, 1922, in Hartford, CT; son of Louis Peterson, Sr. (a bank employee) and Ruth Peterson (a bank employee; maiden name, Conover); married Margaret Mary Feury, July 21, 1952 (divorced 1961). *Education:* Morehouse College, B.A., 1944; attended Yale University, 1944-45; New York University, M.A., 1947.

*CAREER:* Playwright and screenwriter for film and television. Actor in stage plays, including productions of Edwin Bronner's *A Young American,* 1946, Theodore Ward's *Our Lan',* 1947, and Carson McCullers's *The Member of the Wedding,* 1951; worked as a technician at an insurance company, c.

1960s; affiliated with State University of New York at Stony Brook, Department of Theatre Arts, beginning 1972.

*AWARDS, HONORS:* Benjamin Brawley Award for Excellence in English, 1944; *Take a Giant Step* was named as one of the best plays of 1953-54 by *Burns Mantle Yearbook*.

*WRITINGS:*

*STAGE PLAYS*

*Take a Giant Step* (produced in New York, 1954), Samuel French, 1954.
*Entertain a Ghost,* produced in New York, 1962.
*Crazy Horse,* produced in New York, 1979.
*Another Show,* produced at Stony Brook, New York, 1983.

*FILM SCREENPLAYS*

(With Alberto Lattuada) *The Tempest,* Cinecitta, 1957.
(With Julius Epstein) *Take a Giant Step* (adapted from Peterson's play), United Artists, 1958.

*TELEVISION PLAYS*

"Padlocks," *Danger,* CBS, 1954.
"Class of '58," *Goodyear Theatre,* NBC, 1954.
"Joey," *Goodyear Theatre,* NBC, 1956.
"Emily Rossiter Story," *Wagon Train,* NBC, 1957.
"Hit and Run," *Dr. Kildare,* NBC, 1961.

*SIDELIGHTS:* Louis Peterson established himself with his first play, *Take a Giant Step,* a coming-of-age story featuring a young black man, Spencer, who grows up in a predominantly white, middle-class area and faces the insidious racism meted out by his teachers and schoolmates. The play owes much to Peterson's own experience. He grew up in a largely white section of Hartford, Connecticut, and his parents, like Spencer's, worked in a bank. In a *New York Times* interview with Charles Peck, Peterson described his childhood surroundings as "very pleasant" though he also noted that "there were frictions" among the various ethnic groups in the area.

Beginning when Peterson was very young, his parents stressed that a college education was crucial to his success. Peterson's initial pursuit was music, having played the piano since youth. He shifted his major to English, however, and graduated from Morehouse College in Atlanta in 1944. Another interest was the theatre, and Peterson acted in several plays at Morehouse and later pursued graduate studies in drama at Yale and New York universities.

After obtaining his master's degree, Peterson won a minor role in a Broadway play in 1947. He continued to study acting with

Stanford Meisner at New York's Neighborhood Playhouse School of the Theatre, but maintained his desire to write. While studying acting with Lee Strasberg at the Actors Studio, he also took instruction in play writing from Clifford Odets. Odets mentored Peterson, sometimes working with him through the night.

In 1951, while touring as an actor in Carson McCullers's *The Member of the Wedding,* Peterson began to write *Take a Giant Step,* and he completed the play in 1952. Louis Gossett, Jr., then a high school senior, won the role of Spencer in the Broadway production of Peterson's debut play. Though it closed after just 76 performances, the play received a warm critical reception, and it was named as one of the best plays of 1953-54 by the *Burns Mantle Yearbook*.

Speaking about the play in Peck's *New York Times* interview, Peterson said that he felt "almost defensive" that the play did not address the more blatant forms of racism that were especially prevalent in the Southern United States. But as Steven R. Carter noted in *Dictionary of Literary Biography, Take a Giant Step* addressed "quieter, subtler forms" of racism, including "the racist version of Afro-American history in the 1950s, the overwhelming isolation of blacks living away from other blacks, and the fear that made many black parents seek to hobble proud, gifted children lest their strength provoke white fury."

These issues are played out as Spencer faces challenges and insults from his classmates and his teacher. In response to the instructor's assertion that black slaves were too stupid to gain their own freedom, Spencer calls the teacher ignorant and is subsequently suspended from school. His parents, although they fostered his pride in himself, do not support Spencer fully in his conflict and encourage him to avoid confrontations with whites. In a climactic speech, Spencer's mother tells him: "You think it's easy for me to tell my son to crawl when I know he can walk and walk well? I'm sorry I ever had children." In Carter's opinion, this passage prompts Spencer to modify his behavior; he apologizes to his mother for his actions and later distances himself from his white friends, minimizing the chances of further conflicts.

A later play, *Crazy Horse,* written in the late 1970s, was also semi-autobiographical and also employed the same realistic approach as *Take a Giant Step. Crazy Horse* is the account of a marriage between a black journalist and a white woman which crumbles under the opposition of both spouses' families. Peterson's 1983 work, *Another Show,* depicts a college student's suicide and the fallout experienced by those who knew him. Though several of Peterson's plays have been staged since *Take a Giant Step,* critics have suggested that the playwright's debut has had the most lasting impact of all his writing. "For the public and the critics," Carter wrote in *Dic-*

tionary of Literary Biography, "his most significant work is indisputably his stirring, insightful and sensitive portrayal of a black adolescent modeled on himself in *Take a Giant Step*."

*BIOGRAPHICAL/CRITICAL SOURCES:*

BOOKS

Carter, Steven R., in *Dictionary of Literary Biography*, Volume 76: *Afro-American Writers, 1940-1955*, Gale, 1988, pp. 134-39.
Peterson, Louis, *Take a Giant Step*, Samuel French, 1954.

PERIODICALS

*New York Times*, September 20, 1953, section 2, p. 1; April 10, 1962, section 1, p. 48; November 12, 1979, section 3, p. 13; February 20, 1983.

\*   \*   \*

## PHILLIPS, Caryl 1958-

*PERSONAL:* Born March 13, 1958, in St. Kitts, West Indies. *Education:* The Queen's College, Oxford, B.A. (honours), 1979.

*ADDRESSES: Home*—London, England; St. Kitts, West Indies; and Amherst, MA. *Office*—Department of English, Amherst College, Amherst, MA 01002-5002. *Agent*—Antony Harwood, Curtis Brown Ltd., 162-168 Regent St., London, England WIR 5TB.

*CAREER:* Writer in residence, Factory Arts Center (Arts Council of Great Britain), London, England, 1980-82, University of Mysore, Mysore, India, 1987, and University of Stockholm, Stockholm, Sweden, 1989; Amherst College, Amherst, MA, visiting writer, 1990-92, writer in residence, 1992—. Arvon Foundation, writing instructor, summers, 1983—; visiting lecturer, University of Ghana, June-July, 1990, and University of Poznan, July, 1991; Humber College, visiting writer, August, 1992. Member, Arts Council of Great Britain Drama Panel, 1982-85, British Film Institute Production Board, 1985-88, Bush Theater board, 1985-89, and "The Caribbean Writer" board, United States Virgin Islands, 1989; University of Kent, honorary senior member, 1988. Faber & Faber Inc., consultant editor, 1992. Participant at international conferences and festivals, including the Twelfth Annual Conference of German-Speaking Countries of the New Literatures in English (keynote speaker), Giessen, Germany, 1989, and the Hull International Literature Festival (resident writer), Hull, England, 1992. Reader and lecturer at international venues.

*AWARDS, HONORS:* Fiftieth Anniversary Fellowship, British Council, 1984; Giles Cooper Award, best radio play of the year, British Broadcasting Corp., 1984, for *The Wasted Years;* Malcolm X Prize for Literature, 1985, for *The Final Passage;* Martin Luther King Memorial Prize, 1987, for *The European Tribe;* Young Writer of the Year Award, London *Sunday Times*, 1992; Guggenheim Fellowship, 1992.

*WRITINGS:*

FICTION

*The Final Passage*, Faber & Faber, 1985, Viking, 1990.
*A State of Independence*, Farrar, Straus, 1986.
*Higher Ground*, Viking, 1989, Viking, 1990.
*Cambridge*, Bloomsbury, 1991, Knopf, 1992.
*Crossing the River*, Bloomsbury, 1993, Knopf, in press.

PLAYS

*Strange Fruit* (produced at The Crucible Theatre, Sheffield, England, 1980), Amber Lane Press, 1981.
*Where There Is Darkness* (produced at Lyric Hammersmith Theatre, London, England, 1982), Amber Lane Press, 1982.
*The Shelter* (produced at Lyric Hammersmith Theatre, 1983), Amber Lane Press, 1984.

SCREENPLAYS

*Welcome to Birmingham* (documentary), produced for Central TV, 1983.
*The Hope and Glory*, produced for *Play for Today*, British Broadcasting Corp. (BBC), 1984.
*The Record*, produced for Channel 4, 1984.
*Lost in Music*, produced for *Global Report*, BBC, 1985.
*Playing Away* (produced for *Film on 4*, Channel 4, 1984), Faber & Faber, 1987.

RADIO PLAYS

*The Wasted Years*, produced for Radio 4, BBC, 1984, Methuen, 1985.
*Crossing the River*, produced for Radio 3, BBC, 1985.
*The Prince of Africa*, produced for Radio 3, BBC, 1987.
*Writing Fiction*, produced for Radio 4, BBC, 1991.

RADIO DOCUMENTARIES

*St. Kitts (Pride of Place)*, produced for Radio 4, BBC, 1983.
*Sport and the Black Community*, produced for Radio 4, BBC, 1984.
*No Complaints: James Baldwin at Sixty*, produced for Radio 4, BBC, 1985.

*OTHER*

*The European Tribe* (nonfiction), Farrar, Straus, 1987.

Contributor of articles to periodicals, including *Race Today, Caribbean Review of Books,* and *Bomb Magazine.* Contributor to documentary programs, including *Black on Black,* London Weekend Television (LWT), 1983, and *Bookmark,* BBC, 1984.

*SIDELIGHTS:* The compromised identity of the black West Indian is the common thread that links the writings of Caryl Phillips. In the novels *The Final Passage* and *A State of Independence,* Phillips's main characters wander without firm roots between their native West Indies and England. *Higher Ground,* a trilogy of stories that encompasses a period of two hundred years, examines the lingering consequences of being uprooted from one's homeland through multiple points of view. Each story concerns itself with the survival of individuals adrift in a hostile culture, but the author extends his outlook to include the perspective of a white European female. Phillips again uses contrasting points of view in the historical novel *Cambridge,* telling the story through both the white daughter of a plantation owner and the title character, a slave who had once been an educated "English gentleman of color." Phillips himself was born in the West Indies and raised in England, and he acknowledges in the introduction to his book of essays, *The European Tribe,* that he "felt like a transplanted tree that had failed to take root in foreign soil." *The European Tribe* is the result of Phillips's journeys throughout the world to examine racism and define his own place in a white-dominated society. Known initially as a playwright, Phillips also explores the rootlessness of British West Indians in dramas such as *Strange Fruit.*

In *The Final Passage* Leila Preston intends to emigrate with her baby from their Caribbean island home to England. Although Leila is fleeing from the emotional pain of a bad marriage to Michael (a lazy and unfaithful drunk), she ends up traveling with him after a last-minute reconciliation. "But the new start proves to be a resumption of the old pain," wrote David Montrose in the *Times Literary Supplement.* Despite Michael's promise to reform, he backslides into his old habits. Also, Leila's mother, who had already immigrated to England, is dying in a hospital. "England itself administers further hurts," Montrose pointed out. "Walls carry racist slogans, landlords' signs stipulate 'no coloureds'." After five months, Leila leaves Michael for good and returns home to the West Indies. "Her prospects of serenity remain uncertain, but the outlook at least seems promising," Montrose commented in *Times Literary Supplement,* adding later that Phillips's writing "sustains an atmosphere of emotional adversity." Calvin Forbes, a critic for the *Washington Post Book World,*

noticed that Phillips "is one of the few black writers considering the cross-Atlantic relationship."

John Sutherland summed up Phillips's second novel, *A State of Independence,* in the *London Review of Books* as a work that thematically "deals with the contradictions inherent in being a 'British West Indian'." The narrative takes place on an island modeled closely after St. Kitts, where Phillips was born; Bertram Francis, the main character, arrives home after twenty years spent in England as a scholarship student who failed to reach many of his goals. The island is about to become an independent nation, and, like his homeland, Bertram would like to cast off the last vestiges of his Britishness. However, Bertram soon discovers that his brother has died, his mother bitterly resents his long absence, and an old friend who has risen to the position of deputy prime minister of the new regime thinks little of his scheme to start up a local business. This highly-placed friend reminds Bertram that this "is no longer the island he left," mentioned a reviewer in *Best Sellers,* commenting that "Bertram's own independence has estranged him from the people and the island he once knew." Perceiving the book as a discussion on "the national tensions of post-imperialism," Sutherland stated in the *London Review of Books* that *A State of Independence* "is both a promising and an accomplished work."

The opening story of Phillips's trilogy *Higher Ground* is titled "Heartland" and is, in the words of Charles Johnson of the *Los Angeles Times Book Review,* "a chilling, Kafkaesque parable about the slave trade." The narrator, a shepherd on the West African coast, is taken captive by British traders and sold to one of their associates, who teaches him English as well as the fundamentals of slave trading. Eventually, this nameless narrator cooperates with the British, betraying his fellow Africans. "He is half-slave and half-free, poised in a nightmarish limbo between two cultures," Johnson remarked in the *Los Angeles Times Book Review.* When the narrator does finally defy his captors—unable to tolerate the abuse of a black teenage girl he himself helped to enslave—his dubious freedom is ended for good and he is sold on the auction block. Critic Adam Lively singled out "Heartland" as being "a particularly impressive single sweep of narrative" in the *Times Literary Supplement,* and commented that it "owes its immediacy to [the] strength of visual imagination."

The second part of the trilogy *Higher Ground* is the story "The Cargo Rap," which is told by convict Rudi Williams in letters he writes from prison during the late 1960s. A self-proclaimed Marxist-Leninist and adherent to the Black Power movement, Rudi sends letters home full of political polemic. "Ironically, Rudi's black nationalist tirades to his family against 'race-mixing' and integration are at odds with his uncritical acceptance of (white) Marx and Lenin," Johnson remarked in the

*Los Angeles Times Book Review,* complimenting Phillips for "a fine job of showing the contradictions in Rudi's character."

The trilogy closes with "Higher Ground," about Irina, a Jewish refugee from Poland, who encounters England in much the same way as Phillips's black Caribbean characters. The story is set in the 1950s when, according to Lively in the *Times Literary Supplement,* "the backlash against post-war immigration is beginning to be felt." Irina marries, but attempts to commit suicide after the marriage deteriorates, and is sent to a hospital; it is here that she develops an aversion to further emotional attachments. Upon release from the hospital Irina meets a West Indian named Louis, and they share a sexual encounter, although "their friendship across the gulf of cultures falters," according to Johnson in the *Los Angeles Times Book Review.* Johnson appreciated that the author's "ever growing skill ... does allow us to know Irina and the suffering of the dispossessed, the forgotten."

In *Cambridge,* Phillips not only employs another white woman as a major character, he also writes from her perspective. The diary of Emily Cartwright, the British daughter of a West Indies plantation owner, comprises the bulk of the novel and provides a feminine viewpoint into the institution of slavery. Although she might be considered as liberal for her era because she is revolted by conditions on the plantation, Emily nonetheless believes that Africans—an inferior race in her opinion—were intended by God to work for whites. "Unable to comprehend the negative effects of slavery on both slave and slaveholder, she is convinced it is [the slaveholder's] contact with the slaves that causes the otherwise good Christian white man to behave in repulsive ways," summed up Clarence Major in the *Washington Post Book World.*

Emily's commentary is countered by the journal of an elderly slave known as Cambridge, who has been thrown in jail at the time of the novel for defying his captors. As a teenager he had been Olumide, an African kidnapped by slave traders bound for America. The captain, however, "renames him Tom, like a pet, and keeps him," according to Major in the *Washington Post Book World.* Tom became an educated Christian, named himself David Henderson, and married. When his wife died, he decided to embark on a journey to Africa as a Christian proselytizer, but was kidnapped by the ship's captain and again enslaved. Olumide ultimately received the name Cambridge—a reference to his fluency in English—from the overseer at the plantation in the West Indies where he was enslaved. Cambridge had spent many years in hard servitude by the time Emily makes her visit. When she encounters Cambridge, she resents his attitude, "offended by his speaking the King's English with much flourish, his arrogance in addressing her without permission in terms that suggest an equal standing," stated Calvin Forbes, critic for Chicago *Tribune Books.* Forbes pointed out further that Cambridge, however, "merely asks that the white man act like a Christian gentleman."

In his devotion to Christianity, Cambridge resembles other characters from Phillips's fiction (the shepherd in "Heartland," Bertram in *A State of Independence*) whose identities are split between two irreconcilable worlds. He "is enslaved twice—first in England ... and secondly upon his return as a 'free man of color' to Africa," Forbes commented in Chicago *Tribune Books.* The author's deft handling of his characters elicited praise from reviewers, including Forbes who remarked, "One of the marvels of ... *Cambridge* is how artfully [Phillips] manages to convey in a relatively few pages the frailties of many of the people caught in slavery's web." Major, in the *Washington Post Book World,* was particularly impressed with the character of Emily, declaring that "her nineteenth-century white racist mentality becomes a black author's allegorical and ironic means of making one of the subtlest, but most insistent, statements ever about the troubled and urgent relationships between a particular past and the present, Africa and Europe, justice and injustice."

The dichotomies Major mentions above, "Africa and Europe, justice and injustice," are discussed by Phillips as present-day concerns in *The European Tribe.* As Ashok Bery explained in the *Times Literary Supplement,* Phillips "travelled around Europe for nearly a year in an attempt to understand the forces that had helped to shape him; [*The European Tribe*] comes out of that period." Phillips attempts to reconcile "his divided Afro-British self by examining the Europeans as a Pan-Africanist anthropologist might, treating the French, British, Soviets, and Spanish as a single white tribe determined to keep people of color ... down," Charles R. Johnson remarked in the *Los Angeles Times Book Review.* From visits to countries around the world, Phillips records incidents of racism and intolerance, including the actions of France's National Front party to put a halt on African immigration. In Oslo he was detained by suspicious customs officials; in Detroit he was harassed by police. *The European Tribe,* Johnson concluded, "comprised partly of personal odyssey, partly of political indictment, is too important a book to be ignored."

In plays such as *Strange Fruit,* Phillips's characters struggle with the same doubts over identity that define the people in his novels. The two brothers in *Strange Fruit,* living in England, typify this crisis—one "rejects all non-black values," the other is "torn between 'white' and 'black' values," according to Diana Devlin in *Drama: The Quarterly Theatre Review.* But as Phillips is aware, a simple rejection of "white values" will not resolve the conflict of identity that concerns him; despite the sense of alienation Phillips himself felt in Venice, one of the symbolic capitals of Western culture, he remarked in *The European Tribe* that "we, black people, are an inextricable part of this small continent."

*BIOGRAPHICAL/CRITICAL SOURCES:*

*BOOKS*

Phillips, Caryl, *The European Tribe,* Farrar, Straus, 1987.

*PERIODICALS*

*Best Sellers,* October, 1986, p. 252.
*Drama: The Quarterly Theatre Review,* summer, 1982, p. 52.
*London Review of Books,* April 3, 1986, p. 5.
*Los Angeles Times Book Review,* July 19, 1987, pp. 3, 11;
    October 1, 1989, pp. 2, 11.
*Times Literary Supplement,* March 8, 1985, p. 266; April 10,
    1987, p. 396; June 2, 1989, p. 619.
*Tribune Books* (Chicago), March 1, 1992, sec. 14, p. 6.
*Washington Post Book World,* March 4, 1990, p. 8; February
    9, 1992, pp. 4, 10.

—*Sketch by Scot Peacock*


\*   \*   \*


## PINCKNEY, Darryl 1953-

*PERSONAL:* Born in 1953, in Indianapolis, Indiana. *Education:* Attended Columbia University and Princeton University.

*ADDRESSES: Home*—New York, NY. *Office*—c/oPenguin Books, 375 Hudson St., New York, NY 10014.

*CAREER:* Columbia University, teacher, 1992—; free-lance writer.

*AWARDS, HONORS:* Hodder Fellow at Princeton University; received grants from IngramMerrill Foundation and Guggenheim Foundation; Whiting Writers' Award, Mrs. Giles Whiting Foundation, 1986; Art Seidenbaum Award, *Los Angeles Times,* 1992, for first fiction.

*WRITINGS:*

*High Cotton,* Farrar, Straus, 1992.

Contributor to periodicals, including *New York Review of Books, Vanity Fair, Vogue, Granta,* and *New York Times.*

*WORK IN PROGRESS:* A critical book on African American literature.

*SIDELIGHTS:* The relationship between the narrator of Darryl Pinckney's picaresque novel, *High Cotton,* and its author has caused reviewers to speculate that the narrative is more of a memoir than a work of fiction. *Newsday*'s Jonathan Mandell described the work as "a semi-autobiographical novel of growing up as a member of what W.E.B. DuBois called the 'talented tenth'—the African-American elite, the black middle class." Writing in *New York Review of Books,* Michael Woods lauded Pinckney's book as "delicately, intelligently tracing pieces of an uninvented life. The art is in the selection of the traces and in the angle of vision." In the course of the novel, the first person narrator moves from the sheltered world of his extended family into the white world and eventually into the realm of large historical movements—the civil rights struggle and the politics of black cultural nationalism. Because of the deft handling of the complexities of the narrator's skeptical voice, a diverse historical and cultural span, and racial ambiguity, Pinckney's first novel has been widely praised, and received the 1992 *Los Angeles Times*'s Art Seidenbaum Award for first fiction. Wood commented on the author's style, pointing out that "It can't let go, but it learns to relax, and at its best Pinckney's prose—funny, observant, lyrical, self-deprecating—is as good as any now being written in English."

Pinckney is a member of the fourth generation in his family to be college educated. He told Mandell that "Black life is no longer synonymous with underprivileged." His unusual perspective was commented on by *Washington Post Book World* contributor Henry Louis Gates, Jr.: "Pinckney's relation to black America's literary past is distinguished by an intense, and self-conscious, ambivalence—and he has turned that ambivalence into an advantage both intellectual and literary." Though Pinckney's *High Cotton* is heavily grounded in sociology, Gail Lumet Buckley points out in the *Los Angeles Times Book Review* that the novel also possesses a religious aspect, for it "questions the meaning of human suffering." *New York Times Book Review*'s Edmund White asserted that Pinckney explores dimensions of the American race problem with "excruciating honesty and the total freedom from restraint that [German poet and playwright] Schiller said we find nowhere else but in authentic works of art."

*BIOGRAPHICAL/CRITICAL SOURCES:*

*PERIODICALS*

*Los Angeles Times Book Review,* November 8, 1992.
*Newsday,* March 8, 1992.
*New York Review of Books,* March 26, 1992.
*New York Times,* April 4, 1992.
*New York Times Book Review,* February 2, 1992.
*Times* (London), August 13, 1992.
*Times Literary Supplement,* August 14, 1992.
*Washington Post Book World,* February 23, 1992.

## PINSON, Hermine (Dolorez) 1953-

*PERSONAL:* Born July 20, 1953, in Beaumont, TX; daughter of Robert B. (a surgeon) and Enid D. (a school teacher) Harris; married Donald Pinson (a pre-trial officer), September 10, 1976; children: Leah Courtney. *Education:* Fisk University, B.A., 1975; Southern Methodist University, M.A., 1979; Rice University, Ph.D., 1991.

*ADDRESSES: Home*—24 Bromley Drive, Williamsburg, VA 23185. *Office*—Department of English, College of William and Mary, Williamsburg, VA 23185.

*CAREER:* College of William and Mary, Williamsburg, VA, professor.

*MEMBER:* Modern Language Association, South Central Modern Language Association, Southern Conference on Afro-American Studies, Lambda Iota Tau Literary Honor Society.

*AWARDS, HONORS:* Certificate for Outstanding Teacher, National Geographic Society, Texas Southern University, 1990.

*WRITINGS:*

*Ashe* (poetry), Wings Press, 1992.

Fiction published in *Loss of Ground Note: Women Writing about the Death of their Mothers,* Clothespin Fever Press, 1992, and *Common Bonds: Stories by and about Modern Texas Women,* Southern Methodist University Press, 1990. "Journal Entries" included in *Life Notes,* edited by Patricia Bell-Scott, Norton, forthcoming. Contributor to journals, including *Sage.*

*WORK IN PROGRESS: Girlchild.*

*SIDELIGHTS:* Hermine Pinson, author of a doctoral dissertation on the poet Melvin B. Tolson, shows his influence in her verse, not only in allusions to his epics *Libretto for the Republic of Liberia* and *Harlem Gallery* but in the richness of her resourceful and redolent language and in her wide range of reference. Pinson's poems range from the deceptively simple "Sugar's Blues," with its echo of traditional blues lyrics mingled with the onomatopoeic scatting of trains and bebop saxophone solos, to poems like "From Beaumont to Benin" that show the influence of Marianne Moore's refined and distancing imagism: "yes, it can devour the body/like ashes eat a cigarette/by the millimeter."

Pinson's themes run from portraits of strong black women to montage-like renditions of the spectrum of current social problems: urban decay, racial rioting, and the invasion of drugs.

Critics note that pulsing through her poems is a jazzy vitality and a rhythmic sense of verbal improvisation that propels each poem into a new dimension of feeling, even when the subject of the poem promises to be what is expected. The poetry also is filled with the rhetorics of popular music, the black church, street talk, and the cacophony of media overload, giving her verse a contemporary sound that some reviewers suggest is delightful to read aloud. Like contemporary poets such as Jane Cortez and Nikki Giovanni, Pinson is moving into bringing her poetry to a wider audience through recordings with musical accompaniment.

*BIOGRAPHICAL/CRITICAL SOURCES:*

*BOOKS*

Pinson, Hermine, *Ashe,* Wings Press, 1992.

\*    \*    \*

## PITCHER, Oliver 1923(?)-

*PERSONAL:* Born 1923 (some sources say 1924), in MA. *Education:* Attended Bard College; studied at the Dramatic Workshop of the New School and the American Negro Theatre.

*ADDRESSES:* c/o Eaton, 945 Old Trade Road, Palo Alto, CA 94306.

*CAREER:* Poet, playwright, actor, and drama teacher. Vassar College, Poughkeepsie, NY, teacher of black drama, 1970s; Atlanta University Center, Atlanta, GA, poet-in-residence. Has acted professionally and in college and small theater productions.

*WRITINGS:*

*POETRY*

*Dust of Silence,* Troubador, 1960.

Also author of *Prose Poems.* Contributor to anthologies, including *Beyond the Blues,* edited by Pool, 1962; *American Negro Poetry,* edited by Arna Bontemps, 1963; *New Negro Poets: USA,* edited by Hughes, 1964; *Kaleidoscope,* edited by Hayden, 1965; *3000 Years of Black Poetry,* edited by Lomax and Abdul, 1970; and *The Poetry of Black America,* edited by Adoff, 1972. Contributor of poetry to periodicals, including *Negro Digest, Presence Africaine, The Tiger's Eye, Totem, Points of Light,* and *Umbra.* Editor of *Atlanta University Center Sampler.*

*PLAYS*

*Spring Beginning* (poetic drama; full-length), produced at 115th St. People's Theatre, Harlem, in 1940s.

*Snake! Snake!,* produced at the Poet's Theatre, New York, c. 1961.

*The Bite* (one-act), published in the *Atlanta University Sampler,* 1970.

*The One* (monologue; one-act; produced as a work in progress, Negro Ensemble Company, New York, 1971), published in *Black Drama Anthology,* King & Milner, 1972.

*Shampoo,* published in *Atlanta University Sampler,* number 3, 1972.

Also author of *So How're You Wearing Your Straitjacket?* (one-act play), 1963; *The Daisy* (avant-garde drama; two acts), pre-1975; and *The Meaning of Strings* (one-act drama), pre-1975.

*BIOGRAPHICAL/CRITICAL SOURCES:*

*BOOKS*

Page, James A., *Selected Black American Authors: An Illustrated Bio-Bibliography,* G.K. Hall, 1977, p. 218.

Peterson, Bernard L., *Contemporary Black American Playwrights and Their Plays: A Biographical Directory and Dramatic Index,* Greenwood, 1988, p. 383-384.

Rush, Theressa Gunnels, Carol Fairbanks Myers, and Esther Spring Arata, *Black American Writers Past and Present,* Scarecrow Press, 1975, p. 595.

\*    \*    \*

## PLAATJE, Sol(omon) T(shekisho) 1876-1932

*PERSONAL:* Born October 9, 1876, in South Africa; died June 19, 1932, in South Africa; son of Johannes and Martha Plaatje; married Elizabeth (Lilith) M'belle. *Education:* Attended Lutheran Berlin Missionary School.

*CAREER:* Worked as a messenger in Kimberley, Cape Province, South Africa, 1894-99; court interpreter in Mafeking, Cape Province, beginning in 1898; clerk in Cape civil service, 1899-1902; *Koranta ea Becoana* (Tswana-English newspaper), editor, 1902-10; *Tsala ea Becoana* (title means "Friend of the Tswana"), editor, 1910-13; *Tsala ea Batho* (title means "Friend of the People"), editor, 1913-15. Founder and general secretary of the South African Native National Congress (became African National Congress), beginning in 1912; government lobbyist in the United Kingdom and the United States, rallying against South African racial policies; political activist; writer.

*WRITINGS:*

*Native Life in South Africa,* King, 1916, reissued by Ohio University Press, 1991.

(With Daniel Jones) *A Sechuana Reader, in International Phonetic Orthography,* University of London Press, 1916, reissued by Farnborough, 1970.

*Mhudi: An Epic of Native Life a Hundred Years Ago,* Lovedale, 1930, Heinemann, 1978.

*The Boer War Diary of Sol T. Plaatje,* edited by John L. Comaroff, Macmillan, 1973, reissued as *Mafeking Diary,* Ohio University Press, 1990.

Contributor to numerous South African newspapers.

*TRANSLATOR*

*Sechuana Proverbs, with Literal Translations and Their European Equivalents,* Kegan, Paul, Trench, Trubner, 1916.

William Shakespeare, *Diphosho-phosho* (*A Comedy of Errors*), Morija, 1930.

Shakespeare, *Dintshontsho tsa bo-Juliuse Kesara* (*Julius Caesar*), Witwatersrand University Press, 1937.

*SIDELIGHTS:* Decades before the political reality of apartheid, Sol Plaatje was helping to lead the struggle for reform in South Africa. He served as the first secretary to the South African Native National Congress, which would later be renamed the African National Congress, and authored the first novel in English by a black South African, *Mhudi.* Plaatje was also one of the first historians of his own people, the Barolong of south-central Africa and worked as a translator, newspaper editor, and diarist.

Plaatje—the surname came from a nickname for his father—grew up in a large family near Kimberley, a center of South Africa's diamond industry, which was only beginning to develop at the time of his birth. His family, whose ancestors were among Christianity's earliest converts in southern Africa, sent Plaatje to a missionary school. While Plaatje did not receive much formal education—he was to leave the school at the age of seventeen to begin working for the Kimberley post office—he demonstrated special intelligence by learning eight languages. His native language was Tswana, but the youth soon learned English as well as six other European and African languages. He became one of the elite of his region, marrying into the family of a court interpreter.

Plaatje's first break came when he took a court interpreter job himself in Mafeking in 1898, a year before the city came under siege during the Second Anglo-Boer War. The five-month resistance by British and native forces in Mafeking was one of England's few victories in the war's early stages and consequently received much attention. Plaatje emulated others trapped in the city by keeping and later publishing a personal diary of his experiences during the siege. Many such diaries were printed and given wide distribution, but Plaatje's remained unpublished until 1973. However, the siege changed Plaatje's outlook. In 1902 he left the civil service and became a newspaper editor. Over the next decade he worked on numerous newspapers and joined the group that would become the African National Congress, becoming its secretary.

In 1913, the recently formed Union of South Africa passed the Native Lands Act, which helped lay the foundation for apartheid. Plaatje was one of the strongest opponents of the law, which threatened the property rights of all South African non-whites. Plaatje wrote editorials against the act and joined a deputation of leaders who traveled to Britain to lobby the Empire to repeal the act. The group was unsuccessful, but Plaatje remained in England after World War I broke out. He remained abroad for several years.

Plaatje used his time in England to write three books. *Native Life in South Africa,* considered his most important work, attacked the Native Lands Act. Plaatje's biographer Brian Willan, in the *Dictionary of Literary Biography,* called the work "a wide-ranging defense of African political rights and an often-emotive account of the steps taken over the years by South Africa's rulers to exclude Africans from political power." Willan remarked on the book's "personal, often nostalgic tone." Plaatje's contemporaries, though, especially whites, were most struck by the fact that the work marked the first time a black South African had written a book expounding the claims of Africans.

Plaatje also produced two works on his native language, Tswana, or Sechuana. One, *A Sechuana Reader,* was a linguistic description of the language, written to guard the integrity of the language in the face of a changing world. The other, *Sechuana Proverbs,* which Plaatje translated, was a collection of proverbs in Tswana with English translations and European equivalents where they existed. Soon after the books appeared, Plaatje returned to South Africa briefly, but then left, first for a second deputation to Great Britain and then to the United States, where he met political leader Marcus Garvey and educator and writer W. E. B. Du Bois, among others.

From 1920 until he died in 1932, Plaatje continued his newspaper work, with more success at writing for other papers than in editing his own. He devoted himself more to the Tswana language, producing a new dictionary and translations of six Shakespeare plays, of which only two were published. They were the first translations of Shakespeare into an African language. In 1930, *Mhudi* came out. The work failed to truly make its mark until reissued in 1978, long after Plaatje's death. In fact, Plaatje's impact has only really begun to be assessed in the past decade.

Plaatje is generally considered more a man of letters than an author. He produced a wide variety of work, from diaries to polemical essays and translations to a novel. "A man of deeply conservative instinct," Willan writes in his biography, *Sol Plaatje,* "he drew inspiration from both African and European traditions, and was sustained throughout a life of ceaseless endeavour by a vision of what South Africa could be, given only the freedom to draw upon what he saw as the best of those traditions, created from South Africa's unique historical experience." A newspaper obituary for the former newspaperman in *Umteteli wa Bantu,* quoted by Willan in the biography, described the writer more succinctly: "For Plaatje, scholar and patriot, the most fitting epitaph would be: 'He loved his people.'"

*BIOGRAPHICAL/CRITICAL SOURCES:*

*BOOKS*

*Dictionary of Literary Biography,* Volume 125: *Twentieth Century Caribbean and Black African Writers, Second Series,* Gale, 1993.
Willan, Brian, *Sol Plaatje: South African Nationalist 1876-1932,* University of California Press, 1984.

*PERIODICALS*

*Communique,* Volume 9, number 1, 1984, pp. 3-13.
*English in Africa,* March, 1977, pp. 1-6 and 14; May, 1987, pp. 41-65.
*Journal of Commonwealth Literature,* June, 1973, pp. 1-19.
*University of Witwatersrand Historical and Literary Papers: Inventories of Collections,* Number 7, 1978.

—*Sketch by Gordon Mayer*

*   *   *

## PORTER, Connie (Rose) 1959-

*PERSONAL:* Born 1959 in New York state. *Education:* Attended Louisiana State University.

*CAREER:* Novelist.

*WRITINGS:*

*All-Bright Court,* Houghton, 1991.
*Meet Addy: An American Girl* (young adult), illustrated by Tony Wade, Pleasant Co., 1993.

*SIDELIGHTS:* Connie Porter's widely-praised first novel, *All-Bright Court,* tells the story of Southern blacks who move to a Northern steel town in search of higher-paying work, better living conditions, and a more egalitarian society. In the cruel working conditions of the mill, frequent lay-offs, and dangerously polluted air, the workers and their families find they have only traded one set of hardships for another in the move North. The sense of community is strong in the low-rent apartment complex where the novel is set, and through vignettes centering on the Taylor family, their children, their friends and neighbors, Porter presents the variety of experience of poverty in an American ghetto. Adrian Oktenberg of the *Women's Review of Books* called Porter's work "a novel of vision and integrity, wherein a community is seen whole, embedded in its economics and history, sparing nothing, and whose stories are told with great compassion."

One of the Taylor's sons, Mikey, scores high on an intelligence test, is offered a scholarship to a private school and thus a way out of the cycle of poverty and degradation in which his family is caught. Through his new friends, Mikey is exposed to a wealthy white world, and eventually takes on the speech, and the values, of that other world, becoming ashamed of his family and the way they live. Jonathan Yardly commented in the *Washington Post Book World:* "Porter is sensitive to every nuance of the cultural encounter Mikey undergoes, and portrays each step of his journey with as much clarity as sympathy."

Porter garnered praise for her depiction of both the desperation of the lives of her characters as well as the dignity inherent in their manner of coping. Gary Krist remarked in the *Hudson Review:* "She writes simply but powerfully, and with a command of detail that lends authority to the world she depicts." Writing in the *New York Times,* Michiko Kakutani asserted: "Though her prose is often lyrical, even poetic, [Porter] does not shirk from showing the reader the harsh reality of her characters' daily lives.... Indeed, the emotional power of *All-Bright Court* resides in her finely rendered characters, people who come alive for the reader as individuals one has known first hand."

*BIOGRAPHICAL/CRITICAL SOURCES:*

*BOOKS*

*Contemporary Literary Criticism,* Volume 70, Gale, 1992.

*PERIODICALS*

*American Libraries,* February, 1992, p. 192.
*Belles Lettres,* winter, 1991, p. 7.
*Chicago Tribune,* August 25, 1991, p. 4.
*Detroit Free Press,* September 8, 1991, p. 8P.
*Essence,* September, 1991, p. 50.
*Hudson Review,* spring, 1992, p. 141-42.

*Los Angeles Times Book Review,* October 13, 1991, p. 9; September 6, 1992, p. 11.
*New Yorker,* September 9, 1991, p. 96.
*New York Times,* September 10, 1991, p. C14.
*New York Times Book Review,* October 27, 1991, p. 12; August 16, 1992, p. 32.
*Tribune Books* (Chicago), August 25, 1991, p. 4.
*Washington Post Book World,* August 11, 1991, p. 3; December 1, 1991, p. 3; July 26, 1992, p. 12.
*Women's Review of Books,* April, 1992, pp. 16-17.

\*   \*   \*

## POSTON, Ted
### See POSTON, Theodore Roosevelt Augustus Major

\*   \*   \*

## POSTON, Theodore Roosevelt Augustus Major
## 1906-1974
## (Ted Poston)

*PERSONAL:* Known professionally as Ted Poston; born July 4, 1906, in Hopkinsville, KY; died after a long illness, January 11, 1974, in Brooklyn, NY; son of Ephraim (a newspaper publisher) and Mollie (Cox) Poston; married Miriam Rivers, 1935 (divorced); married Marie Byrd Jackson, 1941 (divorced, 1955); married Ersa Hines, August 21, 1957. *Education:* Tennessee Agricultural and Industrial College (now Tennessee State University), A.B., 1928; attended New York University.

*CAREER: Contender,* Hopkinsville, KY, copy clerk, beginning in 1922; writer for Alfred E. Smith presidential campaign, New York City, 1928; dining car waiter for Pennsylvania Railroad and columnist for *Pittsburgh Courier,* c. 1928-29; *Amsterdam News,* New York City, reporter, 1929-34, city editor, c. 1934-36; writer for Works Progress Administration, c. 1936; *New York Post,* New York City, reporter, c. 1937-72. Traveled to U.S.S.R. as extra for unproduced film *Black and White,* 1932. *Wartime service:* Worked in Washington, DC, from 1940 to 1945 as public relations consultant for National Advisory Defense Commission, Office of Production Management, War Production Board, and War Manpower Commission, and as chief of Negro News Desk in news bureau of Office of War Information.

*MEMBER:* Newspaper Guild (Washington chapter), Omega Psi Phi.

*AWARDS, HONORS:* Heywood Broun Memorial Award from American Newspaper Guild, 1950, for coverage of racial discrimination in a trial in Tavares, FL; George Polk Award from Long Island University, 1950, for coverage of racial discrimination in Florida; award from Irving Geist Foundation, 1950, for coverage of antiblack rioting in Groveland, FL; award from Newspaper Guild of New York, 1950, and Unity Award from Beta Delta Mu, 1951, both for promoting interracial tolerance; award from Black Perspective, 1972; distinguished service medal from City of New York; distinguished service plaques from boroughs of Brooklyn, Bronx, and Queens.

*WRITINGS:*

(Contributor) Paul L. Fisher and Ralph Lowenstein, editors, *Race and the News Media,* Praeger, 1967.
*The Dark Side of Hopkinsville: Stories by Ted Poston,* edited by Kathleen A. Hauke, Univ. of Georgia Press, 1991.

Contributor of stories to periodicals including *New Republic.* Work represented in anthologies, including *The Negro Caravan,* edited by Sterling A. Brown, Arthur P. Davis, and Ulysses Lee, Arno, 1970; *Black Joy,* edited by Jay David, Cowles, 1971; and *The Best Short Stories by Negro Writers: An Anthology From 1899 to the Present,* edited by Langston Hughes, Little, Brown, 1967. Contributor of articles and reviews to periodicals, including *Ebony, Nation, Negro Digest, New Republic, Saturday Review,* and *Survey.*

*SIDELIGHTS:* A reporter for the *New York Post* from the late 1930s until he retired in 1972, Ted Poston was one of the first black journalists to work full-time for a white-owned daily newspaper. He grew up in Hopkinsville, Kentucky, and as a teenager he helped out at his family's weekly, the *Contender,* until the paper became so controversial that it was moved out of town. After earning a bachelor's degree at Tennessee Agricultural and Industrial College in 1928, Poston joined the staff of a prominent black weekly in New York City, the *Amsterdam News.* He advanced to city editor in 1934, but after he helped lead a strike to unionize the *News,* its owners fired him.

A few years later Poston applied for a job at the *Post*—a difficult move, since only two black journalists had ever worked for a white-owned daily in the city. He was promised work if he could find a front-page story for the next day's paper. Doubtful of his prospects Poston took the subway back toward his home in Harlem, and as he left the train he saw a white man pursued by a group of angry blacks. Curiosity aroused, Poston discovered that the white was trying to serve notice of a lawsuit on Father Divine, a charismatic black preacher whose

followers often called him an incarnation of God. The angry crowd represented some of Divine's protectors, known as his "angels." Poston had his story and his reporter's job.

The *Post* assigned him to cover New York City Hall, and as he later told *Editor and Publisher,* journalists there "would look at me as if to say I had a hell of a nerve coming into that white man's province. Whenever there was a breaking story, [they] would go into another room to compare notes." Finally, Poston said, "I got tired of it and began to scoop them on stories. That broke the ice."

Poston stressed that his reporting was not limited to events involving race, and in addition to the city hall beat he was known for exclusive interviews with two of the best-known politicians of his day: Huey Long, controversial political boss of Louisiana, and Wendell Wilkie, 1940 Republican nominee for president. But Poston's most dramatic—and dangerous—work often concerned race relations in the South.

While employed by the *News* he went to Alabama to cover the Scottsboro case, in which a group of young black men was falsely accused of raping two white women. Poston was afraid to appear openly as a black reporter from the North, so he dressed in shabby clothes and attended the trial as an itinerant preacher. When a group of suspicious whites caught him mailing a report to New York City, he calmed them down by producing some false identification that showed he was a minister. (He later recounted the incident in an article for *Negro Digest* entitled "My Most Humiliating Jim Crow Experience.") After Poston attended a similar rape trial in Florida for the *Post* in 1949, a gang of whites chased him out of town; when he covered the 1955 bus boycotts in Montgomery, Alabama, his boss asked him to call New York every night to show he was still alive. Such assignments earned Poston several awards in the 1950s, including the Heywood Broun Award of the American Newspaper Guild.

Over the course of Poston's life at least twenty of his short stories appeared in magazines and anthologies, and in *New Republic* he gained a national audience for several narratives about the plight of black Americans. In "A Matter of Record," for example, a decrepit boxer clings to a press clipping of his past glory; in "The Making of Mamma Harris" a woman leads a strike to unionize a tobacco factory; and in "You Go South" a New Yorker prepares himself for the racial humiliations he will face when he travels to the South.

Many of Poston's short stories are autobiographical accounts of life in Hopkinsville at the Booker T. Washington Colored Grammar School. "Revolt of the Evil Fairies," which appeared in *New Republic* and a number of anthologies, illustrates racial barriers in the South by depicting a school play in which roles are assigned on the basis of skin color. According to the narrator, Good Fairies tend to be children "with straight hair and white folks' features," and Prince Charming and Sleeping Beauty are "*always* light-skinned." "And therein lay my personal tragedy," the narrator continues. "I made the best grades in my class, I was the leading debater, and the scion of a respected family in the community. But I could never be Prince Charming, because I was black." Humiliated by his role as leader of the Evil Fairies, the narrator rebels in the middle of a performance by punching Prince Charming, and the dark- and light-skinned children are soon in open combat. "They wouldn't let me appear in the grand dramatic offering at all next year," the narrator concludes. "But I didn't care. I couldn't have been Prince Charming anyway."

Poston knew that his job on a white-owned daily was an opportunity that few blacks had been allowed to share. He actively encouraged more minorities to follow his lead, and when the *Post* hired minority trainees he monitored their progress and lobbied the paper's publisher to keep them on the staff. When Poston retired in 1972, the journalistic organization Black Perspective honored him both for professional excellence and for his efforts on behalf of other blacks in his field. Poston said he hoped to return to Hopkinsville and write more short stories about his youth, but his health failed and he died in 1974.

Shortly after his death Poston was lauded in the *Washington Post* by Joel Dreyfuss, a young black reporter who had worked with him in New York. Dreyfuss praised Poston's "flowing graceful prose" and skill as a rewrite man, and reminded readers of the inner strength Poston must have possessed to endure the "constant pressure" and "isolation" of his difficult role. The headline on Dreyfuss's story read: "The Loneliness of Being First."

*BIOGRAPHICAL/CRITICAL SOURCES:*

*BOOKS*

*Dictionary of Literary Biography,* Volume 51: *Afro-American Writers from the Harlem Renaissance to 1940,* Gale, 1987.

*PERIODICALS*

*Black Perspective,* spring, 1972.
*Editor and Publisher,* April 29, 1972.
*Jet,* April 30, 1990.
*Negro Digest,* April, 1944; December, 1949.
*Newsweek,* April 11, 1949.
*Washington Post Book World,* July 7, 1991, p. 12.

*OBITUARIES:*

*PERIODICALS*

*New York Times,* January 12, 1974.
*Time,* January 21, 1974.
*Washington Post,* January 19, 1974.

\*     \*     \*

## PRICE-MARS, Jean   1875-1969

*PERSONAL:* Born October 15, 1875, in Grande-Riviere du Nord, Haiti; died March 2, 1969, in Port-au-Prince, Haiti; married Clara Perez, 1930; children: one daughter, two sons. *Education:* Attended University of Dakar, French West Africa.

*CAREER:* Diplomat, educator, and author. Professor and rector of the University of Haiti; member of Haitian Senate; served in Haitian diplomatic service in Germany, the U.S., France, the Dominican Republic, and at the United Nations, and as minister of foreign affairs, beginning in 1900. Founder of Institute of Ethnology, Haiti; president of African Society of Culture.

*MEMBER:* Academie des Sciences d'Outre Mer (Paris, France).

*AWARDS, HONORS:* LL.D. from University of Dakar, French West Africa.

*WRITINGS:*

*Silhouettes de negres et de negrophiles,* Presence Africaine (Paris, France), 1960.
*Antenor Firmin,* [Haiti], 1964.
(With Robert Cornevin) *Ainsi parla l'oncle,* [Montreal, Quebec, Canada], 1973, translated as *So Spoke the Uncle* by Magdaline W. Shannon, Three Continents Press, 1983.

Also author of *Le Sentiment de la valeur personnelle chez Henry Christophe,* 1933, *Formation ethnique: Folklore et culture du peuple haitien,* and *Une Etape de l'evolution haitienne.* Contributor to *Tomorrow,* 1954.

*BIOGRAPHICAL/CRITICAL SOURCES:*

*PERIODICALS*

*Ebony,* July, 1966, p. 98.

**PROVIST, d'Alain**
　See DIOP, Birago (Ismael)


\*　　\*　　\*


**QUAYE, Cofie  1947(?)-**
　(Kofi Quaye)

*PERSONAL:* Some sources spell given name Kofi; born c. 1947 near Apan, Ghana. *Education:* Attended school to ninth grade; self-educated thereafter.

*ADDRESSES:* c/o Macmillan Education, Macmillan Publishers Ltd., 4 Little Essex St., London WC2R 3LF, England.

*CAREER:* Fiction writer; clerk in Registrar General's Office in Accra.

*WRITINGS:*

*FICTION*

*Sammy Slams the Gang,* Moxon Paperbacks, 1970.
*Murder in Kumasi,* Moxon Paperbacks, 1970.
*The Takoradi Kidjackers,* Moxon Paperbacks, c. 1971.
*Foli Fights the Forgers,* Macmillan Education, 1991.

Contributor of stories to periodicals, including *When and Where.*


\*　　\*　　\*


**QUAYE, Kofi**
　See QUAYE, Cofie

# R

## RAMPERSAD, Arnold 1941-

*PERSONAL:* Born November 13, 1941, in Trinidad, West Indies; married in 1985; children: one. *Education:* Received B.A. and M.A. from Bowling Green State University; received M.A. and Ph.D. from Harvard University.

*ADDRESSES: Home*—Princeton, NJ. *Office*—Department of English, Princeton University, Princeton, NJ 08544.

*CAREER:* Stanford University, Stanford, CA, professor of English, 1974-83; Rutgers University, New Brunswick, NJ, professor of English, 1983-88; Columbia University, New York City, Zora Neale Hurston Professor of English, 1988-90; Princeton University, Princeton, NJ, Woodrow Wilson Professor of Literature, 1990—.

*MEMBER:* American Studies Association, Modern Language Association.

*AWARDS, HONORS:* National Book Critics Circle Award nomination for biography, 1986, Anisfield-Wolf Book Award in Race Relations, Cleveland Foundation, 1987, and Clarence L. Holte Prize, Phelps Stokes Fund, 1988, all for *The Life of Langston Hughes,* Volume 1: *1902-1941: I, Too, Sing America;* Pulitzer Prize finalist in biography, 1989, and American Book Award, Before Columbus Foundation, 1990, both for *The Life of Langston Hughes,* Volume 2: *1941-1967: I Dream a World.*

*WRITINGS:*

*Melville's Israel Potter: A Pilgrimage and Progress* (essay), Bowling Green University Popular Press, 1969.
*The Art and Imagination of W. E. B. Du Bois,* Harvard University Press, 1976.

*The Life of Langston Hughes,* Oxford University Press, Volume 1: *1902-1941: I, Too, Sing America,* 1986, Volume 2: *1941-1967: I Dream a World,* 1988.
(Editor with Deborah E. McDowell) *Slavery and the Literary Imagination,* Johns Hopkins University Press, 1989.
(Editor) Richard Wright, *Works,* two volumes, Library of America Series, Literary Classics of the United States, 1991.
(With Arthur Ashe) *Days of Grace: A Memoir,* Knopf, 1993.

Contributor to books, including *Artist and Influence 1986: The Challenges of Writing Black Biography,* Billops, 1987; *Voices and Visions: The Poet in America,* edited by Helen Vendler, Random House, 1987; *Afro-American Literary Study in the 1990s,* edited by Houston A. Baker, Jr., and Patricia Redmond, University of Chicago Press, 1989; *The Harlem Renaissance: Revaluations,* edited by Amritjit Singh, William S. Shriver, and Shantley Brodwin, Garland, 1989; and *African American Writers,* edited by Valerie Smith, Scribners, 1991. Contributor to periodicals, including *American Literature, Yale Review, Southern Review, Steppingstones, Langston Hughes Review, American Literature Forum, Kennesaw Review,* and *Menckeniana: A Quarterly Review.*

*SIDELIGHTS:* American educator, literary critic, and writer Arnold Rampersad is best known for his two-volume biography *The Life of Langston Hughes,* a critically acclaimed study of the leading black poet to emerge from the Harlem Renaissance in the 1920s. The first of the volumes, *I, Too, Sing America,* earned Rampersad the 1988 Clarence L. Holte Prize and the second, *I Dream a World,* received an American Book Award.

Rampersad began his literary career in the late 1960s with the publication of a lengthy essay titled *Melville's Israel Potter: A Pilgrimage and Progress,* an examination of American writer Herman Melville's *Israel Potter: His Fifty Years of*

*Exile.* Among Melville's lesser known works, this short fictionalized narrative concerns a forgotten soldier's struggle for existence in the years following the American Revolution. Though Melville's book received little critical attention at the time of its publication in the 1850s, Rampersad maintains that it is a carefully crafted and effective piece of literature. Critics generally credit Rampersad with presenting in *Melville's Israel Potter* an absorbing and penetrating study of both Melville's character and writing style.

Rampersad's 1976 publication *The Art and Imagination of W. E. B. Du Bois* explores the motivations and views of prominent civil rights activist W. E. B. Du Bois. The author presents Du Bois as a sensitive, imaginative, and passionate thinker who wrote persuasively about the oppression of black Americans. Commenting in the *New Republic* on the impact of *The Art and Imagination of W. E. B. Du Bois* in the realm of black studies, Michael Cooke noted, "Rampersad's is an important and necessary book. Clearly it is the product of wide, patient reading, and the expression of a firm and yet mobile intelligence."

More than half a dozen years of research went into Rampersad's next project, the completion of volume one of *The Life of Langston Hughes.* Subtitled *1902-1941: I, Too, Sing America,* the book spans the first four decades of the controversial black American poet's life. Rampersad combed through six thousand folders of papers and correspondence housed at Yale University and traveled across the United States, the Soviet Union, and southwestern Europe to prepare the volume. He begins by tracing Hughes's formative years: the son of an absentee mother and a cold and self-hating father, Hughes spent most of his early years with his maternal grandmother. Rampersad writes in the first volume: "[Hughes's] first day out he took his dinner, then returned to his seat to stare out of the train window and brood on what he had left behind and the life that awaited him now in Mexico. Cheerlessly he thought of his angry mother and his forbidding father. In particular, he brooded on his father's hatred of blacks." Rampersad theorizes that Hughes's dysfunctional childhood fueled in him a lifelong desire to attain the love and respect of the entire black race. Christopher Hitchens commented in *The Observer:* "Arnold Rampersad's finely written and carefully researched book does not say so explicitly, but makes it clear that Hughes had no talent for politics. He was in effect compelled to take stands."

Rampersad closes the first volume of *The Life of Langston Hughes* at the beginning of 1941, a time when Hughes was depressed, in ill health, and facing financial hardship and public scorn because of the radical poetry—such as "Goodbye, Christ"—he had written in the early 1930s. It ends in with Hughes "broke and ruint," writes Rampersad. Hughes is in a California hospital bed, suffering from an illness he described

as arthritis or sciatica but what others said was a venereal disease. The second volume, subtitled *1941-1967: I Dream a World,* follows Hughes through the height of the civil rights movement in the United States and the growth in popularity of a younger generation of black writers. Focusing on Hughes's use of dialect and lyrical simplicity in his prosaic and poetic portraits of blacks, Rampersad maintains that Hughes's efforts to celebrate the true beauty and voice of black American men and women in his writing actually alienated black intellectuals and critics. Though often praised by white critics as an insightful and sensitive writer of the black experience in the United States, Hughes was scorned by some black intellectuals for allegedly depicting black life in a negative way. Such misunderstanding, implies Rampersad, characterized the writer's entire life.

Rampersad, too, does not shy away from some of the ambiguities and ironies that helped to foster misunderstanding and sometimes scorn toward Hughes. Rampersad addresses the questions of Hughes's sexuality; he deals with Hughes's refusal to admit that there were tremendous social injustices in the Soviet Union even though he came face-to-face with many during a trip to Russia; and he indicates that at the same time Hughes was carrying the banner of socialism he was accepting money from capitalist patrons. According to *Kirkus Reviews,* Rampersad refuses to "beautify" his subject.

Widely regarded as the definitive biography of Hughes, Rampersad's striking two-volume study *The Life of Langston Hughes* earned critical praise for its comprehensiveness and readability. "This may be the best biography of a black writer we have had," lauded David Nicholson in the *Washington Post Book World.* And John A. Williams, writing in the *Los Angeles Times Book Review,* commented: "No other biography of Hughes can match the grace and richness of Rampersad's writing, or his investigative and interpretive abilities.... Writing solidly, with an ear for nuance and an eye that measures out Hughes' place in American literature, Rampersad establishes some important points, often ignored, about the importance of the poet."

*New York Times Book Review* contributor Rita Dove offered unequivocal praise for *The Life of Langston Hughes,* stating, "In his superlative study of ... the most prominent Afro-American poet of our century, Arnold Rampersad has performed that most difficult of feats: illuminating a man who, despite all his public visibility, was quite elusive." In her review of the second volume of the life of Hughes, Dove commended the biographer for candidly representing America's tumultuous racial and political past while deftly portraying the life of a gifted figure in the country's literature: "Mr. Rampersad offers a compelling interpretation of a significant chunk of American cultural history, which makes this biography not only entertaining but essential reading."

Rampersad commented that he sees himself "as a literary historian, someone concerned with the combination of history and literature." Although he does not consider himself primarily a biographer, Rampersad said that a good biography should be readable and have some degree of narrative power while "[adhering] to basic standards of accuracy and documentation, of substantiation by multiple sources in the pivotal areas in a subject's life."

Rampersad is also the author, with Arthur Ashe, of *Days of Grace: A Memoir*. Please refer to Ashe's sketch in this volume for additional sidelights.

*BIOGRAPHICAL/CRITICAL SOURCES:*

*BOOKS*

*Contemporary Literary Criticism,* Volume 44, Gale, 1987.

*PERIODICALS*

*Kirkus Reviews,* July 1, 1986.
*Los Angeles Times Book Review,* September 4, 1988.
*Nation,* January 20, 1932.
*New Republic,* April 6, 1932.
*New York Review of Books,* February 16, 1989.
*New York Times,* September 30, 1986.
*New York Times Book Review,* March 29, 1959; October 12, 1986; October 9, 1988.
*Observer* (London), January 18, 1987.
*Publishers Weekly,* January 15, 1988.
*Washington Post Book World,* January 4, 1987.
*Voice Literary Supplement,* July, 1988.
*Yale Review,* autumn, 1988.

\*   \*   \*

## RANDOLPH, A(sa) Philip 1889-1979

*PERSONAL:* Born April 15, 1889, in Crescent City (one source says Jacksonville), FL; died May 16, 1979, in New York, NY; son of James William (a minister) and Elizabeth (Robinson) Randolph; married in 1914 (one source says 1915); wife's name, Lucille E. (a beauty parlor operator). *Education:* Attended College of the City of New York (now City College of the City University of New York). *Politics:* Socialist. *Religion:* Methodist. *Avocational interests:* Reading (especially William Shakespeare and George Bernard Shaw), baseball, basketball, football, tennis.

*CAREER: The Messenger,* New York City, editor, 1917-25; Rand School of Social Science, instructor, c. 1920; founder and president of International Brotherhood of Sleeping Car Porters, 1925-68, and Negro American Labor Council; president of National Negro Congress; founder of League for Non-Violent Civil Disobedience Against Military Segregation, 1947; vice-president of the American Federation of Labor-Congress of Industrial Organizations (AFL-CIO). Member of New York Mayor Fiorello La Guardia's Commission on Race, 1935, and of New York Housing Authority, 1942.

*MEMBER:* Elks, Masons.

*AWARDS, HONORS:* LL.D. from Howard University, 1941; Spingarn Medal, National Association for the Advancement of Colored People (NAACP), 1942; David L. Clendenin Award, Workers' Defense League, 1944; named honorary vice-chairman of Liberal party, 1946; Presidential Medal of Freedom, 1964.

*WRITINGS:*

*The Negro Freedom Movement,* Lincoln University, American Studies Institute, 1968.
(With Chandler Owen) *The Truth about Lynching: Its Causes and Effects,* Cosmo-Advocate Publishing, 1917.

Contributor to periodicals, including *Opportunity* and *Survey Graphic.*

*SIDELIGHTS:* "With a rich baritone voice that seemed destined to command, an imperturbability under fire, a refusal to bend with the times or the fashions, A. Philip Randolph overcame opposition simply by being himself," began a *Time* magazine tribute to one of the most successful black American labor organizers and civil rights activists. Courteous yet determined, Randolph attacked social and economic injustices in government and industry for more than six decades. He organized the first all-black union that was chartered by the American Federation of Labor (AFL); he campaigned for the desegregation of the defense industry, the military, and the civil service; and he was an early and highly visible leader of the civil rights movement of the 1960s. "[Randolph] confronted the establishment [and was] prepared to shake it to its foundations," asserted Nathan Irvin Huggins in the *New York Times Book Review,* "but always with the aplomb and dignity of a gentleman."

"What was your class at Harvard, Phil?" President Franklin D. Roosevelt jokingly asked Randolph, remarking on the union leader's eloquence and graceful manner. In fact, Randolph had dreamed of becoming a Shakespearean actor but his plan was vetoed by his more realistic parents. Instead he took night classes in economics and political science at the College of the City of New York after traveling north from his home in Florida. Through his studies he learned German philosopher Karl Marx's theory that forms of economic inequality are based on race, and from his father, a Jacksonville minister, he learned of the power of united blacks. Once when a black man accused of a crime was taken to a county jail, Randolph's father called the men of his parish together to stand guard outside the prison to protect the man from a group of angry whites. Through seeing the organized parishioners save a man from lynching and through his readings on racial injustice, Randolph realized that economic and political wrongs could be remedied by cooperation among laborers and unity within racial groups. "From the beginning," stated Huggins, "[Randolph] insisted that blacks would get only what they could take and keep only what they could hold. And the power to take and to keep awaited blacks' willingness to organize themselves with purpose and discipline, for group-interest over self-interest, toward the radical transformation of the American economic system."

In 1917 Randolph and Chandler Owen established *The Messenger: The Only Radical Negro Magazine in America,* a black-oriented monthly. In his editorials he urged black men not to fight in the armed forces during World War I because they would be defending a country that denied them civil rights. In response to Randolph's call, the U.S. Justice Department named *The Messenger* one of the most subversive publications in the nation and Randolph "the most dangerous Negro in America." Previously Randolph had been arrested in Cleveland, Ohio, because of his open opposition to blacks participating in World War I, but he was released after spending two days in the city jail. "He contended," explained writer and poet Langston Hughes in *Famous American Negroes,* "that he was simply agitating for fulfillment of Constitutional guarantees for *all* citizens and protection of law for everybody," not just for black equity.

Randolph stressed that workers, regardless of race, could advance economically and socially through unionizing. He helped organize motion picture operators and garment trade workers, and founded a union of elevator operators. Then in 1925 five members of the fledgling Brotherhood of Sleeping Car Porters (BSCP) asked Randolph to help them organize. Notoriously overworked and underpaid, "the porter has always been poor and menial," observed Murray Kempton in a *New Republic* article. "Segregation created his job; the Pullman Company hired Negroes as porters because Negroes were inexpensive." Although he was not a porter, Randolph was elected president of the union, whose members were earning only $67.50 for 300 to 400 hours of work a month. At first, membership in the union grew slowly because Pullman Palace Car Company strongly opposed the brotherhood and fired workers who were active in the union. Nonetheless, by 1928 more than one-half of the railroad maids and porters were members of the BSCP who were ready to strike if the railroad company refused to consider their demands for higher pay and shorter working hours. The workers' boycott was canceled due to lack of support from other railroad unions, but the struggle between Pullman and the BSCP, which also received little support from the Negro religious community and newspapers, raged for ten years.

Finally in 1934 the amended Railway Labor Act created a national mediation board, composed of railroad management and union representatives, to hear grievances. The membership of the porter's union increased. Three years later Pullman signed a contract with the BSCP giving the employees two million dollars in pay increases and guaranteeing them shorter hours and pay for overtime. By September, 1950, due to union pressure, the 18,000 members of the BSCP worked a monthly average of 205 hours for which they were paid a minimum of nearly $240. Randolph used the brotherhood as an example of what could be attained through cooperation among laborers and showed how such groups could be a stronghold against discrimination within the workers' movement. Yet Huggins maintained that "the Union's ultimate victory was to make Randolph one of the most respected and influential black men since Booker T. Washington."

Randolph emphasized that blacks must organize their own groups, choose their own leaders, and raise their own funds, because only with financial independence could an organization control its direction. With the BSCP he made money by sponsoring picnics, parties, and sporting events rather than accepting the financial patronage of well-intentioned white unions. In 1929, when the BSCP joined the American Federation of Labor (AFL), it was the first all-black union to receive an international charter by that organization. Randolph's critics claimed he compromised the position of the Brotherhood by joining the white-run AFL, but he countered by saying that united laborers would have more bargaining power with industries than an isolated union would. When the AFL merged with the Congress of Industrial Organizations (CIO) in 1955, Randolph was named its first vice-president and he undertook a campaign against prejudice in the unions. Demanding that all chapters—black and white—be desegregated, he insisted that blacks had no more right than whites to exclude a prospective member because of race. George Meany and Lane Kirkland, the former president and former secretary-treasurer of the AFL-CIO, commended Randolph for his evenhandedness in the desegregation of the organization. They were quoted in the *New York Times:* "Even in the darkest days, Phil never lost sight of the goals, the needs, the aspirations of workers—both white and black, male and female."

Believing that organized labor was in a position to make economic demands on businesses that held government contracts, Randolph entered the political arena. With the approach of World War II, Randolph took the opportunity to fight discrimination in the industries producing armaments. Defense companies were not hiring blacks to work in the factories, and after

Randolph met with a number of government leaders to no avail, he threatened to lead 50,000 Negroes to Washington, D.C., in protest against the injustice. President Franklin D. Roosevelt called Randolph to the White House immediately. After a standoff with the union leader, the president signed Executive Order 8802 on June 25, 1941, which established the Fair Employment Practices Committee, banning discrimination in the government and defense industries.

As tensions increased between the United States and the Soviet Union in the late 1940s, President Harry S Truman called for the first peace-time draft in American history. Randolph, again by threatening a massive protest and black resistance to military service, pressured Truman into desegregating the armed forces. Huggins related that Randolph told Truman on March 22, 1948: "The mood among Negroes of this country is that they will never bear arms again until all forms of bias and discrimination are abolished." Truman uttered in response, "I wish you hadn't said that, Mr. Randolph. I didn't like it at all." The following month Randolph testified before the Senate Armed Services Committee, maintaining, "Negroes have reached the limit of their endurance when it comes to going into another Jim Crow Army to fight another war for democracy—a democracy they have never gotten." As with Roosevelt, Randolph pressured Truman into issuing an executive order, this one officially banning racial segregation in the armed services.

Randolph finally did march on Washington in August, 1963. Originally he announced that he would call 100,000 Negroes to the capital in October, 1963, to demonstrate against unemployment, but in the late spring of that year President John F. Kennedy introduced his civil rights bill in Congress. Randolph rescheduled the protest for August so that it would include demonstrating for personal liberties. "There was suddenly the surprising prospect that Congress would debate these bills with thousands of Negroes standing outside," recounted Kempton.

Today Randolph's "March on Washington for Jobs and Freedom in 1963" is better remembered as the massive civil rights demonstration where Martin Luther King, Jr., gave his famous "I Have a Dream" speech before more than 200,000 people. Randolph's star has been eclipsed by more famous leaders of the civil rights movement, especially King. "It's so sad because there are so many young people today for whom that name means very little," observed Benjamin L. Hooks, former director of the National Association for the Advancement of Colored People (NAACP) in the *New York Times,* upon hearing of Randolph's death in 1979. "And yet, for more than forty years, he was a tower and beacon of strength and hope for the entire black community." Kempton concurred, commenting on Randolph's program of passive resistance: "He is a pacifist in a native American tradition; before most members of King's non-violent army were born, he was reminding the

Negro of Thoreau's prescription to cast the total vote with feet and voice along with the ballot."

Even Malcolm X, a leader of the Lost-Found Nation of Islam, the Black Muslims, respected Randolph's accomplishments. Randolph invited the advocate of black separatism from white Western society to join a committee that the union leader was organizing on Harlem's financial problems. Kempton related that when Randolph met with Malcolm X he explained his disagreement with the militant's separatist viewpoint, claiming that blacks and whites had to work together for socioeconomic harmony. He commended the Black Muslims, however, for their fight against drugs and liquor, calling it "the greatest contribution any of us have ever made." Later Malcolm X stated that although all leaders of black communities are muddled, Randolph is the least confused. In the spring of 1963 the Black Muslims put a picture of the pacifist Randolph on the cover of their weekly journal, *Muhammad Speaks.*

A. H. Raskin in *New Leader* also paid tribute to the union organizer and activist, maintaining that "Randolph's triumph paralleled that of Mahatma M. K. Gandhi in India, and it stemmed from the same ability to prevail by dint of an unshakable combination of gentleness and conviction over the entrenched forces of obstructionism." Randolph's strength came from his belief in the inevitability of a reformed society, where all laborers enjoyed equal rights. He often stressed that "we never separated the liberation of the white working-man from the liberation of the black workingman," related a reporter for *Time.* Nonetheless, when Randolph died on the eve of the twenty-fifth anniversary of the Supreme Court's historic decision outlawing segregation in public schools, Americans remembered his role as an agitator for civil rights as well as for his labor organizing. "As an elder statesman, he was a guiding light for a new generation of civil-rights advocates," Dennis A. Williams of *Newsweek* commented. Former U.S. President Jimmy Carter, quoted in the *New York Times,* spoke of Randolph: "His dignity and integrity, his eloquence, his devotion to nonviolence and his unshakable commitment to justice all helped shape the ideals and spirit of the civil rights movement."

*BIOGRAPHICAL/CRITICAL SOURCES:*

*BOOKS*

Adams, Russell L., *Great Negroes, Past and Present,* Afro-American Publishing, 1963.

Anderson, Jervis, *A. Philip Randolph: A Biographical Portrait,* Harcourt, 1973.

Bontemps, Arna Wendell, *One Hundred Years of Negro Freedom,* Dodd, 1961.

Cook, Roy, *Leaders of Labor,* Lippincott, 1966.

Davis, Daniel S., *Mr. Black Labor: The Story of A. Philip Randolph, Father of the Civil Rights Movement,* Dutton, 1972.

Flynn, James J., *Negroes of Achievement in Modern America,* Dodd, 1970.

Hughes, Langston, *Famous American Negroes,* Dodd, 1954.

Quarles, Benjamin, *Black Leaders of the Twentieth Century,* University of Illinois Press, 1982.

Redding, Jay Saunders, *The Lonesome Road: The Story of the Negro's Part in America,* Doubleday, 1958.

Richardson, Ben, *Great American Negroes,* Crowell, 1945, second revised edition, with W. A. Fahey, published as *Great Black Americans,* Crowell, 1976.

*PERIODICALS*

*Crisis,* August/September, 1979.
*Dissent,* fall, 1979.
*Ebony,* May, 1969.
*Journal of Negro History,* fall, 1979.
*Negro History Bulletin,* December, 1964; December, 1971.
*New Leader,* June 4, 1979.
*New Republic,* July 6, 1963.
*Newsweek,* September 30, 1940; June 7, 1948; May 28, 1979.
*New Yorker,* December 2, 1972; December 9, 1972; December 16, 1972.
*New York Times,* April 29, 1940; September 15, 1940.
*New York Times Book Review,* May 27, 1973.
*Time,* September 20, 1937; May 28, 1979.

*OBITUARIES:*

*PERIODICALS*

*New York Times,* May 18, 1979.
*Washington Post,* May 18, 1979.

\*　　\*　　\*

# RASHAD, Johari M(ahasin) 1951-

*PERSONAL:* Name is pronounced "joe-*ha*-ree ra-*shad*"; born March 13, 1951, in Washington, DC; children: Chekesha W. (daughter). *Education:* Howard University, graduated, 1976, doctoral study, 1981—; University of the District of Columbia, M.A., 1981.

*ADDRESSES: Office*—Southwest Station, P.O. Box 70417, Washington, DC 20024-0417.

*CAREER:* U.S. Customs Service, Washington, DC, clerk-typist, 1976; U.S. Civil Service Commission, Washington, DC, personnel data standards specialist, 1977-79; U.S. Office of Personnel Management, Washington, DC, instructor, 1980-86; U.S. Coast Guard Headquarters, Washington, DC, senior training specialist, 1986-90; U.S. Department of the Interior, Bureau of Land Management, Washington, DC, chief of office of employee development, 1990—; writer. Smithsonian Institution, volunteer for Festival of American Folklife, summers, 1981—; Metropolitan Washington Ear (radio station), reader for the blind, 1990—. Produced and performed in the two-woman poetry show *In Love and Trouble,* Howard University, 1982. Career counselor; public speaker, seminar and workshop leader; gives readings from her works.

*MEMBER:* International Communication Association, International Women's Writing Guild, Afro-American Writers Guild, American Association of University Women, American Society for Training and Development, Federally Employed Women, National Writers Union, National Career Development Association, PANDORA (Women Collaborating in Arts and Letters), Washington Independent Writers, Phi Beta Kappa, Delta Sigma Theta, Kappa Delta Pi.

*AWARDS, HONORS:* First place, "Women's Issues" category, Chicago Women in Publishing competition, and grant from the D.C. Commission on the Arts and Humanities and National Endowment for the Arts, both 1992, both for *Steppin' over the Glass.*

*WRITINGS:*

*(R)Evolutions* (poems), Writely So!, 1982.
*Woman, Too* (poems), Writely So!, 1984.
*Steppin' over the Glass: Life Journeys in Poetry and Prose,* Evanston Publishing, 1992.

Author of *Federal Jobhunting Simplified,* 1979. Work represented in anthologies, including *The Afro-American Review,* Howard University Press, 1970; *Synergy: Anthology of DC Blackpoetry,* 1975; and *Adam of Ife: Black Women in Praise of Black Men,* Lotus Press, 1992. Washington correspondent, *Changing Woman,* 1986-89. Contributor of articles, poems, and reviews to periodicals, including *Black Collegian, Class, New Directions, Washington Post,* and *Women's Work.*

*WORK IN PROGRESS: How I Got Over: Secrets of a Successful Single Parent* (nonfiction).

*SIDELIGHTS:* Johari M. Rashad commented: "Overcoming obstacles is an important topic for my work, whether the obstacles are of race, gender, skill, education, or family crisis. This is especially true of my book *Steppin' over the Glass.* I am involved in women's issues, black issues, areas that have to do with personal growth and success."

## RASPBERRY, William J(ames)  1935-

*PERSONAL:* Born October 12, 1935, in Okolona, MS; son of James Lee (a teacher) and Willie Mae (a teacher; maiden name, Tucker) Raspberry; married Sondra Patricia Dodson, November 12, 1966; children: Patricia D., Angela D., Mark J. *Education:* Indiana Central College, B.S., 1958.

*ADDRESSES: Home*—1301 Iris St. N.W., Washington, DC 20012. *Office—Washington Post,* 1150 15th St. N.W., Washington, DC 20017.

*CAREER: Indianapolis Recorder,* Indianapolis, IN, 1956-60, began as reporter, photographer, proofreader, and editorial writer, became associate managing editor; *Washington Post,* Washington, DC, teletypist, 1962, reporter, 1962-64, assistant city editor, 1965, columnist, 1966—. Instructor in journalism at Howard University, 1971-73; commentator for WTTG-TV in Washington, DC, 1973-75; discussion panelist for WRC-TV in Washington, DC, 1974-75; former juror for Robert F. Kennedy Awards; member of Pulitzer Prize Jury, 1975-79, Pulitzer Prize Board, 1980-86; lecturer on race relations and public education. *Military service:* U.S. Army, 1960-62; served as public information officer.

*MEMBER:* National Association of Black Journalists, Capitol Press Club, Gridiron Club, Kappa Alpha Psi.

*AWARDS, HONORS:* Named Journalist of the Year by Capitol Press Club, 1965, for coverage of the Los Angeles Watts riot; several awards for interpretive writing from Washington-Baltimore Newspaper Guild; Liberty Bell Award from Federal Bar Association for "outstanding community service in promoting responsible citizenship"; honorary degrees from Georgetown University, University of Maryland, University of Indianapolis, and Virginia State University.

*WRITINGS:*

*Looking Backward at Us,* University Press of Mississippi, 1991.

Also contributor of articles to numerous magazines and other periodicals, including *Reader's Digest, Nation's Cities Weekly, America, Mother Jones,* and *Conservative Digest.*

*SIDELIGHTS:* Described in a *Time* magazine article as "the Lone Ranger of columnists," William Raspberry is known for taking an independent stance on national and international issues. His thrice-weekly column for the *Washington Post* is nationally syndicated twice a week and has earned him several awards. Once referred to by *Time* as "the most respected black voice on any white U.S. newspaper," Raspberry was still a college student when he began working as a reporter for a

black weekly, the *Indianapolis Recorder,* in 1956. During his four years with the newspaper he worked in almost every journalistic capacity; he was named associate managing editor shortly before being drafted into the U.S. Army in 1960. After completing his service as an army public information officer in Washington, D.C., Raspberry joined the staff of the *Washington Post* in 1962 as a teletypist. "I thought if I did that I could arrange to be discovered, and it worked out that way," he would say later in an interview. "I hadn't ever seen a teletype machine, really, but I didn't tell them that." Within a few months he was promoted to writing obituaries and soon afterward became a reporter on the periodical's city desk.

Raspberry served one year as assistant city editor of the *Washington Post* before taking over in 1966 as columnist of "Potomac Watch," a column that dealt with local issues. He gradually shaped the column to fit his own interests, focusing on local topics once a week while treating broader themes in his two syndicated columns. Raspberry is noted for delving into topics that other columnists have avoided, such as drug abuse, criminal justice, and minority issues. Furthermore, he has developed a reputation, according to *Time,* as the "unofficial ombudsman for local underdogs," occasionally serving as troubleshooter for individuals grappling with government bureaucracy.

In addition to writing his weekly columns, Raspberry has taught journalism at Howard University and has served as commentator and discussion panelist for television stations in Washington, D.C. A member of the Pulitzer Prize Board for several years, Raspberry himself was nominated for a Pulitzer Prize in 1982. He has received numerous awards for his writing, including the Capitol Press Club's Journalist of the Year award in 1965 for his coverage of the Los Angeles Watts riot.

His job at the *Indianapolis Recorder* "constituted my journalism school," he said in an interview. "Before I took the job on that weekly, I really hadn't given any thought to journalism as a career. I was thinking of a number of other possible careers. I was at various times a math major, a history major, an English major, and a preseminarian—all at the same school." Raspberry shrugged off his reputation as an expert on education, criminal justice and drug abuse, saying, "It's in some ways an advantage, I guess, that I'm not expert in anything. What it does is free me up to follow things that catch my interest." He added, "I don't spend much time thinking about the philosophy of column writing: What grand purposes are involved in it, how will I know when I've done my work well. I just do it."

Raspberry realizes his position at the *Washington Post* is a powerful one and believes if he can accomplish something through it, he must. "Sometimes," he said, "officials will solve problems in order to avoid having columns written about them." As far as being a "black columnist" goes, he commented, "I never take into account what a black columnist or black man would say about this issue, what he ought to think about this thing. I write about what makes sense to me about particular public issues, and certainly the fact that I'm black has an influence on what I think makes sense about those issues." "The advantage of writing a newspaper column," he added, "is that you can address issues while they're hot—while they're in the public mind—and that tends to be a fairly fleeting phenomenon. You write a piece for a magazine that has a six-week lead time, and the thing that was of such intense interest at the time you wrote it has been supplanted by some other topic."

His book *Looking Backward at Us,* published in 1991, is a collection of some 50 of Raspberry's columns, primarily from the 1980s, covering such issues as race, family, education, and criminal justice. Raspberry "consistently manages to make himself heard at a reasonable decibel level," comments a reviewer in *Washington Post Book World,* and highlights a comment the columnist made in a commencement address: "Your best shot at happiness, self-worth and personal satisfaction— the things that constitute real success—is not in earning as much as you can but in performing as well as you can something that you consider worthwhile."

*BIOGRAPHICAL/CRITICAL SOURCES:*

*BOOKS*

Raspberry, William J., *Looking Backward at Us,* University Press of Mississippi, 1991.

*PERIODICALS*

*Booklist,* November 15, 1991.
*Time,* September 16, 1974.
*Washington Post,* November 23, 1969; June 25, 1971; September 17, 1971.
*Washington Post Book World,* November 3, 1991.

\*   \*   \*

## REDMOND, Eugene B.   1937-

*PERSONAL:* Born December 1, 1937, in East St. Louis, IL; son of John Henry and Emma (Hutchinson) Redmond. *Education:* Southern Illinois University, B.A., 1964; Washington University, M.A., 1966.

*ADDRESSES: Home*—1925 Seventh Ave., No. 7L, New

York, NY 10026. *Office*—Department of English, California State University, Sacramento, CA 95819.

*CAREER:* East St. Louis Beacon, East St. Louis, IL, associate editor, 1961-62; Monitor, East St. Louis, contributing editor, 1963-65, executive editor, 1965-67, editorial page and contributing editor, beginning in 1967; Southern Illinois University at Edwardsville, East St. Louis branch, teacher-counselor in Experiment in Higher Education, 1967-68, poet-in-residence and director of language workshops, 1968-69; Oberlin College, Oberlin, OH, writer-in-residence and lecturer in Afro-American studies, 1969-70; California State University, Sacramento, professor of English and poet-in-residence in ethnic studies, 1970—.

Visiting writer-in-residence, Southern University and Agricultural and Mechanical College, 1971-72; instructor of Afro-American literature, Oak Park School of Afro-American Thought, Sacramento City College, 1971; visiting lecturer, University of Leiden, summer, 1978; visiting professor and writer, University of Wisconsin, 1978-79; visiting professor, University of Nigeria, 1980; lecturer and reader at other colleges and universities in the United States and Canada. Coordinator of Annual Third World Writers and Thinkers Symposium, 1972—; director of Henry Dumas Creative Writing Workshop, 1974—, and of Interracial-Intercultural Communications through the Arts, East St. Louis School District, 1977. Founder-publisher, Black River Writers Press. Member of board of directors, Olatunji Counseling Educational Center, East St. Louis, and IMPACT. Member of board and chair of publicity, Young Disciples Foundation. Senior consultant, Performing Arts Training Center, East St. Louis, 1967—; consultant, Ghetto Communications Workshop Planners. *Military service:* U.S. Marines, 1958-61.

*MEMBER:* Congress of Racial Equality, American Newspaper Guild, National Newspaper Publishers Association, National Association of African American Educators, California Association of Teachers of English, African Association of Black Studies, California Writers Club, Northern California Black English Teachers Association.

*AWARDS, HONORS:* First prize, Washington University Annual Festival of the Arts, 1965, for poem "Eye in the Ceiling"; first prize of Free Lance (magazine), 1966, for poem "Grandmother"; Literary Achievement Award, Sacramento Regional Arts Council, 1974; Best of the Small Press Award, Pushcart Press, 1976; Poet-Laureate, East St. Louis, IL, 1976; faculty research award, California State University, Sacramento, 1976; California Arts Council grant, 1977; Illinois Arts Council grant, 1977; New York Council on the Arts grant,

1977-78; National Endowment for the Arts creative writing fellowship, 1978.

*WRITINGS:*

*POETRY*

*A Tale of Two Toms, or Tom-Tom (Uncle Toms of East St. Louis & St. Louis),* Monitor, 1968.

*A Tale of Time and Toilet Tissue,* Monitor, 1969.

*Sentry of the Four Golden Pillars,* Black River Writers, 1970.

*River of Bones and Flesh and Blood,* Black River Writers, 1971.

*Songs from an Afro!Phone: New Poems,* Black River Writers, 1972.

*In a Time of Rain and Desire: New Love Poems,* Black River Writers, 1973.

*Consider Loneliness as These Things,* Centro Studi E Scambi Internazionali, 1973.

*The Eye in the Ceiling: Poems,* Harlem River Press, 1991.

*EDITOR*

(And contributor) *Sides of the River: A Mini-Anthology of Black Writings* (fiction and poems), Bethany Press, 1969.

(With Hale Chatfield) *Henry Dumas, Ark of Bones, and Other Stories* (fiction), Random House, 1970.

(With Chatfield) *Poetry for My People,* Southern Illinois University Press, 1970.

Dumas, *Play Ebony, Play Ivory,* Random House, 1974.

Dumas, *Jonoah and the Green Stone,* Random House, 1976.

*Griefs of Joy: Selected Afro-American Poetry for Students,* Black River Writers, 1977.

Dumas, *Rope of Wind, and Other Stories* (fiction), Random House, 1979.

*Knees of a Natural Man: The Selected Poetry of Henry Dumas,* Thunder's Mouth Press, 1989.

*PLAYS*

(Contributor and performer) *The Ode to Taylor Jones,* first produced in East St. Louis at Southern Illinois University Performing Arts Training Center, 1968.

*9 Poets with the Blues,* first produced in Sacramento at California State University, 1971.

*The Face of the Deep,* first produced in Sacramento at California State University, 1971.

*River of Bones,* first produced in Sacramento at California State University, 1971.

*The Night John Henry Was Born,* first produced in Baton Rouge, LA, at Southern University, Little Theatre, 1972.

*Will I Still Be Here Tomorrow?,* first produced in Sacramento at California State University, produced Off-Broadway at the Martinique Theatre, 1972.

*Kwaanza: A Ritual in 7 Movements,* first produced in Sacramento at California State University, December 25, 1973.

*Music and I Have Come Home at Last,* first produced in Sacramento at California State University Outdoor Theatre, 1974.

*There's a Wiretap in My Soup,* first produced in Sacramento at California State University, 1974.

Also author of play, *Shadows before the Mirror,* performed live and on television in Sacramento.

*FOR TELEVISION*

*Cry-Cry, Wind, through the Throats of Horns and Drums: A Jazz Ballet,* KXTV, 1977.

*If You Love Me Why Don't You Know It: A Blues Ballet,* KXTV, 1977.

*CONTRIBUTOR TO ANTHOLOGIES*

*Tambourine,* Washington University Press, 1966.

Clarence Major, editor, *The New Black Poetry,* International Publishers, 1969.

*A Galaxy of Black Writing,* Moore Publishing, 1969.

Arnold Adoff, editor, *The Poetry of Black America,* Harper, 1972.

Abraham Chapman, editor, *New Black Voices,* New American Library, 1972.

Quincy Troupe and Rainer Schulte, editors, *Giant Talk: Anthology of Third World Writings,* Random House, 1974.

Theodore Gross, editor, *open poetry,* Random House, 1975.

*A Documentary History of the Little Magazine since 1950,* Pushcart, 1978.

Ishmael Reed, and others, editors, *Calafia: The California Poetry,* Y'bird, 1979.

*OTHER*

*Drumvoices: The Mission of Afro-American Poetry, A Critical History,* Anchor, 1976.

(Advisor) Angela Lobo-Cobb, editor, *A Confluence of Colors: The First Anthology of Wisconsin Minority Poets,* Blue Reed Press, 1976.

Contributor of poetry and articles to numerous journals and newspapers, including *Focus/Midwest, Fine Arts, Nickel Review, Black Scholar,* and *Triquarterly.* Contributing editor, *Confrontation: A Journal of Third World Literature.*

*ADAPTATIONS:* Redmond has recorded *Bloodlinks* and *Sacred Places,* readings of his poetry with musical accompaniment. A play version of *Drumvoices: The Mission of Afro-American Poetry* was produced in Sacramento at California State University Center Theatre in 1976.

*WORK IN PROGRESS:* Adapting his own work and that of other writers for television.

*SIDELIGHTS:* "A poet, critic, journalist, playwright, and educator, Eugene B. Redmond is counted among the number of significant black literary figures who shaped the black arts movement of the late 1960s," Joyce Pettis writes in *Dictionary of Literary Biography: Afro-American Poets since 1955.* The dominant feature of his poetry, she feels, may be "a marked historical and cultural perspective.... Redmond is very conscious of choosing his allusions, images, and symbols from the black cultural context.... His poetry abounds with direct allusions to spirituals, blues, jazz, soul music, and black musicians. His poetry also shows an indebtedness to folk songs and expressions, the great 'folkloristic trunk' from which Redmond believes black literature stems."

Also notable is Redmond's work as an editor. A friend of the late Henry Dumas (writer and cultural activist in East St. Louis, Illinois), Redmond co-founded Black River Writers Publishing Company and worked with Dumas to develop an audience for poetry in their community. Redmond, the executor of the senior poet's estate, has edited several books by Dumas. But a perhaps greater contribution to the appreciation of black literature is his own *Drumvoices: The Mission of Afro-American Poetry, A Critical History,* "the result of eight years of exhaustive research, travel, interviews, and writing," notes Pettis. "The volume, which surveys black American poetry from 1946 to 1976, is important for students and teachers of Afro-American poetry because it follows a historical perspective, and links the eclipsed African culture with the American culture of the earliest black writers.... Redmond also includes an extensive and helpful bibliography."

Redmond commented: "Motherless and fatherless at age eight, I was raised in part by a grandmother and a group of neighborhood fathers—friends of my older brother and members of the Seventh-Day Adventist Church I attended.... I try to make maximum use of formal training and general experience. At the very center of this writer's life and work is the desire and struggle for Black self-determination and respect for basic humanity." Redmond notes that he has been influenced by "Langston Hughes, Melvin Tolson, Theodore Roethke, Smokey Bill Robinson, Yevgeny Yevtushenko, blues, jazz lyrics, and the movement currently underway." He is "concerned with dynamics of Black Block Voting, Black Language, Third World politics and writings, [and feels] indebted to [Franz] Fanon.... I perform regularly, acting and reading poetry with the Performing Arts Training Center (directed by Katherine Dunham, friend and critic).... [and am] involved with music and basic rhythms—the key to 'style' of Black writing. I also play the percussive instruments.... [I]

acquired speaking knowledge of Japanese while in the Far East with the Marines. [I have also] spent some time in Laos."

*BIOGRAPHICAL/CRITICAL SOURCES:*

*BOOKS*

*Dictionary of Literary Biography,* Volume 41: *Afro-American Poets since 1955,* Gale, 1985.

*PERIODICALS*

*Black Scholar,* November 1, 1976; September, 1977; March, 1981.
*Black World,* September, 1984.
*Village Voice,* October 10, 1974.


                              *    *    *


## REED, Ishmael (Scott) 1938-
## (Emmett Coleman)

*PERSONAL:* Born February 22, 1938, in Chattanooga, TN; son of Henry Lenoir (a fundraiser for YMCA) and Thelma Coleman (a homemaker and salesperson); stepfather, Bennie Stephen Reed (an auto worker); married Priscilla Rose, September, 1960 (divorced, 1970); married Carla Blank (a modern dancer); children: (first marriage) Timothy, Brett (daughter); (second marriage) Tennessee Maria (daughter). *Education:* Attended State University of New York at Buffalo, 1956-60. *Politics:* Independent.

*ADDRESSES: Agent*—Ellis J. Freedman, 415 Madison Ave., New York, NY 10017.

*CAREER:* Writer. Yardbird Publishing Co., Inc., Berkeley, CA, co-founder, 1971, editorial director, 1971-75; Reed, Cannon & Johnson Communications Co. (a publisher and producer of video cassettes), Berkeley, co-founder, 1973—; Before Columbus Foundation (a producer and distributor of work of unknown ethnic writers), Berkeley, co-founder, 1976—; Ishmael Reed and Al Young's *Quilt* (magazine), Berkeley, co-founder, 1980—. Teacher at St. Mark's in the Bowery prose workshop, 1966; guest lecturer, University of California, Berkeley, 1968—, University of Washington, 1969-70, State University of New York at Buffalo, summer, 1975, and fall, 1979, Yale University, fall, 1979, Dartmouth College, summers, 1980-81, Sitka Community Association, summer, 1982, Columbia University, 1983, University of Arkansas at Fayetteville, 1982, Harvard University, 1987, and Regents lecturer, University of California, Santa Barbara, 1988. Judge of National Poetry Competition, 1980, King's County Literary Award, 1980, University of Michigan Hopwood Award, 1981. Chair of Berkeley Arts Commission, 1980 and 1981. Coordinating Council of Literary Magazines, chairman of board of directors, 1975-79, advisory board chair, 1977-79.

*AWARDS, HONORS:* Certificate of Merit, California Association of English Teachers, 1972, for *19 Necromancers from Now;* nominations for National Book Award in fiction and poetry, 1973, for *Mumbo Jumbo* and *Conjure: Selected Poems, 1963-1970;* nomination for Pulitzer Prize in poetry, 1973, for *Conjure;* Richard and Hinda Rosenthal Foundation Award, National Institute of Arts and Letters, 1975, for *The Last Days of Louisiana Red;* John Simon Guggenheim Memorial Foundation award for fiction, 1974; Poetry in Public Places winner (New York City), 1976, for poem "From the Files of Agent 22," and for a bicentennial mystery play, *The Lost State of Franklin,* written in collaboration with Carla Blank and Suzushi Hanayagi; Lewis Michaux Award, 1978; American Civil Liberties Award, 1978; Pushcart Prize for essay "American Poetry: Is There a Center?," 1979; Wisconsin Arts Board fellowship, 1982; associate fellow of Calhoun College, Yale University, 1982; A.C.L.U. publishing fellowship; three New York State publishing grants for merit; three National Endowment for the Arts publishing grants for merit; California Arts Council grant; associate fellow, Harvard Signet Society, 1987—.

*WRITINGS:*

FICTION

*The Free-Lance Pallbearers,* Doubleday, 1967, Avon, 1985.
*Yellow Back Radio Broke-Down,* Doubleday, 1969, reprinted, Bantam, 1987.
*Mumbo Jumbo,* Doubleday, 1972, reprinted, Bantam, 1987.
*The Last Days of Louisiana Red* (Book-of-the-Month Club alternate selection), Random House, 1974.
*Flight to Canada,* Random House, 1976.
*The Terrible Twos,* St. Martin's/Marek, 1982.
*Reckless Eyeballing,* St. Martin's, 1986.
*The Terrible Threes,* Macmillan, 1989.
*Japanese by Spring,* Atheneum, 1992.

NONFICTION

*Shrovetide in Old New Orleans* (essays; original manuscript entitled *This One's on Me*), Doubleday, 1978.
*God Made Alaska for the Indians: Selected Essays,* Garland, 1982.
*Writin' Is Fightin': Thirty-Seven Years of Boxing on Paper,* Atheneum, 1990.
Contributor to numerous volumes, including *Armistad I:*

*Writings on Black History and Culture,* Vintage Books, 1970; *The Black Aesthetic,* Doubleday, 1971; *Nommo: An Anthology of Modern Black African and Black American Literature,* Macmillan, 1972; *Cutting Edges: Young American Fiction for the 70s,* Holt, 1973; *Superfiction; or, The American Story Transformed: An Anthology,* Vintage Books, 1975; and *American Poets in 1976,* Bobbs Merrill, 1976.

EDITOR

(Under pseudonym Emmett Coleman) *The Rise, Fall, and ... ? of Adam Clayton Powell,* Bee-Line Books, 1967.
(And author of introduction, and contributor) *19 Necromancers from Now,* Doubleday, 1970.
(With Al Young) *Yardbird Lives!,* Grove Press, 1978.
(And contributor) *Calafia: The California Poetry,* Y-Bird Books, 1979.
(With Kathryn Trueblood and Shawn Wong) *The Before Columbus Foundation Fiction Anthology,* Norton, 1992.
(With Kathryn Trueblood and Shawn Wong) *The Before Columbus Foundation Poetry Anthology,* Norton, 1992.

POETRY

*catechism of d neoamerican hoodoo church,* Paul Breman (London), 1970, Broadside Press, 1971.
*Conjure: Selected Poems, 1963-1970,* University of Massachusetts Press, 1972.
*Chattanooga: Poems,* Random House, 1973.
*A Secretary to the Spirits,* illustrations by Betye Saar, NOK Publishers, 1977.
*New and Collected Poems,* Atheneum, 1990.

Poetry also represented in anthologies, including *Where Is Vietnam? American Poets Respond: An Anthology of Contemporary Poems,* Doubleday, 1967; *The New Black Poetry,* International Publishers, 1969; *The Norton Anthology of Poetry,* Norton, 1970; *The Poetry of the Negro, 1746-1970,* Doubleday, 1970; *Afro-American Literature: An Introduction,* Harcourt, 1971; *The Writing on the Wall: 108 American Poems of Protest,* Doubleday, 1971; *Major Black Writers,* Scholastic Book Services, 1971; *The Black Poets,* Bantam, 1971; *The Poetry of Black America: Anthology of the 20th Century,* Harper, 1972; and *Giant Talk: An Anthology of Third World Writings,* Random House, 1975.

OTHER

*Ishmael Reed Reading His Poetry* (cassette), Temple of Zeus, Cornell University, 1976.
*Ishmael Reed and Michael Harper Reading in the UCSD New Poetry Series* (reel), University of California, San Diego, 1977.
(Author of introduction) Elizabeth A. Settle and Thomas A.

Settle, *Ishmael Reed: A Primary and Secondary Bibliography,* G. K. Hall, 1982.
*Cab Calloway Stands In for the Moon,* Bamberger, 1986.

Also author, with wife, Carla Blank, and Suzushi Hanayagi, of a bicentennial mystery play, *The Lost State of Franklin.* Executive producer of pilot episode of soap opera *Personal Problems* and co-publisher of *The Steve Cannon Show: A Quarterly Audio-Cassette Radio Show Magazine.*

Contributor of fiction to such periodicals as *Fiction, Iowa Review, Nimrod, Players, Ramparts, Seattle Review,* and *Spokane Natural;* contributor of articles and reviews to numerous periodicals, including *Black World, Confrontation: Journal of Third World Literature, Essence, Le Monde, Los Angeles Times, New York Times, Playgirl, Rolling Stone, Village Voice, Washington Post,* and *Yale Review;* and contributor of poetry to periodicals, including *American Poetry Review, Black Scholar, Black World, Essence, Liberator, Negro Digest, Noose, San Francisco Examiner, Oakland Tribune, Life, Connoisseur,* and *Umbra.* Co-founder of periodicals, *East Village Other* and *Advance* (Newark community newspaper), both 1965. Editor of *Yardbird Reader,* 1972-76, editor-in-chief, *Y'Bird* magazine, 1978-80, and co-editor of *Quilt* magazine, 1981.

*Mumbo Jumbo* was translated into French and Spanish, 1975.

*ADAPTATIONS:* Some of Reed's poetry has been scored and recorded on *New Jazz Poets;* a dramatic episode from *The Last Days of Louisiana Red* appears on *The Steve Cannon Show: A Quarterly Audio-Cassette Radio Show Magazine,* produced by Reed, Cannon & Johnson Communications.

*SIDELIGHTS:* The novels of contemporary black American writer Ishmael Reed "are meant to provoke," writes *New York Times* contributor Darryl Pickney. "Though variously described as a writer in whose work the black picaresque tradition has been extended, as a misogynist or an heir to both [Zora Neale] Hurston's folk lyricism and [Ralph] Ellison's irony, he is, perhaps because of this, one of the most underrated writers in America. Certainly no other contemporary black writer, male or female, has used the language and beliefs of folk culture so imaginatively, and few have been so stinging about the absurdity of American racism." Yet this novelist and poet is not simply a voice of black protest against racial and social injustices but instead a confronter of even more universal evils, a purveyor of even more universal truths.

Reed's first novel, *The Free-Lance Pallbearers,* introduces several thematic and stylistic devices that reappear throughout his canon. In this novel, as in his later works, Reed's first satirical jab is at the oppressive, stress-filled, Western/European/Christian tradition. But in *The Free-Lance Pallbearers,*

the oppressor/oppressed, evil/good dichotomy is not as simple as it first appears. While Reed blames whites, called HARRY SAM in the novel, for present world conditions, he also viciously attacks culpable individuals from different strata in the black community and satirizes various kinds of black leaders in the twentieth century. Reed implies that many such leaders argue against white control by saying they want to improve conditions, to "help the people," but that in reality they are only waiting for the chance to betray and exploit poor blacks and to appropriate power.

Leaders of the black movement at the time of the novel's publication regarded as permissible the ridiculing of the white, Christian Bible, as in this grotesque caricature of St. John's vision and the Four Horsemen of the Apocalypse: "I saw an object atop the fragments of dead clippings. I waded up to my knees through grassy film and the phlegm-covered flags and picked up an ivory music box. On the cover done in mother-of-pearl was a picture of Lenore in her Bickford's uniform. I opened the music box and heard the tape of the familiar voice: ROGER YOUNG IN THE FIRST AT SARATOGA / ROGER YOUNG IN THE NINTH AT CHURCHILL DOWNS / ROGER YOUNG IN THE FOURTH AT BATAVIA / ROGER YOUNG IN THE FIFTH AT AQUEDUCT / ANNOUNCED BY RAPUNZEL." But the inclusion of negative black characters was thought by critics such as Houston Baker, Amiri Baraka, and Addison Gayle to be the wrong subject matter for the times. Reed, however, could never agree to rigid guidelines for including or excluding material from the novel form. As he would say later in *Shrovetide in Old New Orleans* concerning his battle with the critics, "The mainstream aspiration of Afro-Americans is for more freedom—and not slavery—including freedom of artistic expression."

Among the black characters whom Reed puts into a negative light in *The Free-Lance Pallbearers* are Elijah Raven, the Muslim/Black Nationalist whose ideas of cultural and racial separation in the United States are exposed as lies; Eclair Pockchop, the minister fronting as an advocate of the people's causes, later discovered performing an unspeakable sex act on SAM; the black cop who protects white people from the blacks in the projects and who idiotically allows a cow-bell to be put around his neck for "meritorious service"; Doopeyduk's neighbors in the projects who, too stupid to remember their own names, answer to "M/Neighbor" and "F/Neighbor"; and finally Doopeyduk himself, whose pretensions of being a black intellectual render all his statements and actions absurd. Yet Reed reserves his most scathing satire for the black leaders who cater to SAM in his palace: "who mounted the circuitous steps leading to SAM'S, assuring the boss dat: 'Wasn't us boss. 'Twas Stokely and Malcolm. Not us, boss. No indeed. We put dat ad in da *Times* repudiating dem, boss? Look, boss. We can prove it to you, dat we loves you. Would you like for us to cook up some strange recipes for ya, boss? Or tell some jokes? Did you hear the one about da nigger in the woodpile? Well, seems dere was this nigger, boss...."'

The rhetoric of popular black literature in the 1960s is also satirized in *The Free-Lance Pallbearers*. The polemics of the time, characterized by colloquial diction, emotionalism, direct threats, automatic writing, and blueprints for a better society, are portrayed by Reed as representing the negative kind of literature required of blacks by the reading public. Reed's point is that while literature by blacks might have been saying that blacks would no longer subscribe to white dictates, in fact the converse was true, manifested in the very literature that the publishing houses generally were printing at the time.

Furthermore, *The Free-Lance Pallbearers* fully exemplifies Reed's orthographic, stylistic, and rhetorical techniques. He prefers phonetic spellings to standard spellings, thus drawing special attention to subjects otherwise mundane. He also uses capitalization for emphasis, substitutes numerals for words (1 for one) when including number references in the text, borrows Afro-American oral folklore as a source for his characters (as when Doopeyduk acts the part of "Shine" of the old crafty black tale), and utilizes newsflashes and radio voiceovers to comment on the book's action.

In his second novel, *Yellow Back Radio Broke-Down,* Reed begins to use at length Hoodoo (or Voodoo) methods and folklore as a basis for his work. Underlying all of the components of Hoodoo are two precepts: 1) the Hoodoo idea of syncretism, or the combination of beliefs and practices with divergent cultural origins, and 2) the Hoodoo concept of time. Even before the exportation of slaves to the Caribbean, Hoodoo was a syncretic religion, absorbing all that it considered useful from other West African religious practices. As a religion formed to combat degrading social conditions by dignifying and connecting man with helpful supernatural forces, Hoodoo thrives because of its syncretic flexibility, its ability to take even ostensibly negative influences and transfigure them into that which helps the "horse," or the one possessed by the attributes of a Hoodoo god. Hoodoo is bound by certain dogma or rites, but such rules are easily changed when they become oppressive, myopic, or no longer useful.

Reed turns this concept of syncretism into a literary method that combines aspects of "standard" English, including dialect, slang, argot, neologisms, or rhyme, with less "standard" language, whose principal rules of discourse are taken from the streets, popular music, and television. By purposely mixing language from different sources in popular culture, Reed employs expressions that both evoke interest and humor through seeming incongruities and create the illusion of real speech. In *Black American Literature Forum,* Michel Fabre draws a connection between Reed's use of language and his vision of the world, suggesting that "his so-called nonsense

words raise disturbing questions ... about the very nature of language." Often, "the semantic implications are disturbing because opposite meanings co-exist." Thus Reed emphasizes "the dangerous interchangeability of words and of the questionable identity of things and people" and "poses anguishing questions about self-identity, about the mechanism of meaning and about the nature of language and communication."

The historical sense of time in Reed's discourse, based on the African concept of time, is not linear; dates are not generally ascribed to the past, and past events overlap with those in the present. Berndt Ostendorf in *Black Literature in White America* notes that the African time sense is "telescoped," that it contains no concept of a future, only the certainty that man's existence will never end. Reed's version of this concept of synchronicity or simultaneity incorporates a future by positing a time cycle of revolving and re-evolving events but maintains an essentially African concept of the past/present relationship, as characters treat past and present matters as though they were simultaneous.

Syncretism and synchronicity, along with other facets of Hoodoo as literary method, are central to *Yellow Back Radio Broke-Down.* The title is street-talk for the elucidation of a problem, in this case the racial and oligarchical difficulties of an Old West town, *Yellow Back Radio;* these difficulties are explained, or "broke down," for the reader. The novel opens with a description of the Hoodoo fetish, or mythical cult figure, Loop Garoo, whose name means "change into." Loop is a truly syncretic character who embodies diverse ethnic backgrounds and a history and power derived from several religions.

At least one of Reed's themes from *The Free-Lance Pallbearers* is reworked in *Yellow Back Radio Broke-Down,* as Christianity is again unmercifully attacked. Three Horsemen of the Apocalypse are represented by the Barber, Marshall, and Doctor, criminals, hypocrites, and upholders of the one-and-only-way-of-doing-things, that is, the way which materially benefits them; and the fourth Horseman is embodied in the Preacher Reverend Boyd, who will make a profit on guilt with the volume of poetry he is putting together, *Stomp Me O Lord.* Loop calls his own betrayal by other blacks—Alcibiades and Jeff—and his resurrection a parody of "His Passion." The Pope, who appears in Yellow Back Radio in the 1880s, is revealed as a corrupt defender of the white tradition, concerned only with preventing Loop's magic from becoming stronger than his own.

The year 1972 saw the publication of Reed's first major volume of poetry, *Conjure: Selected Poems, 1963-1970,* followed in 1973 by his second collection, *Chattanooga: Poems,* and in 1977 by *A Secretary to the Spirits.* It is really in *Conjure* that Reed fully develops his literary method. Although the poem beginning "I am a cowboy in the boat of Ra" continues an earlier Reed interest in Egyptian symbolism, after this work he lyrically draws his symbols from Afro-American and Anglo-American historical and popular traditions—two distinct, but intertwined sources for the Afro-American aesthetic. "Black Power Poem" succinctly states the Hoodoo stance in the West: "may the best church win. / shake hands now and come out conjuring"; a longer poem "Neo-Hoodoo Manifesto" defines all that Hoodoo is, and thus sheds light on the ways Reed uses its principles in writing, primarily through his absorption of material from every available source and his expansive originality in treating that material.

The theme of *Mumbo Jumbo,* Reed's 1972 novel, is the origin and composition of the "true Afro-American aesthetic." Testifying to the novel's success in fulfilling this theme, Houston Baker in *Black World* calls *Mumbo Jumbo* "the first black American novel of the last ten years that gives one a sense of the broader vision and the careful, painful, and laborious 'fundamental brainwork' that are needed if we are to define the eternal dilemma of the Black Arts and work fruitfully toward its melioration.... [The novel's] overall effect is that of amazing talent and flourishing genius." *Mumbo Jumbo*'s first chapter is crucial in that it presents the details of the highly complex plot in synopsis or news-flash form. Reed has a Hoodoo detective named Papa LaBas (representing the Hoodoo god Legba) search out and reconstruct a black aesthetic from remnants of literary and cultural history. To lend the narrative authenticity, Reed inserts favorite scholarly devices: facts from nonfictional, published works; photographs and historical drawings; and a bibliography. The unstated subtext throughout the book is "My aesthetic is just as good as yours maybe better and certainly is founded on no more ridiculous a set of premises than yours."

At the opening of *Mumbo Jumbo,* set in New Orleans in the 1920s, white municipal officials are trying to respond to "Jes Grew," an outbreak of behavior outside of socially conditioned roles; white people are "acting black" by dancing half-dressed in the streets to an intoxicating new loa (the spiritual essence of a fetish) called jazz. Speaking in tongues, people also abandon racist and other oppressive endeavors because it is more fun to "shake that thing." One of the doctors assigned to treat the pandemic of Jes Grew comments, "There are no isolated cases in this thing. It knows no class no race no consciousness. It is self-propagating and you can never tell when it will hit." No one knows where the germ has come from; it "jes grew." In the synoptic first chapter, the omniscient narrator says Jes Grew is actually "an anti-plague. Some plagues caused the body to waste away. Jes Grew enlivened the host. Other plagues were accompanied by bad air (malaria). Jes Grew victims said the air was as clear as they had ever seen it and that there was the aroma of roses and perfumes which had never before enticed their nostrils. Some plagues arise from

decomposing animals, but Jes Grew is electric as life and is characterized by ebullience and ecstasy. Terrible plagues were due to the wrath of God; But Jes Grew is the delight of the gods." Jes Grew also is reflected in Reed's writing style, which may take on any number of guises, but is intended both to illuminate and enliven the reader.

In the novel, Christianity is called "Atonism," a word with its origin in the worship of the sun-god, Aton, of ancient Egypt. Atonists are forever at war to stamp out Jes Grew, as it threatens their traditions and their power. The word *Atonism* is also a cognate of the word *atone,* with its connotations of guilt. The Atonists do not simply wage war against nonwhites and non-Christians. Anyone who opposes their beliefs is attacked. When a white member of a multi-ethnic gang, Thor Wintergreen, sides with nonwhites, he is first duped and then killed by Atonist Biff Musclewhite. Though Musclewhite is initially being held captive by Wintergreen, the prisoner persuades Wintergreen to release him by giving the following explanation of the Atonist cause: "Son, this is a nigger closing in on our mysteries and soon he will be asking our civilization to 'come quietly.' This man is talking about Judeo-Christian culture, Christianity, Atonism, whatever you want to call it.... I've seen them, son, in Africa, China, they're not like us, son, the Herronvolk. Europe. This place. They are lagging behind, son, and you know in your heart this is true. Son, these niggers writing. Profaning our sacred words. Taking them from us and beating them on the anvil of BoogieWoogie, putting their black hands on them so that they shine like burnished amulets. Taking our words, son, these filthy niggers and using them.... Why 1 of them dared to interpret, critically mind you, the great Herman Melville's *Moby Dick!!*" *Mumbo Jumbo* thus presents a battle for supremacy between powers that see the world in two distinct, opposed ways, with the separate visions endemic to the human types involved: one, expansive and syncretic; the other, impermeable and myopic.

Hoodoo time resurfaces in *Mumbo Jumbo* through a stylistic technique that produces a synchronic effect. Certain chapters which have detailed past events in the past tense are immediately followed by chapters that begin with present-tense verbs and present-day situations; this effect introduces simultaneity to the text, and elicits from the reader a response that mirrors the feeling of the Hoodoo/oral culture. That is, the reader feels that all of the actions are thematically and rhetorically related, because they all seem to be happening in the same narrative time frame. Commenting on his use both of time and of fiction-filled news-flashes, Reed says in *Shrovetide in Old New Orleans* that in writing *Mumbo Jumbo,* he "wanted to write about a time like the present or to use the past to prophesy about the future—a process our ancestors called necromancy. I chose the twenties because they are very similar to what's happening right now. This is a valid method and has been used by writers from time immemorial. Nobody ever accused James Joyce of making up things. Using a past event of one's country or culture to comment on the present."

The close of *Mumbo Jumbo* finds Jes Grew withering with the burning of its text, the Book of Thoth, which lists the sacred spells and dances of the Egyptian god Osiris. LaBas says Jes Grew will reappear some day to make its own text: "A future generation of young artists will accomplish this," says LaBas, referring to the writers, painters, politicians, and musicians of the 1960s, "the decade that screamed," as Reed termed it in *Chattanooga.*

In the course of the narrative, Reed constructs his history of the true Afro-American aesthetic and parallels the uniting of Afro-American oral tradition, folklore, art, and history, with a written code, a text, a literate recapitulation of history and practice. By calling for a unification of text and tradition, Reed equates the Text (the Afro-American aesthetic) with the Vedas, the Pentateuch, the Koran, the Latin Vulgate, the Book of Mormon, and all "Holy" codifications of faith. *Mumbo Jumbo,* which itself becomes the Text, appears as a direct, written response to the assertion that there is no "black" aesthetic, that black contributions to the world culture have been insignificant at best.

As seen in *Mumbo Jumbo,* Reed equates his own aesthetic with other systems based on different myths. Then he insists that his notion of an aesthetic is more humanistic than others, especially those based on Americanized, Christian dogma. Finding its spiritual corollary in Hoodoo, Reed's method achieves a manual of codification in *Mumbo Jumbo.* This code also is used in his next two novels, *The Last Days of Louisiana Red* and *Flight to Canada,* to reaffirm his belief that Hoodoo, now understood as a spiritual part of the Afro-American aesthetic, can be used as a basis for literary response.

*The Last Days of Louisiana Red* consists of three major story lines that coalesce toward the close of the novel to form its theme. The first and main plot is the tale of Ed Yellings, an industrious, middle-class black involved in "The Business," an insider's term for the propagation of Hoodoo. Through experimentation in his business, Solid Gumbo Works, Yellings discovers a cure for cancer and is hard at work to refine and market this remedy and other remedies for the various aspects of Louisiana Red, the Hoodoo name for all evil. When he is mysteriously murdered, Hoodoo detective Papa LaBas appears, and the stage is set for the major part of the action. This action involves participants in the novel's second and third story lines, the tale of the Chorus and the recounting of the mythical Antigone's decisions to oppose the dictates of the state. Antigone is clearly heroic in her actions, but the Chorus also fulfills a significant function by symbolizing black Americans who will not disappear, even though they

are relegated by more powerful forces to minor roles. Never satisfied with this position, black Americans want to be placed where they believe they belong: in the forefront of the action, where they can succeed or fail depending upon their merits. Therein lies Reed's theme in *The Last Days of Louisiana Red.*

In *Flight to Canada* Reed most effectively explores Hoodoo as a force that gives his black protagonists the strength to be hopeful and courageous in the face of seemingly hopeless situations. Canada has, in this novel, at least two levels of meaning. It is, first of all, a literal, historical region where slaves might flee to freedom. Second, it becomes a metaphor for happiness; that is, anything that makes an individual character happy may be referred to as "Canada."

The major plot of *Flight to Canada* involves the escape of Raven Quickskill from his owner, Massa Arthur Swille, and Swille's efforts to return Quickskill to captivity. The historical Canada is the eventual destination where Quickskill and other slaves wish to arrive when they flee from Swille in Virginia, but this historical Canada is not the heaven slaves think, and pray, it will be. Yet in the face of the depressing stories about Canada from his friends Leechfield, Carpenter, Cato, and 40s, Quickskill will not relinquish his dream. For him, Canada is personified beyond the physical plane. Refuting those who would deny or degrade the existence of the Canada that his reading tours have allowed him to see as well as the Canada that he must invent to live in peace, Quickskill reflects: "He was so much against slavery that he had begun to include prose and poetry in the same book, so that there would be no arbitrary boundaries between them. He preferred Canada to slavery, whether Canada was exile, death, art, liberation, or a woman. Each man to his own Canada. There was much avian imagery in the poetry of slaves. Poetry about dreams and flight. They wanted to cross that Black Rock Ferry to freedom even though they had different notions as to what freedom was. They often disagreed about it, Leechfield, 40s. But it was his writing that got him to Canada. 'Flight to Canada' was responsible for getting him to Canada. And so for him, freedom was his writing. His writing was his Hoodoo. Others had their way of Hoodoo, but his was his writing. It fascinated him, it possessed him; his typewriter was his drum he danced to."

In *Flight to Canada* Hoodoo becomes a kind of faith that sustains and uplifts without necessarily degrading those to whom it is opposed. Unable to explain how he has attained success, Quickskill can only attribute his freedom to things unseen. Ultimately, all of the black characters turn to this transcendent vision as their shield against the harsher aspects of reality. As is true with Quickskill when he is confronted with the truth about Canada, the black characters' ability to rely upon the metaphysical saves their lives as well as their dreams. In *The Terrible Twos,* Reed maintains the implicit notions of

Hoodoo, while using his main story line to resurrect another apocryphal tale: the legend of Santa Claus and his assistant/boss, Black Peter. The time frame of the novel is roughly Christmas 1980 to Christmases of the 1990s, and the novel is clearly an allegory on Ronald Reagan's presidency and its consequences, as Reed sees them, in the 1990s. The evil of *The Terrible Twos* is the type that comes from selfishness fed by an exclusive monetary system, such as capitalism. Yet Reed does not endorse any other sort of government now in existence but criticizes any person or system that ignores what is humanly right in favor of what is economically profitable. Santa Claus (actually an out-of-work television personality) exemplifies the way Hoodoo fights this selfish evil: by putting those who were prosperous onto the level of those who have nothing and are abandoned. Santa characterizes American capitalists, those with material advantages, as infantile, selfish and exclusionary because their class station does not allow them to empathize with those who are different: "'Two years old, that's what we are, emotionally—Americans, always wanting someone to hand us some ice cream, always complaining, Santa didn't bring me this and why didn't Santa bring me that.' People in the crowd chuckle. 'Nobody can reason with us. Nobody can tell us anything. Millions of people staggering about passing out in the snow and we say that's tough. We say too bad to the children who don't have milk. I weep as I read these letters the poor children send me at my temporary home in Alaska.'"

In *The Terrible Twos* Reed leaves overt Hoodoo references as a subtext and focuses on the Rasta and Nicolaite myths, two conflicting quasi-religious cults revitalized by Black Power. He also concentrates on the myths of power and privilege created by "the vital people," those who are white and wealthy. However, the racist policies of the Nicolaites are eventually thwarted by inexplicable circumstances that stem from the supernatural powers of Hoodoo and from the Hoodoo notion that time is circular and that therefore the mighty will possibly—even probably—fall.

One device used in the novel is perhaps central in conveying Reed's vision. The first chapter is almost all factual reportage about Christmas and related matters, thus laying the foundation of belief for the fantastic Christmas Reed is about to construct. Yet, in comparison, the facts of Christmas seem as preposterous as the fiction of Christmas: Is it fact or fantasy that around Christmas of 1980 the *Buffalo Evening News* put under the headline "The Wild West is Back in the Saddle Again" the story of "First Actor" campaigning in cowboy attire in the West and a Confederate uniform in the South; is it fact or fantasy that a 6,000-pound ice sculpture of Santa and his reindeer carved by Andrew Young appears in a San Francisco Christmas parade? As John Leonard declares in his *New York Times* review of the book: "Mr. Reed is as close as we are likely to get to a Garcia Marquez, elaborating his own mythology

even as he trashes ours.... *The Terrible Twos* tells many jokes before it kills, almost as if it had been written with barbed wire."

*Reckless Eyeballing* is a bitingly satiric allegory. Ian Ball, a black male writer, responds to the poor reception of his earlier play, *Suzanna,* by writing *Reckless Eyeballing,* a play sure to please those in power with its vicious attacks against black men. ("Reckless eyeballing" was one of the accusations against Emmett Till, the young Chicago black who was murdered in Mississippi in 1953 for "looking and whistling at a white woman.") Tremonisha Smarts, a black female writer whose first name is drawn from a Scott Joplin opera of that title, is alternately popular and unpopular with the white women who are promoting her books. The battle for whose vision will dominate in the literary market and popular culture is fierce, and those critics who have seen in the portrait of Tremonisha a thinly veiled response to the current popularity of feminist writers are probably correct.

In Joplin's opera, the character Tremonisha represents the powers of assimilation into American culture in opposition to the "powers of the Hoodoo men." Thus, not only does Reed's version of the Tremonisha character allude to the original Tremonisha's disagreement with early African American currents, but she also becomes one of the critical forces that Reed has long opposed. More ironically, this allusive connection may be merely a feint, a trick leading critics to believe that Reed is covering the same, familiar Hoodoo ground covered before; actually, he moves in this novel toward unearthing the truly universal structures of Hoodoo, which are rooted in the apocryphal rites of other religions.

For example, the name of the character Abiahus in *Reckless Eyeballing* is a variant of the Hebrew "Lilith," and the name helps to remind the reader of the legend of the amulet used when Hebrew women gave birth to ward off child-stealers. Reed found the connections between the shared traditions of Judaism and Hoodoo in *The Legends of Genesis* by Hermann Gunkel, in David Meltzer's magazine *TREE,* and in Mike Gold's *Jews without Money,* the last of which includes a description of a Jewish woman similar to the Mambos and Conjure Women of Hoodoo origin. Reed thus reminds readers that Hoodoo is ever-changing by constantly absorbing materials from diverse cultures. He also warns his readers that he, too, is ever-changing and that a sure way to be misled is to believe that one has Hoodoo's concepts (and Reed's) pinned down as to their "one true" meaning.

Syncretic and synchronic in form, Reed's novels focus most often on social circumstances that inhibit the development of blacks in American society. As satire is usually based on real types, the writer draws in part from history and the news to satirize America's cultural arrogance and the terrible price paid by those who are not "vital people," members of the dominant culture or the moneyed class. His assertion, in a *Review of Contemporary Fiction* interview with Reginald Martin, that Hoodoo is "solidly in the American tradition" is supported by his collation of myth, fact, and apocryphal data into a history; from that history, a method or aesthetic is drawn not only for formulating art and multi-ethnic cultural standards but also for developing a different and more humane way of experiencing and influencing the world.

*BIOGRAPHICAL/CRITICAL SOURCES:*

*BOOKS*

Bellamy, Joe David, editor, *The New Fiction: Interviews with Innovative American Writers,* University of Illinois Press, 1974.

Bruck, Peter, and Wolfgang Karrer, editors, *The Afro-American Novel since 1960,* B. R. Bruener (Amsterdam), 1982.

Chesi, Gert, *Voodoo: Africa's Secret Power,* Perlinger-Verlag (Austria), 1979.

*Contemporary Literary Criticism,* Gale, Volume 2, 1974, Volume 3, 1975, Volume 5, 1976, Volume 6, 1976, Volume 8, 1980, Volume 32, 1985.

*Conversations with Writers,* Volume 2, Gale, 1978.

*Dictionary of Literary Biography,* Gale, Volume 2: *American Novelists since World War II,* 1978, Volume 5: *American Poets since World War II,* 1980, Volume 33: *Afro-American Fiction Writers after 1955,* 1984.

Klinkowitz, Jerome, *Literary Subversions: New American Fiction and the Practice of Criticism,* Southern Illinois University Press, 1985.

Martin, Reginald, *Ishmael Reed and the New Black Aesthetic Critics,* Macmillan (London), 1987.

O'Brien, John, *Interviews with Black Writers,* Liveright, 1973.

O'Donnell, Patrick and Robert Con Davis, editors, *Intertextuality and Contemporary American Fiction,* Johns Hopkins University Press, 1989.

Ostendorf, Berndt, *Black Literature in White America,* Noble, 1982.

Reed, Ishmael, *The Free-Lance Pallbearers,* Doubleday, 1967.

Reed, Ishmael, *Yellow Back Radio Broke-Down,* Doubleday, 1969.

Reed, Ishmael, *Conjure: Selected Poems, 1963-1970,* University of Massachusetts Press, 1972.

Reed, Ishmael, *Mumbo Jumbo,* Doubleday, 1972.

Reed, Ishmael, *Chattanooga: Poems,* Random House, 1973.

Reed, Ishmael, *The Last Days of Louisiana Red,* Random House, 1974.

Reed, Ishmael, *Flight to Canada,* Random House, 1976.

Reed, Ishmael, *A Secretary to the Spirits,* NOK Publishers, 1977.

Reed, Ishmael, *Shrovetide in Old New Orleans,* Doubleday, 1978.

Reed, Ishmael, *The Terrible Twos,* St. Martin's/Marek, 1982.

Reed, Ishmael, *Reckless Eyeballing,* St. Martin's, 1986.

Rush, Theresa Gunnels, Carol Fairbanks Myers, and Ester Spring Arata, *Black American Writers Past and Present: A Biographical and Bibliographical Dictionary,* Scarecrow, 1975.

Settle, Elizabeth A., and Thomas A. Settle, *Ishmael Reed: A Primary and Secondary Bibliography,* G. K. Hall, 1982.

Stebich, Ute, *Haitian Art,* Abrams, 1978.

*PERIODICALS*

*Afriscope,* May, 1977.

*American Book Review,* May/June, 1983.

*American Poetry Review,* May/June, 1976; January/February, 1978.

*Arizona Quarterly,* autumn, 1979.

*Arts Magazine,* May, 1967.

*Berkeley News,* April 10, 1975.

*Black American Literature Forum,* Volume 12, 1978; spring, 1979; spring, 1980; fall, 1984.

*Black Books Bulletin,* winter, 1976.

*Black Creation,* fall, 1972; winter, 1973.

*Black Enterprise,* January, 1973; December, 1982; April, 1983.

*Black History Museum Newsletter,* Volume 4, number 3/4, 1975.

*Black Scholar,* March, 1981.

*Black Times,* September, 1975.

*Black World,* October, 1971; December, 1972; January, 1974; June, 1974; June, 1975; July, 1975.

*Changes in the Arts,* November, 1972; December/January, 1973.

*Chicago Review,* fall, 1976.

*Chicago Tribune Book World,* April 27, 1986.

*Critical Inquiry,* June, 1983.

*Essence,* July, 1986.

*Fiction International,* summer, 1973.

*Harper's,* December, 1969.

*Iowa Review,* spring, 1982, pp. 117-131.

*Journal of Black Poetry,* summer/fall, 1969.

*Journal of Black Studies,* December, 1979.

*Journal of Negro History,* January, 1978.

*Los Angeles Free Press,* September 18, 1970.

*Los Angeles Times,* April 29, 1975.

*Los Angeles Times Book Review,* April 20, 1986; June 4, 1989; April 14, 1991, p. 10.

*MELUS,* spring, 1984.

*Mississippi Quarterly,* winter, 1984-85, pp. 21-32.

*Mississippi Review,* Volume 20, numbers 1-2, 1991.

*Modern Fiction Studies,* summer, 1976; spring, 1988, pp. 97-123.

*Modern Poetry Studies,* autumn, 1973; autumn, 1974.

*Nation,* September 18, 1976; May 22, 1982.

*Negro American Literature Forum,* winter, 1967; winter, 1972.

*Negro Digest,* February, 1969; December, 1969.

*New Republic,* November 23, 1974.

*New Yorker,* October 11, 1969.

*New York Review of Books,* October 5, 1972; December 12, 1974; August 12, 1982; January 29, 1987; October 12, 1989, p. 20.

*New York Times,* August 1, 1969; August 9, 1972; June 17, 1982; April 5, 1986.

*New York Times Book Review,* August 6, 1972; November 10, 1974; September 19, 1976; July 18, 1982; March 23, 1986; May 7, 1989; April 7, 1991, p. 32.

*Nickel Review,* August 28-September 10, 1968.

*Obsidian: Black Literature in Review,* spring/summer, 1979; spring/summer, 1986, pp. 113-127.

*Parnassus: Poetry in Review,* spring/summer, 1976.

*Partisan Review,* spring, 1975.

*People,* December 16, 1974.

*PHYLON: The Atlanta University Review of Race and Culture,* December, 1968; June, 1975.

*Postmodern Culture,* May, 1991.

*Review of Contemporary Fiction,* summer, 1984; spring, 1987.

*San Francisco Review of Books,* November, 1975; January/February, 1983.

*Saturday Review,* October 14, 1972; November 11, 1978.

*Southern Review,* July, 1985, pp. 603-614.

*Studies in American Fiction,* Volume 5, 1977.

*Studies in the Novel,* summer, 1971.

*Times Literary Supplement,* May 18, 1990, p. 534.

*Twentieth Century Literature,* April, 1974.

*Village Voice,* January 22, 1979.

*Virginia Quarterly Review,* winter, 1973.

*Washington Post Book World,* March 16, 1986; June 25, 1989, p. 4; November 12, 1989, p. 16; April 14, 1991, p. 12; January 26, 1992, p. 12.

*World Literature Today,* autumn, 1978; autumn, 1986.

\*     \*     \*

## RICE, Mitchell F.  1948-

*PERSONAL:* Born September 11, 1948, in Columbus, GA; son of Joseph M. Rice (a professor); married Cecelia Hawkins (a teacher), September 12, 1970; children: Colin C., Melissa E. *Education:* California State University, Los Angeles, B.A., 1970, M.S., 1973; Claremont Graduate School, Ph.D., 1976.

*ADDRESSES: Office*—Room 3171, CEBA Building, Louisiana State University, Baton Rouge, LA 70803.
*CAREER:* Southwest Texas State University, San Marcos,

professor, 1977-85; Louisiana State University, Baton Rouge, professor, 1985—. President and owner, Management Development and Training Consultants; member of executive board, Urban League of Greater Baton Rouge.

*MEMBER:* American Political Science Association, American Society for Public Administration, Conference of Minority Public Administrators (president, 1991-92), American Public Health Association.

*WRITINGS:*

(With Woodrow Jones) *Contemporary Public Policy Perspectives and Black America,* Greenwood Press, 1984.

(With J. Owens Smith and Jones) *Blacks and American Government,* Kendall/Hunt, 1987, second edition, 1992.

(With Jones) *Black American Health,* Greenwood Press, 1987.

(With Jones) *Health Care Issues in Black America,* Greenwood Press, 1987.

(With Jones) *Health of Black Americans from Post Reconstruction to Integration,* Greenwood Press, 1990.

Contributor of more than fifty articles to journals in public administration, medicine, and the social and health sciences.

*WORK IN PROGRESS: Public Policy and the Black Hospital;* research on minority business development and government set-aside programs.

*SIDELIGHTS:* Mitchell F. Rice once commented: "Black Americans must fully understand the role and importance of politics and public policy in order to grow professionally, politically, and economically. My writings and research attempt to analyze various public policies and their impact on the black community."

\*     \*     \*

## RICH, Matty  1971-

*PERSONAL:* Given name, Matthew Satisfield Richardson; born November 26, 1971, in Brooklyn, NY; son of Beatrice Richardson. *Education:* Attended John Jay College and New York University.

*ADDRESSES: Agent*—Michael Gruber, William Morris Agency, 1350 Avenue of the Americas, New York, NY 10019; Terrie Williams, 1841 Broadway, Suite 914, New York, NY 10023.

*CAREER:* Screenwriter, director, and producer of motion pictures.
*AWARDS, HONORS:* Special jury prize, Sundance Film Fes-

tival, 1991, for *Straight out of Brooklyn;* NOVA Award, most promising director, Producer's Guild of America, 1992; Independent Spirit Award, 1992; NAACP's Special Award for Filmmaking.

*WRITINGS:*

(And director) *Straight out of Brooklyn* (screenplay), HBO Home Video, 1991.

Also author and director of *Ray Mercer vs. Tommy Morrison Pre-fight Profiles,* for TVKO/Time Warner Sports; author of the nonfiction work *Short-term and Long-term Thinking.*

*WORK IN PROGRESS: The Forty Thieves,* a screenplay; scripts for *Red Hook,* an hour-long television drama being developed for Fox.

*SIDELIGHTS:* While still a teenager, Matty Rich served as screenwriter, director, and producer of *Straight out of Brooklyn,* his autobiographical film depicting a young man's desperate attempt to escape his violent, crime-ridden environment. *Detroit News* film critic Susan Stark deemed Rich's coming-of-age story "terrifying and tragic." For Rich, such a description was also appropriate for his life. *Straight out of Brooklyn*'s main character was based on Rich's best friend, Lamont, who died of an untreated kidney problem while in a juvenile home. The filmmaker's aunt and uncle both died on Rich's birthday (she had a heart attack in a hospital, he was robbed and shot at a bus stop on his way to see her), and each of the six friends he had as an adolescent also died. Rage about the senselessness of these happenings served as a motivating factor for his screen venture. Rich explained to Richard Corliss in *Time,* "I wasn't interested in film because I love film or some director.... I was angry that everybody around me got destroyed, and I wanted to show that everyday struggle."

Rich began making *Straight out of Brooklyn* when he was seventeen years old and employed ingenious methods to pay for the project. Using his sister and mother's credit cards, he financed a short trailer that was featured on a New York radio station, hoping to solicit investors for the movie. By chance, he also met Jonathan Demme, Academy Award-winning director of 1991's *Silence of the Lambs,* who was impressed with Rich's vision and helped him procure funding from television's Public Broadcasting Service (PBS-TV). Made on a budget of $300,000, *Straight out of Brooklyn* was featured at both the Cannes and Sundance film festivals and met with critical and box-office success.

In *Straight out of Brooklyn,* protagonist Dennis Brown lives in a low-income Brooklyn housing project. His father, a Vietnam veteran, is a gas station attendant who blames his economic position on racism and vents his frustrations by drink-

ing to excess and beating his defeated wife who, in turn, tries to shrug off the bruises. This fighting wears on Dennis; he anticipates his father's frequent rages with dread, but attributes both parents' actions to their seemingly inescapable socioeconomic position. In a desperate attempt to halt the cycle of violence and hopelessness, Dennis masterminds a money-making scheme to leave the projects. Along with his friends Larry—played by Rich—and Kevin, Dennis robs a local drug dealer. With a briefcase of money, he dreams of a new life in a safe environment with his family and girlfriend. Rich, however, shows that the problem of poverty cannot be mended with superficial tactics. *Straight out of Brooklyn* ends with Dennis fearing reprisal from the drug dealer and witnessing a family tragedy.

Reviewers and audiences generally lauded Rich's uncompromising portrait of ghetto life in *Straight out of Brooklyn.* Some deemed the work more powerful because of its unhappy ending. Several critics judged Rich's camera work somewhat unpolished, but felt that the emotion and gritty vision he brought to the screen made up for shortcomings in technique. A *Newsweek* writer asserted, "*Straight out of Brooklyn* is a blunt instrument, but that's one reason it works.... The violence feels immediate and random. The wrong people die for the wrong reasons; life goes on unaffected." A *Rolling Stone* contributor noted that Rich "carved an unshakable movie out of his rage."

Rich garnered the immediate attention of movie moguls with his first film venture, and he welcomed the acclaim *Straight out of Brooklyn* received. The director explained to *Premiere* contributor David Sternbach, "I worked hard for it, and I deserve the recognition of being an up-and-coming filmmaker. I'm not a boy genius. I'm just a young man who had something to say, who wanted to express it on film." Rich, however, puts the attention in perspective: In *Time* he admitted, "If I hadn't done this movie, I'd be just another black kid on the street with a gold tooth and a funny haircut."

*BIOGRAPHICAL/CRITICAL SOURCES:*

*PERIODICALS*

*Detroit Free Press,* June 23, 1991, pp. 1G, 6G; June 28, 1991, pp. 1D, 3D.
*Detroit News,* June 20, 1991, pp. 1C, 3-4C; June 28, 1991, pp. 3D, 9D.
*Ebony,* November, 1991, pp. 156-164.
*Elle,* June, 1991, pp. 60-61.
*Newsweek,* May 27, 1991, p. 58.
*New York Times Magazine,* July 14, 1991, pp. 15-19, 38, 40, 44.

*Premiere,* July, 1991, pp. 20, 26-27.
*Rolling Stone,* June 13, 1991, p. 108.
*Time,* June 17, 1991, pp. 64-68.


\*   \*   \*


## RICHARDS, Beah
### (Beulah Richardson)

*PERSONAL:* Born in Vicksburg, MS; married Hugh Harrell; *Education:* Dillard University, New Orleans, Louisiana; San Diego Community Theater.

*ADDRESSES: Agent*—Jack Fields & Associates, 9255 Sunset Boulevard, Suite 1105, Los Angeles, CA 90069.

*CAREER:* Stage and film actress; playwright. Appeared in numerous Off-Broadway and other stage productions, including *Take a Giant Step,* 1956, *A Raisin in the Sun,* and *The Miracle Worker,* 1959, *Purlie Victorious,* 1961, *The Amen Corner* and *Arturo Ui,* 1963, *The Little Foxes,* 1967, *One Is a Crowd,* 1970, *A Black Woman Speaks,* 1975, *Iago—An Evening with Beah Richards,* 1979. Appeared in films, including *Take A Giant Step,* 1959, *The Miracle Worker,* 1962, *Gone Are the Days,* 1963, *Guess Who's Coming to Dinner,* 1967, *Hurry Sundown,* 1967, *In the Heat of the Night,* 1967, *The Great White Hope,* 1970, *The Biscuit Eater,* 1972, *Mahogany,* 1975, *Inside Out,* 1986, *Big Shots,* 1987. Appeared in television programs, including *Hawaii Five-O,* 1969, *The Bill Cosby Show,* 1970-71, *Just an Old Sweet Song,* 1976, *Roots: The Next Generations,* 1979, *The Sophisticated Gents,* 1981, and *As Summers Die,* 1986.

*MEMBER:* Actors' Equity Association, Screen Actors Guild, Congress of Racial Equality, NAACP.

*AWARDS, HONORS: Best Plays* citation and Theater World Award, both 1964, for *The Amen Corner;* nominated for Tony Award for best dramatic actress, American Theatre Wing, 1965, for *The Amen Corner;* Academy Award nomination for best supporting actress, Academy of Motion Picture Arts and Sciences, 1967, for *Guess Who's Coming for Dinner;* All-American Press Association Award, 1968; inducted into Black Filmmakers Hall of Fame, 1974; Emmy Award for outstanding guest performer in a comedy or drama series, Academy of Television Arts and Sciences, 1988, for *Frank's Place.*

*WRITINGS:*

*A Black Woman Speaks and Other Poems* (includes *A Black Woman Speaks,* one-act dramatic monologue, first produced in Chicago, 1950; published in *Freedomways* under name Beulah Richardson, 1964), Inner City Press,

1974.
*One Is a Crowd,* first produced in Los Angeles, CA, 1970. Work represented in anthologies, including *Nine Plays by Black Women,* 1986.


\*   \*   \*


## RICHARDSON, Beulah
### See RICHARDS, Beah


\*   \*   \*


## RIVE, Richard (Moore)   1931-1989

*PERSONAL:* Surname rhymes with "leave"; born March 1, 1931, in Cape Town, South Africa; died June 4, 1989, in Elfindale, South Africa; son of Nancy (Ward) Rive. *Education:* Hewat Training College (now Hewat College of Education), Cape Town, South Africa, teacher's diploma, 1951; University of Cape Town, B.A., 1962, B.Ed., 1968; Columbia University, M.A., 1966; Oxford University, D.Phil., 1974. *Avocational interests:* Mountain climbing, coaching track athletes.

*ADDRESSES: Home*—31 Windsor Park Ave., Heathfield 7800, Cape Town, South Africa.

*CAREER:* Former teacher of English and Latin at South Peninsula High School, Cape Town, South Africa; affiliated with Harvard University, Cambridge, MA, 1987; Hewat College of Education, Cape Town, lecturer in English, became head of department of English, 1988-89.


*AWARDS, HONORS:* Farfield Foundation fellowship to travel and study contemporary African literature in English and French, 1963; Fulbright scholar, 1965-66, and Heft scholar, 1965-66; named Writer of the Year for South Africa, 1970, for "The Visits"; African Theatre Competition Prize, British Broadcasting Corp. (BBC), 1972, for *Make Like Slaves.*

*WRITINGS:*

(Editor and contributor) *Quartet: New Voices from South Africa,* Crown, 1963.
*African Songs* (short stories), Seven Seas, 1963.
(Compiler) *Modern African Prose,* Heinemann, 1964, reprinted, 1982.
*Emergency* (novel), introduction by Ezekiel Mphahlele, Faber & Faber, 1964, Collier Books, 1970.
*Selected Writings: Stories, Essays, and Plays,* Ad Donker (Johannesburg), 1977.

*Writing Black* (autobiography), D. Philip, 1982.

*Advance, Retreat: Selected Short Stories,* D. Philip, 1983, St. Martin's Press, 1989.

*"Buckingham Palace," District Six,* D. Philip, 1986, Ballantine, 1987.

*Emergency Continued* (novel), D. Philip, 1990.

(With Tim Couzens) *Seme: The Founder of the ANC,* Africa World Press, 1992.

Also author of the stage play *Make Like Slaves,* 1972. Contributor to anthologies, including *Darkness and Light: An Anthology of African Writing,* edited by Peggy Rutherford, Drum Publications (Johannesburg), 1958, published as *African Voices,* Grosset, 1959; *An African Treasury: Articles, Essays, Stories, Poems by Black Africans,* edited by Langston Hughes, Crown, 1960; *Poems from Black Africa,* edited by Hughes, Indiana University Press, 1963; *Modern African Stories,* edited by Ellis Ayitey and Ezekiel Mphahlele, Faber & Faber, 1964; *Pan African Short Stories,* edited by Neville Denny, Thomas Nelson, 1965; *African Writing Today,* edited by Mphahlele, Penguin, 1967; *Anthologie de la litterature negro-africaine: Romanciers et conteurs negro-africains,* Volume 2, edited by Leonard Sainville, Presence Africaine, 1968; and *The African Assertion: A Critical Anthology of African Literature,* edited by Austin J. Shelton, Jr., Odyssey Press, 1968. Contributor to periodicals in Africa, Europe, Asia, New Zealand, and the United States. Assistant editor, *Contrast* (literary quarterly).

Rive's work has been translated into twelve languages, including Russian.

*SIDELIGHTS:* Richard Rive, a native of Cape Town and the son of a black American father and a South African mother of mixed heritage, often writes of the injustices of apartheid with "delightful humor where one would expect bitterness and anger," notes Kofi Anyidoho in *World Literature Today.* Rive's specialty lies in presenting "the ironies inherent in racial relationships," acknowledges Robert L. Berner in a *World Literature Today* review of *Selected Writings: Stories, Essays, and Plays.* Rive also uses multiple images and themes to unify his fiction writing. In the *Journal of the New African Literature and the Arts,* Bernth Lindfors describes Rive's style as "characterized by strong rhythms, daring images, brisk dialogue, and leitmotifs (recurring words, phrases, images) which function as unifying devices."

In 1964 Rive wrote *Emergency,* which focuses on the declaration of a state of emergency in Cape Town, South Africa. In the introduction to the novel, Ezekiel Mphahlele comments that "the novelist in the South African setting has to handle material that has become by now a huge cliche, violence, its aftermath, and the response it elicits. In this he travels a path

that has many pitfalls." By focusing on the humanity of his characters so they are neither "tiny" nor "poetic," Mphahlele feels that Rive "has avoided these pitfalls."

In 1982, Rive published *Writing Black,* an autobiographical series of sketches and essays which is supplemented by information on other African American writers. Concerning the work, Anyidoho says, "Rive's design rarely abandons us to the singular beauty or horror of the individual episode or sketch." Instead of focusing on the meaning of each separate instance, in *Writing Black* Rive demonstrates the "larger patterns of converging significance."

Rive later wrote *"Buckingham Palace," District Six,* which dramatizes the oppressive actions of the apartheid government in Cape Town. In relating the story of the inhabitants of District Six, a "colored" slum slated for demolition by the government, Rive "brilliantly intensifies their tragedy by homing in on their humorous humanity rather than on their eventual dispersal," comments a *Publishers Weekly* reviewer. Rive's talent, according to William Walsh in the *Times Educational Supplement,* allows him to "keep in productive balance irony bordering on despair" and characters that demonstrate the humor and strangeness of the human condition. William Finnegan, in the *New York Times Book Review,* criticizes some of these characters and situations, remarking that those based on "worn-smooth issues ... sink nearly to the level of a television sitcom." Nevertheless, Finnegan finds that the novel "gains sudden, almost headlong momentum and a genuine power" when describing the "war" of the government against District Six.

In *Advance, Retreat: Selected Short Stories,* Rive, according to Tony Eprile in the *New York Times Book Review,* presents some his "finest stories and provides a loose chronology of the mixed-race population's evolving consciousness." Returning in the early stories to his District Six roots, Rive depicts the street life in this once multiracial section of Cape Town. But Eprile believes that "Rive's real strengths come through in the stories that focus on the pain of racial awareness." In the story "Resurrection," Rive describes the funeral of a dark-skinned woman of mixed race, all but one of whose children turned out white. Mavis, the black daughter, recalls how she refused to comfort her mother when she complained of being ignored by her white children: "Don't you understand that you are black and your bloody children are white! Jim and Rosie and Sonny are white! And you made me black. You made me black!... Ma, why did you make me black?" With these works, Eprile comments that "Richard Rive's historical place in the development of South African literature is assured. This human, sharply observant collection of stories shows his is a voice to be discovered by each new reader, a voice that lingers long after one has read the stories."

Rive's final novel, *Emergency Continued,* is a sequel to *Emergency.* In this book, Rive has devised a novel within a novel to tell the story of a part-time writer and schoolteacher, Andrew Dreyer. Maya Jaggi in the *Times Literary Supplement* describes Dreyer as "a political activist during an earlier state of emergency twenty-five years before [who] lives quietly in a prosperous 'Coloured' suburb [of Cape Town], having opted for a life of 'cultivated withdrawal' into a career and family concerns." Dreyer's political consciousness is reawakened when he must search for his son who is on the run from the security police. The story is told through letters to a former colleague and chapters of a novel Dreyer is writing. At one point in the book Rive writes, "I am going to quote the words of a banned man, which are illegal in this country only for those who dare not to listen to them.... 'It is not I who am here in the dock, but the illegal South African government. It is not I who am being sentenced to imprisonment, but the members of the apartheid regime. It is not I who will languish in jail, but the perpetrators of racialism who are ... jailing themselves. I go willingly to serve my sentence because I know that I represent the future of this country. And one thing you cannot do, you cannot jail the future.'" On June 4, 1989, Rive was found beaten and stabbed to death at his home near Cape Town, South Africa.

*BIOGRAPHICAL/CRITICAL SOURCES:*

*BOOKS*

Rive, Richard, *Advance, Retreat: Selected Short Stories,* St. Martin's Press, 1989.
Rive, *Emergency,* introduction by Ezekiel Mphahlele, Collier Books, 1970.
Rive, *Writing Black,* D. Philip (Cape Town), 1982.

*PERIODICALS*

*Ariel,* April, 1985.
*Canadian Literature,* winter, 1990
*Chicago Tribune,* June 6, 1989.
*Choice,* December, 1991.
*Current Writing in Southern Africa,* October, 1989.
*Index on Censorship,* December, 1984.
*Journal of the New African Literature and the Arts,* fall, 1966.
*New Statesman,* April 15, 1988.
*New York Times,* June 5, 1989.
*New York Times Book Review,* October 4, 1987; January 17, 1988; January 7, 1990; January 27, 1991; August 25, 1991.
*Publishers Weekly,* June 12, 1987; October 20, 1989.
*South African Literary Journal,* December, 1980; December, 1981; July, 1983; December, 1983; September, 1985.
*Times Educational Supplement,* August 21, 1987.
*Times Literary Supplement,* April 1, 1965; August 2, 1991.

*Transition,* February, 1966.
*World Literature Today,* spring, 1978; summer, 1982; summer, 1990; winter, 1992.

\*   \*   \*

## ROBINET, Harriette Gillem   1931-

*PERSONAL:* Surname is pronounced "ro-bi-*nay*"; born July 14, 1931, in Washington, DC; daughter of Richard Avitus (a teacher) and Martha (a teacher; maiden name, Gray) Gillem; married McLouis Joseph Robinet (a health physicist), August 6, 1960; children: Stephen, Philip, Rita, Jonathan, Marsha, Linda. *Education:* College of New Rochelle, B.S., 1953; Catholic University of America, M.S., 1957, Ph.D., 1963. *Politics:* Democrat. *Religion:* Roman Catholic. *Avocational interests:* Pets, bird watching, growing plants (especially orchids), knitting, crocheting, sketching.

*ADDRESSES: Home and office*—214 South Elmwood, Oak Park, IL 60302.

*CAREER:* Children's Hospital, Washington, DC, bacteriologist, 1953-1954; Walter Reed Army Medical Center, Washington, DC, medical bacteriologist, 1954-1957, research bacteriologist, 1958-1960; Xavier University, New Orleans, LA, instructor in biology, 1957-58. Civilian food bacteriologist, U.S. Army Quartermaster Corps, 1960-1961.

*MEMBER:* Children's Reading Roundtable; Society of Children's Book Writers and Illustrators; Black Literary Umbrella.

*WRITINGS:*

*Jay and the Marigold* (juvenile), illustrated by Trudy Scott, Children's Press, 1976.
*Ride the Red Cycle* (juvenile), illustrated by David Brown, Houghton, 1980.
*Children of the Fire* (juvenile), Maxwell Macmillan International, 1991.
*Mississippi Chariot* (juvenile), Atheneum-Macmillan, forthcoming.

Contributor to magazines.

*SIDELIGHTS:* Influenced by observations of her disabled son as well as by her black slavery roots, Harriette Robinet provides insight in her juvenile works into children's struggles and victories over physical and emotional obstacles. As a *Kirkus Reviews* commentator asserts, Robinet depicts "the sheer concentration conveyed, and the self faith" of her young protagonists.

Robinet's first book, 1976's *Jay and the Marigold,* portrays an eight-year-old boy who, like Robinet's own son, is handicapped by cerebral palsy. His inability to communicate clearly or control his physical movements make him an outsider, until he is befriended by a new student. According to Karen Harris in *School Library Journal,* "the story likens Jay to a marigold which manages to bloom under the most unfavorable conditions."

The author's associations with handicapped children are drawn upon in *Ride the Red Cycle,* her 1980 work. An illness which resulted in brain damage has confined Jerome Johnson, an eleven-year-old boy, to a wheelchair. Jerome's dream is to ride a tricycle, even though he cannot walk, and after a summer of trying, he finally succeeds on Labor Day. "Simply written," declares a *Horn Book* reviewer, the "story conveys not only Jerome's physical struggle but his emotional one to achieve individuality and self-respect."

Robinet's 1991 *Children of the Fire* describes the changing reactions of a young orphan to the Chicago fire of 1871. The protagonist, Hallelujah, is a black orphan whose mother was a runaway slave. At first, Hallelujah is enthusiastic about the fire, thinking it a spectacle. Her perspective changes drastically, however, after she sees the once-stately courthouse destroyed and after she assists a young, lost white child. "No reader will doubt," proclaims Joanne Schott in *Quill and Quire,* "that Hallelujah's experiences in the Chicago fire are great enough to work changes in her."

A contributor to *Bulletin of the Center for Children's Books* believes that Robinet "has clearly done a great deal of research, and many of the historical details are of interest" in *Children of the Fire.* The comment affirms the author's ability to provide a moving story based on both historical fact and personal experience. Robinet's books reflect the many handicapped children and adults who, as cited in *Something about the Author,* "have shared some of their anger, dreams, and victories" with her.

*BIOGRAPHICAL/CRITICAL SOURCES:*

*BOOKS*

*Something about the Author,* Gale, Volume 27, 1982, p. 173.

*PERIODICALS*

*Bulletin of the Center for Children's Books,* September, 1991, p. 20.
*Horn Book Magazine,* June, 1980, p. 303.
*Kirkus Reviews,* July 15, 1980, pp. 911-12.
*Quill and Quire,* January, 1992, p. 34.
*School Library Journal,* January, 1977, p. 84.

# RODGERS, Carolyn M(arie) 1945-

*PERSONAL:* Born December 14, 1945, in Chicago, IL; daughter of Clarence and Bazella (Colding) Rodgers. *Education:* Attended University of Illinois, 1960-61; Roosevelt University, B.A., 1965; University of Chicago, M.A., 1983. *Religion:* African Methodist Episcopal.

*CAREER:* Young Mens Christian Association, Chicago, IL, social worker, 1963-68; Columbia College, lecturer in Afro-American literature, 1968-69; University of Washington, Seattle, instructor in Afro-American literature, summer, 1970; Albany State College, Albany, GA, writer in residence, 1972; Malcolm X College, Chicago, writer in residence, 1972; Indiana University, Bloomington, instructor in Afro-American literature, summer, 1973.

*MEMBER:* Organization of Black American Culture Writers Workshop, Gwendolyn Brooks Writers Workshop, Delta Sigma Theta.

*AWARDS, HONORS:* First Conrad Kent Rivers Memorial Fund Award, 1968; National Endowment for the Arts grant, 1970; Poet Laureate Award, Society of Midland Authors, 1970; National Book Award nomination, 1976, for *how i got ovah: New and Selected Poems*; Carnegie Award, 1979; PEN awards.

*WRITINGS:*

*POETRY*

*Paper Soul,* Third Would Press, 1968.
*Songs of a Blackbird,* Third Would Press, 1969.
*2 Love Raps,* Third Would Press, 1969.
*Now Ain't That Love,* Broadside Press, 1970.
*For H. W. Fuller,* Broadside Press, 1970.
*For Flip Wilson,* Broadside Press, 1971.
*Long Rap/Commonly Known as a Poetic Essay,* Broadside Press, 1971.
*how i got ovah: New and Selected Poems,* Doubleday/Anchor, 1975.
*The Heart as Ever Green: Poems,* Doubleday/Anchor, 1978.
*Translation: Poems,* Eden Press, 1980.
*Finite Forms: Poems,* Eden Press, 1985.

*CONTRIBUTOR*

Ahmed Alhamsi and Harun K. Wangara, editors, *Black Arts,* Broadside Press, 1969.
Arnold Adoff, editor, *Brothers and Sisters,* Macmillan, 1970.
Orde Coombs, editor, *We Speak as Liberators,* Dodd, 1970.
Ted Wilentz and Tom Weatherley, editors, *Natural Process,* Hill & Wang, 1970.

Gwendolyn Brooks, editor, *Jump Bad,* Broadside Press, 1971.

Dudley Randall, editor, *The Black Poets,* Bantam, 1971.

Woodie King, editor, *Blackspirits,* Random House, 1972.

Richard A. Long and Eugenia W. Collier, editors, *Afro-American Writing,* New York University Press, 1972.

William R. Robinson, editor, *Nommo,* Macmillan, 1972.

Adoff, editor, *The Poetry of Black America,* Harper, 1973.

Stephen Henderson, editor, *Understanding the New Black Poetry,* Morrow, 1973.

*Black Sister,* Indiana University Press, 1983.

Amiri Baraka, editor, *Confirmation Anthology,* Morrow, 1984.

Mari Evans, editor, *Black Women Writers (1950-1980): A Critical Evaluation,* Doubleday/Anchor, 1984.

Also contributor to *No Crystal Stairs,* 1984.

OTHER

(Editor) *Roots* (anthology), Indiana University Press, 1973.

*A Little Lower Than Angels* (novel), Eden Press, 1984.

Former reviewer for Chicago *Daily News* and columnist for Milwaukee *Courier.*

WORK IN PROGRESS: *Rain,* short stories; *Arise,* a novel.

SIDELIGHTS: "Carolyn Marie Rodgers is best known as one of the new black poets to emerge from the Chicago Organization of Black American Culture during the 1960s," writes Jean Davis in a *Dictionary of Literary Biography* essay. Calling her "one of the most sensitive and complex poets to emerge from this movement and struggle with its contradictions," Bettye J. Parker-Smith suggests in Mari Evans's *Black Women Writers (1950-1980): A Critical Evaluation* that Rogers has been "instrumental in helping create, and give a new definition or receptive power to, poetry as a Black art form." Although Rodgers's poetry has always concerned the search for self, it has evolved from a militant, sociological perspective to a more introspective one. Davis indicates that while Rodgers has spent most of her career as a poet in her native Chicago, she has gained national recognition for "her thematic concerns with feminist issues, particularly those affecting the black woman in a changing society." Angelene Jamison asserts in her essay, also in *Black Women Writers (1950-1980),* that like "most of the Black women poets of the last twenty years [who] are casually referred to only as by-products of the New Black Arts Movement," Rodgers still awaits both the attention her work deserves, as well as her "appropriate place in literature."

Rodgers began writing "quasi seriously" as an outlet for the frustrations of her year at college, as she recalls in an interview with Evans in *Black Women Writers (1950-1980);* she later participated in the Organization of Black American Culture's Writers Workshop and soon became part of the prolif-

ic black arts movement of the 1960s. Rodgers's "theological and philosophical approach to the ills that plague Black people ... and her attempts to master an appropriate language to communicate with the masses of Black people" suggest to Parker-Smith that she is "an exemplar of the 'revolutionary poet'." Rodgers, who considers her work both art as well as polemic, tells Evans that she has no distinctly defined political stance and that she feels literature "functions as a type of catharsis or amen arena" in the lives of people: "I think it speaks not only to the political sensibility but to the heart, the mind, the spirit, and the soul of every man, woman, and child." Noting that Rodgers's poetry voices varied concerns, including "revolution, love, Black male-female relationships, religion, and the complexities of Black womanhood," Jamison declares that "through a skilfully uncluttered use of several literary devices, she convincingly reinterprets the love, pain, longings, struggles, victories, the day-to-day routines of Black people from the point of view of the Black woman. Gracefully courageous enough to explore long-hidden truths, about Black women particularly, her poetry shows honesty, warmth, and love for Black people." Commenting about the "intensely personal" aspect of Rodger's poetry, Parker-Smith believes that this autobiographical element helps one to more easily comprehend her work. Rodgers "struggles to affirm her womanliness," but hasn't the strength to "move beyond those obstacles that threaten the full development of Black womanhood," Parker-Smith explains. "For her, there are three major dilemmas: the fear of assimilating the value system of her mother, which interferes with claiming an independent lifestyle of her own; the attempt to define her 'self' by the standards of the social system responsible for creating her own and her mother's condition; and the search for love (a man) that will simultaneously electrify and save her."

Rogers's first volume of poetry, *Paper Soul,* "reflects the duality of an individual struggling to reconcile complex realities, dilemmas, and contradictions," says Davis, who recognizes a thematic shift in her second volume of poetry, *Songs of a Blackbird.* Davis suggests that the former addresses "identity, religion, revolution, and love, or more accurately a woman's need for love," whereas the latter deals with "survival, street life, mother-daughter conflict, and love." Indicating that these poems are increasingly concerned with "the black woman poet as a major theme," Davis states that "questions of identity for the poet remain connected with relationships between black men and women but become more centrally located in the woman's ability to express herself." While finding Rodgers's poetry from the late 1960s "vivid and forceful," Davis notes that these first two volumes were not unanimously praised: "Nor did the young poet win unqualified acceptance as a significant new voice among black poets." She states, for instance, that Dudley Randall and Haki Madhubuti had "reservations about her language and her rendering of black speech." Davis posits, however, that Rodgers's "use of speech patterns and of lengthened prose-like lines was an attempt at breaking away from the restrictions of conventional forms and modes, and most especially from those considered appropriate for women poets." Inasmuch as "theme and language" were the general hallmarks of the black art movement from this period, Parker-Smith believes that "the use of obscenities and Black speech patterns" was especially courageous for female artists. Although acknowledging a certain inconsistency in the language of her early poetry, Davis believes that "Rodgers nonetheless had an eye for the contradictions of black experience, particularly the revolutionary or militant experience of the 1960s." And, despite their initial objections to her work, says Davis, poets and critics such as Madhubuti, Randall, and Gwendolyn Brooks, "nonetheless ... recognized her genuine talent and remarked her development."

In Rodgers's *how i got ovah: New and Selected Poems,* written in the mid-1970s, though, she exhibits "a clarity of expression and a respect for well-crafted language," states Davis, who perceives "humor, sincerity, and love" in the autobiographical poems about "black revolution, feminism, religion, God, the black church, and the black family, especially the mother." Similarly, Hilda Njoki McElroy writes in *Black World:* "It is obvious that Carolyn Rodgers loves her craft and her people. *How I got Ovah* is a result of this love match. It is an important literary contribution containing many aspects of human frailty/achievement, love/hate, positive/negative, funny/sad, beautiful/ugly which makes it deeeeep, very deeeeep." Suggesting that these poems "reveal Rodgers's transformation from a ... militant Black woman to a woman intensely concerned with God, traditional values, and her private self," Davis adds that "although her messages often explore social conflict, they usually conclude with a sense of peace, hope, and a desire to search for life's real treasure—inner beauty."

Parker-Smith describes what she refers to as the "two distinct and clear baptisms" that Rodgers's work has experienced: "The first can be viewed as being rough-hewn, folk-spirited, and held 'down at the river' amid water moccasins in the face of a glaring midday sun; the climax of a 'swing-lo-sweet-chariot' revival." Parker-Smith indicates that Rodgers's early work, which is "characterized by a potpourri of themes," exemplifies this period and "demonstrates her impudence, through the use of her wit, obscenities, the argumentation in her love and revolution poems, and the pain and presence of her mother." Parker-Smith points out that Rodgers "questions the relevance of the Vietnam War, declares war on the cities, laments Malcolm X, and criticizes the contradictory life-style of Blacks. And she glances at God." Although this was a time when Rodgers "whipped with a lean switch, often bringing down her wrath with stinging, sharp, and sometimes excruciating pain," Parker-Smith suggests that "the ribald outcry, the incongruity and cynicism that characterize the first period are links in Rodgers' chain of personal judgments—her attempts

to come to grips with 'self'—and with the Black Arts Movement as a whole."

"The second baptism takes place just before Carolyn Rodgers is able to shake herself dry from the first river," Parker-Smith continues: "This one can perhaps be classified as a sprinkling and is protected by the blessings of a very fine headcloth. It is more sophisticated. It is cooler; lacks the fire and brimstone of the first period. But it is nonetheless penetrating." During this time, Rodgers moved from Third World Press to a larger commercial publishing house; and, according to Parker-Smith, having broken with the Organization of Black American Culture as well, Rodgers "moved back inside her once lone and timid world." Considering *how i got ovah* and *The Heart as Ever Green: Poems* to exemplify this second phase, Parker-Smith finds that Rodgers closely examines "the revolution, its contradictions, and her relationship to it." Rodgers also "listens to her mother's whispers" and "embraces God," says Parker-Smith, who concludes that "it is impossible to separate the poet's new attitude toward religion from her attitude toward revolution (the one seems to have evoked the other), they have converged to assist her in her continuous search for 'self'." And although Parker-Smith suggests Rodgers did not take her craft seriously enough in the early poetry, she believes that "a more developed talent" emerges in the second period, revealing "growth and strength and a higher level of clarity, with a new level of sophistication."

Identity and potentiality are central themes in Rodgers's work; and according to Davis, "the evolving feminism" in her poetry is but "a natural extension of her reflections on herself and her world." "I see myself as becoming," Rodgers tells Evans. "I am a has-been, would perhaps, going to be. Underneath, I'm a dot. With no i's." Davis suggests that "determination to grow and to be is the most prevalent idea" in Rodgers's *The Heart As Ever Green,* where "the themes of human dignity, feminism, love, black consciousness, and Christianity are repeated throughout." Rodgers expresses to Evans that "honesty in vision and aspect" are most important to her in her work; and suggesting that the "level of honesty in her work [is] indicative of her own freedom," Jamison believes that "in a variety of idioms ranging from the street to the church, she writes about Black women with a kind of sensitivity and warmth that brings them out of the poems and into our own lives." Jamison adds that "clearly, her artistry brings these women to life, but it is her love for them that gives them their rightful place in literature. The love, the skill, indeed the vision, which she brings to her poetry must certainly help Black women rediscover and better understand themselves."

"It is impossible to assess the actual merit of Carolyn Rodgers' achievements at this point," says Parker-Smith. "And it is difficult to see where she will go from here. She has changed from a rebel to a religious loyalist, but a religious loyalist of a peculiarly different state was present from the start.... Her frantic search for love, the constant battle with her mother, the ambiguity about religion, are factors that run wild in her soul." Davis remarks that Rodgers has witnessed changes both in herself and her work: "In the beginning of her career, she reveals, 'I was just a writer out here just writing. Then I went to an orientation of Black (Negro) work and then I wrote with a message, a sociological orientation. Actually, I've come full circle to a certain extent. I don't write the same message.'" Although survival represents a dominant theme in her stories and poetry, Davis adds that Rodgers "interweaves the idea of adaptability and conveys the concomitant message of life's ever-changing avenues for black people whom she sees as her special audience." Davis relates Rodgers's statement about her writing being "for whoever wants to read it... one poem doesn't do that. But I try to put as many as I can in a book. A poem for somebody young, religious people, the church people. Just people. Specifically, Black people. I would like for them to like me." Rodgers acknowledges to Evans that the direction of her writing has "indeed" changed in the last decade: "My focus is on life, love, eternity, pain, and joy. These matters are cared about by Brown people, aren't they?"

*BIOGRAPHICAL/CRITICAL SOURCES:*

*BOOKS*

*Dictionary of Literary Biography,* Volume 41: *Afro-American Poets Since 1955,* Gale, 1985.
Evans, Mari, editor, *Black Women Writers (1950-1980): A Critical Evaluation,* Doubleday-Anchor, 1984.

*PERIODICALS*

*Black Scholar,* March, 1981.
*Black Would,* August, 1970: February, 1976.
*Chicago Tribune,* November 19, 1978.
*Negro Digest,* September, 1968.
*Washington Post Book World,* May 18, 1975.

\*     \*     \*

## ROGERS, Joel Augustus  1880(?)-1966

*PERSONAL:* Born September, 1880 (some sources say 1883), in Jamaica, West Indies; immigrated to the United States, 1906; naturalized citizen, 1917; died January, 1966, in New York, NY; son of Samuel and Emily Rogers. *Education:* Self-educated.

*CAREER:* Historian, journalist, newspaper columnist, and writer. Correspondent and columnist for *Pittsburgh Courier,*

Pittsburgh, PA; free-lance journalist. *Military service:* Served in British army for four years.

*MEMBER:* American Geographical Society, American Academy of Political Science, Societe d'Anthropologie (Paris, France).

*WRITINGS:*

*From Superman to Man,* M. A. Donohue, 1917.
*As Nature Leads: An Informal Discussion of the Reason Why Negro and Caucasian are Mixing in Spite of Opposition,* M. A. Donohue, 1919.
*The Approaching Storm and How It May Be Averted: An Open Letter to Congress and the 48 Legislatures of the United States of America,* self-published, 1920.
*The Maroons of the West Indies and South America,* self-published, 1921.
*The Ku Klux Klan Spirit: A Brief Outline of the History of the Ku Klan Past and Present,* Messenger, 1923.
*World's Greatest Men of African Descent,* self-published, c. 1931.
*100 Amazing Facts about the Negro, with Complete Proof: A Short Cut to the World History of the Negro,* F. Hubner, 1934, revised and enlarged edition, 1957, revised edition, Sportshelf, 1963.
*Real Facts about Ethiopia,* self-published, c. 1935.
*World's Greatest Men and Women of African Descent,* self-published, 1935.
*Sex and Race: Negro-Caucasian Mixing in All Ages and All Lands,* three volumes, self-published, 1940-44.
*World's Great Men of Color,* two volumes, self-published, 1946-47, edited and introduced by John Henrik Clarke, Macmillan, 1972.
*Nature Knows No Color Line: Research into the Negro Ancestry in the White Race,* Helga M. Rogers, 1952.
*Africa's Gift to America: The Afro-American in the Making and Saving of the United States,* self-published, 1959, published with new supplement, *Africa and Its Potentialities,* Sportshelf, 1961.
*Facts about the Negro,* Lincoln Park Studios, 1960.
*She Walks in Beauty* (novel), Western, 1963.
*Selected Writings of Joel Augustus Rogers,* edited by Kinya Kiorgozi, Pyramid, 1989.

Also author of novels *Blood Money,* 1923, and *The Golden Door,* 1927. Contributor to periodicals, including *Freedomways, American Mercury, Survey Graphic,* and *Journal of Negro History.* Author of special feature, "Your History from the Beginning of Time to the Present," *Pittsburgh Courier,* 1940.

*SIDELIGHTS:* Joel Augustus Rogers was, for more than fifty years, a prominent black journalist and historian. Rogers became a journalist for the *Pittsburgh Courier* and was assigned to cover the coronation of the Emperor of Ethiopia in 1930. He was subsequently assigned to cover the Italo-Ethiopian War in 1935, and became the first Black war correspondent in the history of the United States. In the 1950s he went on to publish numerous books on African American history. According to a *Negro Almanac* reviewer, Rogers's researches were extraordinary "at a time when Negro historians were virtually non-existent in the U.S."

*BIOGRAPHICAL/CRITICAL SOURCES:*

*BOOKS*

*Negro Almanac,* Bellwether, 1971.

*PERIODICALS*

*Library Journal,* November 1, 1992, pp. 47, 49.

* * *

## ROTIMI, (Emmanuel Gladstone) Ola(wale) 1938-

*PERSONAL:* Born April 13, 1938 in Sapele, Nigeria; son of Samuel Enitan and Dorcas Oruene (Addo) Rotimi; married Hazel Mae Gaudreau in 1965; children: Enitan, Oruene, Biodun Ola, Jr., Bankole. *Education:* Boston University, B.F.A., 1963; Yale University, M.F.A., 1966.

*ADDRESSES: Home*—Lagos, Nigeria. *Office*—Department of Creative Arts, University of Port Harcourt, P.M.B. 5323, Port Harcourt, Rivers State, Nigeria.

*CAREER:* University of Ife, Ife, Oyo State, Nigeria, research fellow, 1966-75, acting head of Department of Dramatic Arts, 1975-77; University of Port Harcourt, Port Harcourt, Rivers State, Nigeria, head of Department of Creative Arts and arts director, 1977—; playwright. Director of plays, including his own *The Gods Are Not to Blame,* 1968, *The Prodigal,* 1969, and *Holding Talks,* 1970, Adegoke Durojaiye's *Gbe-Ku-de,* 1969, and Aime Cesaire's *La Tragedie d'Henri Christophe,* 1971. Recorded *Ola Rotimi of Nigeria* for Voice of America, 1978.

*MEMBER:* African Writers Association, Association of Nigerian Authors, Society of Nigerian Theatre Artists.

*AWARDS, HONORS: Our Husband Has Gone Mad Again* was selected by Yale University as the major play of the year, 1966; first prize in international playwriting competition spon-

sored by *African Arts* magazine, 1969, for *The Gods Are Not to Blame;* first prize in Oxford University Press play-writing competition, 1969, for *Our Husband Has Gone Mad Again;* first prize at fourth Nigerian National Festival of the Arts, 1974, for creation and direction of dance-drama *And Man Brought the First Woman.*

*WRITINGS:*

*PLAYS*

*To Stir the God of Iron* (three-act), produced in Boston, MA, 1963.
*Our Husband Has Gone Mad Again: A Comedy* (three-act, produced in New Haven, CT, 1966) Oxford University Press, 1977.
*The Gods Are Not to Blame* (three-act; based on Sophocles' *Oedipus Rex,* produced in Ife, Nigeria, 1968), Oxford University Press, 1971.
*Kurunmi: An Historical Tragedy* (three-act, produced in Ife, Nigeria, 1969), Oxford University Press, 1971.
*The Prodigal* (dance-drama), produced in Ife, Nigeria, 1969.
*Holding Talks: An Absurdist Drama* (produced in Ife, Nigeria, 1970), Oxford University Press, 1979.
*Ovonramwen Nogbaisi: An Historical Tragedy in English* (three-act, produced in Ife, Nigeria, 1971), Oxford University Press, 1974.
*If* (produced at the University of Port Harcourt, 1979), Heinemann Educational Books, 1983.
*Hopes of the Living Dead* (produced at the University of Port Harcourt, 1984), Spectrum, 1988.
*Everyone His/Her Own Problem,* broadcast on British Broadcasting Corporation (BBC) African Theatre, London, 1987.

*OTHER*

*Statements towards August '83,* Kurunmi Adventures, 1983.
*African Dramatic Literature: To Be or to Become?,* University of Port Harcourt, 1991.

Contributor to *Introduction to Nigerian Literature,* edited by Bruce King, Evans/Africana, 1971; *The Living Culture of Nigeria,* edited by Saburi O. Biobaku, Thomas Nelson, 1976. Contributor to periodicals, including *Nigeria Magazine* and *Interlink.*

*WORK IN PROGRESS:* A dictionary of Nigerian Pidgin English; *In Praise of Poverty,* a collection of original short stories on the psycho-emotional resilience of the poor in an uncaring society.

*SIDELIGHTS:* One of the most successful Nigerian playwrights writing in English, Ola Rotimi effectively conveys to both Nigerian and foreign audiences the culture and concerns of the African peoples. He specifically addresses the historical and political problems of Nigeria in a bold, sweeping style that, critics say, engrosses audiences in his productions.

Set in Nigeria, Rotimi's first play, *To Stir the God of Iron,* was performed in 1963 by the Afro-American Dramatic Society of Boston University while Rotimi was a student there. Rotimi's next play, *Our Husband Has Gone Mad Again*—a politico-domestic comedy—was performed in 1966 at Yale University, where it was named the major play of the year. After earning his master's of fine arts degree in 1966 from Yale University, Rotimi returned to Nigeria to take up a research fellowship at the University of Ife. While there he composed his highly successful *The Gods Are Not to Blame,* based on Greek philosopher Sophocles' *Oedipus Rex,* which he directed first at the Ori Olokun Cultural Centre in Ife in 1968 and later at London's Drum Arts Centre in 1978. *The Gods Are Not to Blame* is considered remarkable in its use of broken verse and powerful African imagery. At the second Ife Festival of the Arts in 1969, Rotimi presented *Kurunmi* and *The Prodigal. Kurunmi,* considered one of his best works, is an epic play about the nineteenth-century Ijaiye War and a biting commentary on the Nigerian Civil War. In *Holding Talks,* a 1970 absurdist drama, Rotimi exposes the irrationality of man's obsession with "talking" in situations that clearly demand action. *Ovonramwen Nogbaisi,* produced in 1971 at the fourth Ife Festival of the Arts, indicts British imperialism for its role in the downfall of the Benin Empire, a highly organized kingdom in West Africa overtaken by the British in 1897. Provoked by Nigeria's socio-political inequities, Rotimi composed *If,* a 1979 play that concerns the predicament of ordinary contemporary Nigerians trying to cope with adverse social and political circumstances following the war. *Hopes of the Living Dead,* which premiered in 1984 to widespread critical acclaim and has since been revived twice, uses the historic rebellion of lepers against the British colonial administration in Nigeria at the turn of the century as a metaphor to articulate the striving and aspirations of the ordinary peoples of present-day Nigeria. Rotimi's radio play, *Everyone His/Her Own Problem,* broadcast over the British Broadcasting Corporation's overseas services in 1987, recounts the universal preoccupation of man grappling with personal problems of one kind or another.

According to Joel Adedeji in *Dictionary of Literary Biography,* "Rotimi's genius and significance as a dramatist lie in his successful modification of traditional dramatic form and content and his creation of a language appropriate to the mass audience he wishes to address.... His importance will emerge with time, for he will continue to develop new ways of articulating political ideas through the medium of popular theater."

Rotimi once commented: "A play—for that matter, any work of art—must aim at transcending the purlieus of sheer aesthetics. Ultimate fulfillment comes to the artist when he realizes his work is being seriously discussed, that references or lessons are being drawn, that interpretations are being argued over, that new meanings are being adduced and rationalized, that topical analogies are being discovered. This, to my mind, is the enduring value, the consummation of the artistic expression. My creative passion as a playwright is for an accessible people's theatre informed by that which also impels it—namely, the spasms of the socio-political tendons of Africa yesterday, today, and tomorrow. As a director, my pictorial trademark is a preference for a convoluting concourse of juxtaposed, variegated happenings: a conjuration of the rhythm and agitations of existence in these (African) parts of our universe."

*BIOGRAPHICAL/CRITICAL SOURCES:*

*BOOKS*

*African Literature Today,* Heinemann Educational Books, 1982.
*Dictionary of Literary Biography,* Volume 125: *Twentieth-Century Caribbean and Black African Writers,* Gale, 1993.
*New West African Literature,* Heinemann Educational Books, 1979.

*PERIODICALS*

*Bulletin of Black Theatre,* winter, 1972.

\*     \*     \*

## ROWAN, Carl Thomas  1925-

*PERSONAL:* Born August 11, 1925, in Ravenscroft, TN; son of Thomas David (a lumber stacker) and Johnnie (Bradford) Rowan; married Vivien Louise Murphy, August 2, 1950; children: Barbara, Carl Thomas, Jeffrey. *Education:* Attended Tennessee State University, 1942-43, and Washburn University, 1943-44; Oberlin College, A.B., 1947; University of Minnesota, M.A., 1948.

*ADDRESSES: Home*—3116 Fessenden St. N.W., Washington, DC 20088. *Office*—1220 19th St. N.W., Washington DC 20036.

*CAREER: Minneapolis Tribune,* Minneapolis, MN, copy writer, 1948-50, staff writer, 1950-61; U.S. Department of State, Washington, DC, deputy assistant secretary for public affairs, 1961-63; U.S. ambassador to Finland, based in

Helsinki, 1963-64; director of United States Information Agency (USIA), 1964-65; Chicago *Sun-Times* (formerly Chicago *Daily News*), Chicago, IL, columnist for Field Newspaper syndicate (formerly Publishers Hall Syndicate), 1965—. National affairs commentator on "The Rowan Report," heard nationally on radio five days a week; political commentator for radio and television stations of Post-Newsweek Broadcasting Company; regular panelist on "Agronsky & Co.," a nationally syndicated public affairs television show; frequent panelist on "Meet the Press." Former member of U.S. delegation to the United Nations. *Military service:* Served in U.S. Navy during World War II.

*AWARDS, HONORS:* Sidney Hillman Award, 1952, for best newspaper reporting; Sigma Delta Chi Awards, 1953, for coverage of school desegregation cases before the U.S. Supreme Court, 1954, for coverage of the conference in Bandung, Indonesia; distinguished achievement award, regents of University of Minnesota, 1961; communications award in human relations, Anti-Defamation League of B'Nai B'rith, 1964; Contributions to American Democracy Award, Roosevelt University, 1964; Liberty Bell Award, Howard University, 1965; named Washington journalist of the year, Capital Press Club, 1978; American Black Achievement Award, Ebony magazine, 1978, for contributions to journalism and public communication; recipient of twenty-nine honorary degrees from colleges and universities, including Oberlin College, Notre Dame University, Howard University, University of Massachusetts, Temple University, Atlanta University, and Clark University.

*WRITINGS:*

*South of Freedom,* Knopf, 1952.
*The Pitiful and the Proud,* Random House, 1956.
*Go South to Sorrow,* Random House, 1957.
*Wait Till Next Year: The Life Story of Jackie Robinson,* Random House, 1960. *Just Between Us Blacks,* Random House, 1974.
*Breaking Barriers: A Memoir,* Little, Brown, 1991.
*Dream Makers, Dream Breakers: The World of Justice Thurgood Marshall,* Little, Brown, 1993.

Also roving editor of *Reader's Digest.*

*SIDELIGHTS:* The *Washington Post* called Carl Thomas Rowan "the most visible black journalist in the country." Rowan's nationally syndicated column runs three times weekly in various newspapers and he is a frequent lecturer and commentator on public affairs radio and television programs. His other accomplishments include government appointments in the presidential administrations of John F. Kennedy and Lyndon B. Johnson, whom he considered "the single greatest human rights and civil rights President America has ever known."

In a *Washington Post Book World* review of Rowan's autobiography, *Breaking Barriers,* Nicholas Lemann wrote that Rowan shined brightest as a journalist in the 1950s, when he covered the desegregation struggles in the South, including the Montgomery bus boycott and the integration crisis in Little Rock, the Suez Crisis and the Vietnam War for the *Minneapolis Tribune.* Rowan got some choice assignments overseas, like Indonesia and India, and befriended Dr. Martin Luther King and Eleanor Roosevelt. "He had that great journalist's ability to seem to be everywhere important," Lemann wrote.

In *Breaking Barriers,* Rowan writes about his poverty-stricken childhood in McMinnville, Tennessee, peppering the account with heart-wrenching anecdotes, like sucking milk from the teats of a cow when he was so hungry he could barely think. Quite by accident, Rowan recounts, he was chosen as a candidate for an officer's job in the United States Navy while he was a student at Tennessee State University. The Navy sent a call for candidates to the wrong school, intending it to go to the University of Tennessee instead. But Rowan served honorably in the Navy during World War II as a member of a small corps of black naval officers. When he returned, he finished college at Oberlin in Ohio and went on to study journalism in Minnesota.

Lemann calls Rowan "vivid, toughminded, funny and impassioned" in *Breaking Barriers,* a "race crusader, not a professional curmudgeon." The memoir is full of political punditry but also significant moments in history as seen through the eyes of a man who crusaded on behalf of blacks but held his own in the Establishment. Rowan talks about President Johnson and Ronald Reagan, the latter a man he felt was indifferent to the plight of all minorities. Lemann points out in his review that Rowan seems to be much more comfortable discussing the civil rights era in post-World War II years than the struggles of blacks since the early 1960s.

In the book, Rowan stops telling his life story around his fortieth birthday, which coincided with his resignation from Johnson's National Security Council. Lemann speculated that Rowan's leap into the highly public life of a commentator, TV figure, lecturer and columnist leaves him little time for the assignments he took as a young man when, Rowan recalled, his "journalistic hormones were raging." "Rowan's role as a writer, before he went into government—showing an unknowing audience the conditions in which blacks lived—probably was better suited to the making of that kind of contribution than the commentator's role he has played since 1965 has been," Lemann wrote.

*BIOGRAPHICAL/CRITICAL SOURCES:*

*PERIODICALS*

*Los Angeles Times Book Review,* January 26, 1992.
*New York Times Book Review,* January 26, 1992, p. 24.
*Publishers Weekly,* December 7, 1992, p. 47; January 18, 1993, pp. 444-445.
*Washington Post,* October 28, 1978.
*Washington Post Book World,* December 23, 1990.

\*   \*   \*

## ROY, Jacqueline 1954-

*PERSONAL:* Born January 2, 1954, in London, England; daughter of Namba (a painter, sculptor, and novelist) and Yvonne (an actress and teacher; maiden name, Shelly) Roy. *Education:* University of North London, B.A., 1989; University of Leeds, M.A., 1990. *Politics:* Labour.

*ADDRESSES: Home*—49 Salford Rd., London SW2 4BL, England. *Office*—Manchester Metropolitan University, Lower Ormond St., Manchester M15, England. *Agent*—Rosemary Sandberg, 44 Bowerdean St., London SW6 3TW, England.

*CAREER:* Manchester Metropolitan University, Manchester, England, lecturer, 1992—; writer.

*MEMBER:* Society of Authors.

*WRITINGS:*

(Editor) Namba Roy, *No Black Sparrows: A Vivid Portrait of Jamaica in the 1930s,* Heinemann, 1989.
*Soul Daddy,* HarperCollins, 1990.
*King Sugar,* HarperCollins, 1993.

Also author of the short stories "A Family Likeness" and "Joshua's Friend."

*WORK IN PROGRESS: Fat Chance,* a novel; research in black British women's writing.

*SIDELIGHTS:* Jacqueline Roy commented: "I was born in London of an English mother and a Jamaican father, and this inevitably raises questions of cultural identity, which I try to explore in my fiction. My late father, Namba Roy, was also a writer. He was a Maroon, a people originally composed of escaped slaves who fled to the mountains in Jamaica and established a community there, which tried to hold on to Afri-

can traditions. In Africa, the oral tradition is of great importance, and histories, both personal and public, were usually passed on by word of mouth. For this reason, the storyteller has always been a valued member of the community, and the role was passed down through the generations. My father was the storyteller for the Maroons, and although he had settled in England, when he died it was hoped that at least one of his children would succeed him. Therefore, writing is particularly important in my family; my brother and sister are writers too. In addition to producing my own fiction, I edited my father's novel, *No Black Sparrows.* This increased my sense that writing was a family tradition.

"At school, I was very aware of the lack of interest in Afro-Caribbean history and culture, and partly for this reason, I left without taking A-levels; like many young people, I was not sure what an all-white curriculum could say to me and much of the teaching seemed irrelevant. I worked in various places. At one point I cut cheese in a local supermarket—a job I really wasn't too good at. Customers asking for a quarter pound usually ended up with at least twice that! Working in a bookshop was a lot more interesting than this, but my real ambition was still to write, and I spent my spare time writing stories for all age groups from small children to adults.

"Eventually, bored with shop work, I decided to take a degree in English at the Polytechnic of North London (now the University of North London). The course included studies of African, West Indian, and Indian literature, and I found it exciting and stimulating. On graduating, I went on to do an M.A. in Commonwealth Literature at Leeds University. While at the poly, I wrote *Soul Daddy,* which explored identity on two levels: firstly, the need for a racial and/or cultural identity, and secondly, the wish to create an identity within the family. Twinship featured strongly and was a device for looking at the way in which we see ourselves and how this often changes and develops as other people come into our lives. I wanted to show that the family structure is not stable or fixed but fluctuates, just as the social structure does.

"*King Sugar,* my second book for teenagers, concerns Alex, a young actress who gets a part in a West End production. She plays Poll, a young slave, and as she gets into the role, Poll seems to appear to her. Poll says that the way she is presented in the play is inaccurate, and she wants to tell her story. As Alex listens, she is forced to question versions of history and to ask herself whose story the play is telling—that of the masters, or that of the slaves? Just as sugar is central to the life of a Caribbean slave, it is also central to Alex's life—she has diabetes and is not sure if Poll is a ghost or a symptom of her illness. Alex has a friend called Denise, who becomes the target of the right wing extremists who operate in the area in which the girls live. Denise's victimization, as well as her resilience, show Alex that life is still a struggle for Afro-Caribbeans, but that courage and the will to survive are part of her inheritance.

"*Fat Chance* is for a slightly younger age group (ten to thirteen). It is about the friendship between two misfits, Jasper and Tessa, who are despised and disliked at school and who offer hope to each other. Tessa is overweight and believes slimness is the key to popularity. As she diets and gets thinner, her friendship with Jasper suffers, but he stands by her and helps to prevent her from slipping into anorexia nervosa.

"My books are mainly about young women and the expectations they believe they must meet, whether these are social or personal or relating to the family. For black youngsters, the problems are particularly intense because expectations of them are either very low and negative, or very high, by way of compensation.

"My particular interests are Caribbean and Afro-American women's fiction and the role of women in society in general.

Toni Morrison is my favorite writer for adults, and for young people's authors I like Rosa Guy and Marlene Phillip. I also like music—everything from soul and reggae to jazz and classical. Aretha Franklin and Laura Nyro are my favorite singers. I enjoy walking and wish I had a dog, as they're so much fun to take out, but that's difficult in British cities—there aren't enough places for them to run. I also love street markets; the bustle, the color, and the variety make them exciting places to be. I have a large collection of teddy bears, which have virtually taken over the house, and more books than I've got space for. My favorite foods are chocolate and ice cream, though I'm trying to cut back on the chocolate!

"I have just begun to teach in higher education. I had such a good experience of degree work as a mature student that I'd like to be able to pass on some of the skills and interests I developed. Education is an invaluable tool in voicing social and political concerns, and it is something which is often denied to the black and/or underprivileged communities. It is therefore vital to ensure that it does not remain in the hands of the privileged few."

# S

**SAGAYE, Gabra Madhen**
   **See GABRE-MEDHIN, Tsegaye (Kawessa)**

*   *   *

## ST. OMER, Garth 1931-

*PERSONAL:* Given name, Roland E. Garth St. Omer Bush; born January 15, 1931, in Castries, Saint Lucia, British West Indies. *Education:* University of West Indies, Jamaica, received honors degree; Graduate School of Fine Arts Columbia University, M.F.A., 1971; Princeton University, Ph.D, 1975.

*ADDRESSES:* c/o Heinemann Education Books, 22 Bedford Square, London WC1B 3HH, England.

*CAREER:* Writer. English language assistant in lycees in Dax and Albi, France, 1959-61; Apam Secondary School, Ghana, instructor in French and English, 1961-66; full-time writer of fiction in England and the West Indies, 1966-69; English Department of University of California, Santa Barbara, associate professor, beginning in 1975, became professor of English.

*AWARDS, HONORS:* Writing Grant, London Arts Council, 1967; Columbia University fellowship, 1969-71; Ford Foundation fellowship, 1969-73; Princeton University fellowship, 1971-75.

*WRITINGS:*

*A Room on the Hill* (novel), Faber, 1968.
*Shades of Grey* (contains two novellas, "The Lights on the Hill," and "Another Place, Another Time"), Faber, 1968, *The Lights on the Hill* was reprinted separately by Heinemann, 1986.

*Nor Any Country* (novel), Faber, 1969.
*J-, Black Bam and the Masqueraders* (novel), Faber, 1972.

Contributor of story "Syrop" to the anthology *Introduction 2: Short Stories by New Writers,* Faber, 1964.

*SIDELIGHTS:* Garth St. Omer squarely fits in that tradition of West Indian writers that include his countryman, Nobel poet Derek Walcott, also of Saint Lucia. St. Omer's customary allusions to Walcott in the opening of his works illustrate the influence of his fellow writer and West Indian. The works of both men evoke the aftermath of colonial rule—particularly its dismantled system of brutality—that invincibly shackles their protagonists to small island life. As Walcott observes in his saga *Omeros:* "Their condition / the same, without manacles. The chains were subtler, / but they were still hammered out of the white-hot forge / that made every captor a blacksmith."

From the time of his first publication (the short story "Syrop," which established his writing career), St. Omer's treatment of the hero has developed into a progressive search for material success and a meaningful life. That "Syrop" is the only story of St. Omer's which embodies the tragic death of its hero is significant to this underlying narrative development. Syrop dies caught in the propellers of a passing ship while diving for pennies on the very day he is hired by a fishing crew and the day before his brother's release from jail.

In subsequent works, St. Omer's heroes act more as observers of themselves in relation to the tragedies that surround them. John Lestrade, in St. Omer's first novel, *A Room on the Hill,* is haunted by the failures, misfortunes, and untimely deaths of those with whom he was once intimate. He feels increasingly suffocated by the "poisonous air of the island," by the "failures" who return to consummate their failure, by everything he cannot himself escape. His past is always cross-cut into his present, and though he can never go back, he can never escape that going back, as the narrator observes: "The wheel of his life had come full circle. He had resumed his somnambulistic existence."

In this respect, St. Omerian heroes are, typically, young males from broken, dysfunctional families. Born and conditioned by the urban poverty of post-colonial small-island life, "supported by no weight of tradition or lineage," their lives ultimately reflect their sense of malaise: the psychological paralysis they incur despite their material possibilities. Self-consumed in their search for identity, their isolation subverts their ability to find fulfillment in life.

Stephenson, the protagonist in *Lights on the Hill,* reflects the characteristic traits of the St. Omer outsider: aloof and alienated. Standing at the window of his room he imagines the expectations of his fellow schoolmates as they move about the campus and prismatically sees their excitement and pleasure in terms of his own disturbing alienation: "For all, certainly there was the excitement and pleasure of change.... From his room he looked out at his mates like a rat on the piece of driftwood he had scampered on to." The protagonists of St. Omer's other works, including Derek Charles of *Another Place, Another Time,* John Lestrade of *A Room on the Hill,* and Peter Breville of *Nor Any Country* and *J—Black Bam and the Masqueraders,* resemble the character of Stephenson in that each can be characterized as "restless, always dissatisfied, hovering on the fringe, avoiding the center or the depths."

St. Omer's story-telling is not action packed; his stories retrace the inaction of the protagonists, and because the events of the past continually disrupt St. Omer's linear narrative, the motives for their paralysis, like their hopes for the future, are never fully realized. The narrator in *Lights on the Hill* observes Stephenson's manner of recounting events: "It seemed, as he related them, that no single part of the recital was complete without what preceded or followed it. And so, after a while, he broke off his disjointed, interrupted and backward-moving narrative and began at the beginning."

The introduction to *Lights on the Hill* points out that "the individuality of temperament is impressed on the reader's consciousness before we know fully the personal history and social circumstances" and that "something is left over that is open to varying interpretations which cannot be finally resolved." Recuperating the past, for St. Omer, means reaching into the unreachable "vulnerability and subservience" of colonial third world peoples, and the "exploitative brutality practiced by the economically superior power." St. Omer writes, "to go back a step behind each action or phase of life" is like "a traveller going back along the line of imprints of his feet in the sand."

*BIOGRAPHICAL/CRITICAL SOURCES:*

*BOOKS*

St. Omer, Garth, *A Room on the Hill,* Faber, 1968.
St. Omer, Garth, *The Lights on the Hill,* Heinemann, 1986.
Walcott, Derek, *Omeros,* Farrar, Straus, 1989.

*PERIODICALS*

*Books and Bookmen,* February, 1969, p. 52.
*Guardian Weekly,* January, 2, 1969, p. 14; May 15, 1969, p. 15.
*Listener,* May 8, 1969, p. 656; July, 1972, p. 89.
*New Statesman,* May 9, 1969, p. 665; June 30, 1972, p. 914.
*Observer* (London), May 4, 1969, p. 34; June 25, 1972, p. 30.
*Spectator,* May 9, 1969, p. 620.
*Times Literary Supplement,* May 29, 1969, p. 589; August 25, 1972, p. 985.
*World Literature Today,* spring, 1987, p. 342.

—*Sketch by Robert C. Anderson*

\*   \*   \*

## SALAAM, Kalamu ya 1947-
(Vallery Ferdinand III)

*PERSONAL:* Original name, Vallery Ferdinand III; name legally changed, c. 1971; born March 24, 1947, in New Orleans, LA; son of Vallery and Inola (Copelin) Ferdinand; married Tayari kwa Salaam; children: five, including a daughter named Asante. *Education:* Attended Carlton College, 1964-65, and Southern University, 1968-69; Delgado Junior College, A.A.

*ADDRESSES: Home*—1708 Tennessee, New Orleans, LA 70117.

*CAREER:* Free Southern Theater, New Orleans, LA, writer, artist, and actor, 1968-71, director, BLKARTSOUTH ensemble; *Black Collegian,* New Orleans, founding member, 1970— , began as managing editor, became editor at large, 1983—. New Orleans Jazz and Heritage Foundation, New Orleans, director; Ahidiana, New Orleans, co-founder, 1973-84; Southern delegate to Sixth Pan-African Conference in Tanzania, 1974; North American Zone Organizing Committee for the second World Black and African Festival of Arts and Culture, member of board of directors; senior partner in Bright Moments (a public relations firm). *Military service:* U.S. Army, 1965-68.

*MEMBER:* Afrikan Liberation Support Committee, People Defense Coalition (New Orleans-based chairman).

*AWARDS, HONORS:* Richard Wright Award, *Black World* (now *First World*), 1971, for literary criticism; Deems Taylor Award, American Society of Composers, Authors, and Publishers (ASCAP), 1981 and 1989, for excellence in writing about music; two first place Unity awards in Media, Lincoln University of Missouri; George Washington award, Freedom's Foundation at Valley Forge, "for an outstanding individual contribution reflecting the ideals of human dignity and the principles of a free society"; Deep South Writer's Contest Award for prose, 1986; "Best of Fringe" award, *Manchester Evening News,* for 1987-88 production of *Black Love Song #1;* first place award, CAC Region New Play Competition, 1990.

*WRITINGS:*

(Under name Vallery Ferdinand III) *The Blues Merchant: Songs for Blkfolk* (poetry), BLKARTSOUTH (New Orleans), 1969.

*Hofu ni kwenu: My Fear Is for You* (poetry and essays), Ahidiana (New Orleans), 1973.

*Pamoja tutashinda: Together We Will Win* (poetry), Ahidiana, 1974.

*Ibura* (poetry and fiction), illustrations by Arthrello Beck, Jr., Ahidiana, 1976.

*Tearing the Roof off the Sucker: The Fall of South Afrika* (treatise), Ahidiana, 1977.

*South African Showdown: Divestment Now* (treatise), Ahidiana, 1978.

*Nuclear Power and the Black Liberation Struggle* (pamphlet), Ahidiana, 1978.

*Revolutionary Love* (poetry and essays), drawings by Douglas Redd, photographs by Kwadwo Oluwale Akpan, Ahidiana-Habari, 1978.

(With wife, Tayari kwa Salaam) *Who Will Speak for Us? New Afrikan Folk Tales* (juvenile), Ahidiana, 1978.

*Herufi: An Alphabet Reader* (juvenile), Ahidiana, 1978.

*Iron Flowers: A Poetic Report on a Visit to Haiti* (poetry), Ahidiana, 1979.

*Our Woman Keep Our Skies from Falling: Six Essays in Support of the Struggle to Smash Sexism and Develop Women* (essays), Nkombo (New Orleans), 1980.

*Our Music Is No Accident,* Nkombo, 1987.

*What Is Life?,* Third World Press, 1992.

PLAYS

*The Picket* (one-act), produced in New Orleans at Free Southern Theater, 1968.

*Mama* (one-act), produced in New Orleans at Free Southern Theater, 1969.

*Happy Birthday, Jesus* (one-act), produced in New Orleans at Free Southern Theater, 1969.

*Black Liberation Army* (one-act), produced in New Orleans at Free Southern Theater, 1969.

*Homecoming* (one-act), produced in New Orleans at Free Southern Theater, 1970.

*Black Love Song #1* (one-act), produced in New Orleans at Free Southern Theater, 1971.

*The Quest* (one-act), produced in New Orleans at BLKART-SOUTH, 1972.

*Somewhere in the World (Long Live Asatta),* produced in New Orleans by Art For Life Theater Company, 1982.

Also author of *Cop Killer* (one-act), produced in 1968; *Song of Survival* (with Tom Dent; one-act), produced in 1969; and *The Destruction of the American Stage,* 1972.

OTHER

Contributor to anthologies, including *What We Must See: Young Black Storytellers,* edited by Orde Coombs, Dodd & Mead, 1971; *We Be Word Sorcerers: Twenty-five Short Stories by Black Americans,* edited by Sonia Sanchez, Bantam Books, 1973; *Black Theatre, U.S.A.,* edited by James V. Hatch and Ted Shine, Free Press, 1974; and *Black Southern Voices,* edited by John Oliver Killens and Jerry W. Ward, Jr., Meridian, 1992. Contributor to periodicals, including *Black Scholar, Nkombo, Black World, Callaloo, Encore, Journal of Black Poetry, Negro Digest* and *Nimrod.* Editor and publisher of *Expression;* co-editor and publisher of *Nkombo;* contributing editor of *Culture;* advisory editor of *First World.*

*SIDELIGHTS:* Kalamu ya Salaam is one of the most prolific writers of the South. He has received awards for both his fictional works and literary criticism, and has founded numerous publications and organizations. His roles as activist, editor, poet, playwright, prose writer, critic and speaker are intertwined.

Salaam was born became attracted to social politics while still in junior high school. He joined the Afrikan Liberation Support Committee and numerous other coalitions formed to promote the freedom of African Americans and African nationals. Taking part in protests of the 1960s civil rights movement, he worked to register blacks to vote. His Army service came in the middle of his college studies, ending in June of 1968. In 1969, after being expelled from New Orleans' Southern University for his participation in student demonstrations, Salaam completed an associate of arts degree in business administration from a junior college.

Salaam worked as a director, actor, writer and artist with the Free Southern Theater from 1968 to 1971. During his tenure the company performed seven of his one-act plays. The Theater's community workshop adopted the title BLKART-SOUTH and became a source of nurturing for Salaam, publishing numerous volumes of his poetry. As a playwright and poet, Salaam's work weds his strong ideology with his love of art. His artistic philosophy is that art ought to contain a social agenda; he seeks through his own art to mobilize the strength and unity of the black world community for the sake of its own betterment.

A staunch feminist, Salaam writes extensively about the significance of the family, and the complementary roles of men and women within family. In his 1976 work, *Ibura,* dedicated to his mother, he criticizes the unaware black man who does not see that the black woman is "something special, miraculous or wonderful." And in *Our Women Keep Our Skies from Falling,* a 1980 collection of essays, Salaam exhorts the reader to do as he has done and shed the "skin of the sexist social system," ultimately to end the oppression of women. In "Rape: A Radical Analysis from an African American Perspective," Salaam describes four types of rape which parallel an integral, socially-accepted sexist dogma by which we live. He argues for the education of women in all facets of the economic and social arena. His goal is to "Smash Sexism and Develop Women," as Arthenia J. Bates Millican notes in the *Dictionary of Literary Biography.*

In other works, Salaam uses words to fight cruelty worldwide. He argued for divestment in South Africa, and disparaged the oppression of Haitian blacks. His work, *Iron Flowers: A Poetic Report on a Visit to Haiti* was published in 1979, a decade before mainstream America began a serious debate on the plight of Haitian refugees. According to Millican, "Salaam has shared his energy, vision, and spirit with people all over the world in almost every level of human intellectual endeavor. His readers look forward to hearing more from him."

*BIOGRAPHICAL/CRITICAL SOURCES:*

*BOOKS*

*Dictionary of Literary Biography,* Volume 38: *Afro-American Writers after 1955: Dramatists and Prose Writers,* Gale, 1985, p. 231-39.
Killens, John Oliver, and Ward, Jerry W. Jr., editors, *Black Southern Voices,* Meridian, 1992, pp. 326-45.
Salaam, Kalamu ya, *Ibura,* Ahidiana, 1976.
Salaam, Kalamu ya, *Our Women Keep Our Skies from Falling: Six Essays in Support of the Struggle to Smash Sexism and Develop Women,* Nkombo, 1980.

*PERIODICALS*

*Small Press Review,* August, 1980, p. 14.

## SAMKANGE, S. J. T.
See SAMKANGE, Stanlake (John Thompson)

\*   \*   \*

## SAMKANGE, Stanlake (John Thompson) 1922-1988
### (S. J. T. Samkange)

*PERSONAL:* Born March 11, 1922, in Mariga, Rhodesia (now Zimbabwe); died March 6, 1988, of heart and lung ailments, in Harare, Zimbabwe; son of T. D. (a Methodist cleric) and Grace C. Samkange; married Tommie Marie Anderson (a professor of psychology), February 6, 1958; children: Stanlake John Mudavanhie, Harry Mushore Anderson. *Education:* University College of Fort Hare, B.A., 1948; University of South Africa, B.A. (honors), 1951; Indiana University, M.Sc. in Ed., 1958, Ph.D., 1968. *Politics:* African Nationalist. *Religion:* Methodist.

*CAREER:* Political activist, businessman, educator, publisher, and author. Director of companies in Salisbury, Rhodesia (now Zimbabwe), 1958-65; honorary organizing secretary, Nyatsime College, Rhodesia; teacher of history at Northeastern University, Boston, MA, for twelve years; teacher at Tennessee State University, Nashville, TN, 1967-68; associate professor, 1968-69, then professor, 1969-71, at Fisk University, Nashville; political adviser to Bishop Abel Muzorewa of United African National Council, Rhodesia, 1977-79; director of publishing house, Zimbabwe, beginning in 1979. Lecturer in Afro-American Studies at Harvard University. Also worked variously as a journalist, publisher of business paper, and director of public relations firm.

*AWARDS, HONORS:* Herskovits Award from African Studies Association, 1970, for *Origins of Rhodesia.*

*WRITINGS:*

*The Chief's Daughter Who Would Not Laugh,* Longmans, Green, 1964.
*On Trial for My Country* (novel), Heinemann, 1966.
*Origins of Rhodesia,* Heinemann, 1968, Prager, 1969.
*African Saga: A Brief Introduction to African History,* Abindgon, 1971.
*The Mourned One,* Heinemann, 1975.
*Year of the Uprising,* Heinemann, 1978.
(With wife, Tommie Marie Samkange) *Hunhuism or Ubuntuism: A Zimbabwe Indigenous Political Philosophy,* Graham Publishing (Salisbury, Zimbabwe), 1980.
(Under name S. J. T. Samkange) *What Rhodes Really Said about Africans,* Harare Publishing House (Harare, Zimbabwe), 1982.

*Christ's Skin Colour: Was He a White or Black Man?,* Harare
    Publishing House, 1983.
(Under name S. J. T. Samkange) *The Origin of African Na-
    tionalism in Zimbabwe,* Harare Publishing House, 1985.
*Among Them Yanks,* Harare Publishing House, 1985.
(Under name S. J. T. Samkange) *On Trial for That U.D.I.: A
    Novel,* Harare Publishing House, 1986.
(Under name S. J. T. Samkange) *Oral History: The Zvimba
    People of Zimbabwe,* Harare Publishing House, 1986.

*SIDELIGHTS:* Stanlake Samkange was politically involved
in the liberation of British-ruled Rhodesia for approximately
three decades, until it became the independent republic of
Zimbabwe in 1979. He worked for the African People's Union
under Joshua Nkomo and also for the United African National Council as Bishop Abel Muzorewa's political adviser from
1977 to 1979. After Rhodesia's independence, Samkage
opened Harare Publishing House in Zimbabwe.

*BIOGRAPHICAL/CRITICAL SOURCES:*

*BOOKS*

Zell, Hans M., and others, *A New Reader's Guide to African
    Literature,* Holmes & Meier, 1983.

*PERIODICALS*

*New York Times,* March 9, 1988, p. B6.

*       *       *

## SAMPSON, Henry T(homas)   1934-

*PERSONAL:* Born April 22, 1934, in Jackson, MS; son of
Henry T. and Esther Sampson; children: Martin Todd, Henry
T. III. *Education:* Purdue University, B.S. (chemical engineer-
ing), 1956; University of California, Los Angeles, M.S. (en-
gineering), 1961; University of Illinois at Urbana-Champaign,
M.S. (nuclear engineering), 1965, Ph.D., 1967.

*ADDRESSES: Home*—1501 Espinosa Circle, Palos Verdes
Estates, CA 90274. *Office*—Director, Planning STP, Aerospace Corp, 125/1270 P.O. Box 92957, Los Angeles, CA
90274.

*CAREER:* U.S. Naval Weapons Center, China Lake, CA, research chemical engineer, 1956-61; Aerospace Corp., El
Segundo, CA, project engineer, 1967-81, Planning and Operations Space Test Program, director, 1981—. Co-inventor
of Gamma-electric cell; holder of patents related to solid rocket
motors and conversion of nuclear energy into electricity; pi-

oneered study of internal ballistics of solid rocket motors using high-speed photography. Consultant on and producer of
documentary films on early black filmmakers and films. Lecturer for Pioneer Black Filmmakers. Member of board of directors of Los Angeles Southwest College Foundation; technical consultant to Historical Black Colleges and Universities
Program.

*AWARDS, HONORS:* Fellow of U.S. Navy, 1962-64, and
Atomic Energy Commission, 1964-67; Black Image Award
from Aerospace Corp., 1982; Blacks in Engineering, Applied
Science, and Education Award from Los Angeles Council of
Black Professional Engineers, 1983.

*WRITINGS:*

*Blacks in Black and White: A Source Book on Black Films,*
    Scarecrow, 1977, second edition, Scarecrow, 1993.
*Blacks in Black Face: A Source Book on Early Black Musi-
    cal Shows,* Scarecrow, 1980.
*The Ghost Walks: A Chronological History of Blacks in Show
    Business, 1865-1910,* Scarecrow, 1988.

Contributor to *New Grove Dictionary of American Music in
the United States.*

*WORK IN PROGRESS:* Continuing research on black films
and black musical shows.

*SIDELIGHTS:* To voice the histories of the African American experience is to address its silence; to fill, in stages, its
history, and to emancipate the conditions of oppression and
the silenced voices of a history; to hear the misrepresented
speak into the void of the stereotype is to enlighten the present;
to remember the language that silences. The ghost, says Henry T. Sampson in his 1988 book *The Ghost Walks,* has enlarged
its meaning, has even greater significance today: "Many of
the old stereotypes of bygone years, although much more
subtle, are still deeply imbedded in today's popular entertainment. THE GHOST WALKS."

The stereotypes of major Hollywood films paled in the segregated black moviehouse of Sampson's hometown, Jackson,
Mississippi, where as a youngster he first saw independently
produced films featuring all-black casts. These early experiences instilled an interest that was to grow in contrast to the
disproportionate lack of available subject materials in major
trade journals. Subsequently, Sampson discovered, as he
writes in *Blacks in Black and White,* the best accounts of
historical black films could be found in back issues of black
newspapers "which included not only detailed facts but also
critical and editorial comments which gave an important black
perspective of the events as they happened." His source books
on black entertainment rely on interviews, memoirs, reviews

and the critical commentary of the period, and make no claim to interpretive or critical commentary; rather he prefers that the people involved "tell their own story."

By the early 70s, Sampson was gathering materials on "all aspects of independent black film production before 1950, including films, producers and performers." This project resulted in *Blacks in Black and White: A Source Book on Black Films*. Since that time Sampson has branched out encompassing all forms of popular entertainment, from minstrel shows, burlesque, and vaudeville, to the circus and musical comedy. In a parallel move, he explored the business end of show business: booking agencies, music publishing, and the ownership and operation of theatres by African Americans, a movement that fostered the development of a black film industry during the 1920s. These histories are the subject of his two most recent works *Blacks in Black Face: A Source Book on Early Black Musical Shows,* its development from 1910-1940 and *The Ghost Walks: A Chronological History of Blacks in Show Business, 1865-1910.*

*Blacks in Black and White: A Source Book on Black Films* is, precisely that, a compilation of little known facts about independent black film production. Beginning with The Lincoln Motion Picture Company, "the first film company in the history of the United States to produce and distribute films of and by Negroes portraying themselves in other than humiliating burlesque and slapstick comedies," Sampson details the industries development through the peak years as well its decline. In accomplishing his task he reviewed 15,000 weeklies of the period, interviewed black performers who performed in the films and gained access to private collections of black cinema memorabilia. Beyond the wealth of documentation, *Blacks in Black and White* contains synopses of 126 films and credits, 72 brief biographies of performers, and details about film companies, both black and white, organized to produce and distribute black films for black audiences. Special emphasis is given to the African American producers that greatly influenced the growth of the industry. These synopses provide some knowledge of thematic changes in the black enterprises over the years, especially those having racial connotation.

In the chapter on Oscar Micheaux and The Micheaux Film Corporation, *Blacks in Black and White* highlights a man considered one of cinema's most interesting and controversial filmmakers. Oscar Micheaux's Film Corporation became the most successful black independent film company of its era, operating continuously from 1918 through the 1930s. During this period, he was responsible for the production and distribution of over 30 black-cast films throughout America and Europe. Micheaux, known to his contemporaries as a consummate entrepreneur and businessman, produced, marketed, and often wrote the books on which his films are based. He "felt

that his films should depict accurately the social, economic and political conditions under which the black man existed in America," according to Sampson in the book. Consequently, his films proclaim the milieu of unemancipation: lynchings and criminal conviction, the purchase of property by blacks, intraracial relationships, and the treatment of black women by white males.

In a quite different vain, *The Ghost Walks: A Chronological History of Blacks in Show Business, 1865-1910* and *Blacks in Black Face: A Source Book on Early Black Musical Shows* form a compendium of black show business from its origins through 1940. *Blacks in Black Face* offers a composite picture of empowerment and contribution. Sampson amplifies the much neglected history of black show producers, famous black theatres, musical comedy shows, and the personalities that populated the stages of black theatres throughout America and abroad. Little known personalities like comedian Marshall Rogers and dancer Juanita Stinnette, producer Jesse Shipp, and innumerable others re-emerge to shape and populate the black stages of history. *Blacks in Black Face* offers documentation of the marketing of black show business, the detail focusing on the little known history played by black entrepreneurs in engineering its successes. This body of information reveals the enormity of difficulties entrepreneurs faced on the business end: The purchase and management of playhouses, the production of shows, as well as the organization of touring circuits for road shows.

*The Ghost Walks* chronicles the history of black entertainment, from the end of the Civil War when blacks stepped from the plantation to the stage to discover a pre-existent history of black images diffused by whites in burnt cork makeup— blackface. Identified by Sampson in the book as "Ethiopian Delineators" because they "purported to give a *true* delineation of slave amusements on Southern Plantations," they perpetuated the long tradition of racial stereotyping. Those in power obviated the nature of their role as oppressors by caricaturing black servitude and propagating that image as though servility was some trait inherent in the object oppressed. In addition, the African American's past was obscured, as a voice revised its history and rearranged its face.

With this perspective, Sampson's documentation frames the early appearance of these black minstrels and the significance of minstrelsy in raising the black performer from amateur to professional within the oppressor's genre. performers like Bert Williams, considered by black critics to be the greatest "natural" delineator of his time, Black Patti, Sissieretta Jones, Tim Moore, who 40 years later would become famous for his role as Kingfish on the *Amos and Andy* TV show, and the great poet and lyricist Paul Laurence Dunbar.

Sampson's histories gather in their wake the emerging cross currents of cultural development within the African American community—from an illiteracy rate of seventy percent in 1870 to a rate of less than fifty percent twenty years later. The appearance of black weeklies like the *Indianapolis Freeman* closely reflects the transformations of black society during this period. Sampson's documentation illuminates the parallel development evident in show business where theatre critics like the founder and owner of the *Indianapolis Freeman,* Elwood Knox, or Harry Bradford, and Sylvester Russell captured the spirit of the times. Their writings document a self-awareness and an expressive capacity that goes far beyond entertaining. They emphasized the values of empowerment that reflected their readership amid the maelstrom of change.

In this respect the reviews of Sylvester Russell are of particular value. Russell, a singer and performer, possessed a thoroughgoing knowledge of all aspects of theatre. He was the first to condemn, in print, the common use of demeaning barbarisms in the caricaturing of his race as an insult and an injustice. In his reviews he protested vigorously against the writing of the so called "coon song," as in the sheet music cover for the song title "Niggah Loves His Possum."

Sampson articulates the paradoxical nature of African American entertainment in *The Ghost Walks:* the first 45 years "ended on a combined note of triumph and tragedy." Although these progenitors transformed the face of the entertainment industry, the popularity of blacks and whites in blackface was a major factor in the legitimization of the "negative stereotypes that eventually became a deeply embedded theatrical tradition," one which now reenacts the cultural and linguistic myopia of our present reality—the ghost walks.

*BIOGRAPHICAL/CRITICAL SOURCES:*

*BOOKS*

Sampson, Henry T., *Blacks in Black and White: A Source Book on Black films,* Scarecrow, 1977.
Sampson, Henry T., *The Ghost Walks: A Chronological History of Blacks in Show Business,* Scarecrow, 1988.

*PERIODICALS*

*American Reference Books Annual,* Volume 9, 1978, p. 486; Volume 12, 1981, p. 474; Volume 20, 1989, p. 513.
*Black Books Bulletin,* Volume 7, 1981, p. 52.
*Booklist,* April 15, 1978, p. 1378; September 1, 1981, p. 66.
*Choice,* Volume 14, 1978, p. 1508; Volume 18, 1981, p. 805; Volume, 26, 1988, p. 658.
*College and Research Libraries,* Volume 50, 1989, p. 88.
*Journalism Quarterly,* Summer, 1989, p. 510.
*Phylon,* June, 1981, p. 195.
*Reference and Research Book News,* Volume 3, 1988, p. 22.

*Reference Services Review,* January, 1979, p. 42; summer, 1984, p. 44.
*RQ,* winter, 1978, p. 25.

\* \* \*

## SANCHEZ, Sonia  1934-

*PERSONAL:* Name originally Wilsonia Benita Driver; born September 9, 1934, in Birmingham, AL; daughter of Wilson L. and Lena (Jones) Driver; married Etheridge Knight (a poet); marriage ended; children: Anita, Morani Meusi, Mungu Meusi. *Education:* Hunter College (now Hunter College of the City University of New York), B.A., 1955; post-graduate study at New York University, 1958. *Politics:* "Peace, freedom, and justice."

*ADDRESSES: Home*—407 West Chelten Ave., Philadelphia, PA 19144. *Office*—Department of English/Women's Studies, Temple University, Broad and Montgomery, Philadelphia, PA 19122.

*CAREER:* Writer, activist, and lecturer. Staff member, Downtown Community School, New York City, 1965-67, and Mission Rebels in Action, 1968-69; San Francisco State College (now University), San Francisco, CA, instructor, 1966-68; University of Pittsburgh, Pittsburgh, PA, assistant professor, 1969-70; Rutgers University, New Brunswick, NJ, assistant professor, 1970-71; Manhattan Community College of the City University of New York, assistant professor of literature and creative writing, 1971-73; City College of the City University of New York, teacher of creative writing, 1972; Amherst College, Amherst, MA, associate professor, 1972-75; University of Pennsylvania, Philadelphia, PA, 1976-77; Temple University, Philadelphia, associate professor, 1977, professor of English, 1979—, faculty fellow in provost's office, 1986-87, presidential fellow, 1987-91; University of Delaware, Newark, DE, Distinguished Minority Visiting Professor, fall, 1988; Spelman College, Atlanta, GA, poet-in-residence, 1988-89. Member of literature panel of Pennsylvania Council on the Arts; sponsor of Women's International League for Peace and Freedom.

*AWARDS, HONORS:* PEN Writing Award, 1969; National Institute of Arts and Letters grant, 1970; Ph.D., Wilberforce University, 1972; National Endowment for the Arts (NEA) Award, 1978-79; named Honorary Citizen of Atlanta, 1982; Tribute to Black Womanhood Award, Black Students of Smith College, 1982; Lucretia Mott Award, Women's Way and NEA, 1984; Outstanding Arts Award, Pennsylvania Coalition of 100 Black Women; Community Service Award, National Black Caucus of State Legislatures; American Book Award, Before Columbus Foundation, 1985, for *homegirls & handgrenades;* honorary degrees from Trinity College, 1988, and

Baruch College, 1993; Pennsylvania Governor's Award in the Humanities, 1989, for bringing great distinction to herself and her discipline through remarkable accomplishment.

*WRITINGS:*

*Homecoming* (poetry), Broadside Press, 1969.

*We a BadddDDD People* (poetry), foreword by Dudley Randall, Broadside Press, 1970.

*Liberation Poems,* Broadside Press, 1970.

*It's a New Day: Poems for Young Brothas and Sistuhs* (juvenile), Broadside Press, 1971.

(Editor) *Three Hundred and Sixty Degrees of Blackness Comin' at You* (poetry), 5X Publishing Co., 1971.

*Ima Talken bout the Nation of Islam,* Truth Del, 1972.

*Love Poems,* Third Press, 1973.

*A Blues Book for Blue Black Magical Women* (poetry), Broadside Press, 1973.

*The Adventures of Fat Head, Small Head, and Square Head* (juvenile), Third Press, 1973.

(Editor and contributor) *We Be Word Sorcerers: 25 Stories by Black Americans,* Bantam, 1973.

*I've Been a Woman: New and Selected Poems,* Black Scholar Press, 1978.

*A Sound Investment and Other Stories* (juvenile), Third World Press, 1979.

*Crisis in Culture—Two Speeches by Sonia Sanchez,* Black Liberation Press, 1983.

*homegirls & handgrenades* (poems), Thunder's Mouth Press, 1984.

(Contributor) Mari Evans, editor, *Black Women Writers (1950-1980): A Critical Evaluation,* introduction by Stephen Henderson, Doubleday-Anchor, 1984.

*Under a Soprano Sky,* Africa World, 1987.

*PLAYS*

*Sister Sonji* (first produced with *Cop and Blow* and *Players Inn* by Neil Harris, and *Gettin' It Together* by Richard Wesley, as *Black Visions,* Off-Broadway at New York Shakespeare Festival Public Theatre, 1972), published in *New Plays from the Black Theatre,* edited by Ed Bullins, Bantam, 1969.

*The Bronx Is Next* (first produced in New York City at Theatre Black, October 3, 1970), published in *Cavalcade: Negro American Writing from 1760 to the Present,* edited by Arthur Davis and Saunders Redding, Houghton, 1971.

*Uh Huh; But How Do It Free Us?* (first produced in Chicago, IL, at Northwestern University Theater, 1975), published in *The New Lafayette Theatre Presents: Plays with Aesthetic Comments by Six Black Playwrights, Ed Bullins, J. E. Gaines, Clay Gross, Oyamo, Sonia Sanchez, Richard Wesley,* edited by Bullins, Anchor Press, 1974.

*Malcolm/Man Don't Live Here No Mo',* first produced in Philadelphia, PA, at ASCOM Community Center, 1979.

*I'm Black When I'm Singing, I'm Blue When I Ain't,* first produced in Atlanta, GA, at OIC Theatre, April 23, 1982.

Contributor of plays to *Scripts, Black Theatre, Drama Review,* and other theater journals.

*CONTRIBUTOR TO ANTHOLOGIES*

Robert Giammanco, editor, *Potero Negro* (title means "Black Power"), Laterza, 1968.

Le Roi Jones and Ray Neal, editors, *Black Fire: An Anthology of Afro-American Writing,* Morrow, 1968.

Dudley Randall and Margaret G. Burroughs, editors, *For Malcolm: Poems on the Life and Death of Malcolm X,* Broadside Press, 1968.

Walter Lowenfels, editor, *The Writing on the Wall: One Hundred Eight American Poems of Protest,* Doubleday, 1969.

Arnold Adoff, editor, *Black Out Loud: An Anthology of Modern Poems by Black Americans,* Macmillan, 1970.

Lowenfels, editor, *In a Time of Revolution: Poems from Our Third World,* Random House, 1970.

June M. Jordan, editor, *Soulscript,* Doubleday, 1970.

Gwendolyn Brooks, editor, *A Broadside Treasury,* Broadside Press, 1971.

Randall, editor, *Black Poets,* Bantam, 1971.

Orde Coombs, editor, *We Speak as Liberators: Young Black Poets,* Dodd, 1971.

Bernard W. Bell, editor, *Modern and Contemporary Afro-American Poetry,* Allyn & Bacon, 1972.

Adoff, editor, *The Poetry of Black America: An Anthology of the 20th Century,* Harper, 1973.

J. Chace and W. Chace, *Making It New,* Canfield Press, 1973.

Donald B. Gibson, editor, *Modern Black Poets,* Prentice-Hall, 1973.

Stephen Henderson, editor, *Understanding the New Black Poetry: Black Speech and Black Music as Poetic References,* Morrow, 1973.

J. Paul Hunter, editor, *Norton Introduction to Literature: Poetry,* Norton, 1973.

James Schevill, editor, *Breakout: In Search of New Theatrical Environments,* Swallow Press, 1973.

Lucille Iverson and Kathryn Ruby, editors, *We Become New: Poems by Contemporary Women,* Bantam, 1975.

Quincy Troupe and Rainer Schulte, editors, *Giant Talk: An Anthology of Third World Writings,* Random House, 1975.

Henry B. Chapin, editor, *Sports in Literature,* McKay, 1976.

Brooks and Warren, editors, *Understanding Poetry,* Holt, 1976.

Ann Reit, editor, *Alone amid All the Noise,* Four Winds/Scholastic, 1976.

Erlene Stetson, editor, *Black Sister: Poetry by Black American Women, 1746-1980,* Indiana University Press, 1981.

Amiri and Amina Baraka, editors, *Confirmation: An Anthology of African-American Women,* Morrow, 1983.

Burney Hollis, editor, *Swords upon this Hill,* Morgan State University Press, 1984.

Jerome Rothenberg, editor, *Technicians of the Sacred: A Range of Poetries from Africa, America, Asia, Europe and Oceania,* University of California Press, 1985.

Marge Piercy, editor, *Early Ripening: American Women's Poetry Now,* Pandora (London), 1987.

Paul Lauter, editor, *The Heath Anthology of American Literature, Volume 2,* Heath, 1990.

Patricia Bell-Scott, editor, *Double Stitch: Black Women Write about Mothers and Daughters,* Beacon Press, 1991.

Laurie G. Kirszner and Stephen R. Mandell, editors, *Literature: Reading, Reacting, Writing,* Harcourt, 1991.

*Out of This World: The Poetry Project at the St. Mark's Church in-the-Bowery, An Anthology, 1966-1991,* Crown, 1991.

Arthur P. Davis, editor, *The New Cavalcade, Volume 2,* Harvard University Press, 1992.

Margaret Busby, editor, *Daughters of Africa: International Anthology of Literature by Women from the Queen of Sheba to the Present Day,* Thorsons, 1992.

Grace Cavalieri, editor, *WPFW 89.3 FM Poetry Anthology,* Bunny and the Crocodile Press, 1992.

Poems also included in *Night Comes Softly, Black Arts, To Gwen with Love, New Black Voices, Blackspirits, The New Black Poetry, A Rock Against the Wind, America: A Prophecy, Nommo, Black Culture,* and *Natural Process.*

*RECORDINGS*

*Sonia Sanchez,* Pacifica Tape Library, 1968.

*A Sun Lady for All Seasons Reads Her Poetry,* Folkways, 1971.

*Sonia Sanchez and Robert Bly,* Blackbox, 1971.

*Sonia Sanchez: Selected Poems, 1974,* Watershed Intermedia, 1975.

*IDKT: Capturing Facts about the Heritage of Black Americans,* Ujima, 1982.

*OTHER*

Also author of *Shake Down Memory* and *Continuous Fire.* Work represented in *Black Women of Antiquity,* edited by Ivan Van Sertima, Transaction Books, 1988. Columnist for *American Poetry Review,* 1977-78, and *Philadelphia Daily News,* 1982-83. Contributor of poems to *Minnesota Review, Black World,* and other periodicals. Contributing editor to *Black Scholar* and *Journal of African Studies.* Contributor of articles to numerous journals, including *Journal of African Civilizations.*

*SIDELIGHTS:* Sonia Sanchez is often named among the strongest voices of black nationalism, the cultural revolution of the 1960s in which many black Americans sought a new identity distinct from the values of the white establishment. C. W. E. Bigsby comments in *The Second Black Renaissance: Essays in Black Literature* that "the distinguishing characteristic of her work is a language which catches the nuance of the spoken word, the rhythms of the street, and of a music which is partly jazz and partly a lyricism which underlies ordinary conversation." Her emphasis on poetry as a spoken art, or performance, connects Sanchez to the traditions of her African ancestors, an oral tradition preserved in earlier slave narratives and forms of music indigenous to the black experience in America, as Bernard W. Bell demonstrates in *The Folk Roots of Contemporary Afro-American Poetry.* In addition to her poetry, for which she has won many prizes, Sanchez has contributed equally well-known plays, short stories, and children's books to a body of literature called "The Second Renaissance," as Bigsby's title reflects.

Sanchez reached adulthood in Harlem, which only thirty years before had been the cradle of the first literary "renaissance" in the United States to celebrate the works of black writers. Political science and poetry were the subjects of her studies at Hunter College and New York University during the fifties. In the next decade Sanchez began to combine these interests into one activity, "the creat[ion] of social ideals," as she wrote for a section about her writings in *Black Women Writers (1950-1980: A Critical Evaluation,* edited by Mari Evans. For Sanchez, writing and performing poetry is a means of constructive political activism to the extent that it draws her people together to affirm pride in their heritage and build the confidence needed to accomplish political goals. Yet the terms of "black rhetoric," or words by themselves, are not enough, she says often in poems and interviews. Biographers cite her record of service as an educator, activist, and supporter of black institutions as proof of her commitment to this belief. Writing in the *Dictionary of Literary Biography,* Kalamu ya Salaam introduces Sanchez as "one of the few creative artists who have significantly influenced the course of black American literature and culture."

Before Sanchez became recognized as a part of the growing black arts movement of the 1960s, she worked in the Civil Rights movement as a supporter of the Congress of Racial Equality. At that time, like many educated black people who enjoyed economic stability, she held integrationist ideals. But after hearing Malcolm X say that blacks would never be fully accepted as part of mainstream America despite their professional or economic achievements, she chose to base her identity on her racial heritage. David Williams reports that the title of her first book, *Homecoming,* announces this return to a sense of self grounded in the realities of her urban neighborhood after having viewed it for a time from the outside through the lens of white cultural values. In the title poem, "Sanchez presents the act of returning home as a rejection of fantasy and an acceptance of involvement," notes Williams in an essay for *Black Women Writers (1950-1980)*. For the same reasons, Sanchez did not seek a New York publisher for the book. She preferred Dudley Randall's Broadside Press, a publisher dedicated to the works of black authors, that was to see many of her books into print. Reacting to the poems in *Homecoming,* Johari Amini's review in *Black World* warns that they "hurt (but doesn't anything that cleans good) and [the] lines are blowgun-dart sharp with a wisdom ancient as Kilimanjaro." Haki Madhubuti's essay in *Black Women Writers (1950-1980)* comments on this effect, first remarking that "Sanchez ... is forever questioning Black people's commitment to struggle," and later pointing out that she is "forever disturbing the dust in our acculturated lives."

One aspect of her stand against acculturation is a poetic language that does not conform to the dictates of standard English. Madhubuti writes, "More than any other poet, [Sanchez] has been responsible for legitimizing the use of urban Black English in written form.... She has taken Black speech and put it in the context of world literature." Salaam elaborates, "In her work from the 1960s she restructured traditional English grammar to suit her interest in black speech patterns"—a technique most apparent, he feels, in *We a BaddDDD People.* In one poem cited by Madhubuti, which he says is "concerned with Black-on-Black damage," Sanchez predicts that genuine "RE VO LU TION" might come about "if mothas programmed / sistuhs fo / good feelings bout they blk / men / and I / mean if blk / fathas proved / they man / hood by fightin the enemy." These reviewers explain that by inserting extra letters in some words and extra space between lines, words, and syllables within a poem, Sanchez provides dramatic accents and other clues that indicate how the poem is to be said aloud.

The sound of the poems when read aloud has always been important to Sanchez. Her first readings established her reputation as a poet whose energetic performances had a powerful effect on her listeners. She has visited Cuba, China, the West Indies, Europe, and more than five hundred campuses in the United States to give readings, for which she is still in demand. Of her popularity, Salaam relates, "Sanchez developed techniques for reading her poetry that were unique in their use of traditional chants and near-screams drawn out to an almost earsplitting level. The sound elements, which give a musical quality to the intellectual statements in the poetry, are akin to Western African languages; Sanchez has tried to recapture a style of delivery that she felt had been muted by the experience of slavery. In her successful experimentation with such techniques, she joined ... others in being innovative enough to bring black poetry to black people at a level that was accessible to the masses as well as enjoyable for them."

Sanchez is also known as an innovator in the field of education. During the sixties, she taught in New York City's Downtown Community School and became a crusader and curriculum developer for black studies programs in American colleges and universities. Materials on black literature and history were absent from the schools she had attended, and she has worked to see that other young people are not similarly disenfranchised. Opposition to this goal has often complicated her career, sometimes making it difficult for her to find or keep teaching positions; nevertheless, Sanchez has fought to remain in the academic arena to shape and encourage the next generation. She has written two books for her children—*The Adventures of Fat Head, Small Head, and Square Head* and *A Sound Investment and Other Stories*—for reasons she expressed to interviewer Claudia Tate in *Black Women Writers at Work:* "I do think that it's important to leave a legacy of my books for my children to read and understand; to leave a legacy of the history of black people who have moved toward revolution and freedom; to leave a legacy of not being afraid to tell the truth.... We must pass this on to our children, rather than a legacy of fear and victimization."

Because she takes action against oppression wherever she sees it, Sanchez has had to contend with not only college administrators, but also the Federal Bureau of Investigation (FBI), and sometimes fellow members of political organizations. Reviewers note that while her early books speak more directly to widespread social oppression, the plays she wrote during the seventies give more attention to the poet's interpersonal battles. For example, *Uh Huh; But How Do It Free Us?* portrays a black woman, involved in the movement against white oppression, who also resists subjection to her abusive husband. This kind of resistance, writes Salaam, was not welcomed by the leaders of the black power movement at that time.

Sanchez resigned from the Nation of Islam after three years of membership. She had joined the Nation of Islam in 1972 because she wanted her children to see an "organization that was trying to deal with the concepts of nationhood, morality, small businesses, schools.... And these things were very important to me," she told Tate. As Sanchez sees it, her contribution to the Nation was her open fight against the inferior status it assigned to women in relation to men. Believing that cultural survival requires the work of women and children no less than the efforts of men, Sanchez felt compelled to speak up rather than to give up the influence she could exert through public readings of her poetry. "It especially was important for women in the Nation to see that," stated Sanchez, who also told Tate that she has had to battle the "so-called sexism" of many people outside the Nation as well.

Thus Sanchez became a voice in what Stephen E. Henderson calls "a 'revolution within the Revolution'" that grew as black women in general began to reassess their position as "the victims not only of racial injustice but of a sexual arrogance tantamount to dual-colonialism—one from without, the other from within, the Black community," he writes in his introduction to Evans's book. This consciousness surfaces in works that treat politics in the context of personal relationships. Sanchez told Tate, "If we're not careful, the animosity between black men and women will destroy us." To avoid this fate, she believes, women must refuse to adopt the posture of victims and "move on" out of damaging relationships with men, since, in her words recorded in the interview, "If you cannot remove yourself from the oppression of a man, how in the hell are you going to remove yourself from the oppression of a country?"

Consequently, *A Blues Book for Blue Black Magical Women,* written during her membership in the Nation, examines the experience of being female in a society that "does not prepare young black women, or women period, to be women," as she told Tate. Another section tells about her political involvements before and after she committed herself to the establishment of ethnic pride. In this book, as in her plays and stories, "Sanchez uses many of the particulars of her own life as illustrations of a general condition," writes Salaam. He offers that Sanchez "remains the fiery, poetic advocate of revolutionary change, but she also gives full voice to the individual human being struggling to survive sanely and to find joy and love in life." *Love Poems* contains many of the haiku Sanchez wrote during a particularly stressful period of her life. An interview she gave to *Black Collegian* disclosed that she had been beset by the problems of relocation, illness, and poverty. Writing haiku allowed her to "compress a lot of emotion" into a few lines, which helped her to stay sane. Under the circumstances, she also felt that there was no guarantee she would have the time to finish longer works. The poems in these two books are no less political for their being more personal, say reviewers. "The haiku in her hands is the ultimate in activist poetry, as abrupt and as final as a fist," comments Williams. In Salaam's opinion, "No other poet of the 1960s and 1970s managed so masterfully to chronicle both their public and personal development with poetry of such thoroughgoing honesty and relevant and revelatory depth."

Madhubuti says of the poet, "Much of her work is autobiographical, but not in the limiting sense that it is only about Sonia Sanchez." For example, in her well-known story "After Saturday Night Comes Sunday," a woman on the verge of madness finds strength to break out of a painful liaison with a drug abuser without herself becoming trapped in self-pity or alcoholism. "It's not just a personal story," the poet, who has survived divorce, told Tate. "It might be a personal experience, but the whole world comes into it." Readers of all backgrounds can appreciate writings concerned with black identity and survival, she declares in *Black Women Writers at Work,* mentioning that her works have been translated into Europe-

an languages and remarking that "you don't have to whitewash yourself to be universal." At another point in the interview, she explained why she deliberately pushes her writing beyond autobiography: "We must move past always focusing on the 'personal self' because there's a larger self. There's a 'self' of black people. And many of us will have to make a sacrifice in our lives to ensure that our bigger self continues." In her statement for *Black Women Writers (1950-1980),* she presents her own life as an example of the price that must be paid to contribute to social change: "I see myself helping to bring forth the truth about the world. I cannot tell the truth about anything unless I confess to being a student.... My first lesson was that one's ego always compromised how something was viewed. I had to wash my ego in the needs/ aspiration of my people. Selflessness is key for conveying the need to end greed and oppression. I try to achieve this state as I write."

According to *Detroit News* contributor Carole Cook, the title of the American Book Award winner *homegirls & handgrenades* "underscores the creative tension between love and anger intrinsic to ... young black women poets." Speaking in *Black Women Writers (1950-1980)* of the creative tension between protest and affirmation in her writing, Sanchez declared, "I still believe that the age for which we write is the age evolving out of the dregs of the twentieth century into a more humane age. Therefore I recognize that my writing must serve a dual purpose. It must be a clarion call to the values of change while it also speaks to the beauty of a nonexploitative age." Throughout her poems, Sanchez emphasizes the importance of strong family relationships and exposes the dangers of substance abuse among people who hope to be the vital agents of change, relates Richard K. Barksdale in *Modern Black Poets: A Collection of Critical Essays.* Her message, as he notes, is that the desired revolution will not come about through "violence, anger, or rage;" rather, "political astuteness and moral power" among black people are needed to build the new world. Commenting on the content of the poems as it has broadened over the years, Madhubuti observes that Sanchez "remains an intense and meticulous poet who has not compromised craft or skill for message."

"Her work has matured; she's a much better writer now than she was ten years ago. She has continued to grow, but her will has not changed," states critic Sherley Anne Williams, who told Tate that black women writers as a group have kept their commitment to social revolution strong, while others seem to be letting it die out. In the same book, Sanchez attributes this waning, in part, to the rewards that have been given to black writers who focus on themes other than revolution. "The greatness of Sonia Sanchez," believes Salaam, "is that she is an inspiration." Madhubuti shares this view, concluding, "Sanchez has been an inspiration to a generation of young poets.... Her concreteness and consistency over these many years is noteworthy. She has not bought refuge from day-to-day struggles by becoming a writer in the Western tradition.... Somehow, one feels deep inside that in a real fight, this is the type of black woman you would want at your side."

*BIOGRAPHICAL/CRITICAL SOURCES:*

BOOKS

Bankier, Joanna, and Deirdre Lashgari, editors, *Women Poets of the World,* Macmillan, 1983.
Bell, Bernard W., *The Folk Roots of Contemporary Afro-American Poetry,* Broadside Press, 1974.
Bigsby, C. W. E., editor, *The Second Black Renaissance: Essays in Black Literature,* Greenwood Press, 1980.
*Contemporary Literary Criticism,* Volume 5, Gale, 1976.
*Dictionary of Literary Biography,* Volume 51: *Afro-American Poets since 1955,* Gale, 1985.
Evans, Mari, editor, *Black Women Writers (1950-1980): A Critical Evaluation,* introduction by Stephen E. Henderson, Doubleday-Anchor, 1984.
Gibson, Donald B., editor, *Modern Black Poets: A Collection of Critical Essays,* Prentice-Hall, 1973.
Hartigan, Karelisa V., editor, *The Many Forms of Drama,* University Press of America, 1985.
Randall, Dudley, *Broadside Memories: Poets I Have Known,* Broadside Press, 1975.
Redmond, Eugene B., *Drumvoices: The Mission of Afro-American Poetry, A Critical History,* Anchor, 1976.
Sanchez, Sonia, *We a BaddDDD People,* Broadside Press, 1970.
Tate, Claudia, editor, *Black Women Writers at Work,* Continuum, 1983.
Weixlmann, Joe, and Houston A. Baker, Jr., editors, *Black Feminist Criticism and Critical Theory,* Penkevill, 1988.

PERIODICALS

*Black Creation,* fall, 1973.
*Black Scholar,* May, 1979; January, 1980; March, 1981.
*Black World,* August, 1970; April, 1971; September, 1971; April, 1972; March, 1975.
*Book World,* January 27, 1974.
*CLA Journal,* September, 1971.
*Ebony,* March, 1974.
*Essence,* July, 1979.
*Indian Journal of American Studies,* July, 1983.
*MELUS,* fall, 1985; spring, 1988.
*Negro Digest,* December, 1969.
*New Republic,* February 22, 1975.
*Newsweek,* April 17, 1972.
*Phylon,* June, 1975.
*Poetry,* October, 1973.
*Poetry Review,* April, 1985.
*Publishers Weekly,* October 1, 1973; July 15, 1974.
*Time,* May 1, 1972.

\* \* \*

## SARO-WIWA, Ken 1941-

*PERSONAL:* Born in 1941, in Nigeria.

*CAREER:* Novelist, poet, journalist, publisher, and television script writer.

*WRITINGS:*

*Tambari* (juvenile), Longman Nigeria, 1973.
*Letter to Ogoni Youth,* Saros International, 1983.
*Songs in a Time of War,* Saros International, 1985.
*Sozaboy: A Novel in Rotten English,* Saros International, 1985.
*A Forest of Flowers: Short Stories* (juvenile), Saros International, 1986.
*Prisoners of Jebs,* Saros International, 1988.
*Adaku and Other Stories,* Saros International, 1989.
*Four Farcical Plays,* Saros International, 1989.
*On a Darkling Plain,* Saros International, 1989.
*Nigeria: The Brink of Disaster,* Saros International, 1991.
*Pita Dumbrok's Prison,* Saros International, 1991.
*Similia: Essays on Anomic Nigeria,* Saros International, 1991.
*The Singing Anthill: Ogoni Folk Tales,* Saros International, 1991.
*Genocide in Nigeria,* Saros International, 1992.

*"THE ADVENTURES OF MR. B" SERIES*

*Basi and Company: A Modern African Folktale,* Saros International, 1987.
*Mr. B,* illustrated by Peregrino Brimah, Saros International, 1987.
*Basi and Company: Four Television Plays,* Saros International, 1988.
*The Transistor Radio,* Saros International, 1989.
*Mr. B Again,* illustrated by Brimah, Saros International, 1989.
*Mr B. Goes to Lagos,* Saros International, 1989.
*Mr. B Is Dead,* illustrated by Brimah, Saros International, 1990.
*Segi Finds the Radio,* illustrated by Brimah, Saros International, 1991.
*A Shipload of Rice,* illustrated by Brimah, Saros International, 1991.

*SIDELIGHTS:* Ken Saro-Wiwa is becoming internationally known for his acute, often humorous, satires of Nigerian life. Basi, or Mr. B, the main character of his popular series of young adult novels, has been likened to such folk heroes as Anansi and Brer Rabbit. A prolific, primarily self-published, author, Saro-Wiwa also writes for Nigerian television and newspapers.

*A Forest of Flowers,* Saro-Wiwa's first collection of short stories, conveys the variety and vitality of Nigerian life through pieces that portray the lives of ordinary people in this populous African country. Critic Graham Hough in the *London Review of Books* commented: "Ken Saro-Wiwa's extremely accomplished collection of short stories stands to Nigeria in something of the same relation as [James] Joyce's *Dubliners* to Ireland. They are brief epiphanies, each crystallising a moment, a way of living, the whole course of a life." In several stories, Saro-Wiwa depicts close-knit families in small village communities in which superstition and tradition rule. The author's vision of the nation's cities is one of heartbreaking corruption and civil strife. In *New Statesman,* Adewale Maja-Pearce remarked: "Although [Saro-Wiwa's] English is at times heavy-handed, his use of pidgin—"rotten English" he calls it—gives some of the stories an unusual and refreshing quality, already evident in his novel *Sozaboy.*"

Saro-Wiwa has produced a series of books based on a comic Nigerian television series entitled "Basi and Company." Basi, or "Mr. B" as he appears in subsequent volumes, is a likeable young man whose unquestioning optimism leads him into and out of all sorts of trouble. By all accounts, the books share the fast-paced action and humorous dialogue of the show, as well as its episodic structure. *School Librarian* contributor Irene Babsky, reviewing *Basi and Company: A Modern African Folk Tale,* the first in "The Adventures of Mr. B" series, noted that "the sights, smells and sheer exuberance of life in an African city are conveyed with zest and loving attention to detail."

Saro-Wiwa's third novel, *Prisoners of Jebs,* is a satirical farce set in an island prison full of writers, journalists, and military, judicial, and governmental personnel from all over Africa. The prison is the continent in microcosm and the corrupt political maneuverings of the inmates resulting in the eventual destruction of the prison offers the author the opportunity to comment on the social and political atmosphere in post-colonial Africa. Based on a weekly column Saro-Wiwa wrote for *Vanguard,* a Nigerian newspaper, the structure of *Prisoners of Jebs* is episodic, and the action closely parallels the contemporary Nigerian political and social scene. Though some critics found Saro-Wiwa's characters lacking in depth, the author was commended for his humorous and precise portrayal of public African life.

*BIOGRAPHICAL/CRITICAL SOURCES:*

*PERIODICALS*

*Contemporary Review,* January, 1988, p. 48.
*London Review of Books,* July 3, 1986, pp. 22-23.
*New Statesman,* July 11, 1986, p. 32; July 28, 1988, p. 44.
*School Librarian,* May, 1988, p. 77.
*Times Literary Supplement,* August 5, 1988, p. 857.

\* \* \*

## SCHUYLER, George Samuel  1895-1977

*PERSONAL:* Born February 25, 1895, in Providence, RI; died August 31, 1977, in New York, NY; son of George (a chef) and Eliza Jane (Fischer) Schuyler; married Josephine E. Lewis (a painter), January 6, 1928 (died, 1969); children: Philippa (deceased). *Education:* Educated in Syracuse, NY.

*CAREER:* U.S. Civil Service, clerk, 1919-20; *Messenger* (magazine), cofounder and associate editor, 1923-28; *Pittsburgh Courier,* Pittsburgh, PA, columnist, chief editorial writer, and associate editor, 1924-66, special correspondent to South America and West Indies, 1948-49, to French West Africa and Dominican Republic, 1958; *Review of the News,* analysis editor, 1967-77. *New York Evening Post,* special correspondent to Liberia, 1931; *National News,* editor, 1932; *Crisis* (magazine), business manager, 1937-44; *Manchester Union Leader,* literary editor. National Association for the Advancement of Colored People (NAACP), special publicity assistant, 1934-35. Member of international committee of Congress for Cultural Freedom, and U.S. delegation to Berlin and Brussels meetings, 1950. President of Philippa Schuyler Memorial Foundation. *Military service:* U.S. Army, 1912-18; became first lieutenant.

*MEMBER:* American Writers Association (served as vice president), American Asian Educational Exchange, American African Affairs Association, Author's Guild.

*AWARDS, HONORS:* Citation of Merit award from Lincoln University School of Journalism, 1952; American Legion Award, 1968; Catholic War Veterans Citation, 1969; Freedoms Foundation at Valley Forge Award, 1972.

*WRITINGS:*

*Racial Intermarriage in the United States,* Haldeman-Julius, 1929.
*Black No More: Being an Account of the Strange and Wonderful Workings of Science in the Land of the Free, A.D. 1933-1940* (novel), Macaulay, 1931, reprinted, with introduction by Charles R. Larson, Collier Books, 1971.

*Slaves Today: A Story of Liberia,* Brewer, Warren & Putnam, 1931, reprinted, McGrath, 1969.

*The Communist Conspiracy against the Negroes,* Catholic Information Society, 1947.

*The Red Drive in the Colonies,* Catholic Information Society, 1947.

*Black and Conservative: The Autobiography of George S. Schuyler,* Arlington House, 1966.

*Black Empire* (novel; part of The Northeastern Library of Black Literature series) Northeastern University Press, 1991.

Also author of *A Negro Looks Ahead,* 1930; *Fifty Years of Progress in Negro Journalism,* 1950; *The Van Vechten Revolution,* 1951; and *The Negro-Art Hokum,* published by Bobbs-Merrill with Langston Hughes's *The Negro Artist and the Racial Mountain.* Contributor to Spadeau Columns, Inc., 1953-62, and to North American Newspaper Alliance, 1965-77. Contributor to the annals of the American Academy of Political Science and to periodicals, including *Nation, Negro Digest, Reader's Digest, American Mercury, Common Ground, Freeman, Americans,* and *Christian* Herald American. Contributing editor to *American Opinion* and *Review of the News.*

*SIDELIGHTS:* George S. Schuyler was a satirist on race relations and was known for upholding the opposite stance from what was popularly held on the subject. His shifting views attacked Marcus Garvey's back-to-Africa movement and civil rights leader Martin Luther King, Jr.'s practice of nonviolence. Black historian John Henrik Clarke was quoted in Schuyler's *New York Times* obituary as saying: "I used to tell people that George got up in the morning, waited to see which way the world was turning then struck out in the opposite direction."

"He was a rebel who enjoyed playing that role," continued Clarke. Schuyler put his wit and sarcasm to work with the publication of *Black No More,* a satirical novel that gave a fictitious solution to the race problem. Through glandular treatments, blacks could take a cream that would eventually turn them white and they would disappear into white society. This novel and other works by Schuyler were initially highly rated by various black leaders, despite the ridicule present in his works that was directed toward some of these spokesmen. Rayford W. Logan, chairman of the department of history at Howard University, stated that "he could cut deeply and sometimes unfairly, but he was interesting to read."

In the early 1960s, however, when the civil rights movement began to gain momentum, civil rights leaders became less enthusiastic about Schuyler, whose positions moved farther right and seemed reactionary to those of most blacks. This era of civil rights proved to be too powerful for Schuyler, and he was soon overtaken completely. "His outlets became more and more limited," remarked George Goodman, Jr., in the *New York Times,* though "he nonetheless continued to champion conservative issues such as the presence of U.S. troops in Southeast Asia."

*BIOGRAPHICAL/CRITICAL SOURCES:*

*BOOKS*

*Dictionary of Literary Biography,* Gale, Volume 29: *American Newspaper Journalists, 1926-1950,* 1984, Volume 51: *Afro-American Writers from the Harlem Renaissance to 1940,* 1987.

Peplow, Michael W., *George S. Schuyler,* Twayne, 1980.

Schuyler, George Samuel, *Black and Conservative: The Autobiography of George S. Schuyler,* Arlington House, 1966.

*PERIODICALS*

*Black American Literature Forum,* Volume 12, 1978.
*Black World,* Volume 21, 1971.
*Books and Bookmen,* Volume 16, 1971.
*Journal of the School of Languages,* Volume 8, 1981-82.
*Library Journal,* December, 1991.
*New York Times Book Review,* Sept 20, 1992.

*OBITUARIES:*

*PERIODICALS*

*AB Bookman's Weekly,* November 21, 1977.
*New York Times,* September 7, 1977.
*Washington Post,* September 9, 1977.

\*   \*   \*

## SCHWARZ-BART, Simone 1938-

*PERSONAL:* Born 1938, in Guadeloupe, French West Indies; married Andre Schwarz-Bart (a writer), 1961.

*ADDRESSES: Home*—Guadeloupe; and Lausanne, France. *Office*—c/o Editions du Seuil, 27 rue Jacob, Paris 16e, France.

*CAREER:* Writer.

*WRITINGS:*

(With husband, Andre Schwarz-Bart) *Un Plat de porc aux bananes vertes* (title means "A Dish of Pork with Green Bananas"), Seuil, 1967.

(With A. Schwarz-Bart) *La Mulatresse Solitude,* Seuil, 1967, translation by Ralph Manheim published as *A Woman Named Solitude,* Atheneum, 1973.

*Pluie et vent sur Telumee Miracle,* Seuil, 1972, translation by Barbara Bray published as *The Bridge of Beyond,* Atheneum, 1974.

*SIDELIGHTS:* Simone Schwarz-Bart takes her native Guadeloupe and the former slaves who inhabit the island as the subjects for her highly praised novels. Her plots focus on black women in their continuing struggle with racism, superstition, poverty, and the violence of the men with whom they share their lives. Her work has been commended for its depiction of a strongly matrilineal society grounded in an evocative pastoralism.

In her first two novels, co-authored with her husband, Schwarz-Bart depicts female characters driven beyond the fringes of rural society by their sorrow and suffering. *A Dish of Pork with Green Bananas* is narrated by Mariotte, an elderly, crippled, and half-blind woman from Martinique who endures her last days in an asylum for the aged in Paris. In *A Woman Named Solitude,* the main character is driven mad by the horrors she has endured and begins murdering members of the white master-class she encounters on her aimless wanderings through the Guadeloupe countryside.

In Schwarz-Bart's third novel, *The Bridge of Beyond,* her first solo effort, the narrative spans three generations of women as told through the eyes of Telumee, an elderly, illiterate islandwoman who has never ventured more than a few miles from her home. John Updike commented in *Picked-Up Pieces:* "The 'miracle' attached to Telumee's name and present in the French title may be that of the human spirit, with its immortal resilience, its quicksilver moods admirable even when malevolent, its—as the book puts it—*panache.*" Reviewers praised the novel's poetic prose style and its unusual, dream-like structure. *International Fiction Review* contributor J. David Danielson remarked that *The Bridge of Beyond* "is a remarkable book for its stylistic grace and poetic containment of an often brutal reality ... for its example of persistence in the face of injustice and misfortune, and perhaps most of all for its strikingly vivid and authentic evocation of the Antillean Creole world."

*BIOGRAPHICAL/CRITICAL SOURCES:*

*BOOKS*

*Contemporary Literary Criticism,* Volume 7, Gale, 1977.
Updike, John, *Picked-Up Pieces,* Knopf, 1976.

*PERIODICALS*

*International Fiction Review,* January, 1976, pp. 35-46.

*New Republic,* April 6, 1974.
*New Review,* February, 1975.
*New Statesman,* January 10, 1975.
*New Yorker,* August 12, 1974.
*New York Times,* February 19, 1967.
*New York Times Book Review,* February 11, 1973; March 17, 1974.
*Observer,* January 19, 1975.
*Times Literary Supplement,* January 10, 1975.

\*    \*    \*

## SCOTT, Dennis (Courtney)   1939-1991

*PERSONAL:* Born December 16, 1939, in Kingston, Jamaica; died February 21, 1991, after a prolonged illness; married Joy Scott. *Education:* Attended Jamaica College; University of the West Indies, B.A.

*ADDRESSES: Office*—School of Drama, 1 Arthur Wint Drive, Kingston 5, Jamaica.

*CAREER:* Poet, playwright, actor, dancer, theatrical director. Taught English and Spanish at Presentation College, Trinidad, then taught at Kingston College and Jamaica College. Became director of Jamaica School of Drama and Dean of the Four Schools of Cultural Training Centre, Kingston, Jamaica. Performed with National Dance Theater Company of Jamaica. Visiting professor, Yale University, 1983.

*AWARDS, HONORS:* Shubert Playwrighting Award, 1970; Commonwealth fellowship, 1972; International Poetry Forum Award, 1973, for *Uncle Time;* Commonwealth Poetry Prize, 1974; Silver Musgrave Medal, 1974; Prime Minister's Award, 1983, for contribution to art and education; Jamaican Festival Commission bronze and silver medals, for poetry; has received best director awards.

*WRITINGS:*

*POETRY*

*Journeys and Ceremonies,* privately published, 1969.
*Uncle Time,* University of Pittsburgh Press, 1973.
*Dreadwalk: Poems, 1970-78,* New Beacon, 1982.
*Strategies,* Sandberry Press, 1989.

Also contributor to *Seven Jamaican Poets: An Anthology of Recent Poetry,* edited by Mervyn Morris, Bolivar, 1971, and *Poems from "On the Offbeat"; read at the Barn Theatre, October-November, 1966, [by] Mervyn Morris, Basil McFarlane [and] Dennis Scott,* 1966.

*Terminus,* University of the West Indies Extra-Mural Department, 1966.

*Echo in the Bone* (produced in Kingston, Jamaica, at Creative Arts Centre, 1974), published in *Plays for Today,* edited by Errol Hill, Longmans, 1985.

*The Fantasy of Sir Gawain and the Green Knight* (adaptation of medieval poem; first produced in Washington, DC, at Kennedy Center, 1977), O'Neill Press, 1979.

*Dog,* produced in Kingston at Creative Arts Centre, 1978.

Also author of *The Crime of Anabel Campbell,* published in *Caribbean Plays for Playing,* edited by Keith Noel, Heinemann, 1985.

*SIDELIGHTS:* Dennis Scott is a poet and playwright whose works display an unusual and effective use of language. In *Contemporary Poets,* Edward Kamau Brathwaite commented: "You can dip into most of Dennis C. Scott's poems and come up with glories." Proficient in both his native Jamaican idiom and standard English, Scott exemplifies the split nature of the Jamaican people, descendants of slaves, free yet still dominated by the English culture. His poetry includes personal lyrics concerning relationships, political pieces in which the persona speaks as a representative of his people, and poems which express in surreal and magical imagery the human condition.

In *Uncle Time,* Scott's first major collection to appear in the United States, the author displays his ability to incorporate his dual identity as representative black Jamaican man, and as middle-class, educated, performance artist in poems that utilize both the Jamaican idiom and standard English diction and syntax. A reviewer in *Choice* remarked: "The book is of uneven quality, but all the individual poems bear the stamp of originality, interest, and excitement."

Scott's poetry relies heavily on surrealistic imagery to convey the fear and pain of existence in his beautiful but tragic homeland. The persona utilized most often in his first two major collections, *Uncle Time* and *Dreadwalk,* is heraldic, a voice speaking for a whole people. Critics note the magical quality of much of the language in poems in which the poet appears as conjurer or mythological figure. Scott's vision is often apocalyptic, with mortal danger lurking alongside the magic, as in "Infection": "But the cop was frightened,/never having seen a man make a knife/out of moonlight and laughter./So he shot him." In Scott's later works, which are concerned with the recovery and acceptance of the history of his people, the menace of the earlier work is less present, and reviewers note that the voice of the poems is more at peace, sympathetic rather than frightened.

*The Fantasy of Sir Gawain and the Green Knight,* Scott's adaptation of the famous medieval poem concerning one of the knights of King Arthur's Round Table, was commissioned for performance at the Children's Arts Festival in 1977 by a troupe composed of both hearing and deaf actors. Reviewers commended the charm of Scott's rendering of the medieval legend as a fairy tale and noted its appropriateness for a wide range of players. A critic in *Horn Book* concluded: "The terse dialogue is a skillful simplification of the rich complexity of the original story."

Scott has also written a play, *Echo in the Bone,* which presents a wake on a Jamaican plantation as the catalyst for working through the emotional legacy of slavery.

*BIOGRAPHICAL/CRITICAL SOURCES:*

*BOOKS*

*Contemporary Poets,* St. James, 1991.

*Dictionary of Literary Biography,* Volume 125, *Twentieth-Century Caribbean and Black African Writers, Second Series,* Gale, 1993.

*PERIODICALS*

*Callaloo,* summer, 1990, p. 570.

*Choice,* May, 1974, p. 440; March, 1980, p. 85.

*Horn Book,* June, 1980, pp. 314-15.

\*   \*   \*

## SCOTT, Nathan A(lexander), Jr. 1925-

*PERSONAL:* Born April 24, 1925, in Cleveland, OH; son of Nathan Alexander (a lawyer) and Maggie (Martin) Scott; married Charlotte Hanley (a professor of business administration), December 21, 1946; children: Nathan A. III, Leslie Kristin Ashamu. *Education:* Attended Wayne State University, 1940-41; University of Michigan, B.A., 1944; Union Theological Seminary, New York City, M.Div., 1946; Columbia University, Ph.D., 1949.

*ADDRESSES: Home*—1419 Hilltop Rd., Charlottesville, VA 22903. *Office*—Department of Religious Studies, University of Virginia, Charlottesville, VA 22903.

*CAREER:* Virginia Union University, Richmond, dean of chapel, 1946-47; Howard University, Washington, DC, instructor, 1948-50, assistant professor, 1950-53, associate professor of humanities, 1953-55, director of general education program in humanities, 1953-55; University of Chicago, Divinity School, Chicago, IL, assistant professor, 1955-58, associate professor, 1958-64, professor of theology and literature, 1964-72, Shailer Mathews Professor of Theology and Literature, 1972-77; University of Virginia, Charlottesville, professor of English and William R. Kenan, Jr., Professor of Religious Studies, 1976-90, chair of department of religious studies, 1980-86, professor emeritus. Ordained priest in Episcopal Church, 1960; canon theologian, Cathedral of St. James, Chicago, 1966-76. Adjunct professor, University of Michigan, 1969; visiting professor, Gustavus Adolphus College, 1954; fellow, school of letters, Indiana University, 1965-72; Walter and Mary Tuohy Visiting Professor, John Carroll University, 1970. Former trustee of Seabury-Western Theological Seminary, Episcopal Radio-TV Foundation, and Chicago Historical Society.

*MEMBER:* Society for Religion in Higher Education (Kent fellow), Modern Language Association of America, American Academy of Religion (vice-president, 1984; president-elect, 1985; president, 1986), American Academy of Arts and Sciences (fellow, 1979), Society for Values in Higher Education.

*AWARDS, HONORS:* Litt.D. from Ripon College, 1965, St. Mary's College, Notre Dame, 1969, Denison University, 1976, Brown University, 1981, Northwestern University, 1982, Elizabethtown College, 1989, and Wesleyan University, 1989; L.H.D. from Wittenberg University, 1965, and University of the District of Columbia, 1976; D.D. from Philadelphia Divinity School, 1967, Virginia Theological Seminary, 1985, and Kenyon College, 1993; S.T.D. from General Theological Seminary, 1968, and University of the South, 1992; Hum.D. from University of Michigan, 1988.

*WRITINGS:*

*Rehearsals of Discomposure: Alienation and Reconciliation in Modern Literature,* King's Crown Press of Columbia University Press, 1952.

(Editor) *The Tragic Vision and the Christian Faith,* Association Press, 1957.

*Modern Literature and the Religious Frontier,* Harper, 1958.

*The Broken Center: A Definition of the Crisis of Values in Modern Literature* (lecture), National Council of the Protestant Episcopal Church, 1959.

*Albert Camus,* Hillary House, 1962, second revised edition, Bowes & Bowes, 1969.

*Reinhold Niebuhr* (pamphlet), University of Minnesota Press, 1963.

(Editor) *The New Orpheus: Essays toward a Christian Poetic,* Sheed, 1964.

(Editor) *The Climate of Faith in Modern Literature,* Seabury, 1964.

*Samuel Beckett,* Hillary House, 1965, second revised edition, Bowes & Bowes, 1969.

(Editor) *Forms of Extremity in the Modern Novel,* John Knox, 1965.

(Editor) *Four Ways of Modern Poetry,* John Knox, 1965.

(Editor) *Man in the Modern Theatre,* John Knox, 1965.

*The Broken Center: Studies in the Theological Horizon of Modern Literature,* Yale University Press, 1966.

*Ernest Hemingway: A Critical Essay,* Eerdmans, 1966.

(Editor) *The Modern Vision of Death,* John Knox, 1967.

*Craters of the Spirit: Studies in the Modern Novel,* Corpus Publications, 1968.

(Editor) *Adversity and Grace: Studies in Recent American Literature,* University of Chicago Press, 1968.

*The Unquiet Vision: Mirrors of Man in Existentialism,* World Publishing, 1969.

*Negative Capability: Studies in the New Literature and the Religious Situation,* Yale University Press, 1969.

*The Wild Prayer of Longing: Poetry and the Sacred,* Yale University Press, 1971.

*Nathanael West,* Eerdmans, 1971.

*Three American Moralists: Mailer, Bellow, Trilling,* University of Notre Dame Press, 1973.

*The Legacy of Reinhold Niebuhr,* University of Chicago Press, 1975.

*The Poetry of Civic Virtue: Eliot, Malraux, Auden,* Fortress, 1976.

*Mirrors of Man in Existentialism,* Collins, 1978.

*The Poetics of Belief: Studies in Coleridge, Arnold, Pater, Santayana, Stevens, and Heidegger,* University of North Carolina Press, 1985.

*Visions of Presence in Modern American Poetry,* Johns Hopkins University Press, 1993.

Work represented in numerous anthologies, including, *Religious Symbolism,* edited by F. Ernest Johnson, Harper, 1955; *Literature and Belief,* edited by M. H. Abrams, Columbia University Press, 1958; *Symbolism in Religion and Literature,* edited by Rollo May, Braziller, 1960; *The Scope of Grace,* edited by Philip Hefner, Fortress, 1964; *The Search for Identity: Essays on the American Character,* edited by Roger Lincoln Shinn, Harper, 1964; *Comedy: Meaning and Form,* edited by Robert W. Corrigan, Chandler, 1965; *Conflicting Images of Man,* edited by William Nicholls, Seabury, 1966; *Existentialism,* edited by William V. Spanos, Crowell, 1966; *The Shapeless God,* edited by Harry J. Mooney and Thomas Staley, University of Pittsburgh Press, 1968; *Dark Symphony: Negro Literature in America,* edited by James A. Emmanuel and Theodore L. Gross, Free Press, 1968; *Black Expression: Essays by and about Black Americans in the Creative Arts,* edited by Addison Gayle, Jr., Weybright and Talley, 1969; *Five Black Writers: Essays on Wright, Ellison, Baldwin, Hughes, and LeRoi Jones,* edited by Donald B. Gibson, editor, New York University Press, 1970; *The Black*

*Novelist,* edited by Robert Hemenway, C. E. Merrill, 1970; *Cavalcade: Negro American Writing from 1760 to the Present,* edited by Arthur P. Davis and Saunders Redding, Houghton, 1971; *Makers of American Thought,* edited by Ralph Ross, University of Minnesota Press, 1974; *Harvard Guide to Contemporary American Writing,* edited by Daniel Hoffman, Harvard University Press, 1979; *American Writing Today,* edited by Richard Kostelanetz, Whitston, 1991; *Radical Pluralism and Truth: David Tracy and the Hermeneutics of Religion,* edited by Werner G. Jeanrond and Jennifer L. Rike, Crossroad Publishing, 1991; *The Reader's Companion to American History,* edited by Eric Foner and John A. Garraty, Houghton, 1991. Contributor of articles to numerous periodicals, including *Carleton Miscellany, Christianity and Literature, Southern Review, Virginia Quarterly Review,* and *Journal of the American Academy of Religion.* Advisory editor, *Callaloo; Christian Scholar,* co-editor, 1959-67, book review editor, 1960—; *Journal of Religion,* co-editor, 1964-77, member of board of consultants, 1977—; member of advisory board, *Religion and Literature* (formerly *Notre Dame English Journal*).

*BIOGRAPHICAL/CRITICAL SOURCES:*

*PERIODICALS*

*Books Abroad,* winter, 1970.
*Christian Century,* February 19, 1969; May 6, 1970.
*Comparative Literature,* spring, 1968.
*Contemporary Literature,* spring, 1968.
*Georgia Review,* summer, 1969.
*Virginia Quarterly Review,* autumn, 1968.

\*   \*   \*

## SELVON, Sam(uel Dickson) 1923-

*PERSONAL:* Born May 20, 1923, in Trinidad, West Indies; immigrated to England, 1950; immigrated to Canada, 1978; married Draupadi Persaud, 1947 (divorced); married Althea Nesta Daroux, 1963; children: (first marriage) Shelley Sarojini; (second marriage) Michael, Leslie, Debra Jane. *Education:* Attended Naparima College, Trinidad, 1935-39.

*ADDRESSES:* c/o Davis-Poynter Ltd., 20 Garrick St., London WC2E 9BJ, England; c/o Longman Inc., 95 Church St., White Plains, NY 10601.

*CAREER:* Writer. *Trinidad Guardian* (newspaper and weekly magazine), Trinidad, West Indies, journalist, 1946-50; British Broadcasting Corporation (BBC-TV), London, England, journalist, c. 1950; Indian Embassy, London, civil servant, 1950-53; free-lance writer, beginning c. mid-1950s. *Military*

*service:* Royal Navy Reserve, 1940-45; wireless operator patrolling Caribbean Sea on minesweepers and torpedo boats.

*AWARDS, HONORS:* Fellow of the John Simon Guggenheim Memorial Foundation, 1954 and 1968; traveling scholarship from the Society of Authors, London, 1958; Trinidad Government Scholarship, 1962; grants from the Arts Council of Great Britain, 1967 and 1968; Hummingbird Medal of the Order of the Trinity from Prime Minister's Office of the Trinidad and Tobago Government, 1969, for work in Caribbean literature; D.Litt. University of West Indies, 1985, and University of Warwick, 1989.

*WRITINGS:*

*A Brighter Sun* (novel), Wingate, 1952, Viking, 1953.
*An Island Is a World* (novel), Wingate, 1955.
*The Lonely Londoners* (novel), Wingate, 1956, St. Martin's, c. 1957, published as *The Lonely Ones,* Brown, Watson, 1959, published as *The Lonely Londoners,* Mayflower, 1967, Longman, 1972.
*Ways of Sunlight* (short stories), St. Martin's, 1957.
*The Lonely Londoners* (screenplay), British Broadcasting Corporation (BBC) Films, 1958.
*Turn Again Tiger* (novel), MacGibbon & Kee, 1958, St. Martin's, 1959.
*I Hear Thunder* (novel), Wingate, 1962, St. Martin's, 1963.
*Carnival in Trinidad,* Department of Education (Wellington, New Zealand), 1964.
*The Housing Lark* (novel), MacGibbon & Kee, 1965, Three Continents, 1990.
*A Cruise in the Caribbean,* Department of Education (Wellington), 1966.
*A Drink of Water,* Nelson, 1968.
*The Plains of Caroni* (novel), MacGibbon & Kee, 1970.
*Those Who Eat the Cascadura* (novel), Davis-Poynter, 1972.
*Anansi the Spider Man* (television play), BBC, 1974.
(Under name Sam Selvon) *Moses Ascending* (novel), Davis-Poynter, 1975.
*Home, Sweet India* (television play), BBC, 1976.
*Switch* (play), produced in London at Royal Court Theatre, 1977.
(With Horace Ove) *Pressure* (screenplay), British Film Institute, 1978.
(Under name Sam Selvon) *Moses Migrating* (novel), Longman, 1983, published with preface by Moses Aloetta and afterword by Susheila Nasta, Three Continents Press, c. 1992.
*El Dorado West One,* Peepal Tree (Leeds, U.K.), 1988.
(Under name Sam Selvon) *Highway in the Sun and Other Plays,* Peepal Tree (London), 1988.
(Under name Sam Selvon) *Foreday Morning: Selected Prose 1946-1986,* edited by Kenneth Ramchand and Susheila Nasta, Longman, 1989.

Contributor to *Commonwealth,* edited by Anna Rutherford, Aarhus University Press (Aarhus, Denmark), 1971. Contributor to periodicals, including *London Magazine, Nation, Sunday Times* (London), and *Evergreen Review. Turn Again Tiger* has been translated into German; *Moses Ascending* has been translated into Danish.

*RADIO PLAYS*

"Village in the Bambbees," *Tea-Time Talk,* BBC, 1952.
"English Goes Abroad: English as Spoken in the West Indies," *The English Tongue,* BBC, 1955.
"A Multi-Racial Society," *The Changing Caribbean,* BBC, 1960.
*Lost Property,* BBC, 1965.
*Perchance of Dream,* BBC, 1966.
*Rain Stop Play,* BBC, 1967.
*Highway in the Sun,* BBC, 1967.
*You Right in the Smoke,* BBC, 1968.
*El Dorado, West One,* BBC, 1969.
*Bringing in the Sheaves,* BBC, 1969.
*Turn Again Tiger,* BBC, 1970.
*Voyage to Trinidad,* BBC, 1971.
*Those Who Eat the Cascadura,* BBC, 1971.
*Mary, Mary Shut Your Gate,* BBC, 1971.
*Cry Baby Brackley,* BBC, 1972.
*Water for Veronica,* BBC, 1972.
*The Harvest in the Wilderness,* BBC, 1972.
*Milk in the Coffee,* BBC, 1975.
*Zeppi's Machine,* BBC, 1977.

Also author of the radio plays *A House for Teena,* 1965; *Worse Than Their Bite,* 1968; and *Home Sweet India,* 1970. Adapted *The Magic Stick* for radio, from a work by Ismith Khan, 1971.

*SIDELIGHTS:* Award-winning West Indian writer Samuel Selvon captures the spirit of a changing culture in his short stories and novels. The author is a native of Trinidad, an island in the Atlantic located off the northeastern coast of Venezuela, bordering the southern portion of the Caribbean Sea. Acquired by England in 1802, the island did not become part of an independent state until 1962. Selvon's evocations of Caribbean life explore the ramifications of the British influence on Trinidad as well as the racial tensions existing between black Africans and Indians living in the West Indies. Judged by critics to be impassioned, charming, and sometimes ribald works of fiction, the author's writings are noted for their vibrant local color, faithfulness to the Trinidadian dialect, and conversational tone. In an interview with Kenneth Ramschand for *Canadian Literature,* Selvon asserted: "If I have anything significant to say on an issue it is to be found inside my novels and short stories."

A popular short story writer in Trinidad, Selvon was part of the wave of West Indian writers who settled in London in the early 1950s. It is during this period that his first novel, *A Brighter Sun,* garnered considerable acclaim in both England and the United States. Ivan Van-Sertima in *Contemporary Novelists* says that "through a series of commonplace events we see the Indian peasant facing the crucial adjustments in the movement of the life of the land to the life of the town." Selvon is not so much concerned with notions of rapidly disappearing Indian traditions as much as the impact of the complex social transformations and cosmopolitan culture—Chinese, Portuguese, African—upon the Indian mind-set. A humorist, he is quick to satirize the banal and vulgar side of life for a people caught in the rapidity of change that is toppling both the moral and social fabric of its peoples.

It is this havoc—the changing face of Caribbean culture that industrialization and the American way of life wreak upon the island people and their way of life—that Selvon earnestly portrays. Despite some criticism that Selvon dealt too lightly with the problems of illiteracy, racial conflict, poverty, and psychological depression among the villagers, Anthony West, writing in the *New Yorker,* dubs the book "a delightful first novel." West further contends, "Selvon is a writer with a sharp eye; his characters and the world they inhabit have a substantial reality." In an article for the *New York Times Book Review,* Edith Efron explains, "Tiger's drama lies in his superiority of mind and imagination which drives him constantly to transcend the restricted economic and spiritual horizons of his native neighbors."

The story revolves around "John" Tiger and his wife Urmilla, a rural East Indian couple of orthodox Hindu background who, following an arranged marriage, set up housekeeping in a new housing settlement in cosmopolitan Barataria, a short distance outside of Port-of-Spain and a long way from the strict social norms of traditional Hindu life. In this new life they are brought together with and befriended by their predominantly Creole neighbors amid the turbulence of World War II. As Ian Thomson observes in *Books and Bookmen,* "Selvon's point is that this is all for the best." As events unfold, Tiger enters the service of a U.S. firm contracted to build the rather extensive Churchill-Roosevelt Highway. Caught in the exuberance of American "can-do mentality" Tiger invariably falls into the patronizing trap of, as Thomson puts it, "boundless admiration of all things American." Consistent with the American way, though, the opportunism fades with the departure of the government's investment company, leaving the islanders no better off than before. The novel ends with Tiger's realization that "you don't start things over in life," and with that, Tiger, a farmer at heart, returns to preparing the land for raising crops: "Now is a good time to plant corn."

In *Turn Again Tiger,* Selvon resumes the adventures, or more correctly, the misadventures of Tiger and Urmilla precisely where *A Brighter Sun* leaves off. In an attempt to return to their origins by working the land, the Indian couple relocates from Barataria to the territory of Five Rivers, which only compounds their pre-existing disillusionment with suburban life. As Van-Sertima puts it, "here we see the dilemma of the man who is only educated enough to be restless about his condition but can find no direction or stage for any significant extension or expression." As in Selvon's first novel, *A Brighter Sun, Turn Again Tiger* brings home the realization that the hero must contend with the inevitable pitfalls that the realities of life heap on its protagonists. Returning to suburban Barataria once more, Tiger and Urmilla find themselves on the pendulum that swings between urban and rural patterns.

Selvon's 1956 book, *The Lonely Londoners,* was greeted enthusiastically by the *Financial Times* as "the definitive novel about London's West Indians," as the cover of the 1972 edition of the narrative states. Generally regarded as a more mature work than *A Brighter Sun, The Lonely Londoners* is an exploration of clashing cultures. The novel takes place during the years following World War II and focuses on black West Indians living in London at the height of their mass influx into that city. Selvon illuminates the poor living conditions and racial discrimination that the immigrants faced, creating what Whitney Baillett in *New Yorker* hails as "a nearly perfect work of its kind." The critic further proclaims, "This is the blessedly balanced realism that skirts completely the depressing passion of the naturalist novelist—the romance of total misery." In fact, *The Lonely Londoners* is a classical farce, a "picture," observes Van-Sertima, "both hilarious and pathetic, of the plight of West Indian immigrants in London."

*The Lonely Londoners* is composed of a series of loosely connected vignettes that sharply contrast and poke fun at the differences between the mirthful West Indians and their more sober British hosts. A typical portrait sketch can be found in the mocking tone with which Selvon captures the British "wannabe" Harris: "Harris is a fellar who like to play ladeda, and he like English customs and thing, he does be polite and say thank you and he does get up in the bus and the tube to let woman sit down, which is a thing even Englishmen don't do. And when he does dress, you think is some Englishman going to work in the City, bowler and umbrella, and briefcase tuck under arm with *The Times* fold up in the pocket so the name would show, and he walking upright like it is he alone who alive in the world. Only thing, Harris face black." Addressing this style, Dillibe Onyeama in *Books and Bookmen* says that "its chief winning point is in Selvon's brilliant use of West Indian 'pidgin' throughout, in both prose and dialogue, and in the remarkable humour with which he tackles an essentially poignant and moving story of human endurance in the face of extreme hardship and loneliness."

Selvon's sixth novel, *The Housing Lark,* picks up on the issue of white prejudice, depicting the efforts of freewheeling Trinidadians to save enough money to purchase a home and thereby liberate themselves from exploitation by crooked white landlords. *The Housing Lark,* also a comedy, is a touching story in the 'pidgin' dialect of Trinidad. It recounts the often amusing hardships of its hero, a West Indian expatriot, in his search for affordable housing. Portraits of both expatriate West Indians living in London and the people of Trinidad in their native milieu, the short stories in the 1957 collection *Ways of Sunlight* also contain Selvon's signature characters, leading "precarious lives ... with difficulty but also with gusto," according to Rye Vervaet in the *New York Times Book Review.* K. W. Purdy notes in *Saturday Review* that while the tales in the volume "are not notable for dramatic tension," Selvon's character studies—such as that of the wrinkle-faced, space-toothed black farm woman, Ma Procop, "who gripped a dirty clay pipe firmly with her gums ... and smoked cheap black tobacco"—convey "a warming, balanced conviction of the indestructibility of the human spirit." At home in the idiom of the short story, Selvon "sees clearly his gift for farce.... His stories at best have a pointed finish, a rounded artistry lacking in the episodic fragmentation of the novels."

Selvon broke new ground with his 1962 novel *I Hear Thunder,* centering on the educated native bourgeoisie living in the West Indies. In the story, a black Trinidadian returns to the island from London with a medical degree and a white wife. Selvon portrays Trinidad in *I Hear Thunder* as an island where white skin is "more desired than food." Yet color in no way impedes a series of partner-swapping seductions that occur throughout the course of the novel. Some critics complain that Selvon failed to address the complex social consequences of intermarriage—especially during the 1960s. Dion Reilly, writing in the *New York Times Book Review,* ventures that the development of the narrative might be somewhat misleading in its implication that "money and education, more than race or color" are the "important keys to the apparently somewhat skittish social conditions of Trinidad." Still, Reilly concedes, "Selvon writes with great charm and a fresh, earthy naivete."

Despite being faulted for its thin "simple rise-and-fall" plot, as critic Julian Barnes claims in *New Statesman, Moses Ascending,* Selvon's 1975 novel, is generally praised for its beautifully evocative scenes and authentic language. As the raucous narrator bellows early on, "I will knock them in the Old Kent Road with my language alone.... My very usage of English will have them rolling in the aisles." Selvon also gives ample proof of his mastery of farce and comic relief, mercilessly exploiting, for example, the master's role in his mirthful reversal along the racial line as he does in Moses's imperious treatment of his white Man Friday, his musings on the smell of the white man, or his witty takes on the theme of the black man's burden. As Valentine Cunningham puts it in

*Times Literary Supplement,* "Selvon is a comic master, whose wryly bawdy explorations of immigrant dilemmas and daftnesses make for very much greater conviction and irrefutably more telling humanity than the sobersides earnestnesses of the black neo-left or the grim apoplexies of the white far-right."

Moses, whose story begins in *The Lonely Londoners* and who is the newly risen landlord in Shepard's Bush, muses from his penthouse—his memoirs being the center of his concentration—on the goings-on below his residence. These range from the left-wing revolutionaries in the basement, to the god-invoking Asian crooks upstairs, to the livestock-filled backyard, where sheep await ritual slaughter. Swirling and rising with it all is what Barnes calls the "vigour" of the language, which carries the novel: The language is "an ingenious stylistic miscegenation, a knowing and controlled mix of idioms, and an elasticated West Indian grammar."

Selvon explained in the *Canadian Literature* interview that he is more concerned with "the translation of emotions, feelings, and situations" in his works than in the creation of "an epic or saga" documenting West Indian history. "There is more than enough history and drama here for others to do more comprehensive and detailed studies," the author reasoned. Selvon's humorous and optimistic brand of realism—if not entirely representative of the difficulties faced by the natives of Trinidad—brings what West refers to as a "vigor" to the "new literature of the West Indies." Commenting on the value of Selvon's works, Vervaet concludes that the spirited writer "finds both humor and pathos in the human condition," and "he also believes a little in obeah (magic)."

*BIOGRAPHICAL/CRITICAL SOURCES:*

*BOOKS*

*Contemporary Novelists,* edited by Lesley Henderson, St. James Press, fifth edition, 1991, pp. 578-79.

Dance, Daryl Cumber, *Fifty Caribbean Writers: A Bio-Bibliographical Critical Sourcebook,* Greenwood Press, 1986, pp. 439-49.

*Dictionary of Literary Biography,* Volume 125: *Twentieth-Century Caribbean and Black African Writers,* Gale, 1993, pp. 281-90.

Nasta, Susheila, editor, *Critical Perspectives on Sam Selvon,* Three Continents, 1988.

Selvon, Samuel, *A Brighter Sun,* Viking, 1953.

Selvon, *I Hear Thunder,* St. Martin's, 1963.

Selvon, *The Lonely Londoners,* Longman, 1972.

Selvon, *Moses Ascending,* Davis-Poynter, 1975.

Selvon, *Ways of Sunlight,* St. Martin's, 1957.

*PERIODICALS*

*Atlantic Monthly,* March, 1953.

*Books in Canada,* May, 1991, p. 50.

*Books and Bookmen,* July, 1979, p. 63; July, 1986, p. 33.

*Canadian Literature,* winter, 1982.

*Contemporary Novelists,* 1991, p. 578.

*Journal of Commonwealth Literature,* number 1, 1986, p. 131.

*Listener,* January 27, 1972, p. 120.

*New Statesman,* January 14, 1972, p. 53; August 29, 1975, p. 258.

*New Yorker,* February 14, 1953; January 18, 1958.

*New York Times Book Review,* January 18, 1953; November 2, 1958; August 18, 1963.

*Observer* (London), June 7, 1970, p. 31; September 14, 1975, p. 25.

*Saturday Review,* November 15, 1958.

*Times Literary Supplement,* January 31, 1958; April 1, 1965; February 11, 1972; August 29, 1975, p. 961.

*World Literature Today,* winter, 1977, p. 150; autumn, 1984, p. 565; winter, 1991, p. 203.

*        *        *

## SENGHOR, Leopold Sedar 1906-
### (Silmang Diamano, Patrice Maguilene Kaymor)

*PERSONAL:* Born October 9, 1906, in Joal, Senegal (part of French West Africa; now Republic of Senegal); son of Basile Digoye (a cattle breeder and groundnut planter and exporter) and Nyilane (Bakoume) Senghor; married Ginette Eboue, September, 1946 (divorced, 1956); married Collette Hubert, October 18, 1957; children: (first marriage) Francis-Aphang, Guy-Waly (deceased); (second marriage) Philippe-Maguilen (deceased). *Education:* Baccalaureate degree from Lycee of Dakar, 1928; Sorbonne, University of Paris, agregation de grammaire, 1933, studied African languages at Ecole des Hautes Etudes, Paris, 1929-32.

*ADDRESSES: Home*—Corniche Ouest, Dakar, Senegal Republic; 1 square de Tocqueville, 75017 Paris, France. *Office*—c/o Presidence de la Republique, Dakar, Senegal Republic.

*CAREER:* Lycee Descartes, Tours, France, instructor in Greek and Latin classics, 1935-38; Lycee Marcelin Berthelot, St. Maur-des-Fosses, France, instructor in literature and African culture, 1938-40 and 1943-44; Ecole Nationale de la France d'Outre Mer, professor, 1945; French National Assembly, Paris, France, and General Council of Senegal, Dakar, Senegal, elected representative, beginning in 1946; Bloc Democratique Senegalais, Dakar, founder, 1948; French Government, Paris, delegate to United Nations General Assembly in New York City, 1950-51, Secretary of State for scientific research, and representative to UNESCO conferences, 1955-56, member of consultative assembly, 1958, minister-counsellor to Ministry of Cultural Affairs, Education, and Justice, 1959-60, advisory minister, beginning in 1960; City of Thies, Senegal, mayor, beginning in 1956; Senegalese Territorial Assembly, elected representative, beginning in 1957; founder and head of Union Progressiste Senegalaise, beginning in 1958; Mali Federation of Senegal and Sudan, president of Federal Assembly, 1959-60; Republic of Senegal, President of the Republic, 1960-80, Minister of Defense, 1968-69; Socialist Inter-African, chair of executive bureau, 1981—; Haut Conseil de la Francophonie, vice president, 1985—. Cofounder, with Lamine Gueye, of Bloc Africain, 1945; representative for Senegal to French Constituent Assemblies, 1945 and 1946; official grammarian for writing of French Fourth Republic's new constitution, 1946; sponsor of First World Festival of Negro Arts, Dakar, 1966; chair of Organisation Commune Africaine et Malgache, 1972-74; established West African Economic Community, 1974; chair of ECONAS, 1978-79. *Military service:* French Army, infantry, 1934-35; served in infantry battalion of colonial troops, 1939; prisoner of war, 1940-42; participated in French Resistance, 1942-45; received serviceman's cross, 1939-45.

*MEMBER:* Comite National des Ecrivains, Societe des Gens de Lettres, Societe Linguistique de France.

*AWARDS, HONORS:* Numerous awards, including corresponding membership in Bavarian Academy, 1961; International French Friendship Prize, 1961; French Language Prize (gold medal), 1963; International Grand Prize for Poetry, 1963; Dag Hammarskjoeld International Prize Gold Medal for Poetic Merit, 1963; Marie Noel Poetry Prize, 1965; Red and Green International Literature Grand Prix, 1966, German Book Trade's Peace Prize, 1968; associate membership in French Academy of Moral and Political Sciences, 1969; Knokke Biennial International Poetry Grand Prix, 1970; membership in Academy of Overseas Sciences, 1971; membership in Black Academy of Arts and Sciences, 1971; Grenoble Gold Medal, 1972; Haile Selassie African Research Prize, 1973; Cravat of Commander of Order of French Arts and Letters, 1973; Apollinaire Prize for Poetry, 1974; Prince Pierre of Monaco's Literature Prize, 1977; Prix Eurafrique, 1978; Alfred de Vigny Prize, 1981; Aasan World Prize, 1981; election to Academie Francaise, 1983; Jawaharlal Nehru Award, 1984; Athinai Prize, 1985.

Also recipient of Grand Cross of French Legion of Honor, Commander of Academic Palms, Franco-Allied Medal of Recognition, membership in Agegres de Grammaire and

American Academy of Arts and Letters. Numerous honorary doctorates, including those from Fordham University, 1961; University of Paris, 1962; Catholic University of Louvain (Belgium), 1965; Lebanese University of Beirut, 1966; Howard University, 1966; Laval University (Quebec), 1966; Harvard University, 1971; Oxford University, 1973; and from the universities of Ibadan (Nigeria), 1964; Bahia (Brazil), 1965; Strasbourg (France), 1965; Al-Azan (Cairo, Egypt), 1967; Algiers (Algeria), 1967; Bordeaux-Talence (France), 1967; Vermont, 1971; California at Los Angeles, 1971; Ethiopia Haile Selassie I, 1971; Abidjan (Ivory Coast), 1971; and Lagos (Nigeria), 1972.

*WRITINGS:*

*POETRY*

*Chants d'ombre* (title means "Songs of Shadow"; includes "Femme noire" and "Joal"; also see below), Seuil, 1945.

*Hosties noires* (title means "Black Sacrifices"; includes "Au Gouverneur Eboue," "Mediterranee," "Aux Soldats Negro-Americains," "Tyaroye," and "Priere de paix"; also see below), Seuil, 1948.

*Chants pour Naeett* (title means "Songs for Naeett"; also see below), Seghers, 1949.

*Chants d'ombre* [suivi de] *Hosties noires* (title means "Songs of Shadow" [followed by] "Black Sacrifices"), Seuil, 1956.

*Ethiopiques* (includes "Chaka," poetic adaptation of Thomas Mofolo's historical novel *Chaka;* "A New York"; and "Congo"), Seuil, 1956, critical edition with commentary by Papa Gueye N'Diaye published as *Ethiopiques: Poemes,* Nouvelles Editions Africaines, 1974.

*Nocturnes* (includes *Chants pour Naeett,* "Elegie de minuit," and "Elegie a Aynina Fall: Poeme dramatique a plusieurs voix" [title means "Elegy for Aynina Fall: Dramatic Poem for Many Voices"]), Seuil, 1961, translation by John Reed and Clive Wake published as *Nocturnes,* Heinemann Educational, 1969, with introduction by Paulette J. Trout, Third Press, 1971.

*Elegie des Alizes,* original lithographs by Marc Chagall, Seuil, 1969.

*Lettres d'hivernage,* illustrations by Marc Chagall, Seuil, 1973.

*Paroles,* Nouvelles Editions Africaines, 1975.

*Oeuvre Poetique,* Editions du Seuil, 1990, translation and introduction by Melvin Dixon published as *Leopold Sedar Senghor: The Collected Poetry,* University Press of Virginia, 1991.

Contributor of poems to periodicals, including *Chantiers, Les Cahiers du Sud, Les Lettres Francaises, Les Temps Modernes, Le Temp de la Poesie, La Revue Socialiste, Presence Africaine,* and *Prevue.*

*CRITICAL AND POLITICAL PROSE*

(With Robert Lemaignen and Prince Sisowath Youteyong) *La Communaute imperiale francaise* (includes "Views on Africa; or, Assimilate, Don't Be Assimilated"), Editions Alsatia, 1945.

(With Gaston Monnerville and Aime Cesaire) *Commemoration du centenaire de l'abolition de l'esclavage,* introduction by Edouard Depreux, Presses Universitaires de France, 1948.

(Contributor) *La Nation en construction,* [Dakar], 1959.

*Rapport sur la doctrine et le programme du parti,* Presence Africaine, 1959, translation published as *Report on the Principles and Programme of the Party,* Presence Africaine, 1959, abridged edition edited and translated by Mercer Cook published as *African Socialism: A Report to the Constitutive Congress of the Party of African Federation,* American Society of African Culture, 1959.

*Rapport sur la politique generale,* [Senegal], 1960.

*Nation et voie africaine du socialisme,* Presence Africaine 1961, new edition published as *Liberte 2: Nation et voie africaine du socialisme,* Seuil, 1971, translation by Mercer Cook published as *Nationhood and the African Road to Socialism,* Presence Africaine, 1962, abridged as *On African Socialism,* translation and introduction by Cook, Praeger, 1964.

(Contributor) *Cultures de l'Afrique noire et de l'Occident,* Societe Europeenne de Culture, 1961.

*Rapport sur la doctrine et la politique generale; ou, Socialisme, unite africaine, construction nationale,* [Dakar], 1962.

(With Pierre Teilhard de Chardin) *Pierre Teilhard de Chardin et la politique africaine* [and] *Sauvons l'humanite* [and] *L'Art dans la ligne de l'energie humaine* (the first by Senghor, the latter two by Teilhard de Chardin), Seuil, 1962.

(With others) *Le Racisme dans le monde,* Julliard, 1964.

*Theorie et pratique du socialisme senegalais,* [Dakar], 1964.

*Liberte 1: Negritude et humanisme,* Seuil, 1964, selections translated and introduced by Wendell A. Jeanpierre published as *Freedom 1: Negritude and Humanism,* [Providence, RI], 1974.

(In Portuguese, French, and Spanish) *Latinite et negritude,* Centre de Hautes Etudes Afro-Ibero-Americaines de l'Universite de Dakar, 1966.

*Negritude, arabisme, et francite: Reflexions sur le probleme de la culture* (title means "Negritude, Arabism, and Frenchness: Reflections on the Problem of Culture"), preface by Jean Rous, Editions Dar al-Kitab Allubmani (Beirut), 1967, republished as *Les Fondements de l'Africanite; ou, Negritude et arabite,* Presence Africaine, 1967, translation by M. Cook published as *The Foundations of "Africanite"; or, "Negritude" and "Arabite,"* Presence Africaine, 1971.

*Politique, nation, et developpement moderne: Rapport de politique generale,* Imprimerie Nationale (Rufisque), 1968.

*Le Plan du decollage economique; ou, La Participation responsable comme moteur de developpement,* Grande Imprimerie Africaine (Dakar), 1970.

*Pourquoi une ideologie negro-africaine?* (lecture), Universite d'Abidjan, 1971.

*La Parole chez Paul Claudel et chez les Negro-Africains,* Nouvelles Editions Africaines, 1973.

(With others) *Litteratures ultramarines de langue francaise, genese et jeunesse: Actes du colloque de l'Universite du Vermont,* compiled by Thomas H. Geno and Roy Julow, Naaman (Quebec), 1974.

*Paroles* (addresses), Nouvelles Editions Africaines, 1975.

(Contributor) *La Senegal au Colloque sur le liberalisme planifie et les voies africaines vers le socialisme, Tunis, 1-6 juillet 1975* (includes *Pour une relecture africaine de Marx et d'Engels;* also see below), Grand Imprimerie Africaine (Dakar), 1975.

*Pour une relecture africaine de Marx et d'Engels* (includes "Le socialisme africain et la voie senegalaise"), Nouvelles Editions Africaines, 1976.

*Pour une societe senegalaise socialiste et democratique: Rapport sur la politique generale,* Nouvelles Editions Africaines, 1976.

*Liberte 3: Negritude et civilisation de l'universel* (title means "Freedom 3: Negritude and the Civilization of the Universal"), Seuil, 1977.

(With Mohamed Aziza) *La Poesie de l'action: Conversations avec Mohamed Aziza* (interviews), Stock (Paris), 1980.

*Ce que je crois: Negritude, francite, et la civilisation de l'universel,* Bernard Grasset, 1988.

Also author of *L'Apport de la poesie negre,* 1953; *Langage et poesie negro-africaine,* 1954; *Esthetique negro-africain,* 1956; and *Liberte 4: Socialisme et planification,* 1983. Author of four technical works on Wolof grammar. Author of lectures and addresses published in pamphlet or booklet form, including *The Mission of the Poet,* 1966; *Negritude et germanisme,* 1968; *Problemes de developpement dans les pays sous-developpes,* 1975; *Negritude et civilisations mediterraneennes,* 1976; and *Pour une lecture negro-africaine de Mallarme,* 1981. Contributor, sometimes under the pseudonyms Silmang Diamano or Patrice Maguilene Kaymor, of critical, linguistic, sociological, and political writings to periodicals and journals, including *Journal de la Societe des Africanists, Presence Africaine,* and *L'Esprit.*

*OTHER*

(Editor) *Anthologie de la nouvelle poesie negre et malgache de langue francaise* [precede de] *Orphee noir, par Jean Paul Sartre* (poetry anthology; title means "Anthology of the New Negro and Malagasy Poetry in French [preceded by] Black Orpheus, by Jean-Paul Sartre"), introduction by Sartre, Presses Universitaires de France, 1948, fourth edition, 1977.

(With Abdoulaye Sadji) *La Belle Histoire de Leuk-le-Lievre* (elementary school text; title means "The Clever Story of Leuk-the-Hare"), Hachette, 1953, reprinted as *La Belle Histoire de Leuk-le-Lievre: Cours elementaire des ecoles d'Afrique noir,* illustrations by Marcel Jeanjean, Hachette, 1961, British edition (in French) edited by J. M. Winch, illustrations by Jeanjean, Harrap, 1965, adaptation published as *Les Aventures de Leuk-le-Lievre,* illustrations by G. Lorofi, Nouvelles Editions Africaines, 1975.

(Author of introductory essay) *Anthologie des poetes du seizieme siecle* (anthology), Editions de la Bibliotheque Mondiale, 1956.

(Contributor of selected texts) *Afrique Africaine* (photography), photographs by Michel Huet, Clairfontaine, 1963.

(Contributor) *Terre promise d'Afrique: Symphonie en noir et or* (poetry anthology), lithographs by Hans Erni, Andre et Pierre Gonin (Lausanne), 1966.

(Contributor of selected texts) *African Sojourn* (photography), photographs by Uwe Ommer, Arpel Graphics, 1987.

Also author of prose tale *Mandabi* (title means "The Money Order"). Translator of poetry by Mariane N'Diaye. Founder of journals, including *Condition Humaine,* with Aime Cesaire and Leon Gontran Damas, *L'Etudiant Noir,* and, with Alioune Diop, *Presence Africaine.*

*OMNIBUS VOLUMES*

*Leopold Sedar Senghor* (collection of prose and poems; with biographical-critical introduction and bibliography), edited by Armand Guibert, Seghers, 1961, reprinted as *Leopold Sedar Senghor: Une Etude d'Armand Guibert, avec un choix de poemes [et] une chronologie bibliographique, "Leopold Sedar Senghor et son temps,"* Seghers, 1969.

(In English translation) John Reed and Clive Wake, editors and translators, *Selected Poems,* introduction by Reed and Wake, Atheneum, 1964.

*Poemes* (includes *Chants d'ombre, Hosties noires, Ethiopiques, Nocturnes,* and "poemes divers"), Seuil, 1964, fourth edition, 1969, reprinted 1974, new edition, 1984.

*L. S. Senghor: Poete senegalais,* commentary by Roger Mercier, Monique Battestini, and Simon Battestini, F. Nathan, 1965, reprinted, 1978.

(In English translation) *Prose and Poetry,* selected and translated by Reed and Wake, Oxford University Press, 1965, Heinemann Educational, 1976.

(In French with English translations) *Selected Poems/Poesies choisies,* English-language introduction by Craig Williamson, Collings, 1976.

(In French) *Selected Poems of Leopold Sedar Senghor,* edited, with English-language preface and notes, by Abiola Irele, Cambridge University Press, 1977.

*Elegies majeures* [suivi de] *Dialogue sur la poesie francophone,* Seuil, 1979.

(In English translation) *Poems of a Black Orpheus,* translated by William Oxley, Menard, 1981.

*ADAPTATIONS:* Senghor's *Mandabi* was adapted for film by Ousmane Sembene.

*SIDELIGHTS:* President of the Republic of Senegal from the proclamation of that country's independence in 1960 until he stepped down in 1980, Leopold Sedar Senghor is considered, according to *Time,* "one of Africa's most respected elder statesmen." Yet until 1960 Senghor's political career was conducted primarily in France rather than in Africa. He is a product of the nineteenth-century French educational system, a scholar of Greek and Latin, and a member of the elite Academie Francaise, but he is best known for developing "negritude," a wide-ranging movement that influenced black culture worldwide. As the chief proponent of negritude, Senghor is credited with contributing to Africa's progress toward independence from colonial rule and, according to Jacques Louis Hymans in his *Leopold Sedar Senghor: An Intellectual Biography,* with "setting in motion a whole series of African ideological movements." Senghor first gained widespread recognition, however, when his first collection of poetry was published in 1945; he followed that volume with a highly esteemed body of verse that has accumulated numerous prestigious honors, most notably consideration for the Nobel Prize in Literature. Senghor, thus, seems to be, as Hymans suggests, "the living symbol of the possible synthesis of what appears irreconcilable: he is as African as he is European, as much a poet as a politician, ... as much a revolutionary as a traditionalist."

From the outset, disparate elements comprised Senghor's life. He was born in 1906 in Joal, a predominantly Moslem community established by Portuguese settlers on the Atlantic coast south of Dakar, a major Senegalese port and capital of what was then known as French West Africa. Senghor's mother was a Roman Catholic, and through maternal or paternal lines Senghor was related to the Fulani ethnic group, the Mandingo tribe, and the Serer ethnic group—said to provide a connection between Senghor and Serer royalty. His early childhood afforded contact with traditional customs and beliefs, with indigenous poetry, and with the surrounding natural setting. These contacts, critics note, strongly influenced Senghor's later life. As Sebastian Okechukwu Mezu explained in his 1973 study, *The Poetry of Leopold Sedar Senghor:* "This early childhood gave Senghor the material for his lyric poems.... Despite the splendours of political life, perhaps because of the excess of its paraphernalia, [Senghor] comes back to these memories of childhood ... in his poems, events evoked several times in his public speeches and television interviews, images that have become a kind of obsession, romanticized during the years of his absence from Senegal, and because of this process of nostalgic remembrance, taken to be reality itself. Poetic life for Senghor as a result of this becomes a continual quest for the kingdom of childhood, a recovery, a recapture of this idyllic situation."

As a child Senghor demonstrated a lively intelligence and an early ambition to become a priest or a teacher, and was accordingly enrolled in a Catholic elementary school in 1913. The following year he began living in a boarding house four miles from Joal at N'Gasobil, where he attended the Catholic mission school operated by the Fathers of the Holy Spirit. There Senghor was encouraged to disparage his ancestral culture while he learned Latin and studied European civilization as part of a typical nineteenth-century French teaching program. In 1922 he entered Libermann Junior Seminary in Dakar. In his four years there Senghor acquired a sound knowledge of Greek and Latin classics. Obliged to leave the seminary when he was deemed ill-suited to the priesthood, Senghor, disappointed, entered public secondary school at a French-style lycee in Dakar. There he earned numerous scholastic prizes and distinction for having bested white pupils in academic performance. Senghor obtained his secondary school degree with honors in 1928 and was awarded a half scholarship for continued study in France.

In Paris Senghor boarded at the Lycee Louis-le-Grand, where top-ranking French students study for entrance exams to France's elite higher education programs. One of Senghor's classmates was Georges Pompidou, later prime minister and, eventually, president of France. Pompidou exposed Senghor to the works of French literary masters Marcel Proust, Andre Gide, and Charles Baudelaire. During this time Senghor was also influenced by the writings of Paul Claudel, Arthur Rimbaud, and Maurice Barres. Senghor's lycee education in Paris emphasized methodology for rigorous thought and instilled habits of intellectual discipline, skills that Senghor embraced. He meanwhile continued to observe Roman Catholicism and expressed support for a restoration of the French government to monarchy. According to Hymans, Senghor in his student days was considered fully assimilated into Paris's intellectual milieu, which began including political and social liberation movements such as socialism, rationalism, humanism, and Marxism.

Europe was also reassessing African cultural traditions. European writers, artists, and musicians were exploring Africa's cultural wealth and incorporating what they discovered into their own creations. Paris of the late 1920s was permeated with Europe's new cultural appreciation of Africa, and in this atmosphere an exciting period of discovery began for Senghor.

He began meeting with black students from the United States, Africa, and the Caribbean, and soon a friendship grew between Senghor and Aime Cesaire, a writer from the French West Indian territory of Martinique. Another of Senghor's acquaintances was Paulette Nardal, a West Indian and the editor of a journal, *La Revue du Monde Noir.* Published in French and English, the journal was intended to provide a forum for black intellectuals writing literary and scientific works, to celebrate black civilization, and to increase unity among blacks worldwide. Through its editor Nardal, Senghor met West Indian writers Etienne Lero and Rene Maran and read the poetry of black Americans.

In *The New Negro,* an anthology published in 1925, Senghor encountered the works of prominent writers such as Paul Laurence Dunbar, W. E. B. Du Bois, Countee Cullen, Langston Hughes, Claude McKay, Zora Neale Hurston, James Weldon Johnson, and Jean Toomer. The anthology's editor, Alain Locke, was a professor of philosophy at Harvard University and a contributor to *La Revue du Monde Noir;* Senghor met him through Nardal as well. When Senghor, Cesaire, and Leon Gontran Damas, a student from French Guiana, sought a name for the growing francophone interest in African culture, they borrowed from the title of Locke's anthology and dubbed the movement "neo-negre" or "negre-nouveau." These labels were later replaced by "negritude," a term coined by Cesaire. Senghor credits Jamaican poet and novelist Claude McKay with having supplied the values espoused by the new movement: to seek out the roots of black culture and build on its foundations, to draw upon the wealth of African history and anthropology, and to rehabilitate black culture in the eyes of the world. With Cesaire and Darnas, Senghor launched *L'Etudiant Noir,* a cultural journal.

In exalting black culture and values, Senghor emphasized what he perceived as differences between the races. He portrayed blacks as artistic geniuses less gifted in the areas of scientific thought, attributing emotion to blacks and reason to whites. Europe was seen as alien, dehumanized, and dying, while Africa was considered vital, nourishing, and thriving. As racism and fascism swept through Europe in the 1930s, Senghor's attitudes were affected. For a brief period he became disillusioned with Europe in general and abandoned his religious faith. "By Senghor's own admission," Hymans revealed, "the same Romantic anti-rationalism that fathered racism among the Fascists of the 1930s underlay his early reaction against the West." But Senghor observed the increasing turmoil in Europe caused by Fascist regimes in Italy and Germany and understood the dangers of racism. Accordingly he modified his position.

Senghor nevertheless continued to cite what he considered to be differences between the races, such as an intuitive African way of understanding reality. But more importantly, as negritude evolved, he emphasized racial pride as a way of valuing black culture's role in a universal civilization. In this vein, he published an essay in 1939 titled "What the Negro Contributes." Themes that Senghor introduced to negritude at this time included a humanism based on the solidarity of all races, a moderate position that gave primacy to culture and maintained respect for other values. As Senghor told an audience he addressed in Dakar in 1937: "Assimilate, don't be assimilated." He later developed negritude further, however, by working to insure not only that African cultural identity became accessible to blacks worldwide, but that the unique aspects of African life were accorded status in the cultural community of society as a whole. Once African modes of thought and artistic expression are restored to their proper place among the world's cultures, Senghor proposed, then a sort of cultural cross-breeding can occur. This mixing of the races, according to Mezu, was conceived as "a symbiotic union where blacks will bring to the rendezvous of the races their special ... talents." Hymans examined this development of negritude since its inception in the 1930s and quoted Senghor's retrospective assessment of the movement: "Like life, the concept of negritude has become historical and dialectical. It has evolved."

Much of what later informed negritude had yet to be developed when in 1933 Senghor became the first African to obtain the coveted agregation degree. This distinction led to his first teaching position, at the Lycee Descartes in Tours, France. Senghor's new appreciation for Africa, coupled with his estrangement from his homeland, created an internal conflict that found resolution when he began writing poetry. Influenced by the works of Andre Breton and other surrealist writers, Senghor drew on surrealist techniques for his poetic style. Surrealism, with its emphasis on the irrational, depended on a creative process that tapped latent energies and subconscious sources of imagination without drawing a distinction between the fantastic and the real. Senghor found this process similar to traditional African modes of thought and employed it in his poetry. "By adopting the surrealist techniques," Mezu explained, "he was at the same time modern and African: educated and modernist from the white European viewpoint, traditional and faithful to the motherland from the African viewpoint. This dualism, or rather ambivalence, is ever present in Senghor's theories, poetry and actions." Nevertheless, Mezu noted, "there is a difference between the surrealist norm and the Senghorian philosophy. The difference is basically one of degree. For the surrealists, their effort, and an effort only, was to discover the point where reality and dream merge into one. For Senghor ... this principle is already possessed, already a part of the ancestral culture."

The poems Senghor wrote in the late 1930s were later published in the collection *Chants d'ombre.* For the most part, these poems express Senghor's nostalgia for Africa, his sense

of exile, estrangement, and cultural alienation, and his attempt to recover an idealized past. In a style based on musical rhythms, the poet evokes the beauty of the African landscape and peoples, the richness of Africa's past and the protecting presence of the dead, and the innocence and dignity inherent in his native culture. These poems, critics note, celebrate an Africa Senghor knew as a child, one transformed by nostalgia into a paradise-like simplicity. In some of the volume's other poems Senghor laments the destruction of the continent's culture and the suffering of its people under colonial rule. One of the collection's frequently cited pieces, "Femme noir," employs sensual yet worshipful language intended to glorify all black women. In "Joal" Senghor returns to his native village, revisiting places and inhabitants he had once known very well; it is, according to Mezu, "easily one of the most beautiful poems created by Senghor." When *Chants d'ombre* was published in 1945 it was well received in Paris and brought Senghor to public attention as a voice of black Africa. "In recreating the distant continent by verse," Hymans observed, "Senghor helped blaze the trail that led to the phenomenon of negritude."

World War II intervened between the writing of the poems collected in *Chants d'ombre* and their eventual publication. Germany invaded Poland in September, 1939, and Senghor was immediately called to active duty to protect France at the German border. While the holder of a high academic degree is usually made a commissioned officer, Senghor as a black man was made a second-class soldier in the Colonial Infantry. France fell to the German assault in June, 1940, the same month Senghor was captured and interned in a German prison camp. At the time of his capture he was almost shot along with some other Senegalese prisoners, but a French officer interceded on his behalf. While in prison Senghor met African peasants who had been recruited into the French Army, and began to identify with their plight. He wrote a number of poems that he sent by letter to his old classmate and friend Georges Pompidou; they were hand-delivered by a German guard who had been a professor of Chinese at the University of Vienna before the war. These poems later formed the core of Senghor's second published collection, *Hosties noires,* which appeared in 1948.

*Hosties noires* documents Senghor's realization that he was not alone in his exile from Africa, explores his increasing sense of unity with blacks as an exploited race, and elucidates the positive meaning Senghor finds in the sacrifices blacks have made. In poems such as "Au Gouveneur Eboue," which treats a black man's willingness to die for the salvation of the white world, Senghor memorializes blacks fighting for Europe. Elsewhere in *Hosties noires,* Senghor protests the exploitation of black soldiers and attacks western sources of power and violence. In other poems, such as "Mediterranee" and "Aux Soldats Negro-Americains," he rejoices in the common bonds formed with fellow soldiers and with American blacks. And with "Priere de paix" and "Tyaroye" Senghor hopes for unity and peace; while denouncing colonialism, he calls for an end to hatred and welcomes the new life that succeeds death. The collection, according to Mezu, is "the most homogeneous volume of Senghor's poetry, from the point of view not only of theme but also of language and sentiment."

Through the influence of West Indian colleagues Senghor was released from prison in June, 1942, and resumed teaching at the lycee in suburban Paris where he had earlier served as instructor of literature and African culture. He joined a Resistance group and also participated in activities involving colonial students. During the war, negritude had gained momentum, and when *Chants d'ombre* appeared in 1945, a new group of black intellectuals eagerly embraced Senghor's poetry and cultural theories. That year he published the influential essay "Views on Africa; or, Assimilate, Don't Be Assimilated." While in the 1930s Senghor concentrated on cultural rather than political issues, after the war he was encouraged by colonial reforms extended to French West Africans. He decided to run for election as one of Senegal's representatives in the French National Assembly. With Lamine Gueye, Senghor formed the Bloc Africain to involve Senegalese in their political fate. France was forming a new constitution, and in recognition of his linguistic expertise, France's provisional government appointed Senghor the document's official grammarian. Senghor founded the Bloc Democratique Senegalais (BDS) in 1948; throughout the 1950s the BDS dominated Senegalese politics.

Senghor's literary activities also continued. In 1947 he founded, with Alioune Diop, the cultural journal *Presence Africaine.* Along with a publishing house of the same name, *Presence Africaine* under Diop's direction became a powerful vehicle for black writing worldwide. As editor of *Anthologie de la nouvelle poesie noire et malgache de langue francaise,* published in 1948, Senghor brought together contemporary poetry written by francophone blacks. An essay titled "Orphee noir" ("Black Orpheus"), by French philosopher and writer Jean Paul Sartre, introduced the anthology. Sartre's essay outlined the cultural aims of black peoples striving to recapture their heritage. In the process Sartre defined and gained notoriety for the philosophy of negritude, portraying negritude as a step toward a united society without racial distinction. Many consider "Black Orpheus" to be the most important document of the negritude movement.

After 1948 Senghor became increasingly active politically, serving as France's delegate to the 1949 Council of Europe and as a French delegate to the United Nations General Assembly in 1950 and 1951; he won resounding reelection to the French National Assembly in 1951 as well. In 1955 and 1956 Senghor served in the cabinet of French president Edgar

Faure as secretary of state for scientific research and attended UNESCO conferences as a representative of France. While some French-held territories sought independence from colonial rule, often with accompanying violence, Senghor pushed for an arrangement giving French overseas territories equal status in a federation relationship facilitating economic development. He constantly modified his stance while avoiding violence and making small gains. In Dakar in 1953, according to Hymans, Senghor defined politics as "the art of using a method which, by approximations that are constantly corrected, would permit the greatest number to lead a more complete and happy life."

A collection of poems Senghor had been working on since 1948 was published as *Ethiopiques* in 1956. These poems reflect Senghor's growing political involvement and his struggle to reconcile European and African allegiances through crossbreeding, both figurative and literal. The year *Ethiopiques* was published Senghor divorced his African wife to marry one of her friends, a white Frenchwoman; critics have suggested that Senghor's views on cross-breeding represent an attempt to resolve his personal conflict by eliminating the divisive social elements that divided his loyalties. One of *Ethiopiques*'s poems, "Chaka," is a dramatic adaptation of Thomas Mofolo's novel about a Zulu hero who forged and ruled a vast domain in the early nineteenth century. Mezu called "Chaka" Senghor's most ambitious piece." Others have drawn parallels between Senghor's life and the poem's attempt to combine in the character of Chaka both the poet and politician. In "Chaka" Senghor applied his theories about the combination of music, dance, and poetry found in native African art forms. As Mezu noted, "Senghor aimed to illustrate what he considered an indigenous form of art where music, painting, theatre, poetry, religion, faith, love, and politics are all intertwined." In addition to musical and rhythmic elements, native plants and animals also figure prominently in *Ethiopiques,* whose other poems include "A New York," and "Congo."

When France's Fourth Republic collapsed in 1958 and France began to form a new constitution—along with new African policies—Senghor joined the advocates of independence for African territories. The French government, under Charles de Gaulle, appointed Senghor to the consultative assembly that would formulate the new constitution and policies. De Gaulle's proposed constitution, which was adopted in late 1958, accorded French West African territories autonomy within the French Community. At the same time De Gaulle warned Senghor that complete independence for West Africa would mean a cessation of technical and financial aid. In 1959 Senghor countered with the Mali Federation, linking Senegal and the Sudan (now Mali). The Mali Federation proclaimed its independence in June, 1960, but two months later Senegal withdrew and reproclaimed its independence. A Senegalese constitution was drawn up in August, 1960, and the following month Senghor was elected to a seven-year term as president of the new Republic of Senegal. Almost twenty-five years later Senghor told *Time,* "The colonizing powers did not prepare us for independence."

Poems Senghor wrote during the tumultuous years leading up to his election as president of Senegal were published in the 1961 collection *Nocturnes,* which featured a group of love poems previously published as *Chants pour Naeett* in 1949. In *Nocturnes* Senghor ponders the nature of poetry and examines the poetic process. Critics have noted that in this volume, particularly in poems such as "Elegie de minuit," Senghor reveals his regret for time spent in the empty pomp of political power, his nostalgia for his youth, and his reconciliation with death. Mezu called "Elegie de minuit" the poet's "'last' poem."

After 1960, Senghor wrote mainly political and critical prose, tied closely to the goals, activities, and demands of his political life. During this time he survived an attempted coup d'etat staged in 1962 by Senegal's prime minister, Mamadou Dia. The following year Senghor authorized the Senegalese National Assembly to draw up a new constitution that gave more power to the president, elected to five-year terms. Known for his ability to hold factions together, he remained in power, reelected in 1968 and 1973, despite more coup attempts, an assassination plot in 1967, and civil unrest in the late 1960s. Much of Senghor's writing from this era outlines the course he feels Africa must hold to, despite upheavals. Commenting on the instability suffered after African nations achieved independence, Senghor told *Time:* "The frequency of coups in Africa is the result of the backwardness in civilization that colonization represented.... What we should all be fighting for is democratic socialism. And the first task of socialism is not to create social justice. It is to establish working democracies."

According to Hymans, Senghor's brand of socialism, often called the African Road to Socialism, maps out a middle position between individualism and collectivism, between capitalism and communism. Senghor sees socialism as a way of eliminating the exploitation of individuals that prevents universal humanism. Some of Senghor's writings on this topic were translated by Mercer Cook and published in 1964 as *On African Socialism.* Appraising *On African Socialism* for *Saturday Review,* Charles Miller called its selections "exquisitely intellectual tours de force." Senghor's important political writings include *Liberte 1: Negritude et humanisme,* of which portions are available in translation; a work translated by Cook as *The Foundations of "Africanite": or, "Negritude" and "Arabite"; Politique, nation, et developpement moderne; Liberte 3: Negritude et civilization de l'universel;* and *Liberte 4: Socialisme et planification.* In a collection of interviews with Mohamed Aziza published in 1980, Senghor discussed poetry and both his politics and his life. Senghor "comes across in

these interviews as a brilliant, sincere, and steadfast leader who has yet managed to retain a sense of humility," wrote Eric Sellin, reviewing the collection for *World Literature Today.* Sellin continued: "His unswerving fidelity to personal and national programs is more readily understandable in light of his autobiographical introspections about his youth and education." Published as *La Poesie de l'action,* the volume, Sellin concluded, is "an important and interesting book." Later in 1980, Senghor stepped down from Senegal's presidency when his protege, Prime Minister Abdou Diouf, took office.

Senghor is revered throughout the world for his political and literary accomplishments and a life of achievement that spans nearly six decades. He was widely thought to have been under consideration in 1962 for the Nobel Prize in Literature in recognition of his poetic output. When a major English-translation volume devoted to Senghor's body of poetry appeared in 1964, *Saturday Review* likened Senghor to American poet Walt Whitman and determined that the poems represented were "written by a gifted, civilized man of good will celebrating the ordinary hopes and feelings of mankind." The *Times Literary Supplement* called Senghor "one of the best poets now writing in [French]" and marveled at his "astonishing achievement to have combined so creative a life with his vigorous and successful political activities." Senghor was elected to one of the world's most prestigious and elite intellectual groups, the Academie Francaise, in 1983.

When a new collected edition of Senghor's poetry appeared in 1984, Robert P. Smith, Jr., writing in *World Literature Today* identified Senghor as a "great poet of Africa and the universe." Praising the masterly imagery, symbolism, and versification of the poetry, Smith expressed particular admiration for Senghor's "constant creation of a poetry which builds up, makes inquiries, and expands into universal dimensions," and cited an elegy Senghor wrote for his deceased son as "one of the most beautiful in modern poetry." Critics characterize Senghor's poetic style as serenely and resonantly rhetorical. While some readers detect a lack of tension in his poetry, most admire its lush sensuality and uplifting attitude. Offered as a means of uniting African peoples in an appreciation of their cultural worth, Senghor's poetry, most agree, extends across the chasm that negritude, at least in its early form, seemed to have created in emphasizing the differences between races. "It is difficult to predict whether Senghor's poetry will excite the same approbation when the prestige of the President and that of the idealist no longer colour people's view of the man," Mezu acknowledged. "The Senegalese poet will certainly survive in the history of the Black Renaissance as the ideologist and theoretician of negritude." Writing in the *Washington Post Book World,* K. Anthony Appiah sees Senghor's poetry as "an integral part of his political and intellectual career rather than as a free-standing accomplishment demanding separate literary treatment."

Senghor's negritude in its more evolved form refuses to choose between Africa and Europe in its quest for worldwide national, cultural, and religious integration. Himself a synthesis of disparate elements, Senghor, in his role as reconciler of differences, holds to negritude as a median between nationalism and cultural assimilation. "Politically, philosophically, Senghor has been a middle-of-the-roader, a man of conciliation and mediation," Mezu declared, adding: "Negritude should ... be seen as a stage in the evolution of the literature of the black man.... The contemporary trend in African poetry seems to be away from the negritude movement as the racism and colonialism that inspired this literature dies out or becomes less barefaced." Senghor's life, according to Hymans, "might be summarized as an effort to restore to Africa an equilibrium destroyed by the clash with Europe." For those who see contradictions in Senghor's effort over more than five decades, Hymans observed that "one constant in his thought appears to surmount the contradictions it contains: universal reconciliation is his only goal and Africa's only salvation."

*BIOGRAPHICAL/CRITICAL SOURCES:*

*BOOKS*

Blair, Dorothy S., *African Literature in French,* Cambridge University Press, 1976.

Bureau de Documentation de la Presidence de la Republique, *Leopold Sedar Senghor: Bibliographie,* second edition, Fondation Leopold Sedar Senghor, 1982.

*Contemporary Literary Criticism,* Volume 54, Gale, 1989.

Crowder, Michael, *Senegal: A Study in French Assimilation Policy,* Oxford University Press, 1962.

Guibert, Armand, *Leopold Sedar Senghor: L'Homme et l'oeuvre,* Presence Africaine, 1962.

Hymans, Jacques Louis, *Leopold Sedar Senghor: An Intellectual Biography,* University Press, Edinburgh, 1971.

Kesteloot, Lilyan, *Comprendre les poemes de Leopold Sedar Senghor,* Saint Paul Classiques Africain, 1987.

Markovitz, Irving Leonard, *Leopold Sedar Senghor and the Politics of Negritude,* Atheneum, 1969.

Mezu, Sebastian Okechuwu, *The Poetry of Leopold Sedar Senghor,* Fairleigh Dickinson University Press, 1973.

Moore, Gerald, *Seven African Writers,* Oxford University Press, 1962.

Neikirk, Barend van Dyk Van, *The African Image (Negritude) in the Work of Leopold Sedar Senghor,* A. A. Balkema 1970.

Nespoulous Neuville, Josiane, *Leopold Sedar Senghor: De la tradition a l'universalisme,* Seuil, 1988.

Rous, Jean, *Leopold Sedar Senghor,* J. Didier, 1968.

Saint Cheron, Francoid de, *Senghor et la terre,* Sang de la Terre, 1988.

Saravaya, Gloria, *Langage et poesie chez Senghor,* L'Harmattan, 1989.

Vaillant, Janet G., *Black, French and African: A Life of Leopold Sedar Senghor,* Harvard University Press, 1990.

*PERIODICALS*

*Black World,* August 14, 1978.
*Callaloo,* winter, 1990.
*Ebony,* August, 1972.
*Essence,* September, 1987.
*French Review,* May, 1982.
*Maclean's,* February 24, 1986, p. 22.
*New York Review of Books,* December 20, 1990, p. 11.
*Saturday Review,* January 2, 1965.
*Time,* June 9, 1978; January 16, 1984.
*Times Literary Supplement,* June 11, 1964.
*Washington Post Book World,* July 5, 1992, p. 2.
*World Literature Today,* spring, 1965; autumn, 1978; summer, 1981; winter, 1985; summer, 1990, p. 540.

\*   \*   \*

## SEROTE, Mongane Wally 1944-

*PERSONAL:* Born May 8, 1944, in Sophiatown, South Africa; married Pethu Serote. *Education:* Columbia University, M.F.A., 1979.

*ADDRESSES: Home*—28 Penton Street, P.O. Box 38, London N1 9PR, England. *Agent*—Jane Gregory Agency, Riverside Studios, Crisp Road, Hammersmith, London W6 9RL, England.

*CAREER:* Department of Arts and Culture, African National Congress, London, cultural attache, 1986—. Copywriter for advertising agency, Johannesburg; Medu Arts Ensemble, Gaborone, Botswana, staff member. Poet, novelist, short story writer, and playwright.

*AWARDS, HONORS:* Ingrid Jonker prize, 1973; Fulbright scholarship.

*WRITINGS:*

*POETRY*

*Yakhal'inkomo,* Renoster, 1972.
*No Baby Must Weep,* Donker, 1975.
*Tsetlo,* Donker, 1975.
*Behold Mama, Flowers,* Donker, 1978.
*The Night Keeps Winking,* Medu Art Ensemble, 1982.
*Selected Poems,* edited by Mbulelo Vizikhungo Mzamane, Donker, 1982.

*A Tough Tale,* Kliptown Books, 1987.
*Third World Express,* Philip, 1992.

Contributor of poetry to periodicals, including *Classic* and *Bolt.*

*PROSE*

*To Every Birth Its Blood,* Raven Press, 1981.
*On the Horizon,* foreword by Raymond Suttner, Congress of
   South African Writers, 1990.

*SIDELIGHTS:* Mongane Wally Serote wrote in *Southern African Review of Books:* "Writing, which is a segment of culture which is life itself, cannot be divorced from economics or politics. It is how societies are organized that says how they will eradicate ignorance. It is for all these issues ... that I can say that the first commitment of any writer is to politics; the second, which makes the writer, is in writing."

Serote is best known as a poet, and as such he is considered one of the foremost black South African poets of his generation. His poetry is strongly political in its subject and in its form; Serote's reliance on the repetitive structure of song makes his poetry ideal for recitation, an important factor in South Africa where it is estimated that half the adult black population is illiterate. Serote writes in English, a language associated with his country's oppressors but distinguished from the Afrikaans of the current South African regime. His novel *To Every Birth Its Blood* extends the themes of his poetry in its depiction of the variety of responses to political and cultural oppression.

Serote's poetry documents the struggles, hopes, and despair of people suffering under apartheid. His poems gain much of their emotional intensity through striking imagery, evocative metaphors, and repetition. Reviewers have noted that what has sometimes been taken for stylistic innovation in Serote's poetry is often a hybrid of African oral traditions, the language of the urban black townships of South Africa, and Western poetic conventions such as the panegyric and the elegy. It is this aspect of Serote's skill as a poet that allows him to address his white oppressors as well as his own community, and to write self-reflexive poems concerning the role of the poet in South African society as a cultural freedom fighter.

Serote has especially been commended for his sensitivity to the complex role of women in a traditionally male-dominated society. Children, too, play a pivotal role in Serote's poetry, being the most innocent of the victims of apartheid and the focal point of hope for change for the black people of South Africa. As Serote's poetry has evolved, it has moved away from the despair of his earlier works through defiance toward hope for the future.

In the novel, *To Every Birth Its Blood,* Serote surveys several generations of black South Africans and their responses to life under apartheid. The first half of the novel centers on Tsietsi Molope, a black journalist who is imprisoned, beaten, and tortured by police, then released back to his life in Alexandra, a black township near Johannesburg. William Finnegan, writing in the *New York Times Book Review,* described Molope as "alienated, humane, inept and chronically depressed; he seeks his solace in booze and jazz." The interior monologue that dominates this half of the work documents the chaotic, despairing nature of Molope's humiliation and defeat, which is exacerbated by his arbitrary arrest and equally unexplained release.

As the novel progresses, Serote introduces other characters who become radicalized as the apartheid government increases its pressures on the black population of the country: Molope's parents are slowly politicized by their visits to his brother, a political prisoner; Molope's nephew belongs to the generation whose uprising in 1976 ushers in a new era in black South African response to apartheid. The second half of the novel focuses on these young revolutionaries, and Serote portrays their violent protests and the equally violent response by the authorities with intense dramatic effect. L. Tremaine, reviewing *To Every Birth Its Blood* for *Choice,* commented: "No other South African novelist articulates the interactions between the collective and the personal dramas of oppression and revolution more searchingly or with a more nearly equal mix of commitment and compassion."

*BIOGRAPHICAL/CRITICAL SOURCES:*

*PERIODICALS*

*Choice,* March, 1990, p. 1155.
*The New York Times Book Review,* May 7, 1989, p. 38.
*Southern African Review of Books,* February-May, 1990.

\*   \*   \*

## SEYMOUR, A(rthur) J(ames) 1914-

*PERSONAL:* Born January 12, 1914, in Georgetown, British Guiana (now Guyana); son of James Tudor (a land surveyor) and Philippine (Dey) Seymour; married Elma E. Bryce, July 31, 1937; children: Ann Seymour Boys, Joan, Margaret Seymour Outridge, James T., Guy, Philip. *Education:* Attended high school in Georgetown, British Guiana. *Religion:* Methodist.

*ADDRESSES: Home*—23 North Rd., Bourda, Georgetown, Guyana.

*CAREER:* Bureau of Public Information, British Guiana, assistant public information officer, 1943-54; Government Information Services, Georgetown, British Guiana, chief information officer, 1954-62; Caribbean Organization, San Juan, Puerto Rico, development officer for information and cultural collaboration, 1962-64; Demerara Bauxite Co., Ltd., Mackenzie, Guyana, community relations officer, 1965-70; Guyana Bauxite Co., Ltd., Georgetown, public relations officer, 1970-73; Ministry of Information, Culture, and Youth, Georgetown, cultural relations adviser, 1973—. Director of creative writing for Guyana's Institute of Creative Arts, 1974-79. Lecturer at University of Puerto Rico, 1963, and at University of Brasilia, Federal University of Bahia, and Catholic University of Fluminense, all 1973; visiting professor of journalism, University of Western Ontario, 1979; lecturer in Brazil, the U.S. Virgin Islands, Cuba, and England. Secretary of British Guiana Union of Cultural Clubs, 1943-50; literary coordinator of Caribbean Festival of the Creative Arts, 1972—; chair of National Commission for Research Materials on Guyana, and deputy chair of National History and Arts Council and National Trust, all 1973—. Participant in international conferences of United Nations Educational, Scientific, and Cultural Organization. Broadcasted weekly literary programs in the 1950s; conducts writers' workshops.

*MEMBER:* International PEN, British Guiana Writers' Association (past president), Caribbean Conservation Association.

*AWARDS, HONORS:* Golden Arrow of Achievement from president of Guyana, 1970, for services to literature; D.Litt., University of the West Indies, 1983.

*WRITINGS:*

*POETRY*

*Verse,* Daily Chronicle (Georgetown, British Guiana), 1937.
*Coronation Ode,* privately printed, 1937.
*More Poems,* Daily Chronicle (Georgetown), 1940.
*Over Guiana Clouds,* Demerera Standard, 1945.
*Sun's in My Blood,* Demerera Standard, 1945.
*Six Songs,* privately printed, 1946.
*The Guiana Book,* Argosy, 1948.
*Seven Poems,* privately printed, 1948.
*We Do Not Presume to Come,* privately printed, 1948.
*Leaves from the Tree,* Kyk-over-Al, 1951.
*Water and Blood: A Quincunx,* Kyk-over-Al, 1952.
*Ten Poems,* Argosy, 1953.
*Three Voluntaries,* privately printed, 1953.
*Variations on a Theme,* privately printed, 1961.
*Selected Poems,* privately printed, 1965, reprinted, Labour Advocate Job Print, 1983.
*A Little Wind of Christmas,* privately printed, 1967.
*Monologue,* privately printed, 1968.

*Patterns,* privately printed, 1970.
*I, Anancy,* privately printed, 1971.
*Black Song,* privately printed, 1972.
*The Legend of Kaieteur,* Carifesta, 1972.
*Passport,* privately printed, 1973.
*Song to Man,* privately printed, 1973.
*A Bethlehem Alleluia,* privately printed, 1974.
*Italic,* privately printed, 1974.
*City of Memory,* privately printed, 1974.
*Images Before Easter,* privately printed, 1974.
*Mirror,* privately printed, 1975.
*A Song for Christmas,* privately printed, 1975.
*Tomorrow Belongs to the People,* privately printed, 1975.
*Love Song,* privately printed, 1975.
*For Nicolas Guillen,* Guyana Lithographic Co., 1976.
*Georgetown General,* National History and Arts Council, 1976.
*Lament for Jacqueline Williams and Raymond Persaud,* privately printed, 1976.
*My Resurrection Morning,* privately printed, 1976.
*Shape of the Crystal,* privately printed, 1977.
*Images of Majority: Collected Poems, 1968-78,* Labour Advocate Printery, 1978.
*Religious Poems,* privately printed, 1980.
*Lord of My Life,* privately printed, 1981.
*Poems for Export Only,* privately printed, 1982.
*AJS at 70: A Celebration on His 70th Birthday of the Life, Work, and Art of A. J. Seymour,* edited by Ian McDonald, [Guyana], 1984.

*SHORT STORIES*

*Nine Short Stories from "Kyk-over-Al,"* privately printed, 1981.

*NONFICTION*

*A Survey of West Indian Literature,* Kyk-over-Al, 1950.
*Window on the Caribbean,* privately printed, 1952.
*Edgar Mittelholzer: The Man and His Work,* National History and Arts Council (Georgetown, Guyana), 1968.
*An Introduction to Guyanese Writing,* National History and Arts Council (Georgetown), 1971.
*Looking at Poetry,* privately printed, 1974.
*I Live in Georgetown* (lectures and essays), Labour Advocate Printery, 1974.
*Cultural Policy in Guyana,* United Nations Educational, Scientific, and Cultural Organization, 1977.
*Nine Caribbean Essays,* privately printed, 1977.
*Family Impromptu,* privately printed, 1977.
*A National Cultural Policy for the British Virgin Islands,* Unesco, 1979.
*The Making of Guyanese Literature,* privately printed, 1979.
*Studies in West Indian Poetry,* privately printed, 1981.

*What God is Saying to Caribbean Man in His Poetry,* privately
   printed, 1981.
*The Poetry of Frank A. Collymore,* privately printed, 1982.
*The Poetry of Phyllis Shand Allfrey,* privately printed, 1982.
*Studies of Ten Guyanese Poems,* privately printed, 1982.

*EDITOR*

*The Miniature Poets,* Kyk-over-Al, Series A, 1951, Series B,
   1952.
*An Anthology of West Indian Poetry,* Kyk-over-Al, 1952, re-
   vised edition published as *The Kyk-over-Al Anthology of
   West Indian Poetry,* 1957.
*An Anthology of Guianese Poetry,* Kyk-over-Al, 1954.
*Themes of Song,* privately printed, 1959.
(With wife, Elma Seymour) *My Lovely Native Land,* illustrated
   by Leila Locke, Longman, 1971.
*New Writing in the Caribbean,* Carifesta, 1972.
*Independence Ten: Guyanese Writing, 1966-1976,* Govern-
   ment of Guyana, 1977.
*A Treasury of Guyanese Poetry,* privately printed, 1980.
(With E. Seymour) *Dictionary of Guyanese Biography,*
   [Guyana], 1984.

*OTHER*

*Caribbean Literature* (radio talks), privately printed, 1951.
*Growing Up in Guyana* (first volume of autobiography),
   Labour Advocate Printery, 1976.
*Pilgrim Memories* (second volume of autobiography), private-
   ly printed, 1978.
*Thirty Years a Civil Servant* (third volume of autobiography),
   privately printed, 1982.
*The Years in Puerto Rico and Mackenzie* (fourth volume of
   autobiography), privately printed, 1983.

Author of introduction to *Dictionary of Guyanese Folklore,*
1975. Contributor to anthologies, including *Schwarz Orpheus*
(Munich), and *You'd Better Believe It,* Penguin. Editor of
"Miniature Poet Series," Kyk-over-Al, 1945-61; editor of *Kyk-
over-Al* (literary magazine), 1945-61, editor with Ian McDonald, 1984—; poetry editor of *Kaie,* 1965. Seymour's manuscripts are housed at the National Library, Georgetown.

*WORK IN PROGRESS:* Study of the cultural development of
Guyana.

*BIOGRAPHICAL/CRITICAL SOURCES:*

*BOOKS*

*Fifty Caribbean Writers: A Bio-Biographical Critical Source-
   book,* Greenwood Press, 1986, pp. 451-55.

*PERIODICALS*

*Association for Commonwealth Literature and Language
   Studies Bulletin,* November, 1982, pp. 42-54.
*New World (Fortnightly),* April, 1965, pp. 31-39.
*Wilson Quarterly,* spring, 1982, p. 145.
*World Literature Written in English,* April, 1976, pp. 246-52.

\*   \*   \*

## SHANGE, Ntozake 1948-

*PERSONAL:* Original name Paulette Linda Williams; name
changed in 1971; name pronounced "En-to-zaki Shong-gay";
born October 18, 1948, in Trenton, NJ; daughter of Paul T. (a
surgeon) and Eloise (a psychiatric social worker and educator) Williams; married second husband, David Murray (a
musician), July, 1977 (divorced). *Education:* Barnard College,
B.A. (with honors), 1970; University of Southern California,
Los Angeles, M.A., 1973; graduate study, University of Southern California. *Avocational interests:* Playing the violin.

*ADDRESSES: Home*—231 North Third St., No. 119, Phila-
delphia, PA 19106. *Office*—The Maryland Institute, 1300 Mt.
Royal Ave., Baltimore, MD 21217. *Agent*—c/o St. Martin's
Press, 175 Fifth Ave., New York, NY 10010.

*CAREER:* Writer, performer, and teacher. Faculty member in
women's studies, California State College, Sonoma Mills
College, and the University of California Extension, 1972-75;
artist in residence, New Jersey State Council on the Arts, creative writing instructor, City College of New York; associate
professor of drama, University of Houston, beginning in 1983.
Lecturer at Douglass College, 1978, and at many other institutions, such as Yale University, Howard University, Detroit Art
Institute, and New York University. Dancer with Third World
Collective, Raymond Sawyer's Afro-American Dance Company, Sounds in Motion, West Coast Dance Works, and For
Colored Girls Who Have Considered Suicide (Shange's own
dance company); has appeared in Broadway and Off-Broadway productions of her own plays, including *For Colored
Girls Who Have Considered Suicide/When the Rainbow Is
Enuf,* and *Where the Mississippi Meets the Amazon.* Director
of several productions including *The Mighty Gents,* produced
by the New York Shakespeare Festival's Mobile Theatre,
1979, *A Photograph: A Study in Cruelty,* produced in Houston's Equinox Theatre, 1979, and June Jordan's *The Issue* and
*The Spirit of Sojourner Truth,* 1979. Has given many poetry
readings.

*MEMBER:* Actors Equity, National Academy of Television
Arts and Sciences, Dramatists Guild, PEN American Center,

Academy of American Poets, Poets and Writers, Women's Institute for Freedom of the Press, New York Feminist Arts Guild, Writers' Guild.

*AWARDS, HONORS:* Obie Award, Outer Critics Circle Award, (Audience Development Committee (Audelco) Award, Mademoiselle Award, and Tony, Grammy, and Emmy award nominations, all 1977, all for *For Colored Girls Who Have Considered Suicide/When the Rainbow Is Enuf*; Frank Silvera Writers' Workshop Award, 1978; *Los Angeles Times* Book Prize for Poetry, 1981, for *Three Pieces*; Guggenheim fellowship, 1981; Medal of Excellence, Columbia University, 1981; Obie Award, 1981, for *Mother Courage and Her Children*; Pushcart Prize; Nori Eboraci Award, Barnard College, 1988; Lila Wallace-Reader's Digest Fund annual writer's award, 1992; Paul Robeson Achievement Award, 1992; Arts and Cultural Achievement Award, National Coalition of 100 Black Women, Inc. (Pennsylvania chapter), 1992; Living Legend Award, National Black Theatre Festival, 1993; Claim Your Life Award, WDAS-AM/FM, 1993; Monarch Merit Award, National Council for Culture and Art, Inc..

*WRITINGS:*

*For Colored Girls Who Have Considered Suicide/When the Rainbow Is Enuf: A Choreopoem* (first produced in New York City at Studio Rivbea, July 7, 1975; produced Off-Broadway at Anspacher Public Theatre, 1976; produced on Broadway at Booth Theatre, September 15, 1976), Shameless Hussy Press (San Lorenzo, CA), 1975, revised edition, Macmillan, 1976.

*Sassafrass* (novella), Shameless Hussy Press, 1976.

*Melissa & Smith,* Bookslinger Editions, 1976.

*A Photograph: A Study of Cruelty* (poem-play), first produced Off-Broadway at Public Theatre, December 21, 1977, revised edition, *A Photograph: Lovers in Motion* (also see below), produced in Houston, TX, at the Equinox Theatre, November, 1979.

(With Thulani Nkabinde and Jessica Hagedorn) *Where the Mississippi Meets the Amazon,* first produced in New York City at Public Theatre Cabaret, December 18, 1977.

*Natural Disasters and Other Festive Occasions* (prose and poems), Heirs, 1977.

*Nappy Edges* (poems), St. Martin's, 1978.

*Boogie Woogie Landscapes* (play; also see below; first produced in New York City at Frank Silvera Writers' Workshop, June, 1979, produced on Broadway at the Symphony Space Theatre, produced in Washington, DC, at the Kennedy Center), St. Martin's, 1978.

*Spell #7: A Geechee Quick Magic Trance Manual* (play; also see below), produced on Broadway at Joseph Papp's New York Shakespeare Festival Public Theater, July 15, 1979.

*Black and White Two Dimensional Planes* (play), first produced in New York City at Sounds in Motion Studio Works, February, 1979.

*Mother Courage and Her Children* (an adapted version of Bertolt Brecht's play), first produced Off-Broadway at the Public Theatre, April, 1980.

*Three Pieces: Spell #7; A Photograph: Lovers in Motion; Boogie Woogie Landscapes* (plays), St. Martin's, 1981.

*A Photograph: Lovers in Motion,* Samuel French, 1981.

*Spell #7: A Theatre Piece in Two Acts,* Samuel French, 1981.

*Sassafrass, Cypress & Indigo: A Novel,* St. Martin's, 1982.

*Three for a Full Moon* and *Bocas,* first produced in Los Angeles, CA, at the Mark Taper Forum Lab, Center Theatre, April 28, 1982.

(Adapter) Willy Russell, *Educating Rita* (play), first produced in Atlanta, Ga., by Alliance Theatre Company, 1982.

*A Daughter's Geography* (poems), St. Martin's, 1983, reissued 1991.

*See No Evil: Prefaces, Essays and Accounts, 1976-1983,* Momo's Press, 1984.

*From Okra to Greens: Poems,* Coffee House Press, 1984.

*From Okra to Greens: A Different Kinda Love Story; A Play with Music and Dance* (first produced in New York City at Barnard College, November, 1978), Samuel French, 1985.

*Betsey Brown: A Novel,* St. Martin's, 1985.

(Writer of foreword) Mapplethorpe, Robert, *The Black Book,* St. Martin's, 1986.

*Three Views of Mt. Fuji* (play), first produced at the Lorraine Hansberry Theatre, June, 1987, produced in New York City at the New Dramatists, October, 1987.

*Ridin' the Moon in Texas: Word Paintings* (responses to art in prose and poetry), St. Martin's, 1987.

(Contributor) Feiffer, Jules, *Selected from Contemporary American Plays: An Anthology,* Literacy Volunteers of New York City, 1990.

*The Love Space Demands: A Continuing Saga,* St. Martin's, 1991.

*Three Pieces,* St. Martin's Press, 1992.

Also author of *Some Men* (poems in a pamphlet that resembles a dance card), 1981. Author of the play *Mouths* and the operetta *Carrie,* both produced in 1981. Has written for a television special starring Diana Ross, and appears in a documentary about her own work for WGBH-TV (Boston). Work represented in several anthologies, including *"May Your Days Be Merry and Bright" and Other Christmas Stories by Women,* edited by Susan Koppelman, Wayne State University Press, 1988; *New Plays for the Black Theatre,* edited by Woodie King, Jr., Third World Press, 1989; *Breaking Ice: An Anthology of Contemporary African American Fiction,* edited by Terry McMillan, Penguin, 1990; *Yellow Silk: Erotic Arts and Letters,* edited by Lily Pond and Richard Russo, Harmony Books, 1990; *Daughters of Africa: An International An-*

*thology,* edited by Margaret Bushby, Pantheon, 1992; *Erotique Noire—Black Erotica,* edited by Miriam DeCosta-Willis, Reginald Martin, and Roseann P. Bell, Anchor, 1992; *Resurgent: New Writing by Women,* edited by Lou Robinson and Camille Norton, University of Illinois Press, 1992; and *Wild Women Don't Wear No Blues: Black Women Writers on Love, Men and Sex,* edited by Marita Golden, Doubleday, 1993. Contributor to periodicals, including *Black Scholar, Third World Women, Ms.,* and *Yardbird Reader.*

*ADAPTATIONS:* A musical-operetta version of Shange's novel *Betsey Brown* was produced by Joseph Papp's Public Theater in 1986.

*WORK IN PROGRESS: In the Middle of a Flower,* a play; a film adaptation of her novella *Sassafrass;* a novel.

*SIDELIGHTS:* Born to a surgeon and an educator, Ntozake Shange—originally named Paulette Williams—was raised with the advantages available to the black middle class. But one by one, the roles she chose for herself—including war correspondent and jazz musician—were dismissed as "no good for a woman," she told Stella Dong in a *Publishers Weekly* interview. She chose to become a writer because "there was nothing left." Frustrated and hurt after separating from her first husband, Shange attempted suicide several times before focusing her rage against the limitations society imposes on black women. While earning a master's degree in American Studies from the University of Southern California, she reaffirmed her personal strength based on a self-determined identity and took her African name, which means "she who comes with her own things" and she "who walks like a lion." Since then she has sustained a triple career as an educator, a performer/director in New York and Houston, and a writer whose works draw heavily on her experiences and the frustrations of being a black female in America. "I am a war correspondent after all," she told Dong, "because I'm involved in a war of cultural and esthetic aggression. The front lines aren't always what you think they are."

Though she is an accomplished poet and an acclaimed novelist, Shange became famous for her play, *For Colored Girls Who Have Considered Suicide/When the Rainbow Is Enuf.* A unique blend of poetry, music, dance and drama called a "choreopoem," it was still being produced around the country more than ten years after it "took the theatre world by storm" in 1975. Before it won international acclaim, *For Colored Girls,* notes Jacqueline Trescott in the *Washington Post,* "became an electrifying Broadway hit and provoked heated exchanges about the relationships between black men and women.... When [it] debuted, [it] became the talk of literary circles. Its form—seven women on the stage dramatizing poetry—was a refreshing slap at the traditional, one-two-three-act structures." Whereas plays combining poetry and

dance had already been staged by Adrienne Kennedy, Mel Gussow of the *New York Times* states that "Miss Shange was a pioneer in terms of her subject matter: the fury of black women at their double subjugation in white male America."

Shange's anger was not always so evident. "I was always what you call a nice child," she told *Time* magazine contributor Jean Vallely. "I did everything nice. I was the nicest and most correct. I did my homework. I was always on time. I never got into fights. People now ask me, 'Where did all this rage come from?' And I just smile and say it's been there all the time, but was just trying to be nice."

Shange's childhood was filled with music, literature, and art. Dizzy Gillespie, Miles Davis, Chuck Berry, and W.E.B. Du Bois were among the frequent guests at her parents' house. On Sunday afternoons Shange's family held variety shows. She recalled them in a self-interview published in *Ms.:* "my mama wd read from dunbar, shakespeare, countee cullen, t.s. eliot. my dad wd play congas & do magic tricks. my two sisters & my brother & i wd do a soft-shoe & then pick up the instruments for a quartet of some sort: a violin, a cello, flute & saxophone. we all read constantly. anything. anywhere. we also tore the prints outta art books to carry around with us. sounds/images, any explorations of personal visions waz the focus of my world."

However privileged her childhood might have seemed, Shange felt that she was "living a lie." As she explained to *Newsday* reviewer Allan Wallach: "[I was] living in a world that defied reality as most black people, or most white people, understood it—in other words, feeling that there was something that I could do, and then realizing that nobody was expecting me to do anything because I was colored and I was also female, which was not very easy to deal with."

Writing dramatic poetry became a means of expressing her dissatisfaction with the role of black women in society. She and a group of friends, including various musicians and the choreographer-dancer Paula Moss, would create improvisational works comprised of poetry, music, and dance, and they would frequently perform them in bars in San Francisco and New York. When Moss and Shange moved to New York City, they presented *For Colored Girls* at a Soho jazz loft, the Studio Rivbea. Director Oz Scott saw the show and helped develop the production as it was performed in bars on the Lower East Side. Impressed by one of these, black producer Woodie King, Jr., joined Scott the stage the choreopoem Off-Broadway at the New Federal Theatre, where it ran successfully from November, 1975, to the following June. Then Joseph Papp became the show's producer at the New York Shakespeare Festival's Anspacher Public Theatre. From there, it moved to the Booth Theatre uptown. "The final production at the Booth is as close to distilled as any of us in all our art forms can make it," Shange says of that production in the introduction to *For Colored Girls,* published in 1976. "The cast is enveloping almost 6,000 people a week in the words of a young black girl's growing up, her triumphs and errors, [her] struggle to be all that is forbidden by our environment, all that is forfeited by our gender, all that we have forgotten."

In *For Colored Girls,* poems dramatized by the women dancers recall encounters with their classmates, lovers, rapists, abortionists, and latent killers. The women survive the abuses and disappointments put upon them by the men in their lives and come to recognize in each other, dressed in the colors of Shange's personal rainbow, the promise of a better future. As one voice, at the end, they declare, "i found god in myself / and i loved her / ... fiercely." To say this, remarks Carol P. Christ in *Diving Deep and Surfacing: Women Writers on Spiritual Quest,* is "to say ... that it is all right to be a woman, that the Black woman does not have to imitate whiteness or depend on men for her power of being." "The poetry," says Marilyn Stasio in *Cue,* "touches some very tender nerve endings. Although roughly structured and stylistically unrefined, this fierce and passionate poetry has the power to move a body to tears, to rage, and to an ultimate rush of love."

While some reviewers are enthusiastic in their praise for the play, others are emphatically negative. "Some Black people, notably men, said that ... Shange broke a taboo when her *For Colored Girls* ... took the theatre world by storm," Connie Lauerman reports in the *Chicago Tribune.* "[Shange] was accused of racism, of 'lynching' the black male." But the playwright does not feel that she was bringing any black family secrets to light. She told Lauerman, "Half of what we discussed in *For Colored Girls* about the dissipation of the family, rape, wife-battering and all that sort of thing, the U.S. Census Bureau already had.... We could have gone to the Library of Congress and read the Census reports and the crime statistics every month and we would know that more black women are raped than anyone else. We would know at this point that they think 48 per cent of our households are headed by single females.... My job as an artist is to say what I see."

If these conditions are unknown to some, Shange feels it is all the more important to talk about them openly. Defending her portrayal of the acquaintance who turned out to be a rapist, she told interviewer Claudia Tate that men who deal with the issues by saying they have never raped anyone trouble her: "Maybe we should have a Congressional hearing to find out if it's the UFOs who are raping women.... After all, that is a denial of reality. It does *not* matter if you did or not do something.... When is someone going to take responsibility for what goes on where we live?" In the same interview, printed in *Black Women Writers at Work,* Shange explained that she wrote about Beau Willie Brown, a war veteran who is on drugs

when he drops two small children off a high-rise balcony, because she "refuse[s] to be a part of this conspiracy of silence" regarding crimes that hurt black women.

Some feminist responses to the play were negative, reports *Village Voice* critic Michele Wallace, who suspects "that some black women are angry because *For Colored Girls'* exposes their fear of rejection as well as their anger at being rejected. They don't want to deal with that so they talk about how Shange is persecuting the black man." Sandra Hollin Flowers, author of the *Black American Literature Forum* article "'Colored Girls': Textbook for the Eighties," finds most inappropriate the charges that Shange portrays black men as stupidly crude and brutal. "Quite the contrary, Shange demonstrates a compassionate vision of black men—compassionate because though the work is not without anger, it has a certain integrity which could not exist if the author lacked a perceptive understanding of the crisis between black men and women. And there is definitely a crisis.... This, then is what makes *Colored Girls* an important work which ranks with [Ralph] Ellison's *Invisible Man,* [Richard] Wright's *Native Son,* and the handful of other black classics—it is an artistically successful female perspective on a long-standing issue among black people."

"Shange's poems aren't war cries," Jack Kroll writes in a *Newsweek* review of the Public Theatre production of *For Colored Girls.* "They're outcries filled with a controlled passion against the brutality that blasts the lives of 'colored girls'—a phrase that in her hands vibrates with social irony and poetic beauty. These poems are political in the deepest sense, but there's no dogma, no sentimentality, no grinding of false mythic axes." Critic Edith Oliver of the *New Yorker* remarks: "The evening grows in dramatic power, encompassing, it seems, every feeling and experience a woman has ever had; strong and funny, it is entirely free of the rasping earnestness of most projects of this sort. The verses and monologues that constitute the program have been very well chosen—contrasting in mood yet always subtly building."

While Wallace was not completely satisfied with *For Colored Girls* and complained of the occasional "worn-out feminist cliches," she was still able to commend Shange. She wrote: "There is so much about black women that needs retelling; one has to start somewhere, and Shange's exploration of this aspect of our experience, admittedly the most primitive (but we were all there at some time and, if the truth be told, most of us still are) is as good a place as any. All I'm saying is that Shange's *For Colored Girls* should not be viewed as the definitive statement on black women, but as a very good beginning." She continued: "Very few have written with such clarity and honesty about the black woman's vulnerability and no one has ever brought Shange's brand of tough humor and realism to it."

Reviews of Shange's next production, *A Photograph: A Study of Cruelty,* are less positive, although critics are generally impressed with the poetic quality of her writing. "Miss Shange is something besides a poet but she is not—at least not at this stage—a dramatist," Richard Eder declares in a *New York Times* review. "More than anything else, she is a troubadour. She declares her fertile vision of the love and pain between black women and black men in outbursts full of old malice and young cheerfulness. They are short outbursts, song-length; her characters are perceived in flashes, in illuminating vignettes."

Shange's next play, *Spell #7: A Geechee Quick Magic Trance Manual,* more like *For Colored Girls* in structure, elicits a higher recommendation from Eder. Its nine characters in a New York bar discuss the racism black artists contend with in the entertainment world. At one point, the all-black cast appears in overalls and minstrel-show blackface to address the pressure placed on the black artist to fit a stereotype in order to succeed. "That's what happens to black people in the arts no matter how famous we become.... Black Theatre is not moving forward the way people like to think it is. We're not free of our paint yet," Shange told Tate. "On another level, *Spell #7* deals with the image of a black woman as a neutered workhorse, who is unwanted, unloved, and unattended by anyone," notes Elizabeth Brown in the *Dictionary of Literary Biography.* "The emphasis is still on the experiences of the black woman but it is broadened and deepened, and it ventures more boldly across the sexual divide," Eder writes in the *New York Times.* Don Nelson, writing in the *New York Daily News,* deems the show "black magic.... The word that best describes Shange's works, which are not plays in the traditional sense, is power."

To critics and producers who have complained that Shange's theater pieces do not present an easily marketable issue or point, Shange responds that a work's emotional impact should be enough. As she told Tate, "Our society allows people to be absolutely neurotic and totally out of touch with their feelings and everyone else's feelings, and yet be very respectable. This, to me, is a travesty. So I write to get at the part of people's emotional lives that they don't have control over, the part that can and will respond.... *For Colored Girls* for me is not an issue play.... There are just some people who are interesting. There's something there to make you feel intensely. Black writers have a right to do this," she said, although such works are not often rewarded with financial success. She names a number of successful plays that don't have a point except to celebrate being alive, and claims, "Black and Latin writers have to start demanding that the fact we're alive is point enough!" Furthermore, works which rely on emotional appeal reach a larger audience, she maintains in the same interview: "The kind of esteem that's given to brightness/smartness obliterates average people or slow learners from participating ful-

ly in human life. But you cannot exclude any human being from emotional participation."

Shange writes to fulfill a number of deeply felt responsibilities. Describing the genesis of *For Colored Girls*, for instance, Shange told Tate that she wrote its poems because she wanted young black women "to have information that I did not have. I wanted them to know what it was truthfully like to be a grown woman.... I don't want them to grow up in a void of misogynist lies." It is her commitment to break the silence of mothers who know, but don't tell their daughters, that "it's a dreadful proposition to lose oneself in the process of tending and caring for others," she said. The play "calls attention to how male-oriented black women ... [and] women in general are," and how their self-esteem erodes when they allow themselves to be exploited, writes Tate. Says Shange, "When I die, I will not be guilty of having left a generation of girls behind thinking that anyone can tend to their emotional health other than themselves."

Speaking of her works in general, she said, "I think it was Adrienne Rich or Susan Griffin who said that one of our responsibilities as women writers is to discover the causes for our pain and to respect them. I think that much of the suffering that women and black people endure is not respected. I was also trained not to respect it. For instance, we're taught not to respect women who can't get their lives together by themselves. They have three children and a salary check for $200. The house is a mess; they're sort of hair-brained. We're taught not to respect their suffering. So I write about things that I know have never been given their full due.... I want people to at least understand or have the chance to see that this is a person whose life is not only valid but whose life is valiant. My responsibility is to be as honest as I can and to use whatever technical skills I may possess to make these experiences even clearer, or sharper, or more devastating or more beautiful." Women writers should also demand more respect for writing love poems, for seeing "the world in a way that allows us to care more about people than about military power. The power we see is the power to feed, the power to nourish and to educate.... It's part of our responsibility as writers to make these things important," Shange said.

Shange's poetry books, like her theater pieces, are distinctively original. *Nappy Edges,* containing fifty poems, is too long, says Harriet Gilbert in the *Washington Post Book World;* however, she claims, "nothing that Shange writes is ever entirely unreadable, springing, as it does, from such an intense honesty, from so fresh an awareness of the beauty of sound and of vision, from such mastery of words, from such compassion, humor and intelligence." Alice H.G. Phillips relates in the *Times Literary Supplement,* "Comparing herself to a jazzman 'takin' a solo,' she lets go with verbal runs and trills, mixes in syncopations, spins out evocative hanging phrases, variations on themes and refrains. Rarely does she come to a full stop, relying instead on line breaks, extra space breaking up a line, and/or oblique strokes.... She constantly tries to push things to their limit, and consequently risks seeming overenthusiastic, oversimplistic or merely undisciplined.... But at its best, her method can achieve both serious humour and deep seriousness."

In her poetry, Shange takes many liberties with the conventions of written English, using nonstandard spellings and punctuation. Some reviewers feel that these innovations present unnecessary obstacles to the interested readers of *Nappy Edges, A Daughter's Geography,* and *From Okra to Greens: Poems.* Explaining her "lower-case letters, slashes, and spelling" to Tate, she said that "poems where all the first letters are capitalized" bore her; "also, I like the idea that letters dance.... I need some visual stimulation, so that reading becomes not just a passive act and more than an intellectual activity, but demands rigorous participation." Her idiosyncratic punctuation assures her "that the reader is not in control of the process." She wants her words in print to engage the reader in a kind of struggle, and not be "whatever you can just ignore." The spellings, she said, "reflect language as I hear it.... The structure is connected to the music I hear beneath the words."

Shange's rejection of standard English serves deeper emotional and political purposes as well. In a *Los Angeles Times Book Review* article on Shange's *See No Evil: Prefaces, Essays and Accounts, 1976-1983,* Karl Keller relates, "[Shange] feels that as a black performer/playwright/poet, she has wanted 'to attack deform n maim the language that i was taught to hate myself in. I have to take it apart to the bone.'" Speaking to Tate, Shange declared, "We do not have to refer continually to European art as the standard. That's absolutely absurd and racist, and I won't participate in that utter lie. My work is one of the few ways I can preserve the elements of our culture that need to be remembered and absolutely revered."

Shange takes liberties with the conventions of fiction writing with her first full-length novel, *Sassafrass, Cypress & Indigo.* "The novel is unusual in its form—a tapestry of narrative, poetry, magic spells, recipes and letters. Lyrical yet real, it also celebrates female stuff—weaving, cooking, birthing babies," relates Lauerman. Its title characters are sisters who find different ways to cope with their love relationships. Sassafrass attaches herself to Mitch, a musician who uses hard drugs and beats her; she leaves him twice, but goes back to him for another try. To male readers who called Mitch a "weak" male character, Shange replied to Lauerman, "[He] had some faults, but there's no way in the world you can say [he wasn't] strong.... I think you should love people with their faults. That's what love's about." Cypress, a dancer in feminist productions, at first refuses to become romantically involved with

any of her male friends. Indigo, the youngest sister, retreats into her imagination, befriending her childhood dolls, seeing only the poetry and magic of the world. The music she plays on her violin becomes a rejuvenating source for her mother and sisters. "Probably there is a little bit of all three sisters in Shange," Lauerman suggests, "though she says that her novel is not autobiographical but historical, culled from the experiences of blacks and from the 'information of my feelings'."

Critics agree that Shange's poetry is more masterfully wrought than her fiction, yet they find much in the novel to applaud. Writes Doris Grumbach in the *Washington Post Book World,* "Shange is primarily a poet, with a blood-red sympathy for and love of her people, their folk as well as their sophisticated ways, their innocent, loving goodness as much as their lack of immunity to powerful evil.... But her voice in this novel is entirely her own, an original, spare and primary-colored sound that will remind readers of Jean Toomer's *Cane.*" In Grumbach's opinion, "Whatever Shange turns her hand to she does well, even to potions and recipes. A white reader feels the exhilarating shock of discovery at being permitted entry into a world she couldn't have known" apart from the novel.

"There is poetry in ... *Sassafrass, Cypress & Indigo:* the poetry of rich lyrical language, of women you want to know because they're so original even their names conjure up visions," comments Joyce Howe in the *Village Voice. Betsey Brown: A Novel,* "lacks those fantastical qualities, yet perhaps because this semi-autobiographical second novel is not as easy to love, it is the truer book." Betsey is 13, growing into young womanhood in St. Louis during the 1950s. "An awakening sense of racial responsibility is as important to Betsey as her first kiss," relates Patchy Wheatley, a *Times Literary Supplement* reviewer. As one of the first students to be bused to a hostile white school, Betsey learns about racism and how to overcome it with a sense of personal pride. Says the reviewer, "By interweaving Betsey's story with those of the various generations of her family and community, Shange has also produced something of wider significance: a skillful exploration of the Southern black community at a decisive moment in its history."

"Black life has always been more various than the literature has been at liberty to show," comments Sherley Anne Williams in a *Ms.* review. Though she is not impressed with *Betsey Brown* "as a literary achievement," she welcomes this important-because-rare look at the black middle class. In a *Washington Post* review, Tate concurs, and notes the differences between *Betsey Brown* and Shange's previous works: "Shange's style is distinctively lyrical; her monologues and dialogues provide a panorama of Afro-American diversity. Most of Shange's characteristic elliptical spelling, innovative syntax and punctuation is absent from *Betsey Brown.* Missing also is the caustic social criticism about racial and sexual victimization.... *Betsey Brown* seems also to mark Shange's movement from explicit to subtle expressions of rage, from repudiating her girlhood past to embracing it, and from flip candor to more serious commentary." Shange told Dong that she is as angry and subversive as ever, but does not feel as powerless, she said, "because I know where to put my anger, and I don't feel alone anymore."

In *The Love Space Demands,* a "choreopoem" published in 1991, Shange returns to the blend of music, dance, poetry and drama that characterized *For Colored Girls Who Have Considered Suicide.* "I've gone back to being more like myself," Shange explains to *Voice Literary Supplement* interviewer Eileen Myles, "I'm working on my poetry with musicians and dancers like I originally started." Described by Myles as "a sexy, discomfiting, energizing, revealing, occasionally smug, fascinating kind of book," *The Love Space Demands* includes poems on celibacy and sexuality, on black women's sense of abandonment by black men, on a crack-addicted mother who sells her daughter's virginity for a hit and a pregnant woman who swallows cocaine, destroying her unborn child, to protect her man from arrest. The lead poem of the book, "irrepressibly bronze, beautiful & mine," was inspired by Robert Mapplethorpe's photographs of black and white gay men. The artist's task, Shange tells Myles, is "to keep our sensibilities alive.... To keep people alive so they know they can feel what is happening as opposed to simply trying to fend it off." "I would rather you not think about how the poem's constructed but simply be in it with me," she adds. "That's what it's for, not for the construction, even for the wit of it. It's for actual, visceral responses."

*BIOGRAPHICAL/CRITICAL SOURCES:*

*BOOKS*

Betsko, Kathleen and Rachel Koenig, editors, *Interviews with Contemporary Women Playwrights,* Beech Tree Books, 1987.

Christ, Carol P., *Diving Deep and Surfacing: Women Writers on Spiritual Quest,* Beacon Press, 1980.

*Contemporary Literary Criticism,* Gale, Volume 8, 1978, Volume 25, 1983, Volume 38, 1986.

*Dictionary of Literary Biography,* Volume 38: *Afro-American Writers after 1955: Dramatists and Prose Writers,* Gale, 1985.

Shange, Ntozake, *For Colored Girls Who Have Considered Suicide/When the Rainbow Is Enuf,* Shameless Hussy Press, 1975, Macmillan, 1976.

Shange, Ntozake, *See No Evil: Prefaces, Essays and Accounts, 1976-1983,* Momo's Press, 1984.

Squier, Susan Merrill, editor, *Women Writers and the City: Essays in Feminist Literary Criticism,* University of Tennessee Press, 1984.

Tate, Claudia, editor, *Black Women Writers at Work,* Continuum, 1983.

*PERIODICALS*

*African American Review,* spring, 1992; summer, 1992.
*American Black Review,* September, 1983; March, 1986.
*Black American Literature Forum,* summer, 1981; fall, 1990.
*Black Scholar,* March, 1979; March, 1981; December, 1982; July, 1985.
*Booklist,* April 15, 1987; May 15, 1991.
*Chicago Tribune,* October 21, 1982.
*Chicago Tribune Book World,* July 1, 1979; September 8, 1985.
*Christian Science Monitor,* September 9, 1976; October 8, 1982; May 2, 1986.
*Cue,* June 26, 1976.
*Detroit Free Press,* October 30, 1978.
*Ebony,* August, 1977.
*Essence,* November, 1976; May, 1985; June, 1985; August, 1991.
*Freedomways,* Third Quarter, 1976.
*Horizon,* September, 1977.
*Kliatt Young Adult Paperback Book Guide,* January, 1989.
*Library Journal,* May 1, 1987.
*Los Angeles Times,* October 20, 1982; June 11, 1985; July 28, 1987.
*Los Angeles Times Book Review,* August 22, 1982; October 20, 1982; January 8, 1984; July 29, 1984; June 11, 1985; July 19, 1987.
*Mademoiselle,* September, 1976.
*Ms.,* September, 1976; December, 1977; June, 1985; June, 1987.
*New Leader,* July 5, 1976.
*Newsday,* August 22, 1976.
*New Statesman,* October 4, 1985.
*Newsweek,* June 14, 1976; July 30, 1979.
*New York Amsterdam News,* October 9, 1976.
*New York Daily News,* July 16, 1979.
*New Yorker,* June 14, 1976; August 2, 1976; January 2, 1978.
*New York Post,* June 12, 1976; September 16, 1976; July 16, 1979.
*New York Theatre Critics' Reviews,* September 13, 1976.
*New York Times,* June 16, 1976; December 22, 1977; June 4, 1979; June 8, 1979; July 16, 1979; July 22, 1979; May 14, 1980; June 15, 1980.
*New York Times Book Review,* June 25, 1979; July 16, 1979; October 21, 1979; September 12, 1982; May 12, 1985; April 6, 1986.
*New York Times Magazine,* May 1, 1983.
*Plays and Players,* December, 1979.
*Publishers Weekly,* May 3, 1985.
*Saturday Review,* February 18, 1978; May/June, 1985.
*Time,* June 14, 1976; July 19, 1976; November 1, 1976.

*Times* (London), April 21, 1983.
*Times Literary Supplement,* December 6, 1985; April 15-21, 1988.
*Variety,* July 25, 1979.
*Village Voice,* August 16, 1976; July 23, 1979; June 18, 1985.
*Village Voice Literary Supplement,* August, 1991; September, 1991.
*Washington Post,* June 12, 1976; June 29, 1976; February 23, 1982; June 17, 1985.
*Washington Post Book World,* October 15, 1978; July 19, 1981; August 22, 1982; August 5, 1984.
*Wilson Library Bulletin,* October, 1990.

\* \* \*

## SHERMAN, Charlotte Watson 1958-

*PERSONAL:* Born October 14, 1958, in Seattle, WA; daughter of Charles E. Watson and Dorothy Ray (a homemaker; maiden name, Yarbrough) Glass; married David Joseph Sherman (a diagnostic ultrasound applications specialist), June 14, 1980; children: Aisha and Zahida. *Education:* Seattle University, B.A., 1980.

*ADDRESSES: Agent*—Beth Vesel, Sanford Greenberger Associates, 55 Fifth Ave., New York, NY 10003.

*CAREER:* Fiction writer. Instructional assistant, Garvey School, 1987-88; emergency housing coordinator, East Cherry Y.W.C.A., 1989; social worker for Child Welfare Services, 1989-91; mental health specialist, Group Health Cooperative, 1991-92; writing workshop instructor, Y.M.C.A./Seattle Education Center, 1992-93.

*AWARDS, HONORS:* King County Arts Commission Publication Award, 1990; Seattle African-American Women's Achievement Award, 1992; Great Lakes College Association Award, 1992, for *Killing Color.*

*WRITINGS:*

*Killing Color* (short stories), Calyx Books, 1992.
*One Dark Body* (novel), HarperCollins, 1993.

Also contributor to *Fiction and Poetry Anthology of Writings by African-American Women,* HarperCollins, 1993. Contributor to periodicals, including *Calyx, Obsidian,* and *Obsidian II.*

*WORK IN PROGRESS:* Novel scheduled for publication by HarperCollins, 1994; research on women writers, creativity, and mood disorders.

*SIDELIGHTS:* Charlotte Watson Sherman commented: "I am obsessed with exploring the terrain of psychological wounds, particularly the emotional scars of African-Americans. I never knew either of my grandfathers, though both were reputedly ministers. The paternal grandfather was a Baptist preacher; the maternal grandfather was suspected to have been Elijah Muhammed of the Nation of Islam (my mother believes she is one of his many 'outside' children). As a result, elements of the sacred seem to permeate my writing. A close relative's mental illness and my accompanying fears and fascination with those who 'live on the edge' are also motivating forces in my work."

\* \* \*

## SIMONS, Rita Dandridge
### See DANDRIDGE, Rita B(ernice)

\* \* \*

## SINGLETON, John 1968(?)-

*PERSONAL:* Born c. 1968, in Los Angeles, CA; son of Danny Singleton (a mortgage broker) and Sheila Ward (a sales executive). *Education:* University of Southern California, B.A., 1990.

*ADDRESSES: Home*—Baldwin Hills, CA. *Agent*—Bradford W. Smith, Creative Artists Agency, 9830 Wilshire Blvd., Beverly Hills, CA 90212-1825.

*CAREER:* Screenwriter and film director.

*AWARDS, HONORS:* Academy Award nominations, best director and best original screenplay, 1991, both for *Boyz N the Hood.*

*WRITINGS:*

(And director) *Boyz N the Hood* (screenplay), Columbia, 1991.
(And director) *Poetic Justice* (screenplay), Columbia, 1993.

*WORK IN PROGRESS: The Champ,* a television series about a black boxer in South Central Los Angeles, for Home Box Office, scheduled to premiere in 1993; a third film for Columbia.

*SIDELIGHTS:* John Singleton was nominated for an Academy Award for his role as writer and director of the 1991 film *Boyz N the Hood,* which chronicles the struggles of three black friends growing up in South Central, a neighborhood of Los Angeles. While Singleton addresses issues and themes of specific relevance to blacks in *Boys N the Hood,* the motion picture proved commercially successful with diverse audiences. With this venture, Singleton became one of a number of young black filmmakers who redefined mainstream cinema beginning in the mid-1980s. Shunning the traditional Hollywood formula which resolves the conflict happily, artists such as Spike Lee, Matty Rich, and Singleton strive to tell authentic black urban stories in which the problems defy simple solutions. Intrigued by this new cinematic trend, critics as well as audiences have responded favorably to Singleton's work. "No first film in the new wave of films by and about black Americans states the case for the movement's longevity more forcefully than *Boyz N the Hood,*" declared *Detroit News* film critic Susan Stark.

In *Boyz N the Hood,* the main characters—Tre Styles and his friends Ricky and Doughboy—attempt to live through adolescence despite the constant threat of violence and the temptation to profit from the illegal drug business. Opening with the statistic that one out of every twenty-two black males will be murdered—most by other black males—the film emphasizes the difficulty of survival in the "hood" (slang for neighborhood). Singleton believes that the proliferation of black-on-black crime is partially due to the absence of adult male role models in black communities. The author argues in *Boyz* that the chain of violence can only be halted by concerned fathers who set an example for their sons.

Singleton advocates this solution because he is evidence of its success. Although he lived with his mother, Singleton considers the weekends he spent with his father paramount to his development and success as a filmmaker. He believes that having a dream—and a father to encourage it—kept him out of trouble. "A young boy needs a man to show him how to be a man," Singleton stated in *Elle.* "Black men need to be responsible fathers for their sons." The author notes that it was his father who took him to see movies—such as George Lucas's *Star Wars*—leaving him determined at the age of nine to become a filmmaker. In high school Singleton discovered that the film business revolved around screenplays and began working on his writing skills. He enrolled in film school at the University of Southern California, and by the time he graduated he had made a few eight-millimeter films, won several writing awards, and signed a contract with the influential talent company, Creative Artists Agency. Soon after graduation, his screenplay for *Boyz N the Hood* won him a three-year contract with Columbia Pictures.

Singleton accepted the contract, but, fearing that another director would distort his point of view, insisted that he direct

*Boyz N the Hood* himself. "It's my story, I lived it," he explained in *New York Times Magazine.* "What sense would it have made to have some white boy impose his interpretation on my experience?" In *Elle,* he added, "Having a black man directing raw street-life narratives gives them a certain credibility." It was important to Singleton that every aspect of the production be marked by authenticity. After securing the position of director, Singleton hired a nearly all-black crew and solicited three black Los Angeles gang members to help him fine-tune the dialogue and select the wardrobe. Singleton wanted to deliver his message in language that the average black audience member could understand, because, as he expressed in *Interview,* "I made my film for the regular brother off the street." *Time* contributor Richard Corliss noted the success of this venture, calling the film "a harrowing document true to the director's south-central Los Angeles milieu; he paints it black."

*Boyz N the Hood* portrays "a tragic way of life," according to *New York* contributor David Denby. The hood is an inner-city world in which constant gunshots, sirens, and police helicopter searchlights serve as reminders that danger is never far away. Tre Styles adopts this environment as his new home when, as a troubled ten-year-old, he is sent by his divorced mother to live with his father, Furious. As Tre grows up, Furious teaches him responsibility and dignity, making him strong enough to resist the lure of the street and stay in school. Tre counts as his friends athletic, college-bound Ricky and street-smart Doughboy, half-brothers who live with their mother. Transferring her feelings about their respective fathers to her sons, the mother favors Ricky but has little hope for Doughboy. Tre's friendships draw him into a violent confrontation from which he narrowly escapes. At film's end, Tre, guided by his father's example, manages to survive and go to college, while Ricky and Doughboy—who lack a male role model—are killed.

Though Singleton acted as both writer and director for *Boyz N the Hood,* he considers himself primarily a screenwriter. As he related in *New York Times Magazine,* "In this business, you get hired for your vision, and your vision begins with your script. I'm a writer first, and I direct in order to protect my vision." Although *Detroit Free Press* contributor Kathy Huffhines appreciated the fact that "he puts his anger into words, not just camera angles," Singleton considers the visual aspect of his screenplay more important than the spoken element. He remarked in *New York Times Magazine,* "I strive toward saying things visually—that verbal stuff is for T.V." Critics responded positively to Singleton's first writing and directing effort, which they found authentic and effective. *New York Times* contributor Janet Maslin commented, "Singleton's terrifically confident first feature places [him] on a footing with Spike Lee as a chronicler of the frustration faced by young black men growing up in urban settings." Responding to its style, subject matter, and direction, Stark called *Boyz N the Hood* "a smart, smooth, astonishingly authoritative debut piece."

Yet several reviewers, noting the many speeches which Furious Styles imparts to Tre, found the script verbose. Referring to "the ideological burden" of Singleton's script, Stark maintained that the film "is over-stuffed with ideas." *People* contributor Ralph Novak, calling the film "pedantic," expressed, "Every issue is accompanied by a preachy piece of dialogue." Stark, however, believed Singleton was aware of this problem. She asserted that by adding a line in which Furious is compared to a preacher, Singleton "both anticipates and diffuses negative reaction" to Furious's speeches. Some critics also expressed concern about the attitudes toward women in Singleton's film. "In *Boyz N the Hood,*" stated Corliss, "most of the women are shown as doped-up, career-obsessed or irrelevant to the man's work of raising a son in an American war zone." Huffhines observed that Singleton's "diamond-hard belief in the importance of fatherhood shortchanges motherhood" noting, "he's clearly down on Tre's mother for being cooly ambitious." She added, however, that Singleton's obvious respect for his main characters outweighs the problems with the minor characters, and named Singleton "the most impressive" of the year's young black filmmakers.

Singleton followed *Boyz N the Hood* with *Poetic Justice,* a film many reviewers dubbed "Girlz N the Hood"—a description Singleton emphatically denies—before its release. With poetry by Maya Angelou and featuring Janet Jackson as Justice, a young woman who watches the murder of her boyfriend and turns to poetry to work through her pain, the film parallels *Boyz N the Hood* in presenting a scenario of life for young blacks, but differs in many aspects including its focus on the experiences of women.

Singleton is aware that *Poetic Justice* will be measured against *Boyz N the Hood.* The success of *Boyz* and the distinction of being the youngest director and the only black ever nominated for the best director Oscar equal an inordinate amount of pressure for the twenty-five-year-old screenwriter. In an interview for *USA Weekend,* Singleton told Jill Nelson that he takes the responsibility of his work seriously: "When you go to a movie, you're giving up two hours of your life to whoever made that film.... When people go to see my film, I want them to know I'm not about to waste their time." With his success Singleton has found himself in demand as a leader. His opinion was heavily sought after the acquittals in 1992 of the four police officers accused of beating Rodney King in Los Angeles. Singleton refused to accept that role. "I don't speak for nobody except John Singleton," he told Nelson. "I'd be a fool if I tried that, and I'm not a fool. The problem is, you have so many people in leadership positions, and people are so quick to follow. And once that leader falls, movements

end. Everybody should try and be a leader, then work collectively." Singleton remarked that, growing up, he was never afraid to express himself. That fearlessness is the basis for his philosophy. "I used to talk back to my father, and he was big, big, big," the author told Nelson. "My cousins would be all afraid, and I was like: 'What are you all afraid of?' What gives me strength is: What do you have to be afraid of? Nothing.... You do what you do, be polite, never try to do wrong by anybody, but speak your mind. That's my rule."

*BIOGRAPHICAL/CRITICAL SOURCES:*

*PERIODICALS*

*Detroit Free Press,* July 12, 1991, pp. 1C, 4C.
*Detroit News,* July 12, 1991, pp. 1D, 3D; July 20, 1991, pp. 1C, 3C-4C.
*Detroit News and Free Press,* July 14, 1991, pp. 1A, 8A.
*Elle,* June, 1991, pp. 52-61.
*Essence,* November, 1991, pp. 64, 112.
*Interview,* July, 1991, p. 20.
*Newsweek,* July 29, 1991, pp. 48-49.
*New York,* July 22, 1991, pp. 40-41.
*New York Times,* July 12, 1991, pp. C1, C15; July 14, 1991, p. 10.
*New York Times Magazine,* July 14, 1991, pp. 15-19, 38-40, 44.
*People,* July 22, 1991, pp. 14-15.
*Time,* June 17, 1991, pp. 64-68.
*USA Weekend,* July 23-25, 1993, pp. 4-5.
*Wilson Library Bulletin,* October, 1991, pp. 70-71.

\*   \*   \*

## SMART, Ian Isidore 1944-

*PERSONAL:* Born April 4, 1944, in Trinidad; son of Isidore (an attorney) and Myrle Elma Smart; married Buena Isidra Dawkins (a realtor), December 23, 1978; children: Monifa Isidra and Isidore Kamau. *Education:* University College, Dublin, B.A., 1968; National Autonomous University, M.A., 1970; University of California, Los Angeles, Ph.D, 1975.

*ADDRESSES: Office*—Department of Romance Languages, Howard University, Washington, DC 20059.

*CAREER:* Literary critic. University of California, Los Angeles, instructor, 1975-76; University of Arkansas, Fayetteville, assistant professor, 1976-77; Howard University, Washington, DC, assistant professor, 1977-81, associate professor, 1981-84, professor of Spanish, 1984—. Taught English at National Autonomous University, 1970, and French and Spanish at St. James Secondary School, 1970-71.

*MEMBER:* Afro-Hispanic Institute, Modern Language Association, College Language Association.

*WRITINGS:*

*Central American Writers of West Indian Origin: A New Hispanic Literature* (literary criticism), Three Continents, 1984.
(Translator) Carlos Guillermo Wilson, *Short Stories by Cubena,* Afro-Hispanic Institute, 1987.
*Nicolas Guillen: Popular Poet of the Caribbean* (literary criticism), University of Missouri Press, 1990.
(Translator) Nelson Estupinan Bass, *Pastrana's Last River* (novel), Afro-Hispanic Institute, 1992.
*Amazing Connections: Ancient Africa and Contemporary Hispano-Africana Literature,* Karia Press, 1993.

Contributor to periodicals, including *Africa Events, Afro-Hispanic Review, Carribean Review, Cimarron, College Language Association Journal, Journal of African and Comparative Literature, Kentucky Romance Quarterly, Letras Femeninas, Research in African Literatures, Studies in Afro-Hispanic Literature,* and *Western Journal of Black Studies.*

*WORK IN PROGRESS:* A novel scheduled for publication in 1994; a comparative study of popular African-based literary expressions of the Americas in English, Spanish, French, French Creole, and Papiamento.

*SIDELIGHTS:* Literary critic Ian Isidore Smart approaches the writing of English- and Spanish-based Central American and Caribbean authors and poets with a knowledge not only of their literature, but also of their region's popular culture, religion, politics, and the archetypical myths upon which each is founded. In his critical studies of literature, Smart weaves together the beliefs, mores, myths, history, psychology, art, popular songs, and even the humor of each particular country or region as he explains how these factors have influenced the literature he is exploring. Even when he is writing scholarly literary criticism, Smart gives his readers the feel of a country's culture and beliefs as he reviews the literature it produces.

In his critical studies, Smart's thesis is that the demographic, linguistic, and cultural cross-pollination that has occurred throughout the entire Caribbean has begun to produce a distinctive literature in Spanish-speaking Central America that is very similar to that of those Caribbean countries in which English is the sole native language. Similar to the literature that originated in these primarily English-speaking Caribbean/West Indian countries, this new Hispanic literature of Central America is also strongly affected by the essentially African cultural elements that constitute "West Indianness," ac-

cording to Smart. In particular, Smart recounts how these cultural ties to Africa, history, the black experience of social and political oppression, and the evolution of multi-racial cultures affect the language and literature of this part of the world.

In his book *Central American Writers of West Indian Origin: A New Hispanic Literature,* Smart identifies, describes, and explores this emerging and evolving Spanish literature. Written in English, Smart's critical review presents numerous examples in Spanish with extensive English translations by the author. Although Smart discusses many West Indian writers and poets from Central America in this volume, he concentrates on the work of four: Quince Duncan and Eulalia Bernard from Costa Rica and Panamanian writers Gerardo Maloney and "Cubena" (Carlos Guillermo Wilson). Smart writes that in addition to creating a new Hispanic language and literature, this quartet of writers shares many of the same concerns, themes and philosophical questions. Writing in *World Literature Today,* Evelyn Uhrhan Irving stated that "all four [of the authors] have explored the themes of language, identity, religion, exile, the journey, the plantation, *mestizaje* [literally, their "mixed blood experience," or being of different races], and interracial love and mating."

Moving easily between the peculiar cultural expressions of English-speaking and Spanish-speaking African-ancestored new natives of the Caribbean, Central American writers of Caribbean/West Indian ancestry are creating a literature that closely reflects the reality of their present day culture. This is a culture that bridges the heritage of both the New World and those of Africa and Europe, through the proliferation of bilingualism in the media, the arts, and music. In order to truly understand the concerns of these writers and their world, *San Francisco Review of Books* contributor David H. Anthony wrote, "Smart makes fluency in at least two of the region's major languages a precondition for grasping West Indian identity."

Smart's book *Nicolas Guillen: Popular Poet of the Caribbean* is an in-depth study of the life and work of Cuba's late poet laureate. In this comprehensive study, Smart presents a case for bilingualism as a bridge between the cultures of Africa and those of the New World. His provocative pan-Caribbean thesis is that Guillen's uniquely Cuban poetry is enriched by the African traditions that exist in the West Indies. According to Anthony, "Smart uses 'Caribbean' and 'West Indian' interchangeably, embracing a wider world encompassing Spanish, French, and English variants of a chiefly neo-African, thus homogeneous cultural character." Smart believes that the cultural cross-pollination from Africa, Europe and Latin America that has influenced the Caribbean/West Indies now supports that region's own vibrant, distinctive culture.

Smart does not limit the African influence on Guillen solely to poetry, but shows how the late Cuban poet drew upon the vast wealth of inspiration from various Caribbean/West Indian musical forms and their lyrics, including Jamaican reggae; Puerto Rico's *salsa, bomba,* and *plena;* Cuba's *guaguanco, rumba,* and *son;* the *kaiso* from Trinidad; and songs of resistance sung by laborers and the oppressed throughout the Caribbean. Smart describes how Guillen was a loyal, active member of Cuba's communist party from 1937 until his death in 1989. Guillen "never deviated from politically correct positions in his life or in his art," reported *World Literature Today* contributor Ana Maria Hernandez. Using his vast knowledge of the songs of resistance and political rebellion, Smart is able to draw parallels from these sources to Guillen's activity as a member of Cuba's Communist party and the poetry he produced as Cuba's poet laureate.

The effect of music on Guillen's poetry was so strong that it is a major theme throughout *Nicolas Guillen.* Hernandez wrote that "purely literary considerations are not the focus of Smart's analysis, which is mainly concerned with the popular, collective, and even ritualistic aspects of Guillen's poems linking him to other West Indian poets and popular bards." Using examples from popular music, Smart shows how internationally known Caribbean musicians exerted a strong influence on Guillen's poetry. "Colossal in his homeland and in the greater Spanish-speaking and West Indian worlds, Nicolas Guillen even in death has still to find his North American audience," wrote Anthony. "Ian Smart's book will facilitate that process."

*BIOGRAPHICAL/CRITICAL SOURCES:*

*PERIODICALS*

*San Francisco Review of Books,* fall, 1991, p. 45.
*World Literature Today,* spring, 1985, p. 250; autumn 1991, p. 679.

— *Sketch by Mel Wathen*

\* \* \*

## SMITH, Arthur L(ee)
## See ASANTE, Molefi Kete

\* \* \*

## SMITH, Barbara 1946-

*PERSONAL:* Born November 16, 1946, in Cleveland, OH. *Education:* Mount Holyoke College, B.A., 1969; University of Pittsburgh, M.A., 1971.

*ADDRESSES: Office*—Kitchen Table: Women of Color Press, P.O. Box 908, Latham, NY 12110.

*CAREER:* New York University, New York, NY, instructor, 1985; Kitchen Table: Women of Color Press, Latham, NY, director, 1987—. Taught at University of Massachusetts, 1976-1981; visiting professor at Barnard College, 1983, University of Minnesota, 1986, and William Smith College, 1987; artist-in-residence at Hambidge Center for the Arts and Sciences, 1983, Millay Colony for the Arts, 1983, Yaddo, 1984, and Blue Mountain Center, 1985.

*MEMBER:* National Coalition of Black Lesbians and Gays (member of board of directors, 1985—), National Association for the Advancement of Colored People.

*AWARDS, HONORS:* Outstanding Woman of Color Award, 1982; Women Educator's Curriculum Award, 1983.

*WRITINGS:*

*Toward a Black Feminist Criticism,* Out and Out, 1977.
(Editor with Gloria T. Hull and Patricia Bell Scott) *All the Women Are White, All the Blacks Are Men, but Some of Us Are Brave: Black Women's Studies,* Feminist Press, 1982.
(Editor) *Home Girls: A Black Feminist Anthology,* Kitchen Table: Women of Color Press, 1983.
(Editor with Elly Bulkin and Minnie Bruce Pratt) *Yours in Struggle: Three Feminist Perspectives on Anti-Semitism and Racism,* Firebrand Books, 1984.

Also editor, with Gloria T. Hull, of *Conditions Five: The Black Women's Issue,* 1979.

*SIDELIGHTS:* Black American feminist editor and essayist Barbara Smith is known both for editing volumes that concern homosexual black feminism and for being the first writer to characterize relationships between black women in classic black novels as being lesbian. Smith startled the individuals attending the National Conference of Afro-American Writers with a paper that identified relationships between black women in many American novels written between the 1940s and the 1970s as homosexual. Until Smith read her paper, no one had addressed the subject of black lesbianism publicly. Thulani Davis, writing in the *Nation,* stated that the lesbianism Smith says she uncovers in those novels and discusses in her paper is "basically the closeness and mutual support one often finds among women who are brutalized by life, but the word itself [lesbian] brought alarm. How could something lesbian, however amorphous, step out of black culture's shadows and into the acknowledged landmarks of our genius?"

In *Home Girls: A Black Feminist Anthology,* Smith collected essays and stories from 34 black lesbians living in the United States and the Caribbean. The women write about what makes them and their experiences so different from other black women and their experiences; the collection celebrates the contributors' individuality. Smith believes that these differences and the expression and public acknowledgement of them are what add creativity and life to an interdependent culture. Smith argues that the suppression of these differences would destroy the vitality of the culture. She calls for inclusion, rather than exclusion, of people who are different particularly black lesbians.

Few of the contributors to *Home Girls* are skilled writers, but, as Davis commented, their prose "flashes with the bitterness caused by class and color differences in the black community and by the violence visited so regularly on black women." Writing in the *Women's Review of Books,* Gabrielle Daniels stated that "black women who are feminists, who are lesbians, are considered to have 'left' the community. Moreover, since the larger feminist movement is composed of mostly white women, it is cause for more distrust and vitriol leveled against Black feminists." Daniels explained that the "refusal to follow the straight and narrow line as to the role of women in the Black community has generated most of the negative response to Black feminism."

Smith's focus on the social and economic conditions of and prejudices against women of color form the basis of two other anthologies she coedited: *All the Women Are White, All the Blacks Are Men, but Some of Us Are Brave: Black Women's Studies* and *Yours in Struggle: Three Feminists Perspectives on Anti-Semitism and Racism.* In both of these volumes, Smith and her fellow editors enlarge their scope from that solely of the black lesbian to address the sexual, religious, and racial stereotyping to which women of color, and black women in particular, are subjected.

*BIOGRAPHICAL/CRITICAL SOURCES:*

*BOOKS:*

Culley, Margo, editor, *A Day at a Time: The Diary Literature of American Women,* Feminist Press, 1985, pp. 305-9.

*PERIODICALS:*

*Black American Literature Forum,* winter, 1984, p. 175.
*Essence,* May, 1984, p. 60.
*Ms.,* December, 1983, p. 39.
*Nation,* December 24, 1983, p. 671; February 25, 1984, pp. 234-5.
*Women's Review of Books,* March, 1984, pp. 6-7.

## SMITH, Jessie Carney 1930-

*PERSONAL:* Born September 24, 1930, in Greensboro, NC; daughter of James Ampler and Vesona (Bigelow) Carney; married Frederick Douglas Smith, December 2, 1950 (divorced); children: Frederick Douglas, Jr. *Education:* North Carolina Agricultural and Technical State University, B.S., 1950; attended Cornell University, 1950; Michigan State University, M.A., 1956; George Peabody College for Teachers (now George Peabody College for Teachers of Vanderbilt University), M.A.L.S., 1957; University of Illinois, Ph.D., 1964. *Politics:* Democrat. *Religion:* Methodist.

*ADDRESSES: Office*—University Library, Fisk University, 17th Ave., North, Nashville, TN 37203.

*CAREER:* Tennessee State University, Nashville, instructor and head cataloger at library, 1957-60, assistant professor of library science and coordinator of library service, 1963-65; Fisk University, Nashville, professor of library science and university librarian, 1965—, director of library training institutes, 1970-75, 1978. Lecturer at George Peabody College for Teachers of Vanderbilt University, 1969—, Alabama A & M University, 1971-73, and University of Tennessee, 1973-74. Guest lecturer at many colleges and universities, including Cornell University, Howard University, University of Illinois, and Bennett College. Director of numerous institutes, research programs, and internships in black and ethnic studies librarianship, all at Fisk University, all supported by U.S. Office of Education; also director of other publicly funded Fisk University programs related to black American literature. Member of numerous professional committees on libraries, including Reference and Subscription Books Review, 1969-71, 1971-73, Biomedical Library Review, 1972-76, and American Library Association Committee on Accreditation, 1974—. Also member of various task forces and advisory councils, including Tennessee Advisory Council on Libraries, 1971-75, 1989—, Task Force on Cultural Minorities, 1980-82, and Institute for Research in Black Music, 1980—. Evaluator for Tennessee Committee for the Humanities, Inc., on projects for Scarritt College, 1979, Nashville Panel, 1980, and Tennessee State Museum, 1981-82. Consultant to Southern Association of Colleges and Schools, 1968—, Oak Ridge National Laboratory, 1976, U.S. Office for Civil Rights, 1979-80, and Association of College and Research Libraries National Endowment for the Humanities workshops, 1983. Has appeared on local radio and television shows.

*MEMBER:* American Library Association (member of council, 1969-71, 1971-74), Medical Library Association, Association of College and Research Libraries, American Association of University Professors, National Association for the Advancement of Colored People (NAACP), African Studies Association, Links, Inc. (president of Hendersonville area chapter, 1983-87), Southeastern Library Association (member of nominating committee, 1965-66), Tennessee Library Association (vice-chair, 1968-69; chair of college and university section, 1969-70), Beta Phi Mu (vice-president, 1976; president, 1977), Pi Gamma Mu, Alpha Kappa Alpha.

*AWARDS, HONORS:* National Urban League fellow, 1968, 1976; Council on Library Resources fellow, 1969; certificate of achievement from Alpha Kappa Alpha, 1976, for outstanding work in the community and in the library profession; Martin Luther King, Jr., Black Author's Award, 1982; Certificate of Commendation, State of Tennessee House of Representatives and Senate, 1985; Distinguished Scholars Award, United Negro College Fund, 1986; Distinguished Alumni Award, Peabody College of Vanderbilt University, 1987, and Graduate Library of Information Science, University of Illinois, 1990.

*WRITINGS:*

*Bibliography for Black Studies Programs,* Fisk University, 1969.

*A Handbook for the Study of Black Bibliography,* Fisk University Library, 1971.

*Minorities in the United States: Guide to Resources,* School of Library Science, George Peabody College for Teachers, 1973.

*Black Academic Libraries and Research Collections: An Historical Survey,* Greenwood Press, 1977.

(Editor) *Ethnic Genealogy: A Research Guide,* foreword by Alex Haley, Greenwood Press, 1983.

(Editor) *Images of Blacks in American Culture: A Reference Guide to Information Sources,* foreword by Nikki Giovanni, Greenwood Press, 1988.

(Editor with Carrell P. Horton) *Statistical Record of Black America,* Gale, 1990.

(Editor) *Notable Black American Women,* Gale, 1991.

(Editor) *Epic Lives: One Hundred Black Women Who Made a Difference,* foreword by Stephanie Stokes Oliver, Visible Ink Press, 1992.

Author of introductions to *Special Collections in the Erastus Milo Cravath Library,* Fisk University Library, 1966; and *Dictionary Catalog of the Negro Collection of the Fisk University Library,* G. K. Hall, 1974. Author of foreword to *Dominique-Rene de Lerma, Bibliography of Black Music,* Volume 1: *Reference Materials,* Greenwood Press, 1981. Contributor to books, including *The Black Librarian in America,* edited by E. J. Josey, Scarecrow, 1970; *Library and Information Services for Special Groups,* American Society for Information Science in cooperation with Science Associates/International, 1973; *Dictionary of American Library Biography,* Libraries Unlimited, 1978; *Reference Services and Library Education,* edited by Mark Tucker and Edwin S. Gleaves,

Lexington Books, 1982. Contributor to *Bibliographical Control of Afro-American Literature.* Also contributor to *Proceedings of the Workshop on Social Science Approaches to the Study of Negro Culture,* Fisk University, 1968; *Proceedings of the Workshop on Afro-American Culture,* University of Iowa, 1969; *Proceedings of the Workshop on Negro Life and Culture in the Liberal Arts Curriculum,* Fisk University, 1969; *Proceedings of the Black Caucus of the American Library Association and Alabama State University,* Institute for Training Librarians for Special Black Collections and Archives, 1974; and *ALA Yearbook,* 1977-89.

Contributor to professional journals, including *College and Research Libraries, Southeastern Librarian, Black Information Index, Black World,* and *South Carolina Librarian.* Member of editorial board of *Choice,* 1969-72, 1972-75.

*WORK IN PROGRESS: African-American Women in Research Collections.*

*SIDELIGHTS:* Jessie Carney Smith once commented: "Librarian-ship offers tremendous opportunities for research and publication, particularly when the resources needed for such activities are found in the library where the researcher is employed. Fisk University Library and its notable special collections on black themes have been among the various motivating factors that influenced my writing, my consultant work, and my involvement in professional activities for librarians who needed to develop or to enhance their expertise on black and ethnic themes.

"I have difficulty assuming full credit for any of my publications, for I attribute each piece of work to the stimulation of various people who, without realizing it, influenced my development and my writing. I attribute my addiction to work to my father, who considered every moment too precious to waste in unproductivity. I learned from my mother and my maternal grandparents that one must share resources with others, that helpfulness is a gift to be passed along. Educators who shaped my early life in a rural four-room school, and who taught me to speak correctly and to write clearly in elementary school, high school, and college, mean much more to me in retrospect than I realized as they prepared me for a career. My graduate schools helped to cultivate my self-confidence as one who could write professionally, and there, for the first time, I knew that I would soon publish, thus bringing to the forefront the inspiration from everyone who had helped to shape my life.

"I write almost exclusively on black themes because of my experiences, my surroundings, my vision of the need for published information in these areas, and my love for the subjects. I have a similar love for ethnic themes; thus some of my works reflect this interest. Because I am a perfectionist, I work arduously to produce works that reflect high standards. Whether I have been successful or not is very much left to the judgement of my critics and my reviewers.

"Works which hold special meaning for me are *Ethnic Genealogy, Images of Blacks in American Culture,* and *Notable Black American Women.* Writing is a rewarding part of my life, and it provides a balance between professional responsibilities and personal gratification so necessary in the complexities of contemporary society."

*BIOGRAPHICAL/CRITICAL SOURCES:*

*PERIODICALS*

*College and Research Libraries,* summer, 1965.
*Ebony,* June, 1967.

\*    \*    \*

**SNELLINGS, Rolland**
  **See TOURE, Askia Muhammad Abu Bakr el**

\*    \*    \*

**SOWELL, Thomas 1930-**

*PERSONAL:* Born June 30, 1930, in Gastonia, NC; married Alma Jean Parr; children: two. *Education:* Harvard University, A.B. (magna cum laude), 1958; Columbia University, A.M., 1959; University of Chicago, Ph.D., 1968.

*ADDRESSES: Office*—Hoover Institution, Stanford, CA 94305.

*CAREER:* U.S. Department of Labor, Washington, DC, economist, 1961-62; Rutgers University, Douglass College, New Brunswick, NJ, instructor in economics, 1962-63; Howard University, Washington, DC, lecturer in economics, 1963-64; American Telephone & Telegraph Co., New York City, economic analyst, 1964-65; Cornell University, Ithaca, NY, assistant professor of economics, 1965-69, director of Summer Intensive Training Program in Economic Theory, 1968; Brandeis University, Waltham, MA, associate professor of economics, 1969-70; University of California, Los Angeles, associate professor, 1970-74, professor of economics, 1974-80; Urban Institute, Washington, DC, project director, 1972-74; Center for Advanced Study in the Behavioral Sciences, Stanford, CA, fellow, 1976-77; Hoover Institution, Stanford, senior fellow, 1977, 1980—. Visiting professor, Amherst

College, 1977. Columnist for Forbes Magazine, 1991—.
*Military Service:* U.S. Marine Corps, 1951-53.

*WRITINGS:*

*Economics: Analysis and Issues,* Scott, Foresman, 1971.
*Black Education: Myths and Tragedies,* McKay, 1972.
*Say's Law: An Historical Analysis,* Princeton University Press, 1972.
*Classical Economics Reconsidered,* Princeton University Press, 1974.
*Affirmative Action: Was It Necessary in Academia?,* American Enterprise Institute for Public Policy Research, 1975.
*Race and Economics,* McKay, 1975.
*Patterns of Black Excellence,* Ethics and Public Policy Center, Georgetown University, 1977.
(Editor) *American Ethnic Groups,* Urban Institute, 1978.
(Editor) *Essays and Data on American Ethnic Groups,* Urban Institute, 1978.
*Markets and Minorities,* Basic Books, 1981.
(Editor with others) *The Fairmont Papers: Black Alternatives Conference, December, 1980,* ICS Press, 1981.
*Pink and Brown People, and Other Controversial Essays,* Hoover Institution, 1981.
*Knowledge and Decision,* Basic Books, 1983.
*Ethnic America: A History,* Basic Books, 1983.
*The Economics and Politics of Race: An International Perspective,* Morrow, 1983.
*Compassion Versus Guilt, and other essays,* Quill, 1984.
*Marxism: Philosophy and Economics,* Morrow, 1985.
*Civil Rights: Rhetoric or Reality?,* Marrow, 1985.
*Assumptions versus History,* Hoover Institution, 1986.
*Compassion versus Guilt, and Other Essays,* Morrow, 1987.
*A Conflict of Visions: Ideological Origins of Political Struggles,* Morrow, 1987.
*Judicial Activism Reconsidered* (essays), Hoover Institution, 1989.
*Choosing a College: A Guide for Parents and Students,* Perennial Library, 1989.
*Preferential Policies: An International Perspective,* Morrow, 1990.
*Inside American Education: The Decline, the Deception, the Dogmas,* Free Press, 1992.
*Race and Culture: a World View,* Pennsylvania State University Press, 1992.

Work represented in anthologies, including *Readings in the History of Economic Thought,* edited by I. H. Rima, Holt, 1970; and *Discrimination, Affirmative Action and Equal Opportunity: An Economic and Social Perspective,* edited by W. E. Block and M. A. Walker, Fraser Institute, 1982. Author of column for *Forbes,* 1991—. Contributor to numerous periodicals, including *New York Times Magazine, Ethics, American Economic Review, Social Research, Education Digest,*

*Western Review, University of Chicago Magazine, Oxford Economic Papers,* and *Economica.*

*SIDELIGHTS:* Called "a free-market economist and perhaps the leading black scholar among conservatives" by Fred Barnes of the *New York Times Book Review,* Thomas Sowell has written a score of controversial books about economics, race, and ethnic groups. His support for a laissez-faire economic system with few government constraints and his vocal opposition to most of the social programs and judicial actions favored by most other black spokesmen have made him a target for much criticism. Yet, Steven E. Plaut of *Commentary* calls Sowell "one of America's most trenchant and perceptive commentators on the subject of race relations and ethnicity." Davis Holmstrom, writing in the *Los Angeles Times,* maintains that "in the writing of economist Thomas Sowell, scholarship, clarity and genuine information come together as nicely and perfectly as a timeless quote."

Sowell has done extensive research into the economic performance of racial and ethnic groups throughout the world, trying to determine the factors which make some groups more successful than others. He has presented his research findings and the conclusions he has drawn from it in such books as *Race and Economics, American Ethnic Groups, Markets and Minorities, Ethnic America: A History, The Economics and Politics of Race: An International Perspective,* and *Civil Rights: Rhetoric or Reality?* These books have disproven a number of popularly held beliefs while bringing new and potentially valuable information to light. As George M. Fredrickson notes in the *New York Times Book Review,* "Sowell is engaged in a continuing polemic against the basic assumptions of liberals, radicals and civil rights leaders. But the quality of his evidence and reasoning requires that he be taken seriously. His ideological opponents will have to meet his arguments squarely and incisively to justify the kind of policies currently identified with the pursuit of racial equality and social justice."

One of Sowell's most controversial contentions is that a racial or ethnic group's economic success is not seriously hindered by discrimination from society at large. In *The Economics and Politics of Race,* for instance, he gives several examples of minority groups who have fared well despite prejudice against them, and of other groups with little discrimination to over come who have done poorly. The Chinese minorities in South-east Asian countries, despite intense resistance from the native populations, have done very well economically. They often dominate their local economies. European Jews have also faced opposition from majority population groups. Yet they too have performed outstandingly well and enjoy a high level of economic success. On the other hand, Plaut gives an example of underachievement from Sowell's *The Economics and Politics of Race:* "In Brazil and other parts of South America blacks face less racism than do American

blacks.... Yet for all this tolerance, Brazil shows a larger gap in black-white earnings, social position, and education than does the United States."

The key factor in an ethnic group's economic success, Sowell argues, is "something economists refer to as human capital—values, attitudes and skills embodied in a culture," as Stanley O. Williford explains it in the *Los Angeles Times Book Review.* An ethnic or racial group which emphasizes hard work, saving money, and acquiring an education will generally do well whatever the political or social climate. *Newsweek*'s David Gelman notes that Sowell "has a conservative message to impart. Essentially, it is that diligence, discipline and entrepreneurial drive can overthrow the most formidable barriers of poverty and bigotry."

Because of this belief, Sowell argues against continued efforts by the federal government to end racial discrimination, a problem he believes was largely eliminated during the civil rights struggle, and calls instead for a greater emphasis on free market economics. A healthy, growing economy, Sowell believes, does the most good for minority groups who suffer from poverty. As Aaron Wildavsky writes in the *National Review,* "When labor is scarce and the markets for it are competitive, wages go up regardless of the prejudices of employers." Sowell points out in *Civil Rights: Rhetoric or Reality?* that "the economic rise of minorities preceded by many years passage of the Civil Rights Act...[and] that this trend was not accelerated either by that legislation or by the quotas introduced during the seventies," as Tony Eastland reports in the *American Spectator.* Sowell believes that minority groups, Chris Wall writes in the *Los Angeles Times Book Review,* are "crying racism at every turn to divert attention from the fact that their cultures or subcultures may be economically unproductive."

Sowell dismisses much of what black civil rights leaders believe necessary for the betterment of American blacks. He questions, for example, the value for black students of integrated public schools, called for by the Warren Court in the case Brown vs. Board of Education. Joseph Sobran of *National Review* reports that Sowell finds that the court's contention "that segregated schools produced inferior black education... expresses and justifies a destructively paternalistic attitude, according to which a black child can't learn anything except in close proximity to a white one. With forced busing, [Sowell] reflects ironically, the white man's burden has become 'the white *child's* burden—to go forth and civilize the heathen'."

Other government programs, including affirmative action racial quotas and public welfare, are also attacked by Sowell. Sowell is convinced, Nathan Glazer writes in the *New Republic,* "that hardly anything government will do can help blacks and other minorities with high levels of poverty and low levels of educational and economic achievement, and that almost anything government will do will only make matters worse." In a *Choice* review of *Civil Rights,* R. J. Steamer admits that "Sowell's revolutionary view—that government programs such as affirmative action, forced busing, and food stamps will not bring the disadvantaged black minority into the economic and social mainstream and might better be abandoned— will anger many." One such angered critic is Gelman, who claims that Sowell "seems to fault blacks for resting on their grievances instead of climbing aboard the success wagon." But Sowell sees government programs and those who call for them as part of a self-destructive mind-set. The black civil rights establishment, Sowell believes, "represents a thin layer of privileged blacks who have risen socially by echoing liberal ideology, with its view of blacks in general as helpless victims who depend on political favors for whatever gains they can make," Sobran explains.

Sowell's own life story seems to illustrate many of the values he now expounds. Born in North Carolina, Sowell attended a segregated high school where he was at the top of his class. "We never wondered why there weren't any white kids there," he tells Sobran. "We never though we'd be learning more if there *had* been white kids there. In fact, we never *thought* about white kids." A graduate of Harvard University, Columbia University, and the University of Chicago, Sowell went on to hold a number of positions in government and academia before joining the Hoover Institution in 1980. Through it all, Sobran remarks, Sowell has been "matter-of-fact about his race and its bearing on his intellectual life."

The consistent differences between Sowell's views and those of other black commentators, and the differences between those of the political left and right, moved Sowell to examine the underlying assumptions that create this dichotomy. In *A Conflict of Visions: Ideological Origins of Political Struggle,* he describes "two divergent views of man and society that he convincingly contends underlie many of the political, economic and social clashes of the last two centuries and remain very much with us today," as Walter Goodman of the *New York Times* explains. Sowell posits the unconstrained and the constrained views of man. "The unconstrained see human beings as perfectible," Otto Friedrich of *Time* writes, "the constrained as forever flawed." Sowell writes in the book that "the constrained vision is a tragic vision of the human condition. The unconstrained vision is a moral vision of human intentions."

These two visions are, Daniel Seligman writes in *Fortune,* "the mind-sets that originally made [intellectuals] gravitate to some ideas instead of others." Those with an unconstrained view of man, for example, tend to believe that social problems can be ultimately solved, and that man will usually act rationally. Such beliefs can lead to social engineering efforts to correct perceived societal ills. Those with a constrained view of man see him as imperfect and human nature as unchanging. They

often call for a limited government, a strong defense, and strict criminal penalties.

Sowell admits that not all people hold to one or the other vision consistently. And such ideologies as Marxism and fascism are compounds of both the constrained and unconstrained visions. Yet, critics see much of value in Sowell's plan. "Right or wrong in his main thesis," Sobran states, "he is full of stunning insights." "The split between the constrained and the unconstrained," Barnes notes, "works as a framework for understanding social theories and politics." Goodman finds that *A Conflict of Visions* "does lay out styles of thinking that we can readily recognize today in the divisions between left and right." And Michael Harrington, who explains in his *Washington Post Book World* review that "I reject the basic assumptions and the very intellectual framework" of the book, nonetheless concludes that "its insights and *apercus* reveal a serious mind honestly and fairly ... trying to grapple with those visionary premises on which our supposedly objective data are so often based and ordered."

In a later work, *Preferential Policies: An International Perspective,* Sowell argues against equal opportunity hiring and admissions policies, which mandate that employers and school officials judge minority applicants by different, more relaxed, criteria than they judge other applicants. Sowell believes that these policies result in less-qualified candidates gaining preferential treatment over better-qualified candidates and eventually lower the standards by which all individuals are measured. Citing examples from such countries as Sri Lanka, Nigeria, and India, as well as the United States, Sowell contends that preferential policies can be found around the globe.

Adolph L. Reed, Jr., reviewing *Preferential Policies* in the *Washington Post Book World,* found Sowell's thesis unconvincing, stating that "the relation between his examples and his underlying argument—that preferential policies undermine their own objectives and cause more problems then they resolve—is tortured and unconvincing." Andrew Hacker, however, in the *New York Times Book Review,* found that Sowell does make an important point about the effect of these policies, namely that "those who lose out [to preferential policies] are generally lower-middle-class candidates, who adhered to the rules and find themselves displaced by others deemed entitled to exemptions." He added, "Whether in fire departments or on campuses, groups at the end of the queue are being played off against one another—hardly the best way to promote racial amity."

During his career as a leading black economist, Sowell "has spoken out often, with considerable force and eloquence, against many of the assumptions about black life in the United States that are widely held by the black leadership and its white allies," Jonathan Yardley reports in the *Washington Post*

*Book World.* His arguments are beginning to attract converts the black community. As Glazer notes, "One has the impression that increasingly he is heeded, that this unbending analyst is having a greater influence on the discussion of matters of race and ethnicity that any other writer of the past ten years." Harrington, a socialist who admits that he is "utterly at odds" with Sowell's political beliefs, still calls him "one of the few conservative thinkers in America today who is interesting as a theorist."

*BIOGRAPHICAL/CRITICAL SOURCES:*

BOOKS

Sowell, Thomas, *Civil Rights: Rhetoric or Reality?,* Morrow, 1985.
Sowell, Thomas, *A Conflict of Visions: Ideological Origins of Political Struggles,* Morrow, 1987.

PERIODICALS

*American Political Science Review,* June, 1991.
*American Spectator,* July 1984; November, 1990.
*Change,* January, 1990.
*Choice,* September, 1984; November, 1990.
*Commentary,* December, 1983.
*Foreign Affairs,* Volume 70, number 3, 1991.
*Fortune,* March 16, 1987; February 13, 1989.
*Los Angeles Times,* March 22, 1985.
*Los Angeles Times Book Review,* September 6, 1981; January 8, 1984.
*National Review,* October 16, 1981; February 13, 1987; June 25, 1990.
*New Republic,* November 21, 1983; June 11, 1984.
*Newsweek,* August 24, 1981.
*New York Review of Books,* October 12, 1989.
*New York Times,* January 24, 1987.
*New York Times Book Review,* October 16, 1983; January 25, 1987; July 1, 1990.
*Publishers Weekly,* April 27, 1990.
*Time,* March 16, 1987.
*Wall Street Journal,* September 25, 1989.
*Washington Monthly,* June, 1990.
*Washington Post Book World,* April 29, 1984; January 4, 1987; September 9, 1990.
*Wilson Quarterly,* Volume 14, number 3, 1990.

\* \* \*

## SOYINKA, Wole 1934-

*PERSONAL:* Name is pronounced "*Woh*-leh Shaw-*yin*-ka"; given name, Akinwande Oluwole; born July 13, 1934, in Isara, Nigeria; son of Samuel Ayodele Soyinka (a headmaster) and Grace Eniola Soyinka (a teacher). *Education:* Attended University of Ibadan; University of Leeds, B.A. (honors), 1959. *Religion:* "Human liberty."

*ADDRESSES: Office*—Department of Dramatic Arts, University of Ife, Ife-Ife, Oyo, Nigeria. *Agent*—Greenbaum, Wolff & Ernst, 437 Madison Ave., New York, NY 10022.

*CAREER:* Playwright, poet, and novelist. University of Ibadan, research fellow in drama, 1960-61, director of School of Drama, 1967-71; University of Ife, lecturer, professor, 1976-85; University of Lagos, senior lecturer; visiting professor at Cambridge University, Churchill College, 1972-73, University of Sheffield, 1973-74, and at University of Ghana, Institute of African Studies. Director of own theatre groups, Orisun Players and 1960 Masks, in Lagos and Ibadan, Nigeria, and Unife Guerilla Theatre, 1978. Visiting professor at Yale University, 1979-80, and Cornell University, 1986. Acted in and directed plays for stage, film, and radio.

*MEMBER:* International Theatre Institute (president), Union of Writers of the African Peoples (secretary-general), Committee of Writers for Individual Liberty (secretary).

*AWARDS, HONORS:* Rockefeller Foundation grant, 1960; John Whiting Drama Prize, 1966; Dakar Negro Arts Festival award, 1966; Jock Campbell Award, *New Statesman,* 1968, for *The Interpreters;* Nobel Prize for Literature, 1986; named Commander of the Federal Republic of Nigeria by General Ibrahim Babangida, 1986; D.Litt., University of Leeds, 1973, Yale University, University of Montpellier, France, and University of Lagos; Prisoner of Conscience Prize, Amnesty International.

*WRITINGS:*

POETRY

*Idanre and Other Poems,* Methuen, 1967, Hill & Wang, 1968.
*Poems from Prison,* Rex Collings, 1969, expanded edition published as *A Shuttle in the Crypt,* Hill & Wang, 1972.
(Editor and author of introduction) *Poems of Black Africa,* Hill & Wang, 1975.
*Ogun Abibiman,* Rex Collings, 1976.
*Mandela's Earth and Other Poems,* Random House, 1988.

PLAYS

*The Swamp Dwellers* (broadcast on BBC African Service, 1969), produced in London, 1958.
*The Invention,* first produced in London at Royal Court Theatre, 1959.

*The Lion and the Jewel* (first produced at Royal Court Theatre, 1966), Oxford University Press, 1962.

*Three Plays* (includes *The Trials of Brother Jero, The Strong Breed,* and *The Swamp Dwellers*), Mbari Publications, 1962, Northwestern University Press, 1963, published as *Three Short Plays,* Oxford University Press, 1969.

*A Dance of the Forests* (produced in London, England, 1960), Oxford University Press, 1963.

*The Republican,* produced in Ibadan, Nigeria, 1963.

*Five Plays* (includes *The Lion and the Jewel, The Swamp Dwellers, The Trials of Brother Jero, The Strong Breed,* and *A Dance of the Forests*), Oxford University Press, 1964.

*The (New) Republican,* produced in Ibadan, 1964.

*The Road* (produced in Stratford, England, at Theatre Royal, 1965), Oxford University Press, 1965.

*Kongi's Harvest* (produced in Lagos, Nigeria, 1965, produced Off-Broadway, 1968), Oxford University Press, 1966.

*The Strong Breed,* produced in Ibadan, 1966, and Off-Broadway, 1967.

*The Trials of Brother Jero* (one-act; produced Off-Broadway, 1967), Oxford University Press, 1969.

*Madmen and Specialists* (two-act; produced in Waterford, CT, 1970), Methuen, 1971, Hill & Wang, 1972.

*Before the Blackout* (revue sketches; produced in Ibadan, 1965), Orisun Acting Editions, 1971.

(Editor) *Plays from the Third World: An Anthology,* Doubleday, 1971.

*The Jero Plays* (includes *The Trials of Brother Jero* and *Jero's Metamorphosis*), Eyre Methuen, 1973.

*Camwood on the Leaves* (broadcast by Nigerian Broadcasting Corporation, 1960; produced in Lagos, 1982), Eyre Methuen, 1973, published with *Before the Blackout* as *Camwood on the Leaves and Before the Blackout,* Third Press, 1974.

(Adapter) *The Bacchae of Euripides: A Communion Rite* (first produced in London, 1973), Methuen, 1973, Norton, 1974.

*Collected Plays,* Oxford University Press, Volume 1, 1973, Volume 2, 1974.

*Jero's Metamorphosis,* produced in Bristol, England, 1974.

*Death and the King's Horseman* (first produced in Ife, Nigeria, 1976), Norton, 1975.

*Before the Blow-Out,* produced in Ife, 1978.

*Opera Wonyosi* (light opera; produced in Ife, 1977), Indiana University Press, 1981.

*Rice or Rice Scene,* produced in Lagos, 1981.

*Priority Projects,* produced in Ife, 1982.

*A Play of Giants* (produced in New Haven, CT, 1984), Methuen, 1984.

*Six Plays,* Methuen, 1984.

*Requiem for a Futurologist* (produced in Ife, 1983), Rex Collings, 1985.

*Before the Deluge,* produced in Lagos, 1991.

*A Scourge of Hyacinths,* broadcast by BBC Radio 4, 1991.

*From Zia, with Love* (produced in Siena, Italy, 1992), Fountain, 1992.

*"From Zia, with Love," and "A Scourge of Hyacinths,"* Methuen, 1992.

### FOR RADIO

*The Tortoise,* Nigerian Broadcasting Corporation, 1960.

*Broken-Time Bar* (series), WNBS (Lagos), 1961.

*The Detainee,* BBC African Service, 1965.

*Die Still, Rev'd Dr. Godspeak!,* BBC African Service, 1982.

### OTHER

*My Father's Burden* (for television), Western Nigerian Television, 1960.

*Night of the Hunted* (for television), Western Nigerian Television, 1961.

*The Interpreters* (novel), Deutsch, 1965, Collier, 1970.

(Translator) D. O. Fagunwa, *The Forest of a Thousand Daemons: A Hunter's Saga* (novel), Nelson, 1967.

*The Swamp Dwellers* (screenplay), Transcription Centre, 1967.

*Kongi's Harvest* (screenplay), Calpenny-Nigerian Films, 1970.

*The Man Died: Prison Notes of Wole Soyinka,* Harper, 1972.

*Season of Anomy* (novel), Rex Collings, 1973, Third Press/ Okpaku, 1974.

*Myth, Literature and the African World* (essays), Cambridge University Press, 1976.

*Ake: The Years of Childhood* (autobiography), Random House, 1981.

*The Critic and Society,* University of Ife Press, 1982.

*Unlimited Liability Company* (sound recording), Ewuro Productions, 1983.

*Art, Dialogue, and Outrage* (essays), New Horn, 1988.

*This Past Must Address Its Present,* Anson Phelps Stokes Institute, 1988.

*Isara: A Voyage around "Essay,"* (biography of the author's father), Random House, 1989.

*The Search: With Fountain Study Notes and Exercises,* Fountain Publications, 1989.

*The Credo of Being and Nothingness,* Spectrum, 1991.

Also author of commentary for film *Culture in Transition,* produced by Esso World Theatre, 1964; author of scenario for film *Blues for a Prodigal,* produced in Ife, 1985. Contributor to books, including *The Morality of Art,* edited by D. W. Jefferson, Routledge & Kegan Paul, 1969; *Palaver: Three Dramatic Discussion Starters,* Friendship Press, 1971; *And They Finally Killed Him: Speeches and Poems at a Memorial Rally for Walter Rodney (1942-80),* edited by Femi Falana and others, Positive Review, 1980; and *Criticism and Ideolo-*

*gy: Second African Writers' Conference, Stockholm, 1986,*
Scandinavian Institute of African Studies, 1988. Contributor
to periodials, including *Nigerian Herald, Guardian,* and *Black
American Literature Forum.* Co-editor, *Black Orpheus,* 1961-
64; editor, *Transition* (now *Ch'Indaba*), 1974-76.


*SIDELIGHTS:* Wole Soyinka was the first black African writer to win the Nobel Prize for literature and is considered by
many critics as Africa's finest writer. The Nigerian playwright's unique style blends traditional Yoruban folk-drama
with European dramatic form to provide both spectacle and
penetrating satire. Soyinka told *New York Times Magazine*
writer Jason Berry that in the African cultural tradition, the
artist "has always functioned as the record of the mores and
experience of his society." His plays, novels, and poetry all
reflect that philosophy, serving as a record of twentieth-century Africa's political turmoil and its struggle to reconcile tradition with modernization. Eldred Jones states in his book
*Wole Soyinka* that the author's work touches on universal
themes as well as addressing specifically African concerns:
"The essential ideas which emerge from a reading of Soyinka's
work are not specially African ideas, although his characters
and their mannerisms are African. His concern is with man
on earth. Man is dressed for the nonce in African dress and
lives in the sun and tropical forest, but he represents the whole
race."

As a young child, Soyinka was comfortable with the conflicting cultures in his world, but as he grew older he became increasingly aware of the pull between African tradition and
Western modernization. Ake, his village, was mainly populated wth people from the Yoruba tribe, and was presided over
by the *ogboni,* or tribal elders. Soyinka's grandfather introduced him to the pantheon of Yoruba gods and to other tribal
folklore. His parents were key representatives of colonial influences, however: his mother was a devout Christian convert
and his father acted as headmaster for the village school established by the British. When Soyinka's father began urging him to leave Ake to attend the government school in
Ibadan, the boy was spirited away by his grandfather, who
administered a scarification rite of manhood. Soyinka was also
consecrated to the god Ogun, ruler of metal, roads, and both
the creative and destructive essence. Ogun is a recurring figure in Soyinka's work and has been named by the author as
his muse.

*Ake: The Years of Childhood,* Soyinka's account of his first
ten years, stands as "a classic of childhood memoirs wherever and whenever produced," states *New York Times Book
Review* contributor James Olney. Numerous critics have singled out Soyinka's ability to recapture the changing perspective of a child as the book's outstanding feature; it begins in a
light tone but grows increasingly serious as the boy matures

and becomes aware of the problems faced by the adults around
him. The book concludes with an account of a tax revolt organized by Soyinka's mother and the beginnings of Nigerian
independence. "Most of 'Ake' charms; that was Mr. Soyinka's
intention," writes John Leonard of the *New York Times.* "The
last 5O pages, however, inspire and confound; they are transcendent." Olney agrees that "the lyricism, grace, humor and
charm of 'Ake' ... are in the service of a profoundly serious
viewpoint that attempts to show us how things should be in
the community of men and how they should not be. Mr.
Soyinka, however, does this dramatically, not discursively.
Through recollection, restoration and re-creation, he conveys
a personal vision that was formed by the childhood world that
he now returns to evoke and exalt in his autobiography. This
is the ideal circle of autobiography at its best. It is what makes
'Ake,' in addition to its other great virtues, the best introduction available to the work of one of the liveliest, most exciting writers in the world today."

Soyinka published some poems and short stories in *Black
Orpheus,* a highly regarded Nigerian literary magazine, before leaving Africa to attend the University of Leeds in England. There his first play was produced. *The Invention* is a
comic satire based on a sudden loss of pigment by South Africa's black population. Unable to distinguish blacks from
whites and thus enforce its apartheid policies, the government
is thrown into chaos. "The play is Soyinka's sole direct treatment of the political situation in Africa," notes Thomas Hayes
in the *Dictionary of Literary Biography Yearbook: 1986.*
Soyinka returned to Nigeria in 1960, shortly after independence from colonial rule had been declared. He began to research Yoruba folklore and drama in depth and incorporated
elements of both into his play *A Dance of the Forests.*


*A Dance of the Forests* was commissioned as part of Nigeria's independence celebrations. In his play, Soyinka warned
the newly independent Nigerians that the end of colonial rule
did not mean an end to their country's problems. It shows a
bickering group of mortals who summon up the *egungun* (spirits of the dead, revered by the Yoruba people) for a festival.
They have presumed the *egungun* to be noble and wise, but
they discover that their ancestors are as petty and spiteful as
any living people. "The whole concept ridicules the African
viewpoint that glorifies the past at the expense of the present,"
suggests John F. Povey in *Tri-Quarterly.* "The sentimental-
ized glamor of the past is exposed so that the same absurdities may not be reenacted in the future. This constitutes a bold
assertion to an audience awaiting an easy appeal to racial heroics." Povey also praises Soyinka's skill in using dancing,
drumming, and singing to reinforce his theme: "The dramatic power of the surging forest dance [in the play] carries its
own visual conviction. It is this that shows Soyinka to be a
man of the theatre, not simply a writer."

After warning against living in nostalgia for Africa's past in *A Dance of the Forests,* Soyinka lampooned the indiscriminate embrace of Western modernization in *The Lion and the Jewel.* A *Times Literary Supplement* reviewer calls this play a "richly ribald comedy," which combines poetry and prose "with a marvellous lightness in the treatment of both." The plot revolves around Sidi, the village beauty, and the rivalry between her two suitors. Baroka is the village chief, an old man with many wives; Lakunle is the enthusiastically Westernized schoolteacher who dreams of molding Sidi into a "civilized" woman. In *Introduction to Nigerian Literature,* Eldred Jones comments that *The Lion and the Jewel* is "a play which is so easily (and erroneously) interpreted as a clash between progress and reaction, with the play coming down surprisingly in favour of reaction. The real clash is not between old and new or between real progress and reaction. It is a clash between the genuine and the false; between the well-done and the half-baked. Lakunle the school teacher would have been a poor symbol of any desirable kind of progress.... He is a man of totally confused values. [Baroka's worth lies in] the traditional values of which he is so confident and in which he so completely outmaneouvres Lakunle who really has no values at all." Bruce King, editor of *Introduction to Nigerian Literature,* names *The Lion and the Jewel* "the best literary work to come out of Africa."

Soyinka was well established as Nigeria's premier playwright when in 1965 he published his first novel, *The Interpreters.* The novel allowed him to expand on themes already expressed in his stage dramas and to present a sweeping view of Nigerian life in the years immediately following independence. Essentially plotless, *The Interpreters* is loosely structured around the informal discussions among five young Nigerian intellectuals. Each has been educated in a foreign country and returned hoping to shape Nigeria's destiny. They are hampered by their own confused values, however, as well as the corruption they encounter everywhere. Some reviewers liken Soyinka's writing style in *The Interpreters* to that of James Joyce and William Faulkner. Others take exception to the formless quality of the novel, but Eustace Palmer asserts in *The Growth of the African Novel:* "If there are reservations about the novel's structure, there can be none about the thoroughness of the satire at society's expense. Soyinka's wide-ranging wit takes in all sections of a corrupt society—the brutal masses, the aimless intellectuals, the affected and hypocritical university dons, the vulgar and corrupt businessmen, the mediocre civil servants, the illiterate politicians and the incompetent journalists. [The five main characters are all] talented intellectuals who have retained their African consciousness although they were largely educated in the western world. Yet their western education enables them to look at their changing society with a certain amount of detachment. They are therefore uniquely qualified to be interpreters of this society. The reader is impressed by their honesty, sincerity, moral idealism, concern for truth and

justice and aversion to corruption, snobbery and hypocrisy; but anyone who assumes that Soyinka presents all the interpreters as models of behaviour will be completely misreading the novel. He is careful to expose their selfishness, egoism, cynicism and aimlessness. Indeed the conduct of the intellectuals both in and out of the university is a major preoccupation of Soyinka's in this novel. The aimlessness and superficiality of the lives of most of the interpreters is patent."

Neil McEwan points out in *Africa and the Novel* that for all its seriousness, *The Interpreters* is also "among the liveliest of recent novels in English. It is bright satire full of good sense and good humour which are African and contemporary: the highest spirits of its author's early work.... Behind the jokes of his novel is a theme that he has developed angrily elsewhere: that whatever progress may mean for Africa it is not a lesson to be learned from outside, however much of 'modernity' Africans may share with others." McEwan further observes that although *The Interpreters* does not have a rigidly structured plot, "there is unity in the warmth and sharpness of its comic vision. There are moments which sadden or anger; but they do not diminish the fun." Palmer notes that *The Interpreters* notably influenced the African fiction that followed it, shifting the focus "from historical, cultural and sociological analysis to penetrating social comment and social satire."

The year *The Interpreters* was published, 1965, also marked Soyinka's first arrest by the Nigerian police. He was accused of using a gun to force a radio announcer to broadcast incorrect election results. No evidence was ever produced, however, and the PEN writers' organization launched a protest campaign, headed by William Styron and Norman Mailer. Soyinka was released after three months. He was next arrested two years later, during Nigeria's civil war. Soyinka was completely opposed to the conflict, and especially to the Nigerian Government's brutal policies toward the Ibo people who were attempting to form their own country, Biafra. He traveled to Biafra to establish a peace commission composed of leading intellectuals from both sides; when he returned, the Nigerian police accused him of helping the Biafrans to buy jet fighters. Once again he was imprisoned. This time Soyinka was held for more than two years, although he was never formally charged with any crime. Most of that time he was kept in solitary confinement. When all of his fellow prisoners were vaccinated against meningitis, Soyinka was passed by; when he developed serious vision problems, they were ignored by his jailers. He was denied reading and writing materials, but he manufactured his own ink and began to keep a prison diary, written on toilet paper, cigarette packages and in between the lines of the few books he secretly obtained. Each poem or fragment of journal he managed to smuggle to the outside world became a literary event and a reassurance to his supporters that Soyinka still lived, despite rumors to the contrary. He was released in 1969 and left Nigeria soon after, not returning until a change of power took place in 1975.

Published as *The Man Died: Prison Notes of Wole Soyinka,* the author's diary constitutes "the most important work that has been written about the Biafran war," believes Charles R. Larson, contributor to *Nation.* "'The Man Died' is not so much the story of Wole Soyinka's own temporary death during the Nigerian Civil War but a personified account of Nigeria's fall from sanity, documented by one of the country's leading intellectuals." Gerald Weales's *New York Times Book Review* article suggests that the political content of *The Man Died* is less fascinating than "the notes that deal with prison life, the observation of everything from a warder's catarrh to the predatory life of insects after a rain. Of course, these are not simply reportorial. They are vehicles to carry the author's shifting states of mind, to convey the real subject matter of the book; the author's attempt to survive as a man, and as a mind. The notes are both a means to that survival and a record to it." Larson underlines the book's political impact, however, noting that ironically, "while other Nigerian writers were emotionally castrated by the war, Soyinka, who was placed in solitary confinement so that he wouldn't embarrass the government, was writing work after work, books that will no doubt embarrass the Nigerian Government more than anything the Ibo writers may ever publish." A *Times Literary Supplement* reviewer concurs, characterizing *The Man Died* as "a damning indictment of what Mr. Soyinka sees as the iniquities of wartime Nigeria and the criminal tyranny of its administration in peacetime."

Many literary commentators feel that Soyinka's work changed profoundly after his prison term, darkening in tone and focusing on the war and its aftermath. In the *Dictionary of Literary Biography Yearbook: 1986,* Hayes quotes Soyinka on his concerns after the war: "I have one abiding religion—human liberty.... conditioned to the truth that life is meaningless, insulting, without this fullest liberty, and in spite of the despairing knowledge that words alone seem unable to guarantee its possession, my writing grows more and more preoccupied with the theme of the oppressive boot, the irrelevance of the color of the foot that wears it and the struggle for individuality."

In spite of its satire, most critics had found *The Interpreters* to be ultimately an optimistic book. In contrast, Soyinka's second novel expresses almost no hope for Africa's future, says John Mellors in *London Magazine:* "Wole Soyinka appears to have written much of *Season of Anomy* in a blazing fury, angry beyond complete control of words at the abuses of power and the outbreaks of both considered and spontaneous violence.... The plot charges along, dragging the reader (not because he doesn't want to go, but because he finds it hard to keep up) through forest, mortuary and prison camp in nightmare visions of tyranny, torture, slaughter and putrefaction. The book reeks of pain.... Soyinka hammers at the point that the liberal has to deal with violence in the world however much he would wish he could ignore it; the scenes of murder and mutilation, while sickeningly explicit, are justifed by ... the author's anger and compassion and insistence that bad will not become better by our refusal to examine it."

Like *Season of Anomy,* Soyinka's postwar plays are considered more brooding than his earlier work. "Madmen and Specialists" is called "grim" by Martin Banham and Clive Wake in *African Theatre Today.* In the play, a doctor returns from the war trained as a specialist in torture and uses his new skills on his father. The play's major themes are "the loss of faith and rituals" and "the break-up of the family unit which traditionally in Africa has been the foundation of society," according to Charles Larson in the *New York Times Book Review.* Names and events in the play are fictionalized to avoid censorship, but Soyinka has clearly "leveled a wholesale criticism of life in Nigeria since the Civil War: a police state in which only madmen and spies can survive, in which the losers are mad and the winners are paranoid about the possibility of another rebellion. The prewar corruption and crime have returned, supported by the more sophisticated acts of terrorism and espionage introduced during the war." Larson summarizes: "In large part 'Madmen and Specialists' is a product of those months Soyinka spent in prison, in solitary confinement, as a political prisoner. It is, not surprisingly, the most brutal piece of social criticism he has published." In a similar tone, *A Play of Giants* presents four African leaders—thinly disguised versions of Jean Bedel Bokassa, Sese Seko Mobutu, Macias Ngeuma, and Idi Amin—meeting at the United Nations building, where "their conversation reflects the corruption and cruelty of their regimes and the casual, brutal flavor of their rule," discloses Hayes. In Hayes's opinion, *A Play of Giants* demonstrates that "as Soyinka has matured he has hardened his criticism of all that restricts the individual's ability to choose, think, and act free from external oppression.... [It is] his harshest attack against modern Africa, a blunt, venomous assault on ... African leaders and the powers who support them."

In *Isara: A Voyage around "Essay,"* Soyinka provides a portrait of his father as well as "vivid sketches of characters and culturally intriguing events that cover a period of 15 years," Charles Johnson relates in the *Washington Post.* The narrative follows S. A., or "Essay," and his classmates through his years at St. Simeon's Teacher Training Seminary in Ilesa. Aided by documents left to him in a tin box, Soyinka dramatizes the changes that profoundly affected his father's life. The Great Depression that brought the Western world to its knees during the early 1930s was a time of economic opportunity for Africans. The quest for financial gain transformed African culture, as did Mussolini's invasion of Ethiopia and the onset of World War II. More threatening was the violent civil war for the throne following the death of their king. An aged peacemaker named Agunrin resolved the conflict by an appeal to the people's common past. "As each side presents its case, Agunrin, half listening, sinks into memories that unfold his people's collective history, and finally he speaks, finding his voice in a scene so masterfully rendered it alone is worth the price of the book," Johnson claims. The book is neither a strict biography nor a straight historical account. However, "in his effort to expose Western readers to a unique, African perspective on the war years, Soyinka succeeds brilliantly," Johnson comments. *New York Times* reviewer Michiko Kakutani writes that, in addition, "Essay emerges as a high-minded teacher, a mentor and companion, blessed with dignity and strong ideals, a father who inspired his son to achievement."

"Much of Soyinka's work since *Isara* has been an attempt to salvage something of value from the failed hopes of the heirs to the colonialists, and the tone of his writing over the last few years is often desperate," says James Gibbs in the *Dictionary of Literary Biography*. In recent years Soyinka has continued efforts to reduce the accidents on Nigerian roads and has been campaigning to introduce a new system of drivers licenses to curb the problem. Although Gibbs notes that it might seem strange for a writer of Soyinka's status to be campaigning for minor things such as license reforms, he finds the action characteristic of Soyinka's attempts to better Nigerian society in very pragmatic ways. However, Soyinka has also acted on his concerns through creative writing, and *Before the Deluge,* a satirical revue staged in 1991, is one such example. In this production, says Gibbs, Soyinka variously criticizes the gutter press and expresses his disagreement with violent solutions proposed for urban housing problems.

Soyinka's writing continues to verbalize his concern over social issues in *A Scourge for Hyacinths* and *From Zia, with Love.* Gibbs explains that both texts are different versions of the same play, where the first one was written for "a radio audience with limited knowledge of the intricacies of Nigerian politics." The story revolves around the conviction of Miguel Domingo, accused of a crime that, in hindsight, is seen as a capital crime. The plot derives from actual legislation in Nigeria in the 1980s, and it aggravated Soyinka immensely.

Soyinka's work is frequently described as demanding but rewarding reading. Although his plays are widely praised, they are seldom performed, especially outside of Africa. The dancing and choric speech often found in them are unfamiliar and difficult for non-African actors to master, a problem Holly Hill notes in her London *Times* review of the Lincoln Center Theatre production of *Death and the King's Horseman.* She

awards high praise to the play, however, saying it "has the stateliness and mystery of Greek tragedy." When the Swedish Academy awarded Soyinka the Nobel Prize in Literature in 1986, its members singled out *Death and the King's Horseman* and *A Dance of the Forests* as "evidence that Soyinka is 'one of the finest poetical playwrights that have written in English'," reports Stanley Meisler of the *Los Angeles Times.* The citation, says Gibbs, described Soyinka as "a writer who in a wide cultural perspective and with poetic overtones fashions the drama of existence." Soyinka himself did not see the prize as an award meant solely for him as an individual but said that it was a tribute to "all the others who [had] laid the basis and were the source from which [he] could draw." He also saw the award as a means of providing recognition for the African world. Hayes summarizes Soyinka's importance: "His drama and fiction have challenged the West to broaden its aesthetic and accept African standards of art and literature. His personal and political life have challenged Africa to embrace the truly democratic values of the African tribe and reject the tyranny of power practiced on the continent by its colonizers and by many of its modern rulers."

*BIOGRAPHICAL/CRITICAL SOURCES:*

*BOOKS*

Banham, Martin and Clive Wake, *African Theatre Today,* Pitman Publishing, 1976.

Banham, *Wole Soyinka's "The Lion and the Jewel,"* Rex Collings, 1981.

*Contemporary Literary Criticism,* Gale, Volume 3, 1975; Volume 5, 1976; Volume 14, 1980; Volume 36, 1986; Volume 44, 1987.

*Dictionary of Literary Biography Yearbook: 1986,* Gale, 1987.

*Dictionary of Literary Biography,* Volume 125: *Twentieth-Century Caribbean and Black African Writers, Second Series,* Gale, 1993.

Dunton, C. P., *Notes on "Three Short Plays,"* Longman, 1982.

Gakwandi, Shatto Arthur, *The Novel and Contemporary Experience in America,* Heinemann, 1977.

Gibbs, James, editor, *Study Aid to "Kongi's Harvest,"* Rex Collings, 1973.

Gibbs, editor, *Critical Perspectives on Wole Soyinka,* Three Continents, 1980.

Gibbs, editor, *Notes on "The Lion and the Jewel,"* Longman, 1982.

Gibbs, *Wole Soyinka,* Macmillan, 1986.

Gibbs, Ketu Katrak and Henry Louis Gates, Jr., editors, *Wole Soyinka: A Bibliography of Primary and Secondary Sources,* Greenwood Press, 1986.

Goodwin, K. L., *Understanding African Poetry,* Heinemann, 1979.

Jones, Eldred, editor, *African Literature Today, Number 5: The Novel in Africa,* Heinemann, 1971.

Jones, editor, *African Literature Today, Number 6: Poetry in Africa*, Heinemann, 1973.

Jones, *Wole Soyinka*, Twayne, 1973 (published in England as *The Writings of Wole Soyinka*, Heinemann, 1973).

Katrak, Ketu, *Wole Soyinka and Modern Tragedy: A Study of Dramatic Theory and Practice*, Greenwood Press, 1986.

King, Bruce, editor, *Introduction to Nigerian Literature*, Africana Publishing, 1972.

Larson, Charles R., *The Emergence of African Fiction*, revised edition, Indiana University Press, 1972.

Laurence, Margaret, *Long Drums and Cannons: Nigerian Dramatists and Novelists*, Praeger, 1968.

McEwan, Neil, *Africa and the Novel*, Humanities Press, 1983.

Moore, Gerald, *Wole Soyinka*, Africana Publishing, 1971.

Morell, Karen L., editor, *In Person—Achebe, Awoonor, and Soyinka at the University of Washington*, African Studies Program, Institute for Comparative and Foreign Area Studies, University of Washington, 1975.

Ogunba, Oyin, *The Movement of Transition: A Study of the Plays of Wole Soyinka*, Ibadan University Press, 1975.

Ogunba and others, editors, *Theatre in Africa*, Ibadan University Press, 1978.

Palmer, Eustace, *The Growth of the African Novel*, Heinemann, 1979.

Parsons, E. M., editor, *Notes on Wole Soyinka's "The Jero Plays,"* Methuen, 1982.

Pieterse, Cosmo, and Dennis Duerden, editors, *African Writers Talking: A Collection of Radio Interviews*, Africana Publishing, 1972.

Probyn, editor, *Notes on "The Road,"* Longman, 1981.

Ricard, Alain, *Theatre et Nationalisme: Wole Soyinka et LeRoi Jones*, Presence Africaine, 1972.

Roscoe, Adrian A., *Mother Is Gold: A Study in West African Literature*, Cambridge University Press, 1971.

Soyinka, Wole, *The Man Died: Prison Notes of Wole Soyinka*, Harper, 1972.

Soyinka, *Myth, Literature and the African World*, Cambridge University Press, 1976.

Soyinka, *Ake: The Years of Childhood*, Random House, 1981.

Tucker, Martin, *Africa in Modern Literature: A Survey of Contemporary Writing in English*, Ungar, 1967.

PERIODICALS

*America*, February 12, 1983.
*Ariel*, July, 1981.
*Black Orpheus*, March, 1966.
*Book Forum*, Volume 3, number 1, 1977.
*Books Abroad*, summer, 1972; spring, 1973.
*British Book News*, December, 1984; April, 1986.
*Chicago Tribune Book World*, October 7, 1979.
*Christian Science Monitor*, July 31, 1970; August 15, 1970.
*Commonweal*, February 8, 1985.

*Detroit Free Press*, March 20, 1983; October 17, 1986.
*Detroit News*, November 21, 1982.
*Globe and Mail* (Toronto), June 7, 1986; January 6, 1990.
*London Magazine*, April/May, 1974.
*Los Angeles Times*, October 17, 1986.
*Los Angeles Times Book Review*, October 15, 1989.
*Nation*, October 11, 1965; April 29, 1968; September 15, 1969; November 10, 1969; October 2, 1972; November 5, 1973.
*New Republic*, October 12, 1974; May 9, 1983.
*New Statesman*, December 20, 1968.
*Newsweek*, November 1, 1982.
*New Yorker*, May 16, 1977.
*New York Review of Books*, July 31, 1969; October 21, 1982.
*New York Times*, November 11, 1965; April 19, 1970; August 11, 1972; September 23, 1982; May 29, 1986; May 31, 1986; June 15, 1986; October 17, 1986; November 9, 1986; March 1, 1987; March 2, 1987; November 3, 1989.
*New York Times Book Review*, July 29, 1973; December 24, 1973; October 10, 1982; January 15, 1984; November 12, 1989.
*New York Times Magazine*, September 18, 1983.
*Research in African Literatures*, spring, 1983.
*Saturday Review/World*, October 19, 1974.
*Spectator*, November 6, 1959; December 15, 1973; November 24, 1981.
*Time*, October 27, 1986.
*Times* (London), October 17, 1986; April 6, 1987; March 15, 1990.
*Times Literary Supplement*, April 1, 1965; June 10, 1965; January 18, 1968; December 31, 1971; March 2, 1973; December 14, 1973; February 8, 1974; March 1, 1974; October 17, 1975; August 5, 1977; February 26, 1982; September 23, 1988; March 22-29, 1990.
*Tribune Books* (Chicago), November 19, 1989.
*Tri-Quarterly*, fall, 1966.
*Village Voice*, August 31, 1982.
*Washington Post*, October 30, 1979; October 17, 1986; November 10, 1989.
*World*, February 13, 1973.
*World Literature Today*, winter, 1977; autumn, 1981; summer, 1982.

\*   \*   \*

## SPENCER, Anne 1882-1975

*PERSONAL:* Original name, Annie Bethel Scales Bannister; born February 6, 1882, in Henry County, VA; died of cancer, July 27, 1975, in Lynchburg, VA; daughter of Joel Cephus (a saloon owner) and Sarah Louise Scales Bannister; married Edward Spencer (first parcel postman in Lynchburg, VA) in

1901; children: Bethel, Alroy and Chauncey. *Education:* Virginia Seminary and College (graduated from secondary division as class valedictorian), 1899. *Religion:* Methodist and later Baptist. *Avocational interests:* Horticulture, volunteering in community.

*CAREER:* Poet, librarian. Virginia Seminary, Lynchburg, VA, teacher; Jones Memorial Library, Lynchburg, VA, 1923; Dunbar High School branch library, Lynchburg, VA, librarian, 1924-1945.

*WRITINGS:*

Contributor of poems to anthologies, including *The Book of American Negro Poetry,* edited by James Weldon Johnson, 1922; *Negro Poets and Their Poems,* edited by Robert Kerlin, 1923; *American Poetry since 1900,* edited by Louis Untermeyer, 1923; *Caroling Dusk,* edited by Countee Cullen, 1927; *Ebony and Topaz,* edited by Charles S. Johnson, 1927; *The New Negro,* edited by Locke, 1968; *The Poetry of the Negro, 1746-1970,* edited by Langston Hughes and Arna Bontemps, 1970; and *Black Sister,* edited by Stetson, 1981. Contributor of poems to journals, including *Crisis, Palms, Opportunity, Lyric,* and *Survey Graphic.* Forty-two of her poems are reproduced in the appendix of *Time's Unfading Garden: Anne Spencer's Life and Poetry,* edited by J. Lee Greene, Louisiana State University Press, 1977.

*SIDELIGHTS:* According to Sharon G. Dean, writing in the *Dictionary of Literary Biography,* many critics consider Anne Spencer "the most technically sophisticated and modern poet of the Harlem, or New Negro, Renaissance" of the 1920s and 1930s. However, only about 30 of her poems were published during her lifetime, and much of her unpublished work was accidentally destroyed while she was hospitalized shortly before her death. A collection of her papers can be found at the Anne Spencer House Historic Landmark in Lynchburg, VA, and some of her letters are preserved at Yale University's Beinecke Rare Book and Manuscript Library.

*BIOGRAPHICAL/CRITICAL SOURCES:*

BOOKS

*Dictionary of Literary Biography,* Volume 51: *Afro-American Writers from the Harlem Renaissance to 1940,* Gale, 1987, pp. 252-259; Volume 54: *American Poets, 1880-1945,* Gale, 1987, pp. 420-427.
Roses, Lorraine Elena, and Ruth Elizabeth Randolph, *Harlem Renaissance and Beyond: Literary Biographies of 100 Women Black Writers, 1900-1945,* G. K. Hall, 1990, pp. 298-303.

Rush, Theressa Gunnels, Carol Fairbanks Myers and Esther Spring Arata, *Black American Writers Past and Present,* Scarecrow Press, 1975, pp. 678-679.

\* \* \*

**STEINER, K. Leslie**
 **See DELANY, Samuel R(ay, Jr.)**

\* \* \*

**STEPHEN, Felix N. 1925-**

*PERSONAL:* Born 1925 in eastern Nigeria.

*CAREER:* Fiction writer.

*WRITINGS:*

*NOVELETTES*

*The Life Story of Boys and Girls,* Chinyelu Printing Press, 1962.
*How to Play Love,* Njokuandsons, 1963.
*The Trials and Death of Lumumba,* M. Allan Ohaejesi, 1963.
*The Temple of Love,* B.C. Okara and Sons, 1964.
*Pamphlet Literature from Onitsha,* Kraus Reprint, 1965.
*Lack of Money Is Not Lack of Sense,* Chinyelu Printing Press, 1966.

*OTHER*

"The Sweetness of Love," in *The Work of Love* by Cyril Nwakuma Ariruguzo, Ariruguzo and Sons, 1963.

Also author of *How to Speak and Write to Girls for Friendship,* published by Njoko and Sons.

\* \* \*

**STERN, Harold S. 1923(?)-1976**

*PERSONAL:* Born c. 1923; died May 25, 1976.

*CAREER:* Drama critic, magazine editor, and fiction writer.

*MEMBER:* National Academy of Recording Arts and Sciences.

*WRITINGS:*

*Blackland* (novel), Doubleday, 1970.

Drama and nightclub critic for the *Brooklyn Eagle* and drama critic for WNEW-AM. Syndicated columnist for Woman's News Service, North American Newspaper Alliance, Inter-Press Feature Syndicate, and King Features. Contributing editor, *After Dark* magazine; editor, *Youth Beat, Applause,* and *Broadway Sign Post;* entertainment editor, Bell-McClure Syndicate.

*OBITUARIES:*

*PERIODICALS*

*New York Times,* May 30, 1976.

\*    \*    \*

## STONE, Charles Sumner, Jr. 1924-
## (Chuck Stone)

*PERSONAL:* Born July 21, 1924, in St. Louis, MO; son of Charles Sumner and Madalene (Chafin) Stone; married Louise Davis, October 4, 1958; children: Krishna, Allegra, Charles III. *Education:* Wesleyan University, A.B., 1948; University of Chicago, M.A., 1950.

*ADDRESSES: Office*—Philadelphia Daily News, Philadelphia, PA.

*CAREER:* Regional field representative for World Politics and American Foreign Policy adult education discussion programs, 1952-56; Cooperative for American Relief Everywhere (CARE), New York City, overseas representative to Egypt, Gaza, and India, 1956-57; *New York Age,* New York City, editorial consultant, 1957-58, editor, 1958-60; American Committee on Africa, New York City, associate director, 1960; *Washington Afro-American,* Washington, DC, editor, White House correspondent, 1960-63; *Chicago Daily Defender,* Chicago, IL, editor-in-chief, 1963-64; Columbia College, lecturer in journalism, 1963-64; special assistant to U.S. Congressman Adam Clayton Powell, 1965-67; editorial research specialist for U.S. Congressman Robert N.C. Nix, 1968; Trinity College, Hartford, CN, John T. Dorrance Visiting Professor of Government, 1969; National Broadcasting Company, Inc. (NBC-TV), New York City, commentator on *Today* show, 1969-70; Educational Testing Service, Princeton, NJ, director of minority affairs and educational opportunities, 1970-72; Antioch-Putney Graduate School of Education, Philadelphia, PA, lecturer in sociology, 1973; *Philadelphia*

*Daily News* and Universal Press Syndicate, Philadelphia, PA, columnist, 1973—; member of National Workshop on Testing in Education and Employment steering committee, Creative and Visual Arts Panel, American Revolution Bicentennial Commission, and Wesleyan University board of trustees, and Pennsylvania State Board of Colleges and University Directors. *Military service:* U.S. Army Air Forces, 1943-45.

*MEMBER:* National Conference of Black Political Scientists, black Academy of Arts and Letters (fellow and founding member).

*AWARDS, HONORS:* Award for best column of the year from National Newspaper Publishers Association, 1960; named "Journalist of the Year" by Capital Press Club, Washington, DC, 1961; Annual Distinguished Citizen's award from Frontiers International, Inc., Washington, DC, 1963; named "Outstanding Citizen of the Year" by Congress of Racial Equality (CORE), Chicago chapter, 1964; Award of Merit for journalism, from Alpha Phi Alpha, Chicago, IL, 1965; Politician-in-Residence at Morgan State College Institute of Political Education, 1969; named "Alpha Man of the Year" by Alpha Phi Alpha, Philadelphia, PA, 1973.

*WRITINGS:*

(Under name Chuck Stone) *Tell It Like It Is* (essays), Trident, 1968.
*Black Political Power in America,* Bobbs-Merrill, 1968.
*King Strut* (novel), Bobbs-Merrill, 1970.

Work represented in anthologies, including *The Black Power Revolt: A Collection of Essays,* edited by Floyd Barbour, Sargent, 1968. Contributing editor, *Black Scholar;* member of board of advisers, *Contact.*

*SIDELIGHTS:* As an editor and columnist with Black newspapers in three large American cities, Stone has been recognized as an outstanding journalist. A reviewer in *Best Sellers* called his first collection of essays, *Tell It Like It Is,* "a welcome addition to the thoughtful Negro approach to the racial situation in the United States." "Emphasizing Stone's objectivity, the reviewer added: "Stone is neither an Uncle Tom nor a torch-throwing rioter. What he has to say is sound common sense said with trenchant humor and pungent wit."

Oscar A. Bouise noted Stone's "microscopic scrutiny" of the "political panorama" in *Black Political Power in America,* declaring: "He rakes the coals of party politics; he digs into the ashes of big city machines, revealing some interesting secrets of racial, national, religious, and underworld politics. He probes the North; he slaps the South. He lays bare personalities and secret weapons of success in what is revealed as a dirty game of survival of the fittest, the most wily, the most conscienceless—even sometimes the most inhumane." While acknowledging that Stone possesses the "gift of a good journalist: the facile statement," Bouise also observed that this style is "at times too glib for a real historical study" leading Stone into "portraying politicians as extremes." Bouise called *Black Political Power in America* a "book which had to be written" and concluded that "no writer is better equipped than Chuck Stone is for the task." Citing Stone's "facile style,... love of creative language and expression,... keen wit,... dedication to the subject," Bouise said the author's technique "cannot be equalled, let alone surpassed."

Stone's experiences in Washington, first as an assistant to Representative Adam Clayton Powell, then to Representative Robert N.C. Nix, inspired his novel, *King Strut*. Oscar Bouise called it "a hard hitting book" with a "tongue-in-cheek manner." Again he praised Stone as a "stylist of the first order (journalistic, that is)" and labeled him a "heavy-handed, bludgeon-wielding, Swiftian satirist." "This could be a serious book, if it were not so funny," wrote Bouise, "[and] it would be a funny book if it were not so serious."

*BIOGRAPHICAL/CRITICAL SOURCES:*

*PERIODICALS*

*Best Sellers*, February 1; 1968, December 1, 1968; November 15, 1970.
*Washington Post*, July 11, 1969.

\*　\*　\*

**STONE, Chuck**
  **See STONE, Charles Sumner, Jr.**

\*　\*　\*

**STRONG MAN OF THE PEN, The**
  **See OLISAH, Sunday Okenwa**

# T-V

## TATE, Eleanora E(laine) 1948-

*PERSONAL:* Born April 16, 1948, in Canton, MO; daughter of Clifford and Lillie (Douglas) Tate (raised by her grandmother, Corinne E. Johnson); married Zack E. Hamlett III (a photographer), August 19, 1972; children: Gretchen R. *Education:* Drake University, B.A., 1973.

*ADDRESSES: Home*—1203 Carver St., Myrtle Beach, SC 29577. *Office*—Positive Images, Inc., 1203 Carver St., P.O. Box 483, Myrtle Beach, SC 29578. *Agent*—Charlotte Sheedy, Charlotte Sheedy Literary Agency, 145 West 86th St., New York, NY 10024.

*CAREER: Iowa Bystander,* West Des Moines, news editor, 1966-68; *Des Moines Register* and *Des Moines Tribune,* Des Moines, IA, staff writer, 1968-76; *Jackson Sun,* Jackson, TN, staff writer, 1976-77; Kreative Koncepts, Inc., Myrtle Beach, SC, writer and researcher, 1979-81; Positive Images, Inc., Myrtle Beach, SC, president and co-owner (with husband, Zack E. Hamlett III), 1983—. Contributor to black history and culture workshops in Des Moines, IA, 1968-76; giver of poetry presentations, including Iowa Arts Council Writers in the Schools program, 1969-76, Rust College, 1973, and Grinnell College, 1975; free-lance writer for *Memphis Tri-State Defender,* 1977; guest author of South Carolina School Librarians Association Conference, 1981 and 1982; writer-in-residence, Elgin, SC, Chester, SC, and the Amana colonies, Middle, IA, all 1986.

*MEMBER:* National Association of Black Storytellers, Inc. (member of the board, 1988—), Arts in Basic Curriculum Steering Committee, South Carolina Academy of Authors (vice-president of the board of directors, 1988-90; member of the board, 1987—), South Carolina Arts Commission Artists in Education, Concerned Citizens Operation Reach-Out of Horry County, Horry Cultural Arts Council (president of the board of directors, 1990—).

*AWARDS, HONORS:* Finalist, fifth annual Third World Writing Contest, 1973; Unity Award, Lincoln University, 1974, for educational reporting; Community Lifestyles award, Tennessee Press Association, 1977; Bread Loaf Writer's Conference fellowship, 1981; *Just an Overnight Guest* (film) listed among the "Selected Films for Young Adults 1985" by the Young Adult Committee of the American Library Association; Parents' Choice Award, 1987; Presidential Award, National Association of Negro Business and Professional Women's Clubs, Georgetown chapter, 1988; Grand Strand Press Association Award, Second Place, for Social Responsibilities and Minority Affairs, 1988.

*WRITINGS:*

(Editor with husband, Zack E. Hamlett III, and contributor) *Eclipsed* (poetry), privately printed, 1975.
(Editor and contributor) *Wanjiru: A Collection of Blackwomanworth,* privately printed, 1976.
*Just an Overnight Guest,* Dial, 1980.
*The Secret of Gumbo Grove,* F. Watts, 1987.
*Thank You, Dr. Martin Luther King, Jr.!,* F. Watts, 1990.
*Front Porch Stories at the One-Room School,* Bantam/Skylark, 1992.

*CONTRIBUTOR*

Rosa Guy, editor, *Children of Longing,* Bantam, 1970.
*Impossible?* (juvenile), Houghton, 1972.
*Broadside Annual 1972,* Broadside Press, 1972.
*Communications* (juvenile), Heath, 1973.
*Off-Beat* (juvenile), Macmillan, 1974.
*Sprays of Rubies* (anthology of poetic prose), Ragnarok, 1975.
*Valhalla Four,* Ragnarok, 1977.

Contributor of poetry and fiction to periodicals, including *Journal of Black Poetry* and *Des Moines Register Picture Magazine.*

*ADAPTATIONS: Just an Overnight Guest* was adapted as a film starring Fran Robinson, Tiffany Hill, Rosalind Cash, and Richard Roundtree, Phoenix/B.F.A. Films & Video, 1983.

*WORK IN PROGRESS: A Woman for the People,* for adults; *Island Girl,* for juveniles.

*SIDELIGHTS:* Eleanora Tate was born in 1948 in Canton, a small town in northeastern Missouri, where during her early childhood legal segregation was still enforced. She attended first grade in 1954 at the town's one-room grade school for African Americans. The following year her class was integrated into Canton's white school system.

Tate's novels, each focusing on a young African American girl, are set in places she knows well. Her first novel, *Just an Overnight Guest*—told from the view of nine-year-old Margie Carson—takes place in Nutbrush, Missouri, a small town modeled after Canton. In the story Margie becomes angry when her mother invites Ethel Hardisen, a half-black, half-white four year old, to stay with the family for a night. Ethel, Margie said, "broke stuff, stole candy, threw rocks at people. Once she hit me in the back with a piece of concrete." Ethel's visit is mysteriously extended, despite her bad behavior, and Margie begins to see Ethel as competition for her parents' affection. Only at the end of the book does Margie learn that Ethel had been an abused, neglected child, whose father is Margie's irresponsible Uncle Jake.

Tate once explained that she wrote *Just an Overnight Guest* "to add my voice ... to the thought that children's childhoods can be happy if they can learn that they can do anything they set their minds to." The book, moreover, drew praise from critics. Merri Rosenberg of the *New York Times Book Review* wrote, "Eleanora Tate does a fine job presenting the emotional complexities of Margie's initiation into adult life's moral ambiguities.... If she drives home her point with a slightly heavy hand ... [she] has imbued the situation with enough realism to make it plausible." In the *Horn Book* magazine Celia Morris praises Tate for capturing "the nuances of small-town life, the warmth of a Black family struggling with a problem, and the volatile emotions of a young child."

In her second novel, *The Secret of Gumbo Grove,* the setting is similar to Myrtle Beach, South Carolina. The story, explains Tate, is about an eleven-year-old girl, Raisin Stackhouse, who "loves history, but she can't seem to find any positive Black history in her hometown of Gumbo Grove, South Carolina's most famous ocean-side resort, until she stumbles on to an old cemetery owned by her church.... The townspeople aren't too happy with her discovery [of the area's history of racial segregation] ... because they are ashamed with their own families' past." Linda Classen, writing in the *Voice of Youth Advocates,* considers the book important, for it gives "a feeling for life in a black community before blacks had rights, which ... not many young people today can comprehend." In the *Bulletin of the Center for Children's Books,* Betsy Hearne calls the ending, when Raisin is given a surprise community service award, "a bit tidy," although she goes on to say that the book "will be satisfying for young readers, who can enjoy this as a leisurely, expansive reading experience."

Also set in Gumbo Grove is Tate's third novel, *Thank You, Dr. Martin Luther King, Jr.!,* a story narrated by nine-year-old Mary Elouise, who is embarrassed about being black and who spends much of her energy trying to please a conceited, blond-haired classmate. She finds it especially embarrassing when her patronizing, uninformed white teacher effusively praises Martin Luther King, Jr. It eventually falls upon the grandmother to help Mary appreciate her black heritage.

Tate approaches this sensitive story with great care. In the *Bulletin of the Center for Children's Books,* Zena Sutherland, though critical of the book's "repetitive and slow paced" style, praises Tate for not falling prey to racial stereotyping. "One of the strong points of her story," Sutherland says, "is that there is bias in both races, just as there is understanding in both." *Booklist*'s Denise Wilms echoes this view: "Tate tackles a sensitive issue, taking pains to keep characters multidimensional and human."

Tate returns to Nutbrush, Missouri, for her next book, *Front Porch Stories at the One-Room School,* the sequel to *Just an Overnight Guest.* At the beginning Margie and Ethel, now three years older, are lying around on a hot summer night, so bored that their "life is duller than dirt." This problem, however, is solved when the father takes them on a walk to an old, one-room building, formerly the grade school for the town's African American children. The father then begins to tell a number of stories about his childhood, which not only entertain the children but also teach them something important about their heritage. In an afterward to the book, Tate reveals that "most of the stories that [the father] tells...are based on my own actual experiences, or on stories I heard and greatly embellished." Although *Publishers Weekly* found the book "somewhat heavy-handed," with a "stilted dialogue that at times borders on the saccharine," it also praised Tate's "evocative language," which "conjures up rural southern life." The book, moreover, points out Tate's special concern for father-daughter relationships. Tate once remarked: "It has been said little black boys need fathers. I believe little black girls need fathers. I emphasize that. It's something that hasn't been played up in recent years. I see it every day with my husband and my daughter."

BIOGRAPHICAL/CRITICAL SOURCES:

BOOKS

Rollock, Barbara T., *Black Authors and Illustrators of Children's Books: A Biographical Dictionary*, Garland, 1988, p. 115.

PERIODICALS

*Booklist,* April 15, 1990, p. 1636; August, 1992, p. 2014.
*Bulletin of the Center for Children's Books,* June, 1987, p. 199; June, 1990, p. 254.
*Des Moines Register,* March 1, 1981.
*Horn Book,* December, 1980, pp. 643-644.
*Myrtle Beach Sun News,* November 23, 1980.
*New York Times Book Review,* February 8, 1981, p. 20.
*Publishers Weekly,* August 10, 1992, p. 71.
*Voice of Youth Advocates,* August-September, 1987, p. 123.
*Washington Post Book World,* May 10, 1981.

—Sketch by Thomas Riggs

\* \* \*

## TAULBERT, Clifton L(emoure) 1945-

PERSONAL: Born February 19, 1945, in Glen Allan, MS; son of a preacher and Mary Morgan Taulbert; married December 22, 1973; wife's name, Barbara Ann; children: Marshall Danzy, Anne Kathryn.

ADDRESSES: *Office*—Freemount Corporation, 616 South Boston, Suite 302, Tulsa, OK 74119.

CAREER: University Village Inc., Tulsa, OK, administrator, beginning in 1972; Bank of Oklahoma, Tulsa, vice president of marketing; Freemount Corporation, Tulsa, president. Board member, Tulsa United Way, Thomas Gilcrease Museum, Tulsa Goodwill Industry, and the Business Industrial Development Corp, 19; executive board member, Tulsa Metropolitan Chamber of Commerce. National Volunteer, National Arthritis Foundation, 1985. *Military service:* U.S. Air Force, 1964-68; became sergeant.

AWARDS, HONORS: National Management Association (Oklahoma chapter), Manager of the Year, 1989.

WRITINGS:

*Once upon a Time When We Were Colored* (memoir), Council Oak, 1989.
*The Last Train North* (illustrated autobiography), Council Oak, 1992.

SIDELIGHTS: Clifton L. Taulbert emphasizes the bonds of family and community in *Once upon a Time When We Were Colored,* his memoir of growing up in a small Mississippi town during the waning days of segregation. "I did not choose to focus on the grand scheme of conflict between the races. I wanted to tell about the lives of everyday people," Taulbert told Joseph A. Cincotti in the *New York Times Book Review.* Taulbert portrays those close to him—his mother, grandparents, an extended family of aunts and uncles—as people who were "wryly cognizant of segregation but ... decided to enjoy life anyway," wrote Rosemary L. Bray, critic for the *New York Times Book Review.* Recalling his education at the "colored" school fifty miles away and his labor as a field hand during the summers, Taulbert nonetheless presents his childhood in what Bray described as "loving memories." A critic for the *Kirkus Reviews,* pointing out Taulbert's mention of the harsh realities of the era that faced blacks (such as accepting voting as "white folks' business"), called *Once upon a Time When We Were Colored* "a heartfelt testament to a beleaguered people."

A second autobiography, *The Last Train North,* tells of Taulbert's departure from the Mississippi Delta after his graduation with honors from high school and continues through his service in the air force during the 1960s. A notable section of the book depicts the author's first meeting with his preacher father in St. Louis—"the man left the bewildered youth with relatives ... and informed him that they 'probably' would not have a relationship," summed up a critic in *Kirkus Reviews.* In *Publishers Weekly* Genevieve Stuttaford praised *The Last Train North,* declaring that "a sense of optimism infuses this winning illustrated memoir."

BIOGRAPHICAL/CRITICAL SOURCES:

PERIODICALS

*Kirkus Reviews,* May 1, 1989, p. 682; May 15, 1992, p. 662.
*New York Times Book Review,* February 18, 1990, p. 9.
*Publishers Weekly,* May 25, 1992, p. 44.

\* \* \*

## TAYLOR, Mildred D. 1943-

PERSONAL: Born September 13, 1943, in Jackson, MS; daughter of Wilbert Lee and Deletha Marie (Davis) Taylor; married Errol Zea-Daly, August, 1972 (divorced, 1975). *Ed-*

ucation: University of Toledo, B.Ed., 1965; University of Colorado, M.A., 1969.

*CAREER:* Writer. United States Peace Corps, English and history teacher in Tuba City, AZ, 1965, and in Yirgalem, Ethiopia, 1965-67, recruiter, 1967-68, instructor in Maine, 1968; University of Colorado, study skills coordinator, 1969-71; proofreader and editor in Los Angeles, CA, 1971-73.

*AWARDS, HONORS:* First prize in African American category, Council on Interracial Books for Children, 1973, and outstanding book of the year citation, *New York Times,* 1975, both for *Song of the Trees;* American Library Association Notable Book citation, 1976, National Book Award finalist, *Boston Globe-Horn Book* Honor Book citation, and Newbery Medal, all 1977, and Buxtehuder Bulle Award, 1985, all for *Roll of Thunder, Hear My Cry;* outstanding book of the year citation, *New York Times,* 1981, Jane Addams honor, 1982, American Book Award nomination, 1982, and Coretta Scott King Award, 1982, all for *Let the Circle Be Unbroken;* Coretta Scott King Award, 1988, for *The Friendship; New York Times* notable book citation, 1987, and Christopher Award, 1988, both for *The Gold Cadillac;* Coretta Scott King Book Award, 1990, for *The Road to Memphis.*

*WRITINGS:*

*Song of the Trees,* illustrated by Jerry Pinkney, Dial, 1975.
*Roll of Thunder, Hear My Cry,* Dial, 1976.
*Let the Circle Be Unbroken,* Dial, 1981.
*The Friendship* (also see below), illustrated by Max Ginsburg, Dial, 1987.
*The Gold Cadillac* (also see below), illustrated by Michael Hays, Dial, 1987.
*The Friendship and the Gold Cadillac,* Bantam Books, 1989.
*The Road to Memphis,* Dial, 1990.
*Mississippi Bridge,* illustrated by Ginsburg, Dial, 1990.

*ADAPTATIONS: Roll of Thunder, Hear My Cry* was recorded by Newbery Awards Records in 1978, and as a three-part television miniseries of the same title by American Broadcasting Corporation (ABC-TV), 1978.

*SIDELIGHTS:* Many of Mildred Taylor's books reflect her experiences growing up in a racially biased America. Taylor brings a unique perspective to her work; although born in Mississippi, she spent most of her youth in Ohio. "I grew to know the South—to feel the South—through the yearly trips we took there and through the stories told. In those days, ... before the civil rights movement, I remember the South and how it was. I remember the racism, the segregation, and the fear. But I also remember the other South—the South of family and community," Taylor said in her 1988 *Boston Globe-Horn Book* acceptance speech, printed in *Horn Book Magazine.* A

former Peace Corps worker, Taylor is best known for her Newbery Award-winning novel *Roll of Thunder, Hear My Cry.* That book tells the story of the Logans, a black family living in the South during the Depression. Narrated by Cassie, the only Logan daughter, the book shows how the Logans cope with racism and its related injustices and indignities, and remain together as a family. Other volumes, including *Song of the Trees, Let the Circle be Unbroken* and *The Friendship,* continue the Logan history. Taylor's Logan family chronicles "have been hugely popular for two good reasons," Rosellen Brown suggests in the *New York Times Book Review.* "They bring alive a fragment of the history of black life in the Deep South for a generation that doesn't know much about it except, at best, secondhand. And, though Cassie Logan, her family and friends undergo a seemingly endless series of cruel trials at the hand of their white neighbors, Ms. Taylor has better news for us—she paints an appealingly detailed picture of the warm family relations and the embracing communal spirit to remind us that black life, day to day, however troubled, is not the disaster it looks like when it is simplified by sociology."

In her speech accepting the 1977 Newbery Award, published in *Horn Book Magazine,* Taylor commented, "I was blessed with a special father, a man who had unyielding faith in himself and his abilities, and who, knowing himself to be inferior to no one, tempered my learning with his wisdom. In the foreword to *Roll of Thunder, Hear My Cry* I described my father as a master storyteller; he was much more than that. A highly principled, complex man who did not have an excellent education or a white-collar job, he had instead strong moral fiber and a great wealth of what he always said was simply plain common sense. Throughout my childhood he impressed upon my sister and me that we were somebody, that we were important and could do or be anything we set our minds to do or be."

"From as far back as I can remember," Taylor once remarked, "my father taught me a different history from the one I learned in school. By the fireside in our Ohio home and in Mississippi, where I was born and where my father's family had lived since the days of slavery, I had heard about our past.... It was a history of ordinary people, some brave, some not so brave, but basically people who had done nothing more spectacular than survive in a society designed for their destruction. Some of the stories my father had learned from his parents and grandparents, as they had learned them from theirs; others he told first-hand, having been involved in some of the incidents himself. There was often humor in his stories, sometimes pathos, and frequently tragedy; but always the people were graced with a simple dignity that elevated them from the ordinary to the heroic.

"In those intervening years spent studying, traveling, and living in Africa and working with the Black student movement,

I would find myself turning again and again to the stories I had heard in childhood. I was deeply drawn to the roots of that inner world which I knew so well.... In *Roll of Thunder, Hear My Cry* I included the teachings of my own childhood, the values and principles by which I and so many other Black children were reared, for I wanted to show a family united in love and self-respect, and parents, strong and sensitive, attempting to guide their children successfully, without harming their spirits, through the hazardous maze of living in a discriminatory society.

"I also wanted to show the Black person as heroic," she added. When Taylor was ten years old, her family moved into a newly integrated Ohio town; as a result, Taylor was the only black child in her class. As she recalls in an autobiographical article written for *Something about the Author Autobiography Series,* she felt burdened by the realization that her actions would be judged by whites unfamiliar with blacks as representative of her entire race. She was also uncomfortable because her understanding of black history contrasted sharply with that presented in textbooks. In her Newbery speech, Taylor recalled that such publications contained only a "lack-luster history of Black people ... a history of a docile, subservient people happy with their fate who did little or nothing to shatter the chains that bound them, both before and after slavery." Taylor's efforts to tell her classmates what she knew about black history were met with general disbelief. "It is my hope," she would later say, "that to the children who read my books, the Logans will provide those heroes missing from the schoolbooks of my childhood, Black men, women and children of whom they can be proud."

## BIOGRAPHICAL/CRITICAL SOURCES:

### BOOKS

*Children's Literature Review,* Volume 9, Gale, 1985.
*Contemporary Literary Criticism,* Volume 21, Gale, 1982.
*Dictionary of Literary Biography,* Volume 52: *American Writers for*
*Children since 1960: Fiction,* Gale, 1986.
Rees, David, *The Marble on the Water: Essays on Contemporary Writers of Fiction for Children and Young Adults,* Horn Book, 1980.
*Something about the Author Autobiography Series,* Volume 5, Gale, 1988.
*Something about the Author,* Volume 70, Gale, 1993.

### PERIODICALS

*Best Sellers,* February, 1982.
*Bookbird,* March, 1977.
*Children's Books,* November 15, 1981.

*Christian Science Monitor,* November 3, 1976; October 14, 1981; October 5, 1984.
*Commonweal,* November 19, 1976.
*Horn Book,* August, 1975; December, 1976; August, 1977, pp. 401-14; October, 1977; April 1982; March/April 1989, pp. 179-82.
*Language Arts,* May, 1981.
*Los Angeles Times Book Review,* January 3, 1988.
*Modern Maturity,* December 1989-January 1990.
*New York Times,* February 3, 1988.
*New York Times Book Review,* May 4, 1975; November 16, 1975; November 21, 1976; March 19, 1978; November 15, 1981; September 2, 1982; December 11, 1983; November 15, 1987; February 21, 1988; May 20, 1990.
*Publishers Weekly,* July 26, 1985; October 28, 1988; April 13, 1990; July 27, 1990.
*School Library Journal,* December, 1981; September, 1987; March, 1988; April, 1988; January, 1989; June, 1990; November, 1990.
*Times Educational Supplement,* November 18, 1977.
*Times Literary Supplement,* December 2, 1977; March 26, 1982.
*Top of the News,* summer, 1977.
*Washington Post Book World,* February 13, 1977; April 23, 1978; May 10, 1987.
*Wilson Library Bulletin,* March, 1977; March, 1988.

\*   \*   \*

## TEAGUE, Bob
### See TEAGUE, Robert

\*   \*   \*

## TEAGUE, Robert 1929-
### (Bob Teague)

*PERSONAL:* Born October 26, 1929, in Milwaukee, WI; divorced, 1974; children: Adam. *Education:* University of Wisconsin, B.S., 1950.

*ADDRESSES: Agent*—Goodman Associates, 500 West End Avenue, New York, NY 10024.

*CAREER:* Journalist and author. *Milwaukee Journal,* Milwaukee, WI, reporter, 1950-56; *New York Times,* New York City, reporter, 1956-63; National Broadcasting Company, Inc., New York City, newscaster, beginning 1963.

*AWARDS, HONORS:* Recipient of Amistad Award from American Missionary Association for "his dignity and journalistic skill," 1966.

*WRITINGS:*

*UNDER NAME BOB TEAGUE*

*The Climate of Candor* (fiction), Pageant Press, 1962.
*Letters to a Black Boy* (biography), Walker and Co., 1968.
*Live and Off-Color: News Biz,* A & W Publishers, 1982.
*The Flip Side of Soul: Letters to My Son,* William Morrow & Company, 1989.

*CHILDREN'S FICTION; UNDER NAME BOB TEAGUE*

*Adam in Blunderland* (illustrated by Floyd Sowell), Doubleday, 1971.
*Agent K-Thirteen the Super-Spy,* Doubleday, 1974.
*Super-Spy K-Thirteen in Outer Space,* Doubleday, 1980.

*OTHER*

Contributor of articles to periodicals, including *High Fidelity, Musical America, Look, Reader's Digest, Redbook, TV Guide,* and *New York Times Magazine.*

*BIOGRAPHICAL/CRITICAL SOURCES:*

*PERIODICALS*

*Ebony,* November, 1955.
*Newsweek,* October 14, 1968.
*New York Times Book Review,* March 2, 1969.

\* \* \*

## TEISH, Luisah 1948-

*PERSONAL:* Born April 20, 1948, in New Orleans, LA; daughter of Wilson Allen (a longshoreperson) and Serena Scott (a cook); married David G. Wilson (a paralegal), June 21, 1980. *Education:* Attended Pacific University, 1966-68, Reed College, 1968-69, and Southern Illinois University at Edwardsville (Performing Arts Training Center), 1969-70; Open International University, Ph.D., 1993. *Politics:* Global Humanist. *Religion:* Neo-Yoruba.

*ADDRESSES: Office*—Ile Orunmila-Oshun, Box 28, 2550 Shattuck, Berkeley, CA 94704.

*CAREER:* Coalition for the Medical Rights of Women, San Francisco, CA, newsletter writer and editor, 1976; KPFA-Radio, Berkeley, CA, public affairs reporter and news writer, 1976-77; CommonArts Cultural Center, Berkeley, actor, scriptwriter, director, and artistic director, 1977-79; Bay Area Committee for Alternatives to Psychiatry, San Francisco, staff writer, 1979; Experimental Group Young People's Theatre, Oakland, CA, consultant and dance teacher, 1979-80; Women Against Violence in Pornography and Media, San Francisco, coordinator, and writer and presenter of slide shows, 1980; Berkeley Arts Magnet School, California Arts Council resident, 1981-82; Contra Costa College, San Pablo, CA, consultant to drama department and actor, 1983; Institute in Culture and Creation Spirituality, Holy Names College, Oakland, adjunct instructor, 1983—; Richmond Art Center, Richmond, CA, California Arts Council resident, 1984—. African and Caribbean ritual dancer, 1968—; storyteller of international folklore at events including Black History celebrations at the Oakland Museum and African Hunger Benefit, 1976—; *Plexus,* Berkeley, free-lance writer and reviewer, 1979—; works as a free-lance script consultant; dance instructor at institutions including John F. Kennedy University and Omega Institute; lecturer at the California Institute of Integral Studies; speaker at Take Back the Night March and Rally and in the Women's Department, Stanford, University. Priestess of Oshun; co-founder of Ile Orunmila-Oshun.

*MEMBER:* National Black Women's Health Project, Woman Earth Institute, Black Artists and Writers Union, Federation of Southern Women, Feminist Writers Guild, Third World Women's Alliance, Oxfam America.

*WRITINGS:*

*What Don't Kill Is Fattening,* Fantree Press, 1980.
*Jambalaya: The Natural Woman's Book of Personal Charms and Practical Rituals,* Harper, 1985.

Also author of *Carnival of the Spirit: Rituals for the Extended Family,* in press. Contributor to anthologies, including *Culture, Curers and Contagion: Readings for Medical Social Science,* edited by Norman Klein, Chandler & Sharp, 1979; *Take Back the Night: Women on Pornography,* edited by Laura Lederer, Morrow, 1980; *This Bridge Called My Back: Writings by Radical Women of Color,* edited by Cherrie Moraga and Gloria Anzaldua, Persephone Press, 1981; *Voices in the Night: Women Speaking about Incest,* edited by Toni A. H. McNaron and Yarrow Morgan, Cleis Press, 1982; and *Home Girls: A Black Feminist Anthology,* edited by Barbara Smith, Women of Color Press, 1983.

*Jambalaya: The Natural Woman's Book of Personal Charms and Practical Rituals* has been translated into German and Spanish.

*WORK IN PROGRESS: The Dovetail Deck: An African System of Divining, Iyase: Gender Reverence and Rituals,* and *Ayemu: A Transcultural Guidebook to Primal Spiritualities.*

SIDELIGHTS: Autobiographical and spiritual reflections provide the framework for Luisah Teish's *Jambalaya: The Natural Woman's Book of Personal Charms and Practical Rituals*. A priestess of Yoruba (a religion derived from ancient African culture) who grew up in New Orleans, Teish reveals the significance behind black traditions and offers charms and blessings to aid in daily life. Wanda Coleman, writing in the *Los Angeles Times Book Review,* revealed: "*Jambalaya* often explained 'mysteries' from my similar Watts childhood. I frequently gasped or laughed aloud, saying: 'Oh, so that's what *that* was about!'" The most intriguing portion of the book, Coleman acknowledged, was Teish's personal story, although it was "unfortunately, dissatisfyingly sketchy." Despite this (and a criticism that some rituals might not be practical), Coleman believed that "Teish succeeds in illuminating the marvelous and the magic of Africa."

Teish commented: "I am nurturing a spirituality of global unification, a spirituality of peace between the races, the sexes, and the nations. One that respects the Earth and all Her creations, that promotes and respects the creativity of all people. I am interested in humor and adornment, peace and celebration, healing and understanding."

BIOGRAPHICAL/CRITICAL SOURCES:

PERIODICALS

*Los Angeles Times Book Review,* February 23, 1986, p. 10.

\*    \*    \*

## THELWELL, Michael (Miles) 1939-

PERSONAL: Born July 25, 1939 (one source says 1938), in Ulster Spring, Jamaica; came to the United States, 1959; son of Morris M. (a member of the Jamaican House of Representatives) and Violet (a secretary; maiden name, McFarlane) Thelwell; married; children: Tracey, Todd. *Education:* Attended Jamaica College; Howard University, B.A., 1964; University of Massachusetts, Amherst, M.F.A., 1969.

ADDRESSES: Home—5 Gulf Rd., Pelham, MA 01002. *Office*—Department of Afro-American Studies, University of Massachusetts, Amherst, MA 01002.

CAREER: Jamaica Industrial Development Corp., Kingston, Jamaica, public relations assistant, 1958-59; Student Nonviolent Coordinating Committee (SNCC), Washington, DC, director of Washington office, 1963-64; Mississippi Freedom Democratic Party, Washington, DC, director of Washington office, 1964-65; University of Massachusetts, Amherst, chair

of W. E. B. Dubois department of Afro-American studies, 1969-1975, associate professor of literature, 1975—.

AWARDS, HONORS: First prize in short story contest, *Story* magazine, 1967, for "The Organizer"; National Foundation on the Arts and Humanities award, 1968, for the essay "Notes from the Delta"; Cornell University, Society for the Humanities fellow, 1969; Rockefeller Foundation literary award, 1969-70.

WRITINGS:

*The Harder They Come* (novel; based on Jamaican film of the same name), Grove, 1980.
*Duties, Pleasures, and Conflicts: Essays in Struggle,* introduction by James Baldwin, University of Massachusetts Press, 1987.

FILM SCRIPTS

*Washington Incident,* Intent Films, 1972.
(With Paul Carter Harrison) *Girl beneath the Lion,* Grove Films, 1978.

OTHER

Also author of introduction and afterword, *Rage,* by Gilbert Moor, Carroll & Graf, 1993. Contributor to books, including *William Styron's Nat Turner.* Contributor to anthologies, including *The Stone Soldier,* Fleet, 1964; *Best Stories by Negro Writers,* edited by Langston Hughes, Little, Brown, 1966; *American Literary Anthology I,* Farrar, Straus, 1968; *Theme Book 10: Text for Sophomores,* edited by Irene Wilson, Glenn, 1970; *Modern College Reader,* edited by Diane Millan, Scribner, 1970; *Cosmos Reader,* Harcourt, 1971; *Black Hands on a White Face,* edited by Whit Burnett, Scribner, 1971; *The Fact of Fiction,* edited by Cydril M. Gulassa, Harper, 1973; *New Black Voices,* edited by Chapman; *An Introduction to Black Literature in America,* edited by Patterson. Also contributor to periodicals, including *Black Scholar, Negro Digest, Spectrum, Massachusetts Review, Partisan Review, Short Story International, Story* magazine, and *Motive.* Member of editorial board, *Massachusetts Review,* 1969—, *Black Scholar,* 1970—, and *Okike,* 1972—.

WORK IN PROGRESS: Two novels on Jamaican society.

SIDELIGHTS: Michael Thelwell, longtime civil rights activist, professor, writer, and editor, moved to the United States from Jamaica in 1959. Author of critical work as well as fiction, he is most famous for his novel *The Harder They Come,* a story roughly based on the 1973 Jamaican movie of the same name. In addition to his innumerable contributions to periodicals and anthologies, he has edited essays and short stories, many addressing civil rights. As a fiction writer, critical essayist, and editor of both literary genres, Thelwell provides his readers with a first hand perspective of the Black experience in First and Third World countries.

*The Harder They Come,* published in 1980, is not a standard novelization of the movie script, written by Perry Henzell and Trevor Rhone. Though Thelwell readily admits that the film was the inspiration for the literary work, he articulates the similarities and differences between the two interpretations of the same story in the novel's preface by writing that both the film and the novel focus on "an event in contemporary Jamaican history which now has passed into legend: the life and exploits of 'Rhygin,' the first and most dramatic of the great ghetto gunmen." The difference between the two versions, however, lies in the novel's capacity to provide more historical and political details "which, because of the inherent limitations of the medium, was beyond the scope of the film." In Thelwell's estimation, the book form equipped him with the opportunity to "preserve, and indeed deepen, the essential character and vision of the film while expanding its historical and cultural range."

The hero of the novel, Rhygin, unfulfilled living in the mountains with his grandmother, ventures off to Kingston to seek fame and fortune as a reggae singer. His dream shatters upon arrival when he encounters homelessness, destitution, and utter despair. Through the course of the narrative, the country boy transforms into a sharp edged survivor who is eventually magnified to larger-than-life proportions as reggae singer, ganja (also known as marijuana) trader, and full fledged gun slinging bandit voicing the rage and frustration of the poverty-stricken shantytown. A dense and textured portrayal of Jamaican peasant life, *The Harder They Come* is, according to Jervis Anderson writing in the *New Republic,* an "authentic and evocative portrait of the Jamaican poor—the rich and sustaining vernaculars of their culture, [and] the sheer heroism of their economic existence." Though the novel emphasizes the hard-edged brutality of squalor in Jamaica, Thelwell manages to convey the simultaneous vitality inextricably linked to the ceaseless beat of the reggae music, the Ras Tafarian movement, and the violence in the streets of Kingston. Because most of the characters in the book communicate in a local dialect, Thelwell provides a glossary of Jamaican terms and idioms that repeatedly surface in the text. In *New York Times Book Review* contributor Darryl Pinckney's estimation, it is this "richness of his characters' language—the rolling, resonant, hypnotic, patois," emerging in the depictions of everyday life—that provides the reader with the most convincing material. Though Rhygin stands as a local hero and mythic figure, his story may also be interpreted as a metaphor for the poorer black world experience and "the Sisyphean nature of their uphill struggle against poverty," writes Anderson. Holly Eley quotes Thelwell in the *Times Literary Sup-*

*plement* as saying that he wrote *The Harder They Come* in an effort "to produce a real Jamaican novel that the people who are the subject might enjoy and recognize themselves and not be embarrassed or offended as they are in the case of Naipaul's books which are for white Western readers not blacks of the West Indies."

In 1987, the University of Massachusetts Press published a collection of essays and short fiction pieces written by Thelwell, titled *Duties, Pleasures, and Conflicts: Essays in Struggle,* that respond, in various ways, to the civil rights movement. Though he is the main contributor to the compilation, the book also gives voice to several other writers and activists whose essays and short stories are not readily available, including James Baldwin, Stokely Carmichael, and Lawrence Guyot. In the preface of the collection, Thelwell describes why he compiled these particular works: Teaching a class on civil rights, his students expressed a sincere fascination for the pieces that were written at the height of the movement, not later in a historical, reconstructive style. The written documents "conveyed—so the students said—a good sense of how my generation perceived itself and its circumstances and what it was struggling for, with, and against. They regretted that the pieces were not collected and generally available. Now they are." Thelwell informs the reader that he did not alter the pieces in any way, although at times he struggled with an impulse to do so. He was tempted to modify the harsh tone of some of the writings, specifically when an "absence of kindness" was directed at a particular and recognizable political figure, but decided that they were opinions linked to a very particular moment in our nation's history and demanded, therefore, to be preserved in their original form. A brief overview of the contributions include an honest criticism of the 1964 March on Washington as an "official" event that was intentionally drained of power and influence because of the government's endorsement; several essays addressing black political power; black life in the American South; a variety of critical essays, including one by James Baldwin; and, closing the collection, Jesse Jackson's presidential bid.

*Duties, Pleasures, and Conflicts* "is an important overview of the civil rights struggle reminding us in vivid terms that it continues today," declares a reviewer in *Publishers Weekly.* Henry Louis Gates, Jr. judges in *Callaloo* that Thelwell "writes with ease, wit, and a high moral seriousness that never descends to mere sermonic *gravitas.* Thelwell's book is, finally, as much about the culture of politics as it is about the politics of culture."

Thelwell creates literature for the types of people who inhabit his fictional world; a novel that they can read, identify with, and honestly enjoy. The Jamaican dialect in *The Harder They Come* might be difficult for some readers to fully appreciate, but Thelwell isn't interested in sacrificing the Jamaican experience. Certainly, outsiders who are seriously interested in learning about another culture can greatly profit from his work. The readers who struggle with the local dialect are undoubtedly rewarded by Thelwell's genuine portrait of Jamaican life. As the author of *Duties, Pleasures, and Conflicts: Essays in Struggle,* he maintains a comparable level of authenticity by leaving the written testimonies entirely preserved. Whether he is the author or the editor, writing fiction or critical analysis, Michael Thelwell presents compelling images of the black experience.

*BIOGRAPHICAL/CRITICAL SOURCES:*

*BOOKS*

*Contemporary Literary Criticism,* Volume 22, Gale, 1982.
Dance, Daryl Cumber, editor, *Fifty Caribbean Writers: A Bio-Bibliographical Critical Sourcebook,* Greenwood Press, 1986, pp. 457-61.
Thelwell, Michael, *The Harder They Come,* Grove, 1980.
Thelwell, Michael, *Duties, Pleasures, and Conflicts: Essays in Struggle,* University of Massachusetts Press, 1987.

*PERIODICALS*

*Callaloo,* summer, 1991, pp. 752-54.
*Library Journal,* October 1, 1979.
*New Republic,* July 19, 1980, pp. 30-32.
*New York Times,* February 1, 1980.
*New York Times Book Review,* June 1, 1980, p. 15.
*Publishers Weekly,* April 4, 1980; January 30, 1987, p. 380.
*Times Literary Supplement,* October 31, 1980, p. 1240.
*Washington Post Book World,* July 27, 1980.

—*Sketch by Sara Bader*

\*   \*   \*

## THOMAS, Joyce Carol   1938-

*PERSONAL:* Born May 25, 1938, in Ponca City, OK; daughter of Floyd Dave (a bricklayer) and Leona (a housekeeper; maiden name, Thompson) Haynes; married Gettis L. Withers (a chemist), May 31, 1959 (divorced, 1968); married Roy T. Thomas, Jr. (a professor), September 7, 1968 (divorced, 1979); children: Monica Pecot, Gregory Withers, Michael Withers, Roy T. Thomas III. *Education:* Attended San Francisco City College, 1957-58, and University of San Francisco, 1957-58; College of San Mateo, A.A., 1964; San Jose State College (now University), B.A., 1966; Stanford University, M.A., 1967.

*ADDRESSES: Home*—Berkeley, CA, and Knoxville, TN. *Agent*—Mitch Douglas, International Creative Management, 40 West 57th St., New York, NY 10019.

*CAREER:* Worked as a telephone operator in San Francisco, CA, 1957-58; Ravenwood School District, East Palo Alto, CA, teacher of French and Spanish, 1968-70; San Jose State College (now University), San Jose, CA, assistant professor of black studies, 1969-72; Contra Costa College, San Pablo, CA, teacher of drama and English, 1973-75; St. Mary's College, Moranga, CA, professor of English, 1975-77; San Jose State University, San Jose, reading program director, 1979-82, professor of English, 1982-83; full-time writer, 1982-89; University of Tennessee, professor of English, 1989—. Visiting associate professor of English at Purdue University, spring, 1983; member of Berkeley Civic Arts Commission.

*MEMBER:* Authors Guild, Dramatists Guild.

*AWARDS, HONORS:* Danforth Graduate Fellow at University of California at Berkeley, 1973-75; Stanford University scholar, 1979-80, and Djerassi Fellow, 1982 and 1983; *Marked by Fire* was named outstanding book of the year by *New York Times* and a best book by American Library Association, both 1982; Before Columbus American Book Award, Before Columbus Foundation (Berkeley, CA), 1982, and National Book Award for Children's Fiction, Association of American Publishers, 1983, both for *Marked by Fire;* Coretta Scott King Award, American Library Association, 1984, for *Bright Shadow.*

*WRITINGS:*

*NOVELS*

*Marked by Fire* (young adult), Avon, 1982.
*Bright Shadow* (young adult), Avon, 1983.
*Water Girl,* Avon, 1986.
*The Golden Pasture* (young adult), Scholastic, Inc., 1986.
*Journey,* Scholastic, Inc., 1988.
(Editor) *A Gathering of Flowers; Stories about Being Young in America,* Harper, 1990.
*When the Nightingale Sings,* HarperCollins, 1992.

*POETRY*

*Bittersweet,* Firesign Press, 1973.
*Crystal Breezes,* Firesign Press, 1974.
*Blessing,* Jocato Press, 1975.
*Black Child,* Zamani Productions, 1981.
*Inside the Rainbow,* Zikawana Press, 1982.
*Brown Honey in Broomwheat Tea,* HarperCollins, 1993.

*PLAYS*

(And producer) *A Song in the Sky* (two-act), first produced in San Francisco at Montgomery Theatre, 1976.

*Look! What a Wonder!* (two-act), first produced in Berkeley at Berkeley Community Theatre, 1976.

(And producer) *Magnolia* (two-act), first produced in San Francisco at Old San Francisco Opera House, 1977.

(And producer) *Ambrosia* (two-act), first produced in San Francisco at Little Fox Theatre, 1978.

*Gospel Roots* (two-act), first produced in Carson, CA, at California State University, 1981.

*When the Nightingale Sings* (two-act), first produced in Knoxville, TN, at Clarence Brown Theatre, University of Tennessee, 1991.

*OTHER*

Contributor to periodicals, including *American Poetry Review, Black Scholar, Calafia, Drum Voices, Giant Talk,* and *Yardbird Reader.* Editor of *Ambrosia* (women's newsletter), 1980.

*ADAPTATIONS: Marked by Fire* was adapted by James Racheff and Ted Kociolek for the stage musical *Abyssinia,* first produced in New York City at the CSC Repertory Theater, 1987.

*WORK IN PROGRESS: Madame,* a fictional play based on the life of Madame C. J. Walker.

*SIDELIGHTS:* Often favorably compared to such prominent black female writers as Maya Angelou, Alice Walker, and Toni Morrison, Joyce Carol Thomas first established her literary reputation as a poet and playwright in the San Francisco Bay area of California. Raised in Oklahoma during the 1940s as the fifth child in a family of nine, Thomas developed an early fascination with storytelling when, during harvest time, sharing anecdotes and exchanging bits of family lore were popular sources of entertainment. Her works reflect this ingrained talent for telling stories; her first book, the 1982 award-winning young adult novel, *Marked by Fire,* earned the author critical acclaim for what *San Francisco Chronicle Book World* reviewer Patricia Holt called Thomas's "ear for language and dialect, her gift for simplicity in description and the absolute authenticity of her setting and characters."

*Marked by Fire* chronicles twenty years in the life of Abyssinia Jackson, beginning with her birth in a cotton field, where she is scarred by a spark from a brush fire. As such, she is "marked for unbearable pain and unspeakable joy," according to Mother Barker, the character who serves as the local healer, spiritual adviser, and, eventually, Abyssinia's mentor. Set in Ponca City, Oklahoma—Thomas's birthplace—the story depicts Abyssinia as an especially bright, happy child who is gifted with an extraordinarily beautiful singing voice. At age ten, however, she loses this gift when an elder member of her church brutally rapes her. The incident brings the prophesied "unbearable pain" and a bitter questioning of her faith in God, but with time—and the support of the women in the close-knit community—Abyssinia gradually recovers from the ordeal. The remainder of *Marked by Fire* traces the heroine's passage into young womanhood and concludes with her decision to follow in Mother Barker's footsteps, attending to the needs of the town's troubled and sick.

The novel met with enthusiastic reviews and became required reading in many high school and university classrooms throughout the United States. "Thomas writes with admirable simplicity and finds a marvelous fairy tale quality in everyday happenings," wrote *New York Times Book Review* critic Alice Childress. Holt declared the book a "hauntingly and beautifully written novel" that "reads with the rhythm and beauty of poetry" and deemed *Marked by Fire* "the kind of novel that *no one* should miss." California's *Peninsula Times Review* writer Charles Beardsley praised Thomas's portrayal of the main character, describing Abyssinia as "drawn full scale, shining forth as an unforgettable individual who welcomes life and thereby experiences as much joy as sorrow, life's ignominy and the grandeur of its heritage." Beardsley added that *Marked by Fire* "is no 'made up' story, but the sensitive distillation of the black experience as seen through the eyes of a remarkable writer."

In *Bright Shadow,* the 1983 sequel to *Marked by Fire,* Abyssinia enters college to prepare for a medical career. She meets and falls in love with Carl Lee Jefferson and, despite initial disapproval from Abyssinia's father, their relationship thrives. Together they endure the painful aftermath of the gruesome murder of Abyssinia's favorite aunt as well as the death of Carl Lee's abusive father, an event that reveals the truth of Carl Lee's ancestry.

Critical reception of *Bright Shadow* did not match that of its predecessor, but was nevertheless recommended in library and publishing journals and won the Coretta Scott King Award offered by the American Library Association in 1984. Thomas plans additional novels for the "Abyssinia" series.

*BIOGRAPHICAL/CRITICAL SOURCES:*

*BOOKS*

*Contemporary Literary Criticism,* Volume 35, Gale, 1985.

*Dictionary of Literary Biography,* Volume 33: *Afro-American Fiction Writers after 1955,* Gale, 1984.

*Something about the Author Autobiography Series,* Volume 7, Gale, 1989.

Yalom, Marilyn, editor, *Women Writers of the West Coast,* Capra Press, 1983.

*PERIODICALS*

*New York Times,* November 30, 1982.
*New York Times Book Review,* April 18, 1982; December 5, 1982; March 18, 1984.
*Peninsula Times Tribune* (California), March 20, 1982.
*Publishers Weekly,* July 25, 1986, p. 191; September 9, 1988, p. 140.
*San Francisco Chronicle Book World,* April 12, 1982.
*School Library Journal,* April, 1986, p. 100; August, 1986, p. 107; October, 1988, p. 165; October, 1990, p. 145.
*Wilson Library Bulletin,* November, 1989, p. S9; April, 1991, p. 129.

\*   \*   \*

## THOMPSON, Era Bell   1905-1986

*PERSONAL:* Born August 10, 1905, in Des Moines, IA; died c. December 30, 1986, in Chicago, IL; buried in Driscoll, ND, according to her wishes; daughter of Stewart C. and Mary (Logan) Thompson. *Education:* Attended University of North Dakota, 1929-31; Morningside College, B.A., 1933, LL.D., 1965; also attended Northwestern University, 1938, 1940, and Medill School of Journalism. *Religion:* Presbyterian.

*ADDRESSES: Home*—2851 Martin Luther King Dr., Apt. 1910, Chicago, IL 60616. *Office*—*Ebony,* 820 South Michigan Ave., Chicago, IL 60605.

*CAREER:* Senior interviewer, U.S. Employment service, 1942-46, and Illinois Employment Service, Chicago, 1946-47; Johnson Publishing Co., Inc., Chicago, IL, associate editor, 1947-51, international editor, 1964-retirement in early 1980s; book reviewer for Chicago and N.Y papers. Member of board of trustees of Hull House, 1960-64; member of North Central Region Manpower Advisory Committee, 1965-67; public member of U.S. Information Agency foreign service selection boards, 1976-86.

*MEMBER:* International Visitors Center, Association for the Study of Afro-American Life and History, National Association for the Advancement of Colored People (life member), Society of Midland Authors (member of board of directors, 1961-75), National Council of Christians & Jews, Zonta Int., Urban League (formerly Chicago Community Art Center), Chicago Young Women's Christian Association (YWCA; board member, 1944-47), Friends of Chicago Public Library (member of board of directors, 1959-60), Writing Chicago

Program, Chicago Press Club, Cancer's Reach to Recovery, American Cancer Reach Committee, Iota Phi Lambda, Sigma Gamma Rho.

*AWARDS, HONORS:* Newberry Library Fellowship, 1945; Bread Loaf Writers Conference fellowship, 1949; Rockefeller fellowship, 1953; Capital Press Club citation, 1961; named Woman of the Year, Iota Phi Lambda, 1965; LL.D., Morning-side College, 1965; Patron's Saints Award, Society of Midland Authors, 1968, for *American Daughter;* L.H.D., University of North Dakota, 1969; Distinguished Alumni Award, Morningside College, 1974; Theodore Roosevelt Roughrider Award, state of North Dakota, 1976, for bringing credit to the state; portrait hung in North Dakota Hall of Fame, 1977; cultural center at the University of North Dakota was named in honor of Era Bell Thompson, 1979.

*WRITINGS:*

*American Daughter,* University of Chicago Press, 1946, revised edition, 1974.
*Africa: Land of My Fathers,* Doubleday, 1954.
(Co-editor with Herbert Nipson) *White on Black,* Johnson Publishing Co., 1963.

Contributor to periodicals, including *Negro Digest, Ebony,* and *Phylon. Negro Digest,* editor, mid 1940s; *Ebony,* co-managing editor, 1951-64, international editor, 1964-retirement in early 1980s.

*SIDELIGHTS:* Era Bell Thompson began her career as an editor and writer in college at North Dakota State University. From the university newspaper, the *Student,* she moved to a magazine office in Chicago where she proofread, wrote advertising copy, and reviewed books written by blacks. These work experiences set the foundation for her lifelong commitment to reporting the black experience on the national and international level. In 1946 she published *American Daughter,* a personal account of growing up female and black in an intolerant and prejudiced country. Less than ten years later, she documented a journey abroad in *Africa: Land of My Fathers,* a detailed account of a black journalist's return to her ancestor's homeland. As international editor for *Ebony* magazine, Thompson travelled to all five continents and returned to the States to publish the stories she collected during her excursions. A successful, confident, and exceedingly motivated woman, she explored racial conflicts in her work in the United States and abroad. Though she was profoundly aware of the barriers that separated both blacks from whites and women from men, she also expressed an optimistic hope that future generations will work together to break down the divisions between the races and the sexes.

Her 1946 autobiography *American Daughter* recounts the first half of her life—a story that is inspiring, eventful, and often humorous. She recollects her childhood years spent on a farm in North Dakota, where her memories maintain an idyllic quality appropriate for such an innocent age. In the farming community there exists little racism, though curiosity motivates the neighbors to scrutinize the family rather closely (her rough hair and white palms attract local attention). It is not until the sweet memories of childhood begin to unravel, her mother dies, her brothers move away, and Era Bell must relocate with her father to Bismarck, that she personally experiences racism. In the city she pursues writing and running and eventually pays her way through a college education. According to Judith Long in a *Nation* book review, Thompson, in the course of her educational and professional pursuits, "crosses and recrosses the [racial} tracks many times, never losing that wit and tenacity," two personality traits "she needs in the Chicago of 1933 where being black, educated, and female are no assets to finding work." Thompson explained in the foreword to *American Daughter* why she wrote this autobiography half way through her life: "Usually an autobiography is written near the end of a long and distinguished career, but not taking any chances, I wrote mine first, then began to live." It is not surprising that the remainder of her life maintained the level of accomplishment and achievement so evident in the pages of her first book.

Her second book, *Africa, Land of My Fathers,* is equally revealing and personal; it documents her journey through eighteen countries in Africa as an American black female journalist who returns to her ancestor's homeland in search of her history. While traveling, she experiences the continent's political problems and discriminating economy that places black Africans at the very bottom of the system; she also has the opportunity to interact with many black Africans, some of whom welcome her with open arms and others who exclude her as a foreigner from a strange land. Because her history roots back to Africa, Thompson alternately reports from the inside, as a black, and the outside, as an American. Ultimately torn between these two positions, she is forced to define her origins. "Africans are my brothers," she writes, "for we are of one race. But Africa, the land of my fathers, is not my home. I am an American—an American by nationality, a citizen of the United States by birth. I owe my loyalty and my allegiance to but one flag. I have but one country."

Thompson was one of the most prominent black women journalists in American history. An ardent feminist (long before the views became politically fashionable), she refused to adhere to the sexist journalistic definitions of "women's stories" and "men's stories." She took great pride in disregarding such repressive expectations and tackled any story in any country that piqued her curiosity. Needless to say, her perspective produced an array of controversial accounts that shattered

previously accepted notions of appropriate "female" journalism. According to an article in *Ebony,* "her study of amalgamation of the races in Brazil was one of the best stories ever done on the 'race problem' in the country that was not supposed to have one, and she was the first to look into the problems of 'brown babies'—the offspring of Black soldiers in Europe and Asia." By broadening the minds of her readers with such stories, Thompson deconstructed both racial and gender barriers.

*BIOGRAPHICAL/CRITICAL SOURCES:*

*BOOKS*

Thompson, Era Bell, *American Daughter,* University of Chicago Press, 1946.
Thompson, Era Bell, *Africa: Land of My Fathers,* Doubleday, 1954.

*PERIODICALS*

*Kliatt,* winter 1987.
*Nation,* June 27, 1987.
*Washington Post Book World,* November 2, 1986.

*OBITUARIES:*

*PERIODICALS*

*Chicago Tribune,* January 1, 1987.
*Detroit Free Press,* January 1, 1987.
*Ebony,* March, 1987.
*Jet,* January 19, 1987.
*New York Times Biographical Service,* January 3, 1987.
*Sun-Times* (Chicago), January 1, 1987.

\*    \*    \*

## TOURE, Askia Muhammad Abu Bakr el 1938-
### (Askia Muhammad Abu Bakr el-Toure, Rolland Snellings)

*PERSONAL:* Name originally Rolland Snellings; name changed c. 1970; born October 13, 1938, in Raleigh, NC; son of Clifford R. and Nancy (Bullock) Snellings; married Dona Humphrey in June, 1966 (divorced); married Helen Morton Hobbs (Muslim name, Halima; a writer and editor) in 1970 (divorced); married third wife, Agila; children: (first marriage) Tariq Abdullah bin Toure, (second marriage) Jamil Abdus-Salam bin Toure. *Education:* Attended Art Students League of New York, 1960-62. *Religion:* Muslim.

*CAREER:* Poet, essayist, artist, editor, and educator. Lecturer in African history, black studies, and creative writing at colleges and universities, including Yale University, Cornell University, Pennsylvania State University, Columbia University, University of California, Berkeley, San Francisco State College (now University), Central State College, and Queens College. *Military service:* U.S. Air Force, 1956-59.

*MEMBER:* Rockefeller Foundation (literary fellow), Omega Psi Phi (literary fellow).

*AWARDS, HONORS:* Modern Poetry Association award, 1952; Columbia University Creative Writing grant, 1969.

*WRITINGS:*

*UNDER NAME ASKIA MUHAMMAD ABU BAKR EL-TOURE, EXCEPT AS NOTED*

(Author of introduction under name Rolland Snellings) *Samory Toure* (illustrated biography), designed by Matthew Meade, illustrated by Tom Feelings, produced by William E. Day, privately printed in New York, 1963.

*Earth: For Mrs. Mary Bethune and the African and Afro-American Women,* Broadside Press, 1968.

(With Ben Caldwell) *JuJu: Magic Songs for the Black Nation* (collection of poetry and prose), Third World Press, 1970.

*Songhai!* (collection of poetry and sketches), introduction by John O. Killens, Songhai Press, 1972.

*From the Pyramids to the Projects: Poems of Genocide and Resistance!,* Africa World Press, 1990.

Also author of the record *Black Spirits,* released by Black Forum. Work represented in anthologies, including *Black Fire: An Anthology of Afro-American Writing,* Morrow, 1968; *Black Arts,* Black Arts, 1969, *Black Nationalism in America,* Bobbs-Merrill, 1970; *Natural Process,* Hill & Wang, 1970; *Black Art, Black Culture,* edited by Joe Goncalves, Journal of Black Poetry Press, 1972; *The Poetry of Black America,* Harper, 1973; and *Understanding the New Black Poetry,* Morrow, 1973. Contributor of poetry and articles to periodicals, including *Black Theatre, Black World, Essence, Freedom-ways, Journal of Black Poetry, Liberation Magazine, Negro Digest, Soulbook,* and *Umbra.* Staff member of *Umbra* magazine, 1962-63; member of editorial board of *Black America,* 1963-65; co-founder of *Afro World* newspaper, 1965; staff member of *Liberator Magazine,* 1965-66; associate editor of *Black Dialogue;* editor-at-large of *Journal of Black Poetry* (now *Kitabu Cha Jua*).

*WORK IN PROGRESS:* A volume of poetry, *Sunrise: A New Afrikan Anthem.*

*SIDELIGHTS:* A historian of African culture and a visionary poet foreseeing a "coming Age of Light" for humanity, Askia Muhammad Abu Bakr el Toure has been a leader of the black aesthetic movement since the early 1960s. The movement, whose influence extends to diverse fields, including poetry, theatre, music, journalism, politics, and religion, seeks to separate the spirit of black people from Western influence and define it in terms of its African origin.

While studying at the Art Students League of New York in the early 1960s, Toure helped compose one of the first books celebrating African heroes and history, *Samory Toure.* Toure collaborated with illustrator Tom Feelings, artist Elombe Brath, and others to produce the illustrated biography of the prominent grandfather of Sekou Toure, who was instrumental in maintaining Guinea's resistance to French domination in the nineteenth century.

After publishing his first book, Toure helped promote numerous journals supporting black awareness, including *Black America,* the black nationalist journal of the Revolutionary Action Movement (RAM), *Liberator Magazine,* and *Black Dialogue.* He eventually became editor-at-large of the *Journal of Black Poetry* (now known as *Kitabu Cha Jua*) after its emergence from *Black Dialogue.* With the newspaper he and author Larry Neal founded in 1965, *Afro World,* Toure helped strengthen the black liberation movement through the documentation of oppression and the analysis of racial injustice in America.

That same year Toure and Neal organized a Harlem Uptown Youth Conference with artists from the Black Arts Repertoir Theatre School, soon after which the Black Arts Theatre opened in Harlem. Black artists, including playwright LeRoi Jones (also known as Amiri Baraka), musicians Sun Ra and Milford Graves, and poets Toure and Neal acted out plays, performed music, and recited poetry in blocked-off streets in New York. Joanne V. Gabbin in *Dictionary of Literary Biography* quoted Toure as recalling: "We would serenade the people on the streets of Harlem, and it made the authorities nervous as hell. We went all over Harlem and brought to its neglected, colonized masses the messages of Black power, dignity, and beauty."

Just as the nation was changing under the influence of the black arts and black liberation movements, Toure's personal life changed in the course of his activities. After moving with his wife, Dona Humphrey, to San Francisco soon after their marriage in 1966, Toure came under the influence of the Nation of Islam. Converting to the Islamic faith, he changed his name from Rolland Snellings to Askia Muhammad Abu Bakr el Toure. In his poem "Extension," published in *JuJu: Magic Songs for the Black Nation* in 1970, Toure praises the Islamic faith as "The TRUTH" that can engender "one large community with open doors [and] open minds." Pressures from his religious, social, and political activities, however, contributed to the strain on his marriage, and Toure and his wife divorced after the birth of their son.

After returning to New York, Toure married Helen Morton Hobbs in 1970, who encouraged Toure in his poetry and his newly embraced religion. Called by her Muslim name, Halima, she is probably the inspirational "woman panther-lithe and tawny, a princess come back to haunt me" in Toure's poem "Al Fajr: The Daybreak," published in *Songhai!* in 1972. They, too, divorced, however, after the birth of a son, and Toure moved to Philadelphia in 1974.

Reviewers admired *JuJu* and *Songhai!*, both collections of the visionary poetry and prose Toure composed during the height of his activity with the black aesthetic movement. *JuJu*, which includes three poems and an essay by Toure and a poem by playwright Ben Caldwell, guides the reader through the black person's "quest for national destiny and [his] spiritual identification with the universe," explained Carolyn F. Gerald in *Black World.* In *JuJu*—the title is a West African word meaning "magic"—Toure's epic poetry links the modern black soul to its African heritage through vibrant imagery and long, polyrhthymic lines that imitate classical black music. Inspired by black instrumentalists like John Coltrane and Milford Graves, Toure equates black music with African magic, believing music to be the most authentic expression of the black soul. He explains his belief in an essay he wrote in the *Journal of Black Poetry* in 1968: "When they stripped us of our obvious African culture (robes, drums, language, religion, etc.), the 'abstract' ... aspect of our culture—our music—was the only thing, in altered form, permitted to remain.... As time passed, the Black Musician became *and remains* the major philosopher, priest, myth-maker and cultural hero of the Black Nation." Praising the intricate form and stirring content of Toure's poetry, Gerald declared that *JuJu* is a collection "well worth buying and reading by all Black people, who stand to gain, in the reading, a greater sense of self."

Reviewer Addison Gayle, Jr., proclaimed in *Black World* that *Songhai!*, like *JuJu*, tells an important "truth: that the strength of Black people lay in a culture outside that of the American, and that [its attainment] is possible only after a return to the values and ethics of our African forefathers." The poetry and prose in *Songhai!*, however, suggests more than simply returning to African origins. In "an imaginative work overflowing with symbols, images, and metaphors of the new African world to come," Gayle pointed out, Toure "envisions the world ... peopled by strong Black men and women equipped with the grace and endurance to survive." Gayle found that in the "coming Age of Light" of which the poet writes in his "Hymn to the People," Toure predicts "a world, where poet and people feed into each other's creative ethos, where all men are

poets, where love and fidelity to the human condition remain sacrosanct."

*BIOGRAPHICAL/CRITICAL SOURCES:*

*BOOKS*

*Dictionary of Literary Biography,* Volume 41, *Afro-American Poets since 1955,* Gale, 1985.
Toure, Askia Muhammad Abu Bakr el, and Ben Caldwell, *JuJu: Magic Songs for the Black Nation,* Third World Press, 1970.
Toure, *Songhai!,* introduction by John O. Killens, Songhai Press, 1972.

*PERIODICALS*

*Black World,* June, 1971, September, 1974.
*Journal of Literary Biography,* Volume 8, 1968.

\* \* \*

## TROUPE, Quincy (Thomas, Jr.) 1943-

*PERSONAL:* Born July 23, 1943, in New York, NY; son of Quincy, Sr., and Dorothy (Marshall Smith) Troupe; married Margaret Porter; children: Antoinette, Tymme, Quincy, Porter. *Education:* Grambling College (now Grambling State University), B.A., 1963; Los Angeles City College, A.A., 1967.

*ADDRESSES: Home*—1925 Seventh Ave., No. 7L, New York, NY 10026. *Office*—Department of Performing and Creative Arts, City University of New York, 130 Stuyvesant Place, Staten Island, NY 10301; and School of the Arts, Writing Division, Columbia University, New York, NY 10027. *Agent*—Marie Brown, 412 West 154th St., No. 2, New York, NY 10032.

*CAREER:* Watts Writers' Movement, Los Angeles, CA, creative writing teacher, 1966-68; *Shrewd* (magazine), Los Angeles, associate editor, beginning 1968; University of California, Los Angeles, instructor in creative writing and black literature, 1968; Ohio University, Athens, instructor in creative writing and third world literature, 1969-72; Richmond College, Staten Island, NY, instructor in third world literature, beginning 1972; instructor at institutions including University of California at Berkeley, California State University at Sacramento, and University of Ghana at Legon; College of Staten Island, City University of New York, New York City, associate professor of American and third world literatures and director of poetry center; Columbia University, New York

City, member of faculty of Graduate Writing Program, 1985—. Director of Malcolm X Center and John Coltrane Summer Festivals in Los Angeles, summers, 1969 and 1970. Has given poetry readings at various institutions, including Harvard University, New York University, Howard University, Yale University, Princeton University, Louisiana State University, Dartmouth College, Oberlin College, Ohio State University, University of Michigan, and Michigan State University. Presenter of lecture and readings series "Life Forces: A Festival of Black Roots" at the Church of St. John the Divine in New York City.

*MEMBER:* Poetry Society of America.

*AWARDS, HONORS:* International Institute of Education grant for travel in Africa, 1972; National Endowment for the Arts Award in poetry, 1978; grant from New York State Council of the Arts, 1979; American Book Award from the Association of American Publishers, 1980, for *Snake-back Solos;* New York Foundation for the Arts fellowship in poetry, 1987.

*WRITINGS:*

(Editor) *Watts Poets: A Book of New Poetry and Essays,* House of Respect, 1968.

*Embryo Poems, 1967-1971* (includes "South African Bloodstone—For Hugh Masekela," "Chicago—For Howlin Wolf," "Profilin, A Rap/Poem—For Leon Damas," "The Scag Ballet," "Midtown Traffic," "Woke Up Crying the Blues," "The Earthquake of Peru; 1970; In 49 Seconds—For Cesar Vallejo, Great Peruvian Poet," "In the Manner of Rabearivello," "Poem From the Third Eye—For Eugene Redmond," and "Black Star, Black Woman"), Barlenmir, 1972, second edition, 1974.

(Editor with Rainer Schulte) *Giant Talk: An Anthology of Third World Writings,* Random House, 1975.

(Author of foreword) Arnold Adoff, editor, *Celebrations: A New Anthology of Black American Poetry,* Follet, 1977.

(With David L. Wolper) *The Inside Story of TV's "Roots,"* Warner Books, 1978.

*Snake-back Solos: Selected Poems, 1969-1977* (includes "Springtime Ritual," "The Day Duke Raised," "La Marqueta," "For Miles Davis," "Up Sun South of Alaska," "Today's Subway Ride," "New York Streetwalker," "Steel Poles Give Back No Sweat," "Ghanaian Song—Image," and "Memory"), I. Reed Books, 1978.

*Skulls Along the River* (poetry), I. Reed Books, 1984.

*Soundings,* Writers & Readers, 1988.

(Editor) *James Baldwin: The Legacy,* Simon and Schuster, 1989.

(With Miles Davis) *Miles, the Autobiography,* Simon and Schuster, 1989.

*Weather Reports: New and Selected Poems,* Writers & Readers, 1991.

Also founding editor of *Confrontation: A Journal of Third World Literature* and *American Rag;* guest editor of black poetry and black fiction issues of *Mundus Artium,* 1973; senior editor of *River Styx,* 1983—. Work represented in anthologies, including *The New Black Poetry,* 1969; *We Speak as Liberators,* 1970; *New Black Voices,* 1972; *Black Spirits,* 1972; *Poetry of Black America,* 1973; and *A Rock against the Wind,* 1973. Contributor to periodicals, including *New Directions, Mundus Artium, Iowa Review, Black World, Callaloo, Essence, Antioch Review, Black Creation, Negro American Literature Forum, Umbra, Mediterranean Review, Concerning Poetry, Sumac, Paris Match, Black Review, New York Quarterly,* and *Village Voice.*

*SIDELIGHTS:* Quincy Troupe is "a poet of great feeling and energy," according to Michael S. Harper, reviewing *Snakeback Solos* in the *New York Times Book Review.* Troupe has also founded and edited magazines such as *Confrontation: A Journal of Third World Literature* and *American Rag,* in addition to having a distinguished academic career. He began teaching creative writing for the Watts Writers' Movement in 1966; his other teaching responsibilities have included courses in black literature and third world literature. Troupe was already an established poet and his scholarly interests had led him to compile *Giant Talk: An Anthology of Third World Writings* with Rainer Schulte when, in 1978, he reached a wider audience with *The Inside Story of TV's "Roots."* The book, which Troupe wrote with David L. Wolper, chronicles the production of the highly successful television miniseries about slavery in America, "Roots," which was based on Alex Haley's book of the same title. Troupe's *Inside Story* has sold over one million copies.

Troupe's first poetic publication came in 1964 when *Paris Match* featured his "What Is a Black Man?" Since then he has contributed poetry to many periodicals in addition to having volumes of his poems published in book form. The first of these, *Embryo Poems,* includes poems which display Troupe's interests in the use of dialect, such as "Profilin, A Rap/Poem—For Leon Damas," and in the area of music, such as "The Scag Ballet," The latter poem depicts the actions of drug addicts as a strange form of dance; another piece likens traffic noises to "black jazz piano." Yet another, "Woke Up Crying the Blues," concerns the assassination of black civil rights leader Martin Luther King, Jr. The sadness the speaker of the poem feels at the loss of "the peaceful man from Atlanta" mingles with the happiness of the news that one of his poems has been accepted for publication, producing a mixture of emotion essential to the singing of a blues song.

*Snake-back Solos,* Troupe's second volume of poetry, takes its title from a local name ("Snakeback") for the Mississippi River, recalled from the poet's childhood in St. Louis. Harper cited such poems as "Today's Subway Ride" in praising

Troupe's descriptions of "the strange reality of familiar scenes." The subway is painted starkly, its unpleasant atmosphere displayed in "pee smells assaulting nostrils/blood breaking wine stains everywhere." Though Harper faulted the repetition of some of *Snake-back Solos,* including "Up Sun South of Alaska," he lauded "Ghanaian Song—Image" and "Memory" as "striking" and concluded that "the strength and economy" of the poet's "best insights ... are about people and places he has internalized and often left behind."

Troupe's academic work has also garnered applause from critics. *Giant Talk* was declared "comprehensive" by Jack Slater in the *New York Times Book Review.* The book, which Troupe edited with Rainer Schulte, contains poems, folk tales, short stories, and novel excerpts by black Americans, native Americans, Hispanic Americans, black Africans, and Central and South Americans. According to Slater, the editors define third world writers as "those who identify with the historically exploited segment of mankind, and who confront the establishment on their behalf"; hence the inclusion of U.S.-born authors along with those native to areas more traditionally identified with the third world. Slater hailed the editors' decision to group the anthologized pieces by concept rather than by geographical area or genre. By using categories like "Oppression and Protest" and "Ritual and Magic," Troupe and Schulte "have managed to lessen the unwieldiness of *Giant Talk*'s scope. The uninitiated reader can, therefore, savor with as much ease as possible bits and pieces of longer works ... as well as enjoy complete works by ... short-story writers and poets."

*James Baldwin: The Legacy,* published after Baldwin's death in 1987, is "a sustained fond retrospect," Nicholas Delbanco remarked in a *Tribune Books* review. The book includes tributes and remembrances "studded with remarkable images that attest to the writer's continuing brilliance" from Maya Angelou, Amiri Baraka, Toni Morrison, Chinua Achebe, and others, Charles R. Larson commented in *Washington Post Book World,* and ends with an interview with Baldwin, conducted by Troupe several weeks before the author's death, which is "spirited and funny at times," *Los Angeles Times Book Review* critic Clancy Sigal noted. Delbanco related Troupe's description of the book: "It is a celebration of the life, the vision and, yes, the death of our good and great, passionate, genius witness of a brother, James Arthur Baldwin."

*BIOGRAPHICAL/CRITICAL SOURCES:*

BOOKS

*Dictionary of Literary Biography,* Volume 41: *Afro-American Poets since 1955,* Gale, 1985.
Troupe, Quincy, *Embryo Poems, 1967-1971,* Barlenmir, 1972.

Troupe, Quincy, and Rainer Schulte, *Giant Talk: An Anthology of Third World Writings,* Random House, 1975.
Troupe, Quincy, *Snake-back Solos: Selected Poems, 1969-1977,* I. Reed Books, 1978.

*PERIODICALS*

*Black Scholar,* March/April, 1981; summer, 1990.
*Freedomways,* Volume 10, number 2, 1980.
*Los Angeles Times Book Review,* April 30, 1989, p. 1.
*Mother Jones,* December, 1989, p. 42.
*Nation,* January 29, 1990, p. 139.
*New York Times Book Review,* November 30, 1975; October 21, 1979; October 15, 1989, p. 97.
*Tribune Books* (Chicago), March 19, 1989.
*Washington Post Book World,* April 16, 1989, p. 1.


*       *       *


## TSEGAYE, Gabre-Medhin
## See GABRE-MEDHIN, Tsegaye (Kawessa)


*       *       *


## TUTUOLA, Amos 1920-

*PERSONAL:* Born 1920, in Abeokuta, Nigeria; son of Charles (a cocoa farmer) and Esther (Aina) Tutuola; married Alake Victoria, 1947; children: Olubunmi, Oluyinka, Erinola. *Education:* Attended schools in Nigeria. *Religion:* Christian.

*ADDRESSES: Home*—Ago-Odo, West Nigeria. *Office*—P.O. Box 2251, Ibadan, Nigeria, West Africa; Nigerian Broadcasting Corp., Ibadan, Nigeria, West Africa; and c/o Federal Radio Corp., Broadcasting House, New Court Rd., Ibadan, Nigeria, West Africa.

*CAREER:* Worked on father's farm; trained as a coppersmith; employed by Nigerian Government Labor Department, Lagos, and by Nigerian Broadcasting Corp., Ibadan, Nigeria. Freelance writer. Visiting research fellow, University of Ife, 1979; associate, international writing program at University of Iowa, 1983. *Military service:* Royal Air Force, 1943-45; served as metal worker in Nigeria.

*MEMBER:* Mbari Club (Nigerian authors; founder).

*AWARDS, HONORS:* Named honorary citizen of New Orleans, 1983; *The Palm-Wine Drinkard and His Dead Palm-Wine Tapster in the Dead's Town* and *My Life in the Bush of*

*Ghosts* received second place awards in a contest held in Turin, Italy, 1985.

*WRITINGS:*

*The Palm-Wine Drinkard and His Dead Palm-Wine Tapster in the Dead's Town,* Faber, 1952, Grove, 1953.
*My Life in the Bush of Ghosts,* Grove, 1954, reprinted, Faber, 1978.
*Simbi and the Satyr of the Dark Jungle,* Faber, 1955.
*The Brave African Huntress,* illustrated by Ben Enwonwu, Grove, 1958.
*The Feather Woman of the Jungle,* Faber, 1962.
*Ajaiyi and His Inherited Poverty,* Faber, 1967.
(Contributor) *Winds of Change: Modern Short Stories from Black Africa,* Longman, 1977.
*The Witch-Herbalist of the Remote Town,* Faber, 1981.
*The Wild Hunter in the Bush of the Ghosts* (facsimile of manuscript), edited with an introduction and a postscript by Bernth Lindfors, Three Continents Press, 1982, second edition, 1989.
(Compiler and translator) *Yoruba Folktales,* Ibadan University Press, 1986.
*Pauper, Brawler, and Slanderer,* Faber, 1987.
*The Village Witch Doctor and Other Stories,* Faber, 1990.

Work also represented in anthologies, including *Darkness and Light: An Anthology of African Writing,* Peggy Rutherford, editor, Drum Publications, 1958; *An African Treasury: Articles, Essays, Stories, Poems by Black Africans,* Langston Hughes, editor, Crown, 1960; *Anthologie africaine et malgache,* Hughes and Christiane Reynault, editors, Seghers, 1962; *Reflections,* Frances Ademola, editor, African Universities Press, 1962, new edition, 1965; *Anthologie de la litterature negroafricaine: Romanciers et conteurs negro africains,* Leonard Sainville, editor, two volumes, Presence Africaine, 1963; *A Selection of African Prose,* W. H. Whiteley, compiler, two volumes, Oxford University Press, 1964; *Modern African Prose,* Richard Rive, editor, Heinemann Educational, 1964; *Modern African Stories,* Ellis Ayitey Komey and Ezekiel Mphahlele, editors, Faber, 1964; *African-English Literature: A Survey and Anthology,* Anne Tibble, editor, Peter Owen, 1965; *Through African Eyes,* Paul Edwards, compiler, two volumes, Cambridge University Press, 1966; *African Writing Today,* Ezekiel Mphahlele, editor, Penguin, 1967; *Political Spider: An Anthology of Stories from "Black Orpheus,"* Ulli Beier, editor, Heinemann Educational, 1969; *African Short Stories: A Collection of Contemporary African Writing,* Charles Larson, editor, Macmillan, 1970.

*ADAPTATIONS:* Kola Ogunmola has written a play in Yoruba entitled *Omuti,* based on *The Palm-Wine Drinkard and His Dead Palm-Wine Tapster in the Dead's Town,* published by West African Book Publishers.

*SIDELIGHTS:* With the publication of his novel *The Palm-Wine Drinkard and His Dead Palm-Wine Tapster in the Dead's Town* in 1952, Amos Tutuola became the first internationally recognized Nigerian writer. Since that time, Tutuola's works, in particular *The Palm-Wine Drinkard,* have been the subject of much critical debate. *The Palm-Wine Drinkard* was praised by critics outside of Nigeria for its unconventional use of the English language, its adherence to the oral tradition, and its unique, fantastical characters and plot. Nigerian critics, on the other hand, described the work as ungrammatical and unoriginal. Discussing the first criticism in his book *The Growth of the African Novel,* Eustace Palmer writes: "Tutuola's English is demonstrably poor; this is due partly to his ignorance of the more complicated rules of English syntax and partly to interference from Yoruba." The second criticism, concerning Tutuola's lack of originality, is based on similarities between Tutuola's works and those of his predecessor, O. B. Fagunwa, who writes in the Yoruba language.

The influence of Fagunwa's writings on Tutuola's work has been noted by several critics, including Abiola Irele, who writes in *The African Experience in Literature and Ideology:* "It is clear that much of the praise and acclaim that have been lavished upon Tutuola belong more properly to Fagunwa who provided not only the original inspiration but indeed a good measure of material for Tutuola's novels. The echoes of Fagunwa in Tutuola's works are numerous enough to indicate that the latter was consciously creating from a model provided by the former." Irele adds, however, "that despite its derivation from the work of Fagunwa, Tutuola's work achieves an independent status that it owes essentially to the force of his individual genius."

Tutuola's genius is described by reviewers as an ability to refashion the traditional Yoruba myths and folktales that are the foundation of his work. Eustace Palmer notes, for instance, in *The Growth of the African Novel:* "Taking his stories direct from his people's traditional lore, he uses his inexhaustible imagination and inventive power to embellish them, to add to them or alter them, and generally transform them into his own stories conveying his own message." O. R. Dathorne comments in an essay published in *Introduction to Nigerian Literature:* "Tutuola is a literary paradox; he is completely part of the folklore traditions of the Yorubas and yet he is able to modernize these traditions in an imaginative way. It is on this level that his books can best be approached.... Tutuola deserves to be considered seriously because his work represents an intentional attempt to fuse folklore with modern life."

In *The Palm-Wine Drinkard,* for example, the Drinkard's quest for his tapster leads him into many perilous situations, including an encounter with the Red Fish, a monster Tutuola describes as having thirty horns "spread out as an umbrella," and numerous eyes that "were closing and opening at the same time as if a man was pressing a switch on and off." Tutuola also amends a traditional tale concerning a Skull who borrows appendages belonging to other persons in order to look like a "complete gentleman" to include references to modern warfare. Tutuola writes: "If this gentleman went to the battle field, surely, enemy would not kill him or capture him and if bombers saw him in a town which was to be bombed, they would not throw bombs on his presence, and if they did throw it, the bomb itself would not explode until this gentleman would leave that town, because of his beauty." Gerald Moore observes in *Seven African Writers* that these descriptions are evidence "of Tutuola's easy use of the paraphernalia of modern life to give sharpness and immediacy to his imagery."

*The Palm-Wine Drinkard* was hailed by critics such as V. S. Pritchett and Dylan Thomas, the latter of whom describes the work in the *Observer* as a "brief, thronged, grisly and bewitching story." Thomas concludes: "The writing is nearly always terse and direct, strong, wry, flat and savoury.... Nothing is too prodigious or too trivial put down in this tall, devilish story." The work also has been favorably compared to such classics as *The Odyssey, Pilgrim's Progress,* and *Gulliver's Travels.* Some critics, however, expressed reservations about Tutuola's ability to repeat his success. According to Charles R. Larson's *The Emergence of African Fiction,* critic Anthony West stated, "*The Palm-Wine Drinkard* must be valued for its own freakish sake, and as an unrepeatable happy hit."

Despite the reservations of critics like West, Tutuola went on to publish several additional works, and while critics are, as Larson observes in *The Emergence of African Fiction,* "a little less awed now than they were in the early 1950's," Tutuola's works continue to merit critical attention. His novel *The Wild Hunter in the Bush of the Ghosts* has been a source of scholarly interest in part because of its unusual publishing history. The book was the first long narrative that Tutuola had written; he finished it in 1948 and sent the manuscript to Focal Press, an English publisher of photography books. It remained there, unpublished, until 1982, when Three Continents Press issued a limited scholar's edition.

Like Tutuola's other early works, *The Wild Hunter in the Bush of the Ghosts* concerns a protagonist who embarks on a long, dangerous journey through the wilderness. Wandering from village to village, the narrator encounters strange, ghostly creatures and experiences ordeals that test his wits and his strength of spirit. After visits to both Heaven and Hell, the hero returns to the earthly world, determined to help his people with the knowledge he has gained from his travels. Critical response to *The Wild Hunter* again centered on Tutuola's unique, fractured syntax. John Haynes, writing in the *Times Literary Supplement,* applauded Tutuola's "tellingly non-standard deploy-

ment of the 'bureaucratese' of his civil service years," and he also commended the author's imaginative style, stating, "Tutuola can always produce any situation he wants whatever, at any point. What compels his reader's interest is neither the 'naivety' of the writing, nor the bizarre ghosts he concocts, but his sheer intensity and worry about his hero's spiritual quest."

Among the more widely reviewed of Tutuola's books is *The Witch-Herbalist of the Remote Town.* Published thirty years after *The Palm-Wine Drinkard,* this book involves a quest initiated by the protagonist, a hunter, to find a cure for his wife's barrenness. The journey to the Remote Town takes six years; along the way the hunter encounters bizarre and sometimes frightening places and people, including the Town of the Born-and-Die Baby and the Abnormal Squatting Man of the Jungle, who can paralyze opponents with a gust of frigid air by piercing his abdomen. The hunter eventually reaches the Remote Town, and the witch-herbalist gives him a broth guaranteed to make his wife fertile. The plot is complicated though, when the hunter, weak from hunger, sips some of the broth.

As with *The Palm-Wine Drinkard,* critical commentary of *The Witch-Herbalist of the Remote Town* focuses in particular on Tutuola's use of the English language. Edward Blishen, for instance, comments in the *Times Educational Supplement:* "The language is wonderfully stirring and odd: a mixture of straight translation from Yoruba, and everyday modern Nigerian idiom, and grand epical English. The imagination at work is always astonishing.... And this, not the bargain, is folklore not resurrected, but being created fresh and true in the white heat of a tradition still undestroyed." *Voice Literary Supplement* critic Jon Parales writes: "His direct, apparently simple language creates an anything-can-happen universe, more whacky and amoral than the most determinedly modern lit." *Washington Post Book World* contributor Judith Chettle offers this view: "Tutuola writes with an appealing vigor and his idiosyncratic use of the English idiom gives the story a fresh and African perspective, though at times the clumsiness of some phrasing does detract from the thrust of the narrative. No eye-dabbing sentimentalist, Tutuola's commentary is clear-eyed if not acerbic, but underlying the tale is a quiet and persistent lament for the simpler, unsophisticated and happier past of his people."

*Africa Today* contributor Nancy J. Schmidt observes that Tutuola's language has become increasingly more like that of standard English over the years. She cites other differences between this work and earlier ones as well. "Tutuola's presence is very evident in *Witch-Herbalist,* but the strength of his presence and his imagination are not as strong as they once were," writes Schmidt, who adds that "neither Tutuola nor his hero seem to be able to take a consistent moral stand, a characteristic that is distinctly different from Tutuola's other narratives." Commenting on the reasons for these differences, Schmidt writes: "They may reflect contemporary Yoruba culture, Tutuola's changing attitude toward Yoruba and Nigerian cultures as well as his changing position in Yoruba and Nigerian cultures, the difficulties of writing an oral narrative for an audience to whom oral narratives are becoming less familiar and less related to daily behavior, and the editorial policies for publishing African fictional narratives in the 1980s."

In the *New York Times Book Review,* Charles Larson likewise notes Tutuola's use of standard English, but maintains that "the outstanding quality of Mr. Tutuola's work—the brilliance of the oral tradition—still remains." Larson concludes: "'The Witch-Herbalist of the Remote Town' is Mr. Tutuola at his imaginative best. Every incident in the narrative breathes with the life of the oral tradition; every episode in the journey startles with a kind of indigenous surrealism. Amos Tutuola is still his continent's most fantastic storyteller."

*BIOGRAPHICAL/CRITICAL SOURCES:*

*BOOKS*

Collins, Harold R., *Amos Tutuola,* Twayne, 1969.
*Contemporary Literary Criticism,* Gale, Volume 5, 1976, Volume 14, 1980, Volume 29, 1984.
Herskovits, Melville J., and Francis S. Herskovits, *Dahomean Narrative: A Cross-Cultural Analysis,* Northwestern University Press, 1958.
Irele, Abiola, *The African Experience in Literature and Ideology,* Heinemann, 1981.
King, Bruce, editor, *Introduction to Nigerian Literature,* Evans Brothers, 1971.
Larson, Charles R., *The Emergence of African Fiction,* revised edition, Indiana University Press, 1972.
Laurence, Margaret, *Long Drums and Cannons: Nigerian Dramatists,* Praeger, 1969.
Lindfors, Bernth, editor, *Critical Perspectives on Amos Tutuola,* Three Continents Press, 1975.
Lindfors, Bernth, *Early Nigerian Literature,* Africana Publishing, 1982.
Moore, Gerald, *Seven African Writers,* Oxford University Press, 1962.
Palmer, Eustace, *The Growth of the African Novel,* Heinemann, 1979.
Tucker, Martin, *Africa in Modern Literature: A Survey of Contemporary Writing in English,* Ungar, 1967.
Tutuola, Amos, *The Palm-Wine Drinkard and His Dead Palm-Wine Tapster in the Dead's Town,* Faber, 1952, Grove, 1953.

*PERIODICALS*

*Africa Today,* Volume 29, number 3, 1982.
*Ariel,* April, 1977.
*Books Abroad,* summer, 1968.
*Critique,* fall/winter, 1960-61, fall/winter, 1967-68.
*Journal of Canadian Fiction,* Volume 3, number 4, 1975.
*Journal of Commonwealth Literature,* August, 1974; August, 1981; Volume 17, number 1, 1982.
*Listener,* December 14, 1967.
*London Review of Books,* April 2, 1987.
*Los Angeles Times Book Review,* August 15, 1982.
*Nation,* September 25, 1954.
*New Statesman,* December 8, 1967.
*New Yorker,* April 23, 1984.
*New York Times Book Review,* July 4, 1982.
*Observer,* July 6, 1952; November 22, 1981.
*Okikie,* September, 1978.
*Presence Africaine,* third trimestre, 1967.
*Spectator,* October 24, 1981.
*Times Educational Supplement,* February 26, 1982.
*Times Literary Supplement,* January 18, 1968; February 26, 1982; August 28, 1987; May 18, 1990.
*Voice Literary Supplement,* June, 1982.
*Washington Post,* July 13, 1987.
*Washington Post Book World,* August 15, 1982.

\* \* \*

**USENI**
   **See PERKINS,   (Useni) Eugene**

\* \* \*

**UZODINMA,   E(dmund) C(hukuemeka) C(hieke)   1936-**

*PERSONAL:* Born in 1936 in Eastern Nigeria. *Education:* Attended Ibadan University; received B.A. from University of London.

*CAREER:* Teacher at Our Lady's High School in Onitsha, Nigeria; principal of Aguata Community Grammar School, Nigeria; writer.

*WRITINGS:*

*Brink of Dawn: Stories of Nigeria,* Longman of Nigeria, 1966.
*Our Dead Speak* (novel), Longman, 1967.

**VAIL, Amanda**
**See MILLER, Warren**

\*    \*    \*

**Van DEBURG, William L.   1948-**

*PERSONAL:* Born May 8, 1948, in Kalamazoo, MI; son of Lloyd E. (a retired newspaper advertising manager) and Cora E. (a homemaker; maiden name, Flaugh) Van Deburg; married Alice Honeywell, July 1, 1967 (divorced February, 1988); married Diane Sommers (a systems analyst), June 17, 1989; children: Marcie, Theodore. *Education:* Western Michigan University, B.A., 1970; Michigan State University, M.A., 1971, Ph.D., 1973. *Politics:* "Continually skeptical, often frustrated, left-of-center democrat." *Religion:* "Theologically conservative, socially radical Protestant." *Avocational interests:* "Aficionado of the country blues, legatee of the Big Bopper."

*ADDRESSES: Home*—4133 Cherokee Dr., Madison, WI 53711. *Office*—University of Wisconsin, 4214 Humanities Bldg., 455 Park St., Madison, WI 53706.

*CAREER:* University of Wisconsin, Madison, WI, assistant professor, 1973-79, associate professor, 1979-85, chair of department, 1981-84, professor of Afro-American studies, 1985—. Consultant to the Educational Testing Service, Center for the Study of Southern Culture, and Smithsonian Institution.

*MEMBER:* Organization of American Historians, Southern Historical Association.

*AWARDS, HONORS:* Fellow, National Defense Education Act, 1970-73 and Danforth, 1975-81; grants from American Philosophical Society, 1974, Alfred P. Sloan Foundation, 1975, and Spencer Foundation, 1979; William F. Vilas Trust, 1986-88.

*WRITINGS:*

*The Slave Drivers: Black Agricultural Labor Supervisors In the Antebellum South,* Greenwood Press, 1979.
*Slavery and Race In American Popular Culture,* University of Wisconsin Press, 1984.
*New Day In Babylon: The Black Power Movement and American Culture,* University of Chicago Press, 1992.

Also contributor of articles and reviews to periodicals, including *South Atlantic Quarterly, Historian, Journal of Popular Culture,* and *Journal of American History.*

*WORK IN PROGRESS: Black Camelot: Afro-American Culture Heroes, 1960-1980,* "a study of black sports heroes, film stars, musicians, and fictional heroes as they relate to the popular culture and the black activism of the 1960s and 1970s."

\*    \*    \*

**Van PEEBLES, Melvin   1932-**

*PERSONAL:* Born August 21, 1932, in Chicago, IL; children: Mario, Meggan, Melvin. *Education:* Graduated from Ohio Wesleyan University.

*CAREER:* Writer, actor, producer of plays, director, and composer. Worked as operator of cable cars in San Francisco, CA, and as a floor trader for the American Stock Exchange. Director of motion pictures, including *Watermelon Man,* 1970. *Military service:* U.S. Air Force; served as navigator-bombardier.

*MEMBER:* Directors Guild of America, French Directors Guild.

*AWARDS, HONORS:* First Prize from Belgian Festival for *Don't Play Us Cheap.*

*WRITINGS:*

*Un ours pour le F.B.I.* (novel), Buchet-Chastel, 1964, translation published as *A Bear for the F.B.I.,* Trident, 1968.
*Un Americain en enfer* (novel), Editions Denoel, 1965, translation published as *The True American: A Folk Fable,* Doubleday, 1976.
*Le Chinois du XIV* (short stories), Le Gadenet, 1966.
*La Fete a Harlem* [and] *La Permission* (two novels; former adapted from the play by Van Peebles, *Harlem Party*), J. Martineau, 1967, translation of *La Fete a Harlem,* published as *Don't Play Us Cheap: A Harlem Party,* Bantam, 1973.
*Sweet Sweetback's Baadasssss Song* (adapted from the screenplay by Van Peebles), Lancer Books, 1971.
*The Making of Sweet Sweetback's Baadasssss Song* (nonfiction), Lancer Books, 1972.
*Aint Supposed to Die a Natural Death* (play; directed by the author and produced in New York City at the Ethel Barrymore Theatre, 1971; adapted from the recordings by Van Peebles, "Brer Soul" and "Ain't Supposed to Die a Natural Death"), Bantam, 1973.
*Just an Old Sweet Song,* Ballantine, 1976.
(With Kenneth Vose, Leon Capetanos, and Lawrence Du Kose) *Greased Lightning* (screenplay; produced by Warner Bros., 1977), Yeah, 1976.

*Bold Money: A New Way to Play the Options Market,* Warner
    Books, 1986.
*Bold Money: How to Get Rich in the Options Market,* Warner
    Books, 1987.
(With Mario Van Peebles) *No Identity Crisis: A Father and
    Son's Own Story of Working Together,* Simon & Schus-
    ter, 1990.

OTHER

*Harlem Party* (play), produced in Belgium, 1964, produced
    as *Don't Play Us Cheap,* directed by the author and pro-
    duced in New York City at the Ethel Barrymore Theatre,
    1972.
(And director) *The Story of a Three Day Pass* (screenplay),
    Sigma III, 1968.
(And director) *Sweet Sweetback's Baadasssss Song* (screen-
    play), Cinemation Industries, 1971.
*Sophisticated Gents* (television miniseries; adapted from *The
    Junior Bachelor Society* by John A. Williams), NBC-TV,
    1981.
*Waltz of the Stork* (play), directed by author and produced in
    New York City at the Century Theatre, 1982.
*Champeeen!* (play), directed by author and produced in New
    York City at the New Federal Theatre, 1983.

Also author and director of *Don't Play Us Cheap* (adapted
from the play by Van Peebles). Also creator of short films,
including "Sunlight," Cinema 16, and "Three Pick Up Men
for Herrick," Cinema 16. Composer for recordings, including "Brer Soul," "Aint Supposed to Die a Natural Death,"
"Watermelon Man" (soundtrack for the motion picture), "Serious as a Heart Attack," "Sweet Sweetback's Baadasssss
Song" (soundtrack for the motion picture), and "Don't Play
Us Cheap" (soundtrack for the motion picture).

SIDELIGHTS: Melvin Van Peebles began his career as an
artist by creating short films. He had hoped that his first film
efforts would lead to a filmmaking opportunity in Hollywood,
but moguls there were unimpressed. Instead of obtaining a
position as a director or even assistant director, he was offered
a job as an elevator operator. Seemingly at a dead end, Van
Peebles suddenly received word from Henri Langlois, an associate of the French Cinematheque film depository who'd
been impressed with Van Peebles's films. Langlois invited
Van Peebles to come to Paris. There, Van Peebles enjoyed
brief celebrity as an avant-garde filmmaker. But he had no
opportunities to pursue filmmaking.

Van Peebles worked for some time as an entertainer in cafes
until he discovered a means by which he could once again take
up filmmaking. In France, one could gain entry into the Directors Guild if he wished to adapt his own French writings.
So Van Peebles, in self-taught French, began writing novels.

His first work, *A Bear for the F.B.I.,* concerned events in the
life of an American middle-class black. Critical response was
favorable, with Martin Levin remarking in the *New York Times
Book Review* that "Van Peebles crystallizes the racial problem with rare subtlety." However, Van Peebles noted that the
subtlety of the novel hindered his chances of being published
in the United States. "I wrote the first work and my 'calling
card,' to establish my reputation so I could get my 'black'
novels published," Van Peebles claimed. "But the publishers
aren't interested unless you either lacerate whites or apolo-
gize to them."

American publishers displayed a similar lack of interest toward Van Peebles's next novel, *The True American,* which
was written in 1965 but not published in the United States until
1976. It is the story of George Abraham Carver, a black prisoner who is accidentally killed by falling rocks. Carver arrives
in Hell and learns that blacks are treated well there. This is
because the majority of Hell's residents are white and, supposedly, the preferential attention the blacks receive causes
the white residents more grief. Despite the "promising"
premise, the novel was reviewed unfavorably in *New Yorker.*
"Unfortunately," wrote the critic, "the book never really lives
up to its promise, largely because of its pasteboard characters,
its meandering plot, and its author's tendency to us a two-ton
sledgehammer to drive home every point he makes about racist
America."

Van Peebles continued to write, though, and produced in rapid
succession a collection of short stories, *Le Chinois du XIV,*
and two short novels, *La Fete a Harlem* and *La Permission.*
At the same time, he was also arranging another film project.
With the financial assistance of the French Ministry of Cultural Affairs and a private citizen, Van Peebles made *The Story
of a Three Day Pass,* a film about a black soldier's encounter
with a French woman. *The Story of a Three Day Pass* attracted substantial audiences in France and, upon its release in the
United States, Van Peebles was in demand in Hollywood.

In 1969, after returning to the United States, Van Peebles
agreed to direct a film written by Herman Raucher entitled
*Watermelon Man.* This film deals with a white insurance agent
who awakens one morning to discover that he's turned into a
black man. "It's authentic stuff," related Van Peebles, "that
laughs with, not at people." Later, he insisted, "I thought I had
to make *Watermelon Man* in order to do the films I really
wanted to do."

Van Peebles's next film, *Sweet Sweetback's Baadasssss Song,*
is probably his best known work to date. He made the film in
three weeks, using nonunion crews while keeping union officials disinterested by spreading rumors that he was making a
pornographic film, something unworthy of their attention.

Hollywood had refused to finance the film after a ready of the screenplay failed to impress studio officials. Fortunately, Van Peebles received a sizeable loan from actor and comedian Bill Cosby which enabled him to complete the film. There was also difficulty promoting the film. Distributors declined to present it, theatres refused to book it, and talk shows refused to host Van Peebles. Eventually, he resorted to promoting it himself by passing out leaflets on street corners. Such determination ultimately paid off for Van Peebles. As a writer for *Time* noted, Van Peebles's "fast talk, plus audience work of mouth, made it a limited success. But that was enough." After the initial success of the film, it was mass-released to more than one hundred theatres and enjoyed brief status as the top money-making film in *Variety.*

The film elicited a variety of critical responses. The story, in which a youth's beating at the hands of two policemen is avenged by a black sex-show performer who murders the officers and escapes to Mexico, enraged some reviewers. Robert Hatch accused him in *Nation* of relying "on rather irresponsible contemporary emotionalism to revitalize stock films he must have seen in his childhood." In the *New York Times* Vincent Canby claimed, "instead of dramatizing injustice, Van Peebles merchandizes it." He also declared that "the militancy of *Sweet Sweetback* is of a dull order, seemingly designed only to reinforce the prejudices of black audiences without in any way disturbing those prejudices." Clayton Riley conceded in the *New York Times,* "The film is an outrage," but then observed that it was "designed to blow minds." He wrote, "Through the lens of the Van Peebles camera comes a very basic Black America, unadorned by faith, and seething with an eternal violence." In the same review, Riley contended, "it is a terrifying vision, the Blood's nightmare journey through Watts, and it is a vision Black people alone will really understand in all its profane and abrasive substance." In his study of black filmmakers published in the 1979 book, *American Film Now: The People, the Power, the Money, the Movies,* James Monaco takes a new look at Van Peebles's 1971 screenplay. "[*Sweet Sweetback's Baadasssss Song*] situates itself squarely in a long and important tradition in Black American narrative art," Monaco writes. "The Sweetback character has been mimicked and repeated a number of times since, but never with such purity of purpose and such *elan.* Van Peebles bent the medium of film to his will. No one else has bent it so far or so well since."

Van Peebles told a *Time* reporter that the film was not just for black audiences. "If films are good," he expressed, "the universality of the human experience will transcend the race and creed and crap frontiers." But he also noted that the film does have some specific messages for blacks. "Of all the ways we've been exploited by the Man, the most damaging is the way he destroyed our self-image," he asserted. "The message of *Sweetback* is that if you can get it together and stand up to the Man, you can win." In a *New York Times* interview, Van Peebles asked a writer, "When's the last time you saw a film in which the black man won in the end?" He then declared, "In my film, the black audience finally gets a chance to see some of their own fantasies acted out—about rising out of the mud and kicking ass."

After the success of *Sweet Sweetback,* Van Peebles was inundated with filmmaking offers from Hollywood studios. However, he insisted that he maintain his independence. "I'll only work with them on my terms," he stated. "I've whipped the man's ass on his own turf. I'm number one at the box office—which is the way America measures things—and I did it on my own. Now they want me, but I'm in no hurry."

Much of Van Peebles's most recent work has been as a playwright. *Aint Supposed to Die a Natural Death,* his first play to be produced in the United States, proved to be a popular one with Broadway audiences. In *Cue,* Marilyn Stasio called it a "tremendously vital musical with a dynamic new form all its own." She also write, "The show is an electrifying piece of theatre without having songs, a book, a story line, choreography, or even standard production numbers—and yet all these elements are on the stage, skillfully integrated into a jolting new experience." And Peter Bailey commented in *Black World* that *Aint Supposed to Die a Natural Death* "presented us with an effective and meaningful evening in the theater. Broadway has never seen anything like it. Van Peebles' characters come alive and make us deal with them on their own terms."

A writer for *Variety* was impressed with the U.S. production of another Van Peebles play, *Don't Play Us Cheap.* The reviewer noted that "this new show does not seem to be infused with hate, and it offers what appears to [be] a racial attitude without foul language, deliberate squalor or snarling ugliness." The same critic observed that "points are made with humor rather than rage and are probably more palatable for general audiences." "*Don't Play Us Cheap* is a somewhat special show," concluded the writer for *Variety,* "probably with greater meaning and appeal for black audiences than for whites." Van Peebles later adapted the play for film.

In 1986, Van Peebles published *Bold Money: A New Way to Play the Options Market,* adding another twist to his variety of writing talents. As a result of losing an interesting wager with a friend, Van Peebles was obliged to take the examination to become an options trader. After failing the exam, Van Peebles became a clerk on the floor of the American Stock Exchange in order to learn enough to pass the exam. As Van Peebles told Laurie Cohen and Fred Mac Biddle in the *Chicago Tribune,* "If I had to find one characteristic that is most symbolic of me, I think I am tenacious."

After trading options for three years and passing the examination, Van Peebles was asked by Warner Books to write a how-to-book on making money in the options market. A critic for *Kirkus Reviews* writes of *Bold Money: A New Way to Play the Options Market* that Van Peebles's "often impudent but prudent text is an excellent choice for rookies seeking a like-it-is introduction to a fast game." A year after his first money book was published he wrote *Bold Money: How to Get Rich in the Option Market*.

*BIOGRAPHICAL/CRITICAL SOURCES:*

*BOOKS*

*Contemporary Literary Criticism,* Gale, Volume 2, 1974, Volume 20, 1982.
Monaco, James, *American Films Now: The People, the Power, the Money, the Movies,* Oxford University Press, 1979.

*PERIODICALS*

*Best Sellers,* October 15, 1968.
*Black World,* April, 1972.
*Chicago Tribune,* March 24, 1986.
*Cue,* October 30, 1971; May 27, 1972.
*Kirkus Reviews,* December 1, 1985.
*Nation,* May 24, 1971.
*Newsweek,* June 6, 1969; June 21, 1971.
*New Yorker,* March 1, 1976.
*New York Times,* May 18, 1969; April 24, 1971; May 9, 1971; September 29, 1981; January 6, 1982.
*New York Times Book Review,* October 6, 1968.
*Saturday Review,* August 3, 1968.
*Time,* August 16, 1971.
*Variety,* May 24, 1971.

\*   \*   \*

# Van SERTIMA, Ivan   1935-

*PERSONAL:* Born January 26, 1935, in Kitty Village, Guyana; son of Frank Obermuller (an administrator and trade union leader) and Clara (Smith) Van Sertima; married Maria Nagy, October 24, 1964; children: Lawrence Josef. *Education:* London School of Oriental and African Studies, London, B.A. (with honors), 1969; Rutgers University, M.A., 1977.

*ADDRESSES: Home*—59 South Adelaide Ave., Highland Park, NJ 08904. *Office*—Department of African Studies, Douglass College, Rutgers University, New Brunswick, NJ 08094.

*CAREER:* Government Information Services (Guyana Civil Service), Georgetown, Guyana, press and broadcasting officer, 1956-59; Central Office of Information, London, England, broadcaster, 1969-70; Rutgers University, Douglass College, New Brunswick, NJ, instructor, 1970-72, assistant professor, 1972-79, associate professor of African studies, 1978—. Nominator for Nobel Prize in Literature, 1976-80. President of *Journal of African Civilizations* Ltd. Inc.

*MEMBER:* African Heritage Association, American Association of University Professors, Caribbean Artists Movement.

*AWARDS, HONORS:* Clarence L. Holte prize, Twenty-first Century Foundation, 1981, for *They Came before Columbus: The African Presence in Ancient America.*

*WRITINGS:*

*River and the Wall* (poems), Miniature Poets, 1958.
*Caribbean Writers: Critical Essays,* New Beacon Books, 1968, Panther House, 1971.
*Swahili Dictionary of Legal Terms,* [Tanzania], 1968.
*They Came before Columbus: The African Presence in Ancient America,* Random House, 1977.
(Editor) *Blacks in Science: Ancient and Modern,* Transaction Books, 1983.
(Editor) *Black Women in Antiquity,* Transaction Books, 1984.
(Editor) *African Presence in Early Europe,* Transaction Books, 1985.
(Editor with Runoko Rashidi) *African Presence in Early Asia,* Transaction Books, 1985.
(Editor) *Great African Thinkers, Volume 1: Cheikh Anta Diop,* Transaction Publishers, 1986.
(Editor) *African Presence in Early America,* Transaction Books, 1987.
(Editor) *Great Black Leaders: Ancient and Modern,* Transaction Publishers, 1988.
(Editor) *Egypt Revisited,* Transaction Publishers, 1985, revised edition, 1991.
(Editor) *The Golden Age of the Moor,* Transaction Publishers, 1991.

Editor of *Nile Valley Civilizations: Proceedings of the Nile Valley Conference, Atlanta, September 26-30,* 1985. Contributor to books, including *Black Life and Culture in the United States,* edited by Rhoda Goldstein, Crowell, 1971; *Enigma of Values,* edited by Anna Rutherford, Dangaroo Press, 1975; *Seminar in Black English,* edited by Tom Trebasso, Lawrence Erbaum Associates, 1976. Contributor to periodicals, including *Inter-American Review.* Editor of *Journal of African Civilizations.*

*WORK IN PROGRESS:* Research on African presence in the art of the Americas.

*SIDELIGHTS:* Ivan Van Sertima is a prolific writer who has published numerous books dealing with African history and influence in the histories of the United States and other countries. He is also a poet and has published a collection of poems titled *River and the Wall. They Came before Columbus* is one of his first publications about African history. In this book Van Sertima argues that African people had a significant impact on the Precolumbian civilizations of the New World. He also claims that black Africans came to the Americas long before they were discovered by Christopher Columbus. He presents as evidence a negroid skeleton found in the Virgin Islands dating back to 1250 A.D., as well as the discovery by archeologists of pyramids in Central America. Other books by Van Sertima include *African Presence in Early Europe* and *Egypt Revisited.*

*BIOGRAPHICAL/CRITICAL SOURCES:*

*BOOKS*

*Contemporary Poets,* St. James Press, 1970, p. 1119.

*PERIODICALS*

*New York Times Book Review,* March 13, 1977, p. 8.

\* \* \*

# VANZANT, Iyanla (Rhonda) 1952-

*PERSONAL:* First name is pronounced "e-yon-la"; born September 13, 1952, in Brooklyn, NY; daughter of Horace Lester Harris and Sarah (Jefferson) Harris; married Charles Vanzant, Jr. (died January, 1984); children: Damon Keith, Gemmia Lynnette, Nisa Camille. *Education:* Medgar Evers College, B.S. (summa cum laude), 1983; Queens College of the City University of New York, J.D., 1988; doctoral studies at Temple University. *Religion:* "Ordained as a Yoruba priestess in 1983." *Avocational interests:* Gourmet cooking, astrology, herbalism, metaphysical healing practices, sewing.

*ADDRESSES: Agent*—Marie Brown Associates, 625 Broadway, New York, NY 10012.

*CAREER:* Federation of Addiction Agencies, Brooklyn, NY, drug rehabilitation counselor, 1972-79; Medgar Evers College, Brooklyn, director of Alumni Affairs, 1983-85; Philadelphia Public Defender's Association, Philadelphia, PA, attorney, 1988-90; Inner Visions Life Maintenance, Philadelphia, founder, director of training, 1990—. Talk show host, WHAT, Philadelphia, PA. Medgar Evers College Center for Women's Development, founding member; African Street Festival, board member, 1988—.

*MEMBER:* Association of Black Journalists, African Women's Sisterhood (Philadelphia branch), National Black Women's Health Project.

*AWARDS, HONORS:* Outstanding community service award, Brownsville Community Development Corporation, 1984.

*WRITINGS:*

*Crowing Glory,* Aaron Press, 1989.
*Tapping the Power Within: A Path to Self-Empowerment for Black Women,* Writers & Readers, 1992.
*Acts of Faith: Daily Meditations for People of Color,* Simon & Schuster, 1993.

Also author of *Interiors: A Black Woman's Healing in Progress,* in press. Contributor of articles to *Essence* and *Health Quest.*

*WORK IN PROGRESS: The Wealth of a Spiritual Woman: A Woman's Guide to Self-Preservation; There's Value in the Valley When You Fall and Think You Can't Get Up.*

*SIDELIGHTS:* Iyanla Vanzant commented: "My writing is dedicated to the evolution and empowerment of women throughout the world, particularly women of color. It is dedicated to my stepmother and best friend Lynnette Harris, who saved me from myself and loved me in spite of myself. It is the legacy I want to leave my grandchildren Oluwa and Asole."

\* \* \*

# VERTREACE, Martha M. 1945-

*PERSONAL:* Born November 24, 1945, in Washington, DC; daughter of Walter Charles Vertreace (a supply officer) and Modena (Kendrick) Vertreace (a supervisor). *Education:* District of Columbia Teachers College (now University of the District of Columbia), B.S., 1967; Roosevelt University, M.A., 1971, M.Ph., 1972; Mundelein College, M.S., 1981. *Politics:* Democratic socialist. *Religion:* Roman Catholic. *Avocational interests:* Knitting, photography, water colors.

*ADDRESSES: Home*—1157 East 56th St., Chicago, IL 60637-1531. *Office*—Kennedy-King College, 6800 South Wentworth Ave., Chicago, IL 60621. *Agent*—James Plath, 1108 North Clinton, Bloomington, IL 61701.

*CAREER:* Kennedy-King College, Chicago, IL, associate professor of English and poet in residence, 1977—. Member of board of trustees of Illinois Writers Review; member of advisory board of *City Magazine;* served as judge for Illinois Arts Council grants and Wisconsin Arts Board grants; served as Ariel judge for Triton College. Minister of Care, Saint Thomas the Apostle Church.

*MEMBER:* National Council of Teachers of English, Illinois Association for Teachers of English, Midwest Modern Language Association of America, Society of Midland Authors.

*AWARDS, HONORS:* Three literary awards from Illinois Arts Council; Excellence in Professional Writing Award, Illinois Association for Teachers of English; Hawthornden International Writers' Retreat fellow, 1992; Writers Center poetry fellow, 1993; Significant Illinois Poet Award, from Gwendolyn Brooks, 1993; National Endowment for the Arts creative writing fellowship, 1993.

*WRITINGS:*

*Second House from the Corner* (poems), Kennedy-King College, 1986.
*Kelly in the Mirror* (juvenile), illustrated by Sandra Speidel, Albert Whitman, 1993.
*Oracle Bones* (poems), White Eagle Coffee Store, in press.

Also author of *Under a Cat's-Eye Moon,* Clockwatch Review Press. Work represented in several anthologies, including *Benchmark: Anthology of Contemporary Illinois Poets,* Stormline Press, 1988; *American Women Writing Fiction,* University Press of Kentucky, 1989; *Mother Puzzles: Daughters and Mothers in Contemporary American Literature,* Greenwood Press, 1989; *The Anna Book,* Greenwood Press, 1993; and *Canadian Women Writing Fiction,* University Press of Mississippi, in press. *Oyez Review,* poetry editor; *Community Magazine,* book review editor; *Class Act,* editor; *Rhino,* co-editor; *Seams Magazine,* member of editorial board. Contributor to literary magazines.

*SIDELIGHTS:* Martha M. Vertreace commented: "I consider myself a poet—writing poetry primarily for the adult audience. My entry into writing children's books was quite by accident. The editor had read some of my poems and decided that I wrote with strong images. She invited me to try to write a picture book.

"When I write, my primary goal is to enjoy the experience. Perhaps, therefore, my work can bring joy to someone else. I write whenever I get the chance. I enjoy working in various forms; consequently, although most of my writing is poetry, I have published short stories, reviews, and critical essays.

"If I spoke of influences on my work, I would think of various poets—Richard Wilbur, Rita Dove, Amy Clampitt, Derek Walcott, Mona Van Duyn, Seamus Heaney—and many others.

"For me, writing is fun, although it is not necessarily easy. I began writing after the sudden death of my father when I was sixteen. It was a way to ease the tension and to focus on something else. I try not to judge my writing by asking whether or not the piece gets published; rather, my concern is that it expresses whatever I am after."

*BIOGRAPHICAL/CRITICAL SOURCES:*

*PERIODICALS*

*Booklist,* April 1, 1993.
*Chicago Tribune,* May 9, 1993, p. 6.
*Publishers Weekly,* March 29, 1993, p. 56.

# W-Y

## WADE-GAYLES, Gloria Jean

*PERSONAL:* Born in Memphis, TN; married Joseph Nathan Gayles; children: Jonathan, Monica. *Education:* LeMoyne College, B.A., 1959; Boston University, M.A., 1962; George Washington University, doctoral work, 1966-67; Emory University, Ph.D., 1981.

*ADDRESSES: Office*—Spelman College, Atlanta, GA 30314.

*CAREER:* Spelman College, instructor, 1963-64, assistant professor, 1984-89, professor of English and women's studies, 1989—; Howard University, instructor in English, 1965-67; Morehouse College, assistant professor, 1970-75; Emory University, graduate teaching fellow, 1975-77; Talladega College, assistant professor, 1977-78. Member of board of directors, WETV 30 and WABE-FM, 1976-77; partner in Jon-Mon Consultants, Inc.

*MEMBER:* Callaloo (member of board of directors, 1977—), College Language Association (member of executive board, 1977—), National Association for the Advancement of Colored People (NAACP), ASNLC, Congress of Racial Equality (CORE), Alpha Kappa Mu National Honor Society, Alpha Kappa Alpha Sorority, Inc.

*AWARDS, HONORS:* Boston University Woodrow Wilson fellow, 1962; Merrill Travel Grant to Europe, Charles Merrill Foundation, 1973; Danforth Fellow, 1974; National Endowment for the Humanities fellow, 1975; Faculty of the Year award, Morehouse College, 1975; Outstanding Young Woman of America, 1975; United Negro College Fund Mellon Research Grant, 1987-88, Liaison with National Humanities Faculty; DuBois Research Fellow, Harvard University, 1990; CASE Professor for Excellence in Teaching for the State of Georgia, 1991.

*WRITINGS:*

*No Crystal Stair: Visions of Race and Sex in Black Women's Fiction, 1946-76,* Pilgrim Press, 1984.
*Anointed to Fly,* Harlem River Press, 1991.
*Pushed Back to Strength: A Black Woman's Journey Home,* Beacon Press, 1993.
*Moving in My Heart: African American Women's Spirituality,* Beacon Press, 1994.

Author of preface to *Sturdy Black Bridges,* Doubleday, 1979. Poetry and articles published in periodicals, including *Essence, Black World, Black Scholar, Callaloo, Liberator, Atlantic Monthly,* and *First World.* Editor, *Clanotes,* 1975—.

\* \* \*

## WALCOTT, Derek (Alton) 1930-

*PERSONAL:* Born January 23, 1930, in Castries, St. Lucia, West Indies; son of Warwick (a civil servant) and Alix (a teacher) Walcott; married Fay Moston, 1954 (divorced, 1959); married Margaret Ruth Maillard, 1962 (divorced); married Norline Metivier (an actress and dancer); children: one son (first marriage), two daughters (second marriage). *Education:* Attended St. Mary's College (St. Lucia); University of the West Indies (Kingston, Jamaica), B.A. 1953.

*ADDRESSES: Home*—(summer) 165 Duke of Edinburgh Ave., Diego Martin, Trinidad and Tobago; (winter) 71 St. Mary's, Brookline, MA 02146. *Office*—Creative Writing Department, Boston University, 236 Bay State Rd., Boston, MA 02215. *Agent*—Bridget Aschenberg, International Famous Agency, 1301 Avenue of the Americas, New York, NY 10019.

*CAREER:* Poet and playwright. Teacher at St. Mary's College, St. Lucia, West Indies, Boys' Secondary School, Grenada, and at Kingston College, Jamaica. Founding director of Trinidad Theatre Workshop, 1959—. Visiting professor at Columbia University, 1981, and Harvard University, 1982; visiting professor in Creative Writing Department of Boston University, 1985—. Also lecturer at Rutgers University and Yale University.

*AWARDS, HONORS:* Rockefeller fellowship, 1957; Jamaica Drama Festival prize, 1958, for *Drums and Colours;* Guinness Award, 1961, for "A Sea-Chantey"; Borestone Mountain poetry awards, 1963, for "Tarpon," and 1976, for "Midsummer, England"; named fellow of the Royal Society of Literature, 1966; Heinemann Award, Royal Society of Literature, 1966, for *The Castaway,* and 1983, for *The Fortunate Traveller;* Cholmondeley Award, 1969, for *The Gulf;* Eugene O'Neill Foundation-Wesleyan University fellowship, 1969; Order of the Humming Bird, Trinidad and Tobago, 1969 (one source says 1979); Obie Award, 1971, for *Dream on Monkey Mountain;* honorary doctorate of letters, University of the West Indies, 1972; Officer of British Empire, 1972; Jock Campbell/New Statesman Prize, 1974, for *Another Life;* Guggenheim fellowship, 1977; named honorary member of the American Academy and Institute of Arts and Letters, 1979; *American Poetry Review* Award, 1979; John D. and Catherine T. MacArthur Foundation grant, 1981; *Los Angeles Times Book Review* Prize in poetry, 1986, for *Collected Poems, 1948-1984;* International Writer's Prize, Welsh Arts Council, 1980; Nobel Prize for literature, 1992; St. Lucia Cross, 1993.

*WRITINGS:*

POETRY

*Twenty-Five Poems,* Guardian Commercial Printery, 1948.
*Epitaph for the Young: A Poem in XII Cantos,* Advocate (Bridgetown, Barbados), 1949.
*Poems,* Kingston City Printery (Jamaica), 1953.
*In a Green Night: Poems, 1948-1960,* J. Cape, 1962.
*Selected Poems* (includes poems from *In a Green Night: Poems, 1948-1960*), Farrar, Straus, 1964.
*The Castaway and Other Poems,* J. Cape, 1965.
*The Gulf and Other Poems,* J. Cape, 1969, published with selections from *The Castaway and Other Poems* as *The Gulf: Poems,* Farrar, Straus, 1970.
*Another Life* (long poem), Farrar, Straus, 1973, second edition published with introduction, chronology and selected bibliography by Robert D. Hammer, Three Continents Press, 1982.
*Sea Grapes,* J. Cape, 1976, slightly revised edition, Farrar, Straus, 1976.
*Selected Verse,* Heinemann, 1976.
*The Star-Apple Kingdom,* Farrar, Straus, 1979.

*The Fortunate Traveller,* Farrar, Straus, 1981.
*Selected Poetry,* selected, annotated, and introduced by Wayne Brown, Heinemann, 1981.
*The Caribbean Poetry of Derek Walcott, and the Art of Romare Beardon,* Limited Editions Club (New York), 1983.
*Midsummer,* Farrar, Straus, 1984.
*Collected Poems, 1948-1984,* Farrar, Straus, 1986.
*The Arkansas Testament,* Farrar, Straus, 1987.
*Omeros,* Farrar, Straus, 1989.

Contributor of poems to numerous periodicals, including *New Statesman, London Magazine, Encounter, Evergreen Review, Caribbean Quarterly, Tamarack Review,* and *Bim.*

PLAYS

*Henri Christophe: A Chronicle in Seven Scenes* (first produced in Castries, St. Lucia, West Indies, 1950, produced in London, England, 1951), Advocate (Bridgetown, Barbados), 1950.
*Harry Dernier: A Play for Radio Production,* Advocate, 1951.
*Wine of the Country,* University College of the West Indies (Mona, Jamaica), 1953.
*The Sea at Dauphin: A Play in One Act* (first produced in Mona, Jamaica, 1953, produced in London, 1960), Extra-Mural Department, University College of the West Indies, 1954.
*Ione: A Play with Music* (first produced in Port of Spain, Trinidad, 1957), Extra-Mural Department, University College of the West Indies, 1957.
*Drums and Colours: An Epic Drama* (published in *Caribbean Quarterly,* March-June, 1961), first produced in Kingston, Trinidad, 1958.
*In a Fine Castle,* first produced in Jamaica, 1970, produced in Los Angeles, CA, 1972.
*Ti-Jean and His Brothers,* first produced in Port of Spain, Trinidad, 1958, produced Off-Broadway at Delacorte Theatre, 1972.
*Malcochon; or, Six in the Rain* (one-act; first produced as *Malcochon* in Castries, St. Lucia, 1959, produced in London under title *Six in the Rain,* 1960, produced Off-Broadway at St. Mark's Playhouse, 1969), Extra-Mural Department, University of West Indies, 1966.
*Dream on Monkey Mountain,* first produced in Toronto, Ontario, Canada, 1967, produced Off-Broadway at St. Mark's Playhouse, 1971.
*Dream on Monkey Mountain and Other Plays* (contains *Dream on Monkey Mountain, Sea at Dauphin, Malcochon; or, Six in the Rain, Ti-Jean and His Brothers,* and the essay "What the Twilight Says: An Overture"), Farrar, Straus, 1970.
*The Joker of Seville* (musical), first produced in Port of Spain, Trinidad, 1974.

*The Charlatan,* first produced in Los Angeles, 1974.

*O Babylon!,* first produced in Port of Spain, Trinidad, 1976.

*Remembrance* (three-act), first produced in St. Croix, Virgin Islands, December, 1977, produced Off-Broadway at The Other Stage, 1979.

*Pantomime,* Port of Spain, Trinidad, 1978, produced Off-Broadway at the Hudson Guild Theater, 1986.

*The Joker of Seville and O Babylon!: Two Plays,* Farrar, Straus, 1978. *Remembrance & Pantomime: Two Plays,* Farrar, Straus, 1980.

*The Isle Is Full of Noises,* first produced at the John W. Huntington Theater, Hartford, CT, 1982.

*Three Plays* (contains "The Last Carnival," "Beef, No Chicken," and "A Branch of the Blue Nile"), Farrar, Straus, 1986.

Also author of "Franklin, a Tale of the Islands," "Jourmard," and "To Die for Grenada."

*CONTRIBUTOR*

John Figueroa, editor, *Caribbean Voices,* Evans, 1966.

Barbara Howes, editor, *From the Green Antilles,* Macmillan, 1966.

Howard Sergeant, editor, *Commonwealth Poems of Today,* Murray, 1967.

O.R. Dathorne, editor, *Caribbean Verse,* Heinemann, 1968.

Anne Walmsley, compiler, *The Sun's Eye: West Indian Writing for Young Readers,* Longmans, 1968.

Orde Coombs, editor, *Is Massa Day Dead?,* Doubleday, 1974.

D.J. Enright, editor, *Oxford Book of Contemporary Verse, 1945-1980,* Oxford University Press, 1980.

Errol Hill, editor, *Plays for Today,* Longman, 1985.

Also contributor to *Caribbean Literature,* edited by George Robert Coulthard; *New Voices of the Commonwealth,* edited by Sergeant; and *Young Commonwealth Poetry,* edited by Peter Ludwig Brent.

*OTHER*

Art and literature critic for *Trinidad Guardian;* feature writer for *Public Opinion* (Jamaica).

*SIDELIGHTS:* Although born of mixed racial and ethnic heritage on St. Lucia, a West Indian island where a French/English patois is spoken, poet and playwright Derek Walcott was educated as a British subject. Taught to speak English as a second language, he grew to be a skilled craftsman in his adopted tongue. His use of the language has drawn praise from critics including British poet and novelist Robert Graves who, according to *Times Literary Supplement* contributor Vicki Feaver, "has gone as far to state that [Walcott] handles English with a closer understanding of its inner magic than most

(if not all) of his English-born contemporaries." In their statement upon awarding Walcott the Nobel Prize for Literature, the Swedish Academy, as quoted in the *Detroit Free Press,* declared, "In him, West Indian culture has found its great poet." Walcott is the first native Caribbean writer to win the prize and in its citation, the Academy noted that "in his literary works, Walcott has laid a course for his own cultural environment, but through them he speaks to each and every one of us."

The major theme of Wolcott's writing is the dichotomy between black and white, subject and ruler, and the elements of both Caribbean and Western civilization present in his culture and ancestry. In "What the Twilight Says," the introduction to *Dream on Monkey Mountain and Other Plays,* Walcott refers to his "schizophrenic boyhood" in which he led "two lives: the interior life of poetry [and] the outward life of action and dialect." Robert D. Hamner in *Derek Walcott* notes that this schizophrenia is common among West Indians and comments further that "since [Walcott] is descended from a white grandfather and a black grandmother on both paternal and maternal sides, he is living example of the divided loyalties and hatreds that keep his society suspended between two worlds."

"As a West Indian ... writing in English, with Africa and England in his blood," Alan Shapiro writes in the *Chicago Tribune Book World,* "Walcott is inescapably the victim and beneficiary of the colonial society in which he was reared. He is a kind of a Caribbean Orestes ... unable to satisfy his allegiance to one side of his nature without at the same time betraying the other." Caryl Phillips describes Walcott's work in much the same way in a *Los Angeles Times Book Review* essay. The critic notes that Walcott's poetry is "steeped in an ambivalence toward the outside world and its relationship to his own native land of St. Lucia."

One often-quoted poem, "A Far Cry from Africa," from *In a Green Night,* deals directly with Walcott's sense of cultural confusion. "Where shall I turn, divided to the vein? / I who have cursed / the drunken officer of British rule, how choose / Between this Africa and the English tongue I love? / Betray them both, or give back what they give?" In another poem, "The Schooner Flight," from his second collection, *The Star-Apple Kingdom,* the poet uses a Trinidadian sailor named Shabine to appraise his own place as a person of mixed blood in a world divided into whites and blacks. According to the mariner: "The first chain my hands and apologise, 'History'; / the next said I wasn't black enough for their pride." Not white enough for whites, not black enough for blacks, Shabine sums up the complexity of his situation near the beginning of the poem saying: "I had a sound colonial education, / I have Dutch, nigger and English in me, / and either I'm nobody or I'm a nation."

It is Walcott, of course, who is speaking, and *New York Review of Books* contributor Thomas R. Edwards notes how the poet suffers the same fate as his poetic alter-ego, Shabine. Edwards writes, "Walcott is a cultivated cosmopolitan poet who is black, and as such he risks irrelevant praise as well as blame, whites finding it clever of him to be able to sound so much like other sophisticated poets, blacks feeling that he's sold his soul by practicing white arts."

Although pained by the contrasts in his background, Walcott has chosen to embrace both his island and colonial heritage. His love of both sides of his psyche is apparent in an analysis of his work. As Hamner notes: "Natured on oral tales of gods, devils, and cunning tricksters passed down by generations of slaves, Walcott should retell folk stories; and he does. On the other hand, since he has an affinity for and is educated in Western classics, he should retell the traditional themes of European experience; and he does. As inheritor of two vitally rich cultures, he utilizes one, then the other, and finally creates out of the two his own personalized style."

Walcott seems closest to his island roots in his plays. For the most part, he has reserved his native language—patois or creole—to them. They also feature Caribbean settings and themes. According to *Literary Review* contributor David Mason, through Walcott's plays he hopes to create a "catalytic theater responsible for social change or at least social identity."

Although a volume of poems was his first published work, Walcott originally concentrated his efforts on the theater. In the fifties, he wrote a series of plays in verse, including *Henri Christophe: A Chronicle, The Sea at Dauphin,* and *Ione.* The first play deals with an episode in Caribbean history: ex-slave Henri Christophe's rise to kingship of Haiti in the early 1800s. The second marks Walcott's first use of the mixed French/English language of his native island in a play. Dennis Jones notes in *Dictionary of Literary Biography Yearbook: 1981* that while Walcott uses the folk idiom of the islands in the play, the speech of the characters is not strictly imitative. It is instead "made eloquent, as the common folk represented in the work are made noble, by the magic of the artist."

In "What the Twilight Says" Walcott describes his use of language in his plays. In particular, he expresses the desire to mold "a language that went beyond mimicry,... one which finally settled on its own mode of inflection, and which begins to create an oral culture, of chants, jokes, folk-songs, and fables." The presence of "chants, jokes, and fables" in Walcott's plays causes critics such as Jones and the *Los Angeles Times*'s Juana Duty Kennedy to use the term "folk dramas" to describe the playwright's best pieces for theater. In *Books and Bookmen* Romilly Cavan observes the numerous folk elements in Walcott's plays: "The laments of superstitious fishermen,

charcoal-burners and prisoners are quickly counter-pointed by talking crickets, frogs, and birds. Demons are raised, dreams take actual shape, [and] supernatural voices mingle with the natural lilting elliptical speech rhythms of downtrodden natives." Animals who speak and a folk-representation of the devil, for example, are characters in the play, *Ti-Jean and His Brothers.*

Walcott's most highly praised play, *Dream on Monkey Mountain,* is also a folk drama. It was awarded a 1971 Obie Award and deemed "a poem in dramatic form" by Edith Oliver in the *New Yorker.* The play's title is itself enough to immediately transport the viewer into the superstitious legend-filled world of the Caribbean backcountry. In the play, Walcott draws a parallel between the hallucinations of an old charcoal vendor and the colonial reality of the Caribbean. Islanders subjected to the imposition of a colonial culture over their own eventually question the validity of both cultures. Ultimately, they may determine that their island culture—because it has no official status other than as an enticement for tourists—is nothing but a sterile hallucination. Or, as Jones notes, they may reach the conclusion at which Walcott wishes his audience to arrive: the charcoal vendor's "dreams connect to the past, and that it is in that past kept alive in the dreams of the folk that an element of freedom is maintained in the colonized world."

Perhaps because of critics' unfamiliarity with the Caribbean reality which Walcott describes in his plays, the author's work for theater has received only mixed reviews in this country. For example, while Walter Goodman writes in the *New York Times* that Walcott's *Pantomime* "stays with you as a fresh and funny work filled with thoughtful insights and illuminated by bright performances," the *New York Times*'s Frank Rich's comments on the same play are not as favorable. "Walcott's best writing has always been as a poet...," Rich observes, "and that judgment remains unaltered by 'Pantomime.' For some reason, [he] refuses to bring the same esthetic rigor to his playwriting that he does to his powerfully dense verse."

In James Atlas's *New York Times Magazine* essay on Walcott, the critic confronts Rich's remarks head on, asserting that the poet would respond to Rich by commenting "that he doesn't conceive of his plays as finished works but as provisional effects to address his own people. 'The great challenge to me,' he says, 'was to write as powerfully as I could without writing down to the audience, so that the large emotions could be taken in by a fisherman or a guy on the street, even if he didn't understand every line.'"

If Walcott's plays reveal what is most Caribbean about him, his poetry reveals what is most English. If he hopes to reach the common man in his plays, the same cannot be said of his poetry. His poems are based on the traditional forms of English poetry, filled with classical allusions, elaborate metaphors, complex rhyme schemes, and other poetic devices. In *New York Times Book Review,* Selden Rodman calls Walcott's poems "almost Elizabethan in their richness." *New York Times*'s Michiko Kakutani also recognized British influences in Walcott's poetry, noting that "from England, [Walcott] appropriated an old-fashioned love of eloquence, an Elizabethan richness of words and a penchant for complicated, formal rhymes. In fact, in a day when more and more poets have adopted a grudging, minimalist style, [his] verse remains dense and elaborate, filled with dazzling complexities of style."

Some critics object that Walcott's attention to style sometimes detracts from his poetry, either by being unsuitable for his Caribbean themes or by becoming more important than the poems' content. Denis Donoghue, for example, remarks in *New York Times Book Review,* "It is my impression that his standard English style [is] dangerously high for nearly every purpose except that of Jacobean tragedy." In Steve Ratiner's *Christian Science Monitor* review of *Midsummer,* the critic observes that "after a time, we are so awash in sparkling language and intricate metaphor, the subject of the poem is all but obscured." Helen Vendler, in the *New York Review of Books,* finds an "unhappy disjunction between [Walcott's] explosive subject ... and his harmonious pentameters, his lyrical allusions, his stately rhymes, [and] his Yeatsian meditations."

More criticism comes from those who maintain that the influence of other poets on Walcott's work have drowned out his authentic voice. While Vendler, for instance, describes Walcott as a "man of great sensibility and talent," she dismisses much of his poetry as "ventriloquism" and maintains that in Walcott's 1982 collection of poems, *The Fortunate Traveller,* he seems "at the mercy of influence, this time the influence of Robert Lowell." Poet J.D. McClatchy also notices Lowell's influence in *The Fortunate Traveller* as well as two other Walcott poetry collections: *The Star-Apple Kingdom* and *Midsummer.* In his *New Republic* review, McClatchy not only finds similarities in the two men's styles but also a similar pattern of development in their poetry. "Like Lowell," the critic notes, "Walcott's mode has ... shifted from the mythological to the historical, from fictions to facts, and his voice has gotten more clipped and severe. There are times when the influence is almost too direct, as in 'Old New England,' [a poem from *The Fortunate Traveller*] where he paces off Lowell's own territory."

Both major criticisms of Walcott's poetry are answered in Sven Birkerts's *New Republic* essay. Birkerts observes: "Walcott writes a strongly accented, densely packed line that seldom slackens and yet never loses conversational intimacy. He works in form, but he is not formal. His agitated phonetic surfaces can at times recall Lowell's, but the two are quite different. In Lowell, one feels the torque of mind; in Walcott,

the senses predominate. And Walcott's lines ring with a spontaneity that Lowell's often lack."

Other critics defend the integrity of Walcott's poems. Poet James Dickey notes in *New York Times Book Review,* "Fortunately, for him and for us,... Walcott has the energy and the exuberant strength to break through his literary influences into a highly colored, pulsating realm of his own." In his *Poetry* review of *Midsummer* Paul Breslin writes: "For the most part,... Walcott's voice remains as distinctive as ever, and the occasional echoes of Lowell register as homage rather than unwitting imitation."

In *Omeros,* whose title is the contemporary Greek word for Homer, Walcott pays homage to the ancient poet, in an epic poem that replaces the Homeric Cyclades with the Antilles. This is home to the main characters, Achille and Philoctete, fishermen who set out on a journey to their ancestral land, the coast of West Africa. The characters' concerns are not the events of the Trojan War, but rather the array of civilization, from African antiquity to frontier America and present-day Boston and London. Half-way through the book, the poet himself enters the narrative. Nick Owchar remarks in the *Los Angeles Times Book Review* that "the message of *Omeros* grows with the poet's entrance." He notes that Walcott's "philosophical intentions never come closer to being realized than when he turns ... criticism on himself. Divestiture, as an artist, is Walcott's forte. He considers his own dangerous use of metaphors: 'When would I not hear the Trojan War / in two fishermen cursing?' he asks near the end. The poet's danger, like every person's, is to distance himself from human suffering by reinterpreting it."

Michael Heyward in *Washington Post Book World* observes: "*Omeros* is not a translation or even a recreation of either of Homer's great epics.... The ancient work it resembles most ... is Ovid's *Metamorphoses,* with its panoply of characters, its seamless episodic structure, and its panoramic treatment of a mythic world both actual and legendary." He concludes, "We are used to encountering the dynamic exploration of politics and history and folk legend in the contemporary novel, the domain—thanks to Rushdie, Marquez, Gaddis and others— of modern epic.... *Omeros* is not a novel and it does not approximate the form of a novel, but it does rival the novel's mastery of a mythic, multi-dimensional narrative. Strenuous and thrilling, it swims against the tide."

Hamner maintains that when dealing with Walcott's poetry the terms assimilation rather than imitation should be used. The critic observes, "Walcott passed through his youthful apprenticeship phase wherein he consciously traced the models of established masters. He was humble enough to learn from example and honest enough to disclose his intention to appropriate whatever stores he found useful in the canon of world literature.... But Walcott does not stop with imitation. Assimilation means to ingest into the mind and thoroughly comprehend; it also means to merge into or become one with a cultural tradition."

The uniqueness of Walcott's work stems from his ability to interweave British and island influences, to express what McClatchy calls "his mixed state" and do so "without indulging in either ethnic chic or imperial drag." His plays offer pictures of the common Caribbean folk and comment on the ills bred by colonialism. His poetry combines native patois and English rhetorical devices in a constant struggle to force an allegiance between the two halves of his split heritage. According to *Los Angeles Times Book Review* contributor Arthur Vogelsang, "These continuing polarities shoot an electricity to each other which is questioning and beautiful and which helps from a vision all together Caribbean and international, personal (him to you, you to him), independent, and essential for readers of contemporary literature on all the continents."

*BIOGRAPHICAL/CRITICAL SOURCES:*

BOOKS

*Contemporary Literary Criticism,* Gale, Volume 2, 1974, Volume 4, 1975, Volume 9, 1978, Volume 42, 1987.
*Dictionary of Literary Biography Yearbook: 1981,* Gale, 1982.
Goldstraw, Irma, *Derek Walcott: An Annotated Bibliography of His Works,* Garland Publishing, 1984.
Hamner, Robert D., *Derek Walcott,* Twayne, 1981.
Walcott, Derek, *Collected Poems, 1948-1984,* Farrar, Straus, 1986.
Walcott, Derek, *Dream on Monkey Mountain and Other Plays,* Farrar, Straus, 1970.
Walcott, Derek, *In a Green Night: Poems, 1948-1960,* J. Cape, 1962.
Walcott, Derek, *The Star-Apple Kingdom,* Farrar, Straus, 1979.

PERIODICALS

*Books and Bookmen,* April, 1972.
*Book World,* December 13, 1970.
*Chicago Tribune Book World,* May 2, 1982; September 9, 1984; March 9, 1986.
*Christian Science Monitor,* March 19, 1982; April 6, 1984.
*Detroit Free Press,* October 9, 1992.
*Georgia Review,* summer, 1984.
*Hudson Review,* summer, 1984.
*Literary Review,* spring, 1986.
*London Magazine,* December, 1973-January, 1974; February-March, 1977.
*Los Angeles Times,* November 12, 1986.

*Los Angeles Times Book Review,* April 4, 1982; May 21, 1985; April 6, 1986; October 26, 1986; September 6, 1987; January 20, 1991.
*Nation,* February 12, 1977; May 19, 1979; February 27, 1982.
*National Review,* November 3, 1970; June 20, 1986.
*New Republic,* November 20, 1976; March 17, 1982; January 23, 1984; March 24, 1986.
*New Statesman,* March 19, 1982.
*New Yorker,* March 27, 1971; June 26, 1971.
*New York Magazine,* August 14, 1972.
*New York Review of Books,* December 31, 1964; May 6, 1971; June 13, 1974; October 14, 1976; May 31, 1979; March 4, 1982.
*New York Times,* March 21, 1979; August 21, 1979; May 30, 1981; May 2, 1982; January 15, 1986; December 17, 1986.
*New York Times Book Review,* September 13, 1964; October 11, 1970; May 6, 1973; October 31, 1976; May 13, 1979; January 3, 1982; April 8, 1984; February 2, 1986; December 20, 1987; June 21, 1992.
*New York Times Magazine,* May 23, 1982.
*Poetry,* February, 1972; December, 1973; July, 1977; December, 1984; June, 1986.
*Review,* winter, 1974.
*Spectator,* May 10, 1980.
*Time,* March 15, 1982; October 19, 1992.
*Times Literary Supplement,* December 25, 1969; August 3, 1973; July 23, 1976; August 8, 1980; September 8, 1980; September 24, 1982; November 9, 1984; October 24, 1986.
*Tribune Books* (Chicago), November 8, 1987.
*TriQuarterly,* winter, 1986.
*Village Voice,* April 11, 1974.
*Virginia Quarterly Review,* winter, 1974; summer, 1984.
*Washington Post Book World,* February 21, 1982; April 13, 1986; November 11, 1990.
*Western Humanities Review,* spring, 1977.
*World Literature Today,* spring, 1977; summer, 1979; summer, 1981; winter, 1985; summer, 1986; winter, 1987.
*Yale Review,* October, 1973.

\*    \*    \*

## WALKER, Alice (Malsenior) 1944-

*PERSONAL:* Born February 9, 1944, in Eatonton, GA, daughter of Willie Lee and Minnie Tallulah (Grant) Walker; married Melvyn Rosenman Leventhal (a civil rights attorney), March 17, 1967 (divorced, 1976); children: Rebecca Grant. *Education:* Attended Spelman College, 1961-63; Sarah Lawrence College, B.A., 1965.

*ADDRESSES: Home*—San Francisco, CA. *Office*—Wild Trees Press, P.O. Box 378, Navarro, CA 95463. *Agent*—Wendy Weil, Julian Bach Literary Agency, 747 Third Ave., New York, NY 10017.

*CAREER:* Writer. Wild Trees Press, Navarro, CA, co-founder and publisher, 1984—. Has been a voter registration worker in Georgia, a worker in Head Start program in Mississippi, and on staff of New York City welfare department. Jackson State College (now University), Jackson, MS, writer-in-residence and teacher of black studies, 1968-69; Tougaloo College, Tougaloo, MS, writer-in-residence and teacher of black studies, 1970-71; lecturer in literature, Wellesley College and University of Massachusetts at Boston, both 1972-73; University of California, Berkeley, distinguished writer in Afro-American studies department, spring, 1982; Brandeis University, Waltham, MA, Fannie Hurst Professor of Literature, fall, 1982. Lecturer and reader of own poetry at universities and conferences. Member of board of trustees of Sarah Lawrence College. Consultant on black history to Friends of the Children of Mississippi, 1967.

*AWARDS, HONORS:* Bread Loaf Writer's Conference, scholar, 1966; first prize, *American Scholar* essay contest, 1967; Merrill writing fellowship, 1967; McDowell Colony fellowship, 1967, 1977-78; National Endowment for the Arts grant, 1969, 1977; Radcliffe Institute fellowship, 1971-73; Ph.D., Russell Sage College, 1972; National Book Award nomination, and Lillian Smith Award, Southern Regional Council, both 1973, for *Revolutionary Petunias and Other Poems;* Richard and Linda Rosenthal Foundation award, American Academy and Institute of Arts and Letters, 1974, for *In Love and Trouble;* Guggenheim Award, 1977-78; National Book Critics Circle Award nomination, 1982; Pulitzer Prize, 1983, and American Book Award, 1983, all for *The Color Purple;* D.H.L., University of Massachusetts, 1983; O. Henry Award, 1986, for "Kindred Spirits."

*WRITINGS:*

*POETRY*

*Once: Poems* (also see below), Harcourt, 1968, reprinted, Women's Press, 1988.
*Five Poems,* Broadside Press, 1972.
*Revolutionary Petunias and Other Poems* (also see below), Harcourt, 1973.
*Goodnight, Willie Lee, I'll See You in the Morning* (also see below), Dial, 1979.
*Horses Make a Landscape Look More Beautiful,* Harcourt, 1984.
*Alice Walker Boxed Set—Poetry: Good Night, Willie Lee, I'll See You in the Morning; Revolutionary Petunias and Other Poems; Once: Poems,* Harcourt, 1985.

*Her Blue Body Everything We Know: Earthling Poems, 1965-1990 Complete,* Harcourt, 1991.

*FICTION*

*The Third Life Of Grange Copeland* (novel; also see below), Harcourt, 1970.
*In Love and Trouble: Stories of Black Women* (also see below), Harcourt, 1973.
*Meridian* (novel), Harcourt, 1976.
*You Can't Keep a Good Woman Down* (short stories; also see below), Harcourt, 1981.
*The Color Purple* (novel), Harcourt, 1982; reissued 1992.
*Alice Walker Boxed Set—Fiction: The Third Life of Grange Copeland; You Can't Keep a Good Woman Down; In Love and Trouble,* Harcourt, 1985.
*To Hell with Dying* (juvenile), illustrations by Catherine Deeter, Harcourt, 1988.
*The Temple of My Familiar* (novel), Harcourt, 1989.
*Possessing the Secret of Joy* (novel), Harcourt, 1992.
*Finding the Green Stone* (juvenile), illustrations by Catherine Deeter, Harcourt, 1991.

*CONTRIBUTOR TO ANTHOLOGIES*

Helen Haynes, editor, *Voices of the Revolution,* E. & J. Kaplan, 1967.
Langston Hughes, editor, *The Best Short Stories by Negro Writers from 1899 to the Present: An Anthology,* Little Brown, 1967.
Robert Hayden, David J. Burrows, and Frederick R. Lapides, compilers, *Afro-American Literature: An Introduction,* Harcourt, 1971.
Toni Cade Bambara, compiler, *Tales and Stories for Black Folks,* Zenith Books, 1971.
Woodie King, compiler, *Black Short Story Anthology,* New American Library, 1972.
Arnold Adoff, compiler, *The Poetry of Black America: An Anthology of the Twentieth Century,* Harper, 1973.
Lindsay Patterson, editor, *A Rock against the Wind: Black Love Poems,* Dodd, 1973.
Sonia Sanchez, editor, *We Be Word Sorcerers: Twenty-five Stories by Black Americans,* Bantam, 1973.
Mary Anne Ferguson, compiler, *Images of Women in Literature,* Houghton, 1973.
Margaret Foley, editor, *Best American Short Stories: 1973,* Hart-Davis, 1973.
Foley, editor, *Best American Short Stories: 1974,* Houghton, 1974.
Michael S. Harper and Robert B. Stepto, editors, *Chants of Saints: A Gathering of Afro-American Literature, Art and Scholarship,* University of Illinois Press, 1980.

Mary Helen Washington, editor, *Midnight Birds: Stories of Contemporary Black Women Authors,* Anchor Press, 1980.

Dexter, Fisher, editor, *The Third Woman: Minority Women Writers of the United States,* 1980.

Patricia Bell-Scott and others, editors, *Double Stitch: Black Women Write about Mothers and Daughters,* Harper, 1993.

*OTHER*

*Langston Hughes: American Poet* (children's biography), Crowell, 1973.

(Editor) *I Love Myself When I'm Laughing ... and Then Again When I Am Looking Mean and Impressive: A Zora Neale Hurston Reader,* introduction by Mary Helen Washington, Feminist Press, 1979.

*In Search of Our Mothers' Gardens: Womanist Prose,* Harcourt, 1983.

*Living by the Word: Selected Writings, 1973-1987,* Harcourt, 1988.

Contributor to periodicals, including *Negro Digest, Denver Quarterly, Harper's, Black World,* and *Essence.* Contributing editor, *Southern Voices, Freedomways,* and *Ms.* Co-editor, with Gladys D. Wilcock, of *The Arte of English Poesie.*

*ADAPTATIONS: The Color Purple* was adapted for film and released by Warner Bros., 1985; the film was directed by Steven Spielberg and received several Academy Award nominations.

*SIDELIGHTS:* "*The Color Purple,* Alice Walker's third [novel], could be the kind of popular and literary event that transforms an intense reputation into a national one," according to Gloria Steinem in *Ms.* Judging from the critical enthusiasm for *The Color Purple,* and the fact that the novel was awarded the Pulitzer Prize for fiction in 1983, Steinem's words have proved prophetic. "Walker ... has succeeded," as Andrea Ford notes in the *Detroit Free Press,* "in creating a jewel of a novel." Peter S. Prescott presents a similar opinion in a *Newsweek* review. "I want to say," he comments, "that *The Color Purple* is an American novel of permanent importance, that rare sort of book which (in Norman Mailer's felicitous phrase) amounts to 'a division in the fields of dread'."

Walker's other books—novels, volumes of short stories, and poems—have not received the attention that many critics think they deserve. For example, William Peden, writing about *In Love and In Trouble: Stories of Black Women* in *The American Short Story: Continuity and Change, 1940-1975,* calls the collection of stories "a remarkable book that deserves to be much better known and more widely read." And while Steinem points out that *Meridian,* Walker's second novel, "is

often cited as the best novel of the civil rights movement, and is taught as part of some American history as well as literature courses," Steinem maintains that Walker's "visibility as a major American has been obscured by a familiar bias that assumes white male writers, and the literature they create, to be the norm. That puts black women (and all women of color) at a double remove."

Jeanne Fox-Alston and Mel Watkins both believe that the appeal of *The Color Purple* is that the novel, as a synthesis of characters and themes found in Walker's earlier works, brings together the best of the author's literary production in one volume. Fox-Alston, in the *Chicago Tribune Book World,* remarks: "Celie, the main character in ... *The Color Purple,* is an amalgam of all those women [characters in Walker's previous books]; she embodies both their desperation and, later, their faith." Watkins states in the *New York Times Book Review:* "Her previous books ... have elicited praise for Miss Walker as a lavishly gifted writer. *The Color Purple,* while easily satisfying that claim, brings into sharper focus many of the diverse themes that threaded their way through her past work."

Walker's central characters are almost always black women; the themes of sexism and racism are predominant in her work, but her impact is felt across both racial and sexual boundaries. Walker, according to Steinem, "comes at universality through the path of an American black woman's experience.... She speaks the female experience more powerfully for being able to pursue it across boundaries of race and class." This universality is also noted by Fox-Alston, who remarks that Walker has a "reputation as a provocative writer who writes about blacks in particular, but all humanity in general."

However, many critics see a definite black and female focus in Walker's writings. For example, in her review of *The Color Purple,* Ford suggests that the novel transcends "culture and gender" lines but also refers to Walker's "unabashedly feminist viewpoint" and the novel's "black ... texture." Walker does not deny this dual bias; the task of revealing the condition of the black woman is particularly important to her. Thadious M. Davis, in his *Dictionary of Literary Biography* essay, comments: "Walker writes best of the social and personal drama in the lives of familiar people who struggle for survival of self in hostile environments. She has expressed a special concern with 'exploring the oppressions, the insanities, the loyalties and the triumph of black women'." Walker explains in a *Publishers Weekly* interview: "The black woman is one of America's greatest heroes.... Not enough credit has been given to the black woman who has been oppressed beyond recognition."

Critics reviewing Walker's first collection of short stories, *In Love and Trouble: Stories of Black Women,* respond favorably to the author's rendering of the black experience. In *Ms.* Barbara Smith observes: "This collection would be an extraordinary literary work, if its only virtue were the fact that the author sets out consciously to explore with honesty the textures and terror of black women's lives. Attempts to penetrate the myths surrounding black women's experiences are so pitifully rare in black, feminist, or American writing that each shred of truth about these experiences constitutes a breakthrough. The fact that Walker's perceptions, style, and artistry are also consistently high makes her work a treasure." Mary Helen Washington remarks in a *Black World* review: "The stories in *In Love and In Trouble* ... constitute a painfully honest, searching examination of the experiences of thirteen Black women.... The broad range of these characters is indication of the depth and complexity with which Alice Walker treats a much-abused subject: the Black woman."

Walker bases her description of black women on what Washington refers to as her "unique vision and philosophy of the Black woman." According to Barbara A. Bannon of *Publishers Weekly,* this philosophy stems from the "theme of the poor black man's oppression of his family and the unconscious reasons for it." Walker, in her interview with the same magazine, asserts: "The cruelty of the black man to his wife and family is one of the greatest [American] tragedies. It has mutilated the spirit and body of the black family and of most black mothers." Through her fiction, Walker describes this tragedy. For instance, Smith notes: "Even as a black woman, I found the cumulative impact of these stories [contained in *In Love and In Trouble*] devastating.... Women love their men, but are neither loved nor understood in return. The affective relationships are [only] between mother and child or between black woman and black woman." David Guy's commentary on *The Color Purple* in the *Washington Post Book World* includes this evaluation: "Accepting themselves for what they are, the women [in the novel] are able to extricate themselves from oppression; they leave their men, find useful work to support themselves." Watkins further explains: "In *The Color Purple* the role of male domination in the frustration of black women's struggle for independence is clearly the focus."

Some reviewers criticize Walker's fiction for portraying an overly negative view of black men. Katha Pollitt, for example, in the *New York Times Book Review,* calls the stories in *You Can't Keep a Good Woman Down* "too partisan." The critic adds: "The black woman is *always* the most sympathetic character." Guy notes: "Some readers ... will object to her overall perspective. Men in [*The Color Purple*] are generally pathetic, weak and stupid, when they are not heartlessly cruel, and the white race is universally bumbling and inept." Charles Larson, in his *Detroit News* review of *The Color Purple,* points out: "I wouldn't go as far as to say that all the male characters [in the novel] are villains, but the truth is fairly close to that." However, neither Guy nor Larson suggests that this empha-

sis on women is a major fault in the novel. Guy, for example, while conceding that "white men ... are invisible in Celie's world," observes: "This really is Celie's perspective, however—it is psychologically accurate to her—and Alice Walker might argue that it is only a neat inversion of the view that has prevailed in western culture for centuries." Larson also notes that by the end of the novel, "several of [Walker's] masculine characters have reformed."

This idea of reformation, this sense of hope even in despair, is at the core of Walker's vision, even though, as John F. Callahan states in *New Republic,* "There is nothing but pain, violence, and death for black women [in her fiction]." Despite the brutal effects of sexism and racism suffered by the characters of her short stories and novels, critics note what Art Seidenbaum of the *Los Angeles Times* calls Walker's sense of "affirmation ... [that] overcomes her anger." This is particularly evident in *The Color Purple,* according to reviewers. Ford, for example, asserts that the author's "polemics on ... political and economic issues finally give way to what can only be described as a joyful celebration of human spirit— exulting, uplifting and eminently universal." Prescott discovers a similar progression in the novel. He writes: "[Walker's] story begins at about the point that most Greek tragedies reserve for the climax, then ... by immeasurable small steps ... works its way toward acceptance, serenity and joy." Walker, according to Ray Anello, who quotes the author in *Newsweek,* agrees with this evaluation. Questioned about the novel's importance, Walker explains: "Let's hope people can hear Celie's voice. There are so many people like Celie who make it, who come out of nothing. People who triumph."

Davis refers to this idea as Walker's "vision of survival" and offers a summary of its significance in Walker's work: "At whatever cost, human beings have the capacity to live in spiritual health and beauty; they may be poor, black, and un-educated, but their inner selves can blossom." Steinem adds: "What ... matters is the knowledge that everybody, no matter how poor or passive on the outside, has ... possibilities inside."

Walker's next novel, *The Temple of My Familiar,* is unconventional in its plot structure, consisting of characters who converse with one another, relating their life stories and those of their ancestors (including some discussion of Celie and Shug from *The Color Purple*). The characters talk of failed loves, racism, sexism, and other personal struggles in a format and voices that have drawn mixed reviews. David Gates, writing in *Newsweek,* refers to the novel as "fatally over-ambitious," noting that its content "encompasses 500,000 years, rewrites Genesis and the Beatitudes and weighs in with mini-lectures on everything from Elvis (for) to nuclear waste (against). Problem is, there are lots of stories but no *story.*" Similarly, David Nicholson, in a review for *Washington Post Book World,* remarks that "the central problem is that [*Temple of My Familiar*] is not a novel so much as it is an ill-fitting collection of speeches.... [It] has no plot in the conventional sense of the word, only a series of strung-together stories in which things happen without rhyme or reason." Nevertheless, several critics admire Walker's novel, finding its dialogues interesting and poetic. Luci Tapahonso, for example, in a review for the *Los Angeles Times Book Review,* suggests that Walker "asks us to suspend learned literary expectations and become part of the evolution of a people," and she praises Walker's representation of oral tradition as powerful. Tapahonso concluded that the novel "is about compassion for the oppressed, the grief of the oppressors, acceptance of the unchangeable and hope for everyone and everything. Alice Walker has written beautifully about dreams, the power of stories—and about the remarkable strength of our own histories." Acknowledging both points of view, Bernard W. Bell writes in the *Chicago Tribune*: "A magical, trans-historical, cross-cultural, multivocal blend of fact and fiction that employs realistic details in the service of fantasy, *The Temple of My Familiar* will delight some and disappoint others."

Walker's fifth novel, *Possessing the Secret of Joy,* centers on Tashi, the young African woman who becomes a lifelong friend to Celie's daughter Olivia and weds Celie's son Adam in *The Color Purple.* Tashi's story centers around the African tradition of clitoral circumcision of 11-year-old females, a ritual Tashi had not undergone upon intervention by Adam's missionary family. After Tashi and Adam fall in love, however, Tashi strives to retain her African identity, particularly when faced with the prospect of moving to the United States with Adam. She decides to be circumcised; the procedure and its side effects are described in vivid, horrific detail. Physically and emotionally mutilated, Tashi goes to the United States, where she begins, in the words of *Los Angeles Times* contributor Tina McElroy Ansa, "her lifelong struggle with the concomitant madness that the clitorectomy brings." Describing the power and importance of *Possessing the Secret of Joy,* Ansa comments that "as she did so stunningly and accessibly in *The Color Purple,* Alice Walker takes her readers into formerly taboo territory—areas of the human soul usually shrouded in silence and shame and fear and anguish." Most critics were struck by the detailed depiction of the circumcision, which was, in the words of *Washington Post Book World* reviewer Charles R. Larson, "graphic enough to make one gag." Nevertheless, critics generally agree with Larson that "Walker has not intended to make her story sensational," but rather hopes to impress upon her readership the physical suffering as well as the emotional duress of a procedure whose "cultural intent ... is absolutely clear: the denial of pleasure for women from all sexual activity." Janette Turner Hospital, writing of Walker's literary skill for the *New York Times Book Review,* finds that the novel has "a mythic strength. Its many voices ... are highly stylized, operatic, prophetic—and powerfully poetic."

Walker's early poetry, as well as the uncollected recent verse, were published in 1991 as *Her Blue Body Everything We Know: Earthling Poems, 1965-1990.* Referring to its wide range of subject matter, a reviewer for *Publishers Weekly* notes that Walker's poetry "brings a woman's wisdom to bear on love, life's unavoidable tragedies, blacks' struggle for equality and justice, and a globe spinning toward eco-suicide." Claiming that the collection "teaches us ... to cherish and celebrate life," *Woman's Review of Books* contributor Adrian T. Oktenberg finds Walker's approach to both spiritual and political revolution and change in the world to be of primary importance, observing that Walker's "poems on Malcolm X, on Christ and others make clear that her revolution would include love and laughter; it would combine 'Justice *and* Hope'."

*BIOGRAPHICAL/CRITICAL SOURCES:*

*BOOKS*

*Concise Dictionary of American Literary Biography (1968-1988),* Gale, 1988.
*Contemporary Literary Criticism,* Gale, Volume 5, 1976, Volume 6, 1976, Volume 9, 1978, Volume 19, 1981, Volume 27, 1984, Volume 46, 1988.
*Dictionary of Literary Biography,* Gale, Volume 6: *American Novelists since World War II,* second series, 1980, Volume 33: *Afro-American Fiction Writers after 1955,* 1984.
Evans, Mari, editor, *Black Women Writers (1950-1980): A Critical Evaluation,* Anchor, 1984.
O'Brien, John, *Interviews with Black Writers,* Liveright, 1973.
Peden, William, *The American Short Story: Continuity and Change, 1940-1975,* second edition, revised and enlarged, Houghton, 1975.
Prenshaw, Peggy W., editor, *Women Writers of the Contemporary South,* University Press of Mississippi, 1984.
Tate, Claudia, editor, *Black Women Writers at Work,* Continuum, 1983, pp. 175-187.

*PERIODICALS*

*American Book Review,* May, 1990, p. 12.
*American Scholar,* winter, 1970-71; summer, 1973.
*Ann Arbor News,* October 3, 1982.
*Atlantic,* June, 1976.
*Belles Lettres,* summer, 1989, p. 37.
*Black Scholar,* April, 1976.
*Black World,* September, 1973; October, 1974.
*Book List,* April 15, 1991.
*California Living,* August 15, 1982, pp. 16-20.
*Chicago Tribune,* December 20, 1985; April 23, 1989, p.5.
*Chicago Tribune Book World,* August 1, 1982; September 15, 1985.
*Christian Science Monitor,* May 4, 1989, p. 13.

*Commentary,* November, 1989, p. 57.

*Commonweal,* April 29, 1977.

*Cosmopolitan,* June, 1992, p. 34.

*Detroit Free Press,* August 8, 1982; July 10, 1988.

*Detroit News,* September 15, 1982; October 23, 1983; March 31, 1985.

*Essence,* July, 1988, p. 71; June, 1991, p. 58; July, 1992, p. 42.

*Freedomways,* winter, 1973.

*Globe and Mail* (Toronto), December 21, 1985.

*Jet,* February 10, 1986.

*Listener,* November 2, 1989, p. 35.

*London Review of Books,* December 21, 1989, p. 19.

*Los Angeles Times,* April 29, 1981; June 8, 1983; July 5, 1992.

*Los Angeles Times Book Review,* August 8, 1982; May 21, 1989.

*Mademoiselle,* July, 1989, p. 72.

*Ms.,* February, 1974; July, 1977; July, 1978; June, 1982; September, 1986; July, 1992, p. 65.

*Nation,* November 12, 1973; December 17, 1983.

*National Review,* June 30, 1989, p. 48; August 3, 1992, p. 48.

*Negro Digest,* September-October, 1968.

*New Leader,* January 25, 1971.

*New Republic,* September 14, 1974; December 21, 1974; May 29, 1989, p. 28.

*New Statesman,* September 22, 1989.

*Newsweek,* June 21, 1982; April 24, 1989, p. 74; June 8, 1992, p. 56.

*New Yorker,* February 27, 1971; June 7, 1976.

*New York Review of Books,* January 29, 1987.

*New York Times,* December 18, 1985; January 5, 1986.

*New York Times Book Review,* March 17, 1974; May 23, 1976; May 29, 1977; December 30, 1979; May 24, 1981; July 25, 1982; April 7, 1985; June 5, 1988; June 28, 1992, p. 11.

*New York Times Magazine,* January 8, 1984.

*Oakland Tribune,* November 11, 1984.

*Parnassus: Poetry in Review,* spring-summer, 1976.

*People,* May 29, 1989, p. 33; July 13, 1992, p. 24.

*Playboy,* June, 1989, p. 32.

*Poetry,* February, 1971; March, 1980.

*Progressive,* August, 1989, p. 29.

*Publishers Weekly,* August 31, 1970; February 26, 1988; March 1, 1991.

*San Francisco Review of Books,* January, 1989, p. 12.

*Saturday Review,* August 22, 1970.

*Southern Living,* April, 1989, p. 120; September, 1989, p. 148; December, 1991, p. 83.

*Southern Review,* spring, 1973.

*Time,* May 1, 1989, p. 69.

*Times Literary Supplement,* August 19, 1977; June 18, 1982; July 20, 1984; September 27, 1985; April 15, 1988; September 22, 1989.

*U.S. News and World Report,* June 3, 1991, p. 51.

*Vogue,* May, 1989, p. 223.

*Wall Street Journal,* May 16, 1989, p. A12.

*Washington Post,* October 15, 1982; April 15, 1983; October 17, 1983.

*Washington Post Book World,* November 18, 1973; October 30, 1979; December 30, 1979; May 31, 1981; July 25, 1982; December 30, 1984; May 7, 1989; July 5, 1992.

*Women's Review of Books,* February, 1989; December, 1991.

*World and I,* October, 1992, p. 366.

*World Literature Today,* winter, 1985; winter, 1986.

*Yale Review,* autumn, 1976.

\* \* \*

## WALKER, Margaret (Abigail) 1915-

*PERSONAL:* Born July 7, 1915, in Birmingham, AL; daughter of Sigismund C. (a Methodist minister) and Marion (Dozier) Walker (a music teacher); married Firnist James Alexander, June 13, 1943 (deceased); children: Marion Elizabeth, Firnist James, Sigismund Walker, Margaret Elvira. *Education:* Northwestern University, A.B., 1935; University of Iowa, M.A., 1940, Ph.D., 1965. *Religion:* Methodist.

*ADDRESSES: Home*—2205 Guynes St., Jackson, MS 39213. *Office*—Department of English, Jackson State College, Jackson, MS 39217.

*CAREER:* Worked as a social worker, newspaper reporter, and magazine editor; Livingstone College, Salisbury, NC, member of faculty, 1941-42; West Virginia State College, Institute, WV, instructor in English, 1942-43; Livingstone College, Salisbury, NC, professor of English, 1945-46; Jackson State College, Jackson, MS, professor of English, 1949—, director of Institute for the Study of the History, Life, and Culture of Black Peoples, 1968—. Lecturer, National Concert and Artists Corp. Lecture Bureau, 1943-48. Visiting professor in creative writing, Northwestern University, spring, 1969. Staff member, Cape Cod Writers Conference, Craigville, MA, 1967 and 1969. Participant, Library of Congress Conference on the Teaching of Creative Writing, 1973.

*MEMBER:* National Council of Teachers of English, Modern Language Association, Poetry Society of America, American Association of University Professors, National Education Association, Alpha Kappa Alpha.

*AWARDS, HONORS:* Yale Series of Younger Poets Award, 1942, for *For My People;* named to Honor Roll of Race Relations, a national poll conducted by the New York Public Library, 1942; Rosenthal fellowship, 1944; Ford fellowship for study at Yale University, 1954; Houghton Mifflin literary fellowship, 1966; Fulbright fellowship, 1971; National Endowment for the Humanities, 1972; Doctor of Literature, Northwestern University, 1974; Doctor of Letters, Rust College, 1974; Doctor of Fine Arts, Dennison University, 1974; Doctor of Humane Letters, Morgan State University, 1976.

*WRITINGS:*

*POETRY*

*For My People,* Yale University Press, 1942.
*Ballad of the Free,* Broadside Press, 1966.
*Prophets for a New Day,* Broadside Press, 1970.
*October Journey,* Broadside Press, 1973.
*For Farish Street Green,* [Jackson, MS], 1986.
(With John Warner) *Apparitions,* Jamestown Pubs., 1987.
*This Is My Century: New and Collected Poems,* University of Georgia Press, 1989.

*PROSE*

*Jubilee* (novel), Houghton, 1965.
*How I Wrote "Jubilee"* (also see below), Third World Press, 1972.
(With Nikki Giovanni) *A Poetic Equation: Conversations between Nikki Giovanni and Margaret Walker,* Howard University Press, 1974, reprinted with new postscript, 1983.
(Author of introduction) *Black Women and Liberation Movements,* edited by Virginia A. Blansford, Institute for the Arts and Humanities, Howard University, 1981.
*Richard Wright: Daemonic Genius,* Dodd, 1987.
*How I Wrote Jubilee and Other Essays on Life and Literature,* edited by Maryemma Graham, Feminist Press, 1990.
(With Thea Bowman) *God Touched My Life: The Inspiring Autobiography of the Nun Who Brought Song, Celebration, and Soul to the World,* Harper, 1991.

*CONTRIBUTOR*

Addison Gayle, editor, *Black Expression,* Weybright and Tally, 1969.
Stanton L. Wormley and Lewis H. Fenderson, editors, *Many Shades of Black,* Morrow, 1969.
Henderson, Stephen, *Understanding the New Black Poetry: Black Speech and Black Music as Poetic References,* Morrow, 1973.

Also contributor to numerous anthologies, including Adoff's *Black Out Loud,* Weisman and Wright's *Black Poetry for All Americans,* Williams's *Beyond the Angry Black.* Contributor to *Yale Review, Negro Digest, Poetry, Opportunity, Phylon, Saturday Review,* and *Virginia Quarterly.*

*SIDELIGHTS:* When *For My People* by Margaret Walker won the Yale Younger Poets Series Award in 1942, "she became one of the youngest Black writers ever to have published a volume of poetry in this century," as well as "the first Black woman in American literary history to be so honored in a prestigious national competition," notes Richard K. Barksdale in *Black American Poets between Worlds, 1940-1960.* Walker's first novel, *Jubilee,* is notable for being "the first truly historical black American novel," according to University of Maryland professor Joyce Anne Joyce, reports *Washington Post* contributor Crispin Y. Campbell. It was also the first work by a black writer to speak out for the liberation of the black woman. The cornerstones of a literature that affirms the African folk roots of black American life, these two books have also been called visionary for looking toward a new cultural unity for black Americans that will be built on that foundation.

The title of Walker's first book, *For My People,* denotes the subject matter of "poems in which the body and spirit of a great group of people are revealed with vigor and undeviating integrity," says Louis Untermeyer in the *Yale Review.* Here, in long ballads, Walker draws sympathetic portraits of characters such as the New Orleans sorceress Molly Means; Kissie Lee, a tough young woman who dies "with her boots on switching blades"; and Poppa Chicken, an urban drug dealer and pimp. Other ballads give a new dignity to John Henry, killed by a ten-pound hammer, and Stagolee, who kills a white officer but eludes a lynch mob. In an essay for *Black Women Writers (1950-1980): A Critical Evaluation,* Eugenia Collier notes, "Using ... the language of the grass-roots people, Walker spins yarns of folk heroes and heroines: those who, faced with the terrible obstacles which haunt Black people's very existence, not only survive but prevail—with style." Soon after it appeared, the book of ballads, sonnets and free verse found a surprisingly large number of readers, requiring publishers to authorize three printings to satisfy popular demand.

Some critics found fault with the sonnets in the book, but others deemed it generally impressive, R. Baxter Miller summarizes in *Black American Poets between Worlds.* "The title poem is itself a singular and unique literary achievement," Barksdale claims. In *Black American Literature: A Critical History,* Roger Whitlow elaborates, "The poem, written in free verse, rhythmically catalogues the progress of black American experience, from the rural folkways, religious practices, and exhausting labor of the South, through the cramped and confusing conditions of the northern urban centers, to what she hopes will be a racial awakening, blacks militantly rising up to take control of their own destinies." Collier relates, "The final stanza is a reverberating cry for redress. It demands a new beginning. Our music then will be martial music; our peace will be hard-won, but it will be 'written in the sky.' And after the agony, the people whose misery spawned strength will control our world. This poem is the hallmark of Margaret Walker's works. It echoes in her subsequent poetry and even in her monumental novel *Jubilee.* It speaks to us, in our words and rhythms, of our history, and it radiates the promise of our future. It is the quintessential example of myth and ritual shaped by artistic genius."

Reviewers especially praise Walker's control of poetic technique in the poem. Dudley Randall writes in Addison Gayle's *The Black Aesthetic,* "The poem gains its force ... by the sheer overpowering accumulation of a mass of details delivered in rhythmical parallel phrases." To cite Barksdale, "It is magnificently wrought oral poetry.... In reading it aloud, one must be able to breathe and pause, pause and breathe preacher-style. One must be able to sense the ebb and flow of the intonations.... This is the kind of verbal music found in a well-delivered down-home folk sermon." By giving the poem a musical rhythm, Walker underscores the poem's message, observes Barksdale: "The poet here is writing about the source of the Black peoples' blues, for out of their troubled past and turbulent present came the Black peoples' song." In this case, Walker steps forward to remind her people of the strength to he found in their cultural tradition as she calls for a new, hopeful literature that can inspire social action.

"If the test of a great poem is the universality of statement, then 'For My People' is a great poem," remarks Barksdale. The critic explains in Donald B. Gibson's *Modern Black Poets: A Collection of Critical Essays* that the poem was written when "world-wide pain, sorrow, and affliction were tangibly evident, and few could isolate the Black man's dilemma from humanity's dilemma during the depression years or during the war years." Thus, the power of resilience presented in the poem is a hope Walker holds out not only to black people, but to all people, to "all the adams and eves." As she once remarked, "Writers should not write exclusively for black or white audiences, but most inclusively. After all, it is the business of all writers to write about the human condition, and all humanity must be involved in both the writing and in the reading."

*Jubilee,* a historical novel, is the second book on which Walker's literary reputation rests. It is the story of a slave family during and after the Civil War, and took her thirty years to write. During these years, she married a disabled veteran, raised four children, taught full time at Jackson State College in Mississippi, and earned a Ph.D. from the University of Iowa. The lengthy gestation, she believes, partly accounts for the book's quality. As she told Claudia Tate in *Black Women Writers at Work,* "Living with the book over a long period of time was agonizing. Despite all of that, *Jubilee* is the product of a mature person," one whose own difficult pregnancies and economic struggles could lend authenticity to the lives of her characters. "There's a difference between writing about some-

thing and living through it," she said in the interview; "I did both."

The story of *Jubilee*'s main characters Vyry and Randall Ware was an important part of Walker's life even before she began to write it down. As she explains in *How I Wrote "Jubilee,"* she first heard about the "slavery time" in bedtime stories told by her maternal grandmother. When old enough to recognize the value of her family history, Walker took initiative, "prodding" her grandmother for more details, and promising to set down on paper the story that had taken shape in her mind. Later on, she completed extensive research on every aspect of the black experience touching the Civil War, from obscure birth records to information on the history of tin cans. "Most of my life I have been involved with writing this story about my great-grandmother, and even if *Jubilee* were never considered an artistic or commercial success I would still be happy just to have finished it," she claims.

Soon after *Jubilee* was published in 1966, Walker was given a fellowship award from Houghton-Mifflin, and a mixed reception from critics. Granting that the novel is "ambitious," *New York Times Book Review* contributor Wilma Dykeman deems it "uneven." Arthur P. Davis, writing in *From the Dark Tower: Afro-American Writers, 1900-1960,* suggests that the author "has crowded too much into her novel." Even so, say reviewers, the novel merits praise. Abraham Chapman of the *Saturday Review* appreciates the author's "fidelity to fact and detail" as she "presents the little-known everyday life of the slaves," their music, and their folkways. In the *Christian Science Monitor,* Henrietta Buckmaster comments, "In Vyry, Miss Walker has found a remarkable woman who suffered one outrage after the other and yet emerged with a humility and a mortal fortitude that reflected a spiritual wholeness." Dykeman concurs, "In its best episodes, and in Vyry, *Jubilee* chronicles the triumph of a free spirit over many kinds of bondages." Later critical studies of the book emphasize the importance of its themes and its position as the prototype for novels that present black history from a black perspective. Claims Whitlow, "It serves especially well as a response to white 'nostalgia' fiction about the antebellum and Reconstruction South."

Walker's next book to be highly acclaimed was *Prophets for a New Day,* a slim volume of poems. Unlike the poems in *For My People,* which, in a Marxist fashion, names religion an enemy of revolution, says Collier, *Prophets for a New Day* "reflects a profound religious faith. The heroes of the sixties are named for the prophets of the Bible: Martin Luther King is Amos, Medgar Evars is Micah, and so on. The people and events of the sixties are paralleled with Biblical characters and occurrences.... The religious references are important. Whether one espouses the Christianity in which they are couched is not the issue. For the fact is that Black people from ancient

Africa to now have always been a spiritual people, believing in an existence beyond the flesh." One poem in *Prophets* that harks back to African spiritism is "Ballad of Hoppy Toad" with its hexes that turn a murderous conjurer into a toad. Though Collier feels that Walker's "vision of the African past is fairly dim and romantic," the critic goes on to say that this poetry "emanates from a deeper area of the psyche, one which touches the mythic area of a collective being and reenacts the rituals which define a Black collective self." Perhaps more importantly, in all the poems, says Collier, Walker depicts "a people striking back at oppression and emerging triumphant."

Walker disclosed in *A Poetic Equation: Conversations between Nikki Giovanni and Margaret Walker* that the poem "Ballad of the Free" in *Prophets* articulates "better than even 'For My People' so much of what I [feel] about black people and the whole movement toward freedom." Davis calls the book "the best poetical comment to come from the civil rights movement—the movement which came to a climax with the march on Washington and which began thereafter to change into a more militant type of liberation effort." Barksdale shares this view; as he comments in *Black American Poets between Worlds,* "Because of her experience, background, and training—her familial gift of word power, her intensive apprenticeship in Chicago's literary workshop in the 1930s, and her mastery of Black orature—her *Prophets* ... stands out as the premier poetic statement of the death-riddled decade of the 1960s. The poems of this small volume reflect the full range of the Black protest during the time—the sit-ins, the jailings, the snarling dogs, the ... lynching of the three Civil Rights workers in Mississippi. All of the poems in the volume touch the sensitive nerve of racial memory and bring back, in sharply etched detail, the trauma and tension and triumphs of that period."

In the same essay, Barksdale relates that Walker's books owe little to her academic life and much to a rich cultural sensibility gained in her youth. "There was ... New Orleans with its ... folk mythology, its music, ... and its assortment of racial experiences to be remembered and recalled." And there was the shaping influence of Walker's parents. Born in Jamaica but educated at Atlanta's Gammon Theological Institute, her father, Sigismund, was a Methodist preacher. Her mother, Marion (nee Dozier), was a musician. "So [the poet] grew up in a household ruled by the power of the word, for undoubtedly few have a greater gift for articulate word power than an educated Jamaican trained to preach the doctrine of salvation in the Black South," Barksdale remarks. In such a home, survival "without mastery of words and language was impossible," he adds, citing Walker's comment. And, given her family background, Walker felt destined for an academic career.

That career was characterized by opposition and difficulty. In the interview with Tate, Walker reflects, "I'm a third-genera-

tion college graduate. Society doesn't want to recognize that there's this kind of black writer. I'm the Ph.D. black woman. That's horrible. That is to be despised. I didn't know how bad it was until I went back to school [to teaching] and found out." With her older children nearing college age, Walker had taken leave from her position at Jackson State University to earn an advanced degree in hope that afterward she would be given more pay. She returned only to be slighted by the administration. Eventually, she developed the school's black studies program, attaining personal fulfillment only during the last years of her career as an educator.

Discouragements of many kinds have not kept Walker from producing works that have encouraged many. *For My People, Jubilee,* and *Prophets for a New Day* are valued for their relation to social movements of twentieth-century America. In 1937, the poem "For My People" called for a new generation to gather strength from a militant literature, and the black literature of the 1960s—including the autobiographies of Malcolm X, Eldridge Cleaver, Huey Newton, and Angela Davis, to name just a few—answered that challenge, suggests C. W. E. Bigsby in *The Second Black Renaissance: Essays in Black Literature.* Her example over the years has also proved to be instructive. This summary of Walker's achievement closes the epilogue of *How I Wrote "Jubilee":* "She has revealed the creative ways in which methods and materials of the social science scholar may be joined with the craft and viewpoint of the poet/novelist to create authentic black literature. She has reaffirmed for us the critical importance of oral tradition in the creation of our history.... Finally, she has made awesomely clear to us the tremendous costs which must be paid in stubborn, persistent work and commitment if we are indeed to write our own history and create our own literature."

Writing that history is central to Walker's unauthorized, but highly personal biography of author Richard Wright. In *Richard Wright, Daemonic Genius,* Walker fashions what Waldo E. Martin, Jr. calls in the *Washington Post Book World* "a fascinating and insightful study of the man and his work.... Walker's work is at once personal and analytical, laudatory and critical. It blends memoir and biography to yield a gripping portrait of Wright and his inner self, notably the demons that tormented him and fed his artistic genius." Charles R. Johnson's review in the *Los Angeles Times Book Review* considers Walker's a "curious mixture of delightful remembrance and disappointing critical analysis." Noting that Walker discussed many factors in Wright's life, Johnson finds, "Sadly, the result of this well-intended critical synthesis is a portrait of Wright that borders at times on character assassination." Johnson praises Walker's account of her relationship with Wright, however, noting that "intertwined with this scathing account of Wright's misogyny and Anglophilia is the fascinating three-year, historical friendship they shared.... Equally valuable is Walker's extensive bibliography, and her treatment of Wright's little-known 24-hour discussion in Paris with the Rev. Martin Luther King Jr." Johnson concludes, despite his criticism, that *Daemonic Genius* is "a book that fans of Wright and Walker will read hungrily, as I did, in a single, spellbound sitting." While voicing reservations about Walker's application of psychoanalytic theory to Wright's work and her failure to explore his "ambivalence toward America," Martin concludes, "Walker has written a most valuable study which demands serious attention."

*BIOGRAPHICAL/CRITICAL SOURCES:*

*BOOKS*

Bankier, Joanna, and Dierdre Lashgari, editors, *Women Poets of the World,* Macmillan, 1983.

Baraka, Amiri, *The Black Nation,* Getting Together Publications, 1982.

Bigsby, C. W. E., editor, *The Second Black Renaissance: Essays in Black Literature,* Greenwood Press, 1980.

*Contemporary Literary Criticism,* Gale, Volume 1, 1973, Volume 2, 1976.

*Dictionary of Literary Biography,* Volume 76: *Afro-American Writers, 1940-1955,* Gale, 1988.

Davis, Arthur P., *From the Dark Tower: Afro-American Writers, 1900 to 1960,* Howard University Press, 1974.

Emanuel, James A., and Theodore L. Gross, editors, *Dark Symphony: Negro Literature in America,* Free Press, 1968.

Evans, Mari, editor, *Black Women Writers (1950-1980): A Critical Evaluation,* Anchor/Doubleday, 1982.

Gayle, Addison, editor, *The Black Aesthetic,* Doubleday, 1971.

Gibson, Donald B., editor, *Modern Black Poets: A Collection of Critical Essays,* Prentice-Hall, 1983.

Jackson, Blyden, and Louis D. Rubin, Jr., *Black Poetry in America: Two Essays in Historical Interpretation,* Louisiana State University Press, 1974.

Jones, John Griffith, in *Mississippi Writers Talking,* Volume 2, University of Mississippi Press, 1983.

Kent, George E., *Blackness and the Adventure of Western Culture,* Third World Press, 1972.

Lee, Don L., *Dynamite Voices I: Black Poets of the 1960s,* Broadside Press, 1971.

Miller, R. Baxter, editor, *Black American Poets between Worlds, 1940-1960,* University of Tennessee Press, 1986.

Redmond, Eugene B., *Drumvoices: The Mission of Afro-American Poetry—A Critical Evaluation,* Doubleday, 1976.

Tate, Claudia, editor, *Black Women Writers at Work,* Continuum, 1983.

Walker, Margaret, *For My People,* Yale University Press, 1942.

Walker, Margaret, *How I Wrote "Jubilee,"* Third World Press, 1972.

Walker, Margaret, and Nikki Giovanni, *A Poetic Equation: Conversations between Nikki Giovanni and Margaret Walker,* Howard University Press, 1974, reprinted with a new postscript, 1983.

Walker, Margaret, *Prophets for a New Day,* Broadside Press, 1970.

Whitlow, Roger, *Black American Literature: A Critical History,* Nelson Hall, 1973.

*PERIODICALS*

*Atlantic,* December, 1942.

*Best Sellers,* October 1, 1966.

*Black World,* December, 1971; December, 1975.

*Books,* January 3, 1973.

*Book Week,* October 2, 1966.

*Callaloo,* May, 1979; fall, 1990, p. 949.

*Christian Science Monitor,* November 14, 1942; September 29, 1966; June 19, 1974; January 12, 1990, p. 13.

*Common Ground,* autumn, 1943.

*Ebony,* February, 1949.

*Freedomways,* Volume 2, number 3, summer, 1967.

*Los Angeles Times Book Review,* February 19, 1989, p. 9.

*National Review,* October 4, 1966.

*Negro Digest,* February, 1967; January, 1968.

*New Republic,* November 23, 1942.

*New York Review of Books,* August 17, 1989, p. 16.

*New York Times,* November 4, 1942.

*New York Times Book Review,* August 2, 1942; September 25, 1966.

*Opportunity,* December, 1942.

*Publishers Weekly,* April 15, 1944; March 24, 1945; December 20, 1991, p. 15.

*Saturday Review,* September 24, 1966.

*Times Literary Supplement,* June 29, 1967.

*Washington Post Book World,* February 9, 1983; April 16, 1989, p. 6.

*Yale Review,* winter, 1943.

\*   \*   \*

# WALTER, Mildred Pitts 1922-

*PERSONAL:* Born September 9, 1922, in Sweetville, LA; daughter of Paul (a log cutter) and Mary (a midwife and beautician; maiden name, Ward) Pitts; married Earl Lloyd Walter (a social worker and civil rights activist), 1947 (died June 11, 1965); children: Earl Lloyd, Jr., Craig Allen. *Education:* Southern University, B.A., 1944; attended California State College, 1950-52; Antioch College, M.Ed., 1977.

*CAREER:* Shipwright helper in Vancouver, WA, 1943-44; City Dye Works, Los Angeles, CA, salesperson, 1944-48; Los Angeles Public Schools, personnel clerk, 1949-52, elementary school teacher, 1952-70; consultant and lecturer on cultural diversity for educational institutions, 1971-73. Civil rights activist for Congress of Racial Equality (CORE), during 1950s and 1960s. Northeast Women's Center, Denver, CO, cofounder and administrator, 1982-86. Delegate to Second World Black and African Festival of the Arts and Culture, Lagos, Nigeria, 1977.

*MEMBER:* Society of Children's Book Writers.

*AWARDS, HONORS:* Runner-up for Irma Simonton Black Award, 1981, for *Ty's One-Man Band;* Parents' Choice awards, 1984, for *Because We Are,* and 1985, for *Brother to the Wind;* Coretta Scott King awards from Social Responsibility Round Table of American Library Association, honorable mention, 1984, for *Because We Are,* honorable mention, 1986, for *Trouble's Child,* winner, 1987, for *Justin and the Best Biscuits in the World.*

*WRITINGS:*

*FICTION FOR YOUNG PEOPLE*

*Lillie of Watts: A Birthday Discovery* (novel), illustrations by Leonora E. Prince, Ritchie, 1969.
*Lillie of Watts Takes a Giant Step* (novel), illustrations by Bonnie H. Johnson, Doubleday, 1971.
*The Liquid Trap,* illustrations by John Thompson, Scholastic, 1975.
*Ty's One-Man Band,* illustrations by Margot Tomes, Four Winds, 1980.
*The Girl on the Outside* (novel), Lothrop, 1982.
*Because We Are* (novel), Lothrop, 1983.
*My Mama Needs Me,* illustrations by Pat Cummings, Lothrop, 1983.
*Brother to the Wind,* illustrations by Diane and Leo Dillon, Lothrop, 1985.
*Trouble's Child* (novel), Lothrop, 1985.
*Justin and the Best Biscuits in the World* (novel), illustrations by Catherine Stock, Lothrop, 1986.
*Mariah Loves Rock* (novel), illustrations by Cummings, Bradbury, 1988.
*Have a Happy ...* (novel), illustrations by Carole Byard, Lothrop, 1989.
*Two and Too Much,* illustrations by Cummings, Bradbury, 1990.
*Mariah Keeps Cool* (novel), illustrations by Cummings, Bradbury, 1990.

*OTHER*

*The Mississippi Challenge* (nonfiction), Bradbury, 1992.

Contributor of articles to periodicals, including *Publishers Weekly. Los Angeles Times,* book reviewer and guest book editor, 1965-68, drama reviewer, 1969-71.

*SIDELIGHTS:* "I think family is everything within the lives of human beings," said Mildred Pitts Walter in an interview. "Not just the nuclear family, but the extended family—grandmothers, uncles, cousins, friends, community, city, country." As an African American born in rural Louisiana in 1922, Walter grew up facing the twin obstacles of poverty and racial prejudice. Drawing strength from her home and community, she went on to a meaningful career as a teacher, civil rights activist, and award-winning children's author. Her books often show how a sense of family and community can enrich anyone's life. "That's how we learn to extend ourselves to people," she observed, "when we have a wonderful foundation in our own family."

Walter began teaching in the Los Angeles schools in the early 1950s. "The children who came to me," she commented, "were open and anxious to learn. They were honest—they said exactly what they meant and they meant what they said—and that is the kind of personality I like best. They gave me a lot in terms of keeping my spirit free." Though Walter believed in work and discipline, she realized that young children need work of a special kind. "If you watch young kittens and cubs, they learn by playing," she stated. Children, she realized, learn in much the same way. "Play is really the work of children," she explained. "It is that way that they learn and grow and develop. Too many of our children are not playing now—they are sitting watching TV; they start them early in reading and sitting at desks. I saw children who were different from that," she declared. "I saw them wanting to learn by playing. And providing that kind of play-work activity for them was the thing that inspired me."

Walter started writing children's books. "I didn't want to do it," she noted. "I didn't think I could become a writer. I was interested in teaching—I was interested in books about and by black people for my students, who were all black." As late as the 1960s, however, hardly any such books existed. One day she found herself talking to Dick Lewis, a book salesman who owned part of the local publishing house of Ward Ritchie Press. "I asked him to meet that need," she recalled in an autobiographical essay. "He suggested that I write those books. I felt he was passing the buck and told him so. He insisted." Soon Walter was at work on *Lillie of Watts: A Birthday Discovery.* The title character, a girl who has just turned eleven, discovers that the love within her family is a source of strength that can help her to cope with money troubles and the other struggles of life in her neighborhood. Praised for her ability to understand and accurately portray the concerns of her characters, Walter followed with a sequel, *Lillie of Watts Takes a Giant Step,* in which Lillie stands up for her heritage by joining a campaign to celebrate the birthday of black leader Malcolm X at her school.

In her interview, Walter offers special advice for aspiring writers: "You have to have more than a story to tell—you have to have a love for telling a story, a love for words to make that story come alive." Comparing writing to carpentry in that there are a lot of basic skills to master before you can do your work with confidence and add the special touches that are distinctively your own, Walter continues, "You have to keep doing pieces of work before you become the *artist*—and that's what every writer strives for."

A writer must also be resilient, Walter learned, because getting published is a continual struggle. After *Lillie of Watts Takes a Giant Step* appeared in 1971, Walter saw the market for her work disappear. "In the late sixties it had been less difficult for writers of color to get published because of the great demand for books by and about them," she explained. "President [Lyndon] Johnson, in his push for equality in education, had pressured Congress to allot a great sum of money for books and other materials for schools serving people of color. In the seventies these programs were drastically cut. Opportunities for black writers lessened."

Walter found that the friendship and support of other writers and editors helped her through the impasse. After moving to Colorado in 1970 she encountered Mary Elting and Franklin Folsom, a pair of well-established children's authors who gave her a scholarship to attend writing workshops and polish her skills. At one such workshop she met Frances Keene, a former editor from New York who introduced her to several colleagues back East. Eventually Walter piqued the interest of a number of New York editors—including several African Americans—who remained willing, despite the times, to encourage writers of color. One editor was Ray Shepard, who worked on reading textbooks for the publishers of *Scholastic* magazine. He asked Walter to write a lively easy reader, which became *The Liquid Trap*—the story of a girl in Louisiana's bayou country who has a suspenseful escape from a quicksand hole. Shepard also showed Walter's work to editors at *Scholastic*'s Four Winds Press, which published general-interest books for children. Four Winds editor Barbara Lalicki encouraged Walter to turn some of her own childhood memories into a storybook for the young. The work was published in 1980 as *Ty's One-Man Band*—Walter's first mass-market children's book in almost ten years.

*Ty's One-Man Band* begins on a hot, slow summer day, when young Ty has "nothing fun to do." He heads for a local pond to cool off in the shade, and there he spots Andro, a one-legged man who apparently travels from place to place with all his belongings in a bag slung over his back. Andro calls himself a one-man band, and he offers to perform if Ty will meet him in town that evening with a few simple items: a washboard, a wooden spoon, a tin pail, and a comb. Ty's family can scarcely accept the story when he rushes home. Doubtful that music could be made with "just those old things," his father lends him what he needs anyway. All Ty's friends laugh at him in disbelief, but then Andro appears and soon has the whole town dancing. At the end of the story, only Ty sees Andro "slip away back into the night," leaving as mysteriously as he came. Reviewers were charmed with *Ty's One-Man Band.* "[It] has a magical quality," said a writer for *Booklist,* hailing the book as "a fine work, with music of its own."

As the 1980s began, Walter focused on writing novels for young people. Her years of struggle and training paid off as she developed a distinctive voice as an author. "If there is any one theme that runs through my work it is the dynamics of choice, courage, and change," she says in her autobiographical essay. "My characters must make choices, and once they have made those choices they have to work them through. That's what life is—making a series of choices—and people who cannot choose for themselves don't grow."

*The Girl on the Outside* shows two teenage girls who gain new maturity by making important moral choices. The novel was inspired by the early years of the civil rights struggle in the 1950s, when the segregated public schools of Little Rock, Arkansas—well-funded for whites and poorly funded for blacks—were integrated by court order to provide an equal education for all children. Set in the fictional town of Mossville, the book has two main characters whose lives gradually intertwine. Eva Collins, with encouragement from her parents and her minister, agrees to become one of the first African American students at Mossville's Chatman High School. As the school year approaches, she dreads the growing anger among the white community but feels duty-bound to fulfill the hopes that her own community has for her; with calm courage, she must prove by her actions that the cause of equality is just. "Most of the students [at Chatman] really have not decided whether they want you there, or not," says a civil rights activist who advises Eva and her friends. "So you must act in a way that, if they have to take sides, they'll choose *our* side." Meanwhile Sophia Stuart, daughter of a wealthy white family, cannot accept the coming of outsiders to the closed, predictable world of her high school. But when Eva arrives at the school steps and prays to God for help as she is attacked by an angry white mob, Sophia is so moved that—much to her own surprise—she helps Eva to safety. Elizabeth Muther of the *Christian Science Monitor* wrote that *The Girl on the Outside* was "well crafted and focused" and "sizzling with details" that young adult readers would enjoy.

In several of Walter's novels, the characters grow as people while they learn about their African American heritage. As the grandfather says in *Justin and the Best Biscuits in the World,* "You must know where you've come from in order to find the way to where you want to go." The title character of *Justin* is a ten-year-old boy whose father has died, leaving him without a man to look up to. Picked on by his sisters because he is clumsy at household chores, he rebels by acting as irresponsible as he dares and declaring that all housework is "women's work." Finally Justin finds a role model in his own grandfather, a black cowboy who takes him to his Missouri ranch and convinces him that cowboys are strong, self-sufficient men partly because they know how to cook their own food and otherwise care for themselves. Justin also learns about the origins of black cowboys: they were freed slaves who braved racist opposition in order to move west, buy land, and run their own farms. The high point of the book comes when Justin and his grandfather attend a black rodeo, where Justin wins several prizes for playing classic farm games like horseshoe pitching and his grandfather wins a cooking prize for "the best biscuits in the world." (The recipe was inspired by Walter's own father—"I guess the idea is really rooted in me," she said, "that fathers make good biscuits.") Justin masters biscuit-making, goes back home, and proves to his sisters that he can take care of himself—even in a kitchen.

*Justin* earned Walter national acclaim when it won the 1987 Coretta Scott King Award. But Walter was unable to attend the meeting where she was granted the prize. An experienced traveler, she had accepted an invitation to visit what was then the Soviet Union and join a march in favor of world peace. "I had to choose between going on the walk or going to the awards ceremony," she recalled. "This was the kind of choice my characters have had to make." So she wrote a speech, which was later read at the ceremony by the editor in chief of the Lothrop publishing house. "What ... is most in keeping with the spirit of the Coretta Scott King Award," the speech asked "accepting the award in person, or putting myself wholly on the line to make a statement that the nuclear arms race must end if we are to survive? My answer came. I chose to walk."

Walter had been traveling since the days of her marriage, part of an ongoing effort to broaden her understanding of people—and of herself. She and her husband "started out by seeing every state in the Union," she asserted. "We would go to all the national parks and everywhere. Then we went to Mexico, Canada, and the Caribbean Islands. We were preparing to go to Africa the year he died. We wanted to know our country very well so that when we went overseas we would have a sense of who we were in terms of being American." Why travel? "Places and people give me a sense of who I am very much," Walter said. "They help me in their differences to see who I really am."

Walter's most important journey probably occurred in 1977, when she first visited Africa as an American delegate to the Second World Black and African Festival of the Arts and Culture (FESTAC). She found that her encounter with Africa, like her work with the civil rights movement, inspired mixed emotions. Her first feeling was elation, because reaching Africa allowed her to vanquish some unpleasant memories of her childhood. As a young girl, she explained in her autobiographical essay, "myths about the inferiority of blackness weighed heavily upon me.... Pictures then showed Africans as uncivilized, half-naked with elongated lips, and with bones in their noses. Scenes from the so-called dark continent provoked nervous, boisterous laughter.... I knew but repressed knowing that I was treated inferiorly because, somehow, I was connected to that place that was so terribly ridiculed." Landing in Africa with the FESTAC delegation refuted all those childhood memories at once. "We were met and surrounded by smiling faces that looked very much like people I already knew, people who were near and dear to me," she recalled. "An overwhelming feeling brought tears of joy as I joined others in our delegation in a chant: 'We're home! We're home!'"

But Walter soon realized that for an American descendant of African slaves, going "home" to Africa was not that simple. African writers, she found, sometimes did not want black Americans to join their groups—how could an American be an African? The African tour guide who showed Walter through a slave-traders' fortress seemed to feel little identification with the Africans who had been kidnapped and forced into slavery in the New World. "The brutal events of slavery," Walter decided, "had created a situation of grief and pain that made it impossible for our African relatives to keep us in mind, to carry memories and hopes of our return. Imagine knowing that thousands were disappearing with no knowledge or word of one return!" Walter concluded that she was not simply "African" or "American," but a unique mixture of the two. "Caught between two cultures," she wrote, "I had an opportunity to choose the best from each." From Africa, Walter chose the spirit of community, a spirit of closeness and unity much like what she knew when she was growing up. In African philosophies, she stated, there is a feeling "that we are one with all living things"—the kind of feeling that caused all the people in her neighborhood to look out for her. "Religion is not a Sunday thing, but an everyday thing, interwoven with your life," just as religious values pervaded her childhood. "Art is interwoven with your life"—just as the people she grew up with could entertain one another with stories, dance, and song. "In America," she continued, "I like the *idea* of freedom, the idea of freedom is a great idea, the idea of democracy is a powerful idea. African Americans have the kind of heritage that could make a powerful community, a powerful statement about what life could be. If we could combine what we bring from the Mother Land with what exists in this new land, we could have it all."

Fulfilling that dream, Walter knows, will be a great struggle—especially for younger African Americans. The obstacles that confronted her in her youth, Walter commented, "were *nothing* like what they see today. We had poverty of course, but we were *together*." Years ago, she said, African Americans "were in small communities. We were an agrarian people, close to the land. We had a warmth, a feeling...." With her whole community urging her to succeed, "I *had* to do it in spite of the Depression." But since then, she continued, "we have come into an urban world where we are alienated—where there is no time to care about other people's children. There seems to be a fear of caring, a fear of knowing what's going on, and our children are suffering from that. They are not given direct care—I mean discipline that comes from the community." As a result, Walter declared, "Our children are suffering. They don't know boundaries in terms of behavior, and they are *longing* for those boundaries. They need maps and there is nobody to give them that, and when you do not have maps on the road you are lost."

"My greatest concern for African Americans," Walter continued, "is that we lose this uniqueness that we have—the spontaneity, the laughter, the loving, and the caring that we as a people always had. That we will lose the idea of the extended family, which goes from the immediate family into the community. My greatest hope, of course, is that those of us who have the knowledge of who we were and are—in terms of caring and supporting and giving our children values—will share what we know with our children and with the world, and make for a peaceful place for all children. I hope that we as African Americans, who came unwillingly to this country but stayed and carved out a way of life that is unique and has wonderful values, will cling to that, and spread it, and share it."

Walter shares the strength of her heritage through her books. In *Have A Happy...,* eleven-year-old Chris and his family find the strength to weather tough economic times as they celebrate Kwanzaa, an African American holiday that commemorates traditional African virtues such as *imani* (faith), *umoja* (unity), and *ujima* (collective work and responsibility). Chris wants a bicycle so he can earn money as a paperboy, but his unemployed father cannot afford it; in accord with the principles of Kwanzaa, relatives chip in to give Chris the bike, and Chris, in turn, helps his father to get a job supervising him and the other news carriers. "I was thinking about children whose parents are out of work," Walter noted. "I wanted them to feel that they were not alone, that this *is* happening, and that they can find strength in wanting to help and support the family."

"There are some wonderful things happening in the realm of children's books," Walter declared—"books that are dealing with real issues, dealing with history, talking directly to children, telling them about things they can really relate to." However, she noted, "all the different cultures are not well represented. Less than one percent of American authors are people of color. In terms of diversity I don't think we have reached the golden age yet." What should be done? "First of all," Walter observed, "we should get some of these diverse people into the publishing business as readers, as receptionists, as editors, as vice presidents. Then the material that is coming from people of color would have a better chance of being read with a different perspective. If you have a friend in the business, or a person who is like you, and they see that you have potential, they can help you—they will take the time." And that's important, for Walter, because children's books are so important. "Children's literature is the only true literature now," she said, because it is willing—unlike many movies, television shows, or books for adults—to teach positive values. "Children's books," Walter declared, "are really the mainstay of our literature."

*BIOGRAPHICAL/CRITICAL SOURCES:*

*BOOKS*

*Children's Literature Review,* Volume 15, Gale, 1988.
Walter, Mildred Pitts, *The Girl on the Outside,* Lothrop, 1982.
Walter, Mildred Pitts, *Justin and the Best Biscuits in the World,* Lothrop, 1986.
Walter, Mildred Pitts, autobiographical essay in *Something about the Author Autobiography Series,* Volume 12, Gale, 1991, pp. 283-301.
Walter, Mildred Pitts, *Ty's One-Man Band,* Four Winds Press, 1980.

*PERIODICALS*

*Booklist,* September 15, 1980, pp. 122-123; November 1, 1983, p. 404; September 1, 1989, p. 82; April 15, 1990, p. 1636.
*Bulletin of the Center for Children's Books,* November, 1982, p. 58.
*Christian Science Monitor,* October 8, 1982, p. B11.
*English Journal,* March, 1972, p. 435.
*Horn Book,* July, 1985, p. 446; March, 1989, p. 212.
*Kirkus Reviews,* July 1, 1988, p. 979; August 1, 1989, p. 1170.
*Library Journal,* February 15, 1970, p. 782.
*New York Times Book Review,* October 12, 1980, p. 39.
*Publishers Weekly,* April 14, 1969, p. 97; July 29, 1988, p 234.
*School Library Journal,* March, 1983, p. 167; October, 1985, p. 188; April, 1990, p. 100.
*Wilson Library Bulletin,* June, 1990, p. 117.

*OTHER*

Walter, Mildred Pitts, interview by telephone with Thomas Kozikowski for *Something about the Author,* August 6, 1991.

\*     \*     \*

## WALTERS, Ronald

*PERSONAL: Education:* Fisk University, B.A., 1963; American University, M.A., 1966, Ph.D., 1971.

*ADDRESSES: Office*—Department of Political Science, 144 Douglass Hall, Howard University, 2441 Sixth St. N.W., Washington, DC 20059.

*CAREER:* Syracuse University, Syracuse, NY, assistant professor of political science, 1968-69; Brandeis University, Waltham, MA, assistant professor of African American studies and head of department, 1969-71; Howard University, Washington, DC, lecturer, 1971-74, associate professor, 1974-79, professor of political science, 1979—, chair of department, 1991-93, director of Social Science Research Center, Institute for Urban Affairs and Research, 1975-78, elected member of board of trustees of the university, 1991. Princeton University, visiting professor, fall, 1985; Harvard University, fellow of Institute of Politics at John F. Kennedy School of Government, spring, 1989; Dartmouth College, national fellow at Center on Inter-Ethnic Conflict, 1991; lecturer at colleges and universities in the United States and abroad. TransAfrica Forum, founding member and chair of board of directors; Social Science Research Council, past chair of committee on African American societies and cultures; Overseas Development Council, member of board of directors, 1991-93; consultant to United Nations Security Council's Special Committee against Apartheid. Member of U.S. symposium delegation, Festival of African Art and Culture, Lagos, Nigeria, 1977; Delegation of Afro-American Leaders, member of delegation in Beirut, Lebanon, 1989; invited guest of the government of Zimbabwe, 1983, World Conference on Sanctions Against South Africa (Paris), 1986, government of Jamaica, 1987, and government of Algeria, 1988; expert, International Conference for Action against Apartheid (Budapest, Hungary), 1985; member of National Rainbow Coalition Delegation to Southern Africa, 1986; toured Germany for U.S. Army, 1988; U.S. Information Agency, American participant in Brazil, 1990, in Japan, 1992. Political analyst for Black Entertainment Television, 1988, and WJLA-TV, 1990.

*MEMBER:* African Heritage Studies Association (past president), National Black Leadership Roundtable, American Po-

litical Science Association (member of council, 1990-92), National Conference of Black Political Scientists, National Congress of Black Faculty (founder, past president, vice president), African Political Science Association.

*AWARDS, HONORS:* Frederick Douglass/W. E. B. DuBois Award, African Heritage Studies Association, 1983; Distinguished Scholar/Activist Award, *Black Scholar,* 1984; Ida B. Wells Award, National Conference of Black School Educators, 1985; Carter G. Woodson Award, Congressional Black Associates, 1986; W. E. B. DuBois Award, National Alliance of Black Political Scientists, 1988, and Ralph Bunche Award, American Political Science Association, 1989, both for *Black Presidential Politics in America.*

*WRITINGS:*

(Editor, with Lucius Barker) *Jesse Jackson's 1984 Presidential Campaign: Challenge and Change in American Politics,* University of Illinois Press, 1989.
*Pan Africanism in the African Diaspora: Concepts of Afro-Centricity,* Wayne State University Press, 1992.

Also author of *South Africa and the Bomb,* 1988, and *Black Presidential Politics in America,* 1989. Contributor of more than eighty articles to scholarly journals.

\*     \*     \*

## WARUK, Kona
## See HARRIS, (Theodore) Wilson

\*     \*     \*

## WASHINGTON, Mary Helen   1941-

*PERSONAL:* Born January 21, 1941, in Cleveland, OH; daughter of David C. and Mary Catherine (Dalton) Washington. *Education:* Notre Dame College, B.A., 1962; University of Detroit, M.A., 1966, Ph.D., 1976.

*ADDRESSES: Office*—Department of English, Boston Harbor College, University of Massachusetts, Boston, MA 02125.

*CAREER:* High school teacher of English in the public schools of Cleveland, OH, 1962-64; St. John College, Cleveland, instructor in English, 1966-68; University of Detroit, Detroit, MI, assistant professor of English, 1972-75, director of Center for Black Studies, beginning 1975; currently associate professor of English, Boston Harbor College, University of Massachusetts, Boston.

*MEMBER:* National Council of Teachers of English, College Language Association, Michigan Black Studies Association.

*AWARDS, HONORS:* Richard Wright Award for Literary Criticism, *Black World,* 1974; Bunting fellow, Radcliffe College.

*WRITINGS:*

(Editor and author of introduction) *Black-Eyed Susans: Classic Stories by and about Black Women* (also see below), Doubleday, 1975.

(Editor and author of introduction and critical notes) *Midnight Birds: Stories by Contemporary Black Women Writers* (also see below), Doubleday, 1980, published in England as *Any Woman's Blues: Stories by Black Women Writers,* Virago Press, 1980.

(Editor and author of introduction and critical notes) *Invented Lives: Narratives of Black Women, 1860-1960,* Doubleday, 1987.

(Editor and author of introduction) *Black-Eyed Susans* [and] *Midnight Birds: Stories by and about Black Women* (revised and selected from *Black-Eyed Susans* [and] *Midnight Birds*), Anchor Books, 1990.

(Editor and author of introduction and commentary) *Memory of Kin: Stories about Family by Black Writers,* Doubleday, 1991.

Contributor of articles and reviews to *Negro Digest, Black World, TV Guide, Legacy,* and *Massachusetts Review.* Contributor to books, including *The Voyage In: Fictions of Female Development,* edited by Elizabeth Abel, Elizabeth Langland, and Marianne Hirsch, University Press of New England for Dartmouth College, 1983; *I Love Myself When I Am Laughing ... and Then Again When I Am Looking Mean and Impressive: A Zora Neale Hurston Reader,* edited by Alice Walker, Feminist Press, 1979; and *Mothering the Mind: Twelve Studies of Writers and Their Silent Partners,* edited by Ruth Perry and Martine Watson Brownley, Holmes & Meier, 1984.

*SIDELIGHTS:* Mary Helen Washington is the editor and author of introductions and critical notes for four valued anthologies containing the work of some of the best African American writers, particularly women writers. In reviews of *Black-Eyed Susans, Midnight Birds, Invented Lives,* and *Memory of Kin,* critics praise Washington for expertly assembling unique and sensitive stories describing the life and plight of black women and families.

*Black-Eyed Susans,* Washington's first anthology, presents writings by such authors as Toni Cade Bambara, Gwendolyn Brooks, Louise Meriwether, Toni Morrison, Jean Wheeler Smith, and Alice Walker. Joyce Carol Oates writes in *Ms.* that *Black-Eyed Susans* "constitutes an indictment of stereotyped thinking." Oates goes on to state that "no one has been so misunderstood, perhaps, as the black woman: she has been defined by others, whether white writers or black men writers, always seen from the outside, ringed in by convenient stereotypes.... What strikes the reader who comes to most of these stories for the first time is the wide range of their humanity. All the protagonists are black women: they are *black* women, black *women,* and fiercely individualistic *persons.* And the fiction that presents them is of a high order, the product of painstaking craftsmanship. There is much anger, and no little despair and heartbreak, but emotion has been kept under control; each of the stories is a work of art, moving and convincing."

Marlene Veach writes in *Best Sellers* that Washington's second book, *Midnight Birds,* "is a collection of stories that revolt against ideologies and attitudes that impress women into servitude. It deals with the real lives and actual experiences of black women, in the hope of demolishing racial and sexual stereotypes." And Margaret Atwood writes in a *Harvard Review* article on *Midnight Birds* that "this is American writing at its finest, by turns earthy, sinuous, thoughtful, and full of power." Atwood continues to explain that the writers included in this collection, Toni Cade Bambara, Alexis De Veaux, Gayl Jones, Toni Morrison, Ntozake Shange, Alice Walker, and others, "know exactly whom they are writing for. They are writing for other black American women, and they believe in the power of their words. They see themselves as giving a voice to the voiceless. They perceive writing as the forging of saving myths, the naming of forgotten pasts, the telling of truths."

According to publicity material released by the publisher, each contribution to *Midnight Birds* was "chosen to reflect the efforts of black women to liberate themselves from the structures and constraints of the past. These are not stories about victims but positive stories of and by those women who have provided models of how to live."

In *Invented Lives* Washington chose to highlight the work of ten women, including Harriet Jacobs, Frances E. W. Harper, Zora Neale Hurston, and Dorothy West, who wrote between the years of 1860 and 1960. Washington stated in a *New York Times Book Review* interview conducted by Rosemary L. Bray that "a lot of people think the tradition of black women writing began in the last 20 years. In fact, black women have been writing about their experiences in America for more than 200 years.... I found black women working as domestics, writers, migrant farmers, artists, secretaries—and having economic and personal problems centering around these jobs."

Henry Louis Gates, Jr. comments in the *New York Times Book Review* that in each author's selection "we hear a black woman *testifying* about what the twin scourges of sexism and racism, merged into one oppressive entity, actually *do* to a human being, how the combination confines the imagination, puzzles the will and delimits free choice. What unites these essays, short stories and novel excerpts is their common themes: 'Their literature is about black women; it takes the trouble to record the thoughts, words, feelings, and deeds of black women, experiences that make the realities of being black in America look very different from what men have written.'"

In what appeared to some commentators as a departure from her usual concerns, Washington features short stories and poetry by both female and male black writers in *Memory of Kin,* which includes works by Ernest J. Gaines, Langston Hughes, Lucille Clifton, Alexis De Veaux, Jamaica Kincaid, and others. With the African American family as its focal point, *Memory of Kin* provides, in the words of *New York Times Book Review* writer Bray, "a very modern look at one of the world's oldest social structures." In addition to praising the literary value of the anthology, Marita Golden, in a review in *Washington Post Book World,* observes that "much of the importance of this book springs from the enduring fascination of sociologists, educators, journalists and 'experts' with the black family." Golden concludes that the anthology is not only a valuable classroom text, but is also "for the dining room and the bedroom as well—where families most often explode, make peace and survive." Although Washington chooses to represent the male perspective in this collection, Golden notes that in Washington's introduction the author maintains *Memory of Kin* is "in many ways ... a woman-centered book and that is because the family has been the central concern of women."

Critics note that although the contributors to Washington's anthologies are all of black heritage, their tales can be understood and appreciated by readers from a wide range of cultures and perspectives. Commenting in particular on the diverse groups of women that Washington's second anthology, *Midnight Birds,* might appeal to, Buchi Emecheta remarks in the *Washington Post* that the collection is "a book that is difficult to fault," and that it "speaks through its admirable selection of stories to black women in particular and to all women in general. The message is clear: it is about time we women start to talking to each other, the white to the black, the black American to her African sister, ironing out our differences. For as Toni Morrison said, 'Because when you don't have a

woman to really talk to, whether it be an aunt or a sister or a friend, that is the real loneliness.'"

*BIOGRAPHICAL/CRITICAL SOURCES:*

*PERIODICALS*

*America,* January 31, 1981.
*Best Sellers,* August, 1980.
*Ebony,* March, 1991.
*Harvard Review,* February, 1981.
*Library Journal,* January 15, 1980.
*Ms.,* March, 1976; July, 1980; January, 1988.
*New York Times Book Review,* October 4, 1987; January 20, 1991, p. 26.
*Publishers Weekly,* December 3, 1979.
*Times Literary Supplement,* October 30, 1981.
*Washington Post,* June 3, 1980.
*Washington Post Book World,* January 7, 1990, p. 12; December 23, 1990, p. 1.

\*    \*    \*

# WATKINS, Gloria 1955(?)- (Bell Hooks)

*PERSONAL:* Born c. 1955; publishes under the name of her great-grandmother, Bell Hooks, to pay homage to the "unlettered wisdom" of her female ancestors. *Education:* Attended Stanford University.

*ADDRESSES: Office*—Department of Afro-American Studies, Yale University, New Haven, CT 06520.

*CAREER:* Social critic, educator, and writer. Yale University, New Haven, CT, assistant professor of Afro-American studies and English, beginning in the middle-1980s.

*WRITINGS:*

*UNDER NAME BELL HOOKS*

*Ain't I a Woman: Black Women and Feminism,* South End Press, 1981.
*Feminist Theory From Margin to Center,* South End Press, 1984.
*Talking Back: Thinking Feminist, Thinking Black,* Between-the-Lines, 1988.
*Yearning: Race, Gender, and Cultural Politics,* Between-the-Lines, 1990.
(With Cornell West) *Breaking Bread: Insurgent Black Intellectual Life,* South End Press, 1991.
*A Woman's Mourning Song,* Writers and Readers, 1992.

*Black Looks: Race and Representation,* South End Press, 1992.

*Sisters of the Yam: Black Women and Self Recovery,* South End Press, 1993.

Also contributor to *Double Stitch: Black Women Write about Mothers and Daughters,* 1992.

*SIDELIGHTS:* Bell Hooks takes an analytical yet impassioned look at how certain factors—black womanhood, feminism, the civil rights movement, critical theory—cooperate and clash in the world at large and within herself. "At her best she exhibits a command of various voices that range from subtle overlays of the personal and historical to a refreshing public forthrightness that stings," writes P. Gabrielle Foreman in the *Women's Review of Books.* "Inevitably, a reader will cheer through one essay and scowl through another."

Born Gloria Watkins, she writes under the name of Bell Hooks, the name of her great-grandmother, in order, according to Paula Giddings in *Ms.,* to "honor the unlettered wisdom of her foremothers." Indeed, it is the unheard voice of black women in general which drives her overall work.

Black women finding their voices within mainstream feminism is the focus of Hooks' first three works: *Ain't I a Woman, Feminist Theory: From Margin to Center,* and *Talking Back. Ain't I a Woman* is her formative work in this regard. She develops her black feminism through an examination of the special oppression under which African American women suffered and still suffer, from slavery until the time of her writing. She finds, in the web of racism, sexism, and classism that make up that oppression, that black and white women are sometimes allies and sometimes at odds. Generally, competitiveness and the white woman's vested interest in classism often drives the wedge of racism between her and her black sisters.

This thesis is further systematized in *Feminist Theory,* in which she clearly states the basic ills of the three "isms": racism, classism, and sexism have at their root the notion of domination which is the basis of the hierarchical—or "authoritarian/bureaucratic" organization—of (at least American) society. This kind of organization is opposed to a consensual/collectivist model which would eradicate the existing forces of control, manipulation, and domination, and thus redefine power throughout society. Being at the bottom of the power structure as it now stands, black women are naturally in the vanguard of liberation from the existing structure, by their very efforts at individual self-determination. They are not, however, recognized as such by mainstream feminist organizations, who see the world with the same hierarchical eyes as do white males, wanting merely to be in their positions. Real feminism, says Hooks, should attack the whole hierarchical system.

In Hooks' third book, *Talking Back,* this paradigm is allowed to play itself out in twenty-three essays on different aspects of the black/feminist connection: from "writing autobiography, teaching women's literature, black homophobia, intimate violence, racist feminists, black porn, and politics at Yale," notes Beverly Miller in *Library Journal.*

Hooks' first three works have sometimes been seen as taking on too many voices to deal with their complex, inflammatory issues. A reviewer for *Publishers Weekly,* for example, notes that "although the author makes perceptive and provocative observations, they are diminished by redundancy and weakened by her doctrinaire Marxist rhetoric." In her review of *Feminist Theory,* Giddings wonders why black women and other women from the margins, since they *are* the vanguard, need to lobby at all to be included in other segments of the feminist movement, appearing to assign "proprietary rights to the same 'privileged' women she criticizes for their narrow perspective." And Patricia Bell-Scott, in the *Women's Review of Books,* admits to reacting defensively to some arguments that run against the feminist grain, and again points to the Marxist flavor as possibly irritating. "However," Bell-Scott continues, "we must keep in mind the author's goal, to enrich feminist discourse and 'to share in the work of making a liberatory ideology,' as we struggle with the uncomfortable issues she raises."

Though all of Hooks' work contains self-examination, her fourth book, *Yearning: Race, Gender, and Cultural Politics,* seems to reassess all her efforts, as well as her various voices. In it she continues to broaden her cultural criticism, using more and more of the theoretical tools available to (and expected from) a cutting-edge, post-modern academic. Critics like P. Gabrielle Foreman find that central to this effort is an essay, "Homeplace: A Site of Resistance," in which Hooks once more returns home to find her "location" of strength, a sense of community in the households set up by black women. This "location" helps her to solidify her base point of view, even as she sets out to examine more of her overall culture, and a black woman's part in it, from more varied and theoretical perspectives. This might be the reason that critics, among them Foreman, see her often contradicting herself and taking on the white feminists' point of view. For Foreman, though, it is her "'intervention' into the politics of post-modern theory and practice that makes *Yearning* so timely and valuable." She tries, for example, to untangle the theories of "Otherness"—the position of outsiders within a culture—that have been primarily produced by insiders or white scholars. This includes their theorizing on "essentialism"—in this case the reality of racial groupings, and the politics of identity based on those groupings. This is a complicated question for Hooks, since blacks can be affected by both sides of this dilemma.

The reassessment of Hooks' "locations" as an African American intellectual continues in *Breaking Bread,* a dialogue with social critic Cornel West. Their discussion ranges over the various crises of the black community, and how marketing to blacks, and depictions of blacks in the media, have contributed to those problems. This theme, which has threaded its way through her earlier work, is enlarged upon in *Black Looks: Race and Representation.* In its twelve chapters, she explores the implicit meaning of black images in phenomena such as advertising, Madonna's music videos, and the Hill-Thomas hearings. Her most serious indictment of the media is that it has further threatened the position of the black woman by selling black males a macho self-image. Widely greeted with approval for its ground breaking breadth and theoretical rigor, this last collection of essays caused a *Library Journal* critic to remark, "Hooks continues to produce some of the most challenging, insightful, and provocative writing on race and gender in the United States today."

*BIOGRAPHICAL/CRITICAL SOURCES:*

*PERIODICALS*

*Black Enterprise,* June, 1992, p. 23.
*Black Scholar,* January, 1983, pp. 38, 46.
*Bookwatch,* July 1989, p. 4; September, 1992, p. 10.
*Choice,* April, 1982, p. 1141; July, 1985, p. 1703.
*Essence,* July, 1989, p. 20.
*Library Journal,* December, 1981, p. 178; March 15, 1985, p. 68; December, 1988, p. 126; July, 1992, p. 109.
*Ms.,* July, 1983, p. 24; October, 1985 p. 25.
*Multicultural Review,* April, 1992.
*New Directions for Women,* January, 1992, p. 22.
*New Statesman & Society,* October 22, 1982, p. 31; November 30, 1990, p. 39.
*Phylon,* March, 1983, p.85.
*Political Science Quarterly,* spring, 1983, p. 84.
*Progressive,* March, 1991, p. 42.
*Publishers Weekly,* November 18, 1988, p.72; November 22, 1991, p.49; June 15, 1992, p. 95.
*Queen's Quarterly,* summer, 1990, p. 318.
*Sight and Sound,* June, 1991, p. 36.
*Village Voice Literary Supplement,* June, 1982, p. 10.
*West Coast Review of Books,* April, 1982, p. 51.
*Women's Review of Books,* February, 1985, p. 3; September, 1991, p. 12.

\* \* \*

## WAYANS, Keenen Ivory 1958(?)-

*PERSONAL:* Born c. 1958, in New York, NY; son of Howell (in sales) and Elvira (a homemaker) Wayans. *Education:* Attended Tuskegee Institute.

*ADDRESSES: Home*—Los Angeles, CA. *Office*—Ivory Way Productions, 5746 Sunset Blvd., Hollywood, CA 90028.

*CAREER:* Comedian, actor, director, producer, and screenwriter. Began career as a stand-up comedian at various comedy clubs in New York City and Los Angeles, CA. Television work includes: actor in *Irene* (pilot), 1981, and *For Love and Honor* (series), 1983-84; coproducer and cowriter of *Robert Townsend and His Partners in Crime* (comedy special), 1987; executive producer and writer of *Hammer, Slammer, and Slade* (comedy pilot), 1990; creator, executive producer, actor, and head writer, *In Living Color* (series), 1990-92; guest on specials, including *Motown Thirty: What's Goin' On!,* 1990, *MTV's 1990 Video Music Awards,* 1990, *Comic Relief V,* 1991, *The Fifth Annual American Comedy Awards,* 1991, and *The American Music Awards,* 1991; guest on series *A Different World, Benson,* and *Cheers.* Film work includes: actor, *Star 80,* 1983; actor and cowriter, *Hollywood Shuffle,* 1987; actor, coproducer, and cowriter, *Eddie Murphy Raw,* 1987; director, actor, and writer, *I'm Gonna Git You Sucka,* 1988; cowriter, *The Five Heartbeats,* 1991.

*MEMBER:* Screen Actors Guild, Directors Guild of America, Screen Writers Guild.

*AWARDS, HONORS:* Emmy Award for outstanding variety, music, or comedy program, American Academy of Television Arts and Sciences, 1990, for *In Living Color;* Emmy Award nominations for outstanding writing in a variety or music program, 1990 and 1991, and outstanding individual performance in a variety or music program, 1991, all for *In Living Color.*

*WRITINGS:*

*SCRIPTS FOR TELEVISION*

(With Robert Townsend) *Robert Townsend and His Partners in Crime* (special), HBO, 1987.
*Hammer, Slammer, and Slade* (pilot), ABC, 1990.
*In Living Color* (series), Fox, 1990-92.

*SCREENPLAYS*

(With Townsend) *Hollywood Shuffle,* Samuel Goldwyn, 1987.
(With Eddie Murphy and Townsend) *Eddie Murphy Raw* (sketch portions), Paramount, 1987.
(And director) *I'm Gonna Git You Sucka,* Metro-Goldwyn-Mayer/United Artists, 1988.
(With Townsend) *The Five Heartbeats,* Twentieth Century-Fox, 1991.

*WORK IN PROGRESS:* Writing comedy film with brother.

*SIDELIGHTS:* The second oldest of ten children, Keenen Ivory Wayans grew up in a household where suppertime was filled with humor and laughter. His ready-made audience afforded him the opportunity to develop his unique brand of comedy and to practice for a career in the entertainment business. After his beginnings as a stand-up comedian, Wayans successfully ventured into acting, directing, and writing for film and television. His work, which often pokes fun at the stereotyping of blacks and their culture, has earned him a devoted public following. From his involvement in films like *Hollywood Shuffle* and *I'm Gonna Git You Sucka* to his creation of the prime-time television comedy series *In Living Color,* Wayans has presented controversial, cutting-edge humor that often catches viewers off guard and finds a mixed critical reception. "I want to be an entity," Wayans told *New York*'s Dinitia Smith, adding "a source of product, people."

Wayans was born and raised in New York City. Early in his life he experienced racism firsthand. For example, on occasion a local white police officer would prompt Wayans and his brother to race each other and then trip them. Even though Wayans and his family were victims of prejudice at times, he told *People* contributors Charles E. Cohen and Vicki Sheff that his mother and father "always built up our self-esteem." Wayans's father had a career in sales, and his mother was a homemaker. The family lived in a tenement in Harlem until Wayans was six years old and then moved into a predominantly white housing project where Wayans was frequently harassed by white teenagers. The children shared three rooms, and for privacy Wayans would retreat into a bedroom closet and dream about his future as an entertainer.

The same year they moved, Wayans realized he wanted to become a comedian after he saw actor and comic Richard Pryor delivering a stand-up performance on television. "He was doing routines about being poor, about looking for money, about being beaten up by the school bully. It was all happening to me at the time," explained Wayans to Smith. His penchant for humor was also fueled by his family, who would practice making each other laugh at dinnertime. Wayans recalled for Smith, "All of us sitting around the table, the food would just fly out of our mouths! We'd love it when someone would get mad. That's where we get the edge to our comedy."

Because of his flare for comedy, Wayans stood out in a crowd at his high school. "I was a tall, gangly, Afro-wearing teenager who figured his best shot at attracting girls was by making them laugh," he confessed to *Hollywood Reporter* writer Christopher Vaughn. Wayans and his younger brother Damon were inseparable, rattling off jokes as a team; they would make up characters and act them out for their friends and family. (Some of these characters later appeared on Wayans's show *In Living Color,* which also starred Damon.) Wayans told

Smith that he stayed away from drugs and alcohol in high school, and he worked long hours as a McDonald's manager to help support his family.

After graduation, Wayans attended Alabama's Tuskegee Institute under a scholarship to study engineering. "I had such culture shock down there.... [Y]ou'd get downtown and it wasn't nothing but a pharmacy and a Goodwill store," recalled Wayans to *Interview* contributor Kevin Sessums. Wayans continued to liberate his comedy in college, and before his senior year began he decided to quit school and follow his dream of becoming a comedian. He began his career in New York City's prominent comedy club, The Improv, where he met then sixteen-year-old actor and comedian Eddie Murphy. Wayans told Smith that he remembers the young Murphy stating, "'I thought I was the only funny black guy in New York. Now I see there are two.'" Later Wayans would help write Murphy's concert film, *Eddie Murphy Raw,* which became the most lucrative concert film made to that date. Wayans also met Robert Townsend, another aspiring young black entertainer, at the Improv. In 1980 Wayans moved to Los Angeles where he continued his stand-up comedy and tried out for parts in motion pictures and television.

Landing only an occasional television role in Los Angeles, Wayans decided to venture into filmmaking, which he believed was also more conducive to his outlandish form of comedy. He told Vaughn that the scarcity of quality acting roles for African Americans in the early 1980s also motivated him to make and act in his own films. Wayans rectified this inequity with Townsend, who had also moved to Los Angeles from New York, in their collaborative 1987 motion picture *Hollywood Shuffle.* Townsend explained the objective for *Hollywood Shuffle* to *Ebony* reporter Marilyn Marshall: "The majority of jobs [acting roles for African Americans] are bogus, [focusing on] stereotypes. Yet people fight for them, and in *Hollywood Shuffle,* I spoke up and said, 'That's not right.' And I tried to do it in a funny way."

A satire, *Hollywood Shuffle* revolves around struggling actor Bobby Taylor, played by Townsend, who must work at a hot dog stand to make enough money to support himself. Taylor perceives that because he is an African American his chances of finding a respectable part in a film are practically nonexistent. Therefore, he auditions and receives the lead role as a pimp in a blaxploitation film—a genre capitalizing on the portrayal of dubious black stereotypes, including pimps, drug dealers, murderers, and thieves. The movie, *Jivetime Jimmy's Revenge,* is being written, produced, and directed by white people. The black actors are trained and coached by whites to act more "black." Disheartened by his role, Taylor imagines himself in satirical situations. For example, he envisions an acting school where black people are taught "black" characteristics by white people; he also becomes Superman, defeats a bully named Jerry Curl (played by Wayans) by confiscating his curl activator, reviews blaxploitation films in a spin-off of Gene Siskel and Roger Ebert's movie review television show, *At the Movies*, stars in a blaxploitation film called *Rambro: First Youngblood*, and becomes a victim of ridicule by the National Association for the Advancement of Colored People (NAACP) for acting in blaxploitation films. Following his dream sequences, Taylor realizes he has doubts about his involvement in *Jivetime Jimmy's Revenge* and quits. He also pleas for the other minority cast members to leave the production. Later he auditions for a more tolerable acting role as a mailman in a commercial.

Although *Hollywood Shuffle* was written by both Townsend and Wayans, the latter received meager recognition from the critics for his contributions. Wayans told Smith, however, that he felt Townsend deserved the greater publicity. Critics were generally positive about the production. In *New Republic* Stanley Kauffmann called *Hollywood Shuffle* a "lively, knowledgeable film." Armond White, a *Film Comment* contributor, found that the movie "offers a shrewd look at Hollywood's benighted attitudes and nonthinking." "*Hollywood Shuffle* is an exhilarating blast of anger and disgust. Much of it is wildly funny," wrote David Denby in his review for *New York*. And a writer for *The Motion Picture Guide* found Townsend and Wayans's film to be "downright hilarious."

Following his success with *Hollywood Shuffle*, Wayans began work on a parody of his own. A satire of blaxploitation films, the movie was released as *I'm Gonna Git You Sucka*. Wayans, who wrote, directed, and acted in the film, also cast two family members, Damon and Kim. Like the earlier movie, Wayans's solo comedy pokes fun at Hollywood stereotyping. He admits to receiving inspiration from the 1980 slapstick film *Airplane!* when creating *I'm Gonna Git You Sucka*. Wayans told Sessums that the movie is not intended to "satiriz[e] black people but bad moviemaking." In the film, Jack Slade, played by Wayans, takes leave from the U.S. Army to return to his hometown of "Any Ghetto, U.S.A." He wants to investigate his brother Junebug's death, which was caused by wearing too many gold chains. When Slade learns of a gold-chain pusher named Mr. Big, he vows to attack the malefactor's operations to avenge his brother's death. He solicits help from former stars of 1970s blaxploitation films, including *Slaughter*'s Jim Brown and *Truck Turner*'s Isaac Hayes. However, the heroes have lost their abilities to battle the bad guys, creating havoc as they trip and set off a number of loaded guns and detonate dynamite before breaking through the window of Mr. Big's offices. Eventually Slade finds himself fighting alone, but with help from his mother his mission succeeds.

In *People* Wayans expounded on his aspirations for his film: "I wanted to do something that was true to its ethnicity but not restricted to it. That's important to me as a black filmmaker because I feel that our society is painted to be more racist than it is." In the eyes of some white critics, his film was regarded as being degrading to blacks. "There is no racial issue," responded Wayans to Vaughn. "*Sucka* is a parody of a genre film." He concluded, "these are white guys trying to tell me, a black man, what is funny to black audiences." When asked by *Rolling Stone* contributor Jill Feldman if his movie was just another blaxploitation film, Wayans reflected: "There's really no such thing as blacksploitation. Blacksploitation is just an action-adventure movie with black men in the lead." Other critics gave *I'm Gonna Git You Sucka* rave reviews. A reviewer for *The Motion Picture Guide* stated that "Wayans keeps the jokes coming fast and thick, never giving the audience time to stop laughing." The critic concluded, "*I'm Gonna Git You Sucka* is on target often enough to make Wayans a talent worth watching." And Stuart Klawans stated in his article for *Nation*, "No joke is too dumb, no pose too embarrassing, in this amiably slapdash and utterly engaging story."

Wayans's film received a favorable reception despite some marketing problems. He told *American Film* contributor Betsy Sharkey that United Artists (UA) "never got beyond the fact that [the movie] was black." Sharkey confirmed Hollywood's bias toward black films through a studio marketing executive who told her: "Historically, there is a belief that black films don't do as well" as white films. She also quoted producer Dale Pollock as saying, "Black films do have an extra burden. They have to be better." Wayans believes such negative attitudes prevailed at UA when it was time to market *I'm Gonna Git You Sucka*. Forecasting that the film would not do well in white areas, UA only promoted the film in predominantly black neighborhoods. Wayans was upset over the UA decision, thinking that the movie should be advertised to white audiences as well. Wayans told Sharkey, "I could have set myself on fire, and it wouldn't have changed their minds." Yet Wayans's film proved successful, grossing nearly seven times its production costs. In Sharkey's article Wayans also commented on how he deals with negative reactions from the film industry. "There are times when you ask yourself, 'What does a black man have to do?'" he related. "But you have to channel those feelings into something productive. Bitterness will kill you." In 1990 when Wayans talked to Cohen and Sheff, he maintained that "this town still has not embraced the black creator."

After attending a screening for *I'm Gonna Git You Sucka*, Fox television network executives enticed Wayans to produce a television program telling him he could have creative reign over the series. Taking the offer, in 1990 Wayans developed a skit format program titled *In Living Color* that has been compared to veteran sketch show *Saturday Night Live*. The show consists of bawdy comedy skits parodying television shows and commercials, motion pictures, black stereotypes and culture, and celebrities, especially prominent black figures. Fox executive Harris Katleman talked about the show's cutting-edge nature to Andrew Feinberg of *TV Guide.* "Two years ago, no one would have aired *In Living Color,*" Katleman opined. "It's too different, too ethnic, and brings up too many issues that standards and practices [censors have] never had to deal with before." "There's nothing subtle about the humor. It's extremely visceral, in-your-face stuff," said *In Living Color* writer John Bowman in Jeffrey Ressner's feature for *Rolling Stone.* Ressner himself concluded his article assessing that "*In Living Color* is about raunch and being raunchy."

*In Living Color* also features dancing by a group called the Fly Girls and performances by guest musicians. Wayans explained to Smith that "*In Living Color* shows people different sides of black life and black culture. It's important that I do it honestly. I don't just show the black bourgeoisie or professionals—or criminals. I try to show every side of black life." The cast mainly consists of black actors. Four of Wayans's nine siblings have appeared on the show—Damon, Kim, and Marlon acted, and Shawn, who was at first the D.J. for the Fly Girls, became a member of the acting team in 1991. Kim Wayans told Cohen and Sheff, "We're a very tight family, almost like the Osmonds"—a family of popular entertainers who had a variety show in the 1970s. According to Cohen and Sheff, "critics tripped over their adjectives with praise" for Wayans's show.

While *In Living Color* has received generally favorable reviews, it has been criticized by some viewers for emphasizing stereotypes. One of the skits that received such concern is "The Homeboy Shopping Network." This sketch, which plays on the stereotype that blacks are hoods, features two young black men who sell stolen goods on a home shopping program. Another skit, "The Equity Express Card: Helping the Right Sort of People," presents a wealthy black man having problems using a credit card. Also, certain skits have proved unsettling to some feminists, including sketches wielding jokes about women's breasts, shaving, and tampon use. In particular, one segment featured a woman's talk show ending with women clawing at each other. Members of the gay community have also voiced complaints, citing the characterizations in the "Men on Film" skit, in which two gay black men review movies. Some viewers feel that these depictions, in which the actors speak with feminine voices and rave about leading men in movies, are supplying a dubious representation of gay people to the public. Wayans responded to the reproachful comments in Harry F. Waters and Lynda Wright's *Newsweek* article: "If the show picked on only one group, I could understand people being uptight. But we get *everybody.*"

In light of *In Living Color*'s controversial nature, Fox network censors actively oversee the writing. Tamara Rawitt, the show's former producer, told Smith: "Usually they jump in the car and come right over during taping." In one instance Wayans shot two versions of a sketch, one racier than the other. The sketch in question was a parody on 2 Live Crew singer Luther Campbell, whose album was banned in several states for being overly sexual. Wayans had hoped the more suggestive version would be chosen, but was disappointed. Wayans did admit to Ressner, however, that he does have certain standards for his comedy. He said that the show would never feature sketches on Nazi skinheads, the Ku Klux Klan, crack cocaine, or AIDS.

Despite these criticisms from viewers and censors, *In Living Color* has been described as a "groundbreaking comedy show" by *Entertainment Weekly* contributors Alan Carter and Juliann Garey. Smith called it "a surprise hit" and also emphasized that the program frequently ranked as one of the top-twenty shows in the Nielsen ratings. Ressner lauded *In Living Color* as being "TV's hottest new comedy show."

After almost three years of producing *In Living Color,* Wayans and Fox officials became entangled in a dispute over the rerun syndication of the show. The program's copyright was scheduled to revert to Wayans during 1993, but in December 1992, Fox declared that they would air the reruns first. Given no time to challenge Fox before they announced their plans, Wayans ultimately decided to leave *In Living Color.* "It was absolutely the most difficult thing I've ever had to do," said Wayans to Carter and Garey. "But I had to. I couldn't condone what they did, and how they did it. No one wanted me to leave, but I couldn't continue in good conscience. I couldn't give them a show that was a certain quality and not have them return that quality." Because of Fox's decision, the other Wayans cast members wanted to leave. Having no obligations to the show, Damon and Marlon left immediately, but Kim and Shawn were required by contract to stay. After departing from *In Living Color,* Wayans revealed he would try to create another comedy show on a different network.

During his career, Wayans has made waves in Hollywood, helping to bring African Americans to the forefront of the entertainment industry. He has not been alone in his efforts, however. Other prominent black males are also working to increase African American participation in quality productions. They include Townsend, Murphy, actor and talk-show host Arsenio Hall, and actor and filmmaker Spike Lee. Calling themselves the "black pack," these five entertainers are best friends and provide support to each other in business. Yet each has made his own name in Hollywood. "I've had to be my own big brother in this business," Wayans related to Cohen and Sheff. "I never talk to people about things. I work them out for myself."

657

*BIOGRAPHICAL/CRITICAL SOURCES:*

BOOKS

*The Motion Picture Guide,* Cinebooks, 1988, pp. 119-120, and 1989, p. 84.

PERIODICALS

*American Film,* July/August, 1989, pp. 22-27, 53-54.
*Ebony,* July, 1987, pp. 54, 56, 58.
*Entertainment Weekly,* January 15, 1993, pp. 6-7.
*Film Comment,* March/April, 1987, pp. 11-14.
*Hollywood Reporter,* January 25, 1989, p. 13.
*Interview,* December, 1988, p. 56.
*Los Angeles Times,* April 15, 1990.
*Nation,* February 13, 1989.
*New Republic,* May 4, 1987, pp. 26-27.
*Newsweek,* May 21, 1990.
*New York,* April 6, 1987, pp. 90-91; October 8, 1990, pp. 29-35.
*People,* December 12, 1988, p. 185; June 11, 1990, pp. 75-76.
*Rolling Stone,* November 3, 1988; April 23, 1992.
*Time,* April 27, 1987, p. 79.
*TV Guide,* June 2, 1990.

\*     \*     \*

## WELSING, Frances Cress 1935-

*PERSONAL:* Born March 18, 1935, in Chicago, IL. *Education:* Antioch College, B.S., 1957; Howard University School of Medicine, M.D., 1962.

*ADDRESSES: Office*—7603 Georgia Ave. NW, Suite 402, Washington, DC 20012.

*CAREER:* Author, psychiatrist. Cook County Hospital, intern, 1962-63; St. Elizabeth Hospital, resident in general psychiatry, 1963-66; Children's Hospital, fellowship child psychiatry, 1966-68; private practice in General Psychiatry, Washington, DC, 1966—, and General and Child Psychiatry, Washington, DC, 1968—; Howard University College of Medicine, assistant professor of pediatrics, 1968-75; Hillcrest Children's Center, clinical director, 1975-76; affiliated with Paul Robeson School for Growth and Development, North Community Mental Health Center, Washington, DC, 1976-90. Has appeared on numerous television and radio shows; lecturer.

*MEMBER:* National Medicine Association (section on psychiatry and behavioral sciences), American Medical Association, American Psychiatric Association.

*WRITINGS:*

*The Isis Papers: The Keyes to the Colors,* Third World Press, 1991.

Also author of *The Cress Theory of Color Confrontation and Racism (White Supremacy),* 1970.

\*     \*     \*

## WEST, Dorothy 1907-

*PERSONAL:* Born June 2, 1907, in Boston, MA; daughter of Isaac Christopher and Rachel West. *Education:* Privately tutored, attended public schools and Girl's Latin School; studied journalism, philosophy at Columbia University; attended Boston University.

*CAREER:* Novelist, editor, short story writer. Founded *Challenge* magazine. Worked as relief investigator in Harlem during 1930s; worked on Federal Writers Project.

*WRITINGS:*

*The Living Is Easy* (novel), Houghton Mifflin, 1948, reprinted in paperback, Feminist Press, 1987.

Contributor of short stories to anthologies, including *The Best Short Stories by Negro Writers: An Anthology from 1899 to the Present,* edited by Langston Hughes, Little, Brown, 1967; *Harlem: Voices from the South of Black America,* New American Library, 1970. Contributor to *Saturday Evening Quill, Opportunity, Messenger,* and *Black World.*

*SIDELIGHTS:* Dorothy West's creations include a well-received novel and dozens of short stories. The literary magazine she founded during the 1930s, *Challenge* (and later *New Challenge*), brought into focus the great talent of the Harlem Renaissance by publishing the work of her friends and colleagues: Langston Hughes, Countee Cullen, Richard Wright, Arna Bontemps, Zora Neale Hurston, Wallace Thurman, and Claude McKay.

West was an only child, the daughter of an ex-slave who became a successful Boston businessman. Early tutoring at home nurtured her literary talent, and her first short story, "Promise and Fulfillment," was published by the *Boston Post* when she was still a youngster. The newspaper had contests for the best stories each week, and she became a regular winner. West submitted a piece to *Opportunity*'s competition and won, with her poet cousin Helene Johnson, second place and a trip to the awards banquet in New York City. West's story, "The

Typewriter," was published in 1926, and it was viewed as an auspicious beginning for a young author.

Critics have compared West's narrative style to that of Russian author Fyodor Dostoyevsky, the author of, among other noted works, *Crime and Punishment* and *The Brothers Karamazov.* Like Dostoyevsky, West probes deeply into the minds of her characters, who face "moral, psychological and social confinement," wrote SallyAnn H. Ferguson in the *Dictionary of Literary Biography* (*DLB*). West also shares a belief in the innocent nature of children, much as the Russian novelist's work reflects.

West lived in New York City and stayed at the YWCA until a fellowship made her residence more secure. It was in New York that she was embraced by a circle of literary intellectuals, including H. L. Mencken, who were beginning to recognize the wealth of talent among black writers. West gained an agent but remained relatively obscure, referring to herself, as quoted in *DLB,* as "the best-known unknown writer of the time." For a time, she dappled in theater, performing a bit part in *Porgy and Bess.* It was writing, however, that remained her central focus. Toward the late 1920s, West's friendships with other leading black writers developed, including one with novelist and editor Wallace Thurman, whom West described in *DLB* as "the most symbolic figure of the Literary Renaissance in Harlem." A group of literary standouts, including West, Langston Hughes, and twenty other blacks, sailed to Russia in 1932 to film *Black and White,* a story of the oppression of American blacks. The project was dropped following accusations of association with Communism.

Despite the movie's demise, West remained in Russia with Hughes. Opinions vary on whether the two were romantically involved. West would propose to Hughes in a 1933 letter, but they were never to marry. West stayed in Russia nearly a year under a film contract before learning of her father's death, upon which time she returned to the United States. Once back in America, West felt guilty for not having written more (at age twenty-five), so she put together the first issue of *Challenge* with forty dollars. The periodical was published quarterly for only a few years, but it contained the best of black literature at the time—the works of Hughes, Bontemps, McKay, Hurston, and her cousin Helene Johnson. In an effort to maintain a high calibre of writing, however, many of the submissions from young and unknown writers were not included. In this respect, West was accused of creating too tame a voice for the black writer, of not taking a chance on the new and innovative literature that was being created in the black community.

When the periodical failed in 1937, a more ambitious version, edited by Richard Wright, was launched. *New Challenge,* however, faced the same financial dilemmas as the original

journal had, and it soon folded. West gained work as a welfare investigator, which inspired "Mammy," a story published in *Opportunity* in 1940. She then participated in the Federal Writers' Project until it ended in the mid-1940s, writing numerous short stories which, for the most part, went unpublished.

West's 1948 novel, *The Living is Easy,* is a semi-autobiographical account depicting, as Ferguson described it in *DLB,* "the economic and psychological prisons upwardly-mobile blacks create for themselves by pursuing false values." The story's central figure is Cleo Judson, a neurotic beauty who marries an older, financially secure man. She then invites her three sisters and their husbands to live with them, leading to the demise of all their marriages. Some critics speculate that the novel is loosely based on the experiences of West's mother, who came from a family of twenty-two children.

Reviewing *The Living Is Easy,* Seymour Krim wrote in the *New York Times* that "the important thing about the book is its abundant and special woman's energy and beat." *Commonweal*'s Florence Codman praised West's Cleo Judson as "the predatory female on the loose, a wholly plausible, tantalizing creature." Reviewing the reissued novel in *Ms.,* Susan McHenry compared West's social commentary to that of Theodore Dreiser and Sinclair Lewis and called the author "a brisk storyteller with an eye for ironic detail." In a 1987 review of the book in the *Times Literary Supplement,* Holly Eley commented that "West's sensitive investigation of issues such as miscegenation, racial heritage and colour consciousness ... is extremely relevant today." West has lived in semi-retirement in Massachusetts, lecturing occasionally and continuing to write short stories. Critics and afficionados hope to read more of her creation, many of which remain unpublished to this day.

*BIOGRAPHICAL/CRITICAL SOURCES:*

*BOOKS*

*Dictionary of Literary Biography,* Volume 76: *Afro-American Writers, 1940-1955,* Gale, 1988, pp. 187-95.
*Harlem Renaissance and Beyond,* G. K. Hall, 1990, pp. 343-46.

*PERIODICALS*

*Commonweal,* June 25, 1948.
*Ms.,* March 1982, pp. 37-38.
*New York Times,* May 16, 1948, p. 5.
*Times Literary Supplement,* April 17, 1987, p. 410.

## WIDEMAN, John Edgar 1941-

*PERSONAL:* Born June 14, 1941, in Washington, DC; son of Edgar and Betty (French) Wideman; married Judith Ann Goldman, 1965; children: Daniel Jerome, Jacob Edgar, Jamila Ann. *Education:* University of Pennsylvania, B.A., 1963; New College, Oxford, B.Phil., 1966; attended the University of Iowa's Writing Workshop, 1966-67.

*ADDRESSES: Office*—Department of English, University of Massachusetts—Amherst, Amherst, MA 01002.

*CAREER:* Howard University, Washington, DC, teacher of American literature, summer, 1965; University of Pennsylvania, Philadelphia, 1966-74, began as instructor, professor of English, 1974, director of Afro-American studies program, 1971-73; University of Wyoming, Laramie, professor of English, 1975-1986; University of Massachusetts, Amherst, professor of English, 1986—. Made U.S. Department of State lecture tour of Europe and the Near East, 1976; Phi Beta Kappa lecturer, 1976; visiting writer and lecturer at numerous colleges and universities; has also served as administrator/teacher in a curriculum planning, teacher-training institute sponsored by National Defense Education Act. Assistant basketball coach, University of Pennsylvania, 1968-72. National Humanities Faculty consultant in numerous states; consultant to secondary schools across the country, 1968—.

*MEMBER:* PEN (member of board), National Humanities Faculty, Association of American Rhodes Scholars (member of board of directors and of state and national selection committees), Phi Beta Kappa.

*AWARDS, HONORS:* Received creative writing prize, University of Pennsylvania; Rhodes Scholar, Oxford University, 1963; Thouron fellow, Oxford University, 1963-66; Kent fellow, University of Iowa, 1966, to attend creative writing workshop; named member of Philadelphia Big Five Basketball Hall of Fame, 1974; Young Humanist fellow, 1975—; PEN/Faulkner Award for fiction, 1984, for *Sent for You Yesterday,* and 1991, for *Philadelphia Fire;* National Book Award nomination, 1984, for *Brothers and Keepers;* John Dos Passos Prize for literature, Longwood College, 1986; honorary doctorate, University of Pennsylvania; MacArthur fellow, Rutgers University, 1993.

*WRITINGS:*

*A Glance Away* (novel), Harcourt, 1967.
*Hurry Home* (novel), Harcourt, 1970.
*The Lynchers* (novel), Harcourt, 1973.
*Damballah* (short stories), Avon, 1981.
*Hiding Place* (novel), Avon, 1981.
*Sent for You Yesterday* (novel), Avon, 1983.

*Brothers and Keepers* (memoirs), Holt, 1984.
*The Homewood Trilogy* (includes *Damballah, Hiding Place,* and *Sent For You Yesterday*), Avon, 1985.
*Reuben* (novel), Holt, 1987.
*Fever* (short stories), Holt, 1989.
*Philadelphia Fire* (novel), Holt, 1990.
*All Stories are True,* Vintage Books, 1992.
*The Stories of John Edgar Wideman,* Pantheon Books, 1992.

Contributor of articles, short stories, book reviews, and poetry to periodicals, including *American Poetry Review, Negro Digest, Black American Literature Forum, Black World, American Scholar, Gentleman's Quarterly, New York Times Book Review, North American Review, Washington Post Book World, Esquire,* and *Vogue.*

*SIDELIGHTS:* John Edgar Wideman has been hailed by Don Strachen in the *Los Angeles Times Book Review* as "the black Faulkner, the softcover Shakespeare." Such praise is not uncommon for this author, whose novel *Sent for You Yesterday* was selected as the 1984 PEN/Faulkner Award winner over works by Bernard Malamud, Cynthia Ozick, and William Kennedy. Wideman attended Oxford University in 1963 on a Rhodes scholarship, earned a degree in eighteenth-century literature, and later accepted a fellowship at the prestigious University of Iowa Writers' Workshop. Yet this "artist with whom any reader who admires ambitious fiction must sooner or later reckon," as the *New York Times* calls him, began his college career not as a writer, but as a basketball star. "I always wanted to play pro basketball—ever since I saw a ball and learned you could make money at it," he told Curt Suplee in the *Washington Post.* Recruited by the University of Pennsylvania, Wideman first studied psychology, attracted by the "mystical insight" he told Suplee that he thought this major would yield. When his subjects of study instead "turned out to be rats" and clinical experiments, Wideman changed his major to English, while continuing to be mainly concerned with basketball. He played well enough to earn a place in the Philadelphia Big Five Basketball Hall of Fame, but, he told Suplee, as his time at the university drew to a close, "I knew I wasn't going to be able to get into the NBA [National Basketball Association]. What was left?" The Rhodes scholarship answered that question. Wideman began to concentrate on his writing rather than sports and did so with such success that his first novel, *A Glance Away,* was published just a year after he earned his degree from Oxford.

The story of a day in the life of a drug addict, *A Glance Away* reflects the harsh realities that Wideman saw and experienced during his youth in Pittsburgh's ghetto, Homewood. And, though the author later resided in other locales, including Wyoming, his novels have continued to describe black urban experiences. He explained to Suplee, "My particular imagination has always worked well in a kind of exile. It fits the insider-outside view I've always had. It helps to write away from the center of the action."

Wideman's highly literate style is in sharp contrast to his gritty subject matter, and although reviews of his books have been generally favorable from the start of his writing career, some critics initially expressed the opinion that such a formal style was not appropriate for his stories of street life. For example, Anatole Broyard praised *The Lynchers* in his *New York Times* review, stating: "Though we have heard the themes and variations of violence before in black writing, *The Lynchers* touches us in a more personal way, for John Edgar Wideman has a weapon more powerful than any knife or gun. His weapon is art. Eloquence is his arsenal, his arms cache. His prose, at its best, is a black panther, coiled to spring." But Broyard went on to say that the book is not flawless: "Far from it. Mr. Wideman ripples too many muscles in his writing, often cannot seem to decide whether to show or snow us.... [He] is wordy, and *The Lynchers* is as shaky in its structure as some of the buildings his characters inhabit. But he can *write,* and you come away from his book with the feeling that he is, as they say, very close to getting it all together." In the *New York Times,* John Leonard commented on the extensive use of literary devices in *The Lynchers:* "Flashback, flashforward, first person, third person, journals, identity exchange, interior monologue, dreams (historical and personal), puns, epiphanies. At times the devices seem a thicket through which one must hack one's weary way toward meanings arbitrarily obscure, a vegetable indulgence. But John Edgar Wideman is up to much more than storytelling.... He is capable of moving from ghetto language to [Irish writer James] Joyce with a flip of the page."

*Saturday Review* critic David Littlejohn agreed that Wideman's novels are very complex, and in his review of *Hurry Home* he criticized those who would judge this author as a storyteller: "Reviewers ... are probably more responsible than anyone else for the common delusion that a novel is somehow contained in its discernible, realistic plot.... *Hurry Home* is primarily an experience, not a plot: an experience of words, dense, private, exploratory, and non-progressive." Littlejohn described *Hurry Home* as a retelling of an American myth, that of "the lonely search through the Old World" for a sense of cultural heritage, which "has been the pattern of a hundred thousand young Americans' lives and novels." According to Littlejohn, Wideman's version is "spare and eccentric, highly stylized, circling, allusive, antichronological, far more consciously symbolic than most versions, than the usual self-indulgent and romantic works of this genre—and hence both more rewarding and more difficult of access." Reviewing the same book in the *New York Times Book Review,* Joseph Goodman stated: "Many of its pages are packed with psychological insight, and nearly all reveal Mr. Wideman's formidable command of the techniques of fiction. Moreover, the

theme is a profound one—the quest for a substantive sense of self.... The prose, paratactic and rich with puns, flows as freely as thought itself, giving us ... Joycean echoes.... It is a dazzling display.... We can have nothing but admiration for Mr. Wideman's talent."

Enthusiastic reviews such as these established Wideman's reputation in the literary world as a major talent. When his fourth and fifth books—*Damballah,* a collection of short stories, and *Hiding Place,* a novel—were issued originally as paperbacks, some critics, such as John Leonard and Mel Watkins, reacted with indignation. Leonard's *New York Times* review used extensive quotes from the books to demonstrate Wideman's virtuosity, and stated, "That [these] two new books will fall apart after a second reading is a scandal." Watkins's *New York Times Book Review* article on the two books, which were published simultaneously, had special praise for the short-story volume, and ends with a sentiment much like Leonard's on the books' binding. "In freeing his voice from the confines of the novel form," Watkins wrote, "[Wideman] has written what is possibly his most impressive work.... Each story moves far beyond the primary event on which it is focused.... Like [Jean] Toomer, Mr. Wideman has used a narrative laced with myth, superstition and dream sequences to create an elaborate poetic portrait of the lives of ordinary black people.... These books once again demonstrate that John Wideman is one of America's premier writers of fiction. That they were published originally in paperback perhaps suggests that he is also one of our most underrated writers." Actually, it was the author himself who had decided to bring the books out as original paperbacks. His reasons were philosophical and pragmatic. "I spend an enormous amount of time and energy writing and I want to write good books, but I also want people to read them," he explained to Edwin McDowell in the *New York Times.* Wideman's first three novels had been slow sellers "in spite of enormously positive reviews," he told Suplee, and it was his hope that the affordability of paperbacks would help give him a wider readership, particularly among "the people and the world I was writing about. A $15.95 novel had nothing to do with that world."

*Damballah* and *Hiding Place* had both been set in Homewood, Wideman's early home, and in 1983 he published a third book with the same setting, *Sent for You Yesterday.* Critics were enthusiastic. "In this hypnotic and deeply lyrical novel, Mr. Wideman again returns to the ghetto where he was raised and transforms it into a magical location infused with poetry and pathos," wrote Alan Cheuse in the *New York Times Book Review.* "The narration here makes it clear that both as a molder of language and a builder of plots, Mr. Wideman has come into his full powers. He has the gift of making 'ordinary' folks memorable." Stated Garett Epps in the *Washington Post Book World,* "Wideman has a fluent command of the American language, written and spoken, and a fierce, loving vision of the people he writes about. Like the writing of William Faulkner, Wideman's prose fiction is vivid and demanding—shuttling unpredictably between places, narrators and times, dwelling for a paragraph on the surface of things, then sneaking a key event into a clause that springs on the reader like a booby trap.... *Sent for You Yesterday* is a book to be savored, read slowly again and again."

When he ventured into nonfiction for the first time with his book *Brothers and Keepers,* Wideman continued to draw inspiration from the same source, Homewood. In this book, Wideman comes to terms with his brother Robby, younger by ten years, whose life was influenced by the street, its drugs, and its crime. The author wrote, "Even as I manufactured fiction from the events of my brother's life, from the history of the family that had nurtured us both, I knew something of a different order remained to be extricated. The fiction writer was a man with a real brother behind real bars [serving a life sentence in a Pennsylvania penitentiary]." In his review in the *Washington Post Book World,* Jonathan Yardley called *Brothers and Keepers* "the elder Wideman's effort to understand what happened, to confess and examine his own sense of guilt about his brother's fate (and his own)." The result, according to the reviewer, is "a depiction of the inexorably widening chasm that divides middle-class black Americans from the black underclass." Wideman's personal experience, added Yardley, also reveals that for the black person "moving out of the ghetto into the white world is a process that requires excruciating compromises, sacrifices and denials, that leaves the person who makes the journey truly at home in neither the world he has entered nor the world he has left."

Wideman has, however, made a home for himself in literary circles, and at the same time has learned from his experience how to handle his success. When *Sent for You Yesterday* won the PEN/Faulkner Award—the only major literary award in the United States to be judged, administered, and largely funded by writers—Wideman told Suplee he felt "warmth. That's what I felt. Starting at the toes and filling up. A gradual recognition that it could be real." Still, the author maintained that if such an honor "doesn't happen again for a long time—or never happens again—it really doesn't matter," because he "learned more and more that the process itself was important, learned to take my satisfaction from the writing" during the years of comparative obscurity. "I'm an old jock," he explained. "So I've kind of trained myself to be low-key. Sometimes the crowd screams, sometimes the crowd doesn't scream."

The narrator of Wideman's 1987 novel, *Reuben,* provides inexpensive legal aid to residents of Homewood. One of his clients is Kwansa, a young black prostitute whose husband, a recovering drug addict, kidnaps and seeks legal custody of their illegitimate child as revenge against her. Another cus-

tomer is Wally, an assistant basketball coach at a local white university who seeks Reuben's counsel for two reasons, one being the killing of a white man in Chicago and the other being his fear that he will be blamed for the illegal recruiting practices of his department. Reviewing the book in *Washington Post Book World,* Noel Perrin characterized Wideman's novels as myths. "In the end," Perrin wrote, "one sees that all the shocks—the murders, the fantasies, burnings, strong words—all of them amount to a kind of metaphor for the psychic damage that human beings do to each other and that is no less hurtful than spread-eagled beating, just less visible to the outer eye."

In *Philadelphia Fire*—which also won the PEN/Faulkner Award, distinguishing Wideman as the first writer to receive the honor twice—Wideman brings together two stories, combining fact in fiction. In the first, he describes the events in Philadelphia when the police, under the direction of black mayor Wilson Goode, bombed the headquarters of an organization known as Move, a group that had defied city eviction notices and was armed with weapons. The police bombing killed six adults and five children, destroyed 53 homes, and left 262 people homeless. Wideman's novel begins with a quote by William Penn, the founder of Pennsylvania, stating his dream that the town would "never be burnt, and always be wholesome." As Chicago *Tribune Books* reviewer Paul Skenazy pointed out, *Philadelphia Fire* tries to make sense of the changes that have occurred since Penn's statement, changes that include poverty and racism and that result in the burning of the Philadelphia neighborhood. The other story being told in the book is that of Wideman's relationship with his son who has received a life sentence for murder. "Few pages of prose," Skenazy said, "carry as much pain as do Wideman's thoughts on his son, his words to him in prison, his feelings of confusion as a father." Skenazy concluded that *Philadelphia Fire* is "about a person, and a nation, losing its grip, destroying the very differences and dissonance that provide spirit, beauty, life." Rosemary L. Bray in the *New York Times Book Review* concurred. "The author takes his readers on a tour of urban America perched on the precipice of hell," Bray wrote, "a tour in which even his own personal tragedy is part of the view."

In 1992, Wideman published *The Stories of John Edgar Wideman,* a volume that combined several earlier story collections, including *Damballah,* originally published in 1981, 1989's *Fever,* and *All Stories Are True* from 1992. Michael Harris wrote in the *Los Angeles Times Book Review* that a comparison between Wideman and Faulkner makes sense "because of the scope of Wideman's project, his ear for voices, ... and the way he shows the present as perpetually haunted by the past." *New York Times Book Review* contributor Michael Gorra also believes the Faulkner comparison is apt. "It is appropriate," Gorra wrote, "because both are concerned with the life of a community over time. It is appropriate because they both have a feel for the anecdotal folklore through which a community defines itself, because they both often choose to present their characters in the act of telling stories, and because in drawing on oral tradition they both write as their characters speak, in a language whose pith and vigor has not yet been worn into cliche." It is Gorra's conclusion that "the more you read John Edgar Wideman, the more impressive he seems."

*BIOGRAPHICAL/CRITICAL SOURCES:*

*BOOKS*

*Contemporary Literary Criticism,* Volume 5, Gale, 1976.
*Dictionary of Literary Biography,* Volume 33: *Afro-American Fiction Writers after 1955,* Gale, 1984.
O'Brien, John, editor, *Interviews with Black Writers,* Liveright, 1973.
Wideman, John Edgar, *Brothers and Keepers,* Holt, 1984.
Wideman, John Edgar, *Philadelphia Fire,* Holt, 1990.

*PERIODICALS*

*American Scholar,* autumn, 1967.
*Christian Science Monitor,* July 10, 1992.
*Journal of Negro History,* January, 1963.
*Los Angeles Times,* November 11, 1987.
*Los Angeles Times Book Review,* April 17, 1983; December 23, 1984; December 29, 1985; September 30, 1990; September 13, 1992.
*Michigan Quarterly Review,* winter, 1975.
*Negro Digest,* May, 1963.
*The New Republic,* July 13, 1992.
*Newsweek,* May 7, 1970.
*New York,* October 1, 1990.
*New York Times,* April 2, 1970; May 15, 1973; November 27, 1981; May 16, 1984; October 29, 1984; September 4, 1986; July 21, 1992.
*New York Times Book Review,* September 10, 1967; April 19, 1970; April 29, 1973; April 11, 1982; May 15, 1983; November 4, 1984; January 13, 1985; December 15, 1985; May 11, 1986; November 30, 1986; November 8, 1987; October 16, 1988; December 10, 1989; September 30, 1990; October 14, 1990; November 17, 1991; June 14, 1992.
*Saturday Review,* October 21, 1967; May 2, 1970.
*Shenandoah,* winter, 1974.
*Time,* October 1, 1990.
*Times* (London), December 6, 1984.
*Times Literary Supplement,* December 21, 1984; January 16, 1987; August 5, 1988; August 23, 1991.
*Tribune Books* (Chicago), December 23, 1984; November 29, 1987; October 28, 1990; November 24, 1991.

*Washington Post,* May 10, 1984; May 12, 1984.
*Washington Post Book World,* July 3, 1983; October 21, 1984; November 15, 1987; October 16, 1988; October 21, 1990.

\*   \*   \*

## WILKINSON, Brenda 1946-

*PERSONAL:* Born January 1, 1946, in Moultrie, GA; daughter of Malcolm (in construction) and Ethel (a nurse; maiden name, Anderson) Scott; divorced; children: Kim, Lori. *Education:* Attended Hunter College of the City University of New York.

*ADDRESSES: Home*—560 West 218 St., New York, NY 10034. *Office*—Board of Global Ministries, 475 Riverside Dr., Rm. 1521, New York, NY 10115.

*CAREER:* Poet and author of books for children.

*MEMBER:* PEN International, Harlem Writers Guild.

*AWARDS, HONORS:* National Book Award nominee, 1976, for *Ludell; Ludell and Willie* was named one of the outstanding children's books of the year by the *New York Times,* and a best book for young adults by the American Library Association, both 1977.

*WRITINGS:*

*Ludell* (first book in trilogy), Harper, 1975.
*Ludell and Willie* (second book in trilogy), Harper, 1976.
*Ludell's New York Time* (third book in trilogy), Harper, 1980.
*Not Separate, Not Equal,* Harper, 1987.
*Jesse Jackson: Still Fighting for the Dream,* edited by Richard Gallin, introduced by Andrew Young, Silver Burdett Press, 1990.
*Definitely Cool,* Scholastic, Inc., 1993.

Also author of poetry and short stories.

*SIDELIGHTS:* Brenda Wilkinson's Ludell trilogy has been praised for its accurate, yet sensitive and compassionate portrayal of rural black life. These books, *Ludell, Ludell and Willie,* and *Ludell's New York Time* follow the life of a poor, young, black child growing up in Waycross, Georgia, in the mid-fifties to early sixties.

In the first volume of this trilogy, Ludell Wilson is left in the care of her grandmother after her mother moves to New York City in search of a better life. L. W. Lindsay writes in the *Christian Science Monitor* that *Ludell* is a "beautiful little novel about a sensitive young girl whose individuality and talent blossom in spite of the abyssmal circumstances under which she has to live and go to school." Addison Gayle notes in *Nation* that "the universe of this novel is alive with innocence, which emanates from the community ... and it is highlighted by the love and care that each black person exhibits toward the other—characteristics of black life from the days of slavery until the present time."

"Unlike many novels of the South, *Ludell* is not a tragedy in any sense, not any angry book, nor is it soft-centered," remarks Cynthia King in the *New York Times Book Review*. "By the end of the book I liked Ludell. I was glad to have known her and her friends."

Wilkinson's second book, *Ludell and Willie,* tells the story of Ludell's teenage years when she falls in love, starts to plan for the future, and experiences the death of her grandmother. Ludell must leave her love, Willie, and her home in Georgia and live with her mother in New York City. *Publishers Weekly* calls *Ludell and Willie* "a brilliant novel." In the *New York Times Book Review* Georgess McHargue comments that "we should be grateful to Ludell and Willie, their families and friends, for living and talking like themselves, thus transcending weighty generalizations about black teen-agers, Southern mores or social justice. I'm looking forward to the next book about Ludell."

*Ludell's New York Time,* the last book in Wilkinson's trilogy, finds Ludell unhappily trying to cope with her separation from her love, while getting reacquainted with her mother, and adjusting to her vastly different life in New York City. "Wilkinson has crafted a special kind of love story with wideranging appeal," believes Jerrie Norris. Writing in the *Christian Science Monitor* Norris comments that "the clash of Ludell's Waycross background with the Harlem of the '60s reveals the social fabric of both places. [Wilkinson writes] with a keen eye for detail and a carefully paced presentation of events to totally involve us with Ludell and her life."

*BIOGRAPHICAL/CRITICAL SOURCES:*

*PERIODICALS*

*Christian Science Monitor,* November 5, 1975; April 14, 1980.
*Ms.,* August, 1980.
*Nation,* April 17, 1976.
*New York Times Book Review,* February 22, 1976; August 3, 1980.
*Publishers Weekly,* February 7, 1977; November 27, 1987, p. 83.
*School Library Journal,* April, 1988, p. 114; May, 1991, p. 101.

## WILLIAMS, Chancellor 1905-

*PERSONAL:* Born December 22, 1905 (one source says 1902), in Bennettsville, SC. *Education:* Howard University, B.A., 1930, and M.A., 1935; attended University of Chicago and University of Iowa, 1935-41; American University, Ph.D., 1949.

*CAREER:* Cheltenham School for Boys, administrative principal, 1935-37; Washington, DC, teacher in public schools, 1939-41; worked in various federal government posts as an economist and statistician, 1941-46; Howard University, instructor in social sciences, 1946-52, professor of history, beginning 1961, retired. Oxford University and the University of London, visiting resident scholar, 1953-54. Has done field research in Ghana in the late 1950s, and in 25 African countries, 1963-64.

*AWARDS, HONORS:* Rosenwald Fellowship, 1931-32; Book Award, Black Academy of Arts and Letters, 1971, for *The Destruction of Black Civilization;* Clarence L. Holte International Biennial Prize, Twenty-first Century Foundation, 1979, "in recognition of his significant and lasting contribution to black heritage."

*WRITINGS:*

*NOVELS*

*The Raven,* Dorrance, 1943, reprinted, AMS Press, 1975.
*Have You Been to the River?,* Exposition Press, 1952.
*The Second Agreement with Hell,* Carlton Press, 1979.

*NONFICTION*

*And If I Were White,* Shaw Publications, 1946.
*The Rebirth of African Civilization,* Public Affairs Press, 1961, revised edition, introduction by Baba Zulu, United Brothers and Sisters Communications Systems, 1993.
*Problems in African History,* Pencraft Books, 1964.
*The Destruction of Black Civilization: Great Issues of a Race from 4500 B.C. to 2000 A.D.,* Kendall-Hunt, 1971, revised edition, Third World Press, 1987.

*OTHER*

Contributor to anthologies, including *Contemporary Sociology,* edited by Joseph Slabey Roucek, Philosophical Library, 1958; *Contemporary Political Ideologies,* edited by Roucek, Philosophical Library, 1961; *The Teaching of History,* edited by Roucek, Philosophical Library, 1967. Also contributor to periodicals, including *Journal of Negro Education* and *Journal of Human Relations.*

*SIDELIGHTS:* In his teaching career and in his writings, including the controversial history, *The Destruction of Black Civilization: Great Issues of a Race from 4500 B.C. to 2000 A.D.,* former Howard University professor Chancellor Williams has labored to reconstruct six millennia of the African past in support of his blueprint for black renewal. In the 1950s, his interest in the social development of blacks drew Williams to the African continent, where momentous changes were taking place, and people were working to create new social structures and to revive old ones. The liberation movements of Africa had a necessary academic component: the study of Africa had to be liberated from Eurocentric bias. African history in particular suffered at the hands of historiographers who saw in it only the story of foreign incursion, conquest and exploitation, and who saw this only from foreign perspectives. Consequently, much of the African experience that preceded those incursions remained hidden, waiting to be rediscovered.

After first undertaking a two-year review of the historical resources on Africa housed in England in the British Museum, at Oxford University and at the University of London, Williams went to Ghana to pursue field research. In Ghana he began his investigation of early African history prior to any significant contact with Asia or Europe. On subsequent trips to the continent he would analyze the cultures of more than one hundred language groups. His study revealed common social patterns across Africa, reflecting concepts of nationhood, of government, of land ownership and of individual rights which stood distinct from any corresponding European concepts. From these ancient African social patterns Williams derived the program for contemporary black revival that forms the heart of his most acclaimed work.

In *The Destruction of Black Civilization,* Williams not only explores six thousand years of past triumphs and defeats, but he speaks to the present situation, proposing a "Master Plan" for black renewal, a plan informed by his meticulous analysis of the history of Africa yet addressed to the African American community. He calls for the establishment of a National Council of Leaders, set up according to the African constitutional principles which he uncovered in his research, which would function as a nation within the nation. Such an organization could unite black America and coordinate efforts at self-empowerment. A unified black America, Williams argues, would provide an example and an inspiration for black Africa in its own crisis of disunity.

Critics, while impressed by the scope of the "Master Plan" Williams outlines in *The Destruction of Black Civilization,* have challenged his arguments on several key points. Odeyo Owiti Ayaga, in a *Black World* review in which Williams's book is compared with two other "reconstructionist" histories of Africa, doubts that such a "nation within a nation" could ever be realized, and points to a precedent: "The National

Black Political Convention ... in March 1972, drafted a national agenda, very similar to that outlined by Professor Williams. But less than a year [later], ... it has been a painful realization that most of it cannot be implemented, or enforced, to any meaningful extent."

Reviewing a revised edition of *The Destruction of Black Civilization* for a later issue of *Black World,* Robert L. Harris, Jr., questions Williams's use of African history as a guide to the present situation. "Although African history can be illuminating and suggestive," Harris writes, "an analysis of Afro-American problems must be based largely on an exploration of conditions in the United States. Williams even admits that the Afro-American situation is unique and not analogous to others. By advising Afro-Americans to establish a bureaucracy influenced by the traditional African constitutional system, he ignores his own caveat."

Despite such objections, Williams's scholarly contributions are readily acknowledged even by his critics. Concluding his review, Harris praises *The Destruction of Black Civilization* for its unequivocal conviction that black salvation will come from self-reliance, and for pointing the way toward that salvation with an analysis sustained by rigorous historical research: "Williams readily acknowledges that his 'Master Plan' is a suggestion, but he also makes it clear that he at least has offered a proposal based on the past. In this, he must be applauded, and his work will certainly serve as a guide for further discussion, dialogue, debate, and analysis."

*BIOGRAPHICAL/CRITICAL SOURCES:*

*BOOKS*

*Dictionary of Literary Biography,* Volume 76: *Afro-American Writers, 1940-1955,* Gale, 1988.

*PERIODICALS*

*Black World,* August, 1973, p. 51; May, 1975, p. 51.
*New York Times,* January 9, 1944.

\*   \*   \*

## WILLIAMS, Denis (Joseph Ivan) 1923-

*PERSONAL:* Born February 1, 1923, in Georgetown, Guyana; son of Joseph Alexander (a merchant) and Isabel (Adonis) Williams; married Catherine Hughes, 1949 (divorced, 1974); married Toni Dixon (a poultry farmer), August 21, 1975 (separated, 1982); children: (first marriage) Janice, Evelyn, Isabel, Charlotte; (second marriage) Miles, Morag, Everard, Rachael,

Denis; Kibileri Wishart Williams. *Education:* Attended Camberwell School of Art, 1946-48; University of Guyana, M.A., 1979. *Politics:* None. *Religion:* Christian.

*ADDRESSES: Home*—13, Thorne's Dr., D'Urban Backlands, Botanic Gardens, Georgetown, Guyana. *Office*—Department of Culture, Ministry of Education, 15 Carifesta Ave., Georgetown, Guyana; and Walter Roth Museum of Anthropology, 65 Main St., P.O. Box 10187, Georgetown, Guyana. *Agent*—John Wolfers, 42 Russel Sq., London W.C. 1, England.

*CAREER:* Central School of Art, London, England, lecturer in art, 1950-57; Khartoum School of Art, Khartoum, Sudan, lecturer in art, 1957-62; University of Ife, Ife, Nigeria, lecturer in African studies, 1962-66; University of Lagos, Lagos, Nigeria, lecturer in African studies, 1966-68; National History and Arts Council, Georgetown, Guyana, art consultant, 1968-74; Ministry of Education, Georgetown, director of art and department of culture, 1974—. Founder and director of Walter Roth Museum. Artist, exhibiting work at numerous art shows and in many one-man exhibitions. Visiting tutor at Slade School of Fine Art, University of London, 1950-52; visiting professor at Makerere University, 1966; visiting research scholar, Smithsonian Institution, 1980. Chairman of National Trust, Georgetown, 1978-88. Member of International Visitor Program, United States Information Agency, 1985.

*MEMBER:* National Commissions for the Acquisition, Preservation, Republication of Research Materials on Guyana.

*AWARDS, HONORS:* Second prize from *London Daily Express* "Artists under Thirty-five" competition, 1955; Golden Arrow of Achievement, government of Guyana, 1973; first prize in National Theatre's mural competition, 1976; Cacique's Crown of Honour, 1989; D.Litt., University of West Indies, 1989; received numerous grants from University of Ife, International African Institute, University of Lagos, Smithsonian Institution, and United Nations Economic, Scientific and Cultural Organization.

*WRITINGS:*

*Other Leopards* (novel), Hutchinson, 1963, reprinted with introduction by Edward Baugh, Heinemann, 1983.
*The Third Temptation* (novel), Calder & Boyars, 1968.
*Giglioli in Guyana, 1922-1972* (biography), National History and Arts Council (Georgetown, Guyana), 1970.
*Image and Idea in the Arts of the Caribbean,* National History and Arts Council, 1970.
*Icon and Image: A Study of Sacred and Secular Forms of African Classical Art,* New York University Press, 1974.
*The Amerindian Heritage,* Walter Roth Museum (Georgetown, Guyana), 1984.

*Habitat and Culture in Ancient Guyana,* Edgar Mittelholzer Memorial Lectures, 1984.
*Ancient Guyana,* Guyana Department of Culture, 1985.
*Pages in Guyanese Prehistory,* Walter Roth Museum of Anthropology, 1988.

Contributor to several books, including *Africa in the Nineteenth and Twentieth Centuries,* edited by Joseph C. Anene and Godfrey N. Brown, Thomas Nelson, 1966; *Sources of Yoruba History,* edited by S. O. Biobaku, Clarendon Press, 1973; *Advances in World Archaeology,* Volume 4, Academic Press, 1985; *Americans Before Columbus,* Smithsonian Institution, in press; and *Handbook of Caribbean Prehistory,* Island Archaeological Museum, in press.

Contributor to *The Dictionary of World Art,* Macmillan; contributor of numerous articles to African studies and anthropology journals, including *Africa: Journal of the International African Institute London, Lagos Notes and Records, Carifesta Forum, Archaeology and Anthropology,* and *Odu: University of Ife Journal of African Studies.* Editor of *Odu,* 1964, *Lagos Notes and Records,* 1967, and *Archaeology and Anthropology,* 1978—.

*WORK IN PROGRESS:* A novel, *The Sperm of God.*

*SIDELIGHTS:* Denis Williams once commented: "A Colonial artist or writer who has received his professional education in Britain and made his first home there is not likely easily to forget that experience. I find that in my own case the experience has proven not only formative, but to a degree even determinative. It seems to have shaped the entire course of my subsequent development. Thus, to me, it is impossible to imagine a career built other than upon the solid foundation of early recognition and acceptance which was accorded to me during the first half of the fifties in London. Paradoxically, however, as Fanon has so perceptively shown, given the circumstances and the day, acceptance on this level was in fact far the most unacceptable, indeed probably the most humiliating, of choices open to the Colonial artist.

"This may explain the rapid and apparently permanent darkness which followed the explosion of Caribbean writing in Britain during the time I was there. Colonial territories were all becoming independent, which was quickly to render the Colonial artist or writer obsolete; for just as national independence seems to have pulled the rug from under the feet of the Colonial writer, new national writers were arising in English- and French-speaking West Africa and in the Caribbean.

"By this time I was myself in Africa writing *Other Leopards,* or trying to resolve some of the problems of identity which provided the theme for that novel. By the time of its completion it was becoming evident that even though the new African literature was being written all around me, and by familiar hands, Africa did not represent the uttermost swing of the pendulum in my reaction from an unwilling acceptance in Europe. Indeed, the African experience tended to reveal to me deeply ingrained attitudes to various aspects of European art, life, and literature that had remained so far undetected. Odd as it may seem, it was very easy to write *The Third Temptation* (in an experimental French idiom) simultaneously with my study of African classical art, which in itself represented an intellectual search for African roots.

"I have since returned to Guyana, and see clearly that such a thing could never take place against my rediscovered background. However, if this means that the pendulum has at last reached its ultimate distance of travel, it is no comfort to realize that my first true Caribbean novel, *The Sperm of God*, has remained unfinished now for over thirteen years."

*BIOGRAPHICAL/CRITICAL SOURCES:*

*BOOKS*

Cartey, Wilfred, *Whispers from the Caribbean: I Going Away, I Going Home,* University of California, Los Angeles, 1991.
Dathorne, O. R., *The Black Mind: A History of African Literature,* University of Minnesota Press, 1974.
Fox, C. J., and Walter Michel, *Wyndham Lewis on Art: Collected Writings, 1913-1956,* Thames & Hudson, 1969.
Moore, Gerald, *The Chosen Tongue,* Longman, 1969.
Ramchand, Kenneth, *The West Indian Novel and Its Background,* Faber, 1974.

*PERIODICALS*

*Daily Express,* April 28, 1955.
*Geo,* May, 1981.
*Science Digest,* November, 1981.
*Science News,* January 24, 1981.

\*   \*   \*

# WILLIAMS, Eric (Eustace) 1911-1981

*PERSONAL:* Born September 25, 1911, in Port of Spain, Trinidad; died of a heart attack, March 29 (one source says March 31), 1981, in St. Anne, Trinidad; son of Thomas Henry (a postal clerk) and Eliza (Boissiere) Williams; married Elsie Ribeiro, c. 1939 (divorced, 1951); married Soy Moyeau, c. 1951 (divorced, 1953); married Mayleen Mook-Soong (a dentist), 1957 (divorced c. 1958); children: Alistair, Pamela (first marriage); Erica (second marriage). *Education:* Attended

Queen's Royal College, 1922-31; St. Catherine's College, Oxford, B.A. (first class honors), 1935, D.Phil. (first class honors), 1938. *Religion:* Roman Catholic.

*CAREER:* Queen's Royal College, Port of Spain, Trinidad, acting master and acting lecturer for the Government Training College for Teachers, 1931; Howard University, Washington, DC, assistant professor, 1939-44, associate professor, 1944-47, professor of social and political science, 1947-55; advisor to Trinidad Government, 1954-55; founded People's National Movement (PNM) in Trinidad, 1956; chief minister and minister of finance, planning, and development of Trinidad and Tobago, 1956-61; first prime minister of independent state of Trinidad and Tobago, 1962-81, also minister of external affairs, 1961-64 and 1973-74, minister of community development, 1964-67, minister of Tobago affairs, minister of national security, and minister of finance, planning, and development, 1967-71, minister for finance, beginning in 1975. Anglo-American Caribbean Commission, consultant to the British, 1943-44, secretary of the Agricultural Committee, 1944-46, consultant, 1946-48, deputy chairman of the Caribbean Research Council and member of commission, 1948-55.

*MEMBER:* Historical Society of Trinidad and Tobago (past president).

*AWARDS, HONORS:* Julius Rosenwald Fellow, 1940, 1942; D.C.L., Oxford University, and LL.D., University of New Brunswick, both 1965.

*WRITINGS:*

*The Negro in the Caribbean,* Associates in Negro Folk Education, 1942, Negro Universities Press, 1969.
*Capitalism and Slavery: The Caribbean,* University of North Carolina Press, 1944, Putnam, 1980.
*Education in the British West Indies,* foreword by John Dewey, Guardian Commercial Printery, 1950.
(Editor) *Documents on British West Indian History,* Trinidad, 1952.
*History of the People of Trinidad and Tobago,* People's National Movement Publishing, 1962, Praeger, 1964.
*Documents of West Indian History,* People's National Movement Publishing, 1963.
*British Historians and the West Indies,* People's National Movement Publishing, 1964, published with preface by Alan Bullock, Scribner, 1967.
*Inward Hunger: The Education of a Prime Minister* (autobiography), Deutsch, 1969, published with an introduction by Denis Brogan, University of Chicago Press, 1971.
*From Columbus to Castro: The History of the Caribbean, 1492-1969,* Deutsch, 1970, Harper, 1971.

*Forged from the Love of Liberty: Selected Speeches of Dr. Eric Williams,* compiled by Paul K. Sutton, Longman Caribbean, 1981.

Also author of published political addresses, including *Federation: Two Public Lectures,* 1956; *Perspectives for the West Indies,* 1960; *Message to the Youth of the Nation,* 1962; *A Review of the Political Scene,* 1966; *Some Historical Reflections on the Church in the Caribbean,* 1973; and *The Energy Crisis, 1973-1974,* 1974. Author of pamphlets, including *Constitution Reform in Trinidad and Tobago,* and *The Historical Background of Race Relations in the Caribbean,* both 1955. Contributor to books, including *Patterns of Progress: Trinidad and Tobago: Ten Years of Independence,* edited by Roy Boyke, Key Caribbean Publications, 1972.

*SIDELIGHTS:* Eric Williams became the first prime minister of Trinidad and Tobago when the two-island nation gained its independence from Great Britain in 1962. Also a respected historian, Williams taught at Howard University in Washington, DC, and published several well-received books on the history of the Caribbean before returning to his native Trinidad to become involved in politics in 1955. There he founded colonial Trinidad and Tobago's first stable political party, the democratic, socialist People's National Movement (PNM). As the PNM gained power and popularity, so did Williams. In 1956, under his leadership, the PNM won a majority of the seats in the colony's legislative council by calling for reforms that included universal and secular education and wider availability of birth control. In accordance with the colonial constitution, the British territorial governor named Williams, as leader of the majority party, chief minister of Trinidad and Tobago. He became prime minister when the colony was made an independent member of the British Commonwealth and remained his nation's highest official until his death in 1981.

William's most famed historical work, *Capitalism and Slavery,* began as his Ph.D. thesis at Oxford University. Labelled "a classic in [its] field" by C. Gerald Fraser in Williams's *New York Times* obituary, the work explored the ways in which slavery contributed to the growth of British capitalism. Williams's scholarship carried over to his political life as well; his public addresses as prime minister delivered in Port of Spain's Woodford Square (many of which were subsequently published), were so full of factual information that the site was nicknamed the "University of Woodford Square."

*From Columbus to Castro: The History of the Caribbean, 1492-1969* is "less a history than an interesting and well-written essay on slavery and sugar-cane cultivation and the effects of their interaction on the peoples of the Caribbean," according to a *Times Literary Supplement* reviewer. The work covers the time span between Christopher Columbus's second voyage to the New World (he brought sugar cane from the

Canary Islands to the region) and Fidel Castro's rule of Cuba. The *Times Literary Supplement* had particular praise for William's handling of "present conditions in the West Indies" and for his "suggestions for the future."

*BIOGRAPHICAL/CRITICAL SOURCES:*

*PERIODICALS*

*Times Literary Supplement,* September 11, 1970.

*OBITUARIES:*

*PERIODICALS*

*Newsweek,* April 13, 1981.
*New York Times,* March 31, 1981.
*Time,* April 13, 1981.

\*　\*　\*

## WILLIAMS, John A(lfred) 1925-
## (J. Dennis Gregory)

*PERSONAL:* Born December 5, 1925, in Jackson, MS; son of John Henry (a laborer) and Ola Mae Williams; married Carolyn Clopton, 1947 (divorced); married Lorrain Isaac, October 5, 1965; children: (first marriage) Gregory D., Dennis A.; (second marriage) Adam J. *Education:* Syracuse University, A.B., 1950, graduate study, 1950-51. *Avocational interests:* Travel (has visited numerous countries), cross-disciplinary studies in "pre-history."

*ADDRESSES: Home*—Teaneck, NJ. *Office*—Department of English, Rutgers University, Newark, NJ 07102. *Agent*—Barbara Hogenson, Lucy Kroll Agency, 390 West End Ave., New York, NY 10024.

*CAREER:* Writer. Case worker for county welfare department, Syracuse, NY; in public relations with Doug Johnson Associates, Syracuse, NY, 1952-54, and later with Arthur P. Jacobs Co.; Columbia Broadcasting System (CBS-TV), Hollywood, CA, and New York City, consultant for television special events programs, 1954-55; Comet Press Books, New York City, publicity director, 1955-56; Negro Market Newsletter, New York City, publisher and editor, 1956-57; Abelard-Schuman Ltd., New York City, assistant to the publisher, 1957-58; American Committee on Africa, New York City, director of information, 1958; *Ebony* and *Jet* (magazines), New York City, European correspondent, 1958-59; Station WOV, New York, special events announcer, 1959; *Newsweek,* New York City, correspondent in Africa, 1964-65; City College of the City University of New York, lecturer in writing, 1968; College of the Virgin Islands, lecturer in African American literature, summer, 1968; Sarah Lawrence College, Bronxville, NY, guest writer, 1972; La Guardia Community College, distinguished professor of English, 1973-74 and 1974-79; Rutgers University, professor of English, 1979—, Paul Robeson Professor, 1990; *National Leader,* Philadelphia, PA, columnist, 1982-83; New York University, Exxon Professor of English, 1986-87. Visiting professor at University of Hawaii, summer, 1974, and Boston University, 1978-79. National Education Television, narrator and co-producer of programs, 1965-66, interviewer on "Newsfront" program, 1968. Special assignments writer and stringer for several American newspapers. Has given lectures or readings at more than one hundred colleges and universities. *Military service:* U.S. Naval Reserve, pharmacist's mate, active duty, 1943-46; served in the Pacific.

*MEMBER:* Authors Guild, Authors League of America, PEN, Textbook Authors Association.

*AWARDS, HONORS:* Award from National Institute of Arts and Letters, 1962; Centennial Medal for outstanding achievement from Syracuse University, 1970; LL.D. from Southeastern Massachusetts University, 1978, Lindback Award, Rutgers University, 1982, for distinguished teaching; American Book Award, Before Columbus Foundation, 1983, for *!Click Song;* U.S. Observer, Twenty-third Premio Casa Awards, 1983; New Jersey State Council on the Arts, 1985.

*WRITINGS:*

*NOVELS*

*The Angry Ones,* Ace Books, 1960, published as *One for New York,* Chatham Bookseller, 1975.
*Night Song,* Farrar, Straus, 1961.
*Sissie,* Farrar, Straus, 1963, published in England as *Journey Out of Anger,* Eyre & Spottiswoode, 1965.
*The Man Who Cried I Am,* Little, Brown, 1967.
*Sons of Darkness, Sons of Light: A Novel of Some Probability,* Little, Brown, 1969.
*Captain Blackman,* Doubleday, 1972.
*Mothersill and the Foxes,* Doubleday, 1975.
*The Junior Bachelor Society,* Doubleday, 1976.
*!Click Song,* Houghton, 1982.
*The Berhama Account,* New Horizon Press, 1985.
*Jacob's Ladder,* Thunder's Mouth, 1987.

*NONFICTION*

*Africa: Her History, Lands, and People,* Cooper Square, 1962.

(Under pseudonym J. Dennis Gregory; with Harry J. Anslinger) *The Protectors: The Heroic Story of the Narcotics Agents, Citizens and Officials in Their Unending, Unsung Battles against Organized Crime in America and Abroad,* Farrar, Straus, 1964.
*This Is My Country Too,* New American Library, 1965.
*The Most Native of Sons: A Biography of Richard Wright,* Doubleday, 1970.
*The King God Didn't Save: Reflections on the Life and Death of Martin Luther King, Jr.,* Coward, 1970.
*Flashbacks: A Twenty-Year Diary of Article Writing,* Doubleday, 1973.
(Author of introduction) *Romare Bearden,* Abrams, 1973.
*Minorities in the City,* Harper, 1975.
(With son Dennis A. Williams) *If I Stop I'll Die: The Comedy and Tragedy of Richard Pryor,* Thunder's Mouth Press, 1991.

*EDITOR*

*The Angry Black* (anthology), Lancer Books, 1962, published as *Beyond the Angry Black,* Cooper Square, 1966.
(With Charles F. Harris) *Amistad I,* Knopf, 1970.
(With Harris) *Amistad II,* Knopf, 1971.
*Yardbird No. 1,* Reed & Young, 1979.
*The McGraw-Hill Introduction to Literature,* McGraw-Hill, 1985, second edition, 1994.
*Way B(l)ack Then and Now: Street Guide to African Americans in Paris, 1849-1992,* Cetlana (Paris, France), 1992.
*Approaches to Literature,* McGraw-Hill, 1993.
*Bridges: Literature Across Cultures,* McGraw-Hill, 1993.

*OTHER*

*The History of the Negro People: Omwale—The Child Returns Home* (for television; filmed in Nigeria), National Education Television, 1965.
*The Creative Person: Henry Roth* (for television; filmed in Spain), National Education Television, 1966.
*Last Flight from Ambo Ber* (play; first produced in Boston, 1981), American Association of Ethiopian Jews, 1984.

Contributor of articles, essays, and fiction to numerous anthologies, including *Harlem: A Community in Transition,* Citadel, 1964; *Best Short Stories of Negro Writers,* Little, Brown, 1967; *Black on Black,* Macmillan, 1968; *Thirty-four by Schwartze Lieb,* Barmier & Nickel, 1968; *How We Live,* Macmillan, 1968; *Dark Symphony,* Free Press, 1968; John Henrik Clarke, editor, *Nat Turner: Ten Black Writers Respond,* Beacon Press, 1968; *The Now Reader,* Scott, Foresman, 1969; *The New Black Poetry,* International, 1969; *Black Literature in America,* Crowell, 1970; *The Black Novelist,* C. E. Merrill, 1970; *Black Identity,* Holt, 1970; *A Native Sons Reader,* Lippincott, 1970; *The New Lively Rhetoric,* Holt, 1970; *Broth-*

*ers and Sisters,* Macmillan, 1970; *Nineteen Necromancers from Now,* Doubleday, 1970; *Black Insights,* Ginn, 1971; *The Immigrant Experience,* Dial, 1971; *Cavalcade,* Houghton, 1971; *Racism,* Crowell, 1971; *An Introduction to Poetry,* St. Martin's, 1972; *Different Drummers,* Random House, 1973; *The City Today,* Harper, 1978; *Mississippi Writers,* Volume 2, University of Mississippi Press, 1986; *Breaking the Ice: An Anthology of Contemporary Afro-American Fiction,* Penguin, 1990; *Calling the Wind,* HarperCollins, 1993; and *Censored Books: Critical Viewpoints,* Scarecrow, 1993.

Contributor of numerous stories and articles to newspapers and magazines, including *Negro Digest, Yardbird, Holiday, Saturday Review, Ebony,* and *New York.* Member of editorial board, *Audience,* 1970-72; contributing editor, *American Journal,* 1972—; contributing editor, *Journal of African Civilizations,* 1980-88.

*ADAPTATIONS: Night Song* was produced as *Sweet Love, Bitter,* Film 2 Associates, 1967; *The Junior Bachelor Society* was filmed for television and broadcast by National Broadcasting Company (NBC-TV) as *Sophisticated Gents* in 1981.

*WORK IN PROGRESS:* Two books, *Trio: Clifford's Blues* and *Colleagues.*

*SIDELIGHTS:* John A. Williams, says *Dictionary of Literary Biography (DLB)* contributor James L. de Jongh, is "arguably the finest Afro-American novelist of his generation," although he "has been denied the full degree of support and acceptance some critics think his work deserves." Part of the reason for this, Williams believes, may be because of racial discrimination. In 1961, for instance, he was awarded a grant to the American Academy in Rome based on the quality of his novel *Night Song,* but the grant was rescinded by the awarding panel. Williams felt that this happened because he was black and because of rumors that he was about to marry a white woman, which he later did. However, Alan Dugan, "the poet who eventually was awarded the prize, courageously made public the issue at the presentation ceremony," explains Jeffrey Helterman, another *DLB* commentator, and the resulting scandal caused the American Academy to discontinue its prize for literature for a time.

Williams's first three novels trace the problems facing blacks in a white society. The books—*The Angry Ones, Night Song,* and *Sissie*—relate attempts of black men and women to come to terms with a nation that discriminates against them. In *The Angry Ones,* for instance, the protagonist Steve Hill "struggles with various kinds of racial prejudice in housing and employment, but the focus [of the novel] is on his growing realization of the way his employers at Rocket Press destroy the dreams of would-be authors," explains Helterman. Like Williams himself, Hill perceives that he is being exploited by a

white-dominated industry in which a black artist has no place. Williams has said that "the plain, unspoken fact is that the Negro is superfluous in American society as it is now constructed. Society must undergo a restructuring to make a place for him, or it will be called upon to get rid of him."

*The Man Who Cried I Am,* a novel that brought Williams international recognition, further explores the exploitation of blacks by a white society. The protagonist, Max Reddick, is a black writer living in Europe, as did Williams for a time. Max is married to a Dutch woman, and he is dying of colon cancer. His chief literary rival and mentor is one Harry Ames, a fellow black author. While in Paris to attend Harry's funeral, Max learns that Harry has in fact been murdered because he had uncovered a plot by the Western nations to prevent the unification of black Africa. Max himself unearths another conspiracy: America's genocidal solution to the race problem—code-named "King Alfred"—which closely resembles Adolf Hitler's "Final Solution."

*The Man Who Cried I Am* escapes the protest novel format of most black literature by putting the situation on an epic scale. Jerry H. Bryant describes the book in *Critique: Studies in Modern Fiction* as "Williams's adaptation of the rhetoric of black power to his own needs as a novelist," calling it "in a sense Williams's *Huckleberry Finn.* It reflects his deep skepticism over the capacity of America to live up to its professed ideals, and a development of deep pessimism about whites in particular and man in general." "What purpose does the King Alfred portion of the novel serve?," asks Robert E. Fleming in *Contemporary Literature.* "In one sense, black people have been systematically killed off in the United States since their first introduction to its shores. Malnutrition, disease, poverty, psychological conditioning, and spiritual starvation have been the tools, rather than military operations and gas chambers, but the result has often been the same. King Alfred is not only a prophetic warning of what might happen here but a fictional metaphor for what has been happening and is happening still," he concludes.

Williams states in his *Contemporary Authors Autobiography Series* entry that he considers 1982's *!Click Song* to be his "very best novel." Like *The Man Who Cried I Am,* the book details the careers of two writers, in this case Paul Cummings and Cato Caldwell Douglass, friends who attended school on the GI Bill after World War II. Cummings is Jewish; it is his reaffirmation of his Jewishness that provides the theme for his novels, and his suicide opens the book. Douglass, on the other hand, is black; his problem, as Jervis Anderson in the *New York Times Book Review* indicates, is to overcome racism in the publishing industry. *Chicago Tribune Book World* contributor Seymour Krim compares the two characters: Cummings "was a more successful competitor, a novelist who had won a National Book Award and all the attention that goes with it, while Cato was forced to lecture for peanuts before Black Studies groups. A further irony is the fact that Cummings was a 'passed' Jew who had only recently declared his real name, Kaminsky, in an effort to purge himself. Purge or not, his writing has gone downhill since his born-again declaration, while his earnings have gone up." Roy Hoffman, writing for the *Washington Post Book World* points out, however, that "as Paul's career skyrockets, his private life goes to shambles. As Cato's career runs into brick walls, his personal life grows ever more fulfilled, ever more radiant."

"*!Click Song* is at least the equal of Williams's other masterpiece, *The Man Who Cried I Am,*" states de Jongh. "The emotional power, the fluid structuring of time, the resonant synthesis of fiction and history are similar. But the novelist's mastery is greater, for Williams's technique here is seamless and invisible." the reviewer concludes. Other critics also celebrate Williams's work; says Krim, "Unlike a James Baldwin or an Amiri Baraka, Williams is primarily a storyteller, which is what makes the reality of Black Rage become something other than a polemic in his hands.... Before [Cato Douglass's] odyssey is ended, we know in our bones what it is like to be a gifted black survivor in America today; we change skins as we read, so to speak, and the journey of living inside another is so intense that no white reader will ever again be able to plead ignorance."

In addition to his novels, Williams has also penned numerous nonfiction books throughout his career. One of his more recent works is *If I Stop I'll Die: The Comedy and Tragedy of Richard Pryor,* which he coauthored with his son Dennis, a former *Newsweek* correspondent. The biography details Pryor's professional life as a stand-up comic and film actor, as well as his personal bout with drugs. "The true merit of this book," asserts critic Ralph Wiley in the *Los Angeles Times Book Review,* "lies in its study of Pryor's personal crucibles—his use of cocaine and his work in film—which the authors put in the context of an industry that for years excluded black people from the creative process and manipulated their images in the final product." The commentator states further that "the authors have not missed the telling point.... Their sensitivities counterbalance their scholarship. They are aware, and sound as clearly as two bells. These are the best compliments a writer can get."

*BIOGRAPHICAL/CRITICAL SOURCES:*

*BOOKS*

Bruck, Peter, and Wolfgang Karrer, editors, *The Afro-American Novel since 1960,* Gruner (Amsterdam), 1982.
Cash, Earl A., *Evolution of a Black Writer,* Third Press, 1975.
*Contemporary Authors Autobiography Series,* Volume 3, Gale, 1986.
*Dictionary of Literary Biography,* Gale, Volume 2: *American Novelists since World War II,* 1978, Volume 23: *Afro-American Fiction Writers after 1955,* 1984.
Muller, Gilbert H., *John A. Williams,* Twayne, 1984.

*PERIODICALS*

*American Spectator,* September, 1991, p. 40.
*Black American Literature Forum,* spring/summer, 1987, pp. 25-42.
*Black World,* June, 1975.
*Bloomsbury Review,* October, 1991, p. 13.
*Chicago Tribune Book World,* April 18, 1982; November 17, 1985.
*Contemporary Literature,* spring, 1973.
*Critic,* April, 1963.
*Critique: Studies in Modern Fiction,* Volume 16, number 3, 1975.
*Detroit News,* June 6, 1982.
*Essence,* November, 1991, p. 40.
*Library Journal,* November 1, 1961; September 15, 1967.
*Los Angeles Times Book Review,* May 9, 1982; November 29, 1987; September 1, 1991, p. 4.
*Nation,* September 18, 1976.
*New Yorker,* August 16, 1976.
*New York Times Book Review,* July 11, 1976; April 4, 1982; October 18, 1987; November 15, 1987.
*Prairie Schooner,* spring, 1976.
*Publishers Weekly,* November 11, 1974.
*Time,* April 12, 1982.
*Washington Post Book World,* March 23, 1982; October 4, 1987.

\*   \*   \*

## WILLIAMS, Juan 1954-

*PERSONAL:* Born April 10, 1954, in Colon, Panama; son of Rogelio L. (an accountant) and Alma Geraldine (a secretary; maiden name, Elias) Williams; married Delise (a social worker), July 1, 1978; children: Antonio Mason, Regan Almena, Raphael Leigh. *Education:* Haverford College, B.A. 1976.

*ADDRESSES: Home*—607 Whittier St. N.W., Washington, DC 20012. *Office*—*Washington Post,* 1150 15th St. N.W., Washington, DC 20071. *Agent*—Rafe Sagalyn, Sagalyn Literary Agency, 8000-B Maple Ridge Rd., Bethesda, MD 20814.

*CAREER: Washington Post,* Washington, DC, columnist and reporter, 1976—; commentator, *Inside Washington* television program; visiting scholar, Brookings Institution, 1992; writer-in-residence, American University, 1992-93.

*AWARDS, HONORS:* Front Page Award from Washington-Baltimore Newspaper Guild and award from Education Writers of America, both 1979, for series on public schools in Washington, DC; named columnist of the year by *Washingtonian,* 1982; DuSable Museum Award, 1985, for political writing; Japan Society fellow, 1991; honorary degrees from State University of New York, Wilmington College, and Medaille College.

*WRITINGS:*

(With the *Eyes on the Prize* production team) *Eyes on the Prize: America's Civil Rights Years, 1954-1965,* introduction by Julian Bond, Viking, 1987.

*WORK IN PROGRESS: Thurgood Marshall,* for Random House.

*SIDELIGHTS:* Juan Williams, a columnist and White House correspondent for the *Washington Post,* became interested in civil rights during a tense period of strife between the administration of U.S. President Ronald Reagan and various civil rights groups. Williams commented: "Born in 1954, I was too young to participate in the civil rights movement but am inspired by it nonetheless." In 1987 his interest found expression in his book *Eyes on the Prize: America's Civil Rights Years, 1954-1965,* which was published in conjunction with a six-part public television series of the same title. Both the series and the book provide an overview of a turbulent struggle in American society, helping those who did not witness its events to understand how the movement began and learn about the wide variety of people who made it finally succeed. Reviewing the book in the *Washington Post Book World,* Roy Reed commended its "compelling narrative and impressive research."

Williams acknowledged a benefit to not having been a part of the civil rights era he wrote about: "I believe I'm sufficiently dispassionate about the events to see them as historically valuable evidence of democracy at work in modern America. That perspective makes me part of a new generation of black writers who feel less compelled to be advocates and, instead, simply recount the truth of the black American triumph."

*Eyes on the Prize* covers events ranging from the Supreme Court's landmark 1954 decision declaring segregation of public schools unconstitutional to the 1965 Voting Rights Act, which guaranteed blacks the right to vote. In the process, the book pays tribute to the thousands of ordinary people who participated in a movement that was physically strenuous, socially daring, and at times life-threatening. Each chapter deals with a specific event or series of events, highlighting both the historically famous participants and the lesser-known ones. Williams acknowledges the human cost of the civil rights movement's victories: the book is dedicated to nineteen men and women known to have died in the struggle during the 1950s and 1960s as well as to others who simply disappeared during the period. As Julian Bond wrote in the book's introduction, *Eyes on the Prize* documents the "thousands of acts of individual courage undertaken in the name of freedom."

*BIOGRAPHICAL/CRITICAL SOURCES:*

*PERIODICALS*

*New York Times Book Review,* January 25, 1987, p. 20.
*Washington Post Book World,* January 11, 1987, p. 4.

\*    \*    \*

## WILLIAMS, Kimmika L(yvette Hawes) 1959-

*PERSONAL:* Born January 7, 1959, in Philadelphia, PA; daughter of Samuel S., Jr. and Lillian Yvonne (Curry) Hawes; children: Essence, Tenasha. *Education:* Howard University, B.A., 1980.

*ADDRESSES: Office*—Writer in Residence, Bushfire Theatre, 52nd and Locust Sts., Philadelphia, PA 19139.

*CAREER: Philadelphia Tribune,* Philadelphia, PA, reporter/columnist, 1984-86; Pennsylvania Prison Society, Philadelphia, instructor, 1985-89; Bob Lott Productions, Philadelphia, scriptwriter, 1986-89; WXPN-FM, Philadelphia, arts host and producer, 1989-90; Village Arts Center, Philadelphia, instructor, 1990—; Walnut Street Theatre, Philadelphia, outreach instructor and actress, 1990—. Writer in residence, Bushfire Theatre.

*MEMBER:* International Women's League for Peace and Freedom, National Black Authors Tour, National Black Storytellers.

*AWARDS, HONORS:* American Poetry Center Grant, Teacher's Fellowship, 1990; Playwright's Fellowship, Theatre Association of Pennsylvania, 1990-91; Artist Grant, Philadelphia Neighborhood Arts Project, 1990.

*WRITINGS:*

*It Ain't Easy to Be Different,* In the Tradition Publishing, 1986.
(Under name Kimmika Williams) *Negro Kinship to the Park,* Selrahc Publications, 1990.

Also author of *The Pack, Halley's Comet,* and *God Made Men Brown,* Selrahc Publications. Contributor to the poetry anthology *On the Move,* edited by Sharon Goodman, In the Tradition Publishing, 1985.

\*   \*   \*

## WILLIAMS, Sherley Anne  1944-
### (Shirley Williams)

*PERSONAL:* Born August 25, 1944, in Bakersfield, CA; daughter of Jessee Winson (a laborer) and Lelia Marie (maiden name, Siler) Williams; children: John Malcolm. *Education:* Fresno State College (now California State University, Fresno), B.A., 1966; Howard University, graduate study, 1966-67; Brown University, M.A., 1972.

*ADDRESSES: Office*—Department of Literature, University of California, San Diego, La Jolla, CA 92093.

*CAREER:* Fresno State College (now California State University, Fresno), Fresno, CA, codirector of tutorial program, 1965-66, lecturer in ethnic studies, 1969-70; Miles College, Atlanta, GA, administrative internal assistant to president, 1967-68; affiliated with Systems Development Corporation, Santa Monica, CA, 1968-69; Federal City College, Washington, DC, consultant in curriculum development and community educator, 1970-72; California State University, Fresno, associate professor of English, 1972-73; University of California, San Diego, La Jolla, assistant professor, 1973-76, associate professor, 1976-82, professor of Afro-American literature, 1982—, department chairman, 1976-82.

*MEMBER:* Poetry Society of America, Modern Language Association.

*AWARDS, HONORS:* National Book Award nomination, 1976, for *The Peacock Poems;* Fulbright lecturer, University of Ghana, 1984; *Dessa Rose* was named a notable book in 1986 by the *New York Times.*

*WRITINGS:*

*Give Birth to Brightness: A Thematic Study in Neo-Black Literature,* Dial, 1972.
(Under name Shirley Williams) *The Peacock Poems,* Wesleyan University Press, 1975.
*Some One Sweet Angel Chile* (poems), Morrow, 1982.
*Dessa Rose: A Riveting Story of the South During Slavery,* Morrow, 1986.
*Working Cotton,* illustrated by Carole Byard, Harcourt, 1992.

Also author of *Letters from a New England Negro,* a full-length drama produced in 1982, *Ours to Make,* 1973, and *The Sherley Williams Special,* 1977, both for television, and *Traveling Sunshine Good Time Show and Celebration,* 1973, a stageshow. Author of introduction to *Their Eyes Were Watching God,* University of Illinois, 1991.

*WORK IN PROGRESS: Dessa Rose,* a screenplay based on her novel; *Meanwhile, in Another Part of the City,* a collection of short fiction.

*SIDELIGHTS:* American critic, poet, novelist and educator Sherley Anne Williams during her early years may have seemed an unlikely candidate for fame. As a girl, she lived in a Fresno, California, housing project, and worked with her parents in fruit and cotton fields. Her father died of tuberculosis before her eighth birthday, and her mother, a practical woman from rural Texas who had tried to discourage Williams's early interest in reading, died when Williams was sixteen. "My friends were what you would call juvenile delinquents. Most of them didn't finish school," and her future, she told Mona Gable in a *Los Angeles Times Magazine* interview, amounted to having children. But a series of events including guidance from a science teacher and the discovery of Richard Wright's *Black Boy,* Ertha Kitt's *Thursday's Child,* and other books by black authors about their lives stimulated her desire to write. "It was largely through these autobiographies I was able to take heart in my life," she told Gable. Williams studied at Fresno State, Fisk, Howard, and Brown Universities before deciding to become a writer and to support herself by teaching. Now a professor of Afro-American literature at the University of California, San Diego, Williams has become well-known for her books of criticism, poetry, and fiction, and is "living an extraordinary life," remarked poet Philip Levine, who had been her mentor at Fresno State.

The publication of *Give Birth to Brightness: A Thematic Study in Neo-Black Literature* in 1972 encouraged Williams to pursue a writing career. The essays are, she says in the book's dedication, "a public statement of how I feel about and treasure one small aspect of Blackness in America," and the collection is dedicated to her son Malcolm. *Give Birth to Brightness* claims that "a shared racial memory and a common future" are the foundations of the new black literature, reports Lillie P. Howard in the *Dictionary of Literary Biography: Afro-American Poets since 1955.* Howard relates that the author's aim is to recreate "a new tradition built on a synthesis of black oral traditions [such as the blues] and Western literate forms." Different from both the Harlem Renaissance (in which black writers spoke to white audiences) and from the literary protests of the 1960s, the new writers "speak directly *to* Black people *about themselves* in order to move them toward self-knowledge and collective freedom;" Williams states that this is achieved in art that presents a "liberating vision" of black life, past and future, that goes beyond protest.

Reviewers found some fault with *Give Birth to Brightness,* but it was generally well-received. Writing in the *New York Times,* Mel Watkins notes, "Miss Williams persuasively demonstrates the commonality of viewpoint that she asserts characterizes neo-black fiction. Moreover, she evokes a real sense of what the street life is about." He takes issue with her portrayal of the street rebel as a symbolic hero, calling it a "dangerous and highly romantic idea" which may not be shared by all blacks, since they, too, may be victimized by streetmen. "Criticisms such as this notwithstanding," he adds, "Miss Williams has written a readable and informative survey of black literature. In using both her knowledge of Western literature and her understanding of black life, she provides insight into the sadly neglected area of reversed values that plays such a significant role in much black literature." Howard comments, "As a first major publication, *Give Birth to Brightness* is impressive."

*The Peacock Poems,* her second published book, was also well-received. The volume of autobiographical poems, some about her early family life, and the balance about her feelings as a single mother, drew a National Book Award nomination for poetry in 1976. Expressing herself in blues poetry, "Williams fingers the 'jagged' edges of a pain that is both hers and ours," Howard observes. She says the poems also assert and demonstrate "the therapeutic regenerative powers" of the traditional black music. Blues also shapes the poems in *Some One Sweet Angel Chile.* One of its sections looks at the life of blues singer Bessie Smith. "Singing the blues gave Smith a temporary lifeline which sustained her through all her sufferings," Howard relates. Other sections depict experiences of black women after the Civil War and in more recent times. Williams explains the focus of her early work in an interview with Claudia Tate, published in *Black Women Writers at Work:* "I wanted specifically to write about lower-income black women. . . . We were missing these stories of black women's struggles and their real triumphs. . . . I wanted to write about them because they had in a very real sense educated me and given me what it was going to take to get me through the world."

Two economically disadvantaged women tell their stories in Williams's first novel and most highly acclaimed book, *Dessa Rose.* The book begins with the memories of its title character, a whip-scarred, pregnant slave woman in jail for violent crimes against white men. Dessa recalls her life on the plantation with her lover, a life that ended when he was killed by their master. In turn, Dessa had killed the master, was arrested and chained to other slaves in a coffle, from which she escaped, again by violence to her white captors. Tracked down and sentenced to die after the birth of her child, who would be valuable property to the whites, Dessa is interviewed by Adam

Nehemiah, a white author who expects to become famous when he publishes the analysis of her crimes. When asked why she kills white men, Dessa replies evenly, "Cause I can."

After Dessa escapes again, Rufel Sutton, a white woman in economic distress, provides refuge for her and other runaway slaves simply because she can. Marcia Gillespie, contributing editor to *Ms.* magazine, notes that Rufel breastfeeds Dessa's newborn infant for the same reason, and because the alternative is too severe for her to consider. "As a result of this extraordinary bond, the two women achieve one of the most intricate and ambivalent relationships in contemporary fiction," Elaine Kendall remarks in the *Los Angeles Times.* In a scam designed by the runaways, Rufel earns money for a new life, selling them as slaves, waiting for them to escape, and selling them again. All goes well until the end, when Dessa is arrested by the enraged Nehemiah, but the two women elude his grasp with the aid of a female officer who is sent to verify Dessa's identity by examining her scars. When the group disbands, Rufel goes off to prosperity in the East; the blacks go west to the hardships of prejudice on the frontier. "Thus has Sherley Anne Williams breathed wonderful life into the bare bones of the past," believes *New York Times* reviewer Christopher Lehmann-Haupt. "And thus does she resolve more issues than are dreamed of in most history textbooks."

*Dessa Rose,* Gable writes, "was an instant critical success. There were favorable reviews in the *Washington Post,* the *Boston Globe, Ms.* and a number of other publications. Writing in the *New York Times,* David Bradley called it 'artistically brilliant, emotionally affecting and totally unforgettable.'" Also "one of the biggest hits of the literary season," the book commanded a third printing only months after its debut and six figure amounts for paperback and film rights—unusual for a first novel, Gable reports. "What makes 'Dessa Rose' such an unlikely commercial hit—and what prompted the *New York Times* to give it two glowing reviews and place it for two weeks on its influential recommended reading list—is the book's unflinchingly realistic portrayal of American slavery," Gable suggests. For instance, the sexual exploitation of black men and women that was common to the condition of slavery is fully drawn here, say reviewers, in "a plot dealing with all the [sadism and lust] that Harriet Beecher Stowe [author of *Uncle Tom's Cabin*] did not dare to mention," as London *Times* reviewer Andrew Sinclair phrases it. Furthermore, notes Jane Perliz in the *New York Times Book Review,* Williams intends Dessa's rebellion, based on an actual uprising led by a pregnant slave in 1829, to refute the myth that black women were the passive collaborators of abusive masters under the system.

These realities, not apparent in *Gone with the Wind,* were also absent from William Styron's *Confessions of Nat Turner,* a novel about a slave revolt leader that enraged Williams because it suggested that Turner's rebellion was motivated by his lust for a white woman. With *Dessa Rose*, "Williams not only wanted to challenge Styron's ... view of slavery, which she believes dismissed the brutal social and political conditions that led to Turner's revolt, but to show up the 'hypocrisy of the literary tradition' by detailing the strengths of black culture," Gable relates. That resilience, Williams told her, was the ability to build strong family relationships despite slavery's attack on the black family.

Williams told Gable she also hoped the novel would "heal some wounds" made by racism left in the wake of slavery. In her view, she explained, fiction is one way to conceive of "the impossible, ... and putting these women together, I could come to understand something not only about their experience of slavery but about them as women, and imagine the basis for some kind of honest rapprochement between black and white women." Michele Wallace, writing in the *Women's Review of Books,* notes, for example, the change in Dessa's feelings for Rufel when she realizes that white women, too, are raped by white men. Wallace adds, "*Dessa Rose* reveals both the uniformities and the idiosyncracies of 'woman's place,' while making imaginative and unprecedented use of its male characters as well. Sherley Anne Williams's accomplishment is that she takes the reader someplace we're not accustomed to going, some place historical scholarship may never take us— into the world that black and white women shared in the antebellum South. But what excites me the most, finally, about this novel is its definition of friendship as the collective struggle that ultimately transcends the stumbling-blocks of race and class."

*BIOGRAPHICAL/CRITICAL SOURCES:*

*BOOKS*

*Dictionary of Literary Biography,* Volume 41: *Afro-American Poets since 1955,* Gale, 1985.

Fisher, Dexter and Robert B. Stepto, editors, *Afro-American Literature: The Reconstruction of Instruction,* Modern Language Association of America, 1979.

Henderson, Stephen, *Understanding the New Black Poetry,* Morrow, 1973.

Tate, Claudia, editor, *Black Women Writers at Work,* Continuum, 1983.

Williams, Sherley Anne, *Give Birth to Brightness: A Thematic Study in Neo-Black Literature,* Dial, 1972.

Williams, Sherley Anne, *Dessa Rose,* Morrow, 1986.

*PERIODICALS*

*Black American Literature Forum,* fall, 1986.
*Black Scholar,* March, 1981.
*Black World,* June, 1976.

*Commonweal,* December 3, 1982.
*Essence,* August, 1986; December, 1986.
*Los Angeles Times,* July 23, 1986; August 8, 1986.
*Los Angeles Times Book Review,* July 4, 1982.
*Los Angeles Times Magazine,* December 7, 1986.
*Ms.,* September, 1986.
*New Yorker,* September 8, 1986.
*New York Times,* July 8, 1982; July 12, 1986.
*New York Times Book Review,* August 3, 1986.
*Publishers Weekly,* February 19, 1982; May 30, 1986; October 3, 1986.
*Times* (London), March 19, 1987.
*Virginia Quarterly Review,* spring, 1976.
*Washington Post Book World,* August 3, 1986.
*Women's Review of Books,* Volume 4, number 1, October, 1986.

\* \* \*

## WILLIAMS, Shirley
## See WILLIAMS, Sherley Anne

\* \* \*

## WILSON, August 1945-

*PERSONAL:* Born in 1945 in Pittsburgh, PA.

*ADDRESSES: Home*—St. Paul, MN. *Agent*—c/o Dutton, 375 Hudson St., New York, NY 10014.

*CAREER:* Writer. Black Horizons Theater Company, St. Paul, MN, founder and director, beginning in 1968; scriptwriter for Science Museum of Minnesota.

*AWARDS, HONORS:* Award for best play of 1984-85 from New York Drama Critics Circle and Antoinette Perry ("Tony") Award nomination from League of New York Theatres and Producers, both 1985, and Whiting Writers' Award from the Whiting Foundation, 1986, all for *Ma Rainey's Black Bottom;* Outstanding Play Award from American Theatre Critics, 1986, Pulitzer Prize for drama, Tony Award for best play, and award for best Broadway play from Outer Critics Circle, all 1987, all for *Fences;* John Gassner Award for best American playwright from Outer Critics Circle, 1987; named Artist of the Year by *Chicago Tribune,* 1987; award for best play from New York Drama Critics Circle and Tony Award nomination, both 1988, for *Joe Turner's Come and Gone;* Pulitzer Prize for drama, 1990, for *The Piano Lesson;* award from Black Filmmakers Hall of Fame, 1991.

*WRITINGS:*

*Jitney* (two-act play), first produced in Pittsburgh, PA, at Allegheny Repertory Theatre, 1982.

*Ma Rainey's Black Bottom* (play; first produced in New Haven, CT, at Yale Repertory Theatre, 1984; produced on Broadway at Cort Theatre, October, 1984), New American Library, 1985.

*Fences* (play; first produced at Yale Repertory Theatre, 1985; produced on Broadway at 46th Street Theatre, March, 1987), New American Library, 1986.

*Joe Turner's Come and Gone* (play; first produced at Yale Repertory Theatre, 1986; produced on Broadway at Barrymore Theatre, March, 1988), New American Library, 1988.

*The Piano Lesson* (play; first produced at Yale Repertory Theatre, 1987; produced on Broadway at Walter Kerr Theatre, 1990), Dutton, 1990.

*Three Plays* (contains *Ma Rainey's Black Bottom, Fences,* and *Joe Turner's Come and Gone*), University of Pittsburgh Press, 1991.

*Two Trains Running* (play; first produced at Yale Repertory Theatre, 1991; produced at Walter Kerr Theatre, 1992), Dutton, 1992.

Also author of play *Fullerton Street* and the book for a stage musical about jazz musician Jelly Roll Morton. Poetry represented in anthologies, including *The Poetry of Blackamerica.* Contributor to periodicals, including *Black Lines* and *Connection.*

*WORK IN PROGRESS:* A screenplay adaptation of *Fences.*

*SIDELIGHTS:* August Wilson has been hailed since the mid-1980s as an important talent in the American theatre. In 1968 he first became active in the theatre by founding—despite lacking prior experience—the Black Horizons Theatre Company in St. Paul, Minnesota. Recalling his early theatre involvement, Wilson described himself to the *New York Times* as "a cultural nationalist ... trying to raise consciousness through theater."

In St. Paul Wilson wrote his first play, *Jitney,* a realistic drama set in a Pittsburgh taxi station. *Jitney* was accepted for workshop production at the O'Neill Theatre Center's National Playwrights Conference in 1982. This brought Wilson into contact with other playwrights. Inspired, he wrote another play, *Fullerton Street,* but this work failed to strengthen his reputation.

Wilson then resumed work on an earlier unfinished project, *Ma Rainey's Black Bottom,* a play about a black blues singer's exploitation of her fellow musicians. This work, whose title role is named after an actual blues singer from the 1920s, is set in a recording studio in 1927. In the studio, temperamental Ma Rainey verbally abuses the other musicians and presents herself—without justification—as an important musical figure. But much of the play is also set in a rehearsal room, where Ma Rainey's musicians discuss their abusive employer and the hardships of life in racist America.

*Ma Rainey's Black Bottom* earned Wilson a return to the O'Neill Center's play writing conference in 1983. There Wilson's play impressed director Lloyd Richards from the Yale Repertory Theatre. Richards worked with Wilson to refine the play, and when it was presented at Yale in 1984 it was hailed as the work of an important new playwright. Frank Rich, who reviewed the Yale production in the *New York Times,* acclaimed Wilson as "a major find for the American theater" and cited his ability to write "with compassion, raucous humor and penetrating wisdom."

Wilson enjoyed further success with *Ma Rainey's Black Bottom* after the play came to Broadway later in 1984. The *Chicago Tribune*'s Richard Christiansen reviewed the Broadway production as "a work of intermittent but immense power" and commended the "striking beauty" of the play's "literary and theatrical poetry." Christiansen added that "Wilson's power of language is sensational" and that *Ma Rainey's Black Bottom* was "the work of an impressive writer." The London *Times*'s Hill agreed, calling Wilson "a promising new playwright" and hailing his work as "a remarkable first play."

Wilson's subsequent plays include the Pulitzer Prize-winning *Fences,* which is about a former athlete who forbids his son to accept an athletic scholarship, and *Joe Turner's Come and Gone,* which concerns an ex-convict's efforts to find his wife. Like *Ma Rainey's Black Bottom,* these plays underwent extensive rewriting. Guiding Wilson in this process was Lloyd Richards, dean of Yale's drama school and director of the school's productions of Wilson's plays. "August is a wonderful poet," Richards told the *New York Times* in 1986. "A wonderful poet turning into a playwright." Richards added that his work with Wilson involved "clarifying" each work's main theme and "arranging the material in a dynamic way."

Both *Fences* and *Joe Turner's Come and Gone* were praised when they played on American stages. The *New York Times*'s Frank Rich, in his review of *Fences,* wrote that the play "leaves no doubt that Mr. Wilson is a major writer, combining a poet's ear for vernacular with a robust sense of humor (political and sexual), a sure instinct for cracking dramatic incident and passionate commitment to a great subject." And in his critique of *Joe Turner's Come and Gone,* Rich speculated that the play "will give a lasting voice to a generation of uprooted black Americans." Rich contended that the work was "potentially its author's finest achievement yet" and described it as "a teeming canvas of black America ... and a spiritual allegory."

Wilson's next play, *The Piano Lesson,* added to his stature with another Pulitzer Prize, won before the play ever reached Broadway. A largely realistic play, it focuses on a family conflict over an heirloom piano. Berniece Charles's slave ancestors were traded for it, and another family member carved African-style portraits of them on it. Later Berniece's father died reclaiming it. Now Berniece's brother Boy Willie wants to sell it to buy farmland, and the issue threatens to tear the family apart. Reviewing a pre-Broadway production of *The Piano Lesson* in a 1989 *Time* article, Henry judged it Wilson's "richest" play yet. Some were less enthusiastic, specifically questioning Wilson's use of the supernatural at the end of the drama. Opining that *The Piano Lesson* did not measure up to Wilson's earlier work, Robert Brustein of *New Republic* suggested that the playwright should "develop the radical poetic strain that now lies dormant in his art." Despite perceived weaknesses, however, critics applauded Wilson's strengths in humor and language. And Henry, who also admitted flaws in the play's ending, nonetheless maintained that "already the musical instrument of the title is the most potent symbol in American drama since Laura Wingfield's glass menagerie" in a classic play by Tennessee Williams.

In 1992 a new Wilson play, *Two Trains Running,* came to Broadway, depicting the lives of patrons of a run-down diner in the late 1960s. With a quiet central plot involving the pending sale of the diner, the play seemed more a "slice of life" to critic Henry than the kind of explosive conflict of some of Wilson's previous plays. In contrast, Henry wrote, *Two Trains Running* is a "delicate and mature work" that shows Wilson "at his lyrical best." The play touches on troubled black urban youths, the low self-esteem of some black women, injustices perpetrated by whites, and problems in the ways blacks treat each other, among other subjects. Reviewing the play for the *New Yorker,* Mimi Kramer found "something awe-inspiring" about a play so focused on race and black character. "All the same," she added, "I like my August Wilson a little subtler." Victor Dwyer, on the other hand, called *Two Trains Running* "a dramatic glimpse into the life of black America" in his *Maclean's* review. Praising the language of the play, which he felt sometimes achieves "musical eloquence," David Ansen of *Newsweek* characterized it as "thematically rich."

Throughout his career Wilson has stressed that his first objective is in getting his work produced. "All I want is for the most people to get to see this play," he told the *New York Times* while discussing *Joe Turner's Come and Gone.* Wilson added, however, that he was not opposed to having his works performed on Broadway. He told the *New York Times* that Broadway "still has the connotation of Mecca" and asked, "Who doesn't want to go to Mecca?" In his 1988 *Time* article, Henry noted how Wilson's attitude differs from that of some of his predecessors. "Wilson is not a 'black' playwright in the sense the term was applied in the confrontational 1960s and '70s,"

Henry wrote. "He movingly evokes the ev burden of slavery but without laying on guilt rangues." By 1992 Wilson's lyrical approach according to Henry, "the foremost American his generation."

*BIOGRAPHICAL/CRITICAL SOURCES:*

BOOKS

*Black Literature Criticism,* Gale, 1992.
*Contemporary Literary Criticism,* Gale, Vo
Volume 50, 1988, Volume 63, 1991.
*Drama Criticism,* Volume 2, Gale, 1992.

*PERIODICALS*

*Chicago Tribune,* October 15, 1984; June 8
ber 17, 1987; December 27, 1987.
*Chicago Tribune Book World,* February 9, 1
*Ebony,* January, 1985.
*Los Angeles Times,* November 24, 1984; No
April 17, 1987; June 7, 1987; June 8, 198
February 6, 1988.
*Maclean's,* May 28, 1990, p. 62; May 18, 1
*Nation,* April 18, 1987, p. 518; June 11, 1990,
8, 1992, p. 799-800.
*New Republic,* May 21, 1990, pp. 28-30.
*Newsweek,* April 6, 1987; April 11, 1988,
1992, p. 70.
*New York,* April 6, 1987, pp. 92, 94.
*New Yorker,* April 6, 1987, p. 81; April 11, 19
30, 1990; April 27, 1992, p. 85.
*New York Times,* April 11, 1984; April 13, 1
1984; October 22, 1984; May 6, 1986
June 20, 1986; March 27, 1987; April
1987; April 17, 1987; May 7, 1987; Dec
December 11, 1987.
*Saturday Review,* January/February, 1985.
*Theater,* fall-winter, 1984, pp. 50-55.
*Time,* April 6, 1987, p. 81; April 27, 1987;
pp. 77-78; January 30, 1989, p. 69; Ap
65-66.
*Times* (London), November 6, 1984; April 1
1987.
*Washington Post,* May 20, 1986; April 15, 19
October 4, 1987; October 9, 1987.

\* \* \*

**WILSON, Carletta 1951-**
**(Sundaira Morninghouse)**

*PERSONAL:* Born April 14, 1951, in Philad

*ion:* Cheyney University, B.A.; University of Washington, L.S. *Avocational interests:* Travel, genealogy, the blues and rld music, dance, visual arts.

*DRESSES: Home*—P.O. Box 28483, Seattle, WA 98118-43.

*REER:* Writer and librarian.

*MBER:* Society of Children's Book Writers and Illustra-s.

*RITINGS:*

*DER PSEUDONYM SUNDAIRA MORNINGHOUSE*

*ghtfeathers: Black Goose Rhymes,* Open Hand, 1989.
*bari Gani? What's the News?,* Open Hand, 1992.

*HER*

ntributor to *Poetry Works! The First Verse,* Modern Cur-ulum Press, 1993.

*ORK IN PROGRESS: Where I Live Is a Beautiful Place,* ems.

*DELIGHTS:* Carletta Wilson commented: "Sundaira orninghouse is my *nom de plume.* Sundaira is a name cre-d from beginnings and light. For example, *sun... day... Ra.* is in honor of the Egyptian sun god Ra and also the Phila-phia jazz musician Sun Ra. I work to shine a little light in world of children's literature—particularly in terms of lit-ture written with children of African descent in mind. And , not only these, because all children are invited to explore beauty which is African in this world. I love the wonder words and the worlds they explore. I invite my readers into dance, into the chant. My work as a children's librarian, useum educator, and art and creative writing teacher has lped and inspired me in this effort. I also publish poetry and tion under my given name—work that is intended for adult aders."

*OGRAPHICAL/CRITICAL SOURCES:*

*RIODICALS*

*blishers Weekly,* September 7, 1992, p. 65.

**WITHERSPOON, Naomi Long**
**See MADGETT, Naomi Long**

\*      \*      \*

## WOODSON, Carter G(odwin)   1875-1950

*PERSONAL:* Born December 19, 1875, in New Canton, VA; died April 3, 1950, in Washington, DC; buried in Lincoln Memorial Cemetery, Suitland, MD; son of James Henry and Anne Eliza (Riddle) Woodson. *Education:* Berea College, B.L., 1903; attended the Sorbonne, 1906; University of Chicago, A.B., 1907, M.A., 1908; Harvard University, Ph.D., 1912. *Avocational interests:* Reading, travel, tennis.

*CAREER:* Historian, 1910-50. Railroad construction laborer and coal miner, 1892-94; schoolteacher in Winona, WV, 1898-1900; Douglass High School, WV, principal, 1900-03; schoolteacher in Philippines, 1903-07, and at M Street High School (later Dunbar High School), Washington, DC, 1909-18; Armstrong Manual Training School, Washington, DC, principal, 1918-19; Howard University, dean of School of Liberal Arts, 1919-20; West Virginia Collegiate Institute (now West Virginia State College), dean, 1920-22. Editor and founder of *Journal of Negro History,* 1916-50, and *Negro History Bulletin,* 1937-50; founder and chair of the board of Associated Publishers, Inc., 1921-50. Founder of Negro History Week (which evolved into Black History Month observed every February in the U.S.), 1926.

*MEMBER:* Association for the Study of Negro Life and History (now the Association for the Study of Afro-American Life and History; founder and executive director, 1915), National Association for the Advancement of Colored People (life member), American Negro Academy, American Teachers Association (life member).

*AWARDS, HONORS:* Carnegie Corporation grant, 1921; Laura Spelman Rockefeller Memorial grants, 1921 and 1926; Spingarn Medal, National Association for the Advancement of Colored People (NAACP), 1926; Social Science Research Council award, 1928; Rockefeller Foundation grants, 1929 and 1930; doctor of laws degree from Virginia State College, 1939; Carter Godwin Woodson Public School No. 160 in Baltimore, MD, named in his honor, 1953; Carter G. Woodson Junior High School in Washington, DC, dedicated November 19, 1956; elected to the Ebony Hall of Fame, 1958; Carter G. Woodson Houses (senior citizen housing) established in Brooklyn, NY, 1969; Carter G. Woodson Professorship in Negro History established at Berea College, 1973; a bronze marker was erected at Woodson's birthplace in New Canton, VA, by the Association for the Study of Afro-American Life

and History on December 19, 1975 (the hundredth anniversary of his birth); Dr. Carter G. Woodson Regional Library dedicated in Chicago, IL, December 19, 1975; Woodson House (his home and office) in Washington, DC, was placed on the national register as a historical landmark in 1976; a 20-cent stamp bearing Woodson's likeness was issued by the United States Postal Service in conjunction with Black History Month, February 1, 1984; the mayor of Huntington, WV, formed the Carter G. Woodson Memorial Committee to fund scholarships in his name, 1986; the Black History National Recreation Trail was dedicated in honor of Woodson, February, 1988.

*WRITINGS:*

*Education of the Negro Prior to 1861,* Putnam, 1915, Ayer, 1991.

*A Century of Negro Migration,* Association for the Study of Negro Life and History, 1918, AMS Press, 1970.

*History of the Negro Church,* Associated Publishers, 1921, reprinted, 1992.

*The Negro in Our History,* Associated Publishers, 1922, revised edition, 1990.

*Free Negro Owners of Slaves in the United States in 1830,* Associated Publishers, 1924, reprinted, Association for the Study of Afro-American Life and History, 1990.

*Free Negro Heads of Families in the United States in 1830,* Association for the Study of Negro Life and History, 1925, reprinted, 1978.

(Editor) *Negro Orators and Their Orations,* Associated Publishers, 1925, reprinted, 1986.

(Editor) *The Mind of the Negro as Reflected in Letters Written During the Crisis, 1800-1860,* Association for the Study of Negro Life and History, 1926, reprinted, 1987.

*Negro Makers of History,* Associated Publishers, 1928, reprinted, Chadwyck-Heale, 1987.

*African Myths, Together with Proverbs: A Supplementary Reader Composed of Folk Tales from Various Parts of Africa,* Associated Publishers, 1928, reprinted, Golden Press, 1968.

(With J. H. Harmon and Arnett G. Lindsay) *The Negro as a Business Man,* Association for the Study of Negro Life and History, 1929, reprinted, McGrath, 1969.

*The Rural Negro,* Association for the Study of Negro Life and History, 1930, reprinted, 1987.

(With Lorenzo J. Greene) *The Negro Wage Earner,* Association for the Study of Negro Life and History, 1930, reprinted, AMS Press, 1970.

*The Mis-education of the Negro,* Associated Publishers, 1933, reprinted, Winston-Derek, 1990.

*The Negro Professional Man and the Community, with Special Emphasis on the Physician and the Lawyer,* Association for the Study of Negro Life and History, 1934, reprinted, Johnson, 1970.

*The Story of the Negro Retold,* Associated Publishers, 1935, reprinted, 1959.

*The African Background Outlined: or Handbook for the Study of the Negro,* Association for the Study of Negro Life and History, 1936, reprinted, New American Library, 1969.

*African Heroes and Heroines,* Associated Publishers, 1939, reprinted, 1969.

(Editor) Francis J. Grimke, *The Works of Francis J. Grimke,* four volumes, Associated Publishers, 1942.

Contributor of numerous articles to periodicals, including *Southern Workman, Journal of Negro History,* and *Negro History Bulletin.*

*SIDELIGHTS:* A man of humble origins—he came from a large, poor family and both his parents were former slaves—Carter G. Woodson became a giant in the field of African American studies. He established himself as an authority with the publication of his first book, *Education of the Negro Prior to 1861,* in 1915. A study of the changes in quality of instruction offered to blacks, the book received acclaim from critics. One commentator, quoted by Edward L. Cox in *Dictionary of Literary Biography,* found *Education of the Negro* "a work of profound historical research, full of interesting data on a most important phase of race life which has heretofore remained unexplored and neglected." Woodson went on to pen more than fifteen additional works throughout the course of his career. Among these is 1933's *Mis-education of the Negro,* in which the author returned to education, a subject about which he harbored strong feelings. In the volume Woodson criticizes the "educated Negroes," who maintain an "attitude of contempt toward their own people because in their own as well as in their mixed schools they are taught to admire the Hebrew, the Greek, the Latin and the Teuton and to despise the African." Woodson goes on in *The Mis-education of the Negro* to advocate the instruction of the black student "about his race and its history and such training of his special gifts as will restore in him both individual and racial self-respect." "As far as Woodson was concerned," Cox explained, "a revamping of the entire American educational system, especially of its curriculum, was essential if blacks were to make any meaningful progress in the United States."

In addition to writing numerous pioneering books and holding a variety of academic posts, Woodson established the following: a professional association, two periodicals, and a publishing company. The Association for the Study of Negro Life and History provided a focus for black intellectuals to explore and promote their heritage. The *Journal of Negro History,* still published today, provided an outlet for serious scholarship. Because he also wanted a more popular medium for the layperson, he established the *Negro History Bulletin,* a vehicle designed to make significant research accessible even to school children. Finally, his Associated Publishers, Inc., allowed him and his fellow historians to disseminate their findings in book form at a time when few established publishers were interested in the subjects which attracted Woodson.

Although he never saw to fruition one of his planned projects, an *Encyclopaedia Africana*, he did, according to Cox, firmly establish himself as one of the twentieth century's premier American historians. "He made an indelible impression on the minds of a whole generation of American historians and educators," Cox declared. "The study, writing, and teaching of American history has not been the same since Woodson successfully countered the ignorance and misinformation that had surrounded the contributions of blacks to the building of the United States."

*BIOGRAPHICAL/CRITICAL SOURCES:*

*BOOKS*

*Dictionary of Literary Biography,* Volume 17: *Twentieth-Century American Historians,* Gale, 1983, pp. 458-65.

Goggin, Jacqueline A., *Carter G. Woodson and the Movement to Promote Black History,* University of Rochester, 1984.

Greene, Lorenzo J., *Working with Carter G. Woodson, The Father of Black History: A Diary, 1928-1930,* edited with an introduction by Arvarh E. Strickland, Louisiana State University Press, 1989.

McKissack, Patricia, and Frederick McKissack, *Carter Godwin Woodson: The Father of Black History,* Enslow, 1991.

Page, James A., editor, *Selected Black American Authors,* G. K. Hall, 1977, pp. 300-01.

Ploski, Harry A., and James Williams, editors, *Reference Library of Black America,* Afro-American Press, 1990, p. 1021.

Rollock, Barbara T., *Black Authors and Illustrators of Children's Books, A Biographical Dictionary,* Garland, 1988, p. 126.

Romero, Patricia W., *Carter G. Woodson: A Biography,* Ohio State University, 1971.

Scally, M. Anthony, *Carter G. Woodson: A Bio-Bibliography,* Greenwood Press, 1985.

Scally, M. Anthony, *Walking Proud: The Story of Dr. Carter Godwin Woodson,* Associated Publishers, 1983.

Thorpe, Earl E., *Negro Historians in the United States,* Fraternal Press, 1958.

Woodson, Carter G., *The Mis-education of the Negro,* Winston-Derek, 1990.

Young, James O., *Black Writers of the Thirties,* Louisiana State University Press, 1973, pp. 13-20, 111-20.

*PERIODICALS*

*American Historical Review,* October, 1984.

*Black Collegian,* January-February, 1974.

*Ebony,* February, 1980; February 1983.

*Harlem Weekly,* February 2-8, 1983.

*Jet,* February 25, 1985.

*Journal of Negro History,* January, 1951; January, 1956; April, 1957; April, 1966; January, 1973.

*National Black Monitor,* March, 1977.

*National Medical Association Journal,* September, 1970.

*Negro History Bulletin,* May, 1950; February, 1960; January-February, 1977; January-March, 1981; October, 1982; January-March, 1984.

*New York Amsterdam News,* March 6, 1982, p. 22.

*New York Daily Challenge,* December 11, 1974, p. 5.

*Pan African Journal,* spring, 1974.

*Sepia,* February, 1976.

*Survey,* October, 1933.

*OBITUARIES:*

*PERIODICALS*

*Afro-American* (Baltimore), April 8, 1950, p. 1; April 15, 1950, p. 7.

*Chicago Defender,* April 8, 1950, p. 1; April 15, 1950, p. 4.

*Journal of Negro History,* July, 1950, pp. 344-48.

*National Negro Health News,* April-June, 1950, p. 16.

*New York Age,* April 8, 1950, p. 3.

*New York Amsterdam News,* April 8, 1950, p. 1, 6.

*Pittsburgh Courier,* April 8, 1950, p. 1; April 15, 1950, p. 11.

\* \* \*

## WRIGHT, Jay 1935-

*PERSONAL:* Born May 25, 1935, in Albuquerque, NM; son of Mercer Murphy Wright (a mechanic and jitney driver) and Leona Dailey; married September 15, 1968; wife's name, Lois. *Education:* Attended University of New Mexico; University of California, Berkeley, B.A., 1961; further study at Union Theological Seminary, 1961-62; Rutgers University, M.A., 1967.

*ADDRESSES: Home and office*—R.R.1, Box 236, Piermont, NH 03779.

*CAREER:* Poet, playwright, and educator. Butler Institute, Guadalajara, Mexico, instructor in English, 1964; Foster D. Snell and Company Chemical Abstracts, New York City, abstract writer, 1967-68; Tougaloo College, Tougaloo, MS, writer-in-residence, 1968; Talledega College, Talledega, AL, poet-in-residence, 1969-70; Texas Southern University, Houston, writer-in-residence, 1970; Yale University, New Haven,

CT, visiting lecturer, 1975-76, assistant professor, 1976-79; University of Utah, Salt Lake City, visiting associate professor, 1983; University of Kentucky, Lexington, visiting professor, fall semesters, 1983, 1984; University of North Carolina at Chapel Hill, visiting professor, spring, 1986; Dartmouth College, Hanover, NH, visiting professor, 1989-93; Washington University, St. Louis, MO, Visiting Hurst Professor, spring, 1992. *Military service:* U.S. Army Medical Corps, c. 1955-57.

*AWARDS, HONORS:* Rockefeller Brothers theological fellowship, 1961; MCA creative writing fellowship, 1963; National Endowment for the Arts grant, 1967; Woodrow Wilson/National Endowment for the Arts Poets-in-Concert fellowship, 1967; Hodder fellow in Playwriting, Princeton University, Princeton, NJ, 1970-71; Joseph Compton creative writing fellowship, Dundee University, Dundee, Scotland, 1972-73; Ingram Merrill Foundation award, 1974; Guggenheim fellowship, 1974-75; American Academy and Institute of Arts and Letters Literature Award, 1981; Oscar Williams and Gene Derwood Award, 1985; MacArthur fellow, 1986-1991.

*WRITINGS:*

*POETRY*

*Death as History,* Kriya Press, 1967.
*The Homecoming Singer,* Corinth, 1971.
*Soothsayers and Omens,* Seven Woods, 1976.
*Dimensions of History,* Kayak, 1976.
*The Double Invention of Komo,* University of Texas Press, 1980.
*Explications/Interpretations,* University of Kentucky Press, 1984.
*Selected Poems of Jay Wright,* edited and introduced by Robert B. Stepto, afterword by Harold Bloom, Princeton University Press, 1987.
*Elaine's Book,* University Press of Virginia, 1988.
*Boleros,* Princeton University Press, 1991.

Work represented in poetry anthologies, including *New Negro Poets: U.S.A.,* edited by Langston Hughes, Indiana University Press, 1964; *For Malcolm: Poems on the Life and Death of Malcolm X,* edited by Dudley Randall and Margaret Burroughs, Broadside Press, 1967; *The Poetry of Black America,* edited by Arnold Adoff, Harper, 1972; *Understanding the New Black Poetry,* William Morrow, 1973; *The Best American Poetry,* Scribner's, 1989; *Every Shut Eye Ain't Asleep,* Little, Brown, in press. Contributor of poems to numerous periodicals, including *Negro American Literature Forum, Evergreen Review, Hiram Poetry Review, Nation, Yale Review, Massachusetts Review, Kenyon Review, Tri-Quarterly, Harper's,* and *New Republic.*

*PLAYS*

*Welcome Back, Black Boy,* produced by University of California, Berkeley, May, 1961.
*Balloons: A Comedy in One Act,* Baker's Plays, 1968.

Also author of the plays *Love's Equations* (mythical drama; one-act), published in *Callaloo,* 1983; *The Death and Return of Paul Batuta* (mythical/historical drama; one-act), published in *Hambone,* 1984; *The Adoration of Fire* (mythical drama; one-act), published in *Southern Review,* 1985; *A Sacred Impurity: Death's First Invention* (ritual; one-act), published in *Hambone,* 1987; *Daughters of the Water,* published in *Callaloo,* 1987; *The Delights of Memory, 1: Lily* and *The Delights of Memory, 2: Doss,* both published in *Callaloo,* 1991; *The Delights of Memory, 3: LeRoi,* published in *Hambone,* 1991.

Also author of an unpublished four-play series consisting of *The Unfinished Saint, Part One; The Unfinished Saint, Part Two; Death as History, Part One;* and *Death as History, Part Two.* Also author of *The Hunt and Double Night of the Wood, Homage to Anthony Braxton* (one-act), *The Crossing* (mythical drama; one-act), *The Final Celebration, Crossing the Second River, The Abandoned Eye,* and *The Delights of Memory, 4 and 5,* all unpublished.

Also author of radio plays, including *The Death of Mr. Parker,* and *Woman with Charm,* produced by WPFA, Berkeley, CA.

Also contributor to literature anthologies, including *Black Fire,* edited by LeRoi Jones and Larry Neal, Morrow, 1968; *New Black Voices,* edited by Abraham Chapman, New American Library, 1972; *Heath Anthology of American Literature,* D. C. Heath, 1990; *Harper American Literature,* HarperCollins, in press. Contributor to *The Chant of Saints: A Gathering of Afro-American Literature, Arts and Scholarship,* edited by Michael S. Harper and Robert Stepto, University of Illinois Press, 1979.

*OTHER*

Author of introduction to *Poetry for My People,* by Henry Dumas, edited by Hale Chatfield and Eugene Redmond, Southern Illinois University Press, 1970; contributor of essays to periodicals and anthologies.

*WORK IN PROGRESS: Transformations,* a book of poetry.

*SIDELIGHTS:* Jay Wright is a contemporary black American poet whose work is acknowledged for its evocative language, introspective tone, and mythological imagery. He is the author of plays, essays, and books of poetry which focus on a rediscovery of the African American heritage through historical study and personal experience. His poetry, often autobiographical and allegorical in nature, has been compared by some critics to the works of T. S. Eliot, Walt Whitman, and Hart Crane, and shows the various artistic influences of Dante, Nicholas Guillen, Alejo Carpenter, St. Augustine, and the West African griots—entertainers whose recitals include tribal histories and genealogies. A recurring theme in Wright's poetry is the attempt to overcome a sense of exclusion, whether from society or from one's cultural identity, and to find growth and unity through a connection between American society (the experience of the present) and African traditions (the heritage of the past). Ultimately, as a *Choice* reviewer expressed it, Wright searches for "a new point of origin" for a wider African American cultural identity. Weaving together the mythology and culture of many lands, Wright's poetry heavily reflects the influence of his birthplace in the American Southwest, as well as the heritage of his African ancestry. His poems explore history from this multicultural standpoint and often take the form of allegorical journeys and spiritual quests wherein the persona finally achieves growth.

Wright was born in 1935 in New Mexico, and spent his childhood in Albuquerque and his teen years in San Pedro, California. The early exposure to Mexican, Spanish, and Navajo cultures provided by his upbringing in the Southwest has proved to have a lasting effect on his poetry, as geography and culture have become major themes in his work. For a short time after high school, Wright played baseball in the Arizona/Texas and California State Leagues, and he briefly studied chemistry at the University of New Mexico. Before the term was over, however, Wright joined the United States Army, serving for three years in the Medical Corps. After his discharge, he attended the University of California, earned his bachelor's degree in 1961, won a Rockefeller Brothers theological fellowship, and studied for one semester at Union Theological Seminary. Wright went on to Rutgers University to complete his masters degree in comparative literature in 1967, and a year later was awarded a Woodrow Wilson/National Endowment for the Arts Poets-in-Concert fellowship which enabled him to tour the South. In that same year, 1967, he published his first chapbook of poems, titled *Death as History.* Around this time Wright published a play, *Balloons: A Comedy in One Act,* and in 1970 he was granted a Hodder fellowship in playwriting from Princeton University in 1970. One of his previous plays, *Welcome Back, Black Boy,* had been produced in California.

Wright's first major published collection, 1971's *The Homecoming Singer,* established his reputation as a gifted poet. The theme of bridging past and present, settings that enhance discovery, and meditations on feelings of exclusion from society or personal identity are all evident in these early poems. Geographical settings become backdrops for the autobiographical persona's spiritual, emotional, and intellectual growth. "[The] individual poems ... are firmly grounded in well-defined geographical settings" that function not simply as atmosphere, explained Phillip M. Richard in the *Dictionary of Literary Biography,* but "as symbolic renderings of the persona's inner state." Themes are further explored through experience in such poems as "The Hunting Trip Cook," where a young boy struggles with anger mixed with affection toward his father, who serves as cook on a white man's hunting trip; "Wednesday Night Prayer Meeting," in which a young man questions the relevance of traditional religion; and "Beginning Again," the final poem of the book, which ends with a homecoming and a promise for the future.

Reviewers of *The Homecoming Singer* were largely enthusiastic, and Wright was christened "a major poet of this era" by Eugene B. Redmond in *Drumvoices: The Mission of Afro-American Poetry, A Critical History,* as quoted by Richard. Critics especially admired Wright's use of syntax and rhythm: "His verse resembles prose," wrote David Kalstone in the *New York Times Book Review,* "yet the lines pause at points where he branches out with participles and oddities of syntax to discover what energies are available in worlds he can't belong to. The rhythms—there are few full stops—deceive us into sharing others' dreams." The reviewer concluded, "It is hard to know where Wright will go from here—and important to find out." Robert B. Shaw in *Poetry* admired Wright's Mexican scenes, his "seeking, questioning" meditations and, especially, the final dream vision of the poem, which he described as "one of the more eloquent evocations of an American muse that I have read."

Wright published *Homecoming Singer* while living in Mexico, where he remained from 1968 until 1971. He then moved to Scotland, where he resided from 1971 until 1973, before publishing two volumes of poetry in 1976: *Soothsayers and Omens* and *Dimensions of History.* Wright's interest in the importance of African mythology to the continuity of black awareness (spanning all the way back to Africa) is developed in these works, and is connected to the theme of individual growth achieved through spiritual quest. In *Soothsayers and Omens,* for example, the persona is a seeker on a personal, spiritual quest in a Mexican setting, while in *Dimensions of History* the speaker of the poem is an African dyeli, the tribal historical archivist who explores the collective values of the tribe. "Haunting and evocative, *Soothsayers and Omens* powerfully reveals the Afro-American sense of participation in a tradition and world view other than that in which blacks live in America," declared Richard, "and most successfully of all Wright's books, it assimilates a mythological world view to personal experience." Similarly, Richard noted, Wright incorporates experience in the use of collages in *Dimensions of History* to "dramatize the musical, artistic, or ritualistic acts which the persona wishes to present as the embodiments of spiritual tradition."

The underlying mythology in both *Soothsayers and Omens* and *Dimensions of History* is based on African religions. *Soothsayers and Omens* focuses on the cosmology of the Dogon, which relies heavily on numerology, the process of creation, and symbols, some of which are associated with such material elements as earth, air, fire and water. The doctrine is usually taught by a "Nani," a spiritual instructor in Dogon mythology. Since unity is a crucial concept in Wright's poetry, there is a definite correlation between the spiritual and the physical world in his work. "For Wright," Richard pointed out, "ideas reside primarily in things; thus his poetry frequently focuses on the ritual objects and acts of the native American and African cultures which he finds to be the wellsprings of those spiritual traditions." Wright's researches into West African mythology include the religions of the Dogon and Bambara of Mali, the Komo (an all-male community of the Bambara), and the tribes of Akan and Nuer. Wright acknowledges that he is the "beneficiary" of, among others, French anthropologist Marcel Griaule, whose expeditions to Dakar, Mali, Chad, and Cameroon have provided insight into the African mythology which is the dominant motif of much of Wright's work.

Many reviewers praised the clarity of Wright's poetic vision in *Soothsayers and Omens* and *Dimensions of History*. E. Ethelbert Miller in *Library Journal* proclaimed that "Wright's explorations into African philosophy and the poems that result must be considered bridges healing the wounds that exist within the souls of black Americans." Others pointed to Wright as a "learned" and "mythological" poet, one who is, in Richard's words, "conversant in anthropology, the philosophy of science, and the European literatures of the Renaissance and the Middle Ages." Richard concluded that "Wright's poetry is, in large measure, the fruit of this extensive scholarly enterprise." John Hollander in *Times Literary Supplement* called the works "allegorical at many levels," and Harold Bloom in *The New Republic* asserted that *Dimensions of History* is "the year's best book of poems from a small press."

In 1980 Wright published *The Double Invention of Komo*. This work is, according to many critics, his "most ambitious book," a complex succession of poems following the Komo initiation rites of the African Bambara people. The ritual is a series of instructions into the "central intellectual, spiritual, and social values of [Komo] culture," wrote Richard. The first section of the book deals with the preparation of the initiate for the ceremony, including a dance in which the creation of the world is dramatized; the second section details the actual ceremony, a ritual involving four signs delineating the values of the tribe. According to Komo beliefs, the initiate ultimately realizes that everything in creation is interlinked. The autobiographical element in this work is distinctive because Wright's own literary history is allegorized into the story. *The Double Invention of Komo* is Wright's "intellectual biogra-

phy," asserted Richard. He "uses the dialogue between ritual celebrant and initiate as a means of situating speeches by or addresses to writers and thinkers central to the poet's development." The persona's dialogue in the poem, then, serves as a synopsis of Wright's own literary quests for knowledge, and includes debates with, among others, Dante and St. Augustine, and spiritual journeys to Italy, Germany, Mexico, the United States, and France. Isidore Okpewho added in *Callaloo* that *The Double Invention of Komo* "closes one phase of [Wright's] poetic output ... [that is,] to establish the sources of his black consciousness by a careful and steady archaeology of knowledge."

Typical of critical reactions to *The Double Invention of Komo* was that of John Hollander in the *Times Literary Supplement*, who declared the work a "considerable achievement of a major imagination." Judith McPheron in *Library Journal* described the poetry as "chant-like" and "oracular," but puzzled over the tone, and remarked that "while the poems seem to cling to some large, ritual pattern, it doesn't become quite clear to the reader." Okpewho, however, asserted that "there is no doubt that [Wright] has continued to address himself ... to concerns that are peculiarly American in the broadest sense.... [He] has endeavored to inscribe the African sources of his people into the American cultural soul." And Richard judged the work "an important book in terms of its artistic and cultural ambition."

In 1984 Wright found a publisher for *Explications/Interpretations*, a book of poetry he had written prior to 1980's *The Double Invention of Komo*. As is the case here, Wright often wrote his poetry some years before it was actually published. *Explications/Interpretations* is somewhat easier to understand than some of Wright's previously published poetry, but, according to some reviewers, is just as "spellbinding" as his other works. *Explications/Interpretations* is evidence of Wright's increasing maturity as a poet, said J. N. Igo, Jr. in *Choice*. Calling him "an astonishing poet," Igo asserted that Wright's poetry is "vital, genuine, fresh, and haunting, to be reread and reread."

Two of Wright's recent works, *Elaine's Book* and *Boleros*, experiment with the use of speech, dialect, and setting. *Elaine's Book*, Wright's 1988 publication, was written as a birthday gift for his wife's sister. The language of the poems varies from standard English, to black vernacular, to Spanish. "This volume is Jay Wright at his best," wrote R. G. O'Meally in *Choice*. The poems are "far-reaching in mythic and historic reference yet dramatically in the here and now." A *Virginia Quarterly Review* critic concluded "Wright's language ... is sinuous, beautiful. This is a book worth puzzling over for a long time." Like *Elaine's Book*, Wright's *Boleros*, published in 1991, is multicultural in voice and location. Unlike his previous works, however, there is a tendency in *Boleros* to create words in a "sensual" exploration of the volume's central question: "What is love's habitation...?" M. Waters in *Choice* recommended the book for its "resplendent and evocative language."

*Selected Poems of Jay Wright,* produced in 1987, is an anthology of Wright's previously published works, with an introduction by Robert B. Stepto and an afterword by poetry critic Harold Bloom. The collection is "superb," wrote R. G. O'Meally in *Choice,* "for it brings together the strongest poems of one of America's strongest poets." Numerous reviewers, however, cautioned that Wright is a complex poet. Shaw confessed in *Poetry* that "I have found in this book some poems I was moved by, a great many more I was intrigued by, but not many that I am certain I understand." Critic John Hollander in *Times Literary Supplement* designated Wright "the most intellectual and the most imaginatively serious and ambitious black American poet I know of.... He is also the most difficult." Another commentator, Jack Shreve in *Library Journal,* insisted: "Wright is an intellectual poet, a poet's poet.... Tackling Wright's poetry is no mean task," but may be rewarding. Many reviewers, such as Richard, advised careful rereading, so that the reader might be "assimilated into the world of the poem." Further, Hollander specified that understanding Wright's poems "will take ... the imaginative and moral work that poetry, rather than merely eloquent verse, requires of its readers." This often involves paying careful attention to the author-provided notes, and familiarizing oneself with the references or sources cited in the glossaries to help interpret the work. Finally, the works as a whole are comprehensive in nature, with each volume of poetry building upon the themes presented in the previous one. In a 1983 interview with Charles H. Rowell in *Jay Wright: A Special Issue, Callaloo,* the poet suggested a reading of his major works in the following planned sequence and as chronologically written: *The Homecoming Singer, Soothsayers and Omens, Explications/Interpretations, Dimensions of History,* and *The Double Invention of Komo.*

*BIOGRAPHICAL/CRITICAL SOURCES:*

BOOKS

*Dictionary of Literary Biography,* Volume 41: *Afro-American Poets since 1955,* Gale, 1985, pp. 350-60.
Kutzinski, Vera, *Against the American Grain: Myth and History in William Carlos Williams, Jay Wright, and Nicholas Guillen,* Johns Hopkins University Press, 1987.
Redmond, Eugene B., *Drumvoices: The Mission of African-American Poetry, A Critical History,* Anchor Press, 1976.
Stepto, Robert B., *The Chant of Saints: A Gathering of Afro-American Literature, Art, and Scholarship,* University of Illinois Press, 1979.

PERIODICALS

*Callaloo,* fall, 1983 (special issue dedicated to Jay Wright); summer, 1991, pp. 692-726.
*Choice,* October, 1980; December, 1984, p. 563; April, 1988, p. 1249; December, 1989, p. 636; March, 1992, p. 1082.
*Hambone,* fall, 1982.
*Library Journal,* February 1, 1977, p. 390; May 15, 1980, p. 1170; July, 1987, p. 82.
*New Republic,* November 20, 1976, pp. 23, 26; November 26, 1977, p. 26.
*New York Times Book Review,* July 30, 1972, pp. 4, 15.
*Poetry,* April, 1988, pp. 45-47.
*Times Literary Supplement,* January 30, 1981, p. 115.
*Virginia Quarterly Review,* summer, 1989, p. 98.

—*Sketch by Linda Tidrick*

*   *   *

## WRIGHT, Sarah E(lizabeth) 1928(?)-

*PERSONAL:* Born December 9, 1928 (one source says 1929), in Wetipquin, MD; daughter of Willis Charles (an oysterman, barber, farmer, and musician) and Mary Amelia (a homemaker, barber, farmer, and factory worker; maiden name, Moore) Wright; married Joseph G. Kaye (a composer); children: Michael, Shelley. *Education:* Attended Howard University, 1945-49, and Cheyney State Teachers College (now Cheyney State College), 1950-52; also attended writers' workshops at University of Pennsylvania and New School for Social Research.

*ADDRESSES: Home*—780 West End Ave., Apt. 1-D, New York, NY 10025. *Agent*—Roberta Pryor, International Famous Agency, 1301 Avenue of the Americas, New York, NY 10019.

*CAREER:* Writer. Worked as teacher, bookkeeper, and office manager.

*MEMBER:* Authors Guild, Authors League of America, International PEN, Harlem Writers Guild (past vice-president).

*AWARDS, HONORS: Baltimore Sun* Readability Award, 1969, for *This Child's Gonna Live;* McDowell Colony fellowships, 1972 and 1973; New York State Creative Artists Public Service Award for Fiction, and Novelist-Poet Award, Howard University's Institute for the Arts and Humanities' Second National Conference of Afro-American Writers, both 1976.

*WRITINGS:*

(With Lucy Smith) *Give Me a Child* (poetry; includes Wright's "To Some Millions Who Survive Joseph Mander, Sr."), Kraft Publishing, 1955.

*This Child's Gonna Live* (novel), Delacorte, 1969.

*A. Philip Randolph: Integration in the Work Place,* edited by Richard Gallin, introduced by Andrew Young, Silver Burdett Press, 1990.

Work represented in anthologies, including *The Poetry of Black America; The Poetry of the Negro, 1946-1970; Beyond the Blues;* and *Poets of Today.* Contributor of essays, reviews, and poetry to journals, including *Freedomways* and *American Pen.*

*WORK IN PROGRESS:* A sequel to *This Child's Gonna Live;* a collection of verse, tentatively entitled *Why Do I Have Corns on My Feet?;* a screenplay adaptation of *This Child's Gonna Live.*

*SIDELIGHTS:* Sarah E. Wright distinguished herself as an important writer with her 1955 verse collection *Give Me a Child,* which she wrote with Lucy Smith, and her 1969 novel *This Child's Gonna Live.* Her contributions to *Give Me a Child* reveal a humanist perspective on life. Direct and dramatically charged, Wright's verses address both the despair of the black American and the faith in humanity that oppressed blacks must nonetheless maintain to continue living in a biased society. Wright's best-known poem is probably "To Some Millions Who Survive Joseph Mander, Sr.," which embodies many of her themes. The poem was inspired by the death of a black man who drowned while attempting to save a white person. Wright uses the death to dramatic advantage, asserting that it serves as an inspiring indication of humanism and compassion and urging readers to adopt Mander's compassion.

Two years after publishing *Give Me a Child,* Wright moved to New York City and became involved with various organizations of black writers. Among those groups was the Harlem Writers' Guild, in which she was particularly active from 1957 to 1972. Late in that period she wrote *This Child's Gonna Live,* a stylistically daring novel about a black couple's struggle to overcome poverty and strife in a destitute community. Using flashbacks and stream of consciousness, Wright fashioned a moving account of desperate lives. Among the most memorable characters in the work is Mariah, the mother who tends three children—all in various stages of malnutrition—while also contending with oppressive economic conditions, a sexist husband, and pious, hypocritical neighbors. For its ambitious techniques and compelling drama, *Give Me a Child* was deemed by critics to be a major literary achievement.

*BIOGRAPHICAL/CRITICAL SOURCES:*

*BOOKS*

*Dictionary of Literary Biography,* Volume 33: *Afro-American Fiction Writers after 1955,* Gale, 1984.

Redmond, Eugene, *Drumvoices: The Mission of Afro-American Poetry,* Doubleday, 1976.

Schraufnagel, Noel, *From Apology to Protest: The Black American Novel,* Everett/Edwards, 1973.

*PERIODICALS*

*Best Sellers,* August 1, 1969.
*Harper's,* December, 1969.
*Negro Digest,* August, 1969.
*New York Times Book Review,* June 29, 1969; May 3, 1987, p. 41, col. 1.
*Times Literary Supplement,* October 16, 1969.

\* \* \*

## WRIGHT, Stephen Caldwell 1946-

*PERSONAL:* Born November 11, 1946, in Sanford, FL; son of Joseph Caldwell (an accountant) and Bernice Ida Wright (a writer). *Education:* St. Petersburg Junior College, A.A., 1967; Florida Atlantic University, B.A., 1969; Atlanta University, M.A., 1972; Indiana University of Pennsylvania, Ph.D., 1983. *Religion:* Baptist. *Avocational interests:* Antiques, travel.

*ADDRESSES: Home*—127 Langston Dr., Sanford, FL 32771. *Office*—Seminole Community College, 100 Weldon Blvd., Sanford, FL 32773. *Agent*—Fletcher and Bernary, P.O. Box 72A, Sanford, FL 32772.

*CAREER:* Crooms High School, Sanford, FL, instructor of English and head of department, 1969-70; Clark College, Atlanta, GA, student teacher, 1971-72; Seminole Community College, Sanford, professor of English and Black American history, 1972—.

*MEMBER:* National Council of Teachers of English, College Language Association, Middle Atlantic Writers Association, Gwendolyn Brooks Writers Association (founder), National Association for the Advancement of Colored People, Langston Hughes Society, Zora Neale Hurston Society.

*AWARDS, HONORS:* First Superior Poet, Florida Poetry Festival, 1969; three fellowships, Institute for Services to Education, 1971-72; Gwendolyn Brooks Poetry Award, 1984; Illinois Salutes Award, 1992.

*WRITINGS:*

POETRY

*First Statement: A Collection of Poems,* Celery City Press, 1983.

*Poems in Movement,* Celery City Press, 1984.

*Making Symphony: New and Selected Poems,* Middle-Atlantic Writers Association Press, 1987.

*Talking to the Mountains,* Christopherr-Burghardt, 1988.

*Circumference: An Evolution of Homage,* Christopherr-Burghardt, 1989.

*The Chicago Collective: Poems for and Inspired by Gwendolyn Brooks,* Christopherr-Burghardt, 1990.

*Out of the Wailing: A Collection of Poems,* Christopherr-Burghardt, 1992.

*Inheritance: Poems,* Cloverdale Library, 1992.

Also author of *How a Tulip Blossoms: Women as Revelation,* 1985. Contributor of poetry to periodicals.

OTHER

Contributor to *New Visions: Fiction by Florida Writers,* Arbiter Press, 1989. Reviewer for National Endowment of the Humanities, 1981.

*WORK IN PROGRESS:* A collection of short stories; collected poems.

*SIDELIGHTS:* Stephen Caldwell Wright commented: "The being of anything is not momentary nor complete. It is long-time-consuming and always growing to completeness. Creation is no exception to this process of Being. Therefore, in the process of Becoming, poetry is motion. It is, naturally enough, energy—physical as well as spiritual. The wealth of humankind is measured by one's ability or willingness to be true to one's convictions and to the higher callings of one's ultimate consciousness. The poet responds to this duty, and in so doing, seeks to eradicate barriers."

*       *       *

## WYNTER, Sylvia 1928-

*PERSONAL:* Born May 11, 1928 (one source says 1932), in Holguin Oriente Province, Cuba; daughter of Percival and Lola Maude (Reed) Wynter; married, c. 1955 (divorced); husband's surname, Isachsen (a Norwegian pilot); married Jan Carew (a writer), c. 1960 (marriage ended, July, 1971); children: Annemarie, Christopher. *Education:* King's College, University of London, B.A. (with honors), 1949, M.A., 1953.

*ADDRESSES: Office*—Stanford University, Department of Spanish and Portuguese, Stanford, CA 94305.

*CAREER:* Worked variously as an actor, dancer, and writer in Europe, 1954-59; British Broadcasting Corporation (BBC), commentator, writer, and translator, 1958-62; University of the West Indies, Jamaica, lecturer in Hispanic literature, 1963-74; University of California, San Diego, lecturer in Hispanic literature, 1974-76, coordinator of the Literature and Society Program; Department of Spanish and Portuguese, Stanford University, professor of Spanish and chair of African and Afro-American Studies, 1977—.

*WRITINGS:*

*The Hills of Hebron: A Jamaican Novel,* Simon & Schuster, 1962.

*Black Midas* (juvenile; adaptation of Jan Carew's novel), illustrated by Aubrey Williams, Longmans, 1970.

*Jamaica's National Heroes* (nonfiction), National Commission (Kingston, Jamaica), 1971.

(With Annemarie Isachsen) *Rody and Rena, The Sea Star Readers,* Jamaica Publishing House, 1975.

PLAYS

(With Jan Carew) *The University of Hunger,* BBC, 1961, televised as *The Big Pride,* BBC, 1962.

*Ssh ... It's a Wedding* (musical), produced in Jamaica, c. 1961.

(With J. Carew) *Miracle in Lime Lane,* produced in Spanish Town, Jamaica, at Folk Theatre, 1962.

*Brother Man* (adaptation of Roger Mais's novel), produced in Jamaica, 1965.

*1865 Ballad for a Rebellion* (epic story of Morant Bay Rebellion), produced in Jamaica, 1965.

(Translator) Francisco Cuevas, *Jamaica Is the Eye of Bolivar,* Vantage Press, 1979.

(With Alex Gradussov) *Rockstone Anancy* (Jamaican Pantomime), produced in Jamaica, 1970.

OTHER

Contributor to anthologies, including *Out of the Kumbla: Caribbean Women and Literature,* African World Press, 1990. Also contributor to journals, including *Jamaica Journal 2* and *Jamaica Journal 4, Savacou 5, Caribbean Studies,* and *New World Quarterly 5.*

*SIDELIGHTS:* West Indian author Sylvia Wynter is perhaps best known for her belief in the validity of folk culture. In his essay on Wynter in *Fifty Caribbean Writers,* Victor L. Chang notes that as early as the late 1960's the author publicly took to task such well-known male Caribbean literary critics as W. I. Carr, Louis James, Wayne Brown, John Hearne, Cameron

King, and Mervyn Morris for privileging European culture over West Indian folk culture in their critical writings. Chang further states that Wynter claims that for her the folk culture represents "the only living tradition in the Caribbean," and that any authentic national literature could come only from the life of the West Indian peasant.

*The Hills of Hebron,* published in 1962, was a literary milestone, for as Janice Lee Liddell points out in her essay published in the anthology *Out of the Kumbla: Caribbean Women and Literature,* Wynter was "the first Black woman novelist from the English-speaking Caribbean." The story, set in rural Jamaica, centers around a religious folk group, the New Believers, who follow their leader Moses Barton from the worldly village of Cockpit Center to the hills of Hebron in search of spiritual salvation and a better life. When Moses dies, a struggle for power ensues. Obadiah Brown, in the midst of a severe drought, takes over the leadership and vows celibacy for one year and a day in a covenant with God to protect the Hebronites. But Miss Gatha, Moses' widow, wants the leadership for her own son, Isaac, who is away at school. So when it becomes obvious that Rose, Obadiah's wife, is indeed pregnant, Obadiah is dismissed as a hypocrite, and Miss Gatha assumes temporary leadership as she awaits her son's return. Finally, it is revealed that not only has Isaac raped Rose and is thus responsible for her pregnancy, but has stolen the money that his mother was holding for the New Believers, and will never return to the community. The work ends on a symbolic note of hope when, as Miss Gatha holds her newborn grandson in her arms, the skies open and the rains come down, thus ending the drought.

Although she concedes that the primary thematic concern of this work is certainly not with women, Liddell approaches the work from the perspective of Miss Gatha and the other women whom she sees as living their lives and seeking their identity solely through their roles as wives and mothers. That these women living in what she calls a "patriarchal and patrilineal" society are able to achieve any semblance of autonomy she finds highly unusual and commendable. The primacy that this society places on these "female roles," she suggests, both victimizes and debilitates the Caribbean woman. On that same note, Chang states that although the main character is a man, the work could be called "a woman's novel." He sees the women as demonstrating the "strengths and enduring qualities of the folk culture" and providing "support and sustenance for their men."

*The Hills of Hebron* was met with mixed reviews. The most frequent criticism was that the author attempts to deal with too many issues at once. Kenneth Ramchand in *The West Indian Novel and Its Background* states that "*The Hills of Hebron* is an overloaded work by a West Indian intellectual anxious to touch on as many themes as possible." Chang, writing along

similar lines, believes that "Wynter invests [the work] with so much of her concerns that the medium is too freighted with the message."

On the more positive side, Chang lists other areas in which he believes Wynter achieves "some fine effects" in this work. Citing the language used, Chang explains that while *The Hills of Hebron* is narrated in "Standard English," Wynter captures the "Creole patterns and rhythms" of the folk dialect in the speaking voices of her characters, as well as the "pervasive influence of the King James version of the Bible." He finds commendable the rich "Biblical echoes and allusions" in the place names, character names, and what he calls "near paraphrases [of Biblical events]." Chang also credits the author with being very successful in capturing and depicting rural Jamaica, which he thinks lends the novel "an air of authenticity." And a reviewer in *Library Journal* acknowledges that although "the book is marred by unevenness and a too diverse viewpoint, ... the author's creativity and knowledge of people make it, on the whole, a distinctive and sensitive study of fanaticism."

*BIOGRAPHICAL/CRITICAL SOURCES:*

*BOOKS*

Dance, Daryl Cumber, editor, *Fifty Caribbean Writers: A Bio-Bibliographical Critical Sourcebook,* Greenwood Press, 1986.
Davies, Carole Boyce and Elaine Savory Fido, editors, *Out of the Kumbla: Caribbean Women and Literature,* African World Press, 1990.
Herdeck, Donald E. and others, editors, *A Bio-Bibliographical-Critical Encyclopedia,* Three Continents Press, 1979.
Ramchand, Kenneth, *The West Indian Novel and Its Background,* Faber & Faber, 1970.

*PERIODICALS*

*Library Journal,* July, 1962.
*New York Times Book Review,* July 15, 1962, p. 24.
*Times Literary Supplement,* September 28, 1962, p. 765.

\* \* \*

## YARBROUGH, Camille 1938-

*PERSONAL:* Born in 1938 in Chicago, IL. *Education:* Studied acting and voice in the United States and Australia; attended Roosevelt University.

*ADDRESSES: Office*—246 137th St., New York, NY 10030.

*CAREER:* Employed in dance company of Katherine Dunham; dance instructor at Performing Arts Training center at Southern Illinois University; provided drama workshops at high schools in New York; drama teacher. Actress in plays, including *Trumpets of the Lord, Cities in Bezique, Sambo,* and *To Be Young, Gifted, and Black;* in films, including *Shaft,* 1973; and in television. Singer on tour in United States, Canada, and South America.

*WRITINGS:*

*Cornrows* (poems for children), illustrations by Carole Byard, Coward, McCann & Geoghegan, 1979.
*The Shimmershine Queens* (juvenile fiction), Putnam, 1989.

Also author of additional poetry and songs.

*ADAPTATIONS:* A program of Yarbrough's songs and poetry was presented by Nina Simone at Philharmonic Hall, New York City, in 1972.

\*    \*    \*

## YOUNG, Al(bert James) 1939-

*PERSONAL:* Born May 31, 1939, in Ocean Springs, MS; son of Albert James (a professional musician and auto worker) and Mary (Campbell) Young; married Arline June Belch (a freelance artist), October 8, 1963; children: Michael James. *Education:* Attended University of Michigan, 1957-61; University of California, Berkeley, B.A., 1969. *Politics:* Independent. *Religion:* "Free Thinker."

*ADDRESSES: Office*—University of Michigan, Department of English, 7609 Haven Hall, 505 S. State St., Ann Arbor, MI 48109-1045. *Agent*—Lynn Nesbit, International Creative Management, 40 West Fifty-Seventh St., New York, NY 10019.

*CAREER:* Free-lance musician playing guitar and flute, and professional singer throughout the United States, 1957-64; KJAZ-FM, Alameda, CA, disc jockey, 1961-65; San Francisco Museum of Art, San Francisco, CA, writing instructor, 1967-69; Berkeley Neighborhood Youth Corps, Berkeley, CA, writing instructor and language consultant, 1968-69; Stanford University, Stanford, CA, Edward H. Jones Lecturer in creative writing, 1969-74; screenwriter for Laser Films, New York City, 1972, Stigwood Corporation, London, England, and New York City, 1972, Verdon Productions, Hollywood, CA, 1976, First Artists Ltd., Burbank, CA, 1976-77, and Universal Studios, Hollywood, CA, 1979; director, Associated Writing Programs, 1979—. University of Washing-

ton, Seattle, writer in residence, 1981-82. Yardbird Publishing Cooperative, vice-president. Lecturer at numerous schools, including Massachusetts Institute of Technology, Rhode Island School of Design, University of California, Berkeley, Mills College, University of New Mexico, and University of Michigan.

*MEMBER:* American Association of University Professors, Writer's Guild of America, West, Author's Guild, Author's League of America, American Civil Liberties Union, Committee of Small Magazine Editors and Publishers, Sigma Delta Pi.

*AWARDS, HONORS:* Wallace E. Stegner Creative Writing Fellowship, Stanford University, 1966-77; National Endowment for the Arts grants, 1968, 1969, and 1975; Joseph Henry Jackson Award, San Francisco Foundation, 1969, for *Dancing: Poems;* National Arts Council awards for poetry and editing, 1968-1970; California Association of Teachers of English special award, 1973; Guggenheim fellowship, 1974; Outstanding Book of the Year citation, *New York Times,* 1980, for *Ask Me Now;* Pushcart Prize, Pushcart Press, 1980; American Book Award, Before Columbus Foundation, 1982, for *Bodies & Soul: Musical Memoirs.*

*WRITINGS:*

*NOVELS*

*Snakes: A Novel,* Holt, 1970.
*Who Is Angelina?,* Holt, 1975.
*Sitting Pretty,* Holt, 1976.
*Ask Me Now,* McGraw-Hill, 1980.
*Seduction by Light,* Delacorte, 1988.

*POETRY*

*Dancing: Poems,* Corinth Books, 1969.
*The Song Turning Back into Itself,* Holt, 1971.
*Some Recent Fiction,* San Francisco Book Company, 1974.
*Geography of the Near Past,* Holt, 1976.
*The Blues Don't Change: New and Selected Poems,* Louisiana State University Press, 1982.
*Heaven: Collected Poems 1958-1988,* Creative Arts Book Co., 1989.

*EDITOR*

James P. Girard, *Changing All Those Changes,* Yardbird Wing, 1976.
William Lawson, *Zeppelin Coming Down,* Yardbird Wing, 1976.
(With Ishmael Reed) *Yardbird Lives!,* Grove Press, 1978.

(With Ishmael Reed, and contributor) *Calafia: The California Poetry,* Y'Bird Books, 1979.

*CONTRIBUTOR*

Wallace Stegner and Richard Scowcroft, editors, *Stanford Short Stories, 1968,* Stanford University Press, 1968.
*The Health Introduction to Poetry,* Health, 1975.
John Ciardi and Miller Williams, editors, *How Does a Poem Mean?,* Houghton, 1976.

*OTHER*

*Bodies & Soul: Musical Memoirs,* Creative Arts Book Co., 1981.
*Kinds of Blue: Musical Memoirs,* Creative Arts Book Co., 1984.
*Things Ain't What They Used to Be: Musical Memoirs,* Creative Arts Book Co., 1987.
(With Janet Coleman) *Mingus-Mingus: Two Memoirs,* Limelight, 1991.

Also author of screenplays, *Nigger* and *Sparkle,* both 1972. Contributor of articles, short stories, and reviews to *Audience, California Living, New Times, Rolling Stone, Evergreen Review, Encore, New York Times Book Review, Journal of Black Poetry,* and other periodicals. Founding editor, *Loveletter,* 1966-68; co-editor, *Yardbird Reader,* 1972-76; contributing editor, *Changes,* beginning in 1972, and *Umoja,* beginning in 1973; co-editor and co-publisher, *Quilt,* beginning in 1981.

*SIDELIGHTS:* American poet and novelist Al Young's art destroys "glib stereotypes of black Americans," presenting an image of the black person in "the American tradition of the singular individual," states William J. Harris in the *Dictionary of Literary Biography.* "Not surprisingly," the contributor continues, "[Young's] work illustrates the complexity and richness of contemporary Afro-American life through a cast of highly individualized black characters. Since he is a gifted stylist and a keen observer of the human comedy, he manages to be both a serious and an entertaining author." In his oeuvre, says Harris, Young explores themes of "the beauty of black music and speech, the importance of family love, the dignity and romance of vocation, the quest for identity and the need to come to terms with one's life."

Known for his imaginative style, Young often populates his novels with characters and situations modeled after real-life people and experiences. His first novel, entitled *Snakes,* is the story of MC, a young musician whose successful jazz single, called "Snakes," meets with a modest success in Detroit, his hometown. Eventually, he leaves home for New York in order to start a career as a jazz musician. Like many of Young's characters, MC is black, but the author's interest in him lies not only in his ethnicity, but also in his humanity; as Harris declares, "although it is important that MC ... is undeniably black, it is equally important that he is young and trying to come to terms with who he is." MC faces, among other problems, the bleakness of his Detroit environment, but, as L. E. Sissman points out in the *New Yorker, Snakes* "offers some alternative to hopelessness." Sissman suggests that MC's pursuit of jazz as a vocation "gives his life purpose; it palliates the terrors and disjunctures of the ghetto; it restores his adolescence to a semblance of normal adolescent joy and hope." And Douglass Bolling of *Negro American Literature Forum* concludes that "*Snakes* is clearly a work which seeks to reach out for the universals of human experience rather than to restrict itself to Black protest or Black aesthetic considerations."

Similar statements are made about the main characters of *Who Is Angelina?* and *Sitting Pretty;* according to Jacqueline Adams in the *Christian Science Monitor, Angelina* "represents that classical Everyman figure struggling again conformity, commericalized sentiments, crime, life's insanities and riddles to find peace, happiness, security, honesty, love, beauty, soul." Sidney J. Prettymon, the philosophical janitor and protagonist of *Sitting Pretty,* is, in the opinion of Mel Watkins in the *New York Times Book Review,* "the natural man, with no pretenses, just trying to live with as little chaos as possible and to enjoy the simple pleasures of growing old." Even Durwood Knight, the ex-basketball player hero of *Ask Me Now,* says James A. Steck in the *San Francisco Review of Books,* discovers how "you learn everything there is to know about life no matter what line of endeavour you take up."

Young's 1988 novel *Seduction by Light* focuses on an earthy, middle-aged, black maid named Mamie Franklin. In an interview with *New York Times Book Review* contributor Michael Ross, Young described the character as "fairly avant-garde" and "not afraid to live life as it comes to her." Set in and around Los Angeles, the story follows Mamie as she fends off a couple of young muggers, works for an adulterous Hollywood producer, and copes with the death of her husband and his comic return as a ghost. According to reviewer Robert Ward in *New York Times Book Review,* Mamie is also a representation of "black life in Los Angeles ... something we haven't read much about before." Ward added, however, that the novel's power derives itself more from its "its voice and tone" than its "characters or ... plot."
Calling the *Seduction by Light* "brilliant, funny and sweet," Ward asserted that "Young is a ... gentle philosopher and a man of real sensibility."

Young's fascination with musical rhythms also permeates his writings. Reviewers note that this interest may stem from Young's early career as a jazz musician. Harris states that "dancing and music figure as central metaphors in [Young's] poetry," and his novels, which are also "rich in black language." Not only is music the subject of *Snakes,* notes *Paunch*'s Neil Schmitz, but "the music heard in [the novel] is the music of voices speaking." "It is this elusive sound," he continues, "which hangs Grail-like before MC's imagination throughout *Snakes,* which figures finally as the novel's unifying theme." He concludes, "MC's quest for the right language in his music is a reflection of Young's discovery of the music in his language." Dea Flower remarks in the *Hudson Review,* "I don't know of any other black novel whether the vernacular is used so well [as in *Sitting Pretty*], unless it be in Young's own *Snakes* and *Who Is Angelina?*" The critic is persuaded that "the beauty of Young's vernacular method is that it brings alive a thoroughly engaging human being"; and Sheldon Frank of the *National Observer* notices that *Sitting Pretty* "talks music all the time." "In sum," concludes Harris, "Al Young has captured much of the beauty and complexity of black life and black speech in his impressive and extensive oeuvre."

## *BIOGRAPHICAL/CRITICAL SOURCES:*

### *BOOKS*

Chapman, Abraham, editor, *New Black Voices,* New American Library, 1972.
*Contemporary Literary Criticism,* Volume 19, Gale, 1981.
*Dictionary of Literary Biography,* Volume 33: *Afro-American Fiction Writers after 1955,* Gale, 1984.
O'Brien, John, editor, *Interviews with Black Writers,* Liveright, 1973.
Rush, Theresa Gunnels, Carol Fairbanks Myers, and Esther Spring Arata, *Black American Writers Past and Present: A Biographical and Bibliographical Dictionary,* Scarecrow Press, 1975.

### *PERIODICALS*

*California Living* (Sunday Supplement of *San Francisco Chronicle/Examiner*), May 3, 1970.
*Christian Science Monitor,* March 6, 1975; December 7, 1984.
*Greenfield Review,* summer/fall, 1982.
*Hudson Review,* summer, 1976.
*Kite,* June 9, 1976.
*MELUS,* winter, 1978.
*National Observer,* July 24, 1976.
*Negro American Literature Forum,* summer, 1974.
*New Yorker,* July 11, 1970; August 4, 1980.
*New York Times,* January 23, 1975.
*New York Times Book Review,* May 17, 1970; February 9, 1975; May 23, 1976; July 6, 1980; January 24, 1987; February 5, 1989, pp. 11-12.
*Paunch,* February, 1972.
*Peninsula Magazine,* June, 1976.
*Poetry,* May, 1977.
*San Francisco Review of Books,* August, 1979; September, 1980.
*Saturday Review,* August 22, 1970; March 20, 1976.
*Stanford Observer,* March, 1970.
*Time,* June 29, 1970.
*Times Literary Supplement,* July 30, 1971.
*Washington Post Book World,* May 17, 1970.
*Yale Review,* June, 1970.

# Cumulative Index

## to

## First and Second Editions

(Numeral appearing below refers to edition in which the author's most recent entry appears.)

# C

# D

# E

# F

# G

# H

# X-Y

# Nationality Index
## to
## First and Second Editions

(Authors are listed alphabetically under
country of origin and/or their country of citizenship.
Numeral refers to edition in which the author's most recent entry appears.)

# Gender Index

to

## First and Second Editions

(Numeral appearing below refers to edition in which the author's most recent entry appears.)

## Female

713

# Male

## A

Abdul-Jabbar, Kareem 1947- . . . . . . . . . .  2
Abrahams, Peter (Henry) 1919- . . . . . . . .  1
Achebe, (Albert) Chinua(lumogu) 1930- . . . .  2
Akar, John J(oseph) 1927-1975 . . . . . . . .  2
Al-Amin, Jamil Abdullah 1943- . . . . . . . .  1
Allen, Robert L(ee) 1942- . . . . . . . . . . .  1
Allen, Samuel W(ashington) 1917- . . . . . . .  1
Aluko, T(imothy) M(ofolorunso) 1918(?)- . .  1
Amadi, Elechi (Emmanuel) 1934- . . . . . . .  1
Anderson, Henry L(ee Norman) 1934- . . . . .  2
Anderson, Jervis (B.) 1936- . . . . . . . . . .  2
Andrews, Raymond 1934-1991 . . . . . . . . .  2
Anozie, Sunday O(gbonna) 1942- . . . . . . .  2
Anthony, Michael 1932- . . . . . . . . . . . .  2
Appiah, (K.) Anthony 1954- . . . . . . . . . .  2
Archer, Chalmers, Jr. 1938- . . . . . . . . . .  2
Armah, Ayi Kwei 1939- . . . . . . . . . . . .  1
Asante, Molefi K(ete) 1942- . . . . . . . . . .  2
Ashe, Arthur (Robert, Jr.) 1943-1993 . . . . .  2
Atkins, Russell 1926- . . . . . . . . . . . . .  1
Attaway, William (Alexander) 1911-1986 . . .  2
Aubert, Alvin (Bernard) 1930- . . . . . . . . .  1
Awolowo, Obafemi Awo 1909-1987 . . . . . .  2
Awoonor, Kofi (Nyidevu) 1935- . . . . . . . .  2

## B

Baker, Houston A., Jr. 1943- . . . . . . . . . .  2
Baker, Nikki 1962- . . . . . . . . . . . . . .  2
Baldwin, James (Arthur) 1924-1987 . . . . . .  1
Bankole, Timothy 1920(?)- . . . . . . . . . . .  2
Baraka, Amiri 1934- . . . . . . . . . . . . . .  2
Barrax, Gerald William 1933- . . . . . . . . .  2
Barrett, (Eseoghene) Lindsay 1941 . . . . . . .  2
Bart-Williams, Gaston 1938- . . . . . . . . . .  2
Bebey, Francis 1929- . . . . . . . . . . . . . .  1
Beckham, Barry (Earl) 1944- . . . . . . . . . .  1
Bell, Derrick Albert, Jr. 1930- . . . . . . . . .  2
Bell, James Madison 1826-1902 . . . . . . . .  1
ben-Jochannan, Yosef 1918- . . . . . . . . . .  2
Bennett, George Harold 1930- . . . . . . . . .  1
Bennett, Lerone, Jr. 1928- . . . . . . . . . . .  2
Billingsley, Andrew 1926- . . . . . . . . . . .  2
Bishop, Maurice 1944-1983 . . . . . . . . . .  1
Biyidi, Alexandre 1932- . . . . . . . . . . . .  1

Blassingame, John W(esley) 1940- . . . . . . .  1
Blockson, Charles L(eRoy) 1933- . . . . . . .  2
Boles, Robert (E.) 1943- . . . . . . . . . . . .  2
Bond, Julian 1940- . . . . . . . . . . . . . . .  1
Bontemps, Arna(ud Wendell) 1902-1973 . . .  1
Bradley, David (Henry, Jr.) 1950- . . . . . . .  1
Bradley, Ed(ward R.) 1941- . . . . . . . . . .  1
Braithwaite, (Eustace) F(dward) R(icardo) 1920-  1
Braithwaite, William Stanley (Beaumont)
    1878-1962 . . . . . . . . . . . . . . . . .  1
Branch, William (Blackwell) 1927- . . . . . .  2
Brathwaite, Edward (Kamau) 1930- . . . . . .  2
Brawley, Benjamin (Griffith) 1882-1939 . . .  1
Brew, (Osborne Henry) Kwesi 1928- . . . . . .  2
Brown, Cecil M(orris) 1943- . . . . . . . . . .  1
Brown, Claude 1937- . . . . . . . . . . . . . .  1
Brown, Frank London 1927-1962 . . . . . . .  2
Brown, Lloyd L(ouis) 1913- . . . . . . . . . .  2
Brown, Sterling Allen 1901-1989 . . . . . . .  1
Brown, Wesley 1945- . . . . . . . . . . . . . .  2
Brown, William Anthony 1933- . . . . . . . . .  1
Brutus, Dennis 1924- . . . . . . . . . . . . . .  2
Bryan, Ashley F. 1923- . . . . . . . . . . . . .  2
Bullins, Ed 1935- . . . . . . . . . . . . . . . .  2
Bunche, Ralph J(ohnson) 1904-1971 . . . . . .  2
Busia, Kofi Abrefa 1913(?)-1978 . . . . . . . .  2

## C

Cain, George (M.) 1943- . . . . . . . . . . . .  2
Caldwell, Ben(jamin) 1937- . . . . . . . . . .  1
Cannon, David Wadsworth, Jr. 1911-1938 . .  2
Carew, Jan (Rynveld) 1925- . . . . . . . . . .  2
Carmichael, Stokely 1941- . . . . . . . . . . .  1
Carter, Martin (Wylde) 1927- . . . . . . . . .  2
Cartey, Wilfred (George Onslow) 1931-1992 .  2
Casely-Hayford, J(oseph) E(phraim) 1866-1930  2
Casey, Bernard Terry 1939- . . . . . . . . . .  2
Cesaire, Aime (Fernand) 1913- . . . . . . . . .  2
Chesnutt, Charles W(addell) 1858-1932 . . . .  1
Clark, John(son) Pepper 1935- . . . . . . . . .  1
Clark, Kenneth B(ancroft) 1914- . . . . . . . .  1
Clarke, Austin C(hesterfield) 1934- . . . . . .  1
Clarke, John Henrik 1915- . . . . . . . . . . .  2
Cleaver, (Leroy) Eldridge 1935- . . . . . . . .  1
Cobb, Charles E., Jr. 1943- . . . . . . . . . . .  2
Colter, Cyrus 1910- . . . . . . . . . . . . . .  1

# H

# J-K

# L

# M

# N

# O

# P-Q

# R

# S

# T